THE 1901 EDITIONS OF

THE T. EATON Co. LIMITED.

CATALOGUES

for

SPRING & SUMMER
FALL & WINTER

with an introduction by

JACK STODDART

Published in 1991 by
Stoddart Publishing Co. Limited
34 Lesmill Road
Toronto, Canada
M3B 2T6

Reprinted May 1997

Published in 1970 by The Musson Book Company

Canadian Cataloguing in Publication Data

T. Eaton Co.
The 1901 editions of the T. Eaton Co. Limited catalogues for spring & summer, fall & winter

Reprint. Originally published: Toronto: Musson Book Company, 1970.
ISBN 0-7737-5923-9

1. T.Eaton Co. – Catalogs. 2. Catalogs, Commercial. I. Title.

HF5465.C34E3 1992 381′.029′4 C91-095432-1

See Publisher's note following Introduction for explanation of missing pages.

Printed and bound in Canada

INTRODUCTION

Through the pages of the 1901 Eaton's catalogues the rural and quiet life of Canada in that period comes vividly to life. Some will relive the days of their youth, others will remember the furnishings and equipment they saw stored in their grandmother's attic, and the young will smile and be amused at that very strange and different era.

Canada in 1901 was only 34 years old but already Timothy Eaton had become one of the world's outstanding retail merchants and the famous Eaton's catalogues in most Canadian homes held a position second only to the family bible.

When it was time for the new Eaton's catalogue to arrive young and old waited for their copy at the local post-office or looked down the road eagerly for the rural mail carrier to arrive by horse and buggy or sleigh with the great load of Eaton's catalogues.

All members of the family spent hours enjoying by oil or gas light the fascinating and interesting illustrations and descriptions of items including butter-churns, ostrich feathers, men's fur coats, brass and iron bedsteads, organs, shoo-fly rockers, graphophones, bibles, seal lined underwear, Agnew's heart cure, wigs, ladies' automobile and sealette coats, medical batteries and, of course, Granny's Gift Box of Tom Smith's Toy Crackers.

Long after the new edition of Eaton's catalogue arrived the old one was not easily given up. If the pages were not used to light the wood stove, the complete catalogue was relegated to "the little house out the back".

How could one not buy from Eaton's catalogue when you knew their famous slogan "Money Refunded if Goods Not Satisfactory"? Eaton's introduced this landmark of merchandising and have now used it for more than 100 years.

The early cataloguers were expert in sales psychology. They built confidence in the company, gave explicit details of products, illustrated each page profusely and then on the bottom of most pages gave an extra message that helped lead to the order being made out. Here are a few: "There is only one small profit between our prices and the bare cost of the goods" – "Our prices are always the lowest at which 'Honest Goods' can be made" –

"There is nothing mean or skimped in this lot of Petticoats, they have ample width and proper fulness" – "E.L.S. means extra large size, for stout ladies" – "With few exceptions, all garments shown in this catalogue are produced in our own workrooms, which are the largest, cleanest and best in Canada" and "Mail order customers get the same goods as city customers".

The reader of this catalogue cannot help but relate to-day's high prices with the low prices of 1901. Eaton's finest home-made strawberry jam was only 45 cents for a 5 pound pail and their finest quality smoked hams, from hogs raised on their own farms, was 15 cents a pound. The Labrador refrigerator to store the food in was $6.35. The family ordering in 1901 could get a lady's suit of fancy mixed cheviots for $3.98, a child's white dress 75 cents, a man's navy blue English serge suit $3.50 and a three piece hardwood bedroom suite for $10.25.

While this catalogue will interest most readers it will be especially valuable to collectors of early North American antiques, students, and all who are interested in our early days.

The Publisher wishes to thank The T. Eaton Co. Limited for making the original material available from the Eaton Archives and for their valuable advice and co-operation. Eaton's in 1969 celebrated their centennial and Musson's completed 77 years of publishing. It is fitting that these two early Canadian companies should now make available to all this important piece of Canadiana.

Jack Stoddart

Publisher's Note Regarding This Edition

In this combined edition of the two catalogues for the year 1901 we have, in order to avoid inevitable repetitions, omitted certain pages. However, both indexes have been retained in their entirety and, as a consequence of the aforementioned deletions, if an occasional item is not traceable from one index it will be from the other.

Ladies' Jackets

Sizes in Ladies' Jackets are 32, 34, 36, 38, 40 and 42 inches bust measure; sizes other than our regular **stock can be** supplied at an additional cost of 25 per cent., and are not returnable. When ordering Ladies' Jackets send measurements according to form on page 20.

No. 6206. CHEVIOT SERGE JACKET, colors black, navy, light grey, Oxford grey, brown and green mixtures 2.98

No. 6203. BOX CLOTH JACKET, colors black, navy, fawn, castor and brown, same style as No. 6206 .... 3.98

No. 6213. ETON COAT, made of cheviot homespun, in brown, light grey, dark grey and Oxford grey, lined with serge silk 5.00

No. 6214. JACKET, made of Waterloo cheviot coatings, shades black, Oxford grey, light grey, mid-grey and brown, lined with satin-finished mercerized Italian 5.00

No. 6215. BOX CLOTH JACKET, colors black, navy, fawn, castor and brown, same style as No. 6214 .... 6.75

No. 6216. ETON COAT, made of fine covert coating, shades fawn, castor, brown, navy and black, lined with satin 6.98

No. 6210. JACKET, made of imported covert coatings, colors light fawn, dark fawn, castor, brown, Oxford, navy and black, lined with silk serge 8.50

No. 6210 is not so long as shown in cut.

No. 6219. JACKET, same style as No. 6210, made of camels' hair cheviot, colors dark grey, Oxford and navy blue 6.50

No. 6200. PEBBLE CHEVIOT SERGE COAT, black only, lined with black satin, revers faced with stitched black peau de soie silk 8.50

No. 6217. JACKET, made of fine imported black broadcloth, lined with black satin, collar and fronts faced with silk 10.00

No. 6218. JACKET, made of satin twill Venetian cloth, shades light fawn, dark fawn and black, lined with taffeta silk 12.50

No. 6212. TUCKED BLACK TAFFETA ETON JACKET, finished with stitched broadcloth and black covered buttons, lined with black or white taffeta silk 13.50

No. 6211. JACKET, made of tucked black taffeta silk, finished with stitched straps of satin and fancy braid on collar, lined with white or black silk, as desired 15.00

MONEY CHEERFULLY REFUNDED IF GOODS NOT SATISFACTORY.

LADIES' SUITS.

Sizes in Ladies' Suits are 32 to 42 inches bust measure, Skirt lengths 39 to 43 inches, and waistbands of Skirts 22 to 29 inches. Skirts, unless otherwise stated, are lined with percaline and b und with good quality velveteen. For further particulars and measurement form, see page 20.

Sizes not included n our regular stock cost 25 per cent. extra and are not returnable.

No. 6104. UNLINED SUIT OF FANCY MIXED CHEVIOTS, colors brown, fawn, cadet, dark grey, navy and black, flare skirt, ... 3.98

No. 6105. TAILOR-MADE SUIT, same style as No. 6104, made of English cheviot serge, colors Oxford grey, medium grey, black, navy, royal, brown, and green, unlined flare skirt, coat is lined with mercerized sateen, ... 6.98

No. 6113. ETON SUIT OF CHEVIOT MIXTURES, shades fawn, grey, cadet, navy, and black, jacket lined with silkaline and trimmed with fancy braid 6.50

No. 6107. SUIT OF FANCY MIXED CHEVIOT, colors black, navy, Oxford grey, medium grey, green, and brown, jacket lined with silkaline and trimmed with satin folds, ... 7.50

No. 4100. ETON SUIT OF ALL-WOOL SERGE, in black and navy, has new Paquin sleeves, velvet collar........................ 10.00

No. 6115. ETON HOMESPUN SUIT, colors light, medium, and dark grey, fawn, brown, and green, jacket lined with serge silk.. 10.00

No. 6110. SERGE SUIT, colors black and navy, jacket lined with serge silk, has silk faced revers........................ 11.00

No. 6106. BOX-CLOTH SUIT, colors black, navy, fawn, brown, and castor, jacket lined with silk-finished mercerette, vest of taffeta silk 12.50

The prices we quote are extremely low; they tell a quick, powerful story.

LADIES' SUITS.

Sizes in Ladies' Suits are 32 to 42 inches bust measure; Skirt lengths, 39 to 43 inches, and waistband of Skirts, **22 to 29** inches. Skirts, unless otherwise stated, are lined with percaline and bound with good quality velveteen. For further particulars and Measurement Form, see page 20.

Sizes not included in our regular stock cost 25 per cent. extra and are not returnable.

No. 6102. TAILOR-MADE SUIT, of fine quality English cheviot serge, in black and navy, trimmed with stitched straps of black taffeta silk, jacket lined with taffeta silk and has gilt buttons 13.50

No. 6114. TIGHT-FITTING SUIT, of smooth-faced covert cloth, shades grey, fawn and navy, jacket lined with satin.............15.00

No. 6103. COVERT CLOTH SUIT, colors dark fawn, brown, grey, green and navy, jacket lined with serge silk and has velvet collar 15.00

No. 6111. CAMEL'S HAIR CLOTH SUIT, colors Oxford grey and navy, jacket lined with black satin, suit finished with taffeta silk trimmings 16.50

No. 6109. ALL-WOOL SERGE SUIT, colors black and navy, jacket lined with taffeta silk, has vest and trimmings of taffeta ..17.50

No. 6112. FINE BOX-CLOTH SUIT, colors fawn, castor, navy, green and black, jacket lined with satin, finished with stitching and silk-faced revers 18.50

No. 6108. FINE BROADCLOTH SUIT, colors black, brown and navy, made with black silk vest and trimmed with black silk, closely stitched, and fancy gilt braid, jacket lined with taffeta silk 22.50

The name "EATON" stands for everything that is good and reliable in women's outer garments.

Ladies' Summer Dresses.

Sizes in Ladies' Dresses are 32 to 38 inches bust measure; Skirts 39 to 43 inches long, and waistbands of Skirts 22 to 26 inches. Sizes other than our regular stock can be supplied at a cost of 25 per cent. additional, and are not returnable.

No. 4511. WHITE ORGANDIE DRESS ... 7.50

No. 4512. WHITE ORGANDIE DRESS, trimmed with lace 12.50

No. 4513. WHITE ORGANDIE DRESS, trimmed with lace 15.00

No. 4517. DRESS MADE OF FRENCH PRINTED ORGANDIE, colors pink, blue, heliotrope, grey, red, and black and white, trimmed with lace 10.00

No. 4518. DRESS MADE OF FRENCH PRINTED ORGANDIE, colors pink, blue, heliotrope, grey, red, and black and white, trimmed with lace and velvet ribbon 12.50

No. 4519. FRENCH PRINTED ORGANDIE DRESS, colors pink, blue, heliotrope, and grey and white, trimmed with lace and velvet ribbon 15.00

No. 4520. FRENCH PRINTED ORGANDIE DRESS, colors red, pink, heliotrope, navy, light blue, grey, and black and white, trimmed with lace and velvet ribbon 16.50

No. 4521. SATIN-STRIPED FRENCH PRINTED ORGANDIE DRESS, colors pink, blue, heliotrope, and grey, trimmed with lace and velvet ribbon 19.00

Other style dresses, in white lawn, $2.50, 3.50, 5.00, 7.50 each.

No need to be bothered with dressmakers' worries when you can get dresses like these, ready-made.

Ladies' Ready-Made Dresses.

Sizes in Ladies' Ready-Made Dresses are 32 to 42 inches bust measure; skirt lengths, 39 to 43 inches, and waistbands of skirts 22 to 29 inches. Sizes not included in our regular stock can be supplied at 25 per cent. extra, and are not returnable. When ordering send measurements according to form on page 20.

No. 4500. READY-MADE DRESS, of cheviot serge, colors black and navy, finished with black or white silk front, guipure lace, velvet ribbon and small gilt buttons **12.00**

No. 4501. DRESS, of black and navy cheviot serge, Paquin sleeve, has front and sleeves of tucked black taffeta silk, trimmed with silk velvet, lace insertion and gilt braid **15.00**

No. 4503. READY-MADE DRESS, of English cheviot serge, colors black and navy, trimming of colored taffeta silk, with gilt buttons and braid **13.50**

No. 4504. HOMESPUN DRESS, colors blue and grey, trimmed with silk and lace, with satin bands and gilt buttons **15.00**

No. 4505. READY-MADE DRESS, of nun's veiling, colors black, navy, brown and grey, has white silk and lace trimming, drop skirt made over cambric **16.50**

No. 4506. READY-MADE DRESS, of nun's veiling, colors black, navy, brown and grey, waist trimmed with silk and lace, skirt trimmed with self material **18.50**

No. 4507. READY-MADE DRESS, of nun's veiling, colors black, navy, brown and grey, has lace yoke and trimming of satin bands **20.00**

No. 4508. READY-MADE DRESS, of fine quality English cheviot serge, colors black and navy, has white satin front trimmed with gold braid, waist trimmed with black and gilt braid **20.00**

Order regular sizes of ladies' and children's outer garments. Special sizes cost 25 per cent. extra.

LADIES' DRESS SKIRTS.

Ladies' Dress Skirts are 22 to 29 inches waistband, and 39 to 43 inches long in front. Sizes not included in our regular stock cost 25 per cent. extra, and are not returnable. All Skirts, unless otherwise stated, are lined with percaline and bound with good quality velveteen. Any Skirt illustrated can be supplied with taffeta silk lining, at a cost of $5.00 extra.

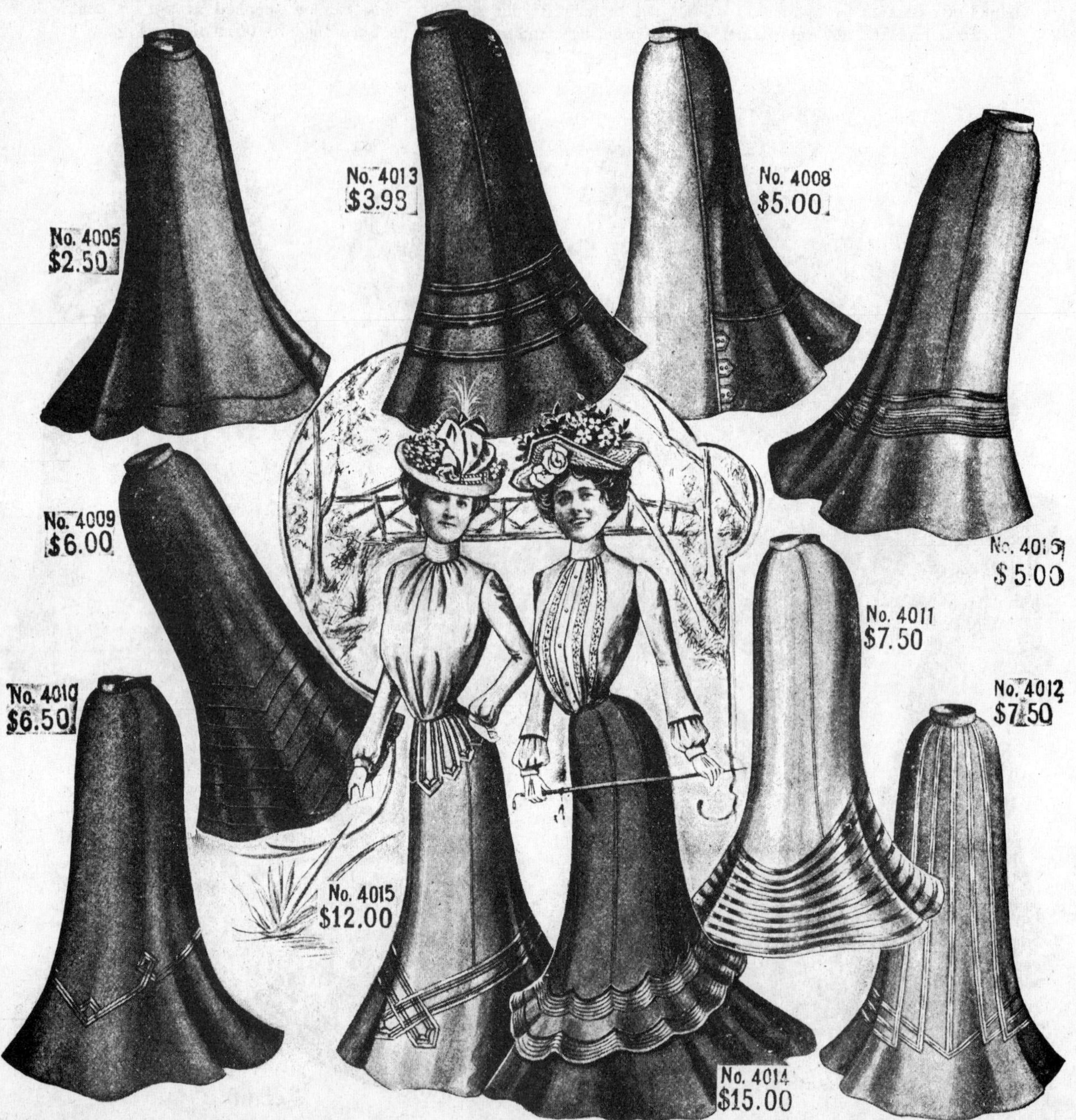

No. 4005. DRESS SKIRT, OF ENGLISH CHEVIOT SERGE, heavy weight, unlined, colors black, navy, fawn, Oxford grey, medium grey, blue, brown, and green mixtures....2.50

No. 4006. DRESS SKIRT, OF ALL-WOOL ENGLISH COATING SERGE, colors black and navy, style as No. 4005 ....3.50

No. 4007. DRESS SKIRT, OF HOMESPUN CHEVIOT, unlined, colors light grey, medium grey, Oxford grey, fawn, brown, blue and black, same style as No. 4005 ....3.98

No. 4013. DRESS SKIRT, MADE OF ENGLISH CHEVIOT HOMESPUN, colors black, navy, brown, green, and medium grey, trimmed with triple-stitched bands of satin, flounce only, lined and interlined 3.98

No. 4008. DRESS SKIRT, of navy, medium and Oxford grey camel's hair cloth, and black pebble serge, new panel front, with flounce. 5.00

No. 4016. DRESS SKIRT, made of black and navy cheviot serge, trimmed with stitched bands of taffeta silk 5.00

No. 4009. CHEVIOT SERGE DRESS SKIRT, in black and navy, five-gore, with corded flounce..6.00

No. 4010. DRESS SKIRT, OF FINE ALL-WOOL ENGLISH CHEVIOT SERGE, black only, made with flounce and trimmed with stitched taffeta silk........ ....6.50

No. 4011. DRESS SKIRT, of black and navy, fine all-wool cheviot serge, trimmed with narrow double-stitched satin bands.......7.50

No. 4012. DRESS SKIRT, MADE OF ROCKWOOD CHEVIOT HOMESPUN, in light, medium, and dark grey, and in black and navy cheviot serge, trimmed with triple-stitched taffeta silk bands................7.50

No. 4015. BLACK BROADCLOTH DRESS SKIRT, trimmed with narrow satin bands and black silk braid 12.00

No. 4014. HIGH-GRADE BLACK BROADCLOTH DRESS SKIRT, flounce is trimmed with stitched taffeta silk, with fancy black silk braid 15.00

Order regular stock sizes; they are made to fit. Special sizes cost 25 per cent. extra.

Ladies' Dress, Walking and Bicycle Skirts.

Walking Skirts are made in lengths 36 to 40 inches, waistbands 22 to 29 inches. Bicycle Skirts, in lengths 35 to 39 inches, waistbands 22 to 29 inches, and Dress Skirts and Wash Skirts, in lengths 39 to 43 inches, waistbands 22 to 29 inches. Sizes not included in our regular stock cost 25 per cent. extra, and are not returnable.

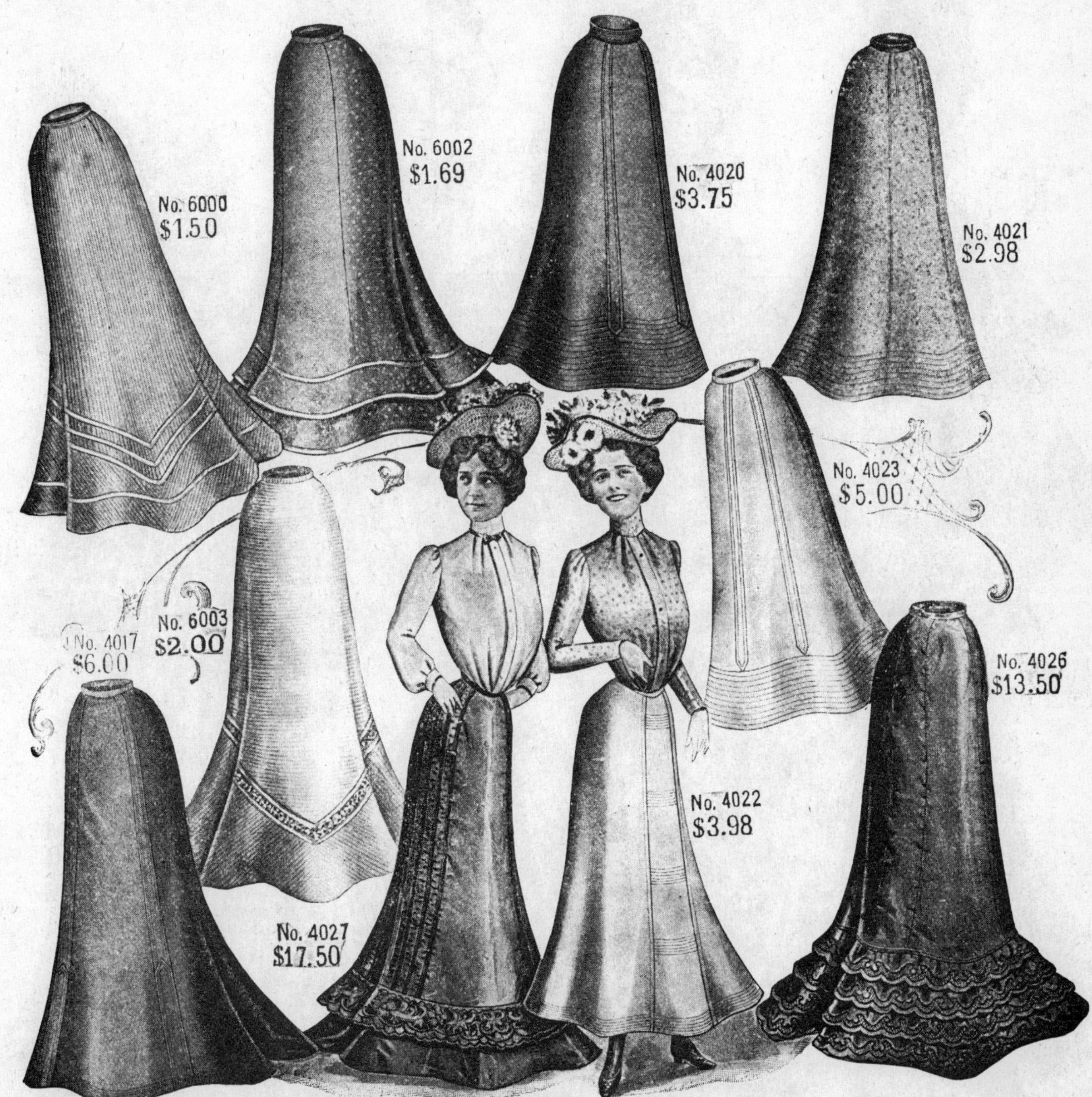

No. 4021. WALKING SKIRT, made of heavy cheviot homespun, unlined, colors black, navy, grey, Oxford grey, brown and green 2.98

No. 4018. BICYCLE SKIRT, same material, style and colors as No. 4021 .... 3.50

No. 4019. BICYCLE SKIRT, OF CHECK-BACK TWEEDS, fawn, brown, blue, light and dark grey mixture, similar style to No. 4021 .... 5.00

No. 4020. WALKING SKIRT, with stitched flounce, made of heavy homespun cheviots, unlined, colors black, navy, brown, green, grey and Oxford 3.75

No. 4024. WALKING SKIRT, OF HEAVY BLACK PEBBLE SERGE, unlined, style as No. 4020 .... 6.50

No. 4022. WALKING SKIRT, OF CAMEL'S HAIR CHEVIOT, unlined, shades grey, Oxford grey and navy 3.98

No. 4023. WALKING SKIRT, OF HEAVY WEIGHT CHECK-BACK TWEEDS, shades light, medium and dark grey, fawn and brown 5.00

No. 6000. WASH SKIRT, of plain black and navy duck, and polka dot duck, in navy and white, and black and white, trimmed with double-stitched bands 1.50

No. 6001. WASH SKIRT, same style as No. 6000, in white pique 2.00

No. 6002. WASH SKIRT, made of polka dot duck, and plain black and navy duck, trimmed with double-stitched straps of duck 1.69

No. 6003. WHITE PIQUE WASH SKIRT, trimmed with white embroidery insertion 2.00

Other styles in white pique, trimmed with insertion, each .... 2.00 to 5.00

No. 4017. DRESS SKIRT, OF COVERT CLOTH, colors fawn, castor, brown, royal, navy and black, unlined, finished with wide stitched straps of same material 6.00

No. 4026. BLACK TAFFETA SILK SKIRT, flounce trimmed with applique embroidery 13.50

No. 4027. FINELY-TUCKED TAFFETA SILK SKIRT, with handsome silk soutache embroidered flounce 17.50

It is always well when ordering to mention a second choice.

LADIES' CAPES.

Sizes 32 to 42 inches bust measure.

No 2106. BLACK SATIN BROCADED CAPE, lined mercerette, length 19 inches... 3.98

No. 2105. BLACK BROCADED SATIN CAPE, same style as No 2106. plainer trimmings, length 18 inches 3.50

No. 2107. BLACK DIAGONAL CLOTH CAPE, length 25 inches 3.98

No. 2109. BLACK CAPE, made of French brocaded cloth, lined mercerette, trimmed with lace and satin ribbon, length 23 inches .. 5.00

No. 2126. BLACK SILK OTTOMAN CAPE, lined mercerette, similar style to No. 2109, length 26 inches......................... 6.50

No. 2113. BLACK CAPE, of jetted braid and lace, made over black silk lining, length 22 inches..................................... 8.00

No. 2110. BLACK CAPE, similar style and materials to No. 2113, length 22 inches 6.50

No. 2114. BLACK BROCADED SILK CAPE, lined India silk, trimmed with lace and satin ribbon, length 27 inches 8.00

No. 2112. BLACK DIAGONAL CLOTH CAPE, unlined, similar style and trimmings to No. 2114, length 27 inches 6.00

No. 2128. BLACK SILK OTTOMAN CAPE, lined India silk, trimmed lace, jet, and satin ribbon, length 27 inches.............. 10.00

No. 2129. BLACK BROCADED SILK CAPE, lined India silk, trimmed with lace and silk ruching, length 26 inches............... 12.00

No. 3400. CHEVIOT CAPE, in black and navy, l'Aiglon collar, length 33 inches........... 3.50

No. 3401. CAPE, same style as No. 3400, in plain broadcloth, colors black, navy, fawn and castor, length 33 inches.................... 6.50

We cannot furnish samples of materials used in Capes illustrated.

SILK WAISTS.

Sizes in Silk Waists are 32 to 42 inches bust measure.

Waists Nos. 5000, 5004, 5007 and 5009 are made in black only, all other numbers are made in black, navy, royal, sky, turquoise, cardinal, cerise, grey, white, pink, old rose, and heliotrope.

No. 5000. TAFFETA SILK WAIST, in black only, front, back, and sleeves are tucked, lined with percaline.......................... 2.98

No. 5004. BLACK TAFFETA SILK WAIST, front, back, and sleeves finished with tucking and fancy hemstitching, Paquin sleeves, ... 3.50

No. 5001. TAFFETA SILK WAIST, in black and colors, has tucked vest, front, back, and sleeves are finished with hemstitching and tucks 5.00

No. 5005. TAFFETA SILK WAIST, in black and colors, front, back, and sleeves finished with new box-plait tucking 5.00

No. 5008. BLACK AND COLORED TAFFETA SILK WAIST, front and back with new box-plaits, hemstitched in black or white.. 5.00

No. 5003. ELEGANT TAFFETA SILK WAIST, in black and colors, elaborately finished with box-plait hemstitching and tucks, front and cuffs trimmed with small buttons, has Paquin sleeves 6.00

No. 5009. BLACK DUCHESSE SATIN WAIST, front, back, and sleeves finished with hemstitching and tucks, has Paquin sleeves, made similar style to No. 5003 50

No. 5002. WAIST made of allover hemstitched taffeta silk, in black and colors, has Paquin sleeves 6.50

No. 5006. FANCY SILK WAIST, made in black and colored taffeta silk, with white silk in yoke and on collar, front, back and sleeves tucked 6.50

No 5007. HEAVY BLACK TAFFETA SILK WAIST, entire garment finished with air cording, has Paquin sleeves 7.50

This page of Silk Waists represents the best values we ever offered. Every garment a perfect model.

LADIES' COLORED SHIRT WAISTS.

Sizes 32 to 42 inches bust measure.

No. 7600. PRINTED PERCALE SHIRT WAIST, assorted colors 50c

No. 7601. PRINTED PERCALE SHIRT WAIST, same style as No. 7600, better quality, stylish patterns..........................75c

No. 7602. HIGHEST GRADE PERCALE SHIRT WAIST, style as No. 7600, assorted stylish patterns, soft buttoned cuff 98c

No. 7603. WOVEN STRIPED MADRAS SHIRT WAIST, assorted colors, same style as No. 7600......... ....98c

No. 7604. SHIRT WAIST, made of Anderson's plain chambray, colors blue, pink, helio and red, style as No. 7600........................98c

No. 7605. SHIRT WAIST, made of plain zephyr, with striped zephyr front, colors blue, pink, red and helio 1.25

No. 7606. SHIRT WAIST, made of Anderson's Scotch zephyrs, colors pink, helio, ox-blood, blue and black 1.25

No. 7607. SHIRT WAIST, made of Anderson's striped Madras, in colors black, ox-blood, helio and blue, new French stock collar 1.69

No. 7608. SHIRT WAIST, made of fancy weave striped Madras, colors blue, pink, helio, ox-blood, and black and white, has new French stock collar, and is finished front and back with tucks 1.98

No. 7609. SHIRT WAIST, of Anderson's organdie Madras, colors blue, pink, ox-blood and helio, trimmed with fine Swiss embroidery 1.98

No. 7610. SHIRT WAIST, made of Anderson's Madras, in plain colors, pink, blue, helio, ox blood, tan and green, made with Swiss insertion front and back.......................2.50

No. 7611. SHIRT WAIST, made of Anderson's organdie Madras, plain colors of blue, pink, ox-blood and helio, front, back and sleeves finished with hemstitching and box-plait tucking.................. ....2.75

No. 7612. NEW STRAIGHT FRONT SHIRT WAIST, made of stylish organdie zephyrs, colors blue, pink, ox-blood, helio and black and white 2.75

No. 7627. BLACK SATEEN WAIST, tucked back and front.................................98c

No. 7628. WAIST, same style as No. 7627, with tucked sleeves, made of fine French cashmere, colors black, navy, heliotrope, cardinal, garnet and plum 1.98

We cannot furnish samples of materials in shirt waists. You run no risk. We refund your money if you are not satisfied.

LADIES' WHITE SHIRT WAISTS.

Sizes 32 to 42 inches bust measure.

No. 7625. WHITE LAWN WAIST, tucked back 75c

No. 7614. WHITE LAWN WAIST, new box-plait tucking 89c

No. 7615. WHITE LAWN WAIST, front and cuffs finished with hemstitched tucking, 1.00

No. 7626. WHITE LAWN WAIST, finished with tucks and embroidery insertion 1.25

No. 7616. WHITE LAWN WAIST, made with new box-plait tucks and Swiss insertion 1.25

No. 7617. WHITE LAWN WAIST, similar style to No. 7616, finished with hemstitched box-plaits and Swiss insertion 1.50

No. 7619. WHITE LAWN WAIST, made with box-plait tucking and valenciennes insertion 1.69

No. 7618. WHITE LAWN WAIST, finished with fine tucking and Swiss insertion 1.69

No. 7624. SHEER WHITE LAWN WAIST, similar style to No. 7619, with tucks and insertion front and back 2.39

No. 7621. SHEER WHITE LAWN WAIST, similar style to No. 7619, with four rows of insertion in front 2.50

No. 7620. WHITE LAWN WAIST, finished with fine Swiss insertion and box-plait tucking 1.98

No. 7622. SHEER WHITE LAWN WAIST, front and cuffs finished with fine tucking and Swiss insertion 2.50

Customers will find it to their advantage to order regular stock sizes. Special sizes cost 25 per cent. extra.

Ladies' Wrappers and Tea Gowns.

Ladies' Wrappers and Tea Gowns are kept in stock in sizes 32 to 42 inches bust measure, front length 57 inches. Special sizes cost 25 per cent. extra and are not returnable.

No. 505. PRINTED PERCALE WRAPPERS, light and dark assorted colors 89c

No. 508. BLACK SATEEN WRAPPERS, same style as No. 505, trimmed with black glacé braid 1.50

No. 504. PRINTED PERCALE WRAPPERS, assorted dark colors, braid trimmed 1.00

No. 500. PRINTED PERCALE WRAPPERS, assorted light colors only 1.25

No. 509. BLACK SATEEN WRAPPERS, same style as No. 500, with black trimming.....1.75

No. 507. PRINTED PERCALE WRAPPERS, assorted dark colors, braid trimmed......1.39

No. 503. PRINTED PERCALE WRAPPERS, assorted colors, braid trimmed 1.50

No. 510. MERCERIZED BLACK SATEEN WRAPPERS, same style as No. 503, trimmed with black satin ribbon 2.25

No. 501. PRINTED PERCALE WRAPPERS, assorted colors, trimmed with braid and cambric insertion 1.69

No. 506. HIGH-GRADE PRINTED PERCALE WRAPPERS, assorted light and dark colors, braid trimmed 2.00

No. 511. FRENCH CASHMERE TEA GOWN, colors black, navy, heliotrope, cardinal, garnet, and plum, lined with percaline, tucked yoke and collar, trimmed with insertion and satin ribbon, back made with watteau plait from yoke 6.95

Our Wrappers have ample width, proper fulness and are sensible styles.

LADIES' PETTICOATS.

Petticoats are kept in stock in lengths 39 to 42 inches, excepting Nos. 2501 and 2502, which are 39 inches long only.

No. 2501. HEAVY PRINTED PERCALE WASH SKIRT, colors blue, pink, helio, navy, and black and white 69c

No. 2502. HEAVY PRINTED PERCALE WASH SKIRT, colors blue, pink, helio, navy, and black and white.................98c

No. 5101. MOREEN PETTICOAT, same style as No. 2502, colors black, cardinal, grey, royal, helio and plum.......................1.50

No. 5102. MOREEN PETTICOAT, colors black, cardinal, grey, royal, helio and plum, trimmed with glacé braid 1.39

No. 5105. MOREEN PETTICOAT, colors black, cardinal, grey, royal, helio and plum, flounce braid trimmed 1.69

No. 5110. MOREEN PETTICOAT, colors black, cardinal, grey, royal, helio and plum, accordion-plaited flounce, with frill............1.69

No. 5107. BLACK MERCERIZED SATEEN PETTICOAT, made with accordion-plaited flounce trimmed with ruching...........1.98

No. 5108. SILK-FINISHED MERCERETTE PETTICOAT, same style as No. 5107, colors black and cardinal.......................2.50

No. 5109. SILK-FINISHED MERCERETTE PETTICOAT, same style as No. 5107, with accordion-plaited flounce of taffeta silk, in black only...............................3.98

No. 5113. BLACK TAFFETA SILK PETTICOAT, style similar to No. 5107, accordion-plaited flounce, with ruching 6.00

No. 5103. MOREEN PETTICOAT, colors black, cardinal, grey, royal, helio and plum, finished with cording 2.00

No. 5104. MOREEN PETTICOAT, colors black cardinal, grey, royal, helio and plum, flounce lined and corded..........................2.50

No. 5106. HEAVY BLACK MOREEN PETTICOAT................................ 3.00

No. 5100. TAFFETA SILK PETTICOAT, with corded flounce, colors black, cardinal, helio, cerise, turquoise and royal blue...........5.00

No. 5111. TAFFETA SILK PETTICOAT, finished with fancy frilling, colors black, cardinal, helio, cerise, turquoise and royal blue....7.50

No. 5112. TAFFETA SILK PETTICOAT, colors black, cardinal, helio, cerise, turquoise and royal blue, accordion-plaited flounce, finished with fancy frilling........................10.00

There is nothing mean or skimped in this lot of Petticoats, they have ample width and proper fulness.

Ladies' Dressing Gowns and Sacques, Misses' Waists, and Bathing Suits.

Ladies' Dressing Sacques are kept in stock in sizes 32 to 42 inches bust measure.
Misses' Waists are kept in stock in sizes 26, 28, 30 and 32 inches bust measure.

No. 605. WHITE LAWN DRESSING SACQUE 75c

No. 606. WHITE LAWN DRESSING SACQUE, trimmed with tucks and embroidery 1.00

No. 607. WHITE LAWN DRESSING SACQUE, with trimming of tucks and valenciennes lace 1.50

No. 608. WHITE LAWN DRESSING SACQUE, trimmed with fine tucks, and valenciennes lace and insertion 2.25

No. 601. EIDERDOWN FLANNEL DRESSING SACQUE, colors cardinal, grey, sky, cream and pink, edges finished with crochet worsted 1.25

No. 602. RIPPLE EIDERDOWN DRESSING SACQUE, same style and color as No. 601, fastened with silk frogs 1.50

No. 603. EIDERDOWN FLANNEL DRESSING ROBE, colors grey, sky, and cardinal, finished with worsted girdle and silk frog fasteners, collar and cuffs bound with satin ribbon, sizes 32 to 42 inches bust, front length 57 inches 4.98

No. 604. RIPPLE EIDERDOWN DRESSING ROBE, same style and colors as No. 603, collar, cuffs and front bound with satin ribbon, sizes 32 to 42 inches bust, front length 57 inches . 6.50

No. 700. MISSES' PERCALE SHIRT WAIST, in pinks, blues, and black and white 50c

No. 701. MISSES' SHIRT WAIST, same style and colors as No. 700, in finer percale 75c

No. 702. MISSES' SHIRT WAIST, of woven striped Madras and plain pink and blue chambray, same style as No. 700 .... 98c

No. 703. MISSES' LAWN WAIST, colors white, pink, sky, red, and navy, tucked and trimmed with Swiss insertion 98c

No. 704. MISSES' SHIRT WAIST, made of pink, blue, and red chambray, with white trimming 1.25

No. 801. BATHING SUIT, of black brilliantine, trimmed with braid 3.50

Other styles in black brilliantine .. 2.50 and 4.00

It is only by producing garments in large quantities that we are able to quote these prices.

Misses' Jackets and Suits

Schedule of Sizes for Misses' Jackets and Suits:

Age	14 years.	16 years.	18 years.
Bust measure	30 inches	32 inches	34 inches.
Length of skirt in front	35 and 36 inches	37 and 38 inches	38 and 39 inches.
Waist-band of skirt	22 to 25 inches	22 to 25 inches	22 to 25 inches.

When ordering Misses' Jackets, state age and bust measure.
When ordering Misses' Suits, state age, bust measure, waist measure and front length of skirt.

No. 6178. MISSES' SUIT, made of English **homespun cheviot, colors black, navy, fawn, brown, green, grey and Oxford grey; coat is lined** with mercerized Italian and trimmed **with** gilt buttons, skirt unlined **6.98**

No. 6179. MISSES' SUIT, made of camel's **hair cheviot,** colors light and dark navy, light **grey and** Oxford grey, imitation collar of **velvet,** trimmed with braid and gilt buttons, **panel** skirt lined with percaline, coat lined **with** mercerized sateen **9.50**

No. 6177. MISSES' SUITS, made of fine quality **covert** coatings, colors light and dark fawn, **brown,** navy, Oxford grey, and black, trimmed with gilt buttons, coat is lined with mercerized Italian, skirt is lined with percaline **11.50**

No. 6175. MISSES' SUIT, made of Rockwood homespuns, pure all-wool material, colors light, medium and dark grey, and brown, also in black and navy all-wool cheviot serges, collar and revers of jacket are faced with satin and embroidered with braid, jacket is lined with taffeta silk, and skirt lined with percaline **13.50**

No. 6176. MISSES' SUITS, made of all-wool English cheviot serge, in black and navy, trimmed with stitched black satin and gilt embroidery, jacket is lined with satin and skirt lined with percaline............... **15.00**

No. 6275. MISSES' CHEVIOT SERGE JACKET, colors black, navy, light grey, Oxford grey, brown, and green mixtures **2.98**

No. 6277. MISSES' COAT, same style as No 6275, made of English covert coating, colors light and dark fawn, navy and black **5.00**

No. 6278. MISSES' BOX COAT, made of high-grade imported covert cloth, colors black, light fawn, dark fawn, brown, royal, and navy, lined with mercerized Italian **6.50**

No. 6276. MISSES' FINE BOX CLOTH COAT, colors light and dark fawn, castor, brown, navy, and black, lined with mercerized Italian, trimmed with small pearl buttons......... **7.50**

Children's Reefers, Coats, and Misses' Skirts

When ordering Children's Reefers, state age.

Misses' Skirts are kept in stock in lengths 26, 28, 30, 32, 34, 36 and 38 inches, waistbands 21 to 25 inches. Sizes not included in our regular stock cost 25 per cent extra, and are not returnable.

No. 6800. NAVY BLUE CLOTH REEFER, trimmed with fancy braid, sizes 2 to 12 years 1.25

No. 6801. NAVY BLUE SERGE REEFER, trimmed with fancy braid, sizes 2 to 12 years 1.69

No. 6802. NAVY BLUE SERGE REEFER, trimmed with fancy braid, sizes 2 to 12 years 2.25

No. 6803. REEFER, made of camel's hair cheviot, colors blue and grey, sizes 2 to 12 years 2.50

No. 6804. REEFER, made of camel's hair cheviot, colors blue and grey, trimmed with fancy braid, sizes 4 to 12 years 3.50

No. 6805. CLOTH REEFER, colors royal, red and fawn, trimmed with fancy braid and contrasting color cloth, sizes 2 to 12 years, 3.50

No. 6807. CHILD'S AUTOMOBILE COAT, made of fawn covert cloth, lined with silk serge, sizes 8, 10 and 12 years 6.98

No. 6808. CHILD'S AUTOMOBILE COAT, made of fawn boxcloth, unlined, same style as 6807, sizes 8, 10 and 12 years 5.00

No. 6806. CHILDS' AUTOMOBILE COAT, made of fawn boxcloth, trimmed with gilt braid and satin straps, lined with silk-finished mercerette, sizes 8, 10 and 12 years 7.50

No. 6076. MISSES' SKIRT, unlined, made of English homespun cheviot, colors black, navy, fawn, brown, green and grey 2.50

No. 6075. MISSES' SKIRT, made of heavy all-wool cheviot serge, in black and navy, same style as No. 6076, unlined 3.50

No. 6077. MISSES' SKIRT, unlined, made of strictly all-wool Rockwood homespun, colors light grey, dark grey, fawn, brown, and green, front trimmed with gilt buttons 3.50

With few exceptions, all garments shown in this Catalogue are produced in our own workrooms, which are the largest, cleanest and best in Canada.

Children's White Dresses, Infants' Cloaks, Etc.

When ordering Children's Dresses, state age.

No. 7502. WHITE NAINSOOK DRESS, yoke of valenciennes and cambric insertion, sizes ½, 1, 2 and 3 years **75c**

No. 7501. WHITE NAINSOOK DRESS, similar style to No. 7502, with two rows of insertion in yoke, sizes ½, 1, 2 and 3 years **50c**

No. 7503. WHITE NAINSOOK DRESS, yoke finished with hemstitching, sizes ½, 1, 2 and 3 years **1.00**

No. 7504. WHITE NAINSOOK DRESS, yoke, sleeves and frills of tucking and hemstitching, sizes ½, 1, 2 and 3 years **1.25**

No. 7506. WHITE NAINSOOK DRESS, same style as No. 7504, finished with Swiss embroidery and insertion, sizes ½, 1, 2 and 3 years.. **1.69**

No. 7505. WHITE NAINSOOK DRESS, trimmed with hemstitching and Swiss insertion, sizes ½, 1, 2 and 3 years **1.50**

No. 7507. WHITE LAWN DRESS, yoke of fancy insertion and fine tucks, with dainty Swiss embroidery trimming, sizes 2, 3 and 4 years **2.00**

No. 7509. WHITE NAINSOOK DRESS, trimmed with Swiss embroidery and insertion, and valenciennes insertion, with fine tucks, sizes ½, 1, 2, 3 and 4 years **2.50**

No. 7511. WHITE NAINSOOK DRESS, frills of dainty Swiss embroidery, yoke of Swiss insertion, with fine tucks, sizes ½, 1, 2 and 3 years **3.00**

No. 7518. GIMP WAIST, of white lawn, sizes 2, 4, 6, 8 and 10 years **1.50**
Similar styles at 59c, 89c, $1.25 and 1.39.

No. 7536. CREAM CASHMERE CLOAK, embroidered with silk **3.00**

Similar styles in cream cashmere, $1.50, 1.69 and 3.98.

Similar styles in cream Bedford cord, $1.25, $1.98 and 2.50.

No. 7538. CHILD'S SHORT COAT, of cream Bedford cord, braid trimmed, back length 22 and 24 inches **1.25**

No. 7539. CHILD'S SHORT COAT, of cream Bedford cord, similar style to No. 7538, trimmed with silk braid and satin ribbon, back length 22 and 24 inches **2.75**

No. 7540. CHILD'S SHORT COAT, of cream Bedford cord, trimmed with satin ribbon, back length 22 and 24 inches **3.98**

 It is always desirable in ordering to mention a second choice, in case we are out of first.

CHILDREN'S DRESSES.

When ordering Children's Dresses, state age.

No. 7519. GINGHAM DRESS, pink, sky, and navy, lace trimmed, sizes 2, 3, 4 and 5 years, ... 59c

No. 7520. GINGHAM DRESS, pink, sky, and navy, trimmed with edging of hemstitched lawn, sizes 2, 3, 4 and 5 years 75c

No. 7523. DRESS, similar style to No. 7520, made of fine quality pink and blue gingham, trimmed with fine tucks and hemstitched lawn, sizes 2, 3, 4 and 5 years 1.25

No. 7522. GINGHAM DRESS, pink, sky, and navy, tucked yoke, sizes 2, 3, 4 and 5 years, ... 98c

No. 7524. DRESS made of plain chambray, colors pink, blue, and red, tucked yoke, with fancy braid trimming, sizes 2, 3, 4 and 5 years, ... 1.39

No. 7526. DRESS, made of plain chambray. colors pink, blue, and red, trimmed with white pique and fancy braid, sizes 2, 3, 4 and 5 years 1.75

No. 7527. LONG-WAISTED DRESS, of fine gingham, colors pink, blue, navy, and red, trimmed with embroidery insertion and elaborate tucking, sizes 2, 3, 4 and 5 years, ... 1.98

No. 7528. GINGHAM DRESS, in pink and blue, trimmed with lace, sizes 6, 8, 10, 12 and 14 years 1.25

No. 7529. GINGHAM DRESS, in pink, navy and light blue, trimmed with fancy braid, sizes 6, 8, 10, 12 and 14 years 1.50

No. 7530. DRESS made of gingham and chambray combination, colors pink, sky, and navy, trimmed with fancy braid, sizes 6, 8, 10, 12 and 14 years 2.00

No. 4600. SAILOR SUIT, made of navy blue all-wool serge, lined throughout, trimmed with soutache braid, kilted skirt, sizes 20, 22, 24 and 26 inches long 3.25

No. 4601. DRESS, made of navy blue all-wool serge, lined throughout, trimmed with straps of silk, sizes 26, 28, 30, 33 and 36 inches long, ... 3.50

Our prices are always the lowest at which "Honest Goods" can be made.

Women's and Children's Waterproof Cloaks.

Women's sizes, 54 to 60 inches long. Children's sizes, 33 to 51 inches long. Measure downwards from back of neck.

No. 2405. WOMEN'S RUBBER-LINED WATERPROOF CLOAK, in fawn, navy, and black paramatta $3.00

No. 2408. WOMEN'S RUBBER-LINED WATERPROOF CLOAK, in navy and black cotton serge, detachable cape...... $3.50

No. 2409. WOMEN'S RUBBER-LINED WATERPROOF CLOAK of cashmere paramatta, black and navy, same style as No. 2408, ... $5.00

No. 2406. WOMEN'S PARAMATTA RUBBER-LINED WATERPROOF CLOAK, colors black, navy, and fawn, velvet collar $4.00

No. 2403. WOMEN'S CASHMERE PARAMATTA WATERPROOF CLOAK, rubber-lined, colors fawn, black and navy, finished with fancy stitching and velvet collar... $7.50

No. 2404. WOMEN'S PARAMATTA WATERPROOF CLOAK, rubber-lined, same style as No. 2403, colors fawn, black and navy.... $5.00

No. 2411. WOMEN'S WATERPROOF CLOAK, made of black and navy cravenette cloth, same style as No. 2403 .... $5.50

No. 2412. WOMEN'S WATERPROOF CLOAK, same style as No. 2403, in Ripley covert cloth, fawn, grey and bronze $6.98

No. 2400. WOMEN'S RUBBER-LINED WATERPROOF CLOAK, made of fawn, black, and navy heavy melton cloth, similar style to No. 2403, with coat sleeves $10.00

No. 2414. LADIES' NEWMARKET COAT, similar style to No. 2403, made of extra heavy weight cravenette waterproof cloth, colors fawn and grey $11.00

No. 2407. WOMEN'S RUBBER-LINED WATERPROOF CLOAK of cashmere paramatta, made with sleeves and detachable cape, with velvet collar, colors black and navy $8.00

No. 2413. Same style as No. 2407, made of black and navy cravenette waterproof cloth, ... $10.00

No. 2410. CHILDREN'S RUBBER-LINED WATERPROOF CLOAK, in fawn and navy paramatta, velvet collar $2.50

"Trade follows the price and the lowest price makes the market."

Cloth Department, Shawls, Measurement Form, Etc.

Men's and Boys' Suitings.

27-inch Halifax tweed, in greys, browns and fawns, 25c, 30c yd.

27-inch Halifax tweed, in fancy mixtures, 30c yd.

27-inch fancy tweed suitings, variety of shades, 30c, 35c, 40c, 50c, 60c yd.

27-inch striped panting tweeds, 35c, 50c, 60c yd.

27-inch all-wool navy blue serge, 25c, 30c, 35c yd.

28-inch English worsted trousering, small neat patterns, $1.00, 1.25 yd.

54-inch English all-wool serge, navy and black, 60c, 75c, $1.00, 1.25, 1.50, 2.00 yd.

56-inch English Clay worsted, black and navy, $1.50, 2.00, 2.50 yd.

56-inch English Clay worsted, black only, fine quality, $3.00 yd.

56-inch English black Venetian worsted, for best wear, $1.50, 2.00, 3.00 yd.

56-inch English Clay worsted, in dark, medium and light grey, $1.50, 2.00, 2.50 yd.

56-inch English worsted suitings, fancy patterns, leading shades, $2.00, 2.50 yd.

Mantle Cloths.

54-inch English cheviot homespuns, colors light and dark grey, navy, black, green, royal, and brown, green and blue mixtures, 60c yd.

54-inch English coating serge, all-wool, light-weight, colors black and navy, 60c yd.

50-inch German homespun cheviots, shades brown, green, royal, navy and Oxford grey, 75c yd.

50-inch all-wool German cheviots, colors royal, fawn and red, 75c yd.

54-inch Waterloo homespun cheviots, shades light, medium and dark grey, black, navy fawn and brown, 80c yd.

54-inch English cheviot serge, light weight, colors black and navy, 80c yd.

50-inch German camels' hair homespun, colors medium and dark Oxford grey, and navy blue 85c yd.

50-inch German box cloth, shades black, light and dark fawn, castor, royal, navy, red, brown and green, $1.25 yd.

54-inch check-back cloths, for walking skirts and bicycle skirts, colors light and dark grey, fawn and brown, $1.35 yd.

50-inch German covert coating, prima quality, colors light and dark fawn, castor, royal, navy, Oxford grey and black, $1.40 yd.

52-inch satin-finished Venetian twill cloth, colors light and dark fawn, castor and black, $2.00 yd.

Samples of any of these cloths can be had for the asking.

Infants' Sacques.

Nos. 1, 2, 3, 4. Infants' hand-made zephyr wool sacques, in all white, and white with pink or blue. No. 1, 50c; No. 2, 65c; No. 3, 75c; No. 4, with silk edging, $1.00.

Nos. 5, 6. Infants' hand-made sacques, new empire style, colors all white, white with pink and white with blue trimming, No. 5, 75c; No. 6, $1.00.

Shawls.

Honeycomb shawls, colors white, grey, black, cardinal, pink and sky, 50c, 75c, $1.00, 1.25, 1.50 each.

Extra fine honeycomb shawls, white only, $2.00, 2.50 each.

Waterproof Cloth.

56-inch English covert coatings, specially adapted for men s light-weight overcoats and suits; cloth is waterproofed by the "Cravenette process," $2.50 yd.

60-inch Cravenette waterproof cloth, light-weight all-wool quality, in black and navy, $1.25 yd.

Measurement Diagram for Suits, Jackets and Skirts.

FRONT AND BACK.—1. All around neck, over dress collar, at bottom of collar.

1 to 2. From bottom of collar to waist line, not too long.

3. Bust measure, all around body, under arms, not too tight. (Take your bust measure well up under the arms around largest part of bust.)

3 to 4. Measurement across bust from armhole to armhole at largest part of bust.

5 to 6. Length of sleeves, inside seam.

7 to 8. Under arm to waist line, not too long. (This measurement should be taken along the line directly underneath the arm.)

8. Size of waist all around.

9 to 10. Length of back from bottom of collar to waist line, not too long.

11 to 12. Across back.

13. Hip measure, around body six inches below waist, not too tight.

Skirt.

14 to 15. Length in front from bottom of skirt belt to desired length.

16 to 17. Length on side from bottom of skirt belt to desired length.

18 to 19. Length in back from bottom of skirt belt to desired length.

(Be careful to have these measurements accurate when ordering suits or skirts.)

Take measurements carefully, and write them down plainly. Be sure to use an accurate tape measure. Do not make any allowance for seams.

When taking measurements, tie a cord around your waist in order that you may see exactly where your waist line is.

Pay particular attention to measurement 9 to 10, which gives the length of back from bottom of collar band to the waist line.

In taking your bust measure, have tape placed around your bust well up under the arms, around largest part of the bust. Do not take the bust measure too tight.

Schedule of Sizes for Ladies' Dresses and Suits.

BUST MEASURE...	32	32	32	32	34	34	34	34	36	36	36	36	38	38	38	38	40	40	40	40	42	42	42	42	JACKET.
LENGTH FRONT...	40	41	42	43	40	41	42	43	40	41	42	43	40	41	42	43	40	41	42	43	40	41	42	43	SKIRT.
WAIST MEASURE.	22	23	22	23	23	24	23	24	24	25	24	25	25	25	26	26	27	27	28	28	28	28	29	29	SKIRT.

Orders for sizes not included in our regular stock require about 5 days to make.

Selected Flower and Vegetable Seeds

These Seeds are put up especially for us by one of the best known Canadian Seed houses, and the satisfaction expressed by our customers in all parts of the country assures us that they are of the highest standard for purity and freshness.

ALL PACKET SEEDS POSTPAID. *NOTE.—Seed orders should reach us before* **May 15th,** *as we do not keep up stock after that date.*

General List of Flower Seeds 12 Packets for 20 Cts.

YOUR SELECTION FROM THE FOLLOWING VARIETIES:

Antirrhinum or Snapdragon, mixed.
Aster, Snowball, white.
" Fireball, crimson.
" Excelsior, mixture.
Bachelor's button.
Balloon vine.
Balsam, Improved Camelia flowered, mixed.
Canary vine.
Canna crozys, mixed.
California poppy.
Candytuft, Snow White.
" mixed.
Carnation, double, mixed.
Climbers, mixed.
Cypress vine.
Chrysanthemums, mixed.
Cockscomb, mixed.
Dianthus, Chinese pinks, mixed.
" double daisy, mixed.
Everlastings, mixed.
Forget-me-not, mixed.
Four o'clock.
Heliotrope.
Hollyhock, double, mixed.
Larkspur, tall, mixed.
Lobelia, mixed.
Marigold, Eldorado, mixed.
Morning glory.
Mourning bride.
Mignonette, sweet.
Musk plant.
Nasturtium, tall, mixed.
" dwarf, mixed.
Nicotiana, white.
Pansy, Snow Queen, white.
" Faust, black.
" Giant Trimardeau, mixed.
Petunia, Grandiflora, mixed.
" fringed, mixed.
Phlox, Drummondi, fringed, mixed.
" " giant, mixed.
Poppy, double, mixed.
Portulaca, mixed.
Stocks, Ten Weeks, mixed.
Sweet Alyssum.
Sweet William, double, mixed.
Sweet Peas, California, mixed.
" English, mixed.
Verbena, mammoth, mixed.
Zinnia, double, mixed.
Wild flower garden, mixed.

For 50c. we will send postpaid 30 PACKETS of VEGETABLE and FLOWER SEEDS. Select from this list.

General List of Vegetable Seeds 10 Packets for 20 Cts.

YOUR SELECTION FROM THE FOLLOWING VARIETIES:

Beans, Improved Golden Wax or Butter.
Beans, Earliest, six weeks.
Beets, Early Eclipse, round.
Beets, Dark Red Egyptian.
Beets, Long Smooth Blood.
Cabbage, Early Winningstadt.
Cabbage, all seasons.
Cabbage, Fottler's Imp. Brunswick.
Carrots, Early Scarlet English Horn.
Carrots, Imp. Danvers, half long.
Carrots, Guerande or Ox-heart.
Cauliflower, Snowball.
Celery, White Plume.
Celery, Golden Self Blanching.
Corn, First of All.
Corn, Stowell's Evergreen.
Citron, for preserving.
Cress or Peppergrass, curled.
Cucumber, Chicago Pickle.
Cucumber, Extra Early White Spine.
Cucumber, Imp. Long Green.
Lettuce, Early Curled Simpson.
Lettuce, Drum Head.
Lettuce, Nonpareil Cabbage.
Muskmelon, Extra Early Hackensack.
Onion, large red, Wethersfield.
Onion, Yellow Globe Danvers.
Onion, White Globe.
Onion, Silverskin Pickling
Parsley, double curled.
Parsnip, Hollow Crown.
Peas, First and Best.
Peas, McLean's Little Gem.
Peas, Champion of England.
Pepper, Improved Bull Nose.
Pumpkin, Large Cheese.
Radish, French Breakfast.
Radish, Rosy Gem.
Radish, Long Scarlet, short top.
Salsify, Mammoth Sandwich Island.
Spinach, Long Standing.
Squash, English Vegetable Marrow.
Squash, Hubbard.
Summer Savory.
Sage, broad leaved.
Turnip, Early Snowball.
Turnip, Purple Top White Globe.
Tomatoes, Early Ruby.
Tomatoes, Livingston's Perfection.
Watermelon, Earliest of All.

Special Collection No. 1.

15 Pkts. of Vegetable Seeds for 25c

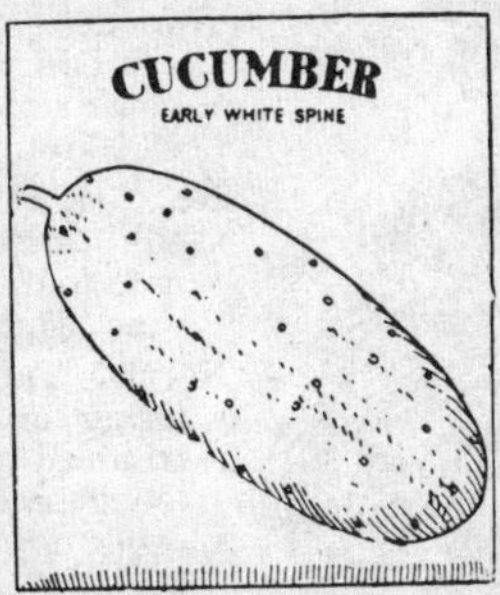

One packet each of the following varieties, postpaid:

Tomatoes, Early Ruby, an excellent early variety.
Pumpkin, Large Cheese, a general favorite.
Cabbage, Early Winningstadt, one of the best.
Onion, Red Wethersfield, the standard red variety.
Cucumber, Early White Spine, fine for slicing.
Lettuce, Early Curled Simpson, one of the best.
Beans, Improved Golden Wax, a bush sort of fine quality.
Spinach, Long Standing, the standard variety.
Parsnips, Hollow Crown, the most successful kind.
Peas, First and Best, very early, dwarf in habit of growth.
Onion, Silverskin, one of the best for pickling.
Carrot, Imperial Danvers, half long, of splendid quality.
Turnip, Early Snowball, a splendid variety.
Beet, Long Smooth Blood, an old favorite.
Watermelon, Earliest of all, unsurpassed in flavor or yield.

SPECIAL COLLECTION NO. 2.

16 Pkts. of Flower Seeds for 25c.

Postpaid.

All Free Blooming Varieties.

Aster, Fireball, crimson.
Nicotiana, white.
California Poppy.
Musk Plant.
Dianthus, Double Daisy, mixed.
Mignonette, Sweet-scented.
Nasturtiums, tall or climbing.
Pansy, Giant Trimardeau, mixed.
Petunia, Fringed, mixed.
Sweet Peas, Royal Gilt Edge, mixed.
Verbena, Mammoth, mixed.
Poppy, double, mixed.
Cypress Vine.
Hollyhocks, double, mixed sorts.
Chrysanthemums, mixed.
Candytuft, white.

STANDARD

LAWN GRASS SEED

One lb. packet, with full directions, "How to Prepare Lawn for Sowing." One pound will sow about 400 square feet of new ground. Price 13c. per packet, or, if to be sent by mail, allow 5c. extra for postage.

RARE SWEET PEAS, NAMED VARIETIES, PUT UP IN OZ. PACKETS.

Per Ounce, 8c., Postpaid.

Three Ounces, "Your Selections," for 20c.

Below we give a list of the best named varieties and finest mixtures, selected from an assortment of over 150 different varieties. These are noted for freedom of bloom, healthy habit of growth and easy culture.

Emily Henderson, a free blooming, strong vigorous variety, pure white.
Countess of Radnor, a beautiful lavender shade tinged with heliotrope, a very choice flower.
Blanche Ferry, large flowers, pink tinted white, a remarkably free blooming variety.
Firefly, bright scarlet, a most brilliant shade and very attractive flower.
Mrs. Chamberlain, white striped crimson, one of the most popular of the new varieties.
Venus, salmon buff shade, a very delicate rare shading.

Mixed varieties Sweet Peas, in 1-oz. and ¼-lb. packets.

English, mixed; this is a charming mixture, including many of the shades and colors found in this popular class of flowers, a selection that is certain to give satisfaction ....
California, mixed; this is selected from the large flowering varieties, and includes over 30 different shades and colors ....

} 1-oz. pkt. either of these mixed varieties ...5c; ¼-lb. ditto..10c Postpaid.

20th Century Trimmed Hats

No. 200. Ladies' Cuba straw dress hats, trimmed chiffon, silk velvet, violets and violet foliage, chiffon facing with velvet folds and violet foliage under brim, $4.25 to $5.50

No. 201. Fancy straw braid turban, brim covered with folds of taffeta silk, trimmed black ribbon, velvet, roses, foliage and buckle, $4.25 to..$5.50

No. 202. Misses' chip or leghorn flop, trimmed, silk ribbon, flowers and foliage, folds of velvet under brim, $3.50 to $4.50

No. 203. Black silk and chiffon toque, with black sequin crown, black flowers and chiffon bow at side, $4.00 to..........................$5.00

No. 204. Stitched silkaline hat, with straw facings, trimmed with silk mechlin net, two ostrich plumes and buckle, flowers on band under brim, $9.00 to $10.50

No. 205. Leghorn flop, trimmed mechlin net overlaid with lace, four ostrich tips, rosette of black ribbon velvet and ornament under brim, $6.00 to $10.00

No. 206. Straw braid dress hat, trimmed taffeta silk, ostrich plumes and buckle, facing of alternate folds of chiffon and velvet, velvet bow on band, $7.25 to..........................$10.00

No. 207. Taffeta silk hat, crown draped, brim and facing of alternate folds of silk and velour, trimmed with large bunch of violets and foliage under brim, $5 50 to.............$6.50

No. 208. Chiffon turban, with flower crown and mount knot of chiffon at side. $4.50 to....$5.50

No. 209. Straw turban, trimmed with folds of taffeta silk and flowers, knot of silk under brim, $3.50 to $4.50

No. 210. Stitched braid hat, with tuscan straw insertion in brim, trimmed with flowers, foliage, chiffon and lace, tucked chiffon facing and large chiffon bows on back band, $5.00 to..$6.00

No. 211. Straw braid toque, trimmed with silk ribbon bow and buckle, flowers and foliage on side band, $5.00 to......................$6.00

No. 212. Straw turban, trimmed with taffeta silk and quill, special.......................$2.19

No. 213. Natural bleach leghorn flop, trimmed with folds of taffeta silk and silk tulle, roses, foliage and buckle, silk bow at back, $4.00 to.. ....$5.50

STATE COLOR WHEN ORDERING. WHEN THIS IS OMITTED WE USUALLY SEND BLACK.

SPECIAL NOTE.

Be sure and state what color you wish to prevail ; and if you desire a touch of any particular shade in the trimmings, state that also.

If possible, send sample of costume the hat is to be worn with.

Your age, complexion and height often help us.

Trimmed Hats

FOR SPRING and SUMMER WEAR.

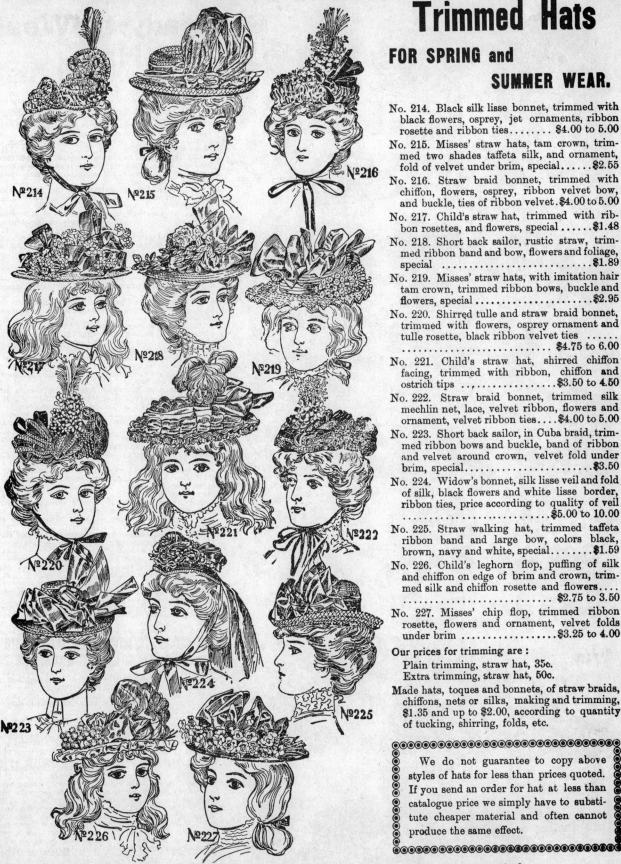

No. 214. Black silk lisse bonnet, trimmed with black flowers, osprey, jet ornaments, ribbon rosette and ribbon ties........ $4.00 to 5.00

No. 215. Misses' straw hats, tam crown, trimmed two shades taffeta silk, and ornament, fold of velvet under brim, special......$2.55

No. 216. Straw braid bonnet, trimmed with chiffon, flowers, osprey, ribbon velvet bow, and buckle, ties of ribbon velvet. $4.00 to 5.00

No. 217. Child's straw hat, trimmed with ribbon rosettes, and flowers, special......$1.48

No. 218. Short back sailor, rustic straw, trimmed ribbon band and bow, flowers and foliage, special $1.89

No. 219. Misses' straw hats, with imitation hair tam crown, trimmed ribbon bows, buckle and flowers, special $2.95

No. 220. Shirred tulle and straw braid bonnet, trimmed with flowers, osprey ornament and tulle rosette, black ribbon velvet ties .... $4.75 to 6.00

No. 221. Child's straw hat, shirred chiffon facing, trimmed with ribbon, chiffon and ostrich tips ....$3.50 to 4.50

No. 222. Straw braid bonnet, trimmed silk mechlin net, lace, velvet ribbon, flowers and ornament, velvet ribbon ties....$4.00 to 5.00

No. 223. Short back sailor, in Cuba braid, trimmed ribbon bows and buckle, band of ribbon and velvet around crown, velvet fold under brim, special.......................$3.50

No. 224. Widow's bonnet, silk lisse veil and fold of silk, black flowers and white lisse border, ribbon ties, price according to quality of veil ....$5.00 to 10.00

No. 225. Straw walking hat, trimmed taffeta ribbon band and large bow, colors black, brown, navy and white, special........$1.59

No. 226. Child's leghorn flop, puffing of silk and chiffon on edge of brim and crown, trimmed silk and chiffon rosette and flowers.... .... $2.75 to 3.50

No. 227. Misses' chip flop, trimmed ribbon rosette, flowers and ornament, velvet folds under brim ....$3.25 to 4.00

Our prices for trimming are :

Plain trimming, straw hat, 35c.
Extra trimming, straw hat, 50c.

Made hats, toques and bonnets, of straw braids, chiffons, nets or silks, making and trimming, $1.35 and up to $2.00, according to quantity of tucking, shirring, folds, etc.

We do not guarantee to copy above styles of hats for less than prices quoted. If you send an order for hat at less than catalogue price we simply have to substitute cheaper material and often cannot produce the same effect.

These cuts are made from the goods and are exactly as represented.

Ready-to-Wear Hats.

No. 228. Henshau, chip braid, trimmed mercerized twill with narrow chip braid on edge, gilt buckle, colors black, navy, castor, pearl, maize and white, trimmed self colors....$1.75
No. 229A. Savoy, fine wool felt fedora, trimmed corded ribbon band and bow, colors black, navy, castor and pearl ...85c
No. 229B. Savoy, ladies' fedora, good quality fur felt, silk ribbon trimmings, colors black, castor and pearl......$1.25
No. 230. Olympia, Milan straw walking hat, trimmed folded band and large knot of taffeta silk, colors black, brown, navy and white, trimmed self colors, except white, which is trimmed black or navy............................$1.45
No. 231. Olympia, fine Milan straw, trimmed corded ribbon band and ornament, colors black, brown and navy....$1.00
No. 232. Mafeking, Japanese straw braid, trimmed mercerized twill in Parisian effects, with narrow straw braid on edge of loops, velvet band, colors black, navy, castor, pearl and white...$1.75
No. 233. Canada, good clear Japanese straw braid, white only, black corded ribbon band and bow, 3-inch crown, 2½-inch brim...50c
No. 234. Eloise, Misses' outing hat, Japanese straw braid, trimmed mercerized satin and gilt ornament, folded band with row white straw braid in centre, colors brown, navy, cardinal, castor, trimmed self colors, and white trimmed navy or cardinal..$1.50
No. 235. Beatrice, misses' hat, chip braid, trimmed mercerized twill, with straw edging, colors white, light blue, maize and castor $2.00
No. 236. Dunbar, Japanese straw braid, trimmed black velvet band and knot, straw quill, in white only $1.25
No. 237. Grandet, chip braid, trimmed mercerized satin and gilt buckle, colors black, white, brown, light navy, maize, castor and pearl, trimmed self colors $1.50
No. 238A. Sagamore, Japanese jumbo braid, 3-inch crown, 2½-inch brim, good clear braid and well made, black corded ribbon band and bow, white only.......................75c
No. 238B. Sagamore, fancy plait Japanese braid, white only, a very clear bleach, black silk ribbon band and bow...$1.00
No. 239. Niagara, extra quality clear split Milan braid, 3-inch crown and 2½-inch brim, double brim, leather sweat and satin linings, in white only, with black or navy silk ribbon band...$2.25
No. 240. Nome, Japanese rough-and-ready braid, trimmed mercerized twill, with straw edging and gilt buckle, colors black or white, trimmed black.........................$1.75
No. 241. Rialto, chip braid, black only, trimmed black and white sateen and gilt buckle...........................$1.50
No. 242. Grandet, chip braid, bow across front and band of same, sateen loop on bow, colors black, light navy, maize, castor, pearl, white..$1.25
No. 243A. Arcade, Japanese straw braid, trimmed mercerized satin and gilt buckle, colors black, light navy, cardinal and castor, trimmed self colors, and white trimmed navy and cardinal $1.75
No. 243B. Arcade, Japanese braid, trimmed mercerized satin, in Persian effect and fancy gilt buckle, colors black, brown, light navy, castor and white...............................$2.25
No. 243C. Landels, same shape as Arcade, lower crown, in rustic straw, colors black or white, trimmed fancy stripe silk knot and gilt buckle, black velvet band $1.00
No. 244A. Child's sailor, Canton straw, row and row effect, colors navy, royal, cardinal and brown, all with white corded ribbon band 45c
No. 244B. Child's sailor, mixed Japanese braid, colors navy, brown, green and cardinal, all with white corded ribbon band 50c
No. 245A. Atlas, Japanese braid, trimmed folded mercerized satin band and gilt buckle on right side, black trimmed black, white trimmed navy or black.....................$1.50
No. 245B. Atlas, fancy plait Japanese braid, in white only, trimmed navy silk band, with white square, gilt buckle on right side $2.00
No. 246. Fielding, fancy chip braid, straw braid loops and gilt buckle, fancy stripe silk band, in black only..........$1.25
No. 247A. Rainbow, Japanese braid, 2¾-inch crown and 2¾-inch brim, black with black band, white with navy or black bands...75c
No. 247B. Rainbow, fine Milan straw, split crown, black with black band, and white with navy, black or white band..$1.25
No. 247C. Rainbow, split Milan straw, double brim, silk ribbon band, black with black band, white with navy, black or white band $1.50
No. 248. L'Aiglon, Japanese braid, trimmed knot of mercerized twill, edged black velvet, straw quill, velvet band and gilt buckle in black, or white trimmed black $1.75
No. 249A. Crescent, rustic straw sailor, corded ribbon band, colors black, brown, navy, self color bands and white with black band, 3-inch crown, 2½-inch brim, special.........29c
No. 249B. Crescent, mottled straw braid, satin ribbon band, colors white mixed with black, navy, cardinal or green. 39c
No. 250. Alhambra, Japanese braid, trimmed mercerized satin fold and knot with gilt buckle, colors black, brown, light navy and castor, trimmed self colors or white trimmed navy, beige or black..........................$1.75

No 228 $1.75 — No 229 .85¢ $1.25 — No 230 $1.45 — No 231 $1.00 — No 232 $1.75 — No 233 .50¢ — No 234 $1.50 — No 235 $2.00 — No 236 $1.25 — No 237 $1.50 — No 238 75¢ $1.00 — No 239 $2.25 — No 240 $1.75 — No 241 $1.50 — No 242 $1.25 — No 243 $1.75-2.25-1.00 — No 244 45¢-50¢ — No 245 $1.50-2.00 — No 246 $1.25 — No 247 $1.25 $1.50 75¢ — No 248 $1.75 — No 249 29¢ 39¢ — No 250 $1.75

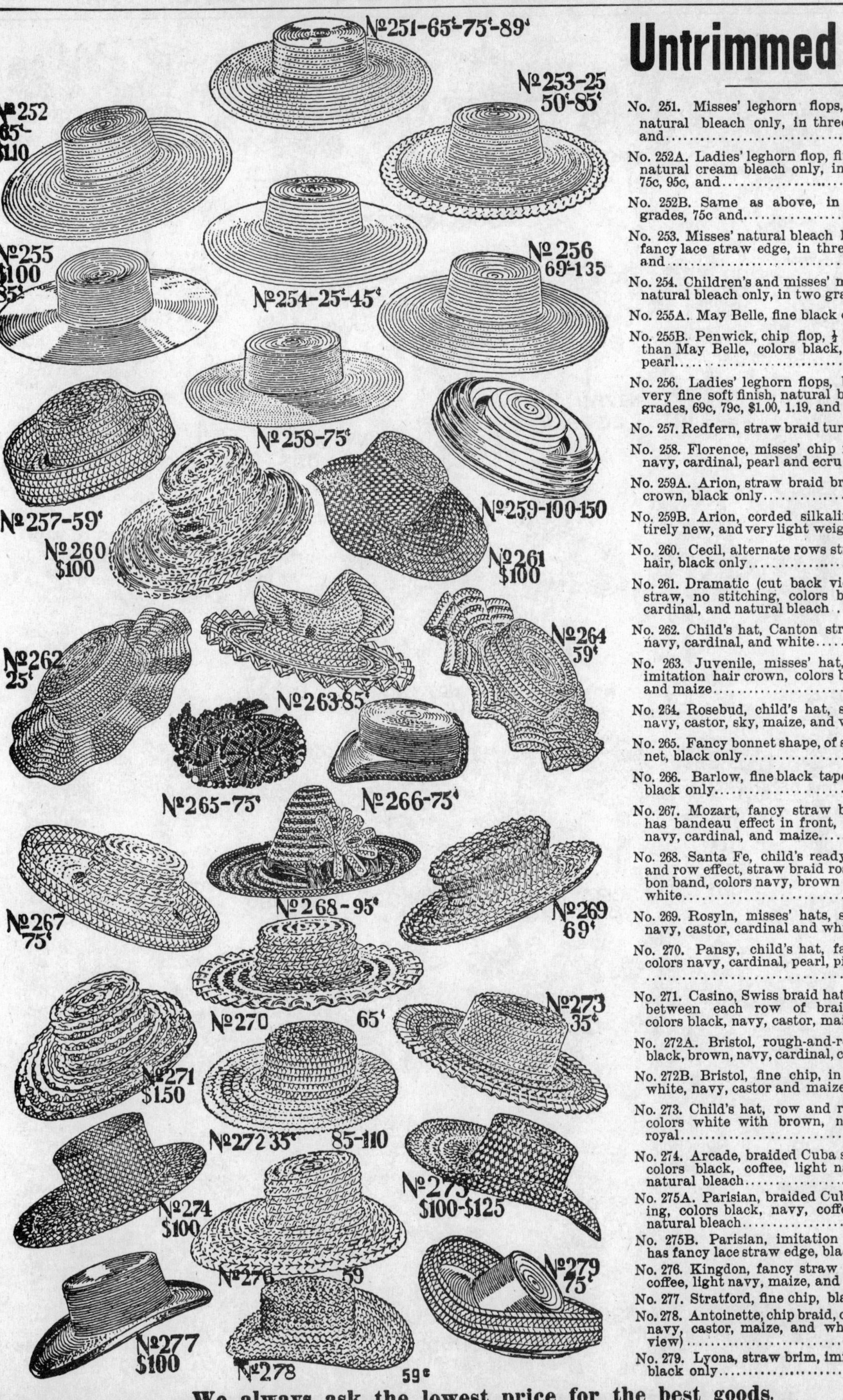

Untrimmed Hats.

No. 251. Misses' leghorn flops, fine soft finish, natural bleach only, in three grades, 65c, 75c and..89c

No. 252A. Ladies' leghorn flop, fine soft finish, and natural cream bleach only, in four grades, 65c, 75c, 95c, and..$1.10

No. 252B. Same as above, in black only, two grades, 75c and..$1.00

No. 253. Misses' natural bleach leghorn flop, with fancy lace straw edge, in three grades, 25c, 50c. and..85c

No. 254. Children's and misses' mountain leghorns, natural bleach only, in two grades, 25c and....45c

No. 255A. May Belle, fine black chip flop......$1.00

No. 255B. Penwick, chip flop, ½ inch higher crown than May Belle, colors black, navy, castor and pearl..85c

No. 256. Ladies' leghorn flops, best Italian make, very fine soft finish, natural bleach only, in five grades, 69c, 79c, $1.00, 1.19, and $1.35

No. 257. Redfern, straw braid turban, black only 59c

No. 258. Florence, misses' chip flop, colors brown, navy, cardinal, pearl and ecru....................75c

No. 259A. Arion, straw braid brim, imitation hair crown, black only..$1.00

No. 259B. Arion, corded silkaline, something entirely new, and very light weight, black only.$1.50

No. 260. Cecil, alternate rows straw and imitation hair, black only..$1.00

No. 261. Dramatic (cut back view) braided Cuba straw, no stitching, colors black, navy, coffee, cardinal, and natural bleach $1.00

No. 262. Child's hat, Canton straw, colors brown, navy, cardinal, and white....................25c

No. 263. Juvenile, misses' hat, straw brim and imitation hair crown, colors black, navy, castor, and maize..85c

No. 264. Rosebud, child's hat, straw braid, colors navy, castor, sky, maize, and white............59c

No. 265. Fancy bonnet shape, of sequin and Brussels net, black only..75c

No. 266. Barlow, fine black tape with straw edge, black only..75c

No. 267. Mozart, fancy straw braid under brim, has bandeau effect in front, colors black, light navy, cardinal, and maize....................75c

No. 268. Santa Fe, child's ready-to-wear hat, row and row effect, straw braid rosette and satin ribbon band, colors navy, brown and cardinal, with white..95c

No. 269. Rosyln, misses' hats, straw braid, colors navy, castor, cardinal and white..............69c

No. 270. Pansy, child's hat, fancy straw braid, colors navy, cardinal, pearl, pink, sky and white, ...65c

No. 271. Casino, Swiss braid hat, with muslin fold between each row of braid, drooping brim, colors black, navy, castor, maize and white..$1.50

No. 272A. Bristol, rough-and-ready straw, colors black, brown, navy, cardinal, castor and white.35c

No. 272B. Bristol, fine chip, in black, 85c; or in white, navy, castor and maize................$1.10

No. 273. Child's hat, row and row effect on brim, colors white with brown, navy, cardinal, or royal..35c

No. 274. Arcade, braided Cuba straw, no stitching, colors black, coffee, light navy, cardinal and natural bleach..$1.00

No. 275A. Parisian, braided Cuba straw, no stitching, colors black, navy, coffee, light blue, and natural bleach..$1.00

No. 275B. Parisian, imitation hair crown, brim has fancy lace straw edge, black only........$1.25

No. 276. Kingdon, fancy straw braid, colors black, coffee, light navy, maize, and pearl............59c

No. 277. Stratford, fine chip, black only.......$1.00

No. 278. Antoinette, chip braid, colors black, brown, navy, castor, maize, and white (cut right side view)..59c

No. 279. Lyona, straw brim, imitation hair crown, black only..75c

We always ask the lowest price for the best goods.

We have very pretty effects in flowers this season.

DESCRIPTION OF FLOWERS.

No. 158. Black satin chrysanthemums, two in packet, 95c.

No. 751. Violet foliage with buds, 20c; also No. 5336, larger packet, shaded leaves and buds, 29c; No. 4580, small packet shaded violet foliage, without buds, 10c.

No. 769. Large packet rose foliage, with buds, 45c; also No. 1508, smaller packet, dark shaded rose foliage and buds, 20c.

No. 771. Shaded geranium foliage, with buds, 35c.

No. 784. Heliotrope, natural shade only, 55c.

No. 788. Muslin asters, in white, pink and mauve, 25c.

No. 812. Muslin rose and bud, with foliage, in white, cream, pink, yellow and dark red, 10c.

No. 1400. Bridal flowers—Orange blossom wreaths, 75c, $1.00, 1.25, 1.50; orange blossom sprays, 75c, $1.00; jessamine sprays, 50c, 75c, $1.00.

No. 1509. Dark shaded ivy foliage, with berries, 25c.

No. 1513. Velvet pansies, in purple, mauve and yellow shaded effects, 15c.

No. 3006. Three muslin crush roses with crimped centres, in white, pink, tea, cerise and dark red, 15c.

No. 4009. Spray of locus with foliage, in white, mauve and violet, 39c.

No. 4106. Muslin daisies and buds, ½ gross in packet, long stems, colors white, pink and white and dark red, 35c.

No. 4185. Muslin carnations and foliage, colors pink, white and pink, and white and mauve, 15c.

No. 4581. Heliotrope foliage, large packet, 19c.

No. 5076. Packet six muslin roses with foliage, colors white, pink, tea, light yellow and dark red, 29c.

No. 5130. Six muslin crush roses, colors white, tea, light yellow, pink and dark red, 25c; also No. 5281, six black satin crush roses with jet centres, 25c.

No. 5151. Six muslin poppies with green centres, colors white, pink, tuscan and red, 25c; also No. 5159, same as above, in silk, colors white, pink, tuscan, violet and red, 50c; or No. 5270, black with black centre, 50c.

No. 5173. Velvet forget-me-nots, light blue only, 25c.

No. 5211. Child's wreath, buttercups, colors white, pink, light yellow and light blue, 15c.

No. 5213. Child's wreath, field daisies, colors white, pink, yellow, light blue and red, 25c.

No. 5218. Large red cherries with foliage, 35c.

No. 5291. Black silk hops, 12 sprays in packet, 50c.

No. 5293. Black satin single violets, 4 dozen in packet, 25c.

No. 5330. Three handsome black silk roses, 65c.

No. 5350. Wild grapes and foliage, large packet, foliage shaded effects, 65c.

No. 5407. Fancy spray violets, with foliage, light natural shades only, 35c.

No. 5419. Three handsome silk roses with foliage, colors cream, pink, tuscan and dark red, 55c.

No. 5462. Packet of single silk violets and buds with foliage, natural shades only, 25c; also No. 207, packet 3 dozen double muslin violets with foliage, natural shades only, 10c.

No. 6132. Packet 1 dozen muslin Marguerites, white only, with brown centres, 15c.

No. 6783. Lily of valley, with foliage, 10c; also No. 5050, larger packet, better quality, 25c, both in white only.

No. 6882. Clover with foliage, colors white, pink and purple, 25c.

No. 7134. Packet 1 gross single linen violets, light and dark natural shades, in packet, 35c.

No. 7562. Muslin apple blossoms with foliage, colors white, white and pink and pink, 25c.

No. 7639. Hawthorne blossoms, in white and pink, and white, large packet, 35c.

No. 7760. Silk hydrangea in shaded effects, white and Nile, light and dark pink, mauve and pink, light and dark violet, 35c.

No. 7943. Wild roses with foliage, colors white and pink, with yellow centres, 35c.

No. 7990. Muslin snowbells with foliage, in white only, with light green shaded centres, 19c.

No. 8095. Muslin lilacs, in white and natural, 15c; or No. 4081, larger packets, white or natural, 25c; also No. 6802, black satin lilacs, 35c.

No. 8096. Velvet cowslips, 4 dozen in packet, yellow only, 15c.

No. 9403. Rose foliage with buds, 19c; or No. 9493, small packet, 10c; also No. 4945, black satin rose foliage with buds, 25c.

MILLINERY TRIMMINGS.

Feathers.

Black single ostrich mounts, range A, 25c, 50c, 75c, $1.00, 1.25, 1.50 each.

Black single ostrich mounts, range B, a smaller mount, extra quality fibre, 25c, 50c, 75c, $1.00, 1.25, 1.50, 2.00, 2.25, 2.75 each.

White and cream single mounts, 25c, 50c, 75c, $1.00, 1.25, 1.50, 2.00, 2.25, 2.75 each.

Leading spring shades in single mounts, 75c, $1.00, 1.50 each.

Tips, Three in a Bunch.

Black ostrich tips, 3 in a bunch, 50c, 75c, $1.00, 1.25, 1.50, 2.00, 2.50, 3.25 bunch.

White and cream tips, 3 in a bunch, 50c, 75c, $1.00, 1.50, 2.00 bunch.

Long Ostrich Plumes.

In black, $1.25, 1.75, 2.25, 2.75, 3.25, 3.75, 4.25, 5.00 each.

In white or cream, $1.75, 2.25, 2.75, 3.25, 3.75 each.

Our Special Ostrich Tips, 3 in a bunch in black, white and colors, very special, 25c bunch.

Ospreys.

Flowing osprey (sold according to number of sprays in mount), black or white, 2-spray mounts, special, 12½c; also 25c, 50c, 75c, $1.00 each.

Bird of paradise osprey, in black, white or natural, 50c, 75c, $1.00, 1.50, 2.00, 2.50, 3.00 each.

Cross osprey, black or white, 25c, 50c, 75c, $1.00, 1.25 each.

Stub osprey, black or white, 25c, 35c, 50c each.

Black ostrich boas, 48 to 52 inches long, $5.00, 6.00, 7.00, 8.00, 9.00, 10.00, 12.00 each.

Black ostrich neck ruffs, 18 inches long with satin ribbon ties, $2.50, 3.00, 3.50, 4.00, 5.00 each.

Maids' Caps.

Fancy maids' caps, 8c, 10c, 12½c, 15c, 20c, 25c each.

Washing caps, 12½c, 15c, 20c, 25c each.

Old Ladies' Dress Caps.

Old ladies' caps, made of black lace and ribbon, ribbon ties, 75c, $1.00, 1.25, 1.50.

Widows' Caps.

Widows' caps, with fall, 75c, $1.00, 1.25, 1.50.

Without fall, 75c, $1.00.

Hat Wires, etc.

Black and colored satin wire, heavy, 5c yd.

Black and white satin wire, medium, 2 yds for 5c; fine, 3 yds for 5c.

Black or white silk block wire, 8-yd ring, for 10c.

Black and white iron wire, 3 yds for 5c; or large ring, 15c.

Black and white flat ribbon wire, card, 10c.

Black and white buckram, 27-inch, 25c yd.

Black and white Paris nets, 24-inch, 15c yd.

Wire shapes in all the correct blocks, plain shapes, 25c; fancy shapes, 35c; Buckram bonnet shapes, 20c.

Bridal and Communion Veils.

Mechlin veils, 72 x 72 inches, handsomely embroidered—

No. 441	$1.00
No. 442	1.25
No. 443	1.50
No. 444	1.75

Mourning Veils and Veiling.

Widows' silk lisse veils, correct styles and sizes, $2.50, 3.00, 4.00, 5.00, 5.50, 6.00 each.

Widows' silk lisse veiling, 42-inch, plain border on both edges, 85c, $1.00, 1.25 yd.

Widows' borders, 10c, 15c, 20c each.

Black crepe, 75c, $1.00, 1.25, 1.50 yd.

Mourning face veils, 35c, 50c, 75c each.

Write us for samples and prices of straw braids and sequin edgings. The latest novelties in these lines in stock during the season.

Millinery Chiffons.

No. H1643. Special millinery chiffon, all silk, 40 inches wide, in black, white, cream only, extra value, 25c yd.

No. H1235. Extra quality pure silk chiffon, 40, 42 inches wide, special semi-stiff finish for millinery purposes, in black, white, cream and all leading spring shades, 39c yd.

Be sure to send enough postage for goods going by Mail.

Muslin Caps.

Instructions for Measurement.

Be sure and state size required.

Measurements in inches for close-fitting caps and bonnet styles are taken from point where tie is fastened to cap, over the head to same point on the opposite side. Sizes, close fitting caps, 12 to 16 inches. Bonnet styles, 14 to 17 inches.

Measurements for children's hats are taken in inches around crown, and sizes are 19, 20, 21 inches.

The misses' hats come in one size only, and we state age they are suitable for.

No. 509. White allover embroidery cap, full lace ruche around front, and double row edging around neck, muslin ties, sizes 12 to 16 inches 50c

No. 518. Embroidered cream cashmere cap, full lace ruche around front, lace edge around neck, ribbon ties, sizes 12 to 16 inches...59c

No. 525. Child's embroidered cream Japanese silk tam, lace ruche across front, silk ties, sizes 19, 20, 21 inches 75c

No. 527. Child's embroidered cream cashmere tam, plain cashmere band finished with cord, elastic under chin, sizes 19, 20, 21 inches, 50c

No. 539. Wash hat, tam, crown of embroidery, corded brim, with rick-rack braid edge, muslin ties, white only, sizes 19, 20, 21 inches, 45c; or No. 544, same style, with plain muslin crown and embroidery crown piece, corded brim, plain edge, white only, sizes 19, 20, 21 inches 35c

No. 548. Hemstitched muslin wash cap, neat embroidery edging all around, wide muslin ties, white only, sizes 13 to 16 inches 75c

No. 553. Fine white muslin French cap, shirred and tucked revers front, trimmed lace edging all around, wide muslin ties, sizes 13 to 16 inches $1.00

No. 581. Child's button crown corded wash hat, rick-rack braid edge, colors white, pink and light blue, sizes 19, 20, 21 inches....55c

No. 590. Embroidered and tucked fine white muslin cap, with valenciennes lace insertion, extra full graduated lace ruche all around, muslin ties, sizes 12 to 16 inches $1.00

No. 619. White embroidery cap, lace top ruche, with baby ribbon loops, lace edge all around, muslin ties, sizes 12 to 16 inches 25c

No. 620. Fine white muslin 30-cord wash cap, hemstitched front, lace edge around neck, muslin ties, sizes 13 to 16 inches 35c

No. 621. White embroidery cap, full graduated lace ruche, with braidene loops, muslin ties, sizes 12 to 16 inches...............35c

No. 623. Embroidered and corded white muslin cap, full net ruche all around, muslin ties, sizes 12 to 16 inches...............55c

No. 624. Fine openwork embroidery cap, white only, very full graduated lace top ruche, with baby ribbon loops, lace edging all around, muslin ties, sizes 12 to 16 inches 50c

No. 625. Fine white muslin cap, two rows hemstitched tucks, with fine cording between, full graduated lace ruche all around, muslin ties, sizes 13 to 16 inches 65c

No. 626. All-over embroidery cap, white only, full lace ruche all around, extra top ruche, with baby ribbon loops, muslin ties, sizes 12 to 16 inches...............................69c

No. 631. Fine white muslin French cap, plain front, with very full plaited lace edging next face, six rows hand tucking, row of feather stitching in centre, with valenciennes lace edging on both sides, muslin ties, sizes 13 to 16 inches $1.25

No. 633. Very fine white Swiss embroidery cap, valenciennes lace ruche and edging, large braidene rosettes, muslin ties, sizes 12 to 16 inches...........................$1.50

Muslin Bonnets.

No. 510. White embroidery bonnet, frill and curtain of same, net ruche and lace edging around face, muslin ties, sizes 14 to 17 inches.......50c

No. 512. White muslin and pique bonnet, double frill and curtain of open-work embroidery, lace edging around face, muslin ties, sizes 14 to 17 inches.................................85c

No. 513. White embroidery bonnet, very full double frill and curtain of same, lace edging next face, muslin ties, sizes 14 to 17 inches.... ....$1.35

No. 514. Fine white embroidery bonnet, top frill and curtain of same, inside frill of crimped muslin edged with lace, lace edging around face, muslin ties, sizes 14 to 17 inches..........$1.50

No. 515. Organdie bonnet, full puff back, trimmed with tuscan straw braid, very full double-fluted frill and curtain edged with lace, inside lace ruche, organdie ties, colors cream, pink and light blue, sizes 14 to 17 inches..........$1.19

No. 516. Cream organdie bonnet, trimmed with gold soutache braid, large bow on top, very full crimped frill and curtain, corded under frill and lace ruche, wide organdie ties, sizes 14 to 17 inches.................................$1.35

No. 517. Cream organdie bonnet, with fancy straw braid body and crown, very full cascaded frill, wide lace edging on frill and curtain, full lace ruche, wide ties, crimped frill around crown and large bow on top, straw braids, come in cream edged tuscan, pink and Nile, sizes 14 to 17 inches $1.65

No. 554. Colored muslin bonnet, shirred and tucked, full puff back, double shirred frills with lace edge, also curtain, full graduated lace ruche, colors white, pink and light blue, wide muslin ties, sizes 14 to 17 inches.................$1.00

No. 555. Fine organdie bonnet, six rows hemstitched tucks around body, double frill edged with lace and three rows tucks on each, bow on top, and back edged with lace, full lace ruche, wide ties with hemstitched ends, colors white, pink and light blue, sizes 14 to 17 inches..$1.50

No. 561. Hemstitched muslin bonnet, frill and curtain of same with lace edging, graduated lace ruche, wide ties, trimmed with satin ribbon bows, in white only, with white, pink or light blue bows, sizes 14 to 17 inches......$2.00

No. 564. Hemstitched muslin bonnet, very full plaited frill and curtain, with fine lace edge, lace edging next face, trimmed baby ribbon loops, wide ties with hemstitched ends, in white only, with white, pink or light blue ribbon loops, sizes 14 to 17 inches...............$2.25

No. 570. Fine organdie bonnet, shirred and wired frill edged fine valenciennes lace, shirred and wired body, with full puff back, large bow on top, wide organdie ties, full graduated lace ruche next face, colors white, pink and light blue, sizes 14 to 17 inches...............$3.00

No. 636. White embroidery bonnet, frill and curtain of same, lace edging next face, white, pink or light blue satin ribbon bow, muslin ties, sizes 14 to 17 inches............................75c

No. 637. White embroidery bonnet, very full fluted frill and curtain, with lace insertion and edging, lace edging next face, muslin ties and bow, sizes 14 to 17 inches...............$1.00

No. 638. Muslin bonnet, with very full cascaded frill, crimped curtain, white lace edging on frill and curtain, colors white, pink and blue, sizes 14 to 17 inches...........................$1.00

No. 639. Fine white muslin bonnet, with cross tucks and fine valenciennes lace insertion, full puff back, body and curtain trimmed narrow straw braid, very full fluted frill edged valenciennes lace, inside lace ruche, muslin ties and bow, sizes 14 to 17 inches...............$1.50

Mail order customers get the same goods as city customers.

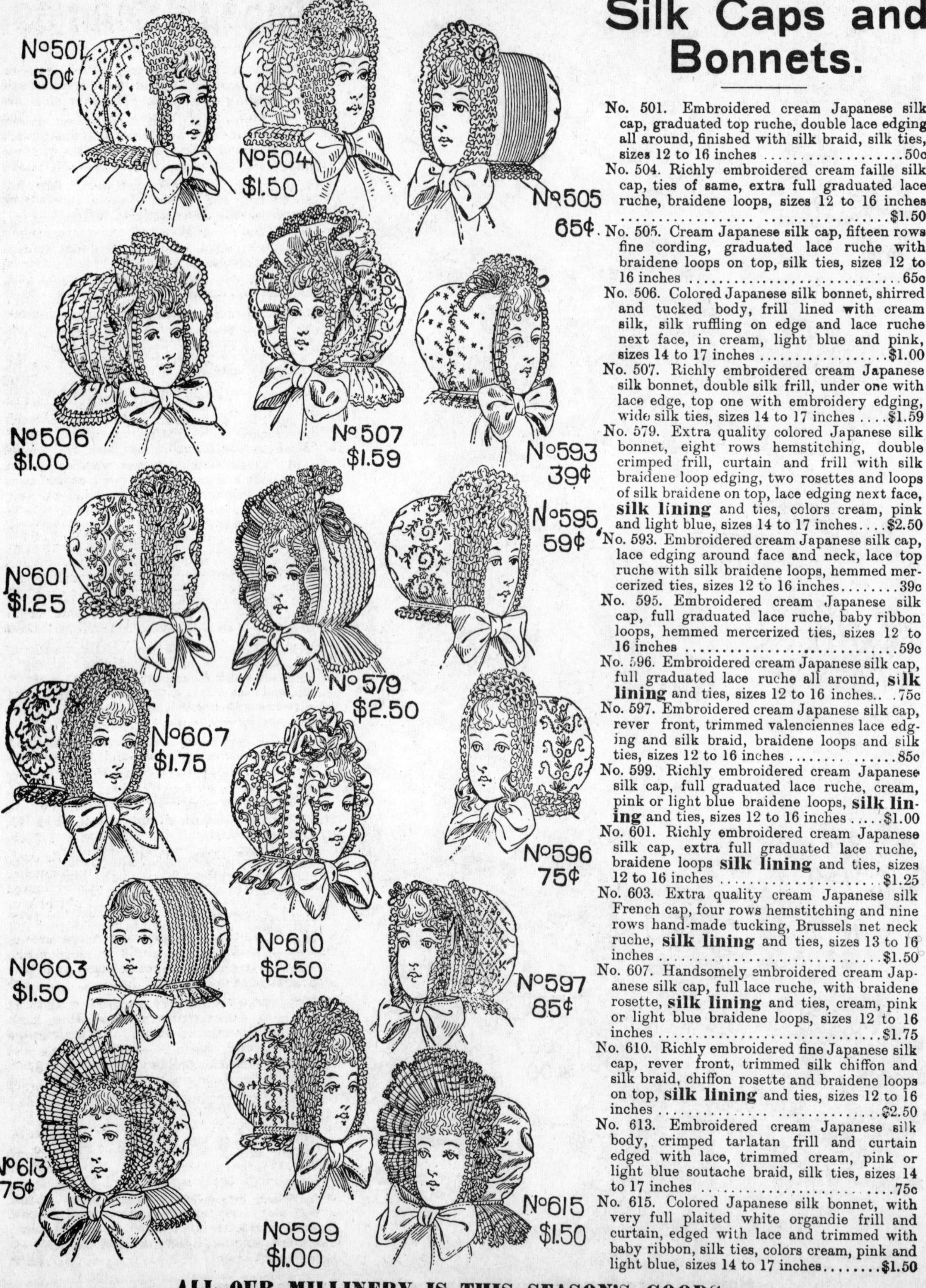

Silk Caps and Bonnets.

No. 501. Embroidered cream Japanese silk cap, graduated top ruche, double lace edging all around, finished with silk braid, silk ties, sizes 12 to 16 inches 50c

No. 504. Richly embroidered cream faille silk cap, ties of same, extra full graduated lace ruche, braidene loops, sizes 12 to 16 inches $1.50

No. 505. Cream Japanese silk cap, fifteen rows fine cording, graduated lace ruche with braidene loops on top, silk ties, sizes 12 to 16 inches 65c

No. 506. Colored Japanese silk bonnet, shirred and tucked body, frill lined with cream silk, silk ruffling on edge and lace ruche next face, in cream, light blue and pink, sizes 14 to 17 inches $1.00

No. 507. Richly embroidered cream Japanese silk bonnet, double silk frill, under one with lace edge, top one with embroidery edging, wide silk ties, sizes 14 to 17 inches $1.59

No. 579. Extra quality colored Japanese silk bonnet, eight rows hemstitching, double crimped frill, curtain and frill with silk braidene loop edging, two rosettes and loops of silk braidene on top, lace edging next face, **silk lining** and ties, colors cream, pink and light blue, sizes 14 to 17 inches.... $2.50

No. 593. Embroidered cream Japanese silk cap, lace edging around face and neck, lace top ruche with silk braidene loops, hemmed mercerized ties, sizes 12 to 16 inches........ 39c

No. 595. Embroidered cream Japanese silk cap, full graduated lace ruche, baby ribbon loops, hemmed mercerized ties, sizes 12 to 16 inches 59c

No. 596. Embroidered cream Japanese silk cap, full graduated lace ruche all around, **silk lining** and ties, sizes 12 to 16 inches.. .75c

No. 597. Embroidered cream Japanese silk cap, rever front, trimmed valenciennes lace edging and silk braid, braidene loops and silk ties, sizes 12 to 16 inches 85c

No. 599. Richly embroidered cream Japanese silk cap, full graduated lace ruche, cream, pink or light blue braidene loops, **silk lining** and ties, sizes 12 to 16 inches $1.00

No. 601. Richly embroidered cream Japanese silk cap, extra full graduated lace ruche, braidene loops **silk lining** and ties, sizes 12 to 16 inches $1.25

No. 603. Extra quality cream Japanese silk French cap, four rows hemstitching and nine rows hand-made tucking, Brussels net neck ruche, **silk lining** and ties, sizes 13 to 16 inches $1.50

No. 607. Handsomely embroidered cream Japanese silk cap, full lace ruche, with braidene rosette, **silk lining** and ties, cream, pink or light blue braidene loops, sizes 12 to 16 inches $1.75

No. 610. Richly embroidered fine Japanese silk cap, rever front, trimmed silk chiffon and silk braid, chiffon rosette and braidene loops on top, **silk lining** and ties, sizes 12 to 16 inches $2.50

No. 613. Embroidered cream Japanese silk body, crimped tarlatan frill and curtain edged with lace, trimmed cream, pink or light blue soutache braid, silk ties, sizes 14 to 17 inches 75c

No. 615. Colored Japanese silk bonnet, with very full plaited white organdie frill and curtain, edged with lace and trimmed with baby ribbon, silk ties, colors cream, pink and light blue, sizes 14 to 17 inches........ $1.50

ALL OUR MILLINERY IS THIS SEASON'S GOODS.

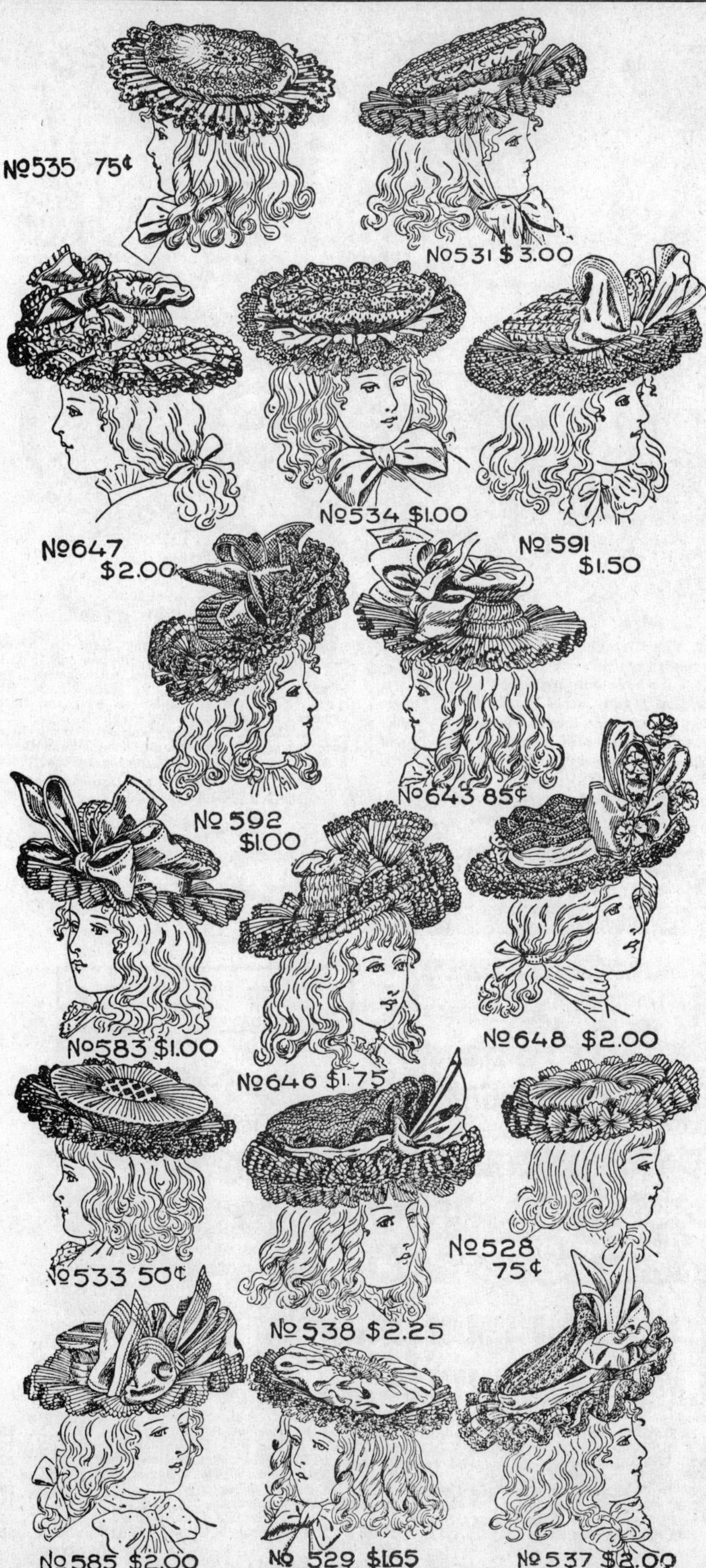

MUSLIN HATS.

No. 528. Silk and tarlatan hat, fluted tarlatan brim, with wired underbrim, crimped silk crown, colors cream, pink, light blue and cardinal, sizes 19, 20, 21 inches 75c

No 529. Japanese silk hat, loose puff crown, with shirred centre, top frill of fluted silk with lace edging, under frill of tarlatan, wired silk underbrim, colors cream, pink, light blue and cardinal, sizes 19, 20, 21 inches $1.65

No. 531. Misses' Japanese silk hat, full puff crown, very full double frills, wired underbrim, colors cream, pink, light blue, cardinal and black, ages 10 to 14 years......................$3.00

No. 533. White lawn hat, full crimped crown with embroidery centre, fluted frill with embroidery edging, wired underbrim, sizes 19, 20, 21 inches. 50c

No. 534. White embroidery hat, full puff crown, top frill of embroidery under one of plain muslin with lace edge, wired underbrim, sizes 19, 20, 21 inches $1.00

No. 535. Fine openwork embroidery hat, white only, puff crown, fluted frill and wired underbrim, sizes 19, 20, 21 inches 75c

No. 537. Fine white muslin and lace hat, crown alternate rows embroidery and valenciennes lace insertion, loose fold muslin around crown, very wide fluted frill with lace edging and insertion, wired tarlatan underbrim, large muslin bow in front, sizes 19, 20, 21 inches $2.00

No. 538. Misses' cream organdie and straw hat, one-piece straw crown, double organdie frill and bow, trimmed with black ribbon velvet and black stitching, wired underbrim, ages 8 to 14 yrs. $2.25

No. 583. Muslin hat, tucked crown, tam effect. large bow across front, crimped frill with lace edge, shirred and wired underbrim, colors white, pink, light blue, maize and cardinal, sizes 19, 20, 21 inches $1.00

No. 585. Fine muslin hat, tam crown effect, with nine rows hemstitched tucks, large bow across front, with four rows hemstitching, plaited muslin frill with wired underbrim, colors white, pink and light blue, sizes 19, 20, 21 inches..$2.00

No. 591. Fine muslin hat, shirred and tucked crown, wired bow, very full double frill with narrow lace edge, wired underbrim, colors white, pink, light blue, cardinal and Nile, sizes 19, 20, 21 inches $1.50

No. 592. Misses' straw hat, top frill of Brussels net with lace edging, under frill of fluted muslin, muslin and net bow, in natural bleached straw, with all white or white with pink, light blue or maize, suitable for ages 7 to 10 years......$1.00

No. 643. Muslin hat, shirred and wired crown, full fluted brim, wired underbrim, large muslin bow across front, colors cream, pink, light blue and cardinal, sizes 19, 20, 21 inches 85c

No. 646. Fine muslin hat, shirred and wired crown, full fluted frill edge with lace, large rosette in front, underbrim of Swiss straw braid in natural bleach colors, white, pink and light blue, sizes 19, 20, 21 inches $1.75

No. 647. Fine muslin hat, band Swiss braid around crown, muslin top, box-plaited frill and rosette, trimmed two rows ½-inch satin ribbon, Swiss braid underbrim, colors cream, pink, light blue and cardinal, ages 8 to 12 years $2.00

No. 648. Straw braid hat, natural bleach straw only, fancy tam crown, muslin twist around crown and bow, spray of flowers in front, muslin ruche with lace edging on edge of brim, colors cream, pink, light blue and cardinal, for ages 8 to 12 years $2.00

WE SELL THE BEST GOODS AT THE LOWEST PRICES.

No. 170. Misses' felt and velveteen tam, trimmed with black braid and two quills, in cardinal, navy, brown and myrtle felt, all with black velveteen 75c
No. 224. Misses' cashmere and velveteen tam, trimmed with white braid, two quills and ribbon bow, in cardinal, navy, brown and myrtle..............69c
No. 322. Childs' straw tam, satin band and bow, with quill, colors navy and white, royal and white, cardinal and white, tan and white, special.........25c

No. 519. Misses' muslin sun-bonnet, full back, ten rows cording around body, double frill of embroidery, colors white, pink and white, light blue and white, sizes 14 to 17 inches....................69c
No. 520. Misses' white muslin sun-bonnet, English style, shirred and corded body, large full frill and curtains edged with lace, sizes 14 to 17 inches...59c

No. 522. Misses' gingham sun-bonnet, three rows white cambric stitched around front, gingham frill, in pink and white, and light blue and white checks, sizes 14 to 17 inches 25c
No. 523. Ladies' garden sun-bonnet, navy and white or brown and white, checked gingham.........25c
No. 542. Misses' velveteen tam, four rows chain stitching in white silk, two quills, buckle and ribbon bow at side, colors cardinal, navy and black....55c

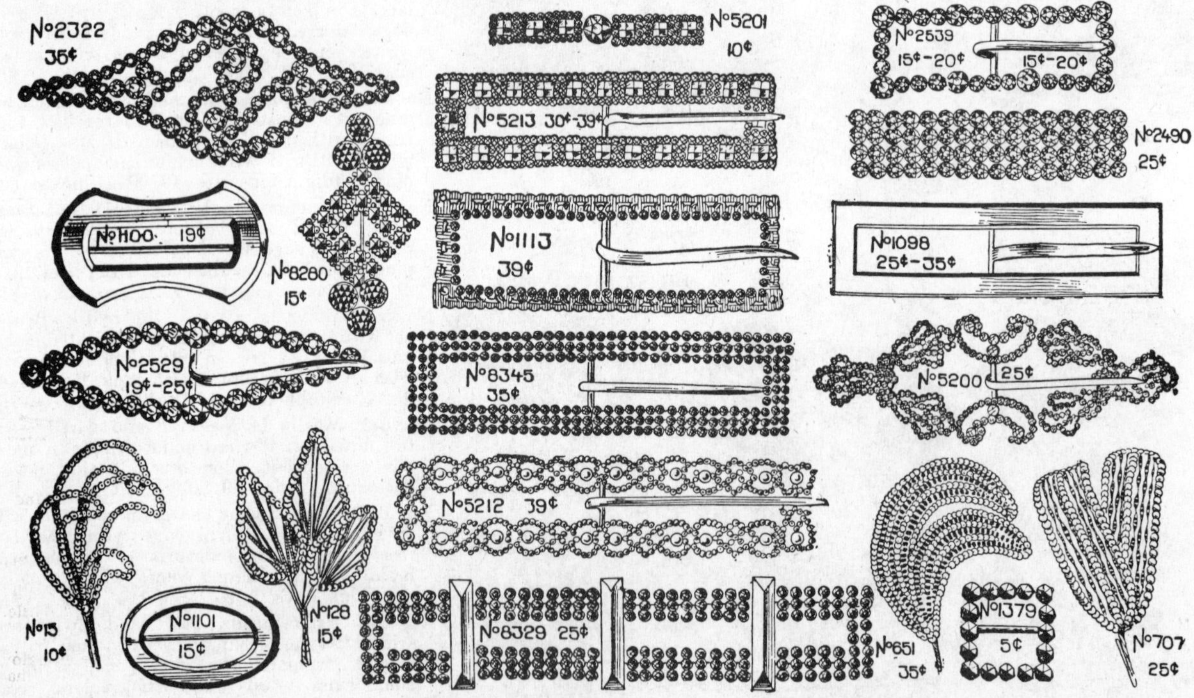

No. 15. Black sequin spray 10c
No. 128. Black sequin and straw spray........... 15c
No. 651. Black sequin and straw mount......... 35c
No. 707. Black sequin and straw mount......... 25c
No. 1098. Gilt buckle, 4 inches long, 25c; also No. 1097, same style, 5½ inches long........... 35c
No. 1100. Gilt slide, heavy effect................. 19c
No. 1101. Gilt slide.............................. 15c

No. 1113. Gilt and steel buckle.................. 39c
No. 1379. Brilliant slide 5c
No. 2322. Brilliant ornament..................... 35c
No. 2490. Brilliant ornament..................... 25c
No. 2529. Brilliant buckle, 4 inches long, 19c; also No. 2527, same style, 5½ inches.................. 25c
No. 2539. Brilliant buckle, 2¾ inches long, 15c; also No. 2536, 4 inches long 20c

No. 5200. Steel buckle............................ 25c
No. 5201. Steel pin, with brilliant in centre...... 10c
No. 5212. Steel buckle, 5 inches long........... 39c
No. 5213. Steel buckle, 4 inches long, 30c; also No. 5214, 5 inches long 39c
No. 8280. Jet pin................................. 15c
No. 8329. Jet buckle, 5 inches long............. 25c
No. 8345. Jet buckle, 4½ inches long 35c

OUR GOODS ARE EXACTLY AS REPRESENTED.

GLOVE DEPARTMENT.

Ladies' Kid Gloves.

B1. Ladies' 2-clasp kid gloves, with embroidered backs, colors in tan, brown, oxblood, white and black, sizes 5¾ to 8, special, 49c pair.

B2. Ladies' 2-clasp fine French kid gloves, made with silk-embroidered backs, colors tan, brown, fawn, mode, oxblood, grey, white, peal grey, black, blue, special, 75c pair.

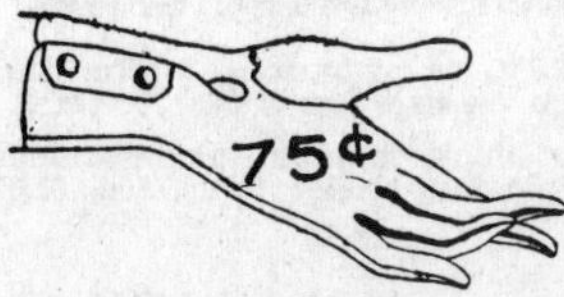

B3. Ladies' 2 large clasp walking gloves, medium weight, made with pique-sewn gusset fingers and Paris points, colors tan, brown, oxblood, grey, fawn, mode, white and black, sizes 5½ to 7½, 75c pair.

B4. Ladies' 2 large dome fine French kid gloves, made from fine choice skins, colors tan, brown, beaver, fawn, oxblood, pearl grey, butter, white, navy, slate and black, sizes 5½ to 7½; this glove is guaranteed in every particular; we buy these gloves in very large quantities to be able to sell them at this price, very special, 85c pair.

B5. Ladies' 2 large dome kid gloves, pique sewn, gusset fingers, medium weight, a perfect walking and shopping glove, colors tan, brown, fawn, mode, grey, oxblood, white, black, pearl grey and butter, sizes 5½ to 7½, $1.00 pair.

B6. Ladies' 2 large dome fine French kid gloves, made from a very fine quality of skins, and our guarantee goes with every pair, colors tan, fawn, mode, brown, grey, pearl grey, cream, new blue, drab, oxblood and black, sizes 5½ to 8, $1.00 pair.

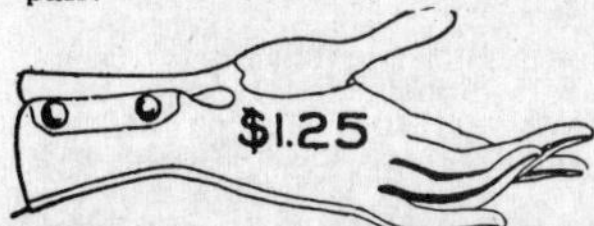

B7. Ladies' 2 large dome fine kid gloves, pique sewn, gusset fingers, medium weight, and guaranteed in every particular, colors in the new tints of brown, fawn, mode, grey, pearl grey, white, cream, tan, oxblood and black, sizes 5½ to 7½, $1.25 pair.

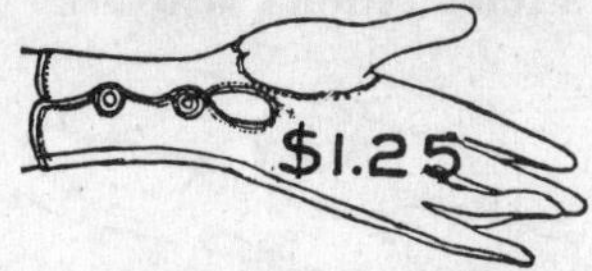

B8. Ladies' fine French kid gloves, pricked seams and narrow silk embroidered backs, made from very choice skins, cut and finish perfect, colors tan, brown, mode, fawn, grey, pearl grey, white, oxblood and black, sizes 5½ to 7½, $1.25 pair.

B9. Ladies' 2 large dome kid gloves, pique sewn, gusset fingers, Paris points, made from the first choice skins, and we guarantee them to hold their shape; colors tan, fawn, mode, grey, beaver, oxblood, pearl grey, white, blue, butter and black, sizes 5½ to 7½, $1.50 pair.

B10. Ladies' 2 large dome heavy kid gloves, made without seams, is a very pretty glove, and is perfect fitting, colors gold, brown and red, sizes 5½ to 7, $1.50 pair.

B11. Ladies' 2 large pearl clasp, set with imitation diamonds, this makes a very pretty effect, colors black, white, pearl, fawn, mode and oxblood, sizes 5½ to 6¾, $2.00 pair.

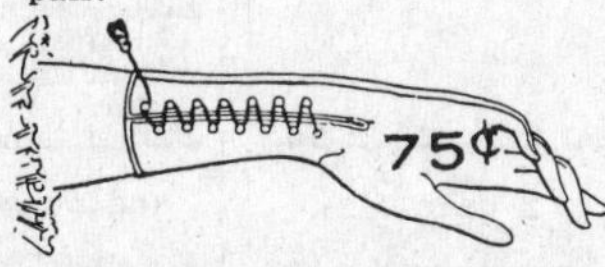

B12. Ladies' 7-hook lacing kid gloves (Roselie), made with 2 rows silk embroidery on back, colors tan, brown, oxblood and black, sizes 5¾ to 8, 75c pair.

B13. Ladies' fine French kid gloves, made with 7-hook lacing, and 1 row silk embroidered backs, color black only, sizes 5½ to 8, $1.00 pair.

Driving Gloves.

B14. Ladies' napa driving gloves, made with spear points and out seams, colors English tan and red tan, sizes 5¾ to 7, $1.50 pair.

B15. Ladies' driving and cycling gloves, made with gauntlet and 1 clasp, sizes 6 to 8, colors tan and red tan, $1.00 pair.

Mocha and Suede Gloves.

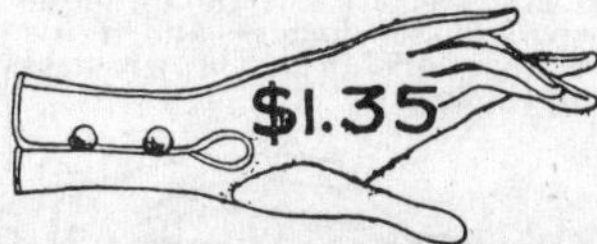

B16. Ladies' 2 large clasp mocha gloves, gusset fingers and Paris points; this is a perfect fitting glove, and wears well, colors tan, brown, beaver, fawn, mode, grey and black, sizes 5½ to 7½, $1.35 pair.

B17. Ladies' 2-clasp mocha gloves, heavy weight, colors tan, grey and black, sizes 5½ to 7½, $1.50 pair.

B18. Ladies' 2-clasp French suede gloves, Paris points, colors black, tan, brown, grey and mode, sizes 5½ to 7½, $1.00 pair.

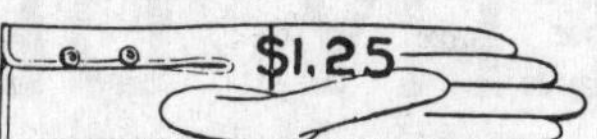

B19. Ladies' 2-clasp French suede gloves, pique sewn, gusset fingers and Paris points, colors tan, fawn, mode, black, grey, sizes 5½ to 7½, $1.25 pair.

B20. Ladies' 2-clasp French suede gloves, very finest make, and perfect-fitting glove, colors in all the new spring tints, sizes 5½ to 7, $1.25 pair.

Chamois Gloves.

B21. Ladies' 2-clasp chamois gloves, white only, sizes 5½ to 7½, 50c pair.

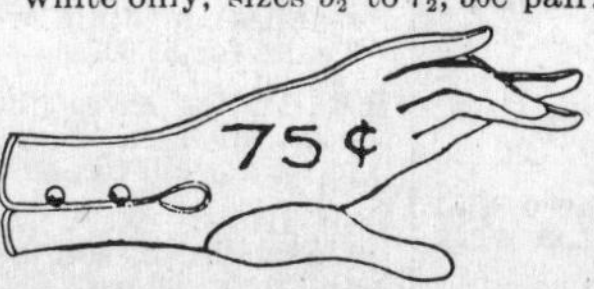

B22. Ladies' 2-dome chamois gloves, in white only, sizes 5¾ to 7½, 75c pair.

Evening Gloves.

B23. Ladies' mousquetaire French suede gloves, colors cream, white and black, button length,

12,	16,	20,	24-inch
$1.50,	1.75,	2.50,	2.75 pair.

Silk Evening Gloves.

B24. Ladies' pure silk gloves, in cream, white and black,

18,	22,	26,	32-inch
50c,	65c,	75c,	$1.00 pair.

B25. Ladies' wedding gloves, made with 4 buttons and silk embroidered backs, sizes 5½ to 8, 50c and 75c pair.

Misses' Kid Gloves.

B26. Misses' 2-dome kid gloves, colors tan, brown and oxblood, sizes 1 to 6, 50c pair.

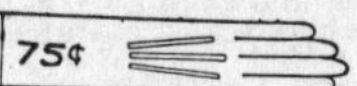

B27. Misses' 2-clasp kid gloves, pique sewn, gusset fingers, embroidered backs, sizes 1 to 6, 75c pair.

Boys' Kid Gloves.

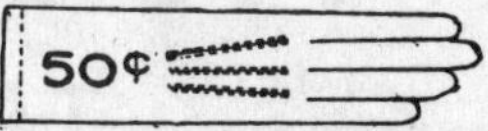

B28. Boys' 2-dome kid gloves, colors tan and brown, self-embroidered backs, sizes 0 to 6, 50c pair.

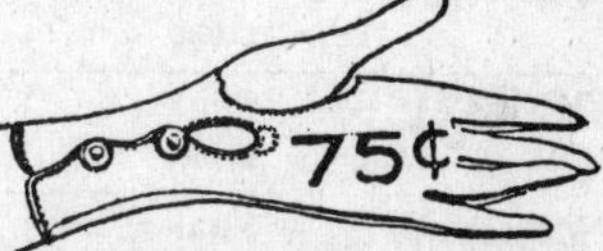

B29. Boys' 2-dome kid gloves, pique sewn and gusset fingers, Paris points, colors tan, brown and red tan, sizes 1 to 6, 75c pair.

Ladies' Silk Gloves.

Please state what size worn in kid gloves when ordering silk, lisle or taffeta gloves.

B30. Ladies' 14-inch pure silk gloves, colors tan, fawn, cream, navy, white and black, 25c pair.

B31. Ladies' 14-inch pure Milanese silk gloves, colors cream, white, black and grey, 35c pair.

B32. Ladies' heavy pure silk gloves, colors black and white only, 50c pair.

B33. Ladies' 14-inch frame-made pure silk gloves, black only, 65c, 75c, $1.00 pair.

WE DO NOT EXCHANGE GLOVES

Ladies' Lisle Gloves.

B34. Ladies' 2-clasp lisle gloves, colors tan, grey and black, 25c pair.

B35. Ladies' lisle gloves, with 2 dome, also 4 pearl buttons, colors tan, slate, white, fawn and black, 35c pair.

B36. Ladies' 4-button, also 2-dome, Milanese lisle gloves, colors tan, beaver, slate, white and black, 45c, 50c pair.

B37. Ladies' 2 large dome finest lisle gloves, with silk-embroidered backs, colors beaver, fawn, grey, white, black, pearl grey and butter, 65c, 75c pair.

B38. Ladies' plain lisle gloves, colors black, fawn and tan, 25c, 35c pair.

Ladies' Taffeta Gloves.

B39. Ladies' 2-clasp taffeta gloves, colors black, tan, fawn, beaver, 25c, 35c, 45c pair.

B40. Ladies' 4 large pearl button taffeta gloves, colors tan, fawn, mode, grey and black, 25c, 35c, 45c pair.

B41. Ladies' plain 13-inch taffeta gloves, colors tan, fawn, mode and black, 15c, 20c, 25c, 35c pair.

Lace Mitts.

B42. Ladies' lisle lace mitts, colors black and white, 15c pair.

B43. Ladies' pure silk lace mitts, black and white, 25c, 35c pair.

Misses' Gloves.

B44. Misses' taffeta gloves, colors tan, brown, white and cream, 15c pair.

B45. Misses' silk taffeta gloves, colors tan, brown, white, navy, red and black, 25c pair.

B46. Misses' 2 large clasp taffeta gloves, colors tan, brown, cream and white, 25c pair.

B47. Misses' 2-dome lisle gloves, colors fawn, mode, tan, white, red and blue, 25c, 35c pair.

B48. Misses' plain silk gloves, colors cream, white, black, red and blue, 25c pair.

Infantees.

B49. Cream, white, red, pink, blue and cardinal infantees, 10c, 15c, 20c, 25c pair.

Men's Gloves.

Men's Kid Gloves.

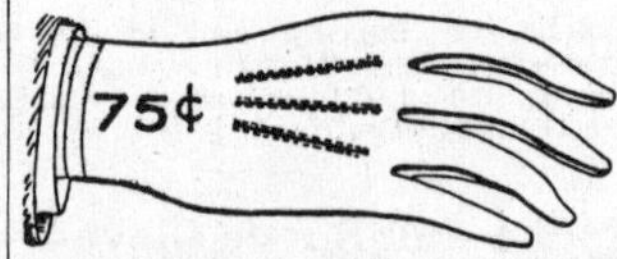

B50. Men's 2-clasp kid gloves, pique sewn, gusset fingers and Paris points, colors tan and brown, sizes 7 to 10, 75c pair.

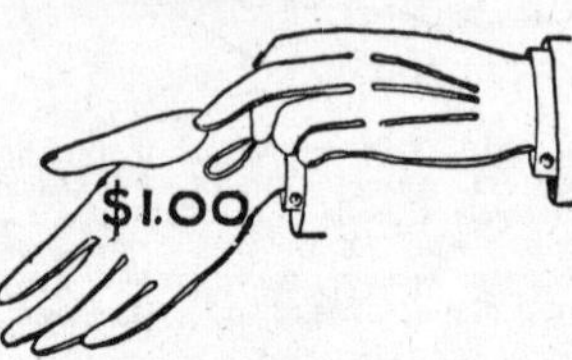

B51. Men's 1-clasp kid gloves, pique sewn, gusset fingers and Paris points; this glove is warranted in fit, finish and wear, colors tan, English red and brown, sizes 7 to 10, $1.00 pair.

B52. Men's 1-clasp fine kid gloves, with gusset fingers, Paris points and pique sewn, colors tan, brown red tans, sizes 7 to 9, $1.25, 1.50 pair.

Men's Mocha Gloves.

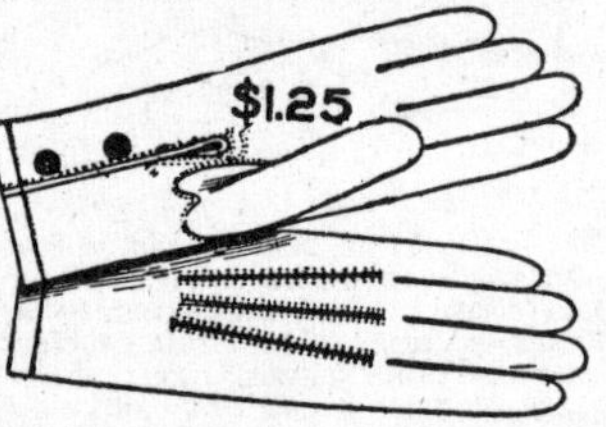

B53. Men's 2-clasp mocha gloves, colors tan, mode, brown and grey, sizes 7 to 9, $1.25 pair.

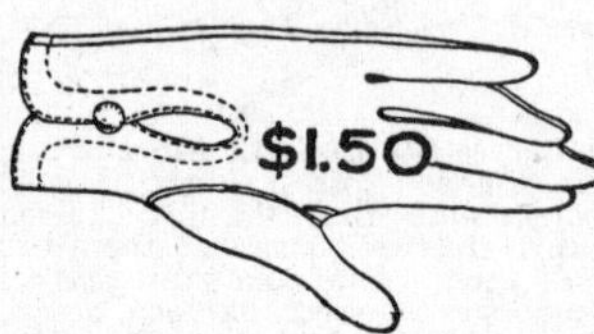

B54. Men's 1-clasp mocha gloves, colors grey and tan only, sizes 7 to 9, $1.50 pair.

B55. Men's 1-clasp kangaroo driving gloves, medium weight, colors tan and red tan, sizes 7½ to 10, $1.00 pair.

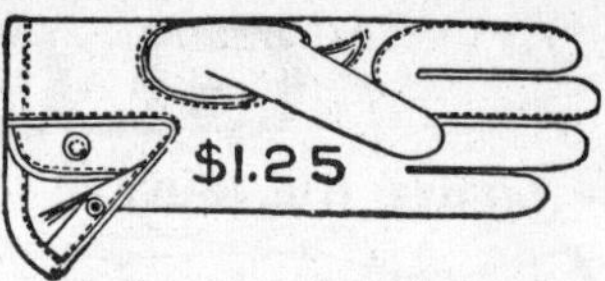

[illegible] Men's 1-clasp kangaroo driving gloves, first and second finger double faced, colors tan and red tan, sizes, 7½ to 10, $1.25 pair.

Men's Lisle Gloves.

B57. Men's lisle gloves, colors black and white, 15c pair.

B58. Men's 2-clasp lisle gloves, colors tan and brown, 25c pair.

Men's Wedding Gloves.

B59. Men's 2-button white kid gloves, sizes 7 to 10, 50c, 75c pair.

B60. Men's fine kid gloves, color light tan, sizes 7 to 10, 75c, $1.00 pair.

Harvest Mitts and Gloves.

B61. Men's mitts, with 1 finger, in oil tan and russet, 10-inch, 25c pair.

B62. Oil tan and russet mitts, with 1 finger, 12-inch, 35c pair.

B63. Men's chrome tan and oil tan harvest gloves, and made with elastic front, 50c pair.

B64. Men's chrome tan and oil tan harvest and driving gloves, with cord and button on back of gloves, 50c pair.

B65. Men's para buck gloves, made with cord and button on back and warranted waterproof, $1.00 pair.

B66. Men's pigskin gloves, heavy weight; this we can recommend for wear, $1.25 pair.

HOSIERY DEPARTMENT.

TABLE OF HOSE.

		Sizes	
Infants'....	Size Shoe Worn	0, 1, 1½, 2, 2½, 3, 3½, 4, 4½, 5	1 to 2 years.
"	" Hose "	4, 4, 4, 4½, 4½, 4½, 4½, 5, 5, 5	
Misses' or Boys' ..	" Shoe "	5, 5½, 6, 6½, 7, 7½, 8, 8½, 9, 9½, 10, 10½	2 to 7 yrs.
..	" Hose "	5, 5½, 5½, 5½, 6, 6, 6, 6½, 6½, 7, 7, 7	
Misses' or Boys' ..	" Shoe "	11, 11½, 12, 12½, 13, 13½, 1, 1½, 2, 2½	7 to 15 yrs.
..	" Hose "	7½, 7½, 7½, 8, 8, 8, 8, 8½, 8½, 8½	
Ladies'	" Shoe "	2½, 3, 3½, 4, 4½, 5, 5½, 6, 6½, 7.	
"	" Hose "	8½, 8½, 8½, 9, 9, 9½, 9½, 10, 10, 10.	

When ordering hosiery be sure to use this table and it will save mistakes. Hosiery will wear much better if the correct size.

Ladies' Plain Black Cashmere Hose.

These hose can be had in the following sizes: 8½, 9, 9½, 10.

B200. Ladies' plain black cashmere hose, full fashioned, double sole, heel and toe, very special, 25c pair.

B201. Ladies' plain black cashmere hose, full fashioned, double sole, heel and toe, high spliced and fine soft finish, 35c, or 3 pairs for $1.00.

B202. Ladies' plain cashmere hose, perfectly seamless, medium weight, soft finish, 35c, or 3 pairs for $1.00.

B203. Ladies' extra fine plain black cashmere hose, full fashioned, double sole, warranted to wear well, 45c, or 3 pairs for $1.25.

B204. Ladies' extra fine black cashmere hose, Llama finish, soft and durable, black heels and toes, 50c pair.

B205. Ladies' plain black cashmere hose, Indiana make, extra soft finish and warranted to give satisfaction, 65c, or 2 pairs for $1.25.

B206. Ladies' extra fine German cashmere hose full fashioned and double sole; this is made from the very finest pure yarns, 75c and $1.00 pair.

B207. Ladies' colored cashmere hose, in cream, cardinal and tan, 35c, or 3 pairs for $1.00; and 50c pair.

Ladies' Ribbed Cashmere Hose.

B208. Ladies' 7/1 ribbed black cashmere hose, special, 19c pair.

B210. Ladies' 4/1 and 2/1 ribbed black cashmere hose, plaited, 20c pair.

B211. Ladies' pure cashmere 2/1 ribbed hose, double heel and toe, seamless heel and toe, 25c pair.

B212. Ladies' 2/1 ribbed black cashmere hose, full fashioned, double sole, heel and toe, 35c, or 3 pairs for $1.00.

B213. Ladies' 1/1 ribbed black cashmere hose, full fashioned, double sole, heel and toe, 35c, or 3 pairs for $1.00.

B214. Ladies' fine quality 2/1 ribbed black cashmere hose, full fashioned, double sole, heel and toe; this is a very special price for this quality, and we guarantee the wear, 40c, or 3 pairs for $1.10.

B215. Ladies' 2/1 ribbed black cashmere hose, full fashioned and double sole, fine soft finish, 45c, or 3 pairs for $1.25.

B216. Ladies' 1/1 ribbed black cashmere hose, full fashioned, double sole, heel and toe, 45c, or 3 pairs for $1.25.

B217. Ladies' 2/1 ribbed black cashmere hose, full fashioned and double sole, heel and toe, high spliced, 50c pair; 65c or 2 pairs for $1.25.

When ordering hosiery use the hosiery table for correct sizes.

Ladies' Embroidered Hose.

B218. Ladies' plain black cashmere hose, embroidered in the newest designs and colors, 35c, 50c, 65c, 75c, $1.00 pair.

Ladies' Opera-Length Hose.

B219. Ladies' opera-length cashmere hose, full fashioned, double sole, made extra long, with wide leg, sizes 8½, 9, 9½, 10, 75c pair.

B220. Ladies' opera-length silk hose, in black only, fine quality, special, $1.50, 2.50 pair.

Misses' Plain Black Cashmere Hose.

B221. Misses' plain black cashmere hose, full fashioned and double soles and knees—
4, 4½, 5, 5½, 6, 6½, 7, 7½, 8, 8½,
15c, 15c, 15c, 15c, 20c, 20c, 25c, 25c, 25c, 25c.

B222. Misses' plain black cashmere hose, full fashioned, double soles, heels, toes and knees—
4, 4½, 5, 5½, 6, 6½, 7, 7½, 8, 8½,
20c, 20c, 20c, 20c, 25c, 25c, 30c, 30c, 35c, 35c.

B223. Misses' extra fine black cashmere hose, full fashioned and made from very fine yarn, double knees and soles—
4, 4½, 5, 5½, 6, 6½, 7, 7½, 8, 8½,
25c, 25c, 25c, 25c, 30c, 30c, 35c, 35c, 40c, 40c.

B224. Misses' plain cashmere hose, in tan, cardinal and cream, full fashioned, double soles—
4, 4½, 5, 5½, 6, 6½, 7, 7½, 8, 8½,
20c, 20c, 20c, 20c, 25c, 25c, 30c, 30c, 35c, 35c.

Misses' and Boys' Ribbed Cashmere Hose.

B225. Misses' and boys' ribbed black cashmere hose, double knees, heels and toes—
4½, 5, 5½, 6, 6½, 7, 7½, 8, 8½, 9, 9½, 10,
12½c, 12½c, 15c, 15c, 20c, 20c, 20c, 20c, 20c, 20c, 20c, 20c

B226. Misses' and boys' 2/1 ribbed black cashmere hose, with heavy 6-fold knees and double soles—
4½, 5, 5½, 6, 6½, 7, 7½, 8, 8½,
20c, 20c, 20c, 20c, 25c, 25c, 25c, 25c, 25c.

B227. Misses' and boys' 2/1 ribbed black cashmere hose, full fashioned—
4½, 5, 5½, 6, 6½, 7, 7½, 8, 8½, 9, 9½, 10,
20c, 20c, 25c, 25c, 30c, 30c, 30c, 35c, 35c, 35c, 35c, 35c.

B228. Misses' and boys' 2/1 ribbed black cashmere hose, full fashioned, double soles, heels, toes and knees, and warranted to wear—
4½, 5, 5½, 6, 6½, 7, 7½, 8, 8½, 9, 9½, 10,
25c, 25c, 30c, 30c, 35c, 40c, 45c, 50c, 50c, 50c, 50c, 50c.

B229. Misses' and boys' 2/1 ribbed extra fine black cashmere hose, full fashioned, double soles, heels, toes, and 6-fold knees—
4½, 5, 5½, 6, 6½, 7, 7½, 8, 8½, 9, 9½, 10,
30c, 30c, 35c, 35c, 40c, 45c, 50c, 50c, 50c, 50c, 50c, 50c.

B230. Misses' and boys' 1/1 ribbed black cashmere hose, double soles, heels and toes—
4½, 5, 5½, 6, 6½, 7, 7½, 8, 8½, 9, 9½, 10,
20c, 20c, 25c, 25c, 30c, 30c, 30c, 35c, 35c, 35c, 35c, 35c.

B231. Misses' and boys' 1/1 ribbed full fashioned black cashmere hose, double soles, heels, toes and knees—
4½, 5, 5½, 6, 6½, 7, 7½, 8, 8½, 9, 9½, 10,
25c, 25c, 30c, 30c, 35c, 40c, 40c, 50c, 50c, 50c, 50c, 50c.

Ladies' Cotton Hose.

B232. Ladies' plain black cotton hose, a good wearer and fast colors, 9c, or 3 pairs for 25c.

B233. Ladies' full fashioned black cotton hose, spliced heels and toes, 10c pair.

B234. Ladies' full fashioned and stainless black cotton hose, double soles, heels and toes, and high spliced, very special, 12½c pair.

B235. Ladies' fine black cotton hose, full fashioned, double soles, heels and toes, spliced, 15c pair.

B236. Ladies' stainless black cotton hose, full fashioned, double soles and extra high spliced ankles, 18c, or 3 pairs for 50c.

B237. Ladies' fast color black cotton hose, fine soft finish, full fashioned and double soles, 20c pair.

B238. Ladies' "gloria" finish black cotton hose; this hose is made from fine soft yarn and does not get hard after washing, every pair guaranteed, special, 25c pair.

B239. Ladies' extra fine "gloria" finish, black cotton hose, made with extra high spliced heels and double soles, 35c, or 3 pairs for $1.00.

Drop-Stitch Cotton Hose.

B240. Ladies' black cotton hose in drop stitch, assorted patterns, full fashioned and double soles, fast black, 18c, or 3 pairs for 50c; 20c, 25c, 35c pair.

Cotton Hose with White Soles.

B241. Ladies' black cotton hose, full fashioned, double soles, heels and toes, high spliced, and made with lower part of foot and heel white; it is cooling on the foot for summer wear, 25c; 35c, or 3 pairs for $1.00; 45c, or 3 pairs for $1.25.

Colored Cotton Hose.

B242. Ladies' tan cotton hose, full fashioned, double soles, in dark colors, 12½c; 18c, or 3 pairs for 50c; 25c pair.

B243. Ladies' balbriggan hose, full fashioned, double soles, heels and toes, 10c; 18c, or 3 pairs for 50c; 25c pair.

B244. Ladies' cream and white cotton hose, full fashioned, and double soles, 15c, 25c pair.

Ladies' Lisle Hose.

B250. Ladies' black lisle hose, full fashioned, double soles, heels and toes, 25c pair.

B251. Ladies black lisle hose, full fashioned, double soles, heels and toes, high spliced, soft finish, 35c, or 3 pairs for $1.00; 45c, or 3 pairs for $1.25; 50c pair.

B252. Ladies' plain white, cream and tan lisle hose, with double soles, 35c, or 3 pairs for $1.00.

Lisle Lace Ankle Hose.

B253. Ladies' black, cream and white lisle hose, with lace ankles, assorted patterns, 35c, 50c pair.

B253½. Ladies' black lace hose, in very pretty patterns, 35c, 50c, 75c, $1.00 pair.

Ladies' Silk Hose.

B254. Ladies' plain black silk hose, 75c, $1.00, 1.25, 1.50, 2.00, 2.50, 3.00 pair.

B254½. Ladies' black lace ankle silk hose, $1.00, 1.25 pair.

Cashmere and Cotton Outside Sizes.

B255. Ladies' "gloria" finish black cotton hose, full fashioned, and high spliced ankles, fine soft finish, and wide legs and feet, 35c, or 3 pairs for $1.00; 45c, or 3 pairs for $1.25.

B256. Ladies' black cashmere hose, full fashioned, double soles, heels and toes; these hose are soft finish, and are made with wide legs and feet, 50c, 65c, 75c pair.

Infants' Cashmere, Lisle, Silk and Cotton Socks.

B257. Black cashmere socks, half length—
4, 4½, 5, 5½, 6, 6½, 7,
15c, 15c, 15c, 15c, 20c, 20c, 20c.

B258. Cream cashmere socks—
4, 4½, 5, 5½, 6, 6½, 7,
15c, 15c, 15c, 15c, 20c, 20c, 20c.

B259. Black cashmere socks, three-quarter lengths—
4, 4½, 5, 5½, 6, 6½, 7,
20c, 20c, 20c, 20c, 25c, 25c, 25c.

B260. Cream cashmere socks—
4, 4½, 5, 5½, 6, 6½, 7,
20c, 20c, 20c, 20c, 25c, 25c, 25c.

B261. Plain tan cashmere socks, half lengths—
4, 4½, 5, 5½, 6, 6½, 7,
15c, 15c, 15c, 15c, 20c, 20c, 20c.

B262. Tan color cashmere socks, with embroidered fronts—
4, 4½, 5, 5½,
25c, 25c, 25c, 25c.

B263. Spun silk socks, in tan colors—
4, 4½, 5, 5½,
35c, 35c, 35c, 35c.

B263½. Cotton socks, in tan, white and black—
4, 4½, 5, 5½, 6, 6½, 7,
12½c, 12½c, 15c, 15c, 20c, 20c, 20c.

Infants' Bootees.

B264. Infants' bootees, in fancy colors, also white, 10c, 15c, 20c pair.

B264½. Infant's bootees, hand made, in cream and fancy colors, 25c, 50c pair.

Misses' Plain Cotton Hose.

B265. Misses' cotton hose, stainless black—
4½, 5, 5½, 6, 6½, 7, 7½, 8, 8½,
10c, 10c, 12½c, 12½c, 15c, 15c, 20c, 20c, 20c.

B266. Misses' black cotton hose, fast black, double soles—
4½, 5, 5½, 6, 6½, 7, 7½, 8, 8½,
12½c, 12½c, 15c, 15c, 20c, 20c, 25c, 25c, 25c.

B266½. Misses' tan cotton hose, full fashioned, double toes, dark colors—
4½, 5, 5½, 6, 6½, 7, 7½, 8, 8½,
10c, 10c, 12½c, 12½c, 15c, 15c, 20c, 20c, 20c.

Misses' Ribbed Cotton Hose.

B267. Misses' 1/1 ribbed cotton hose, fast black—
5, 5½, 6, 6½, 7, 7½, 8, 8½, 9,
10c, 10c, 10c, 10c, 12½c, 12½c, 15c, 15c, 15c.

B268. Misses' 1/1 ribbed black cotton hose, double knees, soles and heels, fast black—
5, 5½, 6, 6½, 7, 7½, 8, 8½, 9,
15c, 15c, 15c, 15c, 20c, 20c, 20c, 25c, 25c.

B269. Misses' 1/1 ribbed black cotton, extra fine quality, and full fashioned—
5, 5½, 6, 6½, 7, 7½, 8, 8½, 9,
20c, 20c, 25c, 25c, 30c, 30c, 30c, 35c, 35c.

B270. Misses' 4/1 ribbed black cotton hose, fashioned, and warranted to wear—
5, 5½, 6, 6½, 7, 7½, 8, 8½, 9,
15c, 15c, 15c, 15c, 20c, 20c, 20c, 25c, 25c.

Boys' Ribbed Cotton Hose.

B271. Boys' 4/1 ribbed cotton hose, extra heavy, and made with seamless feet—
6, 6½, 7, 7½, 8, 8½, 9, 9½, 10,
15c, 15c, 15c, 15c, 15c, 15c, 15c, 15c, 15c.

B272. Boys' ribbed cotton hose, 1/1 rib, medium weight—
5, 5½, 6, 6½, 7, 7½, 8, 8½, 9, 9½, 10,
10c, 10c, 10c, 10c, 12½c, 12½c, 15c, 15c, 15c, 15c, 15c.

B273. Boys' 7/1 ribbed cotton hose, fashioned, and seamless feet, double knees—
5, 5½, 6, 6½, 7, 7½, 8, 8½, 9, 9½, 10,
15c, 15c, 15c, 15c, 20c, 20c, 20c, 25c, 25c, 25c, 25c.

B274. Boys' 7/1 ribbed black cotton hose, full fashioned, double soles and heels, extra fine quality, double knees—
5, 5½, 6, 6½, 7, 7½, 8, 8½, 9, 9½, 10,
20c, 20c, 25c, 25c, 30c, 30c, 30c, 35c, 35c, 35c, 35c.

Men's Cotton and Merino Socks.

These hose may be had in the following sizes: 10, 10½, 11 inches.

B275. Men's cotton socks, in mixed color, blue and brown, 5c, 9c or 3 pairs for 25c.

B276. Men's black cotton socks, double heels and toes, 10c, 12½c, 18c or 3 pairs for 50c, and 25c pair.

B277. Men's tan cotton socks, 12½c, 18c or 3 pairs for 50c, and 25c pair.

B278. Men's balbriggan socks, 12½c, 18c or 3 pairs for 50c.

B279. Men's merino socks, 12½c, 15c pair.

Men's Wool Socks.

B280. Men's merino and wool socks, medium weight, 12½c, 15c, 20c pair.

B281. Men's natural wool socks, double heels and soles, 20c, 25c pair.

B282. Men's fine English natural wool socks, high spliced ankles, 35c or 3 pairs for $1.00.

B283. Men's fine all-wool socks, suitable for summer wear, 20c pair.

B284. Men's heather mixture, medium weight ribbed socks, 35c, 50c pair.

B285. Men's Irish knit socks, ribbed and plain, colors dark, medium and light grey, 35c, 50c pair.

B286. Men's black Irish knit socks, ribbed, splendid wearing, 25c, 35c or 3 pairs for $1.00, and 50c pair.

Men's Plain Black Cashmere Socks.

B287. Men's black cashmere socks, seamless, double heels and toes, 18c or 3 pairs for 50c.

B288. Men's black cashmere socks, seamless, high spliced ankles, double heels and toes, 20c pair.

B289. Men's black cashmere socks, plain double soles, and full fashioned, 25c pair.

B290. Men's plain black cashmere socks, black heels and toes, Llama finish, double heels, toes and soles, 35c or 3 pairs for $1.00; 45c or 3 pairs for $1.25.

Men's Ribbed Black Cashmere Socks.

B291. Men's ribbed black cashmere socks, double soles, heels and toes, 25c pair.

B292. Men's ribbed black cashmere socks, splendid wearing, double soles, 35c or 3 pairs for $1.00; 50c pair.

B293. Men's tan cashmere socks, double heels, soles and toes, fine quality, 35c pair.

Men's Embroidered Cashmere Socks.

B294. Men's fancy embroidered socks, black, embroidered in all the leading shades, 35c or 3 pairs for $1.00, 50c pair.

Boys' Worsted and Wool Hose.

B295. Boys' Irish knit wool hose, ribbed—
6, 6½, 7, 7½, 8, 8½, 9, 9½, 10,
25c, 25c, 30c, 30c, 30c, 35c, 35c, 35c, 35c.

B296. Boys' English wool hose, wide rib and a good wearer—
6, 6½, 7, 7½, 8, 8½, 9, 9½, 10,
30c, 30c, 35c, 40c, 45c, 50c, 50c, 50c, 50c.

SUNSHADES AND PARASOLS.

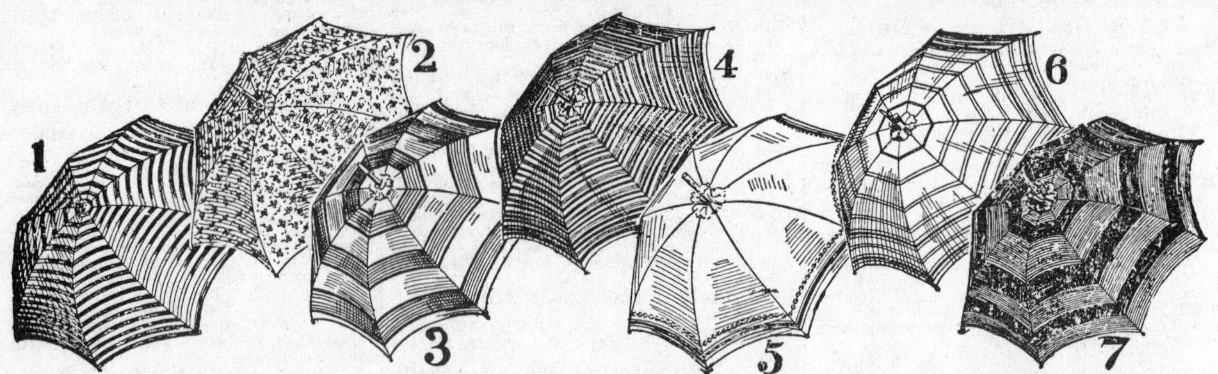

Fancy Sunshades.

No. 1. Cotton cloth, black ground, white stripes; white ground, black stripes, steel rod, 75c.

No. 2. Silk mix, white, cardinal, navy, cadet blue, natural handles, $1.75.

No. 3. Silk mix, black and white, blue and white, cardinal, dark heliotrope, navy, $2.00.

No. 4. Silk mix, white stripes on black, navy, marine, natural sticks, $2.00.

No. 5. Pure silk, hemstitch borders, in white body, with border of navy, heliotrope, sky, pink and grey; black body, black and white border; navy body, navy and white border; natural sticks, $2.50.

No. 6. Pure silk, white ground with stripes, black and grey, black and sky, black and light green, black and heliotrope, natural sticks, $3.50.

No. 7. Pure silk, black, cerise and navy, $4.00.

White Summer Parasols.

Plain white mercerized cloth, white sticks, 75c.

Plain white mercerized cloth, lace insertion, $1.00.

Plain white Japan silk, $1.50.

White, with frill at edge, white sticks, $1.00.

White Japan silk, frill at edge, white sticks, $2.00.

Black Frilled Parasols.

Black Austria, frill at edge, 75c.

Black gloria, frill at edge, $1.00.

Black gloria, two frills, $1.50.

Black satin de chene, frill at edge, $2.00.

Black Japan silk, frill at edge, $2.50.

Black twill silk, frill at edge, $3.00.

Children's Parasols.

Fancy colors, with small frill, 25c, 30c, 35c.

Fancy sateen, with white sticks, 50c.

Austria, pink, sky, white, with frill, 75c.

Pure silk, pink, sky, white, royal, cardinal, with frill, $1.00.

MEN'S AND LADIES' UMBRELLAS.

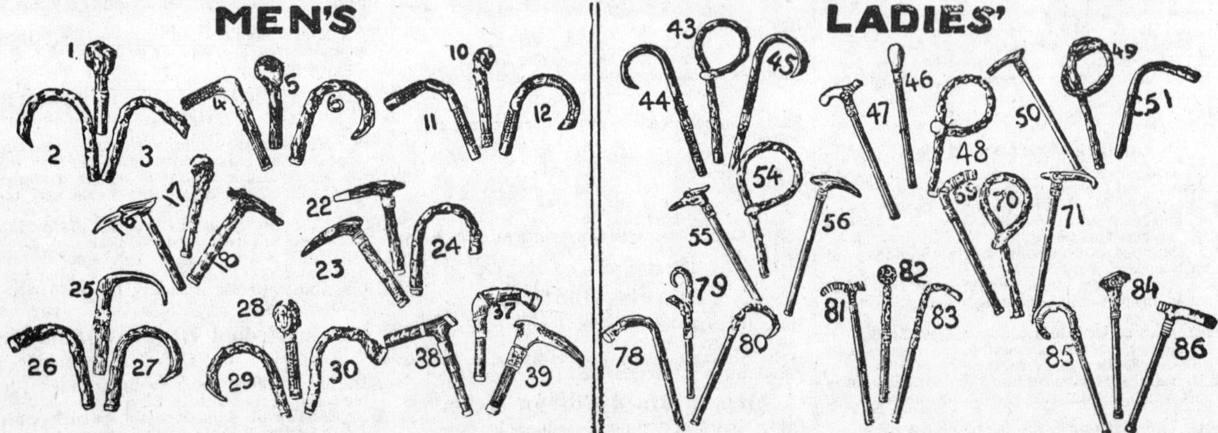

Men's Umbrellas.

Handles 1, 2, 3, wood rod, 25-inch, Austria cloth, 50c.

Handles 4, 5, 6, steel rod, 25-inch, Austria cloth, 75c.

Handles 1, 2, 3, steel rod, 25-inch, gloria cloth, special, $1.00.

Handles 10, 11, 12, steel rod, 27-inch, gloria cloth, extra large size, $1.50.

Handles 16, 17, 18, steel rod, 25-inch, best gloria cloth, $1.50.

Handles 22, 23, 24, steel rod, 25-inch, taffeta silk, cased, $2.00.

Handles 25, 26, 27, steel rod, 25-inch, fine taffeta silk, cased, $2.50.

Handles 28, 29, 30, steel rod, 25-inch, best taffeta silk, cased, $3.00, 4.00.

Handles 37, 38, 39, steel rod, 25-inch, twill silk, tape edge, cased, $5.00, 6.50.

Ladies' Umbrellas.

Handles 43, 44, 45, steel rod, 22-inch, Austria cloth, 50c, 65c.

Handles 46, 47, 48, steel rod, 23-inch, Austria cloth, 75c.

Handles 49, 50, C51, steel rod, 23-inch, fine gloria silk mix, special, $1.00.

Handles 54, 55, 56, steel rod, 23-inch, fine gloria silk mix, $1.25.

Handles 54, 55, 56, steel rod, 23-inch, best gloria silk mix, $1.50.

Handles 69, 70, 71, steel rod, 23-inch, taffeta, silk cased, $2.00.

Handles 69, 70, 71, steel rod, 23-inch, best taffeta, silk cased, $2.50.

Handles 78, 79, 80, steel rod, 23-inch, twill silk, silk cased, $3.50.

Handles 81, 82, 83, steel rod, 23-inch, twill silk, silk cased, $4.00.

Handles 84, 85, 86, steel rod, 23-inch, twill silk, tape edge, silk cased, $5.00, 7.50.

Ribbon Department.

Colored Faille and Satin Ribbons.

No. 1032. Pure silk gros-grain ribbon, satin edge, in colors cream, yellow, buttercup, Nile green, medium green, dark green, coral, old rose, turquoise, lemon, lilac, violet, pink, rose, cerise, bright red, cardinal, dark red, sky blue, medium blue, national blue, navy blue, brown, myrtle green, fawn, white, special make for children's wear, $\frac{1}{2}$-inch, 3c; 1-inch, 5c; $1\frac{1}{2}$-inch, 8c; 2-inch, $12\frac{1}{2}$c; 3-inch, 15c yd.

No. 1075. Gros-grain ribbon, best make, with satin edge, all colors for spring, $\frac{5}{8}$-inch, 5c; 1-inch, 7c; $1\frac{1}{2}$-inch, 10c; $2\frac{1}{2}$-inch, 15c; $3\frac{1}{4}$-inch, 20c yd.

No. 1060. Colored faille ribbon, for children's wear, nice soft quality, with cord edge for shirring, $\frac{3}{4}$-inch, 3c; 1-inch, 5c; 2-inch, 8c yd.

No. 1050. Colored satin ribbon, medium quality, for fancy work, etc., $\frac{7}{8}$-inch, 3c; $1\frac{1}{8}$-inch, 5c; 2-inch, 8c; 3-inch, $12\frac{1}{2}$c yd.

No. 1040. Double-faced satin ribbon, rich quality, for dress trimmings, neckwear, streamers, etc., in all the popular tints, colors and shades for spring of 1901, $\frac{3}{8}$-inch, 4c; $\frac{3}{4}$-inch, 5c; 1-inch, 7c; $1\frac{1}{2}$-inch, 10c; $2\frac{1}{4}$-inch, 15c; 3-inch, 20c; 4-inch, 30c; 5-inch, 35c yd.

Taffeta and Moire Ribbons.

No. 1080. Colored taffeta ribbon, direct from France, for dress trimmings and neckwear, staple colors only, 1-inch, 7c; $1\frac{1}{2}$-inch, 10c; $2\frac{1}{2}$-inch, 15c; 3-inch, 20c; 4-inch, 25c yd.

No. 1085. Colored moire taffeta ribbon, large pattern, in all the staple colors, and white, for streamers, 1-inch, 5c; $1\frac{1}{2}$-inch, 10c; $2\frac{1}{8}$-inch, $12\frac{1}{2}$c; 3-inch, 18c; $5\frac{1}{4}$-inch, 25c yd.

No. 1090. White taffeta ribbon, splendid quality, 4-inch, 20c; 5-inch, 25c yd.

No. 1091. Duchesse satin ribbon, for neckwear, silk one side, satin the other, washable, in colors white, cream, Tuscan, pink, turquoise, old rose, wood rose (new tint), sky blue, navy, Nile, cardinal, mauve, black, very special, $3\frac{1}{4}$-inch, 25c; $4\frac{1}{4}$-inch, 30c yd.

No. 1092. Colored moire ribbon, 4 inches wide, extra special, all colors, 22c yd.

No. 1093. Taffeta ribbon, in two widths only, all the new colors for hat trimming and neckwear, 4-inch, 20c; 5-inch 25c yd.

Black Silk Ribbons.

No. 1014. Black faille ribbon, medium quality, satin edge, $\frac{1}{2}$-inch, 3c; 1-inch, 5c; $1\frac{1}{2}$-inch, 8c; 2-inch, $12\frac{1}{2}$c; 3-inch, 15c yd.

No. 1015. Black gros-grain ribbon, best make, rich heavy quality, $\frac{5}{8}$-inch, 5c; $\frac{7}{8}$-inch, 7c; $1\frac{1}{4}$-inch, 10c; $1\frac{3}{8}$-inch, $12\frac{1}{2}$c; $2\frac{1}{8}$-inch, 15c; $2\frac{3}{4}$-inch, 20c; $3\frac{1}{8}$-inch, 25c; $4\frac{1}{4}$-inch, 30c; 6-inch, 45c yd.

No. 1016. Black gros-grain, plain pearl edge, suitable for mourning, $\frac{1}{2}$-inch, 4c; 1-inch, 7c; $1\frac{1}{2}$-inch, 10c; $2\frac{1}{4}$-inch, 15c; $2\frac{7}{8}$-inch, 20c; $3\frac{1}{4}$-inch, 25c; $4\frac{1}{4}$-inch, 30c yd.

No. 1018. Black moire taffeta ribbon, fine quality, good black, large pattern, $\frac{5}{8}$-inch, $3\frac{1}{2}$c; 1-inch, 5c; $1\frac{5}{8}$-inch, 10c; $2\frac{1}{8}$-inch, $12\frac{1}{2}$c; $2\frac{5}{8}$-inch, 15c; 3-inch, 18c; $3\frac{1}{8}$-inch, 20c; $4\frac{1}{4}$-inch, 25c; 5-inch, 30c; $5\frac{1}{2}$-inch, 35c; $6\frac{1}{4}$-inch, 40c yd.

No. 1019. Black peau de soie, dull finish, suitable for mourning purposes, $\frac{5}{8}$-inch, 5c; 1-inch, 7c; $1\frac{7}{8}$-inch, $12\frac{1}{2}$c; $2\frac{1}{4}$-inch, 15c; 3-inch, 20c; $4\frac{1}{8}$-inch, 30c yd.

Black Satin Ribbons.

No. 1022. Double-faced black satin ribbon, medium quality, $\frac{5}{8}$-inch, 3c; 1-inch, 5c; $1\frac{1}{2}$-inch, 7c; 2-inch, 10c; $2\frac{1}{2}$-inch, $12\frac{1}{2}$c; 3-inch, 15c; 4-inch, 20c yd.

No. 1023. Double-faced black satin ribbon, our best quality, $\frac{1}{2}$-inch, 4c; $\frac{3}{4}$-inch, 6c; 1-inch, 8c; $1\frac{3}{8}$-inch, 10c; $1\frac{3}{4}$-inch, 15c; $2\frac{1}{4}$-inch, 18c; 3-inch, 25c; $4\frac{1}{4}$-inch, 35c; $5\frac{1}{2}$-inch, 45c yd.

No. 1025. Black crape, our best quality, $1\frac{3}{4}$-inch, $12\frac{1}{2}$c; $2\frac{1}{8}$-inch, 15c; $2\frac{1}{2}$-inch, 20c; 3-inch, 25c yd.

No. 1024. Black satin, $4\frac{1}{4}$-inch, 25c; 5-inch, 30c; 6-inch, 35c yd.

No. 1028. Black taffeta ribbon, fine soft quality, $\frac{5}{8}$-inch, $3\frac{1}{2}$c; 1-inch, 5c; $1\frac{3}{4}$-inch, 8c; $2\frac{1}{8}$-inch, 10c; $2\frac{1}{2}$-inch, $12\frac{1}{2}$c; 3-inch, 15c; 4-inch, 20c; $4\frac{7}{8}$-inch, 25c; $5\frac{1}{4}$-inch, 30c; 6-inch, 35c yd.

No. 1029. Black velvet ribbon, linen back, best quality, woven edge, good black, $\frac{1}{8}$-inch, $2\frac{1}{2}$c; $\frac{1}{4}$-inch, 3c; $\frac{3}{8}$-inch, 4c; $\frac{1}{2}$-inch, $4\frac{1}{2}$c; $\frac{5}{8}$-inch, 5c; $\frac{7}{8}$-inch, 7c; $1\frac{1}{8}$-inch, 8c; $1\frac{3}{8}$-inch, 9c; $1\frac{5}{8}$-inch, $12\frac{1}{2}$c; $2\frac{1}{8}$-inch, 18c; $2\frac{7}{8}$-inch, 25c yd.

No. 1037. Black velvet ribbon, linen back, woven edge, $\frac{1}{8}$-inch, 40c; $\frac{1}{4}$-inch, 50c per piece of $17\frac{3}{4}$ yds.

No. 1038. Black velvet ribbon, satin back, best French make, our very best quality, $\frac{1}{8}$-inch, $3\frac{1}{2}$c; $\frac{1}{4}$-inch, 5c; $\frac{1}{2}$-inch, 7c; $\frac{3}{4}$-inch, 9c; $\frac{7}{8}$-inch, $12\frac{1}{2}$c; 1-inch, 14c; $1\frac{1}{4}$-inch, 18c; $1\frac{1}{2}$-inch, 20c; 2-inch, 25c; $2\frac{3}{8}$-inch, 30c; $2\frac{3}{4}$-inch, 35c; 3-inch, 40c yd.

No. 1035. Colored velvet ribbon, satin back, all colors, for waist trimming, $\frac{1}{8}$-inch, 50c; $\frac{1}{4}$-inch, 65c, per piece of $17\frac{3}{4}$ yds.

No. 1036. Colored velvet ribbon, best make, satin back, for dress bows, etc., all the very latest colors, $\frac{1}{8}$-inch, $3\frac{1}{2}$c; 1-inch, $12\frac{1}{2}$c; $1\frac{3}{4}$-inch, 20c; $2\frac{1}{8}$-inch, 25c yd.

No. 1020. Black duchesse satin ribbon, all silk, with satin face, soft rich finish, $\frac{1}{8}$-inch, 5c; 1-inch, 8c; $1\frac{3}{4}$-inch, 15c; $2\frac{1}{8}$-inch, 18c; $2\frac{5}{8}$-inch, 20c; $3\frac{1}{8}$-inch, 25c; $4\frac{1}{8}$-inch, 30c; $5\frac{1}{4}$-inch, 45c yd.

Baby Ribbons.

Baby ribbon, satin faced, faille back, in white, cream, buttercup, yellow, light blue, medium blue, light pink, medium pink, cardinal, violet, lilac, sea green, apple green and black, $\frac{1}{8}$-inch wide, 7 yds for 10c.

Baby ribbon, satin faced, faille back, $\frac{3}{8}$-inch wide, all colors, our leader, 2c yd.

Baby ribbon, $\frac{1}{4}$-inch wide, in double-faced satin, faille, cord edge and moire, white, black, and all colors, 3c yd.

Beltings and Club Colors.

Black belting, medium quality, in heavy cord effect, $1\frac{1}{2}$-inch, $12\frac{1}{2}$c; 2-inch, 15c; $2\frac{1}{2}$-inch, 20c yd.

Black belting, heavy rich quality, our best make, 2 inches wide, 20c yd.

Colored belting, 2-inch, heavy make, in white, cream, cardinal, navy, brown, sky, rose and pink, 20c yd.

Club colors—Varsity: white and royal blue. Dental: sky blue and dark cardinal. Pharmacy: yellow, cardinal and black. Queen's Own: myrtle and cardinal. Trinity Medical: cardinal and black. Trinity University: black and red, 2-inch, 20c yd.

Fancy Ribbons for Neckwear and Millinery Purposes.

Our assortment of fancy ribbons will be the largest and finest we have ever had. The new styles in hats show a large quantity of ribbon, especially taffeta, which comes about 5 inches wide in all the popular colors, 25c yd. Duchesse satin will be worn largely for dress bows and neckwear. There will be an extra large demand for fancies, which will be mostly light colors, and small allover effects, 4, $4\frac{1}{2}$ and $5\frac{1}{4}$ inches, ranging from 15c to 25c yard; also plain centre ribbons with fancy edge, check ribbons, plaids in the new bright colors, and our fine all-silk fancies for hat bows and waist bows, 5 to 7 inches wide, 35c, 50c and 75c yard. Write for samples, and state color, and if plain or fancy required, as the stock is so large we could not very well send samples of every kind.

The Latest Ribbons in the Newest Shades for Spring and Summer Wear.

DRESS GOODS

SPECIAL NOTICE—All Cloths and Heavy Suitings Shrunk and Sponged free of charge if desired. We will not do this unless specially requested to do so when goods are ordered.

Priestley's and Salt's Serges.

Texture and color guaranteed. Shrunk and sponged in the heavier qualities free of charge, if desired.

PRIESTLEY'S ALL-WOOL COATING DRESS SERGE, navy and black only, 42 to 44-inch, 35c, 50c, 65c yd.
PRIESTLEY'S CAMPBELL TWILL DRESS SERGE, smooth finish, navy and black only, 42-inch, 35c, 50c, 65c; 46-inch, 75c, 85c yd.
PRIESTLEY'S SOFT ROUGH FINISH SERGE, navy, 48-inch, 75c, $1.00 yd.
PRIESTLEY'S ESTAMINE SERGE, woolly finish and shower proof, navy, 40-inch, 25c; 41-inch, 35c, 40c; 42-inch, 50c; 48-inch, 75c yd.
SALT'S COATING TWILL DRESS SERGE, good weight, clear finish, navy, 46-inch, 65c; 52-inch, 75c; 54-inch, $1.00 yd.
SALT'S CHEVIOT DRESS SERGE, soft and woolly finish, navy, 50-inch, 85c, $1.25 yd.
SALT'S CHEVIOT DRESS SERGE, smooth soft finish, beautiful suiting weight, navy, 52-inch, $1.00 yd.
SALT'S EXTRA SPECIAL COATING SERGE, in superior finish, fine clear twill, black and navy, 52-inch, 65c yd.

French Serges.

We do not shrink these serges.

FRENCH COATING DRESS SERGE, soft finish, colors fawn, brown, red and navy, 42-inch, 35c yd.
FRENCH COATING DRESS SERGE, fine twill, in staple shades, 42-inch, 50c yd.
FRENCH FLORENTINE SERGE, cashmere twill, navy and black only, 44-inch, 50c yd.

Poplins, Poplinettes, Drap de Paris, Satin Cloths.

FRENCH POPLIN, all wool, plain, in leading shades, 45-inch, 50c, 75c, $1.00 yd.
FRENCH POPLINETTE, a novelty in light weight dress fabric, in all the most stylish shades, 44-inch, 65c yd.
DRAP DE PARIS, a fine diagonal cord, correct material for spring and summer wear, in a select range of colors, 47-inch, 65c yd.
PARISIAN CORD DRESS SUITING, something new, a beautiful finish, in all the leading shades for summer wear, 48-inch, 85c yd.
PRIESTLEY'S SATIN CLOTH, in navy, royal, brown, green, fawn, pearl grey and red, 44-inch, 50c; same shades, heavier weight, 75c yd.

Cashmeres, Henriettas, Nun's Veilings, Cravenettes and Lustres.

FRENCH CASHMERE, all pure wool, in all shades, 40-inch, 25c; 44-inch, 35c yd.
FRENCH HENRIETTA, in silk finish, full range of colors, 46-inch, 50c, 75c yd.
NUN'S VEILING, in colors navy, brown, green and cardinal, 40-inch, 30c yd.
PRIESTLEY'S CRAVENETTE, navy, brown and green, 60-inch, $1.00 yd.
IMPERIAL CRAVENETTE, in navy, medium and dark grey, 60-inch, $1.25 yd.
BRILLIANTINE OR LUSTRE, in staple shades, 42-inch, 35c; 44-inch, 50c; in navy only, 46-inch, 65c, 75c yd.

Salt's Dress Serge,

pure wool, good weight, medium fine twill, fast dye, in black and navy only, 45 inches wide, special, 35c.

Summer or Evening Wear Dress Materials.

FRENCH CASHMERE, in cream and light shades, 40-inch, 25c; 44-inch, 35c yd.
FRENCH HENRIETTA, silk finish, in cream and light shades, 44-inch, 50c yd.
NUN'S VEILINGS, in cream and light shades, 40-inch, 30c, 40c yd.
FANCY DELAINES, in dark and light grounds, with spots and fancy figures, 30-inch, 35c yd.
BRILLIANTINE LUSTRES, cream only, 40-inch, 25c; 44-inch, 50c; 46-inch, 75c; cream and light shades, 42-inch, 35c yd.
CREAM SERGES, including coating twills, cheviots and estamines, 40-inch, 35c; 44-inch, 50c; 46-inch, 75c; 50-inch, $1.00; cream cashmere serge, 44-inch, 50c yd.
AMAZON or LADIES' CLOTH, in cream only, 52-inch, $1.00, 1.25 yd.
WOOL CREPONS, in cream and light shades, 38-inch, 35c.
BEDFORD CORD, in cream only, 42-inch, 50c; 44-inch, 65c; 46-inch, 85c yd.
CHILDREN'S CLOAKINGS, cream honeycomb cloth, all pure wool, 50-inch, $1.00 yd.
FANCY DRESS FABRICS, including all-wool materials, in a variety of designs, cream, also figured brilliantines, in cream and evening shades, 42 to 48-inch, 35c, 50c, 75c, $1.00 yd.
BLOUSING OR WAIST NOVELTIES, in henriettas, albatross and amazons, embroidered with silk spots and other fancy designs, in new shades of light and dark colorings, 39 to 44-inch, 50c, 75c, 85c yd.
GLORIA SILK, with fancy stripe, in beautiful shades of blue, green, brown, cardinal and grenat, makes a handsome waist or evening dress, 44-inch, $1.00 yd.
GLORIA SILK, plain colors, in light and dark shades, beautifully finished material, for summer and evening wear, or blouses, 48-inch, 85c yd.

Fancy Dress Goods and Suitings.

FRENCH WOOL CREPE DE CHENE, in new and fashionable shades, 42-inch, $1.25 yd.
FRENCH SILK AND WOOL POPLINS, new and latest colorings, 44-inch, $1.25, 2.00 yd.

English Costume Cloth,

serge effect, a dressy and stylish fabric, good heavy quality, special for bicycling or walking skirts and costumes, 15 different shades, 52 inches wide, special, 35c.

FRENCH PEBBLE CORD, in select range of shades, including navy, brown, grey, fawn and castor, 46-inch, $1.25 yd.
NEW IMPORTATIONS OF HIGH-CLASS PARISIAN NOVELTIES, consisting of French silk voiles, and a specially select range of patterns, in silk and wool stripes and scroll designs, all new importations, in costume lengths, ranging in price from $10.00 to $15.00.
FRENCH VOILE, fine all-wool texture, suitable for street or evening wear, 44-inch, $1.25 yd.
ENGLISH COVERT SUITINGS, for tailored gowns, in new fawn, green, grey and castor shades, 54-inch, $1.00, 1.50 yd.
GERMAN SPIRAL CORD, two-toned colors, grey, brown, fawn and castor, 48-inch, $1.25 yd.
AMAZON CLOTH, a variety of shades, 46-inch, 65c yd.
FRENCH VENETIAN CLOTH, in carefully selected range of colors, superior finish and special value, 46-inch, 75c yd.
COSTUME CLOTH, sponged and shrunk, good heavy suiting weight, in leading shades, 52-inch, $1.25 yd.
FINE ENGLISH BROADCLOTHS, dark and medium shades, 52-inch, $1.00, 1.25 yd.
GERMAN BROADCLOTHS, correct weight, for tailored gowns, in all new and leading shades, 52-inch, $1.50, 1.75, 2.00 yd.
ENGLISH AND SCOTCH HOMESPUN AND FRIEZES, in a very select variety of weaves and colors, 52 to 54-inch, 75c to $1.50 yd.

Plaids and Checks.

SHEPHERD'S PLAIDS, in black and white, 40-inch, 25c, 35c; 42-inch, 50c yd.
SCOTCH TARTANS AND FANCY PLAIDS, assorted colors, 38-inch, special, 25c; 42-inch, 50c yd.
SCOTCH TARTANS, 100 different clans, special weight and quality, 50-inch, 75c yd.

Low-priced Dress Goods.

AMAZON SUITING, in a variety of shades, extra quality and value, 48-inch, 25c yd.
ENGLISH COSTUME CLOTH, a suitable material for tailored gowns, special, 52-inch, 35c yd.
COVERT SUITING, unspotable, a range of 12 colors, 50-inch, 50c yd.

English Covert Cloth,

unspotable, smooth finish, heavy quality, good range of leading shades, 50 inches wide, an excellent costume cloth, special, 50c.

TWEEDS, in check and mottled effects, 42-inch, 25c, 35c yd.
FANCY BLACK DRESS MATERIALS, in mohair figures and brilliantines, 40-inch, 25c, 35c yd.
SERGE, special, in black and navy only, smooth finish, cheviot twill, 42-inch, 25c yd.

Moreen Skirtings.

PRIESTLEY'S black moreen skirting, 38-inch, 35c, 50c yd.
PRIESTLEY'S colored moreen skirting, in staple colors, 38-inch, 35c, 50c yd.

OUR DRESS GOODS ARE ALWAYS THE LATEST AT LOWEST PRICES.

Black Dress Goods.

In black dress fabrics we carry in stock only makes and qualities that we can conscientiously offer as satisfactory in both wear and dye, in a variety of stylish and carefully selected designs and novelties. PRIESTLEY'S we give the preference, as being of world-wide renown, and the best make and dye produced. Knowing this fact, by arrangements with this noted manufacturer, customers will find THIS STORE THE ONLY ONE in Canada with a full range of these goods direct from the mills, thus saving to buyers here a profit on the mill price on any of Priestley's fabrics bought from us.

FRENCH AND GERMAN makes we also have in great variety.

Priestley's Fabrics.

PRIESTLEY'S black satin cloth, bright dressy finish, 44-inch, 50c, 75c, $1.00 yd.
PRIESTLEY'S black soliel, a rich satin-finished soft cord effect, 42 to 44-inch, 65c, 75c, $1.00 yd.
PRIESTLEY'S black silk and wool eudora, henrietta finish, 41 to 45-inch, $1.00, 1.25, 1.50, 1.75, 2.00 yd.
PRIESTLEY'S black olgana, fine soft finished mourning goods, 42-inch, 85c yd.
PRIESTLEY'S black crepoline wool cord, 43-inch, 65c, 75c, 85c yd.
PRIESTLEY'S black pebble cloth, various weaves, 43-inch, 75c yd.
PRIESTLEY'S black Persian cloth, a diagonal cord, soft finish, 42-inch, 75c, 85c yd.
PRIESTLEY'S black Redfern cord suiting, 44-inch, $1.25 yd.
PRIESTLEY'S black corkscrew cord, fine and different weaves, 42-inch, $1.00 yd.
PRIESTLEY'S black Venetian crepe cloth, 42-inch, 50c, 65c ; 44-inch, 75c, $1.00 yd.
PRIESTLEY'S black wool crepe cloth, 44-inch, $1.00 yd.
PRIESTLEY'S black Espagnol crepe cloth, 46-inch, $1.25 yd.
PRIESTLEY'S black silk and wool crepe cloth, 41-inch, $1.00 ; 46-inch, $1.25 yd.
PRIESTLEY'S black melrose and armure cloths, silk and wool, 45-inch, $1.25, 1.50 yd.
PRIESTLEY'S black drap de Alma, Baritz and crystal cords, 44-inch, $1.25 yd.

Priestley's Black Serges.

PRIESTLEY'S black estamine serge, shower proof, 40-inch, 25c ; 42-inch, 40c, 50c ; 48-inch, 75c yd.
PRIESTLEY'S black cheviot serge, Campbell twill, smooth finish, 42-inch, 35c ; 44-inch, 50c ; 45-inch, 75c ; 48-inch, 85c yd.
PRIESTLEY'S cheviot serge, soft rough finish, 48-inch, 75c, $1.00 yd.
PRIESTLEY'S black coating serge, hard smooth finish, 42 to 44-inch, 35c, 50c, 65c yd.
PRIESTLEY'S black cravenette waterproof, 60-inch, $1.00 yd.

Salt's Serges.

SALT'S black estamine serge, 46-inch, 65c ; 50-inch, 75c yd.
SALT'S black coating dress serge, smooth finish, medium fine twill, 45-inch, 65c ; 52-inch, 75c ; 54-inch, $1.00, 1.25 ; 56-inch, $1.50 yd.
SALT'S black coating serge, fine twill, smooth hard finish, special, 50-inch, 65c yd.
FRENCH black coating serge, soft finish, 42-inch, 35c ; 44-inch, 50c yd.
FRENCH black cheviot, in beautiful soft finish, fine wool, indistinct twill, 50-inch, $1.25, 1.50 yd.
HOMESPUNS, heavy costume weight, rough finish, 50-inch, 85c, $1.00, 1.25 yd.

Black Poplins and Dress Cords.

FRENCH POPLIN CORD, black, 45-inch, 50c ; 47-inch, 75c, $1.00 ; 50-inch, $1.50 yd.
FRENCH WHIPCORD, black, 44-inch, 50c yd.
FRENCH DRAP DE PARIS, black, 46-inch, 65c yd.
REDFERN SUITING, black, in superior finish, 45-inch, 85c, $1.00 yd.
PRIESTLEY'S SILK AND WOOL POPLIN CORD, in black. 44-inch, $2.50, 3.00 yd.
PRIESTLEY'S ONDINE CORD, silk and wool, black, 44-inch, $2.50 yd.
GERMAN CORDS, black, fine all pure wool, comprising poplins, redferns, Venetians, and corkscrews, 50-inch, $1.25, 1.50, 1.75, 2.00 yd.
AMAZON CLOTH SUITING, black, 46-inch, 65c yd.
VENETIAN CLOTH, black, extra value 46-inch, 75c yd.
BROADCLOTH OR LADIES' CLOTH, black, 52-inch, $1.00, 1.25, 1.50 yd ; superior finish, fine quality, 54-inch, $2.00, 2.50, 3.00 yd.

Black Cashmeres, Nun's Veiling, Lustres and Delaines.

FRENCH CASHMERES, black and all wool, 40-inch, 25c ; 45-inch, 35c yd.
FRENCH HENRIETTA, black silk finish, in jet and blue blacks, 45-inch, 50c, 65c, 75c, $1.00 yd.
FRENCH CASHMERE SERGE, black, 44-inch, 50c yd.
NUN'S VEILING, black, 40-inch, 30c, 40c ; 46-inch, 50c yd.
LUSTRE OR BRILLIANTINE, black, 40-inch, 25c ; 42-inch, 35c, 50c ; 44-inch, 65c, 75c, $1.00 yd.
FRENCH DELAINE, black, 42-inch, 35c yd.

Grenadines and French Voiles.

FRENCH VOILE, black, all wool, 40-inch, 75c, $1.00, 1.25 yd.
FRENCH VOILE, black, with fancy mohair stripes, 40-inch, 65c, 75c, 85c, $1.00 yd.
GRENADINES, black, plain, and with fancy mohair stripe, all wool, 40-inch, 85c, $1.00, 1.25 yd.
FRENCH GRENADINES, black, the latest productions of foreign markets in novelties, new and artistic designs in all-wool and silk and wool, ranging in price from 50c to $2.00 yd.
SILK GRENADINES, black, in costume lengths only, all in exclusive designs, $12.00 to $18.00 a costume.

Fancy Black Dress Goods.

FIGURED LUSTRES, black, new, and well-assorted patterns, 42-inch, 50c, 75c yd.
FANCY BROCADES, black, in wool and mohair figures, new weaves, latest designs, 42-inch, 50c, 65c yd.
FANCY BLACK MERCATELLE, in fashionable raised effects, select range of patterns, 42 to 44-inch, 75c, 85c, $1.00 yd.
GERMAN FANCIES, in wool and mohair figures, neat and dressy, 44-inch, 85c, $1.00 yd.
BLACK SILK AND WOOL NOVELTIES, a complete range of nobby and stylish designs in matelasse and blister effects, small, medium, and large patterns, suitable for costumes or separate skirts, widths 42 to 44-inch, $1.25, 1.50, 1.75, 2.00, 2.50 yd.

SILKS AND SATINS.

Plain Colored Silks.

Full range of all colors. Write for samples, stating colors and price :

SATIN MERVEILLEUX, all pure silk, 21-inch, 75c yd.
POPLIN CORDED DRESS SILK, 21-inch, 75c yd.
TAFFETA, all pure silk, 20-inch, 50c yd.
TAFFETA, best French make, wear and quality specially recommended, for waists and linings, 21-inch, 75c yd.
TAFFETA, extra heavy weight, 21-inch, $1.00 yd.

Fancy Waist and Dress Silks.

JAPANESE WASH BLOUSE SILKS, in an excellent range of stripes and fancy checks, 20-inch, special, 35c yd.
TAFFETA SILK, FANCY STRIPES, comprises select range of colors, 20-inch, 50c, 65c yd.
TAFFETA SILK, FANCY STRIPES AND FIGURES, 21-inch, 75c, 85c, $1.00 yd.
SILK BROCADES, evening shades, 21-inch, 75c yd.
SILK AND SATIN BROCADES, all pure silk, 21-inch, $1.00 to $2.00 yd.
SILK AND SATIN BROCADES, black grounds with fancy colored designs, 21-inch, 75c, $1.00 yd.
NEW YORK NOVELTY BLOUSE SILKS, in new and nobby stripe effects, 21-inch, $1.25, 1.50 yd.
TWILLED FOULARD DRESS SILKS, full range of colors, latest New York styles, spot and flower effects, 24-inch, 75c yd.

Plain Colored Satins.

Full range of all colors.

VICTORIA SATINS, 24-inch, 35c, 50c yd.
VICTORIA SATINS, extra fine quality, 21-inch, 65c, 85c yd.
DUCHESSE SATIN, pure silk, special dress quality, wear guaranteed, 21-inch, $1.25 yd.

In writing for Samples, state color and price.

Duchesse and Victoria Satins.

In white, ivory and cream.

DUCHESSE SATIN, all pure silk, 21-inch, $1.25, 1.50 ; 22-inch, $2.00 yd.
VICTORIA SATIN, 24-inch, 40c, 50c yd.
VICTORIA SATIN, extra fine quality, 21-inch 65c, 75c ; 22-inch, 85c, $1.00 yd.

Mousseline de Soie.

MOUSSELINE DE SOIE, in black, white and cream, 46-inch, 65c yd.

Japanese Habutai and Draping Silks.

Full range of plain colors.

JAPANESE HABUTAI, full range of colors, 20-inch, 20c yd.
JAPANESE HABUTAI, Lyons' dyes, taffeta finish, 21-inch, 25c; 23-inch, 35c; 27-inch, 45c yd.
JAPANESE HABUTAI, in white and black, 27-inch, 65c ; 36-inch, 75c, $1.00 yd.

Taffeta Waist, Dress and Lining Silks.

In white, ivory and cream.

PURE SILK, 20-inch, 65c ; 21-inch, 75c ; 22-inch, $1.00 yd.
MOUSSELINE TAFFETA, pure silk, 21-inch, $1.25 yd.

Write for samples.

If you receive more than one of our catalogues, kindly notify us at once.

Dress and Waist Silks.

In white, ivory and cream.

SILK POPLIN CORD, 21-inch, 75c, $1.00 yd.
CRYSTALLINE CORD, 21-inch, 85c yd.
GROSS-GRAIN TAFFETA, pure silk, 21-inch, $1.00 yd.
PEAU DE SOIE, pure silk, 21-inch, $1.25, 1.50 yd.
PURE SILK AND SATIN BROCADES, 21-inch, 75c, $1.00; 22-inch, $1.25, 1.50; 23-inch, $1.75, 2.00; exclusive designs, 24-inch, $2.50, 3.00 yd.
PURE SILK SATIN BROCADES, 21-inch, 50c, 65c yd.

Fancy Black and White Silks.

Samples sent on request; state color, style and price required.
BROCADES, black and white, 21-inch, 75c, 85c, $1.00; 22-inch, $1.25, 1.50 yd.
CHECKED TAFFETA, black and white, 18-inch, 50c; 20-inch, 65c, 75c yd.
STRIPED TAFFETA, black and white, 21-inch, 75c yd.
STRIPED MERVEILLEUX, black and white, 21-inch, 85c, $1.00 yd.

Black Silks.

Write for samples.

BLACK GROS-GRAIN, all pure silk, fine grain, 21-inch, 75c, 85c; 22-inch, medium grain, $1.00; 23-inch, medium grain, $1.25; 23-inch, superior finish, $1.50 yd.
BLACK SILK, GROS DE LONDRE, pure silk, 21-inch, $1.00, 1.25; 22-inch, excellent wearing dress silk, $1.50 yd.
BLACK PEAU DE SOIE AND IMPERIAL LUXOR, all pure silk, reversible, 21-inch, 75c, 85c; bonnet make, 22-inch, $1.00, 1.25; 23-inch, $1.50; 24-inch, $1.75, 2.00 yd.
BLACK FAILLE FRANCAISE, all pure silk, medium cord, 21-inch, 75c, 85c; 22-inch, $1.00, 1.25; 23-inch, $1.50 yd.
BLACK SURAH SILK, pure silk, fine and medium twills, 20-inch, 40c; 21-inch, 50c, 65c; 22-inch, 75c, 85c; 23-inch, $1.00 yd.
BLACK SILK BENGALINES, 21-inch, 75c; 22-inch, $1.00 yd.
BLACK SILK POPLINS, extra wearing quality, 22-inch, $1.25; 23-inch, $1.50 yd.
ROYAL ARMURE, specially adapted for mourning wear, all pure silk, 21-inch, $1.00, 1.25 yd.
BLACK SILK FACONNE, fancy cord, for skirts and trimmings, 21-inch, $1.00 yd.
BLACK ONDINE CORD, heavy, fancy cord, 21-inch, 85c yd.
BLACK TAFFETA DRESS AND LINING SILK, all pure silk, 21-inch, 50c, 65c; 23-inch, 75c, 85c, $1.00, 1.25 yd.
BLACK SATIN MERVEILLEUX, pure silk, bright satin face, specially adapted for skirts and waists, 21-inch, 50c, 65c, 75c, 85c; 22-inch, $1.00, 1.25 yd.
LYONAISE DUCHESSE, dye and wear guaranteed, 25-inch, $1.75, 2.00; 32-inch, $2.25.
IMPERIAL DUCHESSE, all pure silk, 22-inch, $1.25; 25-inch, $1.50 yd.
BLACK SATIN DUCHESSE, soft finish, all pure silk, 22-inch, $1.00 yd.
BLACK INDIA AND JAPANESE HABUTAI SILK, pure silk, 21-inch, 25c; 23-inch, 35c; 27-inch, 45c; 27-inch, Lyon's dyed, very best black, 65c; 36-inch, 85c; 22-inch tucked Japanese silk, 75c yd.

BLACK SILK AND SATIN BROCADES, all new, fancy and exclusive designs, bought by critical experts, pure silk, 21-inch, 65c, 75c; 22-inch, extra value, $1.00; 22-inch, $1.25; 23-inch, $1.50, 1.75; 24-inch, superior weight, $2.00, 2.25 yd.

Black Satin.

Write for samples. State price.

BLACK SATINS.

VICTORIA SATIN, special, 23-inch, 35c yd.
BLACK VICTORIA SATINS, listed below. Special attention of customers is directed to these satins, which are manufactured exclusively for us and are the best that can be procured in these lines, excelling all others in wear. Note this fact: **all are Yarn Dyed.** To know their values notice that color of edge corresponds with color of edge catalogued. We recommend the blue and pink edge to any one wanting a 50c or 65c a yd satin as more than ordinary in quality and value combined. **Order Samples.**

VICTORIA SATIN.

PINK EDGE, black Victoria satin, heavy durable quality for trimmings, linings or blouses, special, 24-inch, 50c yd.
BLUE EDGE, heavy black Victoria satin, a beautiful rich trimming or lining for fur garments or jackets, special, 24-inch, 65c yd.
TERRA-COTTA EDGE, black Victoria satin, heavy fine bright finished quality, for all purposes, special, 24-inch, 75c yd.
GREEN EDGE, black Victoria satin, a model weight of rich superior finish, for trimming or lining purposes, 25-inch, special, 85c yd.
MAUVE EDGE, black Victoria satin, strikingly bright, soft rich pile and heavy weight, 25-inch, special, $1.00 yd.
RED EDGE, very best quality black Victoria satin for purposes requiring an excellent material, 25-inch, $1.25 yd.

Velvets and Velveteens.

When ordering state whether you wish velvet or velveteen cut straight across or on the bias.
ROYAL VELVETEEN, black, 22-inch, 25c yd.
ROYAL VELVETEEN, in black and colors navy, browns, reds, greens, purple, grey and fawn, 23-inch, 35c yd.
ROYALTY VELVETEEN, in black and full range of shades, twilled back, 24-inch, 50c yd.
ROYAL VELVETEEN, specially for dress wear, in black, navy, browns, reds, greens, grey and fawn, 24-inch, 65c, 85c yd.
ROYAL VELVETEEN, special quality, for coats and dresses, in black, 27-inch, $1.00, 1.25 yd.
SILK VELVETS, in navy, browns, reds, greens, grey and fawn, 18-inch, 65c yd.

SILK VELVETS, in well-selected range of shades, 18-inch, $1.00 yd.
SILK VELVETS, in black only, 18-inch, 50c, 75c, $1.00, 1.25 yd.
LYON'S SILK VELVET, superior quality and make, 18-inch, $1.50, 2.00 yd.
CRAPE AND MANTLE VELVET, 32-inch, $1.50, 2.00, 2.50 yd.
SILK COLLAR VELVET, in black, brown and fawn, 20-inch, $2.50 yd.
ARTISTS' MOLESKIN, white, 26-inch, $1.00 yd.

Dress Plush.

ENGLISH SILK DRESS PLUSH, in shades white, cream, pink, sky, Nile, yellow, reds, browns, blues, purple, greens and black, 18-inch, 75c yd.
ENGLISH SILK DRESS PLUSH, in black and colors brown, green, blue, red and purple, 24-inch, $1.00 yd.

Plaiting Department.

We do French accordion plaiting and knife or side plaiting, and for the benefit of customers below may be found a price list showing different widths and prices. When ordering state width of plait required.

PRICE LIST.

French Accordion Plaiting.

	Per Yd.
1 to 5 inches wide	6 cts.
6 to 11 "	9 "
12 to 15 "	12 "
16 to 18 "	16 "
19 to 23 "	20 "
24 to 27 "	25 "
28 to 35 "	30 "
36 to 40 "	35 "
41 to 48 "	40 "

Three yards of material is required to make one yard when plaited. For Skirts, after seaming and hemming, material should measure, for children, 6 to 8 yards; for adult, 22 inches waist measure or over, 10 yards are required. 2c yd extra for hemming.

PRICE LIST.

Knife or Side Plaiting.

	No. 1. Per Yd.	No. 2. Per Yd.
1 to 5 inches wide	5 cts.	2 cts.
6 to 10 "	7 "	5 "
11 to 15 "	12 "	8 "
16 to 20 "	15 "	12 "
21 to 24 "	20 "	17 "
25 to 30 "	30 "	25 "
31 to 40 "	40 "	35 "

Material for above work requires three yards to make one yard plaited, except No. 1, which requires 3½ yards.

PRINTS, MUSLINS AND DRESS GINGHAMS.

VICTORIA LAWN, 45-inch, 8c yd.
VICTORIA LAWN, extra quality, fine even weave, 45-inch, 10c, 12½c, 15c yd.
WHITE INDIA LINEN LAWN, for infants' wear, blousing or dress purposes, without filling, 36-inch, 15c, 20c, 25c, 30c, 35c, 40c yd.
WHITE IRISH LINEN LAWN, beautiful quality, for handkerchiefs and fancy work, 36-inch, 50c, 75c, $1.00, 1.25, 1.50, 1.75 yd.
WHITE IRISH LINEN LAWN, superior qualities, 19-inch, 75c, $1.00, 1.25 yd.
WHITE SCOTCH NAINSOOK, free from dressing, 36-inch, 12½c, 15c, 20c, 25c yd.
WHITE EMBROIDERY CAMBRIC, for ladies' and infants' underwear, 40-inch, 12½c; 42-inch, 15c, 20c yd.

WHITE DIMITY MUSLIN, assorted striped patterns, 28-inch, 12½c; 30-inch, 25c, 30c yd.
WHITE HAIRCORD MUSLIN, for infants' wear, 36-inch, 12½c, 15c, 20c yd.
WHITE JACONET MUSLIN, 36-inch, 12½c, 15c, 20c yd.
WHITE BRILLIANT, small patterns, 30-inch, 12½c, 15c yd.
WHITE MUSLIN, fancy checks, 27-inch, 8c, 10c yd.
FANCY WHITE STRIPE MUSLIN, 26-inch, 8c; 28-inch, 10c, 12½c yd.
WHITE SWISS DRESS MUSLIN, hand worked spots, 30-inch, 20c, 25c; spots and fancy designs, 30-inch, 30c, 35c, 40c, 45c, 50c yd.

WHITE SWISS BOOK MUSLIN, 36-inch, 12½c, 15c, 20c, 25c, 30c, 35c yd.
PLAIN WHITE FRENCH ORGANDIES, 66-inch, 20c, 25c, 30c, 35c, 40c, 50c, 65c, 75c yd.
PLAIN WHITE TARLATAN, 52-inch, 15c, 20c, 25c, 30c, 35c, 40c yd.
COLORED TARLATAN, full range of all leading shades, 52-inch, 15c, 20c yd.
WHITE LAPPET SPOT MUSLIN, 25-inch, 8c; 35-inch, 12½c, 15c; 45-inch, 15c yd.
LENO OR MOSQUITO NET, for screens, candy bags, etc., 60-inch, 8c yd, or 1 piece of 8 yds length for 60c; 40-inch, 6c yd, or 1 piece of 12 yds for 60c.

Our stocks are complete, goods first class and prices just above cost.

Allover Tucks and Insertions.

ALLOVER TUCKED WHITE LAWN, very fine tucks, special, 22-inch, 50c, 65c, 75c yd.
ALLOVER TUCKED WHITE LAWN, extra fine cloth, very small tucks, 25-in., $1.00, 1.25 yd.
ALLOVER EMBROIDERY NOVELTIES, in materials for blouses, yokes and dress fronts, new and elegant productions in embroidered and tucked effects, white, 20-inch, 60c, 75c, 85c, $1.00, 1.25, 1.50; black with white designs, 20-inch, $1.00, 1.25, 1.75 yd.

Tucked and Hemmed Lawns and Nainsook.

WHITE LAWN, plain hem and cluster of tucks, 36 to 40-inch, 15c, 20c, 25c yd.
WHITE LAWN, hemmed and tucked, one row of insertion, 36 to 40-inch, 25c, 30c, 35c; two rows of insertion, 40c, 50c yd.
WHITE NAINSOOK, hemmed and tucked, suitable for infants' dresses, 36 to 40-in., 20c, 25c yd.
WHITE NAINSOOK, hemmed and tucked, one row of insertion, 36 to 40-inch, 25c, 30c, 35c; two rows of insertion, 40c, 50c yd.

Black and Colored Dress Muslins.

WHITE SWISS MUSLIN, with black spot or figure, 30-inch, 35c, 40c, 45c, 50c yd.
BLACK SWISS MUSLIN, with white spot or figure, 30-inch, 35c, 40c, 45c, 50c yd.
BLACK SWISS MUSLIN, with black dot or figure, 30-inch, 30c, 35c, 40c, 45c, 50c, 60c yd.
FANCY EMBROIDERED COLORED SWISS MUSLINS, novelties for summer or evening wear, beautiful striped and small figured effects, make a very attractive waist or dress, 44-inch, 50c, 65c, 85c, $1.25 yd.
PLAIN COLORED SILK ORGANDIES, best French make, full range leading shades, 48-inch, 25c, 35c yd.
PLAIN SILK FRENCH ORGANDIES, in black and white only, 48-in., 30c, 35c, 50c, 65c yd.
PLAIN COLORED COTTON ORGANDIES, select range of leading shades, 30-inch, 25c yd.
PLAIN BLACK COTTON ORGANDIES, 66-inch, 25c, 30c, 40c yd.
FANCY COLORED ORGANDIES, in new and stylish patterns, select range of colorings, 30-inch, 25c, 35c, 45c yd.
PLAIN BLACK LAWN, best aniline black, 45-inch, 15c, 20c yd.

Prints and Ginghams.

Write for Samples.

CANADIAN PRINT, in new fancy patterns, light and dark colorings, fast colors, special, 26-inch, 5c yd.
CANADIAN PRINTS, light and dark grounds, also black and white, in complete range of new patterns, 28-inch, 9c yd.
ENGLISH AND CANADIAN CAMBRICS, best quality, in light ground, navy, best indigo, black and white, full range of new patterns, 32-inch, 11c, 12½c yd.
QUILTING PRINTS, new range of blocked and pieced patterns, 28-inch, 9c yd.
DRESS SATEENS, in navy and black grounds, with new fancy white designs, best indigo blue and aniline black, fine silk finish, 30-inch, 15c, 20c, 25c yd.
PLAIN CAMBRAY, fast colors, in sky, pink, red, fawn and grey, 32-inch, 15c yd.
DRESS GINGHAM, new fancy checks and stripes, light and medium grounds, 30-in., 11c yd
SCOTCH GINGHAM, plaids, checks and fancy stripes, 28-inch, 15c, 20c, 25c yd.
PLAIN WHITE DRESS DUCK, 28-in., 12½, 15c yd
INDIGO BLUE DRESS DUCK, in white designs, in spots and stripes, also plain blue, 27-inch, 12½c yd.
INDIGO BLUE DRESS DUCK, excellent range of fancy white designs, 32-inch, 15c yd.

Dress Flannelettes and Galatea Skirting.

GALATEA SKIRTING, navy ground, with fancy white stripes, 28-inch, 11c, 12½c, 15c yd.
BEST QUALITY ENGLISH GALATEA, satin finish, navy grounds, in stripes, also plain colors, navy, cadet and red, 30-inch, 20c yd.
SALISBURY WRAPPERETTES, complete range of new fancy designs, including spots, stripes and checks, on dark colored grounds, 27-inch, 10c yd.

DRESS LININGS.

Waist and Skirt Linings.

Fast Colors, Reliable Qualities.

CAMBRIC SKIRT LINING, in all colors, 25-inch, 5c yd.
SILESIA SKIRT LINING, in black, brown, slate and fawn, 35-inch, 8c yd.
SILESIA SKIRT LINING, all staple shades, including evening shades, 38-inch, 10c yd.
FAST BLACK LINENETTE SKIRT LINING, 36-inch, 10c; 45-inch, 12½c yd.
CROWN PERCALINE SKIRT LINING, black and colored, 36-inch, 12½c yd.
CROWN PERCALINE WAIST LINING, black and colored 36-inch, 15c yd.
CROWN PERCALINE WAIST LINING, fast black, 36-inch, 12½c, 15c yd.
FERGUSSON'S PERCALINE WAIST LINING, special, fast black, 40-inch, 20c, 25c yd.
SILESIA WAIST LINING, in all colors, 36-inch, 12½c, 15c; special, 40-inch, 20c yd.
SPUN-GLASS AND NEARSILK WAIST LINING, for organdies and light dress materials, in all colors, including fast black, 36-inch, 25c yd.
REVERSIBLE WAIST LINING, one side fast black, other side fancy colors, 36-inch, 20c, 25c yd.

Canvas, Haircloth and Sateens.

HARD BOOK MUSLIN, in black and white, 30-inch, 6c yd.
GRASS CLOTH, black, white and grey, 25-inch, 8c yd.
PURE LINEN DRESS CANVAS, in natural, slate and black, 25-inch, 10c, 12½c, 15c yd.
PURE LINEN DRESS CANVAS, in white only, 25-inch, 12½c, 15c yd.
FRENCH ELASTIC TAILORS' CANVAS, fawn and black, 25-inch, 20c yd.
MILITARY COLLAR CANVAS, black and natural, 36-inch, 20c yd.
AMERICAN COLLAR STIFFENING, in black and white, 25-inch, 20c yd.
WIGAN, in black and white, 27-inch, 10c yd.
HAIRCLOTH, in black and grey, 18-inch, 25c, 35c yd.
FRENCH HAIRCLOTH, in white and grey, 18-inch, 35c yd.

Roman Satins and Sateens.

ROMAN SATIN, permanent silk finish, for waists and linings, in all shades, including black, 31-inch, special, 20c yd.
ROMAN SATIN, in fast black, very special quality, 31-inch, 25c yd.
ROMAN SATIN, superior quality, in all shades, including fast black, 25c yd; in staple shades, 35c yd.
BLACK DRESS SATEENS, all fast blacks, 31-inch, 12½c, 15c, 20c, 25c yd.
PLAIN COLORED DRESS SATEENS, in fast colors, 31-inch, 12½c, 15c, 20c yd.

Suiting and Tailors' Trimmings.

ITALIAN COAT LINING, black only, 54-inch, 25c, 35c, 50c, 65c, 75c, 85c, $1.00 yd.
ITALIAN COAT LINING, in staple colors, browns, fawns, greys, navy, cardinal and green, 54-inch, 35c, 50c yd.
MOHAIR STRIPE SLEEVE LINING, 38-inch, 50c, 65c yd.
FANCY STRIPE SILESIA SLEEVE AND WAISTCOAT LINING, 38-inch, 10c, 12½c, 15c, 20c, 25c yd.
JEAN POCKETING, in drab and black, 32-inch, 18c, 20c yd.
LINEN HOLLAND, in black, cream and slate, 36-inch, 20c, 25c yd.

Turkey Red Cambrics and Jeans.

PLAIN TURKEY RED CAMBRIC, 29-inch, 10c, 12½c, 15c, 20c yd.
PLAIN TWILL TURKEY RED, 32-inch, 10c, 12½c, 15c yd.
WHITE AND DOVE CORSET JEANS, for children's waists, 30-inch, 15c, 20c yd.
WHITE SATIN JEAN, extra fine quality, 28-inch, 50c yd.
COUTILLE JEAN, in white and slate, 54-inch, 50c yd.

LINING SETS.

A simple and easy way to buy linings and trimmings for a dress is to order from the three sets of linings and trimmings quoted below. When ordering give number of set and color required in lining, other trimmings will be sent to match.

Lining Set No. 1

6 yds cambric lining, 5c (skirt)	$0 30
2 " linen canvas, 10c (skirt)	0 20
4 " velveteen binding, 4c (skirt)	0 16
2 " silesia waist lining, 12½c (waist)	0 25
1 set dress bones (waist)	0 05
1 pair dress shields (waist)	0 08
1 single belting (waist)	0 03
1 double belting (skirt)	0 03
1 card hooks and eyes (waist)	0 02
2 spools sewing silk, 5c	0 10
2 " silk twist, 2c	0 04
2 " sewing cotton, 4c	0 08
	$1 34
Linings for waist	$0 55
" " skirt	0 79
	$1 34

Lining Set No. 2 superior quality.

4½ yds double-fold silesia or linenette, 10c (skirt)	$0 45
2 " best linen canvas, 12½c (skirt)	0 25
4 " Brush binding, 6c (skirt)	0 24
2 " percaline or silesia waist lining 15c (waist)	0 30
1 set waist steels (waist)	0 12
1 pair dress shields, size 2 (waist)	0 15
1 single belting (waist)	0 03
1 double belting (skirt)	0 03
1 card hooks and eyes	0 02
2 spools sewing silk, 5c	0 10
2 " silk twist, 2c	0 04
2 " sewing cotton, 4c	0 08
	$1 81
Linings for waist	$0 75
" " skirt	1 06
	$1 81

Lining Set No. 3, linings required for tailor-made suits.

2½ yds silk-finished Italian, 32 inches wide, 25c yd; or 1½ yds 54 inches wide, 50c yd (jacket)	$0 63
1 yd soft tailor canvas (jacket)	0 20
4½ yds silesia linenette or percaline, 12½c (skirt)	0 57
2 " linen canvas, 12½c (skirt)	0 25
4 " Brush binding, 6c (skirt)	0 24
½ oz sewing silk (jacket)	0 18
2 spools cotton (skirt)	0 08
Belting for skirt	0 04
2 sheets wadding (jacket)	0 05
	$2 24
Jacket	$1 06
Skirt	1 18
	$2 24

If jacket is to be tight fitting, 3 yards of featherbone will be required, at 12c yd—36c extra to above suggestion.

Samples of dress goods sent on request. Give us a clear idea what is required.

DRESS TRIMMINGS.

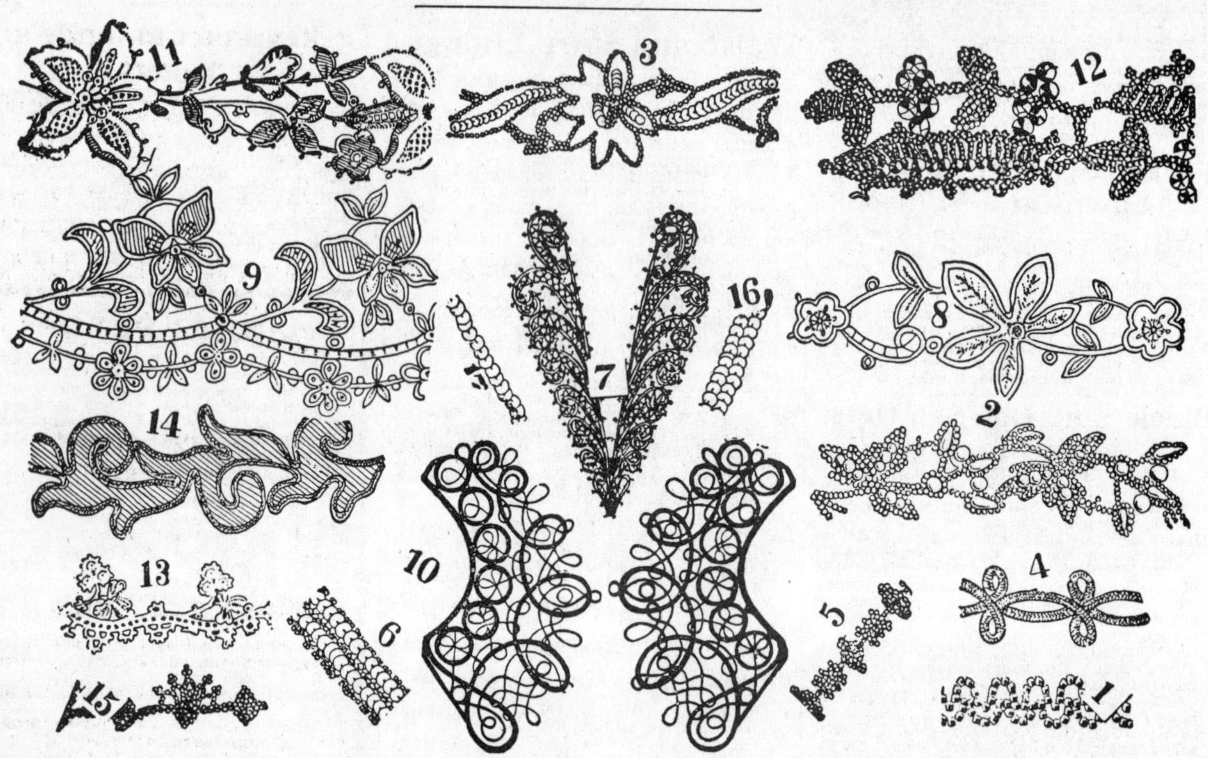

WE give above styles of dress trimmings, making it easy for you to show us what you want. We have something similar in stock to all these patterns, which for convenience in ordering are numbered to correspond with the following list. Please state style number nearest to one required, and state price you wish to pay and color wanted.

Notice when ordering that the more elaborate designs are the most expensive.

1. Black jet, black or colored silk gimp, 5c yd.
2. White pearl passementerie, $1.00 yd.
3. Black or steel sequin, 85c yd.
4. Black or colored mohair gimps, 25c yd.
5. Black jet or colored beaded gimp, 25c yd.
6. Black sequin gimp, 25c yd.
7. Black jet or steel revers, $1.00, 1.50 pair.
8. Black, white or colored silk applique, 65c yd.
9. Black or colored silk applique, $1.25 yd.
10. Black silk and mohair Zouave or bolero jackets, $1.50 to $3.50 each.
11. Colored silk applique, $1.50.
12. Black cut jet or cut steel passementerie, can be separated into sections, $1.00 yd.
13. Black colored or white silk applique, 50c yd.
14. Black taffeta silk applique, $1.00 yd.
15. Black jet gimp, 20c yd.
16. Black sequin gimp, 20c yd.
17. Black steel or white sequin gimp, 15c yd.

BRAIDS AND GIMPS.

BLACK MOHAIR MILITARY BRAID, ⅛ inch, 2c; ¼-inch, 3c; ⅜-inch, 4c; ½-inch, 5c; ⅝-inch, 6c; ¾-inch, 7c; 1-inch, 8c; 1⅛-inch, 10c; 1¼-inch, 12½c; up to 2½-inch, 25c yd.

BLACK WORSTED MILITARY BRAID, ⅛-inch, 2c; up to 2½-inch, 20c yd.

BLACK LOOP EDGE BRAID, ½-inch, 10c, 12½c yd.

BLACK MOHAIR RUSSIA BRAID, ⅛ to ¼-inch, 3c, 4c, 5c, 6c, 7c yd.

BLACK MOHAIR TUBULAR BRAID, ¼ to ⅜-inch, 5c, 6c, 7c, 8c, 10c, 12½c yd.

BLACK WORSTED TUBULAR BRAID, ¼-inch, 3c, 4c, 5c; ⅜-inch, 6c, 7c, 8c, 10c yd.

BLACK MOHAIR BINDING BRAID, ¼-inch, 4c, 5c; ½-inch, 6c, 7c, 8c; ¾-inch, 8c, 10c yd.

BLACK SILK BINDING BRAID, ¼-inch, 4c, 5c; ½-inch, 6c, 7c, 8c; ¾-inch, 8c, 10c yd.

BLACK WORSTED SOUTACHE BRAID, ⅛-inch, 1c, 2c, 3c, 4c yd.

COLORED WORSTED SOUTACHE BRAID, ⅛-inch, 1c yd, or 10c dozen yds.

BLACK OR COLORED SILK SOUTACHE BRAID, ⅛-inch, 3c, or 30c dozen yds; also 5c, or 50c dozen yds.

BLACK AND GOLD (MIXED) FLAT BRAID, ¼-inch, 5c, 10c yd.

CREAM WOOLLEN AND HERCULES BRAID, ⅛-inch, 1c; up to 1½-inch, 10c yd.

WHITE COTTON TRIMMING BRAIDS, ⅛-inch, 1c; ¼-inch, 2c; ⅜-inch, 3c; ½-inch, 4c; up to 1½-inch, 7c yd.

SILVER OR GOLD TINSEL BRAID, ⅛-inch, 5c; 3-16 inch, 7c, 8c; ¼-inch, 10c; ⅜-inch, 12½c; ½-inch, 15c; 1-inch, 25c; up to 2-inch, 50c, 65c yd.

GOLD OR SILVER SOUTACHE BRAID, ⅛-inch, 6c, 8c, 10c yd.

COLORED MILITARY BRAIDS, ¼-inch, 2c, 3c yd; up to 2-inch, 10c, 12½c yd.

BLACK AND COLORED SILK DRESS LACES, 54 inches long, 8c each, or 2 for 15c.

Black Silk and Bead Gimps and Appliques

BLACK BEADED GIMPS, ¼-inch, 3c to 15c; ½-inch, 5c, 8c, 10c, 15c to 35c; ¾-inch, 8c to 40c; 1-inch, 10c to 75c; 1½-inch, 12½c to $1.25; 2-inch, 75c to $2.00; dull jet, 10c, 12½c, 15c, 20c to $1.00 yd.

BLACK SEQUIN GIMPS, ¼-inch, 10c, 12½c, 15c, 20c; ½-inch, 15c, 20c, 25c; ¾-inch, 30c, 35c, 40c; 1-inch, 50c, 65c, 75c, 85c, $1.00; 1½ to 2-inch, 75c, $1.00, 1.25 to 2.00; 3-inch, $3.00 yd.

BLACK JET INSERTION, 1-inch, 20c to 60c; 1½-inch, 50c to $2.00 yd.

BLACK JET FRINGE, 2½-inch, 75c; 3-inch, $1.00; 4-inch, $1.50 yd.

BLACK JET AND STEEL, combined, ½-inch, 25c; 1-inch, 50c, 65c, 75c yd.

BLACK SEQUIN FRINGE, 1-inch, 25c; 1½-inch, 50c, 75c; 2-inch, 85c, $1.00 yd.

BLACK SILK GIMPS, narrow widths, ¼-inch, 5c; ½-inch, 8c, 10c to 35c; ¾-inch to 1½-inch, 10c to $1.50 yd.

BLACK MOHAIR GIMPS, narrow width, 15c 20c to 35c; ¾ to 1-inch, 25c to 50c; 1½ and 2-inch, 60c, 85c; 3-inch, 75c to $1.00 yd.

BLACK TAFFETA SILK APPLIQUE, 1-inch, 50c, 75c; 1½-inch, $1.00, 1.25; 2-inch, $1.50, 2.00 yd.

BLACK SILK APPLIQUE, ½-inch, 25c, 30c, 35c, 40c; ¾-inch, 40c, 50c; 1-inch, 65c, 75c; 1½-inch, 85c, $1.00, 1.25; 2-inch, $1.50, 2.00 yd.

Do not cut ilustrations from Catalogue. Give page and number of article.

Colored Beaded and Silk Gimps.

COLORED BEADED GIMPS, ½-inch, 10c, 15c; ½-inch, 15c to 35c; ¾-inch, 35c to 50c; 1-inch, 40c to 60c; 1½-inch, 75c to $1.50 yd.
CUT STEEL GIMPS, ¼-inch, 10c, 12½c to 20c; ½-inch, 20c to 35c; ¾-inch, 25c to 40c; 1-inch, 40c to 75c; 2-inch, 85c to $1.00 yd.
COLORED SILK GIMPS, ¼-inch, 5c, 8c yd; ½-inch, 8c, 10c, 12½c; ¾-inch, 15c to 35c; 1 and 1½-inch, 40c to 50c yd.
COLORED MOHAIR BRAID PASSEMENTERIE, ½-inch, 15c, 20c to 35c; 1-inch, 25c to 50c; 2-inch, 50c yd.
CREAM SILK GIMPS, ¼-inch, 5c, 8c; ½-inch, 10c, 12½c; 1-inch, 15c to 25c yd.

Evening Wear Trimming.

CREAM OR WHITE SILK APPLIQUE, ½-inch, 25c, 30c, 35c; ¾ and 1-inch, 40c, 50c, 65c, 75c, $1.00; 1½ and 2-inch, $1.25, 1.50, 2.00, 2.50 yd.
WHITE TAFFETA SILK APPLIQUE, 1-inch, 50c, 75c, $1.00; 1½ and 2-inch, $1.50, 2.00, 2.50 yd.
SILK APPLIQUE, in all leading shades, ½-inch, 35c, 40c, 50c; 1-inch, 50c, 75c; 1½-inch to 2-inch, $1.00 to $2.50 yd.
GOLD BRAID PASSEMENTERIE, 1-inch, 50c, 65c, 75c to $1.50 yd.
GOLD AND SILVER TINSEL GIMPS, ½-inch, 5c, 8c, 10c, 12½c; ¾-inch, 15c; 1-inch, 15c, 20c yd.
CREAM OR IVORY SILK FRINGE, 3-inch, 50c, 75c, $1.00 yd.
PEARL AND BEAD FRINGE, 1-inch, 40c, 50c; 2½-inch, $1.25, 1.50 yd.
STEEL FRINGES, ¾-inch, 50c; 2½ and 3-inch, $1.25, 1.50; 4-inch, $2.50 yd.
BLACK SILK FRINGES, 2½-inch, 50c; 3-inch, 75c; 4-inch, $1.00, 1.25; 5 to 6 inches deep, $1.50, 2.00 yd.
WHITE BEAD GIMPS, narrow widths, 10c, 12½c, 15c, 20c yd.
PEARL AND BEAD GIMPS, narrow widths, 20c to 40c; 1-inch, 40c to 75c; 1½-inch, 75c to $2.00 yd.
EMBROIDERED CHIFFON, 20-inch, in black and white, $3.00, 3.50, 4.00, 5.00 yd.
BLACK BEADED NET, 29-inch, $1.00 to 2.50 yd.
BLACK SEQUIN NET, 29-inch, $2.00, 2.50 to 5.00 yd.
WHITE BEADED NET, 29-inch, $1.50, 2.00 to 5.00 yd.
We do not cut samples of allover trimmings.

Ornaments and Garnitures.

WHITE PEARL AND BEAD GARNITURES AND YOKES, 65c, 75c, $1.00 to 3.50 each.
COLORED BEADED GARNITURES OR YOKES, $1.50, 2.00, 3.00 each.
BLACK JET YOKES OR GARNITURES, 75c, $1.00, 1.25, 1.50, 2.00 to 3.50 each.
BLACK JET REVERS, $1.00, 1.25, 1.50, up to 3.50 pair.
BLACK TAFFETA SILK BOLERO JACKETS, $5.00, 6.00 each.
CREAM AND BLACK LACE BOLEROS, $3.50, 4.00, 5.00, 6.00, 7.00 each, suitable for wearing over silk, muslin, or woollen waists.
BLACK BOLERO JACKETS, for front of waists only, in silk or jet, $3.00, 4.00 pair.
CUT STEEL REVERS, $1.50, 2.00 pair.

Skirt Bindings, Belting, Collar Canvas and Dome Fasteners.

Skirt Bindings.

Victoria heavy bias velveteen, with heavy brush edge, skirt binding, in black and all colors, 1½-inch wide, special, 8c yd, or 90c dozen yds.

S. H. & M. bias velvet, with brush edge, skirt binding, all colors, 12c yd, or $1.25 dozen yds.
"Hercules" Amazon brush binding, pure wool, all colors, 6c yd, or 65c dozen yds.
"Leader" brush binding, pure wool, all colors, 4c yd, or 40c dozen yds.

Redfern corded velveteen binding, heavy quality, 1 and 1½-inch, 8c yd, or 90c dozen yds.
Bias velvet binding, in all colors, 1½-inch, 4c yd, or 40c dozen yds.
Black corduroy velvet binding, 1½-inch wide, 5c yd.
Colored worsted skirt braids, 1c yd, or 12c dozen yds.
Black worsted skirt braids, 1c, 2c, 3c, 4c, 5c yd.

Corticelli mohair skirt protector in bunches of 5 yds, black only, 25c bunch.
Corticelli worsted skirt protector in bunches of 5 yds, colors and black, 15c bunch.

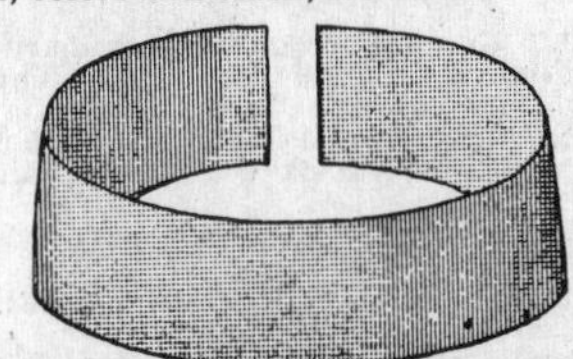

Vorwerk collar stiffener, shaped ready for collars and cuffs, in black or white, 1½-inch, 8c; 2-inch, 10c; 2½-inch, 12½c; 3-inch, 18c yd.
Single waist belting, 3c yd, or 30c dozen yds.
Double skirt belting, 4c yd, or 40c dozen yds.
Black or colored silk lacing cords, ⅛-inch, 2c; 3-16-inch, 4c; ¼-inch, 6c yd.

Featherbone Stock Collars.

Featherbone stock collars, light weight and durable, in two shapes, plain round shape, same width all round, and as cut, deeper at the sides than front.
Featherbone stock foundation collars, in black or white, for covering with silk or other materials, sizes 13, 13½, 14, 14½, 15c each.
Dome fasteners, in black and white, 10c dozen.

Knitting and Crochet Cottons.

The celebrated M. & K. white knitting cotton, Nos. 4 to 20, 5c ball.
Silcotton, substitute for silk crochet thread, in plain and variegated colors, 100 yards on each spool, 5c a spool.

Brilliant crochet thread "Mile End" quality, in all plain and variegated colors, 100 yards on a spool, 5c spool.
Clark's crochet cotton, "Anchor" brand, white only. In ordering, always state size wanted. Sizes 2 to 50, 5c ball, or 55c doz.

Tassels and Cords.

Pompoms, pure silk, all shades, 10c doz.
Pompoms, pure silk, for cushion work, 15c pair, 90c doz.
Silk tassels, all pure silk, all shades, 4c, 15c, 25c, 50c doz.
Fancy cushion tassels, shades to match cords, 4 inches long, 80c for set of 4 tassels.
Silk cushion cord, ½-inch thick, 12½c yd.
Heavy silk cushion cord, variegated, ¾-inch thick, 20c.
Lacing cords for fancy work and bicycle guards, 2c, 4c yd.
Fancy chenille cord, in all shades, 5c, 6c yd.
Fancy variegated cotton cushion cord, ½-inch thick, 10c yd.
New "mercerized" imitation silk, heavy cushion cord, ¾-inch thick, all variegated shades, 12½c yard.

Bath and Dressing Robe Girdles.

Woollen neck cords, to match girdles, in white, red, pink, brown, grey, blue, navy and white, also black, 15c each.
Heavy woollen girdles, in white, red, pink, brown, grey, blue, navy and white, also black, 2 yds long, 60c each.
Heavy cotton bath robe girdles, in white, red, pink, brown, grey, blue, navy and black, 2 yds long, 35c each.

Featherbone.

In boning waists with featherbone, customers will require 2½ to 3 yds.
Featherbone, cambric covered, in lengths of 3 yards, enough to bone a waist, all colors, special, per length, 15c.
Featherbone, twill cover, for waists, all colors, 8c yd, or 85c doz yds.
Tape-covered waist featherbone, in white, drab, black, blue, pink and brown, 10c yd, or $1.00 doz yds.
Featherbone, cotton ribbon, covered, for waists, all colors, 12c yd, or $1.25 doz.
Featherbone, washable, for waists, in white only, 15c yd, or $1.60 doz yds.
Featherbone, silk covered, for waists, all colors, 18c yd, or $2.00 doz yds.
Featherbone, satin covered, for waists, all colors, 25c yd, or $2.75 doz yds.

A FULL LINE OF DRESS SUPPLIES CONSTANTLY IN STOCK.

Featherbone, for collars and revers, 5-cord tape, 10c; 10-cord tape, 15c; 18-cord tape, 20c; 25-cord tape, 25c yd.

Hook and eye featherbone, in grey, white and black only, 12c yd, or $1.25 doz yds.

Featherbone piping cord, in white, black and grey, 3c yd, or 30c doz yds.

Featherbone cable cord, white, black and drab, 5c yd, or 50c doz yds.

Featherbone Duplex skirt bone, black, drab and white, ½-inch, 6c yd, or 60c doz yds.

Skirt featherbone, narrow, in white, black and drab, 6c yd, or 60c doz yds.

Bustle featherbone, 1-inch, 15c yd, or $1.60 doz yds.

Best quality waist whalebone, 36 inches, 20c.

Dress Shields.

The Gem.

REGISTERED.

	Sizes 1	2	3	4	6	
Leader Stockinette	5c	..	..	..	..	pr.
Primrose Stockinette	8c	10c	12½c	..	..	"
Kleinert Stockinette	15c	20c	..	..	..	"
Williamson Stockinette	15c	20c	25c	30c	..	"
The Gem	..	20c	23c	25c	30c	"
The Classique	..	23c	25c	30c	..	"
The Falcon	..	10c	12½c	..	..	"
Velvytte	..	15c	18c	23c	..	"
The Feather Weight, rubber lined	..	15c	20c	23c	30c	"
Japanese Silk, rubber lined	..	23c	25c	..	..	"
The Capsheaf, in black	..	25c	..	..	..	"
The Queen, double lined	..	18c	20c	25c	..	"
The Olympia, odorless	..	20c	25c	30c	35c	"
Onnadoff, self-adjustable without sewing in	..	23c	25c	30c	40c	"

Dress Steels and Bones.

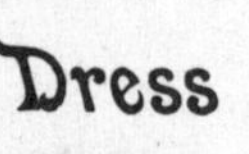

Stays.

Star dress stay, sateen covered, in colors, white, black, drab, special, 5c set.

Brush & Co.'s peerless dress stays, all colors, sizes 6, 7, 8, 9, 15c doz, or set of 9 for 12c.

Crompton's peerless extra sateen-covered dress steels, in all colors, sizes 6, 7, 8, 9, 10c doz.; or set of 9, for 9c.

Crompton's standard dress steels, all colors, sizes 6, 7, 8, 9, 15c doz, or set of 9 for 12c.

Toledo silk-covered dress steels, in colors black and white only, a very superior steel for finest work, sizes 6, 7, 8, 9, 20c doz.

Rubber-tipped sateen-covered dress steels, silk stitched, in all colors, sizes 6, 7, 8, 9, 10c doz, or set of 9 for 9c.

"Superior" satin-covered, rubber-tipped dress steels, in sky, yellow, grey, white, red and black, 10c for set of 9.

Silk, Cotton and Linen Spools.

B. & P. 50-yd machine silk, all shades, 5c spool, or 50c doz.

B. & P. 100-yd machine silk, black only, 10c spool, or $1.00 doz.

B. & P. ½-oz spool machine silk, black only, 18c spool.

B. & P. 10-yd spool twist, all shades, 2c spool.

B. & P. braided yard twist, 6-strand, fawns, greens, browns, greys and black, 2c yd.

Corticelli 50-yd machine silk, all shades, 5c spool, or 50c doz.

Corticelli 10-yd spool twist, all shades, 2c spool.

Corticelli 100-yd machine silk, black only, 10c spool.

Corticelli ½-oz spool machine silk, black only, 18c spool.

Dunbar McMaster's best linen spools, 200 yds, in cream and white, Nos. 30 to 100; black and drab, Nos. 30 to 70, 9c spool.

Barbour's best linen spools, same as above, 9c spool.

Union Jack 100 yds linen spool thread, in cream, black and drab, No. 35 only, 2 spools for 5c.

Dunbar McMaster's linen carpet thread, in drab and black, 4c skein, or $1.15 lb.

"Kerr's" or "Coates'" best quality 6-cord 200-yd cotton spool, in white and black, all numbers, and in colors, size 40 only, 4c spool, or 45c doz.

White basting cotton spools, 1000 yds, white only, Nos. 36 and 40, 10c spool.

BUTTONS.

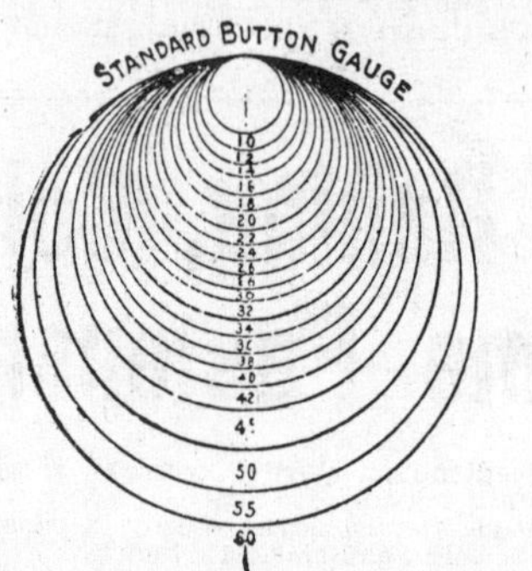

The above gauge represents the exact standard by which all buttons are sized. The following prices indicate the lowest price for the smallest size given in catalogue up to the highest price for the largest size quoted in catalogue only.

Smoked pearl buttons, plain and fancy, 40 to 50 lines, 50c to $2.50 doz.

Natural pearl buttons, plain, sizes 22 to 50 lines, 15c to $1.50 doz.

White pearl buttons, plain rim, sizes 30 to 50 lines, 40c to $1.00 doz.

Fancy smoked pearl and steel buttons, sizes 40 to 50 lines, $1.50, 2.00 doz.

Smoked pearl buttons, plain, sizes 12 to 30 lines, 8c to 50c doz.

Smoked pearl buttons, fancy designs, sizes 16, 18 and 20 lines, 12½c, 15c, 20c doz.

Plain white pearl buttons, 10 to 24 lines, 8c to 25c doz.

Fancy carved white pearl buttons, sizes 12 to 18 lines, 10c to 20c doz.

White ball pearl buttons, with or without shanks, sizes 14 to 18 lines, 15c, 20c, 25c doz.

Pearl shirt buttons, in white and smoked, sizes 14 to 24 lines, 2 and 4 holes, 8c to 20c doz.

Gent's white pearl vest buttons, size 24, 35c doz.

Gilt and Silver Buttons.

Small gilt trimming buttons, with bright polished tops, also dull finish, sizes 12 and 14 lines, 10c, 15c, 20c doz.

Colored pearl trimming buttons, in all dress shades, with or without shanks, size 18, 10c, 12½c doz.

Gilt anchor buttons, for boys sailor suits, etc., sizes 20, 24 and 30 lines, 8c, 10c, 12½c, 15c, 25c doz.

Large plain gilt buttons, for jackets, sizes 30, 36 and 40 lines, 20c, 35c, 50c doz.

Fancy Trimming Buttons.

Real cut steel buttons, small size, 50c, 75c; large size, $1.50, 2.00 doz.

Fancy gilt and steel trimming buttons, small sizes, $1.25; large size, $2.00 doz.

Pressed steel buttons, fancy designs, small sizes, 25c, 50c; large sizes, $1.50, 2.00 doz.

Fancy jet and steel trimming buttons, small sizes, 15c to 35c; large sizes, 40c to $2.00 doz.

Real jet trimming buttons, fancy and plain designs, small sizes, 25c, 35c; large sizes, 75c to $1.50 doz.

Steel effect jet buttons, fancy designs, in small and large sizes, 10c to 75c doz.

Jet effect trimming buttons, fancy and plain, small and large sizes, 10c to 35c doz.

Fancy metal trimming buttons, in all shades, small sizes, 10c to 35c doz.

Fancy ferrets, for ends of ribbons, in fancy patterns, spike-shaped or flat, in gold, silver, jet and oxidized, 10c, 15c, 20c, 25c each.

Fancy Trimming and Belt Buckles.

Smoked pearl trimming buckles, 1-inch long, 15c, 20c each.

Fancy cut steel trimming buckles, 1 to 2 inches long, 15c to 30c each.

Fancy cut steel and enamel belt buckles, newest patterns, 25c to 75c each.

Cut steel belt buckles, large variety, small and large sizes, 25c to 75c each.

Fancy gilt belt buckles, 25c to 75c each.

Horn, Covered and Barrel Buttons.

Ivory buttons, sizes 40 to 50 lines, in all colors, 25c to 40c doz.

Horn buttons, in black and colors, sizes 24 to 50 lines, from 35c to 75c doz.

Ivory coat and vest buttons, in black and variegated colors, vest sizes, 10c, 12½c doz; coat sizes, 12½c, 15c doz.

Covered black coat and vest buttons, with bone edge, sizes 24, 30 and 36 lines, 15c, 20c, 25c doz.

Silk-covered black coat and vest buttons, in sizes 24, 30 and 36 lines, 10c, 15c, 20c doz.

Black silk crochet buttons for trimming, round and flat shapes, 20c to 40c doz.

Small silk-covered buttons, in black and all shades, sizes 12, 14, 18, 20 and 22 lines, 8c, 10c doz.

Black silk-covered barrel buttons, ½-inch long, 20c; 1-inch, 25c; 1½-inch, 35c; 2-inch, 40c per doz.

Black worsted barrel buttons, ½-inch long, 15c; 1-inch, 20c; 1½-inch, 25c; 2 inches, 30c doz.

Silk crochet barrel buttons, in white, grey and black, 60c to 75c doz.

Colored silk barrel buttons, size 1-inch, 30c doz.

Underwear Buttons.

THE SIMPLEX BUTTON
PATENT
COVERED BACKS.

PUT THE BUTTON STRAIGHT ON HEAD OF STUD, THEN PRESS BOTH SIDES WITH EQUAL PRESSURE.

1-DOZEN IN A BOX.

The "Simplex" bachelors' buttons, self-adjustable, easy to put on, won't come off, large and small sizes, 1 doz in a box, 5c per box.

Black metal pant buttons, large and small sizes 3 doz for 5c.

Corset or tape buttons, in boxes, 3 doz in each, 8c box.

Linen underwear buttons, in sets of assorted sizes, 7½ doz each, 8c set.

Linen underwear buttons, in boxes, assorted sizes, 8½ doz each; very superior quality, 20c box,

Linen buttons, in all sizes, size 16, 2½c; sizes 18 and 20, 3c; size 22, 4c; size 24, 5c; size 26, 6c; sizes 28 and 30, 8c doz.

EMBROIDERIES, VEILINGS NETS, LACES, Etc.

Embroideries.

Cambric embroidery, 1-inch, with ½-inch work, 1c yd; 1½-inch, with ¾-inch work, 3c yd.

B5. 3-inch, with 1½-inch work, in cambric and nainsook, 5c yd; also other patterns, 1 to 2½ inches wide, with ½ to 1½-inch work, 5c yd.

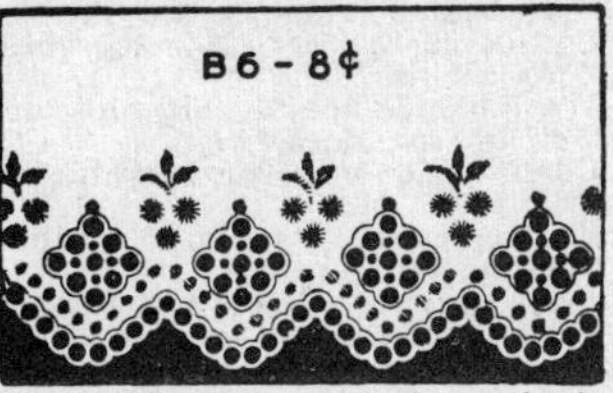

B6. 3-inch, with 1½-inch work, in cambric and nainsook, 8c yd.

B7. 4-inch, with 2-inch work, in cambric only, 10c yd.

B8. 5-inch, with 2½-inch work, in cambric, 12½c yd.

B9. 6½-inch cambric, with 3-inch work, 15c yd.

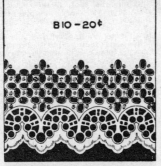

B10. 6-inch, with 3-inch work, cambric only, 20c yd.

Also a large range of patterns, in cambric, 1 to 3½ inches wide, with 1 to 2-inch work, 8c yd; 2 to 5 inches wide, with 1 to 2½-inch work, 10c yd; 2½ to 5½ inches wide, with 1½ to 3-inch work, 12½c yd; 2½ to 8 inches wide, with 1½ to 4-inch work, 15c, 18c, 20c, 22c, 25c yd.

Cambric insertion, 1½-inch, with 1-inch work, 5c, 8c, 10c yd; 1½ to 3-inch, with 1 to 2-inch work, 12½c, 15c, 20c, 25c yd.

Cambric flouncing embroidery for skirts, 6½-inch, with 3-inch work, 15c yd; 8-inch, with 4-inch work, 20c, 25c yd; 9 to 12 inches wide, with 4 to 6-inch work, 35c, 40c, 45c, 50c yd.

Nainsook edging, 1-inch wide, with ½-inch work, 5c, 8c yd; 2-inch, with 1-inch work, 10c yd; 2½ to 3½-inch, with 1¼ to 1¾-inch work, 12½c, 15c, 20c yd; 4 to 6-inch, with 2 to 3-inch work, 25c to 50c yd.

Nainsook insertion, to match embroidery, 10c to 50c yd.

B11. Extra fine nainsook insertion, 2¼-inch, with ¾-inch work, 30c yd.

B12. Extra fine nainsook embroidery, 3-inch, with 1½-inch work, 35c yd.

B13. Extra fine nainsook embroidery, 4½-inch, with 2½-inch work, 75c yd.

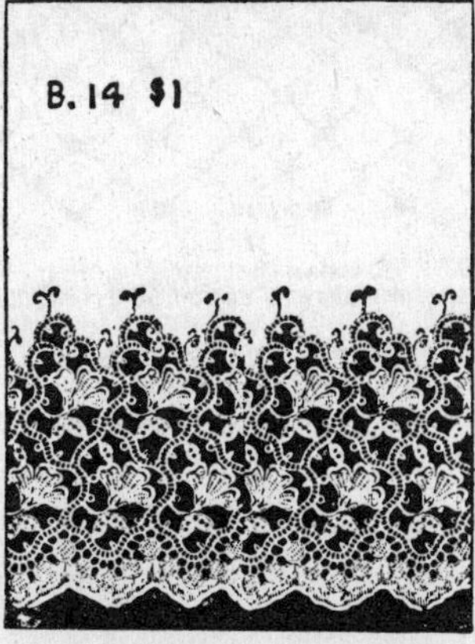

B14. Extra fine nainsook embroidery, 7½-inch, 3¾-inch work, $1.00 yd.

We have also other patterns in fine nainsook sets, 3 widths of embroidery, with insertion to match, 40c to $1.50 yd.

Swiss muslin embroidery, 2-inch, with 1-inch work, 8c yd; 3-inch, 1½-inch work, 10c yd; 4 to 7-inch, 2 to 3½-inch work, 12½c to 50c yd.

Swiss insertion, to match embroidery, 1 to 2½-inch, with ¾ to 1½-inch work, 10c to 40c yd.

Also extra fine Swiss sets, embroidery and insertion to match, 40c to $2.00 yd.

Allover cambric and nainsook embroidery, 20-inch, 35c, 50c, 75c, to $2.25 yd; nainsook only, $2.50, 3.00, 4.00, 5.00 yd.

Fancy Swiss allovers, in lace and embroidery insertions, suitable for waists and yokes, 75c, $1.00, 1.50, 2.00, 2.50 yd.

Allover tucking, in cambric and nainsook, 20-inch, 50c, 65c yd.

27-inch flouncings, in nainsook, Swiss and cambric, 35c, 45c, 50c, 60c, 65c yd; nainsook only, 75c, 85c; 35c, 45c scalloped edges only.

Swiss, with valenciennes insertion, 75c, $1.25 yd.

44-inch skirting, in cambric and nainsook, 35c, 50c, 75c, 85c yd.

White featherstitch braid, 10c, 12½c, 15c, 20c dozen yds.

Colored featherstitched braids, 10c dozen yds.

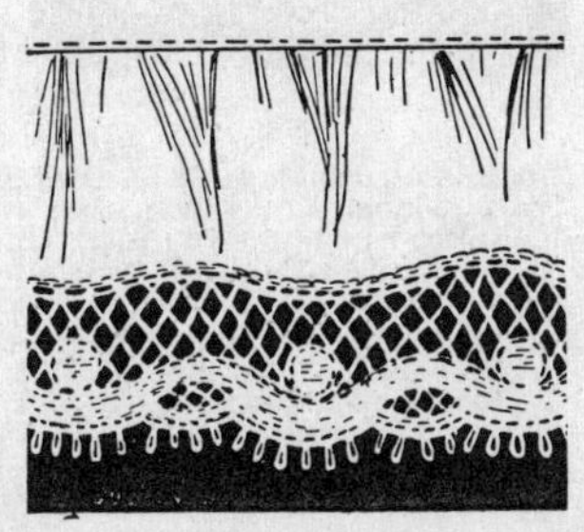

B358.

B358. Plantagenet frillings, suitable for trimming underwear, 5c, 8c, 10c, 12½c, 15c, 20c yd.

B352, 75c yd.

B352. Cream flannel skirting, 36-inch, 75c yd.

B354.

B354. 36-inch, $1.00 yd.

B355.

B355. 36-inch, $1.25: also other designs, at 65c, 75c, $1.00, 1.25 yd.

Cream flannel embroidery, 2-inch, 10c; 3-inch, 12½c, 15c; silk sewn, 2-inch, 15c; 2½-inch, 20c; 3-inch, 25c; 3½-inch, 30c, 35c yd.

Cream cashmere, embroidered with cream silk, 15c, 20c, 25c, 30c yd.

Cream cashmere cloaking, 44-inch, hemmed and embroidered, $1.25, 1.50 yd.

VEILINGS AND NETS.

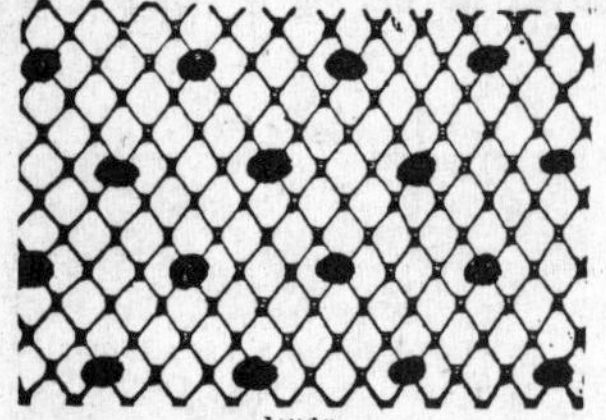

B368.

B368. Tuxedo net veiling, with chenille spot, 18 inches wide, black, brown, navy, ivory, magpie and jackdaw, 25c.

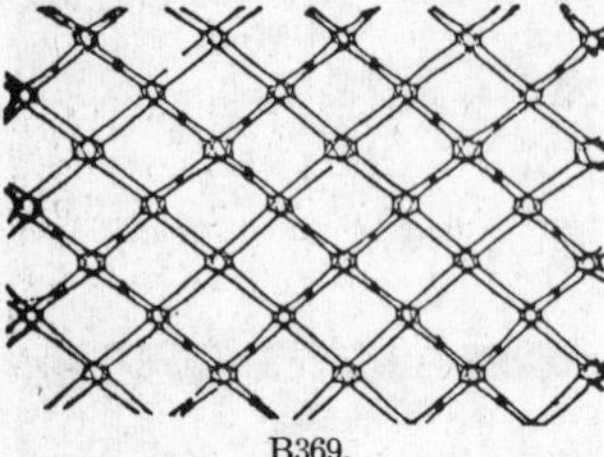

B369.

B369. Fancy mesh tuxedo net veiling, 18-inch, black, brown, navy and ivory, 20c yd.

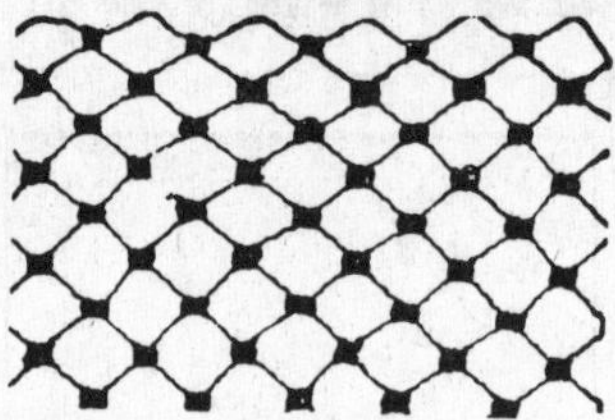

B371.

B371. Russian net veiling, 18-inch, black, brown, navy and ivory, 35c yd.

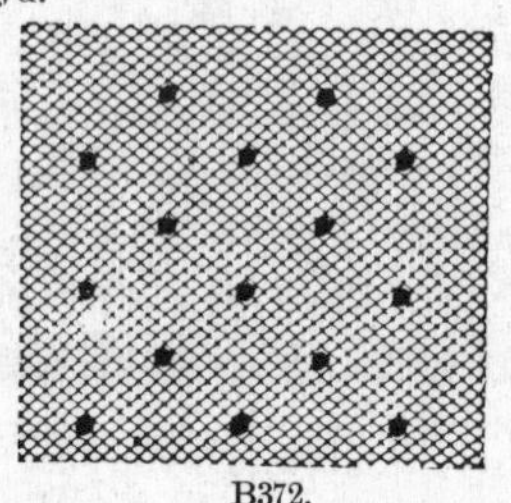

B372.

B372. Tuxedo net veiling, with silk chenille spot, 18-inch, in black only, 50c yd.

Fancy mesh tuxedo net veiling, 18-inch, black, brown, navy and ivory, 15c, 20c, 25c, 35c, 50c yd.

Fancy mesh tuxedo net veiling, with silk chenille spot, 18-inch, black, brown, navy, ivory, magpie and jackdaw, 10c, 12½c, 15c, 20c, 25c, 35c yd.

Russian net veiling, with silk chenille spot, 18-inch, black, brown, navy, ivory, magpie and jackdaw, 15c, 20c, 25c, 35c yd.

Fancy mesh tuxedo and Russian net veiling, in black only, 18-inch, 50c, 65c, 75c, $1.00 yd.

B373. Tuxedo net veils, 18 inches wide and 1 yd long, in black, brown, navy, ivory, magpie, jackdaw, white on navy, and white on brown, 20c each.

Also same style of veil, with heavier border, 35c each.

Silk cambray net, plain black only, 15c, 20c, 25c yd.

Silk cambray net, with chenille spot, 18-inch, black, ivory, brown, navy, magpie and jackdaw, 20c, 25c, 35c yd.

Black silk Brussels net, 14-inch, with neat design and border, 35c, 45c, 50c yd.

Mourning veiling, 14-inch, silk cambray net, with 1-inch hem, 25c yd; finer, 1½-inch hem, 35c yd.

Mourning veils, with neat crepe border, 35c, 45c, 50c each.

Silk chiffon veiling, with satin stripe, both edges, 14-inch, black, ivory, brown and navy, 25c yd.

Silk spotted chiffon veiling, 14-inch, black, brown, navy, ivory, magpie and jackdaw, 35c yd.

Sewing silk veiling, 14-inch, black, brown, navy, ivory and slate, 20c, 25c yd; also 16-inch, 35c yd.

All latest novelties in veilings.

Nets.

Silk mechlin nets, 36-inch, white and black, 20c, 25c, 35c yd; also white, 15c yd.

Colored silk mechlin nets, 36-inch, pink, sky, Nile, apple green, cream, maise, orange, mauve, heliotrope, 25c yd.

Bridal veiling, 72-inch silk cambray net, white, 50c, 65c, 75c; also 108-inch, $1.00 yd.

Black silk Brussels net, 36-inch, 25c, 35c, 50c, 65c, 75c, $1.00, 1.25 yd.

Cotton point d'esprit net, 27-inch, white and cream, 25c, 35c yd.

Cotton zephyr net, 36-inch, white, 15c, 20c yd.

Wash blonde net, 36-inch, white and cream, 25c, 35c, 50c yd.

Confirmation net, 72-inch, white, 45c, 65c yd.

Embroidery or mosquito net, 72-inch, white, 35c, 50c, 60c yd.

Paris or rice net, for stiffening, 22-inch, white and black, 12½c, 15c yd.

DRESS NETS AND LACES.

Black Dress Nets.

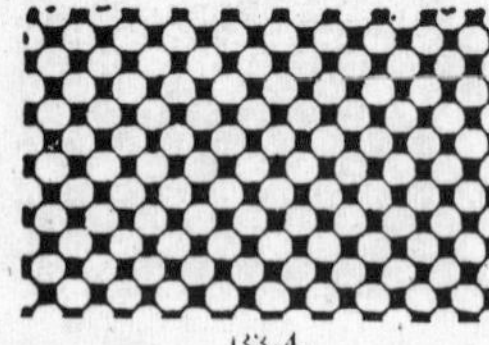

B374.

B374. Black Russian dress net, 45-inch, 50c yd.

Black Russian dress net, 45-inch, 65c, 75c, $1.00 yd.

45-inch silk chantilly dress net, spotted and figured, in neat patterns, $1.00, 1.25, 1.50, 1.75 to 5.00 yd.

54-inch plain black silk brilliantine Brussels net, 75c, $1.00, 1.25 yd.

Black silk point d'esprit, 45-inch, 75c yd.

Fancy Allovers.

These 18-inch allovers specially adapted for yokes, sleeves, trimmings, etc., in chiffon, chantilly and Russian nets.

B375.

B375. 18-inch embroidered chiffon allover, black and ivory, $2.00 yd.

18-inch embroidered chiffon allover, black and ivory, $1.25, 1.50, 1.75, 2.00, 2.50, 3.00 to 6.50 yd.

Dress Nets and Laces.

18-inch Russian net, suitable for yokes and sleeves of dresses, black only, 50c, 65c, 75c, 85c, $1.00, 1.25 to 2.00 yd.

Also chantilly nets, $1.00, 1.25 to 2.50 yd.

27-inch beaded net, $1.00, 1.25, 1.50 yd; also sequin and beaded net, $1.75, 2.00, 2.50, 3.00, 4.00 to 6.25 yd.

27-inch ivory sequin net, $2.00 to 6.00 yd.

N.B.—We do not cut samples off the goods from $2.00 up.

B376.

B376. Silk escurial lace, in black and ivory, 3-inch, 20c; 4-inch, 30c; 6-inch, 50c; 8-inch, 60c yd; insertion to match, 20c yd; also 27-inch allover, $2.25 yd.

Black silk chantilly lace, 3-inch, 5c to 20c; 4-inch, 8c, 10c, 12½c, 15c, 20c, 25c, 35c, 50c; 4 to 8-inch, 12½c to $1.25 yd.

Black Oriental lace, with heavy plauen edge, 50c, 65c, 75c, $1.00, 1.25.

Black Silk Laces.

Black silk Maltese lace (hand-made, special), 1-inch, 20c; 2-inch, 25c; 2¾-inch, 35c; 4-inch, 65c yd.

Black silk patent point lace, 4-inch, 35c; 6-inch, 50c; 7½-inch, 65c yd.

Black silk embroidered chiffon lace, 35c, 50c, 75c, $1.00, 1.25, 1.50 yd.

Narrow black silk chantilly and valenciennes edgings, ½ to ¾-inch, 5c yd, 60c doz yds; ¾ to 1-inch, 8c, 10c, 12½c yd; 1 to 1½-inch, 10c, 12½c, 15c yd; insertions to match, 8c, 10c, 12½c, 15c yd.

Black silk chiffon applique insertion and trimmings, ¾-inch, 25c, 35c; 1-inch, 35c to 65c; 2-inch, 65c to $1.00; 3-inch, $1.25, 1.50 yd.

Black silk plauen applique trimmings, ½-inch, 25c; ¾-inch, 30c, 35c; 1-inch, 50c, 65c; 1½-inch, 75c, $1.00 yd.

Black silk plauen insertion (straight edges), 1-inch, 30c; 1½-inch, 35c, 50c, 65c; 2 to 2½-inch, 85c, $1.00 yd.

Cream Silk Laces.

B377.

B377. Silk lace, in ivory, 2½-inch, 5c, 3-inch, 8c; 4-inch, 10c; 4½-inch, 12½c; 6-inch, 15c yd.

Also similar patterns and widths in black at same price.

Narrow cream silk chantilly and valenciennes edgings, ½ to ¾-inch, 5c yd, 60c doz; ¾ to 1-inch, 8c, 10c, 12½c; 1 to 1½-inch, 10c, 12½c, 15c yd; insertions to match, 8c, 10c, 12½c, 15c yd.

Silk chantilly lace, in white, cream and butter, 1½ to 3-inch, 5c, 8c, 10c, 12½c, 15c; 3 to 5-inch, 10c, 12½c, 15c, 20c to 50c; 4 to 8-inch, 20c to $1.00 yd.

Chiffon laces (evening shades), sky, pink, Nile and ivory, these goods embroidered in ivory, 3-inch, 15c; 5-inch, 20c yd.

Silk embroidered chiffon laces, in ivory, 35c, 40c, 50c, 65c, 75c to $1.50 yd.

B37X.

B37X. Chiffon applique, in black or ivory, 1¾-inch, 50c. Other designs as below.

Chiffon applique, in ivory, ½-inch, 25c; ¾-inch, 30c to 35c; 1 to 1½-inch, 35c to 65c; 2-inch, 75c to $1.00; 2½ to 3½-inch, $1.00, 1.25, 1.50, 1.75 yd.

18-inch embroidered chiffon allover, 85c, $1.00, 1.25 yd.

18-inch silk embroidered chiffon allover, $1.35, 1.50, 1.75, 2.00, 2.25, 2.50 to 7.00 yd.

45-inch cream silk nets, plain and figured, $1.00, 1.50 yd.

Real Maltese lace (bleached), ¾ to 1-inch, 20c; 1 to 1½-inch, 25c; 1½ to 2-inch, 35c; 2½ to 3-inch, 50c, 65c, 75c; 4-inch, $1.00 to 1.50 yd.

Cream silk Bohemian lace (hand-made), 2-inch, 75c, 85c, $1.00; 2½-inch, $1.25, 1.50; 3-inch, $1.50; 4-inch, $1.75 yd.

Real laces, in Honiton, Duchess and Brussels point, $2.50, 3.00, 4.00, 5.00, 6.00 yd, and upwards.

Valenciennes Laces.

NOTE.—These goods are sold by dozen yards only.

B378.

B378. ⅝ inch wide, in white or butter, 12 yds for 15c; in white only, 12 yds for 10c, 12½c.

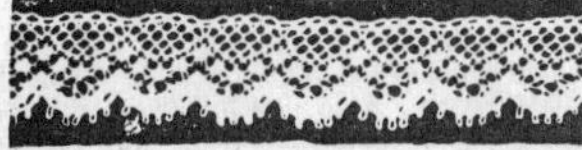

B379.

B379. ½ inch wide, in white or butter, 12 yds, 20c.

B380.

B380. ¾ inch wide, in white or butter, 12 yds for 25c.

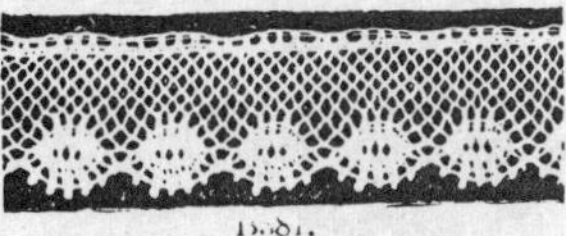

B381.

B381. ¾ to 1¼ inch wide, in white or butter, 12 yds for 35c.

B382.

B382. 1 to 1¼ inch wide, in white or butter, 12 yds for 45c; insertions to match, 10c, 15c, 20c, 25c, 35c doz yds.

Bobbin Net Valenciennes Laces.

B383.

B383. Bobbin net valenciennes insertion, white only, ¾-inch, 3c; 1-inch, 4c yd.

B384.

B384. Bobbin net valenciennes lace, white only, ¾-inch, 3c; 1-inch, 4c; 1½-inch, 5c; 2½-inch, 8c yd.

Also other patterns of bobbin net valenciennes lace, in white or butter, ⅝-inch, 3c, 4c, 5c; ¾-inch, 3c, 4c, 5c; 1-inch, 4c, 5c, 6c, 8c; 1¼-inch, 5c, 8c, 10c, 12½c; 1½-inch, 5c, 6c, 8c, 10c, 12½c; 2-inch, 8c, 10c, 12½c, 15c; 2½-inch, 8c, 10c, 12½c, 15c; 3½-inch, 10c, 12½c, 15c, 20c, 25c, 35c yd.

Bobbin net insertion to match, 3c, 4c, 5c, 8c, 10c, 12½c yd.

Beading valenciennes, in white only, 1-inch, 4c; 1¼-inch, 5c; 2-inch, 8c; 3-inch, 10c yd; insertion to match, 4c yd.

Normandy Valenciennes Laces.

B385.

B385. Normandy valenciennes lace, in ivory, white or butter, 2½-inch, 5c; 4½-inch, 8c; 6-inch, 10c yd; in white only, 7½-inch, 15c; 9-inch, 20c; 11-inch, 25c yd; insertion to match, 5c, 8c, 12½c yd.

Platte valenciennes lace, white or butter, ranging in prices from 8c to 25c yd; different patterns, with insertions to match, 5c, 8c, 10c yd.

Fine Normandy valenciennes lace, in ivory, 1½-inch, 15c; 2-inch, 20c; 2½-inch, 25c; 3½-inch, 35c yd; insertion to match, 10c, 12½c yd.

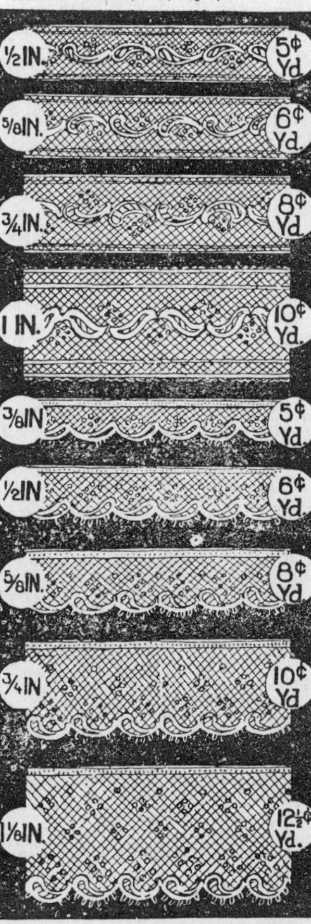

B386.

B386. Finest French (Calais) valenciennes lace and insertion, in white only, prices and widths as cut B386.

French Valenciennes.

Fine French valenciennes lace, in ivory, white or butter, ½-inch, 5c; ¾-inch, 8c; 1¼-inch, 10c; 1¾-inch, 15c; 2½-inch, 20c yd; insertion to match, 5c, 8c, 10c, 15c yd.

B387.

B387. Fine French linen-run valenciennes insertion, in ivory, 1-inch, 10c; 1¼-inch, 15c; 1¾-inch, 20c yd.

B388.

B388. Fine French linen-run valenciennes lace, in ivory, ¾-inch, 10c; 1¼-inch, 15c; 1¾-inch, 20c; 2¾-inch, 25c; 4¼-inch, 35c; 5½-inch, 50c yd.

Valenciennes Allovers.

B389.

B389. 18-inch valenciennes allover, in white, 50c yd; other patterns, 35c to $1.25 yd.

B390.

B390. Galon applique, in ivory, 25c yd; also lace to match galon, 2-inch, 20c; 3½-inch, 35c yd; with insertion, 2-inch, 20c; and 20-inch allover, $1.75 yd.

Maline Laces.

B391.

B391. Fine maline lace, in ivory and butter, ¼-inch, 4c; ½-inch, 5c; ¾-inch, 8c; 1¼-inch, 12½c; 2-inch, 20c yd; insertion to match, 4c, 5c, 8c, 12½c yd.

Point d'esprit laces, 1¼-inch, 8c; 2-inch, 10c; 2½-inch, 12½c; 3-inch, 15c yd; insertion to match, 8c yd.

27-inch point d'esprit net, in white and cream, 25c, 35c yd.

B392.

B392. Fine plain and spotted **footing** with neat valenciennes edge, 1⅛-inch, 4c, 5c; 1¾-inch, 5c, 8c; 2¼-inch, 8c, 10c yd.

Plain footing, with cluster of 3 tucks, 2½-inch, 8c yd.

Plain footing, 1½-inch, 3c; 2½-inch, 5c yd.

Spotted footing, 1½-inch, 5c; 2½-inch, 8c; 3-inch, 10c yd.

White beading, 1-row, 2c; 2-row, 4c; 3-row, 5c yd.

Real hand-made valenciennes lace, ½ to ¾-inch, 25c to 45c yd; insertion to match, 25c, 35c yd.

Oriental Laces.

Fine assortment of Oriental laces, in cream, white and butter, 3-inch, 5c yd.

Oriental lace, in cream, white and butter, 2-inch, 5c; 3-inch, 8c; 3 to 5-inch, 10c, 12½c, 15c; 3 to 8-inch, 20c, 25c, 30c, 35c; 6 to 12-inch, 45c to $1.00 yd.

B393.

B393. Oriental lace, in cream, white, and butter, 4-inch, 10c yd.

Oriental allover, 18-inch, in ivory and ecru, 50c to $2.00 yd.

We buy from the manufacturers and sell at less than wholesale prices.

Plauen Laces.

B394.

B394. Plauen allover, in ivory and ecru, 18-inch, $1.50 yd.
Plauen and guipure allover, 18-inch, in ivory and ecru, 60c, 75c, 85c, $1.00, 1.25, 1.35, 1.50 to 4.00 yd.

B39X.

B39X. Guipure applique, in ivory and ecru, 1-inch 45c yd.
Applique lace, in ecru, ½-inch, 20c; ¾-inch, 25c, 35c; 1-inch, 50c, 65c; 1½ to 2-inch, 65c to $1.00 yd.
A few pretty and neat designs of Russian applique, in linen shade, for dress trimming, 1 to 2½-inch, 85c to $1.50 yd.

Write for prices and widths.

Plauen lace, in ivory and ecru, 3-inch, 35c yd.

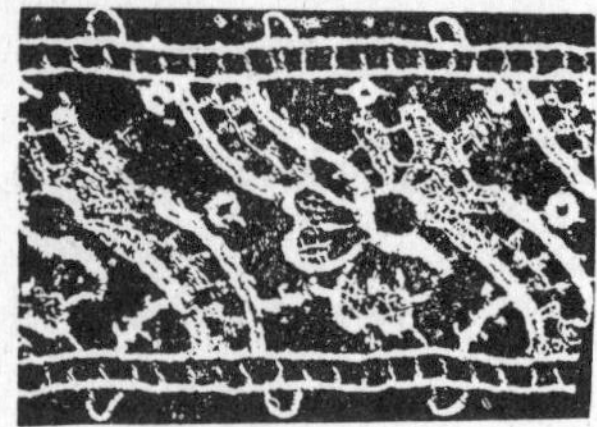

B396.

B396. Plauen insertion, in ivory and ecru, 1½-inch, 20c yd.
Plauen and guipure laces, in ivory and ecru, 3-inch, 25c, 30c, 35c; 4-inch, 35c; 5½-inch, 50c, 65c, 75c; 7 to 9-inch, 75c to $1.50 yd.
Plauen and guipure insertions, in ivory and ecru, ¾-inch, 8c, 10c, 12½c; 1-inch, 10c, 12½c, 15c; 1¼-inch, 15c, 20c; 1½-inch, 15c, 20c, 25c; 2-inch, 25c, 35c, 50c yd.
Heavy plauen edging and insertion to match, 1-inch, 10c; 1½-inch, 12½c, 15c yd.
Extra fine plauen edging and insertion, in ecru, ¾-inch, 25c, 30c; 1-inch, 45c; 1½-inch, 50c, 65c yd.

Renaissance Laces.

Renaissance allover, in ecru, 18-inch, $4.00, 5.00, 5.50, 6.00, 6.25, 10.00 yd.
Renaissance lace, in ecru, 2½-inch, $1.00; 3-inch, $1.35; 4 to 5-inch, $1.50 to 2.50 yd.
Also insertion to match, 2-inch, $1.00; 2½ to 3-inch, $1.25 to 1.75 yd.

Of these we do not cut samples.

Special in cotton Irish point lace, in cream, white and butter, 3-inch, 3c, 5c, 8c; 4-inch, 5c, 8c, 10c, 12½c; 6-inch, 8c, 10c, 12½c yd.
Venice point lace, in white, cream and butter, 3-inch, 5c, 8c; 4-inch, 8c, 10c, 12½c; 5-inch, 10c, 12½c; 6-inch, 15c, 20c yd.

Torchon Laces.

Machine made torchon lace, in a variety of designs, similar to the following:

B397.

B397. Imitation torchon lace, 2-inch, 5c yd.

B398.

B398. Imitation torchon insertion to match, 1½-inch, 5c yd.
Imitation torchon lace, ¾-inch, 3c; 1⅛-inch, 4c; 1⅝-inch, 5c; 2½-inch, 8c yd; insertion to match, ⅝-inch, 3c; 1¼-inch, 4c yd.
German made climax torchon lace, 12 yds on card (these goods we do not sell less than 1 doz yds), linen finish, with plain or pearl edges, ½-inch, 5c; ¾-inch, 8c; 1-inch, 10c; 1¼-inch, 12½c; 1½-inch, 15c card.
Medium make climax torchon lace, good patterns, on cards of 12 yds, ½-inch, 15c; 1-inch, 20c; 1¼-inch, 25c; 1¾-inch, 35c; 2½-inch, 50c card.
Fine climax torchon lace, on cards, ⅜-inch, 25c; ½-inch, 35c; ¾-inch, 50c; 1-inch, 60c card.
Turkey red and white, also navy blue and white, on cards of 12 yds, ½-inch, 5c; ¾-inch, 8c; 1-inch, 10c; 1¼-inch, 15c; 1¾-inch, 20c; 2-inch, 25c card.

Hand-made Torchon Laces.

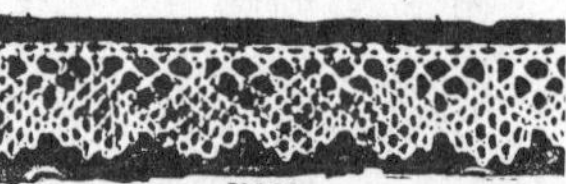

B399.

B399. Special ¾-inch linen hand-made torchon lace, 3c yd.

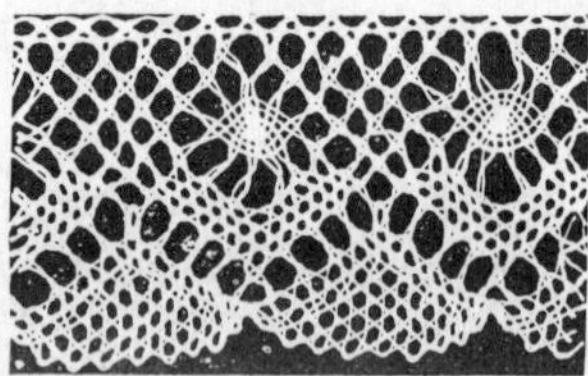

B400.

B400. Heavy 1 to 2-inch linen hand-made torchon lace, 5c yd.

B401.

B401. Linen torchon lace, 1-inch, 10c yd.

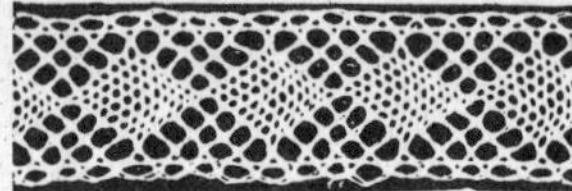

B402.

B402. Linen torchon insertion, 8c yd.

B403.

B403. Linen hand-made torchon lace, 2½ to 3-inch, 15c yd.
Medium make torchon lace, real, ¾-inch, 5c, 8c, 10c, 12½c; 1-inch, 10c, 12½c, 15c; 1½-inch, 10c, 12½c, 15c, 20c, 2-inch, 10c, 12½c, 15c, 20c, 25c; 2½-inch, 12½c, 15c, 20c, 25c, 35c; 3-inch, 15c, 20c, 25c, 35c; 4-inch, 35c yd; insertions to match, 5c, 8c, 10c, 12½c; 15c, 20c, 25c yd.

Heavy linen guipure lace and insertion to match, making a handsome trimming for linen centre-table drapes or curtains. Write for prices and widths.

Extra fine bleached hand-made torchon lace, ⅜-inch, 8c, 10c, 12½c; ½-inch, 10c, 12½c, 15c; ¾-inch, 12½c, 15c, 20c; 1-inch, 15c, 20c, 25c; 1¼-inch, 20c, 25c, 35c; 1½-inch, 25c, 35c; 2 to 2½-inch, 35c, 45c yd; insertion to match, 10c, 12½c, 15c, 20c, 25c, 35c yd.
Cream or black wool yak lace, 1 to 1¼-inch, 8c; 1½ to 2-inch, 10c; 2-inch, 12½c; 2 to 2½-inch, 15c; 2½-inch, 20c; 3-inch, 25c; 3½-inch, 35c yd.

Frillings and Ruchings.

B83. Double edge shirred silk ribbon, ⅜ inch wide, in black, white, cream and all the leading shades, special, 5c yd.
B84. Double edge shirred silk chiffon ruching, ½ inch wide, in black, white, cream, rose, sky, and all the leading shades, 10c yd.
B85. Double edge shirred silk chiffon, 1 inch wide, in black, white, cream, rose, sky, and all the leading shades, 15c yd.
B86. Double edge chiffon ruching, suitable for dress trimmings and finishing yokes, in black, white, cream, and all the leading shades, 35c yd.
B88. Fancy chiffon frillings, in black, white, cream and colors, 15c, 20c, 25c yd.
B89. Something new in lisse frillings, in black, white and cream, 15c, 20c, 25c, 35c yd.
B90. Widows' lisse borderings, in black and white, 15c, 20c, 25c, 35c yd.
Widows' lisse bordering, in double row, 30c yd.
Double ruching for babies' bonnets, in white and cream, 30c yd.
B91. 1-inch muslin frilling, double row, suitable for nurses' caps, in white and cream, 5c yd, or 55c doz yds.
Also tourists' silk cord frilling, in white and cream, 5c yd, or 55c doz yds.
3-inch double ruching, in lisse and chiffon, suitable for neckruffs and cape trimmings, in black only 50c, 65c, 75c, $1.00 yd.

Infants' Bibs.

Infants' lace-trimmed bibs, 6 for 25c.
Quilted bibs, cambric, 5c each.
Fine cambric quilted bibs, with lace or embroidery trimming, new patterns, at 7c each, or 4 for 25c; 9c each, or 3 for 25c; 10c, 12½c, 15c, 20c each; and a special line at 18c each, or 3 for 50c.

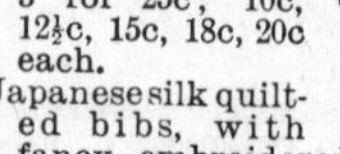

Fine quilted cambric bibs, trimmed with neat embroidery, 25c each.
Silk-faced quilted bibs, lace and embroidery trimming, 9c each, or 3 for 25c; 10c, 12½c, 15c, 18c, 20c each.
Japanese silk quilted bibs, with fancy embroidered design, trimmed with lace or silk embroidery, 25c, 35c, 50c, 75c, 85c, and a special line, 65c each.

Fine hand-made mull bibs, quilted and embroidered, with fancy edges, 35c each, or 3 for $1.00; also same style, 25c, 50c each.

Oilcloth feeders, 5c each.
Oilcloth feeders, larger size, 7c each, or 4 for 25c.
Special line, feeders, large size, 5c each.
Printed feeders, fancy colored designs, 4c each, or 8 for 25c.

Infants' large sized feeders, with fringed and hem-stitched ends, 15c each.
Also a large variety of figured feeders, in crash and linen, 9c each, 3 for 25c; 10c, 12½c each.

Silk Chiffons.

B93. 6-inch silk chiffon band, with satin edges, in black, white, cream, mais, sky, pink, Nile, heliotrope and cardinal, 8c yd.
B94. 14-inch silk chiffon, with satin-striped edges, in black and ivory only, 25c yd.
B95. 41-inch silk chiffon, in black, white, cream, mais, rose, sky, Nile, helio, and all the leading shades, special, 35c yd.
B96. 48-inch silk mousseline de soie, in black, white and cream only, 65c yd.
B97. 4-inch plaited chiffon, in black, white, cream, rose and sky, special, 12½c yd.
B98. 14-inch plaited chiffon, in black, white, cream, rose and sky, special, 25c yd.
B99. 22-inch plaited chiffon, in black, white and cream only, special, 35c yd.

LADIES' NIGHT GOWNS.

SIZES 54, 56, 58 AND 60 INCHES.

1. Cotton, yoke of 6 clusters tucks, lace on neck, down front and sleeves, 35c; E. L. S. 50c

2. Cotton, yoke of fine tucking, frill on neck, down front and sleeves......43c

3. Cotton, yoke of 4 clusters tucks, 2 rows insertion, revers each side, frill on neck and down front, 50c; E.L.S.65c

4. Fine cotton, Empire style, front of insertion and embroidery, collar of insertion and frill................65c

5. Fine cotton, yoke of 6 clusters tucks, 2 rows insertion and frill of embroidery..........................70c

6. Fine cotton, yoke of 4 clusters tucks, 2 rows insertion, embroidery frill ..73c

7. Cotton, yoke of 4 rows insertion, 6 clusters tucks, frill of embroidery, 75c; E. L. S. $1.00

8. Fine cotton, yoke of insertion, revers of embroidery, double frill embroidery down front.......................75c

9. Cotton, 4 rows insertion, double frill of embroidery, 4 rows tucking.....85c

10. Fine cotton, yoke of solid tucking, finished with frill of fine embroidery, $1.00; E. L. S........$1.25

11. Fine cotton, yoke of 4 rows fine insertion, frill of embroidery over shoulder, double frill down front..........$1.00

12. Fine cotton, yoke of fine insertion, embroidery and tucks...........$1.15

13. Fine heavy cotton, yoke finished 4 rows fine tucking, 2 rows insertion, frill of embroidery around yoke and neck, double frill down front....**$1.25**

14. Extra fine cotton, yoke of 4 rows fine insertion, 6 clusters tucks, double frill of embroidery down front, single frill across yoke................**$1.35**

15. Fine cambric, Empress style, front of insertion, beading and lace, revers of beading ribbon and lace **$1.35**

16. Fine cambric, Empire front, 3 rows insertion and embroidery, revers of solid tucking and fine embroidery, $1.50; E. L. S............**$2.00**

E. L. S. means extra large size, for stout ladies.

LADIES' NIGHT GOWNS.

54 to 60 INCHES LONG.—(E. L. S. means Extra Large Size.)

17. Cambric, yoke of tucking, insertion and embroidery $1.50

18. Cambric, yoke of 6 rows insertion, frill of embroidery around yoke, neck and down front $1.75

19. Fine cambric, Empire style, finished fine tucking insertion, frill of embroidery, lapels of insertion and embroidery, $1.65; E. L. S $2.25

20. Fine nainsook, round yoke of 2 rows insertion, puffing and frill of fine embroidery $1.75

21. Fine cambric, collar of insertion, finished with frill of embroidery and insertion, ribbon and embroidery round neck..$2.15

22. Fine nainsook, square yoke of insertion and frill of embroidery $2.25

23. Nainsook, pointed yoke of insertion, beading frill of wide valenciennes lace...$2.25

24. Nainsook, Empire style, fine embroidery insertion and valenciennes lace, short sleeves, 2 frills of lawn with lace....$2.35

25. Nainsook, Empire style, of 2 rows insertion, beading ribbon, insertion and frill of wide embroidery down each side..$2.50

26. Fine nainsook, fancy pointed yoke of solid tucking, finished with insertion, wide frill of embroidery and ribbon, neck of beading ribbon and embroidery, tucked back, $2.75; E. L. S $3.50

27. Nainsook, fancy yoke of tucking, with valenciennes insertion, frill of lawn with valenciennes lace $2.75

28. Nainsook, round yoke of extra valenciennes insertion, beading collar of insertion, beading frill of extra fine wide lace $3.25

29. Nainsook, square neck of insertion ribbon, lawn frills of insertion and valenciennes lace $3.50

30. Nainsook, fancy front of valenciennes insertion, collar finished with insertion and frill of wide lace, beading and ribbon at waist..........................$3.75

31. Fine nainsook round neck, of valenciennes insertion, beading and ribbon, wide frills of lawn with insertion and valenciennes lace $4.00

32. Fine nainsook, Empire front, trimmed to bottom with tucks and insertion, collar of fine insertion, frill of extra fine wide embroidery, sleeves trimmed to match front $8.50

There is no shrinking in the manufacture of these goods.

LADIES' WHITE SKIRTS.

38 TO 40 INCHES LONG.—FLOUNCES FULL.

60. Cotton, deep hem, 1 cluster tucks........25c

61. Cotton, deep frill, with hem and tucks ..50c

62. Cotton, 1 cluster tucks, frill of embroidery 75c

63. Cotton, umbrella finished, with deep frill of embroidery, dust frill $1.00

64. Cotton, 1 cluster tucks, frill finished with 1 row insertion and frill of lace, dust frill $1.10

65. Fine cotton, with umbrella frill, finished with clusters tucks and wide embroidery, dust frill $1.25

66. Cambric, umbrella frill, finished 1 cluster tucks and frill of fine embroidery, dust frill $1.50

67. Cambric, umbrella frill of 3 clusters tucks, 1 row lace insertion and frill of lace, dust frill $1.65

68. Cambric, umbrella frill, finished with extra fine frill of skirting embroidery, 38 to 42 inches long, dust frill $2.00

69. Fine cambric, lawn frill, 2 rows fine valenciennes insertion, frill of valenciennes lace, dust frill, 38 to 42 inches long $2.25

70. Fine cambric, umbrella frill of lawn, with hemstitched tucks, frill of fine embroidery, dust frill, 38 to 42 inches long $2.50

71. Fine cambric, umbrella frill, 2 rows insertion, frill of fine wide embroidery, dust frill, 38 to 42 inches long $2.65

72. Fine cambric, deep umbrella frill, finished with flounce of extra fine wide embroidery, dust frill, 38 to 42 inches long $2.85

73. Fine cambric, deep umbrella frill of finest lawn, 2 rows finest valenciennes insertion and lace under frill, finished with narrow lace, 38 to 42 inches long $3.00

74. Fine cambric, wide umbrella frill, finished with 2 clusters tucks, 2 rows extra fine insertion, frill of extra fine embroidery, dust frill, 38 to 42 inches long $3.50

75. Fine cambric, deep umbrella frill of extra fine lace, finished 3 clusters tucks, 3 rows valenciennes insertion, frill of 1 cluster tucks and frill of valenciennes lace, dust frill, edged with lace, 38 to 42 inches long $4.00

76. Fine cambric, Vandyke frill of finest lawn, with fine valenciennes insertion, finished with frill of fine lace, under frill finished with frill of lace, dust frill, 38 to 42 inches long.. $5.00

These are only a few of the many designs we have in stock. Other prices range as high as $15.00 each.

Any skirt over $1.00 can be had in extra large sizes, 32, 34, 36 waist measure, for 10 per cent. extra.

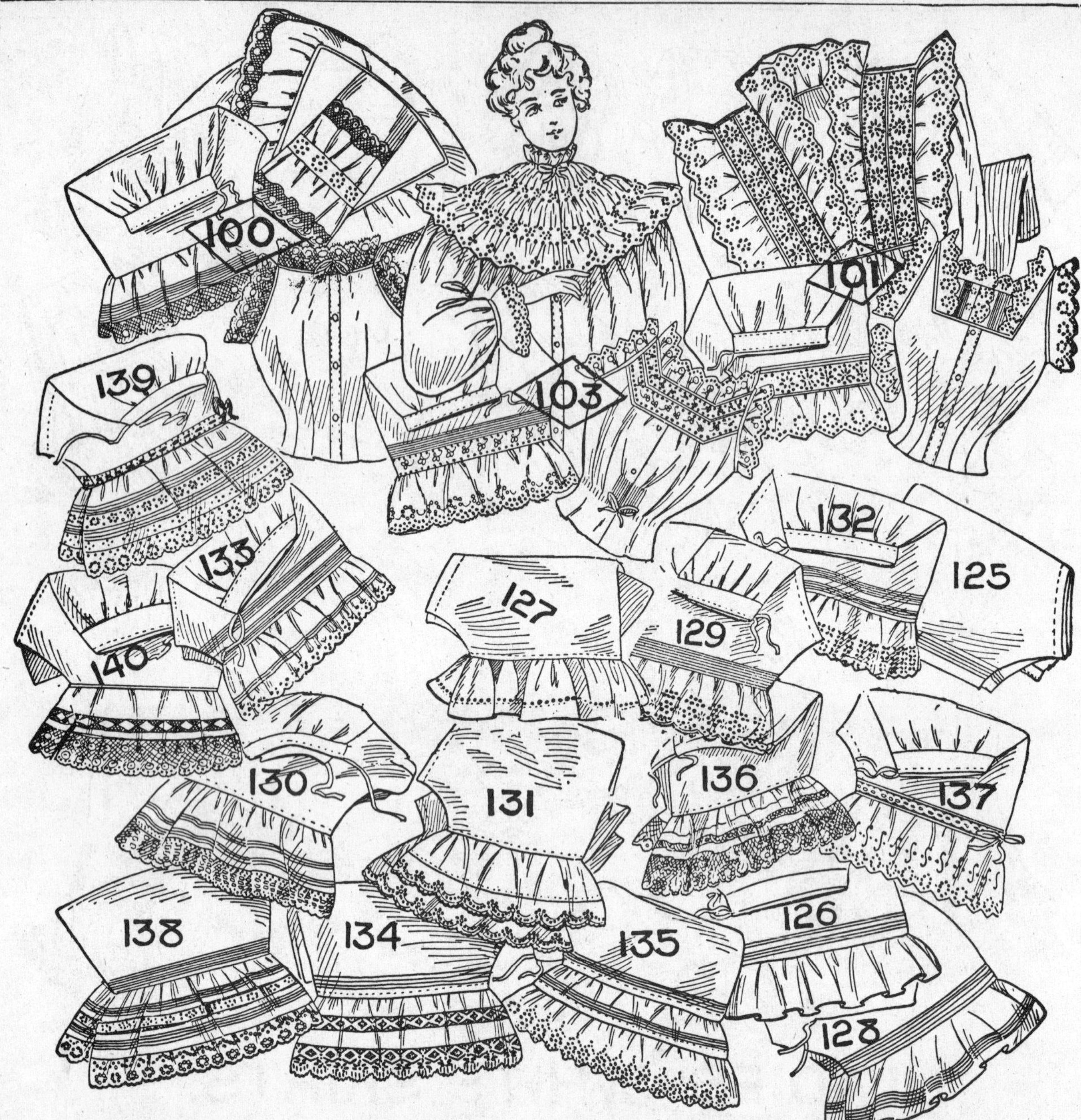

BRIDAL SETS AND DRAWERS.

Gowns, 54 to 60 inches. Drawers, 25 and 27 inches. Corset Covers, 32 to 40 inches.

Bridal Sets.

Set 100. Gown, fine cotton, Empire style, trimmed with insertion, cambric frill and lace. **Drawers,** cambric frill, 1 cluster tucks and lace. **Corset cover,** round neck, trimmed with insertion, beading, ribbon and lace $1.95

Set 101. Gown, fine cotton, Mother Hubbard, front of 4 rows insertion, 4 frills of embroidery. **Drawers,** 1 cluster tucks, 1 row insertion, frill of embroidery. **Corset cover,** square neck, yoke of tucks, 4 rows of insertion, frill of embroidery $2.50

Set 103. Nainsook. **Gown,** round yoke of insertion and puffing, finished with frill of fine embroidery. **Drawers,** 1 cluster tucks, 1 row insertion, frill of embroidery. **Corset cover,** square neck of 2 rows insertion, braid and frill of embroidery $6.00

Other sets, $4.50 to $10.00

Drawers.

25 and 27 inches.

125. Cotton, hem and tuck 12½c
126. Cotton, 2 clusters tucks and wide cambric frilling, 25c; E. L. S 35c
127. Cotton, umbrella frill, hemstitched 30c
128. Cotton, 1 cluster tucks, wide frill, finished with tucks 35c
129. Fine cotton, 1 cluster tucks and wide frill of embroidery 43c
130. Fine cotton, deep umbrella frill, finished with 2 clusters tucks and frill of lace 45c
131. Fine cotton, umbrella frill, finished with fine embroidery, 50c; E. L. S 65c
132. Fine cotton, 2 clusters tucks, frill of fine embroidery 50c
133. Fine cotton, wide umbrella frill, 2 clusters tucks and frill of embroidery 60c
134. Fine cotton, 1 cluster tucks, umbrella frill, finished with 1 row insertion and lace 65c
135. Fine cambric, 1 cluster tucks, umbrella frill, finished with 1 cluster tucks and frill of embroidery, 75c; E. L. S $1.00
136. Cambric, umbrella frill, 1 row valenciennes insertion and frill of lace 85c
137. Cambric, frill of embroidery, with beading and ribbon, $1.15; E. L. S $1.50
138. Fine cambric, 1 cluster tucks, umbrella frill, 2 clusters tucks, 1 row insertion and frill of embroidery $1.50
139. Fine cambric, umbrella frill, 2 clusters tucks, 1 row insertion and frill of embroidery, frill put on with beading and ribbon $2.00
140. Cotton, umbrella frill, with insertion and lace 70c

E. L. S. MEANS EXTRA LARGE SIZE, FOR STOUT LADIES

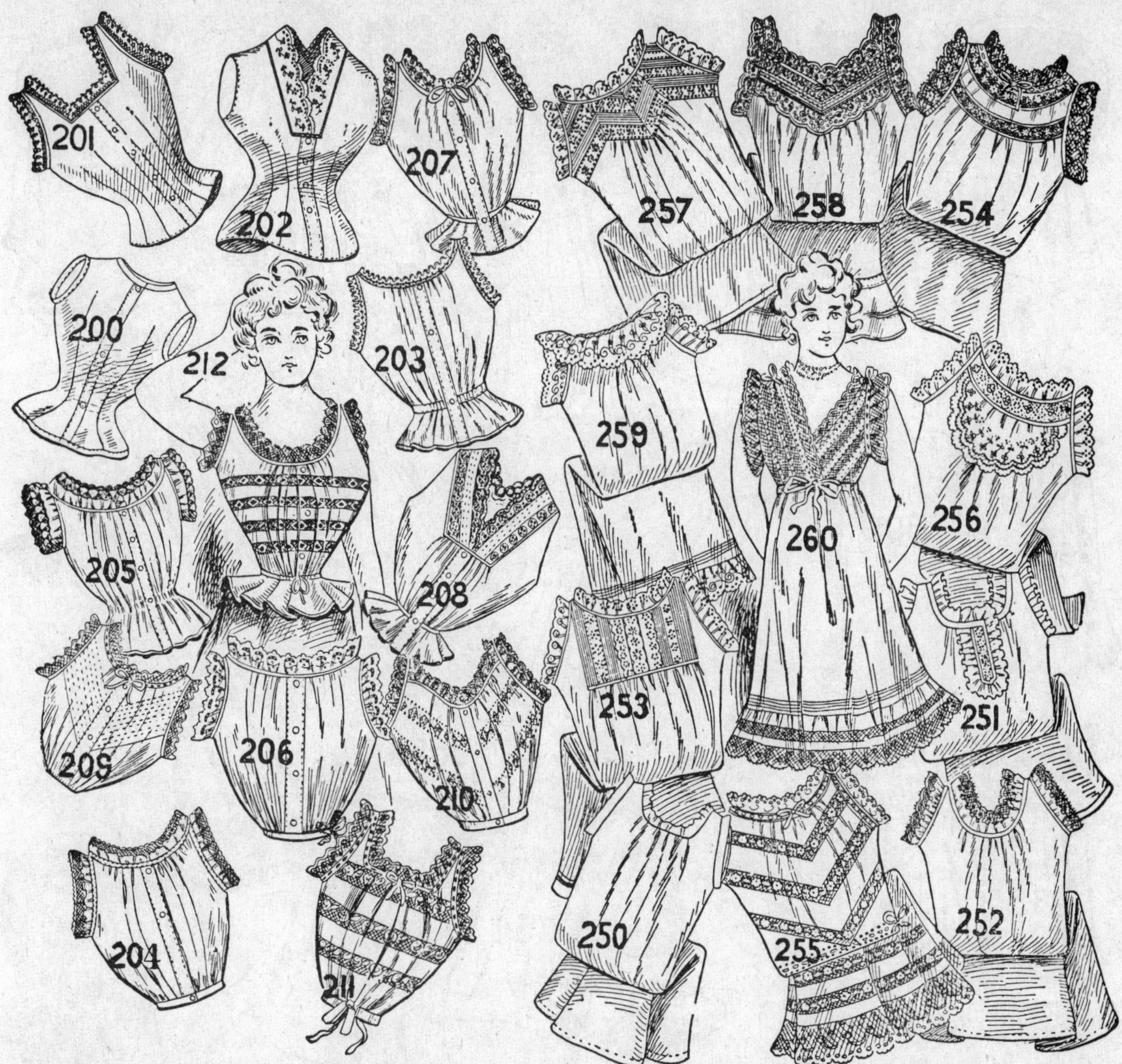

Corset Covers and Chemises.

Corset Covers.

30 to 40 inches.

200. Cotton, plain, with low or high neck......9c
201. Cotton, square neck, lace on neck and arms....................22c
202. Cotton, pointed yoke of wide embroidery.. ....25c
203. Cotton, low neck, French front, embroidery on neck and arms....................35c
204. Cotton, French style, full front neck and arms, with frill and lace....................40c
205. Cotton, frills around neck, finished with lace, full front....................50c
206. Cambric, French style, frill of fine embroidery on neck and arms....................48c
207. Cambric, low neck, full front, frill of embroidery on neck and arms....................55c
208. Nainsook, 1 row valenciennes and Swiss insertion, frill of valenciennes lace, full front 75c
209. Nainsook, full front of hemstitched tucks, beading ribbon and lace on neck........... 85c
210. Nainsook, full front of 2 rows valenciennes insertion, frill of lace on neck and arms..$1.00
211. Nainsook, square neck, front of 3 rows valenciennes insertion, beading ribbon and lace on neck and arms, beading and ribbon at waist....................$1.25
212. Nainsook, low neck, full front of 4 rows valenciennes insertion, neck and arms trimmed with lace....................$1.45

A very large variety not mentioned in catalogue, ranging as high as....................$3.50

42 and 44-inch bust, 25 per cent. extra.

Chemises.

250. Cotton, plain band on neck 12½c
251. Cotton, frilling on neck, arms and around centre-piece of insertion 30c
252. Cotton, frill of lace on neck and arms..45c
253. Cotton, front of tucks and insertion, embroidery on neck and arms....................50c
254. Cambric, round neck, front of 2 rows valenciennes insertion, beading ribbon and lace on neck....................85c
255. Long chemise, fine lawn, 3 rows valenciennes insertion, waist finished with beading and ribbon, beading, ribbon and lace on neck and arms; skirt, 2 rows valenciennes insertion, frill of lace $3.00
256. Fine cambric, front of insertion and embroidery....................$1.00
257. Fine cambric, front of tucking insertion, braid and embroidery $1.50
258. Long chemise, cambric, front of tucking, insertion and embroidery, frill at bottom with tucks....................$1.75
259. Long chemise, cambric, round yoke of embroidery ; skirt, 1 cluster tucks and embroidery $1.25
260. Long chemise, decollete, front of fine valenciennes insertion and lace, waist of beading and ribbon ; skirt, 1 cluster tucks, frill of valenciennes lace and insertion $3.50

We cheerfully refund money if goods are not as represented.

Ladies' Aprons and Children's Pinafores.

Aprons.

300. Lawn, finished with hem and band 15c
301. Gingham, band and sashes, 20c; better quality 28c
302. Lawn, 3 1-inch tucks, wide hem and sashes 25c
303. Fine lawn, fine tucking, band and sashes, 30c; extra wide 40c
304. Fine lawn, 1 row fine insertion, band and sashes, 39c; finished 2 rows insertion 50c
305. Heavy linen, fancy striped border, hem and sashes 35c
306. Gingham, with bib, and straps over shoulders 35c
307. Heavy plain linen, pocket, hem and band 28c
308. Heavy linen, wide hem, yoke band, bib and straps over shoulders 40c
309. Fine linen, yoke band, bib, finished with row fancy braid 39c
310. Blue colored Holland, pocket, bib finished with braid 25c
311. Black sateen, finished with hem, band and sashes, 25c; better quality, with pocket ...35c
312. Lawn, bib of 1 row insertion, finished over shoulders with 1 row insertion and frill of embroidery 28c
313. Lawn, deep hem, bib of insertion and tucks, revers of insertion and embroidery 50c
314. Lawn, bib of tucks, insertion and fine embroidery, revers of tucks, insertion and embroidery 75c
315. Fine lawn, skirt finished with flounce and 2 rows insertion, bib of tucking, insertion and fine embroidery $1.00

Pinafores.

Sizes	1,	2,	3,	4,	5,	6,
Ages	2,	4,	6,	8,	10,	12 years.

350. Lawn, Mother Hubbard, finished with frill of lawn, 28c; finished with frill of embroidery 40c
352. Lawn, Mother Hubbard, finished with insertion and frill of embroidery 50c
353. Lawn, finished with insertion across front, caps of 3 rows insertion and frill of embroidery 65c
354. Lawn, deep waist, finished with embroidery 65c
355. Lawn, deep waist, finished with insertion and lapels of embroidery 75c
356. Fine lawn, Mother Hubbard, neck finished with insertion and fine lace arms and frill finished with lace 75c
358. Fine lawn, front of insertion, tucks and embroidery, lapel of tucks, insertion and embroidery 85c
360. Boys' overalls, blue or pink checked gingham, long sleeves, sizes 1, 2 and 3 years....50c
361. Print pinafores, pink and blue colors, frill of print, Mother Hubbard style, sizes 1 to 6 ....35c

Night Caps.

325. Dusting caps, made of print, dark colors, ...15c
326. Night caps, fine cambric tucks and frill 35c
327. Fine lawn, insertion frill, finished with fine lace 50c

Misses' and Children's White Underwear.

Gowns.

Sizes 1, 2, 3, 4, 5, 6, 7, 8,
Ages 1½, 2½, 4, 5½, 7, 8½, 10, 12 years.

400. White cotton, Mother Hubbard, tucking and lace frill, sizes 1 to 2, 25c; 3 to 4, 28c; 5 to 6, 31c; 7 to 8.................................34c
401. White cotton, yoke of wide tucks, frill each side, around neck and down front, sizes 1 to 2, 32c; 3 to 4, 36c; 5 to 6, 40c; 7 to 8....44c
402. White cotton, yoke of 2 rows insertion, 4 clusters tucks, frill each side and down front, sizes 1 to 2, 35c; 3 to 4, 39c; 5 to 6, 43c; 7 to 8 ....48c
403. Cambric, yoke of hemstitched tucks, embroidery on neck, double frill down front, sizes 1 to 2, 50c; 3 to 4, 55c; 5 to 6, 60c; 7 to 8 ....65c
404. Fine cambric, Empire yoke, lapels of insertion and embroidery, sizes 1 to 2, 75c; 3 to 4, 80c; 5 to 6, 85c; 7 to 8.....................90c

Drawers.

Sizes 1, 2, 3, 4, 5, 6, 7, 8,
Ages 1½, 2½, 4, 5½, 7, 8½, 10, 12 years.

425. White cotton, hem and tucks, sizes 1 to 2, 10c; 3 to 4, 10c; 5 to 6, 11c; 7 to 8..........11c
426. Cotton, 1 cluster tucks, frill of cambric, sizes 1 to 2, 14c; 3 to 4, 16c; 5 to 6, 18c; 7 to 8 ....20c
427. Cotton, 1 cluster tucks, frill of lace, sizes 1 to 2, 20c; 3 to 4, 22c; 5 to 6, 24c; 7 to 8......26c
428. Cotton, 1 cluster tucks, frill of embroidery, sizes 1 to 2, 25c; 3 to 4, 27c; 5 to 6, 29c; 7 to 8 ....32c
429. Cotton, 1 cluster tucks, 1 row insertion and frill of embroidery, sizes 1 to 2, 43c; 3 to 4, 47c; 5 to 6, 52c; 7 to 8 ....57c

Misses' Drawers.

430. White cotton, umbrella frill, finished with tucks and hem, sizes 5, 6, 7, 8..............35c
431. Cotton, umbrella frill, tucks and embroidery, sizes 5 to 8...............................50c
432. Cambric, umbrella frill, 1 cluster tucks, 1 row insertion, frill of lace, sizes 5 to 8......65c

Misses' Skirts.

Sizes 18 to 36 inches.

450. Cotton, 1 cluster tucks and hem, yoke, sizes 18 to 22, 22c; 24 to 30, 24c; 32 to 36....26c
451. Cotton, 1 cluster tucks, frill of cambric, sizes 18 to 22, 33c; 24 to 30, 38c; 32 to 36 ...43c
452. Cotton, 1 cluster tucks, frill of lace, sizes 18 to 22, 55c; 24 to 30, 65c; 32 to 36............75c
453. Cambric, umbrella frill, tucks and frill of lace, sizes 18 to 22, 80c; 24 to 30, 90c; 32 to 36, ...$1.00
454. Cambric, umbrella frill, 1 cluster tucks, frill of embroidery, sizes 18 to 22, 85c; 24 to 30, 95c; 32 to 36 ....$1.10

Children's Skirts.

Ages 1, 2, 3, 4 years.

465. Cotton, waist, 1 cluster tucks and hem..30c
466. Cotton, 1 cluster tucks, frill of lace 50c
467. Cambric, 2 clusters tucks, frill of embroidery 75c
468. Cambric, umbrella frill, 2 clusters tucks, frill of embroidery..........................85c
469. Cambric, 2 clusters tucks, 1 row insertion, frill of embroidery $1.00

Misses' Corset Covers.

Sizes 28, 30, 32 inches.

475. Cotton, round neck, finished with embroidery on neck and arms.........................25c
476. Cotton, square neck, finished with embroidery on neck and arms.....................28c
477. Cambric, pointed yoke of embroidery, finished around arms with embroidery.......43c

It is always cheapest and safest to have your goods sent by Express or Freight.

Outfit No. 1.

600. 2 night slips cambric, pointed yoke of insertion, tuck's and embroidery (85c ea) $1 70
601. 2 night slips, cambric, round yoke of tucks and insertion, frill of embroidery (95c each) 1 90
602. 1 day slip, yoke of insertion, embroidery on neck and around yoke, tucks and insertion in skirt 1 65
603. 1 day slip, cambric, yoke of tucks, insertion and embroidery, skirt, 2 clusters tucks, insertion and embroidery 2 00
604. 1 day slip, nainsook, yoke of 5 rows insertion, frill over shoulder, skirt of insertion, tucks and embroidery 2 15
605. 1 day slip, fine lawn, tucks, Swiss and lace insertion, frill of lace, skirt finished 4 rows insertion, 2 rows Swiss insertion, frill of lace 3 75
606. 2 skirts, cambric, 1 cluster tucks and frill of embroidery (90c each) 1 80
607. 1 skirt, cambric, 1 row insertion, 2 clusters tucks, frill of embroidery 1 10
608. 1 skirt, cambric, tucks, lace, insertion and frill 1 25
609. 2 skirts, fine white flannel, silk embroidered ($1.50 each) 3 00
610. 2 barrowcoats, fine white flannel, elaborately embroidered with silk ($1.50 each) 3 00
611. 12 napkinettes, fine white canton flannel 1 50
612. 4 bands, white flannel, silk embroidered (20c each) $0 80
613. 2 vests, fine all wool, white, buttoned down front (30c each) 0 60

34 pieces $26 20

Each garment can be purchased separately, or the outfit complete for **$24.75.**

Outfit No. 2.

620. 2 night slips, cotton, embroidery trimmed (50c each) $1 00
621. 2 cambric **slips**, embroidery trimmed (65c each) 1 30
622. 1 long slip, cambric, yoke of tucks and insertion, finished with embroidery 0 85
623. 1 cambric slip, 3 rows insertion and tucks, finished with embroidery 1 00
624. 1 long slip, cambric, pointed yoke of insertion, finished with embroidery, tucks and hem 1 25
625. 1 long skirt, cambric, tucks and hem. 0 50
626. 1 white flannelette skirt, deep hem 0 75
627. 1 long skirt, cambric, tuck and embroidery 0 85
628. 1 white flannel skirt, with hem 1 00
629. 1 white flannelette barrowcoat 0 75
630. 1 flannel barrowcoat, plain, with hem. 1 10
631. 12 napkinettes, white canton flannel. 1 50
632. 4 flannel bands, color white, silk embroidered (15c each) $0 60
633. 2 all-wool vests, button front, color white (25c each) 0 50

31 pieces $12 95

This set complete for **$12.00**, or separately at above prices.

Outfit No. 3.

640. 1 slip, cotton, cambric frill $0 45
641. 1 slip, cotton, tucked yoke, cambric frilling 0 50
642. 1 slip, fine cotton, embroidery trimmed 0 50
643. 1 slip, fine cambric, embroidery on neck and sleeves 0 65
644. 1 long skirt, cotton, tucks and hem 0 40
645. 2 long skirts, striped flannelette, deep hem (50c each) 1 00
646. 2 barrowcoats, fancy striped flannelette (50c each) 1 00
647. 2 bands, white flannel, silk embroidery (15c each) 0 30
648. 6 napkinettes, bleached canton flannel 0 60
649. 2 cambric shirts, lace trimmed (12½c each) 0 25

19 pieces $5 65

$5.00 complete, or separately at prices quoted.

We cannot afford to misrepresent our goods. We are in business to stay.

Infants' Slips, Skirts and Barrowcoats.

Infants' Slips.

499. Striped flannelette, pink and white, blue and white 55c
500. White flannelette, tucked front, frill on neck and sleeve, 65c ; same, silk embroidered...75c
501. Cambric, front of solid tucking, and embroidery 85c
502. Cambric, pointed yoke of insertion, tucks and embroidery.......................................$1.00
503. Nainsook, square yoke of 4 clusters tucks, 3 rows valenciennes insertion, frill edged with valenciennes lace; skirt finished deep hem and valenciennes insertion. $1.25
504. Cambric, yoke of tucks, insertion and embroidery, frill of embroidery on skirt.....$1.25
505. Nainsook, pointed yoke extra fine solid tucking, finished with frill of embroidery ; skirt 2 clusters tucks, frill of wide embroidery..$1.50
506. Cambric, yoke of tucks, insertion and embroidery, tucks, insertion and embroidery on skirt $1.50
507. Nainsook, yoke of 6 clusters tucks, 3 rows insertion and braid, wide frill of embroidery .$1.50
508. Nainsook, pointed yoke of valenciennes insertion and tucks, frill of lace, 2 rows insertion, 1 cluster tucks and frill of lace on skirt..$2.00
509. Fine nainsook, yoke of cambric and valenciennes insertion, tucks, frill of embroidery around yoke; skirt 2 clusters tucks, cambric and valenciennes insertion on bias, frill of fine embroidery $2.75
510. Lawn, yoke finished with 4 rows valenciennes insertion, fine nainsook beading frill of lace, skirt finished 3 rows insertion, 2 rows beading and frill of lace..................$2.75
511. Fine lawn, yoke of rows of valenciennes insertion, beading and ribbon, finished with frill of very fine valenciennes lace; skirt 5 clusters tucks, 4 rows valenciennes insertion, frill of fine valenciennes lace............$4.25

Long Skirts.

525. Cambric, 2 clusters tucks, 1 row insertion, frill of embroidery $1.00
526. Cambric, tucks, 2 rows insertion and frill of embroidery, $1.25 ; better qualities. $1.75 to $3.50
527. White flannel, silk embroidered.......$1.25
528. White flannel, deep hem, neatly silk embroidered $1.35

Barrowcoats.

550. White flannel, bound with silk braid..$1.10
551. White flannel, silk-embroidered, silk tape $1.25
552. White flannel, elaborately silk-embroidered, $1.50 ; better qualities.....$1.75 to $3.50

Head Shawls.

575. White flannel, embroidered.............35c
576. White flannel, as cut.....................50c
577. White flannel, embroidered edges and corners 75c
578. White flannel, elaborately embroidered $1.00

Bands.

579. Bands, white flannel, silk-embroidered..20c
580. Bands, white flannel, as cut, silk-embroidered 25c

Diapers.

581. White cotton, embroidered trimmed, each 25c
582. White cotton, as cut, embroidery frilling.38c
583. Rubber diaper, 16 to 26.....................35c
583½. Stockinette diaper, with buttons, 16 to 26 50c
584. Stockinette, with buttons, Canfield, 16 to 26.......................................65c

Bibs.

585. Stockinette, with ties, Canfield..........30c
586. Stockinette, square, with ties............35c
587. Stockinette, large, with ties at waist and neck 50c

Sheets.

588. Stockinette carriage sheet, 18 x 25.......75c
589. Stockinette crib sheet, 28 x 39..........$1.25
590. Stockinette bed sheet, 40 x 62..........$2.50

Aprons.

591. Rubber, 36 inches long, check..........$1.15
592. Stockinette, 36 inches long..........$1.25

SEE OUTFITS FOR EXTRA GARMENTS.

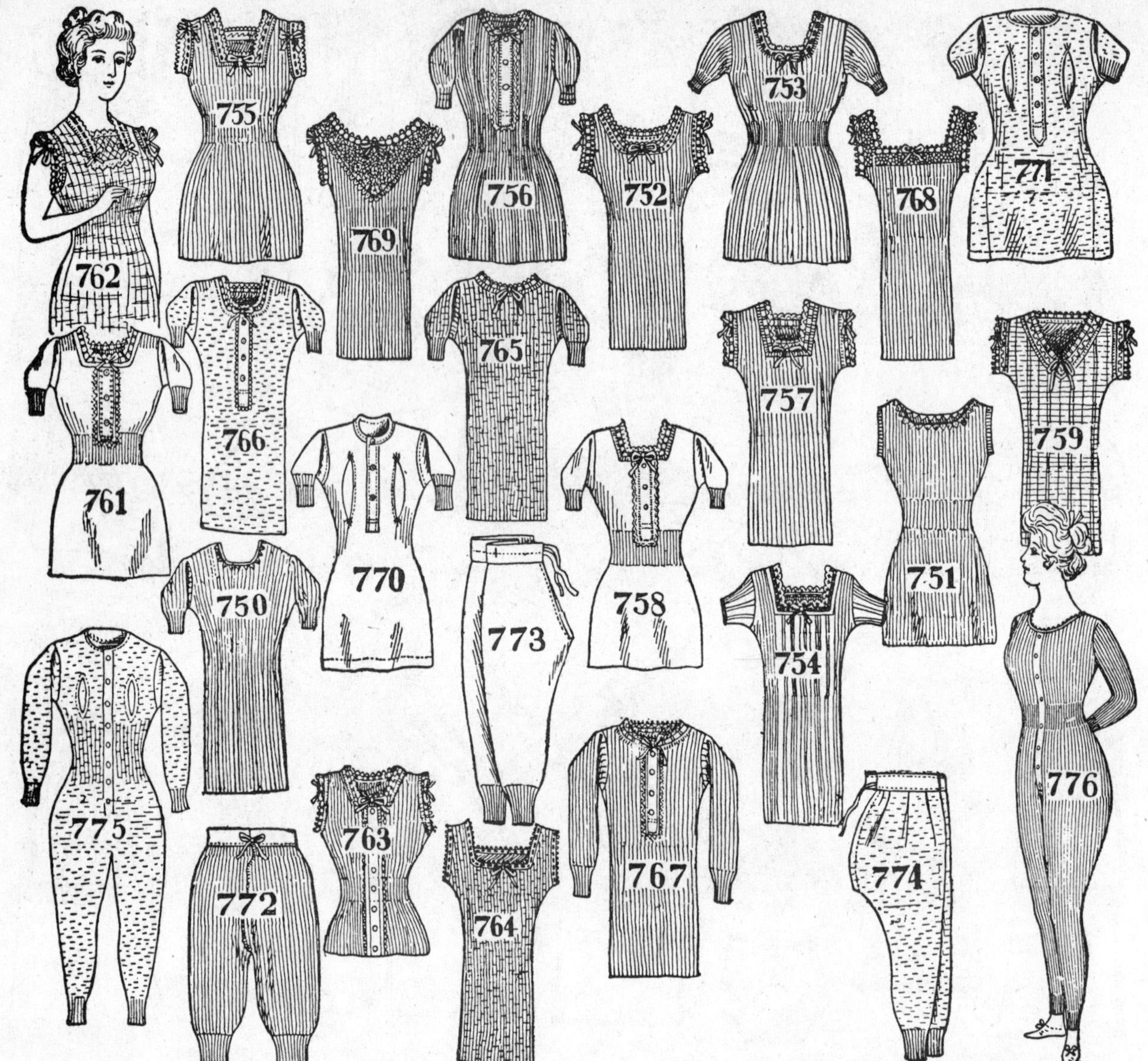

LADIES' WOOLLEN UNDERWEAR.

VEST, 28 TO 38 BUST MEASUREMENT

750. Ribbed cotton, cream, short sleeves......8c
751. Ribbed cotton, shaped, cream, no sleeves, 3 for..25c
752. Fine ribbed, neck and arm, lace trimmed, short sleeves, 10c; long sleeves 12½c
753. Shaped, ribbed, neck trimmed ribbon and lace, short sleeves, 12½c; long sleeves......15c
754. Egyptian yarn, fancy trimmings and ribbons 15c
755. Fine ribbed, shaped, neck and arms trimmed with ribbon and lace, ecru and white......20c
756. Ribbed and shaped, button front, short sleeves, fancy trimmed, ecru, short sleeves, 20c; long sleeves........ ....25c
757. Fine Egyptian yarn, Swiss ribbed, ribbon and lace trimmed...........................25c
758. Fine Egyptian yarn, shaped, silk trimming and ribbon, white and ecru, short sleeves..25c
759. Fancy ribbed, pink and white, striped, silk lace and ribbon..........................30c
761. Lisle thread, fine rib, button front, silk lace and ribbon trimming, white, short sleeves, 40c; long sleeves..................................45c

762. Fancy ribbed, silk and cotton mixture, silk lace on neck and arms, pink and white, and blue and white...................................45c
763. Corset covers, cotton, ribbed, white, 25c; lisle thread, white.........................45c
764. All wool, Swiss, ribbed, neck finished with silk ribbon, white and natural 50c
765. All wool, fine ribbed, medium neck, wool lace and ribbons, white and natural.......60c
766. Fine Swiss, all wool, button front, finished with silk lace and ribbon, short sleeves, white and natural...................................... 65c
767. Ribbed wool, Swiss, button front, long sleeves, silk trimming, white and natural..75c
768. Silk and cotton, ribbed, fancy trimmed, $1.00; better qualities, all silk, in colors, pink, blue and cream, $1.50, 1.75 and..........$2.50
769. Pure silk, fancy trimmed, hand work silk embroidery, pink, blue and cream.........$3.75
770. Balbriggan, button front, short and long sleeves, 35c and.................................50c
771. Fine natural wool, light summer weight, natural color, 75c, $1.00; better qualities in white and natural, short and long sleeves, $1.25 and.......................................$1.50
772. Ribbed cotton drawers, white and ecru, knee and ankle length................................35c
773. Balbriggan drawers, ankle length, 35c and 50c
774. Natural wool drawers ankle length, light summer weight, natural color, 75c, $1.00, 1.25, and 1.50; white, $1.25 and........................$1.50
775. Natural wool combination suits, fine light quality, natural color, $1.25, 1.50, 1.75 and 2.25; white color, $1.75 and..........................$2.25
776. Ribbed cotton combinations, ecru and white, short and long sleeves, knee length.50c
777. Ribbed Swiss drawers, ankle length, cream, pink and blue, $1.75 and..................$2.25
778. Ribbed silk combination suits, short sleeves, ankle length, pink, blue and cream, $2.25 and $2.50
779. Ribbed silk and wool vests, pink, blue, and cream, no sleeves, 65c; short sleeves, 85c; long sleeves..$1.00

Our goods are exactly as represented—high class, low price.

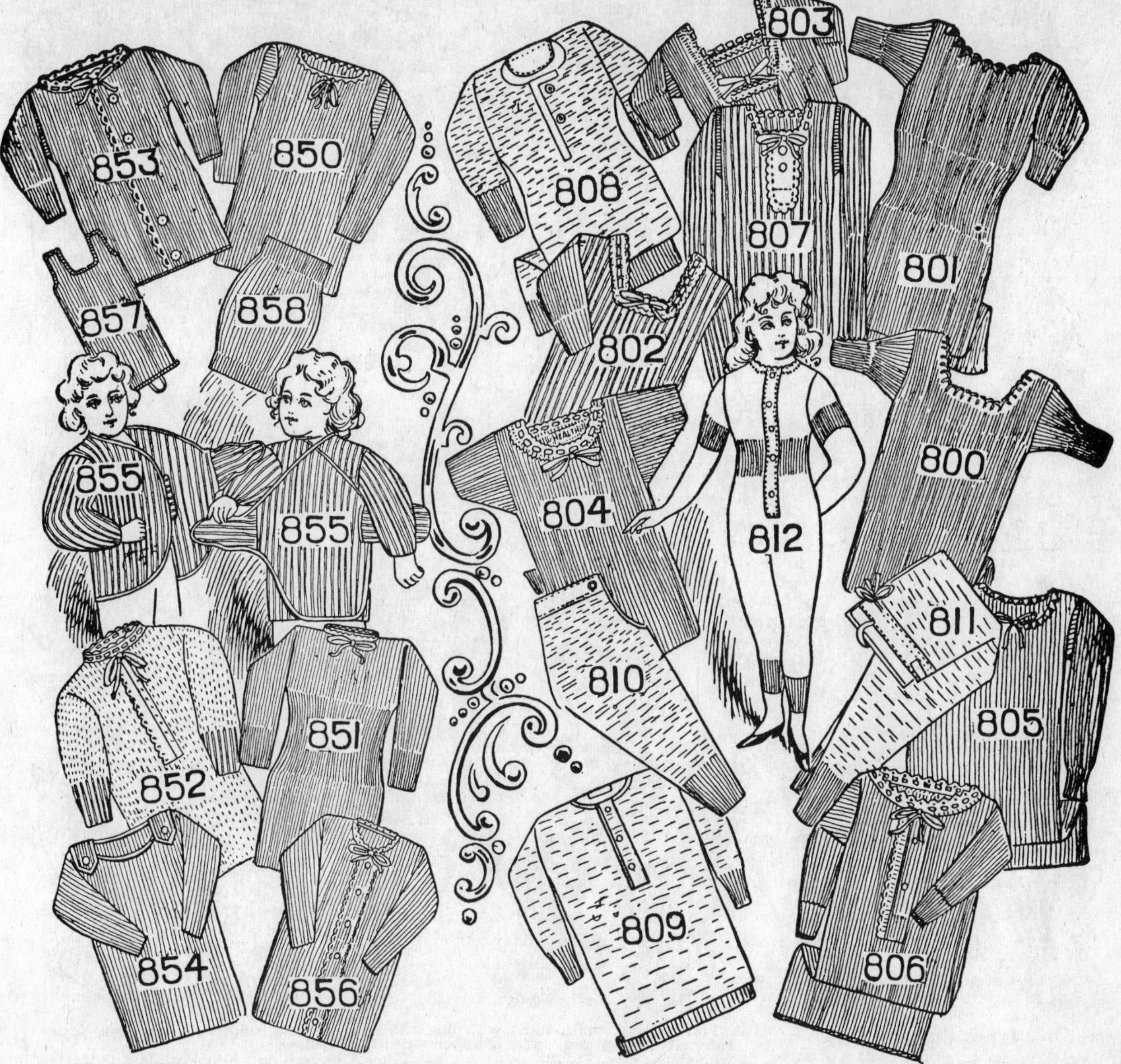

Children's and Infants' Woollen Underwear

Children's Underwear.

Sizes 1, 2, 3, 4, 5, 6, 7,
Ages 2, 4, 6, 8, 10, 12, 14 years.

800. Cotton vests, ribbed, cream color, sizes 1 to 3, 4c; 4 to 6, 5c.

801. Cotton vests, ribbed, cream color, shaped, sizes 1 to 3, 6c; 4 to 6, 8c.

802. Fine Egyptian yarn, short sleeves, colors white and ecru, ribbon and lace trimmed, sizes 1 to 3, 12½c; 4 to 6, 15c.

803. Lisle thread, fine Swiss ribbed, neatly trimmed with lace and ribbon, color white, sizes 1 to 3, 20c; 4 to 6, 25c.

804. Swiss, ribbed, all wool, light weight, ribbons, white and natural, sizes 1 to 3, 25c; 4 to 6, 35c.

805. Ribbed, closed front, wool and cotton, ribbons, natural color, sizes 1 and 2, 25c; 3 and 4, 35c; 5 and 6, 45c.

806. Ribbed, button front, fine merino, natural color, sizes 1 and 2, 30c; 3 and 4, 40c; 5 and 6, 50c.

807. Fine Swiss ribbed, all wool, finest quality, button front, white and natural, short sleeves, sizes 1 and 2, 35c; 3 and 4, 45c; 5 and 6, 55c.

808. Fine plain natural wool, button front, long sleeves, light weight, sizes 1 to 3, 35c; 4 to 6, 45c. Better quality, sizes 1 to 3, 50c; 4 to 6, 60c.

809. Balbriggan vests, cream color, short and long sleeves, button front, sizes 1 to 3, 25c; 4 to 6, 35c.

810. Balbriggan drawers, boys' or girls', ankle length, sizes 1 to 3, 25c; 4 to 6, 35c.

811. Natural wool drawers, boys' or girls', ankle length, natural color, sizes 1 to 3, 35c; 4 to 6, 45c. Better quality, 1 to 3, 50c; 4 to 6, 60c.

812. Combination suit, ribbed, cotton, ankle length, short sleeves, ecru color, sizes 1 to 6, 35c. Better quality, 50c.

Infants' Vests.

Sizes 1, 2, 3, 4,
Ages 3, 6, 12, 18 months.

850. Ribbed, natural merino, closed front, long sleeves—

Sizes	1,	2,	3,	4,
Prices	12½c,	15c,	18c,	20c.

851. Zephyr wool, color white, soft finish, sizes 1 to 4, 25c.

852. Fine merino, natural color, half open front, sizes 1 and 2, 18c; 3 and 4, 22c.

853. Fine merino vests, color white, button all down front, sizes 1 and 2, 25c; 3 and 4, 30c. Better quality, all wool, same style, sizes 1 and 2, 35c; 3 and 4, 40c.

854. Fine all wool, buttons on shoulders, color white, sizes 1 and 2, 50c; 3 and 4, 60c.

855. Reuben's vests, fine pure wool, color white, (see cut for style)—

Sizes	1,	2,	3,	4,
Prices	35c,	40c,	45c,	50c.

856. Fine all wool, imported, button down front, color white, sizes 1 and 2, 60c; 3 and 4, 65c.

857. Infants' bands, ribbed, all wool, straps on shoulders, color white, sizes 1 to 4, 25c.

858. Infants' shaped bands, all wool, white, sizes 1 to 4, 22c.

We guarantee to fill Mail Orders accurately and promptly.

Acme Corsets.

11. Jean throughout, 2 side steels, lace trimmed, white and drab, sizes 18 to 30 .... 28c
13. Jean, sateen stripping, 2 side steels, embroidery, white and drab, sizes 18 to 30 .... 35c
14. Coutil, sateen strips, short hip, lace and ribbons, white and drab, sizes 18 to 30...... 45c
15. White and drab coutil, long waist, sateen strips, silk flossed, sizes 18 to 30 .... 50c
17. White and drab coutil, filled with steel wire, long waist, flossed, sizes 18 to 30 ..... 75c
19. Fine sateen throughout, short hip, single strips, lace and ribbon, sizes 18 to 30 .... 75c
21. Nursing, coutil, steel wire, embroidery, white and drab, sizes 18 to 30 .... 75c
23. High bust, coutil, long waist, steel filled, white and drab, sizes 18 to 30............... 75c
24. Fine sateen, 3-bone, strips fine wire, short hip, with lace, white, drab and black, sizes 18 to 30 .... 85c
28. Sateen, filled with steel wire, lace and ribbon, white and drab, sizes 18 to 30.......... 65c
29. Misses' corsets, coutil, 2 side steels, lace edging, drab and white, sizes 19 to 26 ...... 35c
31. Misses' coutil, sateen stripping, flossed, embroidery, white and drab, sizes 19 to 30.... 50c
35. Fine sateen single strips, filled with fine wire, trimmed with lace, long waist, white and drab, sizes 18 to 30.................... $1.00
37. Summer net, 2-bone, strip of jean, lace edge, sizes 18 to 30 .... 28c
39. Summer net, 3-bone, strip of jean, edge of embroidery, side steels, white, sizes 18 to 30. 38c
41. Summer netting, 3-bone, strip sateen, side steels, lace ribbon, white, sizes 18 to 30...... 50c
53. Fine netting, short, filled with fine wire, baby ribbon top and bottom, sateen strips, white only, sizes 18 to 30.................... 75c
73. Straight front, fine sateen, 3-bone, strip, filled wire, low bust, lace and baby ribbon, white, drab and black, sizes 18 to 30 .... 85c
74. Straight front, fine coutil, sateen strips, steel wire, white and drab, sizes 18 to 30... 75c
75. Straight front, same No. 73, jean, strip sateen, filled with wire, lace and ribbon, white and drab 65c
76. Straight front, jean, 3-bone, strip of sateen, filled with kabo, trimmed lace and baby ribbon, low bust, white and drab, sizes 18 to 30 .... 50c
77. Straight front, fine netting, style as 73, strip of sateen, steel filled, lace and ribbon, white, 18 to 26.. 75c
78. Straight front, netting, style as 74, single strip of sateen, filled with steel, trimmed lace baby ribbon, white sizes 18 to 26........... 75c

B. & C. Corsets.

200. B. & C., straight front, steel filled, jean, drab, broche and white, sizes 18 to 30 .... $1.00
208. B. & C., straight front, featherbone filled, stout figures, drab, white, 18 to 30........ $1.00
209. B. & C., straight front, black sateen, sizes 18 to 26 .... $1.25
210. B. & C., straight front, white batiste, sizes 18 to 26 .... $1.00
204. B. & C., straight front, jean, drab, sizes 18 to 26.................................... 50c
206. B. & C., straight front, summer net, sizes 18 to 26 .... 50c
170. B. & C., nursing, drab, jean, featherbone filled, sizes 18 to 30 .... $1.00
171. Drab or white jean, low bust, short hip, lace ribbon, featherbone filled, 18 to 30. . $1.00
183. Drab jean, long waist, featherbone filled. sizes 18 to 30 .... $1.00
130. Comfort waist, sateen, open or closed hip, or summer net, sizes 18 to 30 .... $1.00
222. Kabo bust perfector, worn with or without corset, white drab jean and summer net. $1.00
220. B. & C. Wright bust form, slender figures, white, drab, jean and summer net......... $2.25

Send waist, bust and height.

P. D. Corsets.

Donita "A."—French coutil 2 side steels, long waist, lace ribbon, drab white, sizes 18 to 30. $1.00
Donita "D."—Coutil, short hip, lace top and bottom, white and drab, sizes 18 to 30 ... $1.25
Donita "K."—Coutil, gored hip, medium waist, lace ribbon, white, drab, 18 to 30.......... $2.50
Donita "M."—Coutil, sateen strips (for stout ladies), spoon clasp, web band, silk embroidered, drab, sizes 22 to 36, $3.00; black.... $3.50

C. C. Corsets.

Magnetic.—Fine sateen, single strips, 5-hook clasp, white and drab, sizes 18 to 28...... $1.25
Yatisi.—Made of Jersey cloth, coraline filled, color ecru, sizes 18 to 30, $1.25; 31 to 36... $1.50
Yatisi Nursing.—Jersey cloth, coraline filled, color ecru, sizes 18 to 30.................. $1.50

When ordering Corsets be careful to give size, style, color and price.

W. B. Corsets.

660. Coutil, 3-bone, strips sateen, short hip, trimmed top and bottom with lace and baby ribbon, white, drab and black, sizes 18 to 30.................................. $1.00

108. Heavy coutil, suitable for stout figures, 3-bone strip, spoon clasp, drab, black and white, sizes 19 to 36 .... $2.00

631. "La Vida," new short Parisian model, perfect fitting, diamond sateen, white, drab and black, handsome lace trimming, short cutaway hip, French bust, graceful, all whalebone, sizes 18 to 30 .... $6.00

499. For short and fully-developed figures, heavy jean, sateen strips, filled with bone wire, long or short waist, drab, sizes 22 to 36 .... $2.50

937. Bias cut, gored over hip, fine sateen, elegant shape, white, drab and black, sizes 18 to 30 .... $1.25

509. "La Vida," imported satin-finished diamond jean, medium waist, Venus back, French model, perfect fitting, white, drab and black, sizes 18 to 30 .... $6.00

115. Fine batiste, light and durable, single strips, short hip, trimmed top and bottom with baby ribbon, white, sizes 18 to 30 .... $1.25

533. Nursing, jean, strips sateen, edge silk embroidery, white, drab and black, sizes 18 to 30 .... $1.00

701. Erect Form, the latest straight-front corset, bias cut, made of jean, gored hip, perfect in shape, colors drab, white and black, sizes 18 to 26.................................. $1.25

702. Erect Form, same style as 701, only made of fine sateen, lace trimmed, white, drab and black, sizes 18 to 26 .... $2.00

962. Erect Form, same style as 701, only made of French coutil, lace trimmed, white, drab and black, sizes 18 to 26.................................. $2.50

703. Erect Form, summer netting, bias cut, same shape as 701, white only, sizes 18 to 30... $1.25

705. Erect Form, fine light batiste, same style as 701, white only, sizes 18 to 30 .... $1.25

965. Erect Form, batiste short, fine lace trimming, gored hips and bust, white only, sizes 18 to 26.................................. $2.25

961. Erect Form, same as 965, only longer, fine batiste, white only, sizes 18 to 30 .... $2.50

Self Reducing, made of imported French coutil, long and short waist, white, drab and fast black sateen, sizes 18 to 36.................. $3.00

The Dowager, for stout figures, heavy coutil, sateen strips, filled with steel wire, white, drab and black, sizes 22 to 30, $2.75; 31 to 36 .... $3.00

R. and G. Corsets.

227. High bust, coutil, sateen strips, medium long waist, white, drab and black, sizes 18 to 30.................................. $1.25

717. Nursing, medium waist, single strips of sateen, white and drab, sizes 18 to 30 ....$1.25

397. Coutil, single strips of sateen, lace and baby ribbon, elegant shape, short hip, white, drab and black, sizes 18 to 30.................. $1.25

601. Straight front, coutil, lace top and bottom, bias cut, white, drab and black, sizes 18 to 30 .... $1.25

604. Straight front, fine batiste or fine netting, single strip, low bust, lace top and bottom, color white, sizes 18 to 30.................. $1.25

297. Heavy jean, with coutil strip, short over hip, lace trimmed, white, drab and black, sizes 18 to 30 .... $1.00

497. Fine sateen throughout, 3-bone strip, short hip, lace at top and bottom, white, drab and black, sizes 18 to 36.................................. $1.60

P. N. Corsets.

454. Heavy jean, abdominal, elastic and lacing on hip, for large people, drab, sizes 20 to 30, $1.75; 31 to 36.................................. $2.00

510. Fine sateen throughout, 3-bone strip, long waist, white, drab and black, sizes 18 to 30 .... $1.75

441. Heavy jean, long waist, silk embroidered, white, drab and black, sizes 18 to 30..... $1.00

493. Heavy jean, sateen strips, 2 side steels, zone waist, white, drab and black, sizes 18 to 30 .... $1.25

458. High bust, coutil, sateen strips, straps over shoulders, white, drab and black, sizes 18 to 30 .... $1.25

F. P. Corsets.

Abdominal, heavy jean, spoon clasp, side lacing, for stout ladies, drab, sizes 20 to 30, $1.50; sizes 31 to 36 .... $1.75

799. High bust, coutil, sateen strips, embroidery edge, straps over shoulders, drab, sizes 18 to 30 .... $1.25

The Erect Form and Straight Front Corsets are in great demand.

WAISTS AND BUSTLES.

LADIES' AND MISSES', CHILDREN'S AND INFANTS'.

Ferris Waists.

223. Misses' or young ladies' waist, fine sateen, plaited bust, ages 13 to 15 years, white and drab, sizes 20 to 26..........$1.25
603. Equipoise waist, fine twill cotton, color white, sizes 20 to 30..........$2.25
220. Ladies' waist, sateen, medium form, long waist, button front, white, drab and black, sizes 19 to 30..........$1.25
319. Ladies' waist, fine sateen, full bust, steel front, colors white drab and black, sizes 19 to 30..........$1.25
230. Ladies' long waist, fine sateen, lace on hip, white, drab and black, sizes 19 to 30......$1.50
215. Misses' waist, 7 to 12 years, laced back, button front, sateen, white and drab, sizes 20 to 26..........$1.15
212. Child's waist, 4 to 6 years, sateen, white and drab, sizes 20 to 26..........$1.00
229. Child's waist, 1 to 4 years, fine sateen, white and drab, sizes 20 to 26..........65c
250. Infants' waist, fine soft material, color white, sizes 20 to 26..........50c

Acme Waists.

911. Misses' waist, 7 to 12 years, fine sateen, laced back, button front, fine corded, white and drab, sizes 20 to 26..........65c
900. Child's waist, white and drab, soft jean, sateen strips, corded, 4 to 7 years, white and drab, sizes 20 to 26..........35c
901. Child's waist, soft jean, button back, color white, 1 to 4 years, sizes 20 to 26..........20c
902. Child's waist, 4 to 7 years, soft jean, button back, white and drab, sizes 20 to 26..........25c
903. Child's waist, 4 to 10 years, fine cambric, full front, white, sizes 20 to 26..........35c
904. Boys' waist, 4 to 7 years, soft jean, button front, white and drab, sizes 20 to 26..........25c
910. Child's waist, soft sateen, small cording, drab and white, 2 to 6 years, sizes 20 to 26..45c
912. Ladies' waist, fine sateen, medium form, long waist, button front, white and drab, sizes 19 to 30..........$1.00
916. Misses' waist, 12 to 17 years, coutil, with sateen strips, lace and baby ribbon, steel clasp front, button on side, lace back, colors white and drab, sizes 20 to 26..........85c

Bustles and Dress Forms.

70. Hygeia dress forms, oval in shape, light and comfortable..........50c
71. Braid wire forms, covered with knitted lace..........50c
72. Imperial hip bustle, made of finest tempered wire, black and white..........60c
73. Combination hip, light and graceful, fine tempered wire..........60c
74. Grecian, fine tempered wire, covered, white and black..........45c
76. Royal hip, fine tempered wire, white and black..........45c
77. La Belle, white tempered wire, covered, white and black..........38c
78. Queen, 2-roll, fine tempered wire..........40c
79. Queen, 3-roll, fine wire..........45c
80. Princess, perfect shape, fine tempered wire..........35c
81. The Gem, fine white wire..........25c
82. The Beauty, fine tempered wire..........22c
83. Empire, best tempered wire..........35c
84. Feather filled, color black..........15c
85. Featherbone, covered with haircloth..........50c
86. Featherbone, white, grey and black..........50c
87. Featherbone, bust forms..........45c
88. Acme belt supporter..........20c
89. Peerless distender..........35c
90. Antiseptic hygienic towels, No. 1, 25c; No. 2, 35c; No. 3..........50c

PREPARE FOR SPRING AND SUMMER BY ORDERING NOW.

Smallwares and Fans.

Summer Fans.

C600. Palm-leaf fans, satin finish, small size, 2c; large size, 3c each.
C601. Paper fans, fancy colored decorations, plain handles, strong and serviceable, 5c, 10c each.
C602. Paper fans, new Parisian and Vienna designs, sixteenth century and floral decorations, 15c, 20c, 25c, 35c each.
C603. Fine linen fans, assorted colors, beautiful decorations, painted sticks, 35c, 50c each.
C604. Black silk fans, 50c each.
C605. American imitation leather folding fans, in plain and decorated, assorted colors, 10c, 12½c, 15c; with leather handles, 20c, 25c each.

Gauze Fans.

They come in white, pink, blue and black.
C606. Gauze fans, beautiful decorations, polished handles, serviceable and pretty, 50c, 75c, $1.00 each.
C607. Gauze fans, hand-painted floral and sixteenth century decorations, hardly two alike; we are continually receiving new designs direct from Paris and Vienna, $1.25, 1.50, 1.75, 2.00, 2.50, 3.00, 3.[illegible] 4.00, 4.50, 5.00 each.

Feather Fans.

C608. Feather fans, "Marguerite" style, feathers both sides, bone handles, in white, pink, blue and black, 65c; large size, 75c, $1.00 each.
C609. Ostrich feather fans, best quality feathers, price according to number and quality of feathers, also style of handles, 3.50, 4.00, 4.75, 5.50, 6.50, 7.00, 8.00 each.

Smallwares.

Battenburg Designs.

They are stamped on colored cambric. The braid is intended to be stitched on, and each pattern can be used many times. Doileys, 5c, 8c, 10c each; cosies, 10c, 12½c, 15c each; handkerchiefs, 10c, 12½c, 15c each; centre-pieces, 12½c, 15c, 20c each; cushion covers, 15c, 20c, 25c each; lace patterns, 10c, 12½c, 15c each; table covers, 35c, 45c; tie ends, 10c, 15c each; yokes, 20c, 25c each; sailor collars, 20c, 25c each; stock collars, 6c, 10c each; bolero jackets, 35c, 40c each; tray cloths, 20c each; curtains, 40c each.

We have just issued a new, complete, illustrated Catalogue of Battenburg and Honiton lace braids, designs, thread, etc. We will be pleased to forward one on application.

Braids.

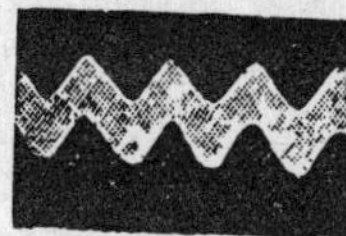

C1. Vandyke or rick-rack braid, 12 yds to bunch, in white, sizes 1, 2, 5c bunch; sizes 3, 4, 5, 6, 10c bunch; in red, blue, navy and black, sizes 1, 2, 5c bunch; sizes 3, 4, 10c bunch; same braid, with picot edge, in white only, sizes 1, 2, 5c bunch; sizes 3, 4, 5, 10c bunch.

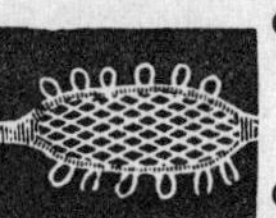

C3. Novelty or antimacassar braid, assorted, Nos. 0, 1, 2, 20c, 25c, 30c doz yds (size of cut is 25c doz yds).
C4. Novelty insertion, 20c, 25c, 35c doz yds.

C5. Feather-edge braid (see cut), sizes 0, 20c doz; size 1, 25c doz; size 2, 30c doz; size 3, 35c doz yds (size of cut is 0).

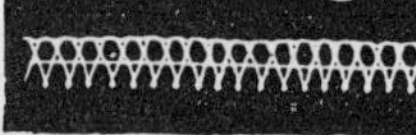

C6. Pearl edging, 10c, 15c, 20c, 45c, 50c doz yds.

C7. Battenburg lace braid, in cream or white, sizes 4, 5, 10c doz yds; sizes 6, 8, 10, 15c doz yds; fine quality braid, in white, sizes 1, 2, 20c doz yds; size 3, 25c doz yds; in cream, size 1, 20c doz yds; sizes 2, 3, 25c doz yds; black silk Battenburg, 35c, 40c, 45c, 50c doz yds.

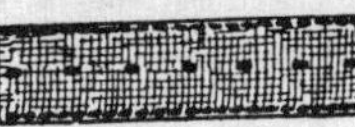

C7½. This cut illustrates a new and pretty Battenburg braid, size 3 only, in cream or white, 35c doz yds.

C8. Gordon braid, for fancy work, in white only, sizes 0, 1, 2, 3, 10c doz yds.
C9. Star braid, white only, for trimming children's dresses, sizes 1, 2, 3, 4, 5c doz yds.
C10. French cotton trimming braid, in white only, assorted widths, 5c bunch of 12 yds; extra width, 10c doz yds.

C11. Honiton braid, English make, according to size and quality, in white, 45c, 50c, 60c, 75c, 95c, $1.20, 1.50, 1.80 doz yds (size of cut is 50c doz yds); in cream, 45c, 50c, 65c doz yds; in black silk, 65c, 75c doz yds.
C12. Honiton insertion, in white, 20c, 25c, 30c, 35c, 45c, 50c, 65c, 95c, $1.20 doz yds; in cream, 25c, 30c doz; in black silk, 50c per doz.
C13. Battenburg rings, in white or cream, assorted sizes, 5c per doz; in silk, black, white, or cream, assorted sizes, 10c per doz.

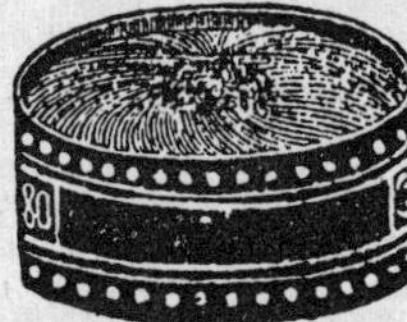

C14. Honiton or Battenburg lace thread, sizes 30 to 200, 4c spool, 3 for 10c; size 300 to 1,500, 5c spool; in cream, 60 to 200, 4c spool, 3 for 10c; 300 to 1,000, 5c spool.

C14½. Coronation braid, in white, red, orange, navy, black and green, 15c bunch of 9 yds.

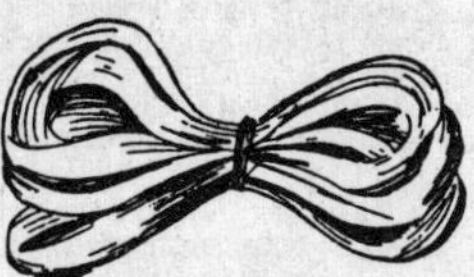

C14½. Tinsel thread, used extensively in making point and Battenburg lace, etc., 8c skein.

French Lace Braids.

C15. French insertion, assorted patterns, white or cream (see cut), 3c yd, 35c doz yds.

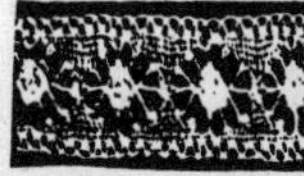

C16. New French insertions, assorted patterns, cream or white (see cut), 50c per doz yds.

C17. New French silk, pearl edging, black or white (see cut), 75c per doz yds.

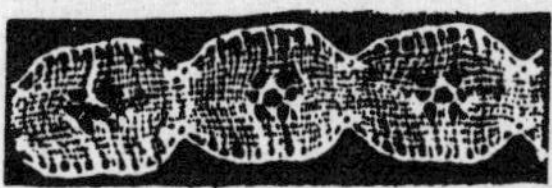

C19. Duchess braid (see cut) cream or white, 45c doz yds; black silk, 95c doz yds.

C20. Black silk insertion, French patterns, 50c doz yds; wider width, 95c doz yds.

Button Hooks.

C21. Steel, with wood or bone handle, 5c, 10c each; steel combination hook and shoe horn, 10c each.
C22. Glove button hooks, 2 for 5c.

Boot and Shoe Laces.

C23. Shoe laces, mohair, ½ inch wide, 27 inches long, black or tan, 3 pairs for 5c; finer quality, 2 pairs for 5c; in silk, 5c, 10c pair; same style, mohair, 45 inches long, black or tan, 3 pairs for 10c.
C24. Boot laces, mohair, 40 inches long, extra strong, black, 5c, 7c doz; better quality, black or tan, fine or heavy quality, 42 inches long, 10c doz; same style, 52 inches long, suitable for bicycle boots, 2 pairs for 5c.
C25. Boot laces, mohair, best quality, banded spiral ends, black or tan, ladies' or gents' sizes, 2 pairs for 5c.
C26. The "Johnston" boot lace, a mixture of Egyptian corded thread and woollen yarn, ladies' or gents', black or tan, 2 pairs for 5c.
C27. Paton's wool boot lace, ladies' or gents', black or tan, 3 pairs for 10c.
C28. Leather boot laces, 36 inches long, single tag, 8c doz; double tag, 10c doz; spiral twist ends, 2 pairs for 5c; imitation porpoise, 5c pair; real porpoise, 8c pair; "White Whale," extra strong, 10c pair.

Boot Buttons—C29. Assorted sizes, 2 boxes for 5c.

Automatic Buttons—C30. Can instantly replace a missing button (see cut), 8c doz.

Binding—C31. Prussian binding for seams, black, 15c doz; white and drab, 20c doz; in silk glaced, white or black, 30c doz yds.
C32. Silk Italian ferret for binding flannel, black and white, 4c yd, 40c doz; colors, 5c yd, 50c doz yds.

Be sure to send enough money for postage.

Glove Laces—C33. Silk glove laces, assorted, browns and black, 5c pair.

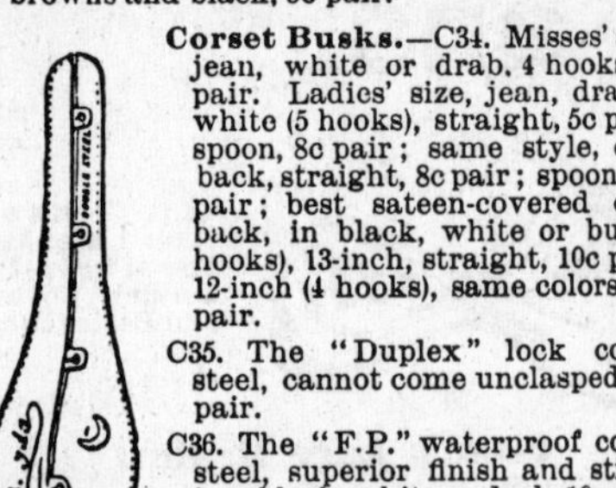

Corset Busks.—C34. Misses' size, jean, white or drab, 4 hooks, 5c pair. Ladies' size, jean, drab or white (5 hooks), straight, 5c pair; spoon, 8c pair; same style, cork back, straight, 8c pair; spoon, 10c pair; best sateen-covered cork back, in black, white or buff (5 hooks), 13-inch, straight, 10c pair; 12-inch (4 hooks), same colors, 10c pair.

C35. The "Duplex" lock corset steel, cannot come unclasped, 10c pair.

C36. The "F.P." waterproof corset steel, superior finish and stitching, black, white or drab, 10c pair. The "Tricora," same style, cork back, 12½c pair.

C37. Kid-covered corset busks, 10c, 12½c, 15c pair.

C38. Side steels, uncovered, 4 for 5c; sateen covered, 20c doz; kid covered, 30c, 40c, 60c doz.

Corset Shields—C39. "Venus" corset shield, prevents corset breaking at waist or hips, 25c pair.

Corset Laces—C40. Round elastic, black or white, 2½ yds, 2 for 5c; flat elastic, 3 for 10c, 5c each; round, satin, 10c each.

C41. Round or flat cotton, 2½ yds, black or white, 6 for 5c; glazed cotton, flat, black, white or drab, 3 for 5c; linen, 2 for 5c.

Chalk—C42. Tailors' marking chalk, black, white or colors, 5c doz.

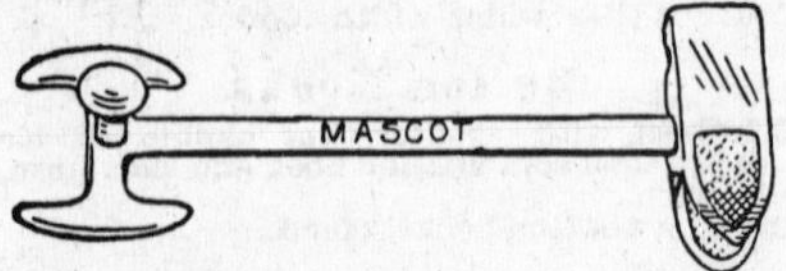

Cuff holders—C43. The "Wizard" cuff holder, 10c pair; the "Mascot" (see cut), 10c pair; the "Washburne," 10c pair.

Crochet hooks—C44. Steel, 2 for 5c, 5c each; wire, reversible, 2 for 5c; bone, 2 for 5c, 5c each; bone, 8 inches long, 5c; 10 inches long, 10c.

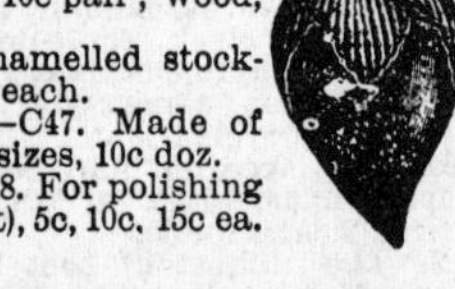

Knitting needles—C45. Rubber, 10c pair; bone, 10c pair; wood, 5c pair.

Darners—C46. Enamelled stocking darners, 5c each.

Dress Weights—C47. Made of lead, assorted sizes, 10c doz.

Emery Bags—C48. For polishing needles (see cut), 5c, 10c, 15c ea.

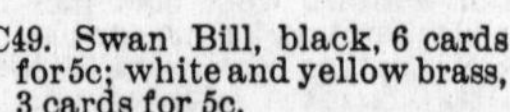

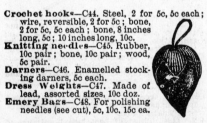

Hooks and Eyes.

C49. Swan Bill, black, 6 cards for 5c; white and yellow brass, 3 cards for 5c.

C50. Improved safety, black or white, 4 cards for 5c; better quality, 2 cards for 5c.

C51. Washable brass safety hook and eye, black or white, 5c card; better quality, 8c card.

C52. The "Francis" hook and eye, black or white, 10c card.

C53. The "Brownie" hook and eye, extra small, for blouses, collars, etc., 10c card.

C54. "Peet's" invisible eyes, black or white, 2 doz for 5c.

C55. Pant hooks and eyes, black or white, 3 doz for 10c.

C56. Vest buckles, japanned, 10c doz.

C57. The ball-and-socket garment fasteners; dressmakers recommend them for plaquets, etc., 10c doz. Small size, better quality, 15c doz.

Hat Wire—C58. Flat, black or white, 6 yds for 5c.
Round, cotton, fine, black or white, 5c roll.
Round, satin, black or white, fine or heavy, 7c roll.

Initial Letters—C59. For marking linen, etc., 4 doz for 5c or 15c gross.

Key Rings—C60. In steel, 3c, 5c each.

Key Chains—C61. In steel, 5c, 10c each.

Mending Wool—C62. "Diamond" quality, made by J. & J. Baldwin, 27 yds on card, in black, white, tan, grey and natural shades, 3 cards, 5c; 17c doz.

C62½. Ball mending wool, fine worsted yarn, black only, 2 balls 5c.

Mending Cotton—C63. On cards, black, white or tan, 4 cards, 5c; in silk, black only, 2 cards, 5c; in ball cotton, black or white, 2 for 5c.

Meshes—C64. In bone, for netting, all sizes, 4c each, 3 for 10c.

Mat hooks—C65. With wood handle, 5c each.

Needles.

C66. Best quality, Abel Morrell's, all sizes, also assorted, 5c paper; cheaper quality, 2 papers 5c.

C67. "Diamond" sewing needles, specially tempered for Canadian trade, all sizes, 5c paper.

THE T. EATON Co. LIMITED
TORONTO CANADA
SCIENTIFIC
NEEDLES
WOOL AND
SMALLWARE
DEPARTMENT

C68. Scientific needles, tapering from the centre, sews easily, all sizes, 5c paper.

Darning Needles—C69. Same quality as our best sewing needles, assorted sizes, 5c paper.

C70. Glove needles, 10c paper.
C71. Between (or tailors') needles, 5c paper.
C72. Chenille needles, 10c paper.
C73. Straw (milliners') needles, 5c paper.
C74. Packing needles, 5c each.
C75. Self-threading needles, 5c paper.
C76. Upholsterers' needles, 5c each.
C77. Machine needles (**always send name and sample of needles required**), 20c doz.
C78. Netting needles, all sizes, 5c each.
C79. Steel knitting needles, all sizes, 3c set.
C80. Rubber and bone knitting needles, 10c pair.
C81. Embroidery needles, 5c pkg.
C82. Carpet needles, 10c paper.

Needle Cases.

C83. An assortment of English sewing needles and darning needles, put up in a fancy case, price according to quality and number of needles, 15c, 25c, 35c each.

Artificial Fruit—C84. Perfect imitation of assorted fruits, such as bananas, pears, peaches, etc., used for pincushion or decorative purposes, 5c each, 50c dozen.

Pin Department.

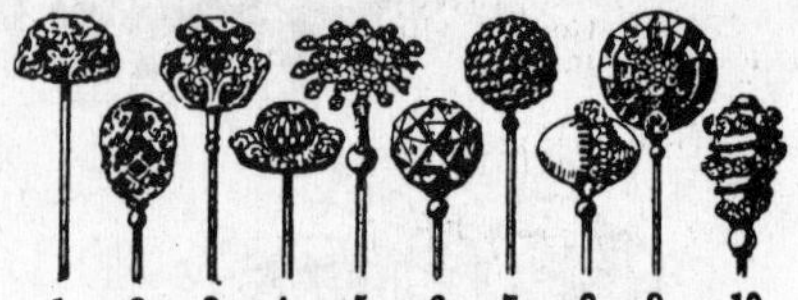

Hat Pins—C85. English steel hat pins, glass tops, 6 or 7 inches long, black or white, 5c dozen, in jet tops, for mourning, 10c doz.

C86. Fancy hat pins, large colored stone settings (see cut No. 1), 5c each; better quality, also in fancy enamel tops, 10c each (see cuts Nos. 2 and 3); with fancy white and colored stone settings, 15c, 20c, 25c (see cut No. 4).

C87. Fancy hat pins, colored stone settings, movable tops (see cut No. 5), 10c, 15c, 25c, 35c each.

C88. Fancy cut glass top hat pins, assorted colors (see cut No. 6), 25c each.

C89. Fancy jet hat pins, French designs (see cut No. 7), 25c, 35c, 50c each.

C90. Fancy hat pins, large colored brilliants, assorted colors, set with small white stones, Parisian designs (see cuts Nos. 8 and 9), 50c, 75c, $1.00; with gold-plated tops, set with white and colored brilliants (see cut No. 10), $1.00, 1.25, 1.50, 1.75, 2.00 each.

NOTE.—For flag and coat-of-arms hat pins see patriotic pins, page 68.

C91. Small fancy gilt lace pins, assorted designs, 2 for 5c; with white and colored unbreakable pearl tops, 10c dozen (see cut).

Sheet Pins—C93. 200 adamantine pins, on sheet, 1c paper; English brass pins, "Diamond" brand, 200 assorted pins, 2 papers for 5c; 250 on sheet, 3c paper; 360 on sheet, 5c paper; 150 extra large size pins, 5c paper.

C94. The "Challenge" brass pin, 360 on sheet extra strong, 5c paper; Taylor's "Queen's Own" brass pins, sizes 1 to 10, 5c paper; The "Ne Plus Ultra" best quality heavy wire brass pins, 360 on sheet, 10c paper; best English steel pins, 360 on sheet, 10c paper.

Bulk Pins—C95. Adamantine, 20c lb; mixed brass, 35c lb; small brass, 40c lb; medium or large size brass, 35c lb; extra small brass ribbon pins, in ¼-lb boxes, 25c.

C96. "Pyramid" pincushion, consisting of 365 pins, put up in a useful form for office or toilet use, 10c.

C97. Large brass blanket pins, 3 papers 10c.

C98. Steel mourning pins, in boxes, ½-oz. box, 5c; 1-oz box, 10c.

C99. Small berry pins, in black, white or assorted, 2 for 5c.

Toilet Pins—C100. glass tops, black or white, contains an assortment of toilet and berry pins, 5c card.

C101. Black or white veiling pins, assorted sizes from 1½ to 2½ inches, also 2½ to 3½ inches, 2 cards for 5c.

C102—Toilet pins, black or white, sizes 2½, 3, 4 or 4½ inches long, all one size on card, 2 for 5c.

C103. Pin cubes, containing 72 pins in all, black and white assorted, or black, white and colored, 5c each; same style, with 144 pins, 10c each.

Belt Supporters and Holders.

Catches for Skirt.

Patented March 4th, 1897.

Supporter.

Gairs' Queen Skirt Support—C104. Prevents skirt from sagging, and shirt waist from slipping up. Pins and hooks are discarded. Full directions with each, 1 belt and 6 catches (enough for 3 dresses), 25c; extra holders, 10c doz.

C105. The **All-ways Ready** shirtwaist holder and skirt supporter, requires no preparation.

of shirt waist or skirt before wearing. It holds both firmly together in perfect position, and leaves the waist-line smooth (see cut), 25c.

C106. Fancy metal belt pins, black or white, 2 for 5c.

C107. Fancy metal belt-holders, black, gilt or silver (see cut), 2 for 5c; better quality, assorted designs, 5c each; leather-covered, assorted colors to match belt, 5c each.

Safety Pins—C108. Lindsay safety pins, sizes 2, 2½, 3, 2 dozen for 5c; The "Columbia" (see cut), nickel-plated, protected points, 3 sizes, 5c dozen; the "Victoria," heavier wire, guarded spring, 8c dozen; the "Clinton," extra strong wire, black or white, small size, 8c dozen; medium size, 10c dozen; large size, 12c dozen.

C109. The "Stronghold" safety pin, with small catch in the pin which prevents it from coming unclasped under any strain, made in 3 sizes, 12c dozen.

C110. Safety-pin book, with two doz. small, medium and large silvered safety pins, 10c book.

C111. Lindsay blanket pins, 3c, 4c, 5c each.

C112. Clinton blanket pins, 4c, 5c each.

C113. The "Climax" pin book case, consisting of 2 dozen assorted sizes in black and white "Climax" safety pins, also 6 dozen best brass pins, put up in a neat paper book, 10c.

C114. **Skirt yokes**, assorted colors, woven in one piece, with lining and buttonholes, 12c each.

C115. **Stilettos**, in bone, 2 for 5c.

C116. **Tailors' Sewing Wax**, 5c each.

C117. **Button Moulds**, assorted sizes, 5c doz.

Twine—C118. White cotton, extra strong, 5c ball; brown twine, 5c, 10c, 12½c ball. Sea Island twine, assorted colors, 5c ball.

Thimbles—C119. White metal, 10c doz.; aluminum, 1c each; heavier metal, 2 for 5c; best quality aluminum, 5c each; steel, 2 for 5c; better quality, 5c each; steel, enamel lined, 2 for 5c; metal, enamel lined, 2 for 5c; celluloid, 2 for 5c; silver finish, 5c each, better quality, extra heavy, 10c each.

C120. The "Iles," solid nickel thimble, armored with ebony, which protects the finger from contact with metal, 10c each.

C121. "Iles" Ivorine thimbles, puncture proof, 5c each.

C122. Tailors' thimbles, steel, 2 for 5c; better quality, 5c each.

C123. Fancy sterling silver thimbles, 25c, 35c, 50c, 75c each.

C124. Tailors' sterling silver thimbles, 25c, 35c each.

These thimbles come in four sizes: misses', small women's, women's, and large women's. Please state size when ordering.

Finger Shields—C125. In celluloid, to protect the forefinger from the thimble or needle, 2 for 5c.

Tape Measures.

C126. Cotton tape measures, 60 inches long, figured both sides (correct measure), 2 for 5c; better quality, linoleum, double-tipped, English standard measure, will not stretch, 5c, 8c, 10c each.

C127. Tailors' tape measures, stitched edge, 60 inches long, ⅝-inch wide, double-tipped, 5c each; better quality, fine sateen cloth, 10c, 15c, 20c each.

C128. Spring tape measures, 36 inches long, 10c each; better quality, 15c, 20c; 40 inches long, 25c; with fine steel wire, made in England, 40 inches long, 40c each; 60 inches long, 85c each; 78 inches long, $1.25 each.

C129. Tape measures for carpenters' or contractors' use, brass bound cases, cotton tape, 25 ft., 25c; 50 ft., 35c; 75 ft., 50c; 100 ft., 75c; same in russet leather case, better quality, linen tape, 50 ft., 75c; 100 ft., $1.00 each.

Tie Clips—C130. The "Au fait" tie holder, for holding the tie in place on shirt or blouse front, 5c each.

C131. **Display** clasps, made of steel, 3 for 5c.

Tatting Shuttles—C132. In white bone or black rubber, extra smooth finish, 10c each.

C133. Bobbins, made of bone, for winding silk, 2 for 5c.

Victoria Plaiter—C133½. Used by leading dressmakers and milliners to make all kinds of trimmings, in plain or fancy patterns; no lady should be without one, 10c each.

Pinking Irons—C134. Assorted sizes (see cut), 10c each.

The Swiss Darner—C135. With this machine a large darn can be made in much less time than the old way. The darn is woven right into the cloth, leaving no lumps or botches in the garment. It mends table cloths, curtains, and fine silks equally as well, and is so simple a child can use it, 20c each.

Tapes—

C136. Bunched tape, assorted widths, 12 pieces, all white or all black, or mixed white and black, 5c, 10c bunch.

C137. Twilled cotton tape, black, white or drab, narrow, medium or wide widths, 5c roll of 12 yds.

C138. Blocked tape, assorted widths, white cotton, 3 for 5c; linen, 3 for 5c.

Tracers—C139. Best steel teeth, sharp and perfect, 5c, 10c, 15c, 25c each.

Splashers—C140. Made of wood splints, decorated, used on wall behind washstand, 5c, 8c, 10c, 15c, 25c each.

Rubber Cuff Protectors—C141. Protects the sleeves when working, keeps light material from being soiled, black or white, 25c pair.

Vapor Bath Cabinets.

Now acknowledged to be a household necessity. Doctors recommend them. Their largely increased sale is sufficient testimony of their worth.

C142. Vapor bath cabinets, made by a reliable manufacturer especially for us, single drill, rubber lined, best material used in construction, wire or wood frame, is 30 inches square and 42 inches high, alcohol heater, lamp, etc., supplied with each cabinet, usually sold at $6.50, our special price, $4.75.

C143. Same style cabinet, with double thickness of cloth, made of antiseptic germ-proof material, will not break or crack easily, trimmings are japanned and will not rust, regular price, $12.50; our special price, $8.25.

Face Steamers—C144. For vapor bath, 75c ea.

NOTE.—We will be pleased to forward further description of vapor baths on application.

The Washburne Patent Fastener—C145. Hose supporters, 10c pair; collar fasteners, 10c each; eyeglass holders, 5c each; drawers supporters, 5c each; bachelors' buttons 2 for 5c; scarf fasteners (see cut) 5c each; pencil holders, 5c each; cuff holders, 10c pair.

The Sahlin Waist Distender.

C146. Gives the wearer that full bust and small waist so much desired, sizes 32 to 40-inch bust, 35c, 50c, 75c each.

Enamelled Wooden-ware.

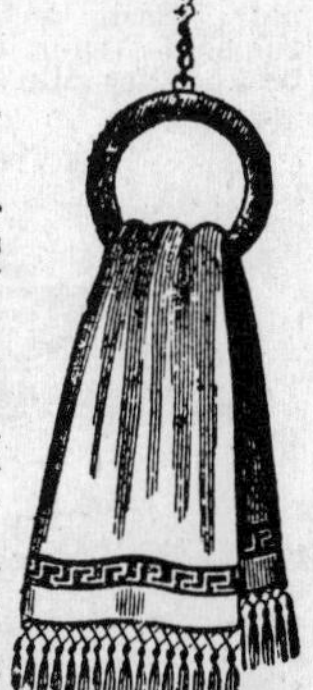

C147. Towel rings, 4-inch or 6-inch in diameter, colors blue, white, pink, yellow and oak, 5c each.

C148. Towel racks, 3 bars, same colors, 5c each.

C149. Towel racks, 18-inch bar, with three rings and brass chain holder attached, same colors, 15c each.

C150. Coat hangers, for keeping coat in proper shape when hanging, 5c each.

C151. Glove or stocking darners, assorted colors, 5c each.

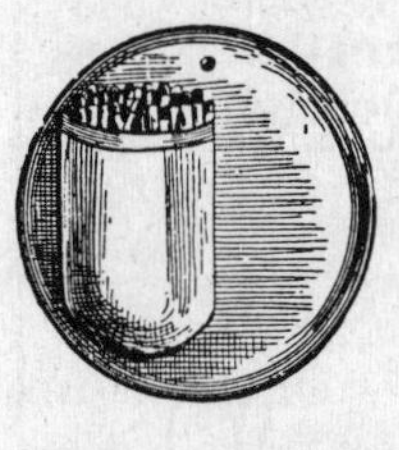

C152. Enamelled match-holders, special, 5c each.

C153. Enamelled tooth-brush holders, 5c each.

Match Scratchers.

C154. Patriotic match scratchers, with picture of British lion under the ensign, with the words, "Strike me and I'm your match," 5c each.

Elastics.

C155. Fancy colored garter elastic, extra strong and durable, special, 5c yd.

C156. French cotton garter elastic, ⅞-inch wide, plaid patterns, 8c yd.

C157. Fancy frilled cotton garter elastic, satin faced, a good strong elastic, 10c yd.

C158. Cotton garter elastic, in black, white and grey, ½-inch, 4c; ⅝-inch, 5c; ¾-inch, 6c; ⅞-inch, 8c yd.

C159. Mercerized cotton garter elastic, black, extra strong web, ½-inch, 5c; ⅝-inch, 6c; ¾-inch, 8c; ⅞-inch, 10c yd.

C160. Silk garter elastic, in black, white and colors, ½-inch, 10c; ⅝-inch, 12½c; ¾-inch, 15c; ⅞-inch, 20c yd.

C161. Fancy silk garter elastic, with frill edge, silk faced, assorted colors, 15c yd.

C162. Fancy frilled garter elastic, pure silk, assorted colors, new shades, 20c, 25c, 30c yd.

C163. Narrow silk elastic, in black and white, 6 cord, 2 yds 5c; 8 cord, 4c yd, 3 yds, 10c; 10 cord, 4c yd.

C164. Round silk elastic, black and white, small, medium and large sizes, 3 yds, 5c.

Arm Bands.

C165. Wool-covered round elastic arm bands, very easy to wear, assorted, plain colors, 5c pair; silk-covered, 10c pair.

C166. Flat silk elastic arm bands, assorted, plain colors, 10c pair.

C167. Cotton elastic arm bands, assorted, plain colors, 5c pair.

C168. Patent ventilated arm bands, fine nickelled steel wire, assorted sizes, 12½c pair

OUR VAPOR BATHS ARE GIVING EXCELLENT SATISFACTION.

C169. Fancy frilled elastic arm bands (see cut), 25c pair.
C170. Sleeve holders, metal catches, silk elastic, 10c pair.

Gents' Garters.

C171. Men's "New York" elastic garters (see cut), Lindsay cloth, tipped clasp, assorted colors, cotton, 20c pair; silk, 30c pair.
C172. Gent's "Boston" garters, with satin web and elastic cord, 30c pair; plain web with rubber-tipped fastener, cotton, 25c pair; best quality silk, 45c pair.

Ladies' Garters.

C173. Ladies' frilled cotton elastic garters, assorted colors, 10c, 15c pair; silk-covered elastic, assorted colors, 25c, 35c pair; pure silk elastic, 50c, 75c pair; sterling silver clasps and slides, $1.25 pair.
C174. Fancy garter buckles, 10c, 15c, 20c, 25c pair.

Garter Lengths.

C175. Garter lengths, ⅔-yd lengths, fancy cotton elastic, 5c; frilled cotton, silk faced, 10c; silk frilled elastic, 15c, 20c, 25c.

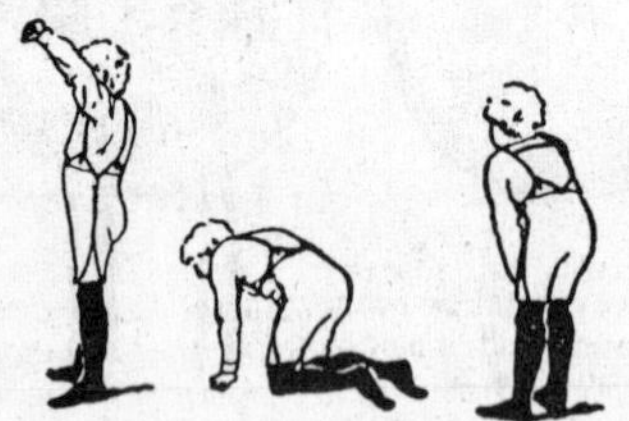

Boys' or Girls' "Suspender Waists."

C176. Holds children's clothing together (see cut). Does not bind the waist, but rather clings to it; may be worn with skirt, waist or blouse, the buttons are placed for trousers or drawers. When ordering state age of child. Sizes for children from 2 to 10 years, 25c each.

Ladies' Side Supporters.

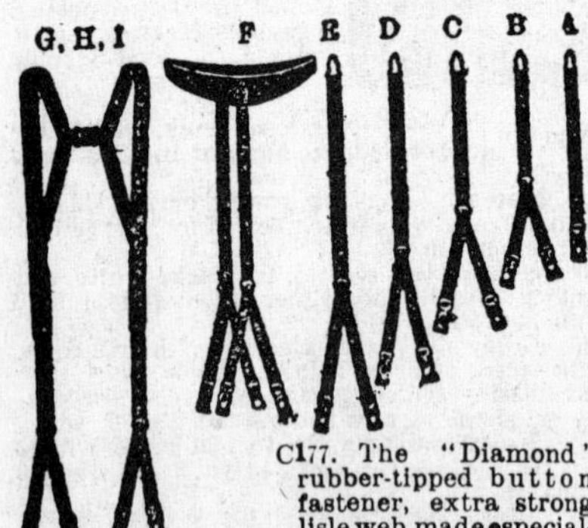

C177. The "Diamond" rubber-tipped button fastener, extra strong lisle web, made especially for us.
(B) Babies', double strap, cotton, 10c pair.
(C) Misses', double strap, cotton, 12½c pair.
(E) Ladies', double strap, cotton, 15c pair.

C178. Ladies' fancy lisle elastic side supporters, assorted colors, rubber-tipped fasteners, ladies', 25c pair; misses', 20c pair; babies', 15c pair.

The "Flexo" rubber-tipped supporter, best quality lisle elastic. The button is so constructed that it will not tear the hose.

C179. (A) Babies', single strap, cotton, 10c pair.
(B) Babies', double strap, cotton, 15c pair.
(C) Children's, double strap, cotton, 18c pair.
(E) Ladies', double strap, cotton, 20c pair.
(F) Ladies', plain belt supporters, 25c pair.

Lindsay Felt Finish Supporter.

C180. (A) Babies', single strap, cotton, 10c, 12½c pair.

(B) Babies', double strap, cotton, 15c; silk, 30c pair.

(D) Misses', double strap, cotton, 20c; silk, 35c pair.

(E) Ladies', double strap, cotton, 20c; silk, 45c pair.

(F) Ladies', plain belt supporters, cotton, 30c; with satin belt and silk elastic, assorted colors, 75c; side supporters, with combination belt, cotton, 35c pair.

GHI. Shoulder brace and hose supporter combined, Lindsay fastener, black or white, ladies', 35c pair; misses', 30c pair; child's, 25c pair.

NOTE.—Silk supporters come in black, white and plain colors.

C181. Ladies' non-elastic garment suspenders, white, 20c pair.

C183.

C182. Ladies' fancy frilled elastic side garters, silk faced, assorted colors (see cut C182), 25c pair; silk elastic, assorted colors, 35c pair; pure silk elastic, nickelled buckle, 65c pair.

C182.

C183. "Hook-on" supporter. It hangs from the corset (see cut C183). The natural position for a supporter to hang. Keeps the corset from protruding in front. In cotton, black or white, 25c pair; better quality, 35c pair; four straps, best lisle web, 50c pair; with silk frilled elastic ends, 75c pair; same style, four straps, $1.00 pair.

C184. The "Marloe" hose supporter, same style as the "Hook-on" with different clasp, in cotton, 35c pair; in cotton frilled elastic, assorted colors, 25c pair; in silk frilled elastic, 50c, 75c, $1.00 pair.

C185. The new "Cast Off" corset supporter, can be adjusted or removed without unfastening the corset, cannot become unfastened accidently, silk finished elastic, assorted colors, 35c pair; pure silk elastic, 75c pair.

C185½. The new "Foster" abdominal hose supporters, gives the wearer that straight military front effect so much desired at present, it has a front pad and supporting bands which push back the entire abdomen, giving the wearer a correct standing position, in black or white, ¾-inch lisle elastic, 60c.

In mercerized silk-frilled elastic, black and colors, 85c.

C187. Safety belt (see cut C187), 25c each.

C188. Children's knee-protectors, stockinette or leather, 25c pair (see cut).

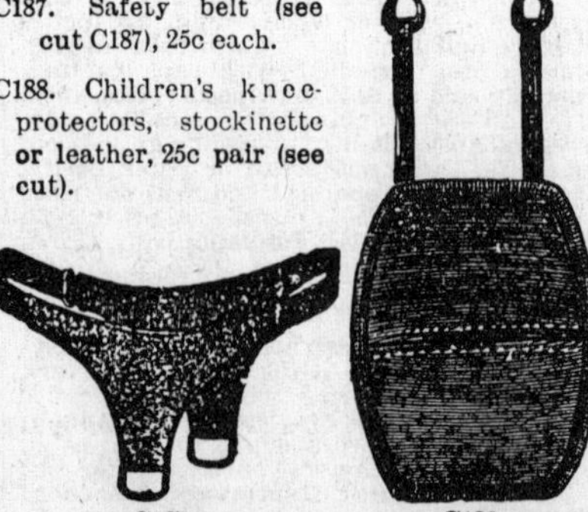

C187. C188.

Shoulder Braces.

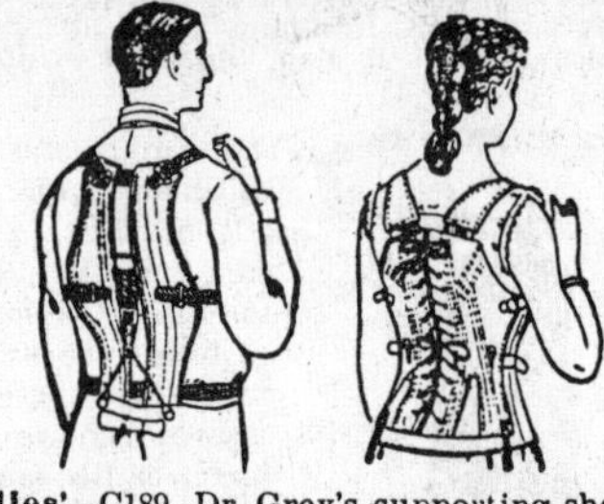

Ladies'—C189. Dr. Grey's supporting shoulder brace, in small, medium and large sizes (see cut), $1.00 each.

Gents'—C190. Dr. Grey's shoulder brace, supports the back from the hips to the shoulder, desirable for men or boys. Made in three sizes, boys', men's and young men's. Always give height and waist measure (see cut), $1.75 per pair.

English Military Brace.—C191. Strengthens and supports the shoulders, back, sides, chest and stomach, and imparts to the wearer an appearance of ease and grace, ladies' or gents', 75c each.

Beads.

C192. Assorted beads, put up in a gauze bag or glass-covered box, 2 for 5c.
C193. Bead necklaces, in white and colored, 10c, 15c, 20c each.

Patriotic Pins.

C194. (A) Brass military hat pins, small and large sizes, with "Canadian Crest," etc., 5c each.
(B and C) British Ensign, or Union Jack, in hat pins, small size top, 5c each; larger size, in hat pins or brooches, 10c each; hard enamel, 15c each; same designs set on square shape gilt metal buckle, special, 25c each; in sterling silver, $1.75 each.
(D and E) British or Dominion coat of arms, in hat pins or brooches, hard enamel, special, 15c each; same designs set in square metal buckle, special, 25c each; in sterling silver, $1.75 ea.
(F) Maple leaf hat pin or brooch, hard enamel, 15c each.
(G) Maple leaf, set in white enamel, with crown, in brooch or hat pin, 15c each; same design in square metal buckle, 25c each; in sterling silver, $1.75 each.
(H) "Royal Arms," in hat pin or brooch, hard enamel, 15c each; in square shape metal buckle, 25c each; same design in hat pin or brooch, in sterling silver, 75c, $1.00 each.

C195. Souvenir buttons of His Majesty King Edward VII., from a famous photograph (this must not be confused with cheap lithographed buttons), 5c each.

C196. Cabinet photographs of King Edward VII., taken from the photograph by Lafayette, copyrighted, a handsome picture, 25c each.

Write us for any goods you desire that are not catalogued.

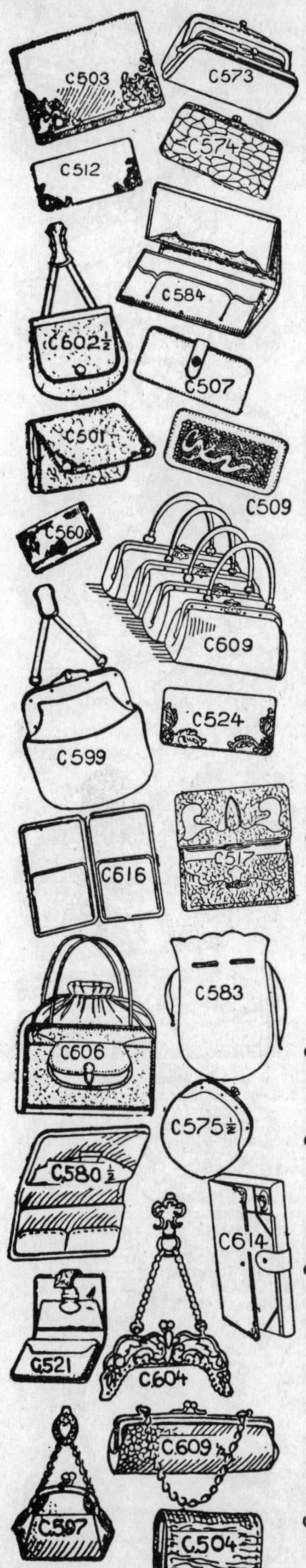

LEATHER GOODS.

Combination Purses

In measuring purses we first give width across the frame, then the depth.

C501. **Small** combination purses, 2¾ x 2, assorted leathers, neat and substantial, 25c; larger size, 3½ x 2½, grain seal, black only (see cut), 25c; better quality, with or without mounting, 35c; in real seal black, 50c; alligator, 60c; large size, real seal, 60c.

C503. Combination purses, in seal grain, stamped leather or imitation alligator, pocket and card case, with or without fancy mountings, (see cut), black or colors, 25c; superior quality and finish, in plain or with silver or oxidized mountings, 35c.

C504. Combination purses, imitation walrus, a very fashionable leather (see cut), square shape, 6 pockets, 35c; better quality and finish, 50c; double frame, large size, 75c; single frame, walrus lined, in black, brown and light grey, new and fashionable, 75c.

C505. Combination purses (see cut), in a large assortment of leathers, such as grain seal, grain morocco, imitation monkey skin, imitation Mexican hand-carved leather (see cut C509), etc., square and long shape (kindly state what shape when ordering), all well-finished goods and special value, for 50c.

C506. **Black** grain seal combination purses, double frame, making 6 separate pockets, 35c; in real seal, 75c.

C507. Combination purses, double frame, black only, same as above, with outside strap and clasp (see cut), 50c; in real morocco two chamois-lined pockets, superior finish, 75c.

C508. **Black** combination purse and card case, square shape, real seal leather, 60c; with polished calf lining, size 4½ x 3, very special, 75c; superior quality, chamois-lined pocket (see cut, C513), our special line, $1.00; better quality in leather and workmanship, $1.25, 1.50, 1.75, 2.50, 2.75; with fancy hand-carved ticket pocket, steel frames, a beautifully finished purse (see cut C517), $3.25, 3.50, 4.00, 5.00.

C509. **Black** seal combination purses, polished calf lining, size 4¾ x 2½, very neat and handy to carry, $1.00; superior quality, chamois lined pocket, $1.25; real seal lining, $1.50.

C510. **Colored** combination purse, in crushed morocco leather, colors brown and green, leather lined, superior finish, 75c; with sterling silver mounts, $1.00.

C511. **Colored** combination purse and card case, in real morocco leather, polished calf lining, in tan, brown and green, $1.00; better quality, tan and brown, $1.50; in real seal, assorted colors, calf lining, $1.00; imitation monkey skin, black, tan, brown and green, calf lining, $1.25; in real seal, brown or green, best polished calf lining, fancy ticket pocket, riveted frame, chamois pocket, a special line, $1.75.

C511½. **Colored** combination purses, beautifully finished goods, some new spring shades, in fashionable leather, such as "Sea Lion," colors grey, brown and mode, $1.50, 1.75, 2.00; "Texas Steer," $3.00, 3.50, 4.00, 5.00.

C514. **Alligator** combination purses, long or square, leather lined, 75c; superior quality and polish, best calf lining, $1.50, 1.75, 2.00; large size, square, "Hornback," $5.00, 6.75, 7.50.

C521. Combination purse and card case, real seal, black only, calf lining, square shape, with outside strap and clasp, $1.50 (see cut); outside clasp both sides, one for change, the other for cards and tickets, gold-plated frame and clasps, black and colors, $2.50.

C524. **Mounted** combination purses, all in sterling silver mounts, new designs; the assortment is so varied it is impossible to give accurate description; they come in black seal and colored morocco, $1.00, 1.25, 1.50. (See cut C512.) Better quality, in alligator, crushed morocco, seal, etc., state the color and leather you want, also the price, we will then use our best judgment in selecting the nearest to your order, prices range at $2.00, 2.50, 3.00, 3.50, 4.00, 4.50, 5.00, 6.00. (See cut C524.)

Clasp Purses.

C526. Children's clasp purses, assorted leathers and colors, 15c.

C527. Ladies' clasp purses, in polished leather and grain morocco, black only, 25c, 35c; in real morocco leather, 50c.

C560. Ladies' clasp purses, grain seal leather, 5 pockets, black only (see cut), special, 25c; larger size, black and colors, superior finish, outside handkerchief pocket, 35c.

C562. Ladies' clasp purses, real seal leather, leather-lined throughout, 75c; better quality, with chamois-lined pocket and calf lining, $1.25, 1.75, 2.00, 2.25.

Finger Purses.

(See cut No. C563½.)

C563½. Finger purses, in grain seal, black only, stamped leather, assorted colors, also suede leather, in brown and grey, inside nickel frames, 50c.

C563¾. Finger purses, real morocco leather, assorted colors, 75c; in real seal, black only, and real morocco, black and colors, calf lining, $1.00; better quality, real seal, chamois pocket, $1.50, 1.75, 2.25.

C565. Initial letters for finger purses, gilt or nickel, 15c each; sterling silver, small size, 25c; large size, 40c.

Chain Purses.

C569. Chain purses (see cut), 25c, 35c, 50c; white chain and finger ring, gate top (see cut C569½) 75c, 85c.

Bag Purses.

C572. Misses' bag shape purses, polished leather, stamped and plain, assorted colors, strong frame (see cut), 10c each; larger size, superior finish, 15c, 20c each.

C573. Bag purse, in black grain seal, chamois lining, also grain morocco, in black and colors, kid lining (see cut), 25c each.

C574. Bag purses, in alligator (see cut), grain morocco, polished leather and grain seal, assorted colors, long and square shapes, 35c; larger size, grain morocco and polished leather, black and colors, double frame, 50c; in real morocco leather, best leather lining, nickel frame, 75c; in real seal, 65c, 85c, $1.00 each.

C575½. Money purses for men, bag shape, made of chamois leather (see cut), 20c, 25c each.

There is only one small profit between our prices and the bare cost of the goods.

Gents' Pocket and Letter Books, etc.

C576. Gents' strap pocket book and bill holder, grain seal, leather lined, 35c.

C577. Gents' strap pocket books, grain morocco, with secret bill holder, leather-lined (see cut), 65c; in real morocco, 75c, $1.00; calf lined, $1.25; in real seal, calf lined, $1.50.

C578. Gents' bill holders, grain seal, leather-lined, size when opened 3¼ x 10½ (see cut), 35c, 50c; in real seal, $1.00; polished calf lining, $1.50; with bill holder and change pocket combined, grain seal, 75c; real seal, superior finish, $1.00, 1.25.

C584. Gents' real morocco letter books, leather-lined card and ticket pocket, $1.00; in real seal, $1.50, 1.75. (See cut.)

C585. Gents' bill books, seal grain, safety bill pocket, size 3¾ x 8 when closed, 75c; in real seal, $2.75.

C586. Gents' bill books, grain seal, size when closed 3½ x 8, $1.00; in real morocco, $1.25, 1.50, 2.00 (see cut); real seal, calf lining, $2.25.

Card Cases.

C579½. Gents' or ladies' card cases, real morocco, morocco lined, 50c; with combination bill holder and memorandum card, 75c.

C580½. Ladies' card cases, grain morocco, morocco lined, 75c; in genuine seal, seal lining (see cut), 85c, $1.00.

C583. Gents' draw-string coin purse, made of chamois leather (see cut), 25c.

C582. Gents' or ladies' stamp and ticket cases, in real seal, morocco or crushed morocco, assorted colors (see cut), 25c each.

Match and Photo Holders.

C588. Gents' leather match holders (see cut), grain seal, with match striker, 35c; in real seal, 50c.

C589. Leather photo holders, grain seal, black only, size 4½ x 6½, to hold 2 photos, 35c; to hold 3 photos, 75c; to hold 6 photos, $1.00.

Music Rolls and Holders.

C563. Music rolls, grain seal, black, 35c; solid leather, black and tan, 40c; polished calf, black, brown, or tan (see cut), 75c; black grain seal, linen lined, $1.00.

C564. Music holders (see cut), seal grain leather, rope handle, nickel trimmings, special, $1.00; polished leather, sateen lining, superior finish, $1.50; genuine morocco, leather handle, satin lined, nickel trimmings, $3.00.

Chatelaines.

C597. Child's chatelaines, grain morocco, bag shape, leather-lined chain chatelaines (see cut), special, 25c; in grain seal and alligator leather chatelaines, 35c.

C599. Ladies' chatelaines, bag shape (see cut), in grain seal, 35c; in real morocco or grain walrus, black or colors, outside pocket, 75c; patent leather, $1.00; in real seal or alligator, $1.25; larger size, real seal front, $1.25, 1.50; same style, real seal throughout, chamois lined, patent clasp, covered frame, $1.75, 2.00, 2.25, 2.50, 3.25; with fancy oxidized or French grey frame and metal chatelaine to match, $3.00, 3.75, 4.00, 4.50, 5.00, 6.00 each. (See cut C602.)

C602½. Ladies' chatelaines, purse shape (see cut), grain seal, black or colors, 35c; better quality, inside chamois pocket, 50c; larger size, 75c, $1.00; same style, real seal faced, $1.50.

C600. Ladies' or misses' real seal chatelaines, bag purse shape, inside chamois-lined pocket, steel frame and chatelaine (see cut), $1.50; larger size, real morocco, $1.75.

Gate and Purse Tops

C603. Gate bag tops (see cut), round top, plain, 25c; with fancy top, 35c, 50c; oblong shape, fancy top, with or without settings, 35c, 50c, 75c, $1.00.

C603½. Purse tops, same style, plain, 25c; fancy top, 50c, 75c.

C604. Bag tops (see cut), in oxidized and French grey, 50c, 75c, $1.00, 1.25.

Shopping Bags.

C605. Child's grain seal shopping bags, outside pocket, leather handle, 15c each.

C606. Ladies' shopping bags, leather grained, sateen cloth tops, outside pocket, leather handle, 25c, 35c (see cut; better quality, 50c; in seal grain leather, 75c; $1.00, 1.25.

C575. String shopping or market bags (see cut), 25c; better quality, 35c.

C608. Ladies' hand bags, in imitation alligator and grain seal, good strong frame, special, 35c; larger size, 50c each.

C609. Ladies' hand bags (see cut), in grain leather, leather lined, nickel frame, leather handle, 7 inches long, black, green or red, $1.00; same style in grain leather, with or without two outside pockets, in black or brown, 8-inch frame, $1.25; 9-inch frame, $1.50; 10-inch frame, $1.75; 11-inch frame, $2.00; same in real seal leather, 8-inch frame, $2.50; 9-inch frame, $2.75; 10-inch frame, $3.00; 11-inch frame, $3.25 each.

C609½. Small leather hand bags, with chain handle (see cut), grain seal, 75c; morocco, $1.25; real seal, $1.50.

C610. Ladies' black silk shopping or opera bags, oxidized gate top, silk cord handle, $1.50.

C579. Boston shopping bags (see cut), in cloth, stripe and check patterns, outside leather strap, leather handle, 75c; leather-covered frame and sides, $1.50; better quality cloth, black only, solid leather ends, $2.00, 2.50.

Travelling Companions.

C580. Gents' or ladies' travelling companions and toilet cases, substantial fittings (see cut), prices according to quality of leather and fittings, also size of case, in grain leather, $2.00, 2.50, 3.00, 3.50; solid leather, superior fittings, $5.00, 6.00, 6.50, 7.50, 9.00, 10.00, 12.00.

C614. **Writing Tablet** in grain seal, brown or black, size 12 x 16, when opened, a handy article for invalids or for travelling purposes (see cut), $1.00.

C582½. **Collar and Cuff Boxes**, sole leather, separate compartments, in tan color (see cut), $1.25.

C615½. Collar and cuff cases, polished leather, perfectly flat, handy to put in satchel when travelling, $1.50 each.

C616. **Cigar cases**, grain leather, nickel frame, book shape (see cut), 75c; solid leather, $1.00, 1.25.

C617. **Cigarette** cases, grain leather, same style as cigar case, 50c, 75c; solid leather, $1.00; real morocco, $1.50.

Mail Order customers always get benefit of reduced prices.

New Spring Belts and Buckles.

BE SURE AND STATE WAIST MEASURE IN ORDERING BELTS.

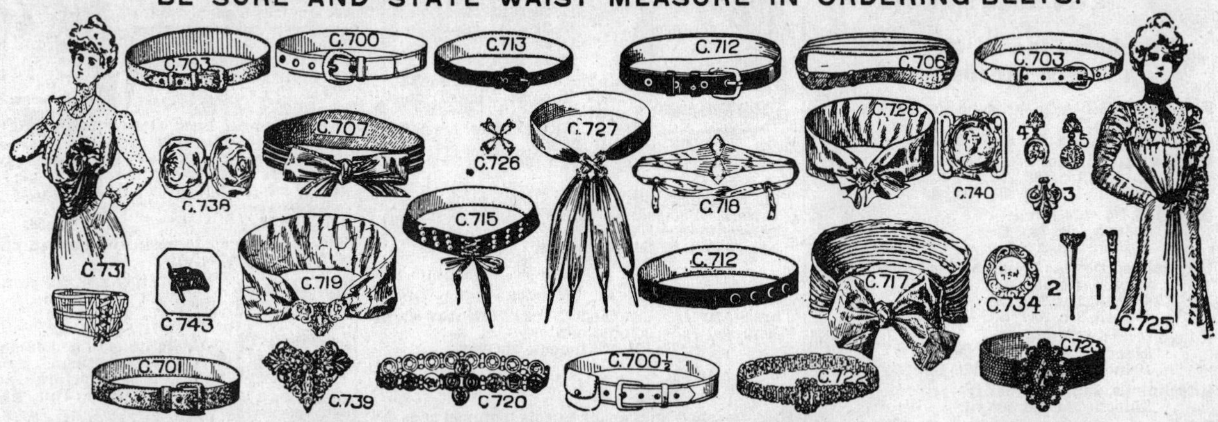

Leather Belts.

C700. Ladies' solid leather belts, polished leather, harness buckle, in black and colors, 13c; same, with covered buckle, 18c (see cut); with pocket attached (see cut C700½), 25c each.

C701. Grain seal belts, stitched edge, leather lined and covered buckle, in black and colors, 25c (see cut); in black only, with pocket attached, 35c each.

C702. Ladies' real morocco leather belts, black and brown, 1 inch wide, very neat, stitched edge, leather lined, 35c; with turned stitched edge, leather lined, black and colors, 50c each.

C703. Ladies' real seal leather belts, black only, 1 inch wide, stitched edge, special, 35c; 1½ inch wide, 50c; with turned stitched edge, 75c; graduated seal belts (see cut), 65c. Real seal pockets for belts, 35c each.

C704. Real alligator leather belts, 1-inch wide, brown only, 65c each.

C705. Suede leather belts, grey or brown, graduated, stitched edge, 50c each.

C706. Graduated leather belts, ribbed back, in patent leather or grain morocco, dome fasteners (see cut), a neat and pretty belt, 75c ea.

C707. Same style, in patent or grain morocco, as C706, with ribbon pulley strings (see cut), 75c each.

C708. White kid belts, covered buckle, 25c, 35c; polished calf, stitched edge, leather lined, straight or graduated, 50c each.

C709. White "keratol" or imitation leather belts, in white, can be easily cleaned with wet sponge, 20c, 25c each.

C710. Ladies' white pique washing belts, fancy buckle, for summer wear, 25c, 35c each.

Patent Leather Belts.

C710½. Black patent leather pulley belts, graduated, satin pulley strings, 35c each.

C711. Patent leather belts, stitched edge, leather lined, 25c; better quality, 1½ inch wide, double turned edge, 75c each.

C712. Patent leather belts, graduated (see cut) with buckle, 25c; better quality, leather lined, 35c; with turned edge, 50c each.

C712½. Patent leather belts, with dome fasteners, graduated (see cut C712) with buttons, 35c; with turned edge, 50c each.

C713. Patent leather belts, shaped to fit the waist (see cut), 35c, 50c ea.

C714. Special line patent leather belts, will wear well and not crack easily, 10c each.

The New Bodice Belt.

C715. New York's latest novelty, made specially to fit the waist when wearing the new "erect form" corset (see cut), in patent leather, leather lined, with gilt buttons, $1.25; without gilt buttons, in patent leather or grain seal, 75c; in black velvet, $1.00 each.

NOTE.—We require exact waist measurement for this belt.

Ribbon Pulley and Buckle Belts.

C716. Ribbon pulley belts, gros-grain ribbon, featherbone sides and back, special, 50c each.

C717. Featherbone corded pulley belts, a handsome belt (see cut), in black taffeta, hemstitched edge, special, 75c; in black moire ribbon, with wide moire pulley strings, $1.00; in taffeta ribbon, wide taffeta pulley strings, with silk fringe edge, black, white or cream, $1.25 each.

C718. The "Golf" style pulley belt (see cut), in black satin ribbon, featherbone stiffened back, special, 50c; better quality ribbon, 75c; in fancy black or white taffeta ribbon, $1.00 each.

C719. Ribbon belts (see cut). We make these up special to your order; look over list of buckles here given, also style and price of ribbon wanted; if colored, send material with which it is to be worn, we will then make your belt to order without extra charge for making.

NOTE.—We can make Nos. C717, C718, in colors, at customer's risk, as we could not exchange if not satisfactory.

Military Belts.

C720. Military button belts, made of brass buttons (see cut), 35c; with velvet ribbon back, 50c each.

C721. Patent leather belts, with gold braid, very fashionable, 35c each.

Metal Girdles.

C722. Fancy metal girdles, gilt or silver (see cut), 25c; with stone setting in buckle, 35c; with stone settings all around, 50c each.

Elastic and Beaded Belts.

C723. Black elastic beaded belts, beaded buckle, 35c; better quality (see cut), 50c, 75c, $1.00, 1.25 each.

C724. Black elastic belts, with fancy metal buckle, 30c; silk elastic, 35c, 40c each.

The New l'Aiglon Belt.

(See figure No. C725.)

C725. A new Parisian novelty, which has caught the popular fancy; it has a pretty effect, and will be worn extensively this spring; in velvet with chenille strings and metal spikes, special, 75c; in velvet, with featherbone lining and velvet or chenille strings, with metal spikes, $1.25; with shaped bodice front for the new "erect form" corset, $1.75; same style, with gold braid trimming, $2.00 each.

The Lorraine Loop for Belts.

C726. The Lorraine belt loop (see cut), is designed to produce a bodice effect to the belt. It requires no sewing, and is adjusted in a minute. It gives the belt a downward tension in front, producing a graceful effect to the figure, in gilt, silver or black, 25c; better quality, 50c each.

C727. The new l'Aiglon belt (see cut), with Lorraine loop attached, in satin ribbon, 75c; with featherbone stiffening, $1.00; same, in velvet ribbon, $1.00; with featherbone stiffening, $1.25 each.

C728. Ribbon belts, black taffeta ribbon, with Lorraine loop (see cut), 50c; better quality, in black and fancy ribbon, 75c, $1.00 each.

C729. Featherbone corded belts, same style as No. C717, with Lorraine loop, in taffeta ribbon, 75c; in moire ribbon, $1.00 each.

C730. Patent leather belts, with Lorraine loop and satin strings, a neat and pretty belt, 75c each.

The New Featherbone Girdle.

(See figure No. C731.)

C731. This girdle is a very useful as well as fashionable dress accessory, as it forms such a connection between the skirt and shirt waist, as to give the appearance of an individual costume. It can be draped to suit the wearer. Being made of featherbone it is convenient of adjustment and easy to wear. We sell the frame with or without draping (see cut), price for frame undraped, 50c; covered with black peau de chene, silk, hemstitched, with rosette, $1.25; in black taffeta silk, $1.75; special colors made to order, which cannot be exchanged.

Ribbon Tips and Spikes.

C732. Ribbon spikes, used for the new l'Aiglon belt, also for dress trimming, in gilt, silver or black, 2 for 5c; and 5c each (see cut 1); better quality, more fancy design (see cut 2). 10c each; larger size, with filigree tops, in plain and with stone settings, 15c, 20c each.

C733. Metal ribbon tips, fashion's latest novelty, worn for collar, belt or dress trimming (see cut C725), in gilt open pattern (see cut 3), 5c, 10c; better quality, in some pretty designs, with or without stone settings (see cuts 4 and 5), 15c, 20c, 25c each.

Pulley Rings.

(See cut C734.)

C734. Pulley rings, in black or nickel, 5c pair; better quality, black, silver or gilt, 10c pair; pearl pulley rings, 15c pair.

Belting.

C735. Black elastic belting, 2 inches wide, cotton, 20c yd; silk, 25c yd; better quality, striped satin, 50c yd.

Buckles.

An entirely new collection of the latest spring novelties. The "Bodice" and "l'Aiglon" being among the newest effects. Gilt will be the leading color.

C736. Fancy metal buckles, open pattern, in black, gilt or silver, with clasp and slide, 10c each.

C737. Fancy metal buckles, oxidized, gilt or black, in some pretty designs, 25c, 35c, 50c; better quality, latest American designs, in plain or with stone settings, 75c, $1.00, 1.50, 2.00, 2.50 each.

C738. Fancy belt buckles, rose pattern, in oxidized or gilt (see cut), 25c, 35c each.

C739. The new "Bodice" shaped belt buckle (see cut), in gilt, open pattern, 25c, 35c, 50c, 75c each.

C740. The "l'Aiglon" belt buckle, the latest Paris novelty, with picture of the "Young Napoleon" or French eagle, in gilt (see cut C740), 50c, 75c each.

C741. Imitation cut steel buckles, 25c, 35c each; genuine French cut steel buckles, $1.00, 1.25, 1.50, 2.00, 2.25 each.

C742. Sterling silver buckles, plain centre, fancy open edge, oval shape, 75c; square shape, $1.00 each; with script monogram 25c extra; block monogram, 25c letter extra.

C743. Coat-of-arms buckles, square shape metal, with hard enamel designs of Dominion or British coat-of-arms, Union Jack ensign or maple leaf (see cut), very special price, 25c; better quality, oval shape, fancy edge, coat-of-arms or maple leaf, $1.00; square shape, sterling silver, gold plated, with flag, coat-of-arms, or maple leaf, $1.75; oval shape metal, in hard enamel British or Dominion coat-of-arms, $1.75; same in sterling silver, gold plated, $2.75 each.

We keep in touch with New York and Paris styles.

Bleached embroidery linen, soft needle finish—
36-inch, at 30c, 40c, 50c, 60c yd.

Fine bleached linen lawn, for handkerchiefs—
36-inch, at 60c, 65c, 75c, 85c, $1.00, 1.25 yd.

Fine quality sheer linen—
30-inch, at $1.35, 1.50, 1.75, 2.00 yd.

Butcher Linens, Hollands, Colored Linens, etc.

Bleached butcher linens, superior quality—
36-inch, 20c, 25c, 30c, 35c.
40-inch, 25c, 30c, 35c, 40c yd.

Unbleached butcher linens—
36-inch, 15c, 18c, 20c, 25c, 30c.
40-inch, 18c, 25c, 30c, 35c yd.

Bleached Dowlas linens—
36-inch, 20c, 25c, 30c.
38-inch, 25c, 30c, 35c yd.

Unbleached Dowlas linens, as used for aprons—
36-inch, 15c, 18c, 20c.
40-inch, 18c, 20c, 25c.
48-inch, 25c, 30c yd.

Rough brown Hollands—
32-inch, 12½c, 15c, 18c, 20c, 22c.
40-inch, 15c, 18c, 20c, 22c, 25c, 30c yd.

Interlinings, superior quality—
38-inch, 20c, 25c, 30c yd.

Bordered apron linens, assorted, in red and blue—
36-inch, 15c, 18c.
38-inch, 18c, 20c yd.

Colored linens, in shades of pink, blue, cream, green, brown, as used for fancy work—
36-inch, 40c yd.

Linen diapers, quality and finish guaranteed—
4/4, 20c, 25c, 30c, 35c yd.

Honeycomb cloth—
27-inch, 25c, 30c, 35c yd.

Stair Linens.

Stair damask, black and grey or brown and grey, with or without red border—
14-inch, 10c   18-inch, 14c
16 " 12½c yd.   20 " 16c yd.

Extra heavy quality stair damasks, assorted, brown and black—
16-inch, 15c   20-inch, 20c yd.
18 " 18c yd.

Stair drill, brown, with red border—
16-inch, 12½c   20-inch 15c
18 " 12½c yd.   22 " 15c yd.

Sanitary Diapers.

Prices subject to change without notice.

Antiseptic bleached cloth, made of specially selected bleached cotton, guaranteed chemically pure and absorbent, soft finish, in sealed packages of 10 yards each—

18 inches wide, 65c piece.
20 " 75c "
22 " 80c "
24 " 85c "
27 " 95c "

Huckaback and Damask Towels.

Half-bleached huckaback union towels, with fringed ends, colored borders—

No. 1, 18 x 35, 17c pair.
" 2, 19 x 37, 19c "
" 3, 20 x 40, 21c "
" 4, 22 x 43, 23c "
" 5, 23 x 43, 25c "
" 6, 24 x 45, 29c "

Bleached, all pure linen, huckaback towels, with fringed ends, colored or plain white borders—

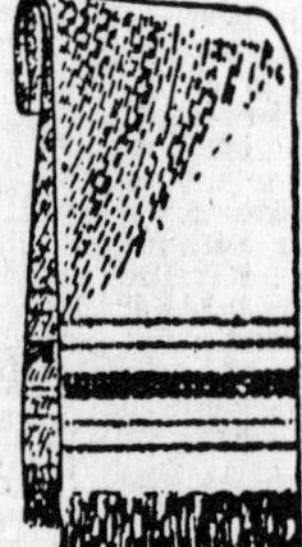
No. 2.

No. 7, 18 x 36 inches, 20c pair.
" 8, 19 x 38 " 25c "
" 9, 20 x 40 " 30c "

No. 11.

Half-bleached huckaback towels, hemmed ends, colored borders, Irish manufacture—
No. 10, 17 x 32, 17c pair.
" 11, 18 x 35, 19c "
" 12, 20 x 40, 23c "
" 13, 21 x 36, 25c "
" 14, 22 x 40, 29c "
" 15, 23 x 44, 40c "

Half-bleached union huckaback towels, fringed, colored or white borders—
No. 16, 20 x 40 inches, 19c pair
" 17, 21 x 44 " 23c "
" 18, 24 x 46 " 25c "

Full bleached pure Irish linen huckaback towels, colored or plain tape borders, fringed—
No. 19, 20 x 40 inches, 29c pair.
" 20, 22 x 42 " 35c "
" 21, 23 x 46 " 40c "
" 22, 23 x 45 " 50c "

Three-quarter bleached huckaback towels, hemmed ends, colored borders—
No. 23, 17½ x 34 inches, 20c pair.
" 24, 19 x 36 " 25c "
" 25, 20 x 37 " 29c "
" 26, 22 x 42 " 38c "

Half-bleached huckaback towels, hemmed ends, colored borders, Irish manufacture—
No. 27, 18 x 35 inches, $1.14 doz.
" 28, 19 x 40 " 1.38 "
" 29, 20 x 42 " 1.50 "
" 30, 22 x 40 " 1.75 "

Full bleached Irish huckaback towels, with fringed ends, colored or plain tape borders—
No. 31, 21 x 41 inches, 33c pair.
" 32, 22 x 45 " 38c "
" 33, 23 x 46 " 40c "

Half-bleached all linen huckaback towels, with fringed ends and colored borders—
No. 34, 22 x 42 inches, 33c pair.

Full bleached huckaback towels, fringed, colored borders, heavy make—
No. 35, 20 x 40 inches, 25c pair.
" 36, 21 x 42 " 29c "
" 37, 24 x 45 " 40c "

Full bleached hemstitched huckaback towels, guaranteed all pure linen, satin damask border and fancy woven designs all over—
No. 38, 21 x 41 inches, 75c pair.
" 39, 21 x 41 " 85c "
" 40, 24 x 45 " $1.00 "
" 41, 26 x 43 " 1.00 "

Fine bleached all linen huckaback towels, fringed, colored borders—
No. 42, 20 x 40 inches, 25c pair.

Heavy crepe or oatmeal linen towels, with fringed ends, colored borders—
No. 43, 18 x 36 inches, 23c pair.
" 44, 20 x 40 " 29c "
" 45, 24 x 42 " 35c "

Check linen glass towels, with fringed ends, red and blue checks—

No. 46, 13 x 26, 10c pair.
" 47, 18 x 36, 12½c "

Three-quarter bleached damask towels, fancy woven centre designs, fringed ends, red, blue, gold or plain white border—

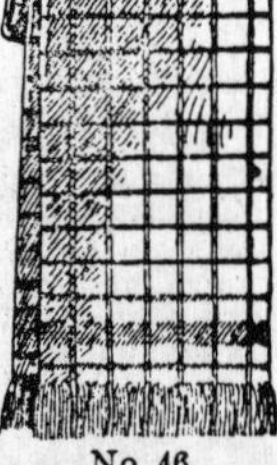
No. 46.

No. 48, 15 x 29, 12½c pair.
" 49, 16 x 32, 17c "
" 50, 17 x 34, 20c "
" 51, 18 x 38, 23c "
" 52, 20 x 40, 29c "
" 53, 22 x 44, 35c "

No. 50.

Half-bleached Scotch damask towels, fringed, solid red borders—
No. 54, 16 x 32, 15c pair.
" 55, 17 x 39, 20c "
" 56, 19 x 44, 23c "
" 57, 20 x 47, 25c "

Half-bleached, all pure linen, damask towels, fringed ends, fancy woven centre designs, solid red borders—
No. 58, 18 x 38, 25c pair.
" 59, 20 x 42, 33c "
" 60, 22 x 44, 38c "

Full bleached satin damask towels, fringed, solid red or white borders, woven designs in centre—
No. 61, 20 x 40, 33c pair.
" 62, 22 x 44, 40c "

Three-quarter bleached damask towels, colored borders, fringed ends—
No. 63, 17 x 34, $1.14 doz.
" 64, 18 x 38, 1.30 "
" 65, 20 x 42, 1.65 "
" 66, 22 x 44, 1.98 "

Fine bleached all linen German damask towels, knotted fringe assorted patterns—
No. 67, 21 x 44 inches, 48c pair
" 68, 22 x 46 " 50c "
" 69, 22 x 47 " 60c "
" 70, 23 x 48 " 75c "

No. 58.

Full bleached satin damask towels, with knotted fringe and openwork—

No. 71.

No. 71, 21 x 43, 50c pair.
" 72, 22 x 46, 60c "
" 73, 23 x 48, 75c "
" 74, 24 x 49, 85c "

Hemstitched linen damask towels, German manufacture, superior satin finish, assorted patterns—
No. 75, 21 x 42, 50c pair.
" 76, 22 x 42, 60c "
" 77, 23 x 44, 75c "

Bleached cotton honeycomb towels, fringed—
No. 78, 14 x 29, 35c doz.
" 79, 15 x 32, 40c "
" 80, 16 x 32, 50c "
" 81, 17 x 35, 60c "
" 82, 20 x 40, 75c "
" 83, 20 x 43, 90c "

Unbleached cotton honeycomb towels, fringed— No. 84, 15 x 28 inches, 35c doz.
" 85, 17 x 30 " 50c "
" 86, 18 x 38 " 60c "

Turkish Bath Towels.

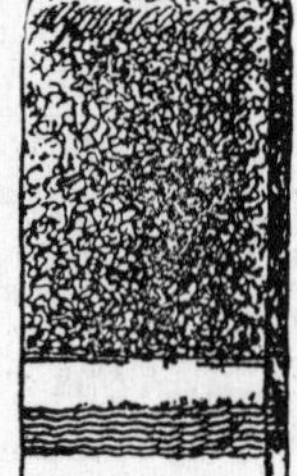
No. 90.

White Turkish bath towels, fringed ends, soft pure finish—
No. 87, 18 x 35, 20c.
" 88, 19 x 40, 25c.
" 89, 21 x 44, 30c.
" 90, 22 x 47, 35c.
" 91, 23 x 48, 40c.
" 92, 24 x 53, 50c.
" 93, 25 x 54, 60c.
" 94, 25 x 56, 65c.
" 95, 25 x 58, 75c.
" 96, 27 x 53, 85c.
" 97, 27 x 56, $1.00.
" 97½, 39 x 58, $1.25 pair.

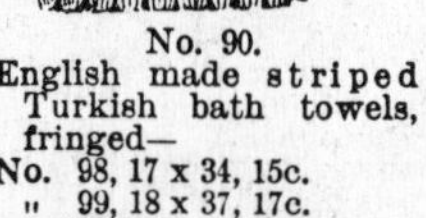

English made striped Turkish bath towels, fringed—
No. 98, 17 x 34, 15c.
" 99, 18 x 37, 17c.
" 100, 20 x 38, 20c.
" 101, 19 x 40, 23c.
" 102, 20 x 42, 25c.
" 103, 20 x 45, 30c.
" 104, 21 x 48, 35c.
" 105, 23 x 50, 40c.
" 106, 24 x 54, 50c.
" 107, 25 x 56, 60c.
" 108, 25 x 58, 75c.
" 109, 25 x 57, 85c.
" 110, 25 x 59, $1.00 pair.

No. 103.

No. 112.

Brown linen Turkish bath towels, fringed—
No. 111, 21 x 41, 45c.
" 112, 21 x 50, 50c.
" 113, 23 x 48, 60c.
" 114, 24 x 50, 75c.
" 115, 26 x 52, 85c.
" 116, 29 x 56, $1.00.
" 117, 26 x 50, 1.10.
" 118, 26 x 53, 1.25.
" 119, 30 x 56, 1.50 pair.

Brown linen Turkish bath towels, with red and white stripe, fringed—
No. 120, 23 x 46, 60c.
" 121, 21 x 48, 75c.
" 122, 24 x 50, 85c.
" 123, 25 x 52, $1.00
" 124, 25 x 54, 1.25
" 125, 28 x 56, 1.50 pair.

It will pay you when ordering to enclose an order for Groceries.

Fancy Linen Department.

Battenburg Lace Centres, Scarfs, Tea Cloths, Doylies, etc.

Battenburg lace centre-pieces, doylies, tea cloths, tray cloths and sideboard scarfs, 5 x 5, 10c, 12½c, 15c; 7 x 7, 15c, 20c, 25c; 9 x 9, 35c, 40c; 12 x 12, 40c, 50c; 14 x 14, 65c, 75c; 19 x 19, 85c, $1.00, 1.25, 1.50 to 3.00; 32 x 32, $3.00, 3.50, 4.00; 36 x 36, $3.50, 4.00, 4.50, 5.00; 20 x 30, $2.50, 2.75, 3.00, 3.25; 20 x 54, $3.50, 4.00, 4.50, 5.00, 6.00; 20 x 70, $4.50, 5.00, 6.00, 7.00 each.

Real renaissance lace centre-pieces, in all the newest designs, 19 x 19, 85c, $1.00, 1.25, 1.50, 1.75, 2.00 each.

Hand-made renaissance lace tea cloths, all new and exclusive designs, 36 x 36, $3.00, 3.50, 4.00, 4.50, 5.00, 5.50, 6.00 each.

Linen centre-pieces, tea cloths, and sideboard scarfs, with deep hand-made renaissance lace edges, 19 x 19, $1.00, 1.25, 1.50; 36 x 36, $2.75, 3.00, 3.25, 3.75, 4.00, 4.50, 5.00; 20 x 60, $3.00, 3.50, 4.00, 4.50 each.

Linen centre-pieces, with real renaissance lace edges, all new designs, 19 x 19, $1.00, 1.25, 1.50, 1.75, 2.00 each.

Hemstitched Irish linen hand-embroidered tea cloths in assorted designs, 36 x 36 inches, $2.50, 3.00, 3.50, 4.00, 5.00 each.

Hemstitched hand-embroidered Irish linen scarfs, 18 x 72 inches, $3.00, 3.50, 4.00, 5.00 each.

Hemstitched linen tray cloths, hand embroidered, 18 x 27 inches, 65c, 75c, 85c, $1.00, 1.25 each.

Hemstitched and Drawn Linens.

Hemstitched Irish linen centre-pieces, doylies, tray clothes, tea cloths, scarfs, pillow shams, with fancy drawn-work—

7 x 7 inches, 8c, 10c.
9 x 9 " 10c, 12½c, 15c.
12 x 12 " 15c, 20c, 25c.
18 x 18 " 20c, 25c, 30c.
20 x 20 " 25c, 30c, 35c, 40c, 50c.
32 x 32 " 50c, 60c, 75c, 85c.
36 x 36 " 60c, 75c, 85c, $1.00, 1.25.
18 x 27 " 25c, 30c, 35c, 40c, 50c.
20 x 30 " 29c, 35c, 40c, 50c, 60c.
18 x 54 " 60c, 65c, 75c, 85c, $1.00.
18 x 72 " 75c, 85c, $1.00, 1.25, 1.50 ea.

Hemstitched plain Irish linen tray or carving cloths—

18 x 27 inches, 23c, 25c, 30c, 35c, 40c, 50c.
20 x 30 " 25c, 30c, 35c, 40c, 50c, 60c ea.

Hemstitched Irish linen scarfs, superior quality

18 x 54 inches, 40c, 50c, 60c, 75c, 85c.
18 x 72 " 50c, 65c, 75c, 85c, $1.00.

Hemstitched plain linen five-o'clock tea cloths, 36 x 36 inches, 50c, 65c, 75c, 85c, $1.00, 1.25 each.

Plain hemstitched linen centre-pieces—

18 x 18 inches, 20c, 25c, 30c, 35c.
20 x 20 " 25c, 30c, 35c, 40c, 50c each.

Hemstitched linen pillow shams, superior quality, with drawn-work—

32 x 32 inches, $1.20, 1.50, 1.75, 2.00 pair.

Damask Tray and Tea Cloths.

Fine bleached German damask tray cloths, with tied fringe and open-work, choice range of new patterns—

18 x 27 inches, 25c, 30c, 35c, 40c.
19 x 28 " 35c, 40c, 45c, 50c.
20 x 30 " 40c, 45c, 50c, 60c, 75c each.

Hemstitched satin damask tray cloths, superior quality and finish, assorted in new damask patterns—

17 x 27 inches, 25c, 30c, 35c, 40c.
19 x 28 " 35c, 40c, 45c, 50c, 60c each.

Bleached linen damask tray cloths, fringed, all pure linen, assorted patterns—

18 x 27 inches, 12½c, 15c.
20 x 30 " 15c, 20c each.

Fine bleached satin damask tea cloths, with knotted fringe and fancy open-work, new designs—

33 x 33 inches, 50c, 60c, 65c.
34 x 34 " 65c, 75c, 85c, $1.00 each.

Hemstitched satin damask tea cloths, superior quality and finish, German manufacture, new designs of open-work—

34 x 34 inches, 75c, 85c, $1.00, 1.25 each.

Damask Napkins and Doylies.

Satin damask doylies, with tied fringe and open-work—

6 x 6 inches, 60c, 75c.
9 x 9 " $1.00, 1.20.
12 x 12 " 1.50, 1.75 doz.

Bleached damask napkins, fringed, assorted patterns—

16 x 16 inches, 60c, 75c, 85c, $1.00.
18 x 18 " 85c, $1.00, 1.20, 1.50.
20 x 20 " $1.00, 1.20, 1.50, 1.75, 2.00 doz.

Cream damask napkins, with red borders, fringed, assorted patterns—

13 x 13 inches, 40c, 50c.
15 x 15 " 50c, 60c, 75c.
17 x 17 " 60c, 75c, 85c doz.

Turkey on white napkins, assorted patterns, fringed, at 40c, 50c, 60c, 75c, 85c doz.

Sideboard Scarfs.

Austrian crepe linen stand and sideboard scarfs, knotted fringe on ends—

16 x 50 inches, 17c each.
16 x 70 " 25c "

German linen crepe bureau or sideboard scarfs, with knotted fringe and openwork ends—

16 x 50 inches, 20c each.
16 x 70 " 29c "

Better quality crepe linen sideboard scarfs, more openwork and knotted fringe—

16 x 50 inches, 25c, 30c, 35c each.
16 x 70 " 35c, 40c, 50c "

German all linen crepe sideboard scarfs, with heavy knotted fringe and openwork ends—

18 x 72 inches, 60c, 65c, 75c each.

Heavier quality crepe linen scarfs, all pure linen, heavy knotted fringe and openwork ends—18 x 72 inches, 75c, 85c, $1.00, 1.25 each.

Fringed satin damask scarfs, full bleached, assorted patterns—

16 x 50 inches, 40c, 50c each.
16 x 68 " 60c, 75c "

Satin damask scarfs, with tied fringe, choice patterns—16 x 68 inches, 75c, 85c each.

Hemstitched satin damask sideboard scarfs, superior quality and finish—

17 x 70 inches, 75c, 85c, $1.00 each.

Applique Cambric Scarfs.

Tamboured and applique scarfs, for dresser, sideboard or toilet covers, fancy openwork centres, scalloped edges—

18 x 36 inches, 35c, 40c, 50c each.
18 x 54 " 50c, 65c, 75c, 85c each.
18 x 72 " 65c, 75c, 85c, $1.00, 1.25 each.

Applique Cambric Covers.

Tamboured and applique covers, with scalloped edges, new designs in fancy openwork centres and corners, Swiss manufacture, assorted patterns—

32 x 32 inches, 50c, 60c, 75c, 85c, $1.00, 1.25 each.

Laundry Bags.

Plain white laundry bags, finished with cord and tassel, stamped, as shown in cut—

19 x 30 inches, 25c each.

Plain white laundry bags, with pink or blue tops, finished with cord and tassel, stamped—

20 x 30 inches, 30c each.

Laundry bags, made of colored art linen, in assorted shades, stamped if required, finished as above—18 x 30 inches, 50c each.

Pincushion Forms.

Pincushion forms, in round, square or heart shape, assorted sizes, 10c each.

Pincushion forms, oblong—

4 x 12 inches, 10c each.
4 x 15 " 12c "
4 x 18 " 15c "
4 x 24 " 18c "
4 x 27 " 20c "
4 x 36 " 25c "

Tea cosy forms, white cambric covered—

12 x 14 inches, Russian down, 25c each.
12 x 14 " mixed " 35c "
12 x 14 " pure " 50c "

Plain white honeycomb toilet covers, with knotted fringe—

26 x 40 inches, 15c, 20c, 25c each.
27 x 45 " 20c, 25c, 30c "

Marseilles toilet covers, plain white—

24 x 43 inches, 20c, 25c, 30c each.
26 x 45 " 25c, 30c, 35c "

Marseilles toilet mats, 5 mats in set, 20c set.

Silk Bolting Cloth.

Silk bolting cloth, as used for fancy work, etc.—
20-inch, $1.00 yd. 40-inch, $2.00 yd.

Duchess Embroidery Hoops.

"The Duchess" embroidery hoop—perfection—does not require winding, the felt cushion on the inside hoop gives the proper tension to hold either light or heavy material tightly and without injury. Nothing could be simpler or more effective. Made of selected wood, lathe turned, with rounded edges and smoothly finished, absolutely true in circle, and guaranteed never to warp out of shape. The felt cushion is secured in a recess of the smaller hoop in such a manner that it can never pull out or become loose. Sizes 5 and 6-inch, 10c set, or $1.10 for package of 1 doz

Japanese Silk Drapes, Scarfs, etc.

Japanese silk drapes, suitable for mantel or piano, with heavy knotted silk fringe, assorted in crimson, olive, Nile, blue, pink, gold, rose, cream, white, etc., richly embroidered with gold thread in the newest designs—

25 x 90 inches, $2.00, 2.25, 2.50, 2.75, 3.00 each.
27 x 100 " 2.75, 3.00, 3.50, 4.00, 5.00 "

Japanese silk drapes, with heavy knotted fringe, assorted in all the newest shades, embroidered in new designs with bullion—

23 x 90 inches, special, $1.75 each.
27 x 100 " " 1.98 "

Satin mantel drapes, with heavy knotted fringe, richly embroidered with silk and gold thread, all new and exclusive designs, assorted in the best shades—

27 x 108 inches, $5.00, 5.50, 6.00, 7.00 each.

Silk mantel or piano drapes, heavy knotted silk fringe, full range of colors, embroidered in new designs with silk and gold thread—

23 x 93 inches, special, $2.50 each.

Japanese silk drapes, richly embroidered in new designs with silk and bullion, full range of the best shades, knotted fringe—

27 x 99 inches, $2.75 each.
27 x 103 " 3.25 "

Japanese silk drapes, knotted silk fringe, embroidered with gold bullion, assorted shades—

23 x 90 inches, special, $1.50 each.

Japanese silk table covers, with knotted fringe, assorted in gold, blue, pink, olive, Nile, crimson, embroidered with gold thread—

36 x 36 inches, $1.25, 1.50, 1.75, 2.00 each.

Japanese silk chair, easel or picture scarfs, with knotted fringe on both ends, embroidered with gold thread in all new designs, assorted in same shades as drapes—

13½ x 36 inches, 35c, 40c each.
15 x 40 " 45c, 50c, 60c each.
18 x 45 " 60c, 75c, 85c, $1.00 each.
20 x 50 " $1.25, 1.35, 1.50 each.

Satin cushion tops, embroidered in handsome designs with silk and gold thread, assorted in all the newest shades—

22 x 22 inches, $1.00, 1.25, 1.50, 1.75, 2.00, 2.25 each.

It is unsafe to send money in an unregistered letter.

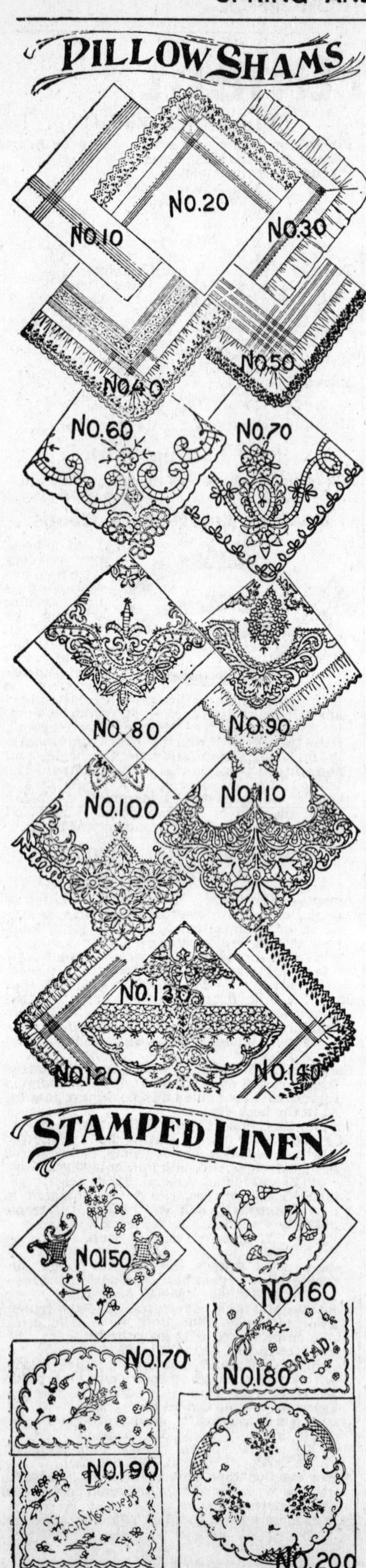

Pillow Shams.

No. 10. Fine cotton tucks and hem, 40c pair.
No. 20. Fine cotton, 1 cluster tucks, frill of embroidery, $1.10 pair.
No. 30. Fine cambric, with cambric frill, 1 cluster of tucks, 85c pair.
No. 40. Extra fine cambric, 2 clusters tucks, 1 row of insertion, frill of embroidery, $2.75 pair.
No. 50. Fine cambric, with embroidery frill, 4 clusters of tucks, $2.00 pair.
No. 60. Applique, with scalloped edge, fancy openwork corners, embroidered in new designs, 65c pair.
No. 70. Applique, with fancy openwork corners and border, fine quality, assorted designs, 80c pair.
No. 80. Fine applique shams, with hemstitched border, fancy openwork centres and corners, $1.50 pair.
No. 90. Extra fine applique shams in new designs of fancy openwork centres and corners, fancy muslin frill, $2.25 pair.
No. 100. Applique shams, openwork centres and corners, Swiss manufacture, neatly embroidered, $1.00 pair.
No. 110. Fine quality, fancy openwork, applique shams, embroidered in assorted designs, $1.50 pair.
No. 120. Fine cambric, 1 cluster tucks, and frill of embroidery, $1.50 pair.
No. 130. Extra fine applique shams, openwork centres, corners and borders, Swiss make, $1.98 pair.
No. 140. Fine cotton, embroidery frill, 1 cluster of tucks, $1.25 a pair.

Stamped Linens.

When ordering stamped linens please state as near as possible the design required.

Stamped linen centre-pieces, buttonhole edge, new designs in conventional and scattered flowers, including pansies, violets, maiden hair ferns, carnations, roses, etc.—
No. 200, 15 x 15, 12½c, 15c. 22 x 22, 30c, 35c.
18 x 18, 15c, 20c. 24 x 24, 40c, 50c.
20 x 20, 25c, 30c.

Stamped linen doylies, designs as above—
No. 160, 4 x 4, 2c, 3c. 9 x 9, 5c, 8c, 10c.
6 x 6, 3c, 5c. 12 x 12, 10c, 12½c, 15c.
8 x 8, 5c, 7c.

Stamped linen tea cosies, buttonhole edge, scattered flowers on honiton designs—
No. 170, 10 x 15-inch, 20c, 25c each.

Stamped photo frames, on fine white linen, in assorted designs—
No. 150. 8 x 10 and 9 x 11, 15c each.

Glove, tie, and handkerchief cases, stamped on fine white linen, buttonhole edge and scattered flowers—
No. 190. Special, 20c each.

Bread cloths, stamped in assorted designs on fine linen—
No. 180. Special, 15c; large size, 20c each.

Hemstitched and drawn linen tray cloths, stamped—
18 x 27, 25c, 30c, 35c, 40c.
20 x 30, 30c, 35c, 40c, 50c, 60c each.

Bleached damask tray cloths, with fringe, stamped—
18 x 27, 15c, 20c. 20 x 30, 20c, 25c each.

Hemstitched and drawn linen tea cloths, stamped in any design required, 36 x 36, 60c, 65c, 75c, 85c, $1.00, 1.25, 1.50 each.

Stamped baby bibs, something dainty, buttonhole edges, and scattered with small forget-me-nots, daisies or rose-buds, special 12½c, 15c each.

Baby's white flannel head shawls, stamped with pretty borders for buttonhole edge and designs in corners, 27 x 27 and 36 x 36, 75c each.

Cotton pillow shams, stamped in a variety of designs, 36 x 36, 19c, 25c pair.

Hemstitched linen pillow shams, stamped, $1.00, 1.20, 1.50, 1.75 pair.

Fine linen hemstitched tray cloths, scarfs, tea cloths, centre-pieces, stamped in assorted designs as required—
Size 18 x 27, 23c, 25c, 30c, 35c, 40c.
" 20 x 30, 25c, 30c, 35c, 40c, 50c.
" 18 x 18, 25c, 30c, 35c, 40c, 50c.
" 36 x 36, 60c, 65c, 75c, 85c, $1.00, 1.25.
" 18 x 54, 60c, 65c, 75c, 85c, $1.00.
" 18 x 72, 75c, 85c, $1.00, 1.25, 1.50 each.

Stamped denim, villa cloth, Holland crash and colored linen cushion tops, in conventional, Bulgarian and floral designs, size 20 x 20, top only, 20c; top, back and frill, 50c each.

Crash cushion tops, stamped, to be embroidered with braid or scattered flower designs, with back and frill, 21 x 21, 50c complete.

Art Embroidery Silks and Fancy Cushion Cords.

Embroidery Silks.

Britannia crochet silk, all shades, 7c spool.
Mayflower crochet silk, pure dye, all shades, 15c spool.
B. & P. rope embroidery silk, all shades, 4c skein, 45c doz.
B. & P. Sicilian embroidery floss, in white, 4c skein, 45c doz.
B. & P. Etching silk, all shades, 3c skein, 30c doz.
B. & P. twisted silks, all shades, 4c skein, 45c doz.
B. & P. Roman floss, all shades, 4c skein, 45c doz.
B. & P. filo floss, all shades, 4c skein, 45c doz.

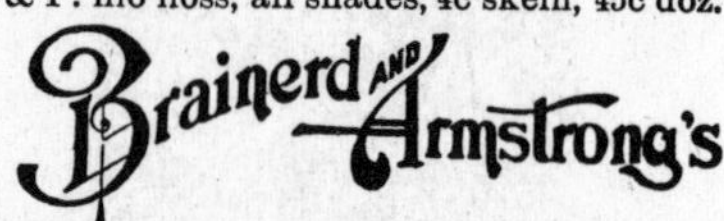

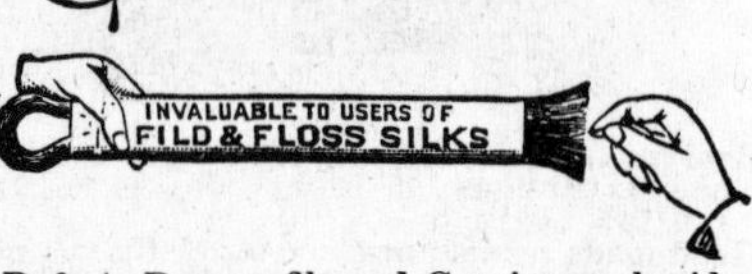

B. & A. Roman filo and Caspian embroidery silks are all put in these patent holders.
B. & A. twisted embroidery silk, all shades, 4c skein, 48c doz.
B. & A. Roman floss, all shades, 5c skein, 50c doz.
B. & A. white Caspian floss, 5c skein, 50c doz.
B. & P. Dresden floss, shaded colors, 4c skein, 45c doz.
Filoselle, all shades, 5c skein, 50c doz.

Belding's and B. & A. knitting or crochet wash silks, all shades, 45c ½-oz spool.
Crochet silk, Belding's Peerless wash silks, 25c ½-oz spool; Corticelli, 25c ½-oz spool.
Crochet silk, Belding's Daisy wash silks, all shades, 25-yd spool, 10c each.

BRAINERD & ARMSTRONG'S

Patent Quill Embroidery

B. & A. quill embroidery silk, all shades, 1c each, 10c doz.

Embroidery Cottons, Linens and Sundries.

Honiton lace thread, in white only, Nos. 500, 600, 700, 800, 5c spool.
Japanese gold thread, for working on silk drapes, etc., 5c, 8c, 12½c, 15c, 18c bunch.
White linen floss, in sizes 0 and 00, 4c skein, 48c doz.
Turkey red tracing cotton, sizes 8, 10, 12, 14, 20c doz.
White, sky, pink and yellow marking cotton, 20c doz.
Barbour's white linen floss, sizes 1, 2, 3, 4, star, 20c doz.
Skein holders for holding embroidery silk, will hold one dozen skeins, 4c each.
Moravian cotton, for padding raised embroidery work, and embroidery initials, etc., 6c ball.
Glove mending silks, in plait of assorted shades, 25c each.
Needlework books, showing lines of shadings on colored plate, 10c each.
Embroidery needles, assorted, sizes No. 7, 8, 9, 5c doz.

Steel Beads, Penelope Canvas and Sheet Celluloid.

Silver steel beads, in bunches of 12 strands, 3 inches long, 18c bunch.
Penelope canvas, used for working Ottoman covers, slippers, etc., 25c yd.
Sheet celluloid, in green, pink, white and blue, 18 inches wide, $1.00 yd.

State clearly on every stamped linen order the design required.

In this department will be found all styles of pincushions, sofa cushions, tea cosies, photo frames, brush and comb cases, handkerchief and tie cravats, shaving cases, towel rings, embroidered centre pieces, doylies, etc.

No. 1. Round pincushion, made in all shades of silk, lace top finished with frill of silk and lace, $1.50 each; embroidered top and ribbon frill, $2.00, 2.50 each.

No. 2. Heart-shaped shaving case, embroidered on white linen, pad of tissue paper and pocket for razor, trimmed with satin ribbon, $1.50 ea.

No. 3. Dainty wide satin ribbon photo frames, with wreath of small flowers and large ribbon bows, 75c each.

No. 4. Large pincushion, with hand-embroidered top and frill of silk and lace, large bow of satin ribbon, $1.50, 2.00 each.

No. 5. Crochet dinner mats, 5 mats to set, $1.75; finer quality, $2.00, 2.25 set.

No. 6. Photo frame, with oval opening, embroidered on white linen, in designs of violets, wild rose, carnations, daisies or forget-me-nots, mounted with glass and brass corners, $1.50; with gilt moulding, $2.00, 2.50 each.

No. 7. Hand-embroidered bookmarks, on white linen, buttonhole edge, mounted on satin ribbon, 50c each.

No. 8. Hand-embroidered doylies, on fine white linen, in assorted floral designs, 9 x 9-inch, 60c, 75c; 12 x 12-inch, 75c, $1.00 each.

No. 9. Round shaving cases, embroidered on white or colored linen in pretty designs, pad of tissue paper and pocket for razor, trimmed with ribbon, $1.50, 2.00 each.

No. 10. Bangle board, suitable for keys, button-hooks, etc., puffing of silk and wide frills of lace, finished with baby ribbon, 75c each.

No. 11. Hanging pincushion, biscuit design, large bows of narrow ribbon, 40c each.

No. 12. Photo frame, with three openings, embroidered on white linen, in designs of violets, roses, forget-me-nots, carnations and sweet peas, finished with glass and brass corners, $2 50, 3.00 each.

No. 13. Tie or handkerchief cases, raised embroidery on fine white linen, in rich floral designs, finished with double frill of silk and lace, $1.50, 2.00; embroidered on bolting cloth, $2.25, 2.50 each.

No. 14. Head rest, made in any shade of silk, with crochet top and silk puffing, satin ribbon frill, "Russian" down form, $2.00, 2.50 each.

No. 15. Knitted tea cosy, made of double Berlin wool, in pink, blue, yellow and green shades, $1.25 each.

No. 16. Hanging pincushion, egg-beater style, richly padded and finished with large bows of ribbon, 40c, 50c each.

No. 17. Hand-embroidered sofa cushions, in our latest designs, finished with two shades of ribbon frill, good forms, $3.50, 4.00, 5.00, 6.00 each.

No. 18. Hand-embroidered tea cosies, on white linen, buttonhole edge, all pretty floral designs, finished with double puffing of silk, $3.50, 4.00 each.

No. 19. Crochet hair receiver, pineapple design, lined with silk, ribbon bows, 50c each.

No. 20. Hand-embroidered centrepieces on white linen, in rich rose, violets, carnations and other floral designs, heavy buttonhole edge, $2.50, 3.00 each; more elaborately worked, $3.50 to 5.00 each.

No. 21. Sofa cushion, with Japanese satin top, embroidered with silk and bullion, finished with frill to harmonize, $3.50 to 5.00 each.

No. 22. Comb and brush cases, made of silk, finished with frill of silk and lace, richly trimmed with satin ribbon, $1.50, 2.00, 2.25 ea.

No. 23. Photo frames, with three openings, embroidered in rich floral designs on white linen, with glass and gilt moulding, $3.00, 3.50 each.

No. 24. Teapot holder, linen, butterfly embroidered in shaded silk, mounted on silk pad, finished with double frill, 75c each.

No. 25. Jewel boxes, made of silk, nicely padded embroidered top of white linen or bolting cloth, in scattered flowers, finished with silk and lace frill, $1.50 each.

No. 26. Tea cosy, made of fine art sateen, double puffing of silk, "Russian" down form, $1.00, 1.25, 1.50 each.

No. 27. Photo frames, embroidered in pretty floral designs on white linen, with glass and brass corners, $2.25, 2.50 each.

No. 28. Watch pockets, with raised embroidery in neat floral designs on white linen, with puffing of silk and baby ribbon, 65c each.

No. 29. Long pincushion, with hand-embroidered linen top, with rich satin ribbon frill, 12-inch, $1.50 each; 15, 18-inch, $2.00 each; 24, 27-inch, $3.00 each.

No. 30. Silk sofa pillow, with Battenburg lace top, finished with ribbon frill, good form, $3.25, 4.00 each.

No. 31. Match receivers, trimmed with baby ribbon, any shade, 40c each.

No. 32. Padded comb and brush tray, with large crochet rings and wide satin ribbon, something quite new for dresser, $1.50, 1.75 each.

No. 33. Handkerchief pocket of black crochet silk rings, puffing of silk, narrow ribbon bows, $1.00 each.

No. 34. Whisk holder, embroidered on white linen, in designs of raised flowers, finished with wide frill of silk and lace, all art shades, 75c, $1.00 each.

No. 35. Bangle board, made of silk, with applique of lace, finished with brass hooks and bows of baby ribbon, 50c each.

No. 36. Round photo frame, embroidered on white or colored linen, in scroll or floral designs, $1.50 each.

No. 37. Towel rings, trimmed with large bows of satin ribbon, any shade, 85c, $1.00 set.

No. 38. Shaving case, embroidered on white linen, lined with silk, pad of tissue paper and pocket for razor, satin ribbon bows, $1.50, 1.75 each.

No. 39. Silk tea cosy, made with three large puffings, Battenburg lace sides, good forms, $2.50, 3.50 each.

No. 40. Dainty tinsel pin balls, richly trimmed with ribbon, 40c, 75c each.

No. 41. Pincushion, fancy ribbon top, any two shades, finished with silk and lace frill, $1.75, 2.50 each.

No. 42. Hairpin glass, neatly trimmed with flowers and clusters of baby ribbon, 35c, 50c each.

Knitted teapot holder, corn-cob shape, any shade, finished with ribbon, 20c each.

Pin balls, embroidered on white linen, in raised designs, in assorted flowers, finished with pins all around and needle case on back, 60c, 75c each.

Hat bands, embroidered on satin ribbon, any shade, 75c each.

Your orders will be accurately and promptly filled.

Cotton Department.

Bleached Cottons.

Best Canadian pure finished bleached cottons, 36-inch, 5c, 6c, 7c, 8c, 10c yd.

Fine English bleached long cloths and shirtings, 36-inch, 8c, 10c, 12½c, 15c yd.

Horrockses' fine bleached cottons, medium and heavy qualities, 36-inch, 10c, 12½c, 15c, 18c yd.

Crewdson's extra fine bleached cottons, medium and light weights, 36-inch, 10c, 12½c, 15c, 18c, 20c yd.

Bleached twill cottons, soft pure makes, 36-inch, 10c, 12½c yd.

Horrockses' and Crewdson's best makes fine bleached twill cottons, 36-inch, 12½c, 15c, 18c, 20c yd.

Cambrics and Nainsooks.

Canadian, American Londsdales and English bleached cambrics, best makes, 36-inch, 10c, 12½c, 15c, 18c, 20c, 25c yd.

Bleached cambrics, best standard makes, in soft or linen finish, 42-inch, 10c, 12½c, 15c, 18c yd.

Fine bleached nainsooks and embroidery cambrics, 40-inch, 15c, 18c, 20c, 25c yd.

Unbleached Cottons.

34-inch plain unbleached cottons, 4c, 4½c, 5c yd.

36-inch unbleached cottons, selected pure cloths, made from round even yarns, 5c, 6c, 7c, 8c, 10c yd.

40-inch fine unbleached cottons, free from sizing, 8c, 10c yd.

36-inch unbleached twill cottons, soft pure makes, 8c, 10c yd.

Sheetings and Pillow Cloths.

Plain unbleached sheeting—
- 64-inch or 7/4 wide, 16c yd.
- 72-inch or 8/4 wide, 16c, 18c, 20c yd.
- 80-inch or 9/4 wide, 20c, 22c yd.
- 90-inch or 10/4 wide, 22c yd.

Twill unbleached sheeting—
- 64-inch or 7/4 wide, 18c yd.
- 72-inch or 8/4 wide, 18c, 20c, 22c yd.
- 90-inch or 9/4 wide, 22c, 24c yd.

Plain bleached sheeting—
- 64-inch or 7/4 wide, 22c yd.
- 72-inch or 8/4 wide, 22c, 24c, 26c, 30c yd.
- 80-inch or 9/4 wide, 24c, 26c, 30c, 35c yd.

Twill bleached sheeting—
- 64-inch or 7/4 wide, 24c yd.
- 72-inch or 8/4 wide, 24c, 26c, 28c, 30c yd.
- 80-inch or 9/4 wide, 26c, 28c, 30c, 35c yd.
- 90-inch or 10/4 wide, 28c, 35c, 40c yd.

Crewdson's fine English bleached sheetings, linen finish, plain or twill—
- 54-inch or 6/4 wide, 25c yd.
- 72-inch or 8/4 wide, 35c yd.
- 80-inch or 9/4 wide, 40c yd.
- 90-inch or 10/4 wide, 50c yd.

Special make bleached plain pillow cotton, round even thread, soft pure finish—

Width,	40,	42,	44,	46 in.
Price,	10c,	11c,	12c,	13c yd.

Horrockses' English bleached plain pillow cotton, fine linen finish—

Width,	42,	45,	48,	54 in.
Price,	15c,	17c,	19c,	21c yd.

Fine bleached circular pillow cotton, pure finish—

Width,	40,	42,	44,	46 in.
Price,	12c,	13c,	14c,	15c yd.

Extra fine English bleached circular pillow cloth, linen finished heavy cotton—

Width,	40,	42,	48 in.
Price,	20c,	22c,	25c yd.

Ginghams and Oxford Shirtings, Galateas, Drills, etc.

Canadian shirting ginghams, in dark blue and brown, solid and broken checks, all fast colors, 27-inch, 7c, 8c; 28-inch, 10c, 12c yd.

Canadian Oxford shirtings, assorted stripe and check patterns, fast colors, 27-inch, 8c, 10c yd.

Heavy English Oxford shirtings, linen finish, in stripe and check patterns, 29-inch, 10c, 12½c, 15c yd.

Extra fine English Oxford shirtings, new patterns, 29-inch, 15c yd.

English stripe galateas, dark blue grounds, all fast colors, 27-inch, 10c, 12½c, 15c yd.

Extra fine English satin-finished skirting, heavy quality, wide, medium and narrow stripe, 30-inch, special, 20c yd.

Fine bleached satin-finished cotton drill, fast colors, 28-inch, 15c, 18c, 20c yd.

Fine bleached satin drill, with narrow red or blue stripes, 28-inch, 15c yd.

Fine English satin drill, in solid light and dark blues, 28-inch, 15c, 18c, 20c yd.

Apron Ginghams.

Apron ginghams, in small and medium checks, dark blue and brown, 27 inches wide, 7c yd.

36-inch apron ginghams, with or without borders, medium and small checks, in brown, dark blue and red, all fast colors, 10c yd.

40-inch apron ginghams, best makes, assorted patterns, small and medium checks, dark blue and brown, fast colors, 12½c yd.

Fine plain colored English apron cloth, in dark grey, pink, fawn, light and dark blue, with deep stripe borders, 40 inches wide, 11c yd.

Cottonades, Denims and Sail Ducks.

Cottonades, in carefully selected qualities, neat checks, large and small stripes, and plain mixtures, 28 inches wide, 12½c, 15c, 18c, 21c, 25c yd.

Denims, in plain blue and brown, 28 inches wide, 10c, 12½c, 15c, 18c, 20c yd.

Unbleached cotton duck, for sails and awnings, best quality, 7-oz, 10c; 8-oz, 12c; 10-oz, 15c; 12-oz, 18c yd.

Hessians or Straw Tickings.

54-inch striped, 10c, 12½c, 15c, 18c yd.

72-inch, plain or striped, 15c, 18c, 20c, 25c yd.

Cotton Tickings.

Cotton tickings, striped patterns, in blue and white, and blue and red, 30-inch, 8c, 10c, 12½c, 15c; 32-inch, 18c, 20c, 22½c; 36-inch, 25c, 30c yd.

Sateen-finished tickings, in fancy stripes, fast colors, 30-inch, 15c; 32-inch, 20c yd.

Potato Bags.

20 x 40-inch, holds 90 lbs, 6½c, 7½c, 8c, 9c each.

Grain Bags.

(Prices subject to change without notice.)

Best Hochelaga makes—
- 2-bushel bags, No. W, $1.80 doz; per 100, $14.00.
- 2-bushel bags, No. X, $2.14 doz; per 100, $16.00.
- 2-bushel bags, No. SB, $2.22 doz; per 100, $17.50.
- 2-bushel bags, No. EB, $2.40 doz; per 100, $19.00.
- 2-bushel bags, No. A, $2.70 doz; per 100, $21.50.
- 2½-bushel bags, No. H, $2.88 doz; per 100, $23.00.

Carpet Warps and Weaving Yarns.

(Prices subject to change without notice.)

Sold only in five-pound packages, best standard makes—

Carpet warps, in light and dark reds, green and orange, one color in each bundle, 5 lbs for $1.15.

White carpet warp, 5 lbs for 95c.

White cotton weaving yarns, Nos. 7, 8, 9, 5 lb bundle, 85c each.

Cheese Cloth and Buntings.

40-inch unbleached cheese cloth, 3½c, 4c, 5c yd.

36-inch bleached butter cloth, 4c, 5c yd.

25-inch, in red, white, orange, yellow, light and dark blue, light and dark green, and pink, 5c yd.

36-inch extra fine American colored bunting, in pink, Nile, green, canary, apple, cream, red, blue, yellow, white, heliotrope and black, 10c yd.

Cotton Batting and Wadding.

Patent roll cotton batting, three qualities—

X brand, 16-oz rolls, 10c each.

XX brand, 16-oz rolls, 11c each.

XXX brand, 16-oz rolls, 12½c each.

Waddings, glazed finish

Dark slate color, in sheets 32 x 36 inches, 24c dozen.

Cream white, in sheets 32 x 36 inches, 24c doz.

Fine American bleached, special for fancy work, 5c per sheet, 50c doz.

Flannel Department.

Grey Union Flannels.

Thoroughly unshrinkable soft pure finished grey union flannel, plain or twill, light and dark shades, 25-inch, 12½c; 27-inch, 15c yd.

Fine pressed finished grey wool flannel, manufactured specially for us, absolutely pure and unshrinkable, light and dark shades, plain and twill, 27-inch, 17c yd.

All-wool grey flannels, thoroughly scoured, very best makes procurable for price, light and dark shades, plain or twill, 25-inch, 17c; 27-inch, 19c yd.

All-wool grey flannel, manufactured of pure yarns, guaranteed entirely free from grease, very smooth and soft in finish, light and dark shades, plain or twill, 27-inch, 25c yd.

Fine all-wool flannel, guaranteed pure all-wool, extra soft pressed finish, light and dark grey shades, plain or twill, 27-inch, 30c yd.

Homespun and Kersey Flannels.

Kersey union flannel, heavy twill, in grey, and black or brown mixtures, 27-inch, 20c yd.

Extra heavy all-wool Kersey twill flannel, for men's heavy shirts, etc, unshrinkable, grey shades only, 27-inch, 25c, 30c yd.

Navy Blue, Scarlet and Natural Flannels.

Medium quality navy blue union flannel, unshrinkable, twill only, 25-inch, 17c; 27-inch, 19c yd.

Special make fine navy blue wool flannel, indigo dye, in plain or twill, 27-inch, 25c yd.

Super all-wool navy blue flannel, guaranteed fast dye, soft pressed finish, plain or twill, 28-inch, 30c, 35c, 40c yd.

Scarlet Yorkshire flannels, warranted all pure wool, soft finish, good clear color, 20-inch, 15c; 22-inch, 20c; 25-inch, 25c; 28-inch, 30c; 30-inch, 35c; 31-inch, 40c; 32-inch, 45c, 50c yd.

Fine all-wool natural color sanitary flannels, guaranteed thoroughly shrunk, soft pure finish, 26-inch, 30c; 28-inch, 35c; 30-inch, 40c; 31-inch, 45c yd.

Cream Flannels.

Fine cream Ceylon flannels, guaranteed unshrinkable, soft pure finish, 28-inch, 20c, 25c, 30c yd.

Fine French plain flannel, made of extra fine yarns, soft smooth finish, all pure wool and warranted unshrinkable, 26-inch, 25c; 31-inch, 30c, 35c, 40c, 45c, 50c; 36-inch, 40c, 45c, 50c, 60c yd.

French cream twill flannel, all pure wool and unshrinkable, soft finish, good clear color, 27-inch, 25c; 31-inch, 30c, 35c, 40c, 45c, 50c yd.

English Saxony flannels, soft pure make, warranted pure all wool, cream shade, 25-inch, 25c; 27-inch, 30c; 30-inch, 35c; 31-inch, 40c, 45c; 32-inch, 50c yd.

Opera and French Printed Flannels.

Plain color fine twill opera flannels, soft in texture and thoroughly fast in color, in black, garnet, cardinal, navy, pink and sky, 27-inch, 30c, 35c yd.

Fine twill French flannels, cashmere finish, with narrow woven stripes and checks, very pretty effects, in mauve, brown, myrtle, grey, pink, scarlet, light blue, navy, cardinal and black, 27-inch, 35c yd.

French twill printed all-wool flannels, specially designed for children's wear, colors pink, navy, sky, scarlet, cream, cardinal, with small polka dot, small and medium stripes, all fast colors, 27-inch, 40c yd.

French printed twill flannels, soft finish pure all-wool fabric, largely used for tea gowns, wrappers, sacques, waists, etc., latest designs and colorings, 27-inch, 50c yd.

Dealing dir ct with manufacturers, we sell you goods at bottom prices.

Boots and Shoes.

Why Not Buy your Footwear by the modern method, without salesmen? Thousands are doing so, why not you? In presenting you with this Catalogue of up-to-date perfect-fitting serviceable Spring Shoes, we have selected just those styles that we trust will particularly interest you and give perfect satisfaction.

Ladies' Boots.

We have pleasure in introducing this season for ladies', gents' and children's wear, genuine Australian glazed kangaroo, tanned by chrome process and is the toughest and longest wearing leather in existence, soft as kid, bright finish, does not peel, and gives comfort to the most tender feet.

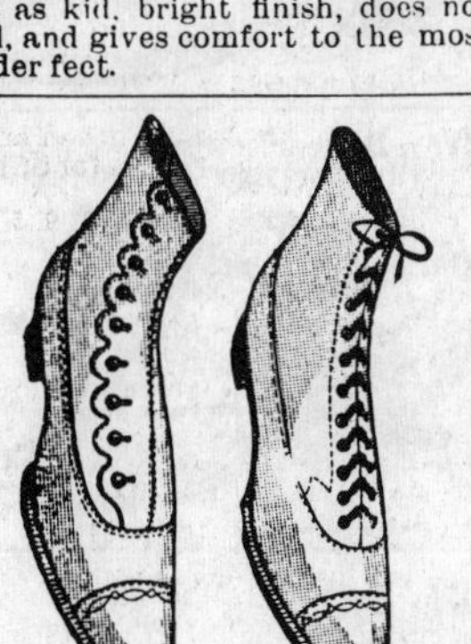

1A.

1A. Glazed kangaroo, buttoned, with the genuine Goodyear welted extension soles, good value at $3.50, sizes 2½ to 7, our price **$2.75**

2A. Laced, same as 1A, sizes 2½ to 7.............................. **$2.75**

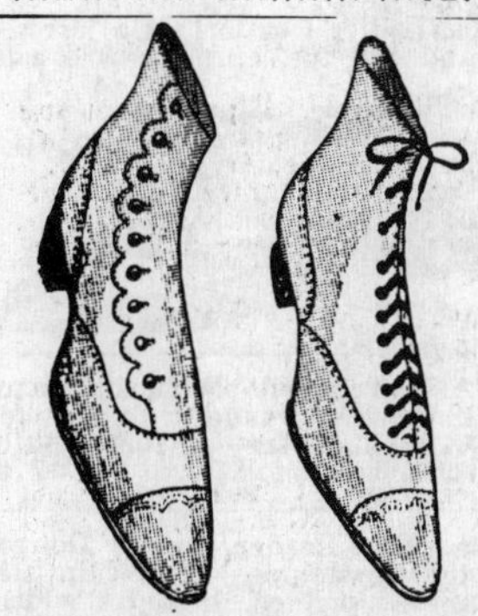

3A.

3A. Ladies' buttoned kangaroo, with medium light McKay sewn soles, sizes 2½ to 7.......................... **$2.25**

4A. Laced, same as 3A, sizes 2½ to 7 .... **$2 25**

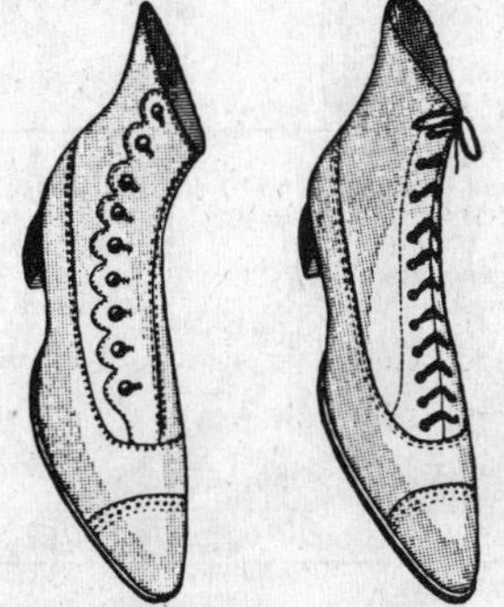

5A. 6A.

5A. Ladies' fine dongola kid, buttoned, McKay sewn soles, with the popular cork inner-sole, cool in summer, just the thing for tender feet, "Walk Easy" style, sizes 2½ to 7, D and E widths .. **$2.50**

6A. Laced, same as 5A, sizes 2½ to 7 .. .. **$2.50**

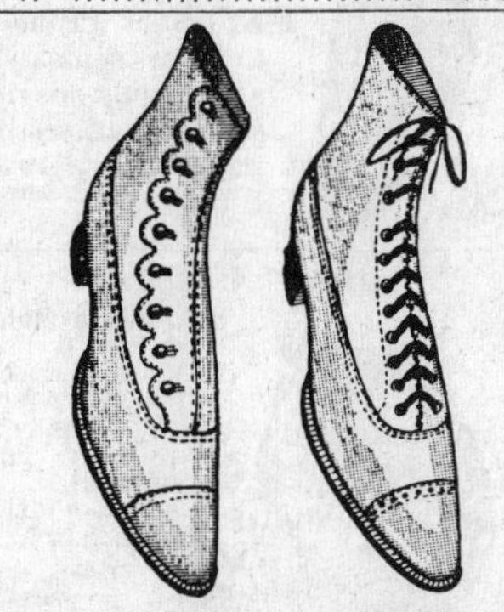

7A. 8A.

7A. Ladies' dongola kid, "Walk Easy," buttoned, with extension soles, sizes 2½ to 7, great value **$2.00**

8A. Laced, same as 7A, sizes 2½ to 7 .... **$2.00**

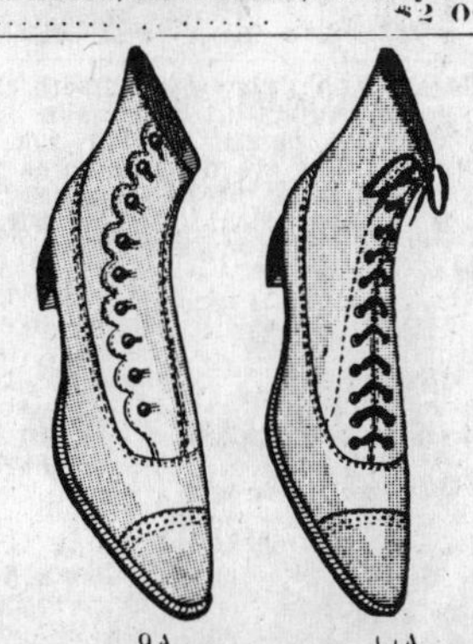

9A. 10A.

9A. Ladies' best quality Brazil kid, buttoned, Goodyear welted extension soles, equal to most $4.00 boots, sizes 2½ to 7, C, D and E widths, our price **$3.00**

10A. Laced, same as 9A, sizes 2½ to 7 .. .. **$3.00**

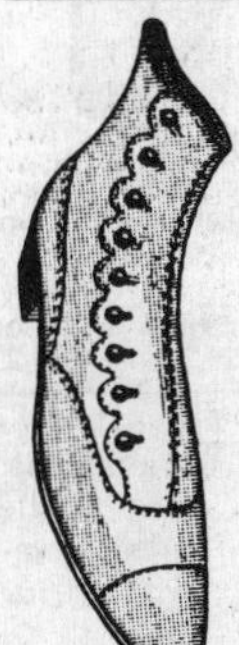

11A. Ladies' choice bright kid, buttoned, with thin turn flexible soles, perfect fitting, sizes 2½ to 7, C, D and E widths **$3.00**

12A. Laced, same as 11A, sizes 2½ to 7, C, D and E widths **$3.00**

11A.

13A. Ladies' patent calf, laced, with Goodyear welted extension soles. We do not warrant patent leather not to crack, but we do warrant this boot splendid value and to ship in good condition, sizes 2 to 7, C and D widths,

$3.00.

14A. Ladies' extra choice vici kid, buttoned, the best boot made in New York State, made by particular people for particular people, Goodyear welted extension, or with light turn soles, cut has welted soles, state which you prefer, sizes 2½ to 8, B, C, D and E widths, none better at $7.00; our price **$4.00**

15A. Laced, same as 14A, only with turn flexible soles. You can can have same with Goodyear welt if you prefer, sizes 2½ to 8, all widths,

$4.00.

16A. Ladies'; this is a very swell patent leather boot, Goodyear welted soles, best American make, warranted the best quality, but not guaranteed not to crack, buttoned or laced, state which you prefer, C, D and E widths, sizes 2½ to 7, usually sold for $6.00, our price

$4.00.

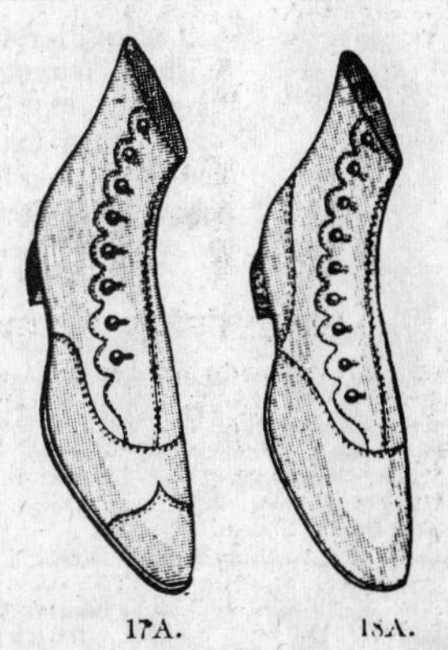

17A. 18A.

17A. Ladies' dongola kid buttoned fat ankle boot, full fitting. You may have same in laced if you prefer, sizes 2½ to 8, E width **$2.00**

18A. Ladies' glazed dongola kid, buttoned, plain wide toe, commonsense shape, sizes 2½ to 8.... **$2.00**

Our Footwear is made by particular people for particular people.

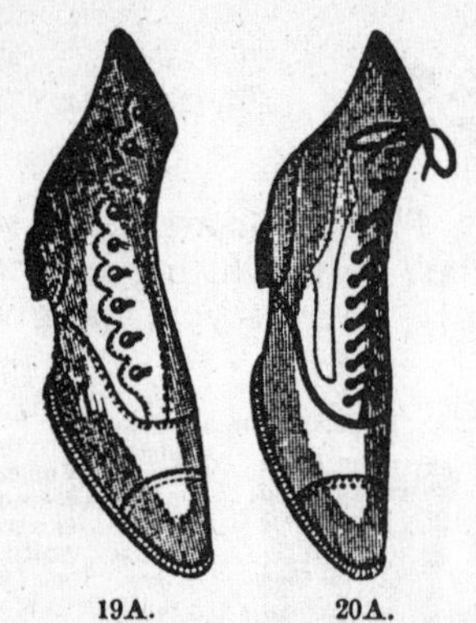

19A. 20A.

19A. Ladies' genuine bright goat kid, buttoned, with Fair stitch, extension soles, best value in Canada, sizes 2½ to 7.................. $1.50

20A. Same quality as 19A, sizes 2½ to 7 ....**$1.50**

21A. 22A.

21A. Ladies' soft glazed kid, buttoned, plain toe, comfort style, with low heel, sizes 2½ to 8. $1.45

22A. Same quality as 21A, sizes 2½ to 8 ....**$1.45**

23A. Ladies' diamond-finished jet black dongola kid, buttoned, with extension soles, looks like a $2.00 boot, sizes 2½ to 7, our price **$1.25**

24A. Same quality, laced, as 23A sizes 2½ to 7........**$1.25**

24A.

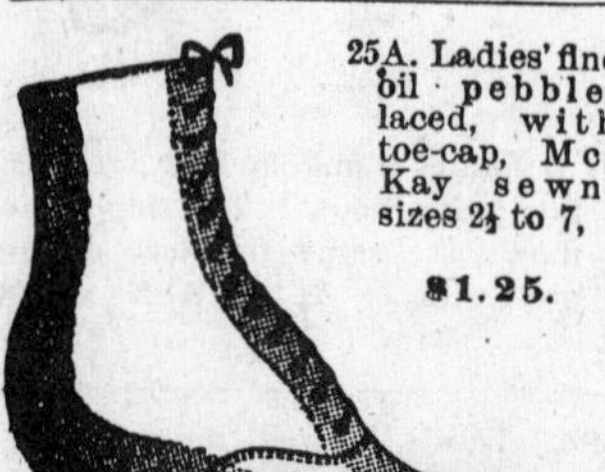

25A. Ladies' fine oil pebble, laced, with toe-cap, McKay sewn, sizes 2½ to 7,

$1.25.

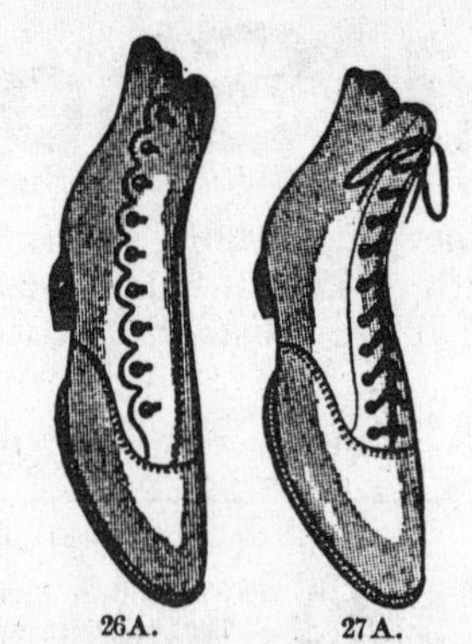

26A. 27A.

26A. Ladies' best quality heavy-weight, oil pebble, buttoned, hard-to-wear-out style, sizes 2½ to 8 ....**$1.20**

27A. Same style as 26A, in laced, sizes 2½ to 8 ....**$1.20**

28A. Ladies', oil buff, laced, with nailed soles, sizes 3 to 7, no half sizes,

95c.

28A.

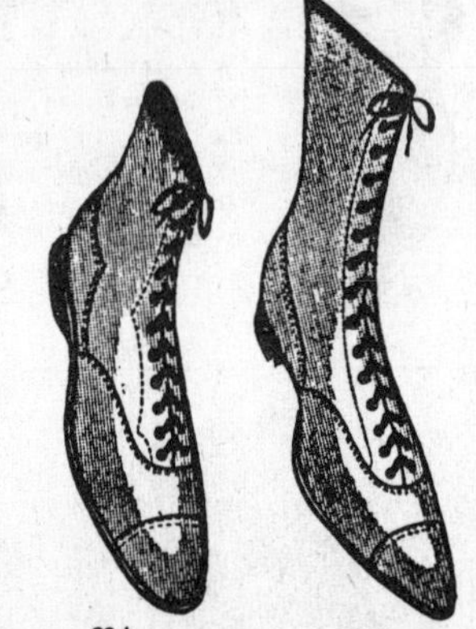

29A. 30A.

29A. Ladies' wedge heel kid boots, buttoned or laced, state which you prefer, sizes 2½ to 6 ....$2.00

30A. Ladies' tan dongola kid bicycle boot, three-quarter length, sizes 2½ to 7.................................$2.00

31A. Ladies' black kid bicycle boot, same as 30A, sizes 2½ to 7...$2.00

32A. Ladies' soft pliable kid elastic side boot, with low heel, full fitting, sizes 3 to 8.......................$1.95

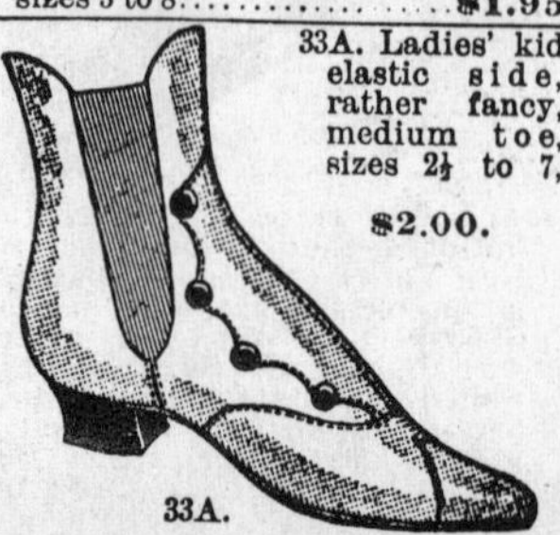

33A. Ladies' kid elastic side, rather fancy, medium toe, sizes 2½ to 7,

$2.00.

33A.

34A. Ladies' plain elastic side Congress, medium fitting, not as wide as 32A, sizes 3 to 8.........**$1.50**

35A. Ladies' goat kid, elastic side, matron style, wide sole and low heel, sizes 3 to 8,

$1.20.

36A. Ladies' Prunella elastic side boot, the old reliable wide turn flexible soles, with low heel, full fitting, sizes 3 to 8.... ....**$1.20**

37A. Ladies' Prunella Congress, same style as 36A, only heavier soles and rather stiff, sizes 3 to 8......**95c**

36A.

Ladies' Oxfords.

38A. Extra choice jet black, best American make with turn flexible soles, very pretty and neat, B, C, D and E widths, sizes 2½ to 7,

$3.00

39A. Patent, very swell, with turn soles, perfect fitting. We don't warrant patent leather not to crack, but we do guarantee this quality to be the best, sizes 2½ to 7, B, C, D and E widths.......**$3.25**

40A. The Flower City shoe, selected Brazil kid, light, neat and very comfortable, turn flexible soles, C, D and E widths, sizes 2½ to 8,

$2.50.

41A. Best selected glazed kid, with Goodyear welted extension soles, a capital walking shoe, C, D and E widths, sizes 2½ to 7,

$2.50.

42A. Soft pliable kid, with light flexible soles, common-sense shape, D and E widths, sizes 2½ to 8,

$2.50.

43A. Genuine kid, Blucher cut, very neat and comfortable, with turn flexible soles. D and E widths, sizes 2½ to 7,

$2.00.

44A. Best selection of dongola kid with Goodyear welted extension soles, D and E widths, sizes 2½ to 7,

$2.00

45A. Very stylish, bright glossy kid, with turn flexible soles, and white kid lining, sizes 2½ to 7. D and E widths,

$2.00

46A. Ladies' Comfort style, low heel, and full toe, turn flexible soles, sizes 2½ to 8,

$2.00.

47A. The old reliable black cloth top, kid foxing, made to fit a fat foot with high instep, turn flexible soles, sizes 2½ to 8 ....$2.00

48A. Our Leader, bright Dongola kid (goatskin), with thin turn soles, kid lined, D and E widths, sizes 2½ to 7,

$1.50.

You don't have to "break in" the "Walk Easy" boot, they fit from the start.

49A. Common Sense, with best dongola kid, low heel and wide toe, flexible soles, sizes 2½ to 8, E width only, $1.50.

50A. Bright soft jet black kid, 2-button strap, flexible soles, very neat and durable, sizes 2½ to 7, $1.50.

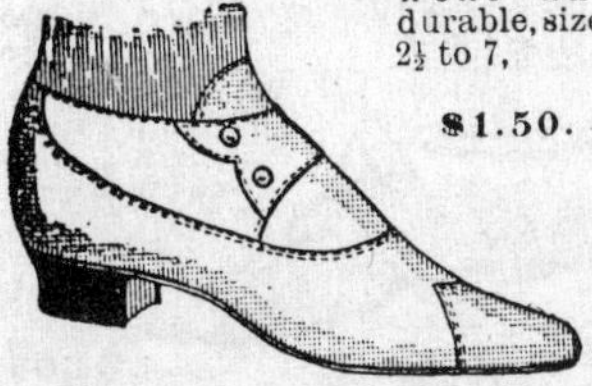

51A. Dongola kid, with extension soles, English walking style, sizes 2½ to 7, $1.50.

52A. Tan goat kid, with turn flexible soles, a neat up-to-date shoe, sizes 2½ to 7, $1.50.

53A. Choice bright kid, with turn soles, well-made, neat and stylish, sizes 2½ to 7, $1.25.

54A. Dongola kid, old ladies' comfort shoe, full fitting, turn flexible soles, sizes 2½ to 8, $1.25.

55A. Genuine goat kid, with turn soles, kid toe-cap, kid-lined, beat it if you can, sizes 2½ to 7, $1.00.

56A. Tan pebble, with rather heavy soles, great value, sizes 3 to 7, no half sizes, 85c.

57A. The milk maid's friend, heavy leather, hard to wear out soles, sizes 3 to 8, no half sizes, 75c.

Ladies' Slippers.

58A. A New York style, very swell, fancy black-beaded vamp and strap, hand-turn soles, the best American make, B, C and D widths, sizes 2½ to 7, $3.00.

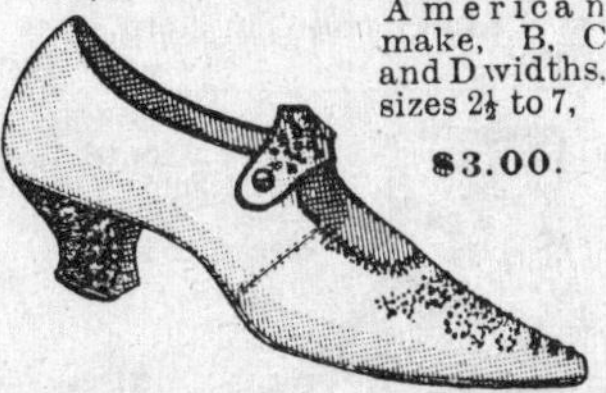

59A. Genuine patent calfskin, with bright kid back, hand-turn soles, sizes 2½ to 7, C and D widths, $2.50

60A. Black beaded strap sandal, very pretty, with turn soles and medium high heels, sizes 2½ to 7, C, D and E widths, $2.50.

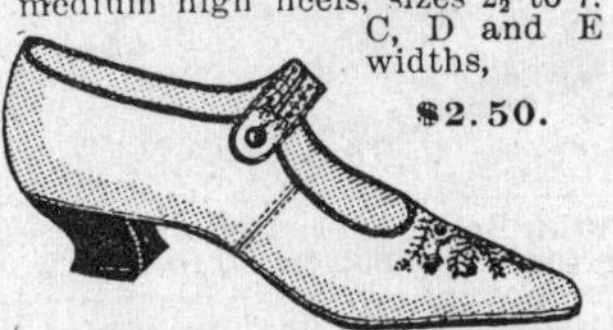

61A. Fine selected American kid, plain, with thin turn soles, very neat and perfect fitting, with wood heels or leather, state which you prefer, C, D and E widths, sizes 2½ to 7, $2.00.

62A. The popular full fitting kid turn flexible soles, one strap sandal, sizes 2½ to 7, D and E widths, $1.75

63A. Our leader, choice glazed kid, one strap, with flexible soles neat, durable and comfortable, sizes 2½ to 7, D and E widths, $1.50.

64A. Bright glazed kid, turn flexible soles, with low heel and plain wide toe, common-sense shape, E width, sizes 2½ to 7, $1.25.

65A. Genuine kid, with flexible soles, kid lined, medium toe and leather heel, great value, sizes 2½ to 7, $1.25.

66A. Solid comfort dongola buskin with elastic over the instep, turn flexible soles, sizes 2½ to 8, $1.20.

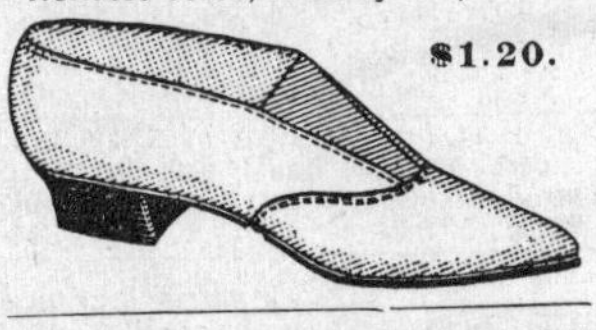

67A. "Snowball," American white kid sandal, with turn soles, kid lined, sizes 2½ to 7, $1.20.

68A. One strap, goat kid, with flexible soles, easy fitting, kid lined, beat it if you can, sizes 2½ to 7, $1.00.

69A. Prunella buskin, flexible soles, fine fitting, low heel, sizes 2½ to 8, $1.00

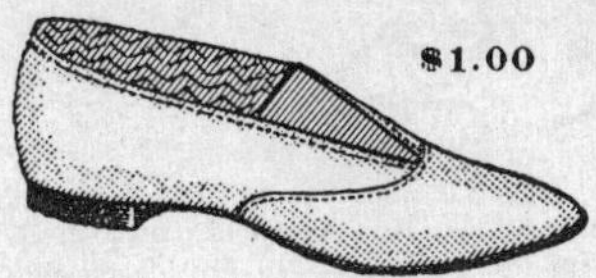

70A. Snowflake white kid sandal, high heel, cotton lined, sizes 2½ to 7, 95c

71A. The housemaid's friend, one-strap sandal, with soles rather thick, can be worn on the street, sizes 2½ to 7, splendid value, 85c

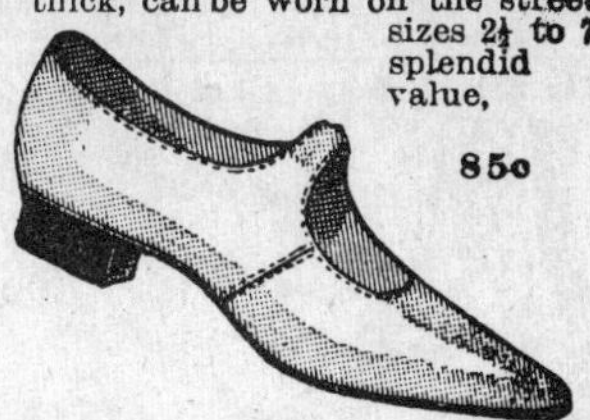

72A. Best imported fancy repp carpet slippers, with leather foxing, a great wearer, sizes 3 to 7, no half sizes............................85c

73A. Fancy carpet, McKay sewn soles and low heels, sizes 3 to 7, no half sizes, 50c.

74A. Prunella buskin, elastic over the instep, sizes 3 to 7, no half sizes, 40c.

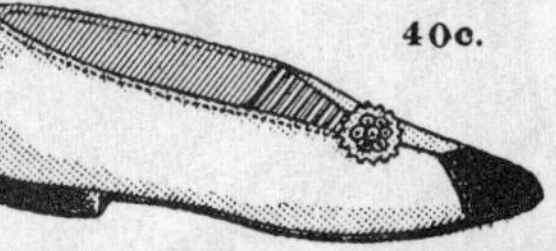

75A. Heavy leather kitchen or outdoor slippers, sizes 3 to 7, no half sizes, 35c.

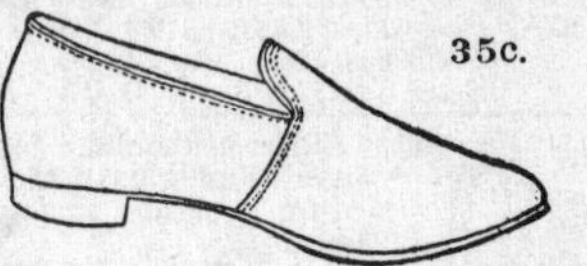

Misses' and Children's Boots.

76A. Genuine kangaroo buttoned, spring heel, little heavier than kid, and will wear better. (For full description of this excellent leather, see page 83.)

Sizes 11 to 2 ..$1.50
Sizes 8 to 10½.. 1.20
Sizes 5 to 7½ .. 1.00

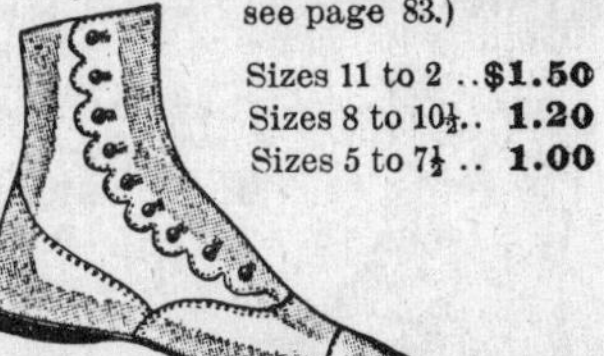

77A. Kangaroo laced, with spring heel,

Sizes 11 to 2........$1,50
Sizes 8 to 10½....... 1.20
Sizes 5 to 7½........ 1.00

78A. Best quality dice calfskin, laced, medium heavy, neat and durable, spring heel,

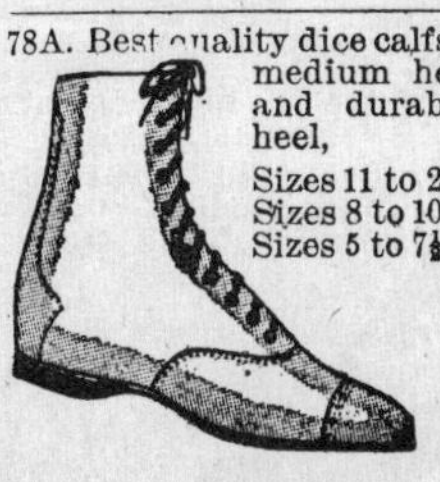

Sizes 11 to 2 ...$1.50
Sizes 8 to 10½ .. 1.25
Sizes 5 to 7½.... 1.00

Our 1901 styles in Footwear are correct in every detail, and will be found very satisfactory.

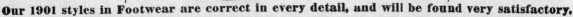

79A. Dice calfskin, buttoned, same style as 78A,
Sizes 11 to 2........$1.50
Sizes 8 to 10½ 1.25
Sizes 5 to 7½........ 1.00

80A. Bright dongola kid (goatskin) buttoned, with medium thick soles and spring heels,
Sizes 11 to 2...$1.50
Sizes 8 to 10½.. 1.25
Sizes 4 to 7½.. 1.00

81A. Laced, same as 80A.
Sizes 11 to 2...... $1.50
Sizes 8 to 10½ 1.25
Sizes 4 to 7½........ 1.00

82A. Fine bright selected kid, buttoned, perfect fitting,
Sizes 11½ to 2 .$1.75
Sizes 8½ to 11 . 1.50
Sizes 5 to 8 .. 1.25

83A. Dice calfskin, buttoned, will give excellent wear, rather heavy soles, spring heels, sizes
11 to 2 ..$1.25
8 to 10½.. 1.00
5 to 7½.. 0.95

84A. Dice calfskin, laced, same as 83A, Sizes 11 to 2 ....$1.25
Sizes 8 to 10½....... 1.00
Sizes 5 to 7½........ 0 95

85A. Dongola kid, buttoned, jet black and glossy, medium weight, spring heel,
Sizes 11 to 2...$1.20
Sizes 8 to 10½... 0.95
Sizes 5 to 7½.... 0.85

86A. Oil pebble grain, iron clad, buttoned, with heavy soles, spring heel, a capital school boot, hard to wear out, sizes
11 to 2...$1.20
8 to 10½.. 0 95
5 to 7½... 0.75

87A. Oil pebble, buttoned, with medium heavy soles, spring heel, great value,
Sizes 11 to 2....$1.00
Sizes 8 to 10½ .. 0.85
Sizes 5 to 7½ .. 0.75

88A. Laced, same as 87A,
Sizes 11 to 2.......$1.00
Sizes 8 to 10½....... 0.85

89A. Little gents' box calfskin, laced, looks like papa's boots, spring heel, sizes 8 to 10½,

$1.20.

90A. Oil pebble grain, little boys' heavy, laced, iron clad, thick soles, hard to wear out, low heel, sizes 8 to 10½,

95c.

91A. Little gents dongola kid, laced, heavy soles and soft uppers, spring heel, sizes 8 to 10,

$1.00.

92A. Best quality Flower City, tan, laced, spring heel, not kept in stock after Aug. 1st, sizes 8 to 10½, $1.50; 5 to 7½ $1.25

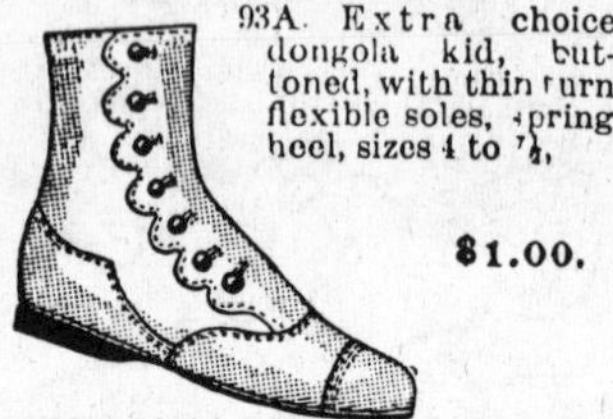

93A. Extra choice dongola kid, buttoned, with thin turn flexible soles, spring heel, sizes 4 to 7½,

$1.00.

94A. Same as 93A, only laced, sizes 4 to 7½.......................$1.00

95A. Fine tan dongola kid, buttoned, same shape as 93A, sizes 4 to 7½, ...$1.15

96A. Same as 95A, only laced, sizes 4 to 7½..........................$1.15

97A. Tan kid, buttoned, with flexible soles, for fat babies, full fitting, spring heel, sizes 3 to 7 .... 85c

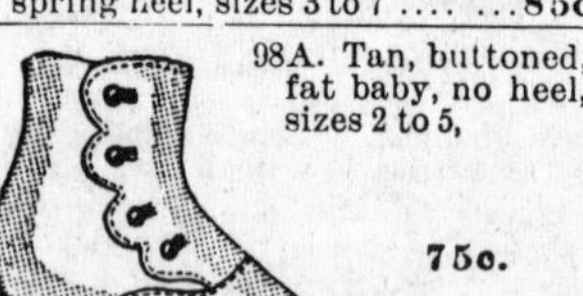

98A. Tan, buttoned, fat baby, no heel, sizes 2 to 5,

75c.

99A. Black dongola kid, buttoned, fat baby style, same shape as cut 97A, spring heel, sizes 3 to 7... 75c.

100A. Fat babies' black kid, buttoned, no heel, sizes 2 to 5............65c

101A. Extra choice American kid, buttoned, with light flexible soles, foot-form shape.
Spring heels, sizes 4 to 8......$1.25
No heels, sizes 2 to 5
$1.00

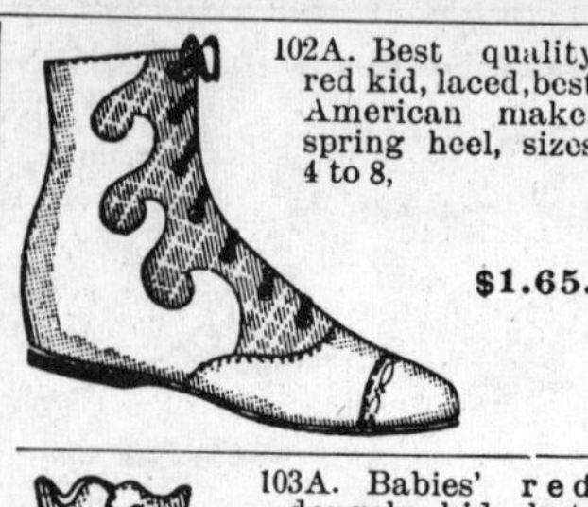

102A. Best quality red kid, laced, best American make, spring heel, sizes 4 to 8,

$1.65.

103A. Babies' red dongola kid, buttoned, with flexible soles, no heels, sizes 2 to 5,

$1.00.

104A. Best selected dongola kid, buttoned, foot-form shape, turn soles, no heels, sizes 2 to 5,

85c.

105A. Same as 104A, in laced, sizes 2 to 5 .... 85c

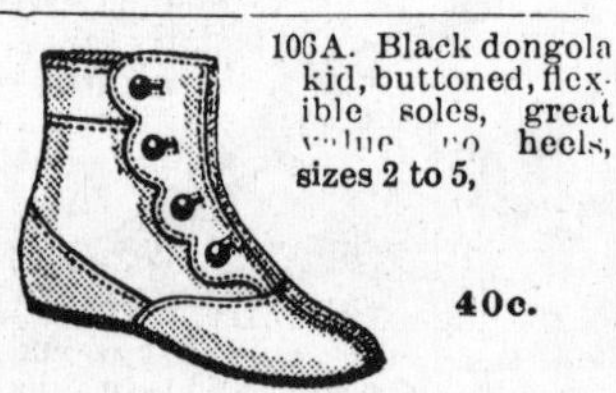

106A. Black dongola kid, buttoned, flexible soles, great value, no heels, sizes 2 to 5,

40c.

107A. Same quality as 106A, only with spring heels, sizes 3 to 7.. 50c

Infants' Soft-Sole Boots and Moccasins.

108A. Black, brown, red, white, pink and blue buttoned, American make, sizes 1 to 4,

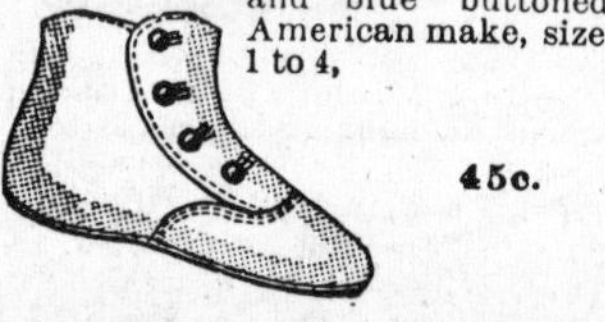

45c.

109A. Brown or black sheepskin, buttoned, low cut, sizes 1 to 4 .... 25c

110A. White, pink, blue and tan colored kid moccasins, sizes 1 to 4 ....20c

Misses' and Children's Oxfords and Slippers

111A.

111A. Babies' dongola kid, ankle strap, turn soles, spring heel, sizes 3 to 7 ....60c

112A. Same as 111A, only without heels, sizes 2 to 5 ....55c

113A. Fine kid, 1-strap sandal, no heel, sizes 2 to 5.... 65c

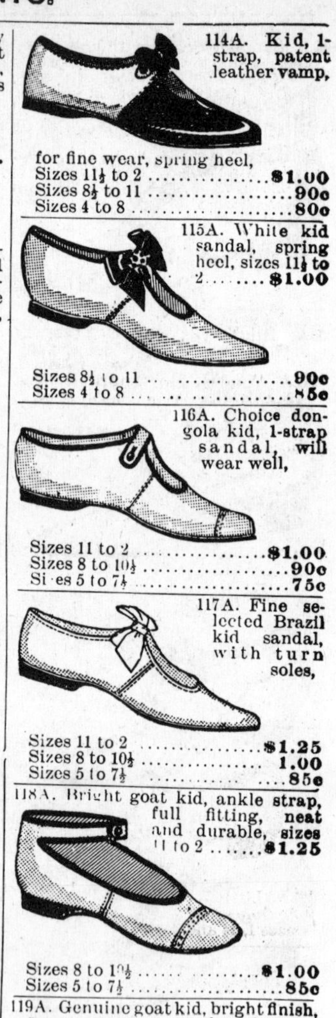

114A. Kid, 1-strap, patent leather vamp, for fine wear, spring heel,
Sizes 11½ to 2 ....$1.00
Sizes 8½ to 11 ....90c
Sizes 4 to 8 ....80c

115A. White kid sandal, spring heel, sizes 11½ to 2......... $1.00
Sizes 8½ to 11 .. ..90c
Sizes 4 to 8 .. ..85c

116A. Choice dongola kid, 1-strap sandal, will wear well,
Sizes 11 to 2 ....$1.00
Sizes 8 to 10½ 90c
Sizes 5 to 7½ 75c

117A. Fine selected Brazil kid sandal, with turn soles,
Sizes 11 to 2 ....$1.25
Sizes 8 to 10½ 1.00
Sizes 5 to 7½ 85c

118A. Bright goat kid, ankle strap, full fitting, neat and durable, sizes 11 to 2 ....$1.25
Sizes 8 to 10½ $1.00
Sizes 5 to 7½ 85c

119A. Genuine goat kid, bright finish, rather heavy soles, 1-strap sandal, sizes 11 to 2,

85c.

Sizes 8 to 10 ....75c
Sizes 5 to 7 ....65c

120A. Tan pebble, Oxford, rather heavy, spring heel, not kept in stock after August 1st, sizes 11 to 2......75c
Sizes 8 to 10 ...... 65c

121A. Bright glazed goatskin, Oxford, with rather heavy soles, spring heel, sizes 11 to 2 ......85c
Sizes 6 to 10½ 75c

122A. Fine selected dongola kid, Oxford, with flexible soles, spring heel, sizes 11 to 2...........$1.00

Our customers in all parts of Canada say our footwear is very reliable.

123A. Best quality selected glazed goat kid, Oxford, with turn soles and spring heels, sizes 11 to 2 $1.25
Sizes 8 to 10½ ... 1.00
Sizes 5 to 7½ ... 85c

124A. Dongola kid, Oxford, same as 123A, only heavier soles, sizes 11 to 2 ... $1.25
Sizes 8 to 10½ ... 1.00
Sizes 5 to 7½ ... 85c

125A. Best imported American tan, Flower City kid, Oxford, turn soles, spring heel, not kept in stock after August 1st, same shape as 123A, sizes 11 to 2 ... $1.50
Sizes 8 to 10½ ... 1.20
Sizes 5 to 7½ ... 1.00

126A. Glazed kid, Oxford, turn soles, with heel, sizes 11 to 2 ... $1.25

127A. Little ladies' fine kid Oxford, flexible soles, kid lined, with heel, sizes 1, 1½ and 2 only ... $1.50

128A. Extra choice black Brazil kid Oxford, kid lining, spring heel, sizes 11 to 2 ... $1.50

Men's Boots.

129A. Patent velour calf, laced, with Goodyear welt, the Packard boot. We do not warrant patent leather, but do warrant this leather the best quality, sizes 5 to 11 ... $4.50

130A. Same quality as 129A, only buttoned, very swell, sizes 5 to 10,

$4.50.

131A. "Bobs" genuine patent calfskin, Goodyear welted, up to date. We don't warrant patent leather not to crack, but we guarantee this boot made by the John McPherson Co., as first-class quality, C, D and E widths, sizes 5 to 10½,

$3.75.

132A. Box calfskin leather lined, Goodyear welted soles, the Packard boot, best American make, D and E widths, sizes 5 to 11 ... $3.75

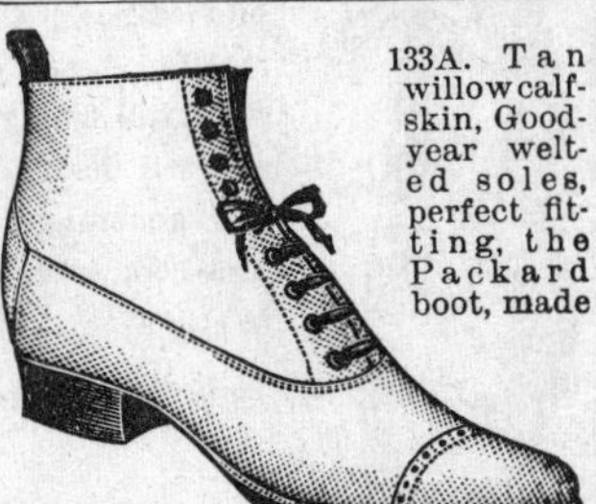

133A. Tan willow calfskin, Goodyear welted soles, perfect fitting, the Packard boot, made by skilled workmen, equal to any $5.00 boot, sizes 5 to 11, D and E widths ... $3.75

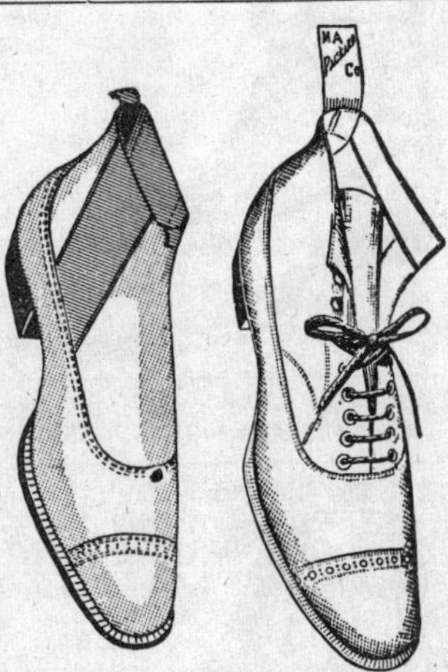

134A. 135A.

134A. Vici kid Congress welted soles, the Packard boot, natural shape, E width, sizes 6 to 11 ... $3.50

135A. Packard box calfskin, laced, with medium weight soles, Goodyear welted, D and E widths, sizes 6 to 11 ... $3.50

136A. Choice black vici kid, laced, medium weight Goodyear welted, Essex toe. The Packard boot, great value at $5.00, sizes 5 to 11, D and E widths, our price, ... $3.50

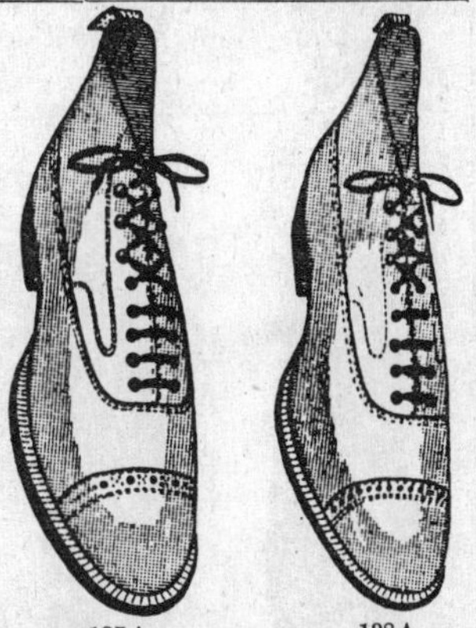

137A. 138A.

Four leaders, made by the John McPherson Co., and warranted to give good satisfaction.

137A. "Patrol," heavy weight, box calfskin, with thick extension soles, a capital walking boot, Goodyear welted soles, sizes 6 to 12 ... $3.50

138A. Genuine box calfskin, "Bobs" shape, very popular, with medium weight sole, C, D and E widths, sizes 5½ to 11 ... $3.00

139A.

139A. Fine selected glazed dongola kid, neat shape, the young man's favorite, genuine Goodyear welts, C, D and E widths, sizes 5½ to 11 .. $3.00

140A. Same as 139A, only with elastic sides, C, D and E widths, sizes 5½ to 11 ... $3.00

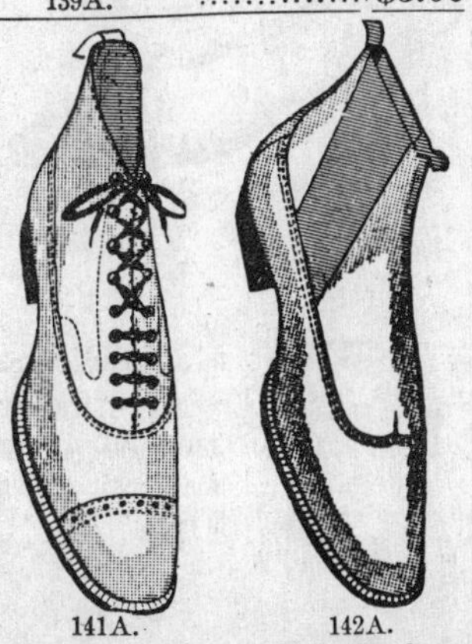

141A. 142A.

141A. Tan willow calfskin, Goodyear welted soles, not kept in stock later than August 1st, sizes 6 to 10 ... $3.00

142A. Genuine glazed Australian kangaroo, Goodyear welted soles, for description see page 83, sizes 6 to 11 ... $3.00

143A. 144A.

143A. Same quality as 142A, only laced, sizes 6 to 11 ... $3.00

144A. Glazed kangaroo, laced, bulldog shape, fine Goodyear welted sole, perfect fitting, see page 83, for particulars, sizes 6 to 11. $3.00

145A. 146A.

145A. Genuine kangaroo laced, Goodyear welted soles, medium toe, very easy for the feet, sizes 6 to 11 ... $3.00

146A. Box calfskin, laced, with welted extension soles, great value, sizes 6 to 11 ... $2.50

147A. Same as 146A, only elastic sides, sizes 6 to 10 ... $2.50

148A.

148A. Black glazed kid, laced, with Goodyear welted soles, just as neat as it looks, sizes 6 to 10,

$2.50.

149A. Tan dongola kid, same style as 148A, only not kept in stock after August 1st,

$2.50.

OUR FOOTWEAR LOOKS WELL, WEARS WELL, AND FITS WELL.

150A. Light weight dongola kid, with turn flexible soles, sizes 6 to 10, **$2.50.**

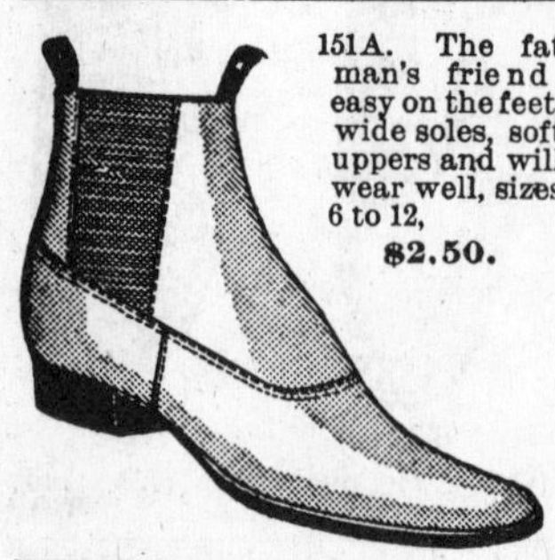

151A. The fat man's friend, easy on the feet, wide soles, soft uppers and will wear well, sizes 6 to 12, **$2.50.**

152A. English kip miners' or farmers' reliable working boot, dust-proof, full-fitting and durable, sizes 6 to 11, **$2.50.**

153A. Klondike, superior quality heavyweight kip, with sole leather, counter soles and heel, covered with large nails, sizes 6 to 11, **$3.75.**

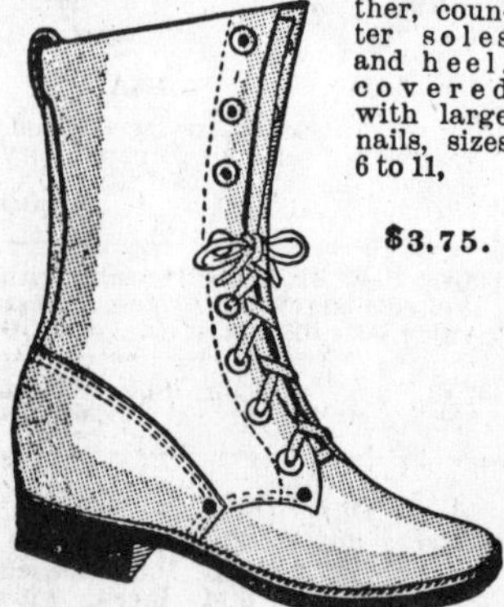

154A. The digger's delight, whole stock, heavy soles, hard to wear out, sizes 6 to 11, **$2.00.**

155A. The "Walk Easy" boot, very popular, with cork inner-sole, cool in summer, easy on tender feet, made from box calfskin, McKay sewn soles. The great demand for this boot enables us to sell it this season, in sizes 6 to 11, for **$2.00**

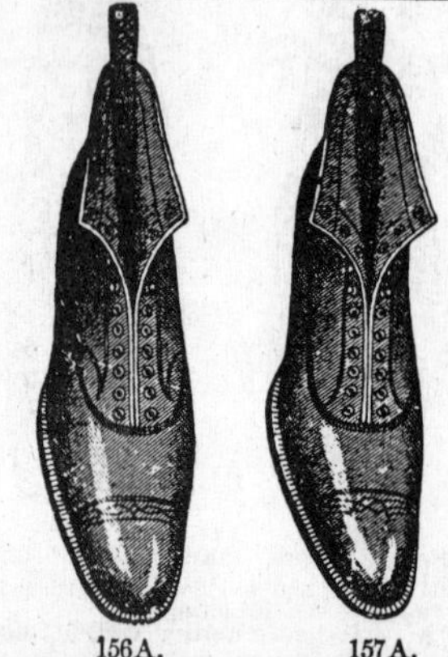

156A. 157A.

156A. Same as 155A, only not quite so full fitting, sizes 6 to 11 **$2.00**

157A. Tan dongola kid, "Walk Easy," medium toe, not kept in stock later than August 1st, sizes 6 to 11 .... **$2.00**

158A. Same as 157A, only black glazed goatskin, "Walk Easy," sizes 6 to 11 .... **$2.00**

159A. Black dongola kid, "Walk Easy," elastic side boot, full fitting, sizes 6 to 11 .... **$2.00**

160A. Solid comfort, wide soles, low heels, made from glazed goatskin, soft and durable, sizes 6 to 11, **$2.00.**

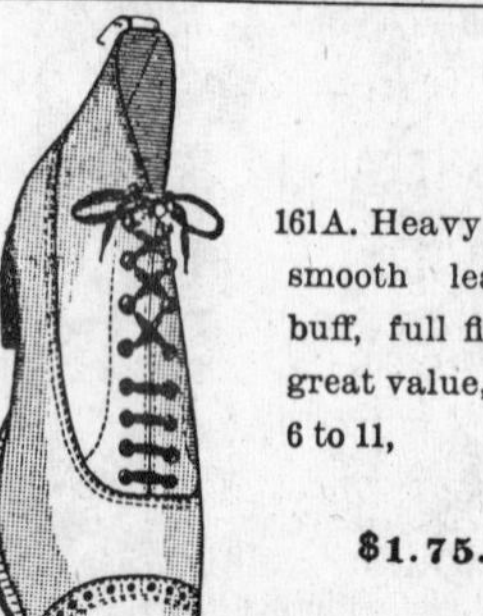

161A. Heavy black smooth leather, buff, full fitting, great value, sizes 6 to 11, **$1.75.**

162A. Iron clad, extra heavy thick soles, dirt proof, bellows tongue, sizes 6 to 11, **$1.75.**

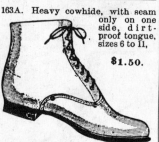

163A. Heavy cowhide, with seam only on one side, dirt-proof tongue, sizes 6 to 11, **$1.50.**

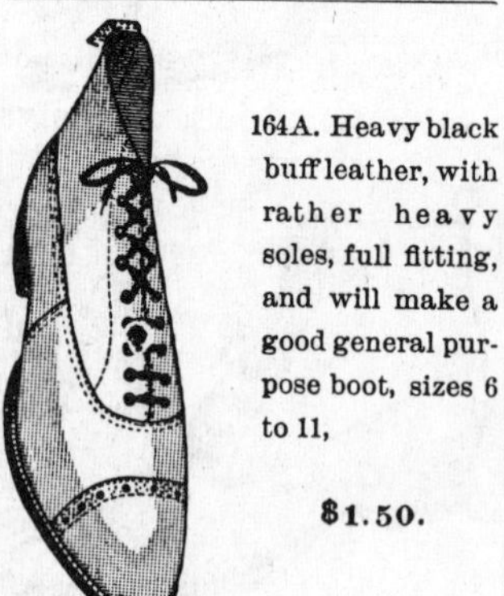

164A. Heavy black buff leather, with rather heavy soles, full fitting, and will make a good general purpose boot, sizes 6 to 11, **$1.50.**

165A. Our "Leader," black buff, with rather heavy soles, full toe, beat it if you can, sizes 6 to 11, **$1.25.**

166A. Same as 165A, only with elastic sides, sizes 6 to 11 .... **$1.25**

167A. The "Working Man's" favorite, dirt proof, easy fitting and durable, sizes 6 to 11, **$1.25.**

168A. "Surprise." We are surprised ourselves that we can sell this neat, durable, medium weight boot, in sizes 6 to 11, for **$1.00**

196A. Heavy every-day boot, wide, well made and excellent value, sizes 6 to 11, **90c.**

Men's Long Boots.

Sizes 6 to 11.

Our long boots are noted for wear and value.

170A. Best quality, extra choice grain kip, full fitting, best value made in a first-class boot, sizes 6 to 11, **$3.20.**

171A. Men's No. 1 grain, military style, long boot, seam up the back, regulation style, sizes 6 to 11. **$3.00**

172A. Men's heavy cowhide long boot, for rough work, sizes 6 to 11 **$2.50**

173A. Men's French calfskin riding boot. The Captain's style, medium weight, sizes 6 to 11 .... **$3.75**

Men's Oxfords.

174A. Black buff, smooth finished, rather heavy sewed soles, sizes 6 to 11; not in stock till May 1st or later than August 1st, **$1.00.**

175A. Genuine goat kid, bright finish, soft and durable, medium heavy sole, not in stock till May 1st, and not later than August 1st, sizes 6 to 11, **$1.25.**

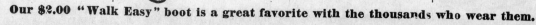

Our $2.00 "Walk Easy" boot is a great favorite with the thousands who wear them.

176A. Extra choice glazed dongola kid, with turn flexible sole, a great seller, always in stock, sizes 6 to 10, **$1.50.**

177A. Our leader, jet black bright goat kid, with extension soles. Not kept in stock till May 1st or later than August 1st, sizes 6 to 11, **$1.50.**

Men's Slippers.

Sizes 6 to 11.

178A. Best quality, fancy repp, upper imported from Germany, will give excellent wear, nothing to equal for comfort and service, plain, 85c.

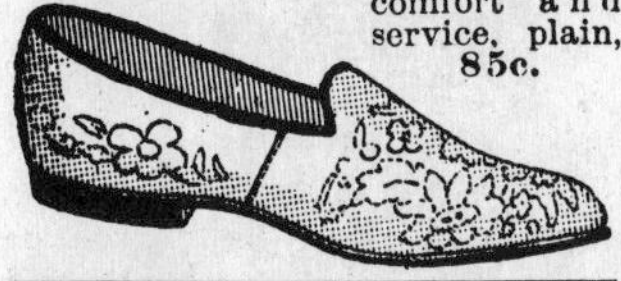

179A. Same quality as 178A, only foxed with leather, a great favorite, **$1 00.**

180A. Fancy leather, imitation of pigskin, neat and comfortable, **$1.00.**

181A. Calf, finegrain, medium heavy, splendid value and a great favorite, **$1.25.**

182A. American Dongola kid, very popular and a great wearer **$1.50**

183A. Superior quality of genuine black Brazil kid, made specially for our trade, with flexible soles ..**$2.00**

184A. Same quality as 183A, in tan kid............................**$2.00**

185A. Boys' pebble calf, with turn flexible soles, leather lined, hard to wear out, sizes 1 to 5............ **$1.20**
Sizes 11 to 13........ **$1.00**

186A. Boy's bright goat kid Oxford, with medium heavy soles. Not kept in stock till May 1st, and not later than Aug. 1st, sizes 1 to 5.... **$1.00**
Sizes 11 to 13, **90c.**

187A. Boys' choice Dongola kid, (genuine goatskin), light weight, flexible soles, suitable for home or street wear, sizes 1 to 5......**$1.50**
Sizes 11 to 13, **$1.35.**

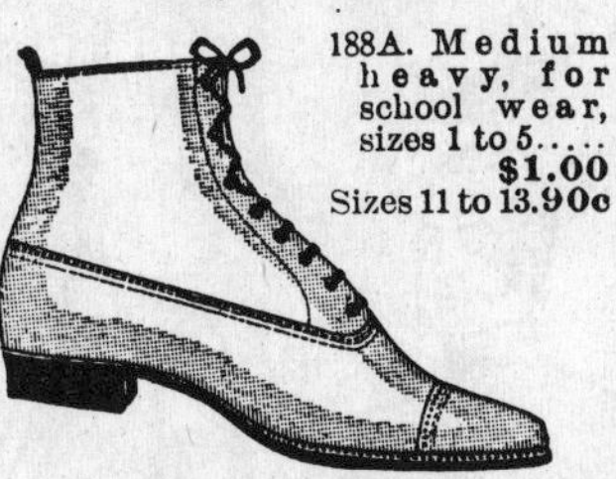

Boys' Boots.

188A. Medium heavy, for school wear, sizes 1 to 5..... **$1.00**
Sizes 11 to 13. **90c**

189A. The favorite black buff, rather heavy and neat, sizes 1 to 5........**$1.25**
Sizes 11 to 13, **$1.15.**

190A. Black buff, with goat kid top, neat, and medium heavy, sizes 1 to 5.....**$1.50**
Sizes 11 to 13, **$1.25.**

191A. Same shape as 190A, only light weight, made from Dongola kid, sizes 1 to 5........................**$1.75**
Sizes 11 to 13.................. **1.50**

192A. The old reliable boys' school boot, neat and heavy, with thick soles, sizes 1 to 5........**$1.50**
Sizes 11 to 13, **$1.25.**

193A. Box calfskin, for best wear, "Walk Easy" shape, sewed soles, Sizes 1 to 5½, **$2.00**
Sizes 11 to 13½, **$1.75**

Sporting Boots and Tennis Shoes.

194A. Men's black pebble grain bicycle boots, sewed soles, not kept in stock till April 15th, and not later than August 1st, sizes 6 to 10, **$1.20**

195A. Tan, pebble grain, same shape as 194A, not in stock till April 15th, and not after August 1st, sizes 6 to 10 ....**$1.35**

196A. Men's brown canvas tennis or lacrosse boots, laced, with rubber soles, sizes 6 to 10..........**95c**
Boys', sizes 1 to 5 ....**85c**

197A. Men's blue or black canvas lacrosse shoes, with rubber soles, sizes 6 to 11 ....**60c**
Boys', sizes 1 to 5 ....**50c**
Youths', sizes 11 to 13 ..**45c**
Children's, sizes 7 to 10....**40c**

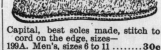

198A. Ladies' black tennis shoes, same style as 197A, only in fine black canvas, sizes 3 to 7 ....**70c**

Rubber Footwear.

We keep the best. For complete list see our Fall Catalogue, No. 45.

Lambs' Wool Soles for Bedroom Slippers.

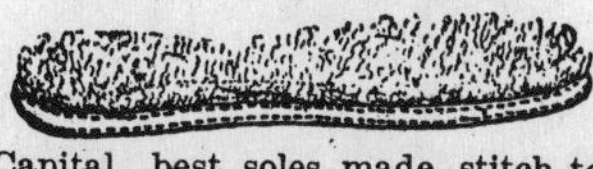

Capital, best soles made, stitch to cord on the edge, sizes—

199A. Men's, sizes 6 to 11 ....**30c**
200A. Ladies', sizes 3 to 7........**20c**
201A. Misses', sizes 11 to 2 ......**20c**
202A. Children's, sizes 2 to 10....**15c**

203A. Cork innersoles, for inside of boots, men's, sizes 6 to 11........**8c**
204A. Ladies', sizes 3 to 7..........**7c**

Neverbreak
TRADE MARK

Shoe laces, finest and best made in the world—

205A. Men's, black, one yard long, ... **2 pairs 5c**
206A. Men's, tan ....**2 pairs 5c**
207A. Ladies', black, 1½ yard long .... **2 pairs 5c**
208A. Ladies', tan, 1½ yard long .... **2 pairs 5c**

209A. Black or tan low-shoe lace, 27 inches long............**3 pairs 5c**

210A. Men's or boys' round leather laces .... **3 pairs 5c**

211A. "Hercules," porpoise, very strong, per pair **7½c**
212A. "Samson," best leather, 36 inches long, per pair **5c**

Sundries.

213A. Button hooks ....**6 for 5c**
214A. Shoe horns, each....... .....**5c**
215A. Black shoe buttons, per doz. **1c**
216A. Half-circle heel plates **2 pairs for** **5c**
217A. Perfumed powder for sweating feet, gives comfort and ease, per package.....................**10c**

Shoe Dressings.

218A. 219A.

218A. Bootlene, for ladies' and children's boots, apply with sponge attached to cork, self shine, best value in Canada, large size bottle **10c**

219A. "Bootlene" combination box of paste and bottle of cleaner, for ladies' and gent's kid, box calf, or patent leather boots, keeps the leather soft, rub to a shine with cloth, our special, black or tan. **10c**

220A. Paste blacking, for men's and boys' boots, shine with brush. This blacking lasts longer and puts a better shine on than any cheap large size boxes, besides preserving the finest leather; try it once and you will use no other..**5c**

221A. Bootlene paste, for ladies' or gent's kid, box calf, or patent leather boots, shine with cloth, same as used with combination, black or tan, state which you prefer, per box. **5c**

Our Shoes are made upon honor and sold upon merit. Try a pair.

Spring and Summer Styles for 1901

THE CLOTH IS ALL THOROUGHLY SHRUNK BEFORE BEING MADE UP.

MEN'S SUITS.

The Linings and Trimmings in our Men's Suits are all of good serviceable materials, and are equal to quality of cloth used.

Men's Single-Breasted Sacque Suits.

36 to 44 inches chest measurement.

As Cut No. 1.

1. Navy blue English serge, lined with Italian cloth.........**3.50**

2. Light and dark brown checked tweed suits, light grey pin check and dark grey with small checked pattern, also navy blue serge suits..............**5.00**

3. Brown, with green tinge and red thread overplaid, all-wool Canadian tweed suit, also small checked pattern, grey and black, well trimmed and finished......................**6.50**

4. All-wool, stylish homespun suits, in light fawn and light or dark grey shades, neatly made..............**7.50**

5. Oxford grey and dark grey with green overplaid, also light grey with green tinge and red thread overplaid, well made and trimmed................**7.50**

6. All-wool stylish tweed suits, light grey check and light brown check with red overplaid, dark brown small check with green tinge, also medium grey small check..................**8.50**

As Cut No. 7.

7. Black and navy blue imported worsted serge, hard finish.**7.50**

8. Imported all-wool black and navy blue, and mid-grey Clay twilled worsted, also navy blue and black worsted serge, silk stitched edges, well tailored and finished..........**10.00**

9. Medium grey with light grey stripes, also dark grey with light grey small check pattern, very stylish..........**10.00**

10. Stylish all-wool suits, made from Oxford grey cheviot-finished tweed, brown and green mixed tweed with red and blue overplaid, also dark grey with light grey small check, worsted-finished tweed..........**10.00**

11. Imported colored worsted suits, black ground with blue and blue-grey ground with black pin check, also small pattern mixed pepper-and-salt color..................**12.50**

12. Worsted-finished tweed suits, Oxford grey, small check patterns, also brown with green tinge with blue and red thread overplaid, fine imported goods best make and finish....**12.50**

13. All-wool imported black and navy blue Clay diagonal worsted suits, also black Venetian-finished worsted, Italian cloth linings, deep French facings, silk-stitched edges......**12.50**

14. Colored worsted suits, made from all-wool imported goods, black and dark blue small check with red thread overplaid, black and grey with green thread overplaid, also Oxford and blue grey, small basket-pattern worsteds, highly tailored..............**15.00**

15. Fine soft finish black vicuna cloth, black Venetian-finished worsted, also black and navy blue Clay diagonal worsted suits, imported all-wool goods, made with deep French facings, perfect make and fit....**15.00**

16. Imported colored worsted suits, black ground with pin check of dark grey, lined with silk serge, also black vicuna cloth, rich soft finish, lined with Skinner's celebrated black satin.................**18.00**

17. West of England Oxford grey cheviot, pure all-wool soft finish material, made with deep French facings, silk serge linings, silk stitched edges, best workmanship..........**20.00**

Single-Breasted Sacque Suits with Double-Breasted Vest.

36 to 44 inches chest measurement.

As Cut No. 18.

18. All-wool tweed, mid-grey with black and red thread overplaid, very stylish..........**7 50**

19. Nobby tweed suits, dark fawn with light brown and red overplaid, greyish green with overplaid of green, grey and green small check with red overplaid, well made and finished..................**8.50**

20. English tweed suits, made from all-wool Oxford grey cheviot, small check, dark grey, worsted-finished tweed, and dark and mid-grey checked tweeds, French facings..**10.00**

21. Worsted-finished tweed suits, black ground, with small dark grey check, also brown with green tinge with red and blue thread overplaid, all-wool imported material, well tailored.........................**12.50**

22. Stylish worsted suit, made of very narrow stripe, black and mid-grey with green tinge, imported West of England goods, silk-stitched edges, very fashionable............**12.50**

Men's Double-Breasted Sacque Suits.

36 to 44 inches chest measurement.

As Cut No. 23.

23. Dark brown and black with red overplaid, serviceable tweed suits, also all-wool blue serge, made neatly..............**5.00**

24. Dark brown, small check with red thread overplaid, also dark grey very small check, fine all-wool tweed suits....**8.50**

As Cut No. 25.

25. Navy blue and black imported worsted serge suits, hard finish, stitched edges....**7.50**

26. Black and navy blue Clay diagonal, also navy blue and black, hard finish worsted serge suits, deep French facings, stitched edges..........**10.00**

27. Uniform Suits, made from imported navy blue hard finish worsted serge, fast indigo dye, cut in 4-button sacque style, eyelet holes for detachable buttons................**10.00**

28. Imported West of England all wool navy blue and black Clay diagonal suits, deep French facings, well tailored and finished.................**12.50**

29. Uniform suits of navy blue beaver cloth, all-wool, indigo dye, imported goods, 4-button sacque style, eyelet holes for detachable buttons, stitched edges..................**15.00**

Men's 3-Button Cutaway or Morning Suits.

34 to 44 inches chest measurement.

As Cut No. 30.

30. Imported black hard finish worsted serge, in 3-button cutaway style, stitched edges.**7.50**

31. West of England all-wool black and mid-grey Clay diagonal worsted suits, deep French facings, silk-stitched edges.....................**10.00**

32. Black vicuna cloth, soft finish, also black Venetian finished worsted and black Clay diagonal worsted, French facings, well tailored......**12.50**

33. Extra choice fine imported black Clay diagonal, black Venetian finished worsted, also soft finish black vicuna cloth, deep French facings, silk-stitched edges..................**15.00**

34. West of England fine wool soft finish black vicuna cloth, lined with Skinner's celebrated satin, deep French facings, highly tailored and finished, perfect in fit..........**20.00**

Full-Dress, Prince Albert and Clerical Suits.

35 to 44 inches chest measurement.

As Cut No. 35.

35. Gent's full dress suits, made from imported black Venetian finished worsted, lined with black satin, edges silk stitched, best finish............**19.00**

As Cut No. 36.

36. Prince Albert suit, all-wool West of England Venetian finished worsted, with or without silk-faced lapels, edges silk-stitched of bound with narrow silk mohair braid, latest style and best workmanship..**19.00**

As Cut No. 37.

37. Clerical suits, made from imported black Venetian-finished worsted, silk-stitched edges......................**18.00**

As Cut No. 38.

38. Tuxedo suits, West of England worsted, Venetian finish, silk-faced collar and roll, edges finished with silk stitching......................**12.50**

Men's Coats and Vests only, Lined.

34 to 44 inches chest measurement.

39. Light and dark Canadian tweeds, and navy blue serge (coat and vest only), single or double-breasted sacque style......................**4.00**

40. Brown and medium or dark grey all-wool tweeds (coat and vest only), single-breasted sacque shape..........**5.00**

41. Navy blue and black serge (coat and vest only), single or double-breasted sacque...**6.00**

42. Single or double-breasted sacque (coat and vest only), in dark and mid-grey and light or dark brown tweeds ..**6.50**

43. All-wool medium and dark grey or brown tweeds and hard finish serges, in single or double-breasted style, coat and vest......................**8.00**

44. Single or double-breasted sacque or 3-button cutaway, in black Clay worsted, silk-stitched edges, coat and vest only......................**8.00**

45. Colored worsted and worsted-finished tweeds, in Oxford grey, plain and check patterns, also brown and grey tweeds, in checks and overplaids, coat and vest, in single-breasted sacque style..................**10.00**

46. Black Clay worsted and black Venetian-finished worsted (coat and vest only), in single-breasted sacque and 3-button cutaway style..................**10.00**

47. Black worsted, in Clay diagonal or Venetian finish, single-breasted sacque or 3-button cutaway style, coat and vest only......................**12.00**

48. Full dress and Prince Albert (coat and vest only), black worsted, Venetian finish.**16.00**

Men's Suits and Overcoats larger than 44 inches chest measurement will cost 50 cents for every additional inch.

All This Season's Productions

WE KEEP ONLY STYLISH WELL-MADE CLOTHING.

Men's Spring Overcoats, Waterproof Coats, Dressing Gowns and House Jackets.

Men's Spring Overcoats.

34 to 44 inches chest measurement.

As Cut No. 49.

49. Oxford grey overcoating, made in single-breasted fly-front style, 39 inches long, self collar **5.00**

50. Mid-grey and black Clay twilled worsted, Chesterfield style, self collar **8.00**

51. Oxford grey cheviot, the fashionable color and style of goods for spring, self collar, made 39 inches in length, silk-faced lapels **8.00**

As Cut No. 52.

52. Box-back overcoat, 35 inches long, made from mid-grey overcoating, self collar **5.00**

53. Fawn covert cloth overcoat, cut in loose box-back style, self collar **8.50**

54. Oxford grey cheviot overcoat, very stylish and fashionable goods, loose box back, 35 inches long, self collar, silk-faced lapels **10.00**

55. Fawn whipcord overcoat, loose box back, self collar, deep French facings **10.00**

56. Black vicuna cloth, rich soft finish, imported goods, cut in box-back style, 35 inches long, self collar, silk-faced lapels **10.00**

57. Box-back overcoats, made from all-wool imported blue-grey cheviot, rich soft finish material, cut 35 inches long, self collar, silk faced ... **12 50**

58. Black and Oxford grey all-wool imported cheviot overcoats, cut in the fashionable box-back style, lined throughout with black satin, self collar.................. **15.00**

59. Box-back overcoat, cut in the latest style and highly tailored, made from West of England, Oxford grey and black cheviot, sleeves and body lined with Skinner's black satin (will not cut) **20.00**

As Cut No. 60.

60. Oxford grey cheviot overcoat, cut 35 inches long, in box-back shape, velvet collar.. **8.00**

61. Priestley's celebrated waterproof covert cloth, made in spring overcoats, box-back style, dark fawn and Oxford grey, Italian linings, velvet collar **12.50**

Waterproof Coats.

36 to 46 inches chest measurement.

As Cut No. 62.

62. Black paramatta cloth waterproof, 24-inch detachable cape, sewn seams **5.00**

63. Black paramatta waterproof coat, with 27 inch detachable cape, rubber-faced bottoms, silk sewn edges and seams ... **8.00**

64. Mid-grey checked tweed, with light brown overplaid, 27-inch detachable fly-front cape, checked linings, sewn seams **8.00**

65. All-wool black paramatta cloth waterproof coat, with sleeves and 30-inch detachable cape, silk-stitched seams and edges, rubber-faced bottoms **10.00**

As Cut No. 66.

66. Inverness waterproof coats, made of black paramatta cloth, 30-inch attached cape, velvet collar, seams and edges silk stitched **10.00**

Paddock Waterproof Coats.

As Cut No. 67.

67. Paddock waterproofs in Oxford grey and dark fawn covert cloth, velvet collar, checked linings, sewn seams......... **5.00**

68. Dark fawn and dark navy blue covert cloth, with checked linings, velvet collar, sewn seams, bottoms faced with rubber **8.00**

69. Imported English covert cloth, in fawn and Oxford grey, single-breasted, with new Raglan shoulder, checked linings, velvet collar, bottoms faced with rubber, sewn seams **10.00**

70. Dark fawn and Oxford grey covert cloth, with checked back; this cloth contains no rubber, but is rendered waterproof by a chemical process; plain shoulders, slash pocket with welt, cuff on sleeve, shoulders and sleeves lined with silk, self collar.............. **12.50**

71. Oxford grey and dark fawn imported covert cloth, checked linings, silk-stitched seams and edges, shoulders and sleeves lined with heavy striped satin, rubber-faced bottoms ... **12.50**

As Cut No. 72.

72. Dark fawn and Oxford grey covert cloth, with checked linings, sewn seams, velvet collar **5.00**

73. Dark grey imported covert cloth, with velvet collar, checked linings, sewn seams, stitched edges **8.00**

74. Raglan style shoulder waterproof coat, double-breasted, light fawn covert cloth, checked linings, velvet collar, silk sewn.................. **10.00**

75. Navy blue and light fawn imported soft Venetian cloth, large buttons, checked linings, velvet collar, silk stitched throughout........... **15.00**

As Cut No. 76.

76. Oxford grey and dark fawn waterproof, covert cloth (without rubber), odorless, Raglan shoulder and pockets, cuff on sleeve, silk-lined shoulders and sleeves, full loose body.. **15.00**

Boys' Cape and Paddock Waterproof Coats.

As Cut No. 77.

77. Blue-black and dark grey paramatta cloth coats, without sleeves, cape attached, sewn seams—

Sizes	26,	28,	30,	32,
	3.50,	**4.00,**	**4.50,**	**4.50.**

As Cut No. 78.

78. Mid-grey and dark fawn covert cloth, checked lining, velvet collar, sewn seams—

Sizes	26,	28,	30,	32,
	3.50,	**4.00,**	**4.50,**	**4.50.**

Boys', Youths', and Men's Dull-finished Rubber Coats and Bicycle Capes.

80. Black rubber coats, dull finished, to fit boys from 4 to 15 years **1.50**

81. Men's dull-finished rubber coats, double breasted, tab to button across throat, 36 to 42-inch chest, $1.50; 44-inch chest **1.90**

82. Heavy weight, dull-finished rubber coats, with snap and ring fasteners, 34 to 44-inch chest **2.50**

83. Extra heavy black dull finish waterproof coats, double sheeting, same on either side, ring and snap fasteners, tab for throat, 36 to 44-inch chest. **4.00**

House Jackets.

34 to 44 inches chest measurement.

As Cut No. 85.

85. Men's house coats, soft eiderdown, with self-checked back, light weight, navy blue ground with overplaid of grey, green and heliotrope check with navy overplaid, green and navy check with blue overplaid, cord edges to match, 34 to 46 inches.. **7.50**

86. Fine blue-grey Venetian cloth house coats, collar inlaid with satin, cuffs satin finished, also small shepherd's plaid pattern, fawn and grey, self-checked lining, cord edges, 34 to 42 inches.................. **8.50**

Men's Dressing Gowns.

As Cut No. 87.

87. Royal blue and black check with black thread overplaid, also crimson and black, worsted finish, edges, cuffs and pockets bound with fancy mohair braid 1 inch wide, silk and wool girdle to match **8.50**

88. Dressing gowns of soft eiderdown, green or navy blue ground with fawn check and large overplaid of grey, also grey with black overplaid, cord edges, girdle to match.. **10.00**

89. Rich stylish eiderdown dressing gown, black ground with large check and overplaid of dark and light grey, cord edges, frog fasteners.... **12.50**

Measurement for Overcoat or Waterproof should be taken around chest, under arms, over the vest.

Our prices are always the lowest at which "Honest Goods" can be made.

Men's Trousers, Bicycle and Summer Clothing.

Men's Bicycle Suits. Coat and Pants Only.

34 to 44 inches chest measurement.

As Cut No. 90

90. Canadian tweed medium dark bicycle suits, double-seated, strap and buckle............3.50

91. Black and grey shepherd's plaid, strap and buckle..............4.50

92. Green and fawn shepherd's plaid, red thread overplaid, self extension cuffs..........................4.50

93. Black and grey tweed, small check, blue thread overplaid; fawn and grey check with green thread overplaid, self extension cuffs .5.00

94. Blue Clay diagonal worsted, self extension cuffs................5.00

95. Dark fawn tweed, red overplaid, light grey, small check, fawn thread overplaid, self extension cuffs..........................6.50

As Cut No. 96.

96. Dark fawn homespun tweed, Norfolk style, extension cuffs..6.50

Men's Bicycle Knee Pants.

29 to 44 inches waist measurement.

As Cut No. 97.

All have double seats and straps on for belt, side and hip pockets.

97. Grey and blue or green and black checked tweed.................1.00

98. Navy blue Clay diagonal worsted, also small grey and black shepherd's check tweed...........2.00

As Cut No. 99.

99. Black and grey shepherd's plaid Canadian tweed................1.50

100. All-wool Canadian tweed, large shepherd's check, grey ground, light blue and black check and large overplaid of green.......2.00

101. Dark fawn tweed, all wool, small check, large red overplaid 2.50

102. Shepherd's plaid pattern, all-wool tweed, in light grey ground, light green check..............3.50

As Cut No. 103.

103. Green and fawn shepherd's plaid Canadian tweed, red thread overplaid...........................1.50

104. Large shepherd's plaid pattern, all-wool Canadian tweed, black and grey check, also light brown and grey check with overplaid of green..........................2.00

105. All-wool tweed, in neat shepherd's check, grey ground, black check.............................3.50

106. Neat hard worsted finished tweed bicycle pants, in small black and grey check with large over-check of black.................4.00

Boys' Bicycle Suits.

As Cut No. 107.

107. Brown and fawn shepherd's plaid tweed bicycle suit, strap and buckle at knee—

27, 28,	29,	30, 31,	32, 33,
2.75.	**3.00.**	**3.25.**	**3.50.**

108. Boys' bicycle suits, dark brown and green small check tweed, red thread over plaid, with strap and buckle—

27, 28,	29,	30, 31,	32,	33,
3.00.	**3.25.**	**3.50.**	**3.75.**	**4.00.**

109. Blue-grey and black check, red thread overplaid, all-wool tweed suits, extension knee pants—

27, 28,	29,	30,	31,	32, 33,
3.50.	**3.75.**	**4.00.**	**4.25.**	**4.50.**

Men's Tennis Suits, Coat and Pants Only.

34 to 44 inches chest measurement.

As Cut No. 110.

110. Light grey or dark fawn plain homespun tweed tennis suits, coat half lined..........................5.00

111. Tennis suit, black ground, narrow grey stripe 5.00

112. Cricket or tennis suit, imported white flannel (London shrunk) 5.00

113. Tennis suit, with vest, coat single breasted, patch pockets, 6.50

114. Single-breasted sacque tennis suit, vest without collar, black ground with blue-grey stripe..7.50

115. White serge cricket suits, soap shrunk 7.50

116. Blue with light grey stripe and black with dark grey stripe, flannel-finished tweed, tennis suit, with vest 10.00

117. White duck pants, size 30 to 44, 75c and 1.00

As Cut No. 118.

118. Tennis suit (coat and pants only), cream with narrow grey stripe, also dark grey with green tint and narrow blue stripe ...5.00

119. Light and dark grey with grey stripe, also mid-grey with green tint and narrow green stripe (coat and pants only)............6.50

120. Dark grey all-wool tweed suit, flannel finish, with narrow grey stripe 10.00

121. Norfolk style coat and pants, mid-grey and light fawn all-wool homespun tweeds, coat lined (as cut No. 96, only long pants)....7.50

Men's Unlined Summer Coats.

34 to 46 inches chest measurement.

122. White drill coats, single-breasted sacque, patch pockets, round or square corners 75c

123. White duck coats, single breasted, square or round corners, patch pockets..........................1.00

124. Black lustre coats, sacque, single breasted 1.00

125. Grey lustre coats...............1.25

126. Blue serge, also grey or black lustre coats, single breasted ..1.50

127. Black Russell cord coats, single-breasted sacque 1.75

128. Black Russell cord coats, sacque-single breasted 2.50

129. Imported navy blue Clay worsted skeleton coats, single-breasted sacque..........................4.00

130. Double-breasted sacque of navy blue Clay worsted, shoulders and sleeves lined 5.00

131. Clerical coats of black Russell cord, square corners...........3.00

Men's Unlined Coats and Vests.

34 to 46 inches chest measurement.

132. Black, mid-grey and navy blue, light weight Clay worsted (coats and vests only), single-breasted sacque..........................5.00

133. Fawn drill shop coat 1.50

134. Long linen duster...........1.75

135. Silver grey lustre, long driving duster 3.00

Boys' and Youths' Summer Coats.

136. Navy blue serge unlined coats—

26, 27, 28.	29, 30,	31, 32, 33,
90c.	**1.00.**	**1.25.**

137. Boys' black lustre coats—

26, 27, 28,	29, 30, 31, 32, 33,
90c.	**1.00.**

138. Grey lustre coats for boys—

26, 27, 28,	29, 30, 31, 32, 33,
1.00.	**1.25.**

139. Navy blue serge unlined coats, edges, pockets, and cuffs trimmed with cream or sky blue cord—

24, 25, 26,	27, 28,	29, 30,	31, 32, 33, 34,
1.25.	**1.50.**	**1.75.**	**2.00.**

140. English all-wool flannel blazers, in red and black, or blue and white stripe—

24, 25, 26,	28, 29, 30,	32, 33, 34,
1.50.	**1.75.**	**2.00.**

Men's Trousers.

31 to 44 inches waist measurement.

As Cut No. 141.

141. Medium and dark grey narrow striped Canadian tweed.......1.00

142. Brown, dark and medium grey striped tweed 1.25

143. Canadian tweed, dark and medium grey stripes............1.50

144. Neat assorted striped worsted, medium and dark colors.......2.00

145. Blue grey, and dark grey, narrow stripes, medium and dark hairline striped tweed...........2.00

146. Striped worsted, light, medium, and dark colors 2.50

147. Narrow striped dark worsted, neat patterns......................3.00

148. Black Clay diagonal and navy blue worsted serge. imported, all wool 3.00

149. Imported worsted, narrow and medium width stripes, dark and medium shades....................3.50

150. Imported black Venetian finished worsted.......... . . 3.50

151. West of England black worsted Venetian, all wool.............4.00

152. Very choice stock of imported all-wool worsted, light, medium, and dark shades, narrow stripes 4.50

Youth's Long Pants.

29 to 31 inches waist measurement.

153. Youths' tweed pants, assorted, dark and medium colors, narrow stripes, $1.00, 1.25, 1.50, 2.00.....2.50

154. Colored striped worsted, dark and light stripes..... .. ..1.75

155. Medium and dark narrow striped worsted...............2.25

Men's Washing Vests.

34 to 44 inches chest measurement.

As Cut No. 156.

156. White duck washing vests, with detachable buttons and collar..75c

157. White duck vests, with collar, detachable buttons 1.00

As Cut No. 158.

158. Washing vests, white duck with blue dot or small figure, also white drill with black check.. . . ...1.25

159. White linen duck vests, no collar, detachable pearl buttons, also imported cream cashmere neat colored checks....................1.50

160. Fancy worsted vests, bronze green, small drab and blue spot, also black ground with slate spot and small figure................2.50

As Cut No. 161.

161. White duck vests, with dot or small figured pattern and checks, double-breasted, no collar......1.25

162. English cream cashmere vests, small dots and neat silk checks, assorted patterns.................1.50

163. Fancy worsted basket pattern, black ground, blue and white spots 2.00

Men's Tweed and Worsted Vests.

164. Light and dark colored Canadian tweed vests................75c

165. All-wool English and Canadian tweed vests, medium and light colors 1.00

166. Black Venetian and Clay twill worsted, also black and navy blue worsted serge.....................1.50

Men's Smocks, Overalls and Aprons.

167. White drill smock, patch pockets, sizes 36 to 44 ....40c

168. Blue denim smock, sizes 36 to 44..............................50c

169. Heavy blue denim smock, sizes 36 to 44..........................75c

170. White drill overalls with bib, front, hip and rule pockets, sizes 32 to 44.........................40c

170A. Blue denim overalls, with or without bib, 3 pockets, sizes 32 to 44..............................50c

170B. Black denim overalls, with bib, 3 pockets..........................65c

170C. Heavy blue denim overalls, with or without bib, 3 pockets..75c

170D. Assorted plain and striped pattern, heavy cottonade overalls, without bib 75c

170E. Grocers' aprons, blue denim or white drill 25c

170F. Surgeons' aprons, butchers' linen, large size.................50c

Our Cutter and Designer visit the leading fashion centres regularly, styles and fashions are right up to date.

THE CLOTH IS ALL THOROUGHLY SHRUNK BEFORE BEING MADE UP.

Youths' Suits.

(Long pants.)

As Cut No. 171.

171. Navy blue serge suits—
32, 33, 34, 35,
3.00. 3.25.

172. Light grey pin check, dark grey small check, and light brown, green tinge, red and green overplaid, tweed suits, also navy blue all-wool serge suits—
32, 33, 34, 35,
4.50. 4.75. 5.00.

173. All-wool Canadian tweed suits, brown with green tinge and red thread overplaid—
32, 33, 34, 35,
6.00. 6.25. 6.50.

174. Navy blue and black imported worsted serge suits, hard finish, also black Clay twill—
32, 33, 34, 35,
7.00. 7.25. 7.50.

175. Light fawn all-wool homespun tweed suits—
32, 33, 34, 35,
6.50. 7.00. 7.50.

176. All-wool tweed, light brown, small check with red overplaid, also dark and blue-grey, small check—
32, 33, 34, 35,
8.00. 8.25. 8.50.

177. Imported navy blue and black worsted serge, also black Clay diagonal worsted and black Venetian-finish worsted—
32, 33, 34, 35,
9.00. 9.50. 10.00.

178. Brown and black pin check with red thread overplaid, all wool, silk-faced lapels—
32, 33, 34, 35,
9.00. 9.50. 10.00.

179. Best black Venetian worsted, pure wool, silk-stitched edges—
32, 33, 34, 35,
10.50. 11.00. 11.50.

Youths' Suits, Single Breasted, with Double-Breasted Vests.

180. All-wool tweed, medium grey with green tinge, red and green thread overplaid—
32, 33, 34, 35,
6.00. 6.25. 6.50.

181. Light green and grey checked tweed, stylish, all wool—
32, 33, 34, 35,
8.00. 8.25. 8.50.

182. Mid-grey and light all-wool tweed, checked pattern, Scotch effect—
32, 33, 34, 35,
8.00. 8.50. 9.00.

183. Black and mid-grey with green tinge, very narrow striped worsted, imported goods—
32, 33, 34, 35,
10.00. 10.50. 11.00.

Youths' Double-Breasted Suits.

As Cut No 184.

184. Dark brown checked tweed, with red overplaid, also all wool navy blue serge—
32, 33, 34, 35,
4.50. 4.75. 5.00.

185. All-wool Canadian tweeds, brown, green tinge, red thread overplaid, also black and grey small check—
32, 33, 34, 35,
6.00. 6.25. 6.50.

186. Navy blue and black hard-finished worsted serge, and navy blue Clay diagonal worsted—
32, 33, 34, 35.
7.00. 7.25. 7.50.

187. Brown and black, red thread overplaid, also black and dark grey pin-checked tweeds—
32, 33, 34, 35,
8.00. 8.25. 8.50.

188. Navy blue Clay diagonal, also black and navy blue hard finished worsted serge—
32, 33, 34, 35,
9.00. 9.50. 10.00.

Boys' Single-Breasted 3-Piece Suits.

As Cut No. 189.

189. Dark Canadian tweed, also navy blue serge suits..........2.50
190. Light grey pin check, dark grey, also brown checked tweeds.. ....3.00
191. Dark brown, fawn and green, also black and grey checked tweed suits..........................3.50
192. Navy blue and black soft finished serge.................3.75
193. Stylish checked tweed suits, fawn and grey, with green overplaid, also dark brown, green overplaid......................4.50
194. Black, Oxford grey and navy blue Clay twill worsted, also navy blue and black worsted serge..5.00
195. Light brown and dark grey, all-wool, small check pattern tweed..........................5.00
196. Black Venetian-finished worsted, and all-wool imported navy blue and black worsted serges, also black and navy blue Clay twill worsteds.......................6.00
197. Worsted-finished tweed, black ground, small grey check, imported..........................6.00
198. Imported all-wool black Clay diagonal worsted, silk-stitched edges..........................6.50

Boys' Single-Breasted 3-piece Suits.

(Double-breasted Vest, no Collar.)

As Cut No. 199.

199. Black and brown pin check, with red thread overplaid, also light grey small check with red overplaid......................5.00
200. Light and dark all-wool grey checked tweeds, very stylish, Scotch effect....................6.00
201. Black and white small pattern shepherd's plaid with overplaid, all-wool, nobby..............6.50
202. Imported colored worsted, black with dark grey small check and green overplaid, very choice..7.50

Boys' Double-Breasted 3-Piece Suits, Short Pants.

27 to 33 inches chest measurement.

As Cut No. 203.

203. Dark Canadian tweed suit, double-breasted.................2.50
204. Light brown and green checked tweed with red overplaid, also brown and grey with red and black overplaid...............3.00
205. Black and grey small check, also grey and green, large checks, with black overplaid..........3.50
206. Navy blue and black soft finished serge, all-wool stock....3.75
207. Black and grey shepherd's plaid, with red overplaid, also dark grey checked tweed with overplaid of green and fawn with grey check, red overplaid......................4.50
208. Light brown and fawn small check with red and fawn overplaid, black and grey small check, also light brown small check with overplaid of red.....................5.00
209. Imported navy blue and black worsted serge, also black and navy blue Clay twilled worsted 5.00
210. Oxford grey worsted finished tweed, indistinct grey stripe pattern all-wool imported goods, also black and navy blue worsted serge suits, hard finish..............6.00
211. Imported fine navy blue Clay twill worsted suits, edges silk stitched, well finished 6.50

Boys' Norfolk Suits (Coats and Pants Only).

28 to 33 inches chest measurement.

212. Norfolk suits, made of light grey and dark fawn homespun tweed, cut with yoke front and back, plaits stitched down 3.50
213. Light fawn homespun, also grey and black small check, red thread overplaid, made with yoke and box plaits........................4.50

Youths' Eton Suits.

28 to 35 inches chest measurement.

As Cut No. 214.

214. Boys' Eton suits, made from imported black Venetian-finished worsted, silk-faced lapels.....10.00

Tuxedo Suits

27 to 33 inches chest measurement.

As Cut No. 215.

215. Boys' Tuxedo suits, of black Venetian worsted, silk-faced collar and roll 7.50

Boys' 2-piece Suits, Single-Breasted.

23 to 28 inches chest measurement.
27 to 28 inches have turned lapels.

As Cut No. 216.

216. Dark grey Canadian tweed, small check pattern 1.50

As Cut No. 217.

217. Canadian tweed suit, of dark grey, small check pattern......2.00

As Cut No. 218.

218. Brown with green tinge and red thread overplaid, also all-wool serge, in navy blue—
23, 24, 25, 26, 27, 28,
2.25. 2.50. 2.75.

219. Brown check with green tinge and overplaid of red—
23, 24, 25, 26, 27, 28,
2.75. 3.00. 3.25.

220. Navy blue worsted serge, hard finish, imported goods—
23, 24, 25, 26, 27, 28,
3.25. 3.50. 3.75.

221. Mid-grey, with blue cast all-wool tweed, green thread overplaid—
23, 24, 25, 26, 27, 28,
3.00. 3.25. 3.50.

As Cut No. 222.

222. Fawn and light brown, small check with red overplaid, also light and blue grey small check, fawn overplaid—
23, 24, 25, 26, 27, 28,
3.50. 3.75. 4.00.

As Cut No. 223.

223. Dark brown and black pin check all-wool tweed, red overplaid, also mid-grey and black imported Clay twilled worsted—
23, 24, 25, 26, 27, 28,
3.50. 3.75. 4.00.

224. Black and navy blue all-wool imported worsted serge, hard finish, also black worsted, Venetian finish—
23, 24, 25, 26, 27, 28,
4.00. 4.25. 4.50.

Boys' Norfolk Suits.

As Cut No. 225.

225. Light grey pin-check tweed, also navy blue serge, plaits stitched down—
23, 24, 25, 26, 27, 28,
2.25. 2.50. 2.75.

As Cut No. 226.

226. Dark fawn and light grey all-wool homespun tweeds, yoke back and front, plaits stitched down—
23, 24, 25, 26, 27, 28,
2.25. 2.50. 2.75.

227. Dark grey and dark fawn homespun tweed, mid-grey and blue-grey check with red overplaid, also light grey tweed, yoke and box plaits—
23, 24, 25, 26. 27, 28,
3.00. 3.25. 3.50.

228. Light grey checked tweed, all wool, Scotch effect, yoke and box plaits—
23, 24, 25, 26, 27, 28,
4.00. 4.25. 4.50.

Double-Breasted 2-Piece Suits.

As Cut No. 229.

229. Brown and green small check tweed, 23 to 28..................2.00
230 Dark grey check, black and fawn shepherd's plaid, grey-blue and brown, small check, with red thread overplaid, also navy blue serge—
23, 24, 25, 26, 27, 28,
2.25. 2.50. 2.75.

231. Dark fawn all-wool homespun, also black and grey small check—
23, 24, 25, 26, 27, 28,
3.00. 3.25. 3.50.

232. Dark brown with green overplaid, also light and mid-grey small check—
23, 24, 25, 26, 27, 28,
3.00. 3.25. 3.50.

233. Dark and light brown pin-check with red overplaid, also dark and mid-grey pin check, lapels silk faced—
23, 24, 25, 26, 27, 28,
3.50. 3.75. 4.00.

234. Navy blue hard worsted serge, all wool, imported stock—
23, 24, 25, 26, 27, 28,
3.25. 3.50. 3.75.

235. Medium grey checked tweed, all wool, Scotch effect, silk-faced lapels—
23, 24, 25, 26, 27, 28,
4.00. 4.25. 4.50.

236. Imported colored worsted suits, black and dark grey, small check with green overplaid, also black and dark blue small check with red overplaid, silk-faced lapels....5.00
237. Navy blue hard finish worsted serge, imported all-wool stock—
23, 24, 25, 26, 27, 28,
4.00. 4.25. 4.50.

Boys' Reefers.

20 to 28 inches chest measurement.

As Cut No. 238.

238. Navy blue serge reefer, brass buttons 1.25
239. All-wool navy blue serge reefer, brass buttons 1.90

As Cut No. 240.

240. Black and navy blue imported Clay twill reefers, black bone buttons 2.50

As Cut No. 241.

241. Dark Oxford grey tweed reefer, with silk-faced lapel 2.50
242. Oxford grey cheviot all-wool fashionable stock, lapels silk-faced 4.00
243. Fawn covert cloth reefer, lapels silk faced 4.50

As Cut No. 244.

244. Oxford grey all-wool cheviot and fawn covert cloth reefer, cuff on sleeves, plaited front, velvet collar 6.00

As Cut No. 245.

245. Navy blue imported Clay twill, with deep sailor collar, trimmed with white or black braid, sizes 20 to 26 only 3.50

Boys' Overcoats.

As Cut No. 246.

246. Oxford grey all-wool soft finish cheviot, box back, silk-faced lapels—
24, 25, 26, 27, 28, 29, 30, 31, 32, 33,
4.50. 4.75. 5.00. 5.25. 5.50.

247. Fawn covert cloth overcoat, box back, vent in cuff, silk-faced lapels, self-collar—
24, 25, 26, 27, 28,
5.50. 5.75. 6.00. 6.25. 6.50.
29, 30, 31, 32, 33,
6.75. 7.00. 7.25. 7.50. 7.75.

The cloth in these goods is bought from the mills, made under our own supervision on our premises.

Nobby, Fashionable Clothing

UP-TO-DATE IN STYLE, FIT AND FINISH.

Boys' Fancy Brownie and Vestee Suits.

SIZES 21 TO 26.

AGES 3 TO 8 YEARS.

NOTE.—These suits are kept in stock in sizes only as catalogued, larger sizes will cost you 10 per cent. more.

Boys' Fauntleroy and Vestee Suits.

21 to 26 inches chest measurement.

As Cut No. 248.

248. Navy blue Fauntleroy soft finish serge, 3 rows black braid, front to match, with 3 rows braid trimming across top **2.00**

As Cut No. 249.

249. Fauntleroy suit, made from blue-grey tweed, with indistinct overplaid of black, also green and brown mixed tweed with red thread overplaid, trimmed with 4 rows black braid..**2.50**

250. Fauntleroy suit of navy blue, soft finish serge, trimmed with 5 rows braid, black and white alternate, front to match with 3 stars **2.50**

As Cut No. 251.

251. Black and blue-grey small check pattern tweed, also light brown small check with brown overplaid, deep collar with 6 rows of navy braid trimming, vest to match, large fancy buttons....................**3.00**

As Cut No. 252.

252. Navy blue hard finish serge Fauntleroy suits, deep collar trimmed with 4 rows of white braid, vest of same material, 4 rows braid top and bottom **3.50**

As Cut No. 253.

253. Stylish Fauntleroy suit of imported hard-finished worsted, navy blue color, sailor collar trimmed with 8 rows of black braid, vest buttoned behind, trimmed with 5 rows of braid top and bottom **4.50**

As Cut No. 254.

254. Handsome suit in Fauntleroy style, navy blue Clay twilled worsted, deep sailor collar with white stars in corners, lapels faced with blue Venetian cloth, trimmed with 10 rows of white braid, gilt buttons.......**4.50**

As Cut No. 255.

255. Boys' vestee suits, all-wool grey narrow striped tweed, silk-faced lapels, cord and olive fasteners, vest of same goods, double breasted, front of same with emblem, anchor and Union Jack **4.50**

As Cut No. 256.

256. Neat stylish suit, vestee style, made of dark fawn Venetian cloth, also in a greyish green Venetian cloth, lapels silk faced, large pearl buttons, back of coat finished with 2-inch plait down back and across waist, vest imitation of double breasted, with collar........... ..**4.50**

As Cut No. 257.

257. Vestee suit, imported very narrow striped worsted, black ground with blue stripe, coat double breasted, round corners, lapels silk faced, red serge front with emblem, vest double-breasted, no collar.......**5.00**

As Cut No. 258.

258. Very choice suit, made in vestee style, black and white shepherd plaid, coat single breasted, vest and front of red serge, white pearl buttons on vest, emblem on front....**5.00**

259. Black and grey very small check tweed suit, vestee style, coat single breasted with round corners, vest of cadet grey Venetian cloth front to match vest, with emblem............**5.00**

As Cut No. 260.

260. Nobby suit, vestee style, Scotch tweed fawn with light brown and green overplaid, coat single breasted, round corners, silk-faced lapels, vest of same material with red silk polka dot, front same with emblem..**5.00**

As Cut No. 261.

261. Scotch tweed vestee suit, fawn and green mixture with fawn and red overplaid, single-breasted coat, lapels silk faced, drab with green cast front with emblem, vest same material as coat, double breasted, without collar...................**5.00**

262. Shepherd's plaid, 3 colors in pattern, black, white and brown tweed, coat single breasted, front of same goods with emblem, vest double-breasted.....**5.00**

As Cut No. 263.

263. New style vestee suit, mid-grey tweed with overplaid of red and blue, small collar, large lapels, collar overlaid with navy blue Venetian cloth, trimmed with 3 rows of white braid and blue and white cord on edge, wide belt and white pearl buttons, vest of blue Venetian, double-breasted, no collar **5.00**

264. Navy blue hard-finish worsted serge, red Venetian overlaid collar, 3 rows black silk braid trimming, red front with 3 rows silk braid, vest double breasted without collar, white pearl buttons...........**6.00**

As Cut No. 265.

265. Vestee suit, blue-grey and black pin-check, coat single breasted, double-breasted vest of bluish drab worsted with white and slate spot, fancy buttons, Venetian cloth front to match vest............ .**6.00**

As Cut No. 266.

266. Fine imported navy blue Clay twill worsted vestee suits, coat single breasted, silk-faced lapels, white serge front, double-breasted vest, olive green with green and heliotrope check, fancy buttons to match **6.50**

Boys' Sailor Suits.

As Cut No. 267.

267. Navy blue serge sailor suits, deep collar, trimmed with gold braid, pants lined.........**75c**

268. Sailor suit of navy blue serge, deep sailor collar, gold braid trimming, lanyard and whistle **1.00**

269. Imported navy blue serge suits, deep sailor collar, braid trimmed, white serge front **1.50**

As Cut No. 270.

270. Boys' sailor suits of navy blue serge, sailor collar, trimmed with 7 rows black braid, serge front with red anchor, button cuffs.. ....**2.00**

As Cut No. 271.

271. Navy blue serge sailor suit, sailor collar, 7 rows of braid trimming, red or blue fronts, fly-front blouse..........**2.50**

As Cut No. 272.

272. Stylish sailor suit, navy blue hard-finish serge, deep collar with 7 rows of narrow black braid and 1 row of ⅜-inch silk braid, front of same, 5 rows trimming, box plait, cuffs to button **3.00**

As Cut No. 273.

273. Fine imported navy blue worsted serge, sailor collar with 8 rows of braid trimming, box plait, cuffs button at wrist, serge front with 5 rows trimming..................**4.00**

As Cut No. 274.

274. Handsome sailor suit of navy blue hard-finish worsted, deep sailor collar of same, also cadet blue Venetian collar separate, 3 rows of white braid trimming, blue front with anchor, black silk tie....**5.00**

As Cut No. 275.

275. Latest style sailor suit, double-breasted blouse, navy blue hard-finish serge, deep collar, front of coat trimmed with black military braid, smooth brass buttons, separate front trimmed with military braid with 2 white stars **4 50**

Man-of-War Suits.

Sizes 21 to 27.

As Cut No. 276.

276. Navy blue soft-finished serge man-of-war suits, regulation collar on full blouse, cream flannel front, lanyard and whistle **3.50**

277. Man-of-war suits, made of fine soft-finished serge, full cut blouse, regulation collar, cream flannel front, lanyard and whistle.................**5.00**

When ordering, be sure the style you require is catalogued in the size you order.

Newest Designs and Serviceable Materials

WE GUARANTEE SATISFACTION OR REFUND YOUR MONEY.

Boys' Washing Blouses, Washing Suits, Knee Pants, and Serge Kilt Suits.

As Cut No. 290.

290. Light and dark fast color print blouses, assorted patterns, sailor collar, suitable for boys or girls from 3 to 10 years of age **25c**

As Cut No. 291.

291. Light and dark colored assorted pattern blouses, deep sailor collar, neatly frilled, sizes 3 to 10 years........ **35c**

292. Boys' blouses, of black sateen, sailor collar, with frill, sizes 3 to 8 years **50c**

As Cut No. 293.

293. White cambric blouses, deep sailor collar, cuffs and collar embroidery trimmed .. **50c**

As Cut No. 294.

294. White cambric blouses, box plait down back, 6 small plaits down front, deep sailor collar, collar, cuffs and front neatly embroidered, sizes 3 to 8 yrs. **75c**

As Cut No. 295.

295. Black sateen blouses, with deep sailor collar, 2 box plaits down front and 1 down back, frill on collar, sizes 3 to 8 years. **75c**

As Cut No. 296.

296. White lawn blouses, wide embroidery on sailor collar and cuffs, 2 rows of embroidery and 1 of insertion down front, full loose blouse, sizes 3 to 8 years. **1.00**

As Cut No. 297.

297. Choice white lawn blouses, sailor collar, trimmed with embroidery and 5 rows of insertion, 2 rows of embroidery and 1 of insertion down front, cuffs trimmed to match, sizes 3 to 8 years **1.25**

As Cut No. 298.

298. Very handsome white lawn blouse, collar, front and cuffs trimmed same style as No. 297, embroidery and insertion of finer quality and wider, sizes 3 to 8 years **1.50**

As Cut No. 299.

299. Striped cambric blouses, full and loose, deep sailor collar, trimmed with white pique, white pique front, sizes 4 to 8 years **50c**

Boys' Shirt Waists.

As Cut No. 300.

300. English cambric shirt waists, assorted colors, striped patterns, plaited fronts, with collar and cuffs, sizes 3 to 8 years **50c**

300A. White and colored English cambric shirt waists, plaited front and back, laundried, sizes 3 to 8 years, with and without collar, $1.00 and **1.25**

Children's Sailor Collars.

301. White and colored drills, neatly trimmed with braid to match, 25c and **35c**

302. Washing circular collars, in white drills with frill, 35c and **50c**

Children's Washing Galatea Kilt Suits.

Ages 1½ to 3½ years.

303. Neat striped galatea kilt suits, dark and light blue stripes and checks........ **50c**

As Cut No. 304.

304. Drill, duck and pique suits, in plain white and khaki, some with belt, sailor collar with white stitching (only with plain front) **75c**

305. Plain khaki, khaki with spot, dark and light blue with white stripes, blue and pink stripes with dot, open front, round collar at back, lanyard and whistle **1.00**

Boys' Washing Suits, Blouse and Short Pants.

22 to 27 inches chest measurement.

As Cut No. 306.

306. Washing suits, in narrow and wide striped galatea, light, medium and dark colors, sailor collar, pearl buttons...... **75c**

As Cut No. 307.

307. Light and dark blue stripe, black and white and blue and white stripes, also khaki and white, plain colors, open front blouses with singlet **1.00**

308. Drill, duck and galatea, large assorted stock, in plain and striped patterns, light blue, khaki and white stripes, also white and khaki plain open front blouses, pearl buttons.................... **1.50**

As Cut No. 309.

309. Boys' sailor suits of brown Holland, deep sailor collar, trimmed with 2 rows narrow white braid and 1 row ½-inch wide, pearl buttons...... **1.00**

As Cut No. 310.

310. Double-breasted brown Holland suit, bone buttons, **1.25**

Boys' Washing Man-of-War Suits.

to 27 inches chest measurement.

As Cut No. 311.

311. White English drill blouse and long pants, blue drill collar trimmed with white.. **2.50**

Highland Kilt Suits.

As Cut No. 312.

312. Highland kilt suits, jacket and vest of blue black velvet, velvet cap to match, sporan, stockings and brooch, plaid skirts with sash, sizes 3 to 7 years **12.50**

Children's Serge Kilt Suits.

Sizes 1½ to 4 years.

As Cut No. 313.

313. Navy blue melton cloth kilt suits, braid trimmed with lanyard and whistle **1.50**

314. Navy blue serge kilt suits, deep sailor collar, braid trimming, separate blouse and skirt attached................ **2.00**

As Cut No. 315.

315. Child's kilt suits, navy blue serge kilt suit, plaited skirts, sailor collar and skirt trimmed with colored braid, $2.50 and **3.00**

As Cut No. 316.

316. Royal blue and cardinal kilt suits, front and skirt plaited, sailor collar neatly trimmed with braid, small buttons on front............ **2.50**

Boys' Knee Pants, Lined.

As Cut No. 317.

317. Navy blue serges, well made, strongly sewn, sizes 22 to 28 inches **25c**

318. Grey and brown mixed Canadian tweeds, side and hip pockets, sizes 22 to 28.... **39c**

319. Navy blue serges, all wool, side and hip pockets, well made, sizes 22 to 28 ...... **60c**

320. Medium and dark Canadian tweed pants, strong pockets, sizes 22 to 28 .... **50c**

321. Oxford grey and light or dark brown Halifax tweeds, sizes 22 to 28 .... **60c**

322. Medium and dark Canadian tweeds, side and hip pockets, sizes 29 to 33 .... **50c**

323. Grey and brown Halifax tweed and navy blue serges, all wool, sizes 29 to 33 ...... **75c**

324. Navy blue and black Clay worsted knee pants, 3 pockets—

22, 23, 24, 25,	26, 27, 28,
75c.	**90c.**
29, 30,	31, 32, 33,
1.00.	**1.25.**

325. All-wool neat stylish pattern tweeds, well made and finished, 3 pockets—

22, 23, 24,	25, 26,	27, 28,
60c.	**75c.**	**90c.**
29, 30,	31, 32, 33,	
1.00.	**1.25.**	

Boys' Knee Pants.

326. Black and navy blue imported hard finish serges, 3 pockets—

22, 23, 24,	25, 26,	27, 28,
75c.	**90c.**	**1.00.**
29, 30,	31, 32, 33,	
1.25.	**1.50.**	

As Cut No. 327.

327. Boys' blue denim brownie overalls, with bib, 5 pockets, **35c**

MEASUREMENT FORM.

STATE DISTINCTLY STYLE WANTED.

1. SINGLE-BREASTED SACQUE. 2. DOUBLE-BREASTED SACQUE. 3. THREE-BUTTONED MORNING CUTAWAY.

Collar to waist, A to B......inches. Whole length to bottom of coat, A to C......inches. Centre of back to shoulder, E........inches. Shoulder to elbow, E to F..........inches. Elbow to hand, F to G..........inches. Inside seam of arm...........inches. Around chest under arms at K.........inches. Waist at L.........inches.

VEST—Length from centre back of neck to bottom in front..........inches. Around chest under arms at K..........inches. Waist at L..........inches.

PANTS—Length of outside seam from waist to heel of boot..........inches. Length of inside seam from crotch to heel of boot, C to D..........inches. Around waist under vest at A ....inches. Around seat at B..........inches. Thigh..........inches.

OVERCOAT—Same as coat (over the vest).

Give Person's Height, Weight and Age.

Always measure the person for whom the clothes are intended.

THE AVERAGE SIZE FOR BOY.—Age 4 is chest 22. Age 5 is chest 23. Age 6 is chest 24. Age 7 is chest 25. " 8 " 26. " 9 " 27. " 10 " 28.

All suits and overcoats over 44 inches chest measurement are 50c additional for every inch. Suits and overcoats are made up in styles only as marked on samples which we send.

Samples sent for the asking of Men's and Boys' Suits, Overcoats and Men's Pants.

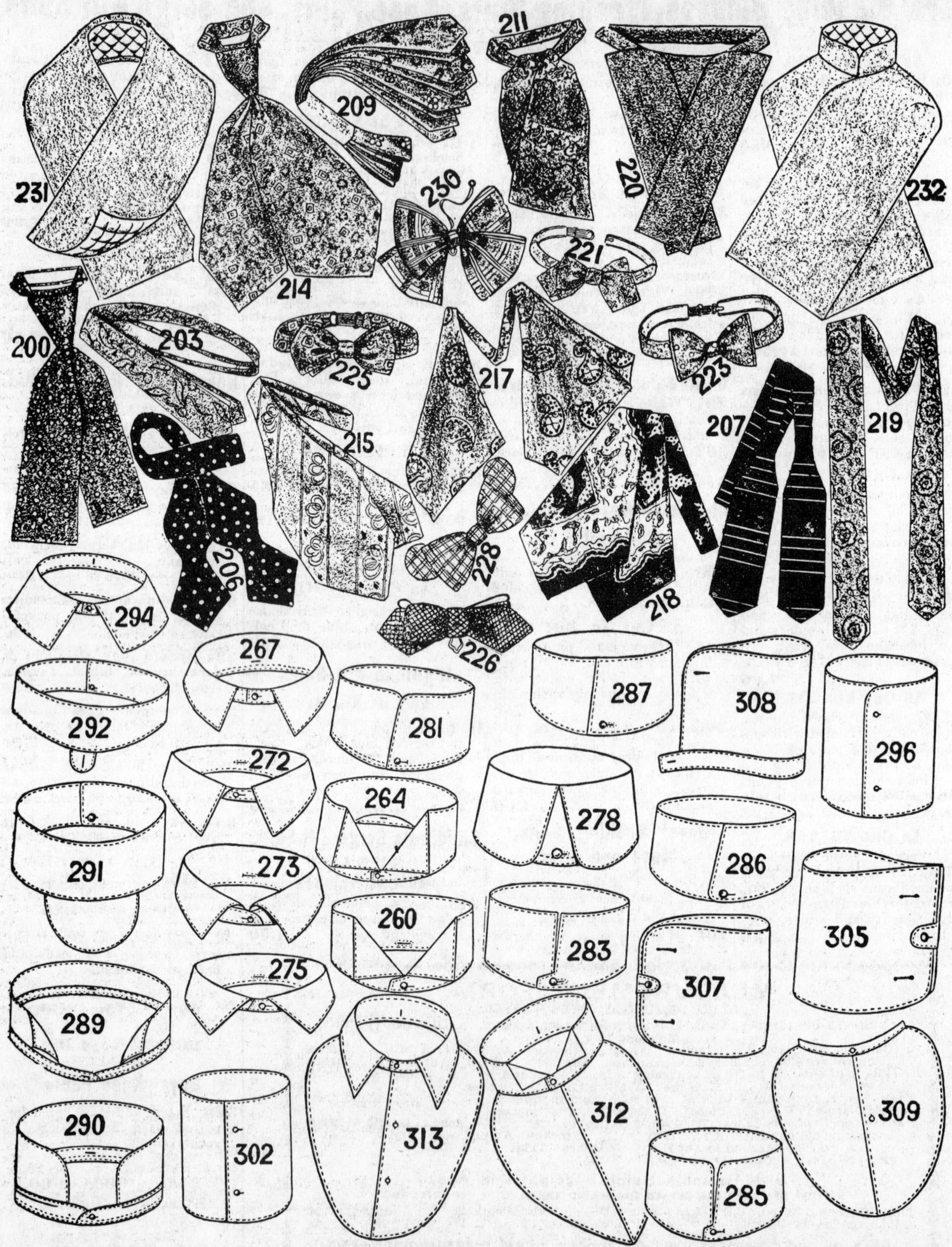

In ordering Neckwear or Collars be sure and give No. of Cut and size of Collar, also depth of Collar if made in d fferent heights.

Men's and Boys' Neckwear.

When ordering Neckwear be sure to tell us the shape you wish, also color preferred.

200. Men's and boys' silk and satin neckties, dark and light colors, as cut 200 .... 12½c

201. Men's and boys' silk and satin neckties, satin lined, in the newest fancy patterns, stripes, polka dots and plain cords, dark and light shades, as cut 200 .... 25c

202. Black silk and satin knot ties, satin lined, as cut 200, 25c 35c

203. Men's and boys' silk and satin neckties, dark and light shades, as cut 203 .... 12½c

204. Men's and boys' silk and satin neckties, satin lined, newest fancy patterns, stripes, polka dots and plain cords, light and dark shades, as cut 203 .... 25c

205. Black silk and satin four-in-hand, satin lined, as cut 203, 25c, ... 35c

206. The "Batwing," newest shape for tying in bow, newest patterns, stripes, polka dots and plain cords, silk both sides, as cut 206 .... 25c

When ordering "Batwing" give size of collar.

207. The "Batwing," straight ends for bow, in all the up-to-date patterns and colors, silk both sides, as cut 207 .... 25c

208. The "Batwing," black silk and satin, to tie in bow, silk both sides, newest shape, as cuts 206 and 207, 25c 35c

209. The "Lombard," to tie in bow, silk and satin all round, newest fancy patterns and colors, light and dark shades and plain cords, as cut 209 .... 25c

210. Black silk and satin, 1¼ inches wide at ends, silk both sides, as cut 209, 25c 35c

211. Silk and satin puff ties, satin lined, newest fancy patterns, stripes, polka dots and plain cords, light and dark shades, as cut 211, ... 25c

212. Silk and satin puff ties, best satin lined, latest American and English patterns and colors, light and dark shades, as cut 211 .... 50c

213. Black silk and satin puff ties, satin lined, fine quality, newest shape, as cut 211, 25c, 35c 50c

214. Silk and satin neckties, best satin lined, neat shape, newest fancy broche patterns and stripes, light and dark shades, as cut 214 .... 50c

215. Fine silk and satin, flowing end shape, newest English and American patterns and colorings, light and dark shades, as cut 215 .... 50c

216. Black silk and satin, large flowing end shape, as cut 215 .... 50c

217. The "Kerchief," for men's and ladies' wear, fine English foulard silk, in fancy patterns and polka dots, light and dark shades, with or without fancy border, as cut 217 .... 50c

218. The "Kerchief," large flowing ends with fancy border, fine English foulard silk, in newest light and dark fancy patterns, as cut 218 .... 75c

219. Fine silk and satin four-in-hand, best satin linings, newest broche patterns, stripes and neat figures, light and dark shades, 2 inches wide, 48 inches long, as cut 219, ... 50c

220. Large flat scarf, to cover the bosom, satin lined, in plain black, plain colored corded silk and polka dot satins, as cut 220, 35c, 50c each.

221. Black silk and satin bows, as cut 221 .... 12½c

222. Silk and satin bow ties, neat fancy patterns, light and dark shades, as cut 221 .... 12½c

223. Silk and satin bow ties, light and dark shades, satin lined, newest fancy patterns, plain cords and polka dots, as cut 223 .... 25c

224. Black silk and satin bows, newest shapes, as cuts 223 and 225, 25c .. 35c

225. Silk and satin bows, neat shapes, latest fancy patterns and stripes, pointed or square ends, light and dark shades, as cut 225 .... 25c

226. Silk and satin shield bows, dark and light shades, for turned-down collars, as cut 226 .... 12½c

227. Black silk and satin shield bow, for turned-down collar, as cut 226, ... 12½c

228. Silk and satin shield bows, for high turned-down collar, the shield is covered with the same silk, newest fancy patterns, polka dots and plain cords, light and dark shades, as cut 228 .... 25c

229. Black silk and satin-covered shield bow, for high turned-down collar, as cut 228, 25c 35c

230. Boys' "Butterfly" bows, with elastic to go around neck, light and dark fancy plaids and stripes, as cut 230 .... 25c

Evening Dresswear.

231. Full dress bosom protectors, black silk and satin, quilted white satin lining, deep shaped back to protect collar, as cut 231, $1.00 .. 1.50

232. Dress shirt bosom protectors, black silk and satin, quilted white satin linings, stand-up collar protector attached, as cut 232, $1.00, ... 1.50

233. White lawn string ties, to tie in bow, 2 for 5c, per doz 25c

234. White lawn string ties, to tie in bow, 5c each, per doz 50c

235. White lawn string ties, to tie in bow, 9c each, or 3 for 25c

236. White lawn bows, with band fastened at back, pointed or square ends, correct shapes, 9c each, or 3 for 25c

237. White lawn bow ties, with band to fasten at back, pointed or square ends 12½c

238. Fine French lawn white bow ties, with band, newest shapes, in pointed or square ends, 18c each, or 3 for 50c

239. Black silk or satin military dress bows, correct shape 20c

240. Black silk string ties, cut bias, ¾ inch wide 10c

241. Black silk string ties, cut bias, ⅝ inch, ¾ inch, ⅞ inch and 1 inch wide 15c

242. Black silk string ties, cut bias, ¾ and 1-inch wide 25c

243. Black silk string ties, cut bias, fine quality, extra long, 1 inch wide, 25c 35c

Summer Washing Ties.

244. Washing string ties, to tie in bow, Madras and Oxford materials, 5c 12½c

245. Reversible pique washing ties, to tie in four-in hand, white, or white with fancy figures and stripes, fast colors 12½c

246. Coachman's flat puff tie, in white corded pique 15c

247. Summer puff ties, made in white pique or fancy percale and Oxford materials 25c

Men's and Boys' Collars and Cuffs.

Men's and Boys' Collars.

260. Men's 4-ply collars, depths 1¾, 2 and 2¼ inches, sizes 14 to 17½, as cut 260, 3 for 25c, each 9c

261. Men's 4-ply linen collars, imported, depths 1½, 1¾, 2, 2¼ and 2½ inches, sizes 14 to 17½, as cut 260, each 12½c

262. Boys' 4-ply collars, depth 1¾ inches, sizes 12 to 13½, as cut 260, 3 for 25c, each 9c

263. Celluloid collars, men's and boys', interlined, depth 2 inches, sizes 12 to 17½, as cut 260 .... 12½c

264. Men's 4-ply best linen, "imported," depths 1½, 1¾, 2, 2¼, 2½, 2¾ inches, sizes 14 to 18½, as cut 264, 3 for 50c, each 18c

265. Boys' 4-ply linen, depth 2 inches, sizes 12 to 13½, as cut 264 .... 12½c

266. Men's American interlined celluloid collars, depth 2 inches, sizes 14 to 18, as cut 264, 3 for 50c, each 18c

267. Men's 4-ply collars, good space, sizes 14 to 17½, as cut 267, 3 for 25c, each 9c

268. Men's 4-ply linen, best quality, sizes 14 to 17½, as cut 267, 3 for 50c, each 18c

269. Boys' 4-ply linen, depth 1¾ inches, sizes 12 to 13½, as cut 267, 3 for 25c, each 9c

270. Boys' 4-ply linen, sizes 12 to 13½, depth 2 in., as cut 267, each 12½c

271. Men's and boys' interlined celluloid collars, sizes 12 to 17½, as cut 267, each 12½c

272. Men's 4-ply linen, long points, sizes 14 to 17½, as cut 272 .... 12½c

273. Men's 4-ply linen, roll front, sizes 14 to 17½, as cut 273 .... 12½c

274. Men's 4-ply best linen, roll front, sizes 14 to 18, as cut 273, 3 for 50c, each 18c

274A. Boys' 4-ply linen, roll front, sizes 12 to 13½, as cut 273 .... 12½c

275. Men's 4-ply linen, cutaway shape, sizes 14 to 17½, as cut 275 . 12½c

276. Men's 4-ply linen, cutaway shape, sizes 14 to 21, as cut 275, 3 for 50c, each 18c

277. Men's American interlined celluloid collars, sizes 14 to 18, as cut 275, 3 for 50c, each 18c

278. Men's 4-ply linen, depths 2 and 2¼ inches, sizes 14 to 17½, as cut 278, ... 12½c

279. Men's 4-ply linen, best imported make, depths 2, 2¼ and 2½ inches, all sizes, 14 to 18, as cut 278, 3 for 50c, each 18c

280. Boys' 4-ply linen, 2 inches deep, sizes 12 to 13½, as cut 278, 2 for. 25c

281. Men's 4-ply collars, depth 2¼ inches, sizes 14 to 17½, imported, as cut 281, 3 for 25c, each 9c

282. Boys' 4-ply collars, depth 2 in., sizes 12 to 13½, as cut 281, 3 for 25c, each 9c

283. Men's 4-ply linen, depths 2, 2¼ and 2½ inches, sizes 14 to 17½, as cut 283 .... 12½c

284. Boys' 4-ply linen, depths 1¾ and 2 inches, sizes 12 to 13½, as cut 283, ... 12½c

285. Men's 4-ply imported linen, depths 2¼, 2½ and 2¾ inches, sizes 14 to 17½, as cut 285, 3 for 50c, each. 18c

286. Men's 4-ply linen, imported, depths 2, 2¼, 2½ and 2¾ inches, sizes 14 to 17½, as cut 286, 3 for 50c, each 18c

287. Men's 4-ply linen, depth 1¾ inches, sizes 14 to 18, as cut 287 .. 12½c

288. Men's American interlined celluloid collars, depth 2 inches, sizes 14 to 18, as cut 287, 3 for 50c, each .. 18c

289. Men's 4-ply linen "fat man's collar," 1½ inches deep, sizes 14 to 21, as cut 289 .... 12½c

290. Men's 4-ply linen coachman's collar, 2¼ inches deep, sizes 14 to 17½, as cut 290 .... 12½c

291. Men's 4-ply linen "clerical," sizes 14 to 18, as cut 291, 3 for 50c, each 18c

292. Men's 4-ply linen "clerical," sizes 14 to 18, as cut 292, 18c each, or 3 for 50c

293. Men's "clerical" interlined celluloid collars, sizes 14 to 18, as cut 292, 3 for 50c, each 18c

294. Boys' Eton collars, with square points, sizes 12 to 13½, as cut 294, ... 12½c

295. Boys' Eton collars, with round points, sizes 12 to 13½, as cut 294, ... 20c

Men's and Boys' Cuffs.

296. Men's 4-ply linen cuffs, sizes 9½ to 11½, as cut 296, pair 15c

297. Men's 4-ply linen cuffs, sizes 9½ to 11½, as cut 296, pair 25c

298. Men's 4-ply linen cuffs, sizes 9½ to 11½, as cut 296, pair 35c

299. Men's interlined celluloid cuffs, sizes 9½ to 11½, as cut 296, pair ... 20c

300. Men's American interlined celluloid cuffs, sizes 9½ to 11½, as cut 296, pair 35c

301. Boys' 4-ply linen cuffs, sizes 8, 8½ and 9, as cut 296, pair 15c

302. Men's 4-ply cuffs, sizes 9½ to 11½, as cut 302, pair 15c

303. Men's 4-ply cuffs, sizes 9½ to 11½, as cut 302, pair 25c

304. Men's 4-ply cuffs, sizes 9½ to 11½, as cut 302, pair 35c

305. Men's 4-ply linen cuffs, sizes 9½ to 11½, as cut 305, pair 15c

306. Men's 4-ply linen cuffs, sizes 9½ to 11½, as cut 305, pair 25c

307. Men's 4-ply linen cuffs, sizes 9½ to 11½, as cut 307, pair 25c

308. Men's 4-ply linen cuffs, sizes 9½ to 11½, as cut 305, pair 35c

Men's and Boys' Dickie Fronts.

309. Men's and boys' 4-ply linen fronts, as cut 309 .... 20c

310. Men's interlined celluloid fronts, length 10½ inches, as cut 309 .... 15c

311. Men's interlined celluloid fronts, length 14 inches, full dress sizes, for waiters, as cut 309 .... 25c

312. Men's and boys' 4-ply linen fronts, sizes 12 to 17½, as cut 312 .... 25c

313. Men's and boys' 4-ply linen fronts, sizes 12 to 17½, as cut 313 .... 25c

Paper Collars.

314. Comet, men's turned-down shape, sizes 14 to 17, per box 10c

315. Opera, boys' turned-down shape, sizes 12 to 13½, per box 8c

IN ORDERING COLLARS GIVE SIZE AND HEIGHT.

Suspenders, Belts, Bathing Suits,

Sweaters, Bicycle Hose, Socks.

Suspenders.

325. Men's heavy elastic web suspenders, leather ends, English make, as cut No. 325, pair ...10c
326. Heavy hand-sewn elastic web suspenders, Saddlers' English make, leather ends, as cut No. 325, pair...25c
327. Men's heavy elastic web suspenders, with double leather cross-back, leather ends, John Bright style, as cut No. 327, pair......15c
Also same style, extra long and heavy, pair...25c
329. Men's elastic web suspenders, mohair ends, drawers supporters, as cut No. 329, pair 15c...25c
331. Men's all-leather suspenders, Argosy style, tan shade, as cut No. 331, pair 25c...40c
333. British Argosy suspenders, solid web, strong and durable, as cut No. 331, pair...50c
334. Military suspenders, solid worsted web, heavy leather ends, strong buckles, elastic back, as cut No. 334, pair...50c
335. Men's fine elastic web suspenders, American Crown make, silk ends, drawers supporters, patent buckles, in black, white, drab and fancy stripes, as cut No. 335...50c
337. French Guyot suspenders, light weight, solid web, elastic back only, in plain black, polka dots and light colors, as cut No. 337, pair...50c
338. American Crown make suspenders, extra heavy elastic web, adjustable back and front, strong leather ends, police and fireman's brace, full size, as cut No. 338, pair...65c
339. Fine elastic web suspenders, roll kid ends, with drawers supporters, dome fasteners, medium shades, as cut No. 339, pair ..50c
341. Fine elastic web suspenders, Crown make, roll kid ends, drawers supporters, black, white and plain colors, guaranteed as cut No. 341, 75c...1.00
341a. Extra fine elastic web suspenders, Crown make, kid ends, plated buckles, best finish, in medium shades, guaranteed, as cut No. 341...1.50
342. Men's and boys' elastic web shoulder braces, strong wire buckles, mohair ends, adjustable, pair...50c
343. Boys' best American Crown make shoulder braces, to fit boys, 6 to 15 years, as cut No. 343, pr. 75c
344. Men's elastic web shoulder braces, strong and durable, silk cord ends, as cut No. 343......1.00
345. Best quality shoulder braces, elastic web, silk ends, patent buckles, Crown make, as cut No. 343...1.50
346. Boys' elastic web suspenders, leather or mohair ends, 24, 27 and 30 inches long, as cut No. 346, pair 10c, 15c...25c
349. Youths' best quality suspenders, roll kid ends, dome fasteners, fine elastic web cross back,...50c

Men's and Boys' Belts.

350. Boys' elastic belts, snake buckles, in plain colors and fancy stripes, as cut No. 350. 10c, 15c. 25c
353. Men's elastic web belts, 3 inches wide, snake buckles, in plain colors and fancy stripes, as cut No. 350...50c
354. Men's plain black silk belts, snake buckles, 2½ inches wide, 50c; 3 inches wide, 75c; and 4 inches wide, as cut No. 350.........1.00
355. Men's black silk sash, with belt attached for summer wear, as cut No. 355...1.00
356. Men's black silk star vest, with watch pocket, imitation button front, fastens at back, as cut No. 356...1.00
357. Men's leather belts, covered buckles, 2¼ inches wide, tan color, as cut No. 357...25c
358. Men's and boys' leather belts, ring sides, steel buckles, in light and dark tan shades, sizes 26 to 44 inches, as cut No. 358, 25c...50c
360. Men's extra fine leather belts, nickel buckle, leather lined, ring sides, sizes 32 to 44 inches, as cut No. 358...75c
361. Men's extra fine leather belts, mocha finish, undressed, leather lined, nickel buckle, sizes 32 to 44 inches, as cut No. 358.........1.00

Men's and Boys' Sweaters and Jerseys.

362. Men's plain ribbed wool sweaters, roll collar, in navy blue only, small, medium, and large sizes, as cut No. 362 ......50c
363. Men's all-wool sweaters, honeycomb stitch, 8 inch roll collar, ribbed skirt and cuffs, also plain rib with stripes around collar, cuffs and skirt, small, medium, and large sizes, in cardinal, navy, black and white, as cut Nos. 362 and 365...75c
364. Men's plain ribbed sweaters, all wool, 8-inch roll collar, close ribbed skirt and cuffs, navy, cardinal, black and white, small medium, and large sizes, as cut No. 362...1.00
365. Men's fine imported all-wool sweaters, roll collar, medium weight, fancy open stitch, navy with white on collar, cuffs, and skirt; navy with red, cardinal with navy, green with red, white with navy, small, medium, and large sizes, as cut No. 365...1.00
367. Fine imported all-wool sweaters, fancy open stitch, deep roll collar, cardinal, navy, black, and green, with white stripes, also white with navy blue stripes, small, medium, and large sizes, as cut No. 367...1.50
368. Men's extra fine imported sweaters, fancy open stitch, roll collar, cardinal, black, navy, green, and white, with 2-inch silk stripes round body, small, medium, and large sizes, as cut No. 368... 2.00
369. Men's all-wool jersey, medium weight, navy blue, 2-inch collar, long sleeves, sizes 34 to 46 inches, as cut No. 369...1.25
370. Men's extra fine imported all-wool cashmere jerseys, with 6-in. roll collar, sizes 34 to 42 inches, as cut No. 369...2.50
371. Fine cashmere gymnasium jerseys, light weight, quarter sleeves, low neck, in black and navy, sizes 34 to 42 inches, as cut No. 371...1.00
372. Men's fine imported all-wool cashmere jerseys, low neck, no sleeves, suitable for canoeing and racing, sizes 32 to 42 inches ..1.50
373. Men's racing or athletic 2-piece suits, all-wool cashmere, low neck, short sleeves, in cardinal, navy and black, sizes small, medium and large, per suit 1.50
374. Men's fine imported combination all-wool cashmere boating or racing suits, double seat, 2-inch stripes around body sizes 34 to 40 inches...2.50
375. Boys' all-wool sweaters, with deep roll collar, navy blue only, to fit boys 5 to 15 years, as cut No. 375...39c
376. All-wool sweaters, roll collar, in navy, cardinal and white, to fit boys from 5 to 15 years, as cut No. 375...50c
377. Boys' all-wool sweaters, roll collar, with stripes around collar, cuffs and skirt, in navy, cardinal and green, sizes to fit boys from 5 to 15 years, as cut No. 375....75c
378. Boys' fine all-wool sweaters, with large sailor collar, in navy, cardinal and black, with stripes on collar, to fit boys from 5 to 15 years, as cut No. 378...75c
379. Boys' extra fine wool sweaters, sailor collar, in navy and cardinal, sizes to fit boys from 4 to 15 years, as cut No. 378...1.00
380. Fine imported all-wool sweaters, fancy open stitch, roll collar, in cardinal, navy, green and white, with different color on collar and cuffs, to fit boys 5 to 15 years 75c
381. Boys' fine imported all-wool sweaters, fancy open stitch, in cardinal, navy, black, green and white, with stripes around body, to fit boys from 5 to 15 years..1.00
382. Boys fine imported all-wool cashmere jerseys, long sleeves, 2-inch collar, in plain navy, navy and white, navy and cardinal stripes, sizes to fit boys from 4 to 15 years, as cut No. 382.......1.50

Bicycle Hose.

383. Men's fine imported footless bicycle hose, heather mixtures, medium weight, fancy roll top, as cut No. 383, pair 50c and.......75c
384. Fine imported all-wool footless bicycle hose, fawn shades, fancy roll top, in the newest designs, as cut 383, pair 1.00
386 Men's imported bicycle hose, heather mixtures, fancy roll top, latest patterns, all sizes, as cut No. 386, 35c, 50c and...75c
387. Extra fine imported bicycle hose, heather mixtures, medium weight, fancy roll top, newest patterns, in neat fancy colors, all sizes, as cut No. 386, pair ...1.00
388. Men's fine imported bicycle hose, in plain black, with deep roll, fancy top, medium weight, all sizes, as cut No. 386, 75c and 1.00
389. Fine all-wool bicycle hose, in plain black, with deep roll, fancy black and white top, all sizes, as cut No. 386. pair 75c, $1.00 and 1.25
390. Men's fine imported all-wool bicycle hose, medium weight, fancy roll top, newest designs, fawn and navy, all sizes, as cut No. 386 1.25
391. Heavy Irish knit golf or bicycle hose, fancy roll top, wide rib, in brown or heather mixtures, all sizes, as cut No. 391, $1.25 ....1.50

Men's Half Hose.

392. Men's heavy cotton socks, mixed colors, as cut No. 392, 5c..9c
393. Men's black cotton socks, double heels and toes, all sizes, as cut No. 392, pair 10c, 12½c, 18c..25c
395. Men's balbriggan socks, double heels and toes, all sizes, as cut No. 392, pair 12½c and...18c
396. Men's tan cotton socks, medium weight, double heels and toes, all sizes, as cut No. 392, pair 12½c, 18c and ...25c
397. Men's black cotton socks, with maco split soles, cool and comfortable for summer wear, all sizes, as cut No. 392, pair......25c
398. Men's black lisle thread socks, Hermsdorf dye, double heels and toes, all sizes, pair 25c and...35c
400. Men's merino and wool socks, summer weight, all sizes, pair 12½c, 15c and...20c
402. Men's natural wool socks, medium weight, all sizes, pair 20c, ...25c
403. Men's fine imported natural wool socks, double heels and toes, spliced ankles, medium weight, all sizes, 35c, or 3 pairs for....1.00
405. Men's black cashmere socks, seamless, all full-fashioned double heels and toes, spliced ankles, all sizes, pair 18c ...25c
407. Men's fine imported plain black cashmere socks, llama finish, double heels, soles and toes, all sizes, 35c pair, or 3 pairs for $1.00; also 45c pair or 3 pairs for....1.25
408. Men's tan cashmere socks, double heels, soles, and toes, medium weight, all sizes, 35c pair, or 3 pairs for...1.00
409. Men's ribbed black cashmere socks, double soles, heels, and toes, all sizes, pair 25c, 35c and......50c
411. Men's imported fine black silk socks, double heels and toes, fast color, all sizes ...75c
412. Men's black cashmere socks, fancy embroidered fronts, seamless, all sizes, as cut No. 412, pair 35c...50c
414. Men's heather mixed imported ribbed wool socks, medium weight, all sizes, as cut No. 414, 35c pair, or 3 pairs for $1.00, and pair...50c
415. Men's Irish knit black socks, ribbed, all wool, soft finish, all sizes, as cut No. 414, pair......25c
416. Men's Irish knit ribbed socks, double heels and toes, seamless, in black, medium, and dark grey, all sizes, as cut No. 414, 35c pair, or 3 pairs for...1.00
417. Extra fine Irish knit wool socks, double heels, soles, and toes, in black, medium and dark grey, all sizes, as cut No. 414........50c

Men's and Boys' Bathing Suits.

420. Men's bathing trunks, dark ground, with fancy stripes, all sizes, each ...25c
421. Men's combination bathing suits, dark ground, with fancy cardinal and white stripes, sizes small, medium, large and extra large, as cut No. 421, per suit...50c
422. Combination bathing suits, navy ground, with fancy cardinal and white stripes around neck, arms and legs, pearl buttons, sizes small, medium, large and extra large, as cut No. 421, per suit 75c
423. Men's plain navy combination swimming suits, no sleeves, made to button on shoulder, pearl buttons, sizes small, medium, large and extra large, per suit......75c
424 Combination bathing suits, no sleeves, in dark navy ground, with white around neck, sleeves and legs, sizes small, medium, large and extra large, per suit......1.00
425. Fine cashmere combination bathing suits, in navy blue and black, fast colors, sizes small, medium, large, and extra large as cut No. 421, per suit...1.50
426. Men's 2-piece bathing suits in navy blue ground with white stripes around neck, arms, and legs, sizes small, medium, large and extra large, as cut No. 426, per suit...1.00
427. Fine cashmere 2-piece bathing suits, navy blue, with white stripes, fast color, sizes small, medium, large and extra large, as cut No. 426, per suit...1.75
428. 2-piece cashmere bathing suits, in plain navy and black, short sleeves, fast colors, small, medium, large and extra large, as cut No. 428, per suit.......1.50
429. Boys' bathing trunks, dark colors, with fancy stripes, all sizes, each...10c
430. Boys' combination bathing suits, dark ground, with fancy stripes, all sizes, to fit boys from 5 to 15 years, as cut No. 430, per suit, 35c and ...50c

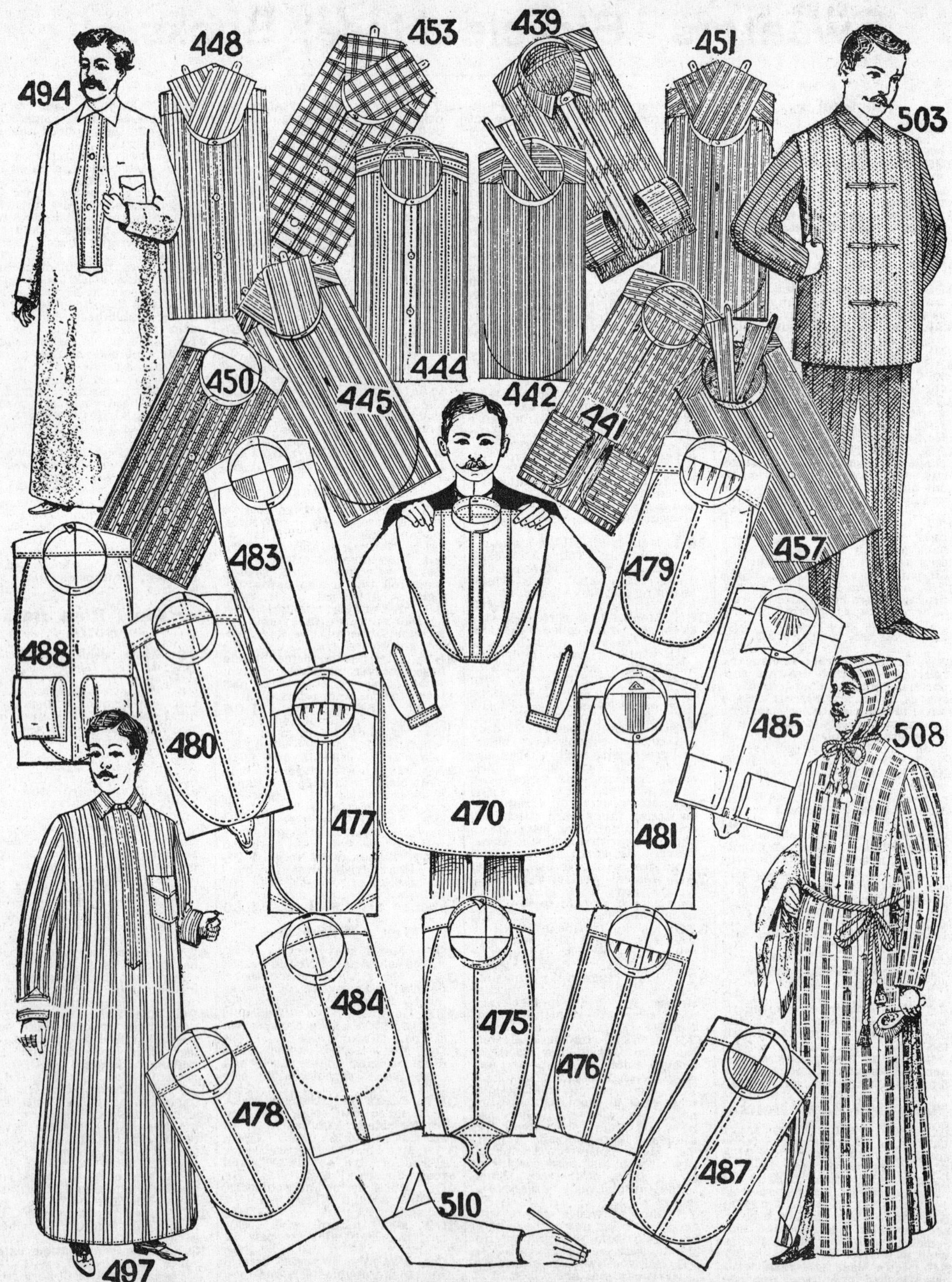

Be sure and give size of Collar worn, also note that some Shirts do not have separate Collars.

Men's Shirts and Night Robes.

Cambric Shirts.

439. Men's colored cambric shirts, open front, collar and cuffs attached, negligee bosom, in neat blue stripes, as cut No. 439, sizes 14 to 17½ **39c**

440. Men's colored cambric shirts, collar and cuffs attached, open front, negligee bosom, blue ground with light stripes, as cut No. 439, sizes 14 to 17½ **50c**

441. Men's colored cambric laundried shirts, open front, cuffs attached, in blue, grey and pink stripes, as cut No 441, sizes 14 to 17½ **50c**

442. Men's fine colored cambric shirts, open back, laundried bosom, one separate turn-down collar, cuffs attached. In this line we have a large assortment of the newest stripes, in light and dark blue and mauve shades, as cut No. 442, sizes 14 to 17½, extra value.. **50c**

443. Men's colored cambric negligee shirts, open front, one separate collar, cuffs attached, in the latest stripes, in blue and mauve shades, sizes 14 to 17½ **50c**

444. Men's zephyr negligee shirts, open front, cuffs attached, laundried neckband, in the latest designs, in stripes and checks, as cut No. 444, sizes 14 to 17½ **50c**

445. Men's fine laundried cambric shirts, open front, long or short bosom, detached link cuffs, in the newest stripes and checks, as cut No. 445, sizes 14 to 18........ **75c**

446. Colored cambric shirts, laundried bosom, open front, or open back and front, reversible link cuffs, in the latest stripes and newest colorings, long or short bosom, as cut No. 445, sizes 14 to 18 ... **1.00**

447. Men's fine cambric shirts, open back, laundried, two separate turn-down collars, detached link cuffs, in the latest American stripes, sizes 14 to 17½........ **75c**

448. Men's fine Scotch zephyr negligee shirts, open front, detached double-end link cuffs, in the newest colorings, in stripes and checks, as cut No. 448, sizes 14 to 18, special value **75c**

449. Fine imported Scotch zephyr negligee shirts, open front, detached double-end link-cuffs, in the newest stripes and checks, as cut No. 448, sizes 14 to 18 .... **1.00**

450. Men's white shirts, with silk fronts, laundried neck and wristbands, in the latest novelties in stripes, checks and plaids, as cut No. 450, sizes 14 to 18........ **75c**

451. Fine cambric shirts, laundried bosom, open back and front, detached double-end link cuffs, in a large assortment of the newest stripes for spring and summer wear, as cut No. 451, sizes 14 to 18 .... **1.25**

452. Fine cambric shirts, laundried bosom, open back and front, detached double-end link cuffs, cushion neckband, in the latest patterns, in blue, mauve and oxblood shades, as cut No. 451, sizes 14 to 18........ **1.50**

453. Fine imported Scotch zephyr negligee shirts, open front, detached link cuffs. These are the newest designs, in blue, mauve and pink stripes, checks and plaids, as cut No. 453, sizes 14 to 18...... **1.25**

454. Fine imported Scotch zephyr negligee shirts, open front, detached, link cuffs, cushion neckband. These are the newest designs, in oxblood, blue, mauve and pink stripes, checks and plaids, as cut No. 453, sizes 14 to 18........ **1.50**

Boys' Shirts and Night Robes.

455. Boys' cambric shirts, collar and cuffs attached, open front, in neat blue stripes, as cut No. 439, sizes 12 to 14 .... **39c**

456. Boys' cambric shirts, open back, laundried bosom, one separate collar, cuffs attached, in the newest blue and mauve stripes, as cut No 442, sizes 12 to 14........ **50c**

457. Boys' cambric shirts, negligee bosom, open front, two separate collars, cuffs attached, in blue and mauve stripes, as cut No. 457, sizes 12 to 14 .... **50c**

458. Boys' fine colored cambric shirts, open front, detached link cuffs, no collars, in the newest stripes, for spring and summer wear, sizes 12 to 14........ **75c**

459. Boys' white shirts, with silk fronts, laundried neck and wristbands, in blue, pink and mauve stripes and checks, sizes 12 to 14 .... **75c**

460. Boys' Scotch zephyr negligee shirts, open front, detached link cuffs, in neat and fancy checks and stripes, newest colors, sizes 12 to 14 .... **75c**

461. Boys' white unlaundried shirts, open back, linen bosom and cuffs, reinforced fronts, heavy cotton, sizes 12 to 13½........ **35c**

462. Boys' fine white unlaundried shirts, open back, fine even thread cotton, linen bosom and cuffs, reinforced fronts, sizes 12 to 13½ .. **50c**

463. Boys' fine white laundried shirts, open back, linen bosom and cuffs, heavy cotton reinforced fronts, sizes 12 to 13½........ **50c**

464. Boys' heavy flannelette night robes, collar attached, pocket yoke and pearl buttons, sizes 10 to 14 .... **50c**

465. Boys' heavy white twilled cotton night robes, collar attached, yoke pocket and pearl buttons, sizes 10 to 14 .... **50c**

White Unlaundried Shirts.

470. Our leader, known as "Eaton's 50c unlaundried shirt," open back, linen bosom, cuffs or wristbands, reinforced front, continuous facings, fine even thread cotton, large full bodies, as cut No. 470, sizes 14 to 21 .... **50c**

471. Men's white unlaundried shirts, open back, reinforced front, cuffs or wristbands, continuous facings, heavy cotton, as cut No. 470, sizes 14 to 17½........ **35c**

472. Men's fine white unlaundried shirts, open back, pure linen, inserted bosom, cuffs or wristbands, fine even thread cotton, patent staying on back and sleeves, reinforced front, continuous facings, as cut No. 470, sizes 14 to 21........ **75c**

473. Our comfort shirt, unlaundried, fine cotton, linen bosom and wristbands, bosom 9½ inches long, sizes 14 to 18, as cut No. 478........ **50c**

474. Men's fine white unlaundried shirts, open front, linen bosom and wristbands, fine cotton, reinforced front, medium size bosom, sizes 14 to 18........ **75c**

475. Men's extra fine white unlaundried shirts, open back, reinforced front, pure Irish linen bosom, wristbands only, fine English cotton, patent staying on back and sleeves, cushion neckband, as cut No. 475, sizes 14 to 18........ **1.00**

NOTE.—Line No. 475 is made in different length sleeves, 31, 33 and 35 inches. Measure from centre of back to end of wristband.

White Laundried Shirts.

476. Men's white laundried shirts, open back, reinforced front, heavy cotton, cuffs or wristbands, continuous facings, as cut No 476, sizes 14 to 17½........ **50c**

477. Men's fine white laundried shirts, open back, reinforced front, linen bosom, cuffs or wristbands, continuous facings, full size bodies, fine cotton, as cut No. 477, sizes 14 to 18........ **75c**

478. "The business shirt," open back, short bosom 9 inches long, linen front and wristbands, as cut No. 478, sizes 14 to 18........ **75c**

479. Men's white laundried shirts, open back, short bosom, linen bosom and wristbands, fine English cotton, as cut No. 479, sizes 14 to 18........ **1.00**

480. Men's laundried white shirts, open back, pure linen bosom, cuffs or wristbands, extra reinforcing around bosom, patent staying on back and sleeves, cushion neckband, fine cotton, as cut No. 480, sizes 14 to 19, extra value at ... **1.00**

481. Men's fine imported white dress shirts, open front, 4-ply linen bosom, cuffs or wristbands, cushion neckband, as cut No. 481, sizes 14 to 18 .... **1.00**

482. White dress shirts, open front, linen bosom and wristbands, as cut No. 481, sizes 14 to 17½........ **75c**

483. Men's white dress shirts, imported make, open front and back, linen bosom and wristbands, superior finish, as cut No. 483, sizes 14 to 18........ **1.00**

484. Laundried white shirts, open front, short bosom, linen bosom and wristbands, imported make, cushion neckband, as cut No. 484, sizes 14 to 18........ **1.00**

485. White laundried shirts, open front, with collar and cuffs attached, linen bosom, as cut No. 485, sizes 14 to 18½........ **1.00**

486. Extra fine white laundried shirts, open back, 4-ply linen bosom and wristbands, cushion neckband, superior finish, sizes 14 to 18.. **1.25**

487. Men's fine imported white laundried shirts, open front and back, medium size bosom, superior finish, linen bosom and wristbands, fine cotton, as cut No. 487, sizes 14 to 17½........ **1.25**

488. Best quality fine imported white dress shirts, open back and front, fine linen bosom, cuffs attached, best finish, extra fine cotton, as cut No. 488, sizes 14 to 17½, each .... **1.50 and 2.00**

White Shirts for Stout Men.

489. Unlaundried shirts, open back, cuffs or wristbands, sizes 16 to 21 .... **50c and 75c**

490. Unlaundried shirts, open back, wristbands, sizes 16 to 18........ **1.00**

491. Laundried shirts, open back, cuffs or wristbands, sizes 16 to 18 .... **75c**

492. Laundried shirts, open back, cuffs or wristbands, sizes 16 to 19½ **1.00**

Night Robes.

493. Heavy white twilled cotton night robes, neatly trimmed or plain, yoke pocket and pearl buttons, 54 inches long, sizes 14 to 19. **50c**

494. White night robes heavy twilled cotton, reinforced front, collar attached, pocket yoke and pearl buttons, 54 inches long, as cut No. 494, sizes 14 to 19........ **75c**

495 Men's fine white twilled cotton night robes, patent front, trimmed with best silk embroidery, full size bodies, 54 inches long, sizes 14 to 19 .... **1.00**

496. Extra fine plain white cotton night robes, made of fine material for summer wear, neatly trimmed, sizes 14 to 19........ **1.00**

497. Men's flannelette night robes, collar attached, yoke pocket and pearl buttons, full size bodies, 54 inches long, pink and blue stripes, as cut No. 497, sizes 14 to 19..... **50c**

498. Men's fine flannelette night robes, good quality, collar attached, yoke pocket and pearl buttons, full size bodies, 54 inches long, as cut No. 497, sizes 14 to 19........ **75c**

499. Flannelette night robes, for large men, made from heavy twilled flannelette, 58 inches long, collar attached, pocket, neat blue and pink stripes, as cut No. 497, sizes 15 to 21........ **1.00**

500. Men's fine imported natural wool night robes, collar attached, pocket and pearl buttons, large loose bodies, 60 inches long, sizes 15 to 19........ **2.50**

501. Fine imported natural wool night robes. This garment is made from the finest and softest wool, collar attached and pocket, large loose bodies, 60 inches long, sizes 14 to 19 .... **3.00**

Pyjama Suits.

502. Men's flannelette pyjama suits, turn-down collar attached, pearl buttons, neat stripes, light, medium and dark shades, sizes 34 to 44-inch chest, per suit **1.25**

503. Pyjama suits, made from fine zephyr material, and flannelette, Ceylon finish, turn-down collar, pearl buttons, in neat and fancy stripes and checks, as cut No. 503, sizes 34 to 46-inch chest, per suit. **1.50**

504. Men's fine silk stripe cashmerette pyjama suits, turn-down collar, frog fasteners, in blue, pink and mauve stripes, as cut No. 503, sizes 34 to 46-inch chest, per suit. **2.00**

505. Pyjama suits, made of fine English unshrinkable flannel, turn-down collar, pearl buttons instead of frog fasteners, in neat stripes, as cut No. 503, sizes 34 to 46-inch chest, per suit........ **2.50**

506. Men's extra fine quality silk stripe cashmere pyjama suits, frog fasteners, turn-down collar, in neat nobby stripes, as cut No. 503, sizes 34 to 44-inch chest, per suit.... **3.00**

507. Men's pyjama suits, made from fine French flannel, turn-down collar, frog fasteners, fly front on pants, in stripes and checks, sizes 34 to 44-inch chest, per suit.... **4.00**

Bath Robes.

508. Men's imported Turkish bath robes, made with hood and girdle, two pockets, in light, medium and dark checks and stripes, lengths 56, 60 and 62 inches, as cut No. 508, each **2.50, 4.00, 5.00, 6.00** and **7.00**

510. Black sateen sleeve protectors, elastic at both ends, as cut No. 510, per pair........ **15c**

Sundries for Mending Purposes.

511. Neckbands, open back or front, sizes 14 to 18, each........ **5c**

512. Wristbands, sizes 9½ to 10½, per pair........ **6c**

513. Cuffs, sizes 9½ to 11, per pair. **10c**

514. Bosoms for open back shirts each........ **10c**

When ordering white shirts state whether you want cuffs or wristbands.

See that the line you select comes in the size you require. Drawers always come 2 in. smaller than the Shirt, unless otherwise requested.

Shirts and Underwear.

Flannelette Shirts.

520. Men's flannelette shirts, collar attached, in neat stripes, sizes 14 to 17 inches, as cut No. 520 ....**25c**

521. Men's flannelette shirts, collar attached, yoke pocket, in neat stripes, sizes 14 to 17½, as cut No. 520 ....**35c**

522. Fine flannelette shirts, collar attached or plain neckband, yoke pocket and pearl buttons, neat stripes, as cut No. 523, sizes 14 to 18..........................**50c**

523. Men's fine Ceylon-finished flannelette shirts, collar attached or plain neckband, new stripes, in light and medium shades, as cut No 523, sizes 14 to 18...........**75c**

Cashmerette and Silk Shirts.

524. Silk stripe cashmerette outing shirts, collar attached, pocket and pearl buttons, in blue, pink and mauve stripes, as cut No. 524, sizes 14 to 18 ....**75c**

525 Men's fine cashmerette shirts, silk stripe, collar attached or sateen neckband, pocket and pearl buttons, light stripes, as cut No. 524, sizes 14 to 18...........**1.00**

527. Fine quality silk-striped cashmere shirts, collar attached, patent front, newest blue, mauve and pink stripes, as cut No. 527, sizes 14 to 18..........**1.50, 2.00**

528. Men's fine silk shirts, collar attached and pocket, patent front, in plain white and blue and pink stripes, as cut No. 527, sizes 14 to 18 each..........**3.00**

529. White French flannel outing shirts, collar attached, pocket and pearl buttons, sizes 14 to 18 ..**1.50**

Sateen, Gingham and Oxford Shirts.

530. Men's black sateen shirts, collar attached and pocket, fast dye, full size bodies, as cut No. 530, sizes 14 to 18 ....**50c**

531. Fine quality black sateen shirts, collar attached, double-stitched seams, as cut No. 530, sizes 14 to 18 ....**75c**

532. Best quality heavy black sateen shirts, collar attached, strong make, as cut No. 530, sizes 14 to 19 ....**1.00**

533. Men's drill or heavy galatea and gingham shirts, attached collar or neckband, strong and durable, as cut No. 533, sizes 14 to 18..........................**50c**

535. Heavy English Oxford shirts, collar attached or plain neckband, as cut No. 533, sizes 14 to 18....**75c**

Knit Top Shirts.

536. Men's grey knit top shirts, laced or buttoned front, medium men's size, as cut No. 536...... ......**35c**

537. Cream knit outing shirts, collar attached, buttoned front, men's size, as cut No. 536.............**43c**

538. Navy blue knit top shirts, laced or buttoned fronts, collar attached, men's size, as cut No. 536 .... **50c**

539. Fine quality navy blue knit top shirts, laced or buttoned front, medium weight, men's size, as cut No. 536 ....**75c**

Men's Flannel Shirts.

540. Grey union flannel shirts, collar attached or silesia neckband, pearl buttons, as cut No. 540, sizes 14 to 18..........................**75c**

541. Grey Campbellford flannel shirts, collar attached or silesia neckband, as cut No. 540, sizes 14 to 18½ **1.00**

542. Men's military flannel shirts, in steel grey shade, collar attached, unshrinkable, as cut No. 540, sizes 14 to 18 ....**1.25**

543. Navy blue Campbellford flannel shirts, collar attached or silesia neckband, pearl buttons, as cut No. 540, sizes 14 to 18½ **1.25**

544. Best navy blue Campbellford flannel shirts, collar attached, patent front, as cut No. 544, sizes 14 to 18 ....**1 50**

545. Unshrinkable English flannel shirts, collar attached or silesia neckband, neat stripes and checks, as cut No. 545, sizes 14 to 18½..**1.25**

546. Best English unshrinkable flannel shirts, collar attached or white sateen neckband, silk stitched, best finish, neat and fancy checks and stripes, as cut No. 545, sizes 15 to 18..........................**2.00**

Boys' and Youths' Shirts.

548. Boys' flannelette shirts, collar attached or plain neckband, neat stripes, sizes 10 to 13½ **25c**

549. Flannelette shirts, collar attached, neat stripes, sizes 12 to 13½ **35c**

550. Boys' shirts, fine Ceylon-finished flannelette, collar attached or plain neckband, pearl buttons, neat blue and pink stripes, sizes 12 to 13½..........................**50c**

551. Fine silk-striped cashmerette shirts, collar attached and pocket, pearl buttons, in light blue, mauve and pink stripes, size 12 to 13½..**50c**

552. Boys' black sateen shirts, collar attached, fast dye, sizes 12 to 13½ **50c**

553. Boys' cream knit outing shirts, laced fronts, collar attached, to fit boys from 5 to 14 years.. ......**43c**

554. Boys' grey flannel shirts, collar attached or silesia neckband, sizes 12 to 13½ **50c**

555. Boys' navy blue Campbellford flannel shirts, collar attached or silesia neckband, sizes 12 to 13½.**75c**

Cardigan Jackets.

556. English cardigan jackets, mohair binding, cuffs to button, black and seal brown shades, medium sizes, as cut No. 556, 75c, $1.00, 1.25, 1.50 ....**2.00**

557. Fine imported English cardigan jackets, worsted finish, mohair binding, black and seal brown shades, as cut No. 556, sizes medium, large and extra large, $1.25, 1.50, 1.75, 2.00, 2.25, 2.50 ....**4.00**

Men's Underwear.

When ordering underwear be careful to see if your size is made in the line you wish, as some lines are not made in all sizes.

Drawers always come 2 inches smaller than shirts, unless instructed otherwise. Note scale of sizes—

Shirts, chest measure—
34, 36, 38, 40, 42, 44 inches.

Drawers, waist measure—
32, 34, 36, 38, 40, 42 inches.

Men's size means, for medium size man, 36 or 38 inch chest measure.

559. Men's double thread balbriggan underwear, natural color and light blue shade, French neck, overlocked seams, as cut No. 559, sizes 34 to 44, each..........................**25c**

560. Men's double thread balbriggan underwear, overlocked seams, pearl buttons, sateen facings, French neck, in fancy stripe, mottled and natural color, as cut No. 559, sizes 34 to 44, each..........**35c**

561. Men's double thread fine balbriggan underwear, overlocked seams, pearl buttons, silk facings, French neck, sizes 34 to 44, as cut No. 559, each **50c**

562. Men's silk-finished balbriggan underwear, extra light weight for the hot summer wear, silk-trimmed, pearl buttons, sizes 34 to 44 inches chest, as cut No. 559, each **75c**

563. Men's fine imported double thread balbriggan underwear, overlocked seams, pearl buttons, silk trimmings, sizes 34 to 46 inches chest, as cut No. 559, each **75c**

564. Men's fine imported balbriggan underwear, gauze weight, pearl buttons, full fashioned, ribbed skirt, silk trimmings, sizes 34 to 46 inches chest, each **1.00**

565. Men's fine imported balbriggan underwear, French neck, pearl buttons, full fashioned, silk trimmings, sizes 34 to 44 inches chest, as cut No. 559, each **1.50**

566. Men's cotton underwear, soft merino finish, French neck, as cut No. 566, medium sizes only.**25c**

567. Men's merino underwear, medium weight, ribbed cuffs and ankles, medium sizes only, as cut No. 566, each..........................**35c**

568. Men's wool merino underwear, summer weight, sateen trimmings, overlocked seams, ribbed skirt and cuffs, small, medium and large sizes, as cut No.566, each **50c**

569. Men's merino underwear, natural shade, beige trimmings, pearl buttons, overlocked seams, ribbed cuffs and ankles, sizes 34 to 44 inches chest, as cut No. 569, each **75c**

570. Men's fine imported all-wool underwear, summer weight, natural shade, overlocked seams, pearl buttons, beige trimmings, sizes 34 to 44 inches chest, as cut No. 570, each **75c**

571. Men's fine natural wool underwear, medium weight, sateen trimmings, overlocked seams, ribbed skirt and cuffs, French neck, sizes 34 to 42 inches chest, as cut No. 570, each **1.00**

572. Men's fine imported natural wool underwear, summer weight, beige trimmings, pearl buttons, overlocked seams, ribbed cuffs and ankles, sizes 34 to 44 inches chest, as cut No. 570, each **1.00**

573. Men's fine imported natural wool underwear, medium weight, full fashioned, pearl buttons, ribbed skirt and cuffs, sizes 34 to 44 inches chest, as cut No. 570, each **1.25**

574. Fine imported natural wool underwear, summer weight, extra fine quality, sizes 34 to 44 inches chest, as cut No. 570, each **1.50**

575. Fine imported fancy striped wool underwear, summer weight, silk trimmed, pearl buttons, sizes 34 to 44 inches chest, as cut No. 575, each..........................**1.25**

576. Men's heavy Scotch wool underwear, shirts double breasted, ribbed skirt and cuffs, sateen trimmings, medium size only, each **75c**

577. Men's heavy Scotch wool underwear, "Turnbull's 16-gauge" unshrinkable full-fashioned, double breasted, winter weight, sizes 34 to 44 inches chest, each **1.25**

578. Men's fine silk uuderwear plain colors, best trimmings, pearl buttons, sizes 34 to 44 inches chest, each **2.50**

579. Men's extra fine pure silk underwear, full fashioned, fancy striped and natural shades, sizes 34 to 44 inches chest, each..........**5.00**

580. Men's imported balbriggan underwear, summer weight, short sleeves, silk trimmings, pearl buttons, sizes 34 to 44 inches chest, each **35c**

581. Men's imported all-wool shirts, summer weight, short sleeves, overlocked seams, pearl buttons, sizes 34 to 44 inches chest, each.**75c**

582. Men's imported fancy striped cotton underwear, summer weight, shirts short sleeves, sizes 34 to 42 inches chest, each **1.00**

583. Men's natural wool bicycle drawers, knee length, double seats, pearl buttons, overlocked seams, sizes 30 to 42 inches **75c**

584. Men's Swiss net undershirts, short sleeves, pearl buttons, sizes 34 to 42 inches chest, each......**25c**

585. Men's fine Swiss net undershirts, with short sleeves, silk trimmings, pearl buttons, all sizes, 34 to 42 inches chest, each......**50c**

Special Sizes for Stout Men.

586. Men's natural wool underwear, medium weight, French neck, overlocked seams, sateen trimmings, sizes 44 and 46 inches chest, as cut No. 586, each **1.25**

587. Men's imported natural wool underwear, summer weight, pearl buttons, beige trimmings, sizes 46, 48 and 50 inches chest, as cut No. 586, each **1.00**

588. Imported natural wool underwear, summer weight, overlocked seams, pearl buttons, best trimmings, sizes 46, 48 and 50 inches chest, as cut No. 586, each **1.50**

Combination Suits.

589. Men's fine imported natural wool combination undersuits, medium weight, overlocked seams, pearl buttons, sizes 32 to 42 inches chest, as cut No. 589, suit......**3.00**

590. Men's fine natural merino combination undersuits, unshrinkable summer weight, perfect fitting, sizes 34 to 44 inches chest, as cut No. 589, suit..........................**4.50**

590A. Men's pure silk combination undersuits, elastic stitch, full fashioned, spliced seats, very best finish, sizes 34 to 40 inches chest, as cut No. 589, suit **10.00**

Chest Protectors and Night Caps.

591. Scarlet flannel chest and back protectors, lined with best quality perforated chamois, as cut No. 591 each **75c**

592. Pure wool body bands, all sizes, according to waist measure, as cut No. 592, each..........................**75c**

593. Men's white cotton night caps, double, medium weight, all sizes, as cut No. 593, each **35c**

Boys' Underwear.

SCALE OF SIZES.

Age	4,	6,	8,	10,	12,	14 years.
Size	1,	2,	3,	4,	5,	6.

594. Boys' underwear, soft merino finish, French neck, ribbed cuffs and ankles, all sizes, each **25c**

595. Boys' balbriggan underwear, overlocked seams, French neck, ribbed cuffs and ankles—

Sizes	1,	2,	3,	4,	5,	6,
Price	25c,	25c,	25c,	35c,	35c,	35c each.

596. Boys' imported balbriggan underwear, shirts short sleeves, drawers knee length, overlocked seams, pearl buttons, all sizes, each **50c**

597. Boys' wool merino underwear, medium weight, sateen trimmings, ribbed skirt and cuffs, all sizes—

Sizes	1,	2,	3,	4,	5,	6,
Price	35c,	35c,	35c,	45c,	45c,	45c each.

598. Fine imported natural wool underwear, summer weight, pearl buttons, overlocked seams, all sizes, each **50c**

599. Boys' imported natural wool underwear, shirts short sleeves, drawers knee length, all sizes, each **65c**

600. Boys' fine imported wool underwear, medium summer weight, overlocked seams, pearl buttons, all sizes, each..........................**1.00**

601. Boys' fine imported combination undersuits, summer weight, button front, unshrinkable, all sizes, as cut No. 601, suit......**1.25**

N.B.—All prices for underwear mean each garment.

Latest Spring Styles in Men's,

OUR CUSTOMERS MAY RELY ON RECEIVING FIRST-CLASS GOODS.

Boys' and Children's Headwear.

1. Men's silk hats, newest styles, finest quality linings and trimmings, as cut No. 1 ....**6.00**

2. Young men's silk hats, special quality silk plush and trimmings, smaller shape than cut No. 1..**5.00**

3. Men's silk hats, fine quality silk plush, very light weight, as cut No. 1 ....**4.00**

4. Men's fur felt stiff hats, best quality silk trimmings, colors black and brown, as cut No. 4 ....**3.00**

5. Young men's fur felt stiff hats, same quality, smaller shape than cut No. 4 ....**3.00**

6. Men's fur felt stiff hats, light weight, fine silk trimmings, black and brown, as cut No. 6.........**2.50**

7. Young men's fur felt stiff hats, same quality, smaller shape than cut No. 6, black, light and dark brown **2.50**

8. Men's fine quality fur felt square crown stiff hats, in black and brown, as cut No. 8 ....**2.50**

9. Men's fur felt stiff hats, new American style, in black, light and dark brown, as cut No. 9......**2.00**

10. Young men's fur felt stiff hats, same quality and shades, smaller shape than cut No. 9.........**2.00**

10A. Men's stiff hats, same quality, but larger shape than cut No. 9, in sizes 7½ and 7⅝...............**2.00**

11. Men's stiff hats, pure fur felt, black and California brown, as cut No. 11...........................**1.50**

12. Young men's hats, same quality and colors, but smaller shape than cut No. 11........................**1.50**

13. Men's fur felt stiff hats, good silk trimming, black and mid brown, as cut No. 13.....................**1.00**

14. Men's soft hats, John B. Stetson's make, black, pearl, nut and bronze, as cut No. 14..............**5.00**

15. Men's black, pearl and brown fur felt soft hats, extra quality, as cut No. 15 ....**3.00**

16. Young men's fedora hats, choice fur felt, smaller shape than cut No. 15.............................**3.00**

17. Men's American shape fur felt soft hats, in black, pearl, light and dark brown, as cut No. 17......**2.50**

18. Young men's fur felt soft hats, same quality and colors, smaller shape than cut No. 17..........**2.50**

19. Men's fine fur felt clerical hats, black only, as cut No. 19..........**2.00**

20. Men's fur felt soft hats, colors black, pearl, light and dark brown, as cut No. 20 ....**2.00**

21. Young men's fur felt soft hats, same quality and colors, but smaller shape than cut No. 20.......**2.00**

21A. Men's fedora hats, black and brown colors, larger shape than cut No. 20, sizes 7½ and 7⅝......**2.00**

22. Men's soft hats, special quality fur felt, in black, pearl, tan and brown, as cut No. 22 ....**1.50**

23. Young men's soft hats, smaller shape, same quality and shades as cut No. 22........................**1.50**

24. Men's English fur felt soft hats, colors black and mid brown, as cut No. 24.............................**1.00**

25. Men's smoke color felt fedora hats, silk trimmings, as cut No. 25 ....**1.00**

26. Men's smoke color felt fedora hats, crown and brim stitched with black silk, as cut No. 25..**1.00**

27. Men's English felt fedora hats, in black and brown colors, as cut No. 25.............................**75c**

28. Men's black and brown felt fedora hats, as cut No. 25......**50c**

29. Men's sombrero felt hats, in black, brown and grey, as cut No. 29..**75c**

30. Men's black sombrero hats, silk bound, as cut No. 29.............**50c**

31. Men's, youths' and boys' plain or fancy colored felt land or water hats, as cut No. 31..............**50c**

32. Men's and youths' fine English felt crush hats, in black and brown, as cut No. 31....................**75c**

33. Men's and youths' black, navy and brown felt crush hats, as cut No. 31.................................**50c**

34. Youths' and boys' fine fur felt stiff hats, latest spring shapes, in black and brown, as cut No. 34.**1.00**

35. Youths' and boys' fine English fur felt crusher hats, in black, brown and grey, as cut No. 35.**1.00**

36. Youths' and boys' fur felt fedora hats, latest spring style, in black and brown, as cut No. 36..... **1.00**

37. Youths' and boys' fine felt fedora hats, neat shape, colors black and brown, as cut No. 36............**75c**

38. Youths' and boys' black and brown felt fedora hats, as cut No. 36.......................................**50c**

39. Ladies' and boys' fawn or dark grey felt fedora hats, crown and brim stitched with black silk, as cut No. 39 ....**75c**

40. Ladies' and boys' fine felt fedora hats, neat small shape, in black and brown, as cut No. 39 ....**50c**

41. Youths' and boys' plain black, navy and brown crush hats, as cut No. 41 ....**50c**

42. Youths' and boys' English felt crush hats, black, navy and brown, as cut No. 41 ....**35c**

43. Boys' felt crusher hats, neat crown, in black and brown, as cut No. 41..................................**25c**

44. Boys' plain navy blue serge and fancy tweed turbans, as cut No. 44 ....**25c**

45. Men's and youths' finest quality Scotch tweed hookdown caps, as cut No. 45 ....**75c**

46. Men's and youths' navy blue worsted serge and tweed hookdown caps, as cut No. 45............**50c**

47. Men's and youths' tweed and navy blue worsted serge hookdown caps, as cut No. 45..................**35c**

48. Men's and youths' Scotch tweed caps, American shape, silk lined, as cut No. 48 ....**75c**

49. Men's and youths' navy blue serge and tweed, American caps, ventilated seams, as cut No. 48.**50c**

50. Men's and youths' tweed and navy serge American shape caps, silk lined, as cut No. 48..........**35c**

51. Men's and youths navy serge and tweed American shape caps, ventilated seams, as cut No. 48.**35c**

52. Men's and youths' imported tweed and navy blue worsted serge American shape caps, as cut No. 48 ....**25c**

53. Ladies' and boys' navy blue serge and fancy tweed caps, American shape, as cut No. 48 ......**35c**

54. Ladies' and boys' navy serge and assorted tweed caps, American style, sateen linings, as cut No. 48...**25c**

55. Men's and youths' navy blue or black worsted serge and assorted tweed hookdown caps, as cut No. 55 ....**25c**

56. Men's and youths' fawn or grey corduroy caps, hookdown style, neat full shape, as cut No. 55...**25c**

57. Men's and youths' worsted serge and tweed hookdown caps, as cut No. 55...**15c**

58. Ladies' and boys' fancy tweed and navy serge hookdown caps, as cut No. 58 ....**35c**

59. Ladies' and boys' navy or black worsted serge and tweed hookdown caps, as cut No. 58 ....**25c**

60. Ladies' and boys' fawn or grey corduroy hookdown caps, as cut No. 58 ....**25c**

61. Ladies' and boys' tweed and navy serge hookdown caps, as cut No. 58.......................................**15c**

62. Ladies' and boys' navy or black serge and tweed varsity caps, as cut No. 62 ....**25c**

63. Ladies' and boys' fawn or grey corduroy varsity caps, silk lined, as cut No. 62 ....**25c**

64. Ladies' and boys' navy serge and tweed varsity caps, as cut No. 62 ....**15c**

65. Ladies' and boys' fancy flannel varsity caps, sateen lined, as cut No. 62..**15c**

66. Boys' navy cloth caps, gilt braid on front, as cut No. 66 ....**15c**

67. Ladies' and boys' blue cloth caps, silk cord on front, as cut No. 66.**19c**

68. Ladies' and boys' navy velvet caps, silk cord on front, as cut No. 66 ....**19c**

69. Ladies' and boys' blue cloth caps, mohair braid band, as cut No. 66..**25c**

70. Ladies' and boys' white duck caps, cream or black braid bands, as cut No. 66.................................**25c**

71. Ladies' and boys' navy serge and cloth caps, plain or fancy braid bands, as cut No. 71................**35c**

72. Ladies' and boys' white duck caps, fancy braid bands, as cut No. 71...**35c**

73. Ladies' and boys' blue beaver cloth and serge caps, silk lined, as cut No. 71...................................**50c**

74. Men's and youth's blue beaver cloth caps, cloth or glazed leather peaks, as cut No. 74..............**25**

75. Men's and youths' fawn or brown pique caps, glazed leather peaks, as cut No. 74 ....**25c**

76. Men's and youths' white duck caps, black braid around band and peak, as cut No. 74 ....**25c**

77. Men's and youths' blue cloth caps, leather or cloth peaks, as cut No. 74...**35c**

78. Men's and youths' white or fawn pique caps, ventilated crown and leather peak, as cut No. 78.....**35c**

79. Men's and youths' white duck caps, cream or black braid band, leather or cloth peaks, as cut No. 79..**50c**

80. Men's and youths' navy serge and beaver cloth caps, cloth or leather peaks, as cut No. 79.....**50c**

81. Men's and youths' blue beaver cloth caps, leather or cloth peaks, as cut No. 79 ....**75c**

82. Men's and youths' blue beaver caps, cloth peaks, as cut No. 79.**1.00**

83. Men's and youths' black silk caps, as cut No. 83.....................**50c**

84. Men's and youths' black Italian cloth caps, as cut No. 83..........**25c**

85. Men's and youths' black silk caps, as cut No. 85......................**50c**

86. Men's and youths' black Italian cloth caps, as cut No. 85............**25c**

87. Men's and youths' black silk caps, as cut No. 87 ....**50c**

88. Men's and youths' black Italian cloth caps, as cut No. 87 ....**25c**

89. Children's Berlin wool toques, plain colors or with fancy striped borders, as cut No. 89.............**25c**

90. Youths' and boys' caps, leather or silk binding, as cut No. 90...**25c**

91. Children's blue, black or brown velvet caps, as cut No. 90......**35c**

92. Youths' and boys' navy caps, silk or leather binding, as cut No. 90.**35c**

93. Youths' and boys' Scotch knit caps, silk or leather binding, as cut No. 90 ....**50c**

94. Children's navy cloth Tam o' Shanters, soft crown, as cut No. 94 ....**25c**

95. Children's white duck Tam o' Shanters, soft detachable top, name on band, as cut No. 94 ....**25c**

96. Children's white or sky blue Tam o' Shanters, soft detachable top, as cut No. 94......................**35c**

97. Children's navy wired top Tam o' Shanters, as cut No. 97.......**25c**

98. Children's blue cloth Tam o' Shanters, wired crown, name on band, as cut No. 97....................**35c**

99. Children's scarlet or myrtle cloth Tam o' Shanters, wired top, named band, as cut No. 97.................**35c**

100. Children's navy velvet Tam o' Shanters, soft top, as cut No. 100 ....**35c**

101. Children's blue cloth Tam o' Shanters, soft top, fancy band, as cut No. 100...............................**35c**

102. Children's scarlet or myrtle cloth Tam o' Shanters, soft crown, as cut No. 100............................ **35c**

103. Children's blue beaver cloth, soft crown Tam o' Shanters, plain or fancy fronts, as cut No. 100..**50c**

104. Children's scarlet cloth Tam o' Shanters, soft crown, plain or fancy silk band, as cut No. 100......... **50c**

105. Children's white duck Tam o' Shanters, soft detachable crown, as cut No. 100 ....**50c**

106. Children's blue beaver cloth or velvet Tam o' Shanters, wired crown, plain or fancy band, as cut No. 106 ....**50c**

107. Children's white duck or cream serge Tam o' Shanters, wired top, as cut No. 106 ....**50c**

108. Children's scarlet cloth tams, wired crown, silk lined, as cut No. 106...**50c**

109. Children's blue beaver cloth, soft crown, Tam o' Shanters, plain or fancy fronts, as cut No. 109..**75c**

110. Children's tan leather Tam o' Shanters, soft top, name on band and silk lining, as cut No. 109 ..**75c**

111. Children's scarlet cloth, soft crown Tam o' Shanters, black silk band, as cut No. 109 ....**75c**

112. Children's navy, black or brown velvet Tam o' Shanters, wired crown, as cut No. 112 ....**75c**

113. Children's blue beaver cloth Tam o' Shanters, wired top, plain or fancy silk band, as cut No. 112...**75c**

114. Children's scarlet cloth Tam o' Shanters, wired crown, silk lining, as cut No. 112 ....**75c**

115. Children's navy or black velvet, wired top, Tam o' Shanters, silk band, as cut No. 112...............**1.00**

116. Children's blue beaver cloth, Tam o' Shanters, wired top, silk lined, as cut No. 112....................**1.00**

117. Children's blue beaver cloth Tam o' Shanters, soft top, plain or fancy band, as cut No. 117.......**1.00**

118. Children's fawn or grey doeskin Tam o' Shanters, soft tops, silk lining, as cut No. 117................**1.00**

119. Ladies' and misses' wool Tam o' Shanters, plain or assorted colors, as cut No. 119 ....**25c**

120. Ladies' and misses' mohair Tam o' Shanters, in plain or assorted colors, as cut No. 119...............**35c**

121. Ladies and misses' mohair knitted Tam o' Shanters, plain colors or fancy patterns, as cut No. 119..**50c**

122. Men's, ladies' and boys' black beaver cloth college caps, as cut No. 122......................................**1.50**

For Hats larger sizes than 7⅜ see Nos. 10A and 21A.

LATEST SPRING STYLES IN MEN'S, BOYS' AND CHILDREN'S HEADWEAR.

123. Men's white straw boaters, black or navy bands, as cut No. 123 .... **25c**

124. Men's Swiss straw boaters, black or navy blue bands, as cut No. 123 .... **25c**

125. Men's white straw boaters, as cut No. 125 .... **35c**

126. Men's Swiss straw boaters, navy blue or black bands, as cut No. 125 .... **35c**

127. Men's white straw boaters, plain navy or black silk bands, as cut No. 127 .... **50c**

128 Men's and youths' rustic straw boaters, plain or fancy bands, as cut No. 127 .... **50c**

129. Men's white Canton straw hats, plain black bands, as cut No. 129 .... **50c**

130. Men's white Canton straw hats, leather sweats and plain bands, as cut No. 129.......... **75c**

131. Men's fine white straw hats, neat shape, plain black or navy blue bands, as cut No. 129 . **1.00**

132. Men's fine Canton or mackinaw straw hats, with plain black bands, as cut No. 129 .... **1 25**

133. Men's white manilla straw hats, with silk band and leather sweats, as cut No. 129 .... **1.5**

134. Men's fancy braid straw boaters, plain or fancy colored silk bands, as cut No. 134 .... **75c**

135. Men's rough straw boaters. American styles, black or navy bands, as cut No. 134 .... **1.00**

136 Men's plain or rough straw boaters, American style, with plain or fancy bands, as cut No. 134 .... **1.25**

137. Men's fancy rough braid straw boaters, plain or fancy colored bands, as cut No. 134 .... **1.50**

138. Men's white Canton and rustic straw boaters, with pure silk bands, as cut No. 138.......... **75c**

139. Men's Canton straw boaters, small or medium shape, silk bands, as cut No. 138 .... **1.00**

140. Men's fine pedal and Canton straw boaters, black or navy bands, as cut No. 138 .... **1.25**

141. Men's fine white pedal and Canton straw boaters, new American styles, black or navy bands, as cut No. 138 .... **1.50**

142. Men's rough straw boaters, in all the leading styles for summer wear, as cut No. 138 .... **2.00**

143. Men's finest quality white Milan straw boaters, neat stylish shape, leather sweats, as cut No. 138 .... **2.50**

144. Men's fine white Canton straw boaters, with ventilated crowns, as cut No. 144 .... **1.50**

145 Men's fine white straw hats, fedora shape, with black or blue bands, as cut No. 145.......... **1.25**

146. Men's white manilla straw hats, fedora style, with black bands, as cut No. 145 .... **1.50**

147. Men's fine manilla straw hats, full-shaped crown and curled brim, black silk band, as cut No. 147 .... **2.00**

148. Men's rough straw fedora-shape hat, fancy plaited bands, and leather sweats, as cut No. 148 .... **2.50**

149. Youths' and boys' mixed or plain white straw boaters, black or blue bands, as cut No. 149.. **15c**

150. Youths' and boys' plain white straw boaters, black or navy bands, as cut No. 149 ...... **19c**

151. Youths' and boys' black and white mixed straw boaters, black bands, as cut No. 151.......... **25c**

152. Youths' and boys' plain white Canton straw boaters, navy or black bands, as cut No. 151 .. **25c**

153. Youths' and boys' rustic straw boaters, plain or fancy bands, as cut No. 151 .... **25c**

154. Youths' and boys' fancy black and white straw boaters, plain black or navy bands, as cut No. 151 .... **35c**

155. Youths' and boys' plain white Canton and Swiss straw boaters, as cut No. 151 .... **35c**

156. Youths' and boys' white Canton straw boaters, plain or fancy bands, as cut No. 156.......... **50c**

157. Youths' and boys' Swiss straw boater hats, plain or fancy bands, as cut No. 156 .... **50c**

158. Youths' and boys' fine white Canton straw boaters, navy blue or black silk bands, as cut No. 156 .... **75c**

159. Youths' and boys' rough straw boaters, plain or fancy bands, as cut No. 156.......... **75c**

160. Youths' white pedal or Canton straw boaters, light weight, navy or black bands, as cut No. 156 .... **1.00**

161. Children's white or fancy colored blue and white straw sailors, as cut No. 161 ...... **12½c**

162. Children's fancy colored navy blue and white straw sailors, navy blue band, as cut No. 161...... **19c**

163. Children's plain white, navy, black or brown Canton straw sailors, navy blue bands, as cut No. 161 .... **19c**

164. Children's fancy colored straw sailors, plain or fancy named band, as cut No. 164 .. **25c**

165. Children's white straw sailors, plain or fancy bands, as cut No. 164 .... **25c**

166. Children's white Canton straw sailors, fancy named or plain satin bands and streamers, as cut No. 166 .... **35c**

167. Children's fancy colored navy blue and white straw sailors, plain or fancy bands, as cut No. 166 .... **35c**

168. Children's white Canton or Swiss straw sailors, plain or fancy bands, as cut No. 166.......... **50c**

169. Children's mixed straw sailors, plain or fancy named bands and streamers, as cut No. 166 .... **50c**

170. Children's white straw sailors, fancy name on band, as cut No. 170 .... **75c**

171. Children's fancy colored navy blue and white straw sailors, plain navy satin or fancy named bands, as cut No. 170.......... **75c**

172. Children's fine white Canton straw sailors, white or navy blue silk bands, as cut No. 170 .... **1.00**

173. Children's fancy colored straw sailors, plain or named satin bands, as cut No. 170 .... **1.00**

174. Children's finest quality white Canton straw sailors, as cut No. 170 .... **1.25**

175. Children's white pedal straw sailors, as cut No. 175 .... **1.25**

176. Children's fine white pedal straw sailors, as cut No. 175 .. **1.50**

177. Children's fancy colored blue and white straw sailors, as cut No. 177 .... **1.50**

178. Children's white pedal straw sailors, plain cream or navy silk bands, as cut No. 177 .... **1.50**

179. Children's fancy colored straw sailors, silk lined, as cut No. 179 .... **1.75**

180. Children's extra fine white straw sailors, round or square crown, and silk lined, as cut No. 180 .... **2.00**

181 Children's finest quality white or mixed straw sailors, roll brim and corded silk band and streamers, as cut No. 180.. .... **2.50**

182. Men's, youths' and ladies' garden or rough straw hats, with wide brims and high crowns **8c, 12½c, 15c**

Mourning Bands.

For wearing on hat—
2 inches wide.......................... **10c**
2½ inches wide **12½c**
3 inches wide **15c**
Elastic arm mourning bands, to pull over sleeve, 4 inches wide **20c**

DIRECTIONS For Head Measurement

Please state distinctly whether felt hat, cap or Tam o' Shanter is for lady, man, youth or child, and measure around the head with a tape-line in the position where the hat or cap is usually worn, find the number of inches, and compare with the scale of sizes, and you will find the exact size. Care should be taken to send the correct size in every case; also state the color and shape, giving the number or corresponding cut in Catalogue. It is impossible to fill your order properly without this information.

Children's sizes run from 6 to 6⅝
Boys' " " " 6¼ " 6⅞
Ladies' " " " 6¼ " 6⅞
Men's " " " 6⅝ " 7⅜

Men's stiff and fedora hats, extra sizes, 7½ and 7⅝, at $2.00 each.

SCALE OF SIZES.

Inch.	Size.	Inch.	Size.	Inch.	Size.
18⅞	6	20⅝	6⅝	22¾	7¼
19¼	6⅛	21¼	6¾	23¼	7⅜
19⅝	6¼	21⅝	6⅞	23⅝	7½
20	6⅜	22	7	24	7⅝
20½	6½	22⅜	7⅛		

OUR DRUG DEPARTMENT

Is replete with all the latest preparations which science has brought forth for the alleviation and cure of diseases. All our dispensing is done by qualified chemists, each prescription being thoroughly checked before leaving the dispensing counter, which makes a perfect safeguard against possible accident. The chemicals which we sell for human use are all chemically pure. We keep agricultural chemicals and chemicals for the arts as well, which are very much cheaper than the pure kinds. When wanting commercial quality kindly state the fact. We do not make a sale for less than 5c. worth of any drug, except where a mixture is made which requires some small quantities in making it up.

Containers Extra.

We charge extra for bottles, tins and other containers where quotation is for **bulk liquids.** The prices of bottles, etc., are

½ to 2-oz. bottles	2c each.
3 " 4 "	3c "
6 " 10 "	4c "
12, 16 or 20-oz bottles	5c "
32 and 40-oz bottles	10c "
80-oz bottles	15c "
80-oz stoppered	25c "
160-oz, 1 gallon bottle	30c "
1-quart tin	13c "
½-gallon tin	15c "
1 "	25c "
2 "	30c "

When pounds are quoted, it means 16 fluid ounces if liquid, and 16 ounces by weight if dry. A pint is 20 fluid ounces, and a gallon 8 fluid pints. Some liquids are sold by weight, such are specially mentioned.

All prices in this list are subject to the fluctuations of the market.

When ordering by letter, state what preparation is required, otherwise a delay occurs.

NOTE.—Where the word "poison" is placed after an item, it is necessary to have physician's prescription accompanying order, which can be repeated if so marked; but where it is a very violent and dangerous poison we require such prescription from physician to accompany each order from you, such as strychnine, morphine, ergot and preparations, arsenic salts (other than Paris green), aconite, red iodide of mercury, cantharides and all poisons in Schedule 1 of Pharmacy Act. We neither sell liquors nor procure them. Female pills, etc., not sold except on physician's prescription.

MAILING NOTE.—Liquids when sent by mail cost about 5c an ounce for postage—that includes weight of bottle and packing. A one-ounce bottle will cost 7c. A 2-ounce bottle will cost 12c, while the larger sizes will cost less, say, as above, 5c per ounce. We give these prices as a guide to you in sending the postage.

A

Acids.

(Acids are all sold by weight.)
Liquid Acid cannot be sent by mail.

Acid, benzoic, Howard's, 20c oz.
" boracic, Howard's, finest powder, 25c lb.
" " fine powder, 20c lb.
" citric, 50c lb.
" oxalic, 15c lb.
" tannic powder, 7½c oz.
" tartaric, powdered, 45c lb.
" acetic, glacial, 5c oz, 40c lb.
" " strong, 20c lb.
" carbolic, 5c oz; 50c lb.
" " crude, light brown, $1.25 gal.
" " " dark brown, $1.00 gal.
" muriatic, pure, 5c oz; 30c lb.
" " spirits of salts, 5c lb.
" nitric, pure, 5c oz; 30c lb; common, 15c lb.
" sulphuric, pure, 30c lb; common, 10c lb.
" " aromatic, 80c lb.
" phosphoric, concentrated, $1.60 lb.
" " dilute, 40c lb.
" salicylic, 7½c oz; $1.00 lb.
Acetanilid (antifebrin), 10c oz.
Aloes, Barbadoes, 30c lb; powdered, 40c lb.
" socotrine, lump or powdered, 80c lb.
Aloin, finest, 10c oz.
Alum, lump, 5 lb 20c; 5c lb; powdered, 5c lb.
" chrome, 30c lb.
" burnt, 40c lb.
Ammonia, carbonate (baking ammonia), 15c lb.
" carbonate resublimed, Howard's, 40c lb.
" chloride (sal ammoniac, lump), 15c lb; in 100-lb lots, 12c lb.
" " granulated, 15c lb; in 100-lb lots, 12c lb.
" " pure powder, 40c lb.
" nitrate, granulated, common, 25c lb.
" " pure, 60c lb.
" sulphate, common, 10c lb; pure, 50c lb.
Annatto, Spanish, 10c oz; $1.60 lb.
Antimony, black, common powder, 15c lb.
" crocus, 40c lb.
" tartrate, 5c oz; 80c lb.
Antipyrine, Knorrs', 75c oz.
Arrowroot, Bermuda, 50c lb; St. Vincent, 25c lb.
Antikamnia powder, $1.35 oz.
" tablets, $1.35 oz.
" and codeia tablets, $1.75 oz.
" quinine and salol tablets, $1.50 oz.
Alkaline antiseptic tablets, Seiler's, 10c oz.
Aristol, $2.25 oz.
Ammonal, $1.50 oz; tablets, $1.50 oz.
Aletris cordial, $1.25 bottle.
Aniseed, whole or powdered, 20c lb.
Areca nuts, 35c lb; powdered, 40c lb.
Armenian bole (Venetian red), 10c lb.
Alcohol, absolute, 10c oz.
" pure, 5c oz; 75c pint.
" methylated, 30c pint.
" wood, 20c pint.
Assafœtida, lump or powder, 5c oz.

B

Beeswax, yellow, best, 60c lb; second, 45c lb.
Beeswax, white, best, 80c lb; second, 60c lb.
Balsam of Canada, 5c oz; 60c lb.
" Copaiba, 7½c oz; $1.00 lb.
" Peru, 20c oz.
" Tolu, 10c oz.
Bismuth, carbonate, 20c oz.
" salicylate, 35c oz.
" subnitrate, 15c oz.
" subgallate, 30c oz.
Borax, lump or powdered, 7c lb; in 100-lb lots, 6c lb.
Burgundy pitch, 15c lb.
Blue vitriol, 10c lb.; in 10-lb lots, 9c lb; 25-lb lots, 8½c lb; 100-lb lots, 7½c lb; barrel, 7c lb.
Brimstone, 5c lb; 5 lbs 20c.

C

Caffeine, citrate, 60c oz.
Camphor, 90c lb; 6c oz.
Camphorated chalk, 20c lb.
Cantharides (poison), 15c oz.
Charcoal, powdered, ordinary, 20c lb.
" " willow, 40c lb.
" animal, powdered, 30c lb.
Carmine, fine, 40c oz; finest, 50c oz.
Calomel, 10c oz.
Cocoa butter, 70c lb; 5c oz.
Cochineal, 5c oz; 40c lb.
Confection senna, 50c lb.
Creasote, common, 10c; good, 15c oz.
" English, 25c oz.
Chloride of lime, 8c lb.
Collodion, 5c oz.
" flexible, 7½c oz.
Cream of tartar crystals, 30c lb; powder, 30c lb.
Capsicum, 2 ozs 5c; 25c lb; ground, 30c lb.
Cudbear, finest, 50c lb; ordinary, 35c.
Caustic points, 10c each.
Currie powder, finest, 10c oz; good, 35c lb.
Creolin, 5c oz; $1.50 bottle.
Cloves, ordinary, 20c lb; powdered, 25c lb.
" Penang, 75c lb.
Cuttle-fish bone, large, 40c lb; powdered, 35c lb.
Chalk, prepared, 15c lb; pink, 20c lb.
" precipitated, 10c lb.
" French cakes, 20c lb; powdered, 10c lb
Creasote carbonate (creasotal), 60c oz.
Cactina pellets, 25c.
Chloroform, pure, Duncan & Flockhart's, 1-lb bottles, by weight, $1.95; methylated, $1.25.
Chloroform, Smith's, pure, $1.35 per lb.
Calvert's carbolic vaporizers, 50c each.

Capsules.

Castor oil, 40-drop, 25c per doz; $1.75 per 100.
Castor oil, 75-drop, 30c per doz; $2.00 per 100.
Cod-liver oil, 40-drop, 25c per doz; $1.75 per 100.
Cod-liver oil, 75-drop, 30c per doz; $2.00 per 100.
Santal oil, 10-drop, 25c doz; 15-drop, 35c doz.
Colocynth (bitter apple) (whole apple), 10c oz.
" pulp, 20c oz.
Copperas, green, 2½c lb; $1.75 per 100 lbs.
" blue, 10c lb; 25-lb lots, 8½c lb; 10-lb lots, 9c lb; 100-lb lots, 7½c lb; barrel, 7c lb.

D

Duotol (guaiacol carbonate), Von Hayden's, $1.00; other makers, 75c oz.
Duncan & Flockart's pill capsules kept in stock.
Dextrine, yellow, 10c lb.

E

Effervescing Preparations.

Granular effervescent—
Citrate of magnesia, 40c lb.
Bishop's citrate of magnesia, 60c lb.
" " caffeine, 45c bottle.
" hydrobromate of caffeine, 75c bottle.
" phenacetine, 25c oz.
" piperazine, 50c oz.
" Vichy salts, 35c bottle.
" lithia citrate, 35c bottle.
Alkalithia (Hay Fever remedy), 25c oz.
Effervescent phosphate of soda, $1.25 lb.; bottle, 10c oz.
Effervescent Vichy, $1.25 lb.; ½-lb. bottle, 45c; 10c oz.
Effervescent Kissingen, $1.40 lb.; ½-lb. bottle, 50c; 10c oz.
Eaton's fruit salts, ½-lb. tin, 20c; 1-lb tin, 35c.

Elixirs.

We carry a full line of the different manufacturers.

Epsom salts, Howard's, 5c lb.
" ordinary, 3 lbs 10c; 100-lb lots, 2c.

Essences.

(Containers extra.)

Essence of aniseed, 5c oz.
" cassia (cinnamon), 5c oz.
" cloves, 5c oz.
" ginger (Jamaica), ordinary strength, 5c oz; strongest, 7½c oz.
" lemon, 5c oz, 60c lb.
" orange, 5c oz, 60c lb.
" peppermint, 5c oz.
" rose, 20c oz.
" ratafia, 5c oz.
" nutmeg, 5c oz.
" vanilla, ordinary strength, 5c oz.
" vanilla, extra fine, 15c oz.

Extracts, Solid.

Extract belladonna (poison), 20c oz.
" cascara sagrada, 20c oz.
" dandelion, 7c oz, $1.00 lb; powdered, 40c oz.

Be sure to send sufficient postage for goods going by Mail.

Extract gentian, 5c oz.
" nux vomica (poison), 40c oz.
" mandrake, 40c oz.
" sarsaparilla (Jamaica), 40c oz.

F

Formalin or formaldehyde, disinfectant, deodorizer, antiseptic, also preservative of food, per oz, 5c; ½-lb bottle, 25c; 1-lb bottle, 50c; 2-lb bottle, 90c.
Fumigating pastiles, red, per oz 5c, or 75c lb.
" " black, 3 ozs 10c, or 50c lb.
" " per box, 10c.
Fuller's earth, lump or powder, 10c lb.
Flake, white, 25c lb.

Fluid Extracts.

We carry a full stock. The following are the principal:

Fluid extract of black haw, 10c oz.
" " blue cohosh, 7½c oz.
" " black cohosh, 10c oz.
" " buchu, 10c oz.
" " cascara sagrada, 7½c oz.
" " cocoa leaves, 15c oz.
" " Culver's root, 10c oz.
" " cascara, aromatic, 7½c oz.
" " " Stearn's, 10c oz.
" " dandelion root, 7½c oz.
" " damiana, 15c oz.
" " gentian, 7½c oz.
" " golden seal, 15c oz.
" " horehound, 7½c oz.
" " kava kava, 15c oz, $2.00 lb.
" " ladyslipper, 12½c oz.
" " life root, 7½c oz.
" " liverwort, 10c oz.
" " mandrake, 7½c oz.
" " pulsatilla, 10c oz.
" " red Peruvian bark, 10c oz.
" " rhubarb, 15c oz.
" " sarsaparilla, 10c oz.
" " " compound, 10c oz.
" " senna, 10c oz.
" " valerian, 7½c oz.
" " wahoo, 10c oz.
" " wild cherry bark, 5c oz.
" " wintergreen, 7½c oz.
" " yellow dock, 10c oz.

G

Glycerine, pure (1.260), 25c lb, by weight.
" 3-oz bottle for 10c.
" Price's, 65c lb.
" " 8-oz bottle, 35c.
" " 4-oz bottle, 20c.
Gelatine, good, 40c lb, 4c oz; fine, 60c lb, 5c oz.
" gold label, 80c lb.; red, 80c lb, 7c oz.
Glue, brown, 12½c lb; amber, 15c lb.
" finest white, 20c lb.
" amber, granulated, 15c lb.
Gold chloride, pure, 15-grain tubes, 60c each.
" and soda, 15-grain tubes, 35c each.
Glauber salts, 5c lb; 3 lbs 10c, 100 lbs. for $2.00.
Guaiacol, carbonate, Von Hayden's, $1.00 oz.
" other makers, 75c oz.
Gutta-percha, crude chips, 15c oz; $2.10 lb.

Gums and Gum Resins.

Gum acacia, best, lump or powder, 7½c oz.
" " good, clean, 5c oz, 70c lb.
" " fair, 2 ozs 5c, 30c lb.
" assafœtida, lump or powder, 5c oz.
" benzoin, lump, 7½c; powder, 10c oz.
" dragon's blood, lump or powder, 5c oz, 70c lb.
" guaiacum, lump, 50c lb; powder, 80c lb.
" galbanum, 15c oz.
" juniper (Sandrach), 50c lb.
" mastich, 7½c oz.
" myrrh, best, lump or powder, 7½c oz.
" shellac, orange, 3 ozs 10c, 40c lb.
" " white, 3 ozs 10c, 50c lb.
" spruce, 10c oz.
" scammony, $1.00 oz.
" tamarac, 10c oz.
" thus, 25c lb.
" tragacanth, best, 7½c oz.
" " powder, 10c oz.
" " good, 5c oz.

H

Herbs, Barks, Roots, etc.

We carry a very complete stock of herbs, The following are the principal:

Arnica flowers, 2 ozs 5c, 30c lb.
Ash berries, prickly, 3 ozs 10c, 50c lb.
Aniseed, whole or powdered, 2 ozs 5c, 20c lb.
Buchu leaves, 2 ozs 5c, 30c lb.
Bugleweed, 2 ozs 5c.
Balmony, 2 ozs 5c.
Burdock root, 2 ozs 5c, 25c lb.
Bayberry, 2 ozs 5c.
Buckthorn bark, 2 ozs 5c.
Barberry, 2 ozs 5c.
Bitter root, 3 ozs 10c.
Bittersweet bark, 2 ozs 5c.
Black cohosh, 2 ozs 5c, 30c lb.
Butternut bark, 2 ozs 5c, 30c lb.
Boneset, 2 ozs 5c, 30c lb.
Blue flag, 2 ozs 5c, 30c lb.
Buckbean leaves, 2 ozs 5c.
Blood root, 2 ozs 5c, 30c lb; powdered, 35c lb.
Blue cohosh, 2 ozs 5c, 30c lb.
Bay leaves, 15c lb.
Celery seed, 20c lb.
Cinchona bark, pale, 40c lb; powdered, 50c lb.
" " yellow, 50c lb; powdered, 60c lb.
" " red, 60c lb; powdered, 70c lb.
Chamomile flowers, 2 ozs 5c, 30c lb.
Cherry bark, wild, 2 ozs 5c, 25c lb.
Comfrey root, 2 ozs 5c.
Catnip, 2 ozs 5c, 30c lb.
Cocoa leaves, 5c oz.
Cubeb berries, 3 ozs 10c, 45c lb; powdered, 50c lb.
Colocynth (bitter apple), 10c oz.
" powdered, 10c oz.
Confection of senna, 3 ozs 10c; 50c lb.
Cascara sagrada bark, 40c lb.
Cassia bark, 20c lb; powdered, 20c lb.
Cascarilla bark, 40c lb.
Cinnamon bark or powder, 5c oz, 80c lb.
Dandelion, 2 ozs 5c, 25c lb.
Elder flowers, 2 ozs 5c.
Elecampane, 2 ozs 5c, 30c lb.
Flax seed, 5c lb, 5 lbs 20c.
Fenugreek, 20c lb.
Golden seal, 5c oz, 60c lb.
Galangal, 2 ozs 5c.
Gall nuts, powdered, 2 ozs 5c, 30c lb.
Gentian, whole or ground, 4 ozs 5c, 15c lb.
" powdered, 3 ozs 5c, 25c lb.
Ginger, Jamaica, bleached, 2 ozs 5c, 35c lb.
" " powdered, 2 ozs 5c, 35c lb.
" African, powdered, 20c lb.
Guaiacum chips, 20c lb.
Horehound, 2 ozs 5c, 30c lb.
Helebore, fresh, powdered, 15c lb.
Indian turnip, 2 ozs 5c.
Juniper berries, 20c lb.
Jalap, powdered, 5c oz.
Licorice root, stick, 20c lb.
" " cut, Russian, 30c lb.
" " powdered Russian, 35c lb.
Lobelia herb, 2 oz 5c, 30c lb.
Mace, powdered or whole, 7½c oz.
Mandrake root, 2 ozs 5c, 25c lb.
Mother root, 2 ozs 5c.
Manna, best flake, 15c oz; good, 10c oz.
Nux Vomica, poison, 30c lb; powder, 35c lb.
Nutmegs, 5c oz; 75c lb; powdered, 7c oz.
Orris root, Florentine, 3 ozs 10c, 45c lb.
" " powdered, 5c oz, 50c lb.
Pennyroyal, 2 ozs 5c, 30c lb.
Pipsissewa (Princess pine), 2 ozs 5c, 30c lb.
Poplar bark, 2 ozs 5c.
Pulsatilla, 2 ozs 5c.
Prickly ash bark, 2 ozs 5c.
" " berries, 3 ozs 10c.
Poppy heads, 3 for 5c.
Quassia chips, 20c lb.
Queen of the meadow, 2 ozs 5c.
Rhubarb, best Turkey, 25c oz.
" " powdered, 25c oz.
" " E. I., 10c oz.
" " " powdered, 10c oz.
Rosemary leaves, 2 ozs 5c, 30c lb.
Rue, 2 ozs 5c.
Senna leaves, best, 2 ozs 5c, 30c lb.
" finest Alexandria, 5c oz.
" powdered, 3 ozs 10c.
Sassafras bark, 20c lb.
Slippery elm bark, 20c lb.
" " ground, 20c lb
" " powdered, 30c lb.
Saffron, American, 5c oz.
" finest Spanish, $1.00 oz.
Skullcap, 2 ozs 5c.
Skunk cabbage, 2 ozs 5c.
Spikenard root, 2 ozs 5c.
Stramonium leaves, 2 ozs 5c, 35c lb.
Seed, coriander, 15c lb; powder, 20c lb.
" fennel, 20c lb; powder, 25c lb.
" cardamon, 10c oz; powder, 10c oz.
" lobelia, powdered, 5c oz, 60c lb.
Sarsaparilla, Jamaica, 5c oz, 80c lb.
" American, 2 ozs 5c, 35c lb.
Sweet flag, 2 ozs 5c.
Serpentary root, 5c oz.
Soap bark, ground, 3 ozs 5c, or 20c lb.
Turmeric, 15c lb, 4 ozs for 5c.
Tamarinds, 20c lb.
Thyme, 2 ozs 5c.
Tonca beans, 15c oz.
Vanilla beans, Mexican, $1.25 oz; Bourbon 85c oz.
Virginia snake root, 5c oz.
Wild cherry bark, 2 ozs 5c, 25c lb.
Witchhazel bark, 2 ozs 5c, 25c lb.
Wintergreen leaves, 2 ozs 5c.
Wormwood, 2 ozs 5c.
Yellow dock, 2 ozs 5c, 25c lb.

NOTE.—When less than half a pound is ordered, the price is by the oz.

I

Iron Salts.

Iron hypophosphite, 20c oz.
Iron, precipitated carbonate, 25c lb.
" saccharated carbonate, 40c lb.
" citrate and quinine, Howard's, 35c oz.
" sulphate, common, 2½c lb; pure, 10c lb.
" reduced, 7½c oz.
" citrate and ammonia, 7½c oz.

We keep all the other salts of iron as well.

Indigo, 10c, 15c oz.
Insect powder, best Dalmatian, 40c lb.
Iodoform, 1-oz bottles, 50c.
Iodine, resublimed, 50c oz.
Iceland moss, 20c lb.
Irish moss, 20c lb.
Isinglass, Russian, 50c oz; Brazil, 35c oz.

J

Jewellers' rouge, 15c and $1.00 lb, 7½c oz.

L

Licorice, Solazzi, 60c lb.
Logwood chips, 3 lbs 10c.
" extract, ¼ lb, 5c; ½ lb, 10c; 1 lb, 18c.
Lactated pepsin, 50c oz.
Lanoline, 7½c oz, $1.00 lb.
Litharge, pure powdered, 15c lb.
Listerine, Lambert's, 30c, 50c, $1.00 bottle; 7½c oz.
Liniment, camphor (camphorated oil), 5c oz.
" camphor compound, 5c oz.
" iodine (poison), 15c oz.
" soap, 5c oz.
" " methylated, 2 ozs for 5c.
Liquid ammonia, household, 10c lb.
" iron, dialysed, 5c oz, 75c lb.
Lithia, citrate, 35c oz.
" salicylate, 35c oz.
Lead sugar of, pure, 50c lb; ordinary, 25c.

Lozenges.

Lozenges, ammonia, chloride and licorice, 5c oz.
" bismuth, 1 grain, 5c oz.
" " and charcoal, 10c oz.
" black currant, 5c oz.
" bronchial, 10c oz.
" charcoal, 10 or 20-grain, 7½c oz.
" carbolic, 5c oz.
" cayenne, 5c oz.
" chlorodyne, 7½c oz.
" cough, 5c oz.
" digestive, 5c oz.
" ginger (strong), 7½c oz.
" guaiacum, 7½c oz.
" " and black currant, 5c oz.
" linseed, licorice and chlorodyne, 5c oz, 50c lb.
" pepsin and bismuth, 15c oz.
" " and charcoal, 7½c oz.
" " and ginger, 12½c oz.
" " charcoal and bismuth, 12½c oz.
" " " magnesia and ginger, 10c oz.
" santonine, 1, 2 or 3-grain, 10c oz.
" sulphur compound, 7½c oz.
" sulphur and cream of tartar, 7½c oz.
" red gum, 20c oz.
" rhubarb, soda and ginger, 7½c oz.
" voice and throat, 5c oz.
" worm, 10c oz.

M

Magnesia citrate 40c, 60c lb.
Magnesia, calcined, 5c oz.
" carbonate, 1-oz blocks, 30c lb, 2 oz for 5c.
Maltopepsin, 50c oz.
Mercury, 5c oz, 75c lb, by weight.
Menthol, crystal, 20c oz.
Musk, finest Canton, 6c grain; good, 4c grain.
Moth camphor, napthaline balls, 6c lb.
Manganese, black oxide, 15c lb.

N

Nitrate of silver, crystals, 80c oz.
" " fused sticks, $1.00 oz.

O

Oils.

(Containers extra.)

Oil, aniseed, 25c oz.
" almonds, sweet, 5c oz ; 70c lb.
" almond, bitter, 75c oz.
" amber, 7½c oz.
" bay, 35c oz.
" bergamont, 25c oz.
" cassia, 20c oz.
" camphor, wood, 20c lb.
" carbolic, 1 in 20, 1 in 40, 1 in 50, 5c oz.
" carraway, 20c oz.
" cedar leaf, 10c oz, $1.20 lb.
" cedar wood, 7½c oz, 80c lb.
" croton, 15c oz.
" citronella, 10c oz.
" cloves, 10c oz.
" cinnamon, true, $1.75 oz.
" cocoanut, 2 ozs 5c ; 25c lb.
" camphorated, 5c oz.
" cod-liver, finest Norwegian, 25c pint ; $1.75 gallon ; 16-oz bottle, 25c.
" castor, 15c pint.
" " Italian, 30c pint.
" " tasteless, 50c pint.
" eucalyptus, 15c oz.
" lemon, 15c oz.
" lavender, common, 10c oz.
" " best, 25c oz.
" linseed, raw, 90c gal.
" " boiled, 95c gal.
" male fern, 20c oz.
" mustard, 75c oz.
" neatsfoot, 25c lb.
" orange, sweet, 25c oz : bitter, 35c.
" olive, best, 5c oz, 65c pint.
" " fine, 3 ozs 10c ; 50c pint.
" " good, 40c pint.
" " union salad, 2 ozs 5c ; 20c pint.
" origanum, 7½c oz.
" peppermint, American, 25c oz.
" Rangoon, 5c oz.
" rose (otto), 2½c drop, $8.50 oz.
" rosemary, 10c oz.
" rhodium, 50c, $1.00, 1.25 oz.
" sassafras, 7½c oz.
" spike, 2 ozs 5c.
" sandalwood, Pears', 50c oz, $6.00 lb.
" sperm, 3 ozs 10c.
" sewing machine, 15c pint.
" turpentine, pure, 5c oz.
" " common, 13c pint, 85c gal.
" tar, 20c lb.
" verbena, 20c oz.
" wintergreen, 25c oz.
" wormwood, 75c oz.

We carry a very complete stock of oils as well as those mentioned above.

Ointments.

Ointment, Peruvian, 15c bottle ; tube, 10c.
" citrine, 5c oz ; dilute, 5c oz.
" belladonna, 10c oz.
" tar, 5c oz, 50c lb.
" white precipitate, 5c oz.
" red precipitate, 5c oz.
" pile, 25c bottle.
" galls and opium, 15c oz.
" carbolic, 5c oz, 40c lb.
" sulphur, 5c oz., 40c lb.
" mercurial "blue," strong, 10c oz.
" " dilute, 5c oz.

P

Pills.

Sugar coated marked by s.c. and g.c. for gelatine coated. Prices quoted are for 100 pills. We cannot sell smaller quantities at same price. 40 pills would be half the price of 100.

Aloes pills, 2, 3 or 4 grs, g.c., 35c per 100.
" and assafœtida, 4 or 5 grs, g.c., 40c per 100.
" and iron pills, 5 grs, 55c per 100.
" nux vomica and belladonna, 50c per 100.
Aloin, strychnine, belladonna and ipecac, 50c per 100.
" strychnine, belladonna and cascara, 50c per 100.
Aperient pills, 60c per 100.
Assafœtida, 3 or 4 grs, 40c per 100.
" and iron, 40c per 100.
Blaud's pills, pink coated, 3 or 5 grs, plain or improved, 20c per 100.
" pills, g.c., 3 or 5 grs, plain or improved, 30c per 100.
Blue pills, ½, 1, 2, 3, 4 or 5 grs, 40c per 100.
Calcium sulphide, 1/20, 1/10, ⅛, 1-5, ¼, ½, 1, 2 or 3 grs, 40c per 100.
Calomel pills, 1/10, ⅛, ¼, ½, 1, 2, 3, 4 or 5 grs, 40c per 100.
Camphor, monobromated, 2 grs, 75c per 100 ; 3 grs, $1.00 per 100 ; 5 grs, $1.50 per 100.

Pills—Continued.

Cascara sagrada extract, 1 gr, 40c per 100 ; 2 grs, 50c ; 3 grs, 60c per 100.
" and nux vomica, 60c per 100.
" nux vomica and belladonna, 60c per 100.
Cathartic compound, improved, 30c per 100.
" " active, 40c per 100.
" " granules, 30c per 100.
Chapman's dinner pills, 40c per 100.
Colocynth compound, 5 grs, 90c per 100.
Damiana extract, 3 grs, 60c per 100.
Evacuant pills, 50c per 100.
Iron and quinine citrate, 1 gr, 35c ; 2 grs, 45c ; 3 grs, 55c ; 5 grs, 65c per 100.
" quinine and strychnine, 70c per 100.
" and strychnine, 60c per 100.
Liver pills, improved, vegetable, 40c per 100.
Migrain pills, 60c per 100.
Morphia pills, on physician's prescription only, ⅛ gr, 45c ; ⅙ gr, 50c ; ¼ gr, 60c ; ½ gr, 75c per 100.
Phenacetine, 2 grs, 75c ; 5 grs, $1.25 per 100.
Phosphorus compound pills, 40c per 100.
" and iron pills, 60c per 100.
" nux vomica and damiana, $1.00 per 100.
" " " iron, 50c per 100.
" zinc and valerian, 60c per 100.
Podophyllin, 1/20, 1/10, ⅛, ⅙, ¼, ½ and 1 gr, 40c per 100.
" compound, 60c per 100.
Quinine sulphate, 1 gr, 40c ; 2 grs, 50c ; 3 grs, 65c 4 grs, 80c, and 5 grs, $1.25 per 100.
Rhubarb compound, 40c per 100.
Strychnine pills (on physician's prescription only), 1/100, 1/60, 1/50, 1/40, 1/32, 1/30, 1/20, 1/16 gr, 40c per 100.
" sulphate pills (on physician's prescription only), 1/200, 1/100, 1/60, 1/50, 1/40, 1/30, 1/20 gr, 40c per 100.
Three valerianates, quinine, iron and zinc, $1.00 per 100.

Besides the above we carry all the different pills, and also different makers' pills.

Potash Salts.

Potash, bicarbonate, 2 ozs 5c, 25c lb.
" " powdered, 2 ozs 5c.
" bromide, 5c oz.
" bichromate, 3 ozs 5c, 20c lb.
" bitartrate (cream of tartar), 30c lb.
" carbonate, 2 ozs 5c, 20c lb.
" chlorate, 2 ozs 5c, 20c lb ; pure, 50c lb.
" " powdered, 2 ozs 5c, 20c lb.
" permanganate, 5c oz, 50c lb.
" caustic, 1-oz bottles, 10c bottle.
" nitrate (saltpetre), 10c lb.
" iodide, 35c oz.
Pyrozone, 3 per cent., 50c bottle.
Parrish's chemical food, 8-oz bottle, 25c.
Phenacetine, Bayer, 40c oz.
Pancreatin, extract, Fairchild's, $1.75 oz.
" Armour's, 90c oz.
Pepsin, English, 25c oz.
" Armour's scale, 90c oz.
" Armour's powder, 90c oz.
" Fairchild's, $1.75 oz.
Pitch, Burgundy, 15c lb.
Pipe clay, 10c lb.
Plaster-of-Paris, fine, 5c lb.
Peroxide of hydrogen, Oaklands' $1.00 bottle.
" " " Harvey's, No. 1, 70c bottle, 7c oz.
" " " Harvey's, No. 2, 40c bt.
" " " Marchand's, ¼-lb bottle, 40c ; ½-lb bottle, 65c ; 1-lb bottle, $1.00.
Platinum chloride, 15-grain tubes, 60c.
Pumice stone, 15c lb ; powdered, 10c lb.
Paris Green, ½-lb boxes, 13c ; 1-lb boxes, 25c. In large quantities a special price will be given.

Powders.

Compound jalap, 5c oz.
" licorice, 20c lb.
" rhubarb, 5c oz.
Aloes and canella (Hiera Picra), 3 ozs 10c.

Plasters.

Belladonna on moleskin, $1.00 per yd.
" plaster on calico, 1 yd rolls, 75c.
" " porous or plain, 7 inches wide, 80c per yd.
Sticking plaster, on calico, 18 inches, 15c per yd.
" " glazed calico, 18 inches wide 20c per yd.
" " finest calico, 18 inches wide, 30c per yd.
Rubber adhesive plaster, ½-inch wide, 10-yard rolls, 45c ; 1-inch, 50c ; 2-inch, 75c roll.
Rubber adhesive plaster, 6 inches wide, 1-yard rolls, 50c yd ; 12-inch, 80c yd.
Menthol plaster, 7 inches wide, 75c yd.
Isinglass plaster, 1-yard rolls, 65c.
All other plasters kept in stock.

Q

"Howard's" Quinine Salts.

Quinine bisulphate, $1.00 oz.
" hydrochloride, $1.25 oz.
" hypophosphite, $1.50 oz.
" sulphate (bulk) 55c oz.
" " (1-oz bottle), 60c oz.
" capsules and pills, 24, 1-gr ; 20, 2-gr ; 15, 3-gr ; 12, 4-gr ; or 9, 5-gr, in a box, 10c.

Per 100 of either pills or capsules—1-gr, 40c ; 2-gr, 50c ; 3-gr, 65c ; 4-gr, 85c ; 5-gr, $1.25.

R

Resorcin, 30c oz.
Resin, yellow, ordinary, 5c lb.
Rochelle salts, 35c lb.
Rose pink, English, 40c lb.

S

Saccharine, $1.00 oz.
Sugar of milk, powdered or crystal, 35c lb.
Salol, 15c oz.
Sulphonal (Bayer's), 60c oz.
Santonine (poison), 40c oz.

Strychnine we do not sell except on physician's order, then price is—

Strychnine, $1.50 oz.
" sulphate, $1.50 oz.
" hypophosphite, $3.00 oz.
Spermaceti, 5c oz.

Silver Salts.

Nitrate of silver crystals, 80c oz.
" " " points, mounted, 10c

Soaps, Medicated.

Ichthyol soap, 35c cake.
Iodide of soda and sulphur soap, 35c cake.
Hydronapthol soap, 35c cake.
Sulphur camphor and balsam of Peru soap, 35c.
Resorcin soap, 35c cake.
Corrosive sublimate soap, 35c cake.
Soft soap, Canadian, 15c lb.
Soap, soft, English, 20c lb.
" " green, 2 ozs, 12½c ; 4 ozs, 25c.
" " " 8 ozs, 35c ; 20 ozs, 65c.
Whale-oil soap, 25c lb.
Castile soap powder, 50c lb.

Other toilet and healing soaps, see "Toilet Soaps."

Sodas.

Bicarbonate of soda, 3 lbs 10c.
Howard's bicarbonate of soda, 20c lb.
Hyposulphite of soda, 5c lb.
Sulphate of soda, Glauber salts, 3 lbs 10c ; Howard's, 5c lb.
Sulphite of soda, 10c lb.
Hypophosphite of soda, 15c oz.
Phosphate soda, granular, 25c ; Howard's, 25c lb.

Spirits.

(Containers extra).

Aromatic spirits of ammonia (sal volatile), 5c oz.
Spirits, camphor, 5c oz, 75c lb.
" juniper, 5c oz, 75c lb.
" sweet nitre, 5c oz, 80c lb ; ordinary, 60c lb.

Stone.

Pumice stone, 15c lb.
" powdered, 10c lb.
Rotten stone, 20c lb.

Sulphurs.

Flower of sulphur, 5c lb, 5 lbs 20c.
Roll sulphur (brimstone), 5c lb, 5 lbs 20c.
Milk of sulphur, 20c lb.
Precipitated sulphur, 40c lb.
Somatose, 60c, $1.10 and 2.00 a tin.

Syrups.

(Containers extra.)

Syrup hypophosphites, 5c oz, 50c lb.
" senna, 3 ozs 10c.
" rhubarb, 3 ozs 10c.
" aromatic, 3 ozs 10c.
" iodide of iron, 5c oz.
" phosphates compound, Parrish's chemical food, 8-oz bottle, 25c.
" squills, 2 ozs 5c.
" wild cherry, 2 ozs 5c.
" Easton's, 5c oz, 70c lb.

T

Tinctures.

(Containers extra.)

Tincture of Aloes, 5c oz, 65c lb.
" Arnica, 5c oz, 65c lb.
" Assafœtida, 5c oz, 75c lb.
" Benzoin compound (Friar's balsam), 5c oz, 80c lb.
" Benzoin simple, 5c oz.
" Buchu, 5c oz, 65c lb.
" Capsicum, 5c oz, 75c lb.
" Catechu, 5c oz, 65c lb.
" Cinchona bark, yellow, 5c oz, 70c lb.
" " compound, 5c oz, 65c lb.
" Digitalis (poison), 5c oz.
" Gentian compound, 5c oz, 50c lb.
" Gelseminum (poison), 5c oz.
" Ginger, 5c oz.
" " strong, 7½c oz.
" Guaiacum, 5c oz, 75c lb.
" Hyoscyamus (poison), 5c oz, 80c lb.
" Iron, 3 ozs 10c.
" Iodine, 7½c oz.
" Lavender compound, 5c oz.
" Myrrh, 5c oz.
" Valerian, 5c oz.
Turmeric, 15c lb, 4 ozs for 5c.
Turpentine, 13c pint, 85c gallon.

Tablet Triturates.

Aloin, belladonna and nux vomica, 30c per 100.
" belladonna and podophyllin, 30c per 100.
" belladonna, strychnine and cascara sagrada, 30c per 100.
" belladonna, strychnine and ipecac, 30c per 100.
" compound, 30c per 100.

Calomel, 1-50, 1-20, 1-10, ⅛, ¼, ½, 1, 2, 3 and 5 grs, 30c per 100.
" and sodium bicarbonate, 30c per 100.
" " " compound, 30c per 100.

Lactated pepsin tablets, 5 grs, 50c oz.
Podophyllin, 1-16, 1-10, ⅛, ¼ and ½ gr, 30c per 100.
Saccharin, ¼ gr, 40c per 100; ½ gr, 75c per 100.
Santonin, ½ gr, 30c per 100; 1 gr, 40c per 100.
" and calomel, 35c per 100.
Sodium salicylate, 5 grs, 40c per 100.

Besides the above enumerated tablet triturates, we carry a full line.

40 tablets at half the price of 100.

W

Wines.

Wine of ipecac, 2 ozs. for 15c.

Wines of aloes, antimony, colchicum, iron, iron bitter, pepsin, quinine, rhubarb, rhubarb sweet, 5c oz.

Whiting (Paris white), 2½c lb, $1.50 per 100 lbs.
White precipitate, 10c oz.

Witch hazel, distilled, 6-oz bottle, 10c; pint bottle, 25c; ½-gallon bottle, $1.00.

Wax, yellow, bees, best, 60c lb; second, 45c.
" white " best, 80c lb; second, 60c lb.
" paraffine, white, 15c lb.

Z

Zinc Salts.

Zinc, oxide, common, 15c lb.
" Howard's, 60c lb.
" Hubbuck's, 60c lb.

Zinc, sulphate, common, 15c lb.
" pure, 25c lb.

Zinc, valerianate, 40c oz.

Heavy chemicals in quantity can be obtained from us. State quality required as well as quantity when writing for prices.

In catalogueing these Drugs, Chemicals and Pharmaceuticals, we aim to give a general list of those usually inquired for, at the same time we carry an immense number which we do not list. Physicians will find our stock up to the B. P. standard, either 1885 or 1898, as may be required, as well as U. S. P.

Patent Medicines.

WE carry a complete assortment of Patent Medicines. The following are a few of the leading lines. They indicate the trend of our prices throughout the entire stock.

A

Allcock's porous plasters, 15c each.
Allen's lung balsam, 17c, 35c, 70c bottle.
Ammonia, household, 10c, 15c bottle.
Acetocura (Coutts' acetic acid), 40c, 70c bottle.
Ayer's sarsaparilla, 70c bottle.
" hair vigor, 65c bottle.
" cherry pectoral, 20c, 40c and 70c.
" pills, 17c box.
Agnew's heart cure, 70c.
" ointment, 30c; pills, 10c.
Abbey's effervescent salt, 20c, 40c.
Arnold's toxin pills, 15c, 50c.
Angier's petroleum emulsion, 35c, 70c.
Agnew's catarrh cure, 40c.
Alpha headache wafers, 18c.
Allenbury's food, No. 1, 45c, 85c.
" " No. 2, 45c, 85c.
" " No. 3, 15c, 30c, 60c.
Armour's extract of beef, 25c, 45c, 85c, $1.60, 3.00
" nutrient wine, $1.00.
" fluid extract of beef, 45c, 75c.
" essence of pepsin, 95c.
" " " pancreatin, 95c.
" extract of red bone marrow, $1.25.
" peptonizing tablets, 25c.
" beef and vegetable tablets, 30c.
Alkalithia, K. & M.'s, $1.15.
Arnold's catarrh cure, 35c.

B

Bynin hypophos., 75c.
" phosph., 75c.
" Amara, 75c.
" liq. malt, 75c.
Bynol, 60c.
Benger's food, for infants and invalids, 50c, 85c.
Belladonna and capsicum plasters, 15c.
Belladonna plasters, 10c, 15c.
Bunion plasters, 10c.
Beef, iron and wine (Lewis'), 50c bottle.
Beef, iron and wine (Wyeth's), 65c bottle.
Beecham's pills, 25c box.
Bovinine, 50c, 75c bottle.
Butter color (Wells-Richardson's), 10c, 18c, 35c,
Blair's rheumatic pills, 35c, 75c.
Bishop's citrate of magnesia, shilling bottles, 25c each; in bulk, 60c lb.
Bragg's charcoal tablets, 30c box.
Burdock blood bitters, 65c; pills, 15c.
Beecham's pills, imported, 25c, 30c.
Brown's chlorodyne, 35c, 90c.
Brown's bronchial troches, 20c.
Bovril, 20c, 35c, 65c, $1.20, 2.00.
" beef cordial, $1.00, large bottle.
Baxter's mandrake bitters, 20c.
Beef peptonoids, powder, 75c tin.
Bromo seltzer, 8c, 23c, 45c, 90c.
Bishop's citrate of lithia (effervescing), 35c bot.
" " caffein " 45c bot
Brown's stainless iodine ointment, 20c.
Bristol's pills, 20c box.
Brandreth's pills, 18c box.
Benson's plasters, 20c.
Braggs' charcoal biscuits, 30c.
Bishop's Vichy salts, 30c.
Bishop's citrate of potash, 35c bottle.
" carbonate of potash, 30c bottle.
" bromide of soda, 30c bottle.
" piperazine, 85c bottle.
" Carlsbad salts, 35c bottle.
" sulphur compound, 30c bottle.
" salicylate of soda, 45c bottle.
" Friedrichshall, 30c bottle.
" phenacetine, 35c bottle.
Bishop's varlets lithia, 3 grain, 35c; 5 grain, 45c.

C

Carter's iron pills, 35c box.
" little nerve pills, 15c box.
" little liver pills, 2 boxes for 25c.
Cockle's pills, 30c.
Chester's catarrh cure, 40c.
Castoria, Pitcher's, 25c bottle.
Chase's catarrh cure, 15c.
Corn plasters, thin, 10c box; thick, 10c box.
Chase's nerve food, 35c; 3 for $1.00.
Chase's ointment, 40c.
Cod-liver oil, finest Norwegian, 8-oz bottle, 15c; 16-oz bottle, 25c; per gallon, $1.75, container 25c extra; 25c pint, bottle 5c extra.
Condition powders, 15c lb. packet.
Castor oil, 5c, 10c, 15c bottle; 20c pint bottle.
" " Italian, 15c bottle, 35c lb bottle.
" " tasteless and odorless, 25c bottle.
Chase's liver and kidney pills, 12½c.
Condy's fluid, red, 30c, 60c; green, 20c.
California syrup of figs, 40c.
Capsules, empty, 10c per 100, any size as numbered: No. 00, holds 8 grs quinine; No. 0, 6 grs; No. 1, 4 grs; No. 2, 3 grs; No. 3, 2 grs; No. 4, 1½ grs; No. 5, ¾ grs.
Chloride of lime, 4c, 8c box.
Celery King, Woodward's, 20c pkg.
Chase's linseed and turpentine, 15c.
Clarke's kola compound, $1.50.
Clarke's blood mixture, $1.00.
Congreve's balsam, 30c, 90c, $1.40.
Clarke's B41 pills, $1.15.
Cuticura resolvent, liquid, 60c, $1.15; dry, $1.15.
" ointment, 50c, $1.00 box.
" plasters, 25c each.
Cactina pellets, 25c.
Candy cascarettes, 10c, 25c, 50c.
Carlsbad salt, powder or crystal, 75c, $1.50.
Chase's liver cure, 35c.
Clarke's aperient pills, 30c.
Citrate of lithia, effervescent (K. & M.), $1.20.
Cascara cordial (P. D. & Co.'s), 75c.
Calvert's carbolic ointment, 35c box.

D

De Jongh's cod-liver oil, 60c bottle.
Dead Shot worm candy, 7½c.
Diamond dinner pills, 18c box.
Dodd's kidney pills, 30c box.
Dodd's dyspepsia tablets, 30c box.
Doan's kidney pills, 35c box or 3 for $1.00.
Datura Tatula asthma cure, 75c.

E

Eaton's effervescing fruit salt is very pleasant to take, per 1-lb tin, 35c; in ½-lb tin, 20c.
Elliman's universal embrocation, 25c, 40c, 70c
Elliman's royal embrocation, 35c and 70c.
Enos' fruit salt, 65c bottle.
Egyptian pile cure, 75c bottle.
Ely's cream balm, 45c.
Egyptian salve, 8c.
Eagar's wine of rennet, 20c.
Edison's obesity salt, $1.15.
" " pills, $1.75.
" reducing compound, $2.50.

Extract of Malt Preparations.

Made from non-alcoholic malt extract.
Extract of—
Malt, plain, 50c bottle.
" and cod-liver oil, 50c bottle.
" cod-liver oil and hypophosphites, 50c bottle.
" cod-liver oil and creasote, 50c bottle.
" and hypophosphites, 50c bottle.
" and hypophosphites, with quinine and strychnine, 75c bottle.
" phosphates, iron, quinine and strychnine, 50c bottle.
" pepsin and pancreatine, 75c bottle.
" and pepsin, 75c bottle.
" pepsin, bismuth and calisaya, 75c bottle.
" kola, celery and cocoa, 50c bottle.
" and iron, 50c bottle.
" tonic (calisaya), 50c bottle.

F

Fellows' syrup, $1.00 bottle.
Furniture polish, 10c bottle.
Fowler's extract wild strawberry, 25c.

G

Gehrig's teething necklaces, 35c each.
Griffiths' menthol liniment, 20c
Greaves' worm syrup, 18c.
Gray's syrup red spruce, 17c and 40c.
Gillett's concentrated lye, 10c tin, 3 for 25c.
Garfield tea, 20c, 40c, 75c.
Godfrey's cordial, 8c.
Gutta-percha enamel for stopping teeth, 5c stick.

Garfield fig syrup, 11c, 18c.
Guy's tonic, 80c bot.
Gibbon's toothache gum, 8c.
Glycerine suppositories (Wyeth's), 25c.

H

Hill's balsam of honey, 8c.
Hall's rheumatic cure, 50c.
Hall's catarrh cure, 60c.
Herb bitters, 15c.
Holloway's pills, 30c, $1.00.
" ointment, 30c, $1.00.
" corn cure, 20c.
Hanson's corn salve, 10c.
Homocea healing ointment, 30c.
Hood's sarsaparilla, 70c; pills, 18c.
Headache powders, 12 in box, 25c.
Hydrogen peroxide, 4-oz 15c; 8-oz, 25c; 16-oz bottle, 40c.
Haarlem oil, 5c.
Horlick's malted milk, 45c, 85c, $3.25.
Hamlin's wizard oil, 40c and 80c.
Haggard's yellow oil, 18c.
" balsam, 18c.
Hanson's junket tablets, 10c.
Hyomei booths, for asthma, 65c; complete, $1.15.
Henches' nourishing meal, 35c.
Horsford's acid phosphates, 60c and $1.20.
Hutch, 7½c, 18c, 35c, 70c.

Horse and Cattle Medicines.

Horseowners and cattlemen will find it to their advantage to have their condition powders, cattle spices, liniments, etc., made up by us. Send your recipes and get prices, etc.

Lewis' cough balls will be found excellent for horses, 50c box.

Lewis' condition powders are the best for both horses and cattle, will promote digestion, give an appetite and good clear skin, 15c lb.

Purgative horse balls, strong, $1.00 box.
" " " mild, 75c box.
Cattle spice, 20c lb.

Humphrey's Homeopathic Specifices and Simples kept in Stock.

J

Johnston's fluid beef extract, 25c, 45c, 75c, $1.25.
Jamaica ginger, Eaton's, 15c bottle.
Japanese catarrh cure, 40c.

K

King's new discovery, small, 40c; large, 75c bot.
King's dandelion pills, English, 35c.
Kay's essence of linseed, 25c, 35c.
Kellog's asthma cure, 20c, 75c.
Kutnow's Carlsbad salts, 90c.
Kendall's spavin cure, 40c, 75c.
K.D.C., 35c, 70c; K.D.C. pills, 18c.
Kennedy's medical discovery, $1.50.
Kilmer's swamp root, 60c, $1.20.
Kepler's extract of malt, 65c.
Karl's clover root tea, 20c and 40c.
Keating's cough lozenges, 30c.
Keating's worm bonbons, 30c box.

L

Liquid peptonoids, 75c.
" and creasote, $1.00.
" and coca, 80c.
Liebig's beef Ramornie, 20c, 35c, 70c.
Listerine, 25c, 50c, $1.00 bottle.
Lane's family medicines, 20c, 40c, 75c.
Lactopeptine, 75c; elixir, 75c.
Lamplough's pyretic saline, 75c.
Liebig's extract beef, 45c, 85c.
Liquid rennet (Wyeth's), 20c.
Little's soluble phenyl, 15c, 25c bottle; phenyl powder, 15c, 25c tin; soluble phenyl, $2.50 gal, 75c qt.
Lemon kali, for drinks, is an effervescing drink, very pleasant and refreshing, especially in the hot summer months, 20c lb.
Lactated food, 18c, 35c, 65c, $2.25.
Laxa liver pills, 20c.
Low's worm syrup, 18c.
Lint in packets, 5c and 10c.
Laxative bromo-quinine tablets, 20c box.

Lewis' Preparations.

Petroleum Emulsion, with hypophosphites of lime and soda. Palatable and easily assimilated; for diseases of the throat and lungs, as well as for building wasted tissues, etc. Price, large bottle (16-oz), 50c.

Herb Bitters.—This packet is composed of blood-purifying herbs, roots and barks, such as sarsaparilla, burdock, cascara, mandrake, etc., and is sufficient to make two quarts of blood-purifying medicine. Price, 15c; sample packet, 5c.

Quinine and Iron Tonic.—12-oz bottle, 25c.

Cascara and Licorice Mixture.—15c, 25c.

Electuary of Sulphur and Cream of Tartar, the old reliable blood-purifying remedy, 15c bottle.

Pile Ointment.—An almost certain cure, and a sure relief for all kinds of piles, 25c bottle.

Peruvian Ointment.—The most antiseptic healing ointment for burns, scalds, cuts, sores, frostbites, and any break of the skin, chap or scald, sore nipples, etc., 15c bottle, 10c tube.

Glycerine, Chlorate of Potash and Iron Mixture—Can be used as a gargle for sore throat and also as an internal remedy for the prevention of dyphtheria, and also for the building up of the system, etc., 10c and 25c bottle.

Quinine Wine—Regular large bottle, 50c.

Rheumatic Wafers—For lumbago or sore back, rheumatism, sciatica, etc., 25c, 50c box.

Indigestion Wafers—A certain relief and a speedy cure for this distressing malady, 25c and 50c.

Headache Wafers—Are an almost instantaneous cure for nervous headache, fulness of the head, etc., 10c, 25c and 50c.

Headache Powders—5c and 25c.

Toothache Drops—5c bottle.

English White Oils—Liniment, 10c.

Salts of Lemon—For removing stains from linens, etc., 5c bottle.

Corn Extractor—15c and 25c bottle.

Bronchial Lozenges—For coughs, colds, etc., 10c box.

Chlorate of Potash—Tablets, 5c box.

Quinine Capsules—1, 2, 3, 4 or 5-gr., 10c box.

Cascara Liver Tablets—15c and 50c box.

Soda Mint Tablets, 10c box.

Rhubarb and Soda—Tablets, 10c box.

Pepsin—Tablets for indigestion, 25c box.

Catarrh Snuff—For catarrh, cold in head, etc., 10c bottle.

Beef, iron and wine. This is a combination of the finest extract of beef with iron, fine sherry wine and aromatics, making one of the nicest and most effectual stimulating tonics and builders that it is possible to make, 50c bottle.

Beef, iron and wine, the same as the 50c bottle with the exception of the sherry wine, which is an imported Spanish wine, but is not as good as the 50c, we sell at 35c a bottle.

Pectoral Balsam of horehound, squills and wild cherry, for coughs and colds, 10c, 25c, 50c bottle.

Children's Cough Syrup of ipecac, squills' wild cherry, tar, horehound tolu, etc., 10c, 25c bottle.

Astringent cordial, for cramps, diarrhœa, cholera, etc., 15c, 25c bottle.

Foot powder, perfumed, will cure blistered, sore feet from almost any cause, hardening them so that they give no further trouble, pain or suffering, 10c, 15c box.

Lewis' emulsion of cod-liver oil with hypophosphites of lime and soda; this emulsion is pleasant to take, and can be recommended as the very best on the market for coughs, colds, debility, loss of flesh and all wasting diseases; it is so prepared that it can be retained by the most delicate stomach; it is not alone the best, but it is the cheapest, because we give a 16-oz bottle for 50c.

Lewis' extract of sarsaparilla, together with cascara, burdock, buchu and other roots and herbs, is a blood purifier and tonic, and will be found very beneficial in cases of chronic constipation, it is purely vegetable. Price, 8-oz bottle, 25c; 16-oz bottle, 50c.

Lewis' compound syrup of hypophosphites of iron, lime, soda, potash, manganese, quinine and strychnine in proper proportions. This is a building tonic, and as it contains all the principal elements of the human system, it is one of the best that can be taken for emaciation and decay of any kind; it is a builder of the tissues, bones and blood; 15c, 25c, 50c bottle.

Lewis' syrup of the hypophosphites without quinine or strychnine, for children, at same prices, viz., 15c, 25c, 50c.

Lewis' Liver Pills, for enlargement and torpidity or sluggishness of the liver, constipation, etc.; boxes of 30 pills, 10c box.

M

M. A. G. mixture of acid and gentian is a liver stimulant, and promotes digestion, as well as being a powerful tonic, 25c bottle.
Mellin's food, 35c, 70c; English, 40c, 75c.
Maltopepsin, 60c; elixir, 80c; tablets, 60c.
Milburn's heart and nerve pills, 35c or 3 for $1.00.
" rheumatic pills, 35c or 3 for $1.00.
Mustard plasters, 10c, 15c, 20c, 25c, 35c.
Menthol plasters, 18c.
Minard's liniment, 15c.
Magnesia citrate, 15c bottle, 40c lb.
" 1-oz blocks, 2 for 5c.
" Lewis' fluid, 12½c bottle.
Morse's Indian root pills, 17c.
Menthol pencils, 10c, 15c, 20c, 25c.
Moller's cod-liver oil, 60c, $1.10.
Menthol inhalers (Wyeth's), 30c.
Maltine with creasote, 80c.
" plain, 75c.
" cod-liver oil, 40c, 75c.
" hypophosphites, 95c.
" pepsin and pancreatine, 95c.
" phosphates, iron, quinine and strychnine, $1.15.
Morse's glycerole of celery, 30c, $1.20 bottle.
Murray's fluid magnesia, 25c.
Montserrat lime juice, 35c, 60c.

N

Neaves' food, 35c.
Nestle's milk food, 2 tins for 75c.
Nasal balm, 35c, 70c.
Norton's chamomile pills, 30c.

O

Orange blossom, 75c.
Olive oil, Ferrari Excelsior Italian brand, 15c, 25c and 45c.
Olive oil, Bertrand's French, 20c, 35c and 65c.
Olive oil, other brands, all edible oils, 10c, 15c, 20c, 25c, 35c, 50c bottle.

P

Powley's ozone, 40c and 85c a bottle.
Perry Davis' pain killer, 18c.
Pettit's eye salve, 20c.
Pond's extract, 40c, 75c.
Peptonizing tubes, 45c.
Paine's celery compound, 70c.
Parrish's syrup or chemical food, 25c.
Paregoric, 2-oz bottle, 10c.
Pink pills (Dr. Williams'), 35c box, or 3 boxes for $1.00.
Putnam's corn cure, 20c.
Pinkham's vegetable compound, 85c.
" pills, 20c.
" compound, in pill form, 85c.
" blood purifier, 85c.
" sanative wash, 20c.
Parmalee's pills, 18c.
Polson's nervoline, 20c.
Phenyo-caffein pills, 20c box.
Pierce's prescription, 70c.
" discovery, 70c.
" pellets, 17c.
" nasal douche, 45c.
" smartweed, 40c.

R

Radway's ready relief, 18c; pills, 18c.
" resolvent, 70c.
Robinson's patent barley, 10c and 20c.
Robinson's groats, 10c and 20c.

S

Sarsaparillas.

Young's sarsaparilla, with iodide of potassium, is the best blood purifier and alterative, as well as the cheapest; price 35c bottle.
Sarsaparilla, Lewis', without iodide of potassium, 25c, 50c bottle.
Sarsaparilla—Ayer's, 70c.
" Hood's, 70c.
" Radway's, 70c.
" Bristol's, 70c.
Sea salt, in bags of about 10 lbs, 12½c.
Sea salt, Tidman's, 20c, 30c, 60c.
Strengthening plasters, 10c.
Stearn's cascara (Kasagra), $1.25 bottle.
South American nervine, 70c.
South American rheumatic cure, 60c; kidney cure, 70c.
Syrup of turpentine, 18c, 35c.
Sulphur fumigators, 5c, 20c.
" lozenges, 12½c box.
Seidlitz powders, 10 in box, 12½c box.
Scott's emulsion, 35c, 70c.

Soothing syrup, Winslow's, 20c.
Steedman's soothing powders, 30c.
Stedman's teething powders, 25c.
Stedman's worm powders, 30c.
Shiloh's consumptive cure, 20c, 40c, 75c.
Spirits camphor, 2-oz bottle, 10c.
Sweet spirits of nitre, 2-oz bottle, 10c.
Sage's catarrh cure, 35c.
Stuart's dyspepsia tablets, 40c, 80c.
" absorbent lozenges, 25c.
" catarrh tablets, 40c, 80c.
" calcium wafers, 40c.

T

Tar, Carolina, 10c tin.
Thomas' eclectric oil, 15c.
Trilene tablets, for cure of corpulency, 85c, $2.60 box.
Tartarlithine tablets, 85c.
" and sulphur tablets, 75c.
Tanglefoot sticky fly paper, 2 for 5c.

V

Vapocresolene, complete with lamp, $1.40.
Vapocresolene, liquid only, 25c, 50c, $1.50 bottle.
Vigrol, Armour's, 30c, 50c, 80c.

W

Waters.

Apenta water, 22c, 30c bottle.
Bilin mineral water, 20c bottle; $7.50 case.
Carlsbad mineral water, 40c bottle, 2 for 75c.
Friedrichshall, 30c, 40c.
Hunyadi Janos, 30c, 40c bottle.
Vichy water, 35c.

Wills' English pills, 18c.
Warner's safe cure, 75c.
Wood's phosphodine, 80c.
Woodward's celery king, 20c.
Wood's Norway pine syrup, 20c.
Wyeth's peptonic pills, 35c.
" liquid malt, 25c.
" peptonate of iron and manganese, $1.00.
" glycerine suppositories, 25c.
" lithia tablets, 3 grs, 25c; 5 grs, 35c.
Wampole's alvenine suppositories, 35c.
" glycerine suppositories, 30c; child's, 25c.
" antiseptic solution, 40c bottle.
" cod-liver oil, 70c.
" syrup, white pine and tar, 15c.

Drug Sundry Department

We carry a very extensive stock of Drug Sundries, and are adding new and improved lines all the time, and frequently renewing all lines.

Acid bottles, with brush, 50c.

Atomizers.

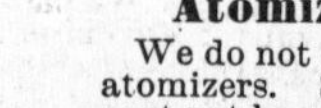

We do not exchange atomizers. Should a part not be perfect, we will make it so, or replace when necessary.
Bronx, No. 1, 1 tip, 35c.
Tyrian, No. 44, water-oil atomizer, small size, 1 tip, 50c.
Tyrian, No. 41, water-oil atomizer, 1 tip, 65c.
Tyrian, No. 42, water-oil atomizer, 2 tips, 75c.
Tyrian, No. 43, water-oil atomizer; 3 tips, 85c.
Vaseline oil-spray producer, 65c; with tube, 75c.
Atomizer bulbs, single, 15c, 20c, 25c each.
Ideal atomizers, 1 tip, red enamelled bulbs. 70c; 2 tips, 80c; 3 tips, 90c.

Absorbent Cottons.

Absorbent cotton, plain, 1-oz packet, 4c.
" " " 2-oz " 7c.
" " " 4-oz " 12½c.
" " " 8-oz " 20c.
" " " 1-lb " 35c.
" " borated, 1-oz packet, 5c; 60c lb.
" " carbolated, 1-oz packet, 5c; 60c lb.

Antiseptic Gauzes.

Boracic acid, moist gauze, per yd, 20c.
Carbolic " " " 20c.
Salicylic " " " 20c.
Iodoform, 5 per cent, moist gauze, per yd, 35c.
" 10 " " " " " 45c.
Iodoform gauze, in packets, 4 per cent., 1 yd, 20c.
" " " 10 per cent., ½-yd, 10c; ½-yd, 15c; 1 yd, 25c.
Iodoform gauze, in packets, 20 per cent., 1 yd, 35c.

Abdominal Supports.

When ordering, give measurements in inches at top, middle and bottom.

The prices are $1.75, 2.00, 2.50 and 3.00. All sizes except extra large or small at each price, that is, sizes from 26 to 38 inches.
Breast pumps, 25c, 35c, 60c.
Bougies, Nos. 1 to 12, best web, 25c.
We do not exchange Bougies or Breast Pumps.

Bent Throat Brushes.

Swabs, 15c, 20c, 25c.
Camel hair pencils, 2c, 3c, 5c.
Bent throat brushes, 10c.

Bandages.

We do not exchange.

Cotton, 6 yds long, 2, 2½, 3 or 3½ inches wide, 3 for 25c, 10c each.
Red Cross bandages, 1 inch wide, 6 yds long, 5c each; 2, 2½, 3 or 3½ inches wide, 6 yds long, 10c each.
Suspensory bandages, 25c, 35c, 50c, 75c, $1.00, 1.25, 1.50.
Rubber bandages, finest quality, 25c oz.
The weights of the first quality in 6-yd lengths are—
2 inches wide, about 7½ ozs, 25c oz.
2½ " " " 9½ " "
3 " " " 11½ " "

Bronze Powders.

For renewing gilt picture frames, gilding ornaments, or any kind of fancy work—
Finest deep gold bronze, 15c oz, $2.00 lb.
Fine " " " 10c oz, $1.40 lb.
Good gold bronze, 5c oz, 70c lb.
Liquid bronze, 10c bottle.
Brilliant gold paint, powder liquid and brush, separate, per box, 15c.
Bottle of liquid for use with bronze or silver powders, for gilding, 2 ozs, 10c; 4 ozs, 15c.
Colored bronze, all shades, green, blue, red, etc., 20c oz.
Aluminum bronze, 15c oz.
Blanco pickerings, in zinc boxes, 15c box.
Blanco refills, 5c tablet.

Beds, Water and Air.

Beds, water and air, from $15.00 to 50.00, according to size and style.

Candles.

Paraffine candles, sets of 14 ozs, 12 or 6 to set, 12½c set.
Parlor wax candles, red, white, blue, green and lavender, 30c doz.
Corn plasters, thin or thick, 10c box.

Corn rubbers, 15c each.

Catheters.

(We do not exchange catheters.)
English style catheters, 15c.
Silk web catheters, 40c.
Catheters, Nos. 1 to 12, best web, 25c; Nos. 4 to 10, soft rubber, 25c.

Cements.

Seccotine, in tubes, mends everything, 15c and 25c.
Blair's cement, 15c bottle.
Kaye's coaguline (English), 15c and 30c bottle.
Crockery mender, 5c bottle.
Glues (see Drug List).

Chamois.

Chamois skins, first quality, are slightly smaller than sizes given, while the second quality, which is, as a rule, a skin that has been cut and sewed up again, is slightly larger. We do not stock the third or inferior qualities. These are all light in color; state whether you want a very soft, thin chamois or a thick one, the prices are as follows. The size is what could be trimmed out of a skin.

The sizes in inches are about, as follows:

10 x 12, 10c each.	19 x 21, 60c each.
13 x 14, 15c "	21 x 25, 70c "
14 x 15, 20c "	22 x 25, 75c "
16 x 17, 25c "	22 x 26, 80c "
16 x 18, 35c "	26 x 26, 90c "
17 x 18, 45c "	23 x 31, $1.15 "

Carriage chamois about 18 x 23, 60c.
Very heavy chamois, yellow, about 22 x 26, 75c.
" " " " " 23 x 28, $1.00.
Droppers, glass, bent or straight, 3c, 5c, 10c each.
Dropper, with protected point, bent or straight, for the eye, 8c.
Eye baths, glass, 10c, 20c.

Ear syringes, glass, 15c.
Ear and ulcer syringes, soft rubber, 20c, 25c.
Ear and nasal douche, 20c.

Electrical Sundries.

Medical Batteries.

We will be pleased to give any information desired in regard to any of the following batteries:

Electro-magnetic batteries, have power generated by hand by turning a handle, these are the finest English goods, at $5.00, 7.00, 10.00 and 12.00.
Capital Duplex, with two cells. Price, $8.00.
Battery coil, cell and handles, on wooden stand, $3.00.
Champion dry cell battery, $3.50.
Climax wet cell battery, $4.00.
Sherman battery, $10.00.
The Criterion battery, $15.00.
Gaiffe's pocket battery, single, $4.50; double, $7.50.
Dr. Spamer's bichromate cell battery, $7.00, 8.00, 11.00, 12.50.
Dr. Glauert's portable double-apparatus for constant and induction current. This is the very best German portable medical battery. Price, $50.00.
Neurotone battery, $7.00.

Electric Batteries, Cells, Bells, etc.

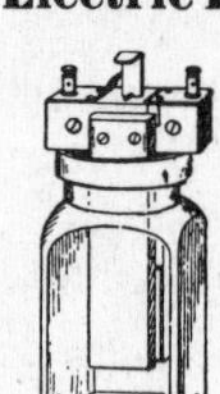

No. 2. Leclanché cell, complete (2 pint), each 40c.
No. 2. Leclanché porous pots, charged, 15c.
No. 2. Leclanché zincs, 7½c.
No. 2. Agglomerate cells (2 pint), 40c.
Carbon plates, 5c.
Zincs, 7½c.
No. 2 Carbon bichromate cells, 35c.
Medical sack cell (Leclanché), 40c.
Carporous cells, complete, 60c.
Window contacts, No. 1, at 30c each.
Door contact, No. 2, at 30c each.
Floor contact (dining-room, etc.), No. 6, $1.00.
Brass door push-buttons, from 50c to $1.50.
Wood, wall or door push-buttons, 2 inches in diameter, 10c; 2½ inches in diameter, 15c; 3 inches in diameter, 20c.
Pear push-buttons, 20c.
Rosette push-buttons, 20c.
China push-buttons, 3-inch, plain, 20c; 3-inch reeded, 25c.
Insulated bell wire, 2/22—Twin wire, one double covered and one single covered and paraffined, 2½c yard; flexible silk-covered cord 2 strand wire, 5c yard.

Dry Cells.

No. 1 A. Round E. & S. dry cell, 60c, and small, 40c.
Midget dry cell, 40c.
Mesco dry cell, 35c.

Bells.

Portable bell set, complete with 12 yards of silk-covered flexible cord, in walnut case, pear-shape push-button and dry cell. This set complete for $3.50.

Best quality electric call bells, 3-inch bell mounted on finely polished back, heavy terminals and best finish, $2.00 each.
The Compact bell, complete with 30 ft of flexible cord, and press button, with 2 E. & S. dry cells, fitted in mahogany case, price $2.75.
Cells for Compact set, 40c each.
The Victoria electric bell, 2½-inch bell, metal case, very strong and compact, 75c each.

The Pygmy, a very small wood backed bell, well made and finished throughout, and very powerful little bell, 1¾ inches in diameter, 50c each.

No. 1987. A 2¾-inch gong, polished walnut cover, with imitation walnut back, very strong, $1.00 each.

No. 1993. Electric bell, 3-inch bell, metal gong, platinum pointed contacts; the movement is cased in polished walnut; price $1.25.

Chemicals for Batteries, Etc.

Sal. ammoniac, granular, 15c lb.
Blue stone or sulphate copper, 10c lb.
Bichromate of potash, 20c lb.
Bisulphate of mercury, 10c oz; $1.40 lb.

Elastic Stockings.

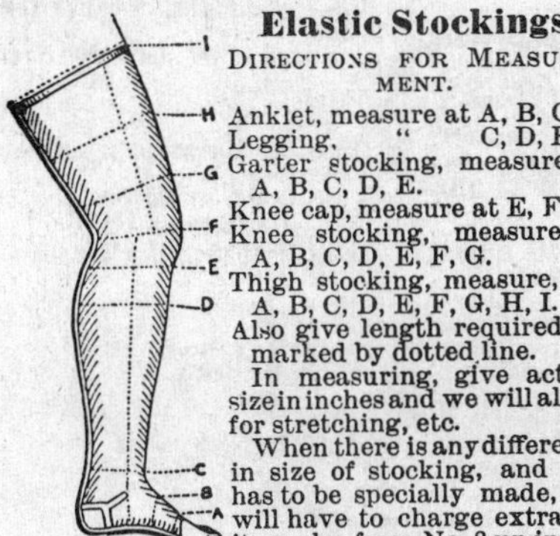

DIRECTIONS FOR MEASUREMENT.

Anklet, measure at A, B, C.
Legging, " C, D, E.
Garter stocking, measure at A, B, C, D, E.
Knee cap, measure at E, F, G.
Knee stocking, measure at A, B, C, D, E, F, G.
Thigh stocking, measure, at A, B, C, D, E, F, G, H, I.
Also give length required, as marked by dotted line.

In measuring, give actual size in inches and we will allow for stretching, etc.

When there is any difference in size of stocking, and one has to be specially made, we will have to charge extra for it, as also from No. 8 up in the regular sizes.

LIST OF PRICES, SINGLE PIECE, FOR REGULAR SIZES NOS. 1 TO 8.

	Silk.	Thread.
Anklet	$0 75	$0 60
Legging	1 00	0 60
Garter stocking	1 50	1 00
Knee cap	1 00	0 60
Knee stocking	2 00	1 40
Thigh stocking	4 00	2 50

Fingerstalls, plain, 5c each.
Fingerstalls, with band, 10c each.
Fingerstalls, very thin rolled, 35c doz.

Flesh and bath gloves, soft or medium hard, 7½c; soft, medium or hard, 10c, 15c; soft, medium, hard and very hard, 20c, 25c pair.

Fumigating pastiles, in bulk, black, 3 ozs for 10c, or 50c lb; red pastiles, 5c oz, or 75c lb.

Foot warmers, stoneware, 60c, 75c and 85c, according to size.

Funnels.

Pressed glass funnels, ribbed, capacity 4-oz, 15c; 8-oz, 20c; 16-oz, 25c; 32-oz, 40c each.

Celluloid funnels, very small, 15c, 20c each.

Glass tubing, assorted sizes, 25c oz, 50c lb.

When small quantities are ordered state whether large or small tubing is required, and if by post send postage for 2 oz for every oz ordered.

Gutta percha stopping for decayed teeth, 5c stick.

Hypodermic Syringes.

Hicks', English, $3.00 and 3.50.
Hypodermic syringes, $1.25, 1.50, 1.75, 2.50.
Hypodermic needles, 10c and 30c each.

Hearing Apparatus.

Ear trumpets, $1.75.
Flexible, covered speaking tubes, $2.50.
Audiphones, $2.00.

Inhalers.

Glass pocket inhalers, 10c each.
Eye protectors, flesh color, right or lef teye, 10c each.
Iodoform, Dredge's hard rubber, 50c.
Insect powder guns, 5c, 10c, 15c.

Invalids' Feeders.

Boat-shaped feeders, 15c, 25c.
Cup-shaped feeders, 15c, 20c, 25c, 35c.

Infants' Feeding Bottles, etc.

We do not exchange these goods.

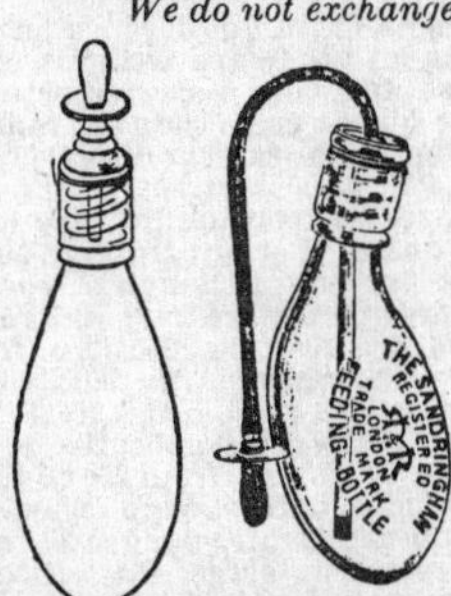

The Baby's Delight boat-shaped feeder, graduated on back, glass screw stopper, with black teat and brush, 20c.

The Canadian, white flint glass feeder, with glass screw cork, black rubber fittings, tube and bottle brush, 15c.

Feeding bottles, with teat on top, 10c.

Maw's old style feeder, boat shape, 25c, 30c, 35c.
Cork top fittings, black rubber, 5c, 8c.
Feeding bottle brushes, 2½c, 5c; tube brushes, 2½c.
Infants' teething rings, ivory, 20c, 25c, 30c, 35c.
" " bone, 5c, 7c.
" soothers, 10c, 15c, 25c, 50c.

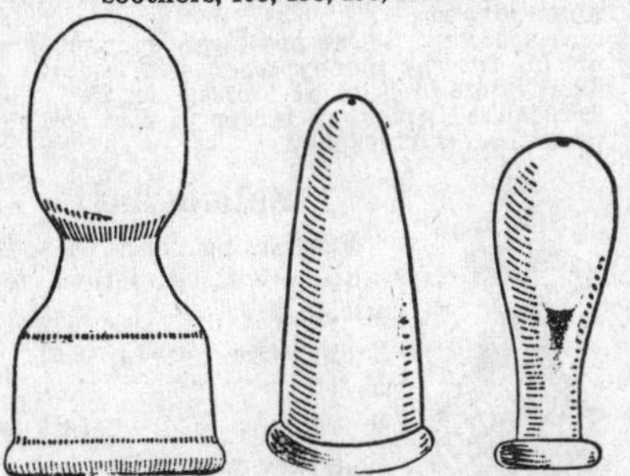

A. B. C.

We do not exchange Teats.

A. Teat for top of bottle, black rubber, 5c.
B. " " black, 3 for 10c.
C. Teats for tube fittings, black, small, 2½c.
C. " " black Para rubber, medium, 3 for 10c; large, 5c.

Mizpah teats with valve, black rubber, 7½c.
Black Para rubber tubing for feeding bottles, 10c yd.
Extra large teats, style B, 5c each.
Lunar caustic, in cocus wood screw-top cases, 10c.
Lint, 75c, $1.00, 1.25 lb.
Lint, in 5c and 10c pkts.

Measure glasses—
Cone shaped, 1-oz, 25c; 2-oz, 30; 4-oz, 35c.
Cup shaped, 8-oz, 50c; 10-oz, 60c; 16-oz, 65c; 20-oz, 85c; 40-oz, $1.25.

Medicine Glasses—
Small, moulded, 5c; large, 10c.
Small, hand-made, 20c; large, 30c.

Milk testers, Heeren's, 50c each.
" Hicks', 40c each.

Wedgwood.

Mortars and pestles; sizes, prices and capacity as follows:

Wedgwood, acid proof, 3 oz, 40c; 3½ oz, 45c; 6 oz, 50c; 8 oz, 60c; 10 oz, 65c; 12 oz, 90c; 1 pint, $1.00; 1½ pints, $1.25; 2 pints, $1.65; 2½ pints, $2.00; 3 pints, $2.50; 5 pints, $3.25; 7 pints, $4.00.

Glass mortars and pestles—
1 oz, 35c; 2 oz, 40c; 4 oz, 50c; 8 oz, 65c; 16 oz, 90c.

The "Natural Body" Brace—C186. Endorsed by leading men of the medical profession for special weaknesses and diseases of women. It is a natural uplifting support, applied where it is needed. **Write for** pamphlet giving full description, also directions for measurement. As they have to be made after order is received, it will take about 10 days to fill orders.

Made in three qualities, special line at $6.00; better quality webbing and metal trimmings, $7.50; fine silk webbing, $10.00.

Nipple shells, 20c and 30c pair.
Nipple shields, glass, with rubber teat, 12½c each.
Nipple shields, rubber, 15c, 25c.
Nail polishers, 25c, 35c, 50c.
Nail files, 5c, 10c, 15c, 25c, 35c.
Oiled silks, $1.25, 1.75 yd.

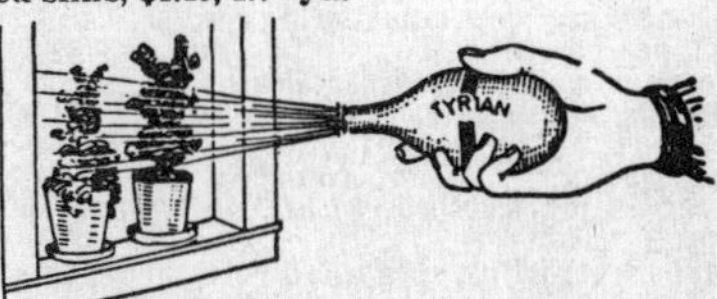

Plant sprinklers, small, 50c; medium, 65c large, $1.00.
Pickering's razor paste, 15c tube.
" blanco, 5c and 15c.

Polishes and Varnishes.

Silver, Metal and Furniture Polishes.

Electro-silicon silver polishing powder, 8c box.
Globe plate powder (German), 15c pkt.
Goddard's plate powder, 15c, 25c.
Gilt-edge metal polish, liquid, 18c.
Zibell's sunshine polishing paste, 20c.
" sunshine metal polish, 20c.
Putz cream metal polishing liquid, 15c.
Globe metal polish, world renowned, 5c, 10c, 25c.
Globe furniture polish, 5c and 10c tin.
Eaton's furniture polish, 6-oz bottle, 10c.
Oakey's Wellington knife polish, 4c, 6c, 8c, 15c and 30c.

Polishes and Varnishes for Stoves and Stovepipes.

Oakey's Nelson's black-lead domes, in boxes of one doz. domes for 15c.
Nonsuch liquid stove polish, 9c bottle.
Enameline stove polishing paste, 7c.
Shino polishing paste for stoves, 7c.
Nonsuch enamel stove paste, 7c.
Nonsuch mirror stovepipe varnish, 12c.
Egyptian stovepipe enamel, 10c and 15c bottle.
Black stovepipe enamel, tins, 10c.
Ebony black stovepipe varnish, 5c tin.

Respirator.

Improved silver-plated wire, 25c.
" cork respirator, 20c.

Syringes, Rubber Goods. Etc.

We do not exchange syringes or other rubber goods; we guarantee them to be in perfect order; should a part be imperfect we will rectify it or replace when necessary.

Rubber Urinals—Male.

Soft rubber, night and day, complete with straps, etc. Price, $1.50, 1.60, 1.75, 2.00, 2.50, 3.00.
Female, day, $3.00 and $3.25.

Hot Water Bottles.

Provincial hot water bottles—
2-quart, 65c.
3-quart, 75c.
4-quart, 85c.

Comfort hot water bottles, finest red rubber, $1.35, 1.60, 1.85, 2.15, 2.50, 3.00, according to size. These we strongly recommend.

Alpha hot water bottles—
2-quart, $1.25.
3-quart, 1.40.
4-quart, 1.60.
5-quart, 1.75.

If you receive more than one copy of our Catalogue kindly notify us.

Omega hot water bottles, 2-quart, $1.00; 3-quart, $1.15; 4-quart, $1.35.
Alpha extra hot water bottle, 2-quart, $1.50; 3-quart, $1.75; 4-quart, $2.00.

Fountain Syringes.

Alpha fountain syringes, heavy wood box, 5-inch pipe, No. 2, $1.50; No. 3, $1.75; No. 4, $2.00; No. 5, $2.25.
Fountain syringes, 3-pipe paper box, No. 2, 60c; No. 3, 65c; No. 4, 75c.
Omega fountain syringe, 3-pipe, No. 2, $1.00; No. 3, $1.25; No. 4, $1.50.
Tyrian globe spray fountain syringe, wood box, 4-pipe, 2-quart, $1.50; 3-quart, $1.75.
Fairbanks' fountain syringes, wood box, 2-quart, $1.25; 3-quart, $1.40; 4-quart, $1.50.
Tyrian success fountain syringe, 3-pipe, card-board box, No. 2, $1.00; No. 3, $1.15, and No. 4, $1.25.
Provincial fountain syringe, 3-pipe, No. 2, 75c; No. 3, 85c; No. 4, $1.00.

Combination Hot Water Bottles and Fountain Syringes.

Globe spray combination, 5-pipe, $2.00 and $2.25.
Alpha combination, 4-pipe, 2-quart, $2.00; 3-quart, $2.25; 4-quart, $2.50.
Omega combination, 3-pipe, 2-quart, $1.50; 3-quart, $1.75; 4-quart, $2.00.
Boston combination fountain syringe, card box, 3 pipes, No. 2, $1.10; No. 3, $1.25; No. 4, $1.35.
Marvel whirling spray, ladies' syringe, $3.00.
Alhambra douche, ladies' syringe, 75c.
Tyrian, ladies' syringe, all soft rubber, and shield, $1.75.

Enema Syringes.

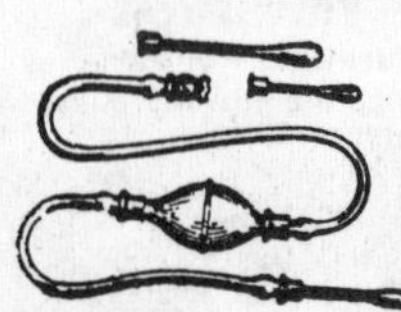

Household, No. 1, with 5 pipes, $1.50; No. 2, 4 pipes, $1.00; No. 3, 3 pipes, 75c.
Omega, 3 pipes, No. 3, $1.00.
Omega, extra, 2 pipes, 75c.
Dominion enema, 35c.
Special enema, 2 pipes, 35c.
English style enema syringe, black rubber bone rectal pipe, with vaginal pipe and shield, $1.25.
The same, made of red rubber, $1.00.
Excelsior enema, 3-pipe, 60c, 75c and 85c.

Syringes.

Glass, male, cork end, ½-oz, 5c; ½-oz, 7c; 1-oz, 10c; 1½-oz, 15c; 2-oz, 20c; female, 1-oz, 15c; 1½-oz, 20c; 2-oz, 25c.
Nickel screw top, male syringes, glass, ½-oz, 7c; ½-oz, 10c; 1-oz, 15c; 1½-oz, 18c; 2-oz, 25c; female, 1-oz, 15c; 1½-oz, 18c; 2-oz, 25c.
Glass droppers, bent or straight, 3c, 5c and 10c.
Glass eye, Pippett's, protected point, bent or straight, 8c; 30 minim, graduated, 35c.
Glass ear syringes, bent or straight, 15c.
Glass nasal syringes, 15c.
Glass and rubber glycerine rectal syringes, 25c, 30c and 60c.
Rubber (hard) glycerine rectal syringe, 35c.

Hard Rubber Syringes.

Ring handle, hard rubber, long nozzle syringe, ½-oz, 20c; ½-oz, 25c; ½-oz, 45c; 1-oz, 65c; 2-oz, $1.25.
Spray nozzle, ring handle syringe, ½-oz, 35c; 1-oz, 60c; 2-oz, $1.00.
Infant's rectal syringe, 2-oz, 20c.
Hard rubber ointment rectal pipes, 35c.
3-dram hard rubber syringe, 30c; 6-dram, 50c.

Soft Rubber Syringes.

Ear syringes, bulb, 20c each.
Soft rubber ear and ulcer syringe, 20c, 25c.
Bulb enema, 1 oz, 30c; 2 oz, 40c; 3 oz, 50c; 4 oz, 60c; 6 oz, 75c; 8 oz, $1.00.
Politzer air bag, 8 oz, $1.25 each.
Powder blower, with hard rubber cannula and receptacle for powder in same, straight or bent, 50c.
Powder blower, with flexible vulcanized cannula, 35c.

Sponge Bags.

No. 1, 10c; No. 2, 12½c; No. 3, 15c; No. 4, 20c; No. 5, 25c; No. 6, 30c; No. 7, 35c; No. 8, 40c.
Sponge nets, 25c.

Sponges.

We do not exchange.

Mediterranean sponges, extra quality; we have a very fine assortment; they are without exception the finest sponges ever imported. The size is smaller for the price than the regular first quality Mediterranean sponges. Our prices are 25c, 50c, 75c, $1.50, 2.00.
Mediterranean sponges "Honeycomb;" are all full form sponges and are not put through the regular bleaching process, although of good light color, some few pieces are very light in color. The prices are 10c, 15c, 25c, 35c, for small toilet and face sponges; large face and bath sponges are 50c, 75c, $1.00, 1.25, 1.50, 2.00.
Fine bleached turkey (silk), 5c, 10c, 15c, 20c, 25c, 30c, 40c, 50c, 60c, 75c, $1.00. At from 25c to 50c you can buy a splendid baby sponge; the 5c, 10c, 15c and 20c line are small sponges fit for surgical use and washing sores, etc.; those from 50c to $1.00 are really fine face sponges, or for any other purpose.
Unbleached wool sponges, 5c, 10c, 15c, 25c, 35c, 50c, 75c. These are very strong soft sponges, suitable for all purposes, viz., toilet, bath, buggy-washing and stable use.
Velvet sponges, 5c, 10c, 15c, 25c, 35c. Are not as strong as the wool, but are good serviceable sponges.
Grass sponges. These are large sponges and are big for the money when size is desired. They range in price at 5c, 10c, 15c, 25c. The unbleached grass are larger in size for the price than the bleached.

Seltzogens.

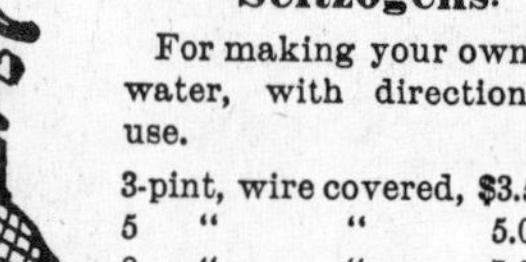

For making your own soda water, with directions for use.

3-pint, wire covered, $3.50.
5 " " 5.00.
8 " " 7.50.

Seltzogen measures—
2-pint .... 20c.
3 " .... 25c.
5 " .... 30c.
8 " .... 35c.

Seltzogen, metal head, with tap, $1.00.

Seltzogen, glass tube, with metal screw, 25c.

Soaps.

Toilet Soaps.

Calvert's prickly heat soap, 10c cake.
" shampoo soap, 30c jar.
" nurses' soap, 12½c cake.
" glycerine carbolic, 15c cake.
" medical carbolic, 25c cake.
" sulphur soap, 15c cake.
" hygienic tar soap, 15c cake.
" " carbolic soap, 15c cake.
" carbolic toilet soap, 15c cake.
Baby's Own soap, 3 cakes for 25c.
Burton's tar soap, 3 cakes for 25c.
Carbolic and glycerine, 3 cakes for 25c.
Pine tar soap, 6 cakes for 20c.
Madam Roy toilet soap, 30c doz.
Colgate's soaps—
Cashmere bouquet, 15c, 25c cake.
Sulphur, 12½c cake.
White castile, 3 cakes for 25c.
Medicated tar, 12½c cake.
White clematis, 3 cakes for 25c.
Oatmeal, 3 cakes for 25c.
Tuscan green castile, 5c.
Bay rum soap, 3 for 25c.
Turkish bath, 80c doz.
Vioris toilet soaps, large, 20c cake.
Vioris toilet soap, special, 5c cake.
Cosmo Buttermilk Soap Co.'s buttermilk soap, 3 cakes for 25c.
Silver plate, 10c cake, 3 cakes for 25c.

Packer's tar soap, 20c cake.
Morse's heliotrope, fine perfumed toilet, 3 cakes for 25c.
Grey oatmeal, 6 cakes for 25c.
Extra fine oatmeal, 3 cakes for 20c.
Turkish bath, 6 cakes for 25c.
Transparent glycerine, 3 cakes for 25c.
Carnation, 6 cakes for 25c.
Floral bouquet, 6 cakes for 25c.
Castile and oatmeal bar, 5c.
Infants' delight, 3 cakes for 25c.
Assorted toilet soaps, 80c doz.
" " " $1.00 "
" " " 50c "
" " " 40c "
Pure castile soap, in cakes, 20c doz.
Virgin castile, 20c doz.
Conti castile soap, 17½c lb.
White imported castile soap, 3 lbs for 25c; 10c, 12½c lb.
Pears' soaps—
Unscented, 10c cake.
Hospital transparent, 12½c cake.
Transparent glycerine, 15c cake.
Scented, 25c cake.
Otto of rose, 60c cake.
Elder flower, 80c, $1.00, 1.20 doz cakes.
Coal tar, 10c cake.
Carbolic, 10c cake.
Fuller's earth, 10c cake.
Dog, 10c cake.
Fairbank's tar soap, 3 cakes for 10c
" copco, 6 cakes for 25c.
Cuticura toilet soap, 25c cake.
Baker's shampoo soap, 25c cake.
Morses' Barclay complexion soap, 30c doz.
Pure white castile soap, in square cakes, 20c doz.

Shaving Soaps.

Williams' barbers' bar, 7c cake, 35c lb.
Williams' barbers' favorite, 8c cake.
Williams' travellers' stick, 25c.
Williams' Yankee shaving cake, 10c.
Williams' luxury shaving cake, 25c.
Pears' shaving sticks, 25c, 35c, 60c.
Cuticura shaving soap, 15c cake.
Colgate's demulcent shaving stick, 18c.
Colgate's shaving cakes, 1 lb bars, 35c.
Taylor's shaving stick, 12½c.
Mitchelsen's shaving cream, 15c and 25c tube.
Pinnacle soap stands, made of rubber, 25c each.

Laundry Soaps.

Lightning ammonia soap, 15c box.
Peerless soft oil soap, 10c a box.
English soft soap, 20c lb.
Canadian soft soap, 15c lb.
Calvert's carbolic soft soap, sample tin, 7½c; 1-lb crocks, 25c each.
Fels' naptha soap, 4 cakes for 25c.
Ammonia powder, washing compound, 5c pkt.
Eaton's bar, black label (about 3 lbs), 15c bar, $2.90 case of 20 bars.
Eaton's bar, red label (about 3 lbs), 12½c bar, $2.50 case of 20 bars.
Eaton's bar, Duchess (about 3 lbs), 10c bar, $2.00 case of 20 bars.
Eaton's electric, 7 cakes for 25c.
Eclipse laundry cake, 6 for 25c.
Morse's mottled, 5 cakes for 25c.
Comfort, 6 cakes for 25c; $4.15 case.
Surprise, 6 cakes for 25c; $4.15 case.
Sunlight, 5c bar.
Pyle's pearline, 4c, 12½c packet.
Gold dust, 3-lb packet for 22c.
Savona, 5c packet.
Borax, lumps or powder, 7c lb.
Sapolio, 3 bars for 25c.
White foam washing compound, 6 packets 25c.
Calvert's paraffine soap, bars of about 1-lb, 10c.
Brooke's monkey brand soap, 5c.
Life Buoy carbolic soap, 5c.

Trusses.

NOTE.—Measurement in inches around top of hips.

New York elastic trusses, from 12 to 44 inches.
N. Y. elastic truss, enamelled pad, single, 80c.
" double, $1.10.
" water pad, single, $1.00.
" double, $1.50.
English trusses, chamois pad, single, 75c; double, $1.00.

If we make any change in filling your order we will write giving full explanations.

Thermometers.

7-inch thermometer, 10c.
8-inch thermometer, 12½c.
10-inch thermometer, fine, 15c.
Glass dairy thermometer, 10c.
Wood-backed thermometer, 15c.
7-inch cabinet wood-backed thermometer, 25c.
8-inch magnifying lens, wood back, 50c.
Barometer and thermometer, cottage, 20c.
Barometer and thermometer, tin panel, 15c.
Barometer and thermometer, polished oak frame, 60c.
Maximum registering thermometer, $1.00.
Minimum registering thermometer, $1.00.
Maximum and minimum combined, $2.50.
Art thermometers, for fancy work, 2-inch, 7c; 2½-inch, 7½c; 3-inch, 8c; 3½ or 4-inch, 10c; 4½ or 5-inch, 13c.
Bath thermometers, Forbes' specification, 15c.

Clinical Thermometers, for Doctors, Nurses, etc.

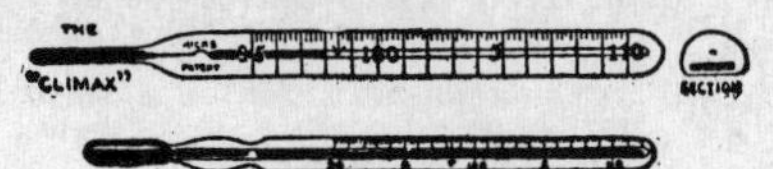

All thermometers sent by post at buyer's risk.
A very good magnifying lens thermometer, 50c.
Veterinary clinical thermometers, 80c, $1.00, 1.50.

Hicks' Clinical Thermometers.

Hicks' ordinary, certified, 75c.
" facilis, " $1.75.
" one minute, " 2.00.
" flat fever " 1.00.
" lens front, " 1.25.

Hicks' ebonite hygenic thermometer, $1.50.
" glass " " $1.50.
" thermometer, stomach use, $2.50.
" surface thermometer, $3.50.
Magnifying thermometers, with certificate of correction, $1.00, 1.25.

Toilet Papers.

500-sheet packets, 5c pkt.
1,000 " 9c "
800 " 7½c "
Unperforated rolls, 800-sheet, 8c; 1,000-sheet 10c roll.
Perforated, 800-sheet, 10c; 1,000 sheet, 12c.
2,000-sheet perforated roll, 17½c; plain, 15c.

Tapers.

For lighting gas, etc., 30 tapers in box for 5c.
Taper holders, 15c and 25c.

PERFUMES AND BRUSHES.

In Cut Glass and Fancy Bottles.

Boxed in the neatest and most elegant box that we could procure. Each bottle has a box to fit it; are filled with Gold Label Perfumes, any odor as listed. The style of the box is as cut, in pale blue, cream, pale green or pink, with gold and contrasting color trimmings.

Price, filled with any Gold Label perfume and boxed, except No. 04892/9.

	Capacity.	Price.
No. 04288/1	½ oz.	$0.40
No. 04662	¾ oz.	0.50
No. 04641	5 oz.	2.50
No. 04855	¾ oz.	1.00
No. 04892/6	1⅛ oz.	0.75
No. 04892/5	¾ oz.	0.60
No. 04892/9	2½ oz.	1.25
No. 04915/1	½ oz.	$0.40
No. 04915/2	1 oz.	0.50
No. 04690	1½ oz.	1.00
No. 04286	1 oz.	0.50
No. 04593/1	½ oz.	0.40
No. 6875/9½	1 oz.	0.75
No. 6875/21	7½ oz.	4.00
No. 0190	1 oz.	0.50

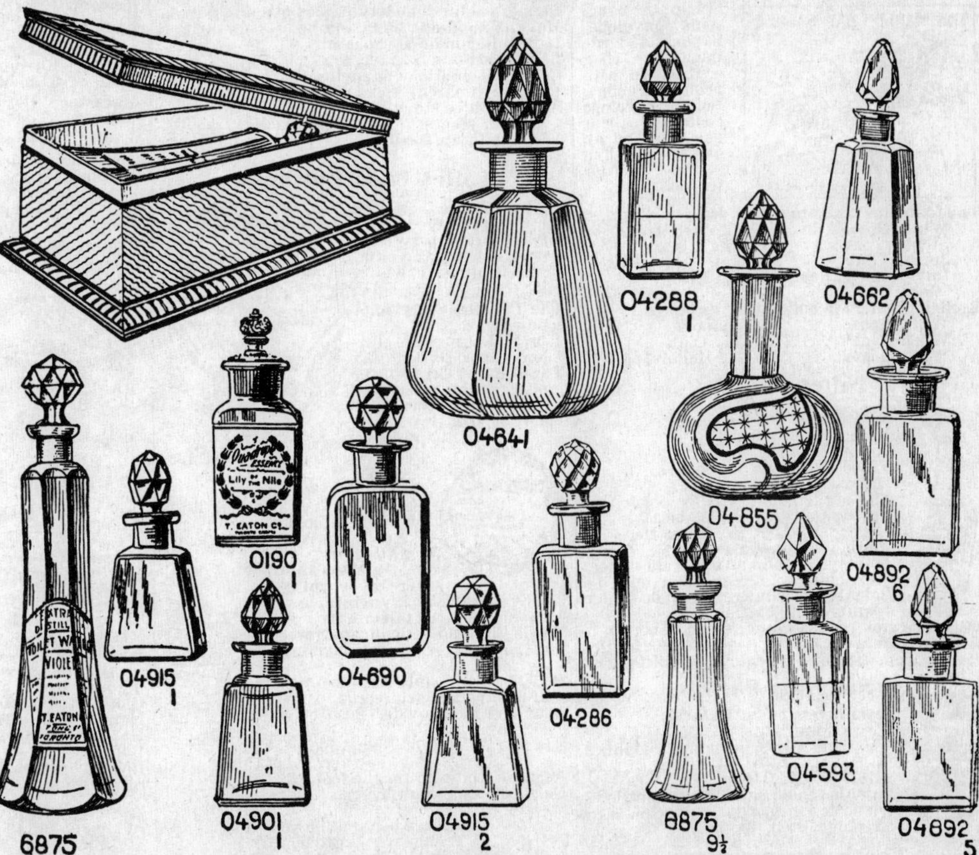

Gold Label Perfume.

Is the very finest quality of perfume, delicate in odor, true to the natural flower and lasting a very long time on whatever it is put. Put up in bottles holding one ounce, with handsome gilt sprinkler, for 50c.

The following is a list of the popular odors:

Parma Violet.
Wood Violet.
Lily of the Valley.
Parisian Bouquet.
White Heliotrope.
Hawthorn Blossom.
Peau d'Espagne.
Heliotrope.
Wallflower.
Opoponax.
Violet.
Magnolia.
Crab Apple.
White Rose.
Musk.
Mignonette.
White Lilac.
Jockey Club.
Stephanotis.
Honeysuckle.
Ylang Ylang.
Mimosa.
Lign Aloe.
Patchouli.
Tea Rose.
Moss Rose.
Sweet Briar.
Ess. Bouquet.
Fougere Royal.
Syringa.
Damask Rose.

Special Odors, in Bulk.

Carnation—Is an idealistic odor of a bouquet of the choicest carnations, price 40c oz.

Canada Bouquet—Is a very fragrant and lasting, at the same time delicate odor of a bouquet of the spring flowers of Canada, price 40c oz.

Reviera Violet—The most fragrant and lasting, while at the same time delicate, odor of sweet violets that is manufactured, 60c oz.

Bulgarian Red Rose—This is a lasting and rich rose perfume, price 60c oz.

Canadian Sweet Violets—Has the true odor of the sweet violets of the woods, price 60c oz.

Bobs' African Bouquet—A very concentrated bouquet odor, price 40c oz.

Pretoria Bouquet—Delicately sweet and lasting, price 40c oz.

Johannesburg Golden Bouquet—Fragrant and very lasting, price 40c oz.

Bouquet of Roses is a rich perfume of roses and does not lose its rose bouquet for a very long time, price 40c oz.

Lily of the Nile—An exquisite lily odor, very fragrant and lasting, 40c oz.

All these odors at 40c are put up as Gold Label style, or in any of the cut glass bottles; those marked 60c an ounce are 20c an ounce higher in price than the prices quoted.

Whenever possible have goods sent by Express or Freight, as it is safer and cheaper.

Blue Label Perfume.

The following list of odors have become very popular. They are not equalled by any on the market for lasting qualities, fragrance of odor, and price. In bulk, 20c oz (bottle extra), or in our regular bottle holding one ounce, with metal sprinkler top, 25c, any of the following odors:

White Rose. Violet.
Lily of the Valley. Ylang Ylang.
New Mown Hay. Wood Violet.
Patchouli. White Lilac.
Crab Apple. Heliotrope.
Jockey Club. Stephanotis.

Little Folks Perfume.

A box of popular perfumes contains fou bottles, and can be had in one odor or four assorted. The odors are—

Jockey Club. White Rose.
White Lilac. Heliotrope.
Wood Violet. Lily of the Valley.

Price, 25c a box.

Perfume Atomizers.

We have many styles of atomizers. When ordering atomizer, give the color desired, and the price. The prices are 20c, 25c, 35c, 50c, 75c, $1.00, 1.25, 3.00, 3.25, 3.50, 4.00, 5.00, 7.50.

Maple Leaf Sachet Powder.

Put up in handsome envelopes having a large Canadian flag embossed and printed in colors, each envelope contains about one-third of an ounce of fine sachet powder for 10c.

The following odors to choose from:

White Rose. White Heliotrope.
Stephanotis. White Lilac.
Jockey Club. Violet.
Lily of the Valley. Japan Iris.
Wood Violet.

Sachet powders in bulk, at 25c an ounce:

White Rose. Stephanotis.
Wood Violet. Jockey Club.
White Lilac. White Heliotrope.

Toilet Waters.

White lilac, 40c, 75c bottle.
Rose, 40c, 75c bottle.
Jockey club, 40c, 75c bottle.
Wood violet, 40c, 75c bottle.
Heliotrope, 40c, 75c bottle.
Lily of the valley, 40c, 75c bottle.
Eau-de-Cologne, 40c, 75c bottle.
Lavender water, 25c, 50c bottle.
Florida water, 35c bottle.
Murray & Lanman's Florida water, 40c bottle.
Colgate's Cashmere bouquet toilet water, $1.00 bottle.
Colgate's violet toilet water, 50c, $1.00 bottle.
Rimmel's aromatic toilet vinegar, 20c, 40c bottle.
Lewis' aromatic toilet vinegar, 4-oz bottle, 25c.

Smelling Salts.

Lewis' lavender salts, 25c, 35c.
Lewis' floral salts, 25c, 35c.
Fancy cut glass bottles of smelling salts, 25c, 35c, 50c, 75c, $1.00, 1.25, 1.50, 1.75, 2.00, 2.50, 3.00.
Crown lavender salts, 35c, 60c bottle.
Aromatic vinegar (for headache, is refreshing, etc.), 25c up.

Tooth Preparations.

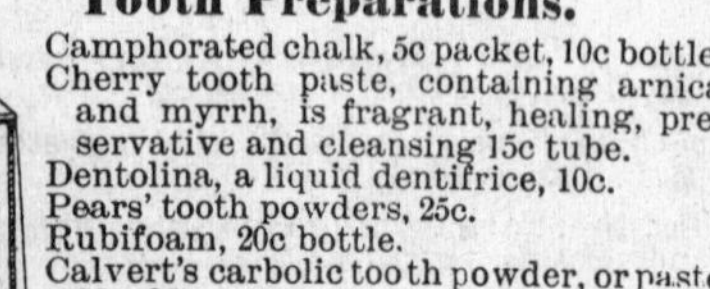

Camphorated chalk, 5c packet, 10c bottle.
Cherry tooth paste, containing arnica and myrrh, is fragrant, healing, preservative and cleansing 15c tube.
Dentolina, a liquid dentifrice, 10c.
Pears' tooth powders, 25c.
Rubifoam, 20c bottle.
Calvert's carbolic tooth powder, or paste 15c, 25c.
Colgate's antiseptic powder, 20c
Teaberry tooth powder, 20c.
Sheffield's dentifrice, 20c.
Antiseptic tooth powder, 10c.
Cracroft's areca nut tooth paste, 20c.
Sozodont, 25c, 65c.
Gosnel's cherry tooth paste, 40c.
Strong's arnica tooth soap, 25c.
Wood's areca nut tooth paste, 18c.

Maw cherry tooth paste, white, 18c; red, 18c. 25c.
Eaton's carbolic tooth paste, 15c.

Skin Preparations.

Lano cream—a true skin food, removing wrinkles by nourishing the skin, 25c tube.
Peruvian ointment, for cuts, scalds, burns, sores, 15c bottle; in tubes, 10c.
Honey and rose, red and white, 10c, 15c.
Cream of almonds and witch hazel for sunburn, wind chaps, etc., 25c bottle.
Lily cream, for the complexion, flesh or white, 25c bot.
Cucumber jelly, 10c tube.
Oriental cream, $1.40 bottle.
Hind's honey and almond cream, 40c bottle.
Cold cream, 15c, 25c pot.
Cold cream, with cucumber and camphor, 20c tube; 15c, 25c pot.
Glycerine and cucumber cream combines the healing properties of the glycerine and the emollient properties of the cucumber in one of the most elegant preparations offered to the public, 25c bottle.
Pepper's sulpholine lotion, 35c bottle.
Hagan's magnolia balm, 60c.
Laird's Bloom of Youth, 40c.
Lanoline cream, 18c, 30c, 40c.
Cocoa butter sticks, 5c each.
Pomade rose (red) sticks, 5c each.
Toilet pumice stone—
Smooth pieces, 3c, 5c, 7½c, 10c each.
Rough lump, 20c lb.

Toilet Face Powders.

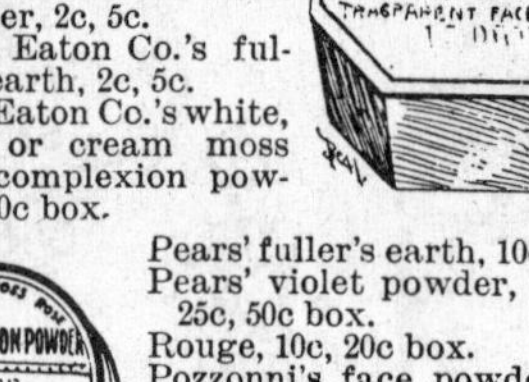

Bloom of Canada, a very highly perfumed, semi-transparent powder, does not dry the skin, in flesh, cream or white, 25c.
The T. Eaton Co.'s violet powder, 2c, 5c.
The T. Eaton Co.'s fuller's earth, 2c, 5c.
The T. Eaton Co.'s white, pink or cream moss rose complexion powder, 10c box.
Pears' fuller's earth, 10c, 20c.
Pears' violet powder, 10c, 15c, 25c, 50c box.
Rouge, 10c, 20c box.
Pozzonni's face powder, flesh or white, 20c, 40c.
Tetlow's gossamer, flesh or white, 20c.
Tetlow's swansdown, flesh, cream or white, 15c.
Tetlow's pearlina, lily white, 5c.
Mennen's borated talcum, 20c.
Lewis' borated talcum, perfumed or carbolated, for chafing, scalding, perspiration, 10c.
Ben Levy's Lablache face powder, flesh, cream or white, 40c.
Saunders' face powder, flesh or white, 25c box.
Saunders' bloom of Ninon, 10c packet.
" white face powder, 10c pkt.
Perfumed powder for the feet, 10c.
Colgate's violet powder, 20c.
" vioris " 20c.
" cashmere bouquet powder, 20c.
" la France rose powder, 20c,
Gelle Frere's almond meal, 10c, 12c, 15c.
" " fleur d'almonde, 20c.

Vaseline and Petroleum Jelly Preparations.

Vaseline, 2-oz bot, blue seal, 5c; 5 oz bot, 10c.
Vaseline pomade, 2-oz bot 10c; 5-oz bot, 20c.
Vaseline oil, perfumed, 20c bottle.
Vaseline, white, perfumed, 2-oz bottle, 15c.
" cold cream, small, 10c; medium, 15c; large, 25c.
" camphor ice, tins, 10c.
" " tubes, 10c.
" pure, ½-lb tins, 20c,
" " 1-lb tins, 35c.
" " 5-lb tins, $1.25.
" " 2-oz bottles, 10c.
" " 5-oz bottles, 20c.
Vaseline, white, collapsible tubes, 10c.
" " 2-oz bottles, 12½c.
" " 5-oz bottles, perfumed, 30c.
" " 1-lb tins, 45c.
" camphorated, 2-oz bottles, 10c.
" carbolated, 2-oz bottles, 10c.
Petroleum jelly, best, screw top bottles, 10c.
" " 2nd quality, 2-oz bottle, 5c.
" " 1-lb tins, 20c.
" " perfumed highly, 10c bottle.
" " carbolated, 10c bottle.
" " camphorated, 10c bottle.

Hair Preparations.

Cantharadine hair tonic is a splendid preparation for preventing the hair from falling; it also promotes the growth, 25c, 50c bottle.
Rum and quinine hair grower. This is an excellent preparation; it promotes the growth of the hair and prevents it from falling. Its continued use will renew the vitality of the hair, and when the roots are not destroyed it will bring on a new growth on apparent baldness, 25c, 50c bottle.
Brilliantine, for softening and making hair glossy, 10c, 20c bottle.
Petroleum pomade for a hair dressing, 10c bottle.
Luby's hair promoter, 40c.
Bay rum, 10c, 15c, 25c, 50c bottle.
Canadian hair dye, 35c.
Barry's tricopherous, 60c.
Edward's harlene, 35c, 70c, $1.25 bottle.
Macassar oil (Rowland's), 85c, $1.75, $3.00.
Alexander's shadeine—
Sample bottles, 12½c; regular, 85c.
Black. Blond.
Brown. Dark brown.
Auburn. Golden.
Light brown.
Pinaud's eau de quinine, 40c, 70c, $1.35
Ko Ko for the hair, 35c, 85c.

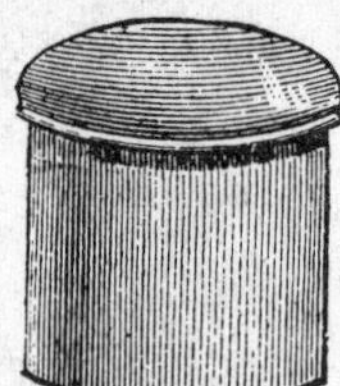

Fancy decorated glass puff boxes, 50c, 75c, $1.00, 1.25; fancy metal, assorted styles and colors, pinks, red and blues predominate, 10c, 15c, 25c, 30c, 35c, 50c, 75c, $1.00, 1.25.

Cloth Brushes.

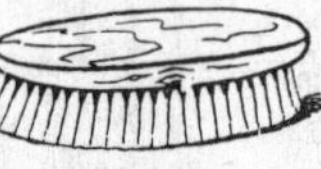
CLOTH.

CLOTH.

Our styles and prices in cloth brushes are many. We have the ordinary cloth brushes, without handles, in all styles and at the following prices:

Cloth brushes, 30c, 40c, 50c, 60c, 75c, $1.00, 1.25.
Handled cloth, 30c, 60c, 75c, $1.00, 1.75, 2.00.
Hat brushes, 15c, 20c, 35c, 50c, 75c.
Bath brushes, 35c, 40c, 50c, 60c, 75c, $1.25.
Bonnet brushes, 20c, 50c, 75c.
Silver brushes, 15c, 20c, 25c, 40c.

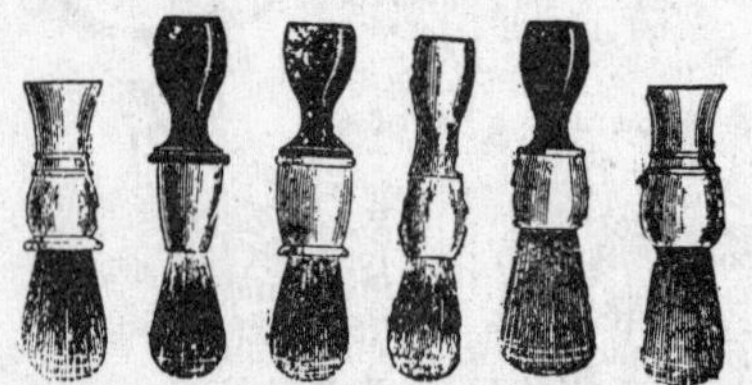

Shaving brushes, bristle, 10c, 15c, 20c, 25c.
Shaving brushes, badger hair, bone handle, 35c, 50c, 60c, 75c, $1.00.
We do not exchange bath or shaving brushes.

Baby Brushes.

Bone handle, 10c, 15c, 20c, 25c, 30c, 35c.
" " decorated, 20c, 25c, 30c, 35c, 40c.
Baby brushes not exchanged.

Hair Brushes.

We do not exchange any toilet brushes, but should you find any imperfection in a brush, we will gladly replace it with a perfect one.

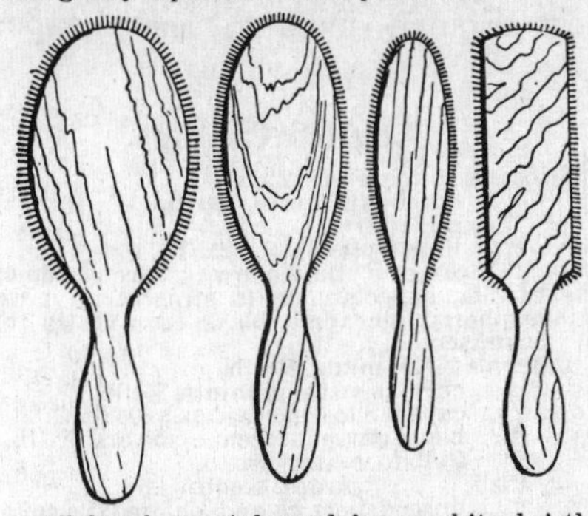

All brushes catalogued have white bristle. The number of rows across brush are indicated by a stroke and the number after it. The following table gives description of brush.

BO means broad oval shape. O, oval.
OO " long oval. Sq, square,
S " short bristle. M, medium long,
VL " very long bristle L, long.
VX " very soft " X, soft stiff.
XX " good stiff " XXX, very stiff.
XXXX " hard penetrating bristle.

Sample of reading of above (there is not a brush of this No.)—

No. 190/9. Sq., S, XXXX, screw back, $2.00.
Reads: No. 190. Brush, 9-row, square shape, short, very hard penetrating bristle, with screw back, $2.00.
No. 978/12. O, S, X, 25c.
No. 1501/7. Sq., S, X, solid, dark or light wood back, 35c.
No. 4300/9. BO, M, X, solid back, light or dark wood, 40c.
No. 14158/9. BO, M, X, solid back, 40c.
No. 4120/9. O, M, XX, olive or cherry back, 50c.
No. 4072/9. OO, M, XX, olive back, solid, 50c.
No. 4180/8. Sq., M, XX, light or dark wood, solid back, 50c.
No. 4381/11. Sq., M, XX, dark wood, solid back, 50c.
No. 448/13. O, M, VX, dark wood back, 2-piece, 50c.
No. 953/8. Sq., M, XXX, light and dark, solid back, 50c.
No. 4920/9. OO, L, VX, light and dark, solid back, 75c.
No. 4189/9. BO, S, XXX, light and dark, solid back, 75c.
No. 5082/9. OO, S, XXX, foxwood, solid back, 75c.
No. 4991/11. BO, M, XX, dark, solid back, 75c.
No. 5469/9. BO, M, XXX, light and dark, solid back, 75c.
No. 509/13. BO, S, XXXX, screwed satinwood back, 75c.
No. T1W/9. BO, Sq., M, XXX, foxwood, solid back, 75c.
No. T10W/9. BO, M, XXX, foxwood, solid back, 75c.
No. T5W/9. OO, M, XXX, foxwood, solid back, 75c.
No. 510/15. O, S, XXXX, screw satinwood back, 85c.
No. 4076/13. BO, M, XXX, fox and olive, solid back, $1.00.
No. 12096/11. O, M, X, fox and olive, solid back, $1.00.
No. 4993/13. BO, M, XXX, fox and olive, solid back, $1.00.
No. 12028/13. L, O, M, X, fox and olive, solid back, $1.00.
No. 12051/11. BO, M, XX, olive wood, solid back, $1.00.
No. 4191/11. BO, M, XXX, cherry wood, solid back, $1.00.
No. 4953/13. BO, M, XX, dark wood, solid back, $1.25.
No. 4193/13. O, M, XXX, satin wood, solid back, $1.25.
No. 4924/13. BO, L, X, light and dark wood, solid back, $1.25.
No. 12084/11. BO, M, X. foxwood, solid back, $1.25.
No. 12409/9. Sq., M, XX, satinwood, solid back, $1.25.
No. 5084/11. OO, S, XXXX, foxwood, solid back, $1.25.
No. T50/9. O, M, XXX, satinwood, solid back, $1.25.
No. T20/11. O, M, XXX, satinwood, solid back, $1.25.
No. T15/11. OO, L, XX, satinwood, solid back, $1.25.
No. 5206/11. Sq., M, XXX, satinwood, solid back, $1.25.
No. 12143/13. O, M, XX, foxwood, solid back, $1.25.
No. 12711/11. O, M, XXX, satin wood, solid back, $1.25.
No. 522/21. O, S, XXX, satinwood, screw back, $1.50.
No. T45/13. O, M, XXX, satinwood, solid back, $1.50.
No. 5470/12. O, M, XX, foxwood, solid back, $1.75.
No. T35/11. O, M, X, satinwood, solid back, $1.75.
No. T40/15. O, L, XX, satinwood, solid back, $2.00.
No. T30/13. O, L, XX, satinwood, solid back, $2.00.
No. 5073/13. Sq., L, XX, olive and foxwood, solid back, $2.00.
No. 5478/13. O, L, XX, dark solid back, $2.50.
No. 3598/15. O, M, XXX, solid satinwood back, $3.00.
No. 12471/11. O, VL, XX, solid satinwood back, $3.00.

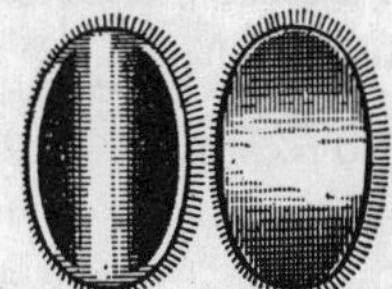

Military brushes, per pair, $1.25, 1.50, 1.70, 2.00, 2.50, 3.00, 3.50.

Cases, 65c and 75c extra.

Ebony Back Brushes.

No. 5617/9. BO, S, XXX, solid ebony, 75c.
No. ET50/9. O, M, XXX, solid ebony, $1.50.
No. ET15/9. OO, L, XX, solid ebony, $1.50.
No. ET45/13. OO, M, XXX, solid ebony, $1.75.
No. E366/15. BO, L, XXX, solid ebony, $3.00.
No. E367/16. BO, L, XXX, solid ebony, $3.00.

Tooth Brushes.

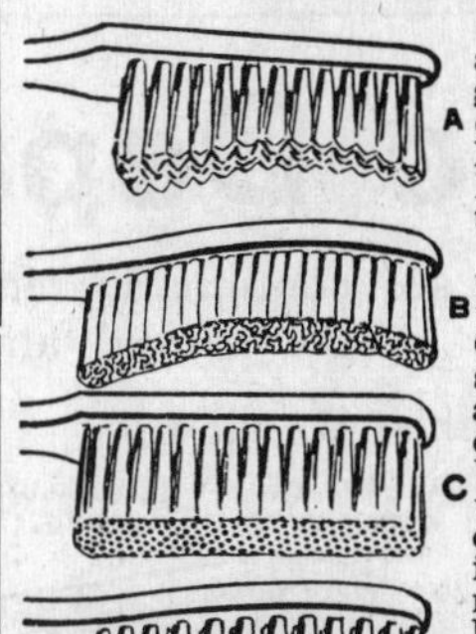

Our tooth brushes are exceptionally good value, and are obtained from the leading English and French manufacturers.

In ordering our 25c tooth brushes, say which shape, A, B, C, or D, and whether serrated or plain, and whether a lady's or gentleman's size. When over 10c, say whether hard, medium or soft bristle is required. We do not exchange tooth brushes, except for faulty manufacture. The prices are as follows: 5c, 10c, 15c, 20c, 25c, 30c, 35c, 40c.

Tooth brushes not exchanged.

Nail Brushes.

Nail brushes, bone back, 10c, 15c, 20c, 25c, 30c, 35c, 40c, 50c, $1.00.

Wood back nail brushes, 10c, 15c, 25c, 30c, 35c, 40c, 50c.

Nail scrubs, fibre, wood back, 2 for 5c, 5c and 3 for 5c.

Whisks.

Enamelled handle, 1-string, 8c; 2-string, 12½c; 3-string, 15c.
Nickel handle, 15c; with ring, 20c.
Barbers' whisk, 15c.
Travellers' or pocket whisk, 10c and 15c.
Little gem whisk, 35c.
Fancy plush shoulder, bone handle, small whisk, 25c; medium, 30c; large, 35c.

Combs.

(Combs not exchanged.)

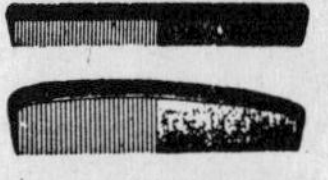

Pocket combs, 5c, 10c, 15c, 20c.
Rubber dressing combs, 5c, 10c, 12½c, 15c, 20c, 25c, 30c, 35c, 40c, 50c, 60c.
Horn dressing combs, 5c, 10c, 15c, 20c, 25c, 35c, 50c, 65c.
Celluloid dressing combs, 10c, 15c, 25c, 35c, 50c, 60c, 75c.

Fine combs, "rubber," 5c, 10c, 15c, 20c, 25c.
Fine ivory combs, 10c, 15c, 20c, 25c, 35c, 50c, 75c.

Fine combs, "horn," 5c, 10c, 15c.
Circular combs, 5c, 10c, 12½c, 15c, 20c.

Soap Boxes.

Celluloid soap boxes, 15c, 25c, 30c and 40c.

Metal soap boxes, 20c, 25c, 30c, 35c.

Mirrors.

Triple mirrors, 25c, 50c, 75c, $1.00, 1.25, 1.50, 1.75, 2.00, 2.50, 3.00, 3.50, 4.00, 5.00.

Shaving mirrors, one side magnifying, the other plain, 50c, 75c, $1.00, 1.50, 2.00, 2.50, 3.00, 3.50.
Folding shaving mirrors, in a variety of styles and sizes, from $1.25, 1.50, 1.75, 2.00.
Folding wire handle, square or oval stand mirrors, all sizes, bevelled edge, wood back, plate mirror, 10c, 15c, 20c, 25c, 30c, 35c, 40c, 50c, 60c, 75c, $1.00, 1.15, 1.25, 1.50.

Square or oval hand mirrors, all sizes, both bevelled edged, plate, crystal white glass, ¾ white bevelled plate, plain or shock glass, at following prices:

Crystal white plate glass, bevelled edge, oval or square, mahogany wood back, mirror, according to size, 20c, 25c, 30c, 35c, 50c, 65c, 75c, $1.00, 1.25, 1.50.
Crystal white, oval or square, olive wood back hand glass, bevelled edge, according to size, 25c, 30c, 35c, 50c, 75c, $1.00.
Oval or square wood handle hand glass, plain glass, 7½c, 10c, 12½c, 15c, 20c, according to size
Metal frame stand mirrors, 5c, 10c, 15c, 20c, 25c, 30c, 35c.
Small magnifying mirror, metal rim, round, 5c.
Black back, imitation ebony, oval and square shape hand mirrors bevelled edge, 25c, 40c, 50c, 60c.
Stand mirrors, wire handle, oval or square, 40c, 50c, 60c, 75c.
Imitation ebony, round hand mirrors, 75c, $1.00, $1.25; also in green and antique oak, at same prices.

Dealing with us gives satisfactory results.

Candies, Etc.

WE carry a very extensive assortment of Candies, from the very finest French down to the cheapest pure sugar goods we can procure.

Chocolate almonds, 40c and 60c lb.
" cinnamon crisps, 30c lb.
Salted almonds, 75c lb.
Crystallized ginger, 30c lb.
Spiced gum drops, extra quality, 40c lb.
Chocolates, vanilla flavor, 30c lb.
" raspberry flavor, 30c lb.
" nougat, 30c lb.
" walnut cream, 30c lb.
" nectar " 30c lb.
" orange " 30c lb.
" lemon " 30c lb.
" black currant cream, 30c lb.
" maple, 30c lb.
" cocoanut, 30c lb.
" strawberry, 30c lb.
" pineapple, 30c lb.
" ginger, 30c lb.
" coffee, 30c lb.
" dipped ginger, 40c lb,
" " pineapple, 40c lb.
" fine flavor, well assorted, 25c lb.
" caramels, best, 25c lb.
" " good, 15c lb.
" Globe, vanilla flavor, 20c lb.
Regal chocolate drops, 20c lb.
Chocolate dates, 20c lb.
Cream almonds, 20c and 30c lb.
Cream burnt almonds, 25c lb.
Sugared almonds, 25c lb.
Lady caramels, 20c lb.
Bon bons, assorted flavors, 20c lb.
Bon bons, finest assorted flavors, 40c lb.
Marshmallow drops, best, 20c lb.
Rock candy, white and pink, 20c lb.
Buttercups, nut centres, best, 20c lb.
" " " good, 15c lb.

Tom Thumb mixture, well flavored, 20c lb.
Cupid's whispers, conversation lozenges, 20c lb.
Gem gum drops, 20c lb.
Crystallized Santa Clara figs, 20c lb.
Peppermint lozenges, 15c lb.
" shrimps, 15c lb.
Nut cream, 15c lb.
Maple walnut bon bons, 12½c lb.
Conversation lozenges, 15c lb.
Chocolate drops, assorted flavors, 15c lb.
Pearls (highly perfumed lozenges), white rose, red rose, musk, wintergreen, chocolate, violet, XXX mint, either assorted or straight, 30c lb.
Cheapest mixed candy, 7c and 8c lb.
Cream mixture, a well assorted mixture, suitable for Xmas trees, etc., this can be done up in ½ and 1 lb. folding boxes, 10c lb.
Silvered nuts, etc., for decorating cakes, etc., 10c oz.; $1.50 lb.
Carraway comfits, smooth, 30c lb.
Carraway comfits, assorted colors, rough, 30c lb.
Silver cachous, 10c oz.; $1.50 lb.
Sugar-coated licorice pellets, 20c lb.

Taffies.

Maple cream, 15c and 20c lb.
" butterscotch, 15c and 20c lb.
Cocoanut cream, pink and white, 15c lb.
Walnut bar, 20c lb.
" rock, 15c lb.
Almond rock, 20c lb.
Cocoanut rock, 15c lb.
Everton rock, 15c lb.
Peanut crisp, 15c lb.
Butter taffy drops, 20c lb.
Peanut squares, 15c lb.
Black currant cream (new), 20c lb.

English Candies.

Gibson's cough drops, 25c lb.
" horehound drops, 25c lb.
" mixed fruits, 25c lb.
" lime fruit tablets, 25c lb.
" Any of the following drops: lemon, vanilla, chocolate, malt, strawberry, plum, raspberry, pineapple, black currant, tip top, butterscotch, 25c lb.
Gibson's XXX mints, 50c lb.
" curiously strong mints, 80c lb.
" cayenne lozenges, 5c oz.; 80c lb.
" black currant lozenges, 5c oz.; 80c lb.
" Coltsfoot stick, 40c lb.
" " drops, 40c lb.
" linseed, licorice and chlorodyne cough lozengers, 5c oz.; 50c lb.
Pascall's lemon barley sugar stick, in small screw top bottles, 20c; large, 35c.
Pascall's raspberry barley sugar stick, bottle, 20c.
Pascall's mixed fruit barley sugar stick, 20c lb.
Pascall's golden maltex, 15c, 25c, 35c and 50c bottle.
Callard & Bowser's butterscotch, 10c and 20c packet.
Callard & Bowser's assorted taffy, 10c and 20c packet.
1-lb box, fine bon-bons and chocolates, 30c.
½-lb " " " " 15c.
1-lb " finest " " 40c.
½-lb " " " " 20c.
1-lb " fine chocolates, 30c.
1-lb " finest " 40c.
½-lb " fine " 15c.
½-lb " finest " 20c.

Photographic Department.

Has Fresh Papers, Plates and Chemicals. We are continually renewing the above, and can strongly recommend them to the careful amateur.

Film Cameras.

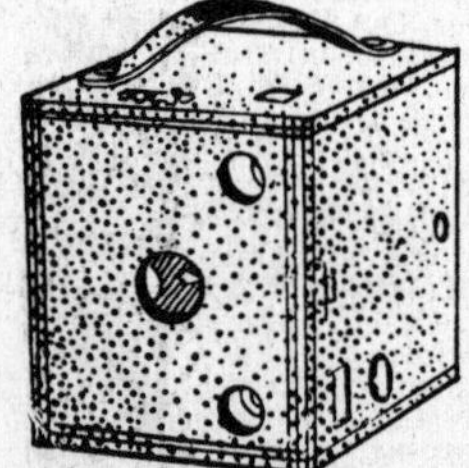

4 x 5 Weno Hawk-Eye.

Dimensions, 5 x 5⅞ x 6½ inches. Size of photo, 4 x 5 inches. Weight, 28 ozs. Capacity, 12 exposures.
With all improvements, loaded, $8.00.
Special sunlight film, 12 exposures, 4 x 5, 90c.
Special sunlight film, 6 exposures, 4 x 5, 45c.

The Weno Hawk-Eye.

Dimensions, 4½ x 4½ x 5½ inches. Size of photo, 3½ x 3½ inches. Weight, 20 ozs. Capacity, 12 exposures.
Weno Hawk-Eye, loaded, $5.00.
Special sunlight film, 6 exposures, 3½ x 3½, 30c.
Special sunlight film, 12 exposures, 3½ x 3½, 60c.

The Tourist Hawk-Eye.

Dimensions, 1½ x 4½ x 6½ inches. Weight, 15 ozs. Size of photo, 3½ x 3½ inches. Capacity, 12 exposures.

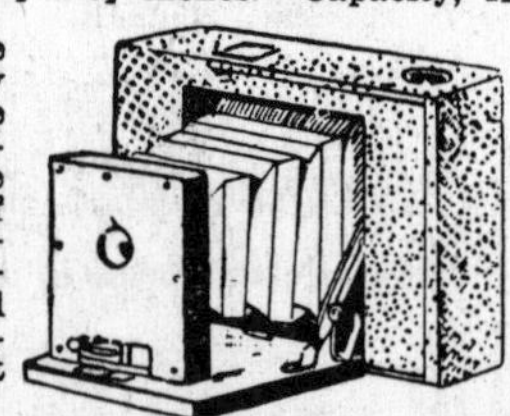

This Hawk-Eye is especially adapted for the cyclist and traveller, who require an instrument of the smallest dimensions possible, so constructed that it can be carried in the pocket or satchel.

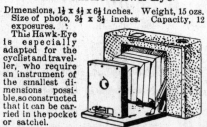

Tourist Hawk-Eye, loaded, $9.00.
Special sunlight film, 6 exposures, 3½ x 3½, 30c.
Special sunlight film, 12 exposures, 3½ x 3½, 60c.
Black sole leather carrying case, $1.25.

4 x 5 Tourist Hawk-Eye.

Dimensions, 2 x 5½ x 8⅞ inches. Weight, 25 ozs. Size of photo, 4 x 5 inches. Capacity, 12 exposures, loaded, $15.00.

4 x 5 Hawk-Eye, Jun.

4 x 5 Hawk-Eye, jun., loaded, $15.00.
Sunlight film, 6 exposures, 4 x 5, 45c.
Sunlight film, 12 exposures, 4 x 5, 90c.

3½ x 3½ Hawk-Eye, Jun.

3½ x 3½ Hawk-Eye, jun., loaded, $8.00.
Sunlight film, 6 exposures, 3½ x 3½, 30c.
Sunlight film, 12 exposures, 3½ x 3½, 60c.
Black sole leather carrying case, $1.25.

Special Tourist Hawk-Eye.

Special Tourist Hawk-eye, loaded, $25.00.
Special sunlight film, 6 exposures, 4 x 5, 45c.
Special sunlight film, 12 exposures, 4 x 5, 90c.
Black sole leather carrying case, $2.00.

Plate Cameras.

Cyclone Senior.

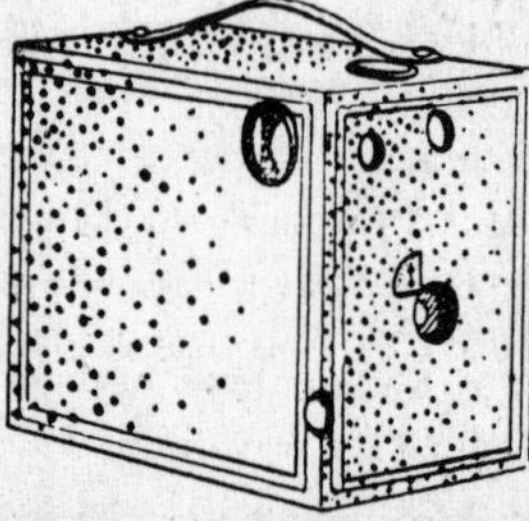

The popularity of this camera is sufficient evidence of its merits. It takes pictures full 4 x 5 inches; has our automatic shutter for time and snapshot exposures, one button answering for both purposes. It is fitted with two large

Our Goods are all of standard quality.

square view finders and two tripod sockets. It accommodates three double plate-holders, with a capacity of six dry plates.
Cyclone Senior, complete with one double plate-holder, $5.00.
Extra plate-holders, $1.00 each.

Poco Cameras.

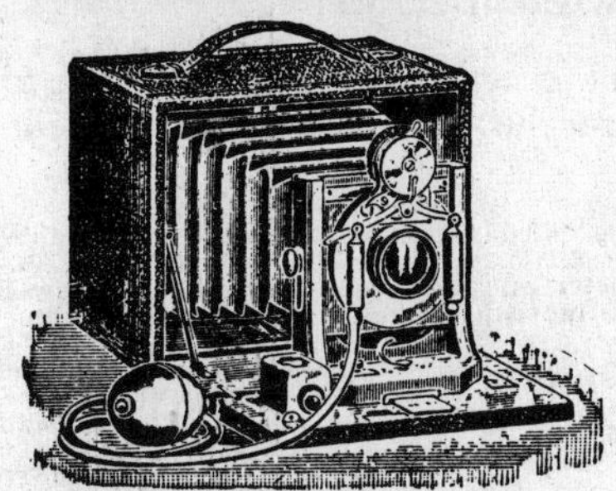

Poco folding camera, Series A. The lens is the high-grade Rochester symmetrical, adapted for all general purposes. The prices:

Complete with Unicum shutter, lens and one dry plate-holder—
Sizes 4 x 5, 5 x 7, 6½ x 8½,
$25.00. 32.00. 40.00.

Complete, B. & L. diaphragm shutter, lens and one dry plate-holder—
Sizes 4 x 5, 5 x 7, 6½ x 8½,
$33.00. 40.00. 50.00.

Complete, with Unicum shutter, Rochester anastigmat lens and one dry plate-holder—
Sizes 4 x 5, 5 x 7. 6½ x 8½,
$50.00. 60.00. 90.00.

Camera, no lens or shutter—
Sizes 4 x 5, 5 x 7, 6½ x 8½,
$15.00. 20.00. 26.00.

Double dry plate-holders—
Sizes 4 x 5, 5 x 7, 6½ x 8½,
$0.75. 1.00. 1.25.

Poco folding camera, Series B. Complete with shutter, Rochester symmetrical lens, rack pinion focusing movement, and one dry plate-holder, 4 x 5, $22.00; 5 x 7, $27.00.
Poco folding camera, series C. Complete with shutter, rapid rectilinear lens, and one dry plate-holder, 4 x 5, $15.00; 5 x 7, $20.00.
Poco D camera, 4 x 5, $15.00; 5 x 7, $16.00.
Poco folding camera, series E, 4 x 5, $10.00; 5 x 7, $14.00.

Cycle Pocos.

Cycle Poco No. 1, complete with Unicum shutters and one dry plate-holder:—
Size 4 x 5 5 x 7
$25.00. $32.00.

Cycle Poco No. 2 is a 4 x 5 camera, having a double symmetrical lens with a Unicum shutter with iris diaphragm. Camera complete with shutter lens, one double dry plate-holder and carrying case, $20.00, and 5 x 7, $25.00.
Cycle Poco No. 3 is a very popular camera, morocco-covered mahogany case, has a Unicum shutter and rapid rectilinear lens. Camera complete with one double plate-holder and carrying case, size 4 x 5, $14.00; 5 x 7, $18.00.
Cycle Poco camera No. 4 has single achromatic lens and all latest adjustments; case is mahogany-covered, with morocco leather. The camera complete with shutter, lens, one double plate-holder and sole-leather carrying case, size 4 x 5, $12.00; size 5 x 7, $16.00.

Cycle Specials.

Cycle special, with Bausch and Lomb shutter and double rectilinear lens and iris diaphragm, together with one double plate-holder in leather carrying case, 4 x 5, $11.50; 5 x 7, $16.00.
4 x 5 double plate-holders, $1.00 each.
5 x 7 double plate-holders, $1.25 each.
Toronto, No. 5, cycle camera, 4 x 5, with Unicum shutter, iris diaphragm, double lens, rack and pinion, and one double plate-holder, $17.50.
Toronto, No. 2, 4 x 5 camera, single achromatic lens, iris diaphragm, Woolensack shutter and one double plate-holder, $10.00.

Chemicals.

Pyrogallic acid, 30c oz.
Hydrochinone, 40c oz.
Eikonogen, 40c oz.
Metol, 75c oz.
Amidol, 65c oz.
Platinum chloride, 15 gr. tubes, 60c each.
Gold chloride, pure, 15 gr. tubes, 60c each.
" " and sodium, 15 gr. tubes, 35c ea.
Sulphite of soda, 10c lb; in 1 lb bottle, 15c.
Hyposulphite of soda, 5c lb; in 1 lb bottle, 10c.
Carbonate of soda, pure, 25c lb.
Sal soda, 3 lbs for 5c.
Bromide of potassium, 5c oz.
Carbonate of potash, 20c lb.
Borax, powdered, 7c lb.
Red prussiate of iron, 10c oz.
Acetate of soda, 10c oz.
Ammonia persulphate, 15c oz.
Soda metabisulphate, 7c oz, 75c lb.
Eikonogen cartridges, box of 10, $1.40 box, 15c each.
Amidol cartridges, $1.40 box, 15c each.
Metol cartridges, $1.40 box, 15c each.
Toning and fixing cartridges, No. 1, 15c each, $1.40 box.
Toning and fixing cartridges, No. 2, 30c each, $2.75 box.

Printing Frames.

Wood—
3¼ x 4¼, or smaller, 15c; 4 x 5, cabinet, 20c; 5 x 7, 25c each.
Metal—
3¼ x 3¼, or 3¼ x 4¼, 25c; 4 x 5, 30c; 5 x 7, 35c each.
Higgins' photo mounting paste, 15c, 25c, 50c bottle.

Tripods.

2-length folding, $1.25.
3-length folding, $2.00.
4-length folding, $2.50.

Films in Rolls of 12 Exposures.

Pocket kodak size, 25c roll.
Folding pocket kodak, 40c roll
Bulls' Eye or Bullet, No. 2, 60c; No. 4, 90c.
No. 4 Cartridge kodak films, in rolls of six exposures, half the price of the rolls of 12 exposures.

Glossy Surface, Mat or Dull Finish Papers.

The Price is by the Small Packet, of whether 1 or 2 dozen sheets, and by the gross. (3½ x 3½ and 3¼ x 4¼ are the same price as 3 x 4.)

Size.	Velox, Glossy or Mat.	Albuma, Glossy.	Etching Mat, Thin, Smooth.	Etching Mat, Heavy, Smooth or Rough	25-sheet Tins French Satin, Jr. Blue Paper.	Nepera-Platino Bromide, Dull.	Cyko Developing Paper.	Actino Printing Out Paper.	Argo Developing Paper.	Disco Printing Out Paper.
	Doz. Grs.	Pkt. Grs.	Doz. Grs.	Doz. Grs.		Doz. Grs.	Doz. Grs.	Doz. Grs.	Doz. Grs.	Pkt. Grs.
3 x 4	20c $2.00	20c $1.00	25c	30c	20c	20c	15c $1.20	15c $1.50	15c $1.00	20c $1.10
Cabinet	30c 2.00	30c 1.50	35c	.. ....	25c	25c	15c 1.50	25c 1.70	20c 1.25	25c 1.20
4 x 5	25c 2.00	25c 1.50	35c	40c	40c	25c	15c 1.55	20c 1.70	15c 1.50	25c 1.20
5 x 7	40c 3.50	50c 3.20	45c	60c	....	40c	30c 3.10	35c 3.30	30c 3.10	30c 2.20
6½ x 8½	.. ..	.. ..	75c	90c	....	....	50c 6.00	... .	... .	... .

PLATES.

The price is for boxes of 1 dozen plates.

Size of Plates.	New York Record.	New York Crescent.	Lumière Extra Rapid.	Hammer	Standard.	Standard Non-Halation Double-Coated.	Standard Orthochromatic.
2½ x 2½	$0.22	$0.22	....	$0.30	....	....	....
3¼ x 3¼	0.30	0.30	....	....	....	....	....
3½ x 3½	0.30	0.30	....	0.30	....	....	....
3¼ x 4¼	0.35	0.35	$0.45	0.35	....	....	....
4 x 5	0.55	0.55	0.70	0.65	$0.50	$0.60	$0.60
4¾ x 6½ Cabinet	0.75	0.75	....	0.85	0.60	....	....
5 x 7	0.85	0.85	1.00	1.10	0.80	0.90	0.90
5 x 8	1.00	....	....	....	....	....	....
6½ x 8½	1.50	....	....	1.65	1.35	....	....
8 x 10	2.25	....	....	2.40	2.00	...	....

4 x 5 Developing outfit, $1.50.

Orders for Cameras and Photo Supplies are accurately filled.

Every Camera is carefully examined and tested before leaving the Department.

When ordering Films always give size of Film and name of your Kodak.

Always give size of picture you intend to make when ordering mounts.

We send a book of full instructions with each Camera.

All Cameras, Kodaks and Photo Supplies are carefully packed for shipment.

WRITE US FOR ANY GOODS YOU NEED AND DO NOT SEE CATALOGUED.

Gentlemen's and Ladies' Watches.

We guarantee every Watch to give satisfaction. ☞ When ordering Watches be sure to mention number and page. Watches are subject to advance without notice.

We always carry every grade of the well-known Waltham watches in every style of case. We also highly recommend our special London watches, and direct your attention to the prices and their excellent time-keeping qualities.

Chatelaine Watches for Ladies.

ALL OPEN FACE.

1205. Special, solid nickel case, plain, genuine American movement, same size as cut, $3.85.

Sterling silver case, plain, polished or engine turned.

1206. Silver case and genuine American movement, $5.25.
1206A. Silver case, neatly engraved, reliable Swiss movement with seconds hand, $5.50.
1207. Silver case and London 7-jewelled movement, nickel, $8.25.
1208. Silver case and London 15-jewelled movement, nickel, $9.50.
1209. Silver case and London 15-jewelled nickel adjusted movement, patent regulator and Brequet hairspring, $11.75.
1210. Silver case and 7-jewelled nickel Waltham or Elgin movement, $9.25.
1211. Silver case and Waltham or Elgin 15-jewelled nickel movement, $12.45.

Gun-metal Watches, Plain.

Chatelaine, same size as cut.

1212. Black gun-metal case and genuine American movement, $5.25.
1212A. Gun-metal case, reliable Swiss movement with seconds hand, $5.00.
1213. Gun-metal case and London 7-jewelled movement, $7.75.
1214. Gun-metal case and London 15-jewelled nickel movement, $9.00.
1215. Gun-metal case and 7-jewelled nickel Waltham movement, $8.75.
1216. Gun-metal case and 15-jewelled nickel Waltham movement, $11.90.

Ladies' 14k Gold-Filled Chatelaine Watches.

Same size as cut above and guaranteed to wear 25 years. Plain, engine turned or handsomely engraved.

1217. Same case and 7-jewelled London nickel movement, $11.35.
1218. Same case and 15-jewelled London nickel movement, $12.75.
1219. Same case and 15-jewelled London nickel movement, patent regulator and Brequet hairspring, $14.50.
1220. Same case and Waltham 7-jewelled nickel movement, with white or blue enamel dial, $11.85.
1221. Same case and 15-jewelled nickel Waltham movement, $14.95.

NOTE.—All **London** watches can be supplied in full open face with seconds hand.

Ladies' Silver Hunting Case, O Size.

Above case can be had plain, polished or engine turned.

1222. Above case and reliable lever, Swiss movement, with seconds hand, $7.00.
1223. Same case and 7-jewelled Waltham movement, $10.00.
1224. Same case and 15-jewelled Waltham movement, $13.50.
1225. Same case and Lady Waltham nickel movement, having 16 jewels, $14.75.
1226. Same case and 7-jewelled London nickel movement, $9.25.
1227. Same case and 15-jewelled London nickel movement, $10.25.
1228. Same case and 15-jewelled London nickel movement, patent regulator and Brequet hairspring, $12.50.
1229. Same case and 17-jewelled London adjusted nickel movement, $16.50.

Any of above cases engraved, $1.00 extra.

Ladies' 14k Gold-Filled Hunting Case, O Size.

We always carry the newest and best filled cases that money can procure. Ladies' 14k gold-filled small-sized case guaranteed for twenty-five years; plain, engine turned or engraved.

1230. Above-case, with London 7-jewelled movement, special value, $13.
1231. Same case, with London 15-jewelled nickel movement, $14.25.
1232. Same case, with highest grade London 17-jewelled fine nickel adjusted movement, reliable, $19.50.
1233. Same case, with Waltham 7-jewelled movement, $13.85.
1234. Same case, with 15-jewelled nickel Waltham movement, $15.75.
1235. Same case, with 16-jewelled special nickel Waltham movement, $19.00.

Ladies' 14k Solid Gold Hunting, O Size.

We always pay special attention to designs in solid gold cases. This case can be had perfectly plain, engine turned, or handsomely engraved.

1236. Above described case, London 7-jewelled movement, $22.00.
1237. Same case, with London 15-jewelled nickel movement, gold settings, patent regulator and Brequet hairspring, $25.75.
1238. Same case, with London special fine nickel adjusted 17-jewelled movement, gold settings, patent regulator, $29.25.
1239. Same case, with a 7-jewelled nickel Waltham movement, $22.75.
1240. Same case, with a 15-jewelled nickel Waltham movement, $25.50.
1241. Above case and 16-jewelled nickel "Lady Waltham" movement, $26.75.
1241½. Above case and Waltham Riverside movement, $36.00.

Ladies' Diamond-Set Watches, 16 Size.

Hunting Case.

Ladies' 14k solid gold, plain polished case, set with genuine diamond, splendid value.

1242. Above case and 15-jewelled nickel London movement, $39.00.
1242A. Same case, with 7-jewel Waltham nickel movement, $37.00.
1243. Same case and 17-jewelled nickel London adjusted movement, $44.00.
1244. Same case and 15-jewelled nickel Waltham movement, $39.00.
1245. Same case and 16-jewelled nickel Waltham movement, $43.75.
1246. Same case and Waltham Riverside 17-jewelled nickel movement, $53.00.

18k gold case, $6.00 extra. Other designs of stone-set cases sent for the asking.
NOTE.—All London movements have exposed winding wheels.

Ladies' Monogram Watches.

Raised Gold Monograms.

Ladies' 14k solid gold, plain hunting case, with a raised gold monogram, any initials on front of case.

1247. The above case fitted with London 15-jewelled nickel movement, $30.00.
1248. Above case, with London 15-jewelled fine nickel movement, patent regulator and Breguet hairspring, $32.25.
1249. Above case, with London 17-jewelled adjusted fine nickel movement, a perfect time-piece, $36.00.
1249A. Above case and 7-jewelled nickel Waltham movement, $29.75.
1250. Above case with a 15-jewelled Waltham movement, $28.90.
1251. Above case with the fine "Royal" 16-jewelled Waltham movement, $33.25.
1252. Above case, with "Riverside" 17-jewelled nickel Waltham movement, adjusted, jewels in gold settings, patent Breguet hairspring and finely finished throughout, $43.25.

NOTE.—Hand-engraved monogram, not raised, $1.00 less.
18k gold cases for any of above $6.00 extra.

We cheerfully refund money if goods are not as represented.

Ladies' 14k Solid Gold Hunting Case, 6 Size.

Ladies' 14k solid gold hunting case watches, regular size, good substantial weight and well made. We have them in engine-turned, plain polished and beautifully engraved designs.

1253. Above case, with 7-jewelled London nickel movement, $24.35.
1254. Same case, with a London 15-jewelled nickel movement, $25.50.
1255. Same case, with London 15-jewelled nickel movement, patent Breguet hairspring and regulator, $28.00.
1256. Same case, with London 17-jewelled fine nickel adjusted movement, jewels in settings, patent Breguet hairspring and regulator, and finely finished, for perfect time, $31.50.
1257. Above case, with 7-jewelled Waltham movement, $24.75; lighter weight case, $20.00.
1258. Same case, with 15-jewelled Waltham nickel movement, $24.75.
1259. Same case, with 16-jewelled fine nickel "Lady Waltham" movement, $27.85.
1260. Same case, with beautiful "Royal" Waltham movement, all the latest improvements, also 16 fine ruby jewels in raised gold settings, adjusted for accurate time, $28.85.
1261. Same case, "Riverside" Waltham, having 17 fine ruby jewels in raised gold settings, patent micrometric regulator and patent Breguet hairspring, exposed pallets, specially suited for presentation, $39.00.

Ladies' 10k Solid Gold Hunting Case, 6 Size.

Engraved Case.

Ladies' 10k solid gold hunting case watches, regular size. These are made plain, engine-turned to garter and shield, or to a shield only, and handsomely engraved in new designs, good heavy cases.

1262. Same case and 7-jewelled nickel London movement, $18.50.
1263. Same case and 15-jewelled nickel London movement, $19.85.
1264. Same case and 15-jewelled nickel London movement, patent regulator, $22.35.
1265. Same case and 17-jewelled adjusted nickel London movement, $25.85.
1266. Same case and 7-jewelled Waltham nickel movement, $18.25.
1267. Same case and 15-jewelled Waltham nickel movement, $20.00.
1268. Same case and 16-jewelled Waltham nickel movement, $23.75.
1269. Same case and 17-jewelled Waltham adjusted "Riverside" movement, $33.75.

Ladies' 14k Gold-Filled Watches.

Ladies' hunting case 14k gold-filled watches, regular size, and guaranteed to wear 25 years, can be had perfectly plain polished, engine-turned to a shield, or handsomely engraved.

1270. Above described case, fitted with London nickel 7-jewelled movement, $12.50.
1271. Same case, fitted with London 15-jewelled nickel movement, $13.60.
1272. Same case, fitted with London 15-jewelled nickel movement, patent regulator, $16.00.
1273. Same case, fitted with London 17-jewelled adjusted movement, made of fine nickel, gold settings and beautifully finished, for accurate time, $19.60.
1274. Same case, with Waltham 7-jewelled nickel movement, $11.50.
1275. Same case, with a 15-jewelled nickel Waltham movement, $13.60.
1276. Same case, with 16 fine ruby jewels, in gold settings, patent regulator and Brequet hairspring, adjusted movement, $16.75.
1277. Same case, with Waltham 16-jewelled nickel movement, named "Lady Waltham," $16.85.
1278. Same case, with a beautiful "Royal" Waltham movement, having 16 fine ruby jewels in gold settings, specially finished throughout and adjusted for accurate time, $17.75.
1279. Same case, with 17-jewelled adjusted fine nickel Waltham movement known as the "Riverside," jewels in raised gold settings, and finely finished throughout, $27.85.

Ladies' Silver-Cased Hunting Watches.

Ladies' silver hunting case watches, made in plain polished or engine-turned.

1280. Silver case and genuine American movement, $6.35.
1281. Silver case and 7-jewelled nickel London movement, $8.25.
1282. Silver case and 15-jewelled nickel London movement, $9.50.
1283. Silver case and 15-jewelled nickel London movement, patent regulator and Breguet hairspring, $11.75.
1284. Above case and 17-jewelled nickel adjusted London movement, $15.50.

1285. Above case and 7-jewelled nickel Waltham movement, $8.50.
1186. Above case and 15-jewelled nickel Waltham movement, $10.35.
1287. Above case and 16-jewelled nickel Waltham movement, $12.65.
1288. Above case and Riverside Waltham movement, having 17-jewelled settings, patent regulator and Breguet hairspring, $23.75.

> Any of above watches can be had in open face for 90c less.
> Engraved case for any of above, $1.00 extra.

The New 12-Size Gentlemen's Watches.

All open face.

The new 12-size watch, the up-to-date gentleman's watch, light in weight, thin in model, perfectly made, an ideal gentleman's watch, 14k gold-filled case, guaranteed to wear 25 years, perfectly plain, engine turned or handsomely engraved.

1289. The above case and London 7-jewelled movement, $13.85.
1290. Same case and London 15-jewelled nickel movement, $15.00.
1291. Same case, with London 15-jewelled adjusted nickel movement, patent regulator and Breguet hairspring, $17.50.
1292. Same case, with highest-grade London 17-jewelled nickel adjusted movement, $20.50.
1293. Same case, with Waltham 7-jewelled movement, $13.50.
1294. Same case, with Waltham 15-jewelled nickel movement, $17.00.
1295. Same case, with "Royal" 17-jewelled nickel movement, $21.50.
1296. Same case and Riverside Waltham movement, 17-jewelled, $28.25.

Hunting Case, $2.00 extra.

12-Size, Open-Face Gun-Metal Cases.

Any 12-size watch from No. 1289 to No. 1296 can be supplied in gun-metal cases for $4.75 less than prices quoted.

12 Size, 14k Solid Gold, Open-Face Case.

1297. 14k solid gold, open-face case, plain or engine-turned with 7-jewelled nickel London movement, $30.
1298. Same case and 15-jewelled nickel London movement, $36.50.
1299. Same case and 17-jewelled nickel London movement, $43.00.
1300. Same case and 7-jewelled nickel Waltham movement, $35.75.
1301. Same case and 15-jewelled nickel Waltham movement, $37.75
1302. Same case and 16-jewelled nickel Waltham movement, $39.50.

Hunting 14k Gold Cases, $5.00 extra.

NOTE.—All London movements have exposed winding wheels.

12-Size, Silver Case, Open Face.

1303. This silver case, open face, plain or engine-turned, genuine American movement, $4.25.
1304. Same case and 7-jewelled nickel London movement, $9.25.
1305. Same case and 15-jewelled nickel London movement, $10.25.
1306. Same case and 17-jewelled nickel London movement, $16.50.
1307. Same case and 7-jewelled nickel Waltham movement, $9.50.
1308. Same case and 15-jewelled nickel Waltham movement, $12.75.

Ladies' Chains.

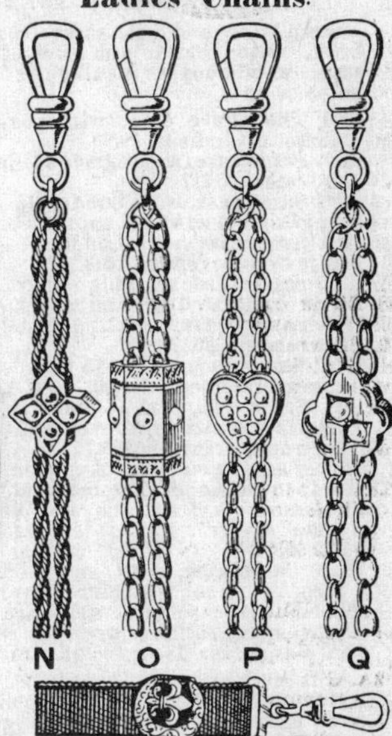

No. N. Rope pattern chain, without slide, solid silver, $3.00; rolled plate, $3.75; 14k soldered chain, 1-10 gold with solid gold jewelled slide, $5.50, 6.00. 10k solid gold, $14.75; heavier, $16.50. 14k, $17.00; heavier, $19.25.

No. O. Medium link pattern, 14k soldered chain, with solid gold jewelled slide, $3.00; heavier links, 1-10 gold filled, $3.75, 4.25, 5.50; 10k solid gold, $14.50; heavier, $17.00; 14k, $16.75; heavier, $19.00; sterling silver without slide, $3.00.

No. P. Neat pattern chain, 1-10 gold filled, 14k soldered link, solid gold jewelled slide, $3.75, 4.25; other patterns, sterling silver, without slide, $1.50, 2.50.

No. Q. Link pattern 14k soldered chain, 1-10 gold filled, with solid gold jewelled slide, $1.75, 2.50, 3.00, 3.75.

No. R. Ladies' long black silk watch guards, rolled plate or sterling silver mounts, 35c; plain black, without mounting, 15c, 20c.

Gentlemen's Open-Face Silver Cases.

3-oz solid silver case

Stem-wind and set, screw bezel and screw back, with gold inlaid locomotive, bicyclist, stag, wood-chopper, sulky and horse, race horse or boat.

1309. The above case, with London 7-jewelled nickel movement, $9.90.
1310. Same case, with London 15-jewelled nickel movement, $11.25.
1311. Same case, with London 15 jewels in settings nickel adjusted movement, $12.90.
1312. Same case, with London 17-jewelled nickel adjusted movement, $17.75.
1313. Same case, with highest grade 17-jewelled nickel adjusted London movement, $29.75.
1314. Same case, with 7-jewelled Waltham movement, $9.75.
1316. Same case, with 15-jewelled nickel Waltham movement, $12.00.
1317. Same case, with 17 jewels in settings, P. S. Bartlett Waltham movement, patent regulator and hairspring, $13.75.
1318. Same case, and Appleton, Tracy Waltham new model movement, $22.00.
1319. Same case and the new Waltham movement, named "Railroader," having 17 jewels, $22.00.
1320. Same case, with new model "Crescent Street" nickel Waltham movement, $27.75.
1321. Same case and new model "C. P. R." movement, 21 fine ruby jewels, $27.50.
1322. Same case, 18-size Waltham "Vanguard," movement, $32.25.

Any of the above can be supplied with 3-oz plain silver case, without the gold inlaying, at $1.00 less than above cases.

Sterling Silver 16-Size Open-Face Watches.

Solid silver case, outside screw back and bezel, thick glass. These cases have been so satisfactory to purchasers that it is unnecessary for us to say further than that they are the strongest and neatest cases made, stem-wind and set. Styles of case: plain or engine turned.

1323. Silver case and genuine American movement, $4.25.
1324. Silver described case, fitted with London 7-jewelled nickel movement, $7.00.
1325. Silver case, with London 15-jewelled nickel movement, $8.25.
1326. Silver case, with London 15 jewels, in gold settings, nickel movements, patent regulator, and Breguet hairspring, beautifully finished, $10.00.
1327. Silver case, with London 17-jewelled nickel movement, patent regulator, and Breguet hairspring, and highly adjusted for accurate time, $15.00.
1328. Silver case, fitted with 7-jewelled Waltham movement, $5.90.

16-Size, Open Face.

1329. Above case, with 15 jewels in settings, nickel Waltham movement, having Breguet hairspring, $10.25.
1330. Above case, with 17 jewels in settings, nickel Waltham movement, patent Breguet hairspring and regulator, double sunk dial, and finely adjusted to heat, cold and all positions, $14.75.

NOTE.—All 16-size London movements have exposed winding wheels, and are of the thinnest model.

Gentlemen's Gun-Metal Watches.

1331. Gentlemen's gun-metal case, with genuine American movement, $2.00.
1331A. Gents' gun-metal watch, American movement, $1.25.
1332. Same case, with Waltham 7-jewelled movement, $6.75.
1333. Same case, with 15-jewelled Waltham movement, $9.25.
1334. Same case, with London 7-jewelled nickel movement, $6.50.
1335. Same case, with London 15-jewelled nickel movement, $7.50.

Watches for Young Men and Boys.

All Open-Face.

1336. The "Eaton" Dollar watch, nickel case, $1.00.
1337. Very reliable strong dust-proof American watch, $1.35.
1338. A good reliable nickel American watch, $2.00.
1339. Solid nickel case, with genuine American movement, thin model, $3.00.
1340. Same case, with 7-jewelled nickel London movement, $5.25.
1341. Same case, fitted with London 15-jewelled movement, $6.50.
1342. Same case, and Waltham 7-jewelled movement, $5.80.
1343. Same case, and Waltham 15-jewelled nickel movement, $8.90.

NOTICE.—All watches quoted in catalogue as American watches are set by pushing down on winding stem, and turn always to the right.

16-Size Gentlemen's Watches.

Gents' 14k Gold-Filled Watches.

Every Watch Guaranteed.

16-Size, Open Face.

Case guaranteed by manufacturer for 25 years' wear.

14k gold-filled case, warranted 25 years, stem wind and set, is screw back and bezel. This is the new model of case which has become so popular lately, does not bulge out the pocket, and in every sense is a perfect gentleman's watch. We have it in plain polished, engine-turned, and handsomely engraved.

1344. The above described case, fitted with London 7-jewelled nickel movement, $11.75.
1345. Same case, fitted with London 15-jewelled nickel movement, $13.00.
1346. Same case, fitted with London 15-jewelled nickel movement, patent regulator and Breguet hairspring, $14.75.
1347. Same case, fitted with London 17-jewelled nickel adjusted movement, $19.75.
1348. Same case, with 7-jewelled Waltham movement, $12.50.
1348½. Same case, with 15-jewelled Waltham movement, patent Breguet hairspring, $15.25.
1349. Same case, with 17 fine ruby jewelled Waltham nickel adjusted movement, having a patent regulator and hairspring, $23.25.
1350. Same case, with Waltham movement, having 17 jewels in settings, patent micrometric regulator, Breguet hairspring, adjusted to heat, cold and positions, $24.75.

NOTE.—Hunting cases for above movements, $4.00 extra.

Gents' 10k Gold-Filled Watches.

Gentleman's 10k gold-filled cases same style as above.

10k gold-filled case, warranted 20 years, stem-wind and set, has a strong glass, is screw back and bezel. This is the new model of case which has become so popular lately, does not bulge out the pocket, and in every sense is a perfect gentleman's watch. We have it in plain polished, engine-turned and handsomely engraved.

1351. Above described case, fitted with London 7-jewelled nickel movement, $9.50.

1352. The same described case, fitted with London 15-jewelled movement, $10.75.
1353. Same case, fitted with London 17-jewelled nickel adjusted movement, $17.50.
1354. Same case fitted with 7-jewelled Waltham movement, $10.00.
1355. Same case, with 15-jewelled Waltham movement, $12.65.
1356. Same case, with 17-jewelled Waltham movement, $17.00.
1357. Same case, and Riverside 17-jewelled nickel Waltham movement, $22.25.

NOTE.—Hunting cases for above, $3.00 extra.

Gentlemen's 14k Solid Gold 16-Size Presentation Watches.

14k solid gold, 33-dwt. case, hinged back and front, thin model, does not bulge out the pocket, made in plain, polished or engine turned.

1358. Above case and London 15-jewelled movement, jewels in settings, $37.75.
1359. Same case and London 17-jewelled adjusted movement, patent regulator and Breguet hairspring, $43.75.
1360. Same case and London new model, 17-jewelled, adjusted to heat, cold and all positions, damaskeened plates, and in every respect a perfect time-piece, $54.25.
1361. Same case and Waltham 15-jewelled nickel movement, $40.50.
1362. Same case and Royal Waltham 17-jewelled nickel Waltham movement, $46.50.
1363. Same case and 17-jewelled Riverside Waltham movement, $52.50.

Hunting cases weigh heavier and will cost $4.00 extra.

Neatly engraved cases can be supplied at an additional cost of $3.00.

Gentlemen's 14k Gold-Filled Cases, 18 size.

Guaranteed to wear and give every satisfaction for 25 years.

Open Face.

14k open-face gold-filled case, stem-wind and stem-set, screw back and screw bezel, dust proof, strong glass. This case is guaranteed to wear and give satisfaction for 25 years, and is the finest filled case made.

1364. Same case, with London 7-jewelled nickel movement, $11.85.
1365. Same case, with London 15-jewelled nickel movement, exposed winding wheels and jewels in plain settings, $13.00.
1366. Same case, with London 15-jewelled nickel movement, exposed counter-sunk winding wheels, Breguet hairspring and patent regulator, jewels in settings, $14.80.
1367. Same case, with 17 jewels in settings, London nickel adjusted movement, $19.65.
1368. Same case, with highest grade London 17-jewelled movement, adjusted to temperature and positions, new patent regulator, $31.65.
1369. Same case, with 17 jewels in settings, Waltham movement, patent regulator and hairspring, $15.25.
1370. Same case, with 7-jewelled Waltham movement, $11.40.
1371. Same case, with 15-jewelled Waltham movement, $13.95.
1372. Same case, with 17 jewels in settings, P. S. Bartlett Waltham movement, patent regulator and hairspring, $15.50.
1373. Same case, with 17 jewels in settings, nickel Waltham movement, patent Breguet hairspring, micrometric regulator, adjusted to heat, cold and all positions, $18.25.
1374. Same case and Waltham new model 17-jewelled nickel adjusted movement, "Railroader," $23.90.
1375. Same case, with "New Model," Appleton, Tracy & Co. nickel Waltham movement, $23.90.
1376. Same case and "New Model," "C.P.R." movement, 21 fine ruby jewels, $28.25.
1377. Same case, with "New model," "Crescent Street," Waltham movement, $29.50.
1378. Same case, with the finest 18-size Waltham movement, "Vanguard," $34.00.

NOTE. – Hunting cases for above movements, $4.00 extra.

Gentlemen's 10k Gold-Filled Cases, 18 size.

10k open face, filled case, stem-wind and set, screw back and bezel, dust-proof, thick glass. In gold-filled cases the main consideration is the quality and their ability to wear well. This point we consider well, and sell only such goods as we can guarantee. These are made perfectly plain, engine-turned, or handsomely engraved, and are guaranteed for 20 years.

1379. The above case, with London 7-jewelled nickel movement, $9.50.
1380. Same case, with London 15-jewelled nickel movement, exposed winding wheels, and jewels in settings, $10.75.
1381. Same case, with London 15-jewelled nickel movement, in settings, exposed counter-sunk winding wheels, patent Breguet hairspring and regulator, $12.50.
1382. Same case, with London 17-jewelled nickel adjusted movement, $17.35.
1383. The same described case, with 7-jewelled Waltham movement, $9.25.
1384. Same case, with 15-jewelled nickel Waltham movement, $12.50.
1385. Same case, with 17 jewels in settings, P. S. Bartlett Waltham movement, patent regulator and hairspring, $13.75.
1386. Same case, with 17 jewels in settings, nickel Waltham movement, patent Breguet hairspring, micrometric regulator, adjusted to heat, cold, and all positions, $16.25.
1387. Same case, with Waltham new model, 17-jewelled nickel adjusted movement, "Railroader," $21.75.
1388. Same case, with Appleton, Tracy nickel movement, $21.75.
1389. Same case, with Crescent Street "New Model" Waltham movement, $27.50.
1389½. Same case and the highest grade 21-jewelled nickel Waltham movement, "Vanguard," $32.00.

Note. — Hunting cases for above movements, $3.00 extra.

Gentlemen's 18-size Open Face Presentation Watches.

14k solid gold 40-dwt. case, hinged back and front, the new up-to-date thin model, made in plain, polished or engine turned, can be supplied with monogram at an additional cost of $2.00.

1390. Above case and London 15-jewelled movement, jewels in settings, patent regulator and Breguet hairspring, $45.00.
1391. Above case and London 17-jewelled movement, jewels in settings, compensating balance, patent regulator, $49.00. Same case and new model 17-jewelled London movement, adjusted to heat, cold and all positions, new patent regulator, $59.75.
1392. Same case and 15-jewelled Waltham movement, nickel, Breguet hairspring, $44.75.
1393. Same case and P. S. Bartlett 17-jewelled nickel Waltham movement, $49.00.
1394. Same case and 21-jewelled new model, "Crescent St." Waltham movement, $59.50.

Hunting cases weigh heavier and will cost $1.00 extra.

Neatly engraved cases can be supplied at an additional cost of $3.00.

Gentlemen's Solid Nickel Cases, 18 size.

Open Face.

Solid nickel case, screw front and back, dust-proof, thick glass, stem-wind and stem-set.

1395. Above case, with London 7-jewelled movement, $5.50.
1396. Same case and London 15-jewelled in settings, nickel movement, patent hairspring and regulator, $6.75.
1397. Same case and London 17-jewelled in settings, nickel, finely adjusted movement, $13.50.
1398. Same case, fitted with genuine Waltham 7-jewelled movement, $6.00.
1399. Same case, fitted with 15-jewelled Waltham movement, $8.00.
1400. Same case, fitted with P. S. Bartlett 17-jewelled adjusted Waltham movement, $9.25.
1401. Same case, fitted with an Appleton, Tracy & Co. "New Model," 17 ruby-jewelled adjusted nickel Waltham movement, $18.00.
1402. Same case and Waltham new model 17-jewelled nickel adjusted movement, "Railroader," $18.00.
1403. Same case, with the new model "Crescent Street" Waltham movement, 21 ruby jewels, gold settings, patent regulator and Breguet hairspring, highly finished throughout, $23.75.
1404. Same case and new model C.P.R., nickel adjusted movement, 21 ruby jewels, $22.50.
1405. Same case and 21-jewelled nickel "Vanguard" Waltham movement, $27.75.

Gentlemen's 18-size Open Face.

Solid silver case, medium weight, screw back and bezel, dust proof, thick glass, and in every way first-class.

1406. Same case and London 7-jewelled movement, $7.25.
1407. Same case and London 15-jewelled movement, $8.75.
1408. Same case and London 15-jewelled movement, nickel, patent regulator, $10.25.
1409. Same case and London 17-jewelled movement, nickel, patent regulator, adjusted jewels in settings, $15.25.
1410. Same case, with 7-jewelled Waltham or Elgin movement, $7.55.
1411. Same case, with 15-jewelled nickel Waltham movement, $9.50.
1412. Same case, with 17-jewelled P. S. Bartlett adjusted Waltham movement, $11.00.
1413. Same case with 17-jewelled nickel adjusted Waltham movement, $14.25.
1414. Same case and Waltham new model movement, 17-jewelled nickel adjusted movement, "Railroader," $19.65.
1415. Same case, with 17 ruby jewels in gold settings, nickel, adjusted Appleton, Tracy & Co. "New Model" Waltham movement, patent Breguet hairspring and micrometric regulator, $19.75.
1416. Same case and 21-jewelled nickel "Vanguard" Waltham movement, $29.50.

GENTS' CHAINS.

Fine Jewellery Quality Guaranteed.

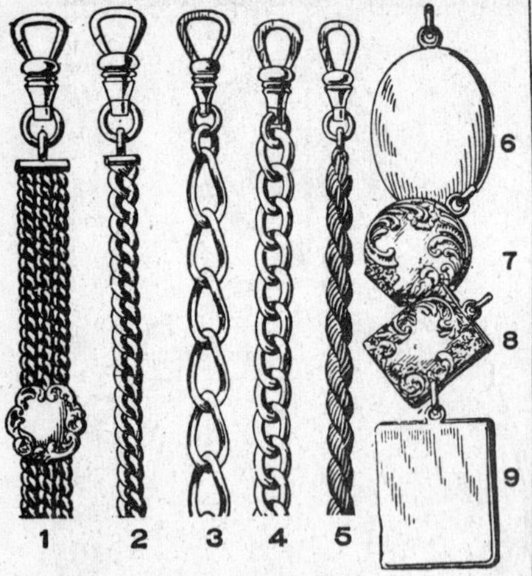

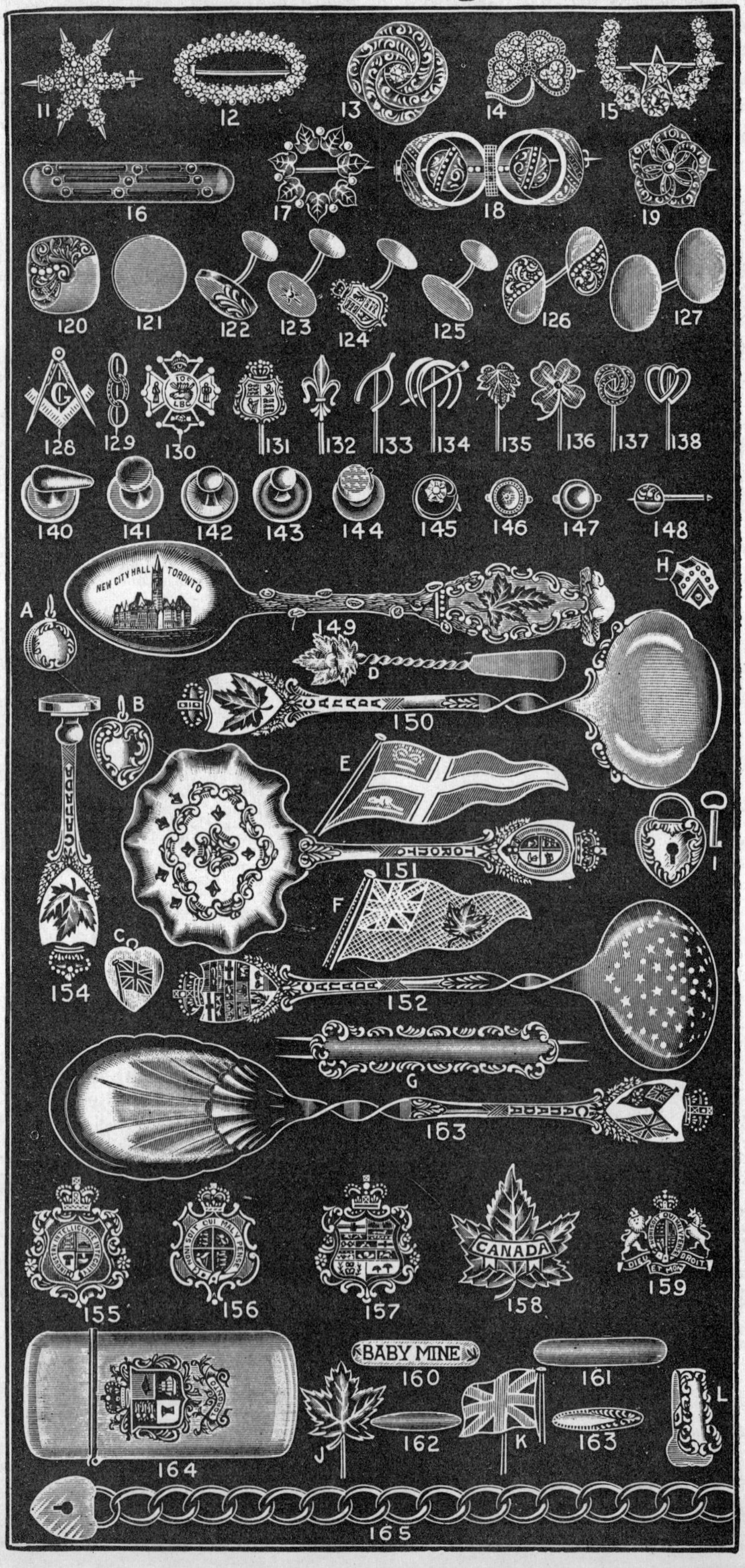

1. Gents' gold-filled watch chain (warranted 10 years), 2-strand, $3.25, 4.25; 3-strand (warranted 15 years), $4.25, 4.75.
2. Gents' 10k solid gold chain, $14.50; heavier, $19.75; 14k, $17.25; heavier, $24.50. Gold-filled, warranted 5 years, $1.00, 1.50; 10 years, $3.25, 3.75.
3. Gents' 10k solid gold watch chain (larger size than cut), $16.75; heavier, $21.50; 14k, $22.50; heavier, $25.50. Gold-filled, warranted 5 years, $1.00, 1.50; 10 years, $3.00; 15 years, $3.75; 20 years, $6.00. Sterling silver, 925/1000 fine, $3.25. White metal throughout, 15c, 25c.
4. Gents' 10k gold watch chain, $15.00; heavier, $19.50; 14k, $21.75; heavier, $27.50. Gold-filled, warranted 5 years, $1.00, 1.50; 10 years, $3.25; 15 years, $3.75, 4.00; chased, $4.50; 20 years, plain, $5.50, 6.00. Sterling silver, $2.25. White metal, same color throughout, 15c, 25c.
5. Gents' 10k gold chain, $14.75; heavier, $17.50; 14k, $16.75; heavier, $21.00. Gold-filled, warranted 5 years, $1.50; 10 years, $2.75; 15 years, $4.50; double chain, $2.75, 3.75. Silver, single chain, $3.00. White metal, same color throughout, 15c, 25c.
6. Gents' 10k solid gold locket, plain, $5.75, 6.50; heavier, $7.75; 14k, $9.00; heavier, $11.00; smaller size, 10k, $5.25; 14k, $8.00. Gold-filled, $1.50. Silver, $2.00.
7. Gents' 10k solid gold locket, plain, $6.00; 14k, $8.00. Gold-filled, style as cut, $1.00, 1.25; plain, $1.50; jewelled-set, $2.00. Silver, plain, $1.50. Rolled plate (as cut), 50c; other designs, compass, etc., 25c, 50c, 75c.
8. Gents' 10k solid gold locket, $5.00; 14k, $7.75. Gold-filled, $1.00, 1.50. Rolled plate, 50c; other designs, signet stone, 75c.
9. Gents' 10k solid gold locket, plain (larger than cut), $7.00; 14k, $10.00; heavier, $11.25; 10k (same size as cut), $6.25; 14k, $8.00. Gold-filled, $1.50. Silver, $2.00.
10. Gents' 10k solid gold mounted, black silk watch guards, $6.50; 14k, $7.50. Rolled plate, 75c, $1.00, 1.25, 1.50; without mounting, 15c, 20c. Hanging fob dress guards, gold-filled mountings, $2.25, 3.25.

10

10A. Sterling silver blouse set, plain or chased, 25c, 50c, 75c.

10B. Gold plated, 15c, 25c; rolled plate, 50c, 75c; gold-filled, $1.00, 1.25; solid gold, $4.00.

10C. Pearl blouse set, 15c, 20c, 50c; white metal, 15c.

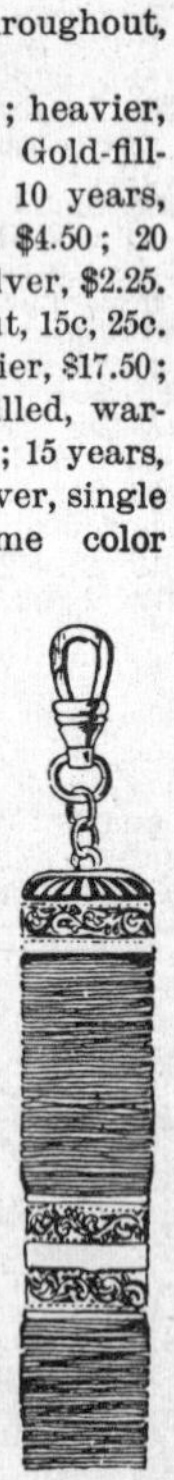

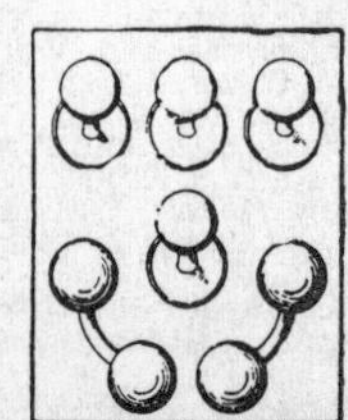

FINEST QUALITY OF REAL PEARLS IN 14K SOLID GOLD.

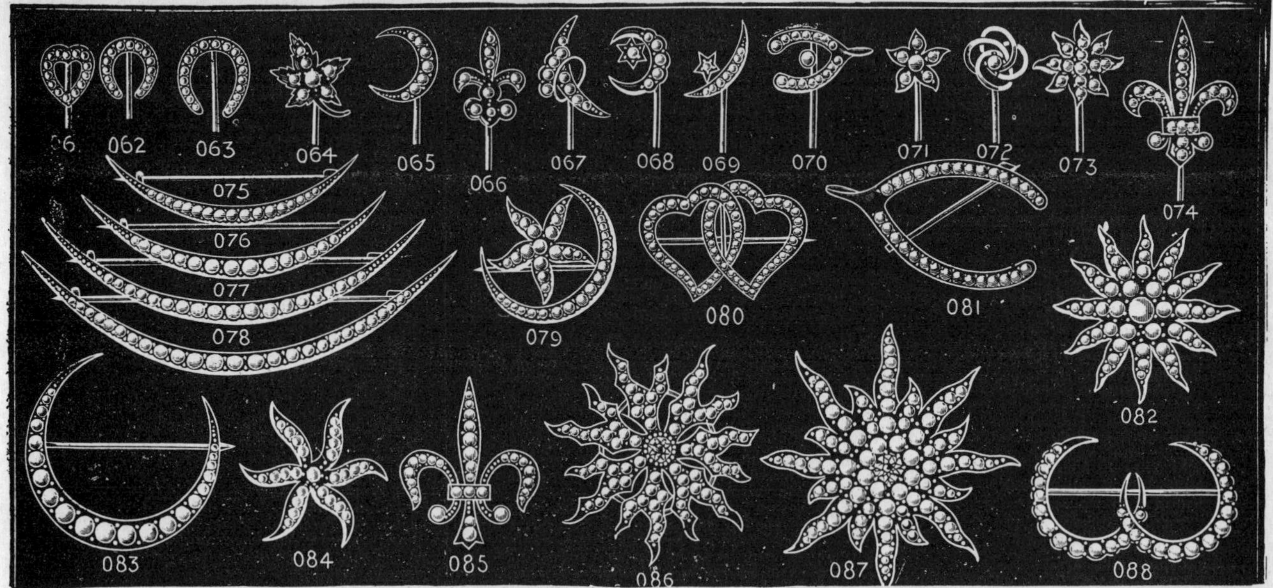

061. 14k solid gold stick pin, pearls $1.75
062. " " " " $1.60
063. " " " " $2.65
064. " " " " $2.50
065. " " " " $2.20
066. " " " " $2.20
067. " " " " $2.40
068. " " " " $1.70
069. 14k solid goldstick pin, pearls $1.40
070. 14k solid gold stick pin, pearls $3.15

071. 14k solid gold stick pin, pearls $1.75
072. " " " " $1.65
073. 14k solid gold stick pin, pearls $2.85
074. " " " " $4.00
075. " " crescent brooch, pearls, $3.20
076. " " " " " $4.25
077. " " " " " $5.75
078. " " " " " $7.85
079. " " crescent and flower, $7.50
080. 14k solid gold double heart brooch, pearls, $7.50

081. 14k solid gold wishbone brooch, pearls, $6.90
082. " " $18.45; smaller size, $10.65.
083. 14k gold, pearls, $10.95; smaller, $6.90, 4.25.
084. 14k solid gold flower brooch, pearls, $7.55.
085. " " fleur-de-lis brooch, pearls, $6.90.
086. " " fancy sunburst brooch doublet and pearls, $17.50; diamond and pearls, $36.00.
087. 14k solid gold sunburst brooch, diamond and pearls, $40.25; smaller, $27.60.
088. 14k solid gold, pearls, $8.45; larger, $13.15.

SEE OPPOSITE PAGE FOR ILLUSTRATIONS.

No. 11. Brooch, 14k, gold filled, set with brilliants, $2.25; rolled plate, $1.75.

No. 12. Brooch, gold filled, set with brilliants, $1.75; with olivine doublets and brilliants, $2.50.

No. 13. Brooch, gold filled, chased coil, with brilliant centre, $1.50; plain coil, with or without setting, $1.25; chased or plain coil, with opal setting, $1.75; solid gold, plain coil, no setting, $4.00; 10k solid gold, 3 diamonds set in centre, $5.95; 14k, $6.90.

No. 14. Brooch, gold filled, clover leaf, with brilliants, $2.00; hard enamelled fronts, in green or black, pearl setting in centre, $1.00, 1.25; larger size, $1.50; gold plated back, green enamel, 35c.

No. 15. Brooch, gold filled, set with brilliants, $1.50; larger size, $2.00.

No. 16. Black mourning brooch, 25c, 35c, 75c; gold front, similar to cut, $1.00; gold plate, 50c.

No. 17. Brooch, gold filled, hard enamelled leaf, with pearls, $1.50; other neat designs, with imitation diamonds, enamelled leaves or cluster settings, $1.25, 1.75, 2.25; with opals, $3.00.

No. 18. Brooch, 14k gold front, $1.50.

No. 19. Brooch, 14k gold filled, set with opal, $1.50, 1.75; solid gold, different settings, $3.75.

No. 120. Cuff buttons, lever backs, fancy tops, gold plate, 25c; rolled plate, 50c, 75c; gold filled, $1.00, 1.25; solid gold top, 10k, ladies', $2.25; larger size, $3.00, 3.50.

No. 121. Cuff buttons, pearl, 25c; silver, ladies', 40c; larger, 50c; rolled plate, 50c; gold filled, $1.50; solid gold top. 10k, ladies', $2.50; larger, $3.00.

No. 122. Cuff links, silver, 35c; rolled plate, 50c, 75c; gold filled, $1.00, 1.25; solid gold, 10k, $3.25.

No. 123. Cuff links, jewel settings, rolled plate, 75c; gold filled, $1.50; solid gold, 10k, $3.50; 14k, $4.75.

No. 124. Cuff links, sterling silver, gold plated, with Toronto, Ontario, Dominion of Canada, British or Scotch coat of arms, in hard enamel, 85c.

No. 125. Cuff links, pearl, 25c; silver, 50c; rolled plate, 50c, 75c; gold filled, $1.00; solid gold 10k, $3.25; 14k, $4.25.

No. 126. Cuff links, silver, 50c; rolled plate, 75c; gold filled, $1.50; solid gold 10k, $3.75; 14k, $4.75.

No. 127. Cuff links, silver, 25c; larger size, 50c; rolled plate, 50c, 75c; gold filled, $1.25; engraved Masonic or Oddfellows' emblem, $1.50; solid gold, 10k, $4.75; 14k, $5.75; solid gold, without emblem, 10k, $3.50, 4.00; 14k, $5.00.

No. 128. Emblem pin, solid gold, Masonic, $1.00; smaller, 65c, 75c; gold filled, 50c.

No. 129. Emblem pin, solid gold, Oddfellows, $1.00; smaller, 65c, 75c; gold filled, 50c.

No. 130. Emblem pin, solid gold, enamelled front, I.O.F., A.O.F., C.O.F., $1.50; other designs, 1.10.

No. 131. Stick pin, sterling silver, gold plated, Toronto, Ontario, Dominion of Canada or British coat of arms, or Scotch arms, in hard enamel on front, 25c.

No. 132. Stick pin, sterling silver, 25c; gold filled, 50c; solid gold, $1.25.

No. 133. Stick pin, sterling silver, 15c; solid gold, 75c; with setting, $1.25.

No. 134. Stick pin, silver, 35c, 50c; solid gold, $1.00.

No. 135. Stick pin, sterling silver, 15c, 25c.

No. 136. Stick pin, sterling silver, clover leaf, 15c, 25c; gold plate, enamelled, 50c, 75c.

No. 137. Stick pin, sterling silver, 25c; gold filled, 50c; solid gold, $1.00, 1.25, 2.00.

No. 138. stick pin, sterling silver, 15c, 25c; brooch, single heart, 25c; double heart, 35c, 50c.

No. 140. Collar button, pointer, gold plated, lever top, celluloid back, 5c each; pearl back, 10c, 15c; silver, 15c; 10k, $1.00; 14k, $1.25.

No. 141. Collar button, gold plated, lever top, celluloid back, for front of neck, 5c, or 6 for 25c.

No. 142. Collar button, gold plated, lever top, pearl back, 5c; rolled plate, 10c, 15c, or 2 for 25c; silver, 15c, or 2 for 25c; bone, 5c, 10c doz; pearl, 10c each.

No. 143. Collar button, one piece button, gold filled, 20c; silver, 15c; 10k, $1.00; 14k, $1.25.

No. 144. Collar button, separable top, with fancy stone top, celluloid back, 8c; pearl back, 10c.

No. 145. Shirt stud, spiral or separable, set with imitation diamond, gold filled, 25c.

No. 146. Shirt stud, set with pearl, gold filled, 25c; mourning stud, 25c; solid gold top, 75c.

No. 147. Shirt stud, plain or chased, 15c; gold filled, 25c; pearl or mourning stud, 15c; solid gold, one piece, 10k, 65c; 14k, 85c; gold filled, 20c.

No. 148. Shirt stud, pipe stem, gold filled, 20c.

No. 149. Souvenir spoons, sterling silver, gold plated, Toronto, Ontario, Dominion of Canada, British coat of arms or Maple Leaf, hard enamel on handle, plain bowl with name of any city or town engraved, or view of new City Hall, Parliament Buildings, University College, Upper Canada College, Metropolitan Methodist Church, or St. Michael's Cathedral in bowl, coffee spoon size, 75c; medium size, $1.00; tea spoon size, $1.50.

No. 150. Cream ladle, sterling silver, gold plated, enamelled handle, coat of arms, same as No. 149, $1.35.

No. 151. Bon Bon spoons, sterling silver, gold plated handles, same coat of arms as No. 149, $1.35.

No. 152. Sugar sifter, sterling silver, gold plated, handles in same coat of arms as No. 149, $1.35.

No. 153. Sugar shell, sterling silver, gold plated, handles same coat of arms as No. 149, $1.35.

No. 154. Letter seal, sterling silver, gold plated, handles in same coat of arm as No. 149, $1.00; other fancy handles, 25c, 50c, 75c, $1.00; with jewel setting on handle, $1.50; monogram on seal, 1 letter, 35c; 2 letters, 50c; 3 letters, 75c.

Nos. 155, 156 and 157. Brooch or hat pin, sterling silver, gold plated backs, hard enamelled fronts, in Toronto, Ontario and Dom nion of Canada or British coat of arms, 50c; smaller size, 25c.

No. 158. Brooch or hat pin, sterling silver, gold plated, Maple Leaf design, in hard enamel, 50c; stick pin, same design, smaller size, 25c.

No. 159. Brooch or hat pin, sterling silver, gold plated back, Royal coat of arms, in hard enamel on front, 75c; large size, $1.00.

Nos. 160 and 161. Baby pin, silver, 50c; gold filled, 50c; solid gold, 10k, $1.50.

Nos. 162 and 163. Cuff pins, sterling silver, 25c ea; gold filled, 50c pr; rolled gold, set of three, 25c, 35c, 50c; solid gold, $1.50, 2.00 pr; set of three, $3.00.

No. 164. Match safe, sterling silver, plain, Toronto, Ontario, Dominion of Canada, or British coat of arms, or Maple Leaf, in hard enamel, the word "Canada" beneath, $1.75; other fancy designs, not enamelled, $1.00, 1.25, 1.50; plain, $1.35.

No. 165. Bracelet, sterling silver or gold filled, baby's size, 75c, $1.00; misses', $1.25, 1.50, 1.75; ladies' size, $2.25, 3.00, 3.75, 4.50, 5.00; solid gold, 10k, $8.50 to 20.00; 14k, $12.50 to 22.00.

A. Locket charm, gold plated, 50c; gold filled, $1.00.

D. Salt spoon, sterling silver maple leaf or coin bowl, gold lined, 35c.

H. Slide for ladies' watch chain, solid gold, assorted stone settings, $1.00, 1.25.

B. Heart, solid gold, $1.00, 1.25, 1.75, 2.00; with stone setting, $1.00, 1.50, 3.00; smaller size, plain, 75c, $1.00.

C. Heart, sterling silver, maple leaf or flag design, 25c; plain, 15c.

E. and F. Brooch or hat pin, sterling silver, hard enamel, 55c, 75c, 95c, according to size.

G. Hat marker, sterling silver, 40c; coat hanger, same design, 60c; engraving, 3c letter.

I. Padlock, for bracelet, sterling silver or gold filled, 45c, 50c; plain, 40c.

J. Stick pin, sterling silver, gold plated, enamelled, with or without word "Canada," 25c.

K. Stick pin, sterling silver, gold plated, Canadian or British flag, enamelled, 25c.

L. Tie clip, sterling silver, 20c; enamelled, 65c.

RINGS THAT WEAR.

EVERY RING GUARANTEED.

BULLOCK'S U.S. STANDARD RING STOCK SCALE 1 2 3 4 5 6 7 8 9 10 11 12 13

Measure the finger with strip of paper; then place same on ring scale and send us the number. Measure from end of cut at left hand side.

01. 14k single stone diamond ring, $12.50.
02. 14k single stone diamond ring, $4.00, 9.75, 15.00.
03. 14k single stone diamond, ruby or emerald ring, $14.50, smaller stone, $11.00.
04. 14k single stone diamond ring, $50.00, smaller stone, $20.00, 25.00, 35.00.
05. 14k single stone diamond ring, $57.00, smaller stone, $25.00, 37.50, 45.00.
06. 14k pearl and 2 doublet ring, ruby, emerald, or sapphire, $5.00.
07. 14k real sapphire and diamond twin ring, $14.00 to 25.00.
07A. 14k diamond twin, from $23.00 to 50.00.
07B. 14k ruby or emerald and diamond twin ring, $18.00 to 50.00.
08. 14k 7 diamond and 1 olivine ring, $40.00 to 60.00.
09. 14k 2 opal and 2 diamond, $7.50.
010. 14k sapphire and diamond twin, $55.00; smaller stones, $22.50, 35.00.
011. 10k 3 pearl and 2 turquoise, or all pearl or turquoise, $4.25.
012. 10k 3 doublets, ruby, emerald or sapphire, $3.75.
012A. 14k 3 diamonds, $50.00; ruby, emerald or sapphire and diamonds, $47.50; smaller stones, $17.50, 25.00, 38.00.
013. 14k 3 opals, $4.75; larger stones, $7.50, 10.00.
014. 14k 2 diamonds and whole pearl, $26.50 to 50.00.
015. 14k single pearl, $9.50; smaller size, special, $6.00.
016. 10k 3 doublets and 4 pearls, $4.50.
016A. 14k 3 doublets and 4 diamonds, $7.00.
017. 14k 2 diamonds and 3 doublets, ruby, sapphire, emerald, $15.75.
018. 14k 4 turquoises and 8 diamonds, $17.25.
019. 14k 5 opal ring, $8.75; larger, $15.00; smaller, $5.00.
020. 14k 3 diamonds and 2 sapphires or rubies, $78.00.
021. 14k 4 diamonds and 2 doublets, ruby, emerald or sapphire, $8.25.
022. 14k 4 whole pearl cluster, $13.75.
023. 14k 8 pearls, 3 opals, 2 doublets, ruby, emerald or sapphire, $5.65.
024. 10k 10 pearls, 3 doublets, ruby, emerald or sapphire, $5.00.
025. 14k 3 pearls, $13.00 to 25.00; smaller stones, $9.00.
026. 14k 8 diamonds, 1 doublet, 2 opals, $9.00.
026A. 14k 8 diamonds, 3 opals, $9.50.
026B. 14k 8 diamonds, 3 doublets, ruby, emerald or sapphire, $8.50.
027. 14k 12 diamonds, 2 doublets, 1 opal, $12.25.
027A. 14k 12 diamonds, 3 doublets, ruby, emerald or sapphire, $11.25.
028. 14k ruby and diamond cluster, $48.00; larger, $100.00; smaller, $35.00.
029. 14k 7 diamonds, 12 olivines, cluster, $36.00.
030. 14k 3 diamonds, 6 olivines, $44.00.
031. 10k ruby, emerald, sapphire, amethyst or topaz, doublet, $1.90; real opal, $2.50.
032. 10k ruby, emerald, sapphire, amethyst or topaz, doublet, $2.25; real opal, $3.50; 14k, $4.75 and 6.75.
033. 10k ruby, emerald, sapphire, amethyst or topaz doublet, $2.75.
033A. 10k real garnet or amethyst, $2.90; large and heavy, $5.50.
034. 10k opal, $8.00 to 20.00; 14k, $10.00 to $25.00.
035. 10k amethyst or garnet, $4.75; carbuncle, $5.75, 6.90, 7.50.
036. 10k carbuncle, $3.75, 4.50, 5.75, 7.50.
037. 10k blood stone or sardonyx, $4.75; Masonic or Oddfellow, $5.25.
038. 10k plain blood stone or sardonyx, $4.75; Masonic or Oddfellow, $5.25.
039. 14k blood stone or sardonyx, $9.75.
040. Solid gold, any initial or society emblem, light, $3.85; heavy, $5.75.
041. 10k child's keeper ring, 50c; heavier pattern, 75c, $1.00.
042. 10k keeper ring, $2.00; heavier, $2.75, 3.50.
043. 10k " $2.50; similar patterns, $1.00 to 4.00.
044. 18k wedding rings, $3.00; heavier, $4.25, 5.25; extra heavy, $6.25.
045. 18k flat band rings, $5.50, 6.75; 14k, $5.00, 6.25; 10k, $4.25, 5.00; raised initial, 85c extra each letter.
046. 10k mizpah ring, $1.90; 14k, $2.25.
047. 14k 1 opal, 2 diamonds and 2 pearls, $4.10.
047A. 10k 3 garnets and 2 pearls, $1.25.
048. 14k 1 ruby, 2 sapphires and 2 diamonds, $5.40.
049. 14k 1 real diamond, ruby, opal, pearl or sapphire, $3.65.
050. 14k 1 real diamond, ruby, opal, pearl or sapphire, $6.00.
051. 10k 3 doublets, ruby, emerald or sapphire, $2.75.
052. 10k 3 garnets and 2 pearls, $1.25; heavier, $1.75.
053. 14k pearl, $4.75; opal or turquoise, $4.25.
054. 10k 3 opals, 4 pearls, $2.75.
055. 14k 4 real diamonds, $3.75.
056. 10k child's ring, sizes 1 to 4, garnets and pearls, 75c; similar, 50c.
057. 10k garnets and pearls, $1.50; smaller, $1.25; larger, $2.20.
058. 10k 3 opals, $1.60; garnets and pearls, 90c.
059. 10k garnets and pearls, $1.75; heavier, $2.25.
060. 10k garnets and pearls, $2.20; medium size, $1.50; smaller, $1.25.

ACCURATE CLOCKS.

H1.

H1. "Can't sleep" alarm clock, nickel finish, American movement, height 5¾ in., alarm rings 5 minutes with one winding, but can be stopped when you want, $1.65.

H2. Small bedroom clock, 1-day, nickel or gilt finish, 2½-in. dial, $1.00.

H3. Same style, with alarm, $1.50.

H4.

H4. Genuine American nickel-finish alarm clock, 3½-in. dial, 75c.

H5. Genuine American nickel-finish alarm clock, 4-in. dial, extra quality, $1.00.

H6. Genuine "Seth Thomas" movement nickel alarm clock, 4½-in. dial, with second hand, our best value, $1.15.

H7.

H7. Handsome alarm clock, height 5 in., nickel finish, with glass sides and gilt front and handle, alarm on bottom, neat design, $2.00.

H8. Same style clock, height 6½ in., with bell alarm or musical alarm which plays 20 minutes, $2.75.

H9.

H9. Fancy gold-plated clock, with porcelain dial, in plain, bright and dull finish, convenient for carriage or boudoir use, $3.25; similar designs, with handle, in larger sizes, $4.25, 5.25.

H10.

H10. Bedroom or boudoir clock, richly gold-plated in ornamental design, handsomely embossed, porcelain dial, American movement, fully guaranteed, $4.50; other designs, $6.50, 7.50.

H11.

H11. Dining-room clock, in walnut or oak finish, cathedral gong strike, 8-day movement, 16 to 18 inches high, $3.75.

H12.

H12. Mantel clock, polished adamantine finish on wood, neatly carved, gilt finish trimmings, 8-day movement, hour and half-hour cathedral gong strike, white dial, height 11 in., base 12½ in., handsome design, $4.75; other similar designs in larger sizes, $5.50, 5.75, 6.00.

H14.

H14. Wall clock, in oak or walnut finish, 32 in. long, regulator style, 12-in. dial, 8-day movement, $6.25; with calendar, $6.75.

H15. Drop-octagon wall clock, in oak or walnut finish, 8-day time, visible pendulum, 21½ in. long, dial same style as cut H14, $4.25; with calendar, $4.75.

H16. Genuine weight regulator, American movement, one of our best timepieces, $14.00.

H13.

H13. Polished wood clock, adamantine finish, with gilt trimmings and feet nicely carved, 8-day movement, hour and half-hour cathedral gong strike, height 11 in. base 16½ in., $6.50; other designs, $7.00, 7.50.

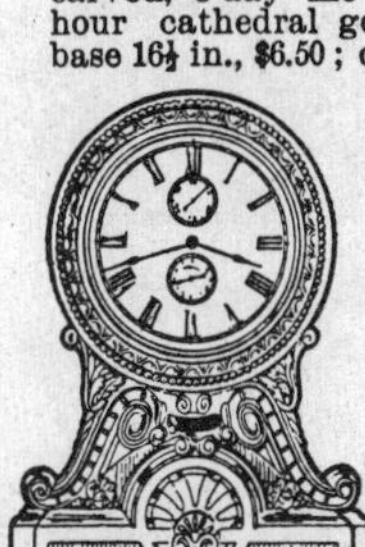
H29.

H29. One-day time, long alarm clock, in metal case, oxidized copper finish, in fancy ornamental design, height 10 in., 4½-in. dial, the alarm rings about 20 minutes with one winding, but can be switched off at pleasure, $3.00.

H17.

Mantel clocks, height 22 in., in oak or walnut finish, gilt decorated glass.

H17. 1-day, strike	$2 25
H18. 1-day, strike, alarm	2 60
H19. 8-day, strike	2 60
H20. 8-day, strike, alarm	3 00
H21. 8-day, cathedral gong strike	3 00
H22. 8-day, cathedral gong strike, alarm	3 25

There is a cheaper grade of these clocks, but we do not handle them and highly recommend above styles.

H23.

Mantel clocks, with thermometer and barometer attachment, in oak or walnut finish.

H23. 8-day, half-hour strike	$3 00
H24. 8-day, half-hour strike, alarm	3 25
H25. 8-day, half-hour gong strike	3 25
H26. 8-day, half-hour gong strike, alarm	3 50

H27.

H27. Enamelled iron clocks, gold-plated trimmings, cream porcelain dial, visible escapement, 8-day, cathedral gong strike, 15 in. long, $9.50.

H28. Same style, without visible escapement, $8.90.

H30.

H30. Dining-room clock, finished in old oak only, 8-day movement, hour and half-hour cathedral gong strike, 6-in. dial, height 21 in., fancy engraved face in gilt, ornamental pendulum, handsome finish and style, $5.75.

OUR CUSTOMERS MAY RELY ON RECEIVING FIRST-CLASS ARTICLES.

Fine Quality of Silverware.

242. Tea set, four pieces, tea pot, sugar bowl, cream jug and spoon holder, bright burnished embossed feet, handles and spout, fancy carved border, spoon holder and cream jug gold lined, with partly shot bead border, handsome design, $23.00; extra tea pot to match, five pieces, $31.50. See cut of teapot, No. 242.

243. Tea set, four pieces, tea pot, sugar bowl, cream jug and spoon holder, satin engraved, bright cut, cream jug and spoon holder gold lined, fancy embossed feet and handles, rococo border, bright burnished lid, $8.75; including extra tea pot, $12.75; same design in bright burnished finish, $10.50; five pieces, $15.00. See cut of teapot, No. 243.

244. Tea set, four pieces, tea pot, sugar bowl, cream jug and spoon holder, new design, top and base bright burnished, satin-finish bowl, shot bead border, handsomely engraved in flower design, embossed handle and spout, cream jug and spoon holder gold lined, best quality, $16.75; see cut teapot, No. 244.

245. Tea set, four pieces, tea pot, sugar bowl, cream jug and spoon holder, satin engraved, fancy spout and handle, bright burnished lid and base, shot bead border, cream jug and spoon holder gold lined, $7.50. See cut of teapot, No. 245.

246. Biscuit jar, of "Wave Crest" ware, bowl in fancy tinted colorings of pink, blue and yellow, bright burnished lid, with scalloped border and shot bead trimming, fancy cord handle, neat design, $3.75.

247. Egg set, six cups and spoons, broken egg pattern, bright burnished base, satin-finished inside, plain bright burnished handle, with receptacle for six spoons, cups and bowl of spoons gold lined, $6.50; four cups and spoons, $5.50; two cups and spoons, $3.50.

248. Tea set, five pieces, tea pot, coffee pot, sugar bowl, cream jug and spoon holder, handsomely engraved with plain burnished shield, heavily embossed feet, lid, handle and spout, rococo border, cream jug and spoon holder gold lined, $34.00; gold-lined slop bowl extra, $4.00.

249. Tilting water pitcher, satin engraved, heavily embossed handle and base, fitted with gold-lined goblet on projected stand, very beautiful design, $10.50; other design, $26.50; pitcher separate, $6.50; heavier design, $13.50.

250. Napkin ring, fancy satin finished, with neat leaf-design stand, neatly engraved in apple blossom pattern, 60c; other designs, 50c, 75c.

251. Napkin ring, broken egg-shell design, with chicken and wishbone on side, satin engraved, 85c.

252. Napkin ring, satin engraved, rococo edge, chicken and wishbone design, with the words "A Sterling Wish" engraved, $1.25.

253. Napkin ring, lyre design, satin finished, engraved, rope-work border, neat design, 85c.

254. Berry dish, on fancy bright finished stand, with shot bead trimming, fancy embossed feet and ornamental handle, dish of fine opalware glass, colored in pink, blue and yellow shades, with ornamental gold flowers, neat shape, $5.00; smaller size dish, in same style, $3.50; other designs, $7.50, 10.00.

255. Tête-à-tête or coffee set, four pieces, tray, tea or coffee pot, sugar bowl and cream jug, plain fluted octagonal pattern, cream jug gold-lined, ebony handles, shot bead border, embossed feet, tray plain satin-finished centre, with shot bead border, $23.00.

256. Cake basket, square shape, bright burnished inside border and satin engraved centre, heavily embossed feet and satin-finished base, shot bead handle and border, very pretty, silver lined, $5.50; gold lined, $6.00; same style with rococo finished border and handle, $4.75 and $5.50; other designs in round shapes, neatly engraved and fancy embossed, $3.00, 3.25, 4.00, 4.50, 5.00, 10.00.

257. Child's mug, in satin finish fancy scroll pattern, embossed handle, fancy border, bright burnished base, gold lined, $2.00; plain design, bright cut, small, 60c; medium, 75c; large, $1.00; other designs, $1.50, 1.85.

258. Card receiver, on bright burnished stand, rococo border on base and top, satin-finish centre, handsomely carved, silver lined, $2.25; gold lined, $2.75.

259. Syrup jug, finished with tray to match, neatly engraved, with rococo border, jug has bright burnished lid, fancy embossed feet, handles and spout, $3.00; other designs, $3.25, 6.00.

260. Individual cruet, fluted stand, satin-finished base, rustic feet, fancy handle, white frosted glass bottles with gold and colored decorations, tops silver plated, strongly made, $2.50; other similar designs, $1.85, 2.00.

261. Bon-bon dish, bright burnished base and plain satin-finished centre, scalloped border, fancy turndown handle, silver lined, $1.50; gold lined, $1.75.

262. Tilting hot water kettle, to match No. 243 tea set, fancy embossed spout and handle, satin finished ornamented stand, bright burnished heater, $9.50; other designs, $15.00.

263. Sugar bowl and spoon holder combined, satin finish, fancy design, bright finished base and lid, with ornamental bird knob, embossed handles, rack for holding twelve spoons around bowl, $3.00; with plain spoons attached, tipped pattern, $5.35; fancy spoons, embossed handles, neat pattern, $5.90; see cut spoons.

264. Salt and pepper sifters, in bright and satin finish, neatly carved salt sifter, has gold-plated top to prevent rust, glass lined, in neat satin-lined box, convenient for mailing, $1.75; smaller size, $1.25 and 1.50.

265. Butter dish, bright burnished base and rim, embossed feet, shot bead border and fancy twisted handles, satin engraved lid and fancy knob, $3.00; same design with bale, $3.50; other similar designs, in satin finish, $2.25, 2.50, 7.00.

266. Dessert set, on fancy stand, sugar bowl, cream jug and spoon, fancy shaped handle, spoon holder on side, satin finish, neatly engraved on sides and stand, cream jug and bowl of spoon gold lined, four fancy embossed feet, bright burnished lid and edges, $4.38.

267. Fern pot, with removable inner dish of bright burnished finish, fancy filigree pattern, four fancy embossed feet, strongly made, $4.00; plainer design, $2.75; other designs, $14.00.

268. Crumb tray and scraper, in fancy carved pattern, satin finish, shot bead edge, bright finished handles, $3.25; other designs, $4.50, 6.00.

269. Salt cellar, white or ruby glass, cut glass pattern, embossed stand, fancy handle and spoon on side, neat design, $1.50.

270. Baking or pudding dish, satin engraved lid and base, fancy embossed feet and handles, separate fine porcelain-lined dish inside, fitted over with extra rim, with fancy rococo border, ornamental knob, $5.75; smaller size, $3.75; other designs, $5.00, 7.50, 9.00.

271. Dessert set, sugar bowl and cream jug, bright burnished finish, shot bead border, both pieces gold lined, $4.75; fitted in fine hinged leather case, satin lined, $6.50.

272. Dinner castor, on high revolving stand, five round bottles of fine glass, engraved, bright burnished edges on stand and satin engraved centre, strong base, ornamented handle, salt, pepper and mustard bottle tops silver-plated, $3.35; same design, with square shaped bottles, $4.25; other plainer designs, special plate, round bottles, $2.25.

273. Waiters, in round and square-shaped styles, satin lined, neatly carved in centre, in flower design, scalloped border, in round shape, 12-inch, $3.50; 15-inch, $4.50; 14-inch tray in square shape, fancy design to match tea set No. 243, with fancy handles, $5.00; other beautiful designs, $7.00; 17-inch, $10.00; 20-inch, $12.50.

274. Cheese dish, satin engraved lid on bright burnished plate, with rococo border, four fancy embossed feet, satin-finished base, bright burnished around knob, $4.00.

275. Pickle cruet, with tongs, ruby tinted glass, gold decorations, fancy embossed stand and handle, $2.25; with straight glass, $1.85; other design with crystal glass, $1.50.

276. Bread tray, oval shaped, in fancy engraved pattern, satin finish, in rococo border, the word "Bread" engraved on centre in large bright letters, $2.25; other design, $2.00.

OUR GOODS ARE ALL OF STANDARD QUALITY.

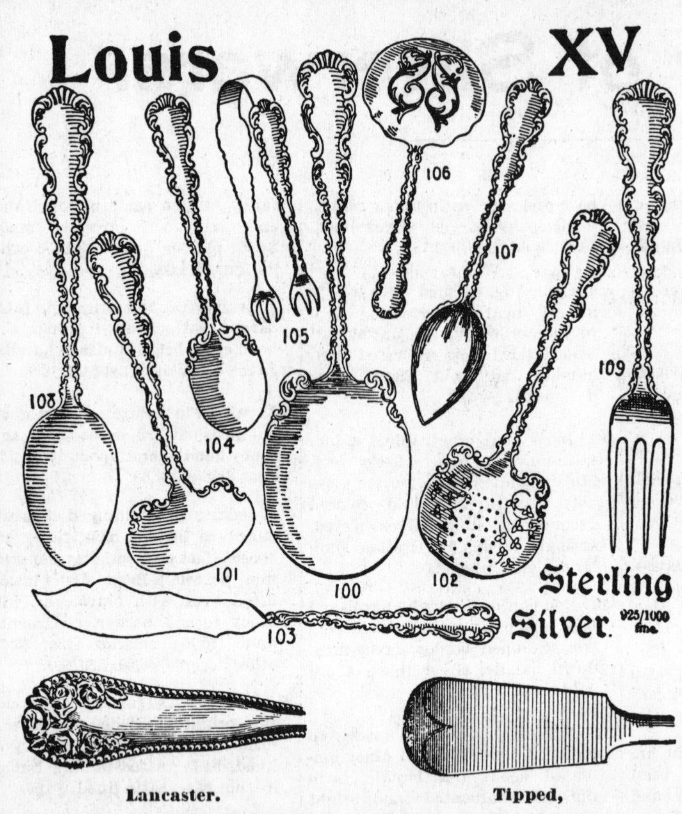

Lancaster. Tipped,

STERLING SILVER TABLEWARE

925/1000 FINE, FULLY GUARANTEED.

	Louis XV.	Lancaster	Tipped.
	Doz.	Doz.	Doz.
108. Coffee spoons, pattern on front only, gilt bowl	$ 3 20	......	......
108. Coffee spoons, standard weight	5 25	$ 6 00	$ 5 50
108. " " " " gilt bowl	6 25	7 00	6 50
108. Tea spoons, medium size, pattern on front only	5 50	......	......
108. Teaspoons, med. size, standard weight	7 50	8 00	7 75
108. " large " " "	9 50	10 25	9 75
108. Dessert spoons, regular size " "	16 50	18 00	17 00
108. Table spoons, " " " "	22 50	24 75	23 00
109. Dessert forks " " " "	16 50	18 00	17 00
109. Table forks " " " "	22 50	24 75	23 00
	Each.	Each.	Each.
100. Berry spoon, large size, silver bowl	$ 4 75	$ 5 00	......
100. " " " " gilt "	5 25	5 75	......
100. " " small silver "	3 25	3 50	......
100. " " " " gilt "	3 75	4 00	......
101. Cream ladle, regular size, silver bowl	2 00	2 25	......
101. " " " " gilt "	2 50	2 75	......
102. Sugar sifter " " silver "	2 50	2 75	......
102. " " " " gilt "	2 75	2 75	......
102A. " " cream ladle or bon bon scoop, gilt bowls	{ 0 85 1 00	....	....
104. Sugar spoon " " silver "	1 00	1 35	......
104. " " heavier gilt "	1 75	1 75	......
105. Sugar or bon-bon tongs, gold tips	1 00	1 35	......
106. Bon-bon or candy scoop, silver bowl	1 00	1 50	......
106. " " " gilt "	1 25	1 75	......
107. Orange spoons, silver bowls	1 00	......	......
107. " " gilt "	1 25	1 35	......
103. Butter knfie, medium size	1 75	2 00	......
103. " " " " heavier	2 25	......	......
110. Mustard spoon, gilt bowl	1 00	1 00	......
111. Cold meat fork	3 75	3 75	......
112. Cheese scoop	1 50	......	......
113. " " larger	2 25	2 50	......
114. Gravy or sauce ladle	3 75	3 75	......
115. Pie knife	5 50	5 50	......
116. Pickle forks	1 25	1 50	......
117. Oyster forks	1 00	1 00	......

SILVER-PLATED FLATWARE

ENGRAVING on Jewellery, Watches, Rings, and Silverware, per letter: script, 3c; Old English or script entwined, 5c; large block monogram, $1.00.

Our Silver-plated Flatware is made by Rogers & Bros., of Waterbury, Conn., Wm. Rogers, of Wallingford, Conn., and other well-known makers. These goods are guaranteed by the makers to be A1, plated on 18 per cent. nickel silver, and warranted to wear from 8 to 12 years in ordinary use.

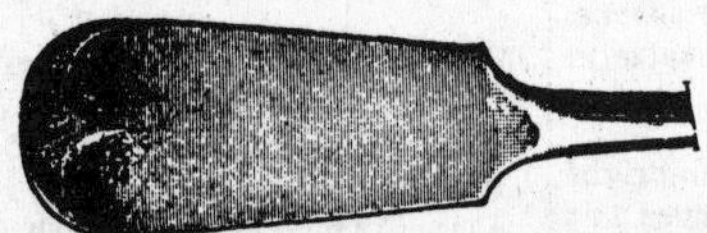

Tipped.

No. 400. Tipped pattern teaspoons, $2.35 doz; dessert spoons, $3.85 doz; dessert forks, $3.85 doz; tablespoons, $4.75 doz; table forks, $4.75 doz.

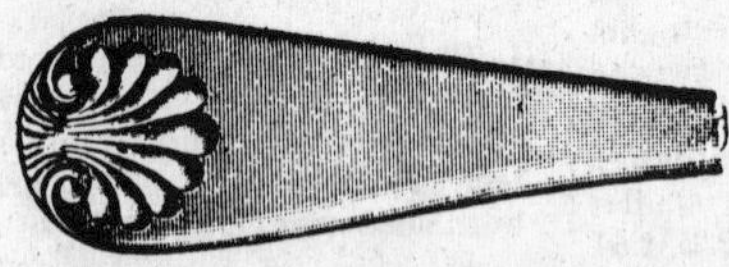

Shell.

No. 401. Shell pattern teaspoons, $2.50 doz; dessert spoons, $4.00 doz; dessert forks, $4.00 doz; tablespoons, $5.00 doz; table forks, $5.00 doz.

Cordova.

No. 402. Cordova pattern teaspoons, $3.00 doz; dessert spoons, $5.20 doz; dessert forks, $5.20 doz; tablespoons, $6.00 doz; table forks, $6.00 doz.

No. 403. Butter knife, 50c each.

No. 404. Sugar shell, gold-lined bowl, 75c each; silver-lined bowl, 50c each.

No. 405. Pie server, Cordova or other patterns, gold blade, $2.25; silver blade, $1.75.

York.

No. 406. York pattern teaspoons, $3.00 doz; dessert spoons, $5.20 doz; dessert forks, $5.20 doz; tablespoons, $6.00 doz; table forks, $6.00 doz.

No. 407. Butter knife, 50c each.

No. 408. Sugar shell, gold-lined bowl, 75c each; silver-lined, 50c each.

The following goods are put up in fancy satin-lined boxes.

No. 409. Berry spoons, Cordova and fancy patterns, with satin-finish bowl, $1.50 each; gold lined, $1.75 each.

No. 410. Salt spoons, 25c each; mustard spoons, 35c each.

No. 411. Coffee spoons, ½ doz in satin-lined case $1.50.

No. 412. Cold meat forks, Cordova or fancy pattern, large size, $1.00 each; small size, 75c each.

No. 413. Tomato and cucumber servers, Cordova and fancy patterns, gold-lined bowl, $1.75 each.

No. 414. Gravy ladle, Cordova and fancy patterns, satin-finish, $1.25 each; gold-lined, $1.75 each.

No. 415. Cream ladle, Cordova and fancy patterns, satin-finished, 85c each; gold-lined, $1.25 each.

No. 416. Pickle fork, Cordova and fancy patterns, 50c each.

No. 417. Oyster ladle, in Cordova and fancy patterns, satin-finish, $2.50 each.

No. 418. Soup ladle, in Cordova or fancy patterns, large size, $3.00 each; small size, $2.50 each.

Child's Knife and Fork Sets.

No. 419. Child's knife, fork and spoon, Cordova pattern, in satin-lined case, $1.00.

No. 420. Child's knife, fork and spoon, fancy pattern, steel knife, 35c, 50c.

Silver-Plated Knives.

Silver-plated knives, warranted 12 dwt. Rogers' make, hand burnished on heavy steel blades.

No. 421. Plain handle, dessert size, $3.75 doz; table size, $4.00 doz.

No. 422. Shell pattern handle, dessert size, $4.50 doz; table size, $5.00 doz.

No. 423. Hollow handle, plain bright finish, dessert size, $5.50 doz; table size, $6.00 doz.

No. 424. Cordova or fancy pattern, hollow handles, soldered with sterling silver, cannot tell them from solid silver, dessert size, $9.50 doz; table size, $11.50 doz.

No. 425. Silver-plated knives, with 6 dwt. of silver on the dozen, will wear for about six years, table and dessert sizes, $2.25 doz.

No. 426. Silver-plated knives, 2 dwt table and dessert sizes, $1.20 doz.

OUR TERMS ARE STRICTLY CASH WITH ORDER.

Pearl Handle Flatware.

No. 428. Table knives, forged steel blades, best English electro-plated, $12.00 doz; forks to match, $10.00 doz.
No. 429. Dessert knives, same quality as cut 428, $10.00 doz; forks to match, $8.00 doz.
No. 430. Fish servers, set knife and fork, best English electro-plate, with silver ferule, fitted in plush-lined case, $5.00.
No. 431. Cake knife, best English electro-plated blade, with saw back and silver ferule, $1.50 each.
No. 432. Bread fork, best English electro-plate, silver ferule, $1.25 each.

No. 433. Butter knives, best electro-plate, fancy engraved blades, with silver ferule, 50c, 75c, $1.00 each.
No. 434. Butter knives, bone handles, with silver ferule, 25c; celluloid handle, 35c each.
No. 435. Pickle forks with silver ferule, 50c, 60c, 75c each.

White Metal.

White metal is the cheapest line of flatware we sell, which we recommend as the best white metal goods made. They will wear white and not turn brassy.
No. 436. Teaspoons, 25c doz; large size, 35c doz; dessert spoons, 55c doz; dessert forks, 55c doz; tablespoons, 65c doz; table forks, 65c doz.

Nickel Silver.

These goods are warranted to wear white and not turn brassy.
No. 437. Teaspoons, tipped pattern, 50c doz; large size, 75c doz; dessert spoons, $1.25 doz; dessert forks, $1.25 doz; tablespoons, $1.50 doz; table forks, $1.50 doz.

Steel Table Cutlery.

Such well-known makers as Joseph Rodgers & Sons, John Derby & Sons, and George Butler, all of Sheffield, need no recommendation from us, as they are all so well-known.

No. 438. Knives only, large size, square ivory handles, riveted, hand-forged steel blades, table, $7.50 and $11.00 doz; dessert size, $5.00 and $7.50 per doz.
No. 439. Knives only, square celluloid handles, hand-forged steel blades, table size, $2.75 and $4.75 doz; dessert size, $2.25 and $3.75 doz.

No. 440. Knives only, round celluloid handles, hand-forged steel blades, table size, $4.50 and $2.50 doz; dessert size, $3.50 and $2.00 doz.
No. 441. Knives only, round celluloid handles, table, $3.25 doz; dessert, $2.75 doz.
No. 442. Knives only, square celluloid handles, table, $2.00 doz; dessert, $1.50 doz.

No. 443. Knives only, buffalo horn handles, bolster ends, table, $3.00 doz; dessert, $2 50 doz.
No. 444. Knives only, stag handles, bolster ends, table, $2.75 doz; dessert, $2.25 doz.

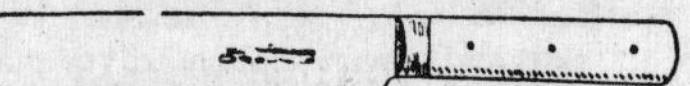

No. 445. Knives only, rosewood and ebony handles, single bolster, table or dessert size, 75c doz.
No. 446. Knives and forks, rosewood and ebony handles, single bolster, 6 knives and 6 forks, $1.25; dessert, $1.15.

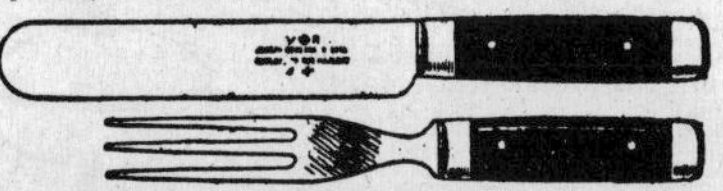

No. 447. Knives and forks, rosewood or ebony, handles, double bolster, 6 knives and 6 forks, table size, $1.75; dessert size, $1.50.
No. 448. Knives and forks, polished buffalo horn handles, forged steel blades, same as cut No. 443, set of 6 knives and 6 forks, table, $2.45; dessert, $2.25; others in same style, table, $1.65; dessert, $1.40 set.
No. 449. Knives and forks, stag handles, with rivet and bolster, hand-forged steel blades, set 6 knives and 6 forks, table, $2.15; dessert, $1.90; different make in same style, table, $1.50 set; dessert, $1.40 set.
No. 450. Knives and forks, rosewood and ebony handles, with patent double bolster, set 6 knives and 6 forks, $1.00.
No. 451. Knives and forks, rosewood and ebony handles, single bolster, finely tempered steel blades, set 6 knives and six forks, 75c.
No. 452. Knives and forks, rosewood and ebony handles, set 6 knives and 6 forks, 50c.

Our Carvers are made by such well-known manufacturers as Joseph Rodgers, and George Butler & Co.

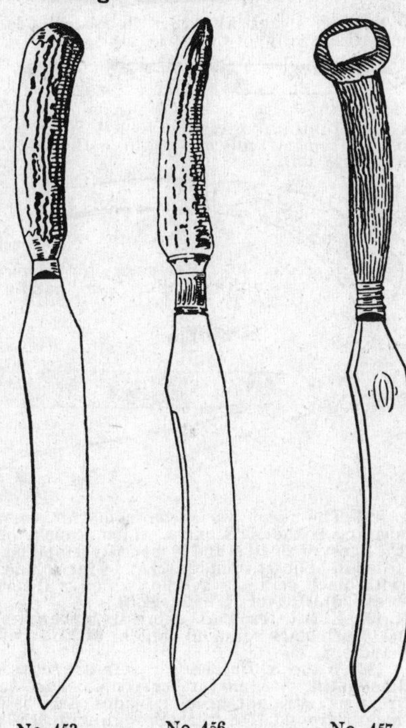

No. 453. No. 456. No. 457.

No. 453. Carving knife and fork, stag horn handles, forged steel blade, 75c; 9-inch blade, $1.00; steel to match, 25c.
No. 454. Carving knife and fork, stag horn handles, forged steel blade, $1.75; steel to match, 50c.
No. 455. Carving knife and fork, stag horn handles, fancy silver ferule, hand-forged steel blade, $2.50; steel to match, $1.25.
No. 456. Carving knife and fork, pointed stag horn handles, fancy silver ferule, hand-forged steel blade, $2.50; steel to match, 75c.
No. 457. Carving knife and fork, fancy stag horn handles with silver ferule, hand-forged steel blade, $2.25; steel to match, $1.25.
No. 458. Carving knife and fork, celluloid handles, square or round, to match table knives Nos. 439 and 440, hand-forged steel blade, $1.75; steel to match, 60c.
No. 459. Carving knife and fork, square ivory handles, to match No. 438 table knives, hand-forged steel blade, $3.75; steel to match, $1.25.

No. 460. Steel, with stag horn handles, 25c and 50c each.

NOTICE.—We furnish satin-lined leather cases for any of the above sets for $1.00 extra.

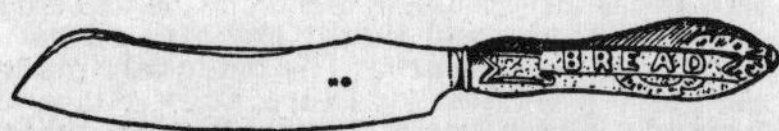

No. 461. Bread knife, hand-carved handle, forged steel blade, 7½-inch, 50c.
No. 462. Bread knife, hand-carved handle, forged steel blade, 6½-inch, 35c each.

No. 462½. Bread knife, saw blade, steel handle, best steel blade, 50c.
No. 463. Bread knife, carved wood handle, Sheffield steel blade, 25c each.

No. 464. Butcher knives, rosewood handle, forged steel blade, 6½-inch, 30c; 7-inch, 35c; 8-inch, 40c; 9-inch, 50c; 10-inch, 60c; 12-inch, 90c each.
No. 465. Paring knife, polished wood handle, with shear steel blade, 10c each.

No. 466. Paring knife, wood handle, steel blade, 5c each.

Scissors.

We have secured the sale of the well-known Heinisch shears, which have been on the market for the past seventy-five years. We can highly recommend them as the best offered for sale, noted for their fine finish and durability.

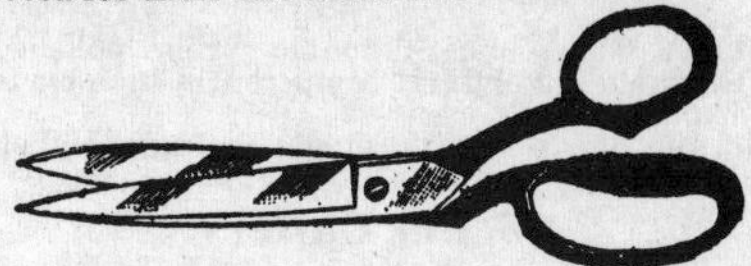

No. 467. Heinisch make, japanned handles, silver-plated blades, bent trimmers, 10-inch, $1.00; 12-inch, $1.25.

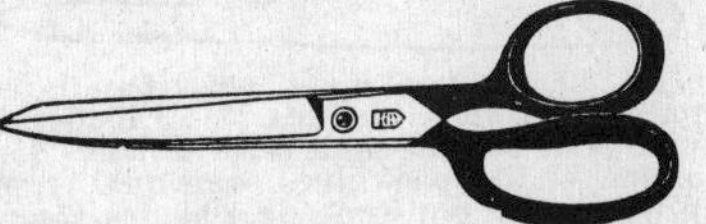

No. 468. Heinisch dressmakers' scissors, 6-inch, 45c; 7-inch, 55c; 8-inch, 65c; 9-inch, 75c.
No. 469. We also handle the well-known Bailey shears, which have been awarded the medal at the Paris Exposition, in competition with the world. They are forged from the best English steel and have nickel-plated handles, 6-inch, 40c; 7-inch, 50c; 8-inch, 60c; 9-inch, 70c; 10-inch, 80c.
No. 470. Dressmakers' scissors, silver-plated, K. & B. make, stamped Rogers, 6-inch, and 7-inch, 25c; 8-inch, 35c; 9-inch, 45c.

No. 471. Ladies' scissors, K. & B. make, solid steel, highly finished and tempered, 5-inch, 55c; 6-inch, 65c; 7-inch, 75c.

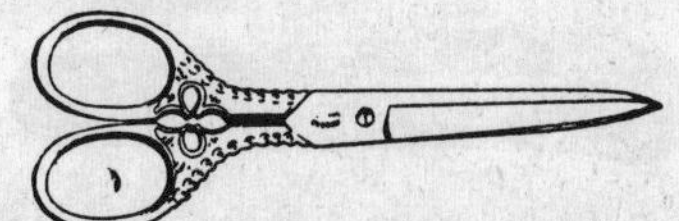

No. 472. Ladies' scissors, fancy handles, 5 and 6-inch, 25c; 6½-inch, 35c.
No. 473. Ladies' fancy work or lace scissors, solid steel, with fine points, 3-inch, 40c; 4-inch, 45c.

No. 447. Ladies' fancy work or lace scissors, solid steel, in swan shape design, fine points, 3-inch, 45c; 4-inch, 50c.
No. 475. Ladies' fancy work or lace scissors, with fine points, 3-inch, 15c; 4-inch, 25c; fancy handle, 35c.

No. 476. Pocket scissors, silver plated, 4-inch 25c; 5-inch, 35c.

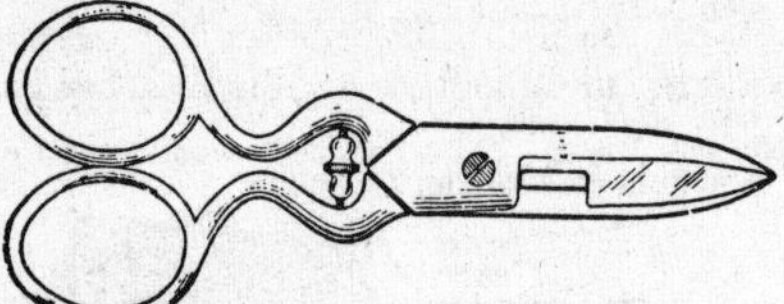

No. 477. Buttonhole scissors, silver plated, 10c; patent extension, 25c, 35c; solid steel, 50c.

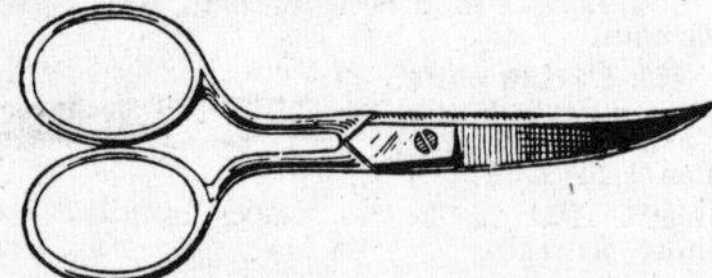

No. 478. Manicure scissors, solid steel, silver plated, 40c, 50c, 60c.

No. 479. Sheep shears, double spring, polished, Sheffield steel, finely tempered, 6½-inch blade, 75c.
No. 480. Sheep shears, single spring, Sheffield steel, finely tempered, 6½-inch blade, 50c.

Pocket Cutlery.

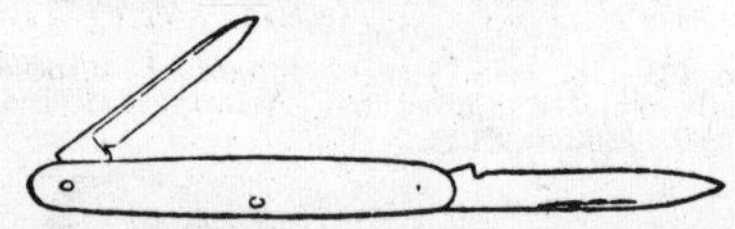

No. 481. Ladies' penknives, pearl handle, bolster or plain ends, 2 blades, 25c; 3 blades, 35c; with bone handle, same style, 2 blades, 15c.
No. 482. Ladies' penknives, same quality, plain pearl handle, plate on side, 2 blades, 25c.
No. 483. Ladies' penknives, 2 blades and nail file on back, neat design in pearl and horn handles, 50c.

No. 484. Gents' pocket knives, same as cut, with stag-horn and bone handles, strongly made, 40c; with bolster, 35c, 50c.
No. 485. Gents' pocket knives, with pearl handles, 2 and 3 blades, 50c, 75c.
No. 486. Gents' pocket knives, horn, 35c; pearl, 50c; with pearl or ivory handles, 3 blades, 75c, $1.00, 1.25.

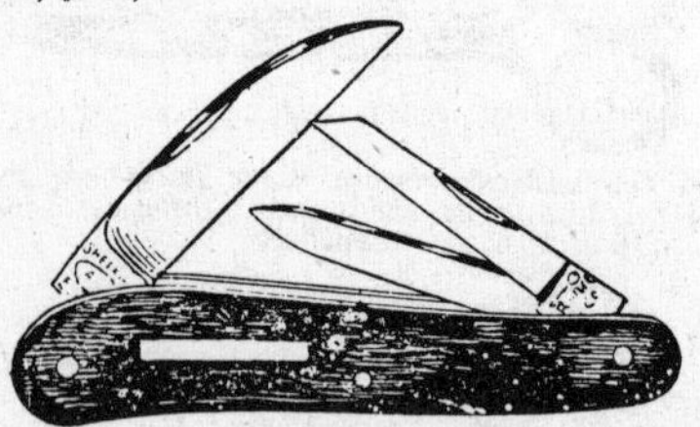

No. 487. Pocket knives, shaped horn handle and shaped blades, plate on side, well made, brass lined, 60c.

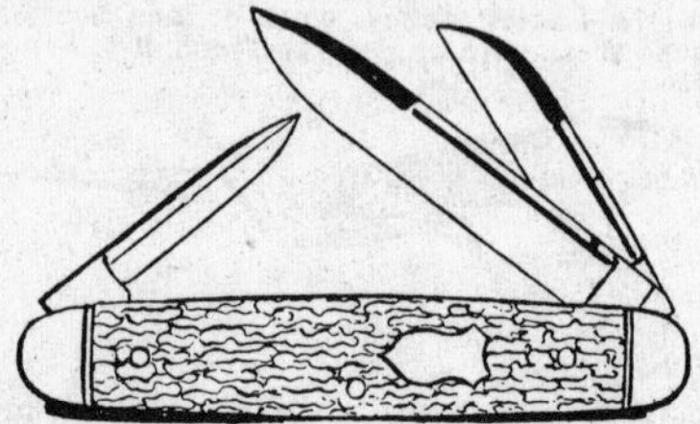

No. 488. This knife is specially made for cattlemen's use, as the steel is of extra quality and will therefore hold an edge longer than the ordinary knife, $1.00.

No. 489. Combination knife, best quality steel, with 2 blades, saw, corkscrew, hoof hook, gimlet, awl, screw-driver, tweezers, sliver hook, plate on side, stag horn handles, $1.50.
No. 490. Men's jack knives, with horn handles, 25c; with stag, bone and buff handles, 40c.
No. 491. Men's jack knives with stag, horn and bone handles, 1 blade, 15c, 30c.

No. 492. Men's jack knives, with bolster ends, made especially for farm use, 40c.

No. 493. Hunting knife, same as cut, 75c.
No. 494. Hunting knife or dirk, in leather case, $1.00, 1.25, 1.50.

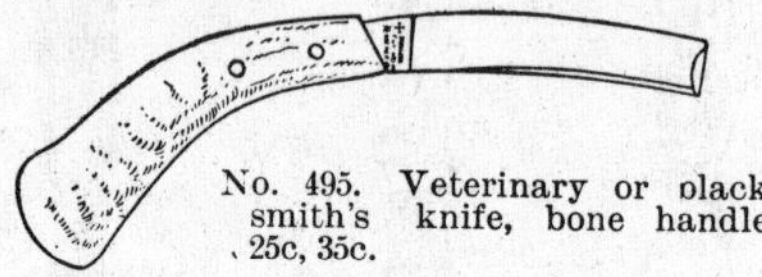

No. 495. Veterinary or blacksmith's knife, bone handle, 25c, 35c.

Razors.

No. 496. The razor we recommend for easy shaving is the K. B. extra, which is made of the finest razor steel and is specially tempered. It is full hollow ground in ½, ⅝ and ¾-inch blade, with black celluloid handle, which will not break, $1.00; ivory handle, $1.50.
No. 497. K. B. extra, made expressly for barbers' use, with black celluloid handle, $1.25; ivory handle, $1.75.
No. 498. Wade & Butcher's razors are so well known they need no further recommendation from us; straight ground blades, 35c; half hollow ground, 75c; full hollow ground, $1.00; ivory handle, $1.50; sizes of the above razors, ½, ⅝ and ¾-inch blades.
No. 499. George Butler & Co. have been manufacturing razors for over 100 years, and turn out one of the best Sheffield razors, ⅝ and ¾-inch blades, with black celluloid handle, $1.25; ivory handle, $2.00.

The "Gem" Safety Razor.

No. 500. The "Gem" safety razor, improved, is a great invention, which renders shaving an easy luxury and totally obviates all danger of cutting the face. The blades are made of the finest steel and are fully concave ground; blades easily removed, and when placed in the handle, which accompanies each razor, can be honed and sharpened as easily as an ordinary razor, $1.50; extra blades for "Gem," $1.00; stropping machines for "Gem," $1.00; strop for safety razor, 50c.

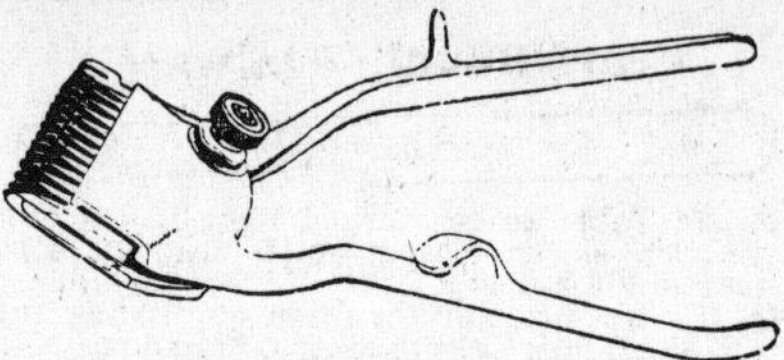

No. 501. Hair clippers, the finest quality made, corrugated back on bottom plate, with invisible springs and ball bearings, $2.15.
No. 502. Hair clippers, hidden spring, $1.75.
No. 503. Hair clippers, coil spring, special, $1.00.

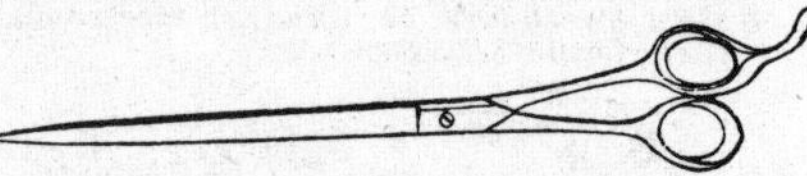

No. 504. Barbers' scissors, Bailey make, finest double shear steel, highly tempered, 8-inch, 75c.

Razor Strops.

All our swing strops are of the finest quality leather.

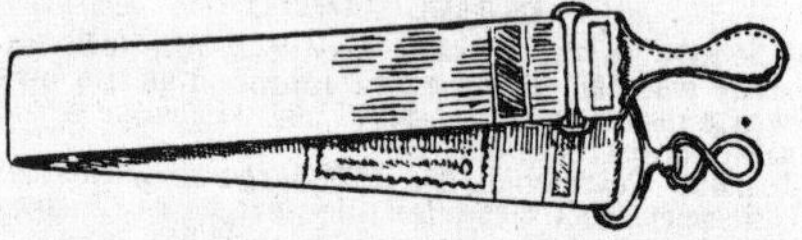

No. 505. Single swing strop, 20 inches long, 20c.
No. 506. Double swing strop, with canvas back and metal handle, 35c.
No. 507. Single, specially prepared leather swing strop, 25c.
No. 508. Double swing strop, specially prepared leather top, canvas back, 50c.

No. 509. Four-sided strop, 25c.
No. 510. Four-sided strop, solid leather, screw adjustment, 50c.
No. 511. Four-sided strop, cushioned, 50c.
No. 512. The celebrated Imperial cushion strop, flat, two sides, 75c.

Salt and Pepper Shakers and Napkin Rings.

No. 513.

No. 514.

No. 513. Salt and pepper shakers, silver plated, nicely chased, 30c pair.
No. 514. Napkin ring, silver plated, nicely chased, 15c each.
No. 515. Wider size, 25c each.
No. 516. Narrower size, 10c each.

Gong Bells.

No. 517. Gong bells, nickel bell, metal base, 35c each.
No. 518. Large double gong, 50c, 75c each.
No. 519. Call table bell, single gong, 35c each.
No. 520. Call bell, touch, 25c each.
No. 521. Small bell, 15c.

Optical Goods.

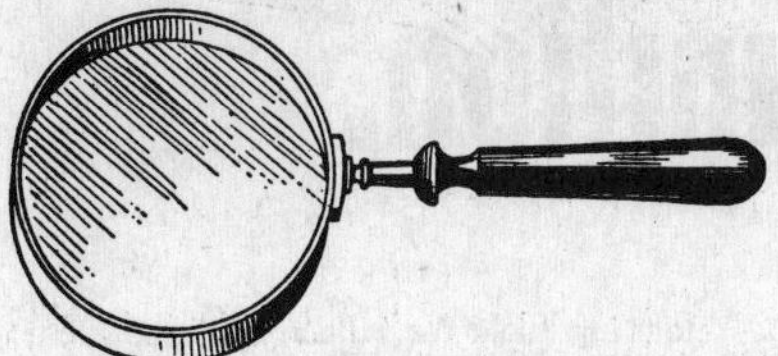

No. 522. Reading glasses, nickel-plated band, with black ebony handles, 2¼-inch, 25c; 2½-inch, 35c; 3-inch, 60c; 3¼-inch, 75c; 3½-inch, 85c; 4-inch, $1.00; 5-inch, $1.25.

No. 523. Botany glasses, nickel-plated case, 1 lens, 15c; 2 lenses, 25c; 3 lenses, 35c; 2 lenses, larger size, 40c; 3 lenses, larger size, 60c.

No. 524. Compasses, gun-metal finished case, open face, 15c, 25c, 35c.

No. 525. Nickel finish or polished brass case, open face, 20c, 25c, 35c, 50c.

No. 526. Nickel finish, hunting case, 35c, 50c, 75c, $1.00; same case, with jewel-set needle, $2.25.

No. 527. Telescopes, 10, 14, 16 and 21-line glasses, in sewn morocco and japanned, 2 to 4 draw, with shade, in leather sling case, $4.75, 5.50, 6.25, 11.00; also 15, 17, 19-line glass, in sewn morocco, with 3 polished brass draws, in case, $3.75, 6.00, 7.75.

No. 528. Marine and field glasses, 19, 21 and 24-line, 12-lens glasses, with flat top, large eye, sewn morocco, with shades, in solid leather sling case, $9.00, 11.00, 13.00.

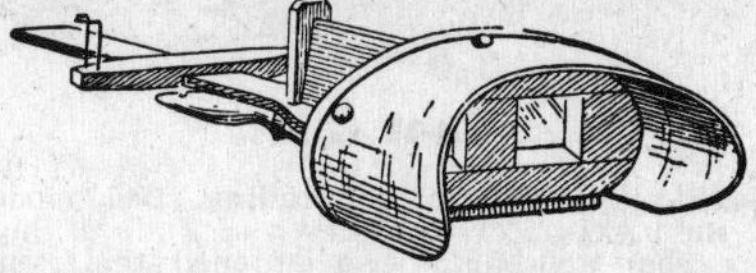

No. 529. Stereoscopes, polished wood, 25c and 50c; better quality, 85c; views, 4c each.

PHONOGRAPHS AND GRAPHOPHONES.

Gem Phonograph.

This machine includes all the latest improvements of a talking machine. It has a handsome oak-finished carrying case and clockwork motor to run two records with one winding. It includes reproducer, recorder, oil can, brush, 10-inch horn, for $10.00; the Standard phonograph, same make, in larger size, with shaving knife attached and 14-inch brass horn, $20.00.

Columbia Graphophone.

TYPE AT.

This make of machine is of medium size and weight, made so as to last a lifetime. It has adjustable case-hardened steel-bushed bearings, and a good machine for home entertainment, easy to operate, price, including recorder, reproducer, speaking-tube, 14-inch aluminum horn and ornamental hand cabinet, $25.00. Records to fit above machines, 50c each or $5.00 per doz. See list.

The "Columbia Grand" (type AC) graphophones, a machine taking the large cylinder, is famous as giving the most natural reproduction of the voice and instrument yet introduced. It runs about 4 records per winding and is fitted with recorder, reproducer, shaving-knife and recording horn, weight of machine 29 lbs. Price reduced to $50.00. Records to fit this machine $1.50 each or $15.00 doz.

We also handle other Grand types at $75.00, $100.00 and $150.00 in both phonographs and graphophones.

For complete outfits for any of above machines write for small catalogue, but always state whether it is a phonograph or graphophone you desire.

Supplies.

Horns.

We recommend hammered brass horns, with spun bells, as they give best production when used with talking machines, 14-inch, 65c; 18-inch, $1.50; 24-inch, $2.25; 30-inch, $3.50; 36-inch, $5.00; 42-inch, $8.00; 48-inch, $10.00; 56-inch, $12.00.

Japanned horns, 10-inch, 20c; 14-inch, 30c; 26-inch, 75c.

Stands and Cranes.

Excelsior combination folding horn stand, can be folded into box 24 inches long and 2½ x 2½ inches square, easy to carry, also to put up and take down, $1.50.

Extension horn crane, can be used on standard phonograph, for horns from 18 to 30 inches, $1.50.

Crane to support 18-inch brass horn for Gem phonograph or type AT Columbia graphophone, 50c.

Carrying Cases.

Canvas-covered box, with pegs for 12 small cylinders, 50c; for 24 small cylinders, $1.00.

Glass for reproducers, 25c, put in free of charge.

Sapphire points for reproducers or recorders, $2.00.

RECORDS.

We reserve the right to substitute where the customer does not give second choice.

It is always best to give two lists.

Following are some of the popular selections, write for latest and complete list. 50c each, or $5.00 per doz. Blank records, $2.50 doz.

Band Records.

1. Selections from "Bohemian Girl."
2. Grand March, from "Tannhauser."
3. Anvil Chorus, from "Il Trovatore."
4. Nearer, My God, to Thee.
5. Selections from "Robin Hood."
6. Bridal March, from "Lohengrin."
7. Georgia Camp Meeting.
8. Jolly Coppersmith (descriptive).
9. El Capitan March.
10. The Bride Elect March.

Orchestra Selections.

11. Selections from "The Charlatan."
12. Return of the Troops, March.
13. Under the Double Eagle, March.
14. March, from "A Runaway Girl."
15. Smoky Mokes, March.
16. At the Circus (descriptive).
17. Down on the Suwanee River (descriptive).
18. Medley, Overture (descriptive with songs).
19. Down on the Old Plantation.

Solos.

20. The Palms.
21. Nearer, My God, to Thee.
22. Soldiers of the Queen.
23. Holy City.
24. Absent Minded Beggar.
25. The Blue and the Grey.
26. And the Parrot Said (comic).
27. A Picture no Artist can Paint.
28. My Wild Irish Rose.
29. My Department Store Girl.
30. A Bird in a Gilded Cage.
31. Little Black Me.
32. Handicap March Song.
33. I Want To Go To-morrow (comic).
34. When Johnnie comes Marching Home.
35. Killarney.
36. Just Because You Made Those Goo-Goo Eyes.

Vocal Trios and Quartettes.

37. Vesper Service.
38. Medley of College Songs.
39. My Lady Lu.

Humorous Talks and Recitations.

40. Casey and the Dude in the Street Car.
41. Casey at the Telephone.
42. Hiram Wilkin's Visit to New York City.
43. The Lightning Rod Agent.
44. Pumpkin Centre Railroad.
45. In a Departmental Store.
46. Uncle Josh Comments on Signs in New York.
47. Uncle Josh on the Bicycle.

Speeches and Orations.

48. The 23rd Psalm and Lord's Prayer.
49. Talmage on Infidelity.

Whistling and Laughing Songs.

50. The Laughing Coon.
51. Turkey in the Straw.

Guns, Rifles, Ammunition.

Shot Guns.

34. Single-barrel, breech-loading, 1901 model, shell extractor, take-down of 2 pieces, high carbon steel barrel, case-hardened steel frame, dull finish, black walnut pistol-grip stock, and hard rubber butt-plate, guards and top lever blued, in 12 and 16 gauge, weight 7 lbs, $7.75.

35. Double-barrel, breech-loading, fine laminated pattern steel barrels, semi-machine made, bar action, rebounding locks, solid plungers, patent fore-end, 8 lbs, 12 and 16 gauge, $10.00; 10 gauge, $11.00.

36. Double-barrel, breech-loading, laminated steel barrels, bar rebounding locks, engraved, polished pistol-grip stock, extension matted rib, solid plungers, rolled shoulders, patent fore-end, circular hammers, left barrel medium choked, 8 lbs, 12 and 16 gauge, $13.50; 10 gauge, $14.00.

37. Same style as No. 36, with Damascus pattern barrels, Greener bolt and Deeley & Edge patent fore-end, 12 and 16 gauge, 30-inch barrels, $15.75; 10 gauge, 32-inch barrels, $16.50.

38. Fine laminated steel barrels, bar rebounding engraved locks, extension matted rib, Greener triple bolt, Deeley & Edge patent fore-end, circular hammers, polished walnut pistol-grip stock, rubber butt and heel plate, left barrel choke bore, 8¼ lbs, 12 gauge, 30-inch barrels, $19.50; 10 gauge, 32-inch barrels, $20.00.

39. Safety hammerless, fine laminated steel barrels, bar rebounding locks, polished walnut pistol-grip stock, extension matted rib, double bolt, Deeley & Edge patent fore-end, rubber heel plate, left barrel choke, 12 gauge, 30-inch barrels, $27.00; 10 gauge, 32-inch barrels, $28.00.

Rifles.

40. Warnant action, walnut pistol-grip stock, polished blued barrel, checkered grip and fore-end, 24-inch barrel, shoots 22 calibre short or long cartridge, $3.25.

40½. Same rifle, in 32 calibre, for short or long cartridge, $3.75.

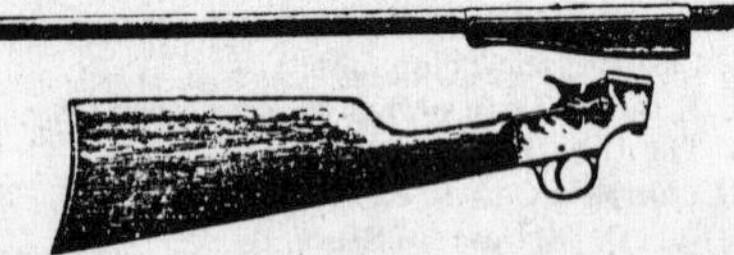

41. Stevens' crack shot rifle, 20-inch barrel, automatic safety lock, with kicking ejector. This rifle is made to shoot 22 calibre cartridges only, and is adapted for this size, weight about 4 lbs, $4.00.

42. Stevens' favorite rifle, is a strong well-made arm, being easy to take down, and will pack in box, length of barrel, 22 inches, half octagon, finely rifled, and is a safety, case-hardened frame, rubber butt plate, weight 5½ lbs. This rifle is made in 22, 25 and 32 calibre, $7.50; with extra Lyman patent sights, $10.00.

43. Take-down Remington action rifles, 22-inch octagon barrel, finely finished, steel butt plate, accurate and handy, highly recommended, in 22 or 32 calibre, $5.00.

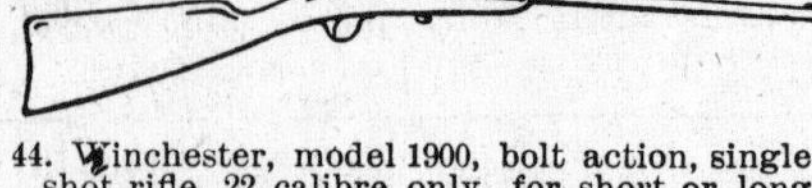

44. Winchester, model 1900, bolt action, single shot rifle, 22 calibre only, for short or long rim fire cartridges. It is neat, well made, and a take-down round barrel, 18 inches long, 2¾ lbs, $5.75.

Winchester Repeating Rifles.

45. Model 1894, 38/55, 26-inch barrels, weight 7¼ lbs., holds 10 shots, round barrel, $16.50, octagon barrel, $18.00.

46. Model 1894, 30/30 smokeless, 26-inch barrels, weight 8 lbs., holds 10 shots, round and octagon barrels, $22.00.

47. Model 1892, 44-calibre, using the 44-Winchester solid head short cartridge, round barrels, holding 15 shots, $16.50; octagon barrels, $18.00; cartridges for this rifle, $2.00 per 100.

Revolvers.

48. Royal rim fire, single action, 7 shots, $1.75.
49. American bulldog double action, rim fire, 7 shots, $2.75.
50. American bulldog double action, centre fire 32 or 38-calibre, takes S. & W. cartridge, $3.00.

Iver Johnson double-action automatic safety hammer revolver, self-cocking, 5-shot, 3-inch barrel, finely nickel plated or blued, everyone guaranteed, centre fire, using S. & W. cartridges. We highly recommend this revolver for accurate and handy shooting.

51. 32-calibre, safety hammer, nickel-plated, $5.90.
52. 32-calibre, safety hammer, blued, $6.60.
53. 32-calibre, safety, hammerless, nickel-plated, $7.15.
54. 32-calibre, safety, hammerless, blued, $7.75.
55. 38-calibre, safety hammer, nickel-plated, $6.15.
56. 38-calibre, safety hammer, blued, $6.85.
57. 38-calibre, safety, hammerless, nickel-plated, $7.35.
58. 38-calibre, safety, hammerless, blued, $7.75.
59. 38-calibre, safety hammer, 6-inch blued barrel, $8.35.
60. 38-calibre, safety, hammerless, 6-inch blued barrel, $9.75.

All Iver Johnson revolvers are as above cut.

Eureka Reloading Tools, 4 pieces.

61. Includes shell extractor, loader, capper and measure, 30c set.

62. Set includes bench closer, recapper, extractor, powder measure, loader including expelling pin and nickel tube, 3-piece cleaning rod with wire scratch brush, swab and wiper, $1.15 per set.

63. Reloading tools for rifle and sporting cartridges, complete set, with bullet mould for 32, S. & W.; 32, W.C.F.; 38, S. & W.; 38, W. C. F.; 44, W.C.F., price, $2.50.

64. Complete set for sporting cartridges, 30, 32/40, 38/55, 38/56, 38/72, 40/60, 40/65, 40/82, 45/60, 45/75, 45/90, Winchester, $3.00 per set; 45/70, U. S. Government, $3.00 per set.

65. Gun grease, 15c tube.

Loaded New Club Shells.

12-gauge, loaded, guaranteed waterproof paper shells, loaded with 3¼ drs. black powder and 1⅛-oz chilled shot, all sizes from BB to No. 10, price, $2.15 per 100.

In 16-gauge, loaded with 3 drs. powder and 1-oz chilled shot, all sizes from 2 to 10, $2.10 per 100.

In 10-gauge, all sizes from BB to No. 8 shot, price, $2.25 per 100.

All our shells are sold 25 in a box only.

Eley's Smokeless Loaded Shells.

In 12-gauge only, any size, 2 to 8, $2.50 per 100.
Empty brass shells, $4.75 per 100.

Empty paper shells in Dominion make, 10 and 12-gauge, 85c per 100.

Empty paper shells in U.M.C. make, for nitro or black powder, in 10, 12 and 16-gauge, $1.00 per 100.

All above shells take No. 2 primers.
Dominion primers, any size, $1.70 per 1000.
U.M.C. primers, any size, $2.00 per 1000.
These are put up in boxes of 250 each.

Rim Fire Cartridges.

BB, Dominion caps, 15c; U.M.C., 22c, 100 in box.

50 in box:
22 short, Dominion, 30c; U.M.C., 35c.
22 long, Dominion, 36c; U.M.C., 42c.
22 shot, Dominion, 70c.
32 shot, Dominion, $1.35.
32 short, Dominion, 60c; U.M.C., 70c.
32 long, Dominion, 70c; U.M.C., 80c.
38 short, Dominion, 95c; U.M.C., $1.10.
38 long, Dominion, $1.10; U.M.C., $1.25.

Centre Fire Cartridges.

32 short, Dominion, $1.00; U.M.C., $1.15 per 100.
32 long, Dominion, $1.10; U.M.C., $1.25.
32 Winchester, solid head, U.M.C., $1.65.
38 short, Dominion, $1.20; U.M.C., $1.40.
38 long, Dominion, $1.30; U.M.C., $1.50.

38 Winchester, solid head, Dominion, $1.40; U.M.C., $2.00.
44 Winchester, Dominion, $1.75; U.M.C., $2.00.
44 bulldog, U.M.C., $1.50.
44 Colt's, U.M.C., $2.10.

All the above cartridges, price by the 100, 50 in box.

Sporting cartridges, 20 in box, 30/30, smokeless, $4.75 per 100.

Winchester, 32/40, $3.60 per 100; all other sizes, $4.50 per 100.

Thin card gun wads, 10-gauge, 25c per 1000; 12 and 16-gauge, 20c per 1000.

Ely's thick felt gun wads, in 10, 12 and 16-gauge, 75c lb., in ½-lb. boxes.

Bibles, Hymn and Prayer Books.

Sizes and Names of Type.

Pearl type is this size.
Ruby type is this size.
Nonpareil type is this size.
Emerald type is this size.
Minion type is this size.
Brevier type is this size.
Bourgeois type is this size.
Long Primer type is this size.
Small Pica type is this size.
Pica type is this size.

Sizes of Books.

16mo is—7 inches x 5 inches.
24mo is—4 " x 5½ "
32mo is—4¾ " x 2¾ "
8vo is—6¾ " x 6 "

Bibles (Oxford Edition).

Pearl, 24mo, cloth, gilt, maps, 25c.

Morocco yapped binding:
- Pearl, 32mo, leather, gilt, maps, 50c.
- Diamond, 32mo, pocket size, 75c.
- Ruby, 16mo, reference maps, 75c.
- Diamond, 32mo, kid lined, $1.00.
- Ruby, 24mo, kid lined, refs., $1.00.
- Minion, 16mo, teachers', $1.00.
- Ditto, kid lined, $1.25.
- Long primer, 16mo, $1.50.
- Emerald, 16mo, teachers', $1.50.
- Emerald, 16mo, kid lined, refs., $1.50.
- Ruby, ditto, teachers', $1.75.
- Emerald, 16mo, India paper, $1.75.
- Emerald, 16mo, kid lined, teachers', $2.00.
- Minion, 8vo, kid lined, concordance, $3.00.
- Long primer, 8vo, silk sewn, teachers', $3.75.
- Minion, 8vo, kid lined, teachers', $4.00.

Revised Bibles (Reference).

Pearl, 16mo, cloth, red edges, 35c.
Bourgeois, 8vo, cloth, red edges, $1.25.
Bourgeois, 8vo, morocco, gilt, $1.50.
Bourgeois, 8vo, " yapped, $1.75.

Bagster's (Teacher's) Bibles.

Morocco yapped.

Minion, 8vo, $1.00.
Long primer, 8vo, linen lined, $1.25.
Minion, kid lined, silk sewn, $2.25.

Family Bibles.

Covers with padded sides and round corners, gold edges, marriage certificates, family records, illustrations and colored maps.

Grained calf binding, with 48 illustrations, concordance, $3.25.
French morocco, pronouncing dictionary of Scripture names, $3.75.
French morocco, gold back and side titles, $4.25.
French morocco, treatises on Bible subjects, etc, $5.00.
French morocco, and new version New Testament, Smith's Bible dictionary, $6.00.

Pulpit Bibles.

French morocco, raised panel, antique, gilt edges, extra large type, 13½ x 11 inches, $8.25.

Prayer Books.

20c, 25c, 35c, 40c, 50c, 60c, 75c, 85c, $1.00, 1.35.

Hymn Books, A. and M.

35c, 50c, 60c.
Large type, cloth, 70c.
Large type, leather, $1.25, 1.40.

Hymns Ancient and Modern, with Music.

Cloth, 65c; leather, $1.00, 1.25.
Large type, cloth, $1.25; leather, $1.85.

Catholic Prayer Books.

Cloth, 15c, 35c; leather, 50c, 65c, 75c, $1.00, 1.25.

Testaments.

Small Size.

Cloth, 10c, 15c.
Leather, 25c, 35c, 50c, 65c, $1.00.
Marked Testaments, 10c, 20c, 45c, 50c.

Presbyterian Book of Praise.

(Words only.)

Black cloth, red edges, 10c.
Paste grain, limp, gilt edges, 35c.
French turkey grain, padded, 60c.
Paste grain, padded, gilt line, 75c.
Arabian morocco, yapped, leather-lined, gilt edges, $1.00.
Alaska seal, limp, silk-sewn, $1.50.
Levant morocco, yapped, $2.00.

Long Primer 24mo.

Larger size, 6 x 3¾ x ¾ inches.

Black cloth, red edges, 30c.
Paste grain, limp, gilt edges, 75c.
Rutland, limp, red and gilt edges, $1.00.
French seal, yapp, round corners, red under gilt edges, $1.25.
Rutland morocco, limp, $1.50.
Alaska, yapp, silk sewn, $2.50.
Alaska seal, yapp, India paper, $3.00.
Levant morocco, yapp, India paper, $4.00.

The Large Type Edition.

Pica, 8vo. On ordinary paper.
Size, 7½ x 4¾ x 1 inch.

Black cloth boards, red edges, 60c.
Paste grain, boards, gilt edges, $1.25.
Seal, yapp, red and gilt edges, $2.25.

Presbyterian Book of Praise, with Tunes.

Emerald type.

Black cloth, boards, red edges, 60c.
Superior cloth, leather back, 90c.
Paste grain, limp, gilt edges, $1.25.
Seal, yapp, round corners, linen-lined, gilt edges, $2.25.
Alaska seal, limp, leather lined, $4.00.

Large Type Edition.

Long Primer, 8vo.
Size, 9 x 6 x 1 inch.

Black cloth, boards, red edges, 90c.
Cloth, leather back, $1.25.
Alaska seal, limp, leather lined, silk sewn, India paper, $5.00.

Bibles and Presbyterian Hymn Books Combined.

Size, 5⅝ x 3½ x 1 inch, pearl type.
Rutland, yapp, r/c, red under gilt edges, 70c.
Paste grain, yapp, padded, 90c.
Size, 5¼ x 3¾ x 1 inch, Ruby type.
French Rutland, yapp, r.c, 80c.
Size, 6 x 4 x 1¼ inches, Ruby type.
French Rutland, yapp, round corners, $1.00.
Seal, yapp, red under gilt edges, $1.50.

On Oxford India Paper.

Size, 5¾ x 4 x ¾ inch.

Aleutian seal, yapp, gilt edges, $1.75.
Aleutian seal, yapp, $2.25.
Alaska seal, yapp, silk sewn, $3.00.
Emerald, morocco, yapped, ref., $3.00.
Emerald, morocco, yapped, ref., India paper, $3.75.
Diamond, morocco, yapped, kid-lined, size, 5 x 3 in, $1.75.
Diamond, morocco, yapped, silk sewn, size, 5 x 3 in, $2.50.

Methodist Hymn Books.

Size, 6 x 4½ x ½ inch, Pearl type.

Cloth, sprinkled edges, 25c.
Roan, " " 40c.
French morocco, gilt edges, limp, 65c.
French morocco, limp, flaps, 75c.
Persian morocco, limp, r.g. edges, leather lined, $1.35.

Size, 7⅜ x 5¼ x ⅝ inch, Brevier type.

Cloth, sprinkled edges, 55c.
French morocco, limp, gilt edges, $1.10.

Size, 6½ x 4½ x 1½ inches, Small Pica.

Cloth, sprinkled edges, 75c.
French morocco, yapped, $1.35.
Persian morocco, kid lined, round corners, red under gold, $1.85.

India Paper Edition.

Old People's Size—Pica type.
Size, 7¾ x 5½.

Egyptian seal, yapped, round corners, red under gold, leather lined, $2.75.

Methodist Hymn and Tune Book.

Size 7½ x 5¾ inches.

Cloth, plain edges, 90c.
Roan, sprinkled edges, $1.25.
Morocco, yapped, gold edges, $1.85.
Morocco, yapped, r.g, edges, $2.75.
Egyptian seal, yapped, India paper, $2.75.

Methodist Hymn Books and Bibles, Combined.

Reference bible, ruby type; hymns, 32mo, pearl type—
No. 01. French morocco, flaps, $1.35.
No. 02½. Persian morocco, flaps, gilt edges, $2.50.
Reference Bible, nonpareil type, India paper; hymns, brevier type, size 7 x 5 x ½ inch; French morocco, limp, yapped edges, $3.50.

Sacred Songs and Solos

750 pieces, Sankey's, music and words—
HH 1. Cloth limp, 65c.
HH 2. Board cover, music, 85c.
FF 1. Cloth limp, large type, $1.00.
FF 2. Cloth boards, large type, $1.15.
FF 3. Bevelled boards, gilt $1.35.
AA2. Words only, 90c per doz.
BB 1. " " 12½c each.
EE1. " " large type, 60c each.

888 pieces by Ira D. Sankey.

AN1. Words only, 10c each.
HN1. Cloth, limp, music, $1.00.
FN1. Cloth, limp, music, $1.25.
FN2. Board cover, music, $1.40.

New Songs and Solos.

Price per single copy—
Canadian Hymnal, words only, 12c.
Canadian Hymnal, revised and enlarged, with music, 50c.
Finest of the Wheat, Nos. 1 and 2, 35c each; 1 and 2 combined, 55c.
Triumphant Songs (board covers), Nos. 1, 2, 3, 4, 5, 35c each; Nos. 1 and 2 combined, 60c.
Sacred Songs, No. 1, 35c; No. 2, 30c.
Songs of Salvation, 25c.
Pentecostal Praises, by W. J. Kirkpatrick and H. L. Gilmour, 35c.
Sifted Wheat, by Gabriel, 35c.
The Seed Sower, by A. F. Myers, 35c.
Songs for Young People, by E. O. Excell, 25c.

Sunday School Lessons.

Notes on the International S. S. Lessons. By Peloubet, $1.00.
Hulburt's Notes on S.S. Lessons, $1.00.
The Gist of the Lessons. A concise exposition of the International Sunday School Lessons for 1901, 25c.
Cruden's Complete Concordance, cloth cover, 75c.

STANDARD SETS.

Charles Dickens (set of 15 vols.)—
Bound in cloth, $4.75.
Silk cloth, gilt titles, illustrated, $6.75.
" full gilt, " $8.25.
½-calf, gilt top and titles, $16.50.

Scott's Waverley Novels, 12 vols.—
Bound in cloth, $4.25.
Silk cloth, gilt titles, $6.25.
Silk cloth, gilt tops and decorations, illustrated edition, $8.25.
½-calf, gilt tops, illustrated edition, $15.00.

Thackeray's Novels, 10 vols.—
Bound in cloth, $2.50.
Silk cloth, illustrated edition, $5.25.

George Eliot's Works—
Bound in cloth, 6 vols., $1.50.
Silk cloth, gilt titles, 6 vols., $2.75.
Silk cloth, gilt tops and titles, 8 vols., $5.00.

Ruskin's Modern Painters, 5 vols, silk cloth, illustrated, $2.50.
J. M. Barrie, silk cloth edition, 7 vols, $2.25.
Conan Doyle, 6 vols, cloth, $1.00.
Macaulay's England, 5 vols., silk cloth, $2.50.
Gibbon's Rome, 5 vols., cloth, $2.50.
Green's England, 5 vols., 16mo, cloth, $1.00.
Green's England, 4 vols., silk cloth, $2.50.

Works of William Shakespeare.

Handy volume Shakespeare, bound in maroon cloth, boxed, 13 vols, $3.00.

Shakespeare's dramatic and poetical works, complete in 39 vols, handy vol. size, limp cloth binding, gilt top and frontispiece, $7.00.

Same edition, paste grain leather, gilt top, $11.50.

Temple edition of Shakespeare, containing notes, each play bound in separate volumes, complete in 40 vols, cloth cover, 30c vol, or $10.50 set; leather cover, 45c vol, or $16.50 set.

The Excelsior 2 Vol. Sets.

Cloth binding. Publisher's price, $1.50; our price, 75c per set.

The Wandering Jew. Eugene Sue.
Life of Christ. Farrar.
French Revolution. Carlyle.
History of Our Own Times. McCarthy.
Essays. Emerson.
Les Miserables. Hugo.

Write us for any published Bible or Hymn Book not listed here.

Uniform 5 Vol. Edition Sets.

Cloth binding. Publisher's price $3.00; our price, $1.50.

Macaulay's England.
Cooper's Sea Tales.
Cooper's Leather Stocking Tales.
Conan Doyle.
Marie Corelli.
Rosa Carey.
Hawthorne

Popular Sets.

Printed on good paper, durably bound in fine book cloth, titles stamped in gold, special price, 90c, postpaid—

Hall Caine, 5 vols.
Rosa Carey, 5 vols.
Cooper's Sea Tales, 5 vols.
Cooper's Leather Stocking Tales, 5 vols.
Marie Corelli, 5 vols.
Hawthorne, 5 vols.
Macaulay's History of England, 5 vols.
Macaulay's Essays and Poems, 3 vols.

POPULAR POETS.

40c ed. is bound in cloth, clear type.
75c is cloth, gilt, large " "
$1.00, padded leather, full gilt edges.
$1.50, " morocco, " "
$2.00, " Nubian, " "

	Cabinet Ed.			Albion Ed.	
	c.	c.	$	$	$
Browning, Mrs....	40	75	1.00	1.50	..
Burns	40	75	1.00	1.50	..
Byron	40	75	1.00	..	..
Campbell	..	..	1.00	..	..
Coleridge	40	..	1.00	..	..
Cowper	40	..	1.00	..	..
Goldsmith	40	..	..	..	..
Hemans, Mrs......	40	75	1.00	1.50	2.00
Keats	40	..	1.00	..	..
Longfellow........	40	75	1.00	1.50	2.00
Milton............	40	75	1.00	1.50	2.00
Moore............	40	75	1.00	1.50	2.00
Scott...	40	75	1.00	1.50	2.00
Shakespeare......	40	75	1.00	1.50	..
Shelley...........	40	75	1.00	1.50	..
Whittier..........	40	75	1.00	1.50	..
Wordsworth......	40	75	1.00	1.50	2.00

Limp Circuit Edition, full gilt edges, Levant grain leather, new designs on side and flap. Regular price, $2 50; our price, $2.00 per vol.

Jean Ingelow. Whittier.
Wordsworth. Scott.
Mrs. Browning. Robt. Browning.
Familiar Quotations.

Padded Morocco edition, full gilt edges with photos. Regular, $3.00; our price, $2.50.

Longfellow. Scott.
Shakespeare. Wordsworth.

Tree calf poets, illustrated edition, price $2.75 per vol.

Mrs. Browning. Wordsworth.
Shakespeare. Shelley.
Scott. Longfellow.

Tennyson's Poems.

Cloth, gilt top, $1.00.
Limp morocco leather edition, $1.25.
" " " round corners, good clear type, $1.50.
Full calf leather, with frontispiece, good clear type, $3.00.
Paste grain leather, complete edition. $2.25.
Padded paste grain leather, complete edition, $2.50.
Library edition, half morocco, complete edition, $2.50.
Tree calf leather, illustrated, complete edition, $3.50.

E. W. Wilcox's Poems.

Poems of Pleasure, cloth, 35c.
Poems of Passion, cloth, 35c.
Maurine, cloth, 35c.

Poems by Whitcombe Riley.

CLOTH.

Riley's Love Lyrics, $1.10.
Afterwhiles, $1.10.
A Child World, $1.10.
Armazindy, $1.10.
Rhymes of Childhood, $1.10.
Neighborly Poems, $1.10.
Green Fields and Running Brooks, $1.10.
Old Fashioned Roses, $1.50.

Robert Browning's Poetical Works.

Camberwell Edition, edited by C. Porter and H. A. Clarke, the only fully annotated, line-numbered edition, 12 vols, cloth, gilt top, boxed, $7.50.
Complete in 1 vol, maroon cloth, $2.50.
Poems, with illustrations by Byam Shaw, cloth cover, gilt top, $1.50.
R. Browning, cloth cover, 85c.

Shakespeare's Poems.

Cloth cover, good clear type, 45c.
Limp leather cover, clear type, $1.25.

Shakespeare's Poems in 6 Vols.

Bound in Russia leather, with case to match, good clear type on India paper, $9.00.

Scott's Poems in 5 Vols.

Bound in paste grain leather, case to match, good clear type, $3.75.
Scott, bound in cloth, case to match, $3.00.

RECENT PUBLICATIONS.

The Voice of the People. Glasgow. Paper, 60c; cloth $1 15
The Redemption of David Corson. Goss. Paper, 65c; cloth 1 10
The Master Christian. Corelli. Paper, 65c; cloth 1 10
Three Men on Wheels. Jerome. Paper, 65c; cloth 1 20
The Farringdons. Fowler. Paper, 65c; cloth.............. 1 25
To Have and To Hold. Mary Johnston. Paper, 65c; cloth 1 20
The Reign of Law. By James L. Allen. Paper, 65c; cloth. 1 10
Prisoners of Hope. By Mary Johnston. Paper, 65c; cloth. 1 20
Biography of a Grizzly. E. S. Thompson. Cloth 1 25
Joan of the Sword Hand. S. R. Crockett. Paper, 65c; cloth 1 10
A Treasury of Canadian Verse. By Theodore H. Rand. Cloth 1 15
Janice Meredith. Ford. Paper, 65c; cloth 1 20
Richard Carvel. Churchhill. Paper, 65c; cloth 1 10
Via Crucis. Crawford. Paper, 65c; cloth...................... 1 25
Sky Pilot. Ralph Connor. Cloth 0 90
Black Rock. " Cloth 0 90
The Habitant. By Drummond. Cloth, 90c; cloth, gilt top, ills. 2 00
David Harum. By E. N. Westcott. Paper, 65c; cloth...... 1 10
Trail of the Sand Hill Stag. By E. S. Thompson. Cloth...... 1 25
Wild Animals I Have Known. By E. S. Thompson. Cloth.. 1 75
Kit Kennedy. By S. R. Crockett. Paper, 65c: cloth...... 1 10
Quisante. By Anthony Hope. Paper, 65c; cloth 1 10
Tennyson: His Art and Relation to Modern Life. By Stopford A. Brooke. Silk cloth 1 40
In the Palace of the King. Crawford. Paper, 65c; cloth 1 10
Tommy and Grizel. By J. M. Barrie. Paper, 65c; cloth.... 1 10
The Hosts of the Lord. By F. A. Steel. Paper, 65c; cloth.. 1 10
Ian Hamilton's March. Winston Churchill. Paper, 65c; cloth 1 10
Dr. North and His Friends. Weir Mitchell. Paper, 65c; cloth 1 10
Eleanor. By Mrs. H. Ward. Paper, 65c; cloth 1 20
Eben Holden. By Bacheller. Paper, 65c; cloth 1 10
The Great Boer War. By Conan Doyle. Cloth......... 1 25
Winsome Womanhood. By Margaret E. Sangster 1 10
Mooswa. By W. A. Fraser. Illustrated by A. Heming. Cloth, gilt top 1 35
The Cardinal's Snuff-Box. By Henry Harland. Paper...... 0 65
A Woman Tenderfoot. By Grace G. Seton-Thompson. Cloth, illustrated............ 1 75
The Ascent of Man. Cloth.... 0 95
The Ideal Life. Cloth 1 00
The Life of Henry Drummond. By Geo. Adam Smith. Cloth, illustrated..................... 1 90
The New Evangelism. Cloth. 1 00

MISCELLANEOUS.

English Literature in the reign of Victoria. Morley $0 60
Victorian Literature: Sixty Years of Books and Bookmen. By Clement Shorter. Cloth 0 70
The Reader's Handbook of Allusions. Ref. Plots and Stories. By Dr. Brewer. Cloth, 1,500 pages 1 90
Life of John G. Paton. Cloth.......................... 0 45
Mackay of Uganda. Cloth.......................... 0 45
The Canadian Lawyer, a handy book for business men, farmers, mechanics, etc. 1 25
House-boat on Styx. Bangs 0 75
Pursuit of House-boat. Bangs 0 75
Cruden's Concordance. Cloth. 0 75
Scottish Clans. Cloth......... 0 75
The Butterfly Book. Holland. 48 colored plates............ .... 2 75
Bird Neighbors. 52 colored plates............................ 2 10
Game Birds and Birds of Prey. By Neltje Blanchon. Illus.. 2 10
The Nuttall Encyclopædia of Universal Information......... 0 75
Looking Forward. By J. R. Miller. Cloth 0 65
Friendship. By Black. Cloth. 0 65
John Ruskin, His Life and Teaching. Matthew 0 40
Dict. of Phrase and Fable. By Dr. Brewer. ½-leather bound 1 35

Popular Works of History.

A Popular History of Greece, from the Earliest Period to the Incorporation with the Roman Empire. By D. Rose. Cloth cover, illustrated 1 00
A Popular History of France, brought down to the First Years of the present Republic. By H. W. Dulcken, Ph.D. Cloth cover, illustrated 1 00
A Popular History of Rome, from the Foundation of the City, B.C. 753, to the Fall of the Western Empire, A.D. 476. By D. Rose. Cloth cover, illustrated 1 00
A Popular History of England, from the Earliest Period to the Diamond Jubilee of Queen Victoria in 1897. By H. W. Dulcken, Ph.D. Cloth cover, illustrated 1 00
History of Our Own Times from 1880 to Diamond Jubilee. By Justin McCarthy. Cloth. 1 50
General Lord Roberts; 41 Years in India. Complete in 1 vol; cloth.................. 2 35
Constitutional History of England. By Hallam. Cloth 1 10
A History of Canada. By Charles G. D. Roberts. Cloth 1 90
Canada (Story of Nation Series). Cloth 1 25
South Africa (Story of Nation Series). Cloth.................. 1 25

Our Historical Studies for Children. Cloth, 50c.

The Children's Study of Ireland. By R. B. O'Brien.
The Children's Study of Scotland. By Mrs. Oliphant.
The Children's Study of Germany. By K. E. Kroeker.
The Children's Study of Greece. By A. Zimmern.
The Children's Study of Rome. By Mary Ford.
The Children's Study of England. By F. E. Cooke.
The Children's Study of Canada. By J. N. McIlwraith.

Large Type Edition of Popular Works.

Price 65c each.

Les Miserables. By Victor Hugo.
The Mysteries of Paris. Eugene Sue.
Charles O'Malley. By Charles Lever.
Count of Monte Cristo. Dumas.
The Wandering Jew. Eugéne Sue.

The World Library.

Regular price, $1.25; our price, 85c.

Plutarch's Lives.
Whiston's Josephus.
Hume's Essays.
Adam Smith's Wealth of Nations.
Hallam's Europe.
Essays. Thomas de Quincey.
Locke's Human Understanding.
Emerson's Works.
Bartlett's Familiar Quotations.
Crabb's English Synonyms.
Millman's History of Jews.
The Conquest of Mexico. By Prescott.
The Conquest of Peru. By Prescott.
Gems of English Poetry.

Chandos Classics.

Silk cloth cover, gilt top. Publisher's price, 70c; our price, 40c.

Eliza Cook's Poems.
Burns' Poems.
Don Quixote.
Vision of Dante.
Johnston's Lives of the Poets.
Hallam's England.
Southey's Life of Wesley.
Pope's Iliad.
Pope's Odyssey.
Eastern Tales.
Pope's Poems.
The Koran.
Works of Horace.
Pepy's Diary.
Half Hours with best authors, complete in 4 vols.
Gems of National Poetry.
Life of Nelson. By Southey.
Gœthe's Faust.
The Spectator.
Dryden's Poems.
Lowell's "
Longfellow's Poems.
Scott's Poems.
Milton's "
Wordsworth's Poems.
Complete Angler.
Schiller's Poems.

Ian Maclaren's Works.

CLOTH.

Beside the Bonnie Brier Bush $0 90
The Days of Auld Lang Syne 0 90
The Mind of the Master....... 1 00
Kate Carnegie 1 00
The Cure of Souls............... 1 00
Companions of the Sorrowful Way. Cloth 0 70
Afterwards. Cloth........... 1 00

Sunday School and Institute Libraries are specially selected.

Books by N. Dwight Hillis.

Cloth Cover.

A Man's Value to Society, $1.00.
The Investment of Influence, $1.00.
Great Books as Life Teachers, cloth, $1.00.

The Blessed Life Series. By F. B. Meyer.

BOARDS, 25c each.

The Shepherd Psalm.
Christian Living.
Present Tenses of Blessed Life.
Future Tenses of Blessed Life.
Key Words of the Inner Life.
Calvary to Pentecost.

Works by Rev. Andrew Murray.

CLOTH.

With Christ	$0 40
Abide in Christ	0 40
Like Christ	0 40
Holy in Christ	0 40
The Spirit of Christ	0 40
The Master's Indwelling	0 40
Jesus Himself	0 25
Love Made Perfect	0 25

The Moody Library.

BOARDS, 25c each.

The Way to God and How to Find It.
Sowing and Reaping.
Pleasure and Profit in Bible Study.
Sovereign Grace.
Secret Power.

The Spirit-Filled Life Series.

CLOTH, 25c each.

The Spirit-Filled Life. MacNeil.
The Christian's Secret of a Happy Life. By H. W. Smith.
A Castaway. By Rev. F. B. Meyer.
In Christ. By Rev. A. J. Gordon.
Absolute Surrender. Murray.
The Overcoming Life. Moody.

Sabbath Library of Books

Paper Covers, 5c each. Postage Extra.

Chonita.
The Days of Mohammed.
A Devotee and a Darling.
Kohath Sloane. J. McNair Wright.
Out of the Triangle. M. E. Banford.
A Double Story. Geo. MacDonald.
Titus. F. M. Kingsley.
Ten Nights in a Bar Room. Arthur.
The Wrestler of Philippi.
A Star in Prison. A. M. Wilson.
Paula Clyde. K. W. Hamilton.
Intra Muros. Mrs. R. R. Springer.
The Young Ditch Rider.
Ruby. A. Lilie Riley.
In League with the Powerful. By E. D. Bigham.
Marti: a Story of the Cuban War.
Ti: a Story of San Francisco's Chinatown.
For the Sake of a Name. Grinnell.

Medical Books.

Gardner's Household, Medicine and Sick Room Guide. Cloth	$2 00
The Doctor at Home and Nurse's Guide Book. Geo. Black, M.B.	0 85
Physical Life of Woman. Napheys	0 80
Transmission of Life. Napheys	0 80
Tokology. Alice B. Stockham	2 25

Books on Etiquette.

Manners for Men. By Mrs. Humphrey. Board cover, 25c.
Manners for Women. 25c.
A Word to Women. 25c.
Etiquette. By Agnes H. Morton. Cloth, 40c.
Letter Writing. By Agnes H. Morton. Cloth, 40c.
Ideals for Girls. By Rev. H. W. Haweis, M.A. Cloth, 60c.
How to be Pretty Though Plain. Boards, 25c.

Cook Books.

Mrs. Beeton's Book of Household Management. Cloth	$1 75
Century Cook Book	1 90
Home Cook Book	0 50
Dr. Chase's New Receipt Book	0 50
Mrs. Rorer's Cook Book	1 45
The Galt Cook Book	1 00
The White House Cook Book	1 00
Mrs. Beeton's Cook Book, 320 pages, with 21 full-page plates	0 30

Elocution Books.

Not Exchanged.

Young Folk's Recitations, 15c.
Shoemaker's Best Selections, Nos. 1 to 26, 25c each.
Wilson's Recit. and Dialogues, 25c.
Dick's Comic Dialogues, 25c.
Choice Dialogues, 25c.
Young Folk's Dialogues, 25c.
McBride's Choice Dialogues, 25c.
Kavanaugh's New Speeches and Dialogues for Children, 25c.
Young Folks' Entertainments, 25c.
Humorous Dial. and Dramas, 25c.
Holiday Selections, 25c.
Temperance Selections, 25c.
Young People's Speaker, 15c.
Entertainments for Young People, 25c.
Good Humor, 25c.
Choice Dialect Reading and Recitations, 25c.
Classic Dialogues and Dramas, 25c.
School-day Dialogues, 25c.
Ideal Drills. By M. Morton, 25c.
Tableaux, Charades and Pantomimes, 25c.

Boys' and Girls' Library Books.

Alcott Series.

CLOTH.

Regular price, 70c; our price, 45c.

Little Men.
Little Women.
Under the Lilacs.
Jimmy's Cruise in the *Pinafore*.
Jack and Jill.
Eight Cousins.
Dred.
Silver Pitchers.
Rose in Bloom.
Old-fashioned Girl.
Lulu's Library.
Spinning-wheel Stories.
Shawl Straps.
Aunt Jo's Scrap Bag.
We and Our Neighbors.
Work and Beginning Again.
Jo's Boys, $1.15.

Pansy Books.

CLOTH.

Regular price, 70c; our price, 55c.

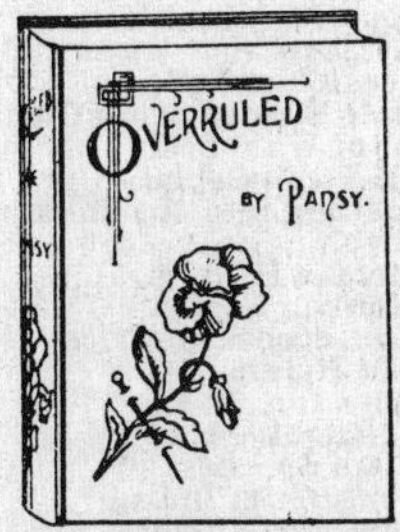

Judge Burnham's Daughters.
Aunt Hannah, Martha and John.
John Remington, Martyr.
Miss Dee Dunmore Bryant.
Stephen Mitchell's Journey.
Wanted.
Twenty Minutes Late.
What They Couldn't.
Making Fate.
Overruled.
As In a Mirror.
Yesterday Framed in To-Day.

The Star Series.

Regular price, 70c; our price, 40c.

CLOTH.

Drayton Hall. Alice Gray.
Golden Ladder. E. Wetherell.
What She Could. "
Wych Hazel. "
Gold of Chickaree. "
The Letter of Credit. "
The End of a Coil. "
Ben Hur. Lew Wallace.
A Daughter of Fife. A. E. Barr.
Between Two Loves. A. E. Barr.
Say and Seal. E. Wetherell.
Without and Within. W. Jay.
Diana. E. Wetherell.
My Desire. "
Nobody. "
A Great Indiscretion. By E. E. Green.
Northward Ho! By Gordon.

Annie S. Swan's Works.

CLOTH.

Briar and Palm	$0 75
Sheila	0 75
Maitland of Laureston	0 75
St. Vedas	0 75
Who Shall Serve	0 75
A Victory Won	0 85
A Bitter Debt	0 85
A Better Part	0 65
Lost Ideal	0 75
Guinea Stamp	0 75
Gates of Eden	0 75
Elizabeth Glen, M.B.	0 85
Ayres of Studleigh	0 60
Carlowrie	0 35
A Foolish Marriage	0 50
A Stormy Voyager	0 85
Home-spun	0 35
Mistaken and Marion Forsyth	0 35
Thomas Dryburgh's Dream	0 35
Robert Martin's Lesson	0 35
The Secret Panel	0 35
Wrongs Righted	0 35
Hazel and Sons	0 35
Twice Tried	0 35
Sundered Hearts	0 35
Shadowed Lives	0 35
Ursula Vivian	0 35
A Divided House	0 35
A Vexed Inheritance	0 35
Kinsfolk	0 85
Mrs. Keith Hamilton	0 85
The Ne'er-do-Weel	0 85
Wyndham's Daughter	0 85

The Chimes Series.

Stories for Girls. By Mrs. Marshall.

Illustrated. In new and attractive binding. Cloth, price, 45c.

Silver Chimes; Story for children.
Daphne's Decision.
Cassandra's Casket.
Poppies and Pansies.
Rex and Regina.
Dewdrops and Diamonds.
Heather and Harebell.
The Roses of Ringwood.
In the Purple.
Eastward Ho!

Agnes Giberne's Stories for Girls.

Illustrated. Handsomely bound in green and gold. Price, 45c.

Enid's Silver Bond.
St. Austin's Lodge.
The Dalrymples.
Number Three Winnifred Place.
Least Said, Soonest Mended.
Sweetbriar.
Aimee.
The Andersons.

Works by Ethel Turner.

Cloth, gilt. Price, 50c each.

"Miss Ethel Turner is Miss Alcott's true successor. The same healthy spirited tone is visible which boys and girls recognized and were grateful for in 'Little Women' and 'Little Men,' the same absence of primness, and the same love of adventure."—*The Bookman.*

The Camp at Wandinong. Illustrated by F. Ewan and others.
Miss Bobbie. Illustrated by Harold Copping.
The Little Larrikin. Illustrated by A. J. Johnson.
Seven Little Australians. Illustrated by A. J. Johnson.
The Family at Misrule (sequel to above). Illustrated by A. J. Johnson.

Books by the Author of "Probable Sons."

Teddy's Button.	Cloth	$0 45
Probable Sons.	Board cover	0 30
The Odd One.	Cloth	0 45
A Thoughtless Seven	"	0 45
On the Edge of the Moor.	"	0 85
Dwell Deep.	Board	0 65
Eric's Good News.	"	0 30
Bulbs and Blossoms	"	0 45
A Puzzling Pair.	Cloth	0 45
His Big Opportunity		0 65

Standard Books for Boys.

Handsome cloth binding, 8vo, fully illustrated.

Regular 75c, for 50c.

Dick Cheveley. By Kingston.
Heir of Kilfinnan. By Kingston.
Off to the Wilds. By Manville Fenn.
The Two Supercargoes. Kingston.
Under the Meteor Flag. By Harry Collingwood.
The Voyage of the Aurora. By Harry Collingwood.
The Three Deserters. By Perelaer.
A Thousand Miles in the Rob Roy Canoe. By John MacGregor.
Blacks and Bushrangers. By E. B. Kennedy.
Sir Ludar. By Talbot Baines Reed.
The Black Bar. Manville Fenn.
Cæsar Cascabel. By Jules Verne.
Tribulations of a Chinaman. Verne.
With Axe and Rifle.
Adrift in the Pacific.
Abandoned. Verne.
The Secret of the Island. Verne.
The Archipelago on Fire. Verne.
Snowshoes and Canoes.
The Marvellous Country.
Hans Brinker; or, the Silver Skates. By Mrs. Dodge.

The latest and purest books for boys and girls.

Boys' and Girls' Library Books.

Henty Books for Boys.

CLOTH, ILLUSTRATED.

Regular price, $1.75; our price, $1.00.

Both Sides of Border.
At Aboukir and Acre.
In Greek Waters.
Thro' Russian Snows.
On the Irrawaddy.
At Agincourt.
With Cochrane the Dauntless.
March on London.
With Frederick the Great.
Condemned as a Nihilist.
No Surrender. A Tale of the Rising in La Vendée.
Won by the Sword. A Tale of the Thirty Years' War.
A Roving Commission; or, Thro' the Black Insurrection of Hayti.
Out with Garibaldi.

Henty Books.

Regular price, $1.00; our price, 70c.

Bonnie Prince Charlie.
By England's Aid.
By Pike and Dyke.
In Freedom's Cause.
The Young Carthaginians.
The Dragon and the Raven
With Clive in India.
With Lee in Virginia.
Captain Bayley's Heir.
The Lion of the North.
Under Drake's Flag.
In the Reign of Terror.
True to the Old Flag.
With Wolfe in Canada.
By Right of Conquest.
St. George for England.
The Bravest of the Brave.
For Name and Fame.
The Cat of Bubastes.
For the Temple.
The Lion of St. Mark.
By Sheer Pluck.
A Final Reckoning.
Facing Death.
Maori and Settler.
One of the 28th.

Henty Books.

Publisher's price, 50c; our price, 25c.

CLOTH.

The Boy Knight.
In Times of Peril.
The Young Buglers.
The Cornet of Horse.
Jack Archer.
Friends Though Divided.
Young Franc-Tireurs.
Out on the Pampas.
Rangers and Regulators. By Capt. Mayne Reid.
Wood Rangers. Mayne Reid.

The Fairy Library.

Ornamental cloth, extra illustrated.

Price, 50 cents.

Golden Fairy Book (profusely illustrated.) By various Authors.
The Blue Fairy Book (profusely illustrated). By Andrew Lang.
The Red Fairy Book (profusely illustrated). By Andrew Lang.
The Green Fairy Book (profusely illustrated). By Andrew Lang.
The Yellow Fairy Book (profusely illustrated). By Andrew Lang.

Young Folks' Natural History, comprising descriptions of animal life, birds, reptiles, etc. By Chas. C. Abbott, M.D. Cloth cover, illustrated, 65c.
Natural History. By Miles. Cloth, illustrated. $1.00.

Young People's Library.

Publisher's price, 50c; our price, 30c

Robinson Crusoe. (70 illustrations.)
Alice's Adventures. (42 illustrations.)
Through the Looking Glass. (50 illustrations.)
The Story of Exploration and Adventure in Africa.
Pilgrim's Progress. (46 illustrations.)
Child's History of England. (80 illustrations.)
Æsop's Fables. (62 illustrations.)
Christopher Columbus. (70 illustrations.)
Swiss Family Robinson. (50 illustrations.)
Gulliver's Travels. (50 illustrations.)
Mother Goose's Rhymes and Stories.
Story of Frozen Seas. (70 illus.)
Wood's Natural History. (80 illus.)
Arabian Nights. (110 illustrations.)
Black Beauty. Anna Sewell.
Flower Fables. Louisa M. Alcott.
Aunt Martha's Corner Cupboard
Water Babies. Charles Kingsley.
Andersen's Fairy Tales. (80 illustrations.)
Child's Life of Christ. (49 illustrations.)
Child's Story of the Bible. (72 illustrations.)
Lives of the Presidents.

Birthday Books.

Birthday Text Books, cloth, 10c, 20c.
" " " Paste grain leather, 25c, 35c, 45c each; padded, 55c, $1.25.

Prizes for Young People.

Cloth Covers, illustrated editions, 19c each.

Wonderful Stories for Children. Hans Andersen.
Fairy Grandmother a London Waif.
The Children of Melby Hall. McKean.
Mark Westcroft Cordwainer. Potter.
A Humble Heroine. L. E. Tiddeman.
Baby John. Author of "Laddie."
The Green Casket. Mrs. Molesworth.
The Bewitched Lamp. "
Little Mary. L. T. Meade.
The Little Knight. Edith C. Kenyon.
Wilfrid Clifford. C. E. Kenyon.
Zoe. Author of "Laddie."
Uncle Sam's Money Box. Mrs. S. C. Hall.
Grandmamma's Pockets. Mrs. S. C. Hall.
Ernest's Golden Thread.
Their Happiest Xmas.

The Evans-Wilson Books.

Publisher's price, 35c; our price, 19c.

Infelice. St. Elmo.
Vashti. Macaria.
Inez. Beulah.
At the Mercy of Tiberius.

Ballantyne's Books for Boys.

Regular price, 35c; our price, 19c.

Away in the Wilderness.
Fast in the Ice.
Chasing the Sun.
Sunk at Sea.
Lost in the Forest.
Over the Rocky Mountains.
Saved by the Life Boat.
The Cannibal Islands.
Hunting the Lions.
Digging for Gold.
The Battle and the Breeze.

The Pioneers.
Wrecked but Not Ruined.

The Elsie Books.

19c each.

By Martha Finley—
Elsie Dinsmore.
Elsie's Holidays at Roselands.
Elsie's Girlhood.
Elsie's Womanhood.
Elsie's Motherhood.
Elsie's Children.
Elsie's Widowhood.
Grandmother Elsie.
Elsie's New Relations.
Elsie at Nantucket.
The Two Elsies.
Elsie's Kith and Kin.
Elsie's Friends at Woodburn.
Christmas with Grandma.
Elsie and the Raymonds.
Elsie Yachting.
Elsie's Vacation.
Elsie at Viamede.
Elsie at Ion.
Elsie at the World's Fair.
Elsie's Journey on Inland Waters.
Elsie at Home.

Pansy Books.

Regular price, 35c; our price, 19c

Four Girls at Chautauqua.
Little Fishers and Their Nets.
Three People.
Echoing and Re-echoing.
Christie's Christmas.
Divers Women.
Spun from Fact.
The Chautauqua Girls at Home.
The Pocket Measure.
Julia Ried.
Wise and Otherwise.
The King's Daughter.
Links in Rebecca's Life.
Interrupted.
An Endless Chain.
Ester Ried.
Ester Ried yet Speaking.
The Man of the House.
Ruth Erskine's Crosses.
Household Puzzles.
Mabel Wynn; or, Those Boys.
Modern Prophets.
The Randolphs.
Flower of the Family.
Pillar of Fire.
Throne of David.
Prince of the House of David.
Naomi.
Mrs. Solomon Smith Looking On.
From Different Standpoints.
A New Graft on the Family Tree.
Profiles.
Sidney Martin's Christmas.
Tip Lewis and His Lamp.
Eighty-seven.
Anna Lee.
Daisy.
Fair God.
Good Wives.
The Hall in the Grove.
John Ward.
Jessamine.
Sevenfold Trouble.
What Katy Did at School.
Queechy.
What Katy Did.
Mabel Vaughan.
Old Helmet.
Ben Hur.
Aunt Jane's Hero.
Basket of Flowers.
One Common-place Day.

E. P. Roe's Works.

Cloth, 19 cents.

An Original Belle.
An Unexpected Result.
Barriers Burned Away.
Driven Back to Eden.
A Day of Fate.
The Earth Trembled.
Found Yet Lost.
A Face Illumined.
From Jest to Earnest.
His Sombre Rivals.
He Fell in Love With His Wife.
Knight of the Nineteenth Century.
Miss Lou.
Near to Nature's Heart.
Opening a Chestnut Burr.
Taken Alive.
Without a Home.
What Can She Do.
A Young Girl's Wooing.

Every Boy's Library.

Regular price, 35c; our price, 19c.

English at the North Pole. Verne.
Five Weeks in a Balloon. "
Round the World in Eighty Days. "
Robinson Crusoe.
Lamb's Tales from Shakespeare.
Adventures in Africa.
The Original Robinson Crusoe.
Great Scholars.
The Ice Desert. Verne.
Mysterious Document. "
Round the Moon. "
Baron Munchausen.
Adventures in Arctic Regions.
True Royalty: Life of the Queen.
Field of Ice. Verne.
Life of Gladstone.
England's Hero: Life of General Gordon.
Nansen and the Frozen North
General Gordon.
Swiss Family Robinson.
Twenty Thousand Leagues Under the Sea.
England's Essayists.
The Sailor Hero.
The Tiger Slayer.
Pirates of the Prairie.
Great Novelists.
Prince Goldenblade.
Notable Women of our Own Time.
Vicar of Wakefield.
Uncle Tom's Cabin.
A Journey into the Interior of the Earth.
Masters in History.
Masterman Ready.
Mission Scenes in Africa.
Life of Nelson.
Doctor's Birthday.
John Bright.
Brilliant Speakers.
Adventures in India.
Among the Cannibals.
From the Earth to the Moon.
On the Track.
The Pirates of the Mississippi.
Adventures of 3 Englishmen and 3 Russians.

Little Stories for Children.

CLOTH.
Regular price, 20c; our price, 15c.
CLOTH.
Regular price, 15c; our price, 10c.
CLOTH.
Regular price, 10c; our price, 7c.

Special care taken in selecting lists of books on travel, history and biography.

Popular Books.

19c Books, attractively bound in cloth, stamped, gilt titles.
25c Books, bound in maroon cloth, gilt tops and titles.
35c Books, large size, 12mo., by exceptionally well known authors.
50c Books bound in silk cloth, gilt tops, illustrated frontispiece.

25c Vade Mecum Series, bound in decorated cloth, ivory finish, illustrated and boxed.

20c Sterling Series, bound in assorted colors of cloth, stamped—an attractive line of standard authors.

20c Pocket Library, marked (*), crimson cloth, gilt titles.

TITLES AND AUTHORS.	(16mo.)	Cts.	Cts.
Abbe Constantine	Ludovic Halevy	20	25
Adventures of a Brownie	Miss Mulock	20	25
Alice in Wonderland	Carroll	20	
Autobiography of Ben Franklin		..	25
*Autocrat of Breakfast Table	Holmes	20	..
Bacon's Essays		20	25
*Browning, E. B., Poems		20	..
Brooke's Addresses		..	25
Balzac's Shorter Stories			25
*Bab Ballads	W. H. Gilbert	20	..
Battle of Life	Dickens	..	25
Confessions of an Opium Eater		20	25
Cranford	Mrs. Gaskell	20	25
Crown of Wild Olives	Ruskin	20	25
Childe Harold	Byron	..	25
Christian Life	Oxenden	..	25
Christie's Old Organ	Walton	..	25
Changed Cross		..	25
Carleton's Farm Ballads		20	..
Discourses of Epictetus		20	25
Drummond's Addresses		20	25
Dream Life	Marvel	..	25
Dog of Flanders	Ouida	..	25
Ethics of the Dust	Ruskin	20	25
*Evangeline	Longfellow	20	25
Greek Heroes	Kingsley	..	25
Heroes and Hero Worship	Carlyle.	20	25
*Hood's Comic Poems		20	
*Hood's Serious Poems		20	..
House of Seven Gables	Hawthorne	20	..
Idle Thoughts of an Idle Fellow	Jerome	20	..
Imitation of Christ	Thomas à Kempis	20	25
Kept for Master's Use	Havergal	..	25
Luck of Roaring Camp	Bret Harte	20	..
Light of Asia	Arnold	..	25
Lays of Ancient Rome	Macaulay	..	25
Lucile	Owen Meredith	..	25
Lalla Rookh	Thomas Moore	25	20
*Lady of the Lake	Scott	20	25
Lamb's Tales from Shakespeare		20	25
*Longfellow's Dante Purgatorio		20	..
* “ “ Inferno		20	..
* “ “ Paradiso		20	
Lowell's Poems		..	25
My Point of View	Drummond	.	25
Marmion	Scott	..	25
Magic Nuts	Molesworth	..	25
Morning Thoughts	Havergal	..	25
Natural Law	Drummond	..	25
*Moore's Irish Melodies		20	..
*Paradise Lost	Milton	20	..
*Professor	O. W. Holmes	20	..
*Poet	“ “	20	..
Pleasures of Life	Lubbock	..	25
*Prince of House of David	Ingraham	..	25
Queen of the Air	Ruskin	20	25
Rip Van Winkle	Irving	..	25
Rab and His Friends	John Brown	20	25
Rasselas	Johnson	20	..
Reveries of a Bachelor	Ik Marvel	20	25
Representative Men	Emerson	20	25
Sartor Resartus	Carlyle	20	25
Sketch Book	Irving	20	25
Story of an African Farm	Schriener	20	..
Steps in Blessed Life	Meyer	..	25
School for Scandal	Sheridan		25
Through the Looking Glass	Carroll	20	25
Thoughts from Marcus Aurelius		..	25
Ten Nights in a Bar-Room	Arthur	20	..
Twice Told Tales	Hawthorne	20	25
Tanglewood Tales		..	25
Undine	Fouque	..	25
Uncle Tom's Cabin	H. B. Stowe	..	25
*Vicar of Wakefield	Goldsmith	20	25
Water Babies	Kingsley	20	25
*Wit and Humor		20	.
Wonder Book	Hawthorne	..	25
Window in Thrums	Barrie	20	25

TITLES AND AUTHORS.	(12mo.)	Cts.	Cts.	Cts.	Cts.
Adam Bede	Geo. Eliot	19	25	..	50
Ardath	Marie Corelli	19	..	..	..
Arabian Nights		19	..	..	..
Æsop's Fables		19	25	..	..
Andersen's Fairy Tales	Andersen	19	25	..	..
A Knight of the 19th Century	Roe	..	25	35	..
Alton Locke	Chas. Kingsley	..	25	..	..
Aunt Jane's Hero	E. Prentiss	..	25	..	..
Alice	Bulwer Lytton	..	25	..	..
Bleak House	Dickens	..	25		..
Barriers Burned Away	E. P. Roe	..	..	35	..
Benjamin Franklin	J. S. C. Abbott	..		35	..
Bernicia	Amelia Barr	..	..	35	..
Brandt and Red Jacket	Eggleston	..	..	35	
Byron's Poems		..	25	..	..
Burns' Poems		..	25	..	..
Beulah	Evans Wilson	..	25	..	..
Beyond Pardon	Bertha Clay	19	..	..	..
Barnaby Rudge	Dickens	..	..	..	50
California and Oregan Trail		..	25	..	50
Child's History of England	Dickens	19	25		50
Christopher	Amelia Barr	..	..	35	..
Captain Kidd	Jno. Abbott	..	..	35	..
Columbus	“ “	..	..	35	..
Cluny McPherson	Amelia Barr	..	..	35	..
Children of Abbey	M. Roche	..	25	..	..
Caxtons	Lord Lytton	..	25	..	..
Creasy's Battles	A. S. Creasy	..	25	..	..
Conquest of Peru	Prescott	..	25	..	..
Count of Monte Cristo	Dumas	19		..	..
Children of New Forest	Maryatt	..	25	..	..
Daisy	Wetherall	.	25	..	..
Deemster	Hall Caine	19	25	..	..
Don Quixote	Cervantes	.	25	..	..
David Copperfield	Dickens	..	25	..	..
Deerslayer	Cooper	19	..	..	..
Donovan	Edna Lyall	19	..	.	50
Dora Thorne	Bertha Clay	19	..	..	..
Duke's Secret	“ “	19	..	..	..
Data of Ethics	Spencer	..	25	..	50
Daniel Deronda	Geo Eliot	..	..	..	50
Day of Fate	E. P. Roe	..	..	35	..
Education	Spencer	..	..	..	50
Earth Trembled	E. P. Roe	..	..	35	..
Enchanted Stone	Louis Hind	..	..	35	..
Ernest Maltravers	Lytton	..	25	..	..
Elsie Venner	O. W. Holmes	..	25	..	..
East Lynne	H. Wood	19	25	..	..
Felix Holt	Geo. Eliot	..	..	..	50
Feet of Clay	Amelia Barr	..	..	35	..
From Jest to Earnest	E. P. Roe	..	25	35	..
Fettered Yet Free	A. Swan	..	..	35	..
First Violin	Fothergill	19	25	..	..
George Washington	J. S. C. Abbott	..	..	35	..
Guy Fawkes	Ainsworth	..	25	..	..
Guy Mannering	Scott	..	25	..	
Grimms' Fairy Tales		19	..	..	..
Grand Mademoiselle	Jas. Farmer	..	..	35	..
Hardy Nor-emen	Edna Lyall	19	..	..	50
Harry Lorrequer	C. Lever	19	25	..	..
Hypatia	Chas Kingsley	19	25	..	
He Fell in Love with His Wife	Roe	.		35	..
His Sombre Rivals	“	..	..	35	..
Home Acre	“	..	..	35	..
Household of McNeil	Amelia Barr	..	..	35	..
Head of the Family	Miss Mulock	..	25	..	
Heart of Midlothian	Scott	..	25		..
History of a Crime	Hugo	..	25		..
Handy Andy	Lover	19		..	..
In the Golden Days	Edna Lyall	19	25		..
Ivanhoe	Scott	19	..	..	50
Irish Idylls	Jane Barlow	..	..	35	..
Jane Eyre	Charlotte Bronte	19	25	..	..
Jess	Rider Haggard	19	.	..	..
John Halifax	Mulock	19	25	.	50
Knight Errant	E. P. Roe	19	25	..	..
Kenilworth	Sir W. Scott	..	25	..	..
Knight of the Nets	Amelia Barr	..	..	35	..
King Solomon's Mine	R. Haggard	19	..	..	..
King's Highway	Amelia Barr	..	..	35	
Lorna Doone	R. D. Blackmore	..	25	..	50
La Salle	J. S. C. Abbott	..	..	35	..
Lilith	Geo. McDonald	..	..	35	..
Lisconnell	Amelia Barr	..	..	35	..
Lone House	“ “	..	.	35	..
Louise de Valliere	Dumas	..	25	..	..
Last Days of Pompeii	B. Lytton	19	25	..	..
Lamplighter	Cummins	19	.	..	..
Last of Mohicians	Cooper	19	.	..	..
Lover or Friend	Rosa Carey	19	..	..	..
Macaria	E. Wilson	..	25	..	..
Montezuma	Eggleston	..	.	35	..
Mabel Vaughan	Cummins	..	25	..	..
Master Man Ready	Capt. Maryatt		25	..	..
Mill on the Floss	Geo. Eliot	..	25	..	50

TITLES AND AUTHORS.	(12mo.)	Cts.	Cts.	Cts.	Cts.
Maids, Wives and Bachelors	Barr	..	..	35	..
Melbourne House	Warner	..	25	..	..
Middlemarch	Geo. Eliot		25	..	..
Micah Clarke	Conan Doyle	19	..	..	..
Mysterious Island	Verne	19	..	..	..
Mary St. John	Rosa Carey	19		..	..
Night and Morning	Lytton	..	25	..	..
Nicholas Nickleby	Dickens	..	25	..	50
Ninety-Three	Hugo	..	25	..	..
Not Like Other Girls	Rosa Carey	19	..	..	..
Near to Nature's Heart	E. P. Roe	..	..	35	..
Oliver Twist	Dickens	..	25	..	50
Opening a Chestnut Burr	E. P. Roe	..	25	35	..
Our Mutual Friend	C. Dickens	19	..	..	..
Original Belle		..	..	35	..
Only the Governess	Rosa Carey	19	..	..	..
Old Ma'm'selle's Secret	E. Marlitt	..	25	..	..
Old Mortality	Scott	..	25	..	..
Origin of Species	Darwin	..	25	..	..
Pickwick Papers	Dickens	..		..	50
Prince House of David	Ingraham	..	25	..	..
Peter Simple	Capt. Maryatt	..	25	..	..
Peter the Whaler	Kingston	..	25	..	..
Pine Needles	Wetherell	..	25	..	..
Paul Clifford	Lytton	.	25	..	..
Paul and Christina	Amelia Barr	..	..	35	..
Peter Stuyvesant	J. S. C. Abbott		..	35	..
Pathfinder	Cooper	19	..	..	..
Prairie		19	..	..	..
Pioneers		19	..	..	..
Princess of the Moor	E. Marlitt	19	..	..	..
Pocahontas	Eggleston	..	..	35	..
Rory O'More	Lover	..	25	..	..
Rifle Rangers	Mayne Reed	..	25	..	..
Robinson Crusoe	Daniel Defoe	19	25	..	..
Romola	Geo. Eliot	..	25	..	..
Rienzi	Lytton	19	..	..	..
Romance of Two Worlds	Corelli	19	..	..	..
Red Eagle	Eggleston	..	..	35	..
Silas Marner	Geo. Eliot	..	..	..	50
Scottish Chiefs	Jane Porter	19	..	..	50
Samantha at Saratoga	M. Holley	19	..	..	..
Seven Lamps of Architecture	Ruskin	..	..	..	50
Scottish Sketches	Amelia Barr	..	..	35	..
She Loved a Sailor	“	..	..	35	..
Singer from the Sea	“	..	..	35	..
Sister to Esau	“	..	..	35	..
Success with Small Fruits	E. P. Roe	..	..	35	..
Snow Bird and Water Tiger		..	..	35	..
Scarlet Letter	Hawthorne	..	25	..	..
Shakespeare Works		..	25	..	..
Swiss Family Robinson	Kingston	19	25	..	..
Scott's Poems		.	25	..	..
Stepping Heavenward	E. Prentice	..	25	..	..
Sign of the Four	Conan Doyle	19	..	..	..
Spy	Cooper	19	..	..	..
Thelma	Corelli	19	25	..	..
Tom Brown's School Days	Hughes	19	25	..	50
Tom Brown at Oxford	“	19	25	..	50
Taken Alive	E. P. Roe	..	..	35	..
Two Captains	C. Russell	..	..	35	..
Toilers of the Sea	Victor Hugo	..	25	..	..
Thaddeus of Warsaw	Jane Porter	19	25	..	..
Throne of David	Ingraham	..	25	..	..
Tale of Two Cities	Dickens	19	..	..	..
Twenty Years After	Dumas	..	25	..	..
Treasure Island	Stevenson	19	..	..	..
Three Musketeers	Dumas	..	25	..	..
Twenty Thousand Leagues	Verne	19		..	..
Uncle Tom's Cabin	Stowe	..	25	..	50
Vendetta	Corelli	19	25	..	..
Vale of Cedars	Aguilar	..	25	..	..
Vashti	E. Wilson	..	25	..	..
Vanity Fair	Thackeray	..	25	..	..
Waverley	Scott	..	25	..	50
Wormwood	Corelli	19	..	..	50
Westward Ho!	Kingsley	..	25	..	50
What Can She Do?	E. P. Roe	..	..	35	..
Without a Home	“		25	35	..
Wine on the Lees	Jno. Steuart	..	..	35	..
Woodruff Stories	L. A. Goulding	..	..	35	..
Wandering Jew	Eugene Sue	..	25	..	..
We Two	Edna Lyall	19	25	..	..
Won by Waiting	“	19	25	..	..
What's Bred in the Bone	Grant-Allen	19	..	..	..
Woman's Friendship	Grace Aguilar	..	25	..	..
Wide, Wide World	Wetherell	..	25	..	..
White Company	Doyle	19	..	..	..
Woman Against Woman	Holmes	19	..	..	..
Wife in Name Only	B. Clay	19	..	..	..
Window in Thrums	J. M. Barrie	19	..	..	..
Wooed and Married	R. Carey	19	..	..	..
Wee Wifie	“	19	..	..	..
Yeast	Kingsley	..	25	..	..
Young Girl's Wooing	E. P. Roe	..	..	35	..

Popular and latest books supplied by us at lowest prices.

Paper-covered Books.

Attract vely bound, each book sewed, thus making a flexible back; printed from clear type on good paper. 10c each; postage, 2c extra.

Arundel Motto. Mary Cecil Hay.
Anna Karénine. Tolstoi.
An American Girl in London. Sarah J. Duncan.
Airy, Fairy Lillian. "Duchess."
Adam Bede. George Eliot.
Afloat in the Forest. Mayne Reid.
Ardath. Marie Corelli.
Beautiful Jim. John Strange Winter.
Bondman. Hall Caine.
Barbara Heathcote's Trial. Rosa Carey.
Countess Daphne. Rita.
Claribel's Love Story. Bertha M. Clay.
Count of Monte Criste. Dumas.
Crooked Path. Mrs. Alexander.
Deemster. Hall Caine.
Donovan. Edna Lyall.
Dorothy's Venture. "Duchess."
Daisy Brooks. Laura Jean Libby.
Donal Grant. Geo. Macdonald.
Dame Durden. "Rita."
Darby and Joan. "
Daughter of an Empress. L. Muhlbach.
Dolores. Mrs. Forrester.
Elaine. Chas. Garvice.
English Orphans. Mary J. Holmes.
East Lynne. Mrs. H. Wood.
Egyptian Princess. George Ebers.
Elizabeth and Her German Garden.
Ernest Maltravers. Lytton.
First Violin. Jessie Fothergill.
Frontier Humor. Palmer Cox.
For Lilias. Rosa Carey.
Gold Elsie. E. Marlitt.
Handy Andy. Samuel Lover.
Hypatia. Charles Kingsley.
Homestead on the Hillside. Mary J. Holmes.
Hidden Perils. Mary Cecil Hay.
Heiress of Cameron Hall. Laura Jean Libby.
Ishmael. Mrs. Southworth.
Idle Thoughts of an Idle Fellow. Jerome.
In the Golden Days. E. Lyall.
Ivanhoe. Scott.
Jane Eyre. C. Bronte.
Jess. H. Rider Haggard.
John Halifax. Miss Mulock.
Kenilworth. Scott.
King Solomon's Mines. H. Rider Haggard.
Lady Hutton's Ward. B. M. Clay.
Lady Valworth's Diamond's. "Duchess."
Knight Errant. Edna Lyall.
Lamplighter. Miss Cummins.
Last Days of Pompeii. Lytton.
Last of the Mohicans. Cooper.
Lena Rivers. Mary J. Holmes.
Lora. W. Heimburg.
Lorna Doone. R. D. Blackmore.
Love's Chain Broken. B. M. Clay.
Lover or Friend. Rosa Carey.
Leslie's Loyalty. Chas. Garvice.
Lorrie, or Hollow Gold. Chas. Garvice.
Leonie Locke. Laura Jean Libby.
Mrs. Geoffrey. "Duchess."
Madolin Rivers. Laura Jean Libby.
Molly Bawn. "Duchess."
My Lord Conceit. Rita.
Mary St. John. Rosa Carey.
Meadowbrook. Mary J. Holmes.
Micah Clarke. Conan Doyle.
Misjudged. W. Heimburg.
My Sister Kate. B. M. Clay.
Mystery of a Hansom Cab. F. Hume.
Ninety-three. Victor Hugo.
Nellie's Memories. Rosa Carey.
Not Like Other Girls. Rosa Carey.
Old Ma'mselle's Secret. E. Marlitt.
Pair of Blue Eyes. B. M. Clay.
Phyllis. "Duchess."
Prisoners and Captives. H. Seton Merriman.
Portia. "Duchess."
Queen Hortense. L. Muhlbach.
Queenie's Whim. Rosa N. Carey.
Reveries of a Bachelor. Ik. Marvel.
Romance of Two Worlds. Marie Corelli.
Rhona. Mrs. Forrester.
Robert Elsmere. Mrs. H. Ward.
Robert Orde's Atonement. Rosa Carey.
Search for Basil Lyndhurst. Rosa Carey.
Self-raised. Mrs. E. D. E. N. Southworth.
Scottish Chiefs. Jane Porter.
St. Cuthbert's Tower. F. Warden.
Samantha at Saratoga. M. Holley.
She. H. Rider Haggard.
Thelma. Marie Corelli.
Thorns and Orange Blossoms. B. M. Clay.
Three Guardsmen. Dumas.
Toilers of the Sea. Victor Hugo.
True Magdalen. Wilkie Collins.
Trumpet Major. Thomas Hardy.
Those Westerton Girls. F. Warden.
Tom Brown's School Days. Hughes.
Thaddeus of Warsaw. Jane Porter.
Uncle Max. Rosa Carey.
Under Two Flags. Ouida.
Uarda. George Ebers.
Vendetta. Marie Corelli.
What's Mine's Mine. Geo. Macdonald.
Wee Wifie. Rosa Carey.
We Two. Edna Lyall.
What's Bred in the Bone. Allen.
When a Man's Single. Barrie.
White Company. Conan Doyle.
Won by Waiting. Edna Lyall.
Wooed and Married. Rosa Carey.
Worth Winning. Mrs. L. Cameron.
Young Mistley. H. Seton Merriman.
Young Mrs. Jardine. Miss Mulock.

Paper-covered Books for Summer Reading.

PRINTED ON HEAVY PAPER, FOR 7c EACH; POSTAGE, 2c EXTRA.

At the World's Mercy. Florence Warden.
At Any Cost. Charlotte M. Braeme.
All for Love of a Fair Face. Laura Jean Libby.
April's Lady. The "Duchess."
Beyond the City. A. Conan Doyle.
Beautiful Ione's Lover. Laura Jean Libby.
Bag of Diamonds, The. George Manville Fenn.
Belle of Lynne. C. M. Braeme.
Blind Fate. Mrs. Alexander.
Called Back. Hugh Conway.
Charlotte Temple. Mrs. Rowson.
Change of Air. Anthony Hope.
Corsican Brothers. Alex. Dumas.
Christie Johnstone. Charles Reade.
Claribel's Love Story. C. M. Braeme.
Crooked Path, A. Mrs. Alexander.
Duchess. "Duchess."
Diana Carew. Mrs. Forrester.
Diana of the Crossways. George Meredith.
Dark House. G. Manville Fenn.
Dreams. Ralph Iron.
Dream Life. Ik. Marvel.
Daisy Brooks. Laura Jean Libby.
Duke's Secret. C. M. Braeme.
Dolly Dialogues. Anthony Hope.
Doris's Fortune. Florence Warden.
Earl's Error. Charlotte M. Braeme.
Elaine. Chas. Garvice.
Fisher Village. Anne Beale.
Fair Women. Mrs. Forrester.
Fiery Ordeal. Charlotte M. Braeme.
Golden Heart, A. C. M. Braeme.
Hon. Mrs. Vereker. "Duchess."
House of the Wolf. Stanley J. Weyman.
Her Only Sin. Charlotte M. Braeme.
The Heir of Linne. Robert Buchanan.
Her Heart's Desire. Chas. Garvice.
Hans of Iceland. Victor Hugo.
Heiress of Cameron Hall, The. Laura Jean Libby.
Hector Servedac. Jules Verne.
House on the Marsh. Florence Warden.
I Have Lived and Loved. Mrs. Forrester.
Junie's Love Test. Laura Jean Libby.
Lord Lisle's Daughter. Charlotte M. Braeme.
Loys, Lord Berresford. "Duchess."
Leslie's Loyalty. Charles Garvice.
Little Rosebud's Lovers. Laura Jean Libby.
Leonie Locke. Laura Jean Libby.
Life's Remorse. "Duchess."
Lord Lynne's Choice. Charlotte M. Braeme.
Little Irish Girl. "Duchess."
Man in Black. Stanley J. Weyman.
Master of the Mine. Robt. Buchanan.
Master of Ballantrae. Robert Louis Stevenson.
Marriage at Sea. Clark Russell.
My Lady Nicotine. J. M. Barrie.
Mystery of Cloomber, The. A. Conan Doyle.
Matt: A Tale of a Caravan. Robert Buchanan.
Merle's Crusade. Rosa N. Carey.
Madolin Rivers. Laura Jean Libby.
Margaret Maitland. Mrs. Oliphant.
Marvel. The "Duchess."
Master Rockafeller's Voyage. Clark Russell.
Mona's Choice. Mrs. Alexander.
My Hero. Mrs. Forrester.
On Her Wedding Morn. Charlotte M. Braeme.
Prince of Darkness. F. Warden.
Put Asunder. Charlotte M. Braeme.
Reveries of a Bachelor. Ik Marvel.
Rogue's Life, A. Wilkie Collins.
Study in Scarlet. A. Conan Doyle.
Shadow of a Sin. C. M. Braeme.
Squire's Darling. C. M. Braeme.
Stage-Land. Jerome K. Jerome.
Sweet is True Love. "The Duchess."
Starling, The. Norman Macleod.
Sign of the Four. A. Conan Doyle.
She's All the World to Me. Hall Caine.
Story of an African Farm. Ralph Iron.
Strange Case of Dr. Jekyll and Mr. Hyde. Robert Louis Stevenson.
Strange Elopement, A. W. Clark Russell.
Struggle for a Heart. Laura Jean Libby.
Three Men in a Boat. Jerome K. Jerome.
Valerie's Fate. Mrs. Alexander.
Wedded and Parted. Charlotte M. Braeme.
Window in Thrums. J. M. Barrie.
When a Man's Single. Jas. M. Barrie.
What Gold Cannot Buy. Mrs. Alexander.
Wife in Name Only. C. M. Braeme.
Woman's War, A. C. M. Braeme.

ORDER YOUR BOOKS EARLY FOR BEST SELECTIONS.

MAGAZINES.

It takes five weeks after we receive your subscription for English magazines for you to receive first copy.

Please state when ordering with what month you wish your subscription to begin.

Prices quoted on application for any of the English or American magazines not mentioned.

The prices are subject to change.

Estimates given to Public Libraries on application.

In ordering single numbers of any magazine, postage is required.

List of 5c Magazines.

	Per Year.
Black Cat	$0.50
Nickell	0.50
Grey Goose	0.50
Ladies' World	0.40

List at 10c.

Munsey's	$1.00
Argosy	1.00
New Illustrated	1.25
Puritan (Am. Edition)	1.00
McClure's	1.00
Ladies' Home Journal	1.00
Cosmopolitan	1.00
Strand	1.15
Pulpit	1.00
Wide World	1.15
Success	1.00
Harmsworth	1 00

Miscellaneous.

	Per Year.
Harper's Bazaar, weekly	$3.75
St. Nicholas	2.75
Outing	2.75
Ladies' Magazine	1.00
NineteenthCentury	4.35
Harper's Monthly	3.75
Etude, new subscribers	1.20
Etude, renewals	1.40
Literary Digest, new subs	2.75
Literary Digest, renewals	$3.00
Sunday Strand	2.00
Weldon's Bazaar of Children's Fashions	0.35
Family Herald	1 65
Review of Reviews, English	1.80
Review of Reviews, American	2 25
Young Ladies' Journal	3.25
Illustrated London News, reprint, weekly	5.75
Illustrated London News, weekly—English edition	9.25
Graphic	9.25
Ladies' Pictorial	8.75
Canadian Magazine	2.00
Boys' Own Paper, monthly	1.50
Girls' Own Paper, monthly	1.50
Pall Mall Magazine	3.50
The Illustrated Milliner	2.40
Weldon's Home Dressmaker	0.35
Weldon's Ladies' Journal	1.00
Scribner's	2.90
Art Amateur	3.60
North American Review	4.35
Lady's Realm	$2.00
Chambers'	2.25
Cassell's	1.35
Leisure Hour	1.50
Outlook	2.90
Pearson's Magazine (Am. Edit.)	1.00
Windsor	2.00
Trained Nurse	1.00
Woman at Home	2.00
Forum	2.75
Girls' Realm	2.00
Captain	1.75
Sunday at Home	1.50
Black and White (American Reprint), weekly	5.75
Truth	2.50
Bon-Ton	3.40
Art-de-la-Mode	3 40
Costume Royal	3 40
Toilettes	2 00
Elite Styles	1 00
Our Home, weekly	1 75
Pearson's, English edition	2 00
Modern Culture	1.00

SCHOOL BOOKS FOR 1901.

Order all School Supplies through our Mail Order Department. Prices will be given on all books not in this list at shortest notice. Postage paid on school books ordered through our Mail Order, excepting Scribblers, Exercise, Copy, Drawing and Blank Books. When ordering books, give name of Author and Publisher when possible.

Dictionaries.

Concise Imperial, half morocco, $2.00; cloth, $1.25.
Student's Standard, $2.25.
Nuttall's Pronouncing, with appendix, 75c.
Webster's English, half leather, $2.25.
" " with Walker's key, $1.00.
Webster's English, 10c, 20c, 35c, 65c.
Handy Vest Pocket Dictionary, leather, 20c; cloth, 13c.
French-English, leather, 35c.
German-English, leather, 35c.
Cassell's French, German, Latin, $1.00 each.
Routledge's French, German, Latin, 40c each.
Liddell & Scott's Greek Lexicon, $1.60

Arithmetics—
New Public School, 20c.
High School, 48c.
Key to High School, $1.50.
Kirkland & Scott's (Revised), 24c.
Hamblin Smith's, 48c.
Prize Problems, 16c.
MacLean's Hints on Teaching Arithmetic, 40c.

Algebras—
High School, Part I., 60c.
" " Part II., $1.20.
Hamblin Smith's, 48c.
McLellan's Elements, 60c.
Todhunter's, for Beginners, 48c.
C. Smith's Elementary, 80c.
Hall and Knight's Elementary, 80c.
Hall and Knight's Higher, $1.60.
Treatise on Algebra. C. Smith, $1.60.

Agriculture—
Public School, by Mills & Shaw, 32c
" " " C. C. James, 25c.
Manitoba Course, Part I., 32c.
" " Part II., 40c.

Book-keeping—
High School Text-book (McLean's), 50c.
Book-keeping and Précis Writing, 52c.
Copp, Clark Book-keeping Blank, No. 14, 20c; No. 8, 30c; No. 9, 40c.
Blank, No. G11, 20c.

Botany—
Spotton's High School, 80c.
" " " Part II., 48c.
Spotton's High School, Manitoba edition, 80c.
Spotton's Botanical Note Book, Part I., 40c.
Spotton's Botanical Note Book, Part II., 48c.

Chemistry—
Remsen Advanced, $3.15.
Remsen, Briefer, $1.35.
High School, 40c.
Advanced, 40c.
Kirkland's Experimental, 48c.
Chemical Note Book, 20c.

Composition—
Composition from Models, 60c.
English Composition, Welsh, 48c.
Practical English and Composition, 40c.
Strang's English Composition, 20c.
Sykes' Elementary English composition, 35c.

Copy Books—
Public School Vertical. By Newland & Rowe. Nos. 1, 2, 3, 4, 5, 6, 6c each.
Public School Vertical. By Casselman. Nos. 1, 2, 3, 4, 5, 6, 6c each.
Business Forms, Vertical, No. 7, 8c.

Drawing Books—
High School Drawing, Nos. 1, 2, 3, 8c each.
Public School Drawing, Nos. 1, 2, 3, 4, 5, 4c each.

English Literature—
Palgrave's Golden Treasury, 40c.
Palgrave's Children's Treasury. Parts I. and II. combined, 40c.
Selections for 1900-1901, by Alexander, cloth, 50c; paper, 40c.

Rolfe's Edition of Shakespeare's Plays, paper cover, 40c—
Richard II.
Macbeth.
Merchant of Venice.
King Lear.
Julius Cæsar.
As You Like It.
Milton's Minor Poems.—Comus, Sonnets, etc., edited by Rolfe, 40c.

French—
La Poudre, 20c.
High School French Grammar and Reader, 80c.
Exercises in French Prose (Squair and Cameron), 60c.
Le Roman d'un jeune Homme pauvre, 56c.
Madame Therese, 48c.
Selections for 1900-1901. By Squair and MacGillivray, $1.00.
Selections for 1900-1901. By Sykes and McIntyre, $1.00.

German—
Germelshausen, 24c.
High School German Grammar with Reader, 80c.
High School German Reader, new edition, 40c.
Baumbach Der Schwiegersohn, 48c.
Elz Er ist nicht eifersüchtig, Wichert, Post Festum, with notes by Vander Smissen, 48c.
Das Kalte Herz, 80c.
Leander's Traumaurian, 80c.
Horning's Exercises in German Prose Composition, 48c.
Eichendorff Aus dem Leben eines Taugenichts und Welhelmi. Einer muss Heiraten und Benedix Eigensinn, with Notes by Osthaus and Vander Smissen, 80c.

Greek—
Homer's Iliad, Book I., 28c.
Elementary Greek Prose Composition (Fletcher and Nicholson), $1.00.
Goodwin's Greek Grammar, $1.65.
White's Beginner's Greek, $1.20.
Demosthenes' Pro Pharmione, $1.60.
Xenophon Anabasis, Book I, 28c.
Homer's Odyssey, XIII. to XVIII., 80c.
Lysias Orationes. By Shuckburgh, 80c.
Lysias Epitaphios. By Snell, 56c.
Lucian, Charon, notes by Heitland, 40c.
Lucian, Vera Historia, notes by Jerram, 32c.

Geography—
Public School Geography, 60c.
High " " 80c.
Modern " Atlas, 60c.
Frye's Complete Geography, $1.50.
Frye's Primary Geography, 75c.
Cornell's First Steps, 45c.
" Primary Geography, 60c.
Moir's Map Geography for junior pupils, 20c.
Geography of British Colonies. By Dawson and Sutherland, 70c.

Geometry—
McKay's Euclid, complete, 60c.
McKay's Euclid, Books I., II., III., 40c.
Todhunter's Euclid, complete, 60c.
Todhunter's Euclid, Books I., II., III., 32c.
Hill's Lessons in Geometry, 70c.
Public School Euclid and Algebra, 20c.
Hamblin Smith's Geometry, 75c.

Grammars—
High School, 60c.
Public School, 20c.

History—
Green's Short History of the English People, $1.20.
High School History of Greece and Rome, 60c.
High School History of England and Canada, 52c.
Public School History of England and Canada, 24c.
Jeffers' History of Canada, 24c.
English and Canadian History Notes, 20c.
New School History of Canada. By W. H. P. Clements, 40c.
Weaver's Canadian History, 40c.
Little Arthur's History of England, 40c.
Moir's British History Notes, 12c.
Creighton's History of Rome, 24c.
Fyffe's History of Greece, 24c.
Tait's Analysis of Green's England, 80c.
Smith's Smaller History of Rome, $1.10.
Oman's History of Greece, $1.30.
Pelham's Outlines of Roman History, $1.20.

Hygiene—
Public School Physiology, 20c.
Physiology, Health Series, No. 1, 24c; No. 2, 40c.

Latin—
Cæsar—With Notes by Henderson or Robertson—
Bellum Britannicum, 40c.
" Gallicum, II., III., IV., 60c.
" " V., 40c.
" " V., VI., 60c.
Henderson and Fletcher's Latin Prose Composition, $1.00.
First Latin, with Reader, 80c.
Latin Reader, 40c.
Primary Latin Book and Reader, by Robertson and Carruthers, new edition, 80c.
Primary Latin Reader, by Robertson and Carruthers, 40c.
Cicero in Catilinam, 48c.
Cicero, Pro Archia, 56c.
Virgil's Æneid—Notes by Henderson or Robertson.
Books I. and II., 40c each.
Horace Odes—
Books I., II., III., IV., 28c each.
Livy, XXI., 28c.

Music—
Educational Music Course, Books I. and II., 8c each; III. and IV., 12c each.
Public School Music Reader, 35c.
High School Music Reader, 60c.

Physics—
High School Physical Science, Part I., 40c; Part II., 60c.
Supplement to High School Physical Science, 28c.
Introduction to Physical Science, 85c.
Physical Science Note Book, 20c.

Reading Books—
Ontario First Primer, 8c.
" Second Primer, 12c.
" " Reader, 18c.
" Third " 24c.
" Fourth " 32c.
Companion to Fourth Reader, 40c.
High School Reader, 48c.
Notes to High School Reader, 40c.
Wells' & Sykes' Notes to High School Reader, 25c.

Students and teachers supplied with latest published book.

School Supplies and Stationery.

Spelling Books—
High School Word Book, 40c.
Public School Word Book, 24c.

Trigonometry—
Hamblin Smith's, 60c.
Locke's Trigonometry, 80c.
Hall and Knight's Elementary, 80c.
High School Trigonometry, $1.15.

Zoology—
Colton's Practical Zoology, 75c.
High School Zoology, 60c.

Mythology—
Bullfinch's Age of Fable, or Beauties of Mythology. Klapp, $1.10.
Murray's Manual of Mythology, revised. W. H. Klapp, $1.10.

Shorthand—
The Phonographic Teacher, 15c.
Key Phonographic Teacher, 15c.
Manual of Phonography, 30c.
Phonographic Reader, 15c.
" Reporter, 50c.
" Dictionary, $1.25.
" " pocket edition, 65c.
Complete Phono. Instructor, $1.25.
Key to complete Phonographic Instructor, 40c.

Teachers' Aids—
Fitche's Lectures on Teaching, 80c.
McLellan's Applied Psychology, 80c.
Sinclair's First Year at School, 40c.
Steps in the Phonic System, 40c.
Millar's School Management, 80c.
Houghton's Physical Culture, 40c.
How Canada is Governed. Bourinot, 90c.
Quick's Educa'al Reformers, $1.20.
Psychology. Baldwin. $1.20.
Education of Man. Froebel, $1.35.
Education from a National Standpoint, $1.20.
Psychology of Number. McLellan and Dewey, $1.20.
Parker's How to Study Geography, $1.20.
Froebel's Educational Laws for Teachers. By Hughes, $1.20.
Teaching Language Arts. Hinsdale, 85c.
Education of the Greek People. Davidson, $1.20.
Old Regime in Canada, under Louis XIV. Parkman, $1.20.
Mottoes and Commentaries of Froebel's Mother Play. Susan E. Blow, $1.20.
Songs and Music of Froebel's Mother Play. Blow. $1.20.
Winners in Life's Race. A. B. Buckley, $1.20.
Life and Her Children. A. B. Buckley, $1.20.
Principles and Practice of Teaching. By Johonnot, $1.20.
La Salle. By Parkman, $1.20.
Methods in Teaching. By J. J. Tilley, $1.20.
History of Education. By Painter, $1.20.
Study of the Child. By Taylor, $1.00.
Canadian Citizenship. By Millar, 50c.
Infant Mind. By Preyer, 80c.
Outline Study of Man. By Mark Hopkins, $1.00.
Symbolic Education. By Blow, $1.20.
The Study of Children. By Francis Warner, $1.10.
Intellectual and Moral Development of the Child. By Compayre, $1.20.
History of Education. By Levi Seeley, $1.10.
Anglo-Saxons and Others. By Aline Gorren, $1.10.

School Maps.

Size 4 x 5 feet, beautifully colored, mounted on cloth rollers, and varnished. Express extra.
Dominion, $3.25.
Ontario, $3.25.
Europe, $3.25.
Asia, $3.25.
Africa, $3.25.
North America, $3.25.
South America, $3.25.
Hemispheres, $3.25.
Mercator's World, $3.25.
England, $3 25.
Scotland, $3.25.
Ireland, $3.25.
Australia, $3.25
United States, $3.25.

Numeral frames, size 8 x 11, 100 balls, 35c. Size 9 x 12, 144 balls, 50c.

"Excelsior" Globes.

Express Extra.

Globe, 6-inch plain wire stand, 25c.
Globe, 6-inch, plain, height 10 inches, wood stand, 90c.
Globe, 9-inch, plain, height 16 inches, bronze stand, $3.75.
Globe, 9-inch, meridian, height 17 inches, bronze stand, $4.75.
Globe, 12-inch, plain, height 20 inches, bronze stand, $5.00.
Globe, 12-inch, meridian, height 21 inches, bronze stand, $6.25.
Globe, 12-inch, plain, height 24 inches, on bronzed plain iron stand, with incline axis, $7.50.
Globe, 9-inch, complete stand, with nickel meridian divided into half-degrees, horizon and hour circle, height 19 inches, $9.00.
Globe, 12-inch, complete, height 18 inches, $8.75.

Atlases.

Imperial Atlas, cloth cover, 65c.
Dominion and Ontario County Atlas, 10c.
Home Reference and Pocket Atlas of the World, containing 46 full-page colored maps, showing every line of railroad and all important cities and towns, size 5½ x 7 inches, 15c.

POSTAGE EXTRA.
For postage add 5c for each quire of paper, and 4c for each package of envelopes. These goods go far cheaper by sending with other goods by express or freight.

Whiting's linen, vellum or satin paper, in cream, blue and heliotrope, pkg of 5 quires, 25c; envelopes to match, 5c.

No.			Paper per Quire.	Envelopes per pkt.
686	Crane's Dresden,	70 lb, white wove,	25c	25c.
28	Crane's extra superfine,	60 " white wove,	18c	18c.
63	" parchment vellum,	70 " cream,	20c	20c.
65½	Hurd's Irish linen	54 " "	10c	10c.
	Whiting's French Organdie, grey and blue Lakewood,		20c	20c.
	Whiting's French Organdie, grey and blue Vassar,		15c	15c.
194	Hurd's satin wove,	60 lb, cream,	10c	10c.
391	Crane's superfine,	60 " pink,	15c	15c.
413	" Venetian repp,	60 " "	18c	18c.
194	" satin wove.	miniature,	10c	10c.
	Eatonia note, fine vellum, plain,		5c	5c.
303	Note paper, cream, ruled, or plain (5-quire, 25c),		5c	5c.
125½	Hurd's Egyptian linen,	12 lb, cream,	8c	10c.
404	Note, commercial, ruled or plain,		6c	7c.
	London Grey paper, 8vo and billet sizes.		7c	8c.
	Silurian (mottled grey), 8vo, plain and billet		5c	5c.
	Foreign note paper,		5c	10c.
	Mourning note, 8vo, plain, narrow, middle broad, extra broad and double broad,		7c	8c.
	London grey, black bordered, as above,		10c	10c.

Writing Tablets.

Postage on tablets, 1 cent per oz.

	Each	Postage extra.
Writing tablets, 80 sheets, small, ruled or plain, blotter cover,	5c	6c.
" 100 " " " " " "	7c	8c.
" 100 " " " " card cover and blotter	10c	10c.
" 100 " large, " " blotter cover,	15c	18c.
" 100 " " " " India linen, blotter cover	13c	14c.
" 100 " " plain standard linen, card cover and blotter,	25c	16c.
" 100 " " plain linen,	25c	14c.
" 80 " " plain olde parchment bond, white,	25c	12c.
" 80 " " overland white,	25c	14c.
" 80 " " parchment cream,	25c	18c.
" 80 " " bond white,	25c	14c.
" 60 " " silurian grey,	15c	10c.

Envelopes.

Envelopes, No. 4, square, good paper, 250 in box, 25c box.
" " 7, white wove, good paper, 500 in box, $1.00 per 1,000.
" " 7, " " " " 500 " 70c per 1,000.
" " 7, " " " " 2c pkg, 40c box of 500.

Typewriting Papers and Supplies.

Postage extra.

Heavy linen laid, $1.00 per ream; 5c quire.
Berkshire linen wove, 75c per ream.
Extra super wove, 60c per ream.
No. 1 Carbon paper, $4.25 per 100 sheets, or 60c doz.
Ribbons, all colors, 80c each, postpaid.
Foolscap paper, 10c quire.
Legal Cap, 15c quire.
Sermon paper, 8c quire; 35c package
Paper wrappers, 50 in book, 12½c.
Butter paper, 50c ream.
Music paper, 35c quire.
Blotting paper, 2 sheets for 5c, or 50c quire.

Exercise Books and Scribblers.

	Each.	Postage extra.
Exercise books, 84 pages, fine manilla cover, 2 for 5c	..	3c ea
Exercise books, 84 pages, press board cover	5c	4c
" " 150 " cloth cover	10c	6c
½ bound, good paper, marginal line board	13c	8c
½ leather bound, good paper, marginal line,	25c	12c
Scribblers, 200 pages, press board cover (3 for 5c)	2c	4c
Scribblers, 300 pages, press board cover,	5c	9c
Reporters' note book, press board cover, oblong, 152 pages, 2 for 5c	..	3c
Reporter's note book, press board cover, oblong, 164 pages	5c	3c.

We carry a full stock of School and Office Supplies

Stationery and Stationery Sundries.

Day Books, Journals, etc.

Postage extra.

Calf, half rough sheep, well bound, 20c per 100 pages; smallest size, 200 pages.
Counter books, from 5c to 25c, best value.
Pass books, 2 for 5c, 5c and 10c each.
500 page letter copying books, 90c.
750 " " " " $1.15.
1000 " " " " 1.35.
Weekly, fortnightly or monthly time-books, 5c each.
Index books, size 4 x 13, 10c each.
Broad index books, 8½ x 13, 20c each.
Housekeeping expense book, 25c.
Portfolio and desk blotting book, 5c and 10c book.

Leather Covered Memos.

Vest Pocket Memos, open at side or end, 10c.
Vest Pocket Memos, indexed, 15c.
Memos, 3 x 5, open at side or end, 15c.
Memos, indexed, 3 x 5, 15c.
Memos, 4 x 6, open at side or end, 20c.
Memos, 4 x 6, indexed, 25c.
Address Books, indexed, 30c, 35c, 45c.
Russian Leather, with clasp, open at end, 3 x 5 and 3½ x 5¾, 75c and $1.00.

Billheads and Blanks.

Billheads, pads of 100 sheets, 10c; post., 11c.
Receipt blanks, 5c, 8c, 10c pad.
Promissory note blanks, 10c for 50 blanks.

Card Engraving.

Postage, 1 cent per oz. extra.

Gents' superfine thick or thin visiting cards (50 in box), 10c box.
Ladies' superfine thick or thin visiting cards (50 in box), 15c and 20c box.
Engraving—
Card plate, name only, 50c.
Card plate, Mr. and Mrs., name only, 65c.
Each additional name, 50c.
Day or address, each 25c.
Lithographing 50 cards from plate, ladies' or gents' (not including cards), 35c; 100 cards, 70c.
Embossing—
Under 5 quires, 12½c per quire.
From 5 quires, 9c per quire.
Envelopes, 9c per package.
Gold stamping—
30c per quire; $4.50 per ream.
Crest, $2.25.
Crest and motto, $4.00 to 6.00.
Monograms, $2.00.

Invitation Cards.

Plain invitation cards, 60c per 100.
Printed at-home cards, $1.00 per 100.
Envelopes to match, 20c per 100.

Wedding Cabinets and Cake Boxes.

Wedding cabinets, containing not less than 50 complete invitations, including printing, $2.25, 2.50 each (printing only, $1.25 each). We do not print less than 50 invitations.
50 cards (cards and name printed), ladies' or gents', 50c; 100 cards, 90c. Postage on 50 cards, 5c extra. We do not engrave or print less than 50 cards.

Wedding cake boxes, 3½x2½-in, 40c doz
" " " 4½x2-in, 50c "

Board files, size 9 x 14½, 35c each.
Shannon board files, complete, with perforator and index, $1.00.
Indices for board files, 4c each.
Bill file hooks, 8c and 10c each.
Bill stick files, 8c and 10c each.
Bill clips, 5c, 10c, 12½c, 15c, 25c each.
Pen racks, 10c each.
Stephen's qt bottle writing fluid, 70c.
" pt " " 45c.
" ½ pt " " 25c.
" ¼ pt " " 10c.
Stephen's copying inks, 25c, 50c, 75c bottle.
Red inks, 5c, 10c bottle.
Mucilage, 5c, 10c, 15c bottle.
Paste, 5c, 10c bottle.
Paste in tubes, 5c, 10c tube.
Le Pages liquid glue, 8c, 10c bottle.
" " " in tins, 15c. 25c, 45c tin.
2½ oz letter balances, 15c.
4 " " " 25c.
8 " " " 35c.
12 " " " 50c.
18 " " " 65c.

Postage paid on the following:

Lead Pencils—
Plain cedar, 5c doz.
Pearl cedar, rubber tips, 10c doz.
Johann Faber's medium grade, 10c doz.
Faber's hexagon pencils, 10c doz.
Faber's pencils, H or HB, 20c doz.
Faber's pencils, all grades, 30c doz.
Faber's, graded, hexagon, 60c doz.
Rubber tips, at 20c, 25c and 30c doz.
Lyra graphite drawing pencils in HB, H, 2H and 3H, compressed lead, 10c each, 3 for 25c.
Colored pencils, 20c doz, or 3 for 5c.
Colored pencils, 60c doz, or 5c each.
Copying pencils in wood, for writing on glass or metal, 4c each.
Indelible copying pencils, in wood, 2 for 5c and 5c each.
Carpenters' pencils, 30c and 60c doz.
Pencil protectors, with inserted rubber tips, 2 for 5c.
Faber's pocket pencils, with nickel pencil protectors, 5c each.
Johann Faber's dermatograph pencil, for writing on the skin, 10c ea.
Slate pencils (in wood), 10c doz.
Programme pencils, assorted colors, 20c doz.
Tassels for pencils, 10c doz.

Gold Pencils and Pens—

Postpaid.

Solid gold pencils, chased or plain, $2.00, 2.50, 3.00, 3.50 each.
Pearl-handled pens, solid gold points, $1.00, 1.25, 1.50, 2.00 2.50.

Paper Cutters—
Pearl blades with sterling silver handles, 25c, 35c, 50c, 75c, $1.00 each.
Hard rubber paper cutters, 15c ea.
Sterling silver pencil holders, 75c, $1.00.

Pen Holders—
Faber's reversible, hard rubber, 15c, 20c, 25c each.
Faber's hard rubber holders, 12½c 15c each.
Cork handles, 8c each.
Cork holder, with wood handle, 5c, 7c each.
Wood handle, covered with cork, 5c each.
Faber's enamelled cedar sticks, 5c each.
Red and black, swell holders, 30c doz.
Plain cedar, swell holders, 20c doz.
Accommodation pen holders, 5c doz.
Mapping pens (6 pens and 1 holder on card), 5c card.

Pens—
292 Eaton's, 25c gross.
292 Gillott's, 45c "
404 " 45c "
303 " 90c "
Eaton's J, 30c "
Mitchell's J, 75c "
Gold J, 75c "
Eaton's Falcon, 30c gross.
Esterbrook's Falcon, 75c gross.
Bank of Montreal, 30c gross.
Bank of England, 30c "
G pens, 30c gross.
Blackstone, Esterbrook, 90c gross.
Judge's quill, " 90c "
Chancellor, " 90c "
Spencerian, No. 1, 90c gross.
Relief, Esterbrook, 90c gross.
Myers' vertical writer, 45c gross.
Ball pointed pens (2½ doz in box), 20c per box.
Waverley pens, box of 1½ doz, 10c.
Pickwick pens, box of 1½ doz, 10c.

Fountain Pens—

Postpaid.

Waterman's Ideal fountain pens, $2.50, 3.50 and 4.00 each; gold mounted, $5.00.
Paul E. Wirt's gold mounted fountain pens, $2.75 and 3.25 ea.
Wirt's No. 1, fine, medium or stub points, $1.50.
Eagle fountain pen, $1.00.
Thumb tacks, 15c and 20c doz.
Paper fasteners, No. 1, 10c gross.
No. 2, 15c "
Eagle compass and divider, 25c each.
Compasses, with pencils attached, 10c each.
Compass sets, at 25c, 35c, 50c set.
Rulers, 15-inch, brass edge, 10c each.
Rulers, 12-inch, brass edge, 8c each.
Rulers, 12-inch, plain edge, 5c each.
Rulers, 12-inch, plain edge, 2c each.
Indelible ink, for rubber stamp, 25c bottle.
Bond's marking ink, 15c bottle.
Payson's indelible marking ink, 20c bottle.
Pencil sharpeners, 3c and 8c each.
Faber's brass pencil sharpener, with reversible knife, 15c each.

Rubber Bands—
Thread, No. 9, 12, 15, 10c, 10c, 10c box.
¼-inch, 0½, 00½, 000½, 8c, 10c, 15c doz.
½-inch 0½, 00½, 000½, 0000½, 12½c, 15c, 20c, 25c doz.
Per pound, boxes, $3.00, all sizes or assorted.
Assorted Boxes Faber's bands, 25c box.
Colored oil mapping crayons, 5c and 8c box.

Rubber Erasers—
Bevel, 1c, 2c, 3c and 5c each.
Circular, 5c each.
Circular eraser, with brush, 8c ea.
Ink and pencil, 8c each.
E. Faber's kneaded eraser, 5c and 8c each.

Postage extra on the following:

Slates, bound, 5 x 7, 8c; 6 x 9, 10c; 7 x 11, 12c each.
Slate pencils in boxes of 100, each, 10c box.
White chalk, 10c box.
Colored chalk, 30c and 60c gross box.
Blackboard erasers, 7c and 9c each.
Rubber stamps, made to order, with name or name and address, 50c and 75c each.

Pencil Boxes.

Postage Extra.

Pencil cases, 10c, 15c, 20c, 25c each.

SCHOOL BAGS.

Postage extra on the following sundries:

Sheepskin bags, 25c, 30c, 35c, 40c, 45c each.
Canvas bags, 35c, 45c each.
Grain leather bags, with strap or handle, in tan, olive or black, 75c each.
Sealing wax, per box, 20c; postage, 4c extra.
Seals for wax, 20c. postage, 3c extra;

Tissue Papers.

Fine crepe tissue, in all shades, 7c, 10c roll; postage, 5c extra.
Plain tissue paper, white, 15c quire; colored, 20c quire.
Shelf paper, perforated and scalloped, in pink, blue, green, yellow and white, 10 yards in piece, 5c; postage, 5c extra.
Fancy crepe paper for lamp shades, 25c roll; postage, 5c extra.

Photo Albums.

Postage Extra.

Photo albums, 75c, $1.00, 1.50, 2.00, 2.50 each.

Unmounted Photo Albums.

Postage Extra.

Unmounted photo books, bound in cloth, size 6 x 7 inches, 25c; 8 x 9 inches, 40c each.
Unmounted photo books, bound in cloth, adjustable covers, interchangeable leaves, size 5 x 7 inches, 85c; 7 x 10 inches, $1.10; 10 x 14 inches, $1.50 each.
Unmounted photo books, leather bound, adjustable cover, interchangeable leaves, size 4 x 5 inches, $1.10; 5 x 7 inches, $1.25; 7 x 10 inches, $1.40 each.

Scrap Albums.

Postage Extra.

Scrap albums, bound in cloth, 35c, 50c, 75c each.
Scrap albums, board cover, 25c each.

Postage Stamp Albums.

Postage Extra.

The International Postage Stamp Album, illustrated with 5,552 engravings of stamps, 160 of arms, 665 of watermarks, 70 portraits of regents, 4,433 quotations of rare stamps, with one map, $1.50 each.
The International Postage Stamp Album, published in three languages, providing for 11,082 postage stamps, cards, envelopes, etc., with 1 map, $1.00 each.
The International Stamp Album, containing 3,330 spaces for all varieties of postage stamps, and giving date of issue, value and color of each stamp, illustrated with 1,816 engravings of stamps, 78 of arms, 105 watermarks, 43 portraits of regents, 50c each.
Illustrated Postage Stamp Album, containing 1,860 engravings of stamps, 57 watermarks, 69 arms and 24 portraits, 25c each.

Orders for wedding stationery and cabinets promptly and accurately filled.

SHEET MUSIC.

SHEET MUSIC.

Lithographed on good paper with attractive title pages. Any selection in this list 5c a copy; regular price 10c.

(1c per copy extra for postage.)

Sheet Music and Music Books Not Exchanged.

VOCAL.

Title	Composer
Bonnie Banks o' Loch Lomon'	Holloway
Good-Bye, Sweet Day	Vannah
He was a Sailor on Board the *Maine*	Jackson
In the Shadow of the Pines	Lang
I Don't Want to Play in Your Yard	Petrie
I Love You if Others Don't	Blandford
Little Rag Doll	Harcourt
My Doll is Bigger'n Your Doll	McClure
Mother's Appeal to Her Boy	H. F. Smith
My Old New Hampshire Home	Von Tilzer
My Old Kentucky Home, Good-Night	Foster
Sweet Bunch of Daisies	Owen
Say that You Forgive Me	Owen
Some Day I'll Wander Back Again	Huntley
Wait, Mr. Postman	Housely
Whose Little Girl are You?	Wheeler
Widow's Plea for Her Son	Hall
What Would You Take for Me, Papa?	Westendorf

INSTRUMENTAL.

Title	Composer
Aunt Ann's Antics (new)	Smith
Black America March	Zickel
Columbian March	Zickel
De Leader of de Coonville Band	Wilmarth
Cuban Liberty	Ramsdell
Cottonfield Dance	Rosenfeld
Frolic of the Brownies	Romaine
Narcissus	Nevin
Star of the Sea	Kennedy

10c; Publisher's Price, 25c.

(1c per copy extra for postage.)

Title	Composer
Coon Hollow Capers, March, Two-Step	Gillis
In the Whirl of Society, Waltzes	Brill
It's the Man Behind the Gun Who Does the Work, Song	Browne
I'd Like to Hear that Song Again	Jefferson
Letter Edged in Black	Nevada

We Carry a Complete Stock of Music.

Some of the More Popular Selections.

Add 1c extra for postage to each of the following.
When ordering please state what voice songs are required for.

VOCAL.

Title.	Composer.	Publisher's Price.	Our Price.
Absent Minded Beggar, The	Kipling & Sullivan.	75c	50c
Always, 2 keys	Horwitz & Bowers	50	23
Asleep in the Deep, Bass and Baritone	Lambe & Petrie	50	23
Asthore, C, A, E, F, G	Bingham & Frotere	60	35
Ave Maria, Cavalleria Rusticana, F, E flat, and C	Mascagni	60	25
Absence Makes the Heart Grow Fonder		50	23
Believe, E flat, and C	Tunnehill & Rosey.	50	23
Because, 2 keys	Horwitz & Bowers	50	23
Better Than Gold	Harris	50	23
Bird in a Gilded Cage	Von Tilzer	50	23
Blue and the Grey	Dresser	50	23
By Your Side	Kuttner	50	23
Calvary, A, C, D	Rodney	50	30
Daddy, F, A	Behrend	40	25
Dixie Kid	Giebel	50	23
Dream of Paradise	Gray	60	35
Ev'ry Race has a Flag but the Coon		50	23
For I Want to be a Soldier	Barnes	50	23
Fairies	Dolores	50	30
Guard While I Sleep	Warrington	25	15
Greeting to the King	Godfrey	40	23
Girl I Loved in Sunny Tennessee	Carter	50c	23c
Heavenly Song, The, A and B flat, G, C	Gray	60	35
Holy City, The, A, B and D flat, C	Adams	75	45
Honey Dat I Love So Well	Freeman	50	23
I Want to Go To-morrow	Sully	50	23
I Can't Tell Why I Love You, But I Do.	Edwards	50	23
I'll Be Your Sweetheart	Dacre	50	23
I'd Leave My Happy Home for You	Von Tilzer	50	23
Just as the Sun Went Down	Udall	50	23
Just One Girl	Udall	50	23
Just Because She Made Dem Goo-Goo Eyes		50	23
Kentucky Babe	Giebel	50	23
Little Black Me	Chattaway	50	23
Little Cotton Dolly	Buck & Giebel	50	23
Lost Chord, F and A flat	Sullivan	50	30
My Hannah Lady	Reed	50	23
My Little Georgia Rose	Roden and Witt	50	23
My Wild Irish Rose	Olcott	50	23
My Tiger Lily	Sloane	50	23
Maple Leaf Forever	Muir	25	10
Never Alone (sacred)	Bullock	35	20
Olcott's Lullaby		50	23
On the Banks of the Wabash	Paul Dresser	50	23
Off to Philadelphia	C. & D. Haynes	50	30
Old Brigade, F, G, A flat, A, B flat		50	30
Priceless Gift, The. E flat, F, G	Gray	60	35
Palm Trees, The. C, B flat, A flat	Faure	50	30
Pliny (Coon Song)	Reid	50	23
Rule Britannia	Arne		10
Strike Up the Band		50	23
Story of the Rose	Mack	50	23
She was Bred in Old Kentucky	Braisted & Carter	50	23
Sweetest Story Ever Told, F and G	Stults	40	23
Soldiers of the Queen	Stuart	50	23
The Rosary	Nevin	50	35
The Recessional	Kipling & De Koven	50	35
Tommy Atkins	Potter	50	25
Where the Sweet Magnolias Bloom		50	23
When Johnny Canuck Comes Home		50	23
You'se Just a Little Nigger		50	23
Zizzy, Zum, Zum		50	23

INSTRUMENTAL.

Title.	Composer.	Publisher's Price.	Our Price.
Absent Minded-Beggar, The, March	Sullivan	75c	50c
Ave Maria, from Cavalleria Rusticana		60	25
Ave Maria, from Cavalleria Rusticana, violin and piano		60	35
Aunt Ann's Antics, Two-Step		25	05
At a Georgia Camp Meeting, Cake Walk	Mills	50	23
Bride Elect, March	Sousa	50	30
Blumenlied, Flower Song	Lange	50	20
Blue and Grey, March	Dresser	50	23
College Song, Lancers		50	23
Charge of the Light Brigade	Paul	50	23
Charlatan, March	Sousa	50	30
Chariot Race, Ben Hur March	Paull	50	23
Colored Major, The	Henry	50	23
Coontown Revels, Cake Walk	Musgrave	50	23
Dance of the Shadows	Newman	50	30
Dawn of the Century	Paul	50	23
Directorate, March	Sousa	50	30
Eli Green's Cake Walk	Koninsky	50	23
El Capitan March	Sousa	50	30
Ev'ry Race has a Flag, March	Heelan & Helf	50	23
Fortune Teller, March	Smith & Herbert	50	23
Fortune Teller, Lancers	Smith & Herbert	50	23
Frangesa March	Costa	50	30
Hail to the Spirit of Liberty	Sousa	50	30
Hands Across the Sea, March	Sousa	50	30
Happy Days in Dixie, March	Mills	50	23
In Old Quebec, Polka	Green	40	23
Janice Meredith Waltzes		50	23
King Cotton, March	Sousa	50	30
La Czarine, Mazurka	Ganne	50	35
Lancers, Medley	Kerry Mills	50	23
Lady of Quality Waltzes		50	23
Loves Dreamland Waltz		60	35
Man Behind the Gun, March	Sousa	50	30
Mendelssohn's Wedding March		50	10
My Rag Time Baby, Two-Step		50	23
Queen's Defenders (just out) March and Two-step		50	23
Relief Column, new March and Two-Step	Smith	50	10
Stars and Stripes Forever, March	Sousa	50	30
Soldier in the Park, March, Two-Step; from "The Runaway Girl"	Van Barr	60	35
Smoky Mokes, Cake Walk	Holzmann	50	23
Simple Aveu (Simple Confession) Romance	Thome	50	30
When Knighthood Was in Flower, Waltzes		50	23
Whistling Rufus	Mills	50	23
Woodland Flowers, Schottische		50	30
Zenda Waltzes	Witmark	50	23

We have the latest and most popular musical selections.

. . . MUSIC BOOKS . . .

NOT EXCHANGED. POSTAGE EXTRA.

Coronet Folio, 49 pieces, for piano or organ, 50c; post., 10c extra.

Royal Folios of Music, Nos. 1, 2 and 3, for piano or organ, each 50c; post, 10c.

Royal March and Two-Step Folio, a collection of 32 popular marches and two-steps, 40c, post., 5c extra.

Royal Pearls, easy for piano or organ, 40c; post., 9c extra.

Superb Folio, popular selections for piano, 50c; post., 9c extra.

Church Voluntaries for Organ or Harmonium, containing 48 select voluntaries, 50c; post., 5c extra.

Wicken's College Album, containing waltzes, schottisches, polkas, lancers, two-steps, etc., 25c; post., 4c extra.

Classic Folios, Vols. 1, 2 and 3, three collections of good classical music, each $1.00; post., 10c.

Modern Pianist, a choice selection by standard composers, 60c; post., 9c.

VOCAL.

New Songs of University of Toronto, paper cover, 70c; post., 7c extra; cloth, 95c; post., 15c extra.

Favorite Song Folio, Nos. 1, 2, 3, 4, 5, and comic, each containing between 70 and 75 popular songs, 35c each; post., 7c extra.

American Song Folio, words and music, 50c; post., 10c extra.

Gems of Scottish Song, 215 Scotch songs, with portrait of Burns, 90c; post., 15c extra.

110 Scotch Songs, popular Scottish songs, with music, 50c; post., 5c extra.

Peerless Song Folio, contains 65 songs, 50c; post., 9c extra.

Royal Song Folio, contains 107 songs, 50c; post., 10c extra.

University of Toronto Song Book, contains 148 choruses, glees, etc., paper, 75c; post., 7c extra; cloth, $1.00; post., 12c extra.

Canadian Patriotic Songs, including "The Land of the Maple," 25c; post., 2c extra.

Superb Song Folio, the latest published, containing 54 new songs, with music, 50c; post., 10c extra.

120 Scotch Songs, a new collection, 50c; post., 5c extra.

Cheerful Voices, 27 action and primary songs, 40c; post., 5c extra

Sacred Song Folio, 57 popular sacred songs, 50c; post., 5c extra.

INSTRUCTION BOOKS.

Bellak's New Method for Piano, paper cover, 25c; post., 3c extra; board cover, 40c; post., 6c extra.

Bellak's Improved Piano Method, No. 2, paper cover, 30c; post., 3c extra; board cover, 40c; post., 6c extra.

Bellak's Improved Organ Method, No. 2, paper, 30c; post., 3c extra; board, 40c; post., 6c extra.

Bellak's Ideal Method for Piano, paper cover, 35c; post., 3c extra; board cover, 50c; post., 6c extra.

Richardson's New Method for Piano, board cover, $1.25; post., 10c extra.

Sydney Smith's Method for Piano, board cover, 65c; post., 8c extra; paper cover, 50c; post., 4c extra.

Gurlitt's Pianoforte Method, paper, 60c; post., 4c extra; boards, 75c; post., 6c extra. Foreign and American fingering.

Louis Plaidy's Technical Studies, foreign and American fingering, 65c; post., 8c extra.

Czerny's Studies in Velocity for Pianoforte, 10c; post., 3c extra.

Czerny's 101 Preparatory Studies, Books 1 and 2 combined, 25c; post., 5c extra.

Winner's Canadian Violinist, a self-instructor, 25c; post., 3c extra.

Winner's Canadian Guitarist, a self-instructor 25c; post., 3c extra.

Winner's New Banjo Method, 30c; post., 3c extra.

Winner's Canadian Method for German Accordion, 30c; post., 3c.

Winner's Guide to German Concertina, 30c; post., 3c extra.

Winner's New Cornet Method, 30c; post., 3c extra.

Winner's Canadian Flutist, a new method, 30c; post., 3c extra.

Winner's Canadian Fifer, a self-instructor, 30c; post., 3c extra.

Winner's Clarionet Method, 30c; post., 3c extra.

Royal Method for Mandolin, 40c; post., 3c extra.

Bassini's Vocal Method, voice cultivation, $1.00; post., 5c extra.

Violin, A Complete Instructor, by Tours, 50c; post., 5c extra.

The Schirmer Library of Musical Classics.

The most carefully prepared edition of the classics published. Tastefully and strongly bound, and lying flat when opened.

Our prices on these books are 40 per cent. lower than publisher's.

When ordering, mention No. of volumes.

No. of Vol.	TITLE.	Pub. Price	Our Price	Postage.
15	Bach, 21 short Preludes and 6 Fugues, paper	60c	36c	06c
16	Bach, 2 and 3-part Inventions (Wm. Mason), paper	60	36	05
1 & 2	Beethoven Sonatas (Bulow-Tebert), 2 vols., paper, each	1 50	90	25
530	Biehl, Elements of Piano Playing, Op. 30	60	36	03
135	Bertini, 12 little Pieces and Preludes, paper	40	24	03
136	" Op. 100, 25 Easy Studies Without Octaves	40	24	03
137	" Op. 29, 24 Studies	40	24	03
138	" Op. 32, 24 Studies (a sequel to Op. 29)	40	24	03
27	Chopin, Waltzes	50	30	06
28	" Mazurkas	1 00	60	14
30	" Nocturnes	75	45	14
29	" Polonaises	75	45	14
31	" Ballads and Impromptus	75	45	14
40	Clementi, 12 Sonatinas, Op. 36, 37, 38	50	30	06
153	Czerny, Op. 139, 100 Progressive Studies without Octaves	50	30	05
378	Czerny, Op. 261, Exercises in Passage Playing	50	30	05
161	" Op. 299, The School of Velocity, complete	60	36	05
148	" Op. 636, Preliminary School of Fingering	50	30	05
146	Czerny, Practical Method for Beginners	50	30	05
154	" The Art of Finger Dexterity, complete	1 25	75	07
325	Gurlitt, Album for the Young	75	45	04
176	Heller, Op. 45, 25 Melodious Studies	1 00	60	09
178	" Op. 47, 25 Studies from Rythm and Expression	1 00	60	09
170	Herz, Scales and Exercises	50	30	04
317	Kohler, Op. 50, First Studies	50	30	04
318	" Op. 157, The Easiest Studies	50	30	04
52 & 53	Kuhlau, Sonatinas, 2 vols., each	50	30	04
341	Liszt, Consolations and Liebestraume	50	30	04
310, 311, 312	Loeschhorn, Op. 65, for beginners, Vogrich, 3 books, each	50	30	04
58	Mendelssohn, Songs without Words	1 00	60	12
65	Mozart, 19 Sonatas (Lebert)	2 00	1 20	23
75	Schubert, Impromptus and Moments Musicals	1 00	60	14
90	Schumann, Album for the Young, Op. 68, and Scenes from Childhood, Op. 15	50	30	04
91	Schumann, Album for the Young, 43 pieces, Op. 68	40	24	03
51	Sonatina Album, 30 Sonatinas and pieces (Kohler)	75	45	10

Publications for Four Hands.

No. of Vol.	TITLE.	Pub. Price	Our Price	Postage.
371	Album. By Haydn, Mozart and others	75	45	07
372	" Four hands, by modern composers	60	36	05
186	Diabelli, Melodious Pieces on 5 notes, Op. 149	50	30	04
188	Diabelli, Pleasures of Youth, 6 Sonatinas on 5 notes, Op. 163	50	30	04

Violin Studies.

No. of Vol.	TITLE.	Pub. Price	Our Price	Postage.
306	Kayser, Op. 20, Elementary Studies, 3 books, each	50	30	04
230	Kreutzer, 42 Studies (E. Singer)	50	30	04
487	Mazas, Book I., Special Studies	60	36	07
364	Schradieck, Scale Studies	75	45	07
297	Pleyel, Op. 8, 6 little duets for 2 violins	50	30	04

Vocal Studies.

No. of Vol.	TITLE.	Pub. Price	Our Price	Postage.
242	Concone, Op. 9, 50 lessons	50	30	04
247	" " 17, 40 " for Contralto	50	30	04
248	" " 17, for Bass	50	30	04

Publications in Schirmer Edition not mentioned in this Catalogue will be supplied to order at 40 per cent. off publisher's price, postage extra.

We carry in stock all Popular Operas. Vocal, Complete, $1.85. Post, 10c extra.

We can supply best vocal or instrumental music books as soon as published.

Butterick Patterns and Books.

No. 4373.

No. 4373.

No. 4373. LADIES' JACKET or SHORT COAT, with fly front and conventional notched collar and lapels. (To be made in straight-around outline at the bottom or with a slight dip at the front and back.) For 34 inches, 3⅜ yards 27 inches wide, or 2⅜ yards 36 inches wide, or 2 yards 44 inches wide, or 1¾ yard 54 inches wide. 9 sizes; 30 to 46 inches, bust. Price, 20 cents or 10d.

No. 4675.

No. 4675.

No. 4675. LADIES' SLIGHTLY FLARED SEVEN-GORED SKIRT, with inverted box-plait at the back. (To be made with a short sweep or in round length, with or without the circular band flounce, and with the conventional or decided dip at the top.) The skirt measures about 4 yards at the foot in the medium sizes and the flounce about 4¼ yards. 20 to 36 inches waist or 37 to 58½ inches hip; 9 sizes. The skirt without the flounce needs, of goods with figure or nap, 4½ yards; without figure or nap, 4¼ yards, each 52 inches wide. The skirt without the flounce needs 4 yards of goods with figure or nap; without figure or nap, 3½ yards, each 52 inches wide, for a lady of 24 inches waist or 41 inches hip measure. Price, 25 cents.

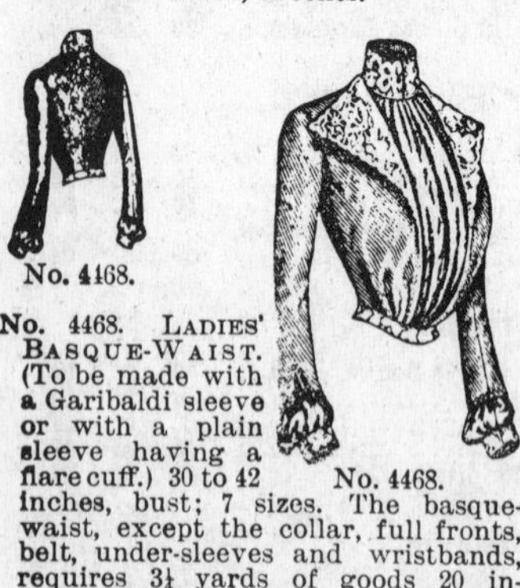

No. 4468.

No. 4468.

No. 4468. LADIES' BASQUE-WAIST. (To be made with a Garibaldi sleeve or with a plain sleeve having a flare cuff.) 30 to 42 inches, bust; 7 sizes. The basque-waist, except the collar, full fronts, belt, under-sleeves and wristbands, requires 3¼ yards of goods 20 inches wide, or 2⅝ yards 27 inches wide, or 1¾ yard 36 inches wide, or 1⅝ yard 44 inches wide, or 1¼ yard 50 inches wide; it needs for the collar, full fronts, belt, under-sleeves, wristbands and for facing the revers, 3⅞ yards 20 inches wide, or 2⅜ yards 27 inches wide, each with ⅞ yard of allover lace 20 inches wide to cover the collar, revers, belt and wristbands, for a lady of 34 inches bust measure. Price, 20 cents.

A full stock of Butterick Patterns always on hand. Orders filled at once.

In sending for children's patterns, *always* send age, and for ladies' patterns always send bust measure under arm, and waist measure.

Descriptions and prices of all patterns we sell are contained in the following FASHION BOOKS:

DELINEATOR, 15c copy; $1.00 Year. Postpaid.

The Glass of Fashion Up-to-Date, issued monthly, 7c a copy, or 60c a year.

Metropolitan Catalogue of Fashions, published quarterly for Spring, Summer, Autumn, and Winter, 25c copy. If ordered by mail, 10c extra for postage.

Bicycle Fashions, 5c copy.

Character and Unique Fashions, 5c copy.

Metropolitan Art Series.

50c copy, Postpaid.

- The Art of Modern Lace-Making.
- The Art of Crocheting.
- The Art of Knitting.
- The Art of Drawn Work.
- The Art of Garment-cutting, Fitting and Making.
- Drawing and Painting.
- Masquerades and Carnivals.
- Wood-carving and Pyrography, or Poker Work.
- Tatting and Netting.
- Fancy and Practical Crochet Work.
- Fancy and Practical Knitting.
- Studies in Modern Lace-Making.

Metropolitan Pamphlet Series.

15c copy. Postpaid.

- Uses of Crepe and Tissue Papers.
- Smocking, Fancy Stitches Cross-Stitch and Darned Net Designs.
- Mother and Babe: Their Comfort and Care.
- Women's Clubs and Societies.
- Child Life: Physical and Mental Development.
- The Perfect Art of Canning and Preserving.
- The Correct Art of Candy-Making at Home.
- Dainty Desserts, Plain and Fancy.
- Extracts and Beverages.
- Bees and Bee-keeping.
- Nursing and Nourishment for Invalids.
- Tableaux, Charades and Conundrums.
- Fancy Drills for Evening Entertainments.
- The Perfect Art of Modern Dancing.
- Wedding and Wedding Anniversaries.
- A Manual of Lawn Tennis.
- Dogs, Cats and other Pets.
- Health—How to be Well and Live Long.
- Birds and Bird-keeping.
- The Decorative Art of Burnt Work.
- Mothers, Sons and Daughters.

The Metropolitan Book Series.

Published by the Butterick Publishing Co. (Limited)
$1.00 copy. Postpaid.

- Good Manners.
- Social Life.
- Home-making and Housekeeping.
- The Pattern Cook Book.
- Beauty: Its Attainment and Preservation.
- The Delsarte System of Physical Culture.
- Needle Craft.
- Needle and Brush.
- Kindergarten Papers.

Metropolitan Handy Series.

25c copy. Postpaid.

- Recitations and How to Recite.
- The Dining Room and Its Appointments.
- Venetian Iron Work.
- Artistic Alphabets for Marking and Engrossing.
- The Home: Its Selection, Management and Preservation.
- Social Evening Entertainments.
- Parlor Plants and Window Gardening.
- Day Entertainments and other Functions.
- Employments and Professions for Women.
- Pleasant Pastimes for Children.
- Pretty Pursuits for Children.
- Art and Ecclesiastical Embroidery.
- How Health Promotes Beauty.
- Women's Colleges and College Life in America and Great Britain.
- Modern Life in England and America.
- Butterick's Correct Cookery.

No. 4128.

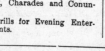

No. 4128.

No. 4128. LADIES' SHIRT-WAIST. (To be made with or without the applied back-yoke.) 30 to 46 inches, bust; 9 sizes. Simplicity is a feature of this shirt-waist, which is shown made of striped gingham with a finish of stitching. The mode is also a desirable one for percale, wash cheviot, pique, etc., and a linen collar may be worn. It needs 3⅛ yards of material 20 inches wide, or 3⅛ yards 27 inches wide, or 2⅜ yards 36 inches wide, or 1¾ yard 44 inches wide, or 1⅝ yard 50 inches wide, for a lady of 34 in. bust measure. Price of pattern, 20 cents.

No. 4592.

No. 4592.

No. 4592. LADIES' RUSSIAN SHIRT-WAIST or BLOUSE, 30 to 42 inches, bust; 7 sizes. This natty blouse is illustrated made of blue and white flannel, with machine stitching and buttons for the finish. It calls for 3¾ yards of goods 20 inches wide, or 3⅛ yards 27 inches wide, or 2½ yards 36 inches wide, or 1⅞ yard 44 inches wide, or 1½ yard 50 inches wide, each with ⅝ yard of contrasting material 27 inches wide for the vest, for a lady of 34 inches bust measure. Price of pattern, 20 cents.

No. 4722.

No. 4722.

No. 4722. LADIES' SLIGHTLY-FLARED FIVE-GORED SKIRT, with inverted box-plait at the back. It measures about 4 yards at the foot in the medium sizes, 20 to 36 inches waist or 37 to 58½ inches hip measure, 9 sizes; at 1s. or 25 cents each.

No. 4563.

No. 4563.

No. 4563. LADIES' SHIRT-WAIST OR BLOUSE, to be made with or without the fitted lining or bust-stay. 30 to 46 inches, bust; 9 sizes. This blouse may be made up in any seasonable fabric. It requires 4 yards of material 20 inches wide, or 3⅛ yards 27 inches wide, or 2 yards 36 inches wide, or 1¾ yard 44 inches wide, or 1⅝ yard 50 inches wide, for a lady of 34 inches bust measure. Price, 20 cents.

We are agents for all the patterns advertised in the Delineator.

TRUNKS AND BAGS.

No. V. Barrel top, metal covered, hardwood slats, good lock and spring clasps, tray and covered hat box, 28-inch, $1.25; 30-inch, $1.80; 32-inch, $2.10; 34-inch, $2.40; 36-inch, $2.70.

No. B. Barrel top, metal covered, iron-covered bottom, iron-bound corners, good lock and spring clasps, tray and covered hat box, 28-inch, $2.15; 30-inch, $2.40; 32-inch, $2.65; 34-inch, $2.90; 36-inch, $3.15.

No. C. Saratoga style, embossed metal covered, iron-covered bottom, iron corner clamps, hardwood slats, fall-in tray, covered boot and hat boxes, 28-inch, $3.00; 30-inch, $3.25; 32-inch, $3.50; 34-inch, $3.75; 36-inch, $4.00.

No. 03. Canvas covered trunk, metal-bound corners, iron-covered bottom, with tray and covered hat box, 28-inch, $2.30; 30-inch, $2.60; 32-inch, $2.90; 34-inch, $3.20; 36-inch, $3.50.

No. A. A square canvas-covered trunk, hardwood slats, iron-bound corners, iron-covered bottom, deep tray with covered hat box, 30-inch, $4.00; 32-inch, $4.25; 34-inch, $4.50; 36-inch, $4.75.

No. 06. Same as No. A, with extra heavy mountings, 30-inch, $4.50; 32-inch, $4.85; 34-inch, $5.20; 36-inch, $5.50.

No. 05. Same as No. 06, with an extra dress tray and bound hardwood slats, 32-inch, $5.75; 34-inch, $6.25; 36-inch, $6.75; 40-inch, $8.00.

No. W. Square canvas-covered trunk, leather bound, brass mounted, 2 outside straps, best lock, and 2 trays, suitable for gent or lady, 30-inch, $8.00; 32-inch, $8.50; 34-inch, $9.00; 36-inch, $9.50; 40-inch, $10.50.

No. E. Ladies' canvas-covered Saratoga trunk, leather bound and brass mounted, extra heavy brass bumpers on corners, 2 outside straps, Yale lock, 2 trays with covered hat boxes, full linen lined, 30-inch, $9.25; 32-inch, $10.25; 34-inch, $11.25; 36-inch, $12.25; 40-inch, $13.25.

No. U. Steel bound, hand riveted, linen lined, two trays, double steel hinges and Yale lock, 32-inch, $8.10; 34-inch, $8.70; 36-inch, $9.30; 40-inch, $11.50. The 40-inch size has 2 outside straps.

No. X. Square canvas trunk, extra heavy brass bound, hinges and mountings riveted on by hand, 2 outside straps, full linen lined, Yale lock, 30-inch, $7.75; 32-inch, $8.25; 34-inch, $9.00; 36-inch, $9.75; 40-inch, $11.25.

No. 03X. Stateroom trunk, canvas covered, steel bound, hardwood slats, iron-covered bottom, shallow tray, with covered boxes, 32-inch, $3.30; 34-inch, $3.60; 36-inch, $3.90.

No. 09. Stateroom trunk, canvas covered, leather bound, brass mounted, full linen lined, iron-covered bottom, 32-inch, $5.25; 34-inch, $5.50; 36-inch, $5.75.

No. D. Canvas-covered stateroom trunk, extra heavy brass mounted, leather bound, iron-covered bottom, 2 outside straps, tray and covered boxes, linen lined, 32-inch, $6.25; 34-inch, $6.50; 36-inch, $6.75; 40-inch, $7.25.

No. 01. Square packing trunk, iron covered, no tray, 28-inch, $1.40; 32-inch, $1.65; 36-inch, $1.90; 40-inch, $2.15.

No. F. Black "Pacific" bag, 14-inch, 55c; 16-inch, 60c; 18-inch, 70c; 20-inch, 80c; 22-inch, 90c; 24-inch, $1.00.

No. O. Gladstone style, pebble grain leather, linen lined japanned frame, brass lock and mountings, 16-inch, $2.00; 18-inch, $2.30; 20-inch, $2.60; 22-inch, $2.90; 24-inch, $3.20.

No. G. Gladstone style, solid cross-grain leather, linen lined, extra heavy japanned frame, brass lock and mountings, 16-inch, $3.75; 18-inch, $4.25; 20-inch, $4.60; 22-inch, $4.95; 24-inch, $5.30.

No. 254. Same as No. G, with leather lining, 18-in., $6.50; 20-in., $7.00; 22-in., $7.50; 24-in., $8.00.

No. P. A canvas telescope, leather bound, and capped corners, wood support in bottom, 16-inch, $1.75; 18-inch, $2.00; 20-inch, $2.25; 22-inch, $2.50; 24-inch, $2.75; 26-inch, $3.00.

No. 86. Leather bound canvas telescope case, riveted edges, three outside straps, 16-inch, $1.00; 18-inch, $1.25; 20-inch, $1.50; 22-inch, $1.75; 24-inch, $2.00; 26-inch, $2.25.

No. 81. Heavy canvas telescope leather, capped corners, riveted edges, 14-inch, 45c; 16-inch, 55c; 18-inch, 65c; 20-inch, 80c; 22-inch, $1.00; 24-inch, $1.10; 26-inch, $1.25.

No. J. Leather club bag, linen lined, japanned frame, brass mountings, 10-inch, 85c; 12-inch, $1.10; 14-inch, $1.35; 16-inch, 1.60; 18-inch, $1.85.

No. T. Solid leather club bag, black, brown or olive, linen lined, brass lock and trimmings, 10-inch, $1.75; 12-inch, $2.00; 14-inch, $2.25; 16-inch, $2.50; 18-inch, $2.75.

No. S. A genuine cross-grain bag, ladies' style, leather lined, leather covered frame, solid brass mounted, this makes a very nobby bag, 14-inch, $4.00; 16-inch, $4.35; 18-inch, $4.70.

No. 78. Gent's bag, same as No. S, with wide bottom, 14-inch, $4.00; 16-inch, $4.35; 18-inch, $4.70.

No. M. Genuine alligator club bag, leather lined, leather covered frame, solid brass mounted, 12-inch, $4.75; 14-inch, $5.35; 16-inch, $6.00; 18-inch, $6.75.

No. 90. Cross-grain leather, imitation leather lined, japanned frame, brass mountings, 14-inch, $2.85; 16-inch, $3.15; 18-inch, $3.45.

No. N. Gent's Victoria club, brown or olive, solid cross-grain leather, leather lined, English frame, hand-sewn, solid brass mountings, 14-inch, $6.50; 16-inch, $7.00; 18-inch, $7.50.

No. L. Paris style, in olive, brown or russet, this is a very heavy and well-made bag, all hand-sewn, heavy leather lined and capped corners, best lock and trimmings, 16-inch, $9.25; 18-inch, $9.75.

No. H. English travelling bags, hand-made, solid cross-grain leather, heavy capped corners, 1½ inch outside straps, best mountings, 18-inch, $12.00; 20-inch, $13.00; 22-inch, $14.00; 24-inch, $15.00; 26-inch, $16.00.

No. 51. Lawyers' brief bags, hand sewn, black pebble grain leather, leather lined, solid brass mountings, 16-inch, $4.35; 18-inch, $4.75.

No. Q. Suit case, made of solid stock, brass mounted, linen lined, capped corners, 22-inch, $4.75; 24-inch, $5.00; 26-inch, $5.50.

No. R. Cabin bag, leather lined, leather-covered frame, brass mountings, 14-inch, $6.25; 16-inch, $6.75; 18-inch, $7.25.

No. 16. Suit case, English frame, best quality stock, corners capped, best brass lock and mountings, 22-inch, $7.00; 24-inch, $7.50; 26-inch, $8.00.

No. 16S. Same as above, but 1½ inches wider, 22-inch, $8.00; 24-inch, $8.75; 26-inch, $9.50.

No. I. Gent's hat box, No. 2 quality, plush lined, russet or olive, $4.00; No. 1 quality, plush lined, $5.75; No. 1 quality, plush lined, will hold two hats, $7.50.

No. K. Shawl straps, 10c, 15c, 20c, 25c, 45c each.

Gladstone bag straps, ¾-inch, 15c; ⅞-inch, 20c ea.

Shoulder straps, with snaps and swivels, ⅝-inch, 20c; ¾-inch, 25c; ⅞-inch, 30c each.

Fibre lunch boxes, 10c, 15c, 20c each.

Address tags, bag size, 5c; trunk size, 10c each.

Whenever possible have goods sent by Express or Freight, as it is safer and cheaper.

HARNESS AND HORSE GOODS DEPARTMENT.

We carry in stock harness suitable for the track, gentlemen's light driving, Surrey, English coupe, light and heavy express, dump cart, light double driving harness, medium double driving harness, double coach, double democrat, double lumber, double knockabout or plow harness—in fact, we carry every kind of harness that is ever called for in the ordinary way, also all the parts necessary to repair your old harness. If you require anything in the harness or horse goods line that you do not see in our catalogue, write us, clearly explaining what is wanted, and we will be pleased to furnish prices, or any other information which you may require.

Single Strap Single Buggy Harness.

No. 105. Bridle, ⅝ inch, box loops, fancy scrolled blinds, good chain front and rosettes, over check; lines, 1 inch, all black or half russet; breast collar wide, single strap, well curved out, and felt lined, with box loops; traces, 1¼-inch, doubled and stitched at ends, buckled to breast collar; saddle, swinging bearer style, 3-inch tree, full padded patent leather skirts, leather lined, 1-inch sewed bearers, good strong shaft tugs and belly bands; breeching, 1⅛-inch body; hip strap, ⅝-inch; side straps ⅞-inch, stuffed crupper. Nickel trimmings and neatly creased, **$10.00** a set; extra for hames and patent leather collar, without the breast collar, **$2.50.**

No. 113. Bridle, ⅝-inch with boxed loops, folded crown, patent leather blinds, round stays, chain front and crystal rosettes, over or side check; lines, 1⅛-inch, half russet or all black; breast collar, well shaped, with boxed loops; traces, 1½-inch, doubled and stitched at ends, and buckled to breast collar; saddle, 3-inch, patent leather jockeys and skirts, Boston metal loops, full padded, No. 1 quality, 1-inch sewn bearers, good strong shaft tugs with boxed loops, sliding belly bands; breeching, 1½-inch seat, ⅝-inch hip straps, boxed loops, ⅞-inch side straps, scalloped back strap with stuffed crupper—

With nickel trimmings...... **$13.50** set
With solid nickel trimmings.. **15.50** "
With genuine rubber " **18.00** "

For hames and patent leather collar on above, without the breast collar, add—

For nickel, $2.75. For rubber, $3.00.

The stock in No. 113 is well finished all the way through, made smooth, with rounded edges, and is a splendid looker.

Doubled and Stitched Single Buggy Harness.

No. 80. **Our Farmers' Special.** This is a real good, strong and good-looking harness, at a very reasonable price. Bridle, ⅝-inch, boxed loop cheeks, neat scrolled patent leather blinds, round stays, over checks, good metal front and rosettes; lines, 1-inch, half russet or all black; breast collar folded, wide, with layer and boxed loops; traces, 1⅛-inch, doubled and stitched, to buckle to breast collar; saddle, 3-inch, full padded, patent leather skirts and jockeys leather lined, 1-inch sewed bearers and shaft tugs, two belly bands to slide; breeching, folded seat with layer, ⅝-inch hip strap, ⅞-inch side straps, stuffed crupper, nickel trimming, $12.00 a set.

For patent leather collar and nickel trimmed hames on above, without the breast collar, add $2.50 to price.

No. 108. **Our Klondike Harness.** This harness is all made of selected stock and well finished all through. Bridle, ⅝-inch, boxed loops, fancy scrolled patent leather winkers, with round stays, good chain front and crystal rosettes, over or side check; lines, 1⅛-inch, with steel spring billets, half russet or all black; breast collar folded and with wide layer, three rows of stitching, boxed loops; traces, 1⅛-inch, double and stitched, buckled to breast collar; saddle, 3-inch tree, patent leather skirts and jockeys, full padded and leather lined, first quality sewed bearers and shaft tugs, folded belly band, with sulky hitch to slide; breeching, 1¾-inch folded seat, with wide layer and three rows of stitching, ⅝-inch hip straps, boxed loops, ⅞-inch side straps, scalloped back strap, stuffed crupper, with nickel trimmings, **$15.00** set; with genuine rubber trimmings, **$18.00**; for hames and patent leather collar, without breast collar, add $3.00 to price.

No. 875. Bridle, ⅝-inch, boxed loop cheeks, large English blinds, round stays, side check, English chain front and rosettes; lines, 1-inch body part, with 1¼-inch folded russet hand parts, and with spring steel billets; breast collar, wide fold with scalloped and raised layer, boxed loops; traces, 1¼-inch double and stitched, raised, to buckle to breast collar; saddle, 3½-inch, patent leather skirts and jockeys full padded and leather lined, first quality sewed bearers and shaft tugs, belly bands folded and with sulky hitch; breeching, folded seat with scalloped and raised layer, with 3 rows of stitching, ¾-inch double and stitched hip straps, boxed loops, 1-inch side straps, scalloped back strap with stuffed crupper sewed on. A very suitable harness for gladstone or phaeton. Solid nickel trimmings only, **$22.00** set; for patent leather collar and full nickel hames without the breast collar, add $3.00 to price.

No. 106. Collar and hame surrey harness. We believe this to be the greatest value ever offered in this kind of harness. It is all cut from good stock, well-finished, and is a very strong as well as a handsome harness. Bridle, ⅝-inch, boxed loop cheeks, large round corner, patent leather blinds, with round stays, fancy chain front and rosettes, side check, Liverpool bit, nose band, medium weight patent leather collar, full nickel hames; traces, 1¼-inch, double and stitched; lines, 1⅛-inch, all black or half russet; saddle, 4-inch, full patent leather skirts and jockeys, full leather lined, 1⅛-inch, sewed bearers to slide, sewed shaft tugs; breeching, 1¾-inch fold, with scalloped and raised layer, ⅝-inch double hip straps, boxed loops, 1-inch side straps, stuffed crupper, nickel trimmings, **$21.00** set.

No. 155. A similar harness to No. 106, but much finer got up, and made of specially selected stock. This harness is made in right up-to-date style and is a beauty, solid nickel or brass trimmings, **$29.00** set.

Light Double Driving Harness.

No. 130. A very stylish harness and a winner at the price. Bridles, ⅝-inch, boxed loop cheeks, neat patent leather blinds, and over or side checks, fancy chain fronts and rosettes; collars half patent, hames full nickel, hame tugs 1¼-inch, with boxed loops; traces, 1¼-inch, double and stitched; pole straps, 1⅛-inch; martingales, 1-inch; light coach pads, with neat housings; lines, all black or half russet; back straps scalloped, stuffed cruppers, nickel trimmings, **$25.00** set.

No. 130½. Same harness as No. 130, only it has breast collars instead of collars and hames, **$20.50** set.

No. 140. Double carriage harness similar to No. 130, but much better and heavier, solid nickel trimmings, **$37.50** set.
Write for full description.

Team Farm Harness.

No. 1. Bridles, ¾-inch harness leather blinds, or open bridles if desired, round stays and side checks, stiff or jointed bits; lines, ⅞-inch, full length, good heavy stock, with snaps; collars, (No. 5) a good strong work collar, open tops, cloth or leather faced; hames, wood, high top, steel bound; hame tugs, 1½ x 18 inches, buckling to trace, with double grip trace buckle, the best heavy harness trace buckle in use; traces, 1½ inch x 6 feet, 3-ply leather, iron cockeyes at ends; martingales, 1½-inch, pole straps, 1½ inch, with snaps; back bands, padded, leather lined, and have fancy housings, hooks and terrets, back straps, hip straps and cruppers, complete with snaps and chain spreaders, **$25.00** set.

No. 1½. Same harness as No. 1, but it also has breechings, **$29.25** set.

No. 2. Same harness as No. 1, but without back bands, and with spider breechings, **$25.75.**

No. 3. A similar harness to No. 1, with following changes: hame tugs, traces, pole straps, martingales are 1¾-inch, lines 1-inch, price, complete, **$26.00.**

No. 3½. Same as No. 3, but with breechings, **$30.25** set.

We give you the same goods and prices as a city customer.

No. 4 Same as No. 3, but without back bands, and with spider breechings, **$26.75** set.

If you do not require collars on any of above team harness, take off $4.00 from price.

The above team harness is a good reliable harness and will give you good service.

No. 165. Special Team Harness. This harness is made expressly for our trade. It is cut from first-class stock, all hand sewn, and will give grand satisfaction. Bridles, ⅞-inch, patent leather blinds, round stays and side checks, face pieces, stiff or jointed bits, lines 1-inch; No. 1 stock, with snaps, collars, cork lined, thong sewn, leather faced; hames, staple, high top, steel bound; hame tugs, 3-ply x 1½-inch, with double grip buckles, martingales 1½-inch, pole straps 1½-inch, with iron slides and snaps; traces, 3-ply, 1½-inch with cock-eyes, back bands padded and with large fancy housings, hooks and terrets, belly bands, heavy folded, back straps, cruppers and hip straps, XC plated trimmings all through, complete with snaps and spreader chains, **$28.50.**

No. 165½. Same harness as No. 165, but it also has breeching, **$32.75.**

No. 166. Same harness as No. 165, but without back bands, and with spider or crotch breechings, **$29.25.**

No. 170. Special team. A similar harness to No. 165, but much heavier, the changes are as follows: Hames are heavy Concorde bolt, traces are 1¾-inch, 3-ply, breast straps and martingales are 1¾-inch, **$30.00** set.

No. 170½. Special. Same as No. 170, but it also has breechings, **$34.25.**

No. 171. Special. Same as No. 170, but without the back bands and with crotch or spider breechings, **$30.75.**

No. 170. Is a very suitable harness for heavy trucking, etc. If you do not require collars on above, take off $4.50 from price.

HARNESS PARTS.

TRACES.

All Traces 6 Feet Long.

Single strap, buggy traces, $1.50, 1.85 pair.
Double and stitched buggy traces, $2.00, 2.50 pair.
3-ply team traces, 1½-inch, $3.00; 1⅝-inch, $4.00; 1¾-inch, $4.50 pair.
1-ply team traces, 2½ inches wide, 3-ply points, $4.00 pair.
2-ply team traces, Manitoba, $4.00 pair.

Team and Single Harness Bridles.

No. 1. Team bridles, blind, $3.75 pair.
No. 1. Team bridles, open, $3.15 pair.
No. 165. Team bridles, blind, $4.35 pair.
No. 105. Single bridle, blind or open, $2.25 each.
No. 108. Single bridle, blind or open, $2.50 each.
No. 113. Single bridle, blind or open, nickel, $2.50; solid nickel, $3.00; genuine rubber, $3.45.
Surrey or coupe bridle, solid nickel or brass, $5.00 each.
No. 1. Single rein riding bridle, full check bit, $1.35 each.
No. 2. Double rein riding bridle, Pelham chain curb bit, a neat strong bridle, $2.80 each.
No. 1. Single work harness breeching, XC plate, $2.85; nickel or brass, $3.25.
No. 1. Team pad breechings, to be used with back bands, $5.75 per set.
No. 2. Team crotch breechings, to be used without back bands, $6.25 set.
Single harness martingales, white rings, 65c each.
Single harness martingales, rubber rings, 75c each.
Team carriage harness martingales, 1-inch, nickel, 60c each.
Team work harness martingales, good heavy stock, 1¼-inch, 35c; 1½-inch, 45c; 1¾-inch, 55c; 2 inch, 75c each.
Team check reins, round, 60c; flat, 45c each.
Buggy harness check reins, overdraw, 60c each.
Side checks, nickel, 60c each.
Team leather fronts, 10c, 12c each.
Team metal fronts, nickel or brass, 20c each.
Light harness fronts, 15c, 18c, 25c, 30c each.
Heavy harness fronts, 30c, 35c, 50c each.
Bridle crowns 25c each.
Throat latches, 15c, 20c each.
Buggy bridle check, parts round, nickel, 50c; genuine rubber, 85c pair.
Team harness rosettes, nickel or brass, 20c pair.
Buggy harness rosettes, glass, 15c, 20c; nickel, 10c; imitation rubber, 25c, 50c pair.
No 1 Team lines, full length, good heavy selected stock, ⅞-inch, $2.45; 1-inch, $2.65; 1⅛-inch, $3.00 set.
Rope plow lines with handles and snaps, hemp, 20c; cotton, 25c pair.
Single driving lines, black or half russet, 1-inch, $1.35; 1⅛-inch, $1.65; 1¼-inch, $2.00 pair.
Single driving lines, 1-inch body part with 1⅛-inch folded russet hand parts. This makes a nice driving line (a sure grip), and is especially suited for ladies' use, $2.65.
Double driving lines, black or half russet, $3.00; full russet, $3.50 pair.
Strap gig saddles, $1.85, 2.25 each.
Gig saddles, full padded, with full patent leather skirts, $3.00, 3.50 each.
No. 106. Harness saddle sliding bearer, $5.50 each.
Team back bands, padded and with fancy housings, $4.00 pair.
Team belly bands, heavy folded, 55c each.
Light harness belly bands, 50c, 70c pair.
Light harness shaft tugs, 55c, 90c pair.
Surrey harness shaft tugs, 75c, $1.00 pair.
Felt gig housings, 20c each.
Felt Express housings, 35c, 50c each.
Felt team back band housings, 25c each.
Patent leather gig housings, 40c, 50c, 65c each.
Heavy felt, for padding harness, 75c square foot.

Interfering Boots, etc.

Ankle boots, 15c, 20c, 25c, 30c each.
" " calf, $1.00 pair.
Shin and ankle boots, $2.00, 2.50 pair.
Knee boots, $2.50, 3.00 pair.
Quarter boots, $2 50, 2.75, 3.00 pair.
Trotting balls, 35c string.
Speeding hobbles, $5.00 set.
Bandages, 50c, $1.50 set of 4.

We have quoted prices on some of the lines of turf boots most in use. If you do not see what you want, write us.

We are Canadian agents for the Air-Cushion Rubber Horseshoe Pads. They reduce concussion to the minimum, cures or relieves all lameness produced or aggravated by jarring on the hard streets and roads. Write us for full particulars.

No. 1 quality white drill sweat pads, brown backs, hair stuffed, large and extra quality, 35c each.
No. 1 quality all-felt sweat pads, 4 springs, heavy felt, 65c each.
Heavy white duck feed bags, ventilated, 75c each.
Leather pipes for chain traces, 50c each.
Buggy or work harness cruppers, 25c each.
Tethering hobbles, good heavy stock, 75c pair.
Kicking straps, $1.25 each.
Weight straps, 7 ft. x 1 inch, 35c each.
" " 12 ft. x 1 inch, 65c each.
Buggy hames, with hame tugs attached, $2.00, 2.25 pair.
Strap breast collars, $2.00, 2.25 each.
Folded " " $2.00, 2.25, 2.50 each.
Express " " $2.85 each.
Double carriage breast collars, with pole strap irons, $5.50 set.
Hip straps, ⅝ and ¾-inch, 15c each; ⅞ and 1-inch, 30c each.
Twin neck yoke straps, 1½-inch $1.60 set.
Carriage harness breast straps, 1⅛-inch, 60c each.
Team " " " 1½-inch, 45c; 1¾-inch, 55c; 2-inch, 75c each.
Team breeching straps, ⅞-inch, 35c; 1-inch, 40c each.
Single breeching straps, ⅞-inch, 23c; 1-inch, 25c; 1⅛-inch, 30c; 1¼-inch, 35c each.
Halter shanks, 1-inch, 22c; 1⅛-inch, 25c; 1¼-inch, 30c each.
Tie lines, with snaps, ⅝-inch, 20c; ¾-inch, 22c; ⅞-inch, 25c.
Hame straps, ⅝-inch, 8c; ¾-inch, 9c; ⅞-inch, 10c; 1-inch, 12c; 1⅛-inch, 15c; 1¼-inch, 18c each.

Collars.

Open or closed top, Scotch, long straw, cloth or leather-faced, $2.85 each. Pipe in Scotch collar, $1.00 extra.

No. 5. Short straw collars, cloth or leather faced, open or closed tops, $2.00 each.

No. 13. Thong sewed, leather-faced, open top, $2.25.

Half patent buggy collar, $2.50 each.

Full patent buggy collar, $3.25 each.
Half " coupe " $3.00 "

Heavy riveted halters, with shanks, 1-inch, 65c; 1¼-inch, 75c each.
Heavy sewed halters, 1-inch, 90c; 1¼-inch, $1.15 each.
Our 1¼-inch sewed halters at $1.15 cannot be duplicated for the money.
1-inch sewed halter, colt size, 90c each.
Adjustable web halter, 25c each.
Rope neck halter, ring and snap, 10c each.

Horse Dandy Brushes.

No. 54. Whisk, dandy, 15c, 20c.
No. 50. Superior whisk, dandy, 25c.
No. 52. Superior whisk, large size, 35c.
No. 53. Superior English, best quality, 45c.

Horse Body Brushes.

No. 44. Leather back OK yellow bristles, 25c.
No. 45. Leather back, yellow bristles, fine quality, 50c.
No. 140. Best quality leather back brush, 85c.
No. 46. Wooden back, mixed hair, black edge, 25c.
No. 47. Wooden back, mixed hair, white edges, 35c.
No. 48. Wooden back, grey bristles, 50c.
No. 60. Wooden back, all bristles, $1.00.
Concorde bolt hames, $1.70, 2.00 set.
Varnished hook hames, $1.20, 1.30 set.
The Success hame fastener, stronger and better than a dozen hame straps, 35c each.
Animal pokes, 25c. 30, 50c each.

Horse Nets.

No. 1. Woven horse covers, covering all over to head. These covers are closely woven of strong material, and have hame and terret holes, especially adapted to keep flies from horses while plowing, threshing, etc., $1.35 each.
No. 2. Climax, heavy team nets, made of extra heavy cord, with leather lashes, covering horse all over to head, $1.25 each.
No. 3. Fancy, heavy team nets, in a large variety of colors, good heavy cord, covering all over to head, $1.25 each.
No. 4. Team nets, heavy cord, colors old gold, brown or salmon, 85c each.
No. 5. Variegated double cord team nets, body and neck, colors blue and lemon, olive and red, and purple and white, $1.00.
No. 6. Buggy nets, body and neck, in a large variety of colors, in old gold and purple, wine and lemon, and black, also in plain brown, olive, and black, $1.00, $1.25 each.
No. 7. Large stallion nets, heavy cord, rounded flank, 1-inch mesh, in assorted colors, old gold with purple tassels, black, and black with white tassels, body and neck, 3 rows of tassels, $2.00 each.
No. 8. Half-inch mesh stallion or show nets, body and neck, in plain colors only, regular beauties, in brown or black, $2.75 each.
No. 9. Buggy flank nets, single heavy cord, in olive and black, old gold and white, and black with lemon, 50c each.
No. 10. Double cord buggy flank nets, in plain brown, old gold, purple and black, 75c each.
No. 11. ¾-inch mesh, double cord flank nets, fancy border, in brown, old gold, purple and black, with assorted tassles, $1.15 each.
No. 12. Extra fancy shell border flank nets, ½-inch mesh, in brown or black, very neat and stylish, $1.50 each.

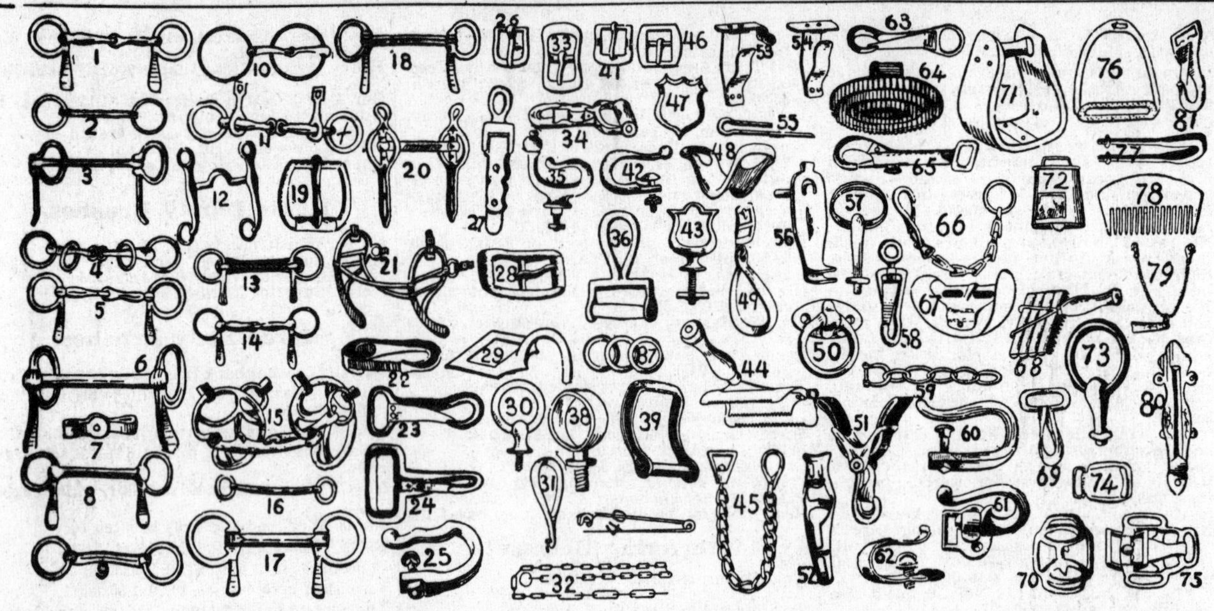

PRICES ON THIS PAGE SUBJECT TO CHANGE WITHOUT NOTICE.

No. 1. Nickel-plated half-cheek snaffle bit, jointed, 20c each.

No. 2. Double-twisted wire scissors bit, severe, 20c each.

No. 3. Solid bar, half-cheek snaffle bit, nickel-plated, stiff or jointed, 30c each.

No. 4. Four ring Wilson bit, in fine XC plate, 20c each; nickel-plated, 50c each.

No. 5. Nickel-plated half-cheek Dexter bit, heavy, jointed, 35c each.

No. 6. Forged-steel Dexter bit, half-cheek, stiff, an extra good bit for the money, $1.00 each.

No. 7. Steel chain repair links, to rivet, absolutely unbreakable, 4c each or 45c doz.

No. 8. Nickel-plated, half-cheek Dexter bit, stiff, 35c each.

No. 9. Rubber-covered mouth team bit, 25c each.

No. 10. Nickel-plated racing bit, large loose rings, jointed, 50c each.

No. 11. The old familiar Rockwell bit, in fine XC plate, 20c; nickel-plated, 50c each.

No. 12. Port riding bit, nickel-plated, without curb chain, 65c each.

No. 13. Flexible rubber half-cheek bit. This bit has a steel chain running through centre, as shown in cut, 50c each.

No. 14. Common team bits, XC plated, stiff or jointed, plain ring ends, 8c each.

No. 15. The imperial bit. This bit positively cures tongue lolling and prevents side-pulling. It will control the most vicious horse, and can instantly be changed to suit the most tender mouth. In fine XC plate, $1.00 each; nickel-plated, $1.50.

No. 16. Steel over-check bit, 10c each.

No. 17. Solid leather mouth bit. This is one of the best bits in use to-day for tender or sore mouths, 65c each.

No. 18. Nickel-plated, double bar, half-cheek snaffle bit, stiff only, 30c each.

No. 19. Single bar, common roller buckle, XC or japanned, ⅝-inch, 10c; ¾-inch, 12c; ⅞-inch, 15c; 1-inch, 18c; 1¼-inch, 20c; 1½-inch, 25c; 1¾-inch, 30c doz.

No. 20. The Liverpool curb bit. Complete with chain curb, nickel-plated, $1.00; solid nickel, $1.75 ea.

No. 21. The famous Jay-Eye-See bit, is considered one of the most effective bits for use on vicious and unruly horses, XC plated, 50c each.

No. 22. Bit snaps, for use on halter bridles, 4c each or 45c doz. The favorite bit snap, opens at both ends, 3c each or 30c doz.

No. 23. German snaps, ⅞ and 1-inch, 2 for 5c, or 25c doz; 1½-inch, 5c each, 50c doz; 1¾-inch, 6c each, 65c doz; 2-inch, 8c each or 90c doz.

No. 24. Champion snaps, ⅞ and 1-inch, 2 for 5c, or 25c doz; 1½-inch, 5c each, 50c doz; 1¾-inch, 6c each, 65c doz; 2-inch, 7c each or 75c doz.

No. 25. The Toronto gig saddle hook, nickel or brass, 10c each or $1.00 doz.

No. 26. Single-bar harness buckle, nickel, wire pattern, ½-inch, 15c; ⅝-inch, 20c; ¾-inch, 25c; ⅞-inch, 35c; 1-inch, 50c doz.

No. 27. Clip cockeyes, for repairing traces, easily put on, 8c each or 90c doz

No. 28. Double bar buckle, with roller, XC or japanned, ½-inch, 10c; ⅝-inch, 12c; ¾-inch, 15c; ⅞-inch, 18c doz.

No. 29. The "Simple" trace carrier, the handiest and simplest device of the kind out, XC plated, 5c pair or 50c doz pairs.

No. 30. Gig saddle terret, wire patterns, nickel or brass, 12c each or $1.25 doz.

No. 31. Chapman side-check swivel, nickel, 15c pair or $1.50 doz pairs.

No. 32. Steel trace chains, length 7 ft. These trace chains are warranted to withstand any strain which a team of horses may subject them to, 35c each.

No. 33. Fancy double bar buckle, nickel or brass, ⅝-inch, 7c; ¾-inch, 8c; ⅞-inch, 9c; 1-inch, 10c; 1¼-inch, 25c each.

No. 34. Breast strap roller snap, heavy, 1½-inch, 20c each or $2.25 doz; 1¾-inch, 25c each or $2.75 doz.

No. 35. Gig saddle post hook, very stylish, in wire or band pattern or C shape, as desired, nickel, 25c each or $2.75 doz.

No. 36. Screw cockeye, 1¼-inch, 4c each or 45c doz; 1½-inch, 5c each or 50c doz; 1¾-inch, 5c each or 50c doz.

No. 37. Martingale or spread rings, composition, in red, white or blue, 5c each or 50c doz; wood, large, in red, white or blue, 5c each or 50c doz; celluloid, white only, 2½-inch, 25c each; 2¾-inch, 30c each; 3-inch, 35c each.

No. 38. Gig saddle terret, band pattern, nickel or brass, 12c each or $1.25 doz.

No. 39. Screw bale or hame tug loops for double-grip trace buckles, 7c each or 75c doz.

No. 40. Large safety-pins for horse blankets, 5c each or 50c doz.

No. 41. Single-bar harness buckle, nickel, band pattern, ½-inch, 15c; ⅝-inch, 20c; ¾-inch, 25c; ⅞-inch, 35c; 1-inch, 50c doz.

No. 42. Gig saddle-hook, wire pattern, nickel or brass, 12c each or $1.25 doz.

No. 43. The "Toronto" fancy terret, very neat, 10c each or $1.00 doz. Refer back to No. 25 for "Toronto" hook to match terret.

No. 44. Steel cattle comb, 15c each.

No. 45. Stallion lead chain, all steel, snap and swivel, 35c each.

No. 46. Fancy double-bar buckle, flat or band style, in brass only, ⅞-inch, 6c; 1-inch, 7c; 1½-inch, 15c each.

No. 47. Fancy ornaments, shield-shape, brass only, ⅞-inch, 5c each or 50c doz; 1-inch, 6c each or 65c doz; 1¼-inch, 7c each or 75c doz; 1½-inch, 8c each or 85c doz; 1¾-inch, 10c each or $1.00 doz; plain nickel spots, ½-inch and ⅝-inch, 1c each or 10c doz; ¾-inch and ⅞-inch, 2c each or 20c doz.

No. 48. Breast strap slides or irons, 1½-inch, 5c each or 50c doz; 1¾-inch, 7c each or 75c doz; 2-inch, 10c each or $1.00 doz.

No. 49. Flexible side-check swivels, for team harness, in fine XC plate or japanned, 5c pair or 50c doz pairs; nickel-plated, for buggy harness, 20c pair.

No. 50. Drop terret, XC plate or japanned, 8c each or 85c doz.

No. 51. The combined breast strap, slide and snap, a very convenient and durable article, 1½ and 1¾-inch, 25c each.

No. 52. Common whip socket, japanned, 5c each or 50c doz.

No. 53. Anti-rattler and bolt holder, steel, 15c pair or $1.75 doz pairs.

No. 54. Anti-rattler, 10c pair or $1.00 doz pairs.

No. 55. Hame clips, 3c each or 30c doz.

No. 56. Tongues for repairing double-grip buckles, easily put on, XC or japanned, 5c each or 50c doz.

No. 57. Hame line rings, with washers, 5c each or 50c doz.

No. 58. Round-eye swivel snap, steel, ¾-inch eye, 4c each or 40c doz.

No. 59. Heel chains for team traces, 1½-inch, 20c each; 1¾-inch, 25c each; 2-inch, 30c each.

No. 60. Gig saddle hook, band pattern, nickel or brass, 12c each or $1.25 doz.

No. 61. Drop hook, XC or japanned, 8c each or 85c doz.

No. 62. "Syracuse" pad hook for team harness, XC plated, 7c each or 75c doz; japanned, 5c each or 50c doz.

No. 63. Round-eye German snaps, ½-inch, 2 for 5c or 25c doz; ⅝-inch, 2 for 5c or 25c doz; ¾-inch, 3c each or 30c doz.

No. 64. "Horse's Friend" curry-comb, 15c each.

No. 65. Bolt snap, ⅞ and 1-inch, 3c each or 30c doz; 1½-inch, 5c each or 50c doz; 1¾-inch, 6c each or 65c doz; 2-inch, 8c each or 85c doz.

No. 66. Steel spreader or rein chain, ring and swivel snap, 8c each or 85c doz.

No. 67. Zinc collar top pad, two sizes, without straps, 25c and 30c each; straps for zinc collar pads, 16c pair.

No. 68. Curry combs, 5 bars, closed back, 6c; 6 bars, closed back, 15c; 6 bars open back, 10c; 6 bars, open back, with mane comb, 18c each.

No. 69. The "Gem" snap, ⅞ and 1-inch, 4c each or 40c doz; 1½-inch, 6c each or 65c doz; 1¾-inch, 7c each or 75c doz; 2-inch, 10c each or $1.00 doz.

No. 70. Trace-carrier, to sew on or to rivet, very strong, 5c each or 50c doz.

No. 71. Wooden stirrups, 25c pair.

No. 72. Cow bells, height 4½-inch, 20c; 5½-inch, 25c; 6½-inch, 35c each. Sheep bells, 10c and 15c each.

No. 73. Hame breast-strap rings, with washers, 5c each or 50c doz.

No. 74. Buckle shields or keepers, nickel or brass, ⅝ and ¾-inch, 8c each or 85c doz; ⅞ and 1-inch, 10c each or $1.00 doz.

No. 75. The double-grip trace buckle, the strongest and handiest trace buckle on the market to-day, in fine XC plate or nicely japanned, 1¼-inch, 10c; 1½-inch, 12c; 1¾-inch, 15c each.

No. 76. Stirrup irons, XC plated, 25c; nickel plated, light, 75c; heavy, 95c pair.

No. 77. Hame staples with washers, 3c each or 30c doz.

No. 78. Horse mane or tail comb, made of horn, very strong, 10c each.

No. 79. Heavy breast chains, snap on one end to shorten chain if necessary, each chain tested, 75c pr.

No. 80. Combined whip and line holder. The handiest thing of its kind in existence, prevents the lines from getting down around horses' feet, and a simple pull releases them at once, 35c; nickel tip, 40c each.

No. 81. All steel snaps, ⅞ and 1-inch, 2 for 5c, or 25c doz; 1½-inch, 5c each or 50c doz; 1¾-inch, 6c each or 65c doz. Curb chains, nickel, 35c; solid nickel, 50c each.

WE CARRY COMPLETE LINES OF HARNESS HARDWARE.

Horse Rain Covers.

Made of heavy 10-oz duck, well oiled.
Loin covers, $1.50 each.
Haine covers, $2.00 each.
Breast covers, $2.25 each.
Rubber horse covers, all over, $3.50 and 4.00 each

Washers.

Leather washers, per box of 5 sets, or 40 washers—

No. 1	—for	$\frac{3}{4}$-inch	axle,		15c	box.
2	"	$\frac{7}{8}$	"	"	15c	"
3	"	1	"	"	20c	"
4	"	$1\frac{1}{8}$	"	"	20c	"
5	"	$1\frac{1}{4}$	"	"	20c	"
6	"	$1\frac{3}{8}$	"	"	25c	"
7	"	$1\frac{1}{2}$	"	"	25c	"

Coil axle washers, can be cut to fit any size axle, 5 coils or 100 washers in each box, 25c box.

Brass or wool collar balls, 45c, 50c pair.

Whips and Whip Lashes.

We have a large and well-selected stock of riding and driving whips, ranging in price from 15c to $3.00. Send to us for any kind of a whip you want.
Straight buggy whips, 15c, 25c, 50c, 75c, $1.00, 1.50, 2.00 each.
Team whips, 25c, 35c, 75c, $1.00, 1.25 each.
Imitation Holly whips, 50c, 75c each.
Genuine " " $1.00, 1.50, 2.00, 3.00 each.
Hickory stocks, with loop, 10c each.
Black-snake stocks, 50c each,
Genuine horse hide lashes, 3 ft, 10c; 4 ft, 15c; 5 ft, 20c; 6 ft, 25c; 10 ft, 60c each.
Riding whips, 25c, 75c each.
Dog whips, 50c, $1.00 each.

Harness Polish, Soap, Oils, etc.

Frank Miller's harness oil, the finest harness oil on the market, pint tins, 35c; quart tins, 50c each.
Boston coach axle oil, 25c pint tin.
F. Miller's coach axle oil, excellent for light or heavy carriages, pint tins, 25c; quart, 45c.
Miller's black harness soap, 20c bar.
Harris' waterproof harness composition, 20c box.
Miller's celebrated harness dressing, the finest in the land, 25c pint.
Miller's carriage top dressing, has no equal for making old tops look new, ½-pint tins, 30c; pint tins, 60c.
Miller's hoof dressing, quart tins, 50c.
Peerless hoof ointment, best healing remedy known, for contracted hoofs it has no equal; also good for cuts, burns, and sores of all kinds, 20c tin.
Diamond axle grease, 5c box.
Mica axle grease, 10c box, or 25c 3-lb pail.

GRANITEWARE, TINWARE, WOODENWARE.

FOR ILLUSTRATIONS SEE OPPOSITE PAGE.

200. Tea kettle, granite, No. 7, 75c; No. 8, 80c; No. 9, 95c; tin, common pit, copper bottom, No. 7, 40c; No. 8, 45c; No. 9, 50c; tin, patent pit copper bottom, No. 7, 55c; No. 8, 65c; No. 9, 75c; No. 10, 80c; copper kettles, nickel-plated, No. 7, 90c; No. 8, $1.10; No. 9, $1.20; No. 10, $2.00.
201. Tin tea or coffee pot, 12c, 15c, 18c.
202. Granite coffee pot, 35c, 40c, 50c, 60c, 65c.
203. Granite tea pots, 30c, 35c, 40c, 50c, 60c, 65c ea.
204. Granite sugar bowl, 40c.
205. Granite tea steeper, 20c, 25c each.
206. Granite milk can, 35c, 45c, 60c, 75c; tin, 20c, 22c, 28c, 30c each.
207. Dinner pails, granite, 50c; tin, round, 15c; tin, oval, 18c each.
208. Creamery cans, with gauge, tap and locking attachment 65c.
209. Japanned water cans, zinc rose, 25c, 35c.
210. Fry pans, granite, No. 7, 25c; No. 8, 30c; No. 9, 35c; steel, No. 7, 25c; No. 8, 30c; No. 9, 35c.
211. Dish pans, granite, 45c, 50c, 60c, 70c, 80c; pressed tin, 28c, 33c, 35c, 45c; pieced tin, handmade, 12c, 15c, 20c each.
212. Toilet jar, tin, japanned, 25c, 40c; granite, $1.15.
212. Chamber pail, granite, $1.00; tin, japanned, 40c, 50c each; galvanized iron, 50c each.
214. Water carrier, tin japanned, oak grained, 75c, $1.00.
215. Water jug, granite, 45c, 55c, 65c.
216. Mug, white granite, 8c, 9c, 10c, 12c.
217. Cuspidor, granite, 30c, 40c; tin, japanned, 10c, 15c.
218. Boilers, medium, tin, copper pit bottom, No. 8, $1.25; No. 9, $1.50; common pit bottom, No. 7, 90c; No. 8, 90c; No. 9, $1.10; No. 10, $1.50.
219. Steamers, No. 7, 20c; No. 8, 22c; No. 9, 25c; No. 10, 30c.
220. Toilet set, tin, japanned, $1.60 oak grained, $1.85; ornamented, $2.50.
221. Roast pans, granite, 45c, 50c; sheet iron, 10c, 12c, 15c and 18c.
222. Infant bath, new style, 28-inch, $1.10; 32-inch, $1.35; 40-inch, $1.75; oval foot bath, 65c, 80c.
223. Wash bowls, granite, 16c, 18c, 22c, 28c, 33c, 35c; tin, 8c, 10c, 15c.
224. Milk pans, granite, 25c, 30c, 35c; pressed tin, seamless, 8c, 10c, 12c.
225. Butter-dish, granite, 25c.
226. Kneading pans, with cover, granite, $1.35; tin, 85c.
227. Cullenders, granite, 35c; heavy tin, 20c.
228. Measures, government stamped, ¼-pk, 30c; ½-pk, 35c; 1-pk, 60c; 2-pk, 75c.
229. Water pails, granite, 55c, 65c; heavy tin, 22c, 28c, 33c; pieced tin, 12c, 17c.
230. Strainer pails, pieced tin, 35c, 40c. The Gem, with removable strainer, 65c.
231. Preserving kettles, granite, 24c, 28c, 32c, 36c, 42c, 50c, 60c, 75c, 90c; pressed tin, 12c, 16c, 20c, 28c, 30c.
232. Covered pails, granite, 22c, 25c, 30c, 40c, 45c; pieced tin, 8c, 10c, 12c, 15c.
233. Victor flour sifters, 12c.
234. Egg timer, 25c each.
235. Lanterns, lift or tilt, 45c; dashboard, with reflector, 65c; extra heavy lantern, 90c; search light, to hang on post, $2.00.
236. Comb case, 15c.
237. Small spirit lamp, asbestos filling, suitable for travelling, etc., 25c, 35c, 50c.
238. Dead shot rat trap, kills instantly, nothing suspicious about it to scare the rats, they are the cheapest and best, 10c each.
239. Frypan, steel, 10c, 12c, 15c, 18c, 20c, 22c, 25c.
240. Set skewers, 15c.
241. Fancy wire toast rack, 35c.
242. Lamp attachments, handy for heating curling tongs, children's food, etc., 10c each.
243. Wire toaster, wooden handle, 10c each.
244. Candle lantern, very handy, without candle, 13c each.
245. Saucepans, lipped, granite, 10c, 14c, 20c, 25c, 30c, 35c, 40c; tin, heavy, 6c, 8c, 10c, 12c, 14c, 16c, 22c, 24c.
246. Tin rice boiler, 25c.
247. Berlin saucepan, with cover, 30c, 40c, 50c, 60c, 70c.
248. Rice boiler, granite, 55c, 75c, 95c, $1.15.
249. Windsor saucepan, granite, with cover, 20c, 30c, 40c, 50c.
250. Straight saucepan, pieced tin, 8c, 10c, 12c, 15c; granite, 30c, 33c, 42c, 50c, 55c, 75c each.
251. Dipper, tin, pieced, 5c, 10c; extra heavy tin, seamless, 17c; granite, 20c.
252. Pudding pans, granite, 12c, 16c, 20c, 25c; tin, seamless, 4c, 6c, 8c, 10c.
253. Flour sieves, tin band, 12c each.
254. Jelly plates, granite, 12c, 15c; tin, 5c, 6c.
255. Novelty bread pans, 6c.
256. Cake moulds, with tube, 4c, 5c, 6c.
257. Paring knife, 5c.
258. Cake moulds, 20c, 25c.
259. Jelly moulds, new style, 18c, 22c.
260. Jelly moulds, copper rim, 35c, 40c, 45c, 65c, 75c, 85c.

Individual jelly moulds, fancy shapes and designs, 5c, 6c, 7c, 10c, 12c, 15c each.

261. Patty pans, assorted shapes, 9c doz.
262. Thumb scoops, tin, 5c; granite, 9c.
263. Candlestick, 5c.
264. Pastry brush, 7c, 10c.

Nutmeg grater, 3c; large vegetable grater, 5c.

265. Biscuit, muffin or corn-cake pans, 6-cup, 12c; 8-cup, 15c; 12-cup, 20c.
266. Asbestos mats, 3c each.
267. Corkscrews, 5c, 10c, 15c; better quality, 25c.
268. Knife trays, embossed, 22c.
269. Machine oilers, 7c; large size, 10c; drip oilers, long spout, 15c.
270. Dinner horns, japanned, 10c.
271. Broilers, self basting, 35c.
272. Dustpans, tin, 5c; japanned, 8c; half covered, 15c.
273. Apple corer, 5c.
274. Cash box, japanned, with tray, good lock, 8-inch, 80c; 9-inch, 90c; 10-inch, $1.00; 11-inch, $1.10; 12-inch, $1.35.
275. Mouse trap, 4-hole, 5c.
276. Milk skimmer, 3c.
277. Spice boxes in tray, 25c.
278. Crumb tray and brush, 25c, 50c, 65c.
279. Edgar nutmeg grater, 10c.
280. Pie crimper and pastry cutter, 5c.
281. Fruit fillers, 6c.
282. Trays, nickel plated, round, 10c, 15c, 35c.
283. Funnel, granite, 10c, 12c, 15c, 20c; tin, 5c, 7c, 8c, 10c.
284. Soap dish, granite, 14c.
285. Stove scraper, 6c.
286. Ladle, granite, 12c; tin, 7c.
287. Soap dish, tin, 9c.
288. Basting spoon, tin, 4c, 5c.
289. Folding wooden table mats, nice finish, alternate light and dark colors, oval shape, 35c set of 3; oblong shape, 25c set of 3.
290. Basting spoon, granite, 7c, 8c, 9c each.
291. Marion Harland's coffee pot:

1 quart size,	1 to	4 cups,	$1.25.
2 " "	3 to	7 "	1.50.
3 " "	4 to	10 "	1.75.

This coffee pot is strong and well made, and is handsomely nickel plated; parts cannot possibly get out of order.

> Prices on this page subject to change without notice.

Brushes.

Shoe brushes—

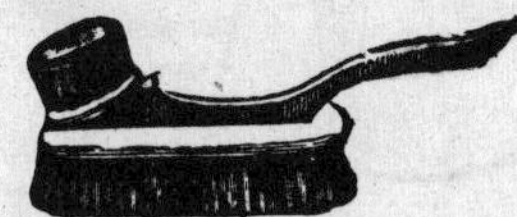

Plain, 15c, 25c each.
Plain top-knot dauber, 15c each.
Plain top-knot dauber, with handle, 10c, 15c, 20c, 25c, 35c, 50c each.
Shoe daubers, 5c each.
Royal shoe dauber, with mud scraper, 20c.
The People's, 15c each.
The Hub, 10c each.

Scrubbing brushes—

Green corn, 5c each.
Whisk root, 8c, 10c, 15c, 20c, 25c each.
White fibre, 5c, 10c each.

Stove brushes—
With handles, double wing, 10c, 15c, 20c, 30c each.
Best quality bristles, 25c, 50c each.
Stove daubers, 5c, 7c, 12c each.

Window brushes—
Round, grey bristles, 25c, 35c, 45c each.
10-ft handles for above window brushes, 15c each.

Banister brushes, single—
Grey hair, 20c, 25c, 30c, 40c each.
Whisk root, 25c each.

Banister brushes, double—
Grey bristle, 30c, 35c, 45c each.

Brooms—Long-handled ceiling brooms, 20c each.
Hair ceiling brooms, complete, with 6-ft handles, 60c, 75c each.
Heather sink scrubs, with wooden handles, 10c each.
Hair brooms, grey centre, handle included, 55c, 75c, 90c each.
Hair brooms, extra quality, 75c, $1.00, 1.25 ea.
Children's toy brooms, 10c, 15c each.

Mops, self-wringing, 25c each.
Mops, common, 10c each.
Hearth dusters, japanned handles, 25c each.
Blacking kits, in imitation leather case, 25c, 30c.

Stable Brooms.

Cane, best quality, hardwood handles, 50c, 60c, 85c.
Split bamboo, with handles, 65c, 75c, 85c each.
Pick handles, 15c each.
Adze handles, 15c each.

If two or three families order together they can save transportation charges.
See Club-order Note, 2nd page Catalogue.

NO ORDER TOO SMALL TO RECEIVE OUR CAREFUL ATTENTION.

Hardware Dept. *All Prices Subject to Change Without Notice*

(For illustrations see opposite page.)

1. Cold handle poker, 10c.
2. Combination corkscrew, knife sharpener, can opener, glass cutter, etc., 5c each.
3. Can opener, 8c.
4. Tack claw, 5c; heavy, 10c.
5. Gate hasps, 5c.
6. Bird-cage bracket, 5c, 8c each.
7. Ceiling hooks, 3-in., 5c, 7c; 9-in., 10c each.
8. Corkscrew, 5c, 10c; heavy, 25c, 35c.
9. Wire on spools, 4c; covered or millinery wire, 4c each.
10. Brass curtain rings, ⅜-inch, 2c doz, 15c gross; ½, ⅜-inch, 2c doz, 20c gross; 7-16, ½, ⅝-inch, 3c doz, 30c gross; ¾-inch, 4c doz, 40c gross; ⅞-inch, 5c doz, 50c gross; 1-inch, 7c doz, 75c gross.
11. Gate hooks and eyes, 2½-inch, 20c doz; 3½-inch, 30c doz; 4-inch, 35c doz; 5-inch, 45c doz.
12. Drapery hooks, 5c, 8c doz.
13. Tolers' bed casters, 10c; Philadelphia casters, metal wheel, 10c; lignum vitæ wheel, 12c set.
14. White porcelain head, picture nails, 20c doz.; fancy, 30c doz.
15. Gimlets, 5c, 10c each.
16. Four-lever padlocks, 35c; six-lever, 50c; eight-lever, 75c each.
17. Picture wire, 25 yds, 10c, 15c, 20c box.
18. Shelf brackets, steel, 4 x 5-inch, 5c pr; 5 x 7-inch, 8c pr; 6 x 8-inch, 10c pr; 7 x 9-inch, 12c pr. These prices do not include screws.
19. Gopher or ground-hog traps, No. 0, no chain, 12c each; No. 1, no chain, 15c each; No. 0, with chain, 15c each; No. 1, with chain, 20c each; No. 1½ with chain, 35c each.
20. Door bolts, light japanned, 4-inch, 5c; 6-inch, 10c; bronzed door bolts, 4-inch, 12c; fancy bronzed, 3-inch, 15c; 4-inch, 18c; heavy japanned, 4-inch, 7c; 6-inch, 10c each.
21. Raisin seeders, 60c each.
22. Drop drawer handles, 5c each.
23. Brass drawer pulls, 5c each.
24. Cast sash lock, 7c; steel sash lock, 10c each.
25. Moulding hooks, 5c, 7c, 10c, 25c doz.
26. Drawer pulls, japanned, 12c doz; bronzed, 24c, 36c doz; brass, 60c doz.
27. Door handles or pulls, 3c; heavy, 5c each.
28. Hinge hasps, 3-inch, 5c; 8-inch, 10c, no screws.
29. Double-pointed tacks, 3c package.
30. Thumb latches, black, japanned, 5c; heavy, 12c; bronzed, 10c.
31. Gate hooks, straight, thick wire, 5c.
32. Door bells, single stroke, or lever, 50c; electric stroke, brass plate, 85c.
33. Cupboard catches, white knob, 7c.
34. " " fancy bronze, 10c.
35. Mortise locks, 20c, 25c, 35c, 40c; rim locks, 15c, 25c, 30c each.
36. Porcelain door knobs, 12c, 25c; bronzed, 45c; brass, 75c each.
37. Clothes-line hooks, japanned, complete with screws, 5c each.
38. Bull snaps, with chain, 40c each.
39. Plasterer's trowel, for family use, 25c; for plasterers, 11-inch, $1.35; 12-inch, $1.50.
40. Wall scrapers, 15c each.
41. Potato forks, 75c.
42. Square-mouthed shovels, 85c.
43. D-handled spade, 85c.
44. Grass hooks, 25c.
45. Door stops, rubber tips, 3c each.
46. 47. Push-button door bell, steady ring, $1.35.
48. Bronzed cupboard turns, 10c each.
49. Brass sash lift, 8c; heavy, 12c each.
50. Steel night latch (as cut), 60c, fits right or left hand doors opening in or out, two keys.
51. Bull ring, copper, 20c each.
52. Tacks in barrels, 2 for 5c.
53. Brick trowel, 9½-inch, 25c; Johnson's 11-inch, 65c; 12-inch, 75c.
54. Electric hay knife, 95c.
55. Scythe, 85c.
56. Snaths, 65c each.
57. Sash lock, solid steel, 10c each.
58. Plumb bobs, 10c, 15c each.
59. Screw eyes, No. 1, 2, 3, 3c doz; No. 4, 5, 6, 4c doz; Nos. 7, 8, 5c doz; Nos. 10, 12, 7c doz.
60. 61. Door spring, 15c; heavy, 20c.
62. Glass cutters, metal handle, 5c, 8c; wood handle, 10c, 15c each.
63. Self-closing spring hinges for screen doors, complete with screws, 15c pair.
64. Machinist's hammer, 45c, 55c, 65c, 75c, 85c.
65. Screw hooks, 4c, 7c, 10c doz; extra large and heavy, 20c, 30c doz.
66. Oil stones, neat wooden case, 15c, 40c; Washita stones, 50c, 60c, 65c, 75c each.
67. Small penknife stones, 5c each; razor hones, 50c, 75c, $1.25, 2.00 each.
68. Horse rasps, Heller, 15-inch, 85c.
69. Nail punch, knurled, 10c.
70. Files, flat bastard, 4-inch, 12c; 5-inch, 13c; 6-inch, 14c; 8-inch, 18c; 10-inch, 24c; 12-inch, 30c; 14-inch, 45c each.
72. Slim taper saw files, 3½-inch, 6c; 4-inch, 7c; 4½-inch, 7c; 5-inch, 8c; 6-inch, 10c; heavier saw, 3½-inch, 7c; 4-inch, 7c; 4½-inch, 7c; 5-inch, 7c; 6-inch, 10c.
73. Tack hammers, 8c, 10c, 12c; household hammers, 25c, 35c; carpenters' hammers, 40c, 60c.
74. Figured cast door hinges, 3 x 2½, 7c; 3 x 3, 8c; 3½ x 3½, 10c; 4 x 4, 12c pair; screws extra.
75. Corner brace, $3.00.
76. Clark's expansion bits, $1.00, 1.50 each.
77. Tape measures, 50 feet, 35c; 66 feet, 65c; metallic wired, English, 50 feet, $1.75; 66 feet, $2.00; 100 feet, $2.75; steel pocket tape measure, 18 feet, $2.50; 25 feet, $3.50 ea.
78. Screw drivers, 2-inch, 7c; 3-inch, 10c; 4-inch, 12c; 5-inch, 15c; 7-inch, 18c; 8-inch, 25c.
79. File handles, 3c each.
80. Tool sets, 10 tools and handle, 50c; varnished handle, 65c.
81. Loose pin butts, 2½ x 2, 5c pair; 2½ x 2½, 5c pair; 3 x 2½, 6c pair; 3½ x 3, 8c pair; 3½ x 3½, 10c pair; 4 x 4, 12c pair, no screws.
82. Saddler's punch, assorted sizes, 10c each.
83. Brad awl, 5c each.
84. Braces, 15c, 35c, 50c, 75c, $1.50; ratchet brace, $1.00, 2.00.
85. Spirit levels and plumb, 18 to 24-inch, 50c; 30-inch, 65c; adjustable plumbs and levels, 30-inch, $1.25; pocket levels, 10c each.
86. Drawknives, 65c.
87. Broad's firmer socket chisels, ¼-inch, 35c; ⅜-inch, 37c; ½-inch, 40c; ⅝-inch, 42c; ¾-inch, 45c; ⅞-inch, 48c; 1-inch, 50c; 1¼-inch, 55c; 1½-inch, 60c; 1¾-inch, 65c; 2-inch, 70c; framing chisels, ¾-inch, 65c; 1-inch, 70c; 1½-inch, 75c; 2-inch, 90c.
88. Iron squares, 25c; steel squares, 85c, $1.25.
89. Sash lifts, 18c, 24c doz.
90. " bronzed, 24c doz.
91. Boys' 12-inch saw, 15c.
92. Meat saw, 40c each.
93. Disston's saws, 22-inch, $1.65; 26-inch, $1.85.
94. Key-hole saw, 25c.
95. Disston's nest of saws, with handle, $1.25.
96. Pruning saws, 50c.
97. Shurley & Dietrich saws, 18-inch, 85c; 20-inch, $1.00; 22-inch, $1.15; 24-inch, $1.25; 26-inch, $1.50; 24-inch rip saw, $1.25; 26-inch, $1.50.
98. Try squares, 4½-inch, 20c; 6-inch, 25c; 7½-inch, 30c; 9-inch, 35c.
99. Carpenters' chalk, red, white or blue, 3 for 5c.
100. Monkey wrenches, 6-inch, 35c; 8-inch, 45c; 10-inch, 50c; 12-inch, 55c; 15-inch, 90c.
101. Sliding T bevels, 8-inch, 25c; 10-inch, 30c; 12-inch, 35c.
102. Adjustable iron planes, smoothing planes, 1¾-in cutter, $1.90; 2-inch cutter, $2.15; jack planes, 14 inches long, 2-inch cutter, $2.35; 18-inches long, 2⅜-inch cutter, $3.00; 22 inches long, 2⅜-inch cutter, $3.50; Stanley's adjustable wood bottom planes, 8 inches long, 1¾-inch cutter, $1.00; handled smooth, 10 inches long, 2⅛-inch cutter, $1.25; jack plane, 15 inches long, 2⅛-inch cutter, $1.25; fore plane, 20 inches long, 2⅜-inch cutter, $1.35; jointer plane, 26 inches long, 2⅜-inch cutter, $1.65.
103. Rules, 1 ft, 4-fold, 5c each; 2 ft, 4-fold, 8c, 15c, 20c, 25c, 35c; 1 ft, 4-fold, calliper rule, 25c.
104. Spoke shave, iron frame, single iron, 15c; double iron, 25c; wood frame, beechwood handle, 2½-inch, 25c; 3-inch, 30c.
105. Light T hinges, without screws, 3-inch, 5c; 5-inch, 6c; 8-inch, 10c pair; heavy T hinges, 5-inch, 12c; 6-inch, 18c; 8-inch, 20c; 10-inch, 25c pair; strap hinges, light, 4-inch, 5c; 5-inch, 6c; 8-inch, 12c pair; corrugated steel hinge, 4-inch, 8c; 5-inch, 10c; 6-inch, 12c; 8-inch, 20c; 10-inch, 25c pair.
106. Gouges, no handle, ¼-inch, 10c; ⅜-inch, 12c; ⅜-inch, 14c; ½-inch, 15c; ⅝-inch, 18c; ¾-inch, 20c; ⅞-inch, 22c; 1-inch, 25c; 1¼-inch, 30c; 1½-inch, 35c; 2-inch, 45c.
107. Stanley's wood bottom planes, smooth, 8 inches long, 1¾-inch cutter, $1.25; 8 inches long, 2-inch cutter, $1.25; handled smooth, 9 inches long, 2-inch cutter, $1.65; jack planes, 2⅛-inch cutter, $1.65; fore planes, 20 inches long, 2⅜-inch cutter, $1.85; jointer plane, 26 inches long, 2⅜-inch cutter, $2.10.
108. Steel dividers, 6-inch, 25c; 8-inch, 35c; 10-inch, 45c each.
109. Bronze lock, spring, 50c, 85c, $1.00.
110. Marking gauge, 5c, 15c, 25c each; mortise gauge, brass thumb-screw, 30c, 35c each.
111. Brass finish lock, 2 keys, 12c each.
112. Cutting pliers, 5-inch, 25c; 5½-inch, 30c; Stubb's line-mans' pliers, 7-inch, $1.50; 8-inch, $1.75.
113. Gas burner pliers, 25c, 65c; single hole, 15c, 60c each.
114. Steel adze, no handle, $1.35, 1.50 each.
115. Cleavers, 25c each.
116. Hunters' axe, 45c each.
117. Hog ringers, 10c each; hog rings, 10c package
118. Flat nose pliers, steel, 4-inch, 15c; 4½-inch, 20c; 5-inch, 20c; extra good, 30c each.
119. Revolving belt punch, 4 cuts, 65c each.
120. Single belt punch, 25c each.
121. Pruning shears, 30c, 50c each.
122. Combination glass cutter, plier, corkscrew, etc., 10c each.
123. Lock, 2 keys, 25c each.
124. Lodi cutting pliers, 5-inch, 15c; 5-inch, extra finish, 30c.
125. Lodi pliers, 4-inch, 5c; 4½-inch, 8c; 5-inch, 10c each.
126. Bronze lock, heavy, 85c, $1.00 each.
127. Broad axe, handled, 5½-inch blade, 85c; 6-inch blade, $1.15 each.
128. Hatchet, 40c, 50c each.
129. Axe, 75c, 95c; boys' axe, 60c each.

Auger bits, 3/16, 15c; 4/16, 15c; 5/16, 15c; 6/16, 18c; 7/16, 18c; 8/16, 18c; 10/16, 20c; 11/16, 22c; 12/16, 25c; 13/16, 27c; 14/16, 30c; 15/16, 33c; 16/16, 35c; 18/16, 40c; 20/16, 45c each.

Auger bits, blued centre—

	3,	4,	5,	6,	7,	8,	9,	10,	11,	12,	13,	14,	15,	16—16ths.
Price,	20c,	20c,	20c,	25c,	27c,	30c,	35c,	40c,	42c,	45c,	50c,	53c,	55c,	60c each.

Car bits—

	4	6,	8,	10,	12—16ths.
Price,	30c,	35c,	45c,	55c,	70c.

Saw set, the Perfect, 50c.
Putty knife, 20c.
Socket chisel handles, 5c, 7c each.
Tanged " " 5c, 8c each.
File handles, 3c.
Jack plane handle, 4c.
Fore " " 6c.
Hand saw " 10c, 50c.

Tanged chisels—

	⅛,	¼,	5/16,	⅜,	½,	⅝,	¾,	⅞	1,	1¼,	1½,	2,
Price,	12c,	12c,	13c,	15c,	18c,	20c,	22c,	25c,	28c,	30c,	35c,	50c.

Centre bits—

	¾,	⅞,	1,	1½,	1¾.
Price,	8c,	8c,	10c,	12c,	15c.

Vises, small, japanned, 15c; tinned, 20c; japanned, 50c; extra heavy, 2¾-inch jaw, opens 4 inches, $2.25 each.
Twine box, to hang, 20c.
Single plane irons, 2-in, 22c; 2⅛-in, 25c; 2¼-in, 28c; 2⅜-in, 30c; 2½-in, 35c.
Whet stone, 5c; round table stone, 15c.
Washer cutter, adjustable, 50c.
Boker's hand vise, 4½-in, 60c.
Callipers, outside, 4-in., 15c; 6-in., 25c; 8-in., 40c.
Cold chisels, 10c, 15c and 25c.
Carpenters' lead pencils, 5c each and 2 for 5c.
Carpenters' pincers, 6-in, 15c; 7-in, 20c; 8-in, 25c.
Boker's or Muller's wire fence pliers, 8-in, 25c; 10-in, 35c.
Punches, ticket, 25c; conductors' punches, 65c, 75c, $2.00.
Screw-driver bits, 10c, 15c each.
Gimlet bits, 7c, 10c each.
Rimer bits, square, ½-in, 10c; half round, ½-in, 10c.
Counter sink bits, ½ to ⅝-in, 10c; rose, 10c.
Ratchet screw-driver, Yankee, 3-in, 45c; 4-in, 55c; 5-in, 65c; 6-in, 70c.
Auger bit sets, in neat wood case, 8 to the set, sizes 4, 5, 6, 8, 10, 12, 14, 16-16ths, $2.00 per set; 13 in a set, $3.00 per set.
Carpenters' tool baskets, lined, 35c each.
Sandpaper, 1c sheet; emery cloth, 5c sheet.
Key-hole saws, 25c, 50c.
Hack saws, 25c; extension, $1.35.
Copper soldering irons, 25c, 50c each.
Solder, 35c per stick; 5c per coil.
Long handle tree pruners, $1.00 each.
Bull dog wrenches, twin, 85c; No. 2, 65c; No. 1, 20c each.
Farriers' pincers, 14-inch, $1.00 each.
Tinsmiths' snips, 35c, $1.65 each.
Upholsterers' hammers, $1.75, 2.00 each.
Butchers' saws, 24-inch, $1.35; 22-inch, $1.25 each.
Boker's butchers' cleavers, 75c; extra fine steel, $1.75 each.
Stylson wrenches, 6-inch, $1.10; 8-inch, $1.50; 10-inch, $1.75 each.
Machinist hammers, round pein, without handle, ½-lb, 35c; 1-lb, 40c; 1½-lb, 50c; 2-lb, 60c each.
Yankee spiral ratchet screw-driver, right hand only, $1.15, 1.35, 1.50; right and left hand, $2.00 each.
Yankee reciprocating drill, $2.75.
Shoemakers' hammers, 35c, 45c each.
Tinners' hammers, 45c and 50c each.
Rabbet plane, iron stock and fence, 8½ inches long, 1½-inch cutter, $1.50.
Rabbet and block plane, detachable side, 7 inches long, 1½-inch cutter, $1.25.
Circular steel plane, can be made either convex or concave, $3.00.
Adjustable tonguing and grooving plane for ⅜-inch to 1¼-inch boards, $2.50.
(The above planes are all of Stanley's best make.)
Mortise lock sets, bronze knobs, 85c; blue black knobs, 60c set.
Shurley & Dietrich's 28-inch rip saw, $1.60; stiff back saw, 12-inch, $1.00.

We can supply all mechanics' and farmers' Tools.

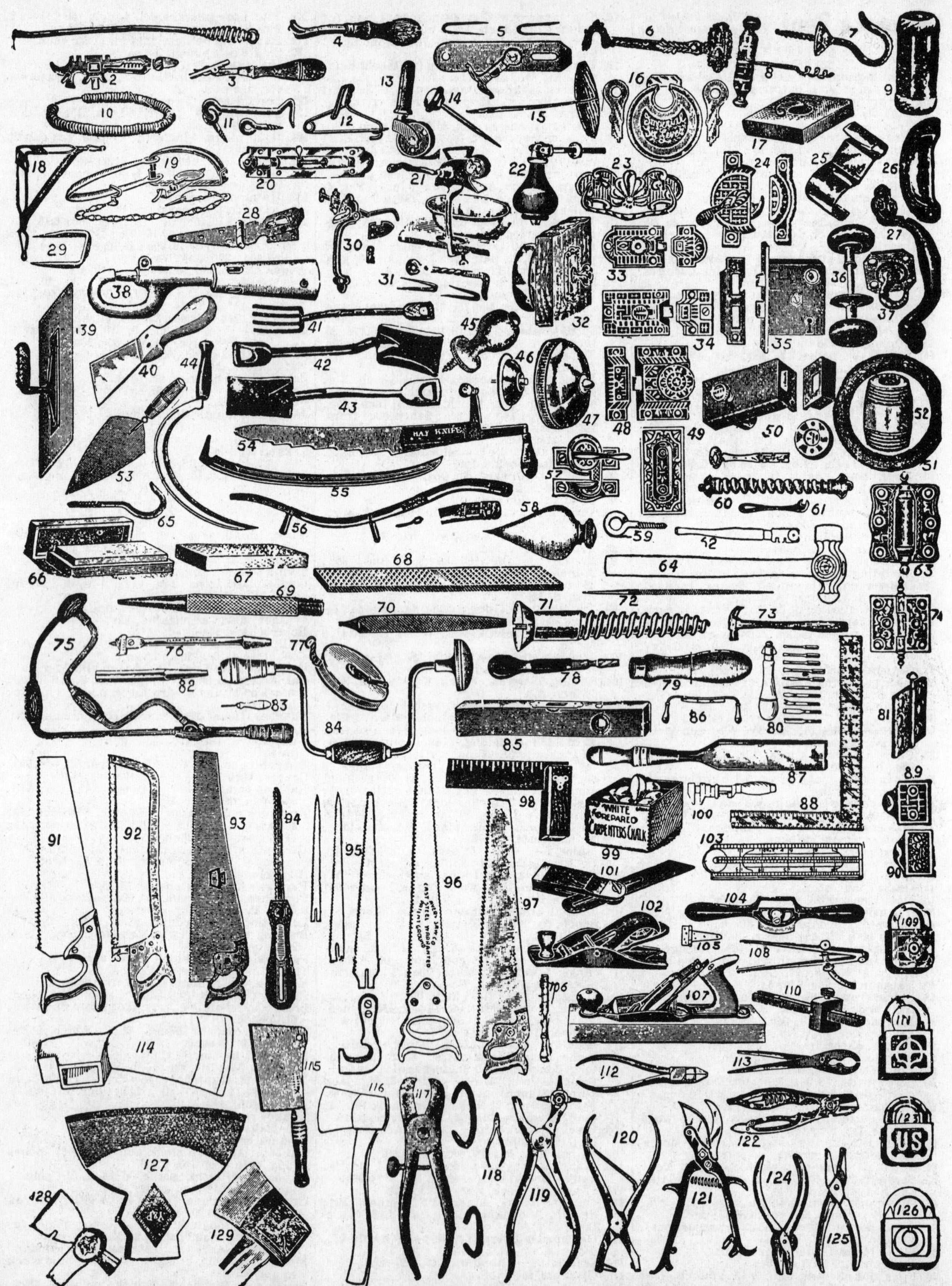

We cannot afford to misrepresent our goods. We are in business to stay.

PREPARE FOR SPRING AND SUMMER BY ORDERING NOW.

Household Furnishings.

FOR ILLUSTRATIONS SEE OPPOSITE PAGE.

400. Leader churn, No. 1, 9 gals, $3.75; No. 2, 15 gals, $4.00; No. 3, 20 gals, $4.75.
401. Wringers, Royal Dominion, $2.50; Leader, $3.00; Paragon, with ball bearings, $3.65.
402. Canadian washer, $3.50.
403. Wood wash tubs, 50c, 60c, 70c, 80c; fibre tubs, 80c, 95c, $1.15, 1.30; wood pails, 15c, 17c; fibre pails, 32c, 40c.
404. Queen mangle, three maple rollers, casters, folding table, best English steel springs, $15.00.
405. Wash board, Globe, 15c; solid back, 20c; toy wash boards, 10c; pastry boards, 25c; toy pastry boards, 10c; bread boards, 35c, 45c, 65c, 75c, $1.25; bosom boards, shaped neck, 12c; sleeve boards, 10c; skirt boards, 25c, 35c; bosom and sleeve boards, combined, or tailor's jack, 35c.
406. Mrs. Potts' irons, polished, consisting of 3 irons, handle and stand, 89c; nickel plated, $1.00.
407. The Dowswell washer, $3.50.
408. Clothes lines, cotton, 50 ft, 15c; 75 ft, 20c; 100 ft, 25c; manilla, 10c.
409. Step ladder with pail rack, 5 ft, 50c; 6 ft, 60c; 7 ft, 75c; pine, extra strong and with patent spreader, 5 ft, 90c; 6 ft, $1.10; 7 ft, $1.35.
410. Grooved butter spades, 5c; butter prints, round, individual, 5c; ½ lb, 20c; 1 lb, 20c; oblong, 1 lb, 25c; butter ladles, 5c; extra fine, 8c; wooden butter knives, 14 inches long, 5c; spice cabinets with glass jars, $1.50.
411. Grocers' scales with side beam, weighing 4 lbs, $2.50; 10 lbs, $3.75.

Tooth picks, box of 1,000, 5c.

412. Dash churns, 6 gallons, $1.50; 8 gallons, $1.75; 10 gallons, $2.00.
413. Folding tub stands, $1.00; folding ironing boards, $1.25.
414. Clothes pegs, 5 doz for 5c.
415. Clothes horse, folding, 4 ft, 35c; 5 ft, 45c; extension, 4 ft, 75c; 5 ft, 90c; 6 ft, $1.00.
416. Towel racks, varnished, 10c, 15c.
417. Clothes arms, 5 bars, 15c.
418. Champion scale, weighing from ½ lb to 240 lbs, $5.00.
419. Platform scales, weighing to 600 lbs, $14.00; to 1,200 lbs, $18.00.
420. Folding coat and hat rack, 10 pegs, 15c; 13 pegs, 30c.
421. Potato masher, 5c.
422. Potato masher, 10c.
423. Cake turner, 8c.
444. Wood spoon, 4c, 5c, 6c, 8c.
445. Cake turner, 5c.
446. Can opener, 5c.
447. Steak pounder and ice shave, 15c.
448. Dover egg beater, 9c; large, 20c.
449. Surprise egg beater, 2c; better quality, 5c.
450. Rolling pin, 5c; enamelled handle, 7c.
451. Maple bowls, 10c, 20c, 25c, 35c.
452. Bucksaws, painted frame, 40c.
453. Coffee mill, 25c, 50c, 75c.
454. Broilers, 12c, 15c, 18c.
455. Toasters, 6c, 8c, 10c, 12c.
456. Tea strainers, 2 for 5c.
457. Tea balls, 15c.
458. Potato masher, 5c.
459. Soap saver, 8c.
460. Empire choppers, with clamp, $1.75, 2.50; to screw on table, $2.00.
461. Axe handles, 10c, 15c.
462. Bird cage springs, 6c; with brass chain, 15c.
463. Brooms, 25c, 35c, 40c.
464. Vegetable skimmers, 5c.
465. Strainer, 6c.
466. Strainer, 12c.
467. Strainer, 10c.
468. Tea strainer, 7c.
469. Gravy strainer, 4c.
470. Salt box, 10c; blacking box with carpet top and metal foot stand, $1.50.
471. Glass rolling pin, can fill with ice, 50c.
472. Lemon squeezer, 15c.
474. Henis' fruit press, 30c.
475. Cup and saucer easel, 10c.
476. Enterprise meat chopper, $1.50, 2.00, 2.50; butcher's size, $3.50; sausage stuffers, for small sizes, 35c each.
477. Knife trays, wood, plain, 10c; varnished and lined, 15c.
478. Spice cabinets, $1.25.
479. Cup and saucer easel, 10c.
480. Double chopper, 10c.
481. Single chopper, 5c.
482. Baskets, 12c, 15c each.

Willow hampers for soiled clothes, square or round, $1.25, 1.75, 2.00 each.

Willow clothes baskets, 55c, 65c, 75c.

Willow clothes baskets, cane handles, 65c, 75c, 85c each.

483. Flower pot bracket, single, 15c; double 30c.
484. Wire teapot stand, 10c.
485. Plate handle, 3c.
486. Heavy chopper, 20c; forged steel, 35c.
487. Soap holder, 10c.
488. Soap holder, 5c.
489. Wire dish cloth, 5c.
490. Feather dusters, 25c, 35c, 50c.
491. Handy truck, $2.00 each.
492. Knife board, 15c.
493. Diamond mop sticks, 10c.
494. Easels, 15c each.
495. Sponge rack, 15c, 25c, 30c.
496. Corn popper, 10c.
497. Dish mop, 5c.
498. Fire shovels, 4c, 10c.
499. Wire clothes line, 50 ft, 20c; 100 ft, 35c.

Wire carpet beater, wooden handle, 10c each.

500. Window cleaner, single, 25c; double, 30c.
501. Wire coat hangers, 3c each.

Belmar suit and skirt hanger, 25c each.

502. Teapot stand, 5c.
503. Towel roller, 12c; better quality, 25c.

Mop cloths, 10c each.

504. Handled wire dish cloth, 10c.
505. Alaska stove lifter, 10c.
506. Stove lifter, 3c each.

Bird Cages.

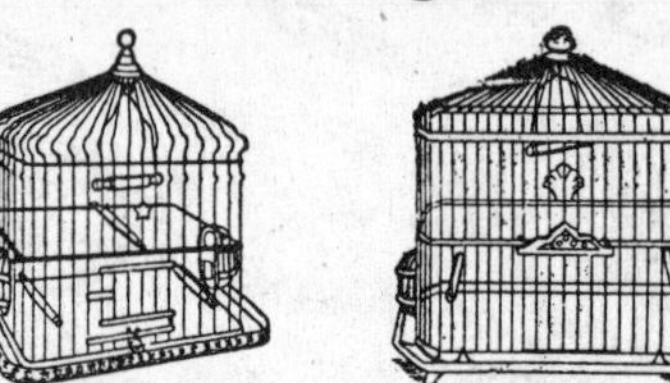

No. 00. Brass, $1.35. No. 10. Japanned, 75c.

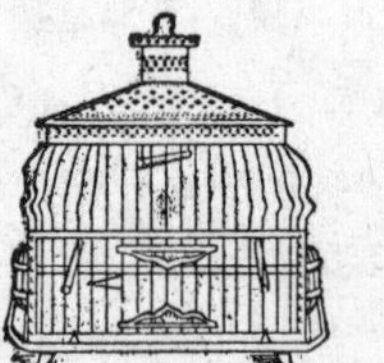

No. 20. Japanned, $1.35.

No. 30. Brass, $2.40.

Japanned bird cages, complete with perches, feed cups and swing, 55c, 65c, 75c, 85c, 90c, $1.00, 1.20, 1.25.

Brass bird cages, our special, a large sized cage, very strong, neat design, with scalloped edge around bottom, $1.35.

Brass cages, $2.00, 2.40, 2.75.
Breeding cages, $1.00 each.
Adjustable brass guards, 45c each.
Opal baths, 5c each.
Opal feed cups, 10c each.
Crystal feed cups, 5c each.
Nests, 6c each.
Brass chain, 5c yard.
Bronze bracket, 5c each.

Parrot Cages.

Round, made of heavy tinned wire.

No. 2. 15¾ x 23½ inches high, $5.25 each.
No. 3. 17½ x 25 inches high, $5.75 each.

Cobblers' Outfits.

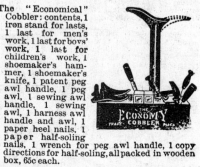

The "Economical" Cobbler: contents, 1 iron stand for lasts, 1 last for men's work, 1 last for boys' work, 1 last for children's work, 1 shoemaker's hammer, 1 shoemaker's knife, 1 patent peg awl handle, 1 peg awl, 1 sewing awl handle, 1 sewing awl, 1 harness awl handle and awl, 1 paper heel nails, 1 paper half-soling nails, 1 wrench for peg awl handle, 1 copy directions for half-soling, all packed in wooden box, 65c each.

The "Bonanza," contents, 1 iron stand for lasts, 1 last for men's work, 1 last for boys' work, 1 last for children's work, 1 shoemaker's hammer, 1 shoemaker's knife, 1 patent peg awl handle and awl, 1 wrench for peg awl handle, 1 pair men's half soles, 1 pair boys' half soles, 1 pair women's half soles, 3 large leather patches for men's shoes, 3 large leather patches for women's shoes, 1 bottle leather cement and directions, 1 package half-soling nails for men's work, 1 package half-soling nails for women's work, 1 copy directions for half-soling, $1.15 each.

These outfits are checked by three different hands, and if you think there is a shortage carefully examine the packing and you will find all goods as listed.

Prices on this page subject to change without notice.

Poultry Netting.

We will not cut less than 4 yards: made of galvanized wire, 2-inch mesh—

12-inch,	2c yard	or $0.90 roll.
18 "	3c "	1.35 "
24 "	4c "	1.90 "
30 "	5c "	2.25 "
36 "	6c "	2.75 "
48 "	8c "	3.65 "
60 "	10c "	4.50 "
72 "	12c "	5.40 "

Roll consists of 50 yards.

Look over these pages carefully; you are sure to find articles you need at prices that will suit you.

Crockery and Glassware Department.

Prices on this page subject to change without notice.

ORDER from the following list as much or as little as you require. Should you want samples of any of the Dinnerware, buy one piece of anything you desire to see, and when it is returned we will refund the money, less the charges.

Dinner and Tea Set Compositions.

40-piece tea sets: 12 tea plates, 12 cups and saucers, 2 cake plates, 1 slop bowl, 1 cream jug.

44-piece tea set: 12 tea plates, 12 cups and saucers, 2 cake plates, 1 teapot, 1 sugar bowl, 1 slop bowl, 1 cream jug.

56-piece tea set: 12 tea plates, 12 cups and saucers, 12 fruit dishes, 2 cake plates, 1 teapot, 1 sugar bowl, 1 slop bowl, 1 cream jug.

100-piece dinner set: 12 tea plates, 12 dinner plates, 12 soup plates, 12 fruit dishes, 12 individual butters, 12 cups and saucers, 3 platters, 1 gravy boat, 1 baker, 2 covered vegetable dishes, 1 pickle, 1 teapot, 1 sugar bowl, 1 slop bowl, 1 cream jug.

112-piece dinner set: 12 tea plates, 12 breakfast plates, 12 dinner plates, 12 soup plates, 12 fruit dishes, 12 individual butters, 12 cups and saucers, 3 platters, 1 gravy boat, 1 baker, 2 covered vegetable dishes, 1 pickle, 1 teapot, 1 sugar bowl, 1 slop bowl, 1 cream jug.

125-piece dinner set: 12 tea plates, 12 breakfast plates, 12 dinner plates, 12 soup plates, 12 fruit dishes, 12 individual butters, 12 cups and saucers, 4 platters, 1 soup tureen, ladle and stand, 1 sauce tureen, ladle and stand, 1 gravy boat, 1 baker, 1 salad, 2 covered vegetable dishes, 1 casserole, 1 pickle, 1 teapot, 1 sugar bowl, 1 slop bowl, 1 cream jug and 1 jug.

No. 12. Meakin's Flo peacock lustre, pattern printed in a handsome decoration, and with very pretty gold tracings on handle—

40-piece tea set......$3.25.
44 " " ...... 3.95.
56 " " ...... 4.50.
100-piece dinner set.. 11.70.
112 " " .. 12.85.
125 " " .. 19.65.

No. 13. Doulton's Albermarle pattern, in a dark blue or pink and green decoration, filled-in colors with heavy gold lines, an exceedingly pretty pattern—

40-piece tea set $3.75. | 100-piece dinner set $13.55.
44 " " 4.40. | 112 " " 14.90.
56 " " 5.25. | 125 " " 23.45.

ORDER WHAT YOU WISH FROM THE FOLLOWING LIST.

PIECES OF DINNER-WARE.	No. 10. UPPER HANLEY'S KING'S BORDER IN BROWN OR GREEN.	No. 11. MEAKIN'S MARGARETTA OR GLORIANA PINK.	No. 12. MEAKIN'S FLO PEACOCK LUSTRE.	No. 13. DOULTON'S ALBERMARLE.	No. 14. HAVILAND'S FRENCH CHINA.	No. 15. OHME'S EGLANTINE CHINA.
Plates, fruit, 5-inch....	$0 55 doz.	$0 85 doz.	$0 80 doz.	$1 00 doz.	$2 25 doz.	$1 35 doz.
" tea, 6-inch......	0 70 "	1 00 "	0 95 "	1 25 "	2 75 "	1 65 "
" breakfast, 7-inch	0 85 "	1 20 "	1 15 "	1 35 "	3 00 "	1 90 "
" dinner, 8-inch ..	1 00 "	1 40 "	1 40 "	1 50 "	3 50 "	2 50 "
" soup, 7-inch	0 85 "	1 20 "	1 15 "	1 35 "	....	....
" " 8-inch	1 00 "	1 40 "	1 40 "	1 50 "	3 50 "	2 50 "
Fruit dishes	0 40 "	0 60 "	0 55 "	0 85 "	1 65 "	1 35 "
Butter pats	0 30 "	0 40 "	0 40 "	0 60 "	1 00 "	0 60 "
After dinner coffees...	....	....	....	....	....	2 00 "
Teacups and saucers ..	1 00 "	1 65 "	1 55 "	1 60 "	4 20 "	2 65 "
Breakfast cups & saucers	....	....	....	....	....	2 65 "
Platters, 9-inch	....	....	....	....	0 65 ea.	....
" 10-inch........	0 20 ea.	0 30 ea.	0 30 ea.	0 50 ea.	0 85 "	0 75 ea.
" 12-inch........	0 30 "	0 50 "	0 45 "	0 60 "	1 10 "	0 95 "
" 14-inch........	0 45 "	0 75 "	0 70 "	0 75 "	1 40 "	1 10 "
" 16-inch........	0 70 "	1 00 "	0 90 "	1 00 "	2 75 "	1 50 "
" 18-inch........	1 00 "	1 40 "	1 30 "	1 50 "	3 75 "	2 75 "
Soup tureen, complete..	2 25 "	3 00 "	2 75 "	3 50 "	†3 50 "	†2 25 "
Sauce " "	0 65 "	1 00 "	0 90 "	1 25 "	*1 75 "	*0 85 "
Gravy boat	0 20 "	0 30 "	0 25 "	0 25 "	1 50 "	0 75 "
Baker................	0 20 "	0 30 "	0 30 "	0 35 "	1 10 "	0 55 "
Salad	0 45 "	0 85 "	0 80 "	1 00 "	1 35 "	1 10 "
Covered vegetable	0 50 "	0 85 "	0 80 "	1 00 "	2 25 "	1 50 "
Casserole	0 50 "	0 85 "	0 80 "	1 00 "	2 25 "	1 50 "
Pickle	0 15 "	0 20 "	0 20 "	0 25 "	....	0 30 "
Teapot	0 35 "	0 45 "	0 40 "	0 35 "	1 35 "	0 55 "
Sugar bowl	0 25 "	0 35 "	0 30 "	0 30 "	0 85 "	0 40 "
Slop bowl	0 10 "	0 15 "	0 15 "	0 20 "	0 35 "	0 25 "
Creamer	0 15 "	0 20 "	0 20 "	0 20 "	0 50 "	0 30 "
Jug, size 6	....	....	....	....	1 35 "	....
" " 12	....	....	....	....	1 10 "	....
" " 24	0 20 "	0 25 "	0 25 "	0 30 "	0 85 "	0 85 "
Bone dishes	....	1 00 doz.	....	0 85 doz.	....	....
Oatmeal	0 65 doz.	1 00 "	....	1 20 "	2 40 doz.	1 65 "
Cake plates	0 15 ea.	0 20 ea.	0 20 ea.	0 25 ea.	0 50 ea.	0 50 "
Celery dishes	....	....	....	....	0 85 "	0 55 "
Notched casserole, with ladle	1 35 "	1 85 "	1 75 "	2 25 "	....	....

*No ladle. †No stand.

No. 10. Upper Hanley's King's border, in brown or green, semi-porcelain, decorated, for ordinary wear surpasses anything we have seen. Prices as per list, or for complete sets, as—

40-piece tea set......$2.25.
44 " " ...... 2.85.
56 " " ...... 3.25.
100-piece dinner set.. 8.25.
112 " " .. 9.10.
125 " " .. 14.15.

No. 11. Meakin's Margaretta and Gloriana pink, is a very dainty pattern, the floral decoration being interlaced with a fine vine pattern with gold tracings. Prices as per list, or in complete sets, as—

40-piece tea set......$3.35.
44 " " ...... 4.15.
56 " " ...... 4.75.
100-piece dinner set.. 12.35.
112 " " .. 13.55.
125 " " .. 20.90.

No. 14. Haviland's fine French china, in four decorations, embossed and scalloped, Louis XVI. shape, beautifully gold stippled handles and edges, decorated in pink apple blossoms, blue, heliotrope, pink floral border on tinting, a very select set of dishes—

40-piece tea set......$8.80.
44 " " ......11.00.
56 " " ......12.65.
100-piece dinner set.. 32.00.
112 " " ..35.00.
121 " " ..48.70.

No. 15. Ohme's fine German china, extra smooth finish, deep scalloped edges, handsomely embossed, pretty floral design, neat gold lines on edges—

40-piece tea set ....$5.85.
44 " " .... 6.80.
56 " " .... 7.15.
100-piece dinner set ....20.90.
112 " " ....22.80.

ALL GOODS CAREFULLY PACKED FREE OF CHARGE

No. 1. Fine English china tea sets, very thin, white with gold lines and sprig in centre, $2.80 for 40 pieces.
No. 2. Semi-porcelain tea sets, with gold band and sprig in centre, $2.39 for 40 pieces.

No. 3. Fine English China tea sets, consisting of 44 pieces, prettily decorated in blue or pink with gold lines, newest style cups and unique-shaped teapot. Composition: 12 tea plates, 12 cups and saucers, 2 cake plates, 1 teapot, 1 sugar bowl, 1 slop bowl, 1 cream jug. Price, complete, $5.50.
No. 4. Similar set to No. 3, but with filled-in colors and gold lines, $6.50 per set.
No. 5. Similar to No. 3, with filled-in colors and heavy gold stippled edges, $8.50 per set.
We also have a nice collection of tea sets at $10.00, 15.00 and 25.00 set.

Brown Rockingham Ware.

Rockingham ware teapots, individual, 8c each.
Teapots, 10c, 15c, 18c, 20c, 22c each.
Jugs, 6c, 7c, 9c, 12c, 15c, 20c each.
Oblong or oval bakers, 6c, 7c, 8c, 10c, 12c, 15c, 20c each.
Round bakers 7c, 8c, 10c, 12c each.
Mixing bowls, 3c, 5c, 7c, 10c, 12c, 15c, 20c, 25c each.
Lipped bowls, 15c, 20c, 25c, 30c each.
Pie plates, 9-inch, 5c; 10-inch, 7c each.
Best English jetware teapots, decorated, flowers and gold lines, 25c, 30c, 35c, 50c each.
Sugar-bowls to match, 25c.
Individual teapots, undecorated, 15c each.
Teapot stands, 15c each.
Jugs, 20c, 25c, 30c each.
Cuspidors, 50c each.
Bed pans, Rockingham, 65c each.
Cane bed pans, 50c each.

Stoneware.

Butter pots, with cover, 1-gal., 25c; 1½-gal., 30c; 2-gal., 40c; 3-gal., 50c; 4-gal., 60c; 5-gal., 75c; 6-gal., 90c each.
Open cream pots, 1-gal., 20c; 2-gal., 30c; 3-gal., 40c; 4-gal., 50c each.
Dutch crocks, 5-lb., 8c; 10-lb., 12c; 15-lb., 18c ea.

Should you require butter pots without covers deduct 5c from 1 and 1½ gals, 10c ea. up to 4 gals., over 4 gals., 15c ea.

Cane Ware, White Lined.

Round bakers, 10c, 12c, 15c each.
Mixing bowls, 10c, 12c, 15c, 20c, 25c each.

Ironstone China.

We carry in our stock nothing but first-quality goods, and every piece warranted not to craze. The goods quoted below are manufactured by J. & G. Meakin, which is a sufficient guarantee of their quality.

The three following cuts represent the three patterns we carry in stock.

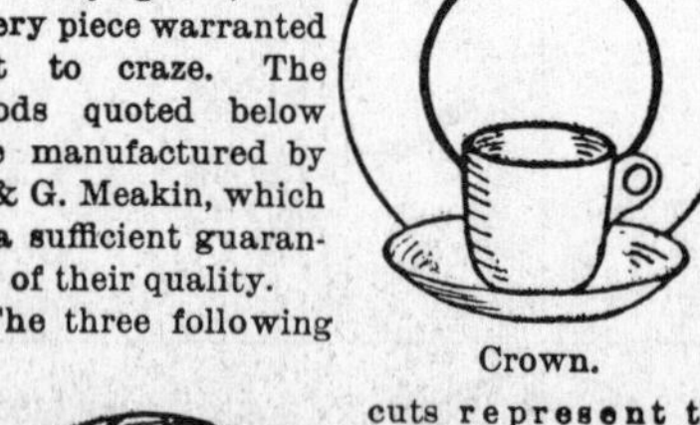

Crown.

Wheat.

In Crown and Astro we carry a full line, but in Wheat pattern we only carry cups and saucers, fruit plates, tea plates, breakfast plates, dinner plates, soup plates, 7 and 8-inch. Prices as follows:

Cups and saucers, 75c doz.
Fruit plates, 5-inch, 45c doz.
Tea plates, 6-inch, 55c doz.
Breakfast plates, 7-inch, 65c doz.
Dinner plates, 8-inch, 75c doz.
Soup plates, 7-inch, 65c doz; 8-inch, 75c doz.
Round fruits, 30c doz.
Individual butter pats, 25c doz.
Bowls, 6c, 8c, 10c each.
Covered vegetable dishes, 45c each.
Platters, 3-inch, 5c; 4-inch, 6c; 5-inch, 7c; 6-inch, 8c; 7-inch, 9c; 8-inch, 10c; 10-inch, 15c; 12-inch, 25c; 14-inch, 35c; 16-inch, 55c; 18-inch, 75c.
Scalloped bowls, 8c, 10c, 12c, 18c, 22c each.
Oval bakers, 2½-inch, 6c; 3-inch, 7c; 4-inch, 8c; 5-inch, 9c; 6-inch, 10c; 7-inch, 12c; 8-inch, 15c; 9-inch, 20c.

Astro.

Jugs, 10c, 20c, 25c, 30c each.
Individual creams, 5c, 6c each.
Ice jugs, 30c each; with bar to hold in ice, 35c each.

Jugs for toilet sets, 35c each.
Basins for toilet sets, 35c each.
Chambers for toilet sets, 30c each.
Covered chambers, 45c each.
3-piece toilet sets, $1.00 per set.
Covers of chambers, 15c each.
Slop jars, no covers, 75c each.
Slop jars, covered, 90c each.
Soap dishes, 25c each.

Toilet Sets.

10-piece toilet sets, in pink, brown or blue, underglaze decorations, printed in one pattern, $2.00 per set.

10-piece toilet sets, in pink, brown or blue, underglaze decorations, printed in one pattern, large rolled edge basin, $2.25 per set.

A fine collection of 10-piece toilet sets in a variety of shapes and designs, at $4.25, 5.50, 6.00, 7.50 and 8.00 per set.

English China, White and Gold.

Gold band and sprig cups and saucers, tea size, $1.20 doz; coffee size, $1.65 doz.
Tea plates, $1.00 doz.
Fruit or bread and butter plates, 85c doz.
Bowls, 15c each.
Bread plates, 15c each.
Cream pitchers, 15c each.

Semi-Porcelain, White and Gold

White, with gold lines and sprig.

Semi-porcelain cups and saucers, tea size, $1.10.
Fruit plates, 5-inch, 65c doz.
Tea plates, 6-inch, 85c doz.
Breakfast plates, 7-inch, $1.00 doz.
Dinner plates, 8-inch, $1.20 doz.
Soup plates, $1.20 doz.
Bowls, 7c, 9c, 12c each.
Bakers, 25c, 30c each.
Vegetables, 75c each.
Platters, 10-inch, 30c; 12-inch, 45c; 14-inch, 65c; 16-inch, 90c.
Gravy boat and stand, complete, 45c ea.
Sauce tureen, 4 pieces, complete with ladle, 85c.
Soup tureen, 4 pieces, complete with ladle, $3.00.

Write us for any goods you need and do not see catalogued

CRYSTAL GLASSWARE.

Our crystal glass is as brilliant as cut glass, and is of the finest quality.

No. 600. Cake stand, 11-inch....................55c
No. 601. Salts and peppers....................5c
No. 602. Cracker jars, each....................35c
No. 603. Hotel sugar bowls and covers..........15c
No. 604. Toothpick holders, each...............5c
No. 605. Individual cream jugs, each...........8c
No. 606. Candlesticks, each....................35c
No. 607. Pitchers, ½-gallon size, each.........50c
No. 608. Tumblers, 8c; with gold, each.........15c
No. 609. Sugar bowls and covers, individual, ea. 8c
No. 610. Goblets, each.........................8c
No. 611. Fruit comports, 9-inch, each..........45c
No. 612. Oil or vinegar bottles, each..........25c
No. 613. Hotel cream jugs, each................15c
No. 614. Footed bowls, 9-inch, each............50c
No. 615. Nappy, 7-inch, 20c; 8-inch, each......25c
No. 616. Berry bowls, oval, each...............25c
No. 617. Celery trays, each....................35c
No. 618. Shakers, salt and pepper, silver-plated top, each....................15c
No. 619. Molasses cans, plated top, each.......35c
No. 620. Pickle jars and covers, each..........20c
No. 621. Tea sets, crystal, 75c; with gold on edges, each....................$1.25
No. 622. Wine glasses, each....................5c
No. 623. Water bottles, each...................50c
No. 624. Tankard jugs, ½-gallon size, 50c; with gold on edges, each..........$1.00
No. 625. Footed jelly bowls, 5-inch, each......15c
No. 626. Cake salvers, 9-inch, each............35c
No. 627. Tall celery, 20c; with gold, each.....35c
No. 628. Custard, each.........................8c
No. 629. Comports, 4½-inch, each...............5c
No. 630. Handled nappies, 5-inch, 10c; 6-inch, ea. 15c
No. 631. Ice cream nappies, 6-inch, each.......8c
No. 632. Plates, 5-inch, each..................6c

ALL GLASSWARE AND CROCKERY CAREFULLY PACKED FREE OF CHARGE.

Notched casserole, $2.00 each.
Butter pats, 40c doz.
Sauce dishes, 45c doz.
China egg cups, white and gold lines, 20c doz.
Soup ladles, 45c each.
Sauce ladles, 25c each.

German China Fruit Sets.

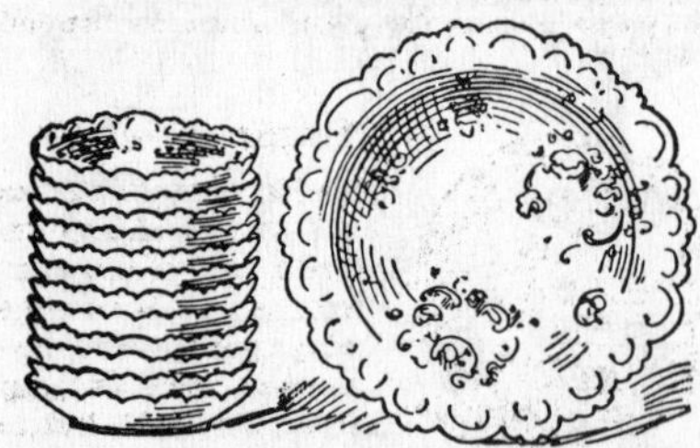

Fine German china fruit sets, consisting of 12 fruit nappies and 1 large bowl, floral decorations and gold lines, $1.10, 1.35, 1.85 set.

Tumblers and Stem Goods.

(For Illustrations See Opposite Page.)

No. 1. Heavy, 50c doz.
No. 2. " 75c doz.
No. 3. " decorated, $1.00 doz.
No. 4. " 8c each.
No. 5. " 9c each.
No. 6. " 5c each.
No. 7. Light, decorated, 20c each.
No. 8. " " 18c each.
No. 9. " " 18c each.
No. 10. " " 15c each.
No. 11. " " 15c each.

No. 12. Light, plain cordial glass, ¾-oz, or 1-oz, $1.65 doz.
No. 13. Light wine glass, 2-oz or 2½-oz, $1.80 doz.
No. 14. " wine glass, 3-oz, $1.65 doz, or claret, 4-oz, $2.00 doz.
No. 15. Light champagne glass, 5-oz, $1.80, or goblet, 7-oz, $2.00 doz.
No. 16. Light champagne, 9-oz, $2.00; 11-oz, $2.00 doz.
No. 17. Light, heavy bottom, 10c each.
No. 18. Light, heavy bottom, 5c each.
No. 19. Heavy, 60c doz.
No. 20. Light, 60c doz.
No. 22. " 60c doz.
No. 23. " 72c doz.
No. 24. " 60c doz.
No. 25. " 60c doz.
No. 26. " 96c doz.
No. 28. " ground bottom, 50c doz.
No. 29. " 35c doz.
No. 30. " will not nest, 84c doz.
No. 31. " 60c doz.
No. 32. Light, needle etched, $1.25 doz.
No. 33. " engraved, $1.00 doz.
No. 34. " " $1.00 doz.
No. 35. " " $1.00 doz.

Table Glassware.

Tea set, consisting of sugar bowl, cream jug, butter dish and spoon holder, 25c set.
Butter dishes, plain, 10c each, cut glass patterns 20c each.
Sugar bowls, with cover, 20c each.
Spoon holders, 15c each.
Vinegar bottles, 15c, 20c, 25c each
Syrup pitchers, spring top, nickelled, 25c, 35c each.
Finger bowls, 15c; genuine cut glass, 25c, 50c, 65c each.
Glass cruets, 4 bottles, 50c, 65c, 75c; 3 bottles, 25c; 2 bottles, 15c each.
Olive dishes, with handle, 10c, 15c each.
Water jugs, 25c, 35c each.
Cream jugs, 10c, 15c each.
Mustard pots, 12c each.
Low fruit dishes, 15c, 20c, and 25c each.
Pickle jars, 15c each.
Salts and peppers, colored and decorated, 10c, 15c each.
Lemonade sets, 6 glasses, 1 large tankard with embossed tray, $1.25.
Individual salts or celery dips, 25c doz.
Table salts open, 5c each.

China Tea Sets.

China tea sets, consisting of sugar bowl, cream jug, spoonholder and butter dish, with heavy gold lines and colored decorations, 60c, 75c, $1.00 set.

Miscellaneous China.

Low candlesticks, 15c each.
Candlesticks, figure attached, 15c, 20c each.
Butter pats, 40c, 50c, $1.00 doz.
Nest eggs, 25c doz.
Bisque match holders, 10c, 15c each.
Bisque figures, 35c each.
Pin trays, 15c, 25c each.
Haviland china, salad or fruit bowls, 50c, 75c, $1.00, 1.25 each.
German china salad or fruit bowls, scalloped edges, 35c, 50c each.
China toothpick holders, 10c each.
French and German china fruit dishes, 85c, $1.00, 2.50 doz.
Biscuit jars, 50c, $1.25 each.
Cheese dishes, $1.00, 1.25, 2.00 each.
Fancy teapots, 75c, $1.00, 1.25 each.
Muffin dishes, $1.00 each.
Marmalade jars, $1.00 each.
Fancy bread or cake plates, perforated handles, 50c each.
Children's white china mugs, floral decorations, 5c, 10c, 15c each.
Spit cups, loose top, plain, 25c; decorated, 35c each.
Invalid cups, boat shaped, 15c each.
Invalid cups, cup shaped, 25c each.
Shaving mugs, gold edge, beautifully decorated, 10c, 15c, 25c each.

Fancy Plates and Cups and Saucers.

Fine French china cups and saucers, gold stippled on handles and edges, prettily decorated in natural flowers, 20c, 25c, 35c each; plates to match above, 20c, 25c each.
Fine German china cups and saucers, gold lined and floral decorations, 50c, 65c each.

Plates to match above, 25c, 50c each.
Cups and saucers, assorted sizes and colors, 10c, 15c, 20c, 25c, 35c, 50c, 65c each.
A fine collection of odd china plates, with gold tracing, 10c, 15c, 25c, 50c, 75c, $1.00 and 1.25 each.

Jugs.

Majolica jugs, holding 1½ pint, 10c; 2 pints, 15c; 2½ pints, 20c. All wine measure.
Semi-porcelain decorated, plain print, 3 sizes, 12c, 15c and 18c; fancy shape, 15c, 18c, 20c each.

Cuspidors.

Fine china cuspidors, tinted in pink, brown and green, with white and gold scalloped border, 50c each.
Floral decoration, satin finished, solid ground, a perfect beauty, 75c each.

Porridge Sets.

Consisting of plate, jug and bowl, gold lined, natural colors, 25c, 35c, 50c per set.

Buying from catalogue has long proved itself to be a success.

Lamps, Gas and Electric Fixtures

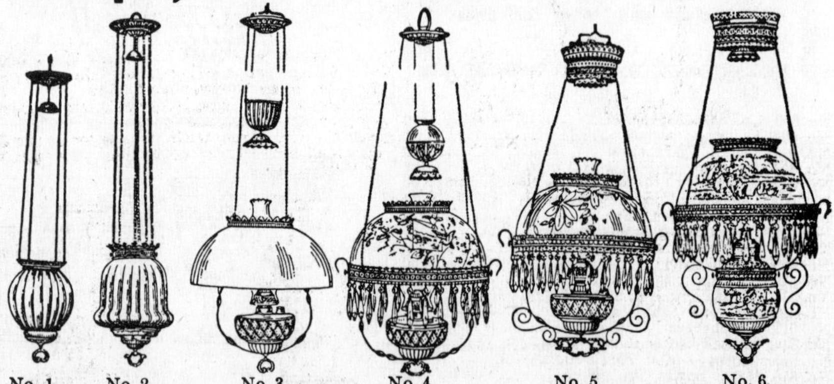

Above cut represents six of our very best lamps. They are very serviceable, as well as ornamental.
No. 1. Hall lamp, gilt lacquered chain and mountings, rose or ruby globe, $1.65.
No. 2. Hall lamp, larger size, gilt lacquered chain and mountings, rose or ruby, $2.50.
No. 3. Hanging lamp, glass fount, large-sized burner, 14-inch plain opal dome-shaped shade, weight balance, brass mountings, $2.25; with decorated shade, $2.50.
No. 4. Hanging lamp, glass fount, brass mountings, weight balance, decorated shade, 30 prisms, $4.30.
No. 5. Hanging lamp, glass fount, with fine gilt lacquered frame, decorated and tinted shade, spring balance, $5.30.
No. 6. Hanging lamp, polished bronze metal, rich gold finish, improved spring extension, length closed 36 inches, extends to 72 inches, removable oil pot, handsome bisque-finished 14-inch dome, shade and fount to match, hand-decorated, centre draught burner, 75 candle-power, can be lighted without removing chimney, 30 crystal prisms, $6.80.

Hall Lamps.

With gilt lacquered chain and mountings, chimney and burner, complete, and very handsome globes, $2.00 each
Fancy brass frames, large fancy globes, large burner and chimney, $3.50, 4.00, 4.50, 5.00 each.

Vase Lamps.

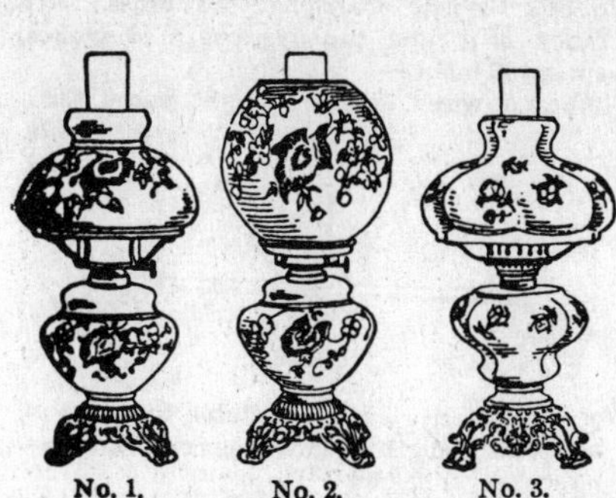

No. 1. No. 2. No. 3.

No. 4. No. 5. No. 6.

No. 1. Brass foot, large-sized burner, 7-inch dome shade, decorated to match fount, tinted in pink or yellow, complete with chimney and wick, $1.00 each.

No. 2. With 6-inch globe, tinted in pink and yellow, $1.25.

No. 3. With 10-inch fluted dome shade, climax burner and chimney, complete, $2.00.

No. 4. With lift-out fount, climax burner, large-sized globe, 23 inches high, decorated in blue and green, $2.75.

No. 5. Large-sized bowl and 10-inch shade, lift-out fount, circular burner, tinted in pink and blue, $3.00.

No. 6. With 10-inch globe, and bowl to match, circular burner, 22 inches high, tinted in green and yellow, $4.50.

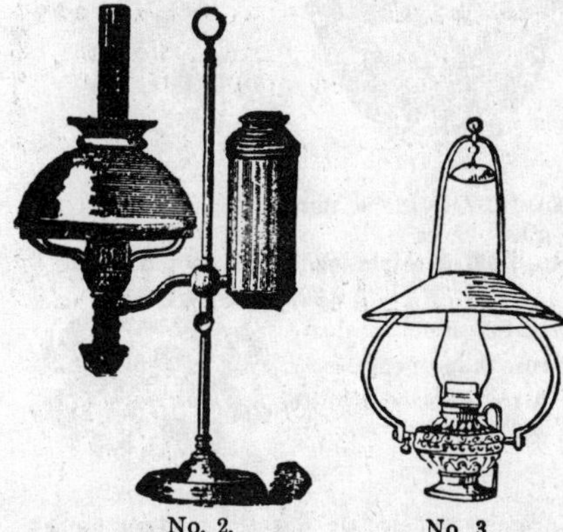

No. 2. No. 3.

No. 2. Students' lamp, nickel-plated, centre draft burner, removable fount, adjustable green shade, $4.25 each.

Sewing or reading lamp, brass, centre draft, circular burner, white shade, $1.95; decorated shade, $2.10 each.

No. 3. Mammoth lamp for store or hall, brass fount, centre draft burner, 300 candle-power, complete with shade, $3.75.

Spring extension for above, $1.50 each extra.

Prices on this page subject to change without notice.

Piano Lamps.

All gilt, onyx top, patent extension rod, with automatic fastener, removable fount, round plain legs, complete with chimney, $8.50 each.

Brass table, onyx top, removable fount, cast bowl and legs, $12.00, 15.00, 20.00 each.

Wrought iron piano lamps, extension rod, removable founts, circular burner, automatic stop, complete with chimney, special, $8.50, 10.00, 12.00 each.

Banquet Lamps.

No. 1. No. 2.

No. 1. Embossed brass, with open-work foot, guaranteed, centre draft burner, complete, with new device for lighting, $1.75, 2.00 each.

Banquet lamp, No. 2, cupid pedestal, fount not detachable, silver or gilt figure, ornamental foot, centre draft burner, complete with chimney, $2.50 each.

Brass Tables.

No. 1. Plain polished legs, onyx, 8 x 8, $5.00 each.
No. 2. Square polished legs, fancy shape onyx, 8 x 8, ornamental lower shelf, $6.50.
No. 3. Heavy cast legs, lacquered, large onyx, very ornamental, $10.00 each.
A variety of designs, with two pieces of onyx, cast legs, ornamental lower shelf, from $12.00 to 50.00 each.

No. 4. No. 5.

No. 4. Glass bowl, iron foot, complete, with large sized burner and fancy engraved chimney, 69c each.

No. 5. Glass bowl, decorated, colored glass pedestal, heavy iron foot, complete, 75c each; No. 5 with flowered chimney, 79c each.

Lamp Shades.

7-inch decorated dome, 35c each.
10-inch dome shades, for vase lamps, plain white opal, 35c; with hand decorations, 50c each.
14-inch dome shades, for hanging lamps, plain white opal, 50c; with hand decorations, fired, 75c and 85c each.
Stiff paper shades, for glass lamps, 5c, 10c and 15c each.

Lamp Globes.

This style of shade has driven silk shades entirely out of the market, and we have some very pretty decorations at prices ranging from 75c, $1.00, 1.25 to 7.00 each.

Bracket Lamps.

No. 1.

Bracket lamps, complete, same as cut No. 1, 65c each.

Lamp brackets for above, 10c, 15c, 30c each.

Fancy lamp bracket, solid brass, as cut No. 2, single swing, extends 12 inches, without burner or glass, $1.00 each.

Double swing, extends 18 inches, $1.25 each.

No. 2.

Lamp Fittings.

Burners, A, or medium size, 7c each; B, or large size, 9c each; Duplex, single, will fit B size collar, 15c each; Duplex, double, will fit B size collar, 25c each.
Lantern burners, 7c each.
Lantern burners, to fit tubular lantern, 12c ea.
Candle wick, 5c ball.
Wick, best quality, A or B size, 3c yd; D size, best quality, 5c yd.
Wick for banquet lamps, 5c each; students' lamps, 2 for 5c; night lamps, 2 wicks for 1c; mammoth lamps, 10c each.
Chimneys, finest lead flint glass, crimped-top, A, or medium size, 4c each; B or D size, 6c each.
Globe chimneys, engraved, for B burner, 10c each.
Lamp glasses, for hall lamps, medium size, 5c; large size, 7c.
Lamp glass, to fit banquet lamp, 10c; to fit students' lamp, 7c; to fit duplex burner, 10c; small size, for night lamps, 2c each.
Auer light chimney, 10c each.
Mammoth glasses, 25c each.
Lantern globes, lead flint, 8c each.
Red lantern globes, 20c each.
Wire frames for silk lamp shades, made in hexagon shapes, with turned-up points, 14-inch, 15c; 16-inch, 15c; 18-inch, 20c; 20-inch, 25c each.
Brass rings to fit on banquet lamps to hold shade, 10c each.
Prisms, 4c each.
Candle shades, fancy stripes and colors, 15c to 50c each.
Holders for same, 5c each.
Reflectors, glass, 6-inch, 15c; 8-inch, 20c; 10-inch, 25c each.

Why not order with your neighbors? Make a Freight shipment of 100 lbs. or over and save charges.

Glass Lamps.

No. 1. No. 2. No. 3. No. 4. No. 5. No. 6. No. 7. No. 8. No. 9. No. 10. No. 11.

No. 1. Complete, with B burner, chimney and wick, 25c each.

No. 2. Complete, with self-filling cap, B burner, chimney and wick, 30c each.

No. 3. Complete, with self-filling cap, handle, B burner, chimney and wick, 35c each.

No. 4. Complete, with handle, A burner, chimney and wick, 20c each.

No. 5. Complete, with handle, A burner, chimney and wick, 25c each.

No. 6. Complete, with A burner, chimney and wick, 25c each.

No. 7. Complete, with A burner, chimney and wick, 30c each.

No. 8. Complete, with B burner, chimney and wick, 35c each.

No. 9. Complete, with B burner, chimney and wick, 40c each.

No. 10. Complete, with B burner, chimney and wick, 45c each.

No. 11. Same as No. 10, but with climax burner, 51c each.

Gas Fixtures.

Length of pendants and gasoliers, 30 or 36 inches.

Our Gas and Electric Fixture Department is one of the finest in Toronto. We are always pleased to furnish estimates and prices of any goods not quoted below for private or public buildings.

Gas Wall Brackets.

Rope pattern—

Stiff, 30c; single swing, 45c; double swing, 65c each.

Square and polished—

Stiff, 50c; single swing, 70c; double swing, $1.15 each.

Hall Lights.

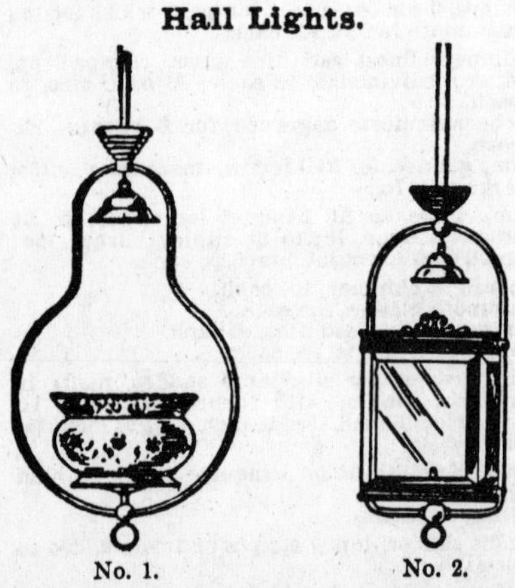

No. 1. No. 2.

No. 1. Fancy brass trimmings, complete with fancy colored globe, $2.10, 2.50, 2.75, 3.00 each.

No. 2. Square lantern, best British plate glass, bevelled edges, an ornament to any hall, $4.50, 5.00, 6.00 each.

Pendants and Chandeliers.

(Prices quoted do not include globes.)

1-light pendant, 60c.

2-light chandeliers, plain, all brass, complete with rings, $1.50.

2-light chandelier, fancy twisted ball and curved arms, $1.75; 3-light, $2.25.

2-light chandeliers, solid brass, complete with rings, prettily curved arms, $2.00; 3-light, $2.75.

Also an assortment of 4 and 5 lights, from $12.00 to 35.00.

Globe holders, 8c each.

Argand burners, 35c each.

Lava gas tips, 15c doz.

The "Crescent" acetylene gas burner, gives as good, if not better, satisfaction, than other burners which cost you more money, ½ and ⅓-foot sizes, price 20c each.

Gem self-lighting gas burner, 35c each.

⅜-inch L cocks, 20c each.

½-inch L cocks, 25c each.

Electric and Combination Fixtures.

Our stock of electric fixtures is complete. Should you desire something in that line, not quoted below, write us for prices. When prices of combination or straight electric fixtures or brackets are quoted "wired" they include wire, sockets and shade holders (not the shades).

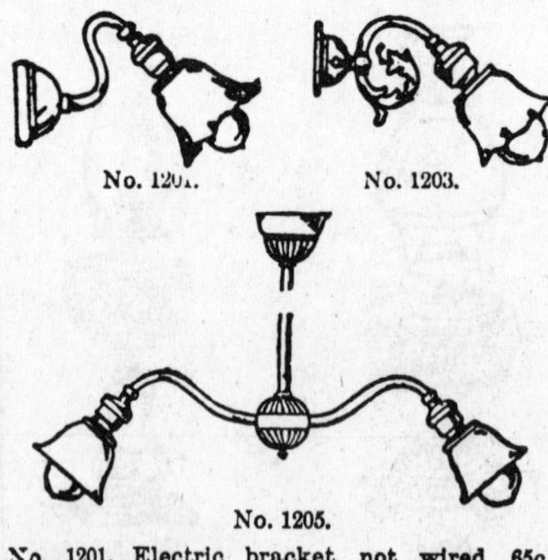

No. 1201. No. 1203.

No. 1205.

No. 1201. Electric bracket, not wired, 65c; wired, $1.05 each.

No. 1203. Electric bracket, not wired, $1.50; wired, $1.90 each.

Electric fixtures required to be more than 36 inches long, 30c per foot extra.

No. 1204. Electric pendant, not wired, 60c; wired, $1.05 each.

No. 1205. Electric chandelier, all brass, with fancy body and canopy, length 36 inches, spread 20 inches—

2-light, not wired, $2.50.	2-light, wired,	$3.25.
3 " " 3.10.	3 " "	4.10.
4 " " 3.70.	4 " "	5.20.

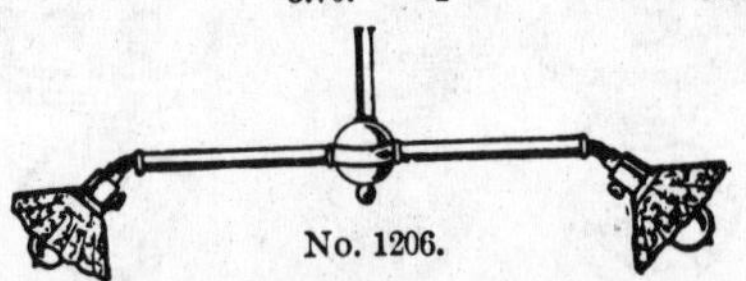

No. 1206.

No. 1206. Electric fixture, suitable for store or hall, plain, length 36 inches, spread 36 inches, no sockets or shades—

2-light, not wired, $3.75.	2-light, wired,	$4.25.
3 " " 4.50.	3 " "	5.50.
4 " " 5.25.	4 " "	6.75.

Electric table lamp, slate base, 10 ft. cord plug attachment, and 10-inch white shade, $1.80; with green shade, $2.20.

Electric portable or table lamp, complete with green tin shades, white enamelled inside, 10 ft cord and plug attachment, $2.80 and $3.80; with adjustable arm, $4.45.

In ordering, always specify style of base required on plug.

Gas Globes.

Gas globes fit 4-inch holder. Electric shades fit 2¼-inch holder.

No. 140.

No. 140E.

No. 140. Gas globe, flaring top, imitation cut glass, 15c each.

No. 140E. Electric shade to match, 15c each.

No. 125. Electric shade, rose shape, very pretty, in red, green and white, 65c each.

No. 125.

Incandescent electric reflector tin, 2¼ x 10 inches, flat, 20c; 2¼ x 10 inches, deep, 20c.

Electric mirror reflectors, 2¼ x 10 inches, flat, 55c; 3¼ x 12 inches, flat, 65c; 3¼ x 18 inches, flat, $1.35; 2¼ x 10 inches, deep, 65c.

We also have a large assortment of gas globes, in white, 20c, 25c, 35c to $1.00 each; colored, 50c, 65c, 85c, $1.25 each.

Combination Gas and Electric Fixtures.

Pendant or drop light, 1 gas and 1 electric, $2.00 and 2.75.

Chandeliers—

2 gas 2 electric,	$4.50.	3 gas 3 electric,	$10.50.
3 " 3 "	5.50.	2 " 2 "	8.25.
2 " 2 "	6.00.	3 " 3 "	11.00.
3 " 3 "	7.50.	2 " 2 "	11.00.
2 " 2 "	8.00.	3 " 3 "	14.00.

Edison key sockets, 20c each.

Edison keyless sockets, 18c each.

Thompson-Houston key sockets, 18c each.

Thompson-Houston keyless sockets, 15c each.

Shade-holders, 2¼-inch, 5c each.

Insulating joints, ⅜ x ½, 50c each.

Insulating tape, Grimshaw, black, $1.50 lb.

Insulating tape, Grimshaw, white, $1.50 lb.

Be sure and send enough money for postage for goods to be sent by Mail

Baby Carriages and Children's Outdoor Goods.

Our wheel goods for the coming season are better than ever. We have spared no pains in our selection, and we may say that the prices are right also.

A. Baby carriage, reed body, upholstered in metallic cloth and plush roll, RO parasol, best quality tinned steel wheels and axles, full-sized wheels, $6.50.

No. 610. Reed body, 16th century finish, large size, fancy front, braided around edge, plush roll, upholstered in Derby cloth, Roman satin parasol, with one frill, $7.50.

C. Our Leader. Reed body, heavy roll around back, curved front, upholstered in plush, MEH parasol, $11. We have carried this carriage for years. We have tried our best to beat it, but we cannot. We buy them in lots of 100 in order to get them to sell at this price. The parasol has two frills instead of one, as shown in the cut.

No. 636. Very handsome design, upholstered in best plush, MEH satin parasol, retinned gearing, foot brake, $15.00.

No. 650. One of our prettiest designs, cut does not do it justice, upholstering, parasol, finish and style the very latest, reed body, 16th century finish, retinned wheels and gearing, RMEF parasol, price only $17.50.

F. This is one of the finest carriages of the year, handsome and attractive, the upholstering the finest, price $22.50.

The cut speaks for itself.

Go-Carts.

Limited space will not allow us to catalogue anything like a full line of Go-Carts. We may draw your attention to the fact that we have the finest selection of adjustable back and front Go-Carts that we can obtain from the leading factories of Canada and the United States.

No. 208. Wicker body, adjustable back and front, moving independently, takes the place of a cheap carriage, without parasol or cushion. $5.10; with parasol and rod, $6.65; complete with parasol and cushion, $7.50.

No. 216. Adjustable back and front, strong springs, fancy reed work, very stylish, plush cushion, satin parasol, with one frill, complete, $13.00.

No. 227. This is a beautiful cart very much prettier than the cut, heavy roll sides, movable back and front, with a two-frilled satin parasol, beautifully upholstered in silk plush, price, complete, $17.00.

Note.—When brown or green upholstering is ordered we are usually able to fill the order same day. Other colors we do not always carry in stock, and it takes from 8 to 10 days to have these made.

Doll Cabs.

No. 100SS. No parasol, 70c.
No. 101SS. With parasol, $1.00.
No. 102SS. No parasol, 75c.
No. 103SS. With parasol, $1.00.
No. 47DS. No parasol, very strong, $1.15.
No. 48DS. Same as No. 47DS, lined, parasol, $1.50.
No. 48DS. Special, upholstered, parasol, $1.75.
No. 116. Lined, fancy parasol, $2.00.

Dolls' Go-Carts.

No. 1½SS. Dolls' go-carts, reed body, seat 7 x 7 inches, 50c.
No. 2½SS. Dolls' go-cart, seat 8 inches, 60c.

Baby Carriers.

No. 3. Shellacked and varnished, no strap, $1.10.

No. 3½. No. 5½.

No. 3½. Same as No. 3, with springs and fenders, no strap, $1.65.
No. 4. Pretty design, high back, fancy wicker, $3.00.
No. 5½. As cut, no strap, $4.25.
Straps for above, 10c each.
Rubber tires on above, $1.00 per set extra.

Boys' Velocipedes.

No. 1. Inside measurement of leg 16 inches, iron tires, $2.00; rubber tires, $3.60.
No. 2. Inside measurement of leg 18 inches, iron tires, $2.25; rubber tires, $4.30.
No. 3. Inside measurement of leg 20 inches, iron tires, $2.50; rubber tires, $5.00.
No. 4. Inside measurement of leg 22 inches, iron tires, $3.00; rubber tires, $6.00.
No. 5. Inside measurement of leg 24 inches, iron tires, $3.25; rubber tires, $6.50.

Girls' Tricycles.

No. 18. For girls, 2 to 4 years, iron tires, $3.80; rubber tires, $6.40.
No. 20. For girls, 3 to 5 years, iron tires, $5.10; rubber tires, $7.60.
No. 1. For girls, 4 to 7 years, iron tires, $6.40; rubber tires, $10.75.
No. 2. For girls, 7 to 10 years, iron tires, $7.60; rubber tires, $12.00.
No. 3. For girls, 10 to 15 years, iron tires, $9.00; rubber tires, $13.25.

Bent Rail Wagons.

No. 1. Body, 10 x 20 inches; wheels, 7 x 10 inches, $1.00.
No. 2. Body, 11 x 22 inches; wheels, 8 x 11 inches, $1.25.
No. 3. Body, 12 x 25 inches; wheels, 10 x 15 inches, $1.75.
No. 7. Hardwood platform, tinned iron railing, $2.50; with fenders, $3.00.
No. 8. Canopy top spring wagon, $4.75.
No. 9. Similar to No. 8, with handles on back, $5.35.
No. 11. Single-seated buckboard, $2.25.
No. 12. Double-seated buckboard, $2.50.

Express Wagons.

No. 14. Box, 9 x 18 inches, $1.00.
No. 14½. Box, 10 x 20 inches, $1.25.
No. 15. Box, 11 x 22 inches, $1.50.
No. 16. Box, 12½ x 25 inches, $1.85.
No 17. Box, 14 x 28 inches, $2.00.

Toy Wheelbarrows.

Pet barrow, wood wheel, 20c.
No. 5. Barrow, 40c each.
No. 6. Body, 9 x 12 x 5 inches high, 50c.
No. 7. Body, 9 x 12 x 5 inches high, long handle, 65c.
No. 8. Body, 11 x 14½ x 5½ inches high, 75c.
No. 9. Body, 13 x 16 x 6 inches high, 90c.

Toy Carts.

Body made of sheet steel—
No. 0. Very neat, 25c.
No. 1. Body, 6 x 10 inches; wheels, 7 inches, 50c.
No. 2. Body, 8 x 12 inches; wheels, 9 inches, 65c.
No. 02. Wood body, 18c.

Baby Carriage Sundries.

Parasols.

No. BAM. Skeleton only, 50c.
No. AG. Skeleton, inside green, 85c.
No. LVD. Roman satin, 1 frill, $1.15.
No. MFT. Roman satin, 1 frill, go-cart size, $1.15.
No. AM. Satin, 1 frill, $2.00.
No. EB. Satin, 1 frill, go-cart size, $2.00.
No. MEH. Satin, 2 frills, $2.75.
No. MJK. Satin, 2 frills, go-cart size, $2.75.
No. JS. Satin, 3 frills, $2.75.
No. ES. Same as LVD, with frill set low, $1.25.
No. RMEF. Satin, with 2 scalloped frills, $3.00.
No. FRM. Satin, 3 frills, $3.25.
White parasol, lace covers, from 75c to $2.50 each.

Go-Cart Beds.

No. A. Derby cloth or Bedford cord, 85c.
No. E. Metallic cloth, $1.00.
No. C. Plush one side, Roman satin frills, $1.50. Velours one side, large size, $1.75.
No. 8. Plush both sides, large size, $3.25.

Carriage Wheels.

Rubber-tired wheels on baby carriages, small size rubber, $1.00 per set extra.
Large-sized rubber tires, $2.00 per set extra.
Baby carriage wheels, $1.40 per set of 4.
Baby carriage wheels, rubber tires, small-sized rubbers, $2.40 per set.
Baby carriage wheels, large-sized rubber, $3.40 per set.

Rods, Straps, Etc.

Parasol rods, 40c each.
Parasol fixtures, 35c each.
Knobs, or TK tops, for parasol rod, 10c each.
Straps for carriages or go-carts, 15c each.
Straps for carriers, 10c each.

We have a very full line of carriages and go-carts, and should you not see what you like in above selection, we will be pleased to make a selection for you somewhat different, if you send us the price you wish to pay and give an idea of the style.

The Etonian Steel Range.

Handsome in appearance, constructed of the very best material, mounted by the most skilled labor, they cannot fail to give complete satisfaction. We may say also that the Etonian is the most economical fuel consumer on the market. The bodies are formed of the very best quality of steel sheets, to which is closely riveted an interlining of asbestos millboard; between main bottom and bottom of stove is a four-inch air space, which protects the floor from over-heating. Add to this a large oven with a perforated loose cast-iron bottom above the sheet-iron oven bottom, also a drop oven door, fitted complete with patent springs, and you have an up-to-date steel range.

No. 0. Etonian, four holes, plain $21.50.

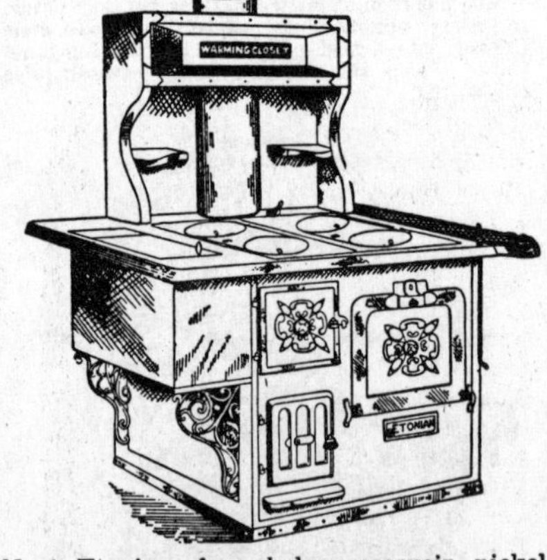

No. 1. Etonian, four holes, reservoir, nickel-plated edges, and ornaments, $30.00.
No. 1½. Etonian, similar to No. 1, but has high warming closet, nicely decorated, $37.50.

The Royal Polished Steel Roaster and Baker.

The Royal Roaster is the latest improved and most perfect utensil of its character on the market. It is unequalled for roasting meats, poultry, game, fish, and for baking bread, biscuits, cake, pudding, etc. The outside pan and cover are made from polished sheet steel, while the inside pan and grate are of the finest bright sheet tin. The inside or dripping pan is kept from contact with the outside pan by four raised indentations in the bottom of the latter, thus forming a perfect air passage, and the burning of gravy and kindred complaints is impossible.

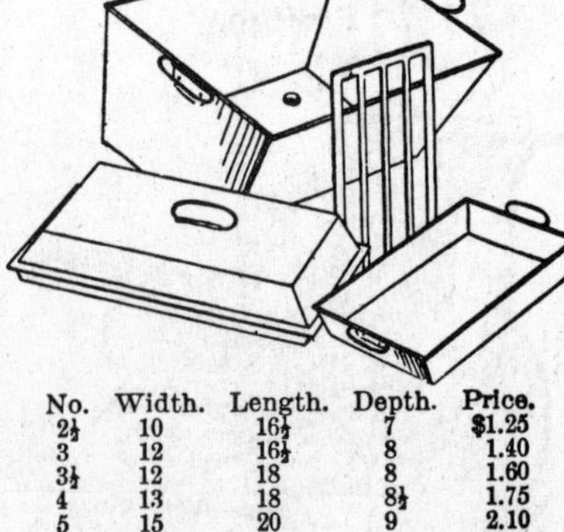

No.	Width.	Length.	Depth.	Price.
2½	10	16½	7	$1.25
3	12	16½	8	1.40
3½	12	18	8	1.60
4	13	18	8½	1.75
5	15	20	9	2.10

Troy Roaster and Baking Pan.

The cheapest, simplest and most effective medium-priced roaster and baker on the market. Very similar to the Royal Roaster and Baker, but of course not so good a quality.

No.	Width.	Length.	Depth.	Price.
6	10	15	7	$0.50
7	10	16½	7	0.70
8	12	16½	8	0.90
9	12	18	8	1.05

NOTE.—In ordering a range, state distinctly whether you want it fitted for coal or wood.

MUSICAL GOODS.

WE DO NOT EXCHANGE MUSICAL GOODS.

Guitars.

The cheapest, most attractive and best-selling styles of guitars ever put on the market.

No. 309. Standard size, imitation mahogany sides and back, colored front, fancy inlaid around sound-hole, imitation ebony finger-board and bridge, pearl position dots, imitation cherry neck, American machine head, $4.00.

No. 111½. Standard size, fine imitation rosewood back and sides, highly polished, fancy strip down back, celluloid bound edges front and back, colored front, fancy ornamental sound-hole, rosewood finger-board and bridge, position dots, imitation mahogany neck, American patent machine head, $6.00.

No. 1. Imperial, antique oak, highly polished mahogany neck, rosewood finger-board and bridge, pearl position dots, inlaid sound-hole, $9.00.

No. 1½. Similar to No. 1, but in concert size, $10.00.

No. 2. Imperial guitar, rosewood, highly polished, similar to No. 1, standard size, $12.00; concert size, $15.00.

Guitar Strings.

Guitar strings, 10c each, 50c per set.

Ideal Mandolins.

Ideal mandolins are of Canadian manufacture, and will, of course, stand our climatic changes much better than foreign importations.

No. 1. Seven ribs, walnut and maple, rosewood finger-board, pearl position dots, inlaid guard-plate, nickel-plated tail piece, $3.50.

No. 2. Nine ribs, mahogany and walnut, rosewood finger-board, pearl position dots, inlaid guard-plate, nickel-plated tail piece, $6.00.

No. 3. Nine ribs, mahogany, rosewood finger-board, pearl position dots, inlaid around sound-hole, celluloid guard-plate, nickel-plated tail piece, $7.50.

Imperial Mandolins.

Imperial mandolins are neither cloth nor paper pasted on the inside, but are constructed on scientific principles, every instrument stamped "Imperial, warranted."

No. 4. Nine bird's-eye maple and rosewood strips, with five colored strips between rosewood cap and side strips, mahogany neck, oval ebony finger-board, pearl position dots, German silver frets, colored wood inlaid around sound hole, inlaid celluloid guard-plate, ebony bridge, nickel-plated tail piece, $9.75.

Mandolin Strings.

Mandolin strings, 3c each, 20c per set.

Violins.

These prices do not include bows.

No. 13. Red or brown shaded, $1.00.

No. 10. Hopf, brown varnish, polished, better quality, $2.00.

No. 33. Conservatory model, amber color, nicely shaded, fine finish, the best violin on the market for the money, $3.00.

No. 100E. Straduarius model, dark amber, shaded, good tone, ebony trimmings, $4.00.

No. 178. Stainer model, bright reddish brown highly flamed and polished, very fine finish and trimmings, $5.00.

No. 886. Paganini concert violin, amber shaded, highly polished, fine tone and finish, $7.00.

No. 313. Conservatory Straduarius, brown and amber shaded, highly polished, fine trimmings, well made and good tone, a splendid instrument, $10.00.

No. 893. Wieniawski violin, D'Artist, dark shaded, engraved on head, elegantly finished and fine tone, $12.00.

Violin Bows.

No. 18. Maple red, black frog, bone button, 25c.

No. 151. Brazil wood, ebony frog, pearl slide, full German silver lined, 50c.

No. 136½. Brazil wood, polished, ebony frog, pearl slide, German silver button and tip, 75c.

No. 145. Brazil wood, octagon polished stick, ebony frog, pearl eye, German silver trimmed, German silver button, leather winding, $1.00.

No. 800. Pernambuco, polished stick, fine ebony polished frog, with pearl eye, full German silver mountings, ivory tip, leather winding, $1.25.

No. 199B. Pernambuco, polished, round stick, fine ebony frog, full German silver trimmed, pearl eye, fine quality, $1.50.

No. 246. Pernambuco, ebony frog, full German silver trimmed, pearl slide and eye, fine quality, $2.00.

Violin Fittings.

Bridges, maple, 3c, 4c, 5c, 8c each.

Pegs, 5c, 7c, 10c each.

Tail pieces, imitation ebony, inlaid with pearl eye, 8c each.

Tail pieces, imitation ebony, inlaid pearl shield, 15c each.

Tail pieces, ebony, inlaid, 3 pearl flowers, 25c ea.

Tail pieces, ebony, highly polished, inlaid with 5 pearl flowers, German silver saddle, 40c each.

No. 11. Chin rests, ebony, with hook, 25c each.

No. 13. Chin rests, ebony, engraved, with German silver tightener, 50c each.

No. 14. Chin rests, ebony, engraved, with 2 German silver tighteners, 75c each.

No. 22. Gutta percha, nickel plated, velvet shoulder rest, improved model Becker, $1.25.

Resin, conservatory, 5c, 10c, 15c each.

Mutes, ebony, 10c; brass, 10c.

Tuning forks, A or C, 10c each.

Combination pitch pipes, A and C, 20c each.

Violin Strings.

Violin strings, 10c each, 40c per set.

Imperial, E, A and D, 20c each; G, 30c each.

Accordions.

No. 65. Miniature size, ebonized frame, open action, nickel keys, one set of reeds, $1.25.

No. 122. Ideal miniature size, ebonized frame, open action, nickel keys, two stops, two sets of reeds, $2.00.

No. 195½. Ideal, ebonized mouldings double bellows, nickel corners and clasps, German silver reeds, open nickel keys, fancy gilt borders, $2.50.

No. 173. Imperial, small size, 10 keys, 2 stops, 3 bass keys, $3.50.

No. 3. Imperial, regular size, ebonized moulding, white enamelled panels, nickel mouldings and nickel protectors, simplex action, bass valves, 8-fold double bellows, leather straps, 10 keys, 2 stops, extra broad steel reeds, $5.00.

Banjos.

No. 5. 16 nickel-plated brackets, nickel-plated rim, wood lined, polished walnut neck, German silver raised frets, calfskin head, nickel-plated tail piece, 11-inch rim, 18-inch finger-board, $5.00.

No. 8. 38 nickel-plated professional brackets, nickel-plated rim, wired edge, highly polished walnut neck, raised German silver frets, inlaid with fancy design of celluloid, calfskin head, imitation ivory pegs and tail piece, 11-inch rim, 18-inch finger-board, $7.50.

No. 101. German silver rim, wired edge, grooved hoop, cherry neck, highly polished, veneered finger-board, inlaid pearl position dot, 20 nickel-plated brackets, $10.00.

Genuine Stewart banjo, 20 professional brackets, polished mahogany neck, N. P. rim, "The Student," $12.00.

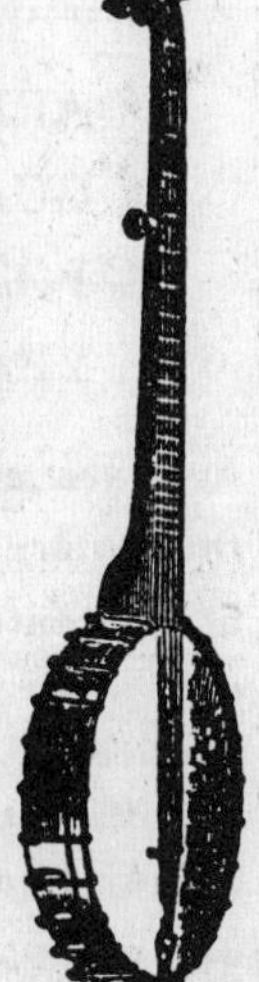

Banjo Strings.

Smooth finish, 25c set.

Imperial quality, finest made, 50c set.

Concertinas, 20 Keys.

No. 1. 20 keys, imitation rosewood, single reed, good quality, $1.00.

No. 21. 20 keys, rosewood, German silver inlaid edges, handsome bellows, double reeds, $2.00.

No. 139. 20 keys, mahogany, ivory keys, imitation leather bellows, Anglo style, $2.50.

Collection of extra quality concertinas, $4.00, 5.00.

Mandolin picks, 7c each.

Autoharp picks, 10c each.

Music stands, "Ideal," umbrella, japanned, $1.00 each.

Metronomes, $3.00; with bell, $3.75.

Nickel-plated music stands, $2.35.

Autoharps.

No. 10. 3 bars, producing 3 chords, $1.95.

No. 20. 4 bars, producing 4 chords, $2.15.

No. 25. 5 bars, producing 5 chords, $2.50.

No. 30. 6 bars, producing 6 chords, concert size, $4.00.

No. 35. 10 stops, producing 10 chords, new covered bar system, a most beautiful instrument, $5.00.

Autoharp strings, plain wire, 5c each; covered strings, 10c each, or per complete set, $1.00. In ordering sets give number of strings required.

Instrument Cases.

No. 2. Violin case, wood, black, swell top, hooks, no lock, $1.25.

No. 3. Same as No. 2, with lock, $1.50.

Mandolin case, canvas, leather bound, flannel lined, $1.75.

Banjo case, canvas covered, leather bound case, $1.75.

Guitar case, canvas covered, leather binding, open at end, full flannel lined, $1.75.

Mouth Organs.

We do not exchange mouth organs.

The mouth organs we sell are all manufactured by M. Hohner, Germany.

No. 0. Ten double holes, brass plates, nickel covers, superior quality, 20c.

No. 1. "Capetown to Pretoria," nickel plated, twenty reeds, put up in neat lidded case, 25c.

No. 1½. Hohner's organ pipe harp, a new novelty, ten single holes, sweet tone, 25c.

No. 5. Midget, Hohner's smallest-size mouth organ, can be covered with one hand, 3 inches long, single reeds, finely nickel-plated, 25c.

No. 6. Grand Symphony, a splendid instrument for professional or amateur players, 20 reeds, 25c.

No. 7. Marine Band, 10 double holes, finely nickel plated, rounded sides, a very sweet-toned instrument, in neat pasteboard case, 25c.

No. 8. Ten single holes, finely nickel plated, rounded covers, very similar to No. 7, put up in handsome satin-lined case, 35c.

No. 9. Special, ten double holes, forty reeds, finely nickel-plated, bevelled edge covers, extra sonorous tone, a grand instrument, 50c.

All our musical instruments are carefully examined before shipment, and guaranteed to be in perfect condition.

Write us for any Musical Instrument required not Catalogued.

Our Organs are made by the most reliable maker in Canada, whose reputation for the manufacture of only strictly high-grade instruments is a guarantee for quality, and our facilities for handling large quantities enable us to sell them at prices which bring them within the reach of all.

The Queen new style cabinet organ, model A, 5 octaves, in F scale, 10 stops, with grand organ and knee swell, 3 sets reeds, made in solid oak or walnut finish .**29.50**

Model B, in oak or walnut finish, 11 stops, with grand organ and knee swell, 4 sets reeds **34.50**

The Empress piano-cased organ, model G, finished in rosewood, mahogany or walnut, handsomely hand-carved and polished; the music rack is one continuous panel, 6 octaves in C scale, 11 stops, grand organ and knee swell, 4 sets reeds......**69.00**

Model H, with 12 stops and 5 sets reeds **75.00**

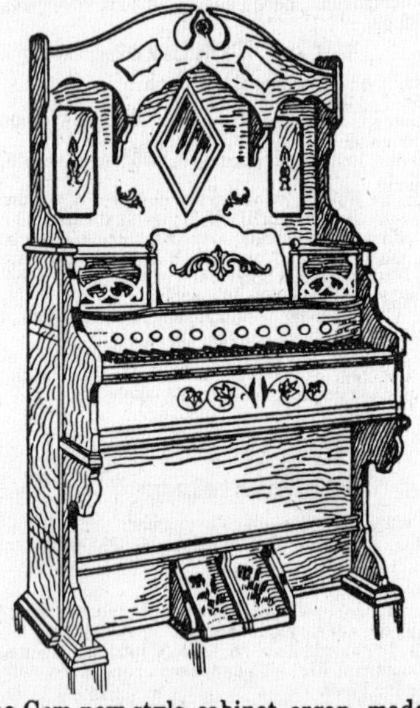

The Gem new style cabinet organ, made in solid walnut or oak, handsomely carved and finished, model C, 5 octaves, F scale, 10 stops, with grand organ and knee swell, 3 sets reeds **42.50**

Model D, 11 stops and 4 sets reeds..**46.00**

These Organs

ARE FULLY GUARANTEED FOR FIVE YEARS

And are shipped direct from the factory at Goderich, a copy of guarantee being affixed to each instrument by the manufacturer.

Satisfaction guaranteed or money refunded.

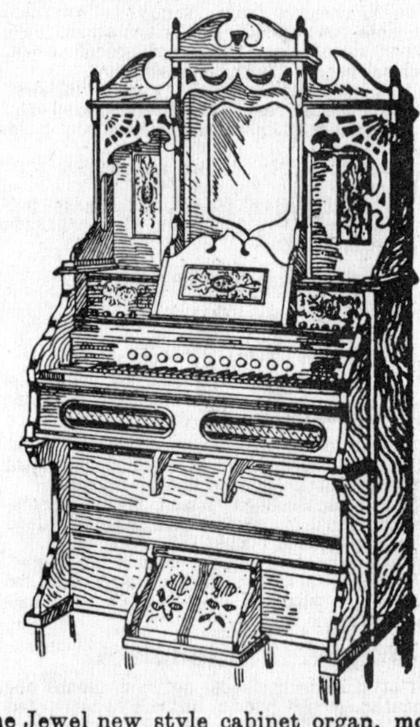

The Jewel new style cabinet organ, model E, made in solid walnut or oak, richly hand carved and ornamented, piano polish finish, compass 5 octaves, 12 stops, F scale, with grand organ and knee swell, 5 sets reeds **52.50**

Model F, 13 stops, 5 sets reeds, F scale **57.50**

No. 5. No. 24.

No. 5. Piano stool, made of hardwood, neat design, fancy turned legs and pedestal, brass claw feet, 14½-inch polished seat, finished in imitation mahogany, rosewood, ebony, curl walnut or oak **2.00**

Made in solid walnut **2.95**

Made in solid mahogany **3.50**

No. 24. Piano chair, a new design, neatly carved and polished, brass feet, seat can be raised to any desired height, made in rosewood, mahogany or walnut finish **3.75**

ORDER EARLY TO SECURE BEST SELECTION.

SEWING MACHINES.

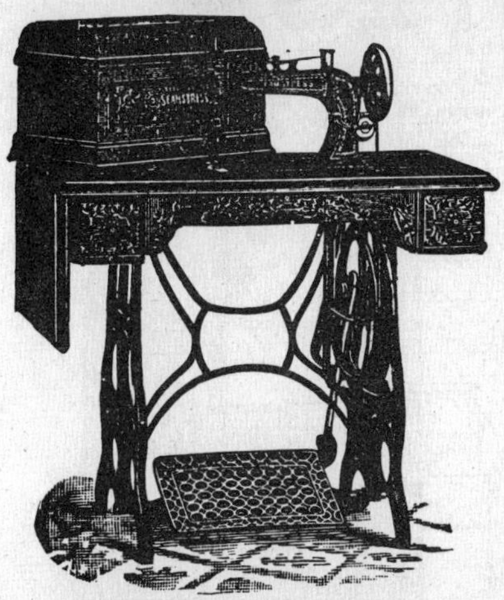

No. 3 Seamstress

THREE DRAWERS (AS CUT)

Finished in Plain Oak, at - - - $21 00
In Quartered Oak, extra finish, at - 22 50

No. 4 Seamstress

FIVE DRAWERS (AS CUT)

Finished in Plain Oak, at - - $22 50
In Quartered Oak, extra finish, at 24 00

No. 4 Drop-Head Seamstress

The machine-head drops out of sight and dust (as cut), leaving a neat table. To open it, raise the drop-leaf and lift the head.

Finished in Quarter-cut Oak, - - $25 50

LEADING FEATURES

OF THE

SEAMSTRESS SEWING MACHINES.

High Arm,
Hardened Steel Bearings,
Light Running,
Rotary Shaft Movement,
Self-Adjusting Working Parts,
Self Threading Shuttle,
Automatic Bobbin Winder,
and the Stand is fitted with the Latest Patent Ball-Bearing Driving Wheel.

Combining Simplicity, Durability, Reliability, Speed, Strength and Beauty.

THE ATTACHMENTS, supplied free with each machine, are of the latest improved pattern, interchangeable and cannot be put on wrong. Constructed to slip on the presser bar, requiring neither screw-driver nor thumb-screw to fasten them. They are made of the best steel, polished and nickel plated. They consist of Ruffler, Tucker, Binder, Under Braider Slide-Plate, Shirring Slide-Plate, 4 Hemmers (assorted widths), Quilter, Thread Cutter, Foot Hemmer, Feller and 2 Screw-Drivers, and 1 dozen Needles.

Not only hundreds, but thousands are in use giving perfect satisfaction. What better evidence of quality could be offered? Remember that

Certificate of Warranty for Five Years

is given with each machine.

Personal instructions are not necessary. A little study of our Illustrated Instruction Book, which is supplied with each machine, will enable the most inexperienced to operate a machine successfully.

Do not judge the quality of the machine by the price we ask for it, but satisfy yourself by careful investigation and comparison, that we can save you some money, and at the same time give you an article that we know to be equal in all respects to any machine on the market regardless of name or price. We do not send out these goods on trial, as the small margin will not allow us to do this, but as on other goods we sell we stand ready to back the goods for all they are worth, and to refund the money you paid if the machine is not equal in *each and every respect* to any machine on the market, regardless of price.

EATONIA

High Arm Sewing Machines

THERE is some demand for a good cheap machine, one that is thoroughly practical and which embodies in its make-up all of the necessary and practical features of a first-class, high-grade machine, but which at the same time is not finished so elaborately or furnished with such expensive equipments, the latter items adding greatly to the cost but not to the utility of the machine for practical purposes.

A complete set of attachments supplied free with each machine.

Its sewing qualities cannot be surpassed. We place the **same guarantee** on it as on our other machines, **that is five years.** The "Eatonia" is so simple in construction that it requires no teacher beyond the printed book of instruction which accompanies each machine.

NOTE.—Needles, Bobbins and all supplies for these machines always kept in stock.

Seamstress Desk Cabinet Closed.

Furnished in Quarter-Sawed Oak and Walnut.

This is the cheapest Desk Cabinet ever offered, quality considered, and by all means the handsomest. It is a beautiful design, hand rubbed and polished, and never fails to please, $37.50.

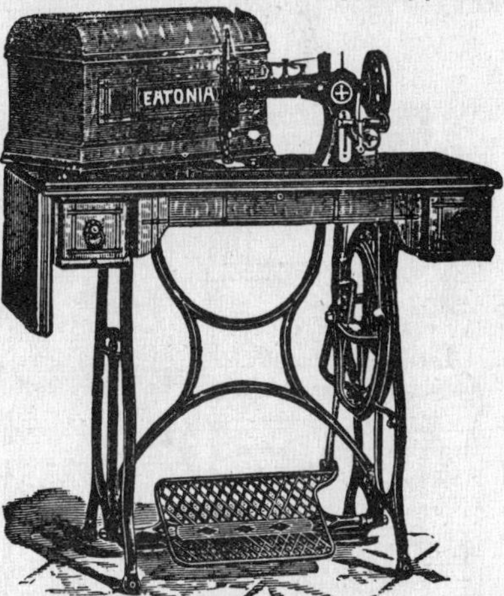

No. 3 Eatonia

Three Drawers (as cut), finished in Oak, at $17.50.

No. 4 Eatonia.—Five drawers, finished in Oak, at $19.00.

No. 4 Eatonia.—Drop-head cabinet, with leaf closed, protecting the machine from dust and making a convenient table when not in use. Finished in Quartered Oak, $22.50.

EXPERT HAND MACHINE.

With the latest triple-action hand gearing. Will do similar work to foot-power machine Fitted with self-threading shuttle and automatic bobbin winder.

GUARANTEED FOR FIVE YEARS

Price, with a full set of attachments, - $11 75
With Walnut Base and bent Walnut Cover, - - - - - - 15 00

If you have a sewing machine send for our Thread Controller, price 10c each.

BEDROOM SUITES.

No. 139. Bedroom suite, hardwood, antique or mahogany finish, bureau has shaped top and legs, with 14 x 24-inch bevel-plate mirror, bedstead, 4 ft 2 in wide, washstand with double doors and drawer, complete with castors..$10.25

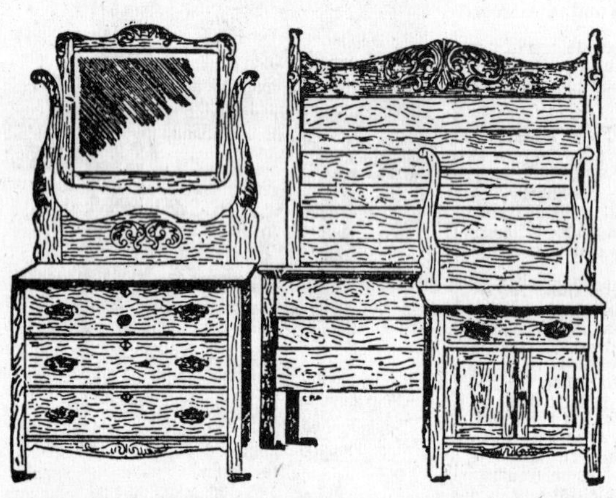

No. 143. Bedroom suite, antique or mahogany finish, neatly carved and well finished, bureau with swell-shaped top, fitted with 20 x 24-inch bevel-plate mirror, bedstead 4 ft 2 in wide, large size washstand.$11.50

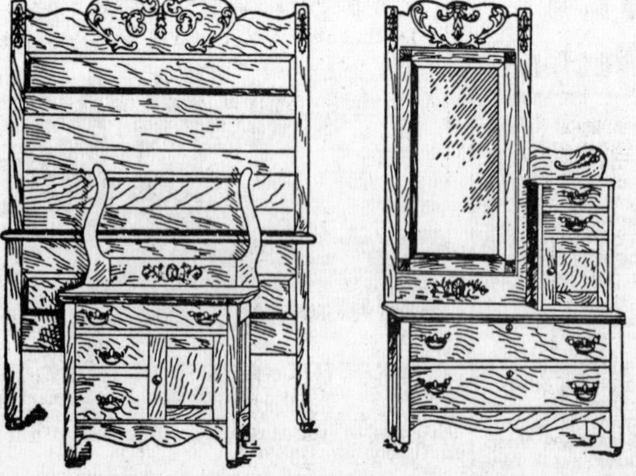

No. 404½. Bedroom suite, in solid oak, golden finish, richly carved, cheval-shaped bureau, fitted with 18 x 36-inch bevel-plate mirror, combination washstand, bedstead 4 ft 2 in wide $17.50

No. 424. Bedroom suite, hardwood, rich antique finish, neatly carved, cheval-shaped bureau with shaped top, fitted with 18 x 36-inch bevel-plate mirror, combination washstand, bedstead 4 ft 2 in wide...$14.50

No. 407. Bedroom suite, made of selected ash, golden finish, neatly carved, bureau 40 in wide, with shaped top, fitted with 20 x 24-inch bevel-plate mirror, combination washstand, bedstead 4 ft 2 in wide $14.25

Same suite, made of birch, mahogany finish 15.00

Same suite, made of solid oak, golden finish....................16.50

No. 419. Bedroom suite, oak, rich golden finish, carved and well finished, bureau has shaped top and swell top drawers, with 22 x 28-inch shaped British bevel-plate mirror, combination washstand, bedstead has quartered oak panels, 4 ft 2 in wide..........................$25.00

 Do not cut illustrations from Catalogue. Give page and number of article.

No. 412. Bedroom suite, solid quartered oak, hand-carved and polished, bureau 44 in. wide, shaped top, 24 x 30-in. British bevel-plate mirror, bedstead 4 ft. 6 in. wide, large combination washstand $28.50

No. 417. Bedroom suite, made of select quarter-cut oak, golden finish, hand-carved and polished, large size bureau, shaped top and drawer front, fitted with 24 x 30-inch British plate shaped bevelled mirror, combination washstand to match, bedstead 4 ft. 4 in. wide $32.50

Separate Bureau and Washstand, suitable to go with Brass or Iron Bedsteads, etc.

Bureau and washstand, as cut No. 139, $8.00; as cut No. 143, $9.25; as cut No. 424, $12.00; as cut No. 407, in ash, $11.35; mahogany finish, $11.90; oak, $13.00; as cut No. 404½, $14.25; as cut No. 419, $20.50; as cut No. 412, $24.00; as cut No. 417, $26.75.

Separate Washstands.

Washstands, antique finish, enclosed, with drawer and doors, splasher back, castered, $2.25.

Washstands, antique finish, combination shape, $2.50; larger size, $2.75, 3.00, 3.25.

Separate Wooden Bedsteads.

No. 81. Bedsteads, head board 3 ft. 6 in. high, single or double size, $2.25.
No. 139. Bedstead, double size, $2.50.
No. 407. " " " ash, $3.50.
No. 407. " " " oak, $4.50.

Folding Mantel Beds.

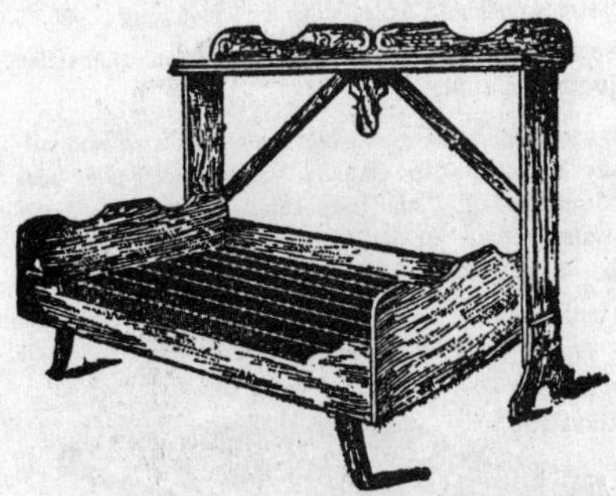

Folding beds, strongly made, with double-woven wire spring mattress attached, inside measure 4 ft. x 6 ft., length over all 6 ft. 8 in., closes up with mattress and bed clothes, made in ash, nicely finished, $6.90; in solid oak, $7.50.

Mixed mattresses to fit above, $2.00, 2.65, 3.25.

Chiffonnieres.

No. 88. Chiffonniere, elm, antique finish, 36 inches wide, 18 inches deep, 56 inches high, with 5 large drawers, $6.50.

No. 88½. Same as No. 88, with 14 x 24 inch bevel-plate mirror, $8.50.

No. 88.

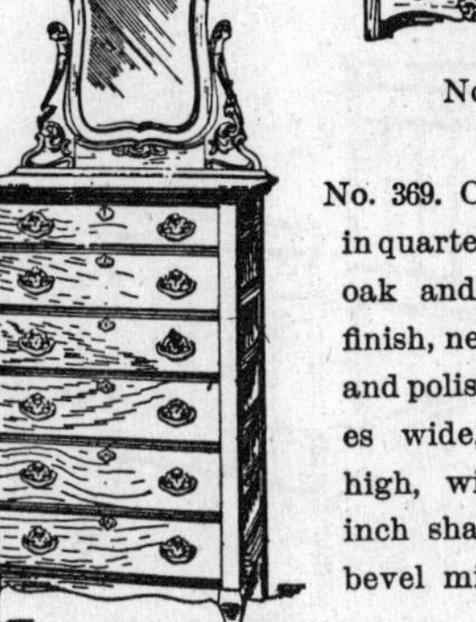

No. 369.

No. 369. Chiffonniere, in quarter-cut golden oak and mahogany finish, neatly carved and polished, 31 inches wide, 72 inches high, with 14 x 16-inch shaped British bevel mirror, $14.25.

No. 5. Five-drawer bureau, hardwood, antique finish, 42 inches wide, 54 inches high, well made and finished, $6.75.

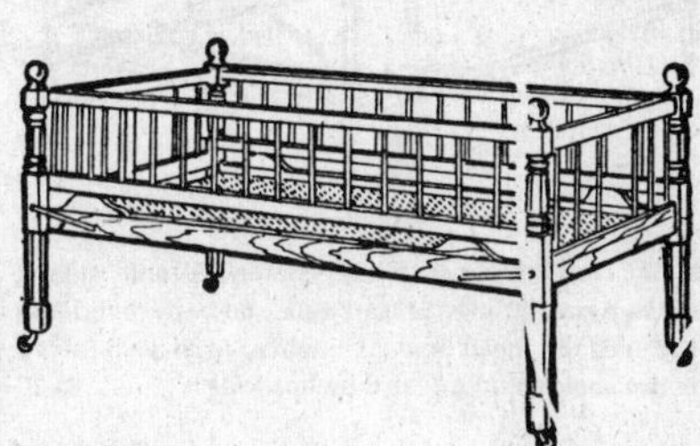

No. 21. Childs' folding cot, hardwood, antique finish, with woven-wire spring bo[illegible], size 2 ft. 4 in. wide, by 4 ft. 6 in. long, $2.90.

No. 92. Bedroom table, hardwood, antique finish, strongly made, 20 x 28-inch top, shaped legs and drawer, $1.40.

Same table, made in solid oak, golden finish, $1.75.

No. 36. Bedroom commode, box shape, 17 x 17 in. square outside measure, 13 x 12 in. square inside measure, made of ash, antique finish $2.00

WE GUARANTEE SATISFACTION OR REFUND YOUR MONEY.

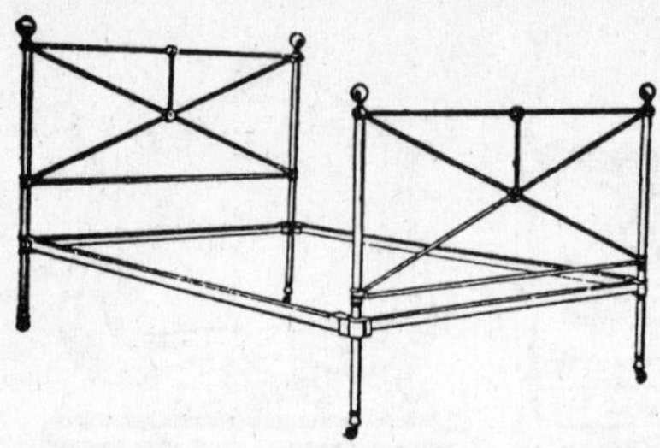

No. 03. Iron bedstead, white enamel, 1-inch pillars, with solid brass caps and knobs, head end 46 inches high, in sizes 3 feet, 3 feet 6 inches and 4 feet 6 inches wide $3.65

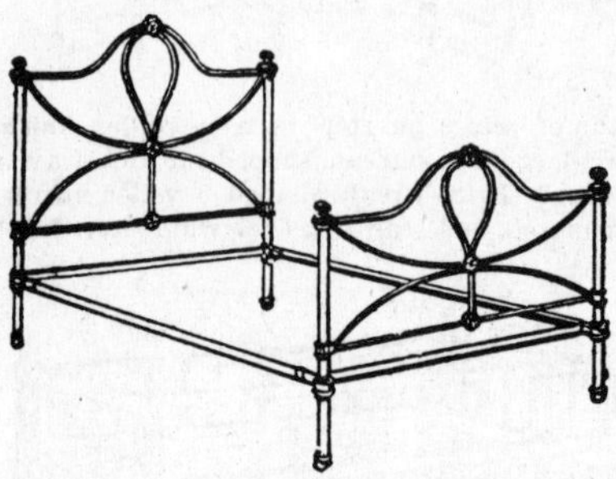

No. 63. Iron bedstead, white enamel, 1-inch pillars, extra heavy filling, brass knobs and caps, height to top rail on head end 52 inches, in sizes 3 feet, 3 feet 6 inches and 4 feet 6 inches wide $4.10

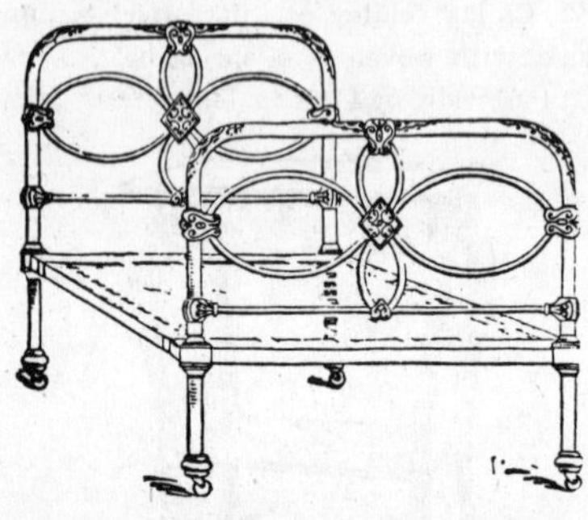

No. 06. Iron bedstead, white enamel finish, with 1-inch posts, with heavy chills and fillings, head end 3 feet 7 inches high, made in sizes 3, feet 3 feet 6 inches and 4 feet 6 inches wide $4.75

No. 401. Iron bedstead, white enamel finish, neat scroll fillings and chills, 1-inch pillars, head end 56 inches high, brass knobs, caps and rosettes, in sizes, 3 feet 6 inches and 4 feet 6 inches wide, $5.40

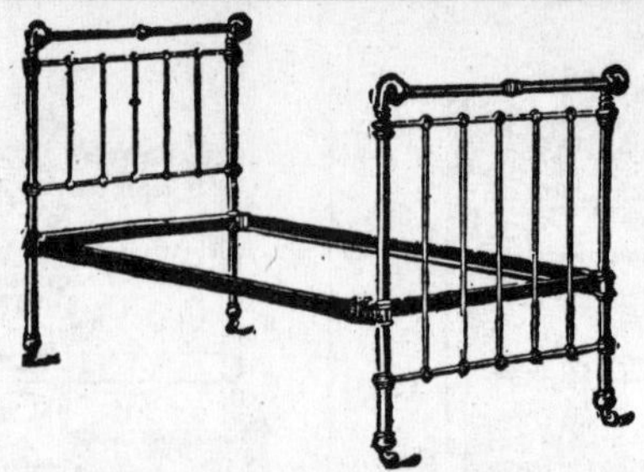

No. 2011. Bedstead, white enamel, with roll top, brass rail, 1-inch pillars, height head end 50 inches, in sizes 3 feet, 3 feet 6 inches and 4 feet 6 inches wide by 6 feet long $7.25

No. 201. Same as No. 2011, with brass knobs instead of roll top $4.90

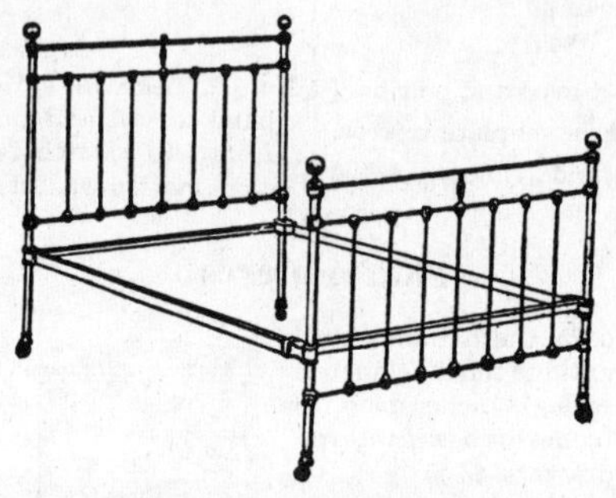

No. 801. Brass and iron bedstead, white enamel finish, 1-inch pillars, with extended foot end, brass rails, knobs and caps, in sizes 3 feet, 3 feet 6 inches and 4 feet 6 inches wide $5.95

Same bed, with extended bow-shaped foot end .. $6.90

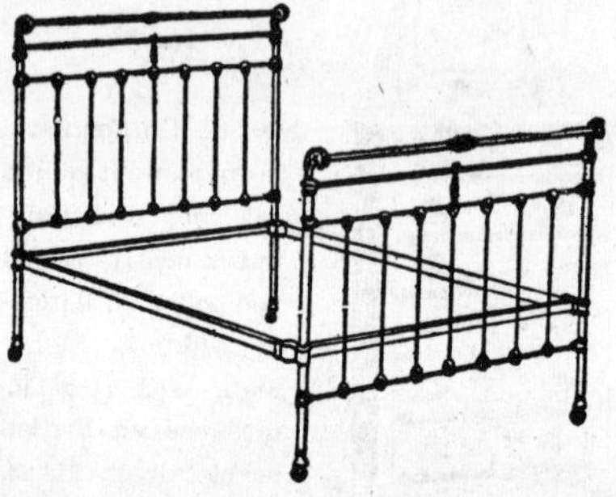

No. 8011. Brass and iron bedstead, white enamel, 1-inch pillars and roll top, extended foot end, double brass rails and mounts, in sizes 3 feet, 3 feet 6 inches and 4 feet 6 inches wide $8.25

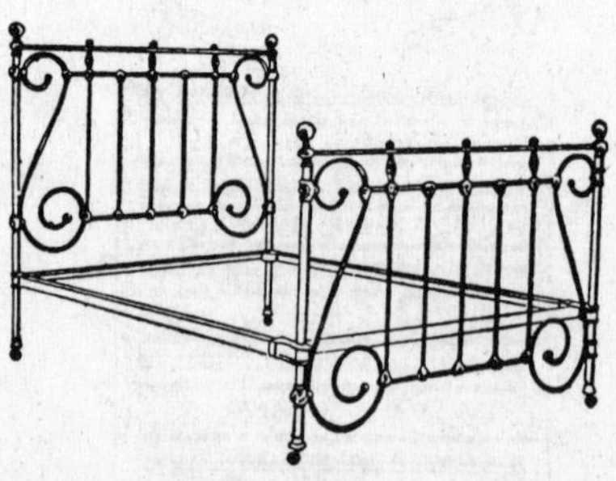

No. 702. Brass and iron bedstead, white enamel finish, 1-inch pillars, heavy scroll fillings, extended foot end, heavy brass rails, knobs and spindles, made in sizes 3 feet 6 inches and 4 feet 6 inches wide $8.90

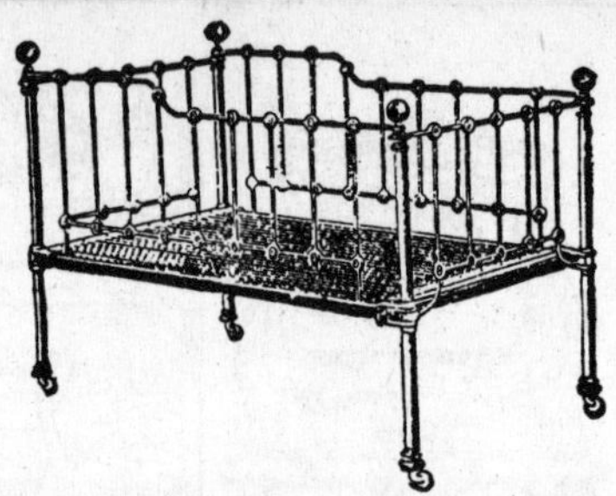

No. 0411. Iron cot, same style as cut No. 140, with woven-wire spring bottom attached, in white enamel finish, 2½ x 4½ ft $6.10

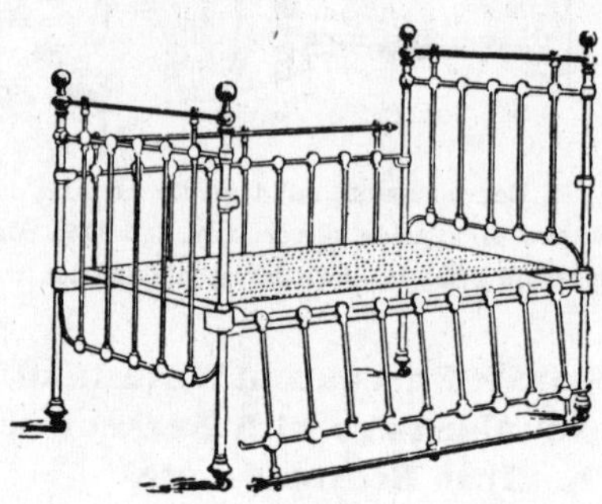

No. 0611. Iron cot, best white enamel finish, with spring bottom and drop sides (as shown in cut), brass rails, knobs and caps, 2 ft. 6 in. by 4 ft. 6 in. long, $9.00; similar cot, without brass rail $7.50

Mixed mattresses, to fit any of above cots, specially made, $1.25, 1.50; best sateen ticking $1.75

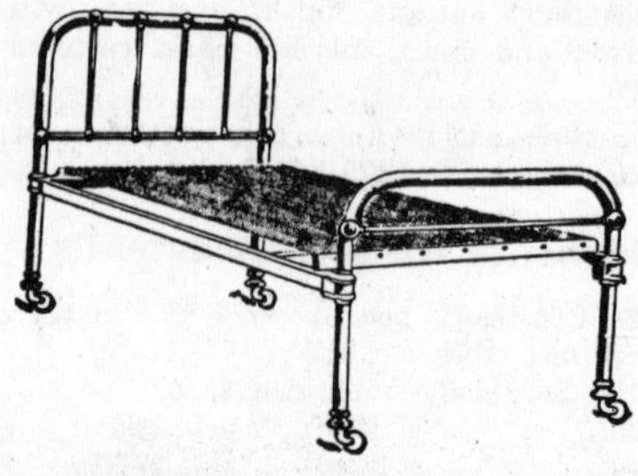

No. 54. Iron bedstead, suitable for institutions, etc., fitted with iron frame, Hercules woven-wire spring mattress, head end 36 inches high, made in sizes 2 feet 6 inches and 3 feet wide by 6 feet long ... $5.75

Special prices for institution bedsteads in quantities quoted on application.

We carry the largest assortment of iron and all-brass bedsteads in Canada, comprising the best productions of Canadian, English and American manufacturers. Prices and description on application. Kindly state about what you require.

Spring Mattresses.

No. 20. Hercules woven wire spring mattress, made of the best steel wire, can be fitted on any iron bed on this page, with heavy angle iron side rails to connect bed together, to fit 3-foot beds, $2.65; 3 feet 6 inches, $2.95 ; 4 feet 6 inches........ $3.60

We guarantee to fill Mail Orders accurately and promptly.

Mattresses.

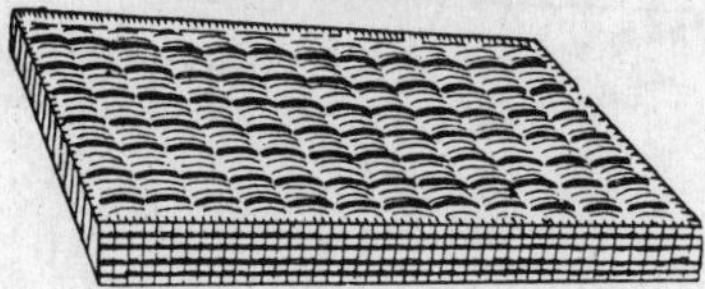

No. 1. Mixed mattresses, seagrass and wool both sides, in sizes 2 ft. x 4 ft., 2 ft. 6 in. x 4 ft. 6 in., $1.25; 3 ft. x 6 ft., $1.90; 3 ft. 6 in. x 6 ft., to 4 ft. 6 in. x 6 ft. $2.00

No. 1S. Mixed mattresses, seagrass centre, and white cotton tops both sides, covered in extra heavy ticking, well made, sizes 3 ft. x 6 ft., $2.75; 3 ft. 6 in. x 6 ft., $2.85; 4 ft. to 4 ft. 6 in. x 6 ft. $2.90

No. 3S. Mixed mattress, covered with sateen ticking, extra well made, well filled with seagrass and white cotton tops both sides, 3 ft. x 6 ft., $2.75; 3 ft. 6 in. x 6 ft., $3.00; 4 ft. to 4 ft. 6 in. x 6 ft. $3.25

No. 3G. Same filling as No. 3S, but with best quality sateen ticking in any of above sizes, extra 25c

Fibre and white cotton mattresses, covered in heavy twill ticking, closely tufted, sizes 3 ft x 6 ft., $4.00; 3 ft. 6 in. to 4 ft. 6 in. x 6 ft. $4.50

Coir hair mattresses, in extra heavy ticking, 3 ft. x 6 ft., $5.75; 3 ft. 6 in. x 6 ft., $6.50; 4 ft. to 4 ft. 6 in. x 6 ft $6.75

Hair mattresses from $8.50 and upwards to $27.50, according to grade, weight, and size.

Mixed mattresses, made in two parts, 35c extra; over 6 ft. long, 25c extra.

When ordering mattresses, state exact size required. For double size we always send 4 ft. 2 in. x 6 ft.

Cradles.

Children's willow cradles, hood tops $1.40

Children's reed cradles, hood tops..$1.90 and 2.25

Pillow Sham Holders.

Sham holder, double size, to fit any wooden bed, double spring brackets 25c

Sham holder, japanned brackets, to fasten on with screws 30c

Tarbox sham holder, to fasten on centre of bed back of pillows, does not fold the shams, "lifts straight up" 60c

Woven Wire Spring Mattresses.

No. 20. Spring mattress, heavy hardwood frame, double weave, with cable and copper wire supports, all sizes $1.40

No. 19. Woven-wire spring mattress, with 6 lock weave bands and 2 copper wire edge supports, all sizes $1.75

No. 23. Woven-wire mattress, very closely woven top, and reinforced with 9 lockweaves, bands and side supports; this we recommend $2.00

Hercules springs, $1.65, $2.25, $3.25.

Springs require to be one inch narrower and one inch shorter than bedstead to fit properly. When ordering double size we always send 4 ft. 1 in. wide by 5 ft. 11 inches long.

Bed Pillows.

No. W. Pillows, wool filled, covered in special ticking, size 20 x 26 in., pair 75c

Mixed feather pillows, $1.10, 1.25, 1.65.

Goose and duck feather pillows .... $2.50.

Goose feather pillows, 5 lb $3.35

Goose feather pillows, 6 lb $4.00

No. 354. Sideboard, hardwood, antique finish, neatly carved, with shaped double top, 46 inches wide, 14 x 24-inch bevel-plate mirror, with two small drawers and double door cupboard $8.00

Same sideboard, with carved panel back in place of mirror $6.50

No. 355. Sideboard, hardwood, dark antique finish, with shaped double top, 46 in. wide, 14 x 24-inch bevel-plate mirror, 1 large and 2 small drawers, and double cupboard, well made and finished $9.35

No. 465. Sideboard, quarter-cut oak, golden polished finish, heavily carved, 48 inches wide, shaped top and drawer 18 x 34-inch British bevel-plate mirror, 1 large and 3 small drawers, 1 lined for cutlery $24.00

No. 363. Sideboard, solid oak, golden finish, heavily carved and polished, swell-shaped top and front, 4 ft. 4 inches wide, with 18 x 36-inch shaped British bevel-plate mirror..$21.00

Same sideboard in quarter-cut golden oak $25.00

No. 474. Sideboard, made of selected ash, golden finish, richly carved, top 48 inches wide, 81 inches high, 15 x 26-inch plate mirror, 2 small and one large drawer, large roomy cupboard, doors are panelled instead of plain as shown in cut $12.50

Same sideboard made of oak, golden finish, ... $16.75

No. 476. Sideboard, made of selected quarter-cut, oak, rich golden finish, hand carved and polished, 4 ft. 6 inches wide, shaped top and swell drawer, 20 x 36-inch British plate bevelled mirror $31.00

If you do not see what you require, write for other designs.

No. 239. Extension table, hardwood, golden finish, top 40 inches wide, with heavy rim and strongly braced legs, extending to 6 ft. long, $4.20 ; extending to 8 ft. long $4.75

No 297. Extension table, hardwood, dark antique finish, top size when closed 42 x 42 in., has 5 heavy turned and fluted legs, which are fastened to top with patent blocks, and can be shipped at a very low freight rate ; extending to 6 ft. long, $5.15 ; extending to 8 ft. long.$5.85

No. 87S. Extension table, hardwood, imitation oak finish, heavy well-braced legs, with fancy embossed carving, top 42 in. wide, extending to 8 ft. long $6.50

Same table, made in solid oak 8.25

No. 272. Extension table, hardwood, golden finish, 42 x 42 in. top, 5 heavily-turned and fluted legs, strongly braced, extending to 8 ft. long $6.60

Same table, in solid oak 8.75

No. 93. Extension table, selected ash, golden finish, top size 3 ft. 8 in. wide, extending to 8 ft. long, with handsome turned and fluted legs, strongly braced, leaves are cleated, which prevents warping, $8.00 ; extending to 10 ft. long....................................$9.00

No. 279. Extension table, solid oak, golden finish, polished top 44 x 44 in., has 5 heavy fancy turned and fluted legs, strongly made, extending to 8 ft. long, $9.85 ; extending to 10 ft. long $11.50

Same table, made in choice quarter-cut golden oak, extending to 8 ft. long, $11.25 ; extending to 10 ft. long $13.00

No. 12. Chair, hardwood, antique finish, strongly made, each 35c

No. 6. Chair, hardwood, antique finish, shaped wood seat, strongly made, brace arms, each 40c

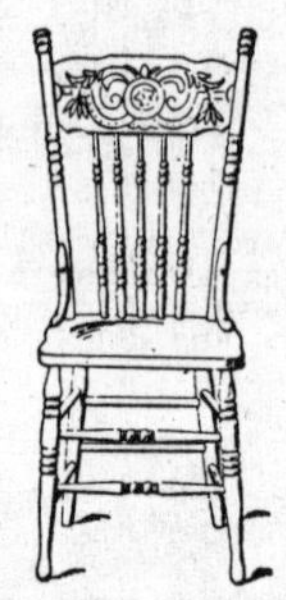

No. 40. Chair, hardwood, antique finish, back is neatly carved, with fancy turned spindles, solid shaped wood seat, brace arms, each....50c

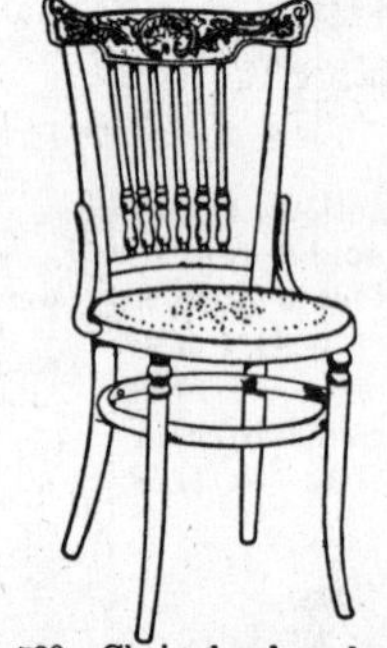

No. 720. Chair, hardwood, antique finish, embossed carved back, brace arms, perforated or impervious veneered seat, legs are strongly bolted to rim and rung, and is shipped K.D., each 80c

No. 700. Chair, hardwood, antique finish, handsomely carved, with impervious veneered seat, strongly made, each 77c

Same chair, with cane seat, each.......................95c

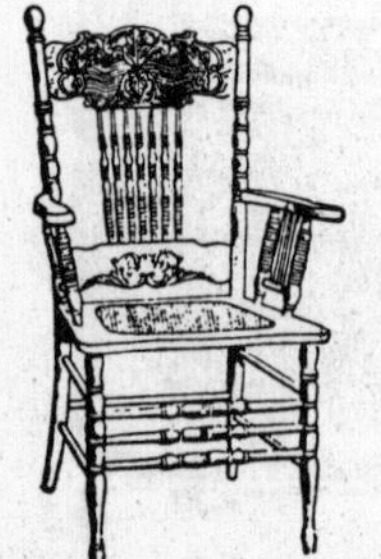

No. 702. Arm chair to match No. 700, impervious seat, each $1.27

Same chair, with cane seat, each.......................$1.40

No. 841. Chair, hardwood, antique finish, embossed carved slat back, brace arms, cane seat, each.. ....$1.00

No. 843. Arm chair to match No. 841, each $1.65

No. 6. Dining-room chair, solid oak or walnut frames, polish finish, with fancy embossed leather cobbler-shaped seat, each $1.65

Same chair, with seat upholstered genuine leather, colors green or maroon, each .$2.00

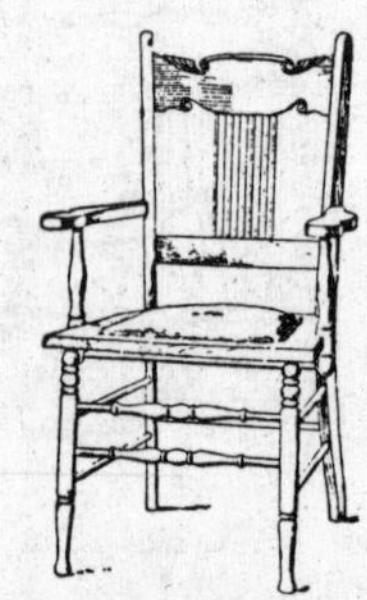

No. 6A. Arm chair, to match No. 6, with embossed leather cobbler-shaped seat, each $2.15

With genuine leather upholstered seat, each $2.55

THESE ARE EXCEPTIONALLY GOOD VALUES.

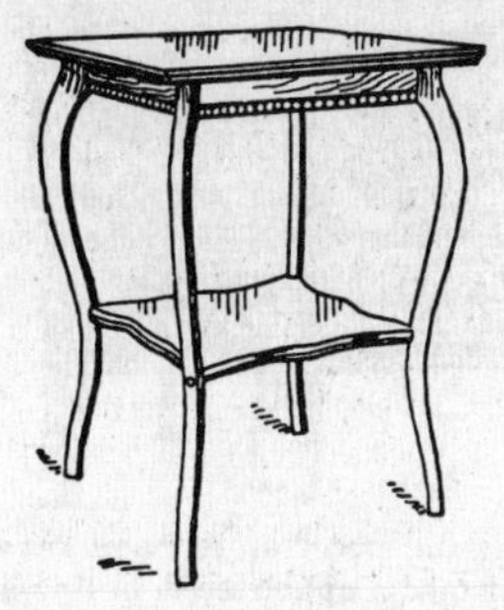

No. 81. Table, hardwood, antique finish, 16 x 16-inch top, shaped legs and shelf 85c
22 x 22-inch top, shaped legs and shelf $1.10

No 447. Parlor table, in solid oak or mahogany finish, 24 x 24-inch top, with fancy turned legs and brass claw feet......................$2.00

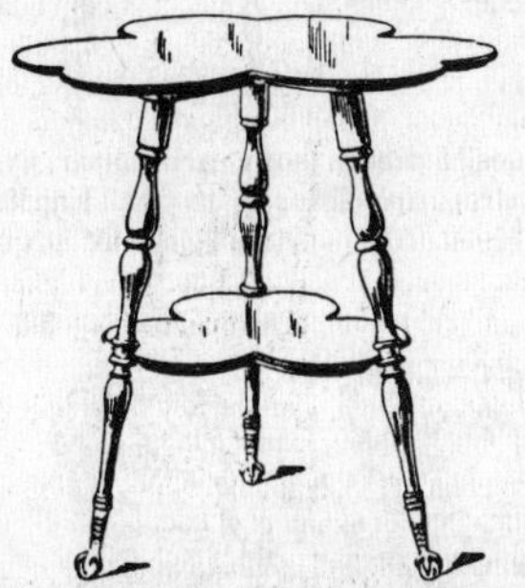

No. 114. Parlor table, in quarter-cut oak and birch, mahogany finish, 25 x 25-inch fancy shaped top, and shelf, well polished $3.35

No. 104. Parlor table, quartered oak or mahogany, hand carved and polished, 24 x 24-inch fancy shaped top and shelf, with brass beading on edges; this is a high-grade table in every particular...........$5.75

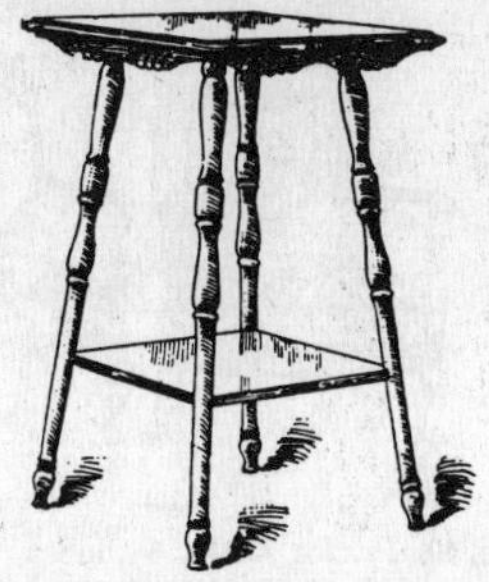

No. 100. Parlor table, with quartered oak top and shelf, or birch, mahogany finish, polished, 18 x 18-inch top, fancy turned legs, can be shipped K.D..................$1.10

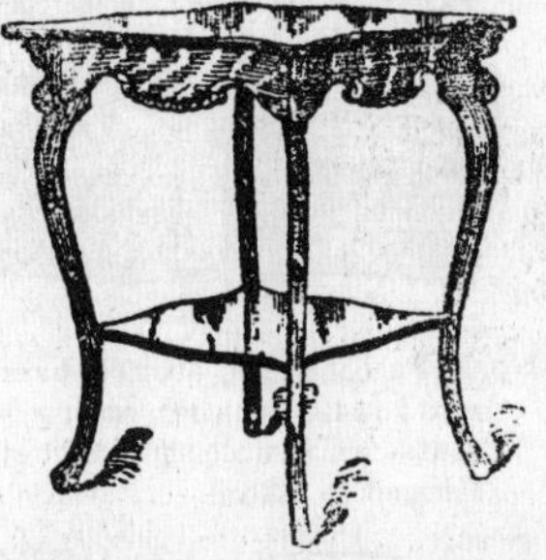

No. 499. Parlor table, quartered oak, golden finish or curly birch, mahogany finish, polished, 24 x 24-inch shaped top and shelf, can be shipped K. D.................$2.95

No. 132. Parlor table, a beauty, made in quarter-cut oak, golden or mahogany finish finely polished, 21 x 29-inch fancy shaped top, brass trimmed around edge $5.00

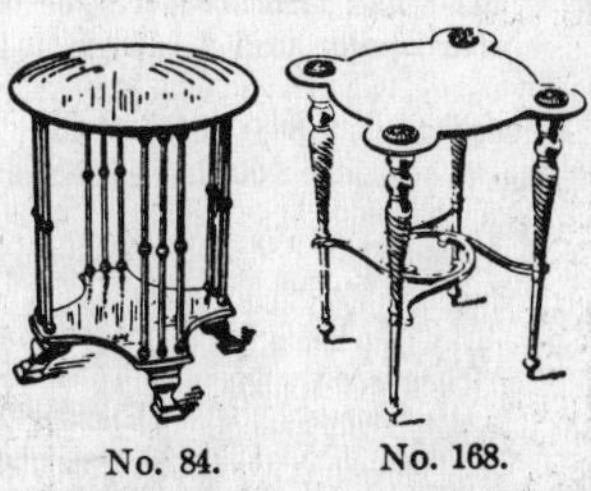

No. 84. No. 168.

No. 84. Jardiniere stand, in quarter-cut golden oak, or mahogany finish, 15 x 15-inch round top, highly polished, 20 inches high......$2.35
No. 168. Jardiniere stand, newest design, in quarter-cut golden oak or mahogany finish, 15 x 15-inch top, and 20 inches high, piano finish.......................... $2.85

No. 16½. Lounge, hardwood, antique-finished frame, upholstered spring seat, in satin russe..$3.95
Upholstered in extra heavy satin-faced tapestry..........................$4.75

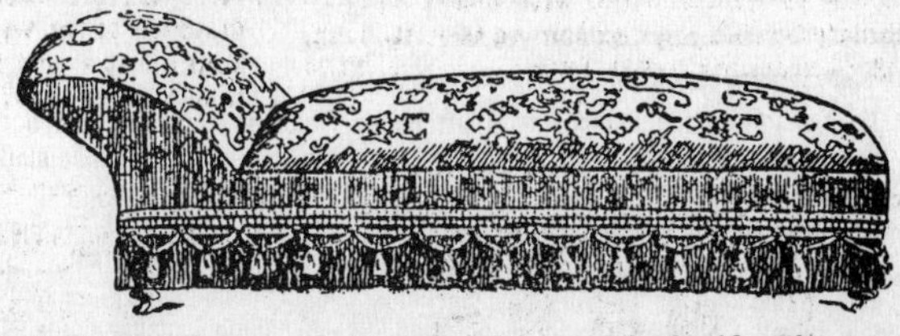

No. 15. Couch, all-over upholstered and fringed both sides the same, a new and very comfortable design, good spring seat well upholstered in French tapestry covering, colors Nile, blue, reseda, terra cotta and crimson $4.85
Same couch, upholstered in fancy figured velours, fringe to match, olive, myrtle, tobac, golden brown and red $6.75

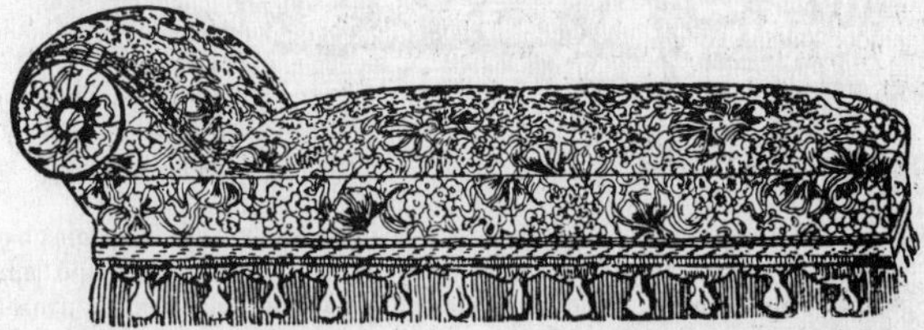

No 19. This couch is our most popular shape, has beautiful sloped head, upholstered with a fine grade of satin-faced tapestry, spring seat, fringed all around $8.00
Upholstered in figured velours $9.25

No. 21. Couch, all-over upholstered, deep tufted top, spring seat, edges and arm, covered in heavy velour covering, colors green, olive, blue, terra cotta and red..$9.50

No. 92. Bed couch, heavy hardwood frame, back can be lowered level with seat, forming a double bed, there is also a wardrobe or box underneath seat for storing bed clothes, etc., upholstered with springs all over, and deeply tufted, in heavy tapestry covering $13.00
Upholstered in figured velours $14.75

SAMPLES OF COVERING MAILED FREE.

No. 10. Parlor suite, the most reliable on the market, in solid walnut or mahogany finished frames, neatly carved and polished, 5 pieces (sofa, arm chairs, arm rocker and 2 reception chairs), upholstered in heavy tapestry covering, silk plush trimmed, good spring seats and plain back........$18.75

Upholstered in fancy figured velour........$21.00

Upholstered in black haircloth........$23.50

No. 11. Parlor suite, upholstered on same frames as No. 10, with first-class upholstering throughout, spring seats and edges double stuffed, and tufted backs—

Upholstered in heavy figured velour........$29.50

Upholstered in silk tapestry........$31.00

No. 247. Parlor suite, 3 pieces (as cut), frames are well made, mahogany finish, highly polished, upholstered in silk tapestry, good spring seats, colors Nile, green, reseda, olive, terra cotta, rose, pink and old gold........$26.00

Upholstered in high-grade silk tapestry........$28.75

No. 761. Parlor suite, 3 pieces (as cut), mahogany-finished frames, with genuine inlaid lines, highly polished, upholstered in high-grade silk tapestry. This makes an elegant 3-piece suit, and upholstered in first-class style........$31.00

PRICES AND DESCRIPTIONS.

Prices and descriptions of other higher-priced suites on application.

We will send samples of coverings used on parlor suites, lounges, easy chairs, etc., on application. Always state price of article you require. Parlor suites can be upholstered in different colors on separate pieces, if so selected, at the same price.

As rugs for Nos. 15 and 2½ suites and rug lounges are made in squares, special sizes to fit, we cannot cut off samples.

We upholster all our own goods and guarantee all work to be first-class, new, fresh and clean. It usually takes from two to three days to make up parlor suites when special colors or coverings are required.

No. 40. Parlor suite, 3 pieces, mahogany finished frames, hand carved and highly polished, thoroughly well made, upholstered in fine silk tapestry, in colors olive, Nile, green, rose, light blue, golden brown, spring seat and edges, buttoned back and bands........$36.00

No. 5. Parlor suite, stuffed over, 5 pieces (sofa, arm chair, arm rocker and 2 ladies' chairs), spring seats and edges, large and comfortable, seats are double-stuffed, well upholstered in heavy figured velour, fringed to match........$31.50

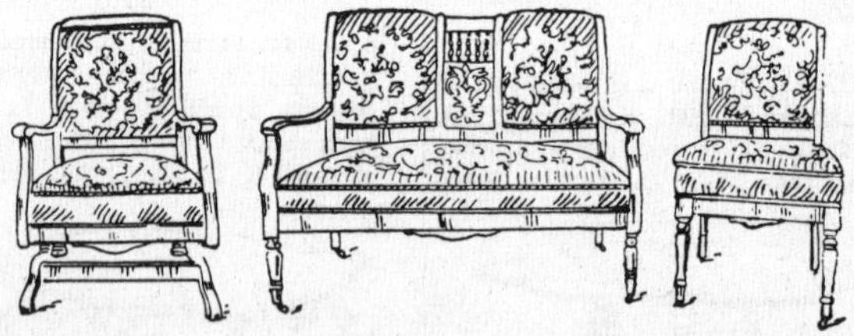

No. 2½. Parlor suite, solid walnut frames, 5 pieces (sofa, arm chair, arm rocking chair and 2 reception chairs), upholstered in best English Wilton rugs, silk plush bands, double-stuffed, spring seat and edges, ...$35.00

Upholstered in satin-faced tapestry........$27.50

No. 15. Parlor suite, 5 pieces, allover upholstered in best Wilton rugs, silk plush trimmed, fringed to match, consisting of sofa, arm chair, arm rocker and 2 reception chairs, spring seats, backs and edges, ...$55.00

In separate pieces: sofa, $18.50; arm rocker, $12.50; arm chair, $12.00; and reception chairs, each........$6.50

No. 8. Five-piece parlor suite, birch, mahogany finish, elaborately hand carved and highly polished, shaped arms strongly braced, suite consists of sofa, arm chair, arm rocker, and two reception chairs, well upholstered with spring seats and edges, double-stuffed, upholstered in fine silk tapestry........$61.50

CHAIRS.

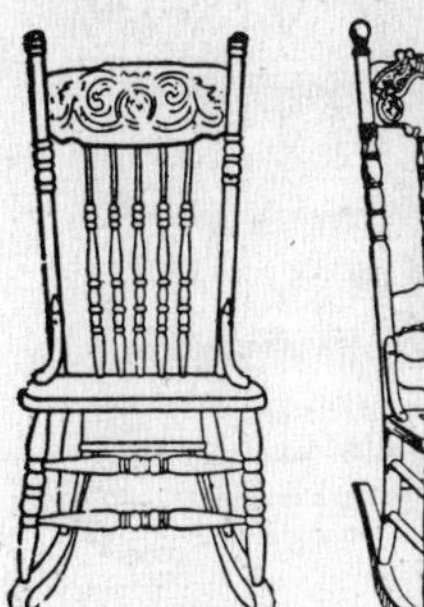

No. 35. Rocking chair, hardwood, antique finish, embossed, carved high back, shaped wood seat 85c

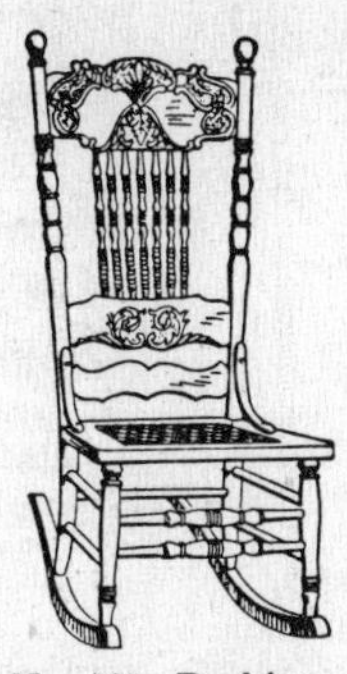

No. 705. Rocking chair, hardwood, antique finish, neatly carved, high back with fancy turned spindles, cane seat $1.25

Same, with impervious veneered seat $1.10

No. 22. Rocking chair, antique finish, large size, high black..........$1.25

Also larger size, with roll seat.................$1.55

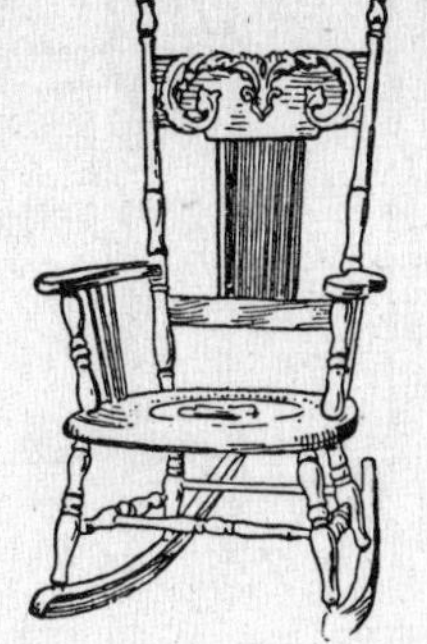

No. 2. Rocking chair, solid oak or mahogany-finished frames, neatly carved and polished, solid leather cobbler-shaped seats $1.90

No. 67. Rocking chair, solid oak or mahogany-finished frame, carved and polished, with embossed leather cobbler-shaped seat . $2.75

No. 4. Rocking chair, larger size, strongly made, shaped arms, in quarter-cut oak and curly birch, mahogany finished, solid and embossed leather cobbler-shaped seats.......$3.90

No. 558. Rocking chair, solid quarter-cut oak and mahogany finish, neatly carved back, solid leather lap-over cobbler seats $4.75

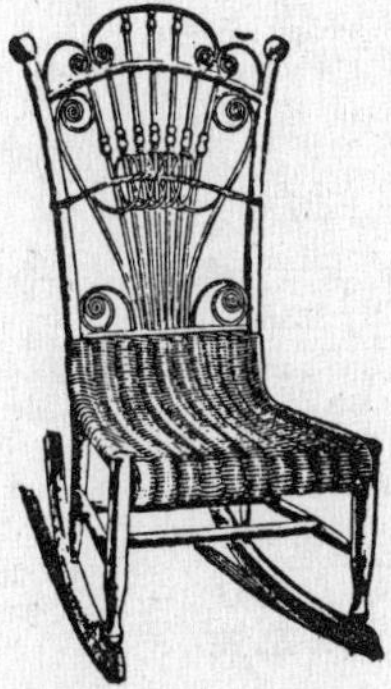

No. 5539. Ladies' rattan rocking chair, 16th century finish...$2.00

Reception chair to match...........$2.00

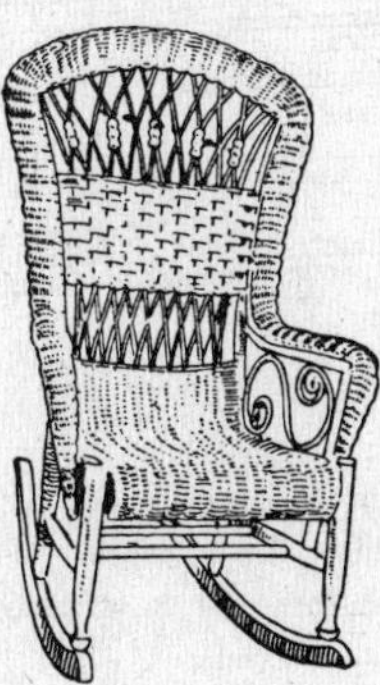

No. 5546. Ladies' large rattan arm rocking chair, 16th century or natural finish ...$3.65

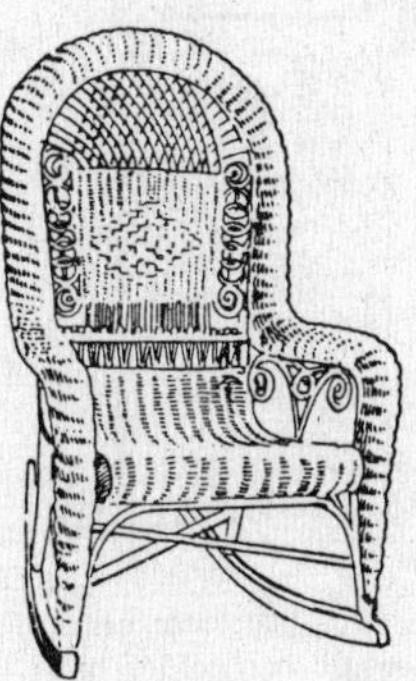

No. 5603. Large rattan arm rocker, with heavy roll edge and seat, 16th century or natural finish $5.25

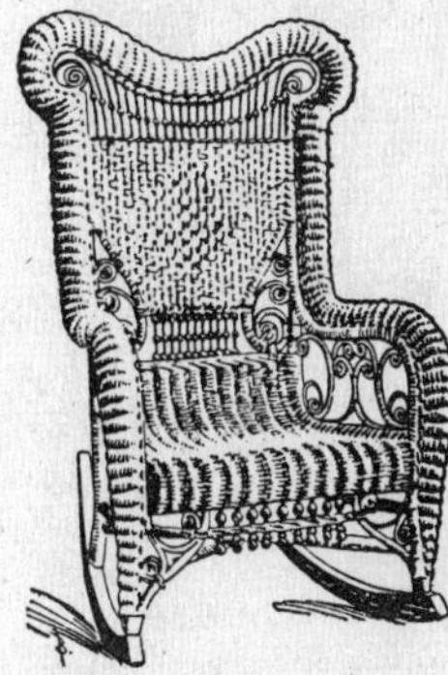

No. 5617. Gents' large-size arm rocking chair, natural or 16th century finish.................$7.75

No. 233. Arm chair, curly birch, rich mahogany finished frame, well polished, fancy carved back upholstered in extra quality silk tapestry covering, spring seat $9.00

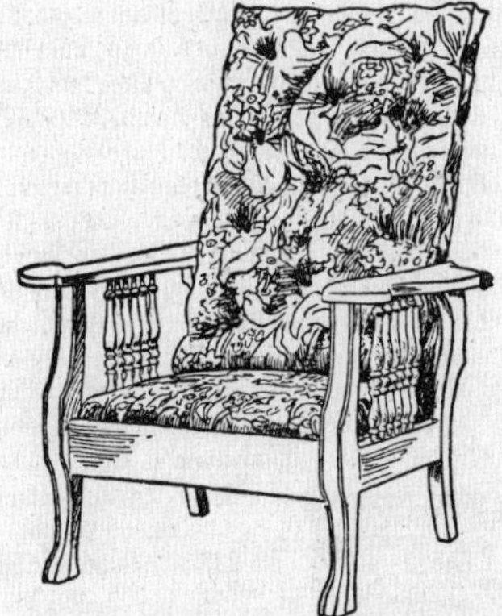

No. 201. Morris chair, golden oak or mahogany finish, polished, heavy shaped legs and arms, spring seat, reversible back cushion, all moss filled, covered in heavy figured velour $10.00

Upholstered in real leather....$15.00

No. 203. Morris chair, golden oak, massively carved and polished, upholstered spring seat, reversible cushion back, covered in fancy figured velour $14.75

Upholstered in real leather....$19.00

Students' easy chairs, hardwood frames, well upholstered in satin russe coverings, hollow seat, $3.85; spring seat, $4.20; in heavy tapestry covers, $4.25; spring seat..$5.25

Students' platform rocking chairs, similar to above, upholstered in satin russe, hollow seat, $5.00; spring seat, $5.50; tapestry covering, hollow seat, $5.75; spring seat $6.25

We will be pleased to send cut of other designs; always state color required and about what price you wish to pay.

No. 209. Music cabinet, in quarter-cut oak and imitation mahogany, 40 in. high, 18 in. wide, 13 in. deep............$3.90

No. 310. Ladies' writing desk, made of oak, golden finish or birch mahogany finish, highly polished, neatly carved, 28 in. wide, 44 inches high......$5.50

No. 275. Parlor cabinet, in birch, mahogany fine polish finish, 34 in. wide, 60 in. high, cabinet in centre, with bent glass door and lined shelves, 3 fancy-shaped British bevel-plate mirrors..........$23.75

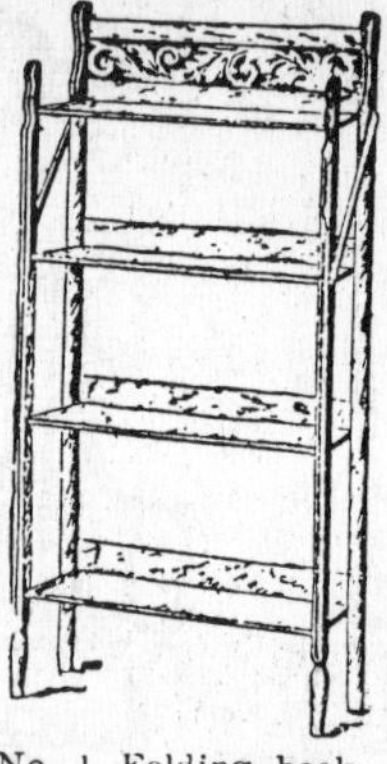

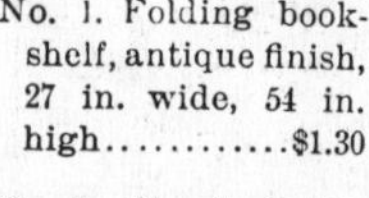

No. 1. Folding bookshelf, antique finish, 27 in. wide, 54 in. high...........$1.30

No. 1½. Bookshelf, similar to No. 1, with three shelves...$1.00

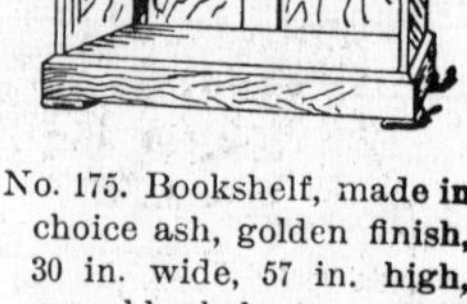

No. 175. Bookshelf, made in choice ash, golden finish, 30 in. wide, 57 in. high, movable shelves......$4.50

Same bookshelf, in solid oak....................$5.25

No. 185. Hall rack, solid quarter-cut oak, polished, 82 in. high, 39 in. wide, fitted with 12 x 20 in. bevel-plate mirror, box seat and lid....$8.25

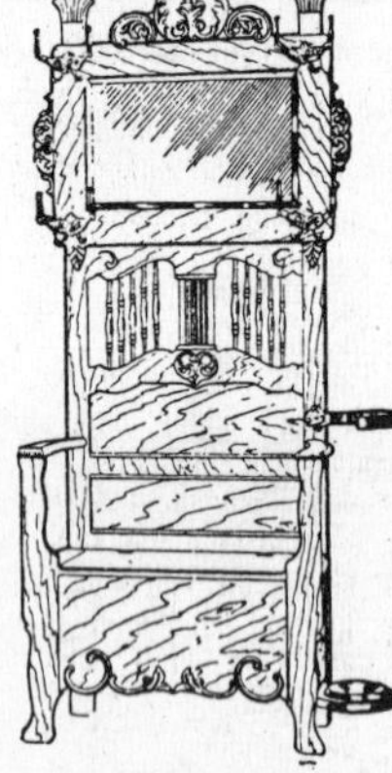

No. 135. Hall rack, quarter-cut oak, golden polish finish, neatly hand carved, 40 inches wide, 79 inches high, with 14 x 24-inch bevel-plate mirror...........$11.25

No. 1047. Library table, quartered oak, golden finish, highly polished, 26 x 48-inch top, with fancy shaped legs, neatly hand-carved........................$9.25

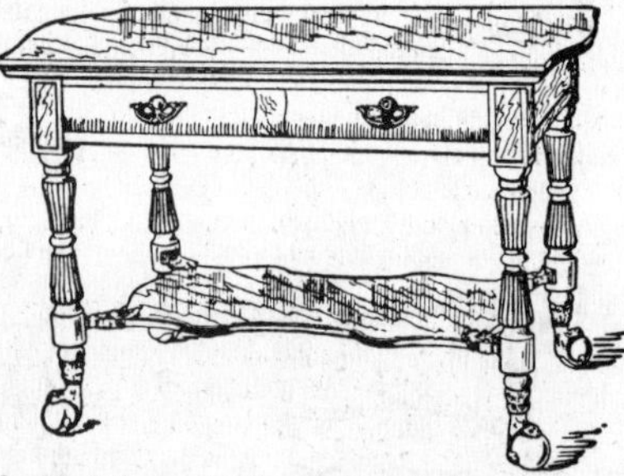

No. 71. Library table, made of select quarter-cut oak, rich golden polish finish, top size 28 x 48 inches, heavy shaped cross-banded rim, fancy turned and fluted legs, with brass claw feet....................................$14.00

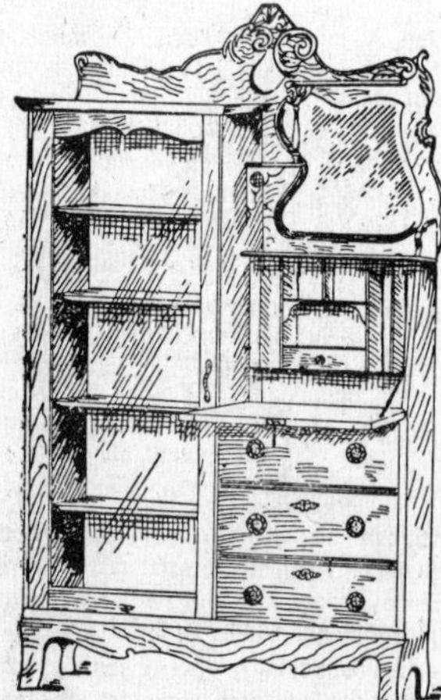

No. 318. Combination secretary and bookcase, quarter-cut golden oak and birch, mahogany finish, extra well polished and hand carved, 41 in. wide, 70 in. high, fitted with 14 x 16-in. shaped British bevel-plate mirror................$18.00

No. 313. Ladies' desk, in quarter-cut oak, golden finish, or mahogany, hand-carved and polished, 30 in. wide, 60 in. high, with 10 x 16 in. British bevel mirror $17.25

Wernicke Elastic Book Case.

The Wernicke Elastic Book Case consists of a series of small compartments, each ingeniously designed to interlock with another in vertical and horizontal arrangement. These, with suitable tops and bases, are the "units" of the system, and are of different depths and heights to suit all sizes of books. They are made in a variety of grades to suit all requirements. The front of each compartment is provided with a dust-proof glass door, which, at its upper corners, hangs on movable pivots, so that it opens outward and upward and can be pushed back over top of the books entirely out of the way.

No. 1.

No. 1. This cut illustrates a base, with compartment and top units, showing the divided shelf construction, whereby vertical expansion with stability, economy of space and good appearance are made possible.

No. 2. This cut shows a double section arrangement of six door units, with "Export" tops and bases. The cases are an ornament in any home or office. Small enough for ten or large enough for 10,000 books. Always complete, but never finished.

No. 2.

PRICES:

Door units, ranging in price from $2.25 to $5.75 each.

Top and base units, ranging in price from $1.50 to 2.50 each.

Write us for Special Catalogue, which fully describes the Wernicke Elastic Book Case, with price list.

DO NOT FAIL TO WRITE FOR SPECIAL CATALOGUE.

No. 456. Office desk, made of choice ash, antique finish, 30 x 48 inches top, separate lock on each drawer, and cupboard fitted for books, $9.50.

No. 106. Office roll-top desk, well made of solid oak, polished, with solid oak writing bed, automatic drawer locks, slides on each side, 48 inches wide, 30 inches deep, 50 inches high. $15.90

No. 104. Office roll-top desk, made in solid oak, golden polish finish, quarter-cut oak writing bed, 50 inches wide, 30 inches deep, 50 inches high, drawers lock automatically, slide on each side, top neatly fitted with pigeon-holes, with 6 enclosed wooden document boxes, ...$20.00

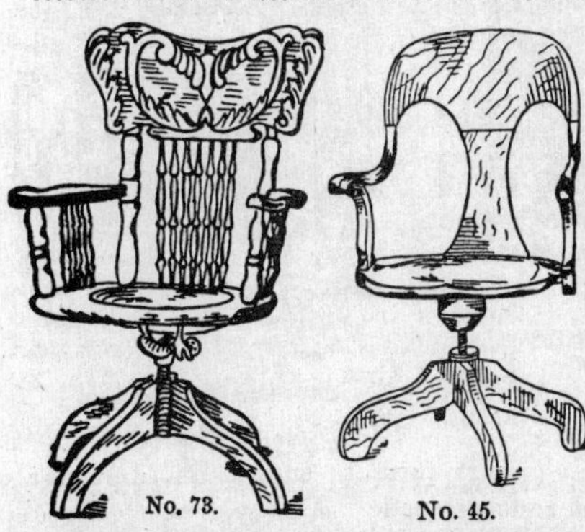

No. 73. No. 45.

No. 73. Revolving and tilting office chair, solid oak, solid leather cobbler-shaped seat, size 15-inch seat, $5.50.

No. 45. Office chair, made of select quarter-cut oak, golden finish, highly polished saddle-shaped seat, $7.10.

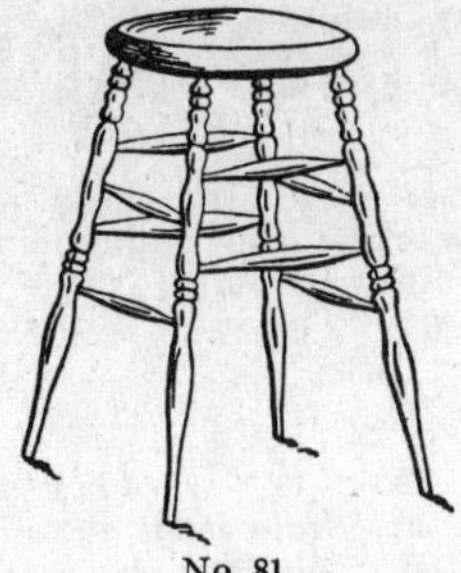

No. 81.

No. 81. Stool, antique finish, hardwood, 24 inches high, wood seat, 50c; 32 inches high, wood seat, 65c; 24 inches high, perforated seat, 60c; 32 inches high, perforated seat, 75c; 24 inches high, cane seat, 65c; 32 inches high, cane seat, 85c.

No. 84. Office stool, similar to No. 81, fitted with revolving seat and screw, raising from 35 inches to 40 inches, perforated seat, $1.60; raising from 35 inches to 40 inches, cane seat, $1.65.

Kitchen Furniture.

Kitchen cabinet, has 2 capacious flour bins, tin lined, made to hold 50 lbs, also 2 large drawers, 1 fitted for spices, 1 for cutlery and linens, Above drawers is 1 large-size sliding baking-board. Top is made of clean basswood, size 28 x 48 inches, heavy turned legs, oil finished, $5.50.

Kitchen tables, unpainted, with drawer, $1.25.

No. 00. Kitchen table, basswood top, maple legs, stained and varnished, bolted-on legs, detached in shipping, 4 feet long, $1.95; 4 feet 6 inches long, $2.20; 5 feet long, $2.30.

Fall-leaf table, antique and dark finish, bolted legs, $3.00.

Kitchen chairs, double rungs, strongly made, not painted, each 30c.

Kitchen chairs, painted yellow, square or bow back, each 34c.

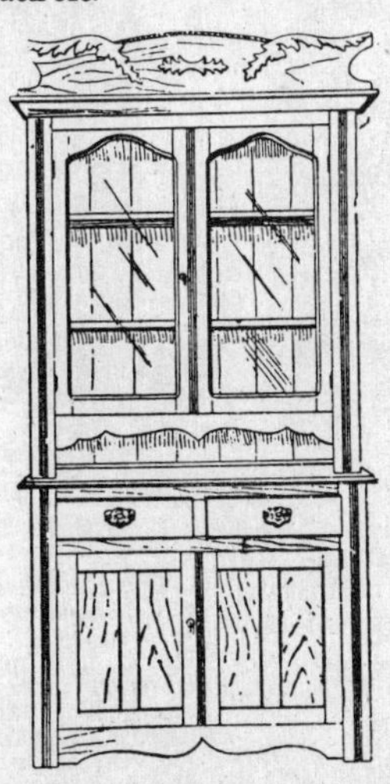

No. 3. Kitchen cupboard, with double glass door top, 2 drawers and cupboard, with shelf 50 inches wide, 7 feet 6 inches high, hardwood, antique finish, $9.75.

No. 59. High chair, hardwood, antique finish, with shaped wood seat 95c

No. 700. High chair, hardwood, antique finish, shaped seat, ... $1.15

No. 702. High chair, solid oak, antique gloss finish, cane seat $1.65

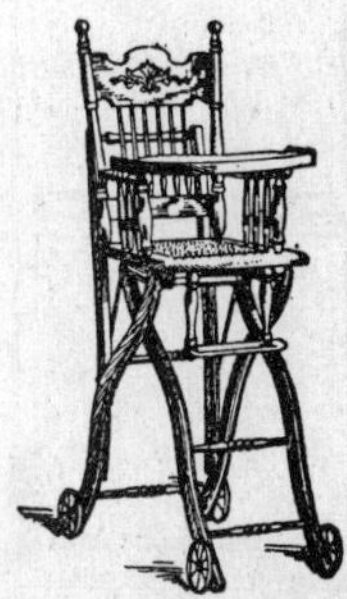

No. 571. Combination high chair, hardwood, antique finish, cane seat, with wheels, can be lowered down to make a carriage $2.25

No. 5330. Rattan high chair, in 16th century finish, swing table, closely woven seat, strong and durable........$2.50

No. 47. Child's kindergarten chair, hardwood, painted red or blue, 12 in. high to seat 39c

No. 42. Child's commode chair, bow back, assorted colors 59c

No. 41. Child's commode chair, square back, lighter make 45c

No. 45. Child's rocking chair, hardwood antique finish, strongly made.. 60c

No. 1. Child's willow commode chair, enclosed stand, with table $1.00

No. 37. Large size bedroom commode chair, high back, with arms, light finish $2.00

The cuts shown in this catalogue do not do justice to any of the furniture, and are merely an outline. The goods are carefully selected from the best values in the market, and we have no doubt that each piece will meet with your highest expectation.

SCREEN DOORS AND WINDOWS.

All our screen doors are made from kiln-dried white pine, with hardwood glued joints, made from 4-inch stock, with 7-inch bottom rail, ⅞ inch thick, nicely moulded. Wire cloth is put in with a key in such a way as to conceal all the rough edges, making the strongest door on the market.

No. 2. Door, dark stain finish—

2/6 x 6/ 6, 2/8 x 6/ 8, 2/10 x 6/10, 3/0 x 7/ 0, 70c each.

No. 2½. Door, with double angle brace, making 5 panels, made in sizes—

2/6 x 6/ 6, 2/8 x 6/ 8, 2/10 x 6/10, 3/0 x 7/ 0, 82c each.

No. 3. Door, oil finish, with fancy brackets, made in sizes—

2/8 x 6/8	90c each.
2/10 x 6/10	90c each.
3/0 x 7/0	90c each.

No. 5. Door, very handsomely made, with fancy bracket corners and spindle crossbar, fine varnish finish, sizes—

2/8 x 6/8	$1.35 each.
2/10 x 6/10	1.35 "
3/0 x 7/0	1.35 "

Spring hinges, 10c, 13c, 15c pair.

Special size doors made to order at an advance of 50c on any of above prices.

Window Screens.

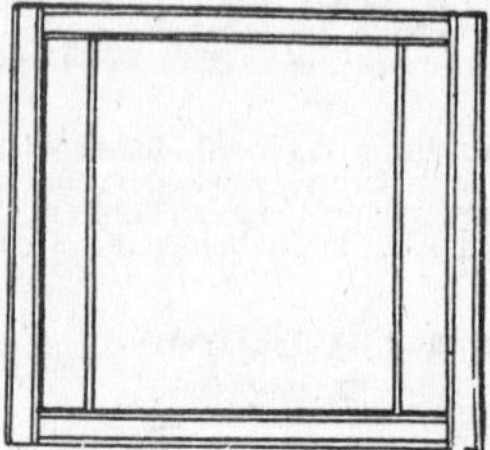

No. 2½. Adjustable window screens, ash or oak frame, oil-finished, with best wire cloth, will fit any window from—

15 inches to	22½ inches wide,	15c each.
20 "	33 " "	18c "
22 "	36 " "	20c "
24 "	44 " "	27c "

Wire Screen Cloth.

18-inch wide,	8c yd.	20-inch wide,	9c yd.
24 "	10c "	26 "	11c "
28 "	12c "	30 "	13c "
34 "	14c "	36 "	15c "
40 "	16c "	42 "	17c "

This cut shows the Perfection sliding screen, with mouldings on which it is raised or lowered from bottom to top of window. These screens are made to order to fit any style of window, and finished in any desired color to match woodwork. Will last a lifetime.

Write us for full description and price list, with directions for measuring.

Refrigerators, screen doors and windows will be in stock from April 1st and during summer months only. Write for full particulars.

REFRIGERATORS.

The Labrador.

The Labrador refrigerators are made of hardwood, antique finish, with bronze lever locks, zinc-lined throughout, all flues are cleanable, improved tin provision shelves with perfect circulation, and a large storage capacity.

No.	L'h. in.	D'h. in.	H't. in.	W'ght. lbs.		Price.
1.	26	17	40	100	single door,	$6.35
2.	28	18	42	115	" "	7.00
4.	32	19	44	130	" "	8.70
6.	36	21	44	150	double "	11.50

The Brantford.

The Brantford refrigerator, made of ash, neatly carved and well finished, fitted with automatic lever locks and patent castors, is constructed with 8 walls, mineral wool filling, cleanable flues, galvanized steel ice rack.

No.	L'h. in.	D'h. in.	H't. in.	W'ght. lbs		Price.
2.	28	19	44	120	single door,	$9.75
3.	30	20	46	135	" "	11.25
7.	36	21	46	160	double "	14.35
11.	30	20	54	160	" "	12.75

No. B.

Single Door Excelsior Refrigerators.

The Excelsior refrigerator is made of ash, antique color, highly finished, with fancy raised panels, has galvanized iron lining throughout, insulated with mineral wool. Provision chamber is large and roomy, doors have polished brass locks and hinges. No. C., same as No. B., but with double doors.

No.	Length. in.	Depth. in.	Height. in.		Price.
B.	32	21	45	single door,	$10.90
C.	38	21	45	double "	14.90

Leonard Cleanable.

The Leonard cleanable refrigerator, the most perfect refrigerator made. All styles and sizes kept in stock, ranging in price from $12.00 to $38.00. **Write us for price list and illustrated description.**

WRITE FOR SUMMER CATALOGUE, READY ABOUT MAY 15TH.

LACE AND NET CURTAINS.

No. 9346. Nottingham lace curtains, 45 inches wide, 3 yds long, colbert edges, white or ivory, pair ..**50c**
No. 9310. 30 inches wide, 2½ yds long, white or ivory, pair **35c**

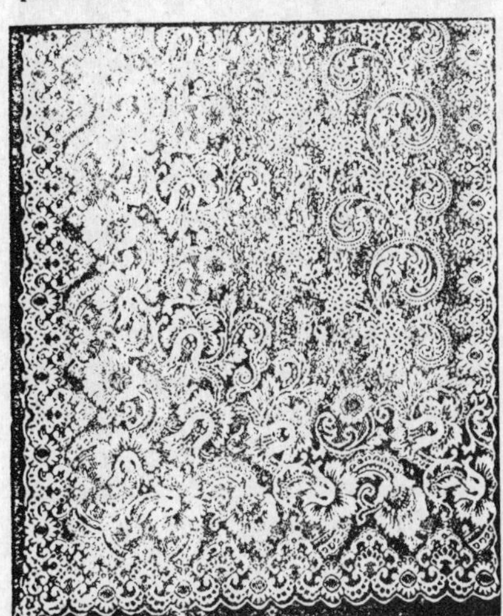

No. 9294. Nottingham lace curtains, 60 inches wide, 3½ yds long, white or ivory, overlocked edges, pair **1.00**

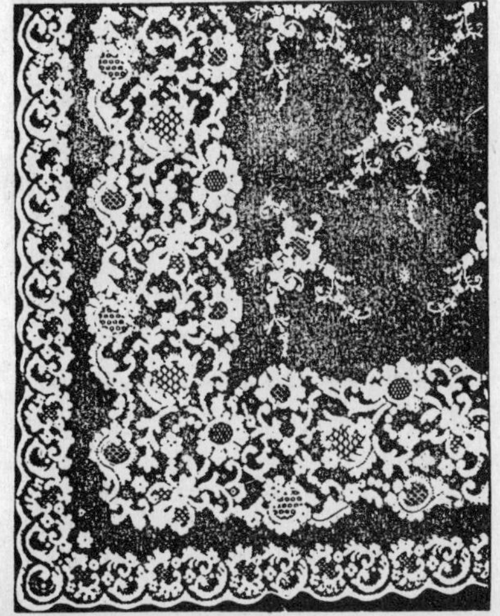

No. 8422. Nottingham lace curtains, 54 inches wide, 3½ yds long, heavy quality, taped edges, white or ivory, pair **1.25**

No. 9341. Nottingham lace curtains, 52 inches wide, 3½ yds long, overlocked edges, white or ivory, pair..**75c**

No. 9368. Nottingham lace curtains, 60 inches wide, 3½ yds long, corded edges, white or ivory, pair.**1.00**

No. 9342. Nottingham lace curtains, 60 inches wide, 3½ yds long, white or ivory, corded edges, pair.1.50

No. 4315. Nottingham lace curtains, 50 inches wide, 3½ yds long, white or ivory, corded edges, pair..**85c**

No. 9254. Nottingham lace curtains, 54 inches wide, 3½ yds long, white or ivory overlocked corded edges, pair 1.25

No. 9354. Nottingham lace curtains 54 inches wide, 3½ yards long, corded edges, white or ivory, pair 1.75

We cannot afford to misrepresent our goods. We are in business to stay.

No. 9376. Nottingham lace curtains, 60 in. wide, 3½ yds long, white or ivory, corded edges, pair........................**2.00**

No. 8863. Nottingham lace curtains, 54 in. wide, 3½ yds long, extra fine, colbert edges, white or ivory, pair........**2.25**

No. 8129. Nottingham lace curtains, 60 in. wide, 3½ yds long, white or ivory, corded edges, pair........................**2.50**

No. 6551. Nottingham lace curtains, 60 in. wide, 3½ yds long, colbert edges, white or ivory, pair......................**3.00**

No. 8734. Nottingham lace curtains, 60 in. wide, 3½ yds long, very fine net, colbert edges, white or ivory, pair... ......**3.50**

No. 4303. Nottingham lace curtains, 60 in. wide, 3½ yds long, colbert edges, white or ivory, pair......................**4.00**
60 in. wide by 4 yds long, pair.......**4.50**

No. 16161. Swiss net curtains, 50 in. wide, 3½ yds long, Irish point and applique work, renaissance effect, white or ivory, pair **2.50**

No. 1147. Swiss net curtains, 50 in. wide, 3½ yds long, white or ivory, pair......**3.00**

No. 10810. Swiss net curtains, 50 in. wide, 3½ yds long, white or ivory, per pair...**3.50**

OUR GOODS ARE BOUGHT DIRECT FROM THE WORLD'S BEST MANUFACTURERS.

No. 15952. Swiss net curtains, 50 in. wide, 3½ yds. long, white or ivory, pair $4.50; 60 in. wide, 4 yds. long, pair **6.00**

No. 15913. Brussels net curtains, 50 in. wide, 3½ yds. long, white only, pair $6.00; 60 in. wide, 4 yds. long, pair **7.50**

No. 189. Renaissance net curtains, 48 in. wide, 3½ yds. long light ivory only, all hand-made, pair **10.00**

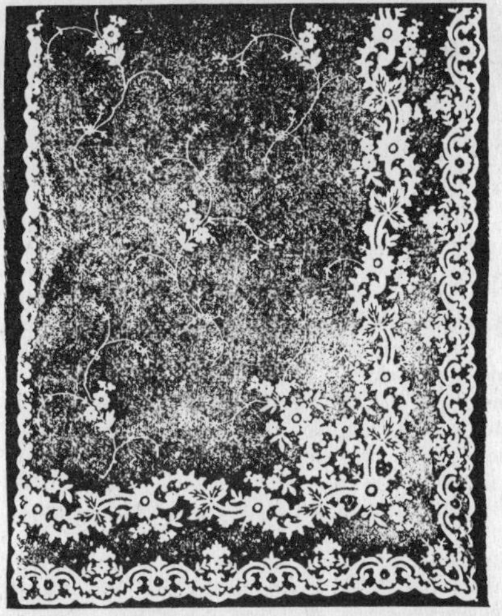

No. 16204. Swiss net curtains, 50 in. wide, 3½ yds. long, white or ivory, pair 5.00; 60 in. wide, 4 yds. long, pair **6.50**

No. 11823. Swiss muslin curtains, tambour work, 50 in. wide, 3½ yds. long, white only, pair .. **2.00**

Lace Curtains.

Scotch lace curtains, 60 in. wide, 4 yds long, extra fine quality, single and double borders, white or ivory, pair $4.00, 4.50, 5.00, 5.50 .. **6.00**

Swiss net curtains, 50 in. wide by 3½ yds. long, Irish point and applique borders, white or ivory, pair $2.50, 3.00, 3.50, 4.00, 5.00 to 10.00; 60 inches wide, 4 yds long, pair $5.50, 6.00, 6.50, 7.00, 8.00 to **12.00**

Brussels net curtains, 50 in. wide, 3½ yds long, white only, pair $4.00, 4.50, 5.00, 5.50, 6.00, 7.00, 8.00, 9.00, 11.00; 60 in. wide, 4 yds long, pair $7.00, 9.00, 14.00 .... **25.00**

Renaissance net curtains, 50 in. wide, 3½ yds long, with heavy linen hand-worked borders, plain centres, in ivory colors only, pair $5.00 5.50, 6.00, 7.00, 10.00 to 25.00; 54 to 58 in. wide, 3½ to 4 yds long, pair $15.00, 18.00, 20.00, 22.50, 25.00, 27.50 .... **35.00**

Point Arabian net curtains, 54 to 60 in. wide, 3½ to 4 yds long, ecru only, with heavy hand-worked lace only and lace and insertion borders, pair $15.00, 18.00, 25.00 to **50.00**

White muslin curtains, 50 in. wide, 3½ yds long, pair $2.00, 2.25, 2.50, 3.00 .... **3.50**

Frilled muslin curtains, 45 to 50 in. wide, 3½ yds long, floral and coin spot, pair $2.50, 2.75.. **3.00**

No. 16066. Brussels net curtains, 50 in. wide, 3½ yds long, white only, pair **4.50**

No. 7871. Battenburg net curtains, 50 in. wide, 3½ yds. long, light ivory only, all hand-made, pair **5.00**

No. 7944. Bobinet curtains, 48 in. wide, 3 yds long, very stylish for bedrooms, etc., made in either point d'esprit or plain net, plain, pair $2.75; spot, pair, $3.00; other qualities up to **7.00**

Our goods are exactly as represented—high class, low price.

CURTAIN NETS, ART MUSLINS, SCREENS, SWEEPERS, ETC.

Sash Curtain Nets.

Swiss Irish point sash curtain nets, white or ivory, 27 to 30 inches wide, single borders, 30c, 35c, 40c, 45c, 50c, 65c yd; double borders, 30 inches wide, 35c, 45c, 50c, 65c yd.
Panel sash nets, Irish point, imitation of renaissance, white or ivory, 18 inches wide, 35c, 40c, 50c yd; 30 inches wide, 65c, 85c, $1.00 yd.
Tambour sash curtain nets, 27 to 30 inches wide, white only, 30c, 35c, 40c, 50c yd.
Brussels sash curtain nets, 27 to 30 inches wide, white only, 35c, 40c, 45c, 50c, 65c, 75c, 85c yd.
Frilled Brussels sash nets, 30 inches wide, white or ivory, frilled on both sides, 75c, $1.00 yd.
Real renaissance sash nets, 27 to 30 inches wide, ivory color only, panel designs, $2.00, 2.50, 3.00, 3.50 yd.
Swiss tambour sash curtain muslins, 30 inches wide, 15c, 18c, 20c and 25c yd.
Frilled curtain muslins, with spot pattern (small and medium), 30 inches wide, 20c, 25c yd.
Nottingham lace curtain nets, white or ecru, 30 and 36 inches wide, 10c, 13c, 15c yd; 45 inches wide, 20c, 25c yd; 50 inches wide, 20c, 25c, 30c, 40c yd.

White Curtain Muslins.

White figured and spot curtain muslins, small, medium and large spots, and a variety of new figured patterns, 36 inches wide, 12½c, 15c yd.
White coin spot muslins, 45 inches wide, in small, medium and large spots, 18c, 20c, 22c yd.
White figured curtain muslins, 45 inches wide, a variety of new patterns, 25c yd.
White curtain muslins, with colored coin spots, 45 inches wide, 20c yd.

White Muslins.

Frilled on both sides, in coin spots, stripes and fancy patterns, 48 inches wide, 35c, 40c yd; frilled on one side, 25c, 35c yd.

Madras Curtain Muslins.

Figured cream Madras curtain muslin, 27 inches wide, 15c yd.
Figured Madras curtain muslin, 45 inches wide, cream, 22c, 25c yd.
Figured Madras curtain muslin, 54 inches wide, white, 40c, 45c yd.

Scrims.

36-inch fancy stripe curtain scrim, cream only, in assorted patterns, 5c, 8c yd; white, 10c yd.
40-inch fancy scrim, cream, 10c, 13c yd.

Plain Scrims.

38-inch plain scrim, cream, 12½c yd.
42-inch plain cream scrim, 20c yd.

Art Drapery Muslins.

Figured art drapery muslin, a large assortment of new patterns and colors, 30 inches wide, 6c, 8c yd; 36 inches wide, 10c, 12½c, 15c yd.
Figured art silkaline, 36 inches wide, a large assortment of new floral patterns and colors, 12½c, 15c yd.
Bordered art muslin, 45 inches wide, 12½c yd; 50 inches wide, 15c yd.

Japanese Crepe Cloths.

Japanese gold-figured crepe cloth, 25 inches wide, a large variety of patterns and colors, 10c yd; 30 inches, 12½c yd.

China Art Drapery Silks.

A large variety of the latest designs and colors in China and Florentine drapery silks, figured, 32 inches wide, 65c, 85c yd.

Furniture Cords and Gimps.

Silk cord, 4c, 7c yd; 45c and $1.00 a piece of 18 yds.

Furniture Gimps.

Cotton, 1c yd, or $1.20 gross.
Silk, 2c yd, or $2.20 gross.
" 3c yd, or $4.00 "
" 5c yd, or $6.50 "
Heavy cotton cord for edging curtains and cushions, assorted colors, 12½c yd.
Silk cord, assorted colors, 20c yd.

Webbing.

Furniture webbing, 2½-inch, 2½c yd; $1.25 a piece about 65 yds.

Cretonnes, Denims, Sateens, Etc.

Our collection of the above goods for this season includes the best qualities and the newest and most handsome patterns of English and American manufacture, the color combinations being simply perfect from the cheapest to the most expensive. To insure satisfaction when ordering, please specify as nearly as possible the colors required. The following ground colors make up some of our stock: Crimson, maroon, olive, fawn, terra cotta, black, blue, electric and myrtle, with rich combinations of other colors combined.

English twilled cretonnes, 27 in. wide, 6c; 29 in. wide, 8c; 30 in. wide, yard, 10c, 12½c, 15c
Extra heavy crepe cretonnes, 30 in., 12½c, 15c; 30 in., yard, 18c 20c
Extra heavy English cretonnes, soft finish, in combinations, 30 in. wide, yard, 10c, 12½c, 15c, 20c.
Reversible twill cretonne, in new combinations of colors, 30 in. wide, yard 12½c
Heavy English reversible crepe-finished cretonnes, 30 in. wide, yard, 15c and 20c

Bordered and Reversible Cretonnes, Suitable for Curtains, etc.

Double-fold reversible cretonnes, colors same as single width, with pretty combination borders—
40 inches wide, 15c, 18c yard.
42 " " 20c, 25c "
44 " " 25c, 30c "
48 " " 25c, 30c, 35c yard.
52 " " 35c, 40c yard.

Special heavy American art cretonne, in the very newest designs, soft pure finish, rich combination of colors, suitable for draperies, furniture covering, etc., 36 in. wide, yard .. 20c

Art Denims.

Heavy plain colored denims, in light and dark blue, myrtle, moss, yellow, terra cotta, red, 36 inches wide, per yd 25c
Genuine printed American denims, in the above colored grounds, in the very newest designs and combinations of colors for this season, used largely for cushions, table covers, curtains, furniture and floor coverings, 36 inches wide, per yd 35c

Villa Cloth.

Villa cloth, self-colors, 36 inches wide, suitable for cushions or drapery purposes; colors garnet, rose, blue, orange, crimson, moss green, yard 20c
Art ticking, self-colors, twilled, soft finish; colors gold, Nile, slate, fawn, pea-green; 36 inches wide, per yard 30c
Art ticking, fancy stripes, light grounds, 36 inches wide, in a full range of new colors and patterns, per yard 30c

Art Sateens.

Figured art sateens, English, French and American manufacture. The following colors will be a guide of what we carry in stock in all qualities: crimson, maroon, olive, fawn, blue, electric, Nile, myrtle, rose, pink, terra cotta and black, with rich combinations of other colors.

30 inches wide, yd 12½c, 15c, 20c, 25c
Fine English art sateen, 31 inches wide, beautiful rich soft finish, choice designs, yard 25c, 30c, 35c, 40c

Turkey Chintz.

Chintz, Turkey red, used principally for comforter covering, in a big range of all new and well selected patterns, per yard, 10c, 12½c, 15c
Special Turkey chintz, 36 inches wide, in a range of new designs, fast colors, per yard 12½c

Screens.

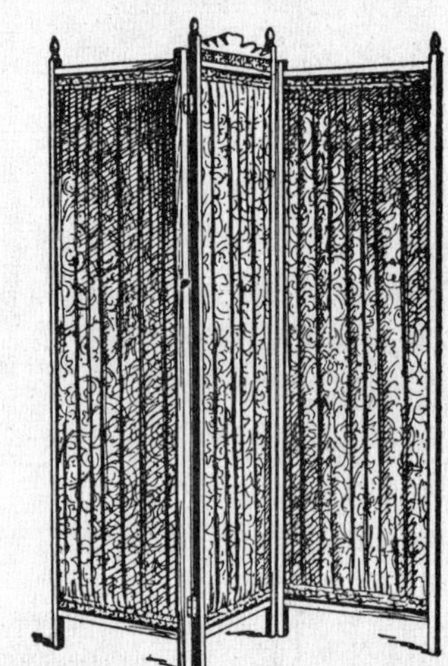

No. 111. Fancy folding screens, 3 panels, each 20 x 66 inches, solid oak frame, strong and durable, filled with figured art silkaline, in assorted colors, $1.95 each; frame only, $1.00.
No. 303. Fancy folding screens, height 62 inches, centre panel 17 x 58, sides 17 x 48, solid oak or mahogany finish, filled with figured art silkaline, assorted colors, $2.95 ea; frame only, $2.00.
No. 0628. Fancy fire screens, single panel, size 24 x 28 inches, frame oak or mahogany, filled with fancy art tapestry subject, $2.95 each; frame only, $1.75.
Japanese 4-panel screens, size of each panel 20 x 60 inches, made of extra strong cotton, painted in rich Oriental designs and colors, $3.50, 4.00, 4.50, 5.00, 7.00 each.
Tapestry panel screens, made any height, with any number of panels, as ordered, frame covered all over with rich floral or figured tapestry panels, prices ranging according to size and quality, from $4.00 to 25.00 each.

Carpet Sweepers.

Bissell's "Champion" sweepers, highly-finished woods, assorted colors, japan, $1.50; nickel, $1.75.
Bissell's "Brunswick" sweepers, durable and finely finished, in assorted woods, $2.00 each.

Bissell's "Grand Rapids" sweepers, cyclo bearings, mahogany and antique oak finish, $2.75 ea.
Bissell's "Gold Medal" carpet sweepers, highly finished wood, nickel trimmings, latest improvements, $3.25 each.

Every article is exactly as represented in this Catalogue.

No. 949. Chenille curtains, 3 yds. long, 32 in. wide, fancy dado and fringe top and bottom, in crimson, blue, terra cotta, brown, olive, bronze, electric, myrtle and fawn, pair... 2.75
36 in. wide, pair 3.25

No. 961. Chenille curtains, 3 yds. long, 44 in. wide, with deep fancy dado and fringe top and bottom, in crimson, terra cotta, myrtle, brown and olive, dark blue and fawn, pr.. 4.75
3½ yds. long, pair.......... 5.50

No. 1321. Chenille curtains, 48 in. wide, 3 yds. long, in self colors, knotted fringe top and bottom and one side, colors red, crimson, terra cotta, brown, myrtle, olive, electric and rose, pair.......... 5.75

No. 968. Chenille curtains, 40 in. wide 3 yds. long, deep fancy floral dado and fringe top and bottom, in blue, crimson, terra cotta, myrtle, olive, fawn, bronze and reseda, pair, ... 4.00

No. 960. Chenille curtains, with deep fancy broken dado, and heavy knotted fringe top and bottom in crimson, terra cotta, myrtle, tan, light blue, dark green, reseda, old red, bronze and olive, 48 in. wide, 3 yds. long, pair.......... 5.50

No. 962. Divided chenille portieres, 3 yds. long, 48 in. wide, in crimson, olive, terra cotta, bronze, myrtle, old red and fawn, each .. 3.25

No. 964. Chenille curtains, 3 yds. long, 42 in. wide, with deep fancy floral dado and fringe top and bottom, in crimson, terra cotta, olive, myrtle, brown, blue and fawn, pair....... 4.25

No. 925. Chenille curtains, handsome allover patterns, in assorted colors and rich combinations, heavy knotted fringe on both ends, 48 in. wide, 3 yds. long, pair.......... 6.00

Reed Portieres.

Japanese string portieres, size 3 feet 6 inches by 9 feet, made in a vast assortment of Oriental colors, designs and qualities, suitable for doors, etc.

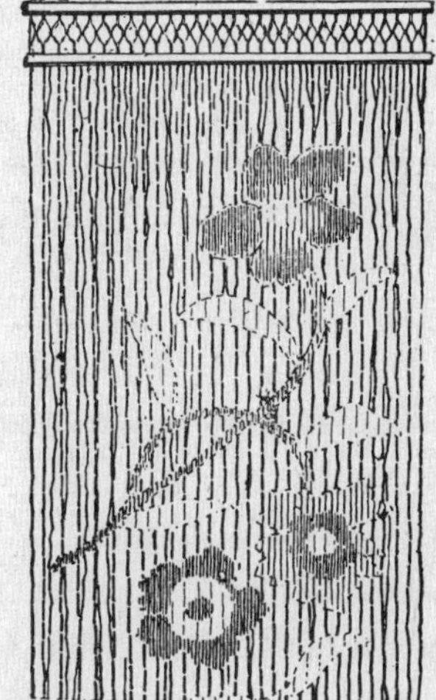

Rice quality, each.......... 1.00, 1.25
Reed quality, each.......... 75c, 1.00
Reed and bead quality, each .... 1.25 to 5.00
Glass, all bead quality, each.......... 6.00

We cheerfully refund money if goods are not as represented.

No. 400. Tapestry curtains, 40 inches wide. 3 yds long, figured allover patterns, in full range of colorings, pair 2.00
48 inches wide, 3 yds long, pair 3.00

No. 531. Tapestry curtains, 42 inches wide by 3 yds long, allover designs, colors crimson, olive, blue, green and rose, pair 3.00

No. 3580. Tapestry curtains, 49 inches wide by 3 yds long, combination colors, crimson, blue, rose, olive and green, pair 3.50

No. 2460. Heavy tapestry curtains, 50 inches wide by 3 yds long, in reversible allover designs, colors crimson, blue, olive, rose and green, pair 4.50

No. 4250. Heavy tapestry curtains, 50 inches wide by 3 yds long, in combination colors of blue, crimson, olive green and rose, very new and effective, pair 5.00

No. 4240. Extra heavy tapestry curtains, in very rich reversible patterns, colors olive, rose, green, blue and crimson, 50 in. wide by 3 yds long, pair...7.50

No. 4530. Bagdad curtains, 50 inches wide by 3 yds long, in combination colors of terra, green, fawn, blue and gold stripes, used for Oriental rooms and dens, pair.... .... 7.75

Prices of Chenille, Tapestry and Silk Portieres.

Plain Shiela curtains, 48 inches wide, 3 yds long, extra heavy quality, with heavy knotted fringe on both ends, colors all-red, empire, olive, reseda, brown and rose, per pair 8.50

Heavy arch portieres, with deep fancy dado and fringe top and bottom, in crimson, terra cotta, fawn, electric, rose and bronze, 3½ yds long, 72 in. wide, per pair..8.50

Very fine chenille curtains, handsome allover designs, assorted colors, heavy knotted fringe top and bottom, 3 yds long, 48 in. wide, per pair, $7.50 ; 3½ yds long, 50 in. wide, per pair, $10.00...........11.00

Extra heavy tapestry curtains, with deep fancy knotted fringe top and bottom, in corded, repp and real tapestry effects, 50 in. wide and 3 yds long, in a variety of new patterns and colors, per pair, $5.00, 6.00, 7.00, 8.50 ....10.00

Heavy Oriental Bagdad curtains, in a variety of new combinations, 48 in. wide, 3 yds long, fringed top and bottom, per pair, $5.00, 6.00, 6.50......... 7.75

Heavy tapestry curtains, 50 inches wide, 3 yds long, in rich Turkish and Oriental designs, reversible, in combination colors, per pair, $8.50, 9.50......10.00

Tapestry couch covers, for loose throws, fringed all round, reversible patterns, in Oriental or Bagdad effects, each $2.50, 4.00, 4.50, 5.50 ....6.50

Japanese rice portieres, size 3½ x 9 feet, each $1.00, 1.25..1.50

Japanese, rattan and bead portieres, in fancy patterns and rich colors, each $1.00, 1.50, 2.25 .... 3.75

No. 107. Rope portieres, made of 3-ply ⅜-in. tinsel cords, size 7 x 8 feet long, made in any combination of colors, with sliding tassels, each $8.00 ....10.00

Upholstery, Curtain Materials, Fringes, Loops, Etc.

Heavy tapestry, satin finish, for coverings or curtains, 48 in. wide, new patterns, colors crimson, blue, olive, green, brown and golden brown, 40c yd.

Heavy cotton French tapestry, strong and durable, suitable for coverings or curtains, 50 in. wide, new patterns, in bronze, olive, electric, blue, terra cotta, crimson and golden brown, 50c yd.

Heavy American and French cotton tapestries, satin finish, 50 in. wide, rich effects, for furniture coverings, in combination colorings, crimson, dark blue, light blue, olive, bronze, terra cotta, gold and brown, 75c yd.

Fancy silk-striped tapestries for curtains and draperies, 50 in. wide, in combinations of cream, Nile and old red; cream, electric, blue and old red; coral, cream, pink and Nile, 65c, 75c, $1.00, 1.25 yd.

Fancy figured Florentine tapestries, in small and medium patterns, for draperies, curtains and upholstery purposes, 50 in. wide, self colors, blue, reseda, Nile, red olive and salmon, $1.00, 1.25 yd.

Heavy French tapestry, for furniture coverings and portieres, 50 in. wide, in rich effects and combination colors, olive and ecru; bronze, Nile and ecru; blue, green, gold and ecru; old red, cream, ecru and olive, $1.00 yd.

Heavy French and Gobelin tapestries, 50 in. wide, real tapestry effects, rich combination colorings, in green, blue, olive, bronze and old red, $1.25 yd.

Silk-faced tapestry, 50 in. wide, new choice designs, in blue, olive, green and red, $1.50 yd.

Heavy silk Palaisean and Sicilian tapestry, 50 in. wide, in olive, brown, blue, crimson, Nile, terra cotta, $1.75 yd.

Fine silk tapestry, reversible, for fine upholstery and silk draperies, 50 in. wide, in a variety of entirely new designs, in olive, electric, crimson, blue, bronze, Nile, $1.35, 1.65 yd.

Fine French and American silk tapestry, for fine upholstering and over draperies, 50 in. wide, in very choice designs and newest colors, olive, terra cotta, gold, blue, bronze and green, $2.50, 2.75, 3.00, 3.50 yd.

Extra fine French and American all-silk tapestry, newest designs and colors, coral, Nile, pink, blue and mode, $4.00, 5.00, 6.50 yd.

Fancy Draping Silks.

Fine silk drapery materials, soft finish, light weight, for arches or mantels, 50 in. wide, reversible, new designs and colorings, electric, gold, Nile, terra cotta, olive, old red and bronze, 75c, $1.00, 1.25, 1.50 yd.

Art Drapery Serges.

Plain art drapery serges, 50 in. wide, in crimson, blue, gold, terra cotta, slate, olive, steel, 45c yd.

All-Wool Damasks.

Figured all-wool damasks, 48 in. wide, for coverings, curtains and draperies, crimson, maroon, blue and olive, 50c yd.

All-wool granite cloth, 50 in. wide, electric and crimson, 75c yd.

Repps.

All-wool repps, in crimson and maroon, 48 in. wide, $1.00 yd.

Furniture Plushes.

Silk plush (Lister's), 24 in. wide, in a full range of new colors, 95c yd.

Plain mohair plush, 24 in. wide, in crimson, $1.00 yd.

Heavy velvet mohair plush, 24 in. wide, in crimson, $1.35, 1.75, 2.00 yd.

Plushette, 50 in. wide, in crimson, blue, gold and olive, 60c yd.

Linen velours for drapes, portieres and upholstery, 50 in. wide, colors electric, old red, Nile, terra cotta, blue, bronze, rose, steel, 85c, $1.10 yd.

Best French linen velours, deep nap, silk effects, colors terra cotta, Nile, electric, coral, bronze, gold and blue, 50 in. wide, $1.35 yd.

Heavy figured velvet velours, new effects, in Nile, blue, bronze and gold, $1.50 yd.

Heavy reversible plain linen velours, for portieres and draperies, 51 in. wide, rich effects in bronze, terra cotta, Nile, copper, blue, salmon, $1.85 yd.

Baize.

Green baize, 36 in., 30c; 52 in., 50c; 72 in., 65c yd.
Red baize, 36 in., 30c; 52 in., 50c; 72 in., 65c yd.

Felt Cloth.

All-wool felt cloths, 72 in. wide, for table covers, fancy work, scarfs, etc., in light and dark shades of crimson, blue, terra cotta, gold, brown, emerald, olive, bronze, black, fawn, rose, 65c yd.

Extra heavy felt cloth, 72 in. wide, in white and other colors, 75c yd.

Haircloth Seating for Furniture Coverings.

Haircloth, 14 in., 40c; 16 in., 45c; 18 in., 50c; 20 in., 55c; 24 in., 70c; 27 in., 85c; 30 in., $1.15. Prices subject to change.

Imitation leather, 50 in. wide, for upholstery purposes, in dark green and brown, 55c yd.

Drapery Fringes.

No. 651. Cotton tassel fringe, full line of colors to match muslin, per yd. 5c

No. 700. Cotton tassel fringe, assorted colors, to match curtain materials, 4½ inches deep, per yd 15c

No. 146. Silk tassel fringe, in colors to match, muslins and silks, 1½ inches deep, per yd. .10c

No. 474. Silk drapery fringe, assorted colors to match muslins and silks, 2½ in. deep, yd., 20c

No. 601. Silk drapery fringe, in colors to match silks and drapery materials, 3 in. deep. yd, 35c

Rug Fringes.

No. 40. Rug fringe, double headed, 4½ inches deep, per yd 13c

Rug fringes, in assorted colors, per yd., 8c, 13c, ... 25c

Furniture Fringes.

No. K84. Furniture fringe, wool, silk covered cord and tassel, 7 inches deep, per yd., 35c, per doz. (24 yd. pieces) $4.00

Cotton furniture fringes, per yd 15c

Worsted and silk furniture fringe, 7½ inches deep, per yd., 35c, 50c $1.35

Silk Curtain Loops.

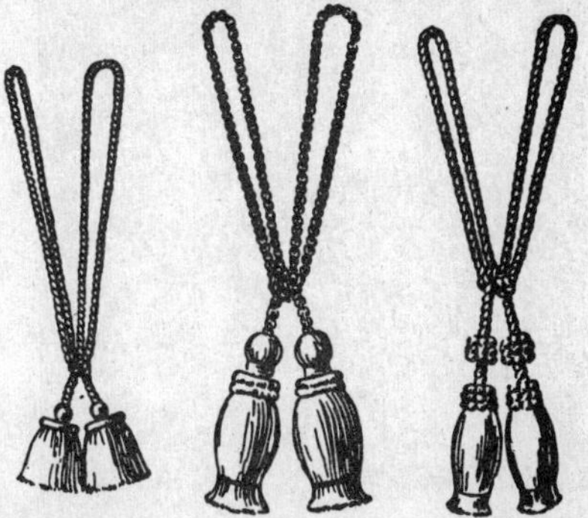

No. 872. No. 208. No. 203.

No. 872. Silk sash curtain loops, 13 inches long, in a full range of colors, per pair 25c

No. 208. Silk curtain loops, 16 inches long, in combination colors, per pair 50c

No. 203. Silk curtain loops, 21 inches long, in combination colors, per pair 75c

Prices of silk curtain loops, per pair, 13c, 25c, 35c, 50c, 75c, $1.00, 1.25, 1.50, 2.00 .... $2.50

Cotton Curtain Loops.

Cotton curtain loops, white or cream, per pair, 8c, 10c, 12c, 15c, 20c 25c

Chenille Curtain Loops.

No. 23. Chenille loops, 20 inches long, in crimson, blue, electric, terra cotta, bronze, olive, gold, fawn and rose, per pair 25c

No 21. Chenille loops, 24 inches long, full range of colors, per pair 50c

Worsted loops for tapestry curtains, in a full range of colors and combinations, per pair, 25c 50c

WHITE DOWN CUSHIONS.

(Covered in white cambric.)

Odorless and Pure.

Comfort, 18 x 18 inches, 25c each.

Russian Down.

16 x 16 inches	$0 30	each.
18 x 18 "	0 40	"
20 x 20 "	0 50	"
22 x 22 "	0 65	"
24 x 24 "	0 75	"

No. 1 Quality.

16 [illegible]6 inches	$0 40	each.
[illegible] 18 "	0 50	"
[illegible] x 20 "	0 75	"
[illegible] x 22 "	0 90	"
24 x 24 "	1 10	"

Fine Quality.

16 x 16 inches	$0 65	each.
18 x 18 "	0 75	"
20 x 20 "	1 00	"
22 x 22 "	1 25	"
24 x 24 "	1 50	"

Extra Fine Quality.

16 x 16 inches	$0 75	each.
18 x 18 "	0 90	"
20 x 20 "	1 25	"
22 x 22 "	1 50	"
24 x 24 "	1 85	"

Cushion Slip Covers.

Made of art silkaline, art cretonnes or sateens, in light or dark colors, with 3½-inch double frill, 18 x 18-inch, each 30c.

No. 1170. Decorated or plain opaque window shades, 37 x 70 in., mounted on spring rollers, complete with pulls, each 35c

No. 190. Plain opaque window shades, 37 x 70 in., mounted on spring rollers, complete with pull, each 30c
Plain oil opaque shades, 37 x 70 in., complete, 40c; 37 x 82 in., each 45c

No. 1136. Fringed oil opaque window shades, 37 x 70 in., mounted on spring rollers, complete with tassel, 55c; 37 x 82 in., 65c each; fringe, per yd...12c

No. 840. Decorated oil opaque window shades, 37 x 70 in., mounted on spring rollers, complete with pulls, 45c; 37 x 82 in., each 50c

PRICES

of plain Standard Opaque or Scotch Holland Window Shades, best quality, in full range of colors, mounted on best Hartshorn rollers, with pulls complete.

WIDTH IN INCHES.

Length	18	21	23	36	41	45	52	59	62	72	82	92	102
	$	$	$	$	$	$	$	$	$	$	$	$	$
3 ft.	0.28	0.31	0.35	0.38	0.43	0.58	0.75	0.90	1.35	1.55	1.90	2 10	2.35
4 "	0.32	0.35	0.40	0.45	0.51	0.69	0.90	1.08	1 53	1.75	2.13	2.37	2.65
5 "	0.35	0.39	0.46	0.51	0.59	0.80	1.05	1.26	1.71	1.95	2.37	2.63	2.95
6 "	0.39	0.44	0.52	0.58	0.68	0.91	1.20	1.45	1.89	2.15	2.60	2.90	3.25
7 "	0.42	0.48	0.58	0.65	0.77	1.02	1.35	1.63	2.08	2.35	2.83	3.17	3.55
8 "	0.46	0.52	0.64	0.72	0.92	1.13	1.50	1.81	2.26	2.55	3.06	3.43	3.85
9 "	0.49	0.57	0.70	0.78	1.00	1.24	1.65	2.00	2.45	2 75	3.30	3.60	4.15
10 "	0.58	0.67	0.82	0.92	1.08	1.35	1 80	2.18	2.63	2.95	3.64	3.87	4.45
11 "	0.61	0.71	0.88	0.99	1.16	1.46	1.95	2.37	2.82	3.15	3.87	4.15	4.75
12 "	0.65	0.75	0.91	1.05	1.25	1.57	2.15	3.15	3.15	3.45	4.10	4.40	5.05

Large shades are mounted on rollers to correspond to size. When measuring, allow 9 inches on net length of window for hem on shade and lap around roller.

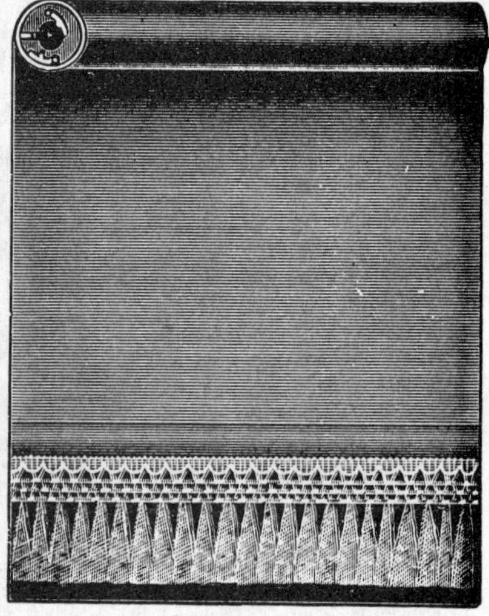

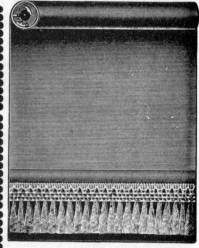

No. 2070. Fringed oil opaque window shades, 37 x 70 in. mounted on spring rollers, complete with tassel, 60c; 37 x 82 in., 70c each; fringe, per yd..13c

No. 870. Fringed oil opaque window shades, 36 x 70 in., mounted, complete with tassels, 50c; 37 x 80 in., 55c each; fringe, per yd 5c

No. 426. Fringed oil opaque window shades, 36 x 70 in., mounted on spring rollers, complete with tassels, 50c; 37 x 82 in., 60c each; fringe, per yd..10c

No. 2001. Best standard oil opaque window shades, 37 x 70 in., complete with spring rollers and tassels, 80c; 37 x 82 in., 90c each; fringe, per yd 18c

No. 3008. Opaque window shades, 36 x 70 inches, cream only, mounted on spring rollers, complete with tassel, 45c each; 37 x 82 inches, 55c each; lace per yard 6c

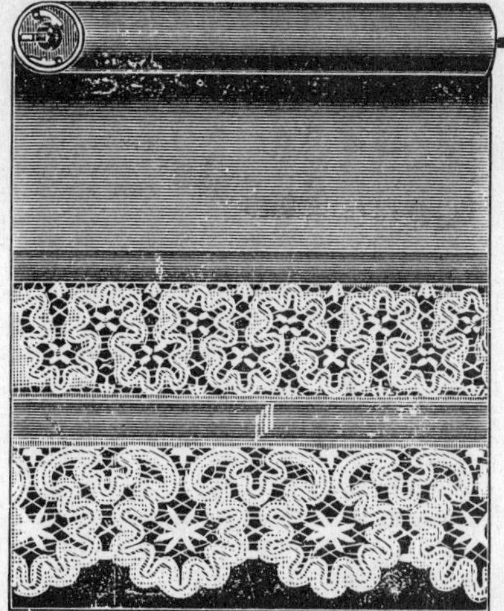

No. 3319. Best standard opaque window shades, size 37 x 70 inches, cream only, mounted on Hartshorn spring rollers, complete with tassel, lace and insertion, 90c each; lace only, 75c each; 37 x 82 inches, 10c extra; lace or insertion, per yard .... $12\frac{1}{2}$c

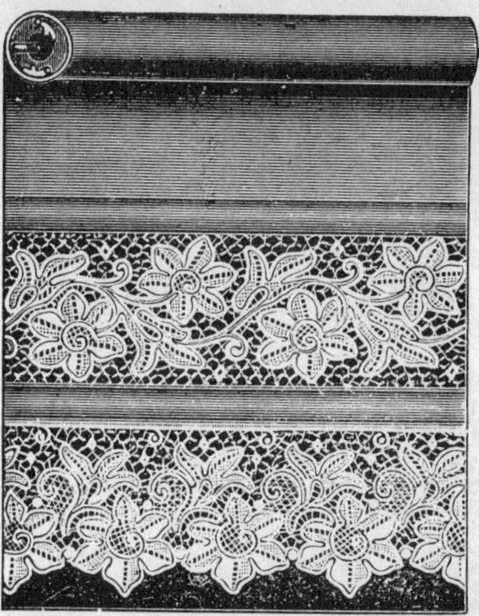

No. 4252. Best standard opaque window shades, size 37 x 70 inches, cream only, mounted on Hartshorn spring rollers, complete with tassel, lace and insertion, $1.25 each; lace only, 95c each; 37 x 82 inches, 10c extra; lace and insertion, each per yard 25c

No. 2606. Oil opaque window shades, 37 x 70 inches, cream only, mounted on spring rollers, complete with tassel, 65c each; 37 x 82 inches, 70c each; with lace only, 37 x 70 inches, 55c each; 37 x 82 inches, 60c each; lace and insertion, each per yard 8c

No. 3762. Best standard opaque window shades, size 37 x 70 inches, cream only, mounted on Hartshorn spring rollers, complete with tassel, lace and insertion, $1.05 each; lace only, 85c each; 37 x 82 inches, 10c extra; lace, per yard, 18c; insertion, per yard 15c

No. 3027. Standard oil opaque or cream Holland window shades, mounted on best roller, complete with tassel, 37 x 70 inches, cream only, $1.90 each; complete with lace only, $1.30 each; 37 x 82 inches, 10c extra; lace and insertion, each per yard 60c

Prices of Window Shades.

Fringed opaque shades, 37 x 70 inches, with spring rollers and tassels, 50c, 55c, 65c, 75c, 85c, 90c, $1.00, 1.10, 1.25 each.

Opaque or Holland shades, with lace and insertion combined, 37 x 70 inches, complete with spring rollers and tassels, 60c, 70c, 85c, $1.00, 1.25, 1.50, 1.75, 2.00, 2.50, 3.00 each; with lace only, 50c, 60c, 70c, 75c, 90c, $1.00, 1.10, 1.25, 1.50, 1.75 each.

Window shade paper, 36 inches wide, in green, 3c yd; extra heavy, 5c yd.

Prices of Fringes and Laces.

Fancy shade fringes, by the yard, 5c, 7c, 10c, 13c, 15c, 18c, 20c, 25c, 30c yd.

Laces, 8c, 10c, 15c, 25c, 30c, 35c, 40c, 50c, 60c, 65c, 75c, 85c, $1.25 yd.

Lace and insertion combined, 16c, 25c, 40c, 50c, 60c, 70c, 80c, $1.00, 1.20, 1.50, 1.70, 2.00, 2.50 yd.

Estimates furnished on best standard opaque window shades in different sizes, trimmed with fringe lace, or lace and insertion; also our combination color shades. Samples sent on application.

Shade Tassels, Silk Trimmed.

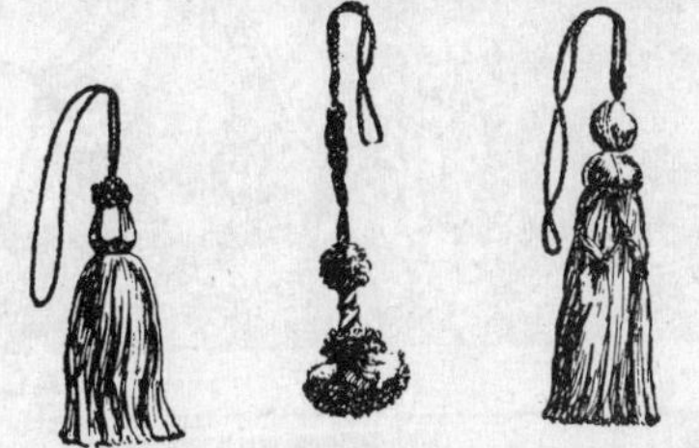

No. 4072, 5c ea. No. 1326, 10c ea. No. 1000, 10c. ea.

Prices of Shade Cloths and Hollands.

Best hand-made opaque shade cloths, in assorted colors.
37, 42, 45, 48, 52, 62, 72, 82, 92 inches wide.
20c, 25c, 33c, 40c, 45c, 55c, 60c, 70c, 85c yard.

John King & Co.'s celebrated Scotch Holland, cream or linen colors, 24-inch, 15c; 30-inch, 20c; 36-inch, 22c; 42-inch, 28c; 48-inch, 33c; 54-inch, 35c; 66-inch, 45c; 72-inch, 50c yd.

White window Holland, 30-inch, 15c; 32-inch, 16c; 36-inch, 18c; 38-inch, 20c; 42-inch, 25c.

Dark green Holland, 24-inch, 20c; 30-inch, 22c; 36-inch, 25c; 42-inch, 30c; 48-inch, 35c; 54-inch, 40c; 60-inch, 45c; 72-inch, 50c.

Price per piece of 50 yards on application.

Spring Shade Rollers.

Hartshorn's celebrated spring rollers, $1\frac{5}{16}$ x 42 inches, 10c each; 1 x 42 inches, with brass cap ends, 13c each.

$1\frac{5}{16}$-inch Mascot spring rollers, 8c each.

Hartshorn's spring rollers for larger shades, $1\frac{1}{4}$ x 42 inches, 18c each; $1\frac{1}{4}$ x 48 inches, 20c; $1\frac{1}{4}$ x 54 inches, 25c; $1\frac{1}{4}$ x 60 inches, 30c each.

Tin spring rollers, $1\frac{1}{4}$ in. x 4 ft. 6 in. to 5 ft., 50c; $1\frac{1}{2}$ in. x 5 ft., 75c; $1\frac{1}{2}$ in. x 5 ft. 6 in. to 6 ft., 85c; $1\frac{3}{4}$ in. x 6 ft., $1.00; $1\frac{3}{4}$ in. x 6 ft. 6 in. to 7 ft., $1.10; $1\frac{3}{4}$ in. x 7 ft. 6 in. to 8 ft., $1.20; $1\frac{3}{4}$ in. x 8 ft. 6 in. to 9 ft., $1.25 each; $2\frac{1}{4}$-inch tin rollers for large heavy shades, 35c foot.

Prices of gross lots of rollers on application.

Flags.

BRITISH ENSIGN.

Length.	Width.	Price.
1 ft. 6 in. x	0 ft. 9 in.	each $0.40
2 ft. 3 in. x	1 ft. 1 in.	0.50
2 ft. 6 in. x	1 ft. 3 in.	0.60
3 ft. 0 in. x	1 ft. 6 in.	0.75
3 ft. 6 in. x	1 ft. 9 in.	1.00
3 ft. 0 in. x	2 ft. 0 in.	1.15
4 ft. 6 in. x	2 ft. 3 in.	1.25
5 ft. 0 in. x	2 ft. 6 in.	1.50
6 ft. 0 in. x	3 ft. 0 in.	2.00
7 ft. 6 in. x	3 ft. 9 in.	2.75
9 ft. 0 in. x	4 ft. 6 in.	3.50
10 ft. 6 in. x	5 ft. 3 in.	4.25
12 ft. 0 in. x	6 ft. 0 in.	5.00
13 ft. 6 in. x	6 ft. 9 in.	6.75
15 ft. 0 in. x	7 ft. 6 in.	8.50
18 ft. 0 in. x	9 ft. 0 in.	12.50
21 ft. 0 in. x	10 ft. 6 in.	15.00
24 ft. 0 in. x	12 ft. 0 in.	17.50

(British Ensigns made of Wool Bunting.)

UNION JACK.

Length.	Width.	Price.
1 ft. 6 in. x	0 ft. 9 in.	each $0.40
2 ft. 3 in. x	1 ft. 1 in.	0.50
2 ft. 6 in. x	1 ft. 3 in.	0.60
3 ft. 0 in. x	1 ft. 6 in.	0.75
3 ft. 6 in. x	1 ft. 9 in.	1.00
4 ft. 0 in. x	2 ft. 0 in.	1.15
4 ft. 6 in. x	2 ft. 3 in.	1.25
5 ft. 0 in. x	2 ft. 6 in.	1.50
6 ft. 0 in. x	3 ft. 0 in.	2.00
7 ft. 6 in. x	3 ft. 9 in.	3.00
9 ft. 0 in. x	4 ft. 6 in.	4.00
10 ft. 6 in. x	5 ft. 3 in.	5.50
12 ft. 0 in. x	6 ft. 0 in.	7.50
13 ft. 6 in. x	6 ft. 9 in.	9.00
15 ft. 0 in. x	7 ft. 6 in.	10.50
18 ft. 0 in. x	9 ft. 0 in.	14.00
21 ft. 0 in. x	10 ft. 6 in.	17.50
24 ft. 0 in. x	12 ft. 0 in.	21.00

(Union Jacks made of Wool Bunting.)

CANADIAN FLAG.

Length.	Width.	Price.
3 ft. 0 in. x	1 ft. 6 in.	each $1.50
4 ft. 6 in. x	2 ft. 3 in.	2.50
6 ft. 0 in. x	3 ft. 0 in.	3.00
7 ft. 6 in. x	3 ft. 9 in.	4.00
9 ft. 0 in. x	4 ft. 6 in.	5.00
10 ft. 6 in. x	5 ft. 3 in.	6.00
12 ft. 0 in. x	6 ft. 0 in.	7.50
13 ft. 6 in. x	6 ft. 9 in.	9.50
15 ft. 0 in. x	7 ft. 6 in.	11.00
18 ft. 0 in. x	9 ft. 0 in.	14.75
21 ft. 0 in. x	10 ft. 6 in.	18.00
24 ft. 0 in. x	12 ft. 0 in.	22.00

(Canadian Flags made of Wool Bunting.)

Cotton Flags.

(Mounted on sticks.)

Canadian Ensigns and Union Jacks—

Sizes			
3 x 2 inches,	$0.06 a doz.,	½c each.
6 x 4 "	0.12 "	1c "
8 x 6 "	0.20 "	2c "
12 x 8 "	0.35 "	3c "
20 x 15 "	0.75 "	7c "
24 x 18 "	1.00 "	10c "
28 x 20 "	1.65 "	15c "
36 x 21 "	2.00 "	20c "

Soft Finish Cotton Flags.

Union Jacks (Unmounted)—

Sizes		
14 x 10 inches,	$0.40 a doz.,	4c each.
17 x 15 "	0.60 "	6c "
20 x 13 "	0.70 "	7c "
29 x 16 "	1.00 "	10c "
27 x 25 "	1.25 "	12½c "
35 x 23 "	1.50 "	15c "
50 x 36 "	3.25 "	30c "
72 x 40 "	7.00 "	65c "
72 x 50 "	8.00 "	75c "
90 x 70 "	19.00 "	$1.75 "

Canadian Ensigns (Unmounted)—

Sizes		
13 x 9 inches,	$0.35 a doz.,	3c each.
29 x 16 "	1.00 "	10c "
35 x 22 "	1.50 "	15c "

Silk Flags

UNION JACKS, BRITISH ENSIGNS CANADIAN AND AMERICAN (SILK)

Size.	Each.	Size.	Each.
3 x 2 in.	$0.02	18 x 18 in.	$0.55
6 x 4 in.	0.04	20 x 20 in.	0.65
8½ x 6 in.	0.08	24 x 24 in.	0.75
12 x 8 in.	0.12½	36 x 23 in.	0.85
16 x 10½ in.	0.20	32 x 48 in.	1.25
18 x 12 in.	0.25	60 x 35 in.	2.00
23 x 16 in.	0.35		

ROYAL STANDARD

20 x 20 in....$0.85   24 x 24 in....$0.95

SCOTCH AND IRISH

Size.	Each.	Size.	Each.
6 x 4 in.	$0.04	18 x 12 in.	$0.25
12 x 8 in.	0.12½	36 x 23 in.	0.85

For other sizes in Bunting, Silk, and Cotton Flags, ask for prices.

Wool Bunting, 18 inches wide, in red, white or blue, 20c yard.

AWNINGS.

Directions for Measurements.—Take measurements on the frame—not on stone or brick. For square windows send width and height. For "circle-top windows" send width and height to centre of circle, and height of curve.

For store awnings give number of feet from sidewalk to top where awning is attached, also number of feet awning is required to extend over sidewalk. State if pillars or columns where brackets are to be fastened are in line, and if top of window where awning is attached projects beyond the columns.

Awning Materials.

White ducks, 8 oz, 12½c ; 10 oz, 15c ; 12 oz, 18c yd.

Awning duck, in the newest patterns and colorings, 30 inches wide, 20c yd.

Awning duck, duplex new fancy stripe, extra quality, 22c yd.

Awnings—Sizes and Prices.

Width	Projection	Price	Width	Projection	Price
2½ feet..	3 feet..	$2.35	4 feet..	3½ feet..	$3.10
3 " ..	3 " ..	2.60	4½ " ..	3½ " ..	3.10
3½ " ..	3 " ..	2.60	5 " ..	4½ " ..	3.50
4 " ..	3 " ..	2.70	3 " ..	5 " ..	3.75
4½ " ..	3 " ..	2.85	3½ " ..	5 " ..	3.75
5 " ..	3 " ..	3.00	4 " ..	5 " ..	4.00
2½ " ..	3½ " ..	2.60	4½ " ..	5 " ..	4.15
3 " ..	3½ " ..	2.90	5 " ..	5 " ..	4.25
3½ " ..	3½ " ..	3.00			

These prices include irons, cords, etc.

Estimates and samples of awning material furnished.

Childs' lawn tents, made of best fancy stripe duck.

Sizes.	Prices, complete.
5 x 5 feet	$4.50 each.
7½ x 7½ "	6.00 "
10 x 10 "	11.00 "

Send for Descriptive PRICE LIST, showing different styles of Tents, Flags and Awnings.

WALL TENT.

Length and width.	Height.	Height of wall.	Prices without poles and pins. 8 oz. Ducks.	10 oz. Ducks.	12 oz. Ducks.	Poles and pins extra.
7x 7 ft.	7 ft.	2 ft.	$6.25	$7.25	$8.50	$1.25
7x 9½ "	7 "	2 "	7.25	8.25	10.00	1.35
8x12 "	7½ "	3 "	10.50	11.50	13.50	1.75
9x12 "	8 "	3 "	11.00	12.00	15.00	1.75
10x12 "	8 "	3 "	12.00	13.75	16.50	1.75
10x14 "	9 "	3 "	14.00	16.00	19.50	2.00
12x12 ft.	9 ft.	3½ ft.	$15.50	$18.50	$21.50	$2.00
12x14 "	9 "	3½ "	17.00	19.00	23.00	2.25
12x16 "	9 "	3½ "	19.00	21.00	25.50	2.25
14x14 "	10 "	4 "	20.50	22.50	27.50	2.25
14x16 "	10 "	4 "	22.00	24.50	30.00	2.50

If higher walls are required add 5 per cent. for each additional 6 inches.

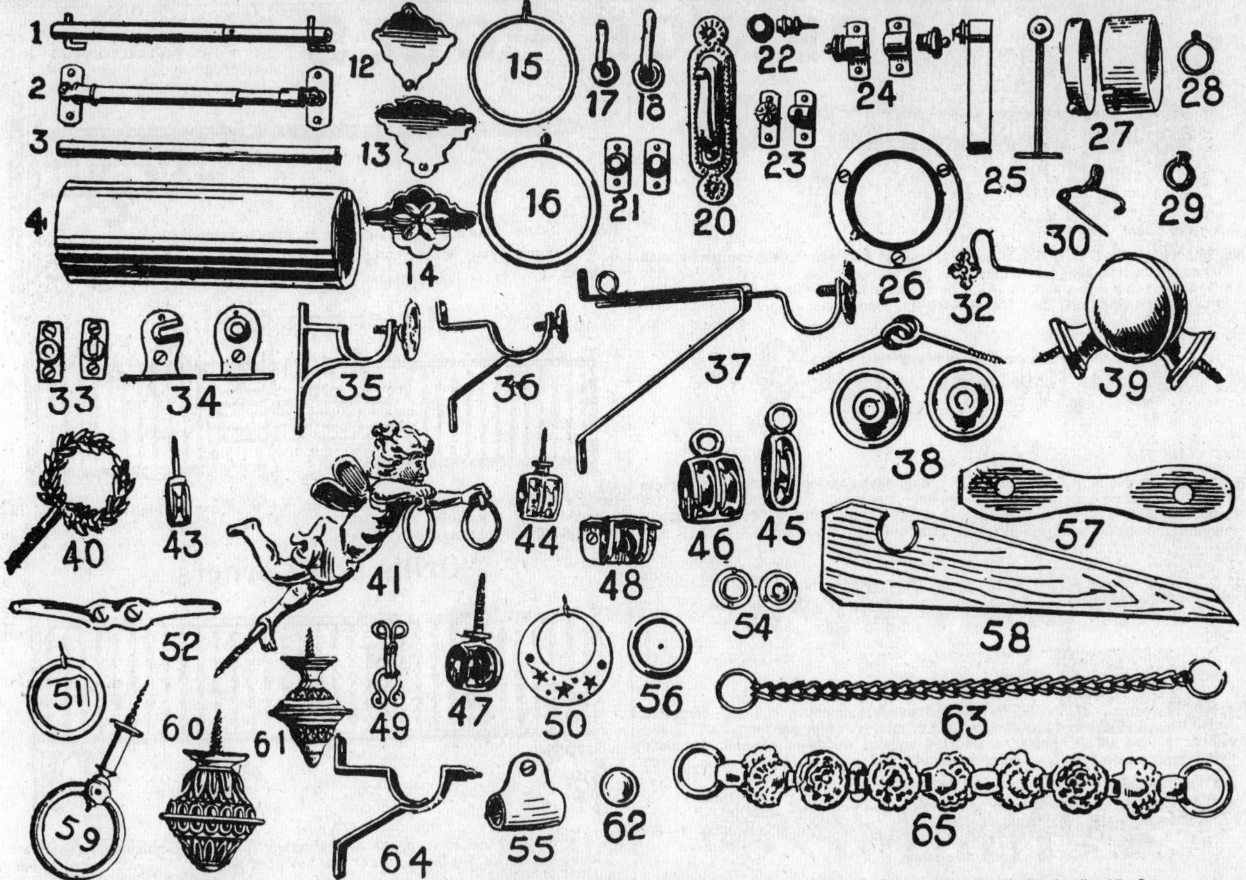

1. ¼-inch brass extension rod, from 23 to 42 inches, with brackets, 10c each.
2. 5/16-inch extension rod, 14 to 24 inches, with brackets, 12c; 24 to 44-inch, 15c each.
3. ½-inch brass rod, 4c ft.
4. ⅝-inch brass rod, 6c ft.
5. 5/16-inch brass-cased tubing, 7c ft.
6. ⅜-inch " " 8c ft.
7. ½-inch " " 10c ft.
8. ¾-inch " " 13c ft.
9. 1-inch " " 20c ft.
10. 1½-inch brass tubing, 25c ft.
11. 2-inch " 35c ft.
12. Brass or nickel stair plates, 12½c doz.
13. " " " 15c doz.
14. " " " 20c doz.
15. American pole rings, 1½-inch, 12c; 2-in, 18c doz.
16. English pole rings, ½-inch, 12c; ¾-inch, 13c; 1-in, 15c; 1¼-in, 18c; 1¾-in, 20c; 2¼-in, 30c doz.
17. Tassel hooks, 3c pair.
18. " 5c pair.
19. " 10c pair.
20. " 12c pair.
21. Vestibule sockets, ¼-inch, 3c; ⅜-inch, 5c pair.
22. Vestibule sockets, ¼-inch, 8c; ⅜-inch, 10c; ½-inch, 15c pair.
23. Vestibule brackets, ¼-inch, 5c; ⅜-inch, 7c pr.
24. Vestibule brackets, ¼-inch, 7c; ⅜-inch, 10c; ½-inch, 15c pair.
25. Extension vestibule brackets, ¼ and ⅜-inch, 15c pair.
26. Pole sockets, 1½-inch, 7c; 2-inch, 10c pair.
27. Pole sockets, ¾-inch, 12c; 1-inch, 13c; 1½-inch, 15c; 2-inch, 25c pair.
28. Vestibule rings, ⅜-inch, 5c; ½-inch, 8c doz.
29. Vestibule rings, ⅜-inch, 8c; ½-inch, 10c doz.
30. Drapery pins, 3c doz, 25c gross.
31. Drapery pins, solid brass, 4c doz; 35c gross.
32. Gordon drapery pins, 12½c doz.
33. Roller brackets for inside shades, 3c pair.
34. Roller brackets, 3c pair.
35. Pole brackets, English brass, ¾ and 1-inch, 12c; 1½-inch, 15c; 2-inch, 18c pair.
36. Pole brackets, American brass, 1 and 1½-inch, 12c; 2-inch, 15c pair.
37. Pole extension brackets, 1-inch, extends from 4 to 7 inches, 18c; 1½ and 2-inch, from 4 to 7 in, 18c; 1½ and 2-inch, from 7 to 12 in, 25c pr.
38. Pole joints (2 links and 4 caps), 1½-inch, 15c; 2-inch, 20c pair.
39. Pole joints, 1½-inch, 30c; 2-inch, 40c pair.
40. Drapery ornament (wreath), 15c each.
41. Drapery ornament (cupid), $2.00, 2.50, 3.50, 4.00, 5.50 each.
43. Screw pulley, brass, ½-inch, 7c; ⅝-inch, 10c ea.
44. Double screw pulley, brass, ⅝-inch, 15c each.
45. Swivel awning pulley, galvanized, ¾-inch, 4c; 1-inch, 5c each.
46. Double swivel awning pulley, galvanized, 1-inch, 5c; 1½-inch, 8c each.
47. Screw stop pulley, ¾-inch, 5c each.
48. Corner stop pulley, ¾-inch, 5c each.
49. Tent hook and eye, galvanized, 15c doz.
50. Crescent shade pull, 1c each.
51. Ring shade pulls, 1c, 2c, 5c each.
52. Line cleat, 4½-inch, 5c; 8-inch, 8c each.
54. Grommets (tent), 3c, 4c, 5c, 15c doz.
55. Awning slide, ½-inch, 7c; ⅝-inch, 10c each.
56. Awning rings, galvanized, ⅜ and ½-inch, 5c 1-inch, 7c doz.
57. Toggles, for guy ropes, 20c doz.
58. Tent pins, 10-inch, 20c; 15-inch, 25c doz.
59. Brass drapery ring, extends 6 inches with 6-inch ring, $1.00 each.
60. Brass pole end, 1½-inch, 10c pair.
61. Brass pole end, 1-inch, 13c pair.
62. Drugget pin, ⅝-inch, 10c; ¾-inch, 12c doz.
63. Curtain chains, 12c pair.
64. Pole bracket, 1½-inch, 5c pair.
65. Curtain chains, 25c pair.

Drapes.

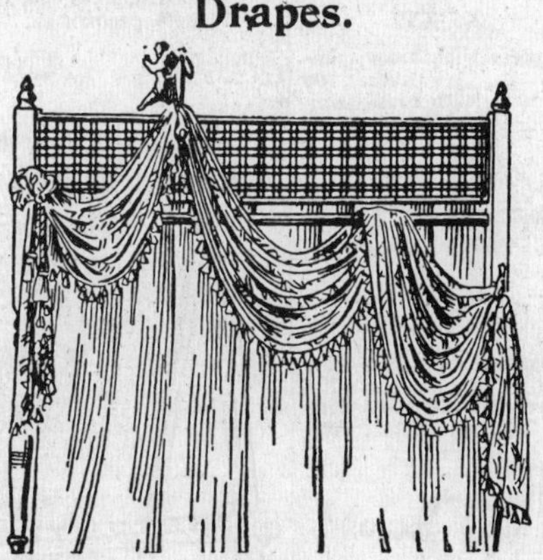

Arch Drape.

This cut is merely a suggestion for draping windows, doors, alcoves, etc. It is the quality of the material that regulates the price. We can originate the designs, and supply any material upon application. It is to work of this kind we give our special attention, and we cordially invite correspondence. This design is for a door 6 ft. wide and 8 ft. high. In ordering, estimate one yard of material to a foot, and three yards more fringe than material.

This cut illustrates a fancy iron lantern with colored glass sides, handsome designs, very strong, well made goods, being the very latest idea for halls, smoking rooms, Moorish rooms or Turkish divans. The bracket is separate from the lantern, but it adds very much to the appearance of each to have both.

No. 135. Fancy iron lanterns with colored glass, in entirely new designs, can be used for halls, Moorish rooms or Turkish divans, each................ $3.50

Other styles and sizes in iron and brass, $2.00 to 7.50 each.

Bracket, $1.50 each.

Mail Order customers always get benefit of reduced prices.

CORNICE POLES

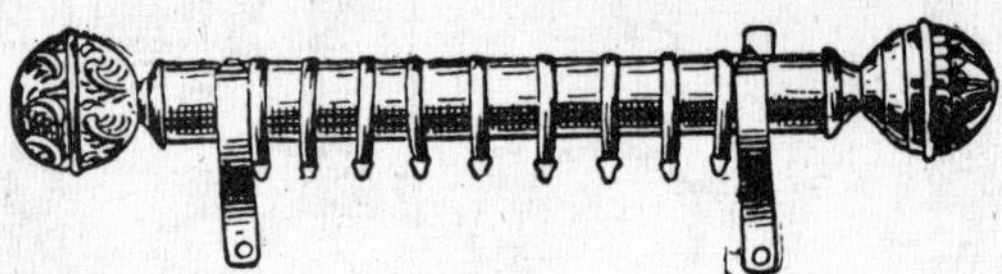

No. 750. No. 156.

No. 750. 1⅜ inch x 5 ft. poles, in cherry, walnut and ash finish, complete with brass trimmings, 23c; trimmings only, per set 15c
No. 156. 1⅜ inch x 5 ft. poles, in oak, cherry, ebony and walnut finish, complete with brass trimmings, 25c; trimmings only, per set 17c

No. 71. No. 374.

No. 71. 1⅜ inch x 5 ft. poles, in oak, mahogany, ebony and walnut finish, complete with brass trimmings, 30c; trimmings only, per set 22c
No. 374. 1⅜ inch x 5 ft. poles, in oak, rosewood, walnut and sycamore, complete with brass trimmings, 55c; trimmings only, per set 40c

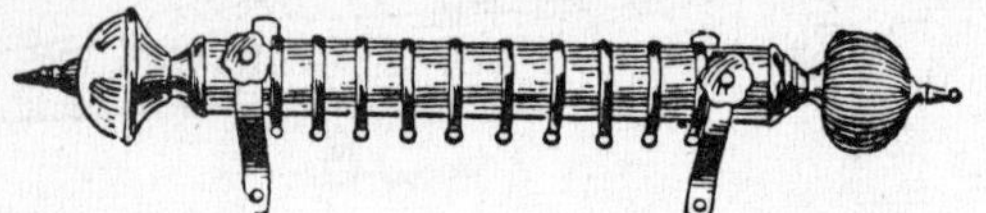

No. 500. No. 349.

No. 500. 1⅜ inch x 5 ft. poles, in assorted woods and white enamel, complete with brass and silvered trimmings, 60c; trimmings only, per set 45c
No. 349. 1⅜ inch x 5 ft. poles, in assorted colored woods or enamel, complete with brass trimmings, 50c; trimmings only, per set 40c

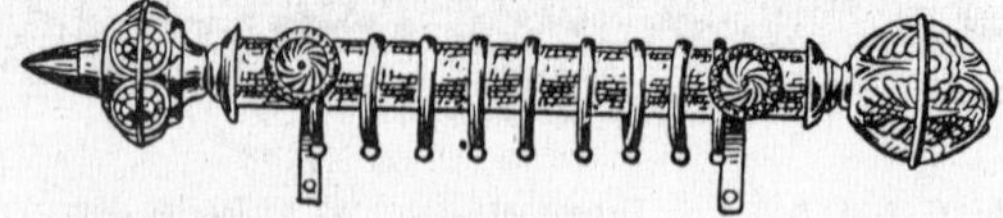

No. 507. No. 331.

No. 507. 1⅜ inch x 5 ft. poles, in assorted woods, complete with English brass trimmings, 85c; ends only, per pair .... 3[illegible]c
No. 331. 1⅜ inch x 5 ft. poles, in assorted woods, complete with English brass trimmings, 80c; ends only, per pair 30c

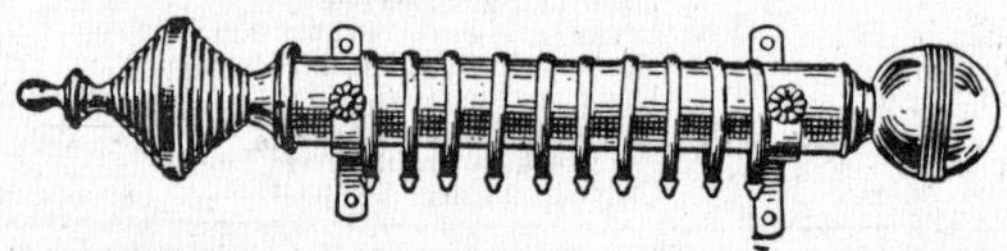

No. 464. No. XX2.

No. 464. 2 inch x 5 ft. poles, in assorted woods, complete with brass trimmings, 95c; trimmings only, per set 70c
No. XX2. 2 inch x 5 ft. poles, in assorted woods, complete with brass trimmings, 65c; trimmings only, per set 40c

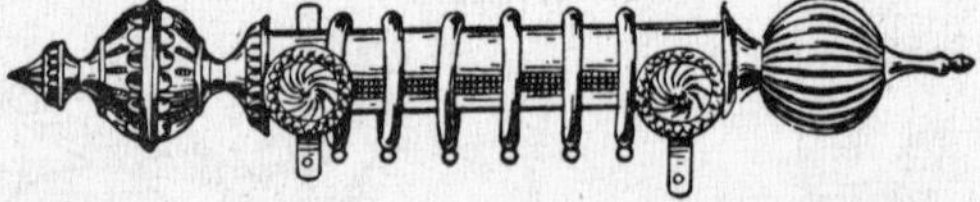

No. 8255. No. 8253.

No. 8255. 2 inch x 5 ft. poles, in assorted woods or enamel, complete with English brass trimmings, $1.45; ends only, per pair 70c
No. 8253. 2 inch x 5 ft. poles, in assorted woods or enamel, complete with English brass trimmings, $1.60; ends only, per pair 90c

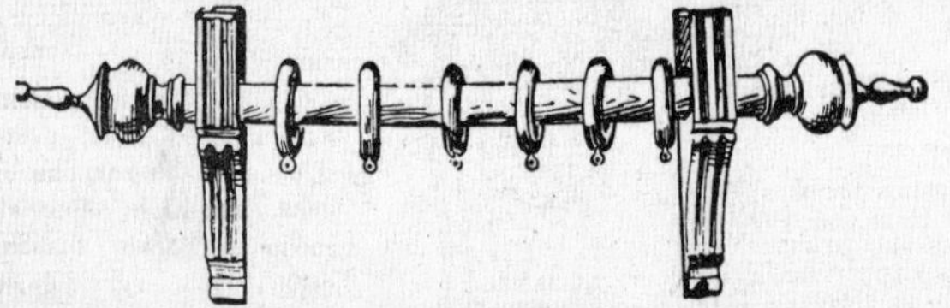

No. 80. 1½ inch x 5 ft. poles, extra finish, in assorted colors, complete with wood trimmings, 60c; trimmings only, per set 45c
No. 80. 2 inch x 5 ft. poles, extra finish, in assorted colors, complete with wood trimmings, $1.10; trimmings only, per set 70c

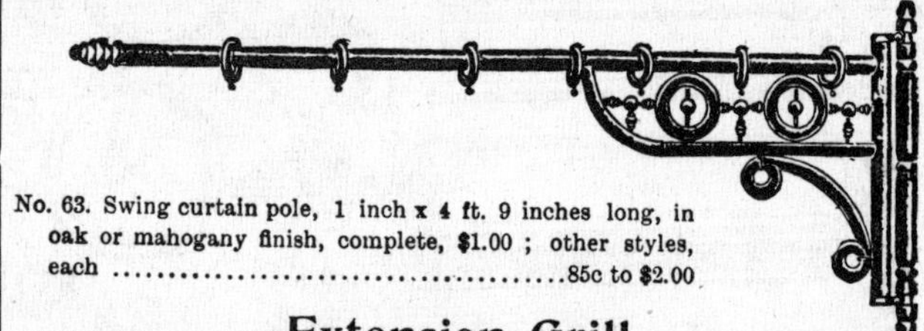

No. 63. Swing curtain pole, 1 inch x 4 ft. 9 inches long, in oak or mahogany finish, complete, $1.00; other styles, each .... 85c to $2.00

Extension Grill.

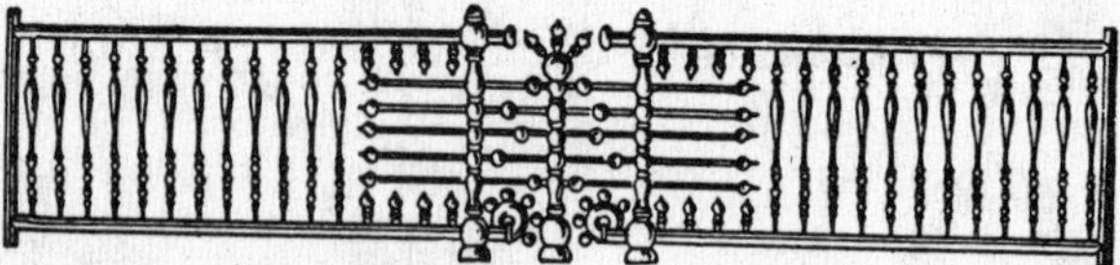

No. 404X. *Extension grill, for doors or arches, solid oak or mahogany finish,* 12 inches deep, 8 spindles to a foot, length 5 feet, extending to 6 feet, $3.00; length 6 feet, extending to 7 feet $3.50

Grills and Corners.

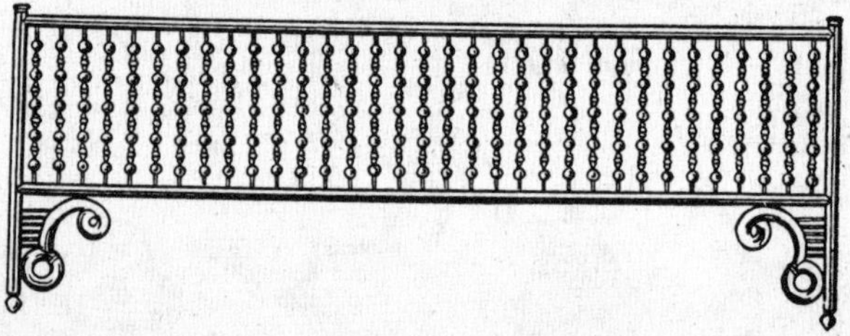

No. 432. Grill, 12 inches deep, oak or mahogany finish, 5 spindles to a foot, 35c foot; 8 spindles, 50c foot; corner brackets, per pair 80c

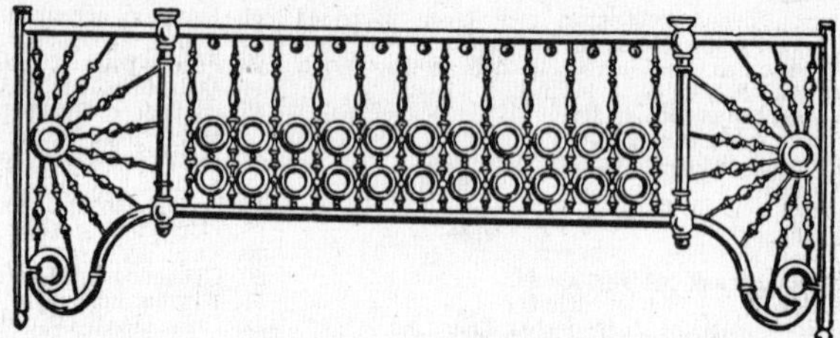

No. 416. Grill, solid oak or mahogany finish, 12 inches deep, 85c foot; corner brackets, per pair $5.75

Curtain Stretcher.

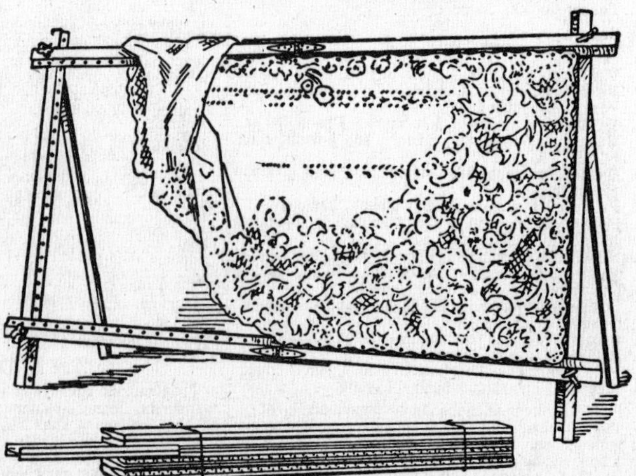

FRAME FOLDED FOR STORING OR SHIPPING

Curtain stretcher, size 6 feet x 12 feet, made with hinges to fold, complete, without legs, each, $1.35; with legs, each $2.00

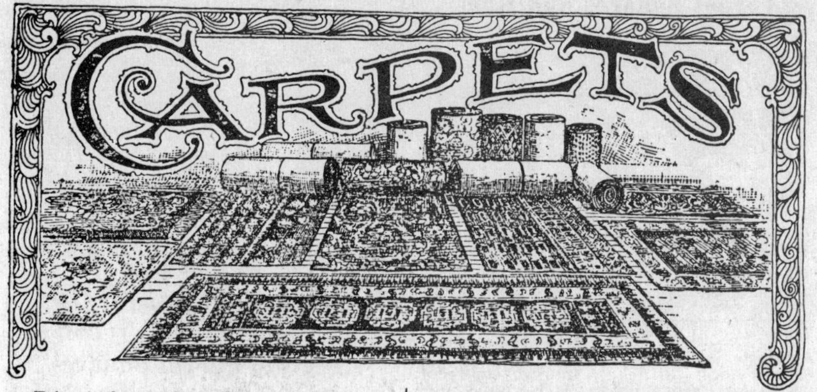

Directions for Measuring.

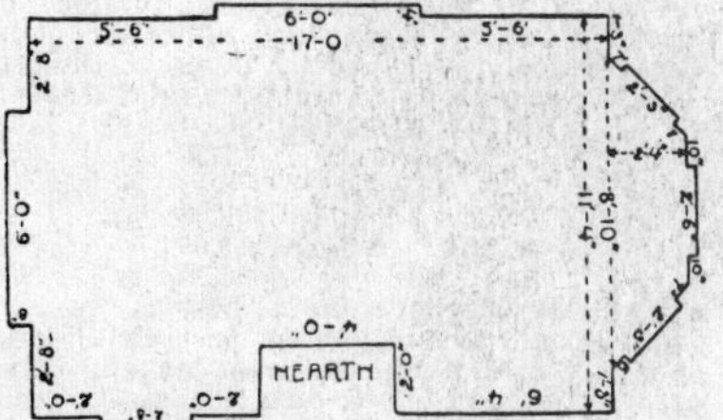

You cannot be too particular in taking measurements for carpets, especially so if they are to be bordered, as bordered carpets cannot be turned under, and should fit exact. (Make no allowances.) Always draw a diagram of rooms if carpets are to be bordered. It is not necessary to draw to a scale. Give all measures on all lines exact to ½ inch, also the total length and width of room in centre and through folding doors (if any), and see if the total of the short or broken measures agree with the through measures. Draw a straight line across jogs and bay windows, and you will have an accurate base to work from. Locate all doors and jogs and give the depth of each, so we can sew on carpet or filling for same if desired; also designate front of rooms and state which way you wish breadths to run. When the room is of such a size as to require a fraction of a breadth (in addition to the full breadths used) we will be obliged to piece it in one or two places, unless you are willing to pay for a full breadth. In such cases state same on your order, and we will send balance of the breadth with the carpet. If for several connecting rooms, make a plan of same all on one sheet. By being careful in taking measures and seeing that they prove before sending in the order, you will perhaps save the delay of our sending back the plan for remeasurements, as we will not cut the carpets unless the measures prove correct.

In measuring circular or winding stairs, always measure on wall or long side.

NOTE.—When ordering carpets not estimated on by us, allow at least one yard extra for waste in matching pattern on each room. If carpet can be cut with less waste, money will be refunded. Delay in despatch will be avoided by carefully carrying out above instructions.

Carpet Sample Department.

Samples showing qualities and colors of any line of goods in this department, with the exception of rugs, squares and crumbcloths, will be cheerfully sent upon application. As these samples are valuable to us, we would ask that they be returned after inspection. Mark the pattern you select on pin ticket attached, and give number of same on order sheet to prevent any misunderstanding.

Prices for Sewing Carpets.

Sewing all carpets, 3c yard, with an additional charge of 5c for each mitre on bordered carpets.

Axminster Carpets.

English Axminster carpets—our range of these strictly high-grade goods for this season excels by far any of our previous efforts. Everything that is newest and most artistic in designs from the looms of the most noted makers in England are represented, beautiful conventional and geometrical designs in dainty self-colored effects of blues, greens, rose-du-barre or chintz, specially adapted for fine drawing, reception or sitting rooms and the rich Oriental designs with the heavier coloring of reds, greens, blues, etc., for the dining-room, library, hall or stairs, with ⅝ borders and ¾ stairs to match, splendid values, per yard, $1.50 and 2.00. 4/4 stairs to match, per yard, $2.50 and 3.50.

Wilton Carpets.

English Wilton carpets—our importations of these well-known floor coverings have been on an unusually large scale, all that is newest and best in designs and color combinations to be found in the British markets are here. We specially recommend this carpet for its exceptional wearing quality for banks, public halls, offices or private residences, made with ⅝ border and ¾ stair to match, per yard, $1.25, 1.50 and 2.00.

Velvet Carpets.

For those who wish the rich effect of the Axminster or Wilton carpet at a much more moderate price we recommend this popular carpet. We show a large range of beautiful designs with all the latest color combinations of greens, blues, terra cotta, crimson, fawn and ecru shades with ⅝ borders and ¾ stairs to match, great values, per yard, $1.00 and 1.15.

English Brussels.

English Brussels carpets. We desire to draw special attention to our range of these popular carpets as the greatest of care has been paid to their selection; it contains the best that time, money or long experience could buy from the leading English makers, the designs being especially handsome with all the latest color combinations suitable for any room or hall, with ⅝ borders and ¾ stairs to match, exceptional values, per yard, 75c, 90c, $1.00, 1.15 and 1.25.

Tapestry Carpets.

Our importation of these goods for this season is particularly attractive, special attention having been paid to their selection, which show a marked improvement in style, finish and general effect, which represents the production of the leading British manufacturers, especially in the four best grades which for effective design and color combinations equals the best Brussels, with ⅝ border and ¾ stair to match, 50c, 55c, 65c, 80c per yard.

Cheaper grades of tapestry carpet, 30c, 35c, 40c, 45c per yard.

Mottled tapestry carpets at 25c per yard.

Tapestry Stair Carpets.

27-inch, 35c, 40c, 45c, 50c, 55c, 65c, 80c yard.
22 " 30c, 35c, 40c, 50c yard.
18 " 25c, 30c, 35c yard.

Information, estimates and quality samples sent on application.

Ingrain Carpets—All Wool.

Our stock of reversible ingrain carpets contains a full range of the best English and domestic made goods, in beautiful designs and color combinations suitable for sitting rooms, bedrooms or halls, and shrewd buyers tell us that nowhere else can they find the same great values.

"Victorian" brand, best 3-ply reversible all-wool carpets, full 36 inches wide, a splendid range of choice patterns with the newest colorings of olive green, sage, blue, terra cotta, red, etc., at $1.00 per yard.

Best English 2-ply reversible all-wool, 36 inches wide, specially recommended for its great wearing qualities, a big range of new up-to-date designs and color combinations at 85c per yard.

"Venice" brand best Canadian 2-ply all-wool carpets at 75c per yard.

"Trafalgar" brand, superfine 2-ply all-wool carpet, 36 inches wide, a large assortment of new designs and colorings of maroon, olive, brown, fawn and ecru shades, excellent value at 65c per yard.

Ingrain Carpets—All-wool Filling.

"Brunswick" brand, a cotton warp, best wool filled carpet, made 36 inches wide, the finest imported Scotch yarns used in the filling of this carpet which can be recommended to hold its color and wear well, a large and well assorted range of choice patterns with new color combinations of green and ecru, fawn and brown, blue and white, etc., at 55c per yard.

Ingrain Carpets—"Union."

"Nassau" brand, best extra super union reversible carpet, 36 inches wide, at 40c yard.

"Kitchener" brand, heavy union carpet, reversible, 36 inches wide, at 30c yard.

"French" brand, special line, good quality union carpet, 35 inches wide, a large range of good designs with all the new colorings, per yard, 25c.

Also a complete range of church carpets. Samples sent on application.

Hemp Carpets.

Fancy stripes, 32-inch, 10c; 33-inch, 12½c; 34-inch, 15c; 35-inch, 18c yard.

Heavy fancy stripes, 35½-inch, 20c, 25c; 54-inch, 38c; 72-inch, 50c yard.

Fancy floral designs, reversible patterns, 33-inch, 15c; 35½-inch, 20c; 36-inch, 25c; 54-inch, 38c; 72-inch, 50c yard.

Hemp Stair Carpets.

Fancy stripe, 18-inch, 8c, 10c, 15c; 22-inch, 12½c, 15c, 20c yard.

China and Japanese Mattings.

China and Japanese mattings in great variety, in plain white and fancy checks, inlaid designs and fancy colored and damask patterns. These goods are in great demand for bedrooms, dining-rooms and upper halls, being neat in appearance and more durable than carpet at the same price.

China mattings, jointed every two yards at back, in fancy check patterns, 36 inches wide, 10c, 12½c yard.

Jointless China mattings, in plain white and fancy checks, 15c, 20c, 25c yard.

Damask patterns, extra heavy, jointless and reversible, 30c yard.

Japanese cotton warp mattings, jointless and reversible, inlaid and fancy carpet and other patterns, 15c, 20c, 25c, 30c, 40c yard.

Cocoa Mattings.

Natural color in all the standard widths.

No. 5. 18-inch, 22½c; 27-inch, 35c; 36-inch, 42½c yard.

No. 9. 18-inch, 27½c; 27-inch, 42½c; 36-inch, 52½c yard.

No. A. Calcutta hard twist, 18-inch, 35c; 27-inch, 52½c; 36-inch, 65c yard.

Wider widths, up to 72 inches, made to order in quantities of not less than 20 yards, at proportionate prices.

String Mattings.

Heavy string mattings, fancy patterns, 36 inches wide, 25c, 35c yard.

Extra heavy quality, plain, 27-inch, 25c; 36-inch, 35c yard.

Plain centre, with fancy border, or in fancy check patterns, 18-inch, 18c; 22-inch, 23c; 27-inch, 27c; 36-inch, 35c yard.

Zinc and Rubber Matting Ends.

Zinc ends for cocoa and other mattings, with copper rivets to fasten, 18-inch, 13c; 27-inch, 18c; 36-inch, 25c each.

Knapp's patent rubber binding, 2 inches wide, for cocoa and other mattings, in 18-inch, 27-inch, 36-inch, 54-inch, 72-inch lengths, 20c foot.

4-inch heavy webbing, for binding mattings, 4c yard.

Stair Pads, Carpet Lining and Felt Paper.

Best quality novelty stair pads, for 36-inch carpet, $1.50 doz; for 27-inch carpet, $1.00 doz; for 22-inch carpet, 90c doz.

Best underlaid felt carpet lining, taped both sides, 36 inches wide, 7c per yard.

Superior carpet lining, 5c yard.

Standard carpet lining, 4c yard.

Felt paper (16 ozs. to yard), 3c yard.

Linoleums and Floor Oilcloths.

Inlaid linoleum is specially recommended for any place where there is hard wear, the colors going right through to canvas, made in 2-yard widths only, in a complete range of new floral, block, tile and parquetry designs. Best quality, $1.10 and 1.25 square yard.

No. 2 quality inlaid linoleum, in similar designs, 90c square yard.

Linoleums in 2 and 4 yard widths, best English and Scotch makes, floral, block and inlaid effects, patterns painted over hard cork composition, suitable for kitchen, dining-rooms, lower halls, bath-rooms, etc., 50c and 60c square yard.

Linoleums, 2 yards wide only, floral, block and inlaid designs, 35c, 40c and 45c square yard.

Plain Brown Linoleums.

2 and 4 yards wide.

No. 1 quality, 90c square yard; 6-inch border to match (key pattern), 25c lineal yard; 9-inch border to match (key pattern), 35c lineal yard.

No. 2 quality, 75c square yard; 6-inch key border, 20c lineal yard; 9-inch key border to match, 30c lineal yard.

No. 3 quality, 55c per square yard; 6-inch key border to match, 15c lineal yard; 9-inch key border to match, 25c lineal yard.

Plain Cork Carpet.

A thicker form of linoleum, suitable for nurseries, school rooms, offices, public buildings, or any place where it is desirable to lessen noise; 2-yard widths only.

No. 1 quality, $1.00 square yard; 9-inch key border to match, 35c lineal yard.

No. 2 quality, cork carpet, 75c square yard; 9-inch key border to match, 25c lineal yard.

No. 3 quality cork carpet, 65c square yard.

Passage and stair linoleums, key borders and plain centres, 18-inch, 20c, 25c; 22-inch, 25c, 32c; 27-inch, 30c, 38c; 36-inch, 40c, 50c yard.

Stair Linoleums.

Best quality stair linoleum, made very pliable to bend over steps, plain centre with scroll border, 18-inch, 50c; 22-inch, 60c; 27-inch, 70c; 36-inch, $1.00; 45-inch, $1.25 yard.

Floor Oilcloths.

Our large range of patterns in these goods excels anything we have ever shown before.

	36-in.	45-in.	54-in.	72-in.	90-in.	
No. 1	40c,	50c,	60c,	80c,	$1.00	yard.
" 2	30c,	38c,	45c,	60c,	75c	"
" 3	25c,	32c,	38c,	50c,	..	"

Floor oilcloth, 3 and 4 yards wide, 45c and 55c square yard.

Passage and stair oilcloths, floral and small neat patterns, with fancy borders, 18-inch, 11c and 16c yard; 22-inch, 13c, 19c yard; 27-inch, 16c, 24c yard.

Oilcloth mats, bordered, light and medium colors—Size, 36 x 36 inches, 40c each.

"	36 x 54	"	60c	"
"	45 x 45	"	65c	"
"	54 x 54	"	90c	"
"	54 x 72	"	$1.20	"
"	72 x 72	"	1.60	"
"	72 x 90	"	2.00	"
"	90 x 90	"	2.50	"

Brass and Zinc Oilcloth Bindings.

Zinc binding, including corners and nails, 4 yds, 12½c; 5 yds, 15c; 6 yds, 20c; 8 yds, 25c.

Brass binding, 4 yards, 20c; 5 yards, 25c; 6 yards, 30c; 8 yards, 40c.

Corrugated rubber stair treads, for hotels and public buildings, cut any size to order. Write for samples and estimates.

Corrugated rubber matting, 36 inches wide, ⅛ inch thick, $2.00 yard.

NOTE.—Estimates and samples of Linoleums and Oilcloths sent on application.

Carpet Squares and Rugs.

Axminster carpet squares, best quality woven in one piece, with 18-inch interwoven border; with the advent of hardwood floors and fancy parquet borders these rugs are becoming more popular every season. We carry a beautiful range of Oriental, medallion and floral designs, which for beauty, richness of coloring and wearing qualities cannot be surpassed—

Size 4 ft.	5 inches	x 6 ft.	6 inches,	$9.50	each.
" 6 "	6 "	x 9 "	8 "	20.00	"
" 7 "	6 "	x 10 "	3 "	25.00	"
" 8 "	8 "	x 10 "	10 "	30.00	"
" 9 "	0 "	x 12 "	0 "	35.00	"
" 9 "	10 "	x 13 "	1 "	40.00	"
" 10 "	11 "	x 14 "	3 "	50.00	"

Second grade Axminster carpet squares, good range of new designs, with all the latest colorings—

Size 4 ft.	5 inches	x 6 ft.	6 inches,	$6.50	each.
" 6 "	6 "	x 9 "	8 "	13.50	"
" 7 "	6 "	x 10 "	3 "	16.75	"
" 8 "	8 "	x 10 "	10 "	20.00	"
" 9 "	10 "	x 13 "	1 "	27.50	"
" 10 "	11 "	x 14 "	3 "	35.00	"

Heavy English Wilton carpet squares, with 22-inch interwoven borders, a large assortment of beautiful designs, in colors of greens, blues, crimson and brown shades—

Size 9 ft.	0 inches	x 10 ft.	6 inches,	$19.00	each.
" 9 "	0 "	x 12 "	0 "	22.50	"
" 11 "	3 "	x 12 "	0 "	27.00	"
" 11 "	3 "	x 13 "	6 "	31.00	"

Cuts of Axminster squares, showing colors and patterns, sent on application. When writing for them please state size of rug wanted.

Velvet Carpet Squares.

Velvet pile carpet squares, made by the famous house of John Crossley & Sons, Ltd., Halifax, all woven in one piece, with 22-inch interwoven border, a splendid range of artistic designs and color combinations from the leading designers in England—

Size 4 ft.	6 inches	x 6 ft.	6 inches,	$5.50	each.
" 5 "	4 "	x 7 "	8 "	9.00	"
" 6 "	9 "	x 9 "	8 "	13.50	"
" 7 "	5 "	x 10 "	10 "	18.00	"
" 8 "	9 "	x 11 "	0 "	23.50	"
" 9 "	9 "	x 12 "	8 "	30.00	"
" 10 "	9 "	x 14 "	0 "	37.50	"

Brussels Squares.

Heavy English Brussels carpet squares, with 18 and 22-inch interwoven border, a complete range of new artistic designs and colorings of crimson and blue, brown and tan, bronze and ecru, sage and ecru—

Size 9 ft.	0 inches	x 10 ft.	6 inches,	$14.00	each.
" 9 "	0 "	x 12 "	0 "	16.00	"
" 11 "	3 "	x 12 "	0 "	20.00	"
" 11 "	3 "	x 13 "	6 "	22.50	"
" 11 "	3 "	x 15 "	9 "	26.50	"

Tapestry Carpet Squares.

Best quality tapestry carpet squares, with 18-inch interwoven borders, Brussels patterns and colors—

Size	3 x 3	yards,	$8.50	each.
"	3 x 3½	"	9.75	"
"	3 x 4	"	11.00	"
"	3 x 4½	"	12.50	"
"	3½ x 4	"	13.50	"
"	4 x 4	"	14.50	"
"	3½ x 4½	"	15.00	"
"	4 x 4½	"	16.50	"

Second quality tapestry carpet squares—

Size	3 x 3	yards,	$6.00	each.
"	3 x 3½	"	7.00	"
"	3 x 4	"	8.00	"
"	3½ x 3½	"	8.00	"
"	3½ x 4	"	9.50	"
"	4 x 4	"	10.75	"
"	4 x 4½	"	12.00	"
"	4 x 5	"	13.75	"

Japanese Rugs and Squares.

Best quality Japanese rugs and squares, good Oriental designs and colorings—

Size 1 ft.	6 inches	x 3 ft.	0 inches,	40c	each.
" 2 "	2 "	x 4 "	6 "	85c	"
" 2 "	6 "	x 5 "	0 "	$1.00	"
" 3 "	0 "	x 6 "	0 "	1.50	"
" 4 "	0 "	x 7 "	0 "	2.50	"
" 6 "	0 "	x 9 "	0 "	4.50	"
" 7 "	6 "	x 10 "	6 "	6.50	"
" 9 "	0 "	x 9 "	0 "	6.75	"
" 9 "	0 "	x 12 "	0 "	9.00	"
" 10 "	0 "	x 14 "	0 "	12.00	"
" 12 "	0 "	x 15 "	0 "	15.00	"

Hall Strips.

Size 3 ft.	0 inches	x 9 ft.	0 inches,	$2.25	each.
" 3 "	0 "	x 12 "	0 "	3.00	"
" 3 "	0 "	x 15 "	0 "	3.75	"

Ingrain Carpet Squares.

Best 2-ply all-wool carpet squares, "Sackville brand, woven in one piece, with 18-inch interwoven border, a splendid range of good designs, including some very effective medallions, in colors of green, blue, terra-cotta, crimson, brown, fawn and ecru mixtures—

Size,	2½ x 3	yards,	$6.00	each.
"	3 x 3	"	7.25	"
"	3 x 3½	"	8.50	"
"	3 x 4	"	9.50	"
"	3½ x 4	"	11.25	"
"	4 x 5	"	16.00	"

"Brunswick" carpet squares, best all-wool filling, cotton warp, colors as fast as all-wool, specially adapted for bedroom carpets, a well-assorted range of up-to-date designs and color combinations, in the following sizes—

Size	2½ x 3	yards,	$4.50	each.
"	3 x 3	"	5.50	"
"	3 x 3½	"	6.25	"
"	3 x 4	"	7.25	"
"	3½ x 4	"	8.50	"
"	4 x 5	"	12.00	"

"Omdurman" carpet squares, extra super union quality, everything that is newest and best in designs and colorings is represented in our range of these squares—

Size	2½ x 3	yards,	$3.00	each.
"	3 x 3	"	3.50	"
"	3 x 3½	"	4.25	"
"	3 x 4	"	4.75	"
"	3½ x 4	"	5.50	"
"	4 x 5	"	8.00	"

Reversible linen crumb cloths, in floral and block patterns, with appropriate borders, in two qualities, as follows:

Size in feet and inches.

	Black pattern on white ground		Brown pattern on white ground.	
5/7 x 6/10,	$1.25	each.	$1.00	each.
5/7 x 8/7	1.50	"	1.25	"
7/ x 8/7	2.00	"	1.75	"
7/ x 10/	2.25	"	2.00	"
8/6 x 10/	2.75	"	2.50	"
8/6 x 11/6	3.25	"	3.00	"
10/ x 11/6	3.75	"	3.50	"

Plain Durries and Felt for Rug Surrounds.

Plain durries, all-wool, 36 inches wide, best English make, in shades of green, terra cotta, crimson and blue, $1.00 per yd.

Plain felt, special heavy quality, 50 inches wide, in shades of old gold, green, blue, terra cotta, crimson and olive, 80c yd.

Best quality English Wilton or Dag-Dag rugs, made by John Crossley & Sons, Halifax, England, fine soft all-wool pile, Persian and floral designs, in very rich blending of colors—

Size	13 x 30	inches,	fringed ends,		$1.25	each.
"	13 x 36	"	"	"	1.50	"
"	18 x 36	"	"	"	1.90	"
"	18 x 36	"	"	sides,	2.25	"
"	36 x 36	"	"	ends	3.75	"
"	27 x 54	"	"	"	4.25	"
"	36 x 63	"	"	"	6.25	"
"	36 x 72	"	"	"	7.25	"

Your orders will be accurately and promptly filled.

Wall Paper Department.

THE above cut shows our SPECIAL DESIGN, made for our trade exclusively. IT CANNOT BE BOUGHT ELSEWHERE. We selected this design from many others owing to its suitability for any room or hall, it is made in Glimmers, Gilts, and Embossed Gilts. Following is the description, etc.:

No. 1103. Glimmers, blue, fawn, and red grounds, design in colors to harmonize with each shade of ground, 6c single roll.

9-inch match border, 2c yd.

No. 1103. Plain gilts, Nile-green, blue, grey, and rich green grounds, designs in gilt and colors to harmonize with each shade of ground, 8c single roll.

9-inch match border, 2½c yd.

No. 1103. Embossed gilt, buff, crimson, and emerald green grounds, design in gold and colors to harmonize with each shade of ground, basket weave embossing, 10c single roll.

9-inch match border, 3c yd.

THE LATEST AND MOST DESIRABLE AMERICAN, ENGLISH, CANADIAN AND JAPANESE WALL PAPERS are represented in our stock. New colors and choice designs, which are pleasing to the eye and correct from the decorative standpoint, nowhere in Canada can the assortment be equalled.

Ungrounded wall papers, large selectoin of designs and colors, for kitchens and attic rooms, 3c, 4c roll.

Match borders, 6 and 9 inches wide, 1c, 1½c yd.

White blanks, floral and set figure patterns, buff, blue, green and terra cotta colors, suitable for any appartment, 5c, 6c, 7c roll.

Match borders, 9 inches wide, 1½c, 2c, 2½c yd.

Glimmers, printed on heavy stock, floral, chintz and bold striking designs, red, green, blue and cream colors, suitable for bedrooms, sitting-rooms and stores, 7c, 8c, 10c roll.

Match blended borders, 18 inches wide, 4c, 5c, 6c yd.

Gilt wall papers in an immense variety of designs, terra cotta, olive, blue, pink, green and buff grounds, with designs in gilt and colors to harmonize with each color of ground, suitable for any room or hall, 8c, 10c, 12½c roll.

Match borders, 9 inches wide, 2c, 2½c, 3c yd.

Rich blended borders, 18 inches wide, 6c, 8c, 10c yd.

American gilt wall papers, colonial stripes, empire and floral designs, blue, brown, yellow and green colors, for sitting rooms, bedrooms and halls, 17c, 20c, 25c roll.

Rich blended borders, 18 inches wide, 12½c, 15c, 17c yd.

American and Canadian embossed gilts, rococo, conventional and scroll designs, red, green, blue, brown and cream colors, basket weave and ribbed embossings, for halls, dining rooms and sitting rooms, 12½c, 15c roll.

Match blended borders, 9 inches wide, 4c, 5c yd.

American and Canadian embossed gilts, Louis XIII., renaissance, tapestries and conventional scrolls, French grey, coffee brown, crimson, sage green, old blue and ivory, for drawing rooms, libraries, halls and dining rooms, 15c, 17c, 20c, 25c, 35c roll.

Match borders, artistically blended, 18 inches wide, 12½c, 15c, 17c, 20c yd.

Special embossed gilts, 21 inches wide, Flemish, renaissance, floral, Louis XV., and brocaded effects, forest green, new blue, olive, ivory and crimson colors, 30c, 35c, 50c, 75c roll.

Match blended borders, 18 and 21 inches wide, 15c, 17c, 20c, 25c, 30c yd.

Plain Ingrains.

Ingrain wall papers, 30 inches wide, 16 oz. weight, 8 yds to roll.

Our selection of colors comprises the newest colors in greens, olive, blues, terra-cottas, pinks, old rose, flesh and straw, 12½c roll.

Rich crimsons, 20c, 25c roll.

Match flitter and gilt ceilings, 17c, 20c roll.

Rich blended borders, 18 inches wide, 10c, 12½c, 15c, 17c yd.

Choice American ingrains, new blue, moss green, coffee, terra-cotta, flesh, straw and apple green colors, 17c, 20c roll.

Match ceilings, 25c roll.

Rich blended and relief borders, 18 inches wide, 15c, 17c, 20c, 25c yd.

English Tile Wall Papers

English washable tiles, unsurpassed in durability for kitchens, bathrooms and pantries, 10c, 12½c, 15c, 17c, 20c roll.

English and American varnished washable tiles, natty designs, blue, green, red and brown colors, 25c, 30c, 35c, 40c roll.

Japanese Wall Papers.

The latest Japanese designs, rich and effective colors, for dados and wall decorations, prices ranging from 40c to $1.50 yd.

RULES FOR MEASURING A ROOM.

To find number of single rolls required, multiply distance round room by height, taking out 20 sq ft for each opening, and divide by 30. To find quantity for ceiling, multiply length by width and divide by 30.

For 30-in. plain ingrains divide by 60, result will be number of rolls required.

N. B.—Wall papers are sold by the single roll, but put up in double rolls, as they then cut to better advantage.

Price for border is for a single strip the width of border, and one yard long.

Whole rolls of paper will be exchanged, provided we still have the same in stock, but we will not exchange borders or trimmed papers or paper if the line is out of stock.

Before returning paper left over please send samples to us, so that we can inform you if paper is still in stock; by doing this you may save charges.

Samples mailed free upon application. State what priced papers you wish, width of border and color effect desired, to enable us to make suitable selection.

Ceiling papers same price as walls they match, with exception of ingrains.

If you receive more than one of our catalogues, kindly notify us at once.

Brushes, Paints and Mouldings.

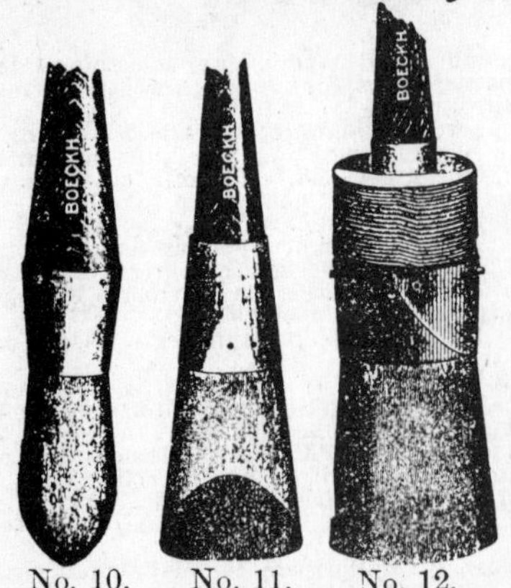

No. 10. No. 11. No. 12. No. 13. No. 14. No. 15. No. 16. No. 17.

Brushes.

No. 10. Round sash tools, tin bound, pure bristles, 8c, 11c, 16c, 23c, 28c ea.

No. 11. Flat sash tools, tin bound, pure bristles, 11c, 15c, 20c, 28c each.

No. 12. Oval paint, pure white bristles, plain, 17c, 23c, 28c; bridled, 2/0, 40c; 4/0, 60c; 5/0, 75c; 8/0, $1.20 each.

Columbia, black, oval, plain, 23c, 25c, 35c, 55c; bridled, 5/0, 75c; 7/0, $1.10; 8/0, $1.25; 9/0, $1.40 each.

No 13. Chiselled flat varnish, tin bound, pure white bristles, 1-inch, 10c; 1½-inch, 15c; 2-inch, 23c; 2½-inch, 28c; 3-inch, 40c each.

No. 14. Standard flat paint, mixed, 25c, 30c, 40c; pure bristles, plain, 45c; bridled, 75c, $1.00 each.

Tip-top flat paint, black bristles, 45c, 55c, 80c each.

No. 15. Painters' dusters, 40c, 50c each.

No. 16. Paper layers, pure bristles, single thick, 10-inch, 50c; 12-inch, 75c; double thick, 10-inch, 80c; 12-inch, 95c each.

Combination paper layers, pure bristles, 12-inch, 95c each.

No. 17. Kalsomine brushes, mixed, 45c, 55c, 80c, $1.25; pure bristles, $1.35, 1.65, 1.80, 2.15, 2.75, 3.50 each.

Whitewash brushes, mixed, 18c, 22c, 25c, 30c each.

Whitewash heads, mixed, pure bristles, $1.00, 1.20, 1.40 each.

Room Mouldings.

1½-inch American room moulding (as cut), blended colors, crimson and gilt; blue, cream and gilt; green, pink and gilt, 3½c foot.

1½-inch Canadian room mouldings, in fancy colors and gilt, colors to match any shade of wall paper, 3c foot.

2-inch American room moulding (as cut), blended colors, crimson, olive and gilt; green and gilt; sage, cream and gilt, 4½c foot.

2-inch Canadian room mouldings, large assortment of fancy color and gilt, to harmonize with our new shades of wall paper, 4c foot.

1-inch fancy color and gilt, blended, cream, blue, green and terra cotta, 2c and 2½c foot.

1-inch, plain burnished gilt, 3c; 1½-inch, 4c foot.

1½-inch, polished antique oak, 3c foot.

OUR ROOM MOULDING COLORS are fast and will not rub or run when damp. When 100 or more feet of the same pattern and color is bought we make a reduction in price of 25c per 100 feet.

Paints.

Pure prepared paints. One gallon properly applied will cover 200 square feet with two coats. Color card sent on application.

Ordinary colors and floor paints, ½-pint tins, 11c; 1-pint, 22c; 1-quart, 35c; ½-gallon, 70c; 1-gallon, $1.40 each.

Shutter greens and vermilion colors, ½-pint tins, 18c; 1 pint, 33c; 1 quart, 50c each.

Fancy enamel paints for decorative work, pink, rose, light and dark green, red, black, yellow, blue and white, ¼-pint tins, 15c each.

White, ½-pint tins, 25c; 1-pint, 45c each.

Ivory and white bath enamel, ½-pint tins, 30c each.

"G" stovepipe enamel, prevents rust and is unaffected by water, for stovepipes, radiators and registers, ½-pint tins, 20c; 1-pint, 35c each.

No. 20. "Our Favorite" gold enamel paint, put up in boxes, with brush and liquid for mixing, small size, 18c; large size, 30c ea.

No. 20.

Japanese gold paint, ready for use, with brush, 20c each.

Gold bronze, per oz, 15c; per lb, $2.00.

Silver and copper bronze, per oz, 18c; per lb, $2.50.

Oil wood-stains, for re-staining furniture and woodwork, imitation mahogany, oak, walnut and cherry. ½-pint tins, 15c; 1-pint, 25c; 1-quart, 40c each.

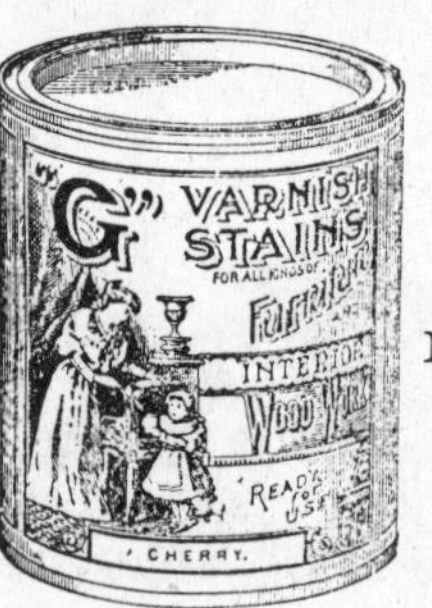

No. 21.

No. 21. Varnish stains, in imitation mahogany, rosewood, oak, walnut and cherry, ½-pint tins, 18c; 1-pint, 35c; 1-quart, 60c each.

Furniture varnish, ½-pint tins, 11c; 1-pint, 18c; 1-quart, 30c each.

Oak varnish, ½-pint tins, 16c; 1-pint, 28c; 1-quart, 45c each.

White varnish, same price as the oak.

White lead, 1-lb tins, 12c; 5-lb, 55c 12½-lb, $1.10 each.

Prepared kalsomine, blue, flesh, cream, green and terra cotta colors, 5-lb package, 20c each.

"G" furniture polish not only cleans, but gives the furniture a beautiful and lasting gloss, 4-oz bottle, 10c; 8-oz, 20c ea.

Wax and Finishes for Hardwood Floors.

Johnson's paste-wood filler, for new work only, 1 lb properly applied will cover 40 square feet. 1-lb tin, 12c; 25-lb can, $2.25 each.

Johnson's prepared wax, 1 lb will cover 300 square feet, 1 coat, put up in 1-lb, 2-lb and 5-lb tins, per lb 40c.

Johnson's floor finish, for natural woods, 1-quart bottle, 75c.

Johnson's floor restorer, will clean and restore the finish of hardwood floors, 1-pint bottle, 75c; 1-quart bottle, $1.25.

Johnson's natural wood renewer, for removing stains and discolorations, 1-quart bottle, 75c.

Steel shavings for rubbing down floors, per lb, 50c.

Johnson's weighted brushes, for polishing floors, 15-lb, $2.50; 25-lb, $3.00 each.

PREPARE FOR SPRING AND SUMMER BY ORDERING NOW.

Picture Department.

English strip etchings, size 12 x 22, pretty landscape scenes, framed with 1-inch oak moulding, 50c each.

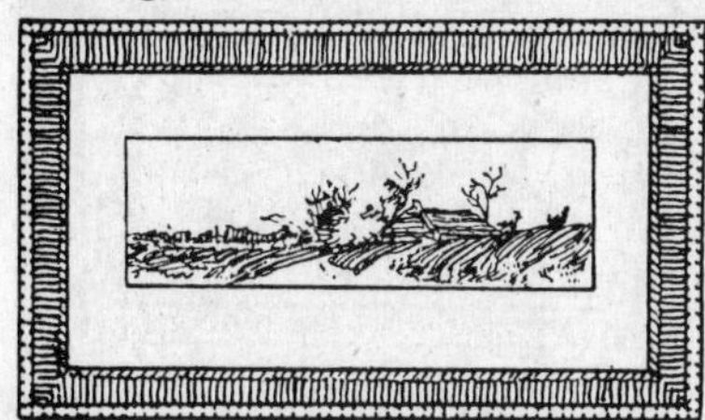

Artist-signed etchings, size 17 x 26, framed with 2-inch fancy oak moulding, with steel lining, $1.00; size 14 x 28, framed with 1½-inch polished ivory moulding, with gilt beading, $1.00 each.

Sepia colored etchings, choice selection of American landscape and water scenes, 3-inch Flemish brown moulding, with gilt strap inside, size 12 x 18, $1.75; 14 x 25, $2.25 each.

Steel-plate engravings (framed as cut), good assortment of standard subjects, such as The Combat, A Plunge for Life, Haying Time, The Life-Boat, Hunters at Rest, The Halt, and others, framed with 3-inch fancy oak moulding, with steel lining, sizes ranging from 28 x 34 to 30 x 40, $4.75 each.

Steel plate engravings, good selection of religious, military, marine and landscape subjects, sizes ranging from 22 x 27 to 30 x 40, framed with fancy walnut, oak and gilt mouldings, 3 and 4 inches wide, with 1-inch steel or gilt lining, $5.00, 5.50, 6.00, 7.50, 10.00 and 12.00 each.

Colored steel-plate engravings, choice and new military, figure and landscape subjects (sizes and complete description sent on application) framed to suit pictures, with heavy fancy oak and gilt Florentine mouldings, with gilt linings, $13.50, 15.00, 18.00, 20.00, 24.00 and 25.00 each.

Artotypes (framed as cut), size 18 x 24, St. Cecilia, Napoleon in 1806, and many other figure and landscape subjects, framed with 1½-inch polished oak moulding, 50c each.

Standard American artotypes, large assortment of figure, landscape and marine subjects, size 11 x 14, framed in 1-inch oak mouldings, 25c; 16 x 20, framed in 2-inch fancy oak moulding, with steel lining, 95c; 20 x 24, framed with 2½-inch oak moulding, with steel lining, $1.35; 22 x 28, framed in 3-inch fancy polished oak moulding, with steel lining, $2.00 each.

English photogravures, size 11 x 14, large assortment of landscape and figure subjects, framed with 1-inch fancy gilt moulding, $1.00 each.

Photogravures (framed as cut) platinum and sepia colored, size 15 x 20 and 16 x 22, choice landscape, marine and figure subjects, framed with 3-inch black and wax brown Florentine frames, burnished tips and solid corners, $3.50 each.

Colored pictures, in fancy color and gilt mouldings, landscape, figure and fruit subjects, size 11 x 14, 1-inch moulding, 25c; 16 x 20, 2-inch moulding, 50c; 20 x 24, 3-inch moulding, 75c; 22 x 28, 4-inch moulding, $1.25 each.

Yard pictures, size 8 x 36, colored flower and fruit subjects, framed with 1-inch white enamel and gilt and 1-inch plain gilt mouldings, 75c each.

Imported carbon photos, mounted on white pebbled mats, framed with 3-inch burnished gilt moulding, or 3-inch hardwood moulding, Flemish brown finish with burnished tips, choice landscape and marine scenes, size 12 x 19, $2.50; 14 x 23, $3.50 each.

Hand-colored pastels, landscape and water scenes, size 12 x 20, fitted with gilt mats, framed with 1-inch gilt moulding and brass corners, $2.25; 14 x 17, gilt mat with oval opening, framed with 1-inch gilt moulding and brass corners, $2.75; 16 x 24, olive and grey mats, framed with 2-inch gilt moulding and brass corners, $4.50; 18 x 26, gilt mat, oval opening, framed with 2-inch burnished gilt moulding, with solid brass burnished corners, $7.50 each.

Imitation pastels, colored fruit and landscape subjects, framed in fancy color and gilt mouldings, size 11 x 14, 1-inch moulding, 25c; 16 x 20, 2-inch moulding, 50c; 20 x 24, 3-inch moulding, 75c; 22 x 28, 4-inch moulding, $1.25 each.

French oil paintings (as cut), size 9 x 11, choice collection of handsomely colored figure and landscape subjects, framed with 2-inch high back Florentine gilt moulding, $3.25 each.

Artist-signed water colors (framed as cut), selected landscape and water scenes, fitted with 2-inch gilt mats, framed with 1-inch Florentine gilt moulding, sizes 11 x 14 and 8 x 18, $1.75; 8 x 26 and 10 x 22, $2.75 each.

Fancy table medallions, gilt frames, fancy brass corners, large assortment of figure subjects, size 6 x 8, 30c, 50c each.

Table medallions (as cut), photo colored, burnished gilt frames, neat brass corners, large assortment of subjects, size 7 x 9, 65c each.

Table medallions, size 8 x 10, plain and colored, large assortment of the newest subjects, gilt frames, with relief corners, 80c, $1.00 each.

Fancy table medallions (as cut), choice collection of head and figure subjects, handsomely colored, 1-inch gilt frame, with overlaid corners, size 11 x 14, $1.25 each.

Fancy table medallions, in a large variety of styles and subjects, sizes 10 x 13 and 11 x 14, solid brass and burnished corners, $1.75, 2.25, 2.75, 3.25 each.

Wall medallions, plain and colored, in a variety of designs, ranging in size from 13 x 17 to 16 x 20, framed with fancy gilt mouldings, projecting and overlaid corners, $2.25, 3.25, 3.50, 4.25, 5.00, 6.00, 7.50, 10.00 each.

Carbon and platinotype pictures, heads and fancy figure subjects, oval and oblong shapes, framed with black, grey and Flemish brown mouldings, $3.50, 4.00, 5.00, 7.50 each.

Picture Framing.

Our assortment of sample mouldings comprises the newest patterns, colors and finish. All kinds of frame moulding can be cut and mitred for any size picture ready to be put together, thus making smaller parcels and saving freight.

Four days are required for making complete frames. When ordering with other goods please state if we may hold them and ship with frames, or ship separately.

To find length of moulding required for frame, measure the four sides of picture, and allow eight times the width of moulding for waste in mitreing. We do not send out samples of frame mouldings.

The following is a list of prices for frames cut and mitred any size, or put together, without glass; all of the sizes given can be shipped at once from the mouldings illustrated below:

No. 2109. Combination frame, 2½-inch shaded oak outside, 3 inches deep roll shell gilt in side, size 16 x 20, 75c 18 x 22, 80c; 20 x 24 85c; 22 x 27, 95c each

No. 2959. Combination frame, 2½-in., fancy polished oak outside, 1½ inch roll gilt centre, 1-inch plain burnished gilt, and 1-inch figured gilt inside sizes 16 x 20, $1.65; 18 x 22, $1.80; 20 x 24, $2.00; 22 x 27, $2.20 each.

No. 2108. High back gilt, 3 inches wide, with fancy relief edge, burnished inside line, size 16 x 20, $2.00; 18 x 22, $2.20; 20 x 24, $2.40; 22 x 27, $2.65 each.

All the above frames have been specially selected for enlarged portraits in crayon, water color, sepia and pastel.

Glass for above frames, 16 x 20, 15c; 18 x 22, 20c; 20 x 24, 25c; 22 x 28, 30c each.

1-inch oak, antique and plain, 3c foot; carved, 4c foot; 1½-inch, plain or shaded, 4c foot; carved, 6c foot; 2-inch, plain or shaded, 6c foot; carved, 8c foot; 2½-inch, plain or shaded, 7c foot; carved, 10c foot; 3-inch, plain or shaded, 9c foot; carved, 14c foot; 4-inch, plain or shaded, 12c foot; carved, 18c foot.

Linings suitable for the same, in steel or gilt, ½-inch, 3c; ¾-inch, 4c; 1-inch, 5c foot.

Bone black and grey black mouldings, plain, 1-inch, 4½c; 1½-inch, 5c; 2-inch, 6c; 2½-inch, 7c; 3-inch, 8c foot.

Bone black and grey black mouldings, carved, with gilt ornament, 1-inch, 8c; 2-inch, 9c; 2½-inch, 12c; 3-inch, 18c foot.

Dark green mouldings, plain, ½-inch, 4c; 1-inch, 5c; 2-inch, 6c; 2½-inch, 8c; 3-inch, 9c foot.

Dark green mouldings, carved, with gilt ornament, ½-inch, 7½c; 1-inch, 10c; 2-inch, 13c; 2½-inch, 15c; 3-inch, 18c foot.

Mahogany, fancy carved, ½-inch, 6c; 1-inch, 15c; 2-inch, 18c foot.

Imitation mahogany, with gilt ornament, 1-inch, 7½c; 1½-inch, 10c; 2-inch, 15c; 2½-inch, 18c foot.

Fancy colored mouldings, in gilt and white, pink, gilt and white; blue, gilt and white; green, gilt and white; and olive green and gilt, 1-inch, 5c; 1½-inch, 6c; 2-inch, 7c; 2½-inch, 8c; 3-inch, 9c; 4-inch, 11c foot.

Flat or shell gilt mouldings, 1-inch, 4c; 1½-inch, 5c; 2-inch, 6c; 2½-inch, 7c; 3-inch, 8c; 4-inch, 10c foot.

Plain gilt mouldings, with ornamented edge, suitable for oil paintings, 1½-inch, 12c; 2-inch, 15c; 2½-inch, 18c; 3-inch, 23c; 4-inch, 30c foot.

Fancy Florentine mouldings, with open-work edge, in gilt, or olive green and gilt, 1-inch, 10c; 1½-inch, 12c; 2-inch, 14c; 2½-inch, 18c; 3-inch, 25c foot.

Ebony, black and brown wax mouldings, with gold burnished tips, 1-inch, 12c; 2-inch, 15c; 2½-inch, 18c; 3-inch, 20c foot.

Photos Enlarged.

Photos enlarged in crayon, water colors, sepia, and pastel. It takes from 6 to 10 days to enlarge photos. When ordered with other goods we will hold orders, unless otherwise instructed. All photos sent to be enlarged will be taken care of and returned with the enlargement.

Enlarged crayons, 16 x 20, $1.15; 18 x 22, $1.45; 20 x 24, $1.70; 22 x 27, $2.00 each.

Water colors, mounted on stretchers, 16 x 20, $2.00; 18 x 22, $2.50; 20 x 24, $2.75; 22 x 27, $3.00 each.

Enlargements made in sepia, same price as water colors.

Pastels, mounted on stretchers, 16 x 20, $2.75; 18 x 22, $3.25; 20 x 24, $3.75; 22 x 27, $4.25 each.

Pastels, very best finish, 16 x 20, $4.50; 18 x 22 $5.00 each.

Photo Frames.

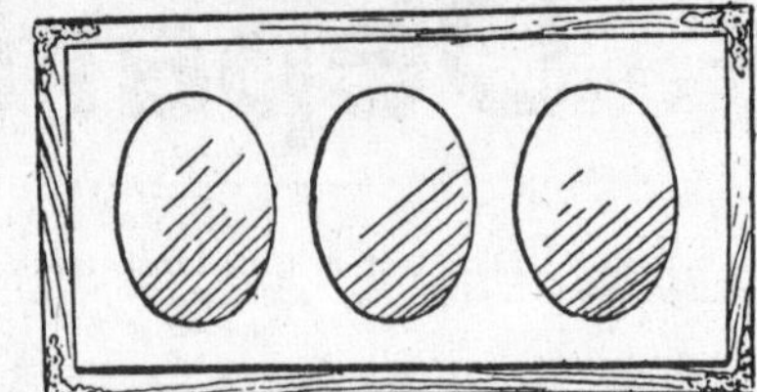

The latest styles in photo frames, ½-inch, black, white enamel, gilt and light and dark oak, fitted with plain and fancy colored mats, oval and square openings—

Size 8 x 10, 1 opening, 30c; 8 x 12, 2 openings, 40c; 8 x 16, 3 openings, 50c; 8 x 21, 4 openings, 60c; 8 x 26, 5 openings, 75c.

Miniature photo frames, in bronze, with burnished tips, oval and square shapes, with easel backs, 25c, 35c, 40c, 50c each.

Cabinet photo frames, in bronze, with burnished tips, fancy Florentine designs, 65c, 75c, $1.00, 1.25, 1.50 each.

Miniature photo frames, guaranteed quadruple gold plate, oval and square shapes, with easel backs, 90c, $1.15, 1.25, 1.40 and 1.75 each.

Cabinet photo frames, guaranteed quadruple gold plate, newest designs, fancy Florentine edge, oval and square shapes, $2.25, 2.50, 2.75, 3.25, 3.75, 4.25 and 4.75 each.

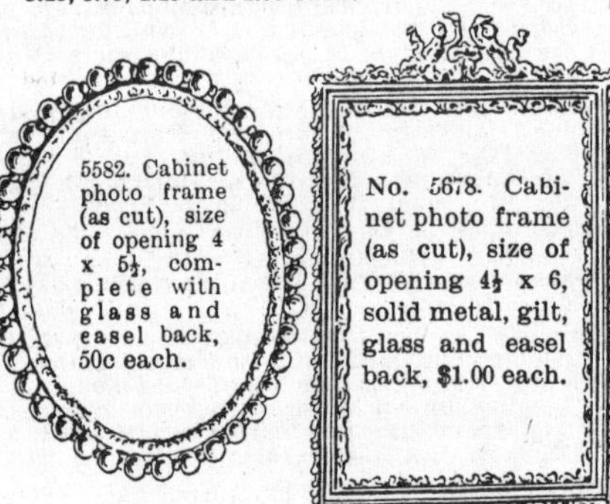

5582. Cabinet photo frame (as cut), size of opening 4 x 5½, complete with glass and easel back, 50c each.

No. 5678. Cabinet photo frame (as cut), size of opening 4½ x 6, solid metal, gilt, glass and easel back, $1.00 each.

7538. Cabinet photo frame (as cut), size of opening 5 x 7, solid metal, gilt with burnished ornaments and tips, glass and easel back, $1.35 each.

Mirrors.

No. 217. Mirrors, framed in 1-inch reeded moulding, oil finish, size 6 x 9, 12c; 8 x 10, 15c; 9 x 12, 18c; 10 x 14, 20c ea.

No. 215. Mirrors, arch top, framed with 2-inch walnut stained moulding and narrow gilt lining, size 7 x 9, 25c; 8 x 10, 30c; 9 x 12, 35c; 10 x 14, 45c; 10½ x 17, 55c; 12 x 18, 60c; 12 x 20, 65c; 13 x 22, 75c; 14 x 24, 85c each.

No. 271. Special line German plate mirrors, size 9 x 12-inch, 1-inch polished oak frame, 55c; 10 x 14, 1½-inch oak moulding, 75c; 10 x 17, 1½-inch oak moulding, $1.15; 12 x 18, 1½-inch, moulding, $1.35; 12 x 20, 1½-inch moulding, $1.60; 12 x 20, bevelled, 1½-inch moulding, $1.85; 14 x 24, 2-inch moulding, $2.75; 20 x 24, 2½-inch moulding, $3.68; 18 x 36, 2½-inch moulding, $5.25; 18 x 40, 2½-inch moulding, $6.00 each.

Wall Pockets.

Bamboo wall pockets, light, durable, size 14 x 15 inches, 35c each.

Oak wall pockets, strong and well made, size 15 x 17 inches, 50c each.

Wall pockets, white enamel and gilt, imitation pastel in front, with glass, size 16 x 19½, 65c ea.

No. 24135. Wall pockets (as cut), green bronze, tipped with silver, very handsome design, pretty colored scenes in front, with glass, size 17 x 24, 75c each.

Easels.

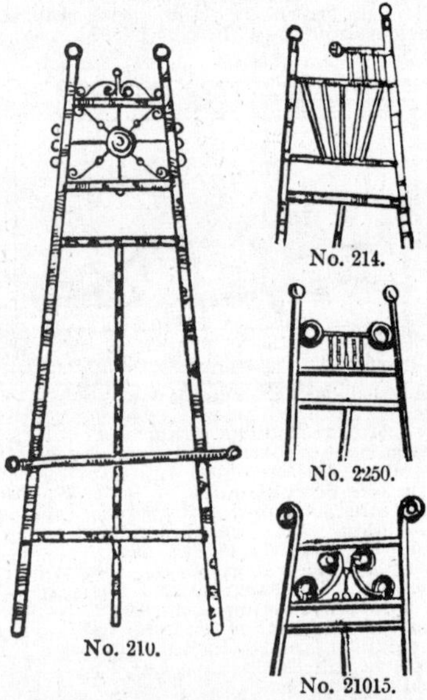

No. 214.

No. 2250.

No. 210.

No. 21015.

Bamboo easels, neat and strong, 60 inches high, 50c; bamboo easels, ornamented, 66 inches high, 65c, 85c each.

No. 214. Bamboo easel (as cut), 66 inches high, new design and well made, 75c each.

No. 210. Bamboo easel (as cut), 66 inches high, handsome design and durable, $1.15 each.

Oak easels, plain, 60 inches high, 50c; ornamented with brass trimmings, and adjustable rests, 66 inches high, 75c, $1.25, 1.50 and 2.25 ea

No. 2250. Oak easel (as cut), 60 inches high, polished oak, fancy top, adjustable rests, 90c each.

No. 21015. Oak easel (as cut), 62 inches high, polished oak, fancy top, brass trimmings and adjustable rests, $1.75 each.

Picture Wire.

(25 yards to a coil.)

Tinned, No. 0, 4c; No. 1, 7c; No. 2, 10c; No. 3, 15c; No. 4, 20c; No. 5, 25c coil.

Gilt, No. 11, 35c; No. 12, 40c; No. 13, 50c coil.

Picture Nails.

Brass-headed nails, 2½ inches long, 5c doz; porcelain slide-head nails, 15c doz; fancy colored slide-head nails, 25c doz.

Brass Moulding Hooks.

Made to fit 1-inch, 1½-inch and 2-inch mouldings, 10c, 18c, 25c, 30c, 35c and 40c doz.

CONDENSED INDEX TO DEPARTMENTS.

A

B

C

D

E

F

G

H

I

J

K

INDEX.

If you do not see in this List or Catalogue the goods you require, kindly write us.

For Sporting and Summer Goods, Write for Summer Catalogue—READY MAY 15TH.

FALL & WINTER
1901 - 1902

FOR PRICES OF THESE
GARMENTS SEE LAST
PAGE OF CATALOGUE

THE T. EATON Co. LIMITED

190 YONGE St. TORONTO CANADA

Instructions for Shoppers by Mail.

Follow instructions on this page, and we guarantee satisfaction or refund money.

☛ This Catalogue cancels all former prices

1. Our Terms—Net cash with order.

2. How to Send Money—

The **best way** is by Express Money Order.

Cost of Express Money Orders—

$5.00 and under	3c.	Over $30.00 to $50.00	15c.
Over 5.00 to 10.00	6c.	" 50.00 at same rate.	
" 10.00 " 30.00	10c.		

The **next best way** is by Post Office Orders, or Postal Notes.

Cost of Post Office Orders—

If not exceeding	$2.50,	3c.	Over $40.00 and up to	$50.00,	20c.
Over $2.50 and up to	5.00,	4c.	" 50.00 "	60.00,	24c.
" 5.00 "	10.00,	6c.	" 60.00 "	70.00,	28c.
" 10.00 "	20.00,	10c.	" 70.00 "	80.00,	32c.
" 20.00 "	30.00,	12c.	" 80.00 "	90.00,	36c.
" 30.00 "	40.00,	15c.	" 90.00 "	100.00,	40c.

Postal Notes from 20c to 40c, cost 1c; from 50c to $2.50, cost 2c.
We also accept bank drafts.
If none of the above ways are convenient, send by registered letter carefully sealed.
Do not send money unregistered. It is unsafe.
For amounts smaller than $1.00, and over 20c, use Postal Notes whenever possible.
If absolutely necessary to send stamps, send those of large denominations.
Do not send 2c stamps or silver, if you can avoid it.

3. How to Write an Order—

Write distinctly.
Use our Order Forms if possible. We supply them free.
Give your name in full, using Mr., Mrs., or Miss.
Give Post Office, County and Province.
State exact amount of money sent.
State how and where goods are to be shipped: Freight, Express, or Mail.
Order each article on a separate line.
Give size, quantity, color, price, page and number of Catalogue.
When ordering from samples attach your choice to the Order Sheet.
Give second and third choice, if possible.
Where any goods are sold out we will substitute, using our best judgment, unless you tell us not to.

4. À nos Clients Français—

Nous préférons que vous nous écriviez en Anglais, mais si vous ne pouvez pas, alors veuillez écrire distinctement en Français. En envoyant vos ordres mentionnez toujours la page du Catalogue et le numéro de l'article.
Pour les commandes par la poste ajoutez l'argent en plus pour le port et 5 cents pour l'enregistrement.

5. Cost of Sending by Express or Freight—

When possible, have your goods sent by Freight or Express, as it is usually cheaper.
The railway companies guarantee safe delivery.
Parcels weighing over 2 pounds and under 25 pounds, will generally go cheaper by Express, and over 25 pounds, cheaper by Freight.
When ordering by Freight, try to order enough goods to make your shipment reach 100 pounds.
The first 100 pounds will cost no more than 25 pounds.
If the weight is 100 pounds or over, you are charged for at the actual rate only, at the rate per pound.
A shipment put up in two or more parcels or cases, does not cost any more than if put up in one parcel.
The charge is not by the number of parcels, but by the total weight.
When goods are to be shipped to a Flag Station (where there is no agent), sufficient money must be allowed to prepay charges, otherwise they will be sent to the nearest regular station.
To a regular station, charges can be paid on arrival of goods.
We have no special rates.
We make no charges for cases or packing.
Do not sign for goods if damaged.

6. Cost of Sending by Mail—

(Postage must be prepaid by customer.)
On general merchandise one cent per ounce, or 16c per pound.
On books (printed), one cent per four ounces.
On music (in book or sheet form), blank books and photo albums, one cent for two ounces.
Notepaper, or pads and envelopes, one cent per ounce.
The limit of weight is 5 pounds, and the limit of size is 30 inches in length by one foot in width or depth.
Should goods weigh more than 5 pounds, they can be put in two or more parcels.
Always enclose sufficient for postage and **5c.** extra for safe delivery. (See No. 7, "Delivery Guarantee.")
If not enough is sent to pay all the postage, we will omit some of the goods, send them by Express, or delay goods by writing for necessary balance.
If too much money is sent it will be returned.

7. Delivery Guarantee—

5c extra with each order over $1.00 guarantees safe delivery of your goods if they are to be sent by mail.
We will deduct 5c from your remittance for above purpose unless otherwise instructed.
Unless 5c extra is enclosed you run your own risk.
Goods sent by freight or express are guaranteed safe delivery by the companies who carry them.

8. Club Orders—

Two or more persons can *reduce Transportation Charges* by making up an order of 100 pounds or over, having goods sent in one shipment to one address.
We parcel and tag each order separately.
Each order must be written on a separate sheet, just the same as any other order.
State on each as follows: "Enclose with Mr.......'s order"—giving the name of the person to whom the goods are to be shipped.
The person to whom the goods are to be shipped must write shipping instructions fully in his letter, and state what orders are to be enclosed.
All orders must be mailed at one time.

9. Send for Samples—

We send samples of cut goods free; but you must always state color, quality and price you wish to pay.
When ordering from samples, attach your choice to the Order Form separate from other samples.
Make a second and third choice, if possible.
When returning the unused samples send them in separate envelope tied, not sealed.
Attach a one cent stamp for every four ounces.
Do not enclose correspondence.

10. Delays and Complaints—

If you do not hear from us within a reasonable time after sending an order or receiving goods, or if the goods are not satisfactory write us, giving date of your order and order number, if possible; state where and when you mailed, how addressed, amount of money sent and whether by Express Money Order, Post Office Order, cheque, cash or stamps.
If by registered letter, Post Office Order or Postal Note, give number.
Send copy of your order as near as possible.
If goods are short state what received and in how many parcels.
All claims must be made within 5 days after goods are delivered.

11. Exchanging Goods—

We will exchange or refund money for goods if not satisfactory, if returned at once and in good condition, with the following exceptions:

Goods made to order according to measurement.
Cut goods sent according to samples.
Gloves that have been worn.
Veils, hair or toilet goods, such as brushes and combs.
Rubber goods, such as hot water bags, syringes, etc.
Goods not catalogued which have been procured specially to your order.

12. How to Return Goods—

Enclose bills for goods returned, but no correspondence.
Pack securely and address to us.
Write your name and address in left hand corner, with the word "from" before it.
Prepay charges cheapest way.
Write us separately, giving full particulars.
If bills are lost, state how and when goods were purchased.

13. Special Notice—

We will not hold for instructions bargains or goods advertised at special prices in Toronto daily papers.
Shipping instructions must accompany money.
Be sure to send sufficient for postage on goods by mail.
Hats should be sent by express. They may be crushed in the mails, and we are not responsible.
Daily we receive letters with money but no name or address. We hold them till claimed.
Only printed matter (not ordinary correspondence) will go for one cent in an open envelope.
We employ no agents.
No goods held unless paid for.

14. Estimates

Will be promptly furnished for outfitting Hotels, Boarding Houses, Camps, Steamboats, etc.

Address all communications to—

THE T. EATON Co. LIMITED,
190 YONGE STREET,
TORONTO, CAN.

LADIES' COSTUMES AND DRESSES.

Sizes in Ladies' Ready-Made Dresses are 32 to 42 inches bust measure; skirt lengths, 39 to 43 inches, and waistbands of skirts 22 to 29 inches. Sizes not included in our regular stock can be supplied at 10 per cent. extra.
When ordering send measurements according to form on page 84.

No. 4529. LADIES' DRESS, made of black and navy cheviot serge, bodice is trimmed with applique lace and velvet ribbon, and has front of black or white taffeta silk **11.00**

No. 4527. LADIES' DRESS, made of albatross cloth, colors black, navy, grey and old rose, front and cuff of black or colored taffeta silk; trimmed with silk gimp and strappings of ribbon velvet, yoke of applique lace **12.50**

No. 4524. LADIES' DRESS, made of albatross cloth, colors black, navy, grey and old rose, trimmed with black velvet ribbon and silk applique lace, and has black or colored taffeta silk front, with tucks **12.50**

No. 6170. LADIES' DRESS, made of black and navy pebble serge, has pipings and trimmings of black taffeta silk, with fancy braid, bodice is lined with silkaline **13.50**

No. 4526. LADIES' CHEVIOT SERGE DRESS, colors black and navy, bodice trimmed with narrow velvet ribbon and applique lace, with front of black or colored taffeta silk. **14.00**

No. 4528. LADIES' STYLISH DRESS, of black and navy cheviot serge; skirt has flaring frills, finished with rows of tucking; bodice is finished with fine tucks and lace applique, and has front of black or colored taffeta silk..... **15.00**

No. 6172. LADIES' ENGLISH CHEVIOT SERGE DRESS, colors black and navy; bodice is lined with black taffeta silk and has vest of peau de soie silk, finished back and front with tucks; skirt is trimmed with wide-stitched strap of peau de soie silk and narrow satin bands.. **15.00**

No. 4525. LADIES' BROADCLOTH DRESS, colors black, navy, fawn, brown, red and grey, trimmed with narrow velvet ribbon, bodice has black or colored taffeta silk front, covered with chiffon and applique lace........... **16.50**

No. 6171. LADIES' BROADCLOTH DRESS, colors black, navy, fawn and grey, bodice is lined with taffeta and has collar and vest of peau de soie silk; skirt is trimmed with stitched velvet band with peau de soie pipings **16.50**

LADIES' SUITS.

Sizes in Ladies' Suits are 32 to 42 inches bust measure; skirt lengths 39 to 43 inches, and waistbands of skirts 22 to 29 inches. Skirts, unless otherwise stated, are lined with percaline and bound with good quality velveteen. Sizes other than our regular stock cost 10 per cent. extra. For further particulars and measurement form, see page 84.

No. 6138. LADIES' SUIT, of fancy mixed cheviots, colors black, navy, fawn, brown, cadet, and dark grey, jacket lined with Egerton sateen **6.98**

No. 6135. LADIES' SUIT, made of fancy mixed cheviots, colors black, navy, fawn, brown, grey, blue and Oxford, jacket lined with Egerton sateen, skirt trimmed with narrow satin folds **7.50**

No. 6140. LADIES' WALKING SUIT, made of English cheviot mixtures, colors medium grey, Oxford grey, black, navy, green and brown, skirt is unlined, coat is lined with mercerized Italian **8.00**

No. 6142. LADIES' SUIT, made of fine quality worsted cheviot, colors black and navy, jacket is lined with silk serge, skirt and jacket are trimmed with taffeta silk straps **10.00**

No. 6159. LADIES' SUIT, made of Rockwood homespun, shades light grey, medium grey, Oxford grey and brown, also black and navy cheviot, strictly all-wool material; the jacket is lined with silk serge.......... **10.00**

No. 6150. LADIES' SUIT, made of all-wool worsted cheviot serge, colors black and navy; coat is lined with black taffeta silk and has silk facings; the skirt and coat are trimmed with stitched taffeta silk bands.......... **12.00**

No. 6148. LADIES' SUIT, made of all-wool cheviot serge, colors black and navy, jacket is lined with heavy black satin **12.50**

No. 6149. LADIES' SUIT, made of high grade English pebble serge, colors black and navy, jacket has silk facing and is lined with black taffeta silk **12.50**

No. 6141. LADIES' SUIT, made of heavy all-wool worsted cheviot, in black and navy; jacket is lined with good wearing black satin and has silk facings **13.50**

LADIES' SUITS.

Sizes in Ladies' Suits are 32 to 42 inches bust measure; skirt lengths 39 to 43 inches, and waistbands of skirts 22 to 29 inches. Skirts, unless otherwise stated, are lined with percaline and bound with good quality velveteen. Sizes not included in our regular stock cost 10 per cent. extra. For further particulars and measurement form see page 84.

No. 6137. LADIES' BLACK BOX-CLOTH SUIT, with taffeta silk vest; the coat is lined with good quality black taffeta silk, and the trimming is of black taffeta and silk rings **15.00**

No. 6146. LADIES' SUIT, made of high-grade English worsted cheviot serge, colors black and navy; jacket is lined with good taffeta silk, is faced with peau de soie, and has velvet collar; the trimming is of silk-stitched taffeta silk.................................... **15.00**

No. 6147. LADIES' SUIT, made of fine all-wool tucked cheviot serge, colors black and navy; jacket is lined with heavy black satin, with silk facings; skirt has drop lining of mercerized Italian, with four small ruffles **15.00**

No. 6160. LADIES' SUIT, made of choice all-wool English worsted cheviot, colors black and navy; jacket is lined with heavy black taffeta silk and trimmed with silk velvet ribbon.................................... **16.50**

No. 6169. LADIES' SUIT, made of fine all-wool broadcloth, colors black, navy, brown, castor and royal blue; jacket is lined with heavy taffeta silk, the trimming is velvet stitched, and silk bands.................................... **17.50**

No. 6145. LADIES' SUIT, made of fine all-wool tucked cheviot serge, colors black and navy; jacket is lined with heavy black taffeta silk, and skirt has drop lining with deep accordion-plaited taffeta silk ruffle; suit is trimmed with stitched taffeta silk **18.50**

No. 6162. LADIES' FINE COVERT CLOTH SUIT, colors black, navy, royal blue and Oxford grey, jacket has heavy satin lining, skirt and jacket are trimmed with taffeta silk and fancy braid **20.00**

No. 6168. LADIES SUIT, made of choice black French pebble cheviot; jacket is lined with heavy black taffeta silk, and the skirt has drop lining with accordion-plaited ruffles of black taffeta, the trimming is black taffeta bands and silk crochet rings **20.00**

No. 6161. LADIES' SUIT, made of fine all-wool cheviot, in black only, lined throughout with heavy black taffeta silk; skirt has drop lining with accordion-plaited ruffle, trimmed with stitched satin, with narrow satin straps **25.00**

LADIES' JACKETS

Sizes in Ladies' Jackets are 32, 34, 36, 38, 40 and 42 inches bust measure, and length of sleeve (inside seam) 18½ inches. Sizes other than our regular stock can be supplied at an additional cost of 10 per cent.
When ordering, send measurements according to form on page 84.

No. 6240. HEAVY FRIEZE JACKET, colors black, navy, Oxford, medium grey, light grey, fawn and brown, has velvet collar 3.50

No. 6270. ENGLISH BEAVER CLOTH JACKET, colors black, navy, fawn and brown, revers finished with stitching 3.98

No. 6271. ENGLISH BEAVER CLOTH JACKET. colors black, navy, fawn, brown and green, sacque back 4.00

No. 6263. BEAVER CLOTH JACKET, colors black, navy, fawn, brown, green and red, lined throughout with mercerized sateen, has velvet collar 5.00

No. 6269. ALL-WOOL ROCKWOOD FRIEZE JACKET, colors black, navy, Oxford, light grey, medium grey, fawn, brown and blue, has box back 5.00

No. 6272. BEAVER CLOTH JACKET, colors black, navy, brown and fawn, lined throughout with silkaline 5.00

No. 6273. HEAVY CHEVIOT JACKET, colors Oxford, navy, brown, fawn, green, light grey and medium grey, lined throughout with mercerized sateen, revers, collar and cuffs trimmed with velvet applique 6.00

No. 6241. HEAVY ALL-WOOL FRIEZE JACKET, colors black, navy, brown, blue mixture, Oxford, medium grey, light grey and fawn, lined throughout with silkaline, has velvet collar and pipings 6.50

No. 6249. ALL-WOOL ENGLISH BEAVER CLOTH JACKET, colors black, navy, brown, green, light fawn and dark fawn, lined throughout with silkaline, has velvet collar 6.50

No. 6242. FINE BEAVER CLOTH JACKET, colors black and navy, lined throughout with silkaline, fastened with large pearl buttons, sacque back 7.50

LADIES' JACKETS.

Sizes in Ladies' Jackets are 32, 34, 36, 38, 40 and 42 inches bust measure, and length of sleeve (inside seam) 18½ inches. Sizes other than our regular stock can be supplied at an additional cost of 10 per cent.

When ordering, send measurements according to form on page 84.

No. 6259. HEAVY ALL-WOOL FRIEZE JACKET, colors black, navy, Oxford, medium grey, fawn, brown and blue, lined throughout with satin, has sacque back 7.50

No 6266. FINE ENGLISH KERSEY CLOTH JACKET, colors black, navy, light fawn, dark fawn, brown and green, lined throughout with silk serge, sacque back.......... 8 00

No. 6258 PRESTON KERSEY CLOTH JACKET, colors black and navy, lined throughout with satin, has velvet collar and pearl buttons, back finished with wide stitched straps 8.50

No. 6264. BEST QUALITY PRESTON CHEVIOT JACKET, colors dark grey and Oxford, lined throughout with black satin, revers faced with black peau de soie silk, has velvet collar and black covered buttons.. 8.50

No 6243. FINE ALL-WOOL KERSEY CLOTH JACKET, colors black, navy, light fawn, dark fawn, and castor, lined throughout with satin, box back finished with wide straps, velvet collar and large pearl buttons.... 10.00

No. 6265. ALL-WOOL ROCKWOOD FRIEZE JACKET, colors black, navy, Oxford, dark grey, fawn and brown, lined throughout with satin, has straps of self and velvet trimmings, pearl buttons 10.00

No. 6268 FINE ALL-WOOL KERSEY CLOTH JACKET, colors black, navy, light fawn and dark fawn, lined throughout with heavy satin, collar and revers faced with finely stitched velvet, pearl buttons 10 00

No. 6257. FINE ENGLISH KERSEY CLOTH JACKET, colors black, navy, light fawn and dark fawn, lined throughout with satin, finished with stitching, has pearl buttons, box back........ 11.00

No. 6261. FINEST ALL-WOOL KERSEY CLOTH JACKET, colors black, light fawn and dark fawn, new collar, trimmed with rows of stitching and straps of material, lined throughout with satin, has pearl buttons........ 12.50

No. 6262. FINEST ALL-WOOL KERSEY CLOTH JACKET, colors black, navy, light fawn and castor, lined throughout with good quality satin, revers, pockets and bottom of coat trimmed with stitched velvet, has pearl buttons, box back........ 14.00

Ladies' Automobile and Sealette Coats.

Sizes in Ladies' Jackets are 32, 34, 36, 38, 40 and 42 inches bust measure, and length of sleeve (inside seam) 18½ inches. Sizes other than our regular stock can be supplied at an additional cost of 10 per cent.

When ordering, send measurements according to form on page 84.

No. 6247. LADIES' AUTOMOBILE COAT, made of English kersey cloth, colors black, navy, light fawn and dark fawn, lined throughout with silk serge, has pearl buttons, box back, length 35 inches **10.00**

No. 6246. LADIES' AUTOMOBILE COAT, made of good quality Preston cheviot, colors Oxford and medium grey, lined throughout with heavy black satin, box back, is fastened with large pearl buttons, length 36 inches **12.00**

No, 6248. LADIES' AUTOMOBILE COAT, made of heavy all-wool Rockwood frieze, colors black, navy, Oxford, medium grey and fawn, lined throughout with good quality satin, has box back, is fastened with pearl buttons, length 43 inches **13.50**

No. 6256. BLACK SILK SEALETTE COAT, body lined with quilted satin, sleeves satin lined **10.00**

No. 6251. BLACK SILK SEALETTE COAT, body lined with quilted mercerette, sleeves lined mercerette........................ **10.00**

No. 6254. EXTRA QUALITY BLACK SILK SEALETTE COAT, body lined with quilted satin, sleeves satin lined................ **13.50**

No. 6252. GOOD QUALITY BLACK SILK SEALETTE COAT, body lined with quilted mercerized sateen, sleeves lined with mercerized sateen.............................. **11.50**

No. 6255. EXTRA QUALITY BLACK SILK SEALETTE COAT, body lined with quilted satin, sleeves satin lined................. **15.00**

No. 6250. GOOD QUALITY BLACK SILK SEALETTE COAT, body lined with quilted satin, sleeves satin lined, revers, collar and cuffs finished with silk soutache braiding. **15.00**

No. 6253. GOOD QUALITY BLACK SILK SEALETTE COAT, body lined with quilted satin, sleeves satin lined **18.50**

Ladies' Waists and Raglan Coats.

Raglan Coats are made 32 to 42 inches bust measure. When ordering, send bust measure and length of back. Measure downward from back of neck. Bust measure only is required for Waists.

No. 6300. LADIES' RAGLAN COAT, made of medium weight vicuna cheviot, colors grey, Oxford and black, has silk velvet collar and cuffs 9.50

No. 6301. LADIES' RAGLAN COAT, made of heavy weight vicuna cheviot, colors light grey, dark grey, and Oxford grey, silk velvet collar, has satin-lined raglan sleeves.... 10.00

No. 6302. LADIES' RAGLAN COAT, made of heavy weight vicuna cheviot, colors light grey, dark grey, and Oxford grey, sleeves are satin lined 10.00

No. 6303. LADIES' LIGHT WEIGHT RAGLAN COAT, made of fine quality all-wool covert cloth, shades fawn, navy and Oxford grey, sleeves and body are lined with satin, collar is of silk velvet 15.00

No. 6304. LADIES' LIGHT WEIGHT NEW-MARKET, made of high grade covert cloth, shades Oxford grey, black and navy, has silk velvet collar, body and sleeves lined with heavy black satin 18.50

No. 5051. LADIES' BLACK MERCERIZED ITALIAN WAIST, front and back corded, lined throughout with percaline.......... 1.39

No. 5047. LADIES' WAIST, made of finest black satin-finished mercerized Italian, front, back and sleeves finished with fine tucks, trimmed with silk-covered buttons 2.75

No. 5049. LADIES' SILK-EMBROIDERED FLANNEL WAIST, colors black, navy, sky, pink, cardinal, old rose, tan and lavender, lined throughout 3.00

No. 5050. LADIES' FLANNEL WAIST, colors black, navy, royal, cardinal, old rose, green, light blue and cream, front and back finished with fancy stitching and trimmed with silk-covered buttons, lined throughout 3.00

No. 5052. LADIES' TAFFETA SILK WAIST, colors black, navy, royal, sky, turquoise, cardinal, cerise, grey, white, pink, old rose and helio, finished with tucks and hemstitching, and silk-covered buttons 5.00

No. 5045. LADIES' GUARANTEED BLACK TAFFETA SILK WAIST, front, back and sleeves finished with tucks and hemstitching, trimmed with black silk-covered buttons, lined with percaline............ 8.50

No. 6910. CHILD'S BEAVER CLOTH GRETCHEN COAT, colors navy, green, red and royal blue, braid trimmed, sizes 4 to 12 years, length, 27-inch, $4.00; 30-inch, $4.50; 33-inch, $5.00; 36-inch, $5.50; 39-inch 6.00

SILK WAISTS

Sizes in Silk Waists are 32 to 42 inches bust measure. Waist No. 5030 is made in black only, all other numbers are made in black, navy, sky, turquoise, old rose, cardinal, cerise, royal, white, pink and heliotrope.
All waists illustrated are lined throughout.

No. 5033. TAFFETA SILK WAIST, in black and colors, front, back and sleeves are tucked 3.00

No. 5036. TAFFETA SILK WAIST, in black and colors, front, back and sleeves finished with tucks and hemstitching........... 3.75

No. 5039. TAFFETA SILK WAIST, in black and colors, front and back tucked and hemstitched.............................. 4.50

No. 5037. TAFFETA SILK WAIST, in black and colors, front, back and sleeves finished with cording and hemstitching 5.00

No. 5040. TAFFETA SILK WAIST, in black and colors, has hemstitched vest, back, front and sleeves finished with hemstitching and clusters of tucks 5.00

No. 5038. TAFFETA SILK WAIST, in black and colors, collar and cuffs tucked, back, front and sleeves prettily finished with clusters of hemstitching and tucks 5.00

No. 5030. BLACK DUCHESSE SATIN WAIST, front, back, and sleeves finished with clusters of tucks, trimmed with black silk covered buttons 6.00

No. 5035. BLACK AND COLORED TAFFETA SILK WAIST, finished all over with fine tucking, bolero effect with stitched strap of self, trimmed with silk covered buttons, new collar 6.00

No. 5034. TAFFETA SILK WAIST, in black and colors, back, front and sleeves finished with fine tucking and hemstitching, new collar and tie, trimmed with black silk covered buttons 6.50

No. 5042. HEAVY TAFFETA SILK WAIST, in black and colors, collar, cuffs and deep yoke back and front finely tucked, trimmed with straps of self, and small silk covered buttons 7.50

No. 5041. FANCY SILK WAIST, made in black and colored taffeta silk, white silk cuffs and yoke, finished with narrow straps of self color silk, trimming of fine tucks and small buttons 8.50

LADIES' WAISTS.

Sizes 32 to 42 inches bust measure.

No. 201. BLACK SATEEN WAIST, finished back and front with small box-pleat tucking, unlined 98c

No. 203. CASHMERE WAIST, colors black, sky, cardinal, garnet, cream, heliotrope, old rose and plum, back and sleeves finished with box-pleat tucking, lined throughout......1.50

No. 214. VELVETEEN WAIST, colors black, navy, cardinal, green and plum, finished back and front with box-pleats, unlined 1.75

No. 212. PLAIN BLACK LUSTRE WAIST, finished back and front with large stitched tucks, lined with percaline................1.98

No. 5015. ELEGANT BLACK SATIN-FINISHED MERCERETTE WAIST, trimmed with 71 rows of silk-stitched cording, detachable collar, body lined with percaline 1.98

No. 5031. CASHMERE WAIST, colors black, navy, sky, cardinal, garnet, cream, old rose, plum and heliotrope, finished all over with clusters of fine tucks, lined throughout 2.00

No. 5043. FINE FRENCH FLANNEL WAIST, colors black, navy, royal, cardinal, old rose, blue, green, cream and turquoise, front finished with fine tucks and stitching, lined throughout....................................2.25

No. 5044. WAIST MADE OF SILK-FINISHED MERCERIZED ITALIAN, black only, collar, cuffs and deep yoke finished with cording, back has clusters of cording, trimmed with straps of self, lined with percaline..2.50

No. 5046. WAIST MADE OF ALBATROSS CLOTH, colors black, navy, cardinal, sky and cream, front finely tucked, back finished with clusters of tucks, trimmed with silk-covered buttons, lined throughout.................2.50

No. 213. PLAIN BLACK LUSTRE WAIST, front, back and sleeves finished with fine tucking, lined throughout with percaline 2.50

No. 5024. PLAIN LUSTRE WAIST, colors black and navy, finely tucked all over, lined with percaline.................................2.98

LADIES' DRESS SKIRTS

Ladies' Dress Skirts are 22 to 29 inches waistband, and 38 to 43 inches long in front. Sizes not included in our regular stock cost 10 per cent. extra. All skirts, unless otherwise stated, are lined with percaline and bound with good quality velveteen.

No. 4058. DRESS SKIRT, of English cheviot serge, colors black, navy, fawn, Oxford, medium grey, blue, brown and green mixtures, flare bottom, finished with stitching 3.00

No. 4045. DRESS SKIRT of all-wool homespun, colors blue, brown, medium grey, light grey, Oxford, and blue grey, finished with stitching 3.69

No. 4051. ENGLISH CHEVIOT SERGE DRESS SKIRT, colors black, navy, brown, medium grey and Oxford, trimmed with stitched band of satin, flounce only, lined and interlined 3.98

No. 4044. ALL-WOOL HOMESPUN DRESS SKIRT, colors black, brown, medium grey, blue, Oxford, and blue and grey mixture, trimmed with narrow stitched straps of satin 5.00

No. 4057. DRESS SKIRT, of black and navy fine all-wool cheviot serge, made with flounce and trimmed with stitched taffeta silk .. 5.00

No. 4047. DRESS SKIRT, of black satin amazon cloth, trimmed with stitched bands of satin 6.00

No. 4054. ENGLISH CHEVIOT SERGE DRESS SKIRT, colors black and navy, flounce trimmed with satin pipings 7.50

No. 4040. DRESS SKIRT, of black and navy English pebble serge, flounce finished with rows of stitching 7.50

No. 4041. BLACK BROADCLOTH DRESS SKIRT, corded flounce, finished with stitched strap of self 8.50

No. 4053. DRESS SKIRT, made of black and navy pebble serge, trimmed with narrow satin bands 8.50

Ladies' Dress and Walking Skirts

Ladies' Dress Skirts are 22 to 29 inches waistband, and 38 to 43 inches long in front. Ladies' Walking Skirts are 22 to 29 inches waistband, and 36 to 41 inches long. Sizes not included in our regular stock cost 10 per cent. extra.

All Skirts, unless otherwise stated, are lined with percaline and bound with good quality velveteen.

No. 6012. DRESS SKIRT, of black and navy cheviot serge, has deep flounce trimmed with stitched straps of black taffeta silk..6.50

No. 6011. HEAVY ALL-WOOL COVERT CLOTH DRESS SKIRT, colors black, navy, fawn, brown and Oxford grey, has deep corded flounce 8.50

No. 4050. BLACK BROADCLOTH DRESS SKIRT, finished all-over with tucking, plain flounce trimmed with wide stitched band of taffeta silk 9.00

No. 4052. DRESS SKIRT, of black satin Amazon cloth, made with flounce, trimmed with tucked taffeta silk straps and narrow bands of black satin 10.00

No. 4056. FINE BLACK BROADCLOTH DRESS SKIRT, made with new deep flounce, trimmed with wide straps of self and narrow black satin bands and pipings 12.50

No. 4059. BLACK TAFFETA SILK SKIRT, made with flounce, finished with frill embroidered in silk soutache and point d'esprit 12.50

No. 4064. BLACK TAFFETA SILK DRESS SKIRT, made with deep flounce, embroidered with silk soutache braid and point d'esprit, finished with ribbon ruching ..15.00

No. 4060. ELEGANT BLACK TAFFETA SILK SKIRT, finely tucked, with flounces handsomely embroidered with silk soutache and point d'esprit 18.50

No. 4063. WALKING SKIRT, made of heavy homespun cheviots, unlined, colors black, navy, brown, green, grey and Oxford, stitched around bottom 3.00

No. 4043. WALKING SKIRT, of homespun cheviot, colors black, navy, fawn, brown, blue, medium and Oxford grey, made with flounce, is finished with stitching, unlined 3.98

No. 4062. WALKING SKIRT of black and navy pebble serge, has stitched flounce, seams tailor stitched, unlined 5.00

No. 4061. WALKING SKIRT of check-back tweeds, colors light, medium and dark grey, brown and Oxford, has stitched flounce, unlined 6.50

LADIES' CAPES.

Sizes in Ladies' Capes are 34 to 42 inches bust measure.

No. 2141. BLACK BEAVER CLOTH CAPE, has black Thibet fur collar, length 30 inches 3.98

No. 2142. BLACK BEAVER CLOTH CAPE, has black Thibet fur collar and fronts, length 30 inches 5.00

No. 2143. BLACK BEAVER CLOTH CAPE, same style as No. 2142, with black Thibet fur collar and fronts, length 32 inches 6.50

No. 2146. BLACK WOOL CREPON CAPE, collar and fronts edged with coney fur, lined with wadded and quilted mercerette, length 30 inches 5.00

No. 2151. BLACK VICUNA CLOTH CAPE, trimmed with wide silk-stitched band of satin, edged with black coney fur, length 30 inches 5.00

No. 2131. BLACK SILK PLUSH CAPE, collar and fronts edged with black Thibet fur, lined with silk-finished mercerette, length 30 inches 6.00

No. 2133. BLACK SILK PLUSH CAPE, same style as No. 2133, collar and fronts edged with black Thibet fur, lined with silk-finished mercerette, length 33 inches 7.50

No. 2148. BLACK SILK BROCHE CAPE, has Thibet fur collar, lined throughout with mercerette, length 32 inches 6.98

No. 2132. BLACK SILK PLUSH CAPE, embroidered with jet and mohair braid, collar and fronts edged with black Thibet fur, lined with mercerette, length 30 inches 6.98

No. 4751. BEAVER CLOTH CAPE, colors black, navy, green and crimson, has black Thibet fur collar, finished with rows of stitching, length 34 inches 7.50

No. 2149. BLACK SILK BROCHE CAPE, black Thibet fur collar and fronts, lined with wadded and quilted mercerized Italian, length 32 inches 8.00

No. 4753. BLACK SILK BROCHE CAPE, good quality, has black Thibet fur collar and fronts, lined with wadded and quilted mercerette, length 32 inches 9.50

LADIES' CAPES.

Sizes in Ladies' Capes are 34 to 42 inches bust measure.

No. 4750. HIGH-GRADE ENGLISH BEAVER CLOTH CAPE, colors black, navy, crimson, green, fawn and brown, lined with mercerized Italian, has extra large storm collar of black Thibet fur, and same trimmings down front, length 34 inches........................12.50

No. 4755. LADIES' STREET AND EVENING CAPE, made of fine quality box-cloth, colors black, navy, cardinal, grey, cadet and fawn, trimmed with good quality Thibet fur, has heavy quilted mercerized lining, length 30 inches........................12.50

No. 4754. LADIES' CAPE, made of best quality all-wool black beaver cloth, trimmed with folds of black satin and silk-stitched cording, lined throughout with heavy black satin, length 40 inches........................15.00

No. 4700. KALUGA FUR-LINED CAPE, with covering of box-cloth, colors black, navy, green and crimson, has black Thibet fur collar and fronts, length 30 inches............15.00

No. 4701. LADIES' HAMSTER FUR-LINED CAPE, with fine box-cloth covering, colors black, navy, green, crimson, collar and fronts of black Thibet fur, length 32 inches.... 18.50

No. 4757. LADIES' EVENING CLOAK, made of fine broadcloth, colors black, brown, grey, cadet, cardinal and fawn, has heavy quilted mercerized lining, trimmed with Thibet fur and applique of satin on collar..........20.00

No. 4704. LADIES' GREY AND WHITE SQUIRREL FUR-LINED CAPE, covering of black brocaded cloth, trimmed with black Thibet fur, length 32 inches..............21.00

No. 4710. LADIES' GREY AND WHITE SQUIRREL - LOCK FUR-LINED CAPE, with black brocaded cloth coverings and Thibet fur trimmings, length 32 inches..25.00

No. 4708. LADIES' BEST GREY AND WHITE SQUIRREL FUR-LINED CAPE, has covering of black brocaded matelasse cloth, trimmed with black Thibet fur, length 34 in..32.00

No. 4702. GREY AND WHITE SQUIRREL FUR-LINED CAPE, with fine box-cloth covering, colors black, navy, green and crimson, has black Thibet fur collar and fronts, length 32 inches........................25.00

No. 4712. LADIES' GREY SQUIRREL FUR-LINED CAPE, with black broadcloth covering and fur trimmings of choice Alaska sable, length 32 inches........................37.50

No. 4703. LADIES' HANDSOME CAPE, with best all-grey squirrel lining, covering of rich black Bengaline silk, trimmed with choice Alaska sable, length 32 inches............47.50

No. 4711. LADIES' GREY SQUIRREL FUR-LINED CAPE, has rich brocaded cloth covering, in black, and black and silver, trimmed with Alaska sable fur, length 32 inches.... ....40.00

LADIES' WRAPPERS.

Ladies' Wrappers are kept in stock in sizes 32 to 42 inches bust measure; front length, 57 inches. Special sizes cost 25 per cent. extra.

No. 505. PRINTED PERCALE WRAPPER, light and dark assorted colors, waist lined 89c

No. 700. ENGLISH FLANNELETTE WRAPPER, colors red and black, black and white, and blue and black, waist lined 89c

No. 701. FLANNELETTE WRAPPER, colors black and white, red and white, blue and white, red and black, and blue and black, finished with braid, waist lined 1.00

No. 702. FLANNELETTE WRAPPER, colors black and white, red and white, blue and white, red and black, and blue and black, braid trimmed, waist lined 1.25

No. 703. HEAVY ENGLISH FLANNELETTE WRAPPER, assorted colors, braid trimmed, waist lined 1.39

No. 707. BLACK SATEEN WRAPPER, finished with narrow black satin ribbon, waist lined 1.50

No. 704. AMERICAN SABLE TWILL FLANNELETTE WRAPPER, assorted colors, braid trimmed, waist lined 1.50

No. 705. AMERICAN SABLE TWILL FLANNELETTE WRAPPER, assorted colors, braid trimmed, waist lined 1.75

No. 708. BLACK SATEEN WRAPPER, trimmed with black satin ribbon, waist lined 1.89

No. 706. AMERICAN SABLE TWILL FLANNELETTE WRAPPER, assorted colors, trimmed with black velveteen, finished with velvet ribbon and pearl buttons, waist lined 2.00

No. 709. MERCERIZED BLACK SATEEN WRAPPER, trimmed with black satin ribbon, waist lined 2.50

LADIES' TEA GOWNS, DRESSING GOWNS AND SACQUES.

Ladies' Gowns all come in one length. Order Gowns and Sacques by bust measure.

No. 601. EIDERDOWN FLANNEL DRESSING SACQUE, colors grey, cardinal, sky, cream, and pink **1.25**

No. 602. RIPPLE EIDERDOWN DRESSING SACQUE, colors grey, cardinal, sky, cream, and pink **1.50**

No. 2388. JAPANESE SILK HOUSE JACKET, silk lined with warm interlining and quilted, colors black, navy, cardinal, pink, sky and heliotrope **3.98**

No. 2903. JAPANESE SILK HOUSE JACKET, hand embroidered, has silk lining with quilted wadding interlining, colors black, navy, cardinal, sky, old rose, heliotrope and green. **5.00**

No. 614. JAPANESE SILK HOUSE JACKET, colors black, navy, heliotrope, cardinal, sky, and pink, lined with silk, has wadding interlining, finely machine quilted **9 00**

No. 605. EIDERDOWN FLANNEL DRESSING GOWN, in cardinal or grey **3.98**

No. 603. EIDERDOWN DRESSING GOWN, colors cardinal, grey, sky, and dark green. **4.98**

No. 604. RIPPLE EIDERDOWN DRESSING GOWN, colors cardinal, grey, sky, and dark green **6.50**

No. 2390. JAPANESE SILK HOUSE GOWN, lined with silk, wadded and quilted, colors black, navy, cardinal, pink, sky and heliotrope **8.00**

No. 2782. JAPANESE SILK HOUSE ROBE, colors navy, cardinal, black, green, and sky, lined with silk, wadding interlining quilted, is silk embroidered **10 00**

No. 721. FINE FRENCH CASHMERE TEA GOWN, colors black, navy, cardinal, heliotrope, garnet, and plum, lined with percaline, trimmed with silk ribbon, lace and insertion, collar, yoke and sleeve finished with box-plait tucking, has watteau pleat in back. **8.00**

Ladies', Misses' and Children's Rubber-lined Waterproof Cloaks.

Sizes in Ladies' Waterproof Cloaks are 54, 56, 58, 60 and 62 inches long. Sizes in Misses' and Children's Waterproof Cloaks are 33 to 51 inches long. Measure downward from back of neck.

2405. LADIES' RUBBER-LINED WATERPROOF CLOAK, in fawn, navy and black paramatta 3.00

2408. LADIES' RUBBER-LINED WATERPROOF CLOAK, in navy and black cotton serge, detachable cape 3.50

2409. LADIES' RUBBER-LINED WATERPROOF CLOAK, of cashmere paramatta, black and navy, same style as 2408 .... 5.00

2406. LADIES' PARAMATTA RUBBER-LINED WATERPROOF CLOAK, colors black, navy and fawn, velvet collar 4.00

2403. LADIES' CASHMERE PARAMATTA WATERPROOF CLOAK, rubber-lined, colors fawn, black and navy, finished with fancy stitching and velvet collar 7.50

2404. LADIES' PARAMATTA WATERPROOF CLOAK, rubber-lined, same style as 2403, colors fawn, black and navy 5.00

2407. LADIES' RUBBER-LINED WATERPROOF CLOAK, of cashmere paramatta, made with sleeves and detachable cape, with velvet collar, colors black and navy 8.00

2410. MISSES' AND CHILDREN'S RUBBER-LINED WATERPROOF CLOAK, in fawn and navy paramatta, velvet collar 2.50

Ladies Cravenette Waterproof Cloaks.

Sizes in Ladies' Cravenette Waterproof Cloaks are 54, 56, 58, 60 and 62 inches long. Measure downward from **back** of neck, also send bust measure.

No. 2453. LADIES' CRAVENETTE RAIN CLOAK, colors black, navy, fawn and Oxford grey, velvet collar.......... **5.00**

No. 2454. LADIES' CRAVENETTE RAIN CLOAK, colors black, navy, fawn, Oxford grey and green.......... **5.00**

No. 2455. LADIES' CRAVENETTE RAIN CLOAK, colors black, navy, fawn and Oxford grey, velvet collar.......... **6.00**

No. 2452. LADIES' RAIN CLOAK, made of Priestley's cravenette, in black and navy, velvet collar.......... **6.50**

No. 2450. LADIES' RAIN CLOAK, made of Priestley's cravenette covert cloth, colors fawn, Oxford grey, bronze and blue.......... **8.50**

CRAVENETTE COVERT CLOTH, colors fawn, drab, bronze and Oxford grey, per yard, **1.25** and.......... **2.50**

No. 2456. LADIES' RAIN CLOAK, made of Priestley's cravenette covert cloth, heavy quality, colors black, navy, fawn, green and Oxford grey, bell sleeves, yoke back and velvet collar.......... **10.00**

No. 2451. LADIES' RAIN CLOAK, made of Priestley's best quality heavy weight cravenette covert cloth, colors fawn, green, Oxford grey and brown, velvet collar.......... **12.00**

Misses' Suits, Costumes and Skirts

Schedule of Sizes for Misses' Suits and Costumes:

Age	14 years.	16 years.	18 years.
Bust measure	30 inches	32 inches	34 inches.
Length of skirt in front	35 and 36 inches	36 to 38 inches	37 to 39 inches.
Waistband of skirt	22 and 23 inches	22 to 24 inches	23 to 25 inches.

Misses' Skirts are kept in stock in lengths 32 to 38 inches, waistbands 22 to 25 inches. Sizes not included in our regular stock cost 10 per cent. extra. Skirts, unless otherwise stated, are lined with percaline and bound with good quality velveteen. When ordering Misses' Garments state age, bust measure, waist measure and front length of skirt.

No. 6180. MISSES' SUIT, made of fancy mixed cheviots, colors black, navy, fawn, medium grey, electric and blue mixture; jacket is lined with silkaline **5.00**

No. 6185. MISSES' WALKING SUIT, made of heavy cheviot mixtures, colors black, navy, light grey, medium grey, dark grey, fawn, brown and green; skirt is unlined; jacket lined with mercerized sateen, has velvet collar **7.50**

No. 6181. MISSES' SUIT, made of heavy English cheviot mixtures, colors black, navy, Oxford grey, medium grey, brown and green; the trimming is velvet with fancy braid; jacket is lined with mercerette, flounce only of skirt lined **8.50**

No. 6184. MISSES' SUIT, made of fine all-wool worsted cheviot, in black and navy; jacket is lined with mercerized Italian, and has carved pearl buttons, with velvet collar.. .... **9.50**

No. 6183. MISSES' SUIT, made of heavy all-wool French pebble cheviot, colors black and navy; jacket is lined with mercerized Italian, and the suit is trimmed with stitched bands of black satin **11.00**

No. 6082. MISSES' SKIRT, made of heavy English cheviot mixtures, colors black, navy, brown, green, Oxford grey and medium grey, unlined **2.98**

No. 6081. MISSES' SKIRT, made of heavy English cheviot serge, colors black, navy, grey, Oxford and brown, unlined, tucked flounce **3.50**

No. 6083. MISSES' SKIRT, made of heavy all-wool French pebble serge, colors black and navy, flounce is lined and finished with cording **3.98**

No. 6080. MISSES' SKIRT, made of all-wool worsted cheviot serge, colors black and navy, trimmed with narrow silk bands and silk stitching, with covered buttons, lined with percaline and bound with velveteen...... **4.98**

No. 6187. MISSES' COSTUME, made of Rockwood homespun, in blue, brown, grey, fawn, and Oxford, and in black and navy cheviot serge, has tucked silk yoke with stitched taffeta silk collar.......... **11.00**

No. 6188. MISSES' COSTUME, made of fine quality cheviot serge, colors black and navy, waist is tucked all over, and has sailor collar, trimming is stitched taffeta silk, waist is lined with taffeta silk **12.50**

No. 6186. MISSES' COSTUME, made of fine, all-wool worsted cheviot, colors black, navy, royal, fawn and brown, waist is lined with mercerized sateen, the trimming is wide bands of taffeta silk, with stitching...... **13.50**

MISSES' JACKETS.

Schedule of Sizes for Misses' Jackets:

Age	14 years.	16 years.	18 years.
Bust measure	30 inches.	32 inches.	34 inches.

When ordering Misses' Jackets state age and bust measure.

No. 6285. MISSES' BEAVER CLOTH JACKET, colors black and navy, has storm collar, box back 3.00

No. 6279. MISSES' FRIEZE JACKET, colors fawn, brown, grey, green, Oxford, navy and black, has storm collar, box back 3.50

No. 6280. MISSES' FRIEZE JACKET, colors black, navy, fawn, brown, grey and Oxford, lined throughout with silkaline, has velvet collar, box back 4.75

No. 6288. MISSES' ENGLISH BEAVER CLOTH JACKET, colors black, navy, green, red, royal, fawn and brown, lined throughout with Egerton sateen, finished with velvet pipings 5.00

No. 6286. MISSES' JACKET, made of Preston cheviot, colors black, Oxford, and dark grey, lined throughout with Egerton sateen, has velvet collar 5.25

No. 6284. MISSES' ENGLISH BEAVER CLOTH JACKET, colors black, brown and green, lined throughout with silkaline, has box back, velvet collar 6.00

No. 6290. MISSES' JACKET, made of all-wool Rockwood frieze, colors black, navy, Oxford, light grey, medium grey, fawn, brown and blue mixture, lined throughout with mercerette, has storm collar 6.00

No. 6287. MISSES' ALL-WOOL KERSEY CLOTH JACKET, colors black, navy, fawn, brown and light blue, lined throughout with mercerette, fastened with pearl buttons.. 6 98

No. 6281. MISSES' JACKET, made of Preston vicuna cloth, colors mid grey and Oxford. lined throughout with heavy satin, fastened with pearl buttons, box back 8.00

No. 6283. MISSES' KERSEY CLOTH JACKET, colors black and navy, lined throughout with heavy satin, has pearl buttons and velvet collar, box back, semi-fitting 8.50

No. 6289. MISSES' KERSEY CLOTH JACKET, colors black and navy, lined throughout with satin, fastened with large pearl buttons, box back 9.00

No. 6282. MISSES' FINE ENGLISH KERSEY CLOTH JACKET, colors black, navy, fawn and brown, lined throughout with satin, revers finished with applique of si.k velvet, has pearl buttons, semi-fitting, box back, **10.00**

LADIES' PETTICOATS.

Unless otherwise stated, Ladies' Petticoats are kept in stock in lengths 39, 40, 41 and 42 inches.

No. 5132. MOREEN PETTICOAT, colors black, cardinal, grey, royal, helio and plum..... **1.50**

No. 5124. BLACK MERCERIZED SATIN PETTICOAT **1.69**

No. 5129. MOREEN PETTICOAT, colors black, cardinal, grey, royal, cerise and plum, trimmed with fancy braid **1.75**

No. 5143. BLACK MERCERIZED SATIN PETTICOAT, accordion-pleated flounce, finished with ruching **1.98**

No. 5142. MOREEN PETTICOAT, colors black, royal, grey, cardinal, plum and cerise, flounce lined and trimmed with cording.......... **2.00**

No. 5131. BLACK MERCERETTE PETTICOAT, flounce lined and trimmed with rows of cording **2.25**

No. 5144. SILK-FINISHED MERCERETTE PETTICOAT, black only, accordion-pleated flounce, with ruching **2.50**

No. 5128. MOREEN PETTICOAT, colors black, cardinal, royal, cerise, and helio, has accordion-pleated flounce, trimmed with ruching.... .... **2.50**

No. 5123. BLACK SILK-FINISHED MERCERETTE PETTICOAT, flounce has accordion-pleated frill, trimmed with three ruffles and ruching **2.50**

No. 5130. MOREEN PETTICOAT, heavy quality, colors black, grey, plum, cardinal, royal, cerise and heliotrope, double flounce, accordion-pleated, finished with ruching and narrow frill with cording **3.00**

No. 5140 TAFFETA SILK PETTICOAT, colors black, cardinal, turquoise, navy, royal, cerise and sky, flounce lined.............................. **5.00**

No. 5135. TAFFETA SILK PETTICOAT, black only, flounce has frill trimmed with cording, lined throughout with mercerette.......... **5.00**

No. 5141. TAFFETA SILK PETTICOAT, colors black, cardinal, cerise, helio, old rose and sky, flounce lined.............................. **6.98**

No. 5126. TAFFETA SILK PETTICOAT, colors black, cardinal, cerise, helio, sky and old rose, flounce trimmed with hem-corded frills **7.50**

No. 5125. TAFFETA SILK PETTICOAT, colors black, cardinal, helio, cerise, royal and sky, has accordion-pleated flounce trimmed with frill and ruchings, flounce lined **8.50**

No. 5139. TAFFETA SILK PETTICOAT, colors black, cardinal, cerise, royal, navy, sky and helio, flounce trimmed with ruchings and accordion-pleated ruffle, lining of flounce finished with hemstitched frill.......... **10.00**

Flannelette underskirts, 36, 37 and 38 inches long, 59c and 65c.

Felt petticoats, about 39 inches long, assorted styles and colors, $1.00, 1.25, 1.50, 1.69, 2.00, 2.50, 3.00, 4.00.

Children's Ulsters and Automobile Coats.

Schedule of Sizes for Children's Ulsters

Length, 27 inches; 30 inches; 33 inches; 36 inches; 39 inches.
Age, 4 years; 6 years; 8 years; 10 years; 12 years.

When ordering Children's Ulsters state age and length downward from bottom of collar band (back).
When ordering Children's Automobile Coats state age.

No. 6901. ENGLISH CHEVIOT SERGE ULSTER, colors navy, royal, fawn, brown and green, trimmed with fancy braid, 27-inch, **3.00**; 30-inch, **3.50**; 33-inch, **4.00**; 36-inch, **4.50**; 39-inch, **5.00**; 42-inch, **5.50.**

No. 6902. HEAVY FRIEZE ULSTER, colors Oxford, navy, green, brown, fawn, red, royal and blue mixture, finished with rows of stitching, 27-inch, **3.50**; 30-inch, **4.00**; 33-inch, **4.50**; 36-inch, **5.00**; 39-inch, **5.50**; 42-inch, **6.00.**

No. 6903. HEAVY FRIEZE ULSTER, colors fawn, brown, navy, red and royal, braid trimmed, 27-inch, **4.00**; 30-inch, **4.50**; 33-inch, **5.00**; 36-inch, **5.50**; 39-inch, **6.00**; 42-inch, **6.50.**

No. 6904. BEAVER CLOTH ULSTER, colors **fawn,** brown, navy, royal, red and green, **trimmed** with folds of satin, 27-inch, **4.50**; 30-inch, **5.00**; 33-inch, **5.50**; 36-inch, **6.00**; 39-inch, **6.50**; 42-inch, **7.00.**

No. 6900. ENGLISH BEAVER CLOTH ULSTER, colors fawn, brown, navy, royal, green and red, is trimmed with velvet, fancy braid and small buttons, 27-inch, **5.00**; 30-inch, **5.50**; 33-inch, **6.00**; 36-inch, **6.50**; 39-inch, **7.00**; 42-inch, **7.50.**

No. 6906. HEAVY ALL-WOOL FRIEZE ULSTER, colors blue mixture, fawn, brown, grey, green and navy, trimmed with velvet pipings and pearl buttons, 27-inch, **5.50**; 30-inch, **6.00**; 33-inch, **6.50**; 36-inch, **7.00**; 39-inch, **7.50**; 42-inch, **8.00.**

No. 6907. STYLISH ALL-WOOL KERSEY CLOTH ULSTER, navy only, finished with straps of self, and pearl buttons, 27-inch, **7.00**; 30-inch, **7.50**; 33-inch, **8.00**; 36-inch, **8.50**; 39-inch, **9.00**; 42-inch, **9.50.**

No. 6905. FINE ALL-WOOL KERSEY CLOTH ULSTER, colors fawn, brown, castor, royal and navy, trimmed with folds of satin, and pearl buttons, 27-inch, **9.50**; 30-inch, **10.00**; 33-inch, **10.50**; 36-inch, **11.00**; 39-inch, **11.50**; 42-inch, **12.00.**

No. 6909. CHILD'S AUTOMOBILE COAT, made of heavy all-wool frieze, colors blue, fawn, brown, green, navy and Oxford, trimmings of velvet and braid, 8, 10 and 12 years, **4.50.**

No. 6908. CHILD'S AUTOMOBILE COAT, made of fine all-wool kersey cloth, colors light fawn, dark fawn and red, lined throughout with serge silk, has velvet trimmings and pearl buttons, 8, 10 and 12 years, **8.50.**

CHILDREN'S REEFERS

When Ordering Children's Reefers State Age.

No. 6820. CHEVIOT SERGE REEFER, colors navy, fawn, brown, green and royal, sizes 4 to 12 years 1.69

No. 6815. NAVY BEAVER CLOTH REEFER, trimmed with fancy braid, sizes 4 to 12 years 2.25

No. 6819. CHEVIOT SERGE REEFER, colors navy, green, royal, fawn and brown, lined throughout with mercerized sateen, trimmed with fancy braid, sizes 4 to 12 years 2.69

No. 6812. NAVY BEAVER CLOTH REEFER, trimmed with black mohair and black and gold soutache braid, has gilt buttons, sacque back, sizes 4 to 12 years 2.75

No. 6813. HEAVY FRIEZE REEFER, colors fawn, brown, navy, Oxford, red and royal, trimmed with velvet and fancy braid, sizes 4 to 12 years 3.00

No. 6817. ALL-WOOL FRIEZE REEFER, colors Oxford, green, brown, navy, fawn and blue mixture, has velvet collar and pearl buttons, sizes 4 to 12 years 3.25

No. 6822. ALL-WOOL FRIEZE REEFER, colors fawn, blue, navy and Oxford, trimmed with satin straps and fancy braid, sizes 4 to 12 years 3.75

No. 6814. ALL-WOOL BEAVER CLOTH REEFER, navy only, trimmed with satin straps and fancy braid, sizes 4 to 12 years 3.98

No. 6818. HEAVY BEAVER CLOTH REEFER, colors green, red, royal and navy, trimmed with satin straps, black and gold silk soutache braid and gilt buttons, sizes 4 to 12 years 4.50

No. 6821. ALL-WOOL BEAVER CLOTH REEFER, colors black and navy, lined throughout with good quality black satin, has pearl buttons, sacque back, sizes 4 to 12 years 5.50

No. 6816. ALL-WOOL KERSEY CLOTH REEFER, colors light fawn, dark fawn, red, royal, navy and electric blue, lined with mercerette, trimmed with stitched velvet and pearl buttons, sizes 4 to 12 years...... 6.50

Children's Coats and Dresses, Infants' Long Cloaks, etc.

Children's Coats are made in lengths 22, 24 and 26 inches, for ages 6 months to 4 years. All Coats and Cloaks illustrated on this page have warm and heavy linings.

No. 2137. CREAM SERGE COAT, trimmed with white mohair bearskin cloth and satin ribbon 2.50

No. 2014. CREAM SERGE COAT, trimmed with silk embroidery and white mohair curl cloth 2.75

No. 2007. CREAM BEDFORD CORD COAT, trimmed with white mohair bearskin cloth and satin ribbon 3.25

No. 2229. WHITE MOHAIR BEARSKIN CLOTH COAT 3.50

No. 2217. CREAM BEDFORD CORD COAT, trimmed with cream gimp and white Thibet fur, has pearl buttons 4.00

No. 2236. CREAM BEDFORD CORD COAT, trimmed with white Thibet fur and satin ribbon 5.00

No. 2131. WHITE MOHAIR BEARSKIN CLOTH COAT, extra quality, trimmed with white Thibet fur 5.50

No. 2251. HEAVY SERGE COAT, colors royal blue, cardinal and cadet, trimmed with silk embroidery and white hare fur. 2.50

No. 7551. INFANTS' CREAM COBOURG LONG CLOAK, trimmed with silk embroidery and satin ribbon 2.25

No. 7552. INFANTS' LONG CLOAK, made of cream Bedford cord, trimmed with silk braid 2.69

No. 7553. INFANTS CREAM CASHMERE CLOAK, trimmed with silk embroidery and silk braid 3.00

No. 7554. INFANTS' LONG CLOAK, made of cream Bedford cord, trimmed with silk embroidery, satin ribbon and silk gimp 3.50

No. 2252. CASHMERE DRESS, colors cardinal, pink, sky and cream, trimmed with hemstitching and tucks, yoke lined, sizes 20, 22, 24 and 26 inches long 1.39

No. 4604. SAILOR SUIT, made of navy blue all-wool serge, skirt and waist lined, trimmed with cream braid, kilted skirt, sizes 20, 22, 24 and 26 inches long 3.39

No. 4603. SAILOR SUIT, made of navy blue all-wool serge, trimmed with fancy cream braid, has white cashmere tie, waist and skirt lined, sizes 28, 30, 33 and 36 inches long 3.98

Style A. INFANTS' HAND-MADE ZEPHYR WOOL SACQUES, in all white, and white with blue or pink, **50c** and **75c**; with silk edging **1.00**

Style B. INFANTS' HAND-MADE ZEPHYR WOOL SACQUES, empire style, in all white, and white with pink or blue trimming, **75c** and **1.00**

No. 500. Silk velvet toque, trimmed with drape of ribbon and handsome breast, finished with buckle at side, special $3.75

No. 501. Fine fur-felt dress hat, folds of satin around crown, and fold of velvet on edge of brim, trimmed with two handsome ostrich plumes, finished with knot of satin and velvet in front, price according to size and quality of plumes .... $8.50 to 12.00

No. 502. Silk velvet turban, trimmed standing folds taffeta silk and velvet, velvet drape coming over brim to bandeau and two long curled quills .... $4.25 to 5.00

No. 503. Tucked silk velvet toque, with tucked satin facing, trimmed with handsome long breast and two ornaments, special $5.00

No. 504. Fine fur-felt turban, trimmed standing folds of silk velvet and satin, handsome long breast around left side, velvet knot on side bandeau .... $3.75 to 4.50

No. 505. Gainsborough hat, in silk velvet, shirred velvet brim with tucks on edge, twist of soft satin ribbon around crown, handsome large ostrich plume finished with rosette of soft satin ribbon, completes the trimming .... $7.75 to 10.00

No. 506. Felt dress hat, trimmed soft fold of taffeta silk around crown, fastened with two ornaments at back, handsome long ostrich plume across front completes the trimming, the colorings for this shape are castor, brown, cardinal and pearl, all faced with black or in solid black .... $6.75 to 8.00

No. 507. Dress hat, taffeta silk crown, soft draped velvet brim, trimmed standing folds, of taffeta silk and two handsome long breasts, finished with knot of velvet .... $4.50 to 5.50

No. 508. Fur-felt walking hat, drape of silk velvet on brim and folds of taffeta silk around crown, finished on left side with knot of velvet and fancy quill, special $2.75

No. 509. Silk velvet dress hat, with satin facing, folds of velvet and satin form edge of brim, trimmed with soft satin ribbon, two feather pom-poms and buckle, side bandeau with ribbon bow, special $5.00

No. 510. Tucked felt turban, trimmed large rosette soft satin ribbon and wings, special. $3.50

No. 511. Silk velvet toque, trimmed rosettes of taffeta silk with corded edge, handsome fancy breast and ornament, special.. .... $3.99

No. 512. Silk velvet bonnet, trimmed renaissance lace, soft satin ribbon, paradise osprey and buckle, satin ribbon ties .... $5.00 to 7.00

No. 513. Black silk mourning bonnet, silk and silk lisse folds, ribbon bows and ties, dull jet ornaments .... $3.50 to 5.00

No. 514. Silk and velvet bonnet, tucked silk brim, crown alternate folds of velvet and silk, fancy feather drooping over left side, handsome ornament and velvet ties .... $3.75 to 5.00

No. 515. Widows' bonnets, silk folds and silk lisse veil, white lisse border and ribbon ties, price according to quality of veil .... $5.00 to 10.00

No. 516. Misses' fine felt flop, trimmed wide bow of silk velvet and taffeta silk, special $2.00

No. 517. Child's felt flop, velvet fold on edge of brim, trimmed two shades of ribbon, special $1.75

No. 518. Child's hat, tucked taffeta silk brim with fluted edge, silk velvet crown and silk rosette and ties, special.... $3.50

No. 519. Misses' hat, camel's hair felt, stitched brim and crown, trimmed drape of taffeta silk, knot of silk and velvet and fancy quill, special $2.35

No. 520. Black silk mourning toque, draped crown and brim, with tucks of chiffon around brim, two dull jet ornaments and flowing osprey .... $5.00 to 6.50

No. 521. Black silk mourning hat, soft drape brim and folded crown, trimmed black silk flowers .... $4.75 to 6.00

No. 522. Felt short back sailor, new set brim, trimmed soft drape of taffeta silk rosette of silk velvet, fancy breast on left side, side bandeau with silk bow, special $3.00

No. 523. Felt turban, with drape of silk velvet and taffeta silk, handsome breast on left side, special $2.95

No. 524. Jerome, street hat, silk velvet and taffeta silk, colors black, brown, navy, castor, and cardinal $2.45

No. 525. Hampton, felt outing hat, trimmed drape, satin liberty, in Paisley effects, colors black, brown, navy, castor and cardinal..$2.00

No. 526. Echo, street hat, silk velvet and taffeta silk, colors black, brown, castor and navy $2.50

No. 527. Bernice, camel's hair felt outing hat, trimmed velvet band and knot, felt quill, colors black, brown, pearl and white, trimmed black $1.75

No. 528. Victor, silk velvet dress shape, corded taffeta silk facing, in black only, with black, white, rose, pink or sky blue facings $2.50

No. 529. Odessa, dress hat, stitched felt crown, tucked brim, colors black, brown, castor and pearl $1.75

No. 530. Eureka, fine felt, satin wire on edge, colors black, brown, castor, navy and pearl 75c

No. 531. Wilhelmina, street hat, in silk velvet, with corded taffeta silk crown, colors black, brown, castor, navy and cardinal $2.89

No. 532. Dongola, felt outing hat, trimmed satin band, felt rosette and curled quill, colors navy and pearl, trimmed self colors, castor trimmed brown and brown trimmed castor ..$2.00

No. 533. Linden, camel's hair felt outing hat, trimmed standing folds felt and velvet and curled quill, colors black, brown, navy, cardinal, castor and pearl, all trimmed black......$2.25

No. 534. Argyle, felt outing hat, satin band, felt rosette and curled quill, colors black, pearl and castor $2.00

No. 535. Helena, camel's hair felt, three rows silk cording on edge, colors black, brown, castor, pearl and navy $1.00

No. 536. West Side, silk velvet hat, double edge with tucks of chiffon between, colors black, brown, navy and castor $2.65

No. 537. Rexmere, camel's hair felt, three rows silk cording on edge, colors black, brown, castor, pearl and navy $1.00

No. 538. Langdon, felt outing hat, trimmed drape printed mercerized twill in self colors and curled quill, colors black, brown, castor and pearl...$2.00

No. 539. Hilarius, felt outing hat, satin band, felt rosette, gilt ornament and curled quill, colors black, pearl, castor, brown, navy..$2.00

No. 540. Bohemia, felt outing hat, trimmed satin drape and felt rosettes with satin binding, color, black, navy and pearl, trimmed self colors, castor trimmed brown and brown trimmed castor $2.00

No. 541. Hadley, felt hat, soft tam crown, stitched narrow strips satin, felt rosette and curled quill, colors black, brown, castor, navy and cardinal $2.25

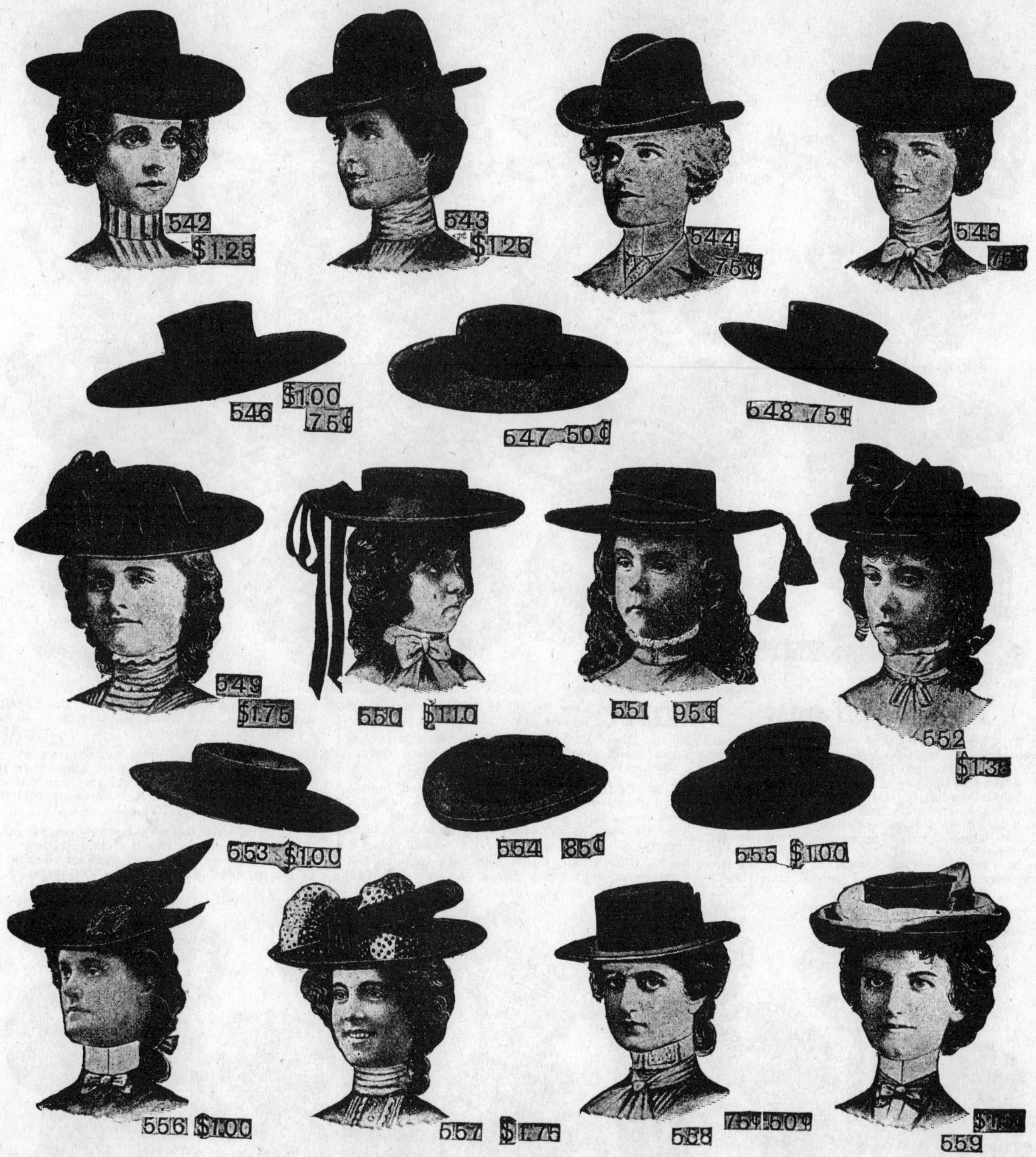

No. 542. Cliffwood, fine soft felt crown, semi-stiff brim with welt edge, silk ribbon band, colors pearl, castor, brown, navy and cardinal $1.25

No. 543. Edna May, fur felt fedora, corded ribbon trimming, colors black, castor and pearl $1.25

No. 544. Claremont, soft felt, corded ribbon band and bow, colors black, brown, navy, castor and pearl 75c

No. 545. Duchess, fine wool felt, set crown, semi-stiff finish, ribbon band and binding, band caught at each side with small gilt buckle, colors black, brown, navy and pearl 75c

No. 546A. Orleans, stitched flop, camel's hair felt, colors black, brown, castor and pearl..$1.00

No. 546B. Empire, fine wool felt flop, colors pearl, castor, brown and navy 75c

No. 547. Flossie, misses' felt flop, colors brown, cardinal, navy, royal and pearl 50c

No. 548. Hampton, fine wool felt, welt edge, set brim, colors black, castor, pearl, brown and cardinal 75c

No. 549. Marion, felt outing hat, trimmed velvet band and felt drape, bound with satin, colors navy, brown, castor and cardinal..$1.75

No. 550. Admiral, child's fine felt hat, white silk binding on edge, satin ribbon band and streamers, colors brown, cardinal, pearl, royal and navy $1.10

No. 551. Edna, felt hat, trimmed white silk cord and tassels, colors cardinal, navy, castor and pearl 95c

No. 552. Valjean, camel's hair felt, liberty satin band and bow, two curled quills, colors black, pearl, castor, brown, navy and cardinal..$1.35

No. 553. Bonnie, fine wool felt, welt edge, colors black, pearl, castor, brown, navy and cardinal $1.00

No. 554. Luzerne, fine felt, welt edge, colors black, brown, navy, pearl and castor......85c

No. 555. Peconic, camel's hair felt, welt edge colors black, brown, castor and pearl $1.00

No. 556. Woodside, stitched felt outing hat, velvet band, ornament and felt quill, colors black, brown, cardinal and navy $1.00

No. 557. Kenwood, felt hat, three folds velvet around crown, wide bow of polka dot satin, finished with strap of velvet and curled quill, colors navy, brown, castor and cardinal..$1.75

No. 558A. York, fine wool felt sailor, welt edge, corded ribbon band, colors black, brown, cardinal, navy and pearl 75c

No. 558B. York, Belgian felt, bound edge, corded ribbon band, colors black, brown and navy only 50c

No. 559. Piazza, fine felt turban, trimmed drape mercerized satin in self color and white, colors black, castor, pearl, brown and navy.. ....$1.50

Hats and Tams.

No. 32. Child's hat, brim of corded silk, tucked velveteen crown, silk ties, colors cardinal, navy and brown, sizes 19, 20, 21 inches, style suitable for children 6 to 10 years $2.25

No. 33. Child's hat, crystal cord silk, trimmed with grey fox, shirred and wired underbrim of Japanese silk and ties of same, colors cardinal, navy and brown, sizes 19, 20, 21 inches, style suitable for children 8 to 12 years $3.00

No. 34. Child's felt tam, bow of felt, quill and embroidered fleur-de-lis, colors cardinal, navy, brown and myrtle, sizes 19, 20, 21 inches, suitable for children 4 to 7 years 29c

No. 35. Misses' tam, best quality velveteen, trimmed two quills, bow and buckle, colors black, brown, navy and cardinal 69c

No. 36. Child's felt tam, crown trimmed corded velvet and white silk cord, two quills, bow and buckle at side, colors navy, cardinal, brown and myrtle, sizes 19, 20, 21 inches, for children 6 to 12 years 45c

No. 39. Child's hats, fluted brim, special quality of velveteen, corded silk crown and bow silk ties, brim is well corded so as to hold shape, colors navy, cardinal and brown, sizes 19, 20, 21 inches, for children 5 to 8 years $1.89

No. 87. Child's hat of faille silk, tucked crown, shirred and wired brim, silk velvet band and crown tip, silk bow, colors light blue, old rose, cardinal and navy, sizes 19, 20, 21 inches, suitable for children 4 to 7 years $1.95

No. 108. Child's hat, bearskin cloth crown, bengaline silk brim and rosette, ties of same, brim is shirred and wired, colors cream and cardinal, sizes 19, 20, 21 inches, suitable for children 4 to 6 years ..$1.50

Ostrich Boas and Ruffs.

Black ostrich boas, as cut E, 48 to 52 inches long, $5.00, 6.00, 7.50, 9.00, 10.00, 12.00 and 15.00 each.

Black ostrich neck ruffs, 18 inches long, with black satin ribbon ties .... $3.00, 3.50, 4.00 and 5.00 each

No. 1208. Neck ruffs, in black silk brilliant, very full and deep ruffling around neck, pleated ends with ruching across bottom $3.75

No. 1214. Neck ruff, in black silk brilliant, neat ruffling around neck, pleated ends with ruching all around $1.69

No. 1215. Neck ruff, in black silk brilliant, new crimped ruffling around neck, pleated ends trimmed with narrow ruching $2.75

No. 2019. Black hackle feather boa, 50 in. long .. 50c

No. 2019B. Black hackle feather neck ruff, 20 inches long, ribbon ties 25c

No. 2039. Black hackle feather boa, 50 inches long, a heavier boa than 2019 ....85c

No. 2040. Black curled hackle feather boa, 54 inches long, a fine full boa........................$1.19

No. 3008. Black hackle feather boa, tipped with natural coque feathers, 48 inches $1.50

No. 3012. Natural coque and black marabou feather boa, 52 inches long, a very full soft boa $2.50

No. 3354. Black hackle feather ruff, with four ends of pointed hackle, 42 inches long 85c

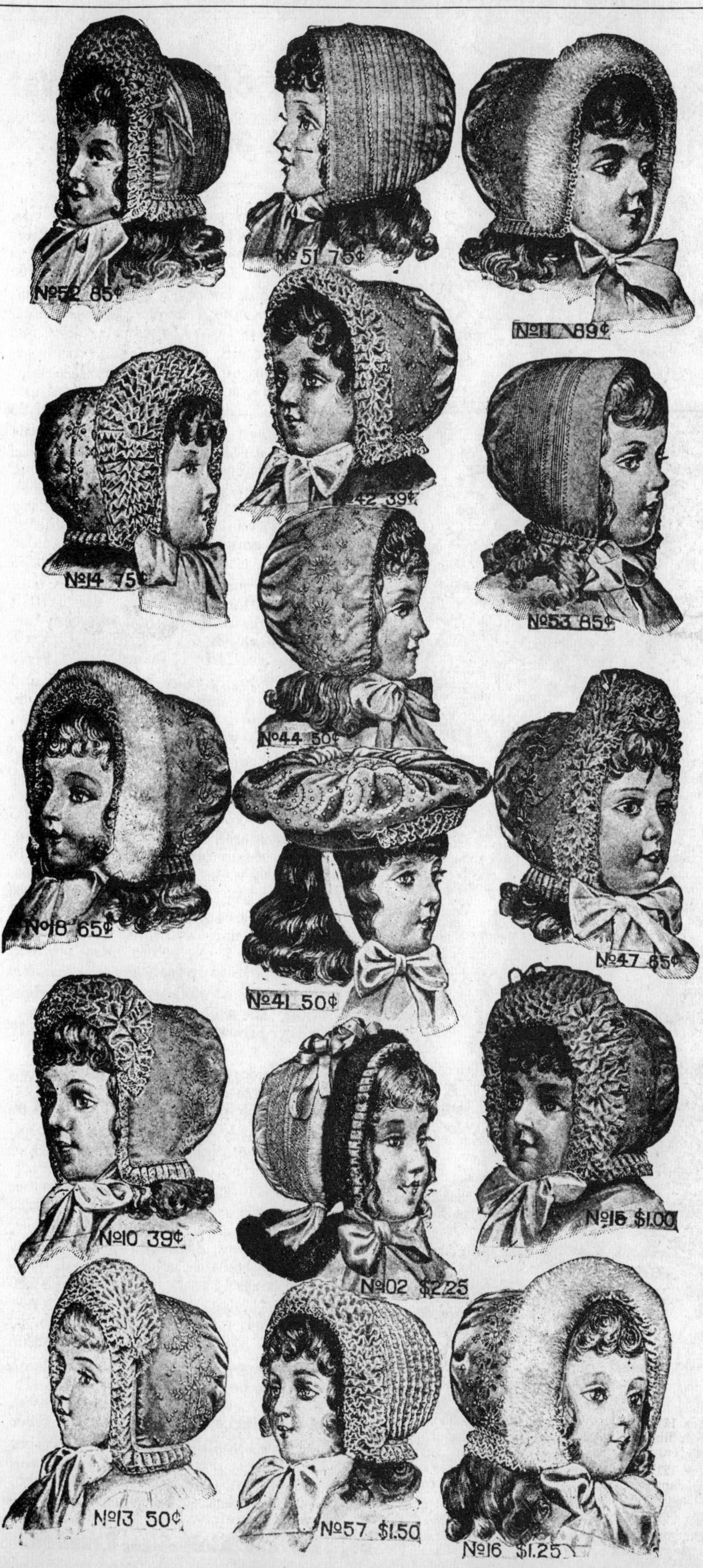

Cream Silk and Cashmere Caps

No. 10. Embroidered cream cashmere cap, lace and net top ruche, lace edge all around, sizes 12 to 16 inches 39c

No. 11. Embroidered cream cashmere cap, swansdown ruche, ribbon ties, sizes 13 to 16 inches 89c

No. 13. Embroidered cream Japanese silk cap, full top ruche, double lace edge all around, hemmed mercerized ties, sizes 12 to 16 inches........................50c

No. 14. Embroidered cream Japanese silk cap, very full graduated lace ruche, silk lining and ties, sizes 12 to 16 inches . . 75c

No. 15. Cream Japanese silk cap, openwork embroidery, very full graduated lace ruche, with braidene loops, silk lining and ties, sizes 12 to 16 inches $1.00

No. 16. Cream Japanese silk cap, very rich openwork embroidery, extra wide swansdown trimming, lace edging all around, finished with silk cord, silk lining and wide silk ties, sizes 12 to 16 inches. . $1.25

No. 18. Embroidered faille silk, cream only, swansdown ruche, silk ties, sizes 13 to 16 inches 65c

No. 41. Cream cashmere Tam o' Shanter, neat embroidery pattern, lace ruche across front, cashmere ties, sizes 19, 20, 21 inches 50c

No. 42. Embroidered cream Japanese silk cap, neat lace ruche, hemmed mercerized ties, sizes 12 to 16 inches.............39c

No. 44. Child's French cap, embroidered cream Japanese silk, finished silk cord on edges, hemmed mercerized ties, sizes 13 to 16 inches........................50c

No. 47. Richly embroidered cream Japanese silk cap, graduated lace and net ruche, with baby ribbon loops, hemmed mercerized ties, sizes 12 to 16 inches........65c

No. 51. Tucked French cap of cream Japanese silk, embroidered revers front, finished with silk cord, silk ties, sizes 13 to 16 inches........................75c

No. 52. Cream Japanese silk cap, with fine cording, double hemstitched tucks on each side of cording, full top ruche and double lace edging all around, finished with silk cord braidene loops on ruche, silk ties, sizes 12 to 16 inches 85c

No. 53. French cap of cream Japanese silk, with fine cording, lace edging next face, sizes 13 to 16 inches 85c

No. 57. Cream Japanese silk cap, tucked and shirred all around, lace ruche, silk ties, sizes 12 to 16 inches..........$1.50

No. 102. Cream satin cap, trimmed two rows valenciennes insertion and narrow satin ribbon bows, nutria fur around face and curtain lace edging next face, ribbon ties, sizes 1', 15 and 16 in $2.25

Colored Silk and Velvet Caps and Bonnets.

No. 21. Velveteen cap, trimmed nutria fur, lace edging next face, mercerized satin ties, colors navy, brown, cardinal and black, sizes 13 to 16 inches 75c

No. 22. Faille silk bonnet, corded frill, graduated lace ruche, colors navy, cardinal, brown and cream, sizes 14 to 17 inches 89c

No. 23. Corded silk and velveteen bonnet, trimmed imitation chinchilla fur, lace edging next face, colors navy, cardinal and brown $1.25

No. 24. Velveteen bonnet, embroidered star, frill is edged and lined with black Japanese silk, puffing around neck and ties of same, cream Japanese silk ruching around face, colors black embroidered cardinal, navy embroidered white, cardinal embroidered black, brown embroidered white, sizes 14 to 17 inches..................................$1.35

No. 25. Crystal cord silk and velveteen bonnet, trimmed fancy silk cord, double frill outside, one of silk inside, frill of cream tarlatan, colors brown, navy, cardinal, myrtle and cream, sizes 14 to 17 inches $1.75

No. 27. Corded silk poke bonnet, frill and curtain edged imitation chinchilla fur, graduated lace ruche next face, colors navy, brown, cardinal and myrtle $1.75

No. 29. Crystal corded silk and velveteen bonnet, full-tucked back, trimmed with grey fox, colors brown, navy and cardinal, sizes 14 to 17 inches $2.25

No. 37. Embroidered cream Japanese silk bonnet, extra wide double frills, frill and curtain has three rows tucks and edged with lace, lace ruche next face, sizes 14 to 17 in ..$2.00

No. 64. Faille silk cap, trimmed with fur and finished with narrow braid, lace edging around face and neck, colors navy, brown, cardinal, sizes 13 to 16 inches 50c

No. 75. Faille silk bonnet, trimmed with rick-rack braid, lace edging next face, colors cardinal, navy, brown and cream, sizes 14 to 17 inches 75c

No. 76. Embroidered cream faille silk bonnet, trimmed slink lamb, lace edging next face, sizes 14 to 17 inches..................$1.00

No. 99. Corded velvet cap with curtain, trimmed imitation chinchilla fur, fur head and ribbon bow on top, ribbon ties, colors cardinal, navy and brown, sizes 13 to 16 inches $1.35

No. 100. Corded velvet bonnet, revers front, trimmed black silk cord and black velvet, black satin ribbon ties, colors cardinal, navy and brown, sizes 14 to 17 inches $1.50

No. 101. Crystal cord silk, trimmed nutria fur, lace edging next face, colors cream, cardinal, navy and brown, sizes 14 to 17 inches..$3.00

No. 103. Felt cap with curtain, clipped lamb ruches, ribbon bow and fur head on top, ribbon ties, colors cardinal, navy and brown, sizes 13 to 16 inches 95c

No. 115. Clipped lamb and felt bonnet, trimmed white silk braid and ribbon bows, silk ties, colors cream, cardinal, navy and brown, sizes 14 to 17 inches..................$1.75

Be Sure and State Size Required.

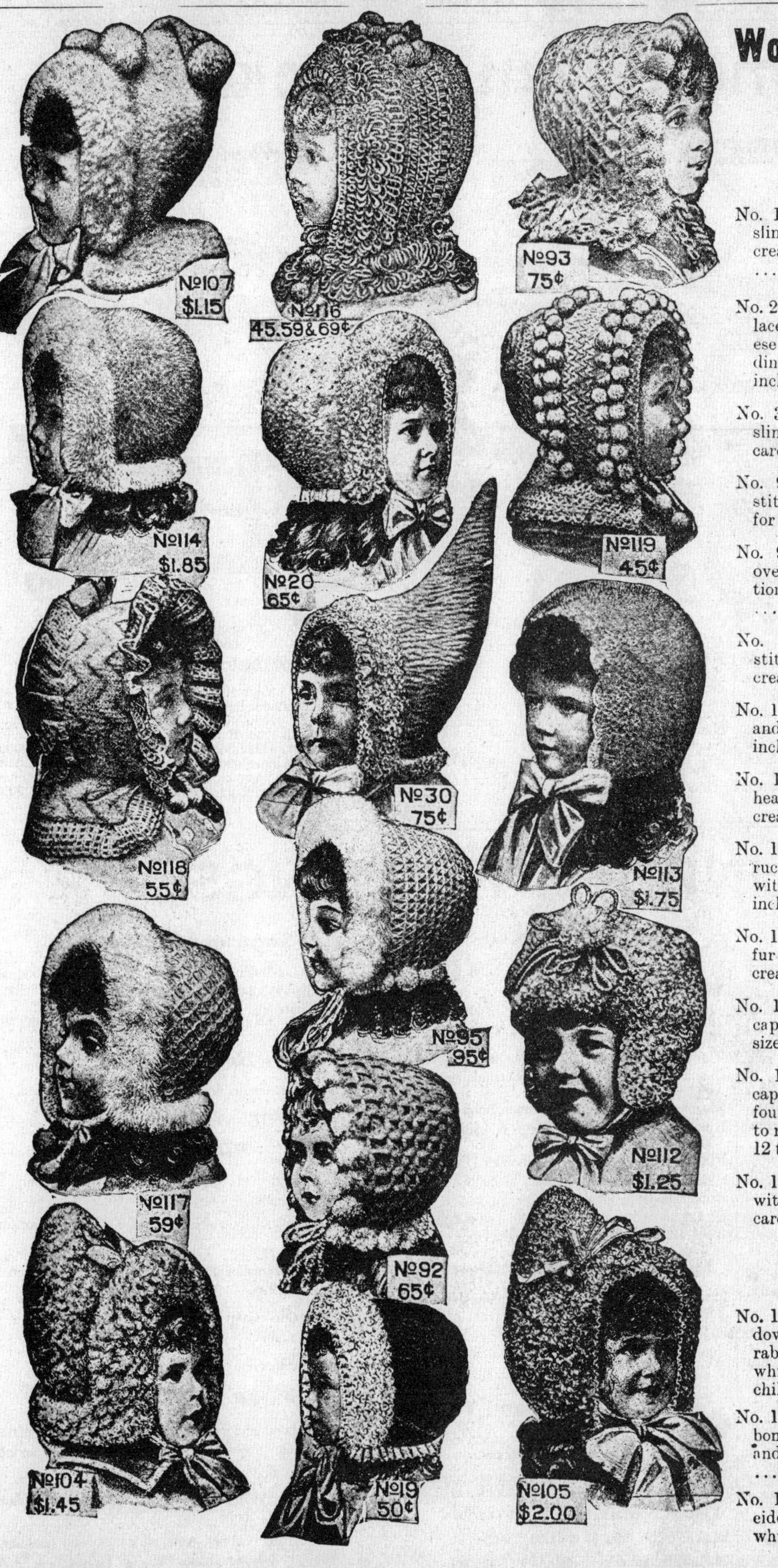

Wool Hoods, Fur and Eiderdown Caps and Bonnets.

No. 19. Ripple eiderdown cap, trimmed slink lamb, mercerized satin ties, colors cream or cardinal, sizes 13 to 16 inches 50c

No. 20. Curl cloth cap, slink lamb trimming, lace edging around face and neck, Japanese silk ties, in cream only, with cardinal, navy or green spot, sizes 13 to 16 inches 65c

No. 30. Ripple eiderdown brownie cap, slink lamb trimming, colors cream or cardinal, sizes 14 to 17 inches 75c

No. 92. Child's zephyr wool cap, overstitched silk braidene, in cream only, for child 1½ to 3 years 65c

No. 93. Zephyr wool cap with curtain, overstitched silk floss and ribbon insertion, in cream only, for ages 2 to 4 years 75c

No. 95. Child's zephyr wool cap overstitched silk floss, swansdown ruche, in cream only, for child 2 to 4 years 95c

No. 104. Clipped lamb bonnet, ribbon bow and ties, cream only, sizes 15 to 17 inches $1.45

No. 105. Slink lamb bonnet, trimmed fur head and narrow ribbon bows, silk ties, cream only, sizes 15 to 17 inches.... $2.00

No. 107. Eiderdown bonnets, clipped llama ruche and balls, colors cream or cardinal with white trimming, sizes 14 to 17 inches $1.15

No. 112. Boys' clipped lamb cap, trimmed fur head and silk cord, ribbon ties, in cream only, sizes 19, 20, 21 inches... $1.25

No. 113. Child's hand-made angora wool cap, Japanese silk ties, white only, sizes 12 to 16 inches $1.75

No. 114. Child's hand-made angora wool cap, swansdown trimming all around, four rows zephyr wool under swansdown to make it firm, Japanese silk ties, sizes 12 to 16 inches.......... $1.85

No. 116. Misses' zephyr wool hood, lined with eiderdown, colors cream, pink, sky, cardinal, garnet, navy and black.

Size 1, 3 to 6 years........ 45c.
" 2, 6 to 12 " .... 59c.
" 3, For misses or ladies.. 69c.

No. 117. Zephyr wool cap, lined with eiderdown, silk flossed and trimmed white rabbit fur, colors white, white and pink, white and sky, white and cardinal, for child 6 months to 2 years.......... 59c

No. 118. Zephyr wool hood, trimmed ribbon bows, colors white, white and sky, and white and pink, ages 4 to 6 years. 55c

No. 119. Zephyr wool hood, lined with eiderdown, colors white, white and pink, white and sky, ages 3 to 5 years...... 45c

Ornaments and Buckles.

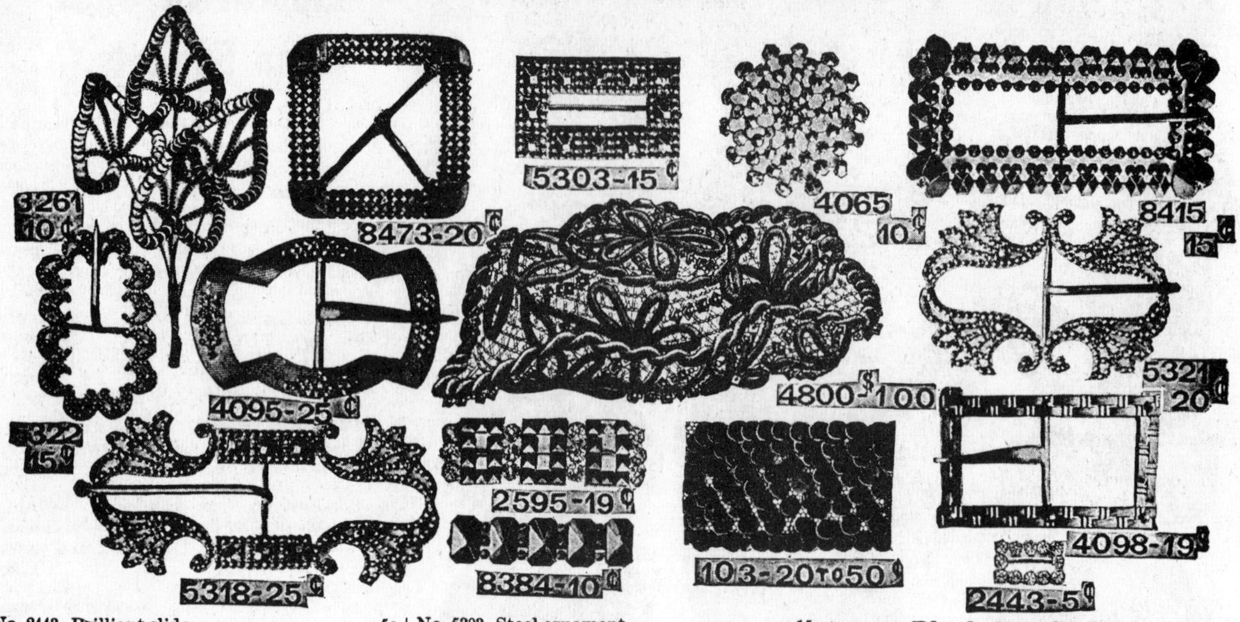

No. 2443. Brilliant slide 5c
No. 2595. Jet and brilliant pin 19c
No. 3261. Sequin and chenille spray, black only 10c
No. 4065. Steel ornaments 10c
No. 4095. Gilt and steel buckle 25c
No. 4098. Gilt buckle 19c
No. 4800. Sequin and chenille bonnet, black only $1.00

No. 5303. Steel ornament 15c
No. 5318. Steel buckle 25c
No. 5321. Steel buckle 20c
No. 5322. Steel buckle 15c
No. 8384. Jet pin 10c
No. 8415. Jet buckle 15c
No. 8473. Jet buckle 20c
No. 103. Black sequin trimming, 1½ inches wide, 20c yd; 1¾ inches wide, 25c yd; 2½ inches wide, 35c yd; 4 inches wide, 50c yd.

Black Sequin Crowns.

No. 2801. 10½ x 10½ inches, Brussels net ground, chenille centre 50c
No. 2464. Round crown, very effective design, 12-inch size, Brussels net ground 75c
No. 2454. Handsome design, 14½ x 14½ inches, Brussels net ground $1.00
No. 2452. Very rich new design, 14½ x 14½ inches, Brussels net ground $1.25

MILLINERY TRIMMINGS.

Millinery Velvets.

Black silk millinery velvet, 18 inches wide, very even close pile, every line a leader at the price. We make a specialty of millinery velvets, and show the best values in Canada, 50c, 69c, 75c, 85c, $1.00, 1.25, 1.50 and 2.00 yd.

50X. Colored silk millinery velvet, 18 inches wide, in following shades: light, medium and dark castor, and same in browns, royal blue, medium and dark navy, light blue, coquelicot red, cardinal, light and medium grey, violet, russe and myrtle green, and turquoise, special value, 65c yd.

No. 60. Colored silk millinery velvet (our leader), in all the new fall tints, as well as staple shades, 18 inches wide, very bright finish, a splendid millinery velvet, $1.00 yd.

Millinery Chiffons.

No. H1643. Special millinery chiffon, all silk, 40 inches wide, in black, white and cream only, extra value, 25c yd.

No. H1235. Extra quality pure silk chiffon, 40, 42 inches wide, special semi-stiff finish for millinery purposes, in black, white, cream and all leading spring shades, 39c yd.

Maids' Caps.

Fancy maids' caps, 8c, 10c, 12½c, 15c, 20c each.

Washing caps, 10c, 12½c, 15c, 20c, 25c each.

Old Ladies' Dress Caps.

Old ladies' caps, made of black lace and ribbon, ribbon ties, 75c, $1.00, 1.25, 1.50.

Widows' Caps.

Widows' caps, with fall, 75c, $1.00, 1.25, 1.50.

Without fall, 75c, $1.00.

Hat Wires, etc.

Black and colored satin wire, heavy, 5c yd.

Black and white satin wire, medium, 2 yds for 5c; fine, 3 yds for 5c.

Black or white silk block wire, 8-yd ring, for 10c.

Black and white iron wire, 3 yds for 5c; or large ring, 15c.

Black and white flat ribbon wire, card, 10c.

Black and white buckram, 27-inch, 25c yd.

Buckram bonnet shape, 20c.

Buckram shapes in turbans, dress hats, etc., 25c and 35c, according to shape.

Bridal and Communion Veils.

Mechlin veils, 72 x 72 inches, handsomely embroidered—

No. 411 .... $1.00
No. 412 .... 1.25
No. 443 .... 1.50
No. 444 .... 1.75

Mourning Veils and Veiling.

Widows' silk lisse veils, correct styles and sizes, $2.50, 3.00, 4.00, 5.00, 5.50, 6.00 each.

Widows' silk lisse veiling, 42-inch, plain border on both edges, 85c, $1.00, 1.25 yd.

Widows' borders, 10c, 15c, 20c each.

Black crepe, 75c, $1.00, 1.25, 1.50 yd.

Mourning face veils, 35c, 50c, 75c each.

Swansdown Trimming.

No. 500. 1-inch swansdown trimming, 25c; 1½-inch, 35c; 2-inch, 50c; 2½-inch, 65c yd.

[NOTE.—Measurement is for fur side, not back.]

Bridal Flowers.

Orange blossom wreaths, 75c, $1.00, 1.25, 1.50.

Orange blossom sprays, 75c, $1.00.

Black Flowers.

010. Single violets, black satin, 3 dozen in packet, 25c.

050. Black silk double violets, 3 dozen in packet, 35c.

060. Black satin roses with jet centres, 6 in a packet, 25c.

070. Black satin roses, good quality, 6 in a packet, 50c.

080. Black silk roses, 3 in packet, 50c.

Colored Roses and Violets.

010. Velvet crush roses, 6 in a bunch in pink, old rose, violet, turquoise and dark cerise, 25c.

020. Single velvet violets, natural shades, 3 doz. in packet, 15c

030. Double velvet and silk violets, natural shades, 3 dozen in packet, 35c.

FANCY FEATHERS, BIRDS AND WINGS.

67. Shaded breast effect, in green, red, fawn and brown colorings 35c
103. Breast effect, curled quill ends, black only . . 19c
3859. Soft quill mount, in two colors, black and white, black and red, red and white, light navy and white, castor and brown 25c
3878. Feather pom-pom, castor, brown, red, black, 25c
3889. Curled aigret, black only 19c
3891. Breast effect, in white tipped black, red tipped black, castor tipped brown, light navy tipped white, black tipped white, and solid black .. 25c
3892. Natural coque tail, black shaded dark green 25c
3900. Fancy side mount, shaded colorings of brown, fawn, cardinal and green 50c
3902. Black breast, fine feathers and well made mount 59c
3912. Breast effect, shaded fawn to castor and tipped dark green, a very effective feather, above coloring only 50c
3918. Curled quill mount, castor, brown, red, light navy, black and white 19c
3964. Handsome blackbird, well cured 75c
3968. Black parrot, fine, clean, well-cured bird, 65c
3969. Pair natural gull wings, medium size, correct shape for the season $1.00
3994. Soft quill mount, tipped black sequin, castor, brown, red, light navy, black and white, 10c
3998. Soft quill, side mount, castor, light blue, brown, grey, red, white and black, all tipped black sequins 19c
4008. Bird and quill mount tipped black sequins, colors castor, brown, red, light navy and black 15c
4022. Fawn bird, with white wings and breast effect, above coloring only 39c
4023. Fancy mount, composed of bird's head and small wings, in two colors, black with castor, brown, red or white 50c
4024. Small blackbird 25c
4457. Black breast effect, with sequins 35c
4518. Pair wings, in white, castor, brown, light navy, red and black 25c
5371. Merle bird, with wings and coque tails, natural dark green shaded effects 69c

OSTRICH FEATHERS AND OSPREYS.

Black single ostrich mounts, range A, 25c, 50c, 75c, $1.00, 1.25, 1.50 ea. A larger mount than style B.
Black single ostrich mounts, range B, style as cut.
Extra quality fibre, 25c, 50c, 75c, $1.00, 1.25, 1.50, 2.00, 2.25 .... 2.75 each
White and cream single mounts, 25c, 50c, 75c, $1.00, 1.25, 1.50, 2.00, 2.25 .... 2.75 each
Leading fall shades in single mounts, 75c, $1.00, ... $1.50 each

Tips, Three in a Bunch.

Black ostrich tips, 3 in a bunch, 50c, 75c, $1.00, 1.25, 1.50, 2.00, 2.50 .... $3.25 bunch
White and cream tips, 3 in a bunch, 50c, 75c, $1.00, 1.50 .... $2.00 bunch
Our special ostrich tips, 3 in a bunch, in black, white and colors, very special .... 25c bunch

Long Ostrich Plumes, as Cut C.

In black, $1.25, 1.75, 2.25, 2.75, 3.25, 3.75, 4.25, ... $5.00 each
In white or cream, $1.75, 2.25, 2.75, 3.25, 3.75 each.

Ospreys.

Flowing osprey (sold according to number of sprays in mount) black or white, 2-spray mounts, special 12½c; also 25c, 50c, 75c .... $1.00 each
Bird of paradise osprey, in black, white or natural, 50c, 75c, $1.00, 1.50, 2.00, 2.50 ...... $3.00 each
Cross osprey, black or white, 25c, 50c, 75c, $1.00, ... $1.25 each
Stub osprey, black or white, 25c .... 50c each

Worn Gloves Not Exchanged.

LADIES' GLOVES.

Postage paid on all Unlined Gloves only.

SEND SIZES AND SHADE REQUIRED WHEN ORDERING GLOVES.

1. 2-dome lamb gloves, colors tan, brown, oxblood, white and black, sizes 5¾ to 8 ....49c, 65c, 69c, 75c
2. 2-dome French kid gloves, colors tan, brown, mode, fawn, oxblood, grey, white, pearl, black and blue, sizes 5¾ to 7½ 75c
3. 2-dome French kid gloves, princess pique sewn, also over-seam, colors tan, brown, mode, grey, oxblood, white, black, pearl and butter, sizes 5½ to 7½ 1.00
4. 2-dome fine French kid gloves, pique sewn, colors tan, brown, mode, fawn, grey, pearl, white, blue, oxblood and black, sizes 5½ to 7½ 1.25
5. 2-dome finest quality French kid gloves, pique sewn, Paris points, colors tan, fawn, mode, grey, beaver, oxblood, pearl, grey, white, blue, butter and black, sizes 5½ to 7 ....1.50
6. 7-hook lacing kid gloves, in black only, sizes 5¾ to 8..........75c, 1.00
7. 2-dome driving gloves, mocha, good to wear, tan and grey colors only, sizes 5¾ to 7 ....1.25
8. 3-pearl button napa driving gloves, Paris points, color English tan, sizes 5¾ to 7 ....1.50
9. 1-dome cuff driving gloves, colors tan and red tan, sizes 6 to 8....1.00

Mocha Gloves.

10. 2-dome mocha gloves, in grey and black only, sizes 5½ to 7½ 1.50

Suede Gloves.

11. 2-dome suede gloves, over-sewn seams, colors black and grey, sizes 5½ to 7½.................1.00, 1.50
12. 2-dome pique sewn suede gloves, colors black and grey, sizes 5½ to 7½.............................1.25, 1.50

Evening Gloves.

13. Mousquetaire suede gloves, colors cream, white, pink, sky, heliotrope and black, sizes 5½ to 7—
Button length, 12, 16, 20, 24,
Price 1.50. 1.75. 2.50. 2.75

13½. Silk evening gloves, colors cream, white and black—
Button length, 18, 22, 26, 32,
Price 50c. 65c. 75c. 1.00

14. Ladies' fur top wool-lined kid gloves, colors tan and brown, sizes 5½ to 7½ 75c, 1.00

14½. 2-clasp mocha gloves, without fur top, wool lined, all sizes ..1.25

15. Elastic and fur top kid mitts, wool lined, colors tan and brown, sizes 5½ to 8.......................75c, 1.00

16. Plain black cashmere gloves, in black only........15c, 20c, 25c, 35c

Also frame made silk plaited goves...................................35c

17. 2-dome cashmere gloves, in black only 25c, 35c, 45c, 50c

18. Ringwood gloves, in assorted colors and patterns, all sizes, ...20c, 25c, 35c, 45c, 50c

Also plain colors, black, white, red and grey 25c, 35c, 50c

19. Plain black wool mitts 20c, 25c, 35c, 45c, 50c

20. Fancy back black wool mitts 35c, 45c, 50c

21. Plain black silk mitts 1.00, 1.25

22. Fancy back black silk mitts 1.50, 1.75, 2.00, 2.25

23. Black and grey imitation astrachan mitts, all sizes 75c, 1.00

MEN'S, BOYS' AND MISSES' GLOVES.

Boys' and Misses' Kid Gloves.

24. Boys' and misses' unlined kid gloves, colors tan, brown and ox-blood, sizes 1 to 6 ....**50c, 75c**

25. Boys' and misses' lined kid gloves, sizes 2 to 6 ....**50c, 65c, 75c, 1.00**

26. Misses' and boys' elastic top kid mitts, tan and brown, sizes 2 to 6 ....**35c, 50c**

27. Misses' fur top lined kid mitts, sizes 2 to 6 ....**50c**

28. Boys' and misses' fancy ring-wood gloves **20c, 25c, 35c, 45c**

29. Boys' and misses' single wool mitts **15c, 20c**
Also double wool mitts **25c, 35c, 45c**

30. Boys' and girls' imitation astrachan mitts, sizes 1 to 6, in grey only **50c, 65c**

Men's Gloves.

31. Men's unlined kid gloves, in white only..................**50c, 75c**

32. Men's kid gloves, unlined, pique-sewn, Paris points, in tan and brown, sizes 7 to 10 ..**75c, 1.00, 1.25**

33. Men's-dome French kid gloves, pique-sewn, colors tan and black, also mocha gloves, in grey only, sizes 7 to 9½ **1.50**

34. Fowns' grip driving gloves, sizes 7½ to 9 ....**2.00**

35. Men's napa tan driving gloves, in tan and red tan colors, sizes 7½ to 10..................**1.00, 1.25, 1.50**

Lined Gloves.

36. Men's lined kid gloves, 1 clasp, colors tan and brown, **50c, 65c, 75c, 1.00**; also in black, **1.00, 1.50**; 2-clasp, with fine wool lining...... ....**75c, 1.00, 1.25, 1.50**

37. Fine kid gloves, with medium weight lining, sizes 7½ to 10 ....**1.00, 1.25, 1.50**

38. Men's outside seamed gloves, colors tan and brown, with wool lining, sizes 7 to 10.. **1.00, 1.25, 1.50**

39. Men's wool lined and fur top kid gloves, tan and brown colors, sizes 7½ to 10 ....**1.00, 1.25**

Mocha Gloves.

40. Men's lined imitation mocha gloves, sizes 7 to 10........**75c, 1.00**
Also men's mocha gloves in tan colors only, sizes 7 to 10 ....**1.25, 1.50, 2.00**

41. Men's lined gloves, with wool top, oil tan colors **50c, 65c**

42. Men's chrome tan lined glove, with strap, **75c**; para buck, **1.10**; calfskin, **1.25**; buckskin **1.50**

43. Men's black leather gauntlet gloves, lined, sizes 7½ to 10 ....**1.00**

44. Men's imitation astrachan gauntlet driving gloves, wool-lined, sizes 7½ to 10 ....**1.00**

45. Men's 1-clasp fur-lined mocha gloves, tan shades only, sizes 7 to 10................................**2.25, 3.00**

46. Men's kid mitts, wool-lined, sizes 7½ to 10..............**50c, 75c, 1.00**

47. Men's mitts, lined and made with one finger........**35c, 50c, 65c, 75c**

48. Men's comfort, roll top leather mitts, wool top **45c**

49. Men's oil tan mitts, lined, made with wool top, also made with elastic top....................**50c, 65c**

50. Men's pigskin mitts, heavy wool lining, special **75c**

51. Men's para buck mitts, wool lined, **1.00**; calfskin, **1.25**; buckskin **1.50**

52. Men's ringwood gloves, in fancy patterns, also in plain black **25c, 35c, 45c, 50c**

Infantees.

53. Infantees, in cream and white **10c, 15c, 20c, 25c, 35c**

Pull-Over Mitts.

54. Men's pull-over mitts, in oil tan, **50c**; chrome tan, **75c**; para buck, **1.00**; calfskin, **1.00**; buckskin..**1.50**

Wool Mitts.

55. Men's wool mitts, hand knit, colored, good heavy mitt **35c**
Also men's plain black double wool mitts **35c, 50c**

FUR DEPARTMENT.

Our Catalogue is not exaggerated, every statement and illustration is a fact of value and reliability. We think you can order from it to better advantage than you can buy in your own town. Hundreds are ordering from it daily and think so too.

Furs are a class of goods most people cannot tell the actual value of. It is important that you should buy from a house of unquestioned reputation. Buying direct from trappers and shippers in the best fur-trading centres of the world, and making our furs on our own premises, enable us to both guarantee their quality and offer them at the lowest prices in the market; no manufacturer of high-grade furs can undersell us. Furs, above everything, must be right; we use nothing but fine skins. Our Sealskins are the very choicest and are dyed by Rice, of London, England. The workmanship and linings are of the very best, and we employ only the very best skilled artists. You are quite safe in selecting any furs you may require from us. Here is your guarantee, "Money refunded if goods are not satisfactory."

FURS REMODELLED INTO THIS YEAR'S LATEST STYLES.

SEALSKIN AND PERSIAN LAMB JACKETS.

32 to 42 inches Bust Measure.

700. SEALSKIN JACKET, 24 inches long, choice selected skins, lined silk-backed satin linings, as cut 700 .... 185.00

701. Same jacket and style, 27 inches long 215 00

702. SEALSKIN, with chinchilla collar and large revers, 21 inches long, as cut 702 .... 250.00

703. SEALSKIN, with Russian sable collar and revers, 24 inches long, as cut 703 .... 350.00

704. PERSIAN LAMB JACKET, 22 inches long, bright glossy curl, best satin linings, as cut 704 ...... 95 00

705. PERSIAN LAMB JACKET, 24 inches long, as cut 704 ...... 100 00

706. PERSIAN LAMB JACKET, 26 inches long, as cut 704 ...... 110.00

707. PERSIAN LAMB JACKET, 24 inches long, collar and revers Alaska sable, as cut 707 .... 110.00

708. PERSIAN LAMB JACKET, 24 inches long, collar and revers Labrador mink, as cut 707 ...... 115.00

Electric Seal, Astrachan, Grey Lamb, and Raccoon Jackets.

32 to 42 inches Bust Measure.

709. **ELECTRIC SEAL JACKET,** 22 inches long, satin-lined, as cut 709 .... **30.00**

710. Same, 24 inches long, as cut 709 .... **32.50**

711. Same, 26 inches long, as cut 709 .... **35.00**

712. **ELECTRIC SEAL,** with Alaska sable collar and revers, 24 inches long, as cut 712 .... **40.00**

713. As 712, only dark Labrador mink collar and revers, 24 inches long **45.00**

714. As 712, only beaver collar and revers, 24 inches long **45.00**

715. BLACK ASTRACHAN JACKET, satin linings, 26 inches long, as cut 715 .... **25.00**

716. BLACK ASTRACHAN JACKET, extra choice, 26 inches long, as cut 715 .... **30.00**

717. BLACK ASTRACHAN JACKET, 26 inches long, as cut 715 .. **35.00**

718. BLACK ASTRACHAN JACKET, 36 inches long, heavy Italian lining, coarse curl, strong pelts, as cut 718 .... **20.00**

719. BLACK ASTRACHAN JACKET, 36 inches long, as cut 718, medium curl **25.00**

720. BLACK ASTRACHAN JACKET, 36 inches long, as cut 718, satin lined, chamois pockets .. **30.00**

721. BLACK ASTRACHAN JACKET, 36 inches long, as cut 718, glossy even curl **35.00**

722. BLACK ASTRACHAN JACKET, 36 inches long, as cut 718, all glossy skins **40.00**

723. BLACK ASTRACHAN JACKET, 36 inches long, as cut 718, extra choice skins **45.00**

724. GREY LAMB JACKET, satin linings, 22 inches long, as cut 724 .... **37.50**

725. DARK RACCOON JACKET, 30 inches long, heavy Italian linings, full furred, as cut 725 .... **35.00**

726. Same, 36 inches long, full furred and evenly matched, as cut 725 .... **45.00**

727. MISSES' AND BOYS' ICELAND LAMB JACKET, satin lined, 26, 28 and 30 inches long, as cut 727 .... **12.00**

728. WOMEN'S WALLABY JACKET, 27 inches long, as cut 725 .... **18.50**

Caperines and Fancy Shoulder Scarfs.

Write for quotations for any Furs you cannot find in this catalogue.

ALL SATIN LINED.

ALL OUR FURS ARE GUARANTEED.

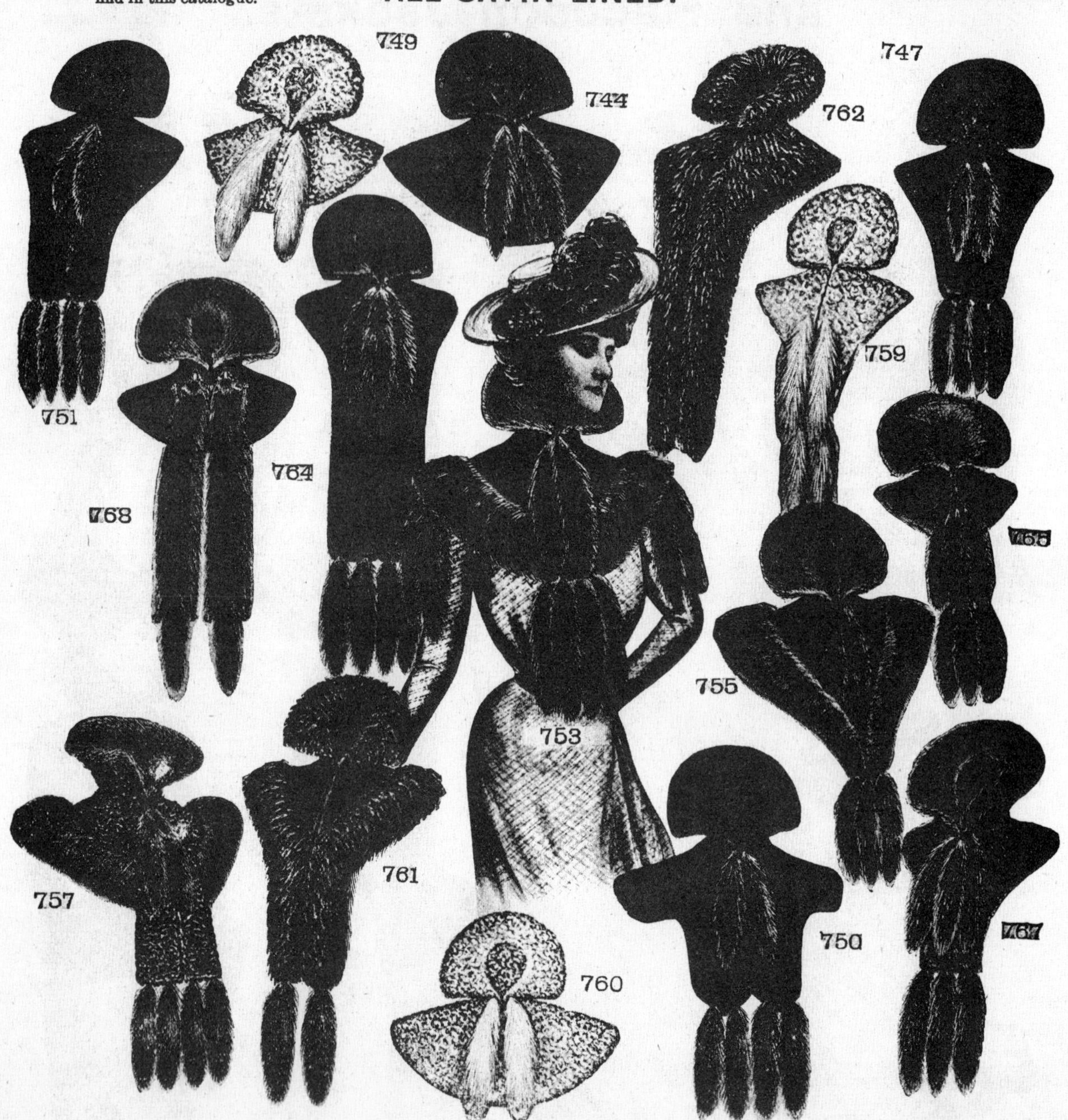

744. BLACK ASTRACHAN, satin-lined, as cut 744 .... **5.00**

745. BLACK OPOSSUM, as cut 744 .... **6.50**

746. ELECTRIC SEAL, as cut 744 .... **7.50**

747. ELECTRIC SEAL, as cut 747 .... **7.50**

748. BEAVERIZED NUTRIA, as cut 747 .... **7.50**

749. MISSES' GREY LAMB, as cut 749 .... **8.00**

750. ELECTRIC SEAL, as cut 750 .... **9.00**

751. ELECTRIC SEAL, as cut 751 .... **10.50**

752. BLACK ASTRACHAN, as cut 751 .... **10.50**

753. ELECTRIC SEAL, with blue opossum trimming, as cut 753 .... **10.50**

754. ELECTRIC SEAL, with black opossum trimming, as cut 753 .... **10.50**

755. ELECTRIC SEAL, with blue opossum trimming, as cut 755 .... **10.50**

756. Same, with black opossum trimming, as cut 755 .... **10.50**

757. ASTRACHAN YOKE and electric seal top collar and trimmings, as cut 757 .... **12.50**

758. ELECTRIC SEAL, with top collar of astrachan and trimmed with astrachan, as cut 757 .... **12.50**

759. GREY LAMB, as cut 759 .... **12.50**

760. GREY LAMB, as cut 760 .... **13.50**

761. ELECTRIC SEAL, trimmed with black Thibet, as cut 761 .... **13.50**

762. BLACK THIBET, as cut 762 .... **13.50**

763. ELECTRIC SEAL, trimmed with South American sable, as cut 753 .... **13.50**

764. ELECTRIC SEAL, as cut 764 .... **13.50**

765. BLACK PERSIAN LAMB, as cut 765 .... **17.50**

766. ALASKA SABLE, as cut 765 .... **17.50**

767. ALASKA SABLE, as cut 767 .... **20.00**

768. ALASKA SABLE and electric seal, as cut 768 .... **20.00**

Caperines and Fancy Shoulder Scarfs

769. ELECTRIC SEAL AND ALASKA SABLE, as cut 769 .... 20.00

770. BLACK PERSIAN LAMB AND ALASKA SABLE, as cut 770 .... 20.00

771. ALASKA SABLE, as cut 771 .... 22.50

772. ELECTRIC SEAL AND ALASKA SABLE, as cut 770 .... 16.50

773. ALASKA SABLE, as cut 773 .... 25.00

774. BLACK PERSIAN LAMB AND ALASKA SABLE, as cut 774 .... 25.00

776. ALASKA SABLE, as cut 776 .... 25.00

777. BLACK PERSIAN LAMB and ALASKA SABLE, as cut 777 .... 30.00

778. DARK CANADIAN MINK, see front and back view, as cuts 778 .... 30.00

779. ALASKA SABLE, as cut 779 .... 30.00

780. BLACK PERSIAN LAMB and ALASKA SABLE, as cut 780 .... 32.50

781. Same, only style as cut 781 .... 32.50

782. ALASKA SABLE, as cut 782 .... 35.00

783. BLACK PERSIAN LAMB and ALASKA SABLE, see back and front view, as cuts 783.... 35.00

784. ALASKA SABLE, as cut 784 .... 37.50

785. ALASKA SABLE, as cut 782 .... 35.00

786. DARK CANADIAN BEAVER, as cut 786 .... **35.00**

787. ALASKA SABLE, as cut 787 .... **40.00**

788. BLACK PERSIAN LAMB AND ALASKA SABLE, as cut 788 .... **45.00**

789. SEALSKIN AND STONE MARTEN, see back and front view of cuts 783 .... **50.00**

790. ALASKA SABLE, same style as cut 790 .... **42.50**

791. DARK LABRADOR MINK, as cut 790 .... **75.00**

Mink, Persian Lamb, Electric Seal, Astrachan Capes

All satin lined. Be careful to give correct measurements and number of cut required.

735 743 742 695 741 729

737. BLACK CONEY CAPES, 27 inches long, as cut 735 ...... 10.00
729. BLACK ASTRACHAN CAPES, 24 inches long, as cut 729 .... 13.50
730. Same, only 27 inches long, as cut 729 .... 16.50
740. WOOL SEAL CAPES, 24 inches long, as cut 735 ...... 16.50
738. BLACK OPOSSUM CAPES, 24 inches long, as cut 735 ..... 20.00
739. Same, only 27 inches long, as cut 735 .... 22.50
735. ELECTRIC SEAL CAPES, 24 inches long, as cut 735 ..... 22.50
736. Same, only 27 inches long, as cut 735 .... 27.50
697. GREY LAMB, 24 inches long, as cut 695 .... 27.50
698. Same, only 27 inches long, as cut 695 .... 32.50

731. BLACK ASTRACHAN CAPES, choice quality, 27 inches long, as cut 729 .... 22.50
732. Same, only 33 inches long, as cut 729 .... 30.00
734. Same, only 36 inches long, as cut 729 .... 35.00
741. ELECTRIC SEAL, and Alaska sable collar, with 2 inches on each side down front, 27 inches long, as cut 741 .... 40.00
695. BLACK PERSIAN LAMB CAPE, bright glossy skins, 24 inches long, as cut 695 .... 75.00
696. Same, only 27 inches long, as cut 695 .... 90.00
742. DARK LABRADOR MINK CAPES, 24 inches long, as cut 742 .... 100.00
743. EXTRA CHOICE LABRADOR MINK CAPES, 33 inches long, as cut 743 .... 200.00

LADIES' MEASUREMENT FORM.

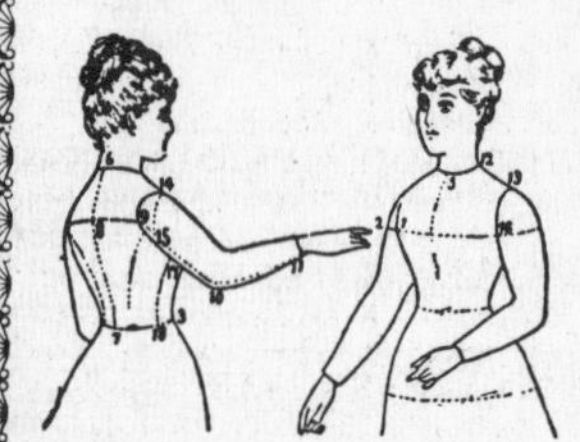

1 to 1—Around bust and back under arms.
2 to 2—Around bust and back over arms.
3 to 3—Around waist.
4 to 4—Around hips.
5 to 5—Around neck.
6 to 7—Length of waist.
8 to 9—Centre of back to shoulder.
8 to 10—Centre of back to elbow.
8 to 11—Centre of back to wrist.
12 to 13—Across shoulder.
14 to 15—Armhole.
1 to 16—Across bust, seam to seam.
17 to 18—Length of waist under arms.
Length of garment.

Ladies' Jackets larger than 42 inches bust will cost more, according to quality of garment.

Ladies' and Misses' Neck Scarfs and Boas

792. ALASKA SABLE, as cut 792 ....**27.50**

793. ALASKA SABLE, as cut 793 ....**20.00**

794. WHITE FOX, as cut 794 ..**15 00**

795. BLUE FOX, as cut 794 ....**15.00**

796. BLACK FOX, as cut 794 ..**15.00**

797. ISABELLA FOX, as cut 794 ....**15.00**

798. FOX MUFF TO MATCH 794, 795, 796, 797, as cut 798 ....**15.00**

799. RED FOX, as cut 794 ......**7.50**

800. FOX MUFF TC MATCH 799, as cut 798 ....**7.50**

801. STONE MARTEN, 56 inches long, as cut 801 ....**35.00**

802. STONE MARTEN, 42 inches long, as cut 802..................**25.00**

803. STONE MARTEN, 36 inches long, as cut 812 ....**17.50**

804. DARK CANADIAN MINK, 10 natural tails, 52 inches long, as cut 804 ....**25.00**

805. Same, 40 inches long, 10 natural tails, as cut 804 ....**20.00**

806. ALASKA SABLE, 54 inches long, as cut 801 ....**18.00**

807. ALASKA SABLE, 50 inches long, as cut 801 ....**16.50**

808. Same, only 44 inches long, as cut 801 ....**15.00**

809. Same, only 40 inches long, as cut 801 ....**12.50**

810. BLACK CUB BEAR, 54 inches long, as cut 810 ....**12.50**

811. DARK CANADIAN MINK, 36 inches long, as cut 811, only 10 tails **13.50**

812. Same, only 30 inches long, 8 tails, as cut 812 ....**10.00**

813. ALASKA SABLE, 30 inches long, as cut 812 ....**10.00**

814. ALASKA SABLE, small shape, 30 inches long, as cut 812 ......**8.50**

815. ALASKA SABLE, 27 inches long, as cut 815........................**7.50**

816. ELECTRIC SEAL, as cut 816 ....**5.00**

817. ALASKA SABLE, as cut 817 ....**5 00**

818. MINK, as cut 817 ....**5.00**

819. BLACK THIBET **BOA**, 54 inches long, as cut 819.........**5.00**

820. WHITE THIBET, 54 inches long, as cut 819 ....**5.00**

821. SABLE RUFF, as cut 821 ..**3.75**

822. MINK RUFF, as cut 821....**4.00**

823. BLACK ASTRACHAN RUFF, as cut 821 ....**2.50**

824. BLACK PERSIAN LAMB RUFF, as cut 821 ....**7.50**

825. GREY LAMB RUFF, as cut 821...**2.25**

826. BLACK OPOSSUM RUFF, as cut 821..............................**2.00**

827. WHITE ICELAND RUFF, as cut 821 ....**1.50**

LADIES' AND MISSES' COLLARS, MUFFS, AND CHILDREN'S FURS

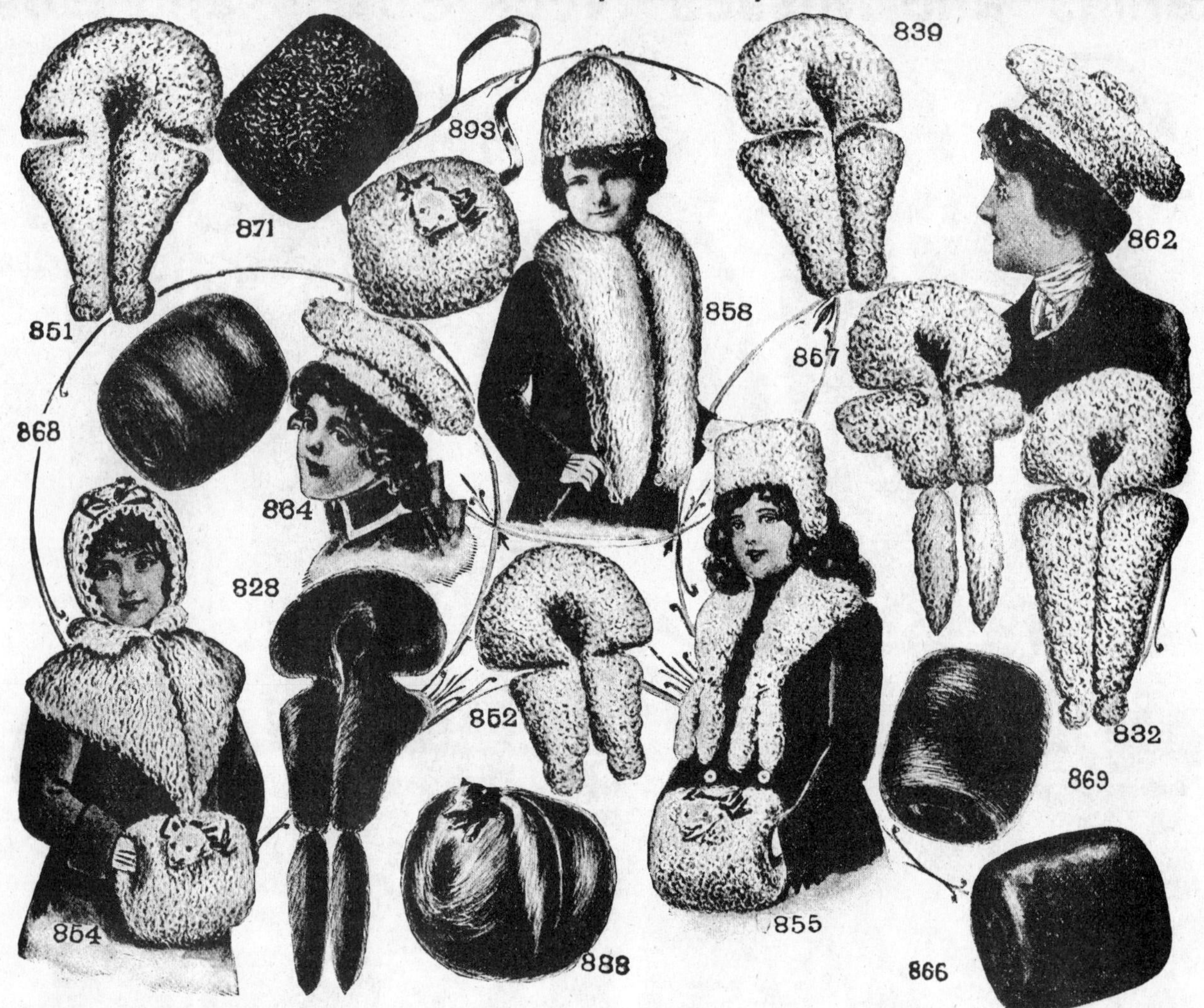

828. **ALASKA SABLE**, as cut 828 .... **17.50**

829. **DARK CANADIAN MINK**, as cut 828 .... **17.50**

830. **BLACK PERSIAN LAMB**, as cut 828 .... **17.50**

831. **DARK CANADIAN BEAVER**, as cut 828 .... **17.50**

832. **GREY LAMB**, as cut 832 .... **6.50**

833. **BEAVERIZED NUTRIA**, as cut 832 .... **5.75**

834. **DARK RACCOON**, as cut 832 .... **5.00**

835. **ELECTRIC SEAL**, as cut 832 .... **5.00**

836. **BLACK ASTRACHAN**, as cut 832 .... **4.50**

837. **BLACK OPOSSUM**, as cut 832 .... **4.50**

838. **FRENCH CONEY**, as cut 832 .... **3.50**

839. **ALASKA SABLE**, as cut 839 .... **15.00**

840. **BLACK PERSIAN LAMB**, as cut 839 .... **15.00**

841. **CANADIAN BEAVER**, as cut 839 .... **15.00**

842. **GREY LAMB**, as cut 839 .... **5.00**

843. **RACCOON**, as cut 839 .... **4.50**

844. **ELECTRIC SEAL**, as cut 839 .... **4.50**

845. **BEAVERIZED NUTRIA**, as cut 839 .... **4.50**

846. **BLACK ASTRACHAN**, as cut 839 .... **3.75**

847. **BLACK OPOSSUM**, as cut 839 .... **3.75**

848. **FRENCH CONEY**, as cut 839 .... **2.50**

849. **IMITATION BLACK PERSIAN LAMB**, as cut 839 .... **2.00**

850. **SEALETTE**, as cut 839 .... **2.00**

851. **MISSES' GREY LAMB**, as cut 851 .... **4.25**

852. **CHILD'S GREY LAMB**, as cut 852 .... **3.75**

853. **MISSES' AND CHILDREN'S ICELAND LAMB**, as cut 852 .... **2.50**

854. **CHILDREN'S ICELAND LAMB SETS**, caperine, muff and cap complete, as cut 854 .... **10.00**

855. **CHILDREN'S GREY LAMB SETS**, collarette, muff and cap complete, as cut 855 .... **12.50**

856. **CHILDREN'S GREY LAMB SETS**, caperine and muff, as cut 854, only no cap **10.00**

857. **CHILDREN'S GREY LAMB CAPERINE**, as cut 857 .... **7.50**

858. **CHILDREN'S WOOL BOAS**, as cut 858, 36 inches **20c**

859. Same, 42 inches **25c**

860. Same, 48 " **35c**

861. Same, 54 " **50c**

862. **LADIES' GREY LAMB TAM O' SHANTER**, as cut 862 .... **4.00**

863. **LADIES' BLACK PERSIAN LAMB**, as cut 862 .... **7.50**

864. **MISSES' GREY LAMB**, as cut 864 .... **3.50**

865. **MISSES' ICELAND LAMB**, as cut 864 .... **2.25**

866. **SEALSKIN MUFFS**, as cut 866 .... **20.00**

867. **CHINCHILLA MUFFS**, as cut 866 .... **25.00**

868. **LABRADOR MINK**, as cut 868 .... **15.00**

869. **ALASKA SABLE**, very choice, as cut 866 .... **10.00**

870. **ALASKA SABLE**, full furred, as cut 869 .... **8.00**

871. **BLACK PERSIAN LAMB**, choice quality, as cut 871 .... **10.00**

872. **BLACK PERSIAN LAMB**, glossy curl, as cut 866 .... **7.50**

873. **STONE MARTEN**, as cut 868 .... **20.00**

874. **DARK CANADIAN BEAVER**, as cut 836 .... **10.00**

875. **BLACK CUB BEAR**, as cut 869 .... **10.00**

876. **BLACK THIBET**, as cut 869 .... **5.00**

877. **WHITE THIBET**, as cut 869 .... **5.00**

878. **ELECTRIC SEAL**, as cut 866 .... **3.50**

879. **BEAVERIZED NUTRIA**, as cut 866 .... **4.00**

880. **DARK RACCOON**, as cut 869 .... **4.00**

881. **GREY LAMB**, as cut 871 .... **3.50**

882. **BLACK ASTRACHAN**, No. 1 quality, as cut 871 .... **3.50**

883. **BLACK ASTRACHAN**, No. 2 quality, strong pelts, as cut 871 .... **2.75**

884. **BLACK OPOSSUM**, as cut 866 .... **2.75**

885. **BLACK CONEY**, as cut 866 .... **2.00**

886. **BLACK IMITATION PERSIAN**, as cut 871 .... **1.75**

887. **SEALETTE**, as cut 866 .... **1.75**

888. **BLACK FOX**, as cut 888 .... **15.00**

889. **WHITE FOX**, as cut 888 .... **15.00**

890. **BLUE FOX**, as cut 888 .... **15.00**

891. **ISABELLA FOX**, as cut 888 .... **15.00**

892. **RED FOX**, as cut 888 .... **7.50**

893. **CHILDREN'S ICELAND LAMB**, as cut 893 .... **1.75**

894. **CHILDREN'S GREY LAMB**, as cut 893 .... **3.00**

Men's, Ladies', Misses' and Boys' Caps, Gauntlets, Adjustable Collars.

Ladies' Gauntlets.

895. SEALSKIN GAUNTLETS, as cut 895 ....20.00
896. DARK LABRADOR MINK, as cut 895 ....13.50
897. DARK CANADIAN BEAVER, as cut 895 ....9.00
898. ALASKA SABLE, as cut 920 ....10.00
899. BLACK PERSIAN LAMB, first choice, as cut 895 ....9.00
900. BLACK PERSIAN LAMB, second choice, as cut 895 ......7.50
901. BLACK PERSIAN LAMB, third choice, as cut 895 ....5.00
902. ELECTRIC SEAL, as cut 895 ....3.75
903. BEAVERIZED NUTRIA, as cut 895 ....4.00
904. GREY LAMB, LADIES', as cut 905 ....4.00
905. GREY LAMB, MISSES', as cut 906 ....3.50
906. GREY LAMB, CHILDS', as cut 906, only smaller 2.50
907. BLACK OPOSSUM, LADIES', as cut 895 ....3.75
908. BLACK ASTRACHAN, first choice, as cut 895 ....4.00
909. BLACK ASTRACHAN, second choice, as cut 895 ....3.00
910. RACCOON, as cut 920 ......4.00
911. MISSES' ICELAND LAMB, as cut 906, only smaller 1.75

Men's Gauntlets.

912. BLACK PERSIAN LAMB GAUNTLET GLOVES, choice quality, as cut 912 ....15.00
913. BLACK PERSIAN LAMB GAUNTLET GLOVES, medium curl, as cut 912 ....12.50
914. BLACK PERSIAN LAMB GAUNTLET GLOVES, strong coarse pelt, as cut 912 ....10.00
915. OTTER GAUNTLET GLOVES, as cut 912 ....20.00
916. OTTER GAUNTLET GLOVES, medium color, as cut 912......15.00
917. DARK CANADIAN BEAVER GAUNTLET GLOVES, as cut 912 ....15.00
918. BEAVERIZED NUTRIA GAUNTLET GLOVES, as cut 912 ....7.50
919. BLACK ASTRACHAN GAUNTLET GLOVES, as cut 912 ....7.50
920. RACCOON GAUNTLET MITTS, as cut 920............ 5.00
921. WOMBAT GAUNTLET MITTS, as cut 920............3.50
922. BLACK ASTRACHAN GAUNTLET MITTS, as cut 920 ....7.50
923. BLACK PERSIAN LAMB GAUNTLET MITTS, as cut 920 ....12.50

Men's Adjustable Collars.

(All as cut 924.)

924. OTTER COLLARS, fine quality, as cut 924............20.00
925. OTTER, medium quality..15.00
926. DARK CANADIAN BEAVER, as cut 924 .... 15.00
927. BLACK PERSIAN LAMB, as cut 924 .... 12.50
928. BLACK PERSIAN LAMB, medium, as cut 924 ....10.00
929. BEAVERIZED NUTRIA, as cut 924....................5.00
930. ASTRACHAN, as cut 924 ..4.00
931. RACCOON, as cut 924 ......5.00

Men's Caps.

932. OTTER, as cut 932 ....16.50
933. OTTER BAND, sealskin top, as cut 933....................16.50
934. DARK MINK, as cut 932..15.00
934A. SEALSKIN, as cut 932..12.50
935. DARK CANADIAN BEAVER, as cut 932 .... 9.00
936. MEDIUM DARK CANADIAN BEAVER, as cut 932 ....7.50
937. BLACK PERSIAN LAMB, choice quality, as cut 937......8.00
938. Same, medium curl, as cut 937 ....6.50
939. Same, smaller curl, as cut 937.5.00
940. BLACK PERSIAN, choice quality, as cut 940 ....8.00
941. BLACK PERSIAN, medium curl, as cut 940 ....6.50
942. BLACK PERSIAN, small curl, as cut 940 ....5.00
943. BLACK PERSIAN, strong coarse pelts, as cut 940 ....3.50
944. BLACK PERSIAN, choice quality, as cut 944..............8.00
945. BLACK PERSIAN, medium curl, as cut 944 ....6.50
946. BALTIC SEAL, as cut 940 ....2.75
947. BALTIC SEAL, as cut 947 ....3.00
948. BALTIC SEAL, as cut 932..2.50
949. BEAVERIZED NUTRIA, as cut 932....................3.00
950. BLACK ASTRACHAN, as cut 937 ....2.75
951. BLACK ASTRACHAN, as cut 947 ....3.00
952. BLACK ASTRACHAN, as cut 940 ....2.75
953. GERMAN OTTER, as cut 932 ....2.50

Ladies', Boys' and Children's.

954. SEALSKIN, as cut 932.....10.50
955. DARK CANADIAN BEAVER, as cut 932................7.50
956. BLACK PERSIAN LAMB, extra choice, as cut 937 ....7.50
957. BLACK PERSIAN LAMB, medium, as cut 937 ....5.00
958. BLACK PERSIAN LAMB, choice, as cut 940 ....7.50
959. BLACK PERSIAN LAMB, medium, as cut 940 ....5.00
960. BLACK ASTRACHAN, as cut 937 ....2.50
961. ELECTRIC SEAL, as cut 932 ....2.50
962. BLACK OPOSSUM, as cut 932....................2.50
963. BEAVERIZED NUTRIA, as cut 932 ....2.50
964. GERMAN OTTER, as cut 932 ....2.00
965. GREY LAMB, choice, as cut 937 ....2.75
966. GREY LAMB, medium, as cut 937 ....2.50
967. GREY LAMB HOOD, as cut 967 ....3.00
968. GREY LAMB TURBAN, with ear laps, as cut 968 ....2.75
969. ICELAND LAMB HOOD, as cut 967....................2.50
970. ICELAND LAMB TURBAN, as cut 968.................. 1.75
971. ICELAND LAMB, WEDGE, as cut 932....................1.50

Directions for Cap Measurement.

MEASURE around the head with a tape-line in the position where the hat or cap is usually worn, find the number of inches, and compare with the scale of sizes, and you will find the exact size. Care should be taken to send the correct size in every case; also state shape, giving the corresponding cut in Catalogue. It is impossible to fill your order properly without this information. Boys' sizes run from 6¼ to 6⅞, men's from 6⅝ to 7⅝, ladies' from 6⅝ to 7⅛.

SCALE OF SIZES

18⅞	6	21⅝	6⅞
19¼	6⅛	22	7
19⅝	6¼	22⅜	7⅛
20	6⅜	22¾	7¼
20½	6½	23¼	7⅜
20⅞	6⅝	23⅝	7½
21¼	6¾	24	7⅝

Larger sizes in caps than 7⅝ will cost more.

Men's Fur-Lined and Fur Overcoats, Sleigh Robes, Hearth and Baby Carriage Rugs.

By buying your Furs from us you buy direct from the manufacturer and save middleman's profit.

Our Furs are made on our premises, under our own supervision.

Men's Coats.

972. MEN'S WALLABY COAT, Italian lining, as cut 972..... 12.50

973. Same, only better quality, as cut 972..... 15.00

974. Same, only extra quality, as cut 972..... 25.00

975. WOMBAT, heavy pelt, as cut 972..... 16.50

976. BLACK RUSSIAN CALF, as cut 972..... 22.50

977. BLACK CORSICAN LAMB, as cut 977..... 19.00

978. BLACK CORSICAN LAMB, extra choice, as cut 977..... 25.00

979. RACCOON COATS, good strong pelts, as cut 972..... 30.00

980. Same, only better quality, as cut 972..... 5.00

981. Same, fuller in fur and better color, as cut 972..... 40.00

982. Same, dark, heavy, and evenly matched, as cut 972..... 45.00

983. Same, extra choice, and full-furred, as cut 972..... 50.00

984. BLACK ASTRACHAN COATS, as cut 977..... 35.00

985. BEAVER SHELL, indigo dye, lined with muskrat body and sleeves, otter collar attached, as cut 985..... 50.00

986. Same, with detachable otter or Persian lamb collar..... 50.00

987. BEAVER SHELL, indigo dye, body and sleeves lined with muskrat, black Persian lamb collar, and trimmed down front with 3-inch black Persian, as cut 987..... 55.00

988. BEAVER SHELL, extra quality otter collar, and body lined with Canadian mink, sleeves lined with chamois and striped satin, chamois pockets, as cut 985..... 90.00

989. Same, only extra quality, in mink lining, as cut 985..... 125.00

990. COACHMAN'S SET, cape, gauntlet and cap, in brown bear-goat, as cut 990..... 25.00

991. Same, only in cub bear, as cut 990..... 65.00

Sleigh Robes.

992. GREY GOAT, lined heavy cardinal plush, size 42 x 66 inches..... 6.00

993. Same, only 52 x 66 inches..... 7.00

994. Same, only 60 x 70 inches..... 8.50

995. WHITE GOAT, 42 x 66 inches..... 6.00

996. Same, 52 x 66 inches..... 7.00

997. Same, 60 x 70 inches..... 8.50

998. BLACK GOAT, heavy plush linings and fast dye, 52 x 66 inches..... 10.00

999. Same, 60 x 70 inches..... 12.50

1000. RED RIVER ROBES, imitation buffalo, with waterproof rubber interlining, plush outside, thoroughly waterproof, 54 x 50 inches..... 6.25

1001. Same, only 62 x 54 inches..... 7.25

1002. Same, only 72 x 54 inches..... 8.25

1003. WOLF ROBES, medium size..... 20.00

1004. Same, only larger size..... 25.00

1005. MUSK-OX ROBES, heavy skins, 65.00 each; pair..... 125.00

Baby Carriage Robes.

1006. GREY GOAT, 33 x 33 inches, as cut 1006..... 1.95

1007. WHITE GOAT, same size, as cut 1006..... 1.95

1008. WHITE SHEEPSKIN, lined with felt, medium grade, as cut 1006..... 1.95

1009. WHITE WOOL, as cut 1006..... 2.50

1010. Same, finer quality, as cut 1006..... 3.00

1011. WHITE WOOL, with shaped head, as cut 1011..... 3.50

1012. WHITE ICELAND LAMB, as cut 1006..... 5.00

1013. WHITE THIBET, as cut 1006..... 10.00

Hearth Robes.

1014. GREY GOATSKIN, 28 x 66 inches..... 2.50

1015. WHITE GOATSKIN, same size..... 2.50

1016. WHITE SHEEPSKIN, same size..... 2.50

1017. BLACK GOATSKIN, same size..... 3.75

Men's, Boys' and Children's Headwear from Maker to Wearer.

WE show nothing but the very latest and fashionable London, Paris and New York styles. We clear out all lines at the end of each season, which allows us to visit personally twice yearly all the European markets. We buy direct from the factories where made, in very large quantities for prompt cash, which puts us on the very best footing to buy at the very lowest prices, and enables us to save you at least from 25 to 50 per cent., according to quality. Try us on a sample order by mail. We take great care in filling and packing your order carefully, and it is quite easy to pack a hat separate or with other goods. Compare Eaton's fur felt $1.00 hat with anything you have paid $2.00 for elsewhere. Our hats are nearly all English make, made on the very latest American blocks. English felt is more serviceable than American felt, being more durable and will not change the color so quick, and consequently will wear much longer. If not satisfactory, your money returned. See Hat Measurement Form, page 47.

300. Men's American silk hats, fine quality silk plush, silk trimmings, calf leather sweats, as cut 300 .... **4.00**

301. Tress & Co., of London, England, silk hats, extra quality silk plush and trimmings, as cut 300 .... **5.00**

302. Men's best grade of Tress & Co.'s silk hats, very best material and trimmings, as cut 300.......... **6.00**

303. "Eaton's" fine fur felt fedora or soft hats, special quality trimmings, colors black and brown, as cut 303 .... **1.00**

304. Men's fur felt fedora hats, latest shape for fall, silk trimmings and leather sweats, colors black and brown, as cut 304 .... **1.50**

305. Young men's fur felt Alpine or soft hats, extra quality trimmings, colors black and brown, as cut 303 .... **1.50**

306. Men's English and American fur felt fedora hats, colors black and brown, as cut 304.......... **2.00**

307. Young men's fedora hats, fur felt, latest style and best quality trimmings, colors black and brown, as cut 303.......... **2.00**

308. Men's English and American fedora hats, fur felt and silk trimmings, colors black and brown, as cut 304.......... **2.50**

309. Young men's fur felt fedora hats, latest shape for fall wear, colors black and brown, as cut 303 .... **2.50**

310. Men's fedora hats, manufactured by Tress & Co., London, England, best quality trimmings, colors black and brown, as cut 304 .... **3.00**

311. Tress & Co., of London, England, fedora hats, only smaller shape, colors black and brown, as cut 304 .... **3.00**

312. Young men's American fur felt fedora hats, made by J. B. Stetson & Co., unbound curl brim, colors black, brown and pearl, as cut 303. .... **3.50**

313. Men's American fur felt soft hats, manufactured by J. B. Stetson & Co., unbound flat brim, colors black, brown, fawn and pearl, as cut 313.......... **5.00**

314. Eaton's fur felt stiff hats, silk trimmings and leather sweats, colors black and brown, as cut 314 .... **1.00**

315. Men's stiff hats, fur felt and silk trimmings, colors black and brown, as cut 314.......... **1.50**

316. Young men's fur felt stiff hats for fall wear, silk binding and leather sweats, colors black and brown, as cut 316.......... **1.50**

317. Men's fine quality fur felt stiff hats, neat fall shape, best quality trimmings, colors black and brown as cut 314 .... **2.00**

318. Young men's fur felt derby hats, newest blocks for fall wear, colors black and brown, as cut 316... **2.00**

319. Men's stiff hats, extra quality fur felt, best silk band and binding and leather sweats, colors black and brown, as cut 314.......... **2.50**

320. Young men's fur felt stiff hats, latest style and best quality trimmings, as cut 316.......... **2.50**

321. Men's stiff hats, manufactured by Tress & Co., London, England, neat full shape, colors black and brown, as cut 316 .... **3.00**

322. Tress & Co., of London, England, fur felt stiff hats, latest block for fall wear, best quality trimmings, colors black and brown, as cut 316 .... **3.00**

323. Men's square crown fur felt stiff hats, silk trimmings and leather sweats, as cut 323 .... **2.50**

324. Clerical hats, special quality fur felt, fine quality trimmings, as cut 324 .... **2.00**

324A. We keep in stock both stiff and fedora shape fur felt hats in extra large sizes, 7½ and 7⅝ **2.00**

English Wool Hats.

325. Men's English felt fedora hats, silk trimmings and leather sweats, in colors black and brown, as cut 325 .... **75c**

326. Men's black and brown felt fedora hats, neat full shape, in colors black and brown, as cut 326, **50c**

327. Men's black and brown felt crush hats, unbound edges and leather sweats, as cut 327 ...... **50c**

328. Men's English felt crush hats, round crown and unbound brim, in colors navy, black or brown, as cut 327 .... **75c**

329. Men's black or brown felt sombrero hats, unbound flat brim and medium high crown, as cut 329, **50c**

330. Men's fine English felt sombrero hats, high narrow crown and flat unbound brim, in colors black, brown or grey, as cut 329, ... **75c**

331. Boys' special quality fur felt Derby hats, extra quality trimmings, in colors black and brown, as cut 331 .... **1.00**

Boys' and Youths' Fedora Hats.

332. Boys' and youths' fur felt crush hats, silk band, unbound edges, and satin lined, in colors black, fawn, brown or grey, as cut 332 .... **1.00**

333. Boys' and youths' fur felt fedora hats, special quality trimmings, in colors black and brown, as cut 333 .... **1.00**

334. Boys' and youths' black or brown felt fedora hats, neat full shape and leather sweats, as cut 333 .... **75c**

335. Boys' English felt fedora hats, neat shape, silk band and binding and leather sweats, in colors black and brown, as cut 333 .... **50c**

Boys' Crush Hats.

336. Boys' and youths' black, navy or brown felt crush hats, raw edge brim and round crown, as cut 336 .... **50c**

337. Boys' English felt crush or knock-about hats, si k band and leather sweat, in colors black, navy and brown, as cut 336 .... **35c**

338. Boys' black or brown felt crush hats, neat full shape," and good quality sweats, as cut 336 ...... **25c**

339. Boys' plain navy blue worsted serge and assorted pattern tweed turbans, as cut 339.......... **25c**

Men's, Ladies', Boys' and Children's Peak, Hookdown, Varsity and College Caps, also Ladies' and Children's Wool and Felt Tam o' Shanters and Toques.

Men's Peak Caps.

340. Men's blue beaver cloth caps, cloth peak and leather sweats, as cut 340 .... 1.25
341. Men's and youths' blue beaver cloth caps, cloth or glazed leather peaks and leather sweats, as cut 340 .... 1.00
342. Men's navy blue beaver cloth caps, glazed leather or cloth peak, as cut 340 .... 75c
343. Men's navy blue beaver cloth or serge caps, leather or cloth peak and silk lined, as cut 343 .... 50c
344. Men's navy blue beaver cloth caps, leather or cloth peak, as cut 343 .... 35c
345. Men's navy blue beaver cloth caps, cloth or glazed leather peaks, as cut 343 .... 25c

Men's American Caps.

346. Men's and youths' plain or fancy pattern tweed and navy blue worsted serge caps, silk lined, as cut 346 .... 50c
347. Men's plain navy blue worsted serge and assorted pattern tweed caps, silk serge lining, as cut 346 .... 35c
348. Men's and youths' assorted pattern tweed and navy blue worsted serge caps, as cut 346 .... 25c

Men's Hookdown Caps.

349. Men's and youths' assorted pattern Scotch tweed caps, as cut 349 .... 75c
350. Men's plain navy blue worsted serge and assorted tweed caps as cut 349 .... 50c
351. Men's assorted pattern tweed and navy blue worsted serge caps, silk serge lining, as cut 351 .... 35c
352. Men's navy blue or black worsted serge and assorted tweed caps, as cut 351 .... 25c
353. Men's and youths' assorted pattern tweed and navy blue worsted serge caps, as cut 351 .... 15c

Men's Silk and Sateen Caps

354. Men's black gros-grain silk college caps, satin lining, as cut 354, 50c
355. Men's black Italian cloth college caps, as cut 354 .... 25c
356. Men's black gros-grain silk 6/4 peak caps, as cut 356 .... 50c
357. Men's black Italian cloth 6/4 peak caps, as cut 356 .... 25c
358. Men's black gros-grain silk polo caps, satin lining, as cut 358 .... 50c
359. Men's black Italian cloth polo caps, as cut 358 .... 25c

Boys' and Ladies' Peak Caps

360. Ladies' and boys' fine blue beaver cloth caps, mohair braid band and silk-lined, as cut 360 .. 50c
361. Ladies' and boys' navy blue beaver cloth caps, mohair braid band and silk serge lining, as cut 360 .... 35c
362. Boys' and ladies' navy blue beaver cloth or serge caps, plain or fancy braid band, as cut 360, 25c
363. Boys' and ladies' black velvet peak caps, gold braid on front, as cut 363 .... 19c
364. Ladies' and boys' navy blue beaver cloth peak caps, silk cord on front, as cut 363 .... 19c
365. Boys' navy blue melton cloth caps, gold cord on front and anchor, as cut 363 .... 15c

Boys' and Ladies' American Caps.

366. Ladies' and boys' fine navy blue worsted serge and assorted pattern tweed caps, silk serge lining, as cut 366 .... 35c
367. Boys' and ladies' assorted pattern tweed and navy blue worsted serge caps, as cut 366 .... 25c

Boys' and Ladies' Hookdown Caps.

368. Boys' and ladies' assorted pattern tweed and navy blue worsted serge caps, silk lined, as cut 368 .... 35c
369. Boys' and ladies' navy blue or black worsted serge and assorted pattern tweed caps and silk serge lining, as cut 368 .... 25c
370. Boys' and ladies' assorted pattern tweed and navy blue worsted serge caps, as cut 368 .... 15c

Boys' Varsity Caps.

371. Boys' plain navy blue or black worsted serge and fancy pattern tweed caps, silk lined, as cut 371 .... 25c
372. Boys' plain or fancy pattern tweed and navy blue worsted serge caps, as cut 371 .... 15c
373. Boys' navy blue or black velvet caps, with fancy ribbon on seams, as cut 371 .... 15c

Boys' Glengarry Caps.

374. Boys' fine Scotch knit Glengarry caps, silk or leather bound and silk bow on side, as cut 374 .... 50c
375. Boys' navy blue and black velvet Glengarry caps, silk tassel on top and silk lined, as cut 374 .... 50c
376. Boys' and youths' Scotch knit Glengarry caps, silk or leather-bound, as cut 374 .... 35c
377. Boys' and youths' Scotch or Glengarry caps, silk or leather bound, as cut 374 .... 25c
377A. Men's, youths' and ladies' black beaver cloth mortar-board or college caps, with large silk tassel on top, as cut 377A 1.25
377B. Men's, youths' and boys' uniform caps, made of fine beaver cloth, straight leather peak, and sweatband, as cut 377B, each 75c, 1.00, 1.25, 1.50

Children's Tam o' Shanters

377C. Children's extra fine navy blue or scarlet cloth wire top Tam o' Shanters, as cut 377C 1.25
378. Children's extra fine navy blue beaver cloth Tam o' Shanters, soft top, with plain black silk band, as tam on boy 1.25
379. Children's navy blue or black velvet Tam o' Shanters, large wired top and plain black silk bands, as tam on boy, or as cut 377C 1.00
380. Children's fine navy blue beaver and scarlet cloth Tam o' Shanters, wired top, plain or fancy bands, as tam on boy, or as cut 377C 1.00
381. Children's fawn doe skin, Tam o' Shanters, soft top, name on band, and silk lined, as cut 381 .... 1.00
382. Children's extra quality navy blue beaver and scarlet cloth Tam o' Shanters, soft top, as cut 381. 1.00
383. Children's navy blue or black velvet Tam o' Shanters, wired top, plain or fancy bands, and silk lined, as tam on girl 75c
384. Children's navy blue beaver or scarlet cloth wire top Tam o' Shanters, as tam on girl 75c
385. Children's tan leather Tam o' Shanters, soft top, name on band, and silk serge lining, as cut 385 .... 75c
386. Children's fine navy blue beaver and scarlet cloth Tam o' Shanters, soft top, plain or fancy bands, as cut 385 .... 75c
387. Children's navy blue or black velvet Tam o' Shanters, wired top, and plain silk bands, as tam on girl 50c
388. Children's fine blue beaver and scarlet cloth Tam o' Shanters, wired top, plain or fancy bands, as tam on girl 50c
389. Children's fine blue beaver and scarlet cloth Tam o' Shanters, soft top, plain or fancy bands, as cut 385 .... 50c
390. Children's navy blue beaver cloth Tam o' Shanters, wired top, plain or fancy named band, as cut 390 .... 35c
391. Children's navy blue velvet Tam o' Shanters, soft top, fancy flag design in front, as cut 385 .... 35c
392. Children's navy blue, scarlet or myrtle cloth Tam o' Shanters, soft top and fancy name on band or plain, as cut 385 .... 35c
393. Children's navy blue cloth Tam o' Shanters, wired top, plain bands, as cut 390 .... 25c
394. Children's navy blue cloth Tam o' Shanters, soft top, name on band or plain, as cut 385 .... 25c
395. Children's fine Berlin wool toques, plain colors, or with fancy striped borders, as cut 395 .... 25c
396. Children's extra large Berlin wool toques, in plain colors, or with fancy striped borders, larger size than cut 395 .... 50c
397. Ladies' and misses' extra fine Scotch wool knitted Tam o' Shanters, in plain colors, also fancy mixed patterns, as cut 397 .... 50c
398. Ladies' and misses' fine Scotch wool knitted Tam o' Shanters, in plain or assorted colors, as cut 397 .... 35c
399. Ladies' and misses' knitted Scotch wool Tam o' Shanters, in plain or assorted colors, as cut 397 .... 25c

MEN'S, LADIES' AND BOYS' HEAVY WINTER CAPS.

Men's Heavy Cloth Winter Caps.

400. Men's heavy blue cloth caps, Manitoba shape, double roll band and heavy sateen lining, as cut 400 .... **25c**

401. Men's navy blue or brown corduroy caps, Manitoba shape, double roll band and heavy lining, as cut 400........ **25c**

402. Men's heavy blue cloth caps with slip band and heavy sateen lining, as cut 402........ **25c**

403. Men's and youths' heavy navy blue or brown corduroy caps, slip band and good sateen lining, as cut 402........ **35c**

404. Men's and youths' heavy frieze caps, slip band and satin lining, as cut 402........ **35c**

405. Men's and youths' heavy blue cloth caps, American slip band with heavy sateen lining, as cut 402........ **35c**

406. Men's and youths' heavy blue cloth caps, American 8/4 slip band style and satin lining, as cut 402 .... **50c**

407. Men's and youths' navy blue cloth caps, American square crown with seams on top, slip band and cloth or leather peak, as cut 407 .... **35c**

408. Men's and youths' navy blue cloth caps, slip band, silk cord and buttons on front and silk lined, as cut 408........ **50c**

409. Men's heavy blue cloth caps, Quebec style, with deep slip band and sateen lining, same shape as cut 409........ **25c**

410. Men's heavy blue cloth caps, Quebec shape, slip band, 2 bows on front and sateen lining, as cut 409 .... **35c**

411. Men's heavy blue cloth caps, Quebec shape, slip band, bow on front and sateen lining, as cut 411 .... **35c**

412. Men's heavy blue cloth caps, Quebec style, with buttons and silk cord on front, slip band to pull down, as cut 412........ **35c**

413. Men's fine blue beaver cloth caps, 2 bows on front, slip band and satin lined, as cut 413........ **50c**

414. Men's extra fine blue beaver cloth caps, Quebec style, with slip band and good quality lining, as cut 413 .... **75c**

415. Men's extra fine blue beaver cloth caps, silk cord and buttons on side, silk bow on front and sateen lining, as cut 415 .... **75c**

416. Men's extra heavy black Mackinaw blizzard-shape caps, with deep cape to pull down and lined with heavy cloth, as cut 416........ **1.00**

417. Boys' heavy blue cloth caps, American style, with slip band and sateen lining, as cut 417 .... **25c**

418. Boys' navy blue cloth, American shape caps, with slip band and good quality sateen lining, as cut 417........ **35c**

419. Boys' heavy blue cloth caps, Quebec shape, deep slip band and good lining, as cut 409 .... **35c**

420. Boys' fine blue beaver cloth caps, Quebec shape, two bows on front, slip band and satin lined, as cut 409........ **50c**

421. Men's heavy Scotch knit Tam o' Shanters, plain or fancy bands, tassel on top, and heavy lining ... **1.00**

Men's Black Imitation Lamb Caps.

422. Men's black imitation lamb caps, good lining, as cut 422........ **25c**

423. Men's and youths' fine black imitation lamb caps, deep crown, sateen lining, as cuts 422, 423 .. **35c**

424. Men's and youths' black imitation lamb caps, bright curl, lined with special quality Italian cloth, as cuts 422, 423, 424........ **50c**

425. Men's and youths' extra quality black imitation lamb caps, large bright curl with black gros-grain silk sweats, and satin lining, as cuts 422, 423 .... **75c**

426. Men's and youths' extra fine black imitation lamb caps, bright glossy curl and best quality lining, as cuts 422, 423........ **1.00**

Men's, Youths' and Ladies' Sealette Caps.

427. Men's, youths' and ladies' sealette caps, Italian cloth sweats and sateen lining, in shapes as cuts 427, 428, 429, 430, 431 .... **50c**

428. Men's, youths' and ladies' fine silk-finished sealette caps, grosgrain silk sweats with satin lining, in shapes as cuts 427, 428, 429, 430, 431 .... **75c**

429. Men's, youths' and ladies' extra fine silk-finished sealette caps, grosgrain silk sweats and special quality satin lining, in shapes as cuts 427, 428, 429, 430, 431 .... **1.00**

Boys' Black Imitation Caps.

432. Boys' or girls' black imitation caps, good full shape, with sateen lining, as cuts 432, 433 .... **25c**

433. Boys' or girls' black imitation caps, neat close curl, with heavy sateen lining, as cuts 432, 433... **35c**

434. Boys' or girls' fine black imitation lamb caps, large bright curl, Italian cloth sweats and sateen lining, as cuts 432, 433 .... **50c**

Boys' and Girls' Grey Imitation Caps.

435. Boys' and girls' grey imitation lamb caps, good full shape crown and sateen lining, as cuts 432, 433, **25c**

436. Boys' and girls' imitation lamb caps, medium large curl, neat shape crown and good quality lining, as cuts 432, 433 .... **35c**

437. Boys' and girls' imitation grey lamb caps, close glossy curl, satin sweatband and lining, as cuts 432, 433 .... **50c**

438. Boys' and girls' extra quality grey imitation lamb caps, neat full crown with special quality lining, as cut 433 only **75c**

Mourning Bands.

For wearing on hat—

2 inches wide **10c**
$2\frac{1}{2}$ " " .... **$12\frac{1}{2}$c**
3 " " **15c**

Elastic arm mourning bands, to pull over sleeve, 4 inches wide..... **20c**

DIRECTIONS For Head Measurement

Please state distinctly whether felt hat, cap or Tam o' Shanter is for lady, man, youth or child, and measure around the head with a tape-line in the position where the hat or cap is usually worn, find the number of inches, and compare with the scale of sizes, and you will find the exact size. Care should be taken to send the correct size in every case; also state the color and shape, giving the number or corresponding cut in Catalogue. It is impossible to fill your order properly without this information.

Children's sizes run from 6 to $6\frac{5}{8}$
Boys' " " " $6\frac{1}{4}$ " $6\frac{7}{8}$
Ladies' " " " $6\frac{1}{4}$ " $6\frac{7}{8}$
Men's " " " $6\frac{5}{8}$ " $7\frac{3}{8}$

Men's stiff and fedora hats, extra sizes, $7\frac{1}{2}$ and $7\frac{5}{8}$, at $2.00 each.

SCALE OF SIZES.

Inch.	Size.	Inch.	Size.	Inch.	Size.
$18\frac{7}{8}$	6	$20\frac{5}{8}$	$6\frac{5}{8}$	$22\frac{3}{4}$	$7\frac{1}{4}$
$19\frac{1}{4}$	$6\frac{1}{8}$	$21\frac{1}{4}$	$6\frac{3}{4}$	$23\frac{1}{4}$	$7\frac{3}{8}$
$19\frac{5}{8}$	$6\frac{1}{4}$	$21\frac{5}{8}$	$6\frac{7}{8}$	$23\frac{5}{8}$	$7\frac{1}{2}$
20	$6\frac{3}{8}$	22	7	24	$7\frac{5}{8}$
$20\frac{1}{2}$	$6\frac{1}{2}$	$22\frac{3}{8}$	$7\frac{1}{8}$		

MEN'S AND BOYS' CLOTHING DEPARTMENT

WE manufacture our own clothing and personally visit Europe twice yearly, and select our cloths from the English, Scotch and Irish mills, together with our domestic tweeds, gathering together from the different firms the most suitable and satisfactory materials both as to wear and appearance. Our stock includes the celebrated Salts' Saltaire Serges, and Campbell Belwarps, Priestley's Cravenette Rainproof Coverts, Mahoney's Irish Blarney Serges, Hawick and Galashiel's Scotch Tweeds. These are all thoroughly examined, steamed and shrunk before being made up on our own premises. These linings, interlinings and trimmings are a very particular feature with us, being graded up according to price and quality of cloth ; even the buttons and thread must be of the best quality. Every garment is examined and inspected thoroughly before leaving our workrooms under our own personal supervision. Our designers and cutters are experts, who thoroughly understand their business and visit the leading fashion centres.

Satisfy yourself by comparing our clothing with what you usually see. Examine the linings and interlinings, the sewing, the staying and workmanship when finished throughout, and you will readily see how much superior **EATON** standard of clothing is. That applies to our low-priced goods as well as our high-grade qualities. Buying and making as we do, and having such a tremendous output for our clothing, permit us to offer clothing values that are not easily equalled. Those who buy from our stock reap the benefit in bigger values and better garments than are usually given for the same money. Back of all we stand with our broad guarantee, "Money refunded if goods are not satisfactory."

TRY US BY MAIL.

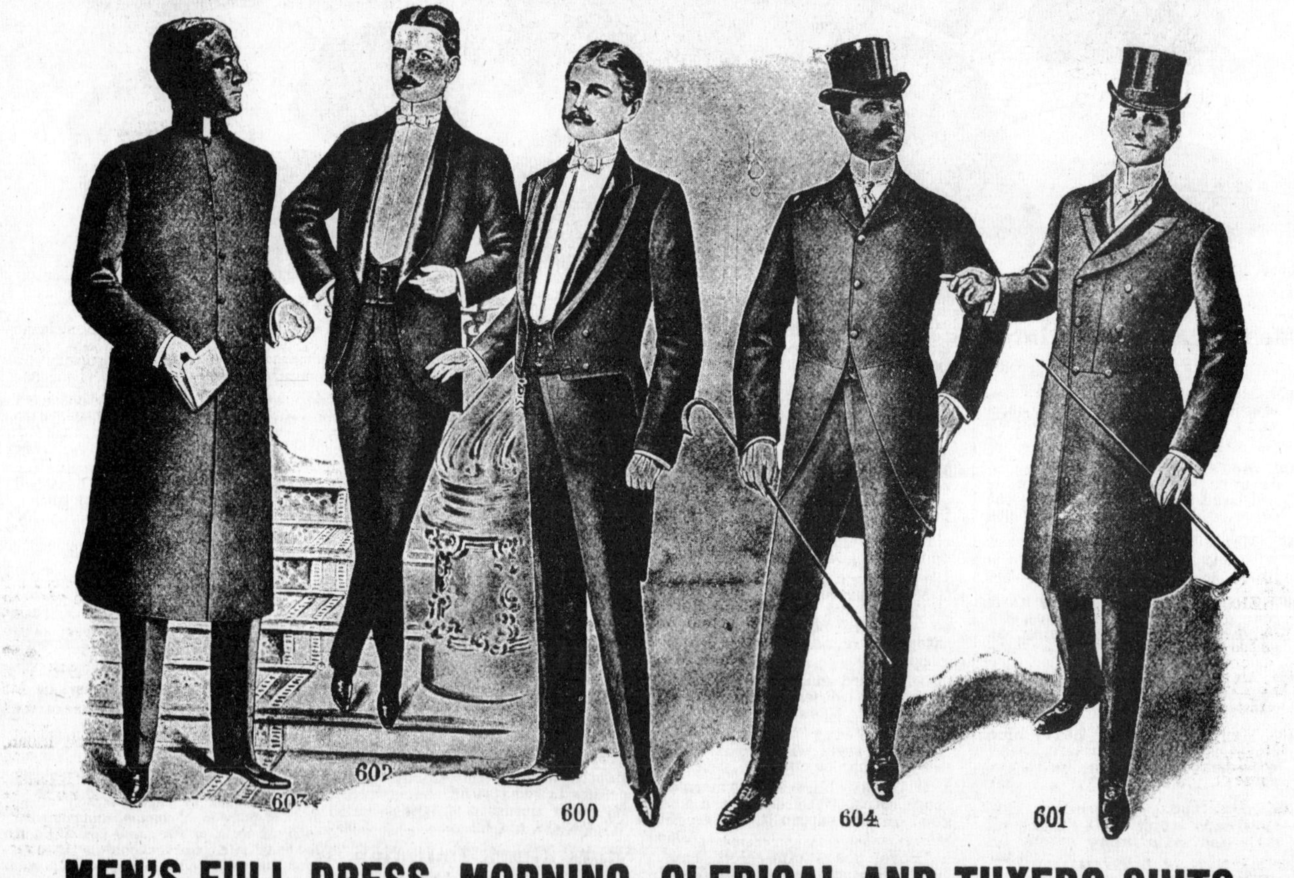

603 602 600 604 601

MEN'S FULL DRESS, MORNING, CLERICAL AND TUXEDO SUITS

35 TO 44 INCHES CHEST MEASURE

600. MEN'S FULL DRESS SUIT, all-wool black Venetian worsted, silk stitched, satin lined, as cut 600 .... **18.00**

601. PRINCE ALBERT SUIT, imported black Venetian-finished worsted, stitched or bound edges, as cut 601 .... **18.00**

602. TUXEDO OR DINNER SUIT, black Venetian worsted, as cut 602 .... **15.00**

603. CLERICAL SUIT made from imported black Venetian-finished worsted, edges silk stitched, as cut 603 .... **18.00**

604. ALL-WOOL BLACK WORSTED SERGE, hard finish, 3-button cutaway suit, as cut 604 .... **7.50**

605. BLACK VENETIAN, also black Clay diagonal worsted, as cut 604 .... **8.50**

606. BLACK AND OXFORD GREY all-wool imported Clay diagonal weave worsted, as cut 604 .. **10.00**

607. PLAIN BLACK VENETIAN-FINISHED WORSTED, also black and Oxford grey cheviot, as cut 604 .... **12.50**

608. IMPORTED OXFORD GREY, also black Clay diagonal worsted, silk sewn, as cut 604 .... **12.50**

609. IMPORTED OXFORD GREY UNFINISHED WORSTED, also black Clay diagonal fine twill, as cut 604 .... **15.00**

610. BLACK VICUNA CLOTH, also black Venetian-finished worsted, as cut 604 .... **15.00**

611. CHOICE ALL-WOOL IMPORTED BLACK VICUNA CLOTH, silk-stitched edges, as cut 604 .... **18.00**

612. BLACK VENETIAN WORSTED, lined with Skinner's celebrated satin, as cut 604 .... **20.00**

MEN'S SACQUE SUITS, SINGLE AND DOUBLE BREASTED.

36 to 44 inches chest measure. Order stock sizes; larger or special garments will cost you 25 per cent. extra.

613. NAVY BLUE ALL-WOOL SERGE, as cut 613 ....5.00

614. BROWN OR DARK GREY ALL-WOOL CHECKED TWEED, as cut 613 ....5.00

615. LIGHT BROWN CHECKED ALL-WOOL TWEED, as cut 613 ....6.50

616. IMPORTED ENGLISH CAMPBELL SERGE, 20-oz, hard finish, blue or black, as cut 616............7.50

617. DARK ALL-WOOL GREY CHECKED TWEED, as cut 616 ....7.50

618. FINE ALL-WOOL DARK BROWN TWEED, with overplaid, as cut 616 ....8.50

619. BLACK CLAY WORSTED, as cut 616 ....8.50

620. BLACK VENETIAN WORSTED, as cut 616 ....8.50

621. HEAVY IMPORTED NAVY BLUE IRISH CELTIC OR TYKE SERGE, 24-oz, indigo dye, as cut 616............10.00

622. FINE IMPORTED CLAY WORSTED, in black Oxford grey or blue, as cut 616 ....10.00

623. DARK GREY BUCKSKIN TWEED, as cut 616 ....10.00

624. IMPORTED SCOTCH TWEED dark grey, as cut 616 ....10.00

625. GREY UNFINISHED WORSTED, as cut 616 ....10.00

626. IMPORTED CLAY WORSTED, in black or blue, as cut 616 ....12.50

627. BLACK VENETIAN IMPORTED ENGLISH WORSTED, as cut 616............12.50

628. HEAVY 24-OZ. OXFORD GREY CLAY WORSTED, as cut 616 ....12.50

629. BANNOCKBURN TWEEDS, dark mixtures, small patterns, as cut 616 ....12.50

630. FINE WEST OF ENGLAND WORSTED, in blue greys, patterns very small neat checks, as cut 616 ....12.50

631. MAHONEY'S IRISH BLARNEY SERGE, navy blue, 25 oz. indigo dye, as cut 616 ....13.50

632. BLACK OR BLUE IMPORTED CLAY WORSTED, indigo dye, as cut 616 ....15.00

633. IMPORTED BLACK WORSTED, Venetian finish, as cut 616 ....15.00

634. HEAVY SCOTCH TWEED SUITS, dark mixtures, in fancy checks, as cut 616............15.00

635. BLACK VENETIAN WORSTED, lined with Skinner's satin, as cut 616 ....20.00

Single-Breasted, with Double-Breasted Vests.

(As cut 636.)

636. DARK ALL-WOOL DOMESTIC TWEEDS, as cut 636 ....6.50

637. CHECKED TWEEDS, with overplaid patterns, dark colors, as cut 636............7.50

638. DARK FINE ALL-WOOL TWEEDS, as cut 636 ....8.50

639. IMPORTED WORSTED, in Oxford grey or brown and green mixtures, check and overplaids, as cut 636 ....10.00

640. SCOTCH TWEED, with overplaid in brown mixture, as cut 636 ....10.00

641. FINE IMPORTED WORSTED, neat checked pattern, as cut 636 ....12.50

642. SCOTCH TWEEDS, in brown or grey mixtures, with overplaids, as cut 636............12.50

Double-Breasted Suits.

(As cut 643.)

643. NAVY BLUE SERGE, as cut 643 ....5.00

644. HEAVY 24-OZ. OXFORD GREY HALIFAX HOMESPUN, as cut 643 ....5.00

645. ALL-WOOL DOMESTIC CHECKED TWEEDS, in grey or brown, as cut 643 ....5.00

646. HEAVY NAVY BLUE CHEVIOT SERGE, as cut 643 ....6.50

647. DARK GREY OR BROWN CHECKED TWEEDS, as cut 643 ....6.50

648. HEAVY IMPORTED CAMPBELL SERGE, 20-oz., hard finish, black or blue, as cut 643........7.50

649. HEAVY ALL-WOOL FRIEZE, in dark Oxford grey, and black, as cut 643............8.50

650. ALL-WOOL TWEEDS, in brown and grey checks, with overplaids, as cut 643 ....8.50

651. ENGLISH CORDUROY, dark brown, heavy rib, as cut 643..10.00

652. IMPORTED NAVY BLUE CELTIC OR TYKE SERGE, 24 oz. indigo dye as cut 643............10.00

653. SCOTCH TWEEDS, in dark grey or brown, with overplaids, as cut 643 ....10.00

653A. BLACK OR BLUE IMPORTED CLAY WORSTEDS, as cut 643 ....10.00

654. BLUE BEAVER OR PILOT CLOTH, as cut 643............12.50

655. IMPORTED SCOTCH TWEED, in dark colors, with overplaid, as cut 643 ....12.50

656. MAHONEY'S IRISH BLARNEY SERGE, navy blue, 25 oz., indigo dye, as cut 643 ....13.50

MEN'S OVERCOATS

34 to 44 inches chest measure. Samples of these Overcoats sent for the asking. No variations from illustrated styles. Ordering otherwise than catalogued will cost you 25 per cent. extra, and will delay your order.

657. BLUE OR BLACK BEAVER CLOTH, as cut 657 .... 5.00

658. BLUE BEAVER, as cut 658 .... 5.00

659. OXFORD GREY CHEVIOT, box back, as cut 659.......... 5.00

660. FINE BLUE AND BLACK BEAVER, as cut 659 .... 7.50

661. HARRIS ROCKWOOD HEAVY GREY CHEVIOT CLOTH, as cut 659 .... 7.50

662. GREY OR BLACK CHEVIOT, light weight, as cut 659.......... 7.50

663. FINE BLACK BEAVER, as cut 657 .... 7.50

664. NAVY BLUE ENGLISH BEAVER, as cut 658 .... 7.50

665. BLACK OR OXFORD GREY CLAY TWILL, light weight, as cut 665.......... 8.00

666. HEAVY OXFORD GREY CHEVIOT CLOTH, as cut 666 .... 8.00

667. IMPORTED OXFORD GREY NAP CLOTH, as cut 659 .... 8.50

668. LIGHT WEIGHT FAWN COVERT OR FAWN WHIPCORD CLOTH, as cut 668 .... 8.50

669. BLACK OR NAVY BLUE BEAVER CLOTH, as cut 659 .... 10.00

670. IMPORTED ENGLISH BEAVER CLOTH, in black only, as cut 657 .... 10.00

671. HARRIS ROCKWOOD CHEVIOT, in Oxford grey shade, as cut 657 .... 10.00

672. NAVY BLUE ENGLISH BEAVER CLOTH, as cut 658 .... 10.00

673. OXFORD GREY CHEVIOT RAGLAN STYLE COAT, as cut 673 .... 10.00

674. IMPORTED GREY CLAY WORSTED, 24 oz., fall weight, as cut 665.......... 10.00

675. BLACK OR NAVY BLUE IMPORTED BEAVER CLOTH, as cut 659 .... 12.50

676. IMPORTED GREY CHEVIOT CLOTH, as cut 659.......... 12.50

676A. TALMA COAT in imported grey cheviot, as cut 666 .... 12.50

677. NAVY BLUE OR BLACK IMPORTED BEAVER CLOTH, as cut 659 .... 15.00

678. IMPORTED BLACK AND OXFORD GREY CHEVIOT CLOTH, as cut 659.......... 15.00

679. MEDIUM GREY OR FAWN HERRINGBONE ALL-WOOL STRIPED TWEED, as cut 673 .... 15.00

680. OXFORD GREY CHEVIOT, self lined, check back, as cut 659 .... 15.00

681. SELF-LINED CHECKED BACK FAWN WHIPCORD, silk piped, as cut 668.......... 15.00

682. ALL-WOOL OXFORD GREY ENGLISH BEAVER CLOTH, as cut 657 .... 15.00

683. LONG BOX BACK COAT, in Oxford grey cheviot, yoke on shoulders and front, as cut 683 .... 15.00

684. OXFORD GREY CHEVIOT COAT, choice goods, as cut 666 .... 15.00

685. IMPORTED CHEVIOT CLOTH, Oxford grey, as cut 666 .... 18.00

686. BLACK ENGLISH THIBET CLOTH, satin lined, as cut 666 .... 20.00

687. IMPORTED GREY CHEVIOT CLOTH, satin lining, as cut 666 .... 20.00

688. CHOICE BLACK IMPORTED THIBET CLOTH, satin lined, as cut 666 .... 25.00

Men's Ulsters, Reefers, Dressing Gowns and House Jackets.

34 to 46 inches chest measure. We sell direct to the wearer, no wholesale profits on materials between the wearer and the mills that weave the cloth.

Men's Ulsters.

689. HEAVY ALL-WOOL CANADIAN FRIEZE, in Oxford grey or black lined with check linings, as cut 689 .... 4.50
690. BROWN OR OXFORD GREY FRIEZE, as cut 690 .... 6.00
691. HARRIS ROCKWOOD HEAVY FRIEZE, in Oxford grey or black, as cut 690 .... 8.00
692. HARRIS ROCKWOOD EXTRA HEAVY 36-OZ. FRIEZE ULSTERS, in seal brown, Oxford grey or black, as cut 690...... 10.00
693. IMPORTED HEAVY BLACK MONTAGNAC CURL CLOTH, checked worsted linings, satin sleeve lining, as cut 690 ...... 18.00

Men's Pea Jackets.

694. BLACK OR BROWN FRIEZE PEA JACKET, storm collar, heavy linings, as cut 694 ...... 4.00
695. BLUE BEAVER, storm collar, Italian linings, as cut 694...... 4.00
696. IMPORTED BLUE NAP, storm collar, heavy linings, as cut 694 .... 4.50
697. HEAVY OXFORD GREY FRIEZE, storm collar, heavy linings, as cut 694 .... 5.00
698. IMPORTED FINE BLUE BEAVER CLOTH, as cut 694, 7.00
699. NAVY BLUE IMPORTED BEAVER CLOTH, as cut 699.. 7.00
700. IMPORTED HEAVY ALL-WOOL BLUE NAP CLOTH, cord edges, deep storm collar, as cut 694 .... 8.00

Dressing Gowns.

701. BLUE BEAVER CLOTH DRESSING GOWN, cord edges and girdle, button front 6.00
702. FAWN AND GREY CHEVIOT GOWNS, bound with cloth binding to match, 4 rows of stitching, button front 7.50
703. FANCY PLAID, with frogs and silk and wool girdle, as cut 703, only neat cloth binding to match 10.00
704. PLAIN FAWN CAMEL'S HAIRCLOTH, checked back cloth to match, with 4 rows of neat silk stitching, with frogs and silk and wool girdle, as cut 703.... 10.00
705. CAMEL'S HAIRCLOTH, in plain and fancy plaids, silk cord edges, as cut 703 .... 12.50
706. FANCY PLAIDS, with reversed plaids on collar, cuffs and pockets, silk frogs on front and silk and wool girdle 15.00
707. FINE PURE CAMEL'S HAIRCLOTH, trimmed to match, as cut 703 .... 18.00
708. INVALID'S GOWN, soft lamb's curl cloth or camel's hair 8.50

House Jackets.

709. SHEPHERD'S PLAID, fancy flannelette, silk cord edge and frogs to match, as cut 709 ... 3.50
710. JAPANESE SILK SMOKING JACKET, quilted throughout. 4.50
711. PLAIN FAWN CAMEL'S HAIRCLOTH, trimmings to match, as cut 709 .... 4.50
712. FANCY PLAIDS, trimmed with silk frogs and silk cord edges 5.00
713. FAWN CAMEL'S HAIRCLOTH, bound with cloth to match, 4 rows of silk stitching, as cut 712, only self collar and cuffs 6.00
714. MYRTLE, MAROON, NAVY VENETIAN CLOTH, satin-bound edges and frogs, as cut 714 .... 7.50
715. FANCY PLAID CAMEL'S HAIRCLOTH, with different plaid on collar, cuffs and pockets, silk cord edges and frogs, as cut 712.............................. 8.50
716. NEAT SHEPHERD'S PLAID, in neat fancy tweed, silk cord edges and silk frogs to match, as cut 709 .... 10.00
717. SILK BROCADE, in black with scarlet, as cut 717............ 12.50
718. PLAIN BLACK WORSTED CASHMERE CLOTH, with white spots, neat and nobby 12.50
719. SILK BROCADED, in black ground with scarlet mixture, as cut 717 .... 15.00
720. LIGHT ELECTRIC BLUE SILK BROCADE, blue ground with white figure, as cut 717 . 20.00
721. INVALID'S SOFT CAMEL'S HAIRCLOTH, in lamb's curl 5.00

MEN'S AND BOYS' WATERPROOF COATS.

36 to 46 inches Chest Measure. These Waterproofs are all imported English make and will not harden (we do not handle any cheap American goods); all sewn seams and stitched edges. Every garment guaranteed to give satisfaction.

Men's Waterproof Cape Coats.

722. BLACK PARAMATTA COAT, 24-inch detachable cape, as cut 722 .... 5.00
723. FINE BLACK PARAMATTA COAT, 27-inch detachable cape, wide and loose, as cut 722 ...... 8.00
724. DARK ENGLISH TWEED, with checked linings, 27-inch detachable cape, as cut 722 ...... 8.00
725. FINE BLACK CASHMERE PARAMATTA, with 30-inch detachable cape, large, loose, serviceable garment, as cut 722 ...... 10.00
726. BLACK CASHMERE PARAMATTA INVERNESS COAT, no sleeves, cape attached, as cut 726 .... 10.00

Paddock Waterproof Coats Without Capes.

727. FAWN COVERT WATERPROOF COAT, velvet collar, checked back, as cut 727 ...... 3.95
728. GREY COVERT WATERPROOF COAT, as cut 727 .... 5.00
729. FAWN COVERT WATERPROOF COAT, as cut 729 ... 5.00
730. FAWN WORSTED COVERT CLOTH COAT, checked, single breasted, as cut 729 .... 8.00
731. GREY WORSTED COVERT WATERPROOF COAT, double-breasted, as cut 727 .... 8.00
732. FAWN COVERT RAGLAN WATERPROOF COAT, double-breasted, as cut 727, only Raglan shoulders and Talma pockets, 10.00
733. GREY COVERT WATERPROOF COAT, single breasted, checked linings, as cut 729 .. 10.00
733A. MEN'S COVERT CLOTH WATERPROOF COAT, with yoke on front and back, cuff on sleeve, paddock back, velvet collar, as cut 733A 10.00
734. OXFORD, GREY AND DARK FAWN COVERT CLOTH COAT, shoulder and sleeve satin-lined, as cut 729 .... 12.50
735. NAVY BLUE AND FAWN BEAVER CLOTH WATERPROOF COAT, double breasted, paddock shape, heavy cloth, and heavy all-wool checked linings, as cut 727 .... 15.00

Rainproof Coats.

(Made free of rubber and odorless, won't stand the wet weather same as a rubber-lined coat

737. FAWN COVERT RAINPROOF CLOTH, odorless, as cut 737, only self collar 10.00
738. OXFORD GREY AND FAWN CRAVENETTE COVERT CLOTH, checked back, as cut 737, only self collar 12.50
739. PRIESTLEY'S CRAVENETTE RAINPROOF COAT, in fine covert cloths, fawn and Oxford grey, lined with all-wool Italian, Talma pockets, as cut 739 .... 15.00

Dull Rubbers, Men's and Boys'.

740. MEN'S DULL-FINISHED RUBBER-SHEETING COAT, double-breasted, 36 to 44 inches 1.75
741. MEN'S DULL-FINISHED RUBBER COAT, with clasps and rings 2.50
742. MEN'S HEAVY DRIVING or FIREMEN'S COAT, with clasps and rings 4.50
743. BOYS' DULL RUBBER-SHEETING COAT, sizes 24 to 32 inches chest measure 1.50
744. BOYS GREY COVERT CLOTH CAPE WATERPROOF COAT, no sleeves, sizes 26-inch chest measure, 3.50; 28-inch, 4.00; 30-inch, 4.25; 32-inch 4.50
745. BOYS' GREY AND FAWN PADDOCK, velvet collar, with sleeves, no cape, checked linings, box back, sizes 26-inch chest measure, 3.50; 28-inch, 4.00; 30-inch, 4.25; 32-inch 4.50
D. FISHERMAN'S OILED CLOTHING, black or yellow, jacket style 1.25
E. Same, in APRON TROUSERS, black or yellow 1.25
F. LONG BLACK OILED COAT 2.25
G. SOUTH-WESTERN HAT to match 50c

Men's and Youths' Trousers, Leather and Mackinaw Coats, Plain and Fancy Vests, Overalls and Smocks, Barbers' and Waiters' Coats.

Men's Trousers.

31 to 44 inches waist measure.

746. Heavy striped Canadian tweed, dark color 1.00
747. Dark grey Canadian striped tweed, 20 oz 1.25
748. Heavy 26-oz. all-wool tweed, dark stripe 1.25
749. Etoffe brown or grey small check pattern, heavy weight .. 1.50
750. Heavy diagonal woven, plain Oxford grey homespun, 28 oz. 1.50
751. Dark Canadian tweed, with grey stripe, medium weight .. 1.50
752. Medium and dark grey, all-wool Canadian tweed 1.75
753. Plain hairline tweed, small neat pattern 2.00
754. Dark all-wool Canadian tweed, with neat stripe 2.00
755. Striped hairline tweed, good heavy all-wool cloth, special .. 2.00
756. Heavy brown corduroy, imported goods 2.50
757. Drab moleskin, strong and well made 2.50
758. Oxford and blue-grey worsted, striped tweed 2.50
758A. Medium weight blue mackinaw 2.25
759. Imported English solid worsted (not backed goods), in neat stripes, special 2.50
759A. Heavy blue black mackinaw lumbermen's trousers 3.00
760. Navy blue English Campbell serge 2.50
761. All-wool colored worsted, in wide and narrow stripe patterns 3.00
762. Imported narrow-stripe black worsted 3.00
763. Plain black Clay twill diagonal worsted 3.00
764. Fancy colored all-wool English worsted, in narrow striped patterns 3.50
765. Plain black Venetian-finished worsted, all wool 3.50
766. Imported worsted, in all black with narrow self stripe 4.00
767. Best imported colored worsted, in narrow stripes, dark, medium and light grey 4.00
768. Venetian-finished worsted, plain black 4.50
769. Extra choice imported worsted, in black, with light grey and blue grey stripes 5.00

Youths' Trousers.

29 to 31 inches waist measure.

770 Dark Canadian tweeds, neat stripe patterns, 1.00, 1.25, 1.50 pair; finer tweeds, 2.00, 2.50 pair; fine imported worsted, in black and colored stripes, 2.50, 3.00, 3.50 pair.

Leather and Mackinaw Coats.

771. Blue mackinaw, lined with Kersey tweed, as cut 771 .... 5.00
772. Blue mackinaw, unlined lumbermen's jackets, with belt, no hood 3.50
773. Black leather coats, lined with striped cottonade, with patent buttons, as cut 773 .... 4.75
774. Black leather coats, lined with drab corduroy, patent buttons, as cut 773 .... 5.75
775. Black leather coats, reversible, leather one side, corduroy the other, turn and wear either side out, patent buttons, as cut 773. 6.50
776. Tan leather coats, reversible, corduroy lined, patent buttons, as cut 773 .... 7.00

Men's Plain and Fancy Vests.

34 to 44 inches chest measure.

778. Odd tweed vests, cut out of remnants .... .75c
779. Tweed vests, in better quality of cloth, as cut 779 .... 1.00
780. Imported black Venetian vests, as cut cut 779 .... 1.50
781. Drab, blue or brown plain corduroy, small cord, as cut 781 .. 1.39
782. Heavy constitutional corduroy, brown, drab or blue, wide cord, as cut 781 .... 1.75
783. Imported narrow ribbed corduroy, brown, blue or drab, with colored silk spots, red flannel lined, as cut 779 .... 1.95
784. Imported fancy mohair vestings, made as cut 779 .... 2.00
785. English corduroy, red flannel lined, brown, blue or drab shades, with colored silk spots, as cut 781 .... 2.50
786. Brown or green ground all-wool fancy checked vestings, with red and blue checks, as cut 786 .... 2.50
787. Dark ground all-wool fancy worsted vests, with light blue figure, as cut 787 .... 3.00
788. All-wool fancy worsted, black ground, with light and dark blue dot, as cut 779 .... 3.00
789. All-wool mohair, cardinal ground, with small black figure, as cut 787 .... 3.00
790. Fancy mohair, basket pattern weave, green and black ground, with red dot, as cut 787 .... 3.50
791. Dark green mohair cloth, with slate colored figure, as cut 787. 3.50

Smocks and Overalls.

Smocks are sizes 36 to 44 chest.
Overalls " " 32 to 44 waist.

578. White drill smocks 40c
579. White drill overalls with bib. 40c
580. Blue denim overalls with bib 50c
581. Blue denim overalls without bib 50c
582. Men's smocks, made of blue denim 50c
583. Striped cottonade overalls without bib 75c
584. Heavy blue denim smocks ... 75c
585. Heavy black overalls, with bib 75c
586. Extra heavy blue denim overalls, without bib 75c
587. Men's overalls, with bib, made of strong heavy blue denim ... 75c
588. Blue denims or white drill aprons 25c
589. White duck bar aprons 35c
590. Surgeons' linen aprons 50c
591. Barbers' white drill coats, round or square corners 75c
592. Barber's white duck coats, round or square corner sacque 1.00
593. Black lustre coats, sacque shape 1.50
594. Better quality black lustre coat 2.00

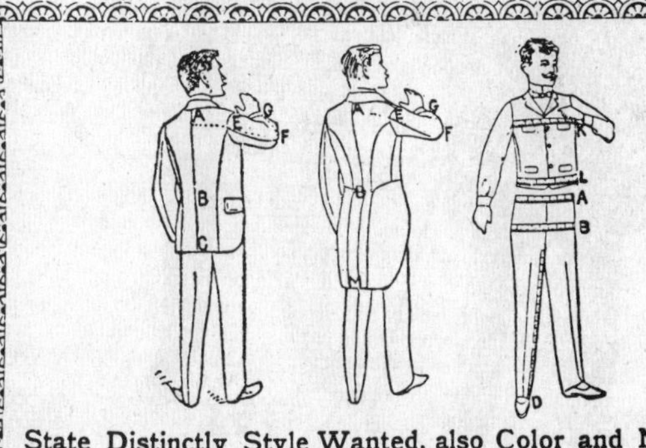

State Distinctly Style Wanted, also Color and Number of Cut.

Single-breasted Sacque Suit ....
Double " " " ....
Three-button Morning Cutaway ....

ALWAYS MEASURE OVER VEST FOR SIZE OF COAT.

Collar to waist, A to B .... inches. Whole length to bottom of coat, A to C .... inches. Centre of back to shoulder, E .... inches. Shoulder to elbow, E to F ...... inches. Elbow to hand, E to G .... inches. Inside seam of arm ...... inches. Around chest under arms at K ...... inches. Waist at L ...... inches.

VEST—Length from centre back of neck to bottom in front ...... inches. Around chest, under arms at K ...... inches. Waist at L ...... inches.

PANTS—Length of outside seam from waist to heel of boot ...... inches. Length of inside seam from crotch to heel of boot, C to D ...... inches. Around waist under vest at A ...... inches. Around seat at B ...... inches.

OVERCOAT—Take measurement for Overcoat around Chest, under arms, over Vest.

Give person's height ...... weight ......

Always measure the person for whom the clothes are intended.

YOUTHS' AND BOYS' OVERCOATS AND ULSTERS.

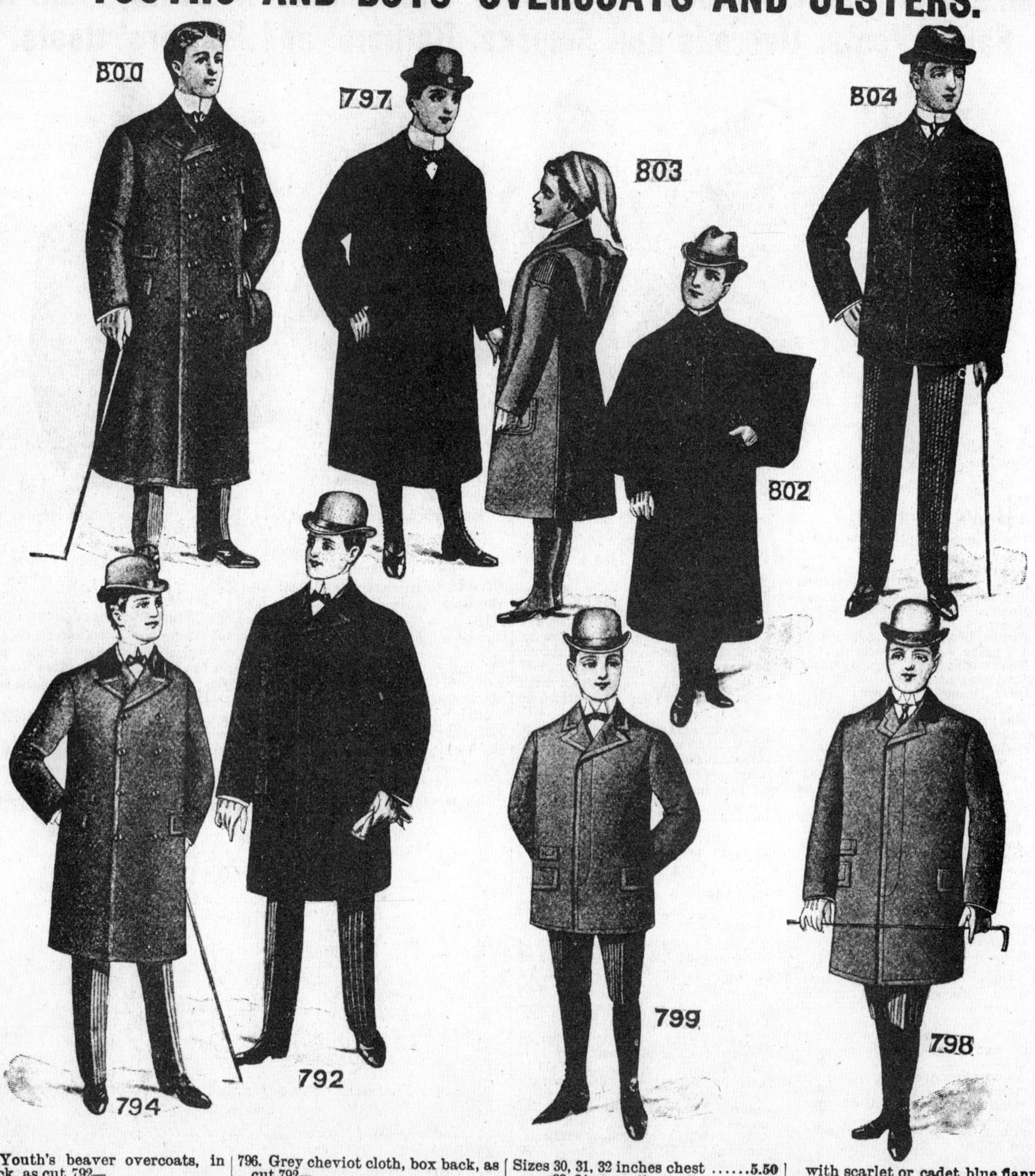

792. Youth's beaver overcoats, in black, as cut 792—

Sizes 29, 30 inches chest..........**4.50**
31, 32 " " **4.75**
33, 34, 35 " " **5.00**

793. Oxford grey cheviot cloth, as cut 792—

Sizes 29, 30 inches chest..........**4.50**
31, 32 " " **4.75**
33, 34, 35 " " **5.00**

794. Blue beaver, as cut 794—

Sizes 29, 30 inches chest..........**4.50**
31, 32 " " **4.75**
33, 34, 35 " " **5.00**

795. Fine imported blue beaver, as cut 792—

Sizes 31, 32, 33 inches chest **7.00**
34, 35 " " **7.50**

796. Grey cheviot cloth, box back, as cut 792—

Sizes 31, 32, 33 inches chest **7.00**
34, 35 " " **7.50**

797. Youth's Raglan overcoats in Oxford grey all-wool cheviot cloth, Italian linings, as cut 797—

Sizes 24, 25, 26 inches chest **6.50**
27, 28, 29 " " **7.00**
30, 31, 32 " " **7.50**
33, 34, 35 " " **8.00**

798. Oxford grey cheviot overcoat, Italian linings, velvet collar, as cut 798—

Sizes 29, 30, 31 inches chest **7.00**
32, 33, 34 " " **7.50**

799. Short box-back Oxford grey cheviot cloth, as cut 799—

Sizes 24, 25, 26 inches chest **4.50**
27, 28, 29 " " **5.00**

Sizes 30, 31, 32 inches chest **5.50**
33, 34 " " **6.00**

800. Ulsters, in black and Oxford grey frieze, as cut 800—

Sizes 26, 27, 28 inches chest **3.50**
29, 30, 31 " " **4.00**
32, 33, 34, 35 " " **4.50**

801. Heavy Harris Rockwood frieze, in Oxford grey and black, as cut 800—

Sizes 31, 32, 33 inches chest **7.50**
34, 35 " " **8.00**

802. Boys' bronze frieze cape overcoats, Italian linings, fly front cape, as cut 802—

Sizes 21, 22, 23, 24 inches chest....**3.50**
25, 26, 27 " " ... **4.00**
28, 29, 30 " " **4.50**

803. Children's Red River hood overcoats, in blue mackinaw, trimmed with scarlet or cadet blue flannel, as cut 803—

Sizes 20, 21, 22, 23 inches chest....**3.50**
24, 25 " " **3.75**
26, 27 " " **4.00**

Fancy wool sash to match, extra.**50c**
Wool toque to match, extra......**50c**

804. Black or brown frieze reefer, heavy linings, as cut 804—

Sizes 31, 32 inches chest..........**3.75**
33, 34, 35 " " **4.00**

805. Navy blue beaver cloth, good linings, as cut 804—

Sizes 31, 32 inches chest..........**3.75**
33, 34, 35 " " **4.00**

806. English nap cloth, navy blue, as cut 804—

Sizes 31, 32 inches chest..........**4.0[illegible]**
33 " " ....**4.2[illegible]**
34, 35 " " ....**4.5[illegible]**

Boys' Norway Reefers or Short Overcoats, and Fancy Reefers.

807. Navy blue imported union English nap, as cut 807—
Sizes 21 to 28 inches chest........1.95

808. Boys' reefers, navy blue nap cloth, brass buttons, velvet collar, as cut 807—
Sizes 20, 21, 22 inches chest 2.25
23, 24 " " 2.50
25, 26 " " 2.75
27, 28 " " 3.00

809. Imported all-wool navy blue English nap cloth, pearl buttons, as cut 807—
Sizes 20, 21 inches chest 3.25
22, 23 " " 3.50
24 " " 3.75
25 " " 4.00
26 " " 4.25
27 " " 4.50
28 " " 4.75

810. Imported navy blue English beaver cloth, pearl buttons, as cut 807—
Sizes 20, 21 inches chest 3.25
22, 23 " " 3.50
24 " " 3.75
25 " " 4.00
26 " " 4.25
27 " " 4.50
28 " " 4.75

811. Navy blue beaver cloth, with checked linings, as cut 811—
Sizes 22 to 28 inches chest 1.98

812. Oxford grey or blue black frieze, heavy linings, as cut 811—
Sizes 22 to 28 inches chest....... 1.98

813. Brown or black frieze Norway reefer, good linings, as cut 811—
Sizes 22, 23 inches chest 2.75
24, 25 " " 3.00
26, 27, " " 3.25
28, 29, " " 3.50
30, " " 3.75

814. Navy blue English nap cloth, as cut 811—
Sizes 22, 23 inches chest 2.75
24, 25 " " 3.00
26, 27, " " 3.25
28, 29, " " 3.50
30, " " 3.75

815. Blue beaver cloth, imported goods, heavy and warm, as cut 811—
Sizes 22, 23 inches chest 2.75
24, 25 " " 3.00
26, 27 " " 3.25
28, 29 " " 3.50
30 " " 3.75

816. Imported Oxford grey cheviot, all-wool cloth, as cut 811—
Sizes 22, 23 inches chest 3.50
24, 25 " " 3.75
26 " " 4.00
27 " " 4.25
28 " " 4.50
29 " " 4.75
30 " " 5.00

817. Heavy navy blue imported English nap cloth, as cut 811—
Size 22 inches chest............ 4.25
23 " " 4.50
24 " " 4.75
25 " " 5.00
26 " " 5.25
27 " " 5.50
28 " " 5.73
29 " " 6.00
30 " " 6.25

818. Oxford grey imported cheviot cloth reefer, made as cut 818, sizes 21 to 26..........................4.50

819. Imported black English beaver cloth, as cut 819, sizes 21 to 26..5.00

820. English cheviot cloth, in Oxford grey shade, as cut 819, sizes 21 to 26 ....5.00

821. Electric blue imported Kersey cloth, as cut 821, sizes 21 to 26..5.00

822. Dark brown English Kersey cloth, as cut 821, sizes 21 to 26..5.00

823. Navy blue imported English beaver cloth, velvet piping, as cut 823, sizes 21 to 26................6.50

824. Imported Kersey cloth in fawn shade, as cut 824, sizes 21 to 26 .... 6.50

825. Electric blue Kersey cloth imported goods, as cut 824, sizes 21 to 26............................. 6.50

826. Kersey cloth reefer, English imported goods, color scarlet, as cut 824. ....6.50

827. Imported fine black montagnac curl cloth, as cut 827, sizes 21 to 26 .... 7.50

827A. Fancy Russian blouse overcoat, in fine scarlet Kersey cloth, best trimmings, as cut 827A, sizes 20 to 26.............................7.50

YOUTHS' SUITS, LONG PANTS.

860. Navy blue serge, all wool, as cut 860—

32	33	34, 35
4.50	**4.75**	**5.00**

861. Dark tweeds, in neat checked patterns, as cut 860—

32	33	34, 35
4.50	**4.75**	**5.00**

862. Heavy all-wool grey diagonal homespun tweed, as cut 862—

32	33	34, 35
4.50	**4.75**	**5.00**

863. All-wool navy blue serge as cut 862—

32	33	34, 35
4.50	**4.75**	**5.00**

864. Dark grey or dark brown checked domestic tweeds, with overplaid, as cut 862—

32	33	34, 35
4.50	**4.75**	**5.00**

865. Heavy all-wool navy blue cheviot serge, as cut 860—

32	33,	34, 35
6.00	**6.25**	**6.50**

866. Light brown all-wool small checked tweeds, with overplaid, as cut 860—

32	33	34, 35
6.00	**6.25**	**6.50**

867. Navy blue cheviot serge, heavy all-wool cloth, as cut 862—

32	33	34, 35
6.00	**6.25**	**6.50**

868. Brown or mid-grey all-wool tweed, with red overplaid, as cut 868—

32	33	34, 35
6.00	**6.25**	**6.50**

869. Oxford or mid-grey all-wool cheviot tweed, green tinted, as cut 862—

32	33	34, 35
6.00	**6.25**	**6.50**

870. Navy blue Campbell's worsted serge, pure wool, as cut 860—

32	33	34, 35
7.00	**7.25**	**7.50**

871. Campbell's all-wool black worsted serge, as cut 860—

32	33	34, 35
7.00	**7.25**	**7.50**

872. Mid-grey or dark grey and green mixed, all-wool tweeds, with red thread overplaid, as cut 868—

32	33	34, 35
7.00	**7.25**	**7.50**

873. Black or navy blue Campbell's worsted serges, as cut 862—

32	33	34, 35
7.00	**7.25**	**7.50**

874. All-wool dark grey checked tweed, as cut 860—

32	33	34, 35
7.00	**7.25**	**7.50**

875. Dark brown checked tweed, with green tint, as cut 862—

32	33	34, 35
7.00	**7.25**	**7.50**

876. Blue grey checked all-wool tweed, neat pattern, as cut 868—

32	33	34, 35
8.00	**8.25**	**8.50**

877. Small check in dark grey tweed with red overplaid, as cut 862—

32	33	34, 35
8.00	**8.25**	**8.50**

878. Black Clay twilled worsted solid all-wool cloth, as cut 860—

32	33	34, 35
8.00	**8.25**	**8.50**

879. Dark brown and green checked tweed, with overplaid, as cut 868—

32	33	34, 35
8.00	**8.25**	**8.50**

880. All-wool dark brown checked Canadian tweed, as cut 862—

32	33	34, 35
8.00	**8.25**	**8.50**

881. Black and navy blue worsted serge, all wool, as cut 881—

32	33	34, 35
8.50	**9.00**	**9.50**

882. Black or navy blue Clay twilled worsted, as cut 881—

32	33	34, 35
9.00	**9.50**	**10.00**

883. Green and grey all-wool tweed, with overplaid, as cut 868—

32	33	34, 35
9.00	**9.50**	**10.00**

884. Navy blue and black worsted serges, all wool, as cut 862—

32	33	34, 35
8.50	**9.00**	**9.50**

885. Heavy all-wool tweed, green and grey mixed checked patterns, as cut 868—

32, 33, 34, 35
10.00

886. Plain black Venetian-finished worsted, as cut 881—

32	33	34, 35
10.00	**10.50**	**11.00**

887. Scotch and English tweeds, in dark and medium colors, checked patterns, as cut 881—

32	33	34, 35
10.00	**10.50**	**11.00**

888. Eton suit, plain black Venetian finished worsted, as cut 888—

Sizes 28 to 35
10.00

889. Oxford grey imported cheviot finished worsted, as cut 868—

32	33	34, 35
9.00	**9.50**	**10.00**

BOYS' THREE-PIECE SUITS, SHORT PANTS

Sizes 27 to 33 inches Chest Measure.

YOU can order your suit, overcoat or trousers by mail just as easily as you can by visiting the store personally. Our goods are all marked in plain figures. Cash and one price only to all. No reduction in prices for large or small quantities. When writing for samples mention whether suit, overcoat or trousers you require are for men or boys. Always make first and second choice when ordering from samples. If goods are ordered in a different style than what sample calls for, it will only cause delay, as goods are only made in styles that samples and Catalogue state. Our sizes in men's suits and overcoats are 34, 35, 36, 37, 38, 39, 40, 42 and 44 inches chest measure. The size of our stock and equipment for filling orders enable us to furnish promptly almost anything you can think of in Ready-to-Wear Clothing. There are no mysteries about our business; our methods are plain, simple and straightforward; our success is based on sound business principles. The perfection of our equipment and the amount of our output enable us to sell close to the cost of production. The sketches on accompanying page will give you an idea of our scientific system of turning out reliable goods.

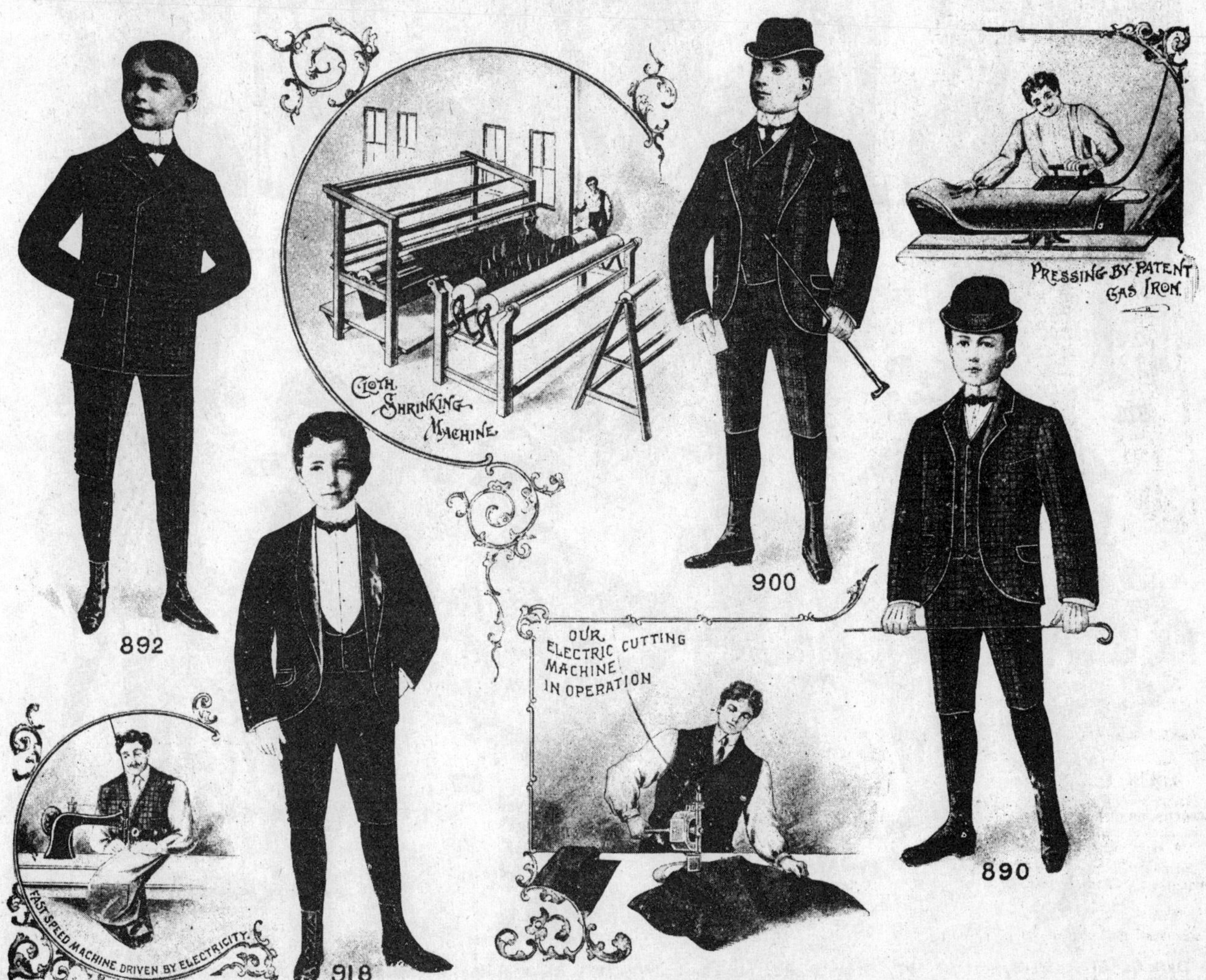

890. Navy blue serge, Italian lined, as cut 890 .... **2.50**
891. Dark Canadian tweeds, neat patterns, as cut 890 .... **2.50**
892. Checked Canadian tweeds, dark colors, as cut 892 .... **2.50**
893. Dark brown or dark grey checked tweeds, as cut 890 .... **3.00**
894. Dark grey or light brown Canadian tweeds, as cut 892 .... **3.00**
895. Dark brown or dark grey checked tweeds, with overplaids, as cut 890 .... **3.50**
896. Heavy all-wool cheviot-finished serge, navy blue, as cut 892 .... **3.50**
897. Brown or grey dark checked pattern Canadian tweed, as cut 892 .... **3.50**
898. Navy blue English serge, as cut 890 .... **3.75**
899. Imported English serge, in navy blue only, as cut 892 .... **3.75**
900. Heavy all-wool tweeds, brown or grey checks, with overplaids, as cut 900 .... **4.50**
901. Light brown, small checked tweed, green tinted, as cut 890 .. **4.00**
902. All-wool dark grey and green check, Italian lined, as cut 892 .. **4.00**
903. Black or navy blue Campbell's worsted serge, as cut 890 ...... **5.00**
904. Mid-grey or dark grey and green mixed, in neat checks, with overplaids, as cut 900 .... **5.00**
905. Navy blue and black imported worsted serge, as cut 892 ...... **5.00**
906. Dark brown mixed tweed, neat patterns, all wool, as cut 892 .. **5.00**
907. Brown and green or Oxford grey checked domestic tweeds, as cut 890 .... **5.00**
908. Pure all-wool dark brown check, with overplaids, as cut 892 .... **5.00**
909. Plain black venetian-finished worsteds, as cut 890 .... **6.00**
910. Blue-grey and black, in a neat check, all-wool cloth, as cut 900 .... **6.00**
911. Imported all-wool navy blue or black worsted serge, as cut 890 .... **6.00**
912. Oxford grey checked English tweed, with overplaids, as cut 892 .... **6.00**
913. Black or navy blue hard worsted serge, as cut 892 .... **6.00**
914. Black Clay diagonal worsted, pure all-wool, as cut 890 .... **6.50**
915. Navy blue or black Clay twilled worsted, as cut 892 .... **6.50**
916. Black venetian-finished worsted, silk stitched edges, as cut 890 .... **7.50**
917. Dark grey striped English tweed, as cut 900 .... **7.50**
918. Boys' tuxedo suits, made of black venetian-finished worsted, as cut 918 .... **7.50**

BOYS' BROWNIE AND VESTEE SUITS.

Sizes 21 to 26 inches chest measure.

THE AVERAGE SIZE FOR BOY

Age 4 is Chest 22.	Age 8 is Chest 26.
" 5 " " 23.	" 9 " " 27.
" 6 " " 24.	" 10 " " 28.
" 7 " " 25.	

919. Dark Canadian tweed, neat pattern, as cut 919 .... **2.50**

920. Plain dark grey tweed, as cut 920 .... **2.50**

921. Navy blue serge, braid trimmed, as cut 919 .... **2.50**

922. Green tinted brown checked Canadian tweed, with red overplaid, as cut 922 .... **3.00**

923. All-wool brown and green checked tweed, as cut 919 ..... **3.00**

924. Dark brown all-wool tweed, neat pattern, as cut 924 .... **3.50**

925. Light and dark brown mixed, small neat pattern, as cut 925 .. **3.50**

926. Mid-grey pin check, with green overplaid, as cut 924 .... **3.50**

927. Greenish-grey pin checked domestic tweeds, trimmings to match, as cut 927 .... **4.00**

928. Black and green pin check tweed, with red overplaid, red front and red trimming on collar, as cut 928 .... **4.00**

929. Scotch effect tweed, all-wool, greyish-green, brown mixed, blue Venetian collar and blue front, as cut 928 .... **4.00**

930. Small check black and grey fancy worsted, red overplaid, as cut 921 .... **4.00**

931. Navy blue imported worsted serge, as cut 931 .... **4.00**

932. Heavy navy blue all-wool cheviot, as cut 932 .... **4.00**

933. All-wool English tweed, in dark brown, neat pattern, as cut 932 .... **4.00**

934. Blue black velvet, black braid trimmings, as cut 934 .... **5.00**

935. Heavy all-wool Scotch tweed, dark green mixed red overplaids, green venetian vest, as cut 935 .... **5.00**

936. Mid-grey striped all-wool English tweed, blue venetian front, as cut 936 .... **5.00**

937. All-wool navy blue worsted serge, silk-faced and fancy silk spot double-breasted vest, as cut 937, ... **5.00**

938. Fancy English worsted, light brown ground with dark brown overplaids, red vest with spots, as cut 938 .... **6.00**

939. Heavy all-wool English tweed, black with grey stripe, red front, as cut 939 .... **6.00**

940. Blue black fancy checked colored English worsted, self-front, as cut 940 .... **6.50**

941. Black and grey small check English worsted tweed, as cut 940 .... **6.50**

942. English tweed, small check, blue grey and black mixed, as cut 942 .... **6.50**

943. Navy blue worsted serge, small stand collar, red front, as cut 943 .... **7.50**

944. Fancy West of England worsted, brown and black mixed, neat small check, red front, as cut 943 .... **7.50**

Boys' Two-Piece Suits, Sailor Suits, Kilt Suits and Knee Pants.

Two-Piece Suits.

Sizes 23 to 28.

945. Navy blue serge, as cut 945..**1.50**

946. Dark Canadian tweed, neat patterns, as cut 945 ....**1.50**

947. Light brown or dark grey Canadian tweed, as cut 945 ....**2.00**

948. Plain Oxford grey or light brown small checked tweed, as cut 948..............................**2.00**

949. All-wool dark grey or dark brown checked tweed, as cut 949—
23, 24 25, 26 27, 28
2.25 2.50 2.75

950. Navy blue serge, all wool, as cut 950—
23, 24 25, 26 27, 28
2.25 2.50 2.75

951. Neat dark checked all-wool Canadian tweed, as cut 950—
23, 24 25, 26 27, 28
2.25 2.50 2.75

952. Navy blue all-wool serge, as cut 948—
23, 24 25, 26 27, 28
2.25 2.50 2.75

953. All-wool navy blue serge, Norfolk suit, as cut 953—
23, 24 25, 26 27, 28
2.25 2.50 2.75

954. Neat dark grey-check all-wool tweed, as cut 953—
23, 24 25, 26 27, 28
2.25 2.50 2.75

955. Heavy navy blue all-wool cheviot serge, as cut 949—
23, 24 25, 26 27, 28
2.50 2.75 3.00

956. Light brown and grey mixed tweed, with overplaid, as cut 953—
23, 24 25, 26 27, 28
3.00 3.25 3.50

957. Dark or light brown checked Canadian tweed, with overplaid, as cut 949—
23, 24 25, 26 27, 28
2.50 2.75 3.00

958. Mid-grey or dark grey and green mixed, neat checked Canadian tweed, as cut 958—
23, 24 25, 26 27, 28
2.50 2.75 3.00

959. Dark brown and green mixed, also greenish grey with overplaid, as cut 949—
23, 24 25, 26 27, 28
3.00 3.25 3.50

960. Dark grey small checked Canadian tweed, as cut 950—
23, 24 25, 26 27, 28
3.00 3.25 3.50

961. All-wool navy blue worsted serge, as cut 950—
23, 24 25, 26 27, 28
3.25 3.50 3.75

962. Navy blue worsted serge, pure wool, imported goods, as cut 953—
23, 24 25, 26 27, 28
3.25 3.50 3.75

963. Very dark brown checked all-wool tweeds, some green-tinted, as cut 963—
23, 24 25, 26 27, 28
3.50 3.75 4.00

964. Very dark grey or dark brown all-wool tweeds, as cut 949—
23, 24 25, 26 27, 28
3.50 3.75 4.00

965. Pure all-wool tweed, black ground, with blue grey small check, as cut 953—
23, 24 25, 26 27, 28
4.00 4.25 4.50

966. All-wool imported navy blue or black Clay twilled worsted, as cut 963—
23, 24 25, 26 27, 28
4.00 4.25 4.50

966A. Plain black venetian-finished worsted, as cut 963—
23, 24 25, 26 27, 28
4.00 4.25 4.50

967. Bannockburn and Galashiel's Scotch tweeds, grey broken checks with overplaids, as cut 953—
23, 24 25, 26 27, 28
3.50 3.75 4.00

968. Fancy small checked worsted, grey and black mixed, as cut 950—
23, 24 25, 26 27, 28
3.50 3.75 4.00

969. Navy blue or black worsted serges and Clay twills, as cut 963—
23, 24 25, 26 27, 28
4.00 4.25 4.50

Sailor and Kilt Suits.

970. Navy blue serge, braid trimmed, pants lined, as cut 970, sizes 21 to 26 ....**75c**

971. Better blue serge, lanyard and whistle, as cut 970, sizes 21 to 26 ....**1.00**

972. Navy blue serge, trimmed with black braid, as cut 970, sizes 21 to 26 ....**1.50**

973. Navy blue serge, braid trimmed, separate front, as cut 973, sizes 21 to 26..................................**2.00**

974. Same, only better quality, as cut 973..................................**2.50**

975. Navy blue hard worsted serge with black braid trimming, as cut 973..................................**4.00**

976. Pure all-wool imported worsted serge in navy blue, as cut 976..**5.00**

977. Man-of-war suits, in navy English serge, as cut 977 ....**3.50**

978. Same, only better quality serge, as cut 977 ....**5.00**

979. Navy blue melton cloth kilted suit, a little plainer than cut 979, sizes 1½ to 3½ years **1.50**

980. Navy blue serge kilt suit, colored narrow braid trimming, as cut 979, sizes 1½ to 3½ years........**2.00**

981. Fine imported serge, navy blue, braid trimmed, as cut 981......**2.50**

982. Very pretty suit, all-wool serge, navy blue, as cut 982 ....**3.00**

983. Highland kilt Scotch suit, blue-black velvet jacket, vest and cap, plaid skirt, sizes 3 to 7 years, as cut 983 ....**12.50**

Knicker Pants, Lined.

984. Navy blue serge, sizes 22 to 28 ....**25c**

985. Brown or grey Canadian tweed, side and hip pockets, sizes 22 to 28 ....**39c**

986. Navy blue all-wool serge, sizes 22 to 28..................................**60c**

987. Halifax tweed, in dark colors, sizes 22 to 28 ....**60c**

988. Dark Canadian tweed, brown or grey, sizes 29 to 33 ....**50c**

989. All-wool navy blue serge, sizes 29 to 33 ....**75c**

990. Neat checked tweeds, in all-wool materials—
22, 23, 24 25, 26, 27 28, 29, 30 31, 32, 33
75c 90c 1.00 1.25

991. Black or navy blue worsted serges—
22, 23, 24 25, 26, 27 28, 29, 30 31, 32, 33
75c 90c 1.00 1.25

992. Brown or drab English corduroy, soft cord—
22, 23, 24 25, 26, 27 28, 29 30, 31 32, 33
75c 90c 1.00 1.25 1.50

993. All-wool serges and checked English tweed—
22, 23, 24 25, 26 27, 28 29, 30 31, 32, 33
75c 90c 1.00 1.25 1.50

994. Blue denim brownie overalls, 5 pockets, bib and straps, sizes 20 to 30..................................**40c**

MEN'S AND BOYS' NECKWEAR AND SILK OR SATIN MUFFLERS

A WORD about our neckties. Our neckwear is all made on our own premises, and is kept strictly up to date in shapes, patterns and quality, as our buyer visits the American and European markets several times yearly, thus securing the very latest fashions from London, Vienna, Paris and New York. Our 25c tie is made out of selected silk and satin, made in full length and large shapes, all satin lined. This is a line we can thoroughly recommend.

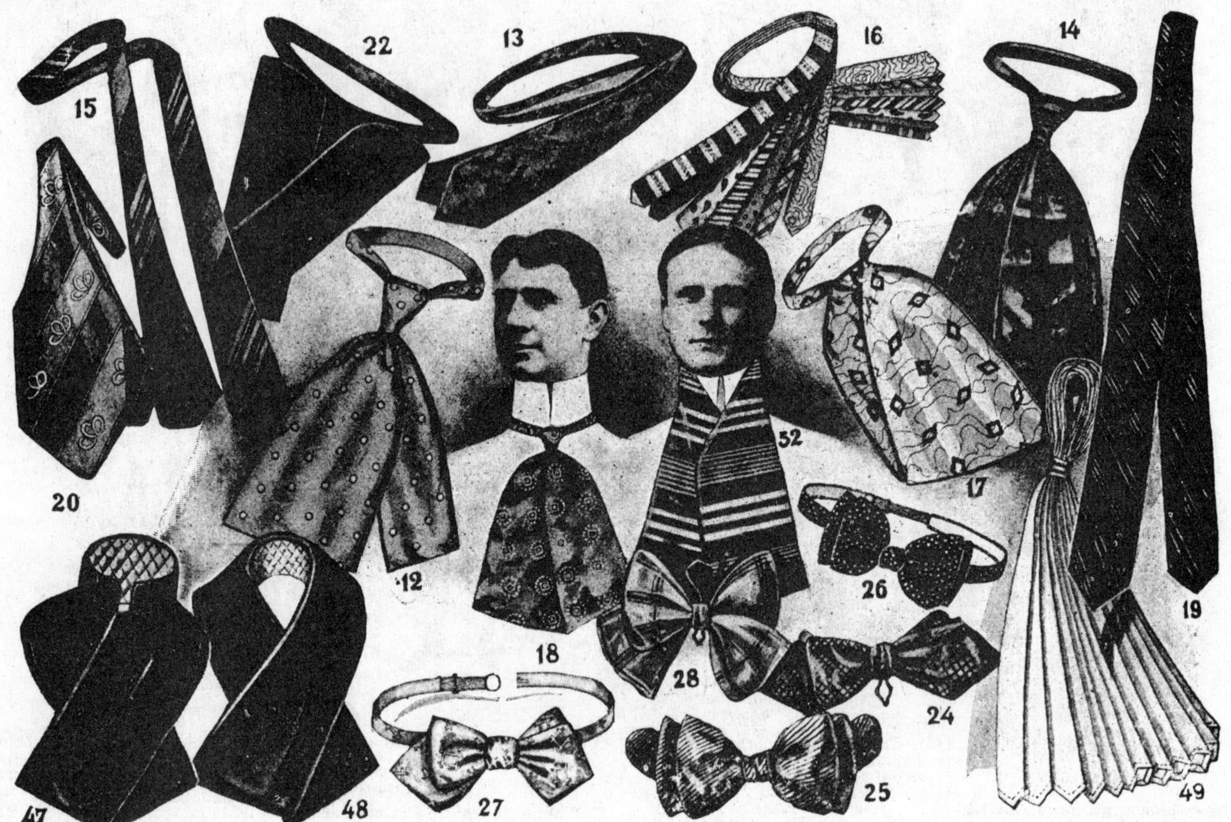

Neckwear.

12. Men's silk and satin neckties, made-up knot shape, dark and light fancy patterns and stripes, as cut 12, each....................12½c
13. Men's silk and satin neckties, four-in-hand shape, dark and light fancy patterns and stripes, as cut 13, each....................12½c
14. Men's silk and satin neckties, satin lined, choice fancy patterns, polka dots, stripes, plain cords, newest patterns, our big seller, as cut 14, each....................25c
15. Men's silk and satin neckties, satin lined, newest fancy stripes, plain cords, polka dots, stripes, our big seller, as cut 15, each ..25c
16. Men's silk and satin club ties, to tie in bow or small four-in-hand, silk all round, newest fancy patterns, stripes, polka dots and plain cords, as cut 16, each...........25c
17. Men's silk and satin puffs ties, satin lined, latest shape, newest fancy patterns, polka dots, stripes and plain cords, as cut 17, each 25c
18. Men's fine imported silk and satin knot ties, latest American and English designs, satin lined, newest fancy patterns, neat figures, stripes, polka dots and plain cords, as cut 18, each....................50c
19. Men's silk and satin derby ties, fine imported Crefeld goods, best satin lined, newest shape, extra long, latest fancy broches, stripes, plain cords and polka dots, as cut 19, each....................50c
20. Men's high-grade neckwear, fine imported silk and satin, latest New York and Crefeld goods, large English flowing-end shape, newest colorings and designs, in stripes, broches, polka dots and plain cords, as cut 20, each....................50c
21. Men's fine silk and satin puff ties, satin lined, fine imported Crefeld quality, latest styles and colorings, stripes, broches, plain cords and polka dots, as cut 17, each......50c
22. Men's flat scarf, to cover the bosom, in black silk and satin, plain cords and polka dots, satin lined, well made, as cut 22, each 35c and....................50c
23. The "Ascot" tie, to tie in puff shape, satin lined, full length, fine silk and satin, in black, plain cords and polka dots, each...........50c

Bow Ties.

24. Silk and satin bow ties, with shield for turn-down collar, light and dark fancy patterns, as cut 24, each....................12½c
25. Fine silk and satin bow ties, with covered shield of same silk, made with pointed or square ends, newest fancy stripes, checks, polka dots, plain cords and neat figures, as cut 25, each....................25c
26. Fine silk and satin bow ties, with band, satin lined, pointed or square ends, newest fancy patterns, stripes, polka dots and plain cords, as cuts 26 and 27, each..........25c
28. Boys' butterfly bows, with elastic to go around neck, in fancy plaids, as cut 28, each....................25c

Black Silk and Satin Neckwear.

29. Black silk and satin knots, satin lined, as cut 14, each...........25c
30. Black silk and satin four-in-hands, satin lined or silk all around, as cut 15, each....................25c
31. Black silk and satin puff ties, satin lined, as cut 17, each 25c, 50c
32. Black silk and satin knot ties, satin lined, as cut 18, each......50c
33. Black silk and satin Derbys, silk all round, as cut 19, each........50c
34. Black silk and satin flowing-end ties, as cut 20, each..............50c
35. Black silk and satin flat scarf, satin lined, as cut 22, each..35c, 50c
36. Black silk and satin shield bows, as cut 24, each....................12½c
37. Black silk and satin shield bows, as cut 25, each....................25c
38. Black silk and satin bows, with band, as cuts 26 and 27, each...25c
39. Black silk Tom Thumb ties, ½ in. wide, each....................10c
40. Black silk Tom Thumb ties, ⅝, ¾, ⅞ and 1 in. wide, each..........15c
41. Black silk Tom Thumb ties, ¾ and 1 in. wide, each.................25c
42. Black silk Tom Thumb ties, 1 in. wide, extra long, each 25c, 35c

Evening Dress-Wear.

43. White lawn bow ties with shield for turn-down collar, 3 for 25c, or each....................9c
44. White lawn dress bows with band, pointed or square ends, large or small shape, 3 for 25c, or each, 9c
45. White lawn dress bow ties, with band, latest shapes, pointed or square ends, each 12½c
46. Best white lawn dress bows, with band, latest shapes, pointed or square ends, 3 for 50c, or each..18c
P.S.—All dress bows put up in small box.
47. Dress shirt bosom protectors, in black silk and satin, heavy quilted satin linings, stand-up collar protector attached, shaped over shoulders, as cut 47 ......1.00, 1.50
48. Dress shirt bosom protectors, black silk and satin, lined with heavy quilted satin, deep-shaped back to protect collar, as cut 48, each 1.00 and....................1.50
49. White lawn string ties, per doz., as cut 49....................25c
50. White lawn string ties, per doz., as cut 49....................50c
51. White lawn string ties, as cut 49, 3 for 25c, or each 9c

Oxford Mufflers.

52. Men's and boys' Oxford mufflers, in black silk and satin, lined with heavy quilted satin, well padded and very warm, worn instead of the large handkerchief, always in place, also worn by ladies, as cut 52, ...75c, 1.00
53. The Oxford muffler for men and boys, in silk and satin polka dots, stripes, plain cords and fancy patterns, as cut 52 ....75c, 1.00

MEN'S AND BOYS' COLLARS AND CUFFS

OUR collars are all made 4-ply. The linen used in our best lines of collars and cuffs is all the very best Irish Bessbrook linen, which insures the wearing quality. Be sure and give depth of collar, also size, and number of cut.

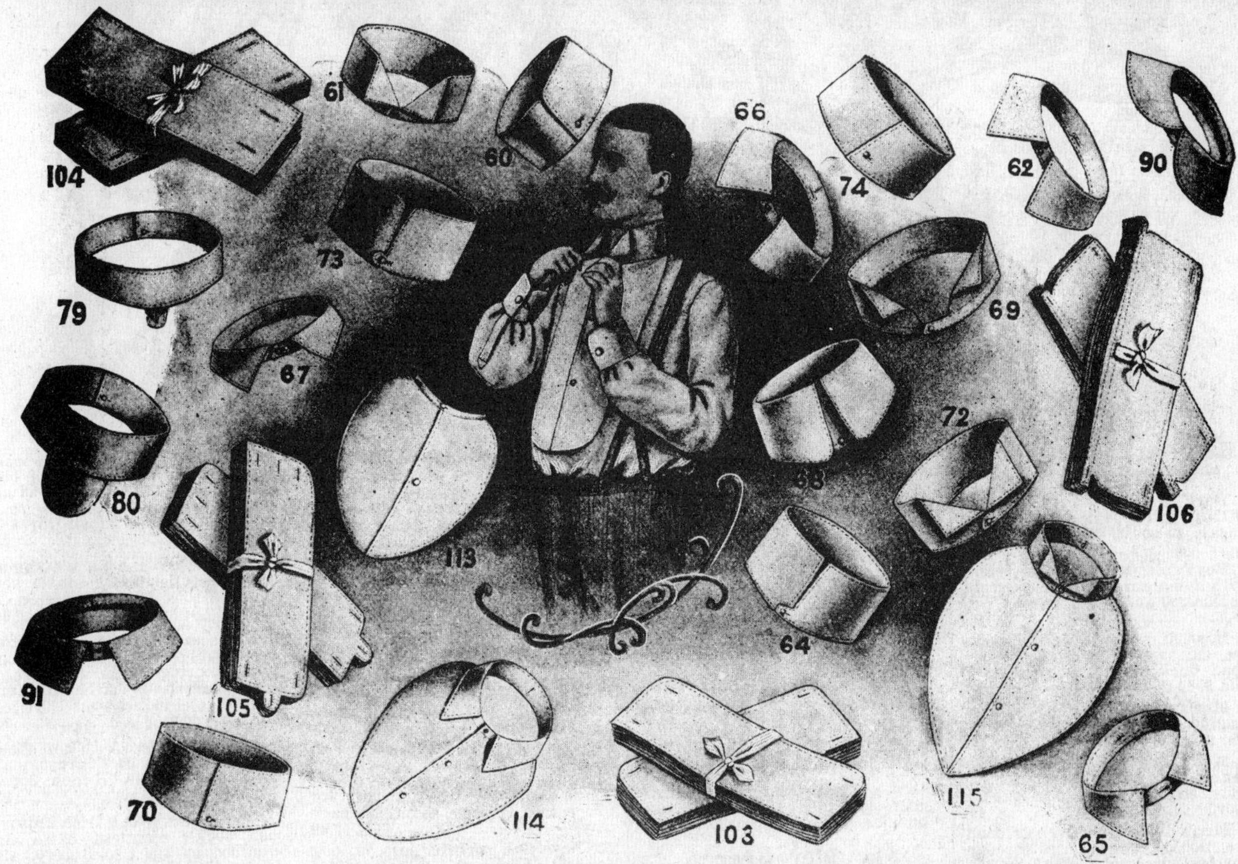

Men's Collars.

60. Men's 4-ply linen collars, depth 2¼-inch, sizes 14 to 17½, as cut 60, 3 for 25c, or each 9c
61. Men's 4-ply collars, depths 1¾, 2, 2¼-inch, sizes 14 to 17½, as cut 61, 3 for 25c, or each 9c
62. Men's 4-ply collars, deep turn-down, sizes 14 to 17½, as cut 62, 3 for 25c, or each 9c
63. Men's 4-ply 1800 linen collars, depths 1½ to 2½-inch, sizes 14 to 17½, as cut 61, each..................12½c
64. Men's 4-ply 1800 linen stand-up collars, depths 2, 2¼, 2½-inch, sizes 14 to 17½, as cut 64, each........12½c
65. Men's 4-ply linen collars, turn-down, long points, sizes 14 to 17½, as cut 65, each 12½c
66. Men's 4-ply linen collars, roll shape, sizes 14 to 17½, as cut 66, each..................12½c
67. Men's 4-ply linen collars, cutaway shape, sizes 14 to 17½, as cut 67, each 12½c
68. Men's 4-ply linen collars, high band shape, depths 2, 2¼-inch, sizes 14 to 17½, as cut 68, each 12½c
69. Dragoon shape, fat man's collar, 4-ply linen, depth 1¾-inch, sizes 14 to 21, as cut 69, each..................12½c
70. 4-ply linen, straight band, depth 1¾-inch, sizes 14 to 18, as cut 70, each..................12½c
71. Coachman's collar, 4-ply linen, with round points, depth 2¼-inch, sizes 14 to 17½, each 12½c
72. 4-ply imported collars, 2100 linen, depths 1½ to 2¾-inch, all sizes, as cut 72, 3 for 50c, or each........18c
73. 4-ply imported collars, best linen, straight standing, with round corners, depths 2¼ to 2¾-inch, sizes 14 to 17½, as cut 73, 3 for 50c, or each 18c
74. 4-ply best imported linen collars, straight band, depths 2 to 3-inch sizes 14 to 18, as cut 74, 3 for 50c, or each..................18c
75. 4-ply best linen turn-down collars, sizes 14 to 21, as cut 62, 3 for 50c, or each..................18c
76. 4-ply best linen collars, cutaway shape, sizes 14 to 19, as cut 67, 3 for 50c, or each 18c
77. 4-ply best linen roll collars, sizes 14 to 18, as cut 66, 3 for 50c, or each 18c
78. 4-ply linen collars, high band style, depths 2¼, 2½-inch, sizes 14 to 17½, as cut 68, 3 for 50c, or each.18c
79. Clerical collars, with small tab, sizes 14 to 18½, as cut 79, 3 for 50c, or each..................18c
80. Clerical collars, with large tab, sizes 14 to 17½, as cut 80, 3 for 50c, or each..................18c

Boys' Collars.

82. 4-ply linen collars, depth 2-inch, sizes 12 to 13½, as cut 60, 3 for 25c, or each 9c
83. 4-ply linen collars, turn down, sizes 12 to 13½, as cut 62, 3 for 25c, or each 9c
84. 4-ply linen collars, depth 1¾-inch, sizes 12 to 13½, as cut 61, 3 for 25c, or each..................9c
85. 4-ply linen collars, depth 2-inch, sizes 12 to 13½, as cut 72, each..12½c
86. 4-ply linen collars, depth 1¾, 2-inch, sizes 12 to 13½, as cut 64, each..12½c
87. 4-ply linen collars, sizes 12 to 13½, as cut 62, each 12½c
88. 4-ply linen collars, sizes 12 to 13½, as cut 63, each 12½c
89. 4-ply linen collars, depth 2-inch, sizes 12 to 13½, as cut 68, each..12½c
90. Eton collars, 4-ply, sizes 12 to 13½, as cut 90, each..................12½c
91. Eton collars, best 4-ply linen, sizes 12 to 13½, as cut 91, 3 for 50c, or each..................18c

Celluloid Collars.

92. Men's and boys' interlined celluloid collars, best Canadian make, depth 2-inch, sizes 12 to 17½, as cut 61, each 12½c
93. Men's and boys' interlined celluloid collars, best Canadian make, sizes 12 to 17½, as cut 62, each..12½c
94. Men's colored celluloid collars, interlined, depth 2-inch, sizes 14 to 17½, as cut 61, each..................12½c
95. Best American interlined celluloid collars, depth 1¾-inch, sizes 14 to 18, as cut 72, 3 for 50c, or each 18c
96. Best American interlined celluloid collars, depth 1¾-inch, sizes 14 to 18, as cut 70, 3 for 50c, or each 18c
97. Best American interlined celluloid collars, sizes 14 to 18½, as cut 67, 3 for 50c, or each 18c
98. Clerical celluloid collars, linen interlined, sizes 14 to 18, as cut 79, 3 for 50c, or each 18c
99. Clerical celluloid collars, linen interlined, the Roman style, narrow double band, to fasten at back, 3 for 50c, or each 18c

Men's and Boys' Cuffs.

100. 4-ply cuffs, sizes 9½ to 11½, as cut 103, pair 15c
101. 4-ply cuffs, sizes 9½ to 11½, as cut 104, pair 15c
102. 4-ply link cuffs, sizes 9½ to 11½, as cut 105, pair..................15c
103. 4-ply linen cuffs, sizes 9½ to 11½, as cut 103, pair..................25c
104. 4-ply linen cuffs, sizes 9½ to 11½, as cut 104, pair..................25c
105. 4-ply linen link cuffs, sizes 9½ to 11½, as cut 105, pair..................25c
106. 4-ply linen link cuffs, sizes 9½ to 11½, as cut 106, pair 25c
107. 4-ply best linen cuffs, sizes 10 to 11, as cut 103, pair..................35c
108. 4-ply best linen cuffs, sizes 10 to 11, as cut 104, pair..................35c
109. 4-ply best linen cuffs, sizes 10 to 11, as cut 105, pair 35c
110. Boys' 4-ply cuffs, sizes 8 to 9, as cut 103, pair 15c
111. Men's interlined celluloid cuffs, best Canadian make, sizes 9½ to 11½, as cut 103, pair 20c
112. Men's interlined celluloid cuffs, best American make, sizes 9½ to 11½, as cut 103 pair..................35c
113. Men's and boys' linen dickey fronts, as cut 113, each..................20c
114. Men's and boys' linen dickeys, collar attached, sizes 12 to 17½, as cut 114, each 25c
115. Men's and boys' linen dickeys, collar attached, sizes 12 to 17½, as cut 115, each..................25c
116. Boys' "Opera" paper collars, turn-down shape, per box of ten 10c
117. Men's "Comet" paper collars, turn-down shape, per box of ten 10c

Men's and Boys' Suspenders, Belts, Socks, Sweaters and Jerseys.

Men's and Boys' Suspenders.

118. Boys' elastic web suspenders, with mohair or leather ends, strong buckle, 24 and 27 inches long, pair 10c

119. Boys' elastic web suspenders, with mohair or leather ends, strong buckles, 27 and 30 inches long, pair 15c

120. Boys' fine elastic web suspenders, silk woven or leather ends, good buckles and well made, 27 and 30 inches long, pair 25c

121. Men's elastic web suspenders, English make, leather ends, as cut 124, pair 10c

122. Men's heavy elastic web suspenders, John Bright style, leather ends, strong buckles, as cut 122, pair 15c

123. Men's fine elastic web suspenders, mohair ends and drawers supporters, wire buckle, double-stitched, as cut 125, pair 15c

124. Men's fine elastic web suspenders, Saddler's English make, leather ends, hand-sewn, strong buckle, as cut 124, pair 25c

125. Men's fine elastic web suspenders, mohair ends and drawers supporters, double-stitched back, wire buckle, black, white, stripes and spots, as cut 125, pair 25c

126. Men's elastic web suspenders, woven silk ends and drawers supporters, fancy slide buckles, as cut 125, pair 35c

127. Men's elastic web suspenders, with roll kid ends and drawers supporters, kid tips, drop fasteners, as cut 132, pair 50c

128. Men's "Guyot" suspenders, best French make, as cut 128, pair. .50c

129. Regulation military suspenders, woollen web, elastic slide back, leather ends 50c

130. Crown make elastic suspenders, silk woven ends and drawers supporters, double-stitched back, patent detachable buckles, pair 50c

131. Police and fireman's suspenders, Crown make, heavy elastic web, leather ends, extra well made and very strong, pair 65c

132. Crown make elastic web suspenders, roll kid ends and drawers supporters, kid tips, drop fasteners, black, white and plain greys, as cut 132, pair 75c

133. Crown make, extra quality elastic web suspenders, roll kid ends and drawers supporters, drop fasteners, fully guaranteed, as cut 134, pair 1.00

134. Crown make, extra quality elastic web suspenders, roll kid ends and drawers supporters, best make and finish throughout, plated buckles, as cut 134, pair. 1.50

135. Men's tan leather belts with ring sides, shaped front, as cut 135, all sizes, each 50c, 75c

136. Men's fine mocha leather belts, with ring sides, shaped front, fine quality, all sizes, as cut 135, each 1.00

137. "Star vests," made of black silk to fasten at the back, watch pocket, all sizes, as cut 137, each 1.00

138. Men's leather braces, Argosy style, good strong leather, as cut 138, pair 25c

139. Men's leather suspenders, Argosy style, heavy quality, strong buckles, as cut 138, pair 40c

Shoulder Braces.

140. Boys' and youths' shoulder braces, elastic web, mohair ends, double crossed back, pair 50c

141. Boys' fine elastic web shoulder braces, Crown make, silk ends, best make, as cut 143, pair 75c

142. Men's elastic web shoulder braces, double crossed back, mohair ends, strong buckles, each 50c

143. Men's elastic web shoulder braces, silk ends, as cut 143, pair 1.00

144. Men's Crown make elastic web shoulder braces, silk ends, well stayed, as cut 143, pair 1.50

Men's and Boys' Sweaters.

145. Men's all-wool sweaters with deep roll collar, stripes around skirt, cuffs and collar or without stripes, in assorted colors, all sizes, as cut 145, each 75c

146. Men's heavy all-wool sweaters, deep roll collar, close ribbed cuffs and skirts, in assorted colors, all sizes, as cut 146, each 1.00

147. Men's fine imported pure wool sweaters, heavy quality, close ribbed skirt and cuffs, deep roll collar, small, medium and large men's sizes, in assorted colors, as cut 146, each 2.00

148. Men's gymnasium jerseys in black jersey cloth, all sizes, as cut 148, each 1.00

149. Men's athletic jersey, 2-inch collar, in plain navy, also 1-inch stripes all sizes, in assorted colors, as cut 149, each 1.25

150. Men's fine imported athletic jersey sweaters, navy blue, 3-inch roll collar, light weight, small, medium and large sizes, as cut 146, each 2.00

151. Men's fine imported athletic jersey sweaters, 8-inch roll collar, extra fine quality, light weight, navy blue, as cut 146, each 2.50

152. Boys' fine all-wool sweaters, deep roll collar, close ribbed cuffs, in navy, cardinal and white, sizes for boys 5 to 14 years, as cut 152, each 50c

153. Boys' fine all-wool ribbed sweaters, deep roll collar, with stripes around collar, cuffs and skirt, in navy, cardinal and green, also plain white, for boys 5 to 14 years, as cut 145, each 75c

154. Boys' fine all-wool ribbed sweaters, deep roll collar, close ribbed throughout, in assorted colors, cuffs and skirt, heavy quality, for boys 4 to 14 years, as cut 145, each 1.00

155. Boys' fine imported jerseys, long sleeves, 2-inch collar, in cardinal and navy, for boys 8 to 15 years, each 1.50

Men's Socks and Bicycle Hose.

156. Men's heavy cotton mixed socks, blue and brown mixed ribbed tops, 3 for 25c, or pair 9c

157. Men's heavy wool socks, grey, full size, pair 10c

158. Medium weight grey wool socks, ribbed top, pair 12½c

159. Heavy wool socks, light and dark grey, pair 12½c

160. Heavy and medium weight, grey wool socks, pair 15c

161. Fine merino socks, medium weight, grey mixtures, sizes 10 to 11 inch., 3 pair for 50c, or pair .. 18c

162. Men's extra heavy ribbed wool socks, suitable for street car men, teamsters, soft and very warm, large size, pair 20c

163. Men's medium weight wool socks, ring top, soft finish, pair. 20c

164. Men's extra heavy Arctic socks, for lumbermen, teamsters, etc., large size, pair 25c

164A. Men's heavy ribbed Irish knit socks, in dark grey shades, sizes 10 to 11-inch, pair 25c

165. Men's black cashmere socks, seamless foot, size 10, 10½ and 11-inch, 3 pair 50c, or pair 18c

166. Men's fine black cashmere socks, fast dye, seamless, sizes 10, 10½ and 11-inch, pair 20c

167. Men's fine black cashmere socks, ribbed or plain leg, double heel and toe, fast dye, sizes 10, 10½ and 11½-inch, as cut 167, pair 25c

168. Men's fine black cashmere socks, full fashioned or seamless foot, close ribbed top, double heel and toe, spliced ankles, sizes 9½ to 11-inch, as cut 167, 3 pair for 1.00, or pair 35c

169. Men's extra fine black cashmere socks, full fashioned double heel, toe and sole, fast black, sizes 10, 10½ and 11-inch, pair 50c

170. Men's pure wool Irish knit socks, heavy ribbed leg, plain feet, extra good wearing goods, seamless, in black, grey and heather mixture, sizes 10 to 11-inch, as cut 170, 3 pair for 1.00, or pair 35c

171. Men's pure wool Irish knit socks, seamless, in assorted greys, plain knit, sizes 10, 10½, 11-inch, 3 pair for 1.00, or pair 35c

172. Men's pure wool Irish knit ribbed socks, seamless, extra fine quality, in black and grey, also plain knit in grey, as cut 170, pair 50c

173. Men's fine black cashmere socks, silk embroidered, full fashioned, double heel and toe, sizes 10, 10½, 11-inch, as cut 173, pair 35c, 50c

174. Men's fine silk socks, full fashioned, close ribbed top, fast black, fine quality, sizes 10, 10½, 11-inch, as cut 174, pair 75c

175. Men's extra fine pure silk socks, double heel, toe and sole, spliced ankles, fine ribbed top, full fashioned, fast black, sizes 10 to 11-inch, as cut 174, pair 1.50

Bicycle Hose.

176. Men's imported ribbed bicycle hose, heather mixed leg with fancy deep turn-over tops, all sizes, as cut 178, pair 50c

177. Men's ribbed black hose, seamless, plain top, sizes 10, 10½, 11-inch, pair 50c

178. Men's ribbed black bicycle hose, with deep turn-over top of black and white, sizes 10, 10½, 11-inch, as cut 178, pair 75c

179. Men's heavy ribbed bicycle hose, heather mixed leg, with deep turn-over fancy top, sizes 10, 10½, 11-inch, as cut 178, pair 75c

180. Men's heavy ribbed bicycle hose, black with fancy black and white top, and heather mixed with fancy top, deep turn-over, sizes 10, 10½, 11-inch, as cut 178, pair 1.00

181. Men's heavy ribbed hunting or golf hose, plain feet, with extra heavy ribbed leg, in light and dark brown mixtures, with fancy turn-over top, sizes 10, 10½, 11-inch, as cut 181, pair 1.25, 1.50

Men's and Boys' White Unlaundried and Laundried Shirts.

WE make all our white shirts with large loose bodies; from size 16-inch neck measure we make extra large bodies. Our cut, fit and style are absolutely perfect. You will find the length and width are in comparison with neck measure, not skimped in any way.

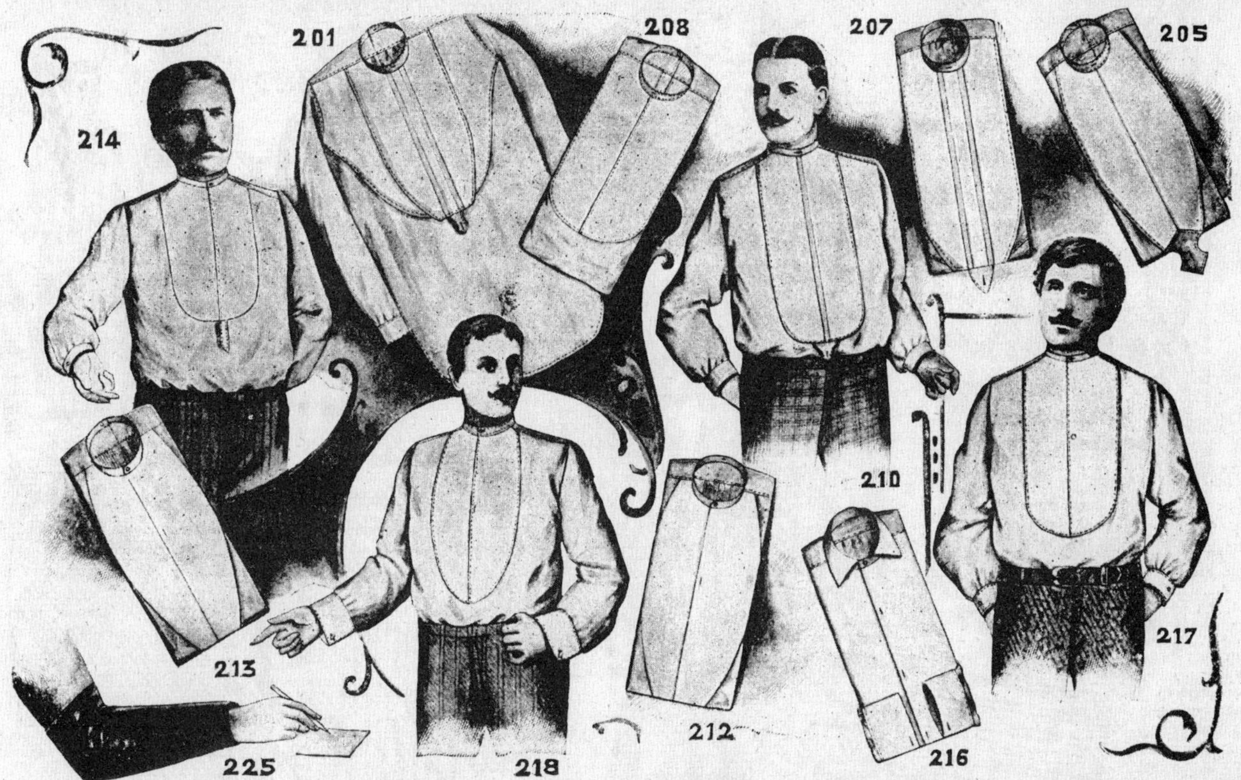

White Unlaundried Shirts.

200. Men's white unlaundried shirts, open back, linen bosom, cuffs or wristbands, reinforced fronts, continuous facings, strong heavy cotton, sizes 14 to 17½ 35c

201. "Our Leader," Eaton's special unlaundried shirt, open back, linen bosom, cuffs or wristbands, reinforced fronts, continuous facings on back and sleeves, fine even thread cotton, full size bodies, as cut 201, sizes 14 to 18............50c

202. Men's fine white unlaundried shirts, short bosom, 9½ inches long, open back, linen bosom and wristbands, large bodies, as cut 208, sizes 14 to 18 ....50c

203. Men's fine unlaundried white shirts, open back, 4-ply linen bosom, cuffs or wristbands, patent staying on back and sleeves, fine English cotton, reinforced fronts, double-stitched seams, large bodies, as cut 201, sizes 14 to 18............75c

204. Men's open front white unlaundried shirts, linen bosom and wristbands, medium size bosom, fine even thread cotton, reinforced fronts, large bodies, as cut 214, sizes 14 to 18 ....75c

205. Our best quality white unlaundried shirt, open back, pure linen inserted bosom, wristbands only, fine English cotton, patent staying on back and sleeves, cushion neckband, well finished, as cut 205, sizes 14 to 18............1.00

NOTE.—This line is made in different length sleeves, 31, 33 and 35 inches. In order to get correct length of sleeve, measure from centre of back to end of wristband.

White Laundried Shirts.

206. Men's laundried white shirts, open back, linen bosom, cuffs or wristbands, strong heavy cotton reinforced front, as cut 207, sizes 14 to 17½, each 50c

207. Fine laundried white shirts, open back, linen bosom, cuffs or wristbands, reinforced fronts, continuous facings, fine medium weight cotton, large bodies, as cut, 207, sizes 14 to 18, each............75c

208. The business shirt, white laundried, with short bosom, 9½ inches long, reinforced fronts, continuous facings, linen bosom and wrist bands only, fine medium weight, cotton, as cut, 208, sizes 14 to 18, ...75c

209. Men's fine white laundried dress shirts, open front, linen bosom and wristbands, one buttonhole in bosom, medium weight cotton, as cut 212, sizes 14 to 17½............75c

210. Men's fine laundried white shirts, open back, pure linen bosom, cuffs attached or with wristbands, extra well made, with cushion neckbands, reinforcing around bosom, fine English cotton, patent staying on back and sleeves, as cut 210, sizes 14 to 18............1.00

211. Men's fine white laundried shirts, open back, short bosom, 10 inches long, linen bosom and wristbands, extra well finished, see cut 208, sizes 14 to 18 ....1.00

212. Men's fine imported white dress shirts, open front, linen bosom, cuffs or wristbands, hand-made buttonholes, fine even thread cotton, cushion neckband, with one or two buttonholes in bosom, large bodies, as cut 212, sizes 14 to 18 ....1.00

213. Men's fine white dress shirts, open back and front, fine imported make, best finish, cushion neckband, hand-made buttonholes, linen bosom and wristbands, as cut 213, sizes 14 to 18 ....1.00

214. Men's fine imported white shirts, with short bosom, 10 inches long, correct shirt for every day wear, open front or open back and front, superior finish, large bodies, linen bosom and wristbands, as cut 214, sizes 14 to 18 ....1.00

215. Men's extra fine white laundried shirts, open back, pure linen bosom and wristbands, cushion neckband, fine even thread cotton, extra well finished throughout, as cut 210, sizes 14 to 18 ....1.25

216. Men's white laundried shirts, open front, collar and cuffs attached, linen bosom, medium weight cotton, large bodies, well finished, as cut 216, sizes 14 to 18 ....1.00

217. Men's fine imported white shirts, open back and front, extra fine cotton linen bosom and wristbands, cushion neckband, superior finish, medium size bosom, as cut 217, sizes 14 to 17½ 1.25

218. Men's fine imported white dress shirts, open back and front, large bosom, cuffs attached, made from cambric cotton, pure linen bosom, superior finish, hand-made buttonholes, cushion neckband, as cut 218, sizes 14 to 17½, each 1.50, 2.00

White Shirts for Stout Men.

219. White unlaundried shirts, open back, wristbands, large bodies, made specially for large men, as cut 201, sizes 16 to 21.....50c and 75c

219A. Extra fine unlaundried white shirts, open back, best quality, wristbands only, we have short, medium or long sleeves, as cut 205, sizes 16 to 18............1.00

220. Fine white laundried shirts, open back, linen bosom and wristbands, large bodies for stout men, as cut 210, sizes 16 to 19½....1.00

Boys' White Shirts.

221. Boys' fine white unlaundried shirts, open back, and linen bosom and cuffs, strong cotton, reinforced fronts, sizes 12 to 13½, in sizes 13 and 13½ we make over size bodies for stout boys............35c

222. Boys' fine unlaundried white shirts, open back, linen bosom and cuffs, fine medium weight cotton, reinforced fronts, continuous facings, sizes 12 to 13½............50c

223. Boys' fine laundried shirts, open back, linen bosom and cuffs, reinforced fronts, strong medium weight cotton, sizes 12 to 14....50c

224. Boys' extra fine white laundried shirts, open back, linen bosom and cuffs, reinforced fronts, continuous facings, fine even thread cotton, superior finish, sizes 12 to 14....75c

Sleeve Protectors.

225. Black sateen sleeve protectors, elastic in both ends, as cut 225, each 15c

Men's and Boys' Colored Cambric Shirts, Night Robes, Pyjama Suits, Bath Robes.

Colored Cambric Shirts.

226. Men's colored cambric shirts, open back, separate turn-down collar, cuffs attached, in neat and fancy stripes, see cut 226, sizes 14 to 17½, each 50c
227. Men's fine colored cambric shirts, open back, with 2 separate collars, detached double-end link cuffs, newest colorings, for fall and winter wear, in neat and fancy stripes, see cut 227, sizes 14 to 18, each 75c
228. Men's colored cambric shirts, open front, detached double-end link cuffs, newest stripes, see cut 228, sizes 14 to 18, each 75c
229. Men's fine colored cambric shirts, open back and front, white neckband, detached double-end link cuffs, newest stripes, for fall and winter wear, see cut 230, sizes 14 to 18, each 1.00
230. Men's fine imported colored cambric shirts, open back and front, detached double-end link cuffs, cushion neckband, the latest English and American patterns, neat and fancy stripes, see cut 230, sizes 14 to 18, each....................1.25
230A. Boys' cambric shirts, laundried bosom, open back, two separate collars, cuffs attached, newest colorings, see cut 226, sizes 12 to 14, each..........................50c

Night Robes, Pyjama Suits and Bath Robes.

231. Men's flannelette night robes, well made, with collar attached, pocket and pearl buttons, yoke, double-stitched seams, full size bodies, 54 inches long, in blue and pink stripes, see cut 231, sizes 14 to 19, each 50c
232. Men's night robes, made from heavy English flannelette, with collar attached, pocket and pearl buttons, yoke, large bodies, 54 inches long, pink and blue stripes, see cut 231, sizes 14 to 19, each..75c
233. Flannelette night robes for large men, made from heavy English flannelette, collar attached, pocket and pearl buttons, large full bodies, 58 inches long, see cut 233, sizes 15 to 21 inch, each................1.00
234. Men's heavy white twilled cotton night robes, neatly trimmed or plain collar attached, pocket and pearl buttons, full size bodies, 54 inches long, yoke, sizes 14 to 19 each 50c
235. Men's white night robes, made from heavy twilled cotton, collar attached, pocket and pearl buttons, reinforced fronts, double stitched seams, large full bodies, 54 inches, as cut 231, sizes 14 to 19 each 75c
236. Men's extra fine white twilled cotton night robes, patent front, trimmed with best silk embroidery, collar attached, and pocket, double stitched seams, large full bodies, 54 inches long, see cut 236, sizes 14 to 19 ....1.00
237. Men's fine imported natural wool night robes, made with collar attached, and pocket, overlocked seams, medium weight, large full bodies, 60 inches long, Stuttgarter sanitary brand, see cut 237, sizes 15 to 19, each......................2.00
238. Men's fine imported natural wool night robes, Stuttgarter sanitary brand; this garment is made from the finest and softest wool, collar attached, pocket and pearl buttons, large full bodies, 60 inches long, see cut 237, sizes 15 to 19, each 3.00

Boys' Night Robes.

239. Boys' flannelette night robes, made from fine quality English flannelette, collar attached, pocket and pearl buttons, in blue and pink stripes, sizes to fit boys 5 to 15 years, see cut 239, sizes 10 to 14-inch collar, each 50c
240. Boys' white twilled cotton night robes, collar attached, pocket and pearl buttons, double stitched seams, sizes 10 to 14-inch collar, each 50c

Pyjama Suits.

241. Men's pyjama suits, made from fine quality flannelette, turn-down collar attached, pocket and pearl buttons, well made throughout, see cut 242, sizes 34 to 46-inch chest measure, per suit 1.25
242. Men's fine Ceylon-finished flannelette pyjama suits, made with collar attached, pocket and pearl buttons, in fancy stripes and checks, see cut 242, sizes 34 to 48-inch chest measure, per suit 1.50
243. Men's fine Ceylon flannel pyjama suits, turndown collar, pocket and pearl buttons, unshrinkable, in neat and fancy stripes, see cut 242, sizes 34 to 46-inch chest measure, per suit 2.00
244. Men's pyjama suits, made from fine English unshrinkable flannel, collar attached, pocket and pearl buttons, in neat and fancy stripes, see cut 242, sizes 34 to 46-inch chest measure, per suit 2.50
245. Men's fine French flannel pyjama suits, made with collar, attached pocket, frog fasteners, fly front on pants, light ground, with neat and fancy stripes, see cut 242, sizes 34 to 44-inch chest measure, per suit 4.00
246. Men's fine silk pyjama suits, extra fine quality, made with turndown collar, frog fasteners, fly front on pants, in oxblood, blue and mauve shades, see cut 242, sizes 36 to 44-inch chest measure, per suit 7.00

Bath Robes.

247. Men's fine imported Turkish bath robes, made with hood and girdle, large full skirts, in light and medium shades, in stripes and checks, as cut 247, small, medium and large sizes, each 2.50 and...4.00
248. Men's imported Turkish bath robes, best qualities, made with hood and girdle, 2 pockets, newest designs and colors, small, medium and large sizes, as cut 247, each 5.00, 6.00 and..................5.00

Sundries for Mending Purposes.

249. Neckbands for white shirts, sizes 14 to 18, each 5c
250. Wristbands, sizes 9½ to 11, per pair 6c
251. Cuffs, sizes 9½ to 11, per pair..10c
252. Linen bosoms for open back shirts, each 10c

Men's and Boys' Flannel and Flannelette Shirts, Heavy Winter and Working Shirts, and Imported Cardigan Jackets.

ALL our flannel and flannelette shirts are made in our own factory, which insures you the best possible value, and also a shirt well made. Our flannel shirts are made from best grades of Campbellford, and are made large in the body. From size 16-inch collar up the bodies are extra large in proportion to the collar worn. All our best flannelette and all flannel shirts are made with double stitched seams, yoke and pearl buttons.

Flannelette Shirts.

265. Men's flannelette shirts, collar attached, blue and pink stripes, sizes 14 to 17 inches, each 25c
266. Men's flannelette shirts, collars attached, and pocket, blue, grey and pink, neat stripes, sizes 14 to 17½ inches, as cut 267, each......35c
267. Men's fine flannelette shirts, collar attached, or plain neckband, neat stripes, in blue, pink and grey, sizes 14 to 18 inches, as cut 267, each 50c
268. Men's Ceylon finished flannelette shirts, collar attached, new stripes, in light and medium shades, sizes 14 to 18-inch collar, as cut 267, each 75c
269. Men's cashmerette shirts, with collar attached, or sateen neckband, light fancy stripes, sizes 14 to 18-inch collar, as cut 267, each..1.00

Sateen, Oxford and Galatea Shirts.

270. Men's black sateen shirts, collar attached, yoke, fast dye, double stitched seams, sizes 14 to 18-inch collar, as cut 271, each 50c
271. Men's fine black sateen shirts, collar attached, and pocket, large body and well made, fast dye, sizes 14 to 18-inch collar, as cut 271 each 75c
272. Men's heavy black sateen shirts, collar attached, best make and finish, sizes 14 to 18-inch collar, as cut 271, each......1.00
273. Men's heavy galatea working shirts, collar attached on neckband, well made, fast color, in plain navy and neat dark stripes, sizes 14 to 18-inch collar, as cut 273, each 50c
274. Men's duck working shirts, with collar attached, navy blue with small polka dot, sizes 14 to 18, as cut 274, each 50c
275. Men's heavy English Oxford shirts, collar attached or plain neckband, light and medium stripes and checks, sizes 14 to 18, as cut 273, each......75c

Knit Top Shirts.

276. Men's grey knit top shirts, laced or buttoned front, medium men's size, each......35c
277. Men's knit top shirts, in navy blue or grey shades, collar attached and pocket, laced or buttoned front, medium sizes, as cut 277, each 50c
278. Men's heavy knit top shirts, in plain navy and dark fancy patterns, laced or buttoned front, also heavy fleece-lined top shirts, buttoned front, in dark stripes, medium sizes, as cut 277, each 75c
278½. Men's fine navy blue knit top shirts, soft quality, medium weight, buttoned front, collar attached, medium sizes, as cut 277, each 1.00

Men's Flannel Shirts.

279. Grey union flannel shirts, collar attached or silesia neckband, sizes 14 to 18, as cut 280, each......75c
280. Grey Campbellford flannel shirts, collar attached or silesia neckband, sizes 14 to 18, as cuts 280 and 275, each 1.00
281. Men's heavy tweed army shirts, collar attached and pocket, pearl buttons, steel grey shade, sizes 14 to 18, as cut 281, each......1.00
282. Men's heavy winter working shirts, made of heavy twilled cloth, collar attached and pocket, pearl buttons, medium grey shade, sizes 14 to 17½, as cut 281, each..75c
283. Navy blue Campbellford flannel shirts, collar attached or silesia neckband, best make and finish, sizes 14 to 18, as cuts 280 and 275, each 1.25
284. Navy blue best Campbellford flannel shirts, collar attached, patent front, pocket, best make, sizes 14 to 18, each......1.50
285. Men's fine English Ceylon flannel shirts, collar attached, or plain neckband, pocket, neat and fancy stripes in light and medium shades, sizes 14 to 18-inch collar, as cuts 286 and 275, each 1.00
286. Men's fine English unshrinkable flannel shirts, collar attached or plain neckband, neat fancy stripes, sizes 14 to 18-inch collar, as cuts 286 and 275, each 1.25
287. Men's fine English flannel shirts, collar attached, best make and finish in neat fancy stripes and checks, sizes 14 to 18-inch, as cut 286, each......1.50
288. Men's best English unshrinkable flannel shirts, collar attached, or sateen neckband, best make and finish, beautiful quality, sizes 15 to 18-inch collar attached, as cuts 286 and 275, each 2.00

Boys' Flannelette, Flannel, Black Sateen and Duck Shirts.

289. Boys' flannelette shirts, collar attached or neckband, fancy stripes, see cuts 267 and 275, sizes 10 to 13½, each 25c
290. Boys' shirts, heavy flannelette, collar attached, yoke, pocket and pearl buttons, double-stitched seams, neat stripes, see cuts 267 and 275, sizes 11½ to 14 inches, each 35c
291. Boys' fine Ceylon-finished flannelette shirts, collar attached or plain neckband, yoke, pocket and pearl buttons, double-stitched seams, in blue and pink stripes, see cuts 267 and 275, sizes 12 to 14 inches......50c
292. Boys' black sateen shirts, collar attached, yoke, double-stitched seams, see cut 271, sizes 12 to 14 inches, each 50c
293. Boy's grey flannel shirts, collar attached or silesia neckband, sizes 12 to 13½ as cuts 280 and 275, each 50c
294. Boys' navy blue all-wool flannel shirts, collar attached or silesia neckband, best make, sizes 12 to 13½, as cuts 280 and 275, each....75c
295. Boys' navy blue duck shirts, with white polka dots, collar attached, fast color, sizes 12 to 13½, as cut 274 ......50c

Men's Cardigan Jackets.

300. Men's heavy English cardigan jackets, 2 pockets, buttoned cuffs, black and dark brown, medium men's size only......75c
301. Men's heavy imported cardigan jackets, two pockets, buttoned cuffs, bound edges and pockets, sizes from 36 to 40 inches chest measure, as cut 301 ...... 1.00
302. Men's heavy English cardigan jackets, two pockets, mohair bound, elastic stitch, dark, sizes 36 to 42, as cut 301 ...... 1.25
303. Men's heavy English cardigan jackets, buttoned cuffs, mohair bound, small, medium, large and extra large sizes, as cut 301....1.50
304. Men's fine English cardigan jackets, worsted finish, elastic stitch, mohair bound, fine quality, sizes medium, large and extra large, as cut 301......2.00, 2.50
305. Men's extra large cardigan jackets, English make, dark brown and black, for very large men, 46 to 50 inches chest measure, as cut 301 ......2.50
306. Men's fine imported cardigan jackets, worsted finish, mohair bound, elastic stitch, beautiful quality, small, medium and large sizes, as cut 301 ......4.00

MEN'S AND BOYS' UNDERWEAR.

Small men's means size about 34 inches chest measure ; medium men's size, about 38 inches chest measure ; OS men's size, about 40 inches chest measure ; XOS men's size, about 42 inches chest measure ; XXOS men's size, **about 44 inches chest measure.**

It is imperative that you find out whether the size you require is made in the line you order. Price is quoted **for single** garment only, not for suit. Mail orders entrusted to us will be filled with care and promptness.

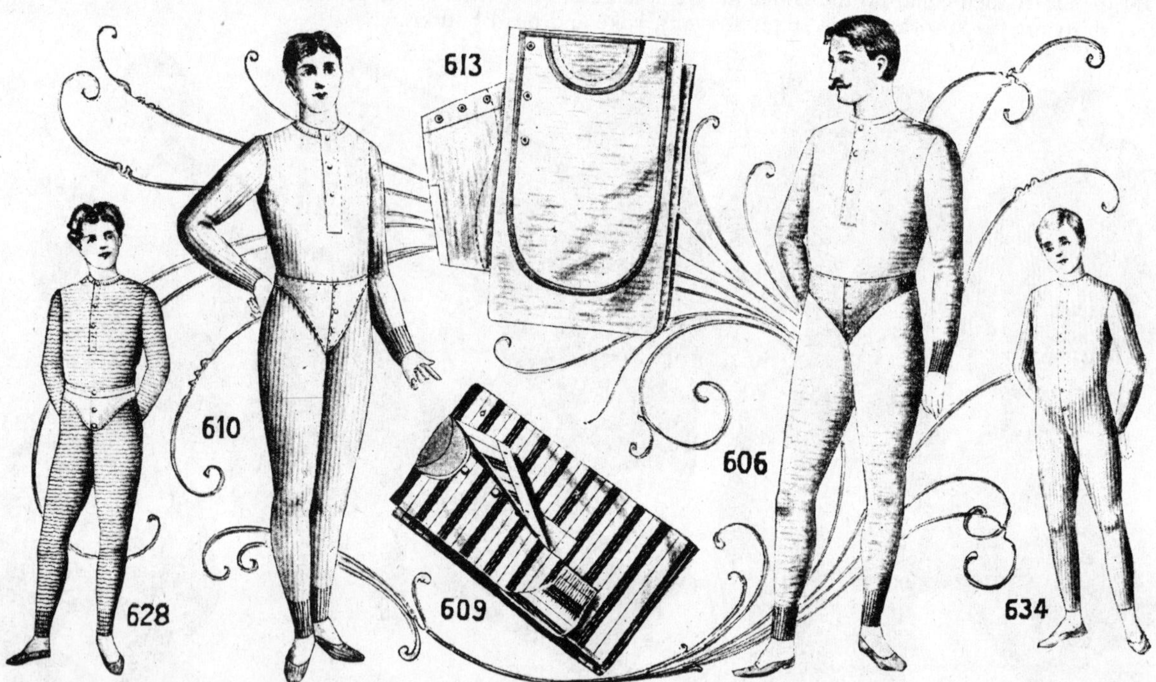

Men's Scotch Wool Underwear.

600. Men's Scotch wool shirts and drawers, ribbed skirt and wristbands, double breasted, in men's sizes, each **39c**

601. Scotch wool shirts and drawers, double breasted, ribbed skirt and cuffs, heavier weight than 600, in small, medium and OS sizes, each **50c**

602. Extra heavy Scotch wool Manitoba shirts and drawers, double breasted, in small, medium and OS sizes, as cut 606, each **50c**

603. Heavy Scotch wool shirts and drawers, double breasted, sateen trimmings, ribbed skirt and wristbands, in small, medium and OS sizes, each **65c**, or, per suit.... **1.25**

604. Same, in 42 and 44 inches, each **75c**

605. Same as 602, in small, medium and OS sizes, double breasted and double back, drawers double body, each **75c**

606. Scotch mottled unshrinkable shirts and drawers, heavy weight, double breasted, sateen trimmings, ribbed skirt and cuffs, in men's sizes, as cut 606, each **75c**

607. Plain Scotch wool shirts and drawers, heavy weight, double breasted, in beige trimmings, good serviceable winter line, small, medium and OS sizes, as cut 606, each **75c**

608. Same as 607, 42 and 44 inches chest measure, each.......... **1.00**

609. Scotch wool, in fancy stripe pattern, double breasted, in small, medium and OS sizes, as cut 609, each **75c**

610. Imported heavy English Scotch wool shirts and drawers, double breasted, double elbows, double knees, double spliced seats, pearl buttons on shirts, Shetland shade, in all sizes, as cut 606, each.... **1.00**

611. Fancy Shetland wool, neat stripe pattern, double breasted, in small, medium and OS sizes, as cut 609, each........................ **1.00**

Men's Heavy Arctic Fleece-Lined Underwear.

613. Heavy Arctic shirts and drawers, double woven back and double over chest, pearl buttons on shirt, all sizes, special, as cut 613, each **50c**

614. Heavy fleece undershirts and drawers, extra heavy weight, overlock seams, French neck, as cut 610, all sizes, each **50c**

615. Arctic fleece-lined shirts and drawers, double woven back and double over chest, overlock seams, very heavy, all sizes, as cut 613, each **65c**, or per suit **1.25**

616. Mottled wool fleece-lined shirts and drawers, nice medium weight, silk trimmings, pearl buttons, overlock seams, all sizes, as cut 606, each........................ **75c**

617. Fine Arctic undershirts and drawers, the fleece is a mixture of silk and wool, fancy stripe pattern, silk trimmings and best finish, very suitable for people troubled with tender skin, medium weight, all sizes, as cut 610, each **1.00**

Men's Heavy Ribbed Scotch Elastic.

618. Blue, grey and flesh ribbed elastic undershirts and drawers, double-breasted, working man's shirt, men's sizes, each.......... **39c**

619. 18-oz. heavy Scotch elastic shirts and drawers, double-breasted, in blue grey, scarlet and flesh colors, men's sizes, each.................. **50c**

620. 20-oz. heavy ribbed Scotch elastic shirts and drawers, OS sizes, in blue grey shade, each **65c**, or per suit........................ **1.25**

Men's Medium or Light Weight Underwear.

621. Merino undershirt and drawers, ribbed skirt and wrists, sateen trimmings, sizes 34 to 42 inches chest measure, as cut 606, each **50c**

622. Double thread balbriggan undershirts and drawers, pearl buttons, suitable for wearing under heavy weight garments, all sizes, each. **50c**

623. Fine merino shirts and drawers, double breasted, ribbed skirt and wristbands, all sizes, as cut 606, each **75c**

624. Medium weight Scotch wool shirts and drawers, double breasted, pearl buttons, ribbed skirt, all sizes, as cut 606, each **75c**

625. Medium weight Scotch wool undershirts and drawers, in scarlet shade, double breasted, ribbed skirt and cuffs, small, medium and OS sizes, as cut 606, each...... **1.00**

626. Men's medium weight natural wool underwear, shirts and drawers, shirts double breasted and back, drawers with double body, as cut 613—

Sizes 34 to 42 chest, each **1.00**
44 and 46 " " **1.25**

627. Men's imported natural merino underwear, shirts and drawers, overlock seams, pearl buttons, medium weight, all sizes, each **1.10**

Boys' Underwear.

Boys' underwear comes in sizes 1, 2, 3, 4, 5, 6, to fit average boys aged 4, 6, 8, 10, 12, 14 years.

628. Boys' medium-weight Arctic undershirts and drawers, overlock seams, very special, as cut 628—

Sizes	1, 2, 3	4, 5, 6
Each	**20c**	**25c**

629. Boys' Arctic undershirts and drawers, heavier weight than 628, overlock seams, French neck, ribbed wrists, as cut 628—

Sizes	1, 2, 3	4, 5, 6
Each	**25c**	**35c**

630. Boys' medium-weight Shetland wool undershirts and drawers, double-breasted, overlock seams, ribbed skirt and wrists, as cut 628—

Sizes	1, 2, 3	4, 5, 6
Each	**35c**	**50c**

631. Boys' heavy Scotch wool undershirts and drawers, double breasted, ribbed skirt and wrists, sateen facings, as cut 628 –

Sizes	1, 2	3, 4	5, 6
Each	**25c**	**35c**	**50c**

632. Boys' Scotch wool undershirts and drawers, double breasted, in natural shades, ribbed cuffs and ankles, as cut 628—

Sizes	1, 2	3, 4	5, 6
Each	**50c**	**65c**	**75c**

633. Boys' Wolsey or Stuttgarter brand of imported natural wool undershirts and drawers, double breasted, full fashioned, pearl buttons, soft and unshrinkable, as cut 628—

Sizes	1, 2, 3	4, 5, 6
Each	**90c**	**1.10**

Boys' Combination Suits.

634. Boy's heavy ribbed combination all-wool undersuits, in natural shade, overlock seams, pearl buttons, unshrinkable, as cut 634—

Sizes	1, 2, 3	4, 5, 6
	1.00	**1.25** per suit.

635. Boys' heavy imported combination undersuits, full fashioned, pearl buttons, ribbed cuffs and ankles, Wolsey brand, as cut 634, all sizes, per suit................ **1.50**

MEN'S EXTRA FINE UNSHRINKABLE UNDERWEAR.

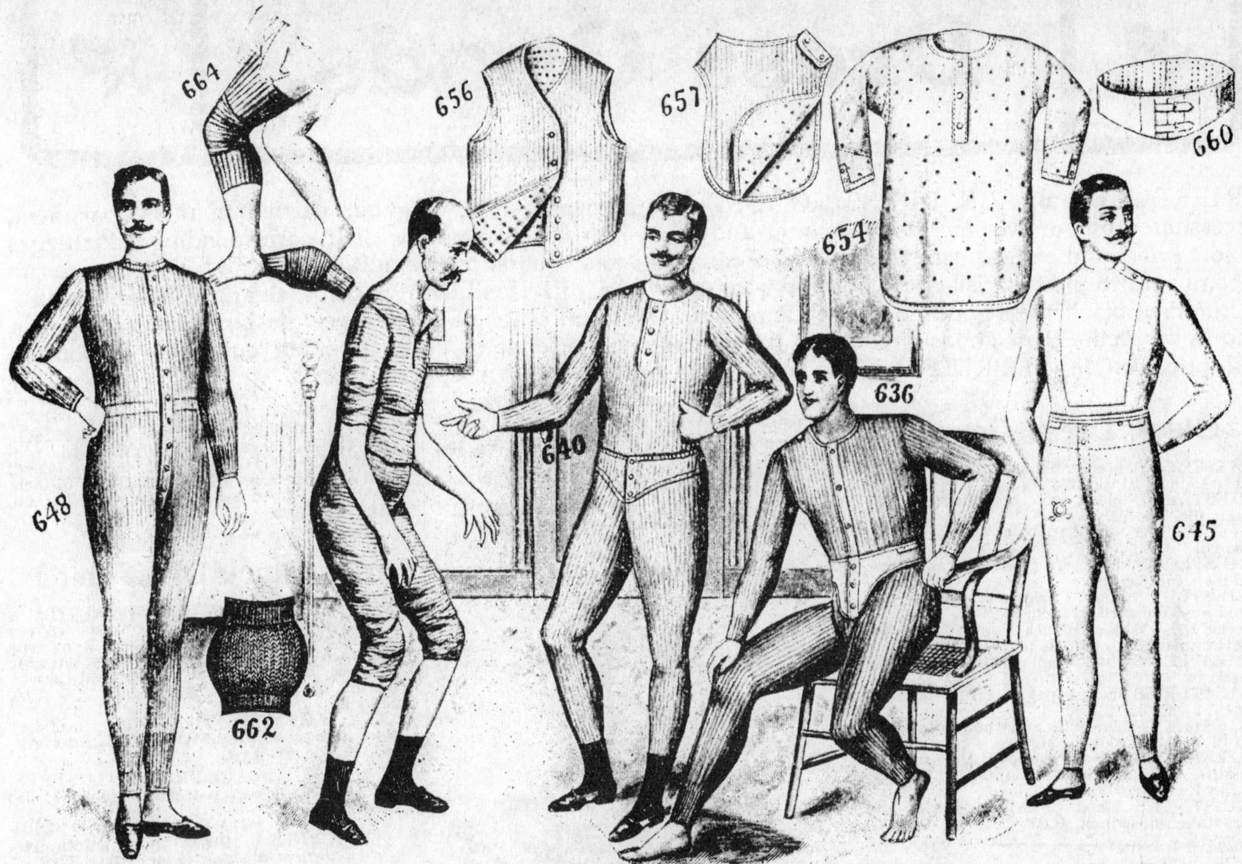

Turnbull's Hand-Made Pure Scotch Wool Unshrinkable Underwear

636. Men's heavy Scotch wool undershirts and drawers in Shetland shade, double breasted, full fashioned, hand knit, ribbed skirts and wrists, Manitoba weight, sizes 34 to 44 chest measure, as cut 636, each 1.00

637. Men's heavy Scotch wool undershirts and drawers, 16 gauge, double breasted, as cut 636.
Sizes 34 to 44 chest, each 1.25
46, 48 and 50 " 1.50

638. Men's extra heavy Scotch wool undershirts and drawers, 14 gauge, double breasted, full fashioned, pearl buttons, ribbed skirt, Shetland shade, as cut 636, sizes 34 to 44 chest measure, each 1.50

639. Men's heavy natural wool undershirts and drawers, 20 gauge, full fashioned, shirts double breasted, spliced seats in drawers, as cut 636.
Sizes 34 to 44 chest, each 2.00
46, 48, 50 " " 2.50

Wolsey Fine Pure Unshrinkable English Underwear.

640. Men's imported natural wool undershirts and drawers, light weight, overlocked seams, pearl buttons, sizes 34 to 44 chest measure, as cut 640, each 1.25

641. Men's imported natural wool undershirts and drawers, full fashioned, double-breasted, ribbed skirt and wrists sizes 34 to 44 chest measure, as cut 640, each 1.50

642. Men's imported natural wool undershirts and drawers, shirts double-breasted and back, drawers double body and spliced seats, sizes 34 to 44 chest measure, each 2.00

643. Men's imported natural wool undershirts and drawers, full fashioned, shirts double-breasted, drawers spliced seats, sizes 34 to 44 chest measure, as cut 640, each 2.00

644. Men's heavy imported natural wool shirts and drawers, shirts double-breasted, drawers spliced seats, full fashioned, beige trimmings, sizes 34 to 44 chest measure, as cut 640, each 2.50

Stuttgarter Sanitary Underwear.

(Recommended by Medical Men.)

645. Men's imported natural wool undershirts and drawers, shirts double-breasted, made to button on shoulder, overlocked seams, pearl buttons, sizes 34 to 44 chest measure, as cut 645, each 1.50

646. Men's imported natural wool undershirts and drawers, medium and heavy weight, double-breasted, made to button on shoulder, overlocked seams, sizes 34 to 44 chest measure, as cut 645, each 1.75

647. Men's heavy imported natural wool undershirts and drawers, double-breasted, made to button on shoulder, overlocked seams, sizes 34 to 44 chest measure, as cut 645, each 2.00

"Knit-to-Fit" Combination Undersuits.

648. Men's natural wool combination undersuits, winter weight, overlocked seams, elastic ribbed stitch, perfect fitting, Turnbull's make, sizes 32 to 44 in. chest measure, as cut 648, per suit 2.50

649. Men's heavy-weight balbriggan combination undersuits, in ecru shades, pearl buttons, ribbed throughout, sizes 32 to 42 in. chest measure, as cut 648, per suit 3.50

650. Men's heavy natural wool combination undersuits, ribbed throughout, full-fashioned, pearl buttons, sizes 32 to 42 in. chest measure, as cut 648, per suit 4.00

651. Men's extra heavy natural wool combination undersuits, double-breasted, shaped and ribbed throughout, sizes 32 to 42 in. chest measure, as cut 648, per suit 5.00

652. Men's pure silk combination undersuits, full-fashioned, elastic ribbed stitch, winter weight, perfect-fitting garment, sizes 32 to 42 in. chest measure, as cut 648, per suit 12.00

Silk and Wool Mixture.

653. Men's imported silk and wool underwear, shirts short double-breasted, full-fashioned, best trimmings, ribbed skirt and wrists, in silver grey shade, sizes 34 to 46 chest measure, as cut 636, per garment 3.00

Chamois Goods, etc.

654. Men's chamois undershirts and drawers, made from selected skins, perforated, pearl buttons, sizes 34 to 44 chest measure, as cut 654, each garment 5.00

655. Men's scarlet flannel vests, lined with chamois skins, full length sleeves, in small, medium and large size, each 4.00

656. Men's scarlet flannel vests, lined with perforated chamois skins, made to button close to neck, pearl buttons, sizes 32 to 44 inches chest measure, as cut 656, each 2.00

657. Men's chamois chest and back protectors, made from fine Saxony flannel, lined with perforated chamois, best quality, size 13 x 11½ in., as cut 657, each 1.00

658. Scarlet Saxony flannel chest and back protectors, lined with perforated chamois, size 10 x 9 in., as cut 657, each 75c

659. Chamois chest protector, with elastic band to go around neck, men's and youths' sizes, each .. 50c

660. Men's scarlet flannel body belt, lined with perforated chamois, shaped around hips, sizes 32 to 42 in. waist measure, as cut 660, each 1.00

661. Men's fibre chamois vest, strong and durable, but light in weight, size 34 to 44 in. chest measure, each 40c

Body Bands, Knee Warmers, etc.

662. Men's natural wool body bands, in white or natural shades, all sizes according to waist measure, as cut 662, each 75c

663. Men's natural wool body bands, shaped with narrow band at back, natural shade only, each 75c

664. Men's natural wool knee caps, shaped, specially adapted to persons suffering from rheumatism, all sizes, from youths' to large men's, as cut 664, per pair 75c

665. Men's imported natural wool night caps, double thread, in medium and large sizes, each 50c

666. Men's white cotton night caps, fine double thread, in medium and large sizes, each 35c

Dress Goods.

PRIESTLEY'S BLACK DRESS GOODS.—The immense stock of goods carried in this department, necessitated by our ever-increasing counter and mail order trade, carries with it corresponding advantages in low prices and endless assortments. We carry in stock guaranteed qualities only and such as we can recommend to prove satisfactory, both in wear and dye. PRIESTLEY'S being the most notable manufacturers of black dress goods, our stock is replete with a full range of their newest designs and plain goods, and as we secure these goods direct from the manufacturer it enables us to give our customers a profit on mill prices on any of PRIESTLEY'S goods. **Samples sent on application.**

Black Dress Goods.

PRIESTLEY'S black silk and wool henrietta, 41 to 45-inch, $1.00, 1.25, 1.50, 1.75, 2.00 yd.
PRIESTLEY'S black wool crepoline cord, 43-inch, 65c, 75c, 85c yd.
PRIESTLEY'S black pebble cloth, 43-inch, 75c yd.
PRIESTLEY'S black soft finish diagonal cord, 42-inch, 75c, 85c yd.
PRIESTLEY'S black Parisian corkscrew, fine and medium cord, 42-inch, $1.00 yd.
PRIESTLEY'S black soleil and satin cloths, fine satin finish, 42 to 44-inch, 65c, 75c, $1.00 yd.
PRIESTLEY'S black Redfern suiting, 44-inch, $1.25 yd.
PRIESTLEY'S black espagnol crepe cloth, 46-inch, $1.25 yd.
PRIESTLEY'S black silk and wool crepe cloth, 41-inch, $1.00; 46-inch, $1.25 yd.
PRIESTLEY'S black melrose and armure cloths, silk and wool, 45-inch, $1.25, 1.50, 1.75 yd.
PRIESTLEY'S black de Alma, Baritz and crystal cord, 42-inch, $1.25 yd.

Priestley's Black Serges.

PRIESTLEY'S black cravenette waterproof, 60-inch, $1.00 yd.

PRIESTLEY'S black cheviot serge, soft, rough finish, 48-inch, 75c, $1.00 yd.

PRIESTLEY'S black shower-proof estamine serge, 40-inch, 25c; 42-inch, 40c, 50c; 48-inch, 75c yd.

PRIESTLEY'S black coating serge, good heavy weight, 42 to 44-inch, 35c, 50c, 65c yd.

Salt's Serges.

SALT'S black Campbell twill coating serge, 60-inch, 50c.

SALT'S black estamine serge, 46-inch, 65c; 50-inch, 75c.

SALT'S homespun cheviots, for tailored suits, rough finish, 50-inch, 85c, $1.00, 1.25 yd.
FRENCH coating twill serge, fine twill, smooth finish, 42-inch, 35c; 44-inch, 50c yd.
FRENCH cheviots, in soft finish and fine all-wool quality, 50-inch, $1.25, 1.50 yd.
SALT'S black dress serge, medium fine twill and smooth finish, 45-inch, 65c; 52-inch, 75c; 54-inch, $1.00, 1.25; 56-inch, $1.50 yd.

Black Cashmeres, Poplins and Cords.

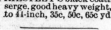

FRENCH CASHMERES, in black, guaranteed all-wool, 40-inch, 25c; 45-inch, 35c yd.

GERMAN HENRIETTA, fine satin finish, in blue and jet black, 45-inch, 50c, 65c, 75c, $1.00 yd.
FRENCH CASHMERE SERGE, in black, very special, 44-inch, 50c yd.
PRIESTLEY'S SILK AND WOOL POPLIN CORD, in black, 44-inch, $2.50 to 3.00 yd.

PRIESTLEY'S ONDINE CORD, silk and wool, black, 44-inch, $2.50 yd.
FINE FRENCH CORDS, in black, and fine all-wool quality, in poplins, Venetians and corkscrews, 50-inch, $1.25, 1.50, 1.75, 2.00 yd.
VENETIAN AMAZON SUITINGS, in black, 46-inch, 65c yd.

FRENCH POPLIN CORDS, in black, 45-inch, 50c; 47-inch, 75c, $1.00; 50-inch, $1.50 yd.
VENETIAN CLOTH, in black, 46-inch, 75c yd.
LADIES' BLACK BROADCLOTH, 52-inch, $1.00, 1.25, 1.50; superior quality, 54-inch, $2.00 to 3.00 yd.

Fancy Black Dress Goods.

BLACK SILK AND WOOL NOVELTIES, a complete assortment of the newest weaves and most stylish designs, in scroll patterns and medium sized blistered effects, suitable for street gowns, and stylish separate skirts, widths 42 to 44-inch, $1.00, 1.25, 1.50, 2.00, 2.25 yd.
BLACK FRENCH NOVELTIES, in fancy wool and mohair figures, neat small designs, 44-inch, 85c, $1.00 yd.

FANCY BLACK FIGURED LUSTRES, in the newest patterns, 42-inch, 50c, 65c yd.

FANCY BLACK GERMAN BROCADES, in all-wool and mohair figures, newest designs, 42-inch, 50c, 75c yd.

Novelty Grenadines.

GRENADINES, black, in plain weaves and fancy stripes and checks, 40-inch, 85c, $1.00, 1.25 yd.
SILK AND WOOL GRENADINES, black, in newest and leading designs, from $1.00 to 3.00 yd.
SILK GRENADINES, in costume length only, $10.00 to 15.00 per costume.
FRENCH BATISTE, in black and all-wool, 40-inch, 85c, $1.00 yd.
FRENCH BATISTE, black, with fancy silk designs, in all-wool and silk and wool, 40-inch, 65c, 75c, 85c, $1.00, 1.25 yd.

Fancy Dress Suitings.

ENGLISH SPIRAL COVERT SUITING, for stylish street costumes, in all the newest shades, 44-inch, 65c yd.
GERMAN COVERT CLOTH, in medium weight, suitable for dresses or travelling gowns, 48-inch, $1.00 yd.
FRENCH REDFERN CLOTH, in bright smooth finish and variety of new shades, 48-inch, 85c yd.
FRENCH VENETIAN CLOTH, in good range of leading shades, very special, 52-inch, 65c yd.
FRENCH VENETIAN, in good heavy weight, suitable for travelling suits, 47-inch, 75c yd.
NEW IMPORTATIONS OF HIGH-CLASS DRESS NOVELTIES, in canvas weaves, camel's-hair suiting and plain worsted suiting, in costume lengths, ranging in prices from $10.00 to 14.00.

FRENCH SILK AND WOOL POPLINETTE, in the most desirable shades for evening wear, 44-inch, $1.25 to 1.50 yd.

FRENCH SILK AND WOOL CREPOLINE, newest materials for evening dresses, in leading shades, 44-inch, $1.50 yd.

Broadcloth Suitings.

FINE ENGLISH BROADCLOTH, in all the leading colors, 52-inch, $1.00 to 1.25 yd.
GERMAN BROADCLOTHS, in medium and heavy weight, for fashionable travelling costumes, 52-inch, $1.50, 1.75, 2.00, 2.50 yd.
GERMAN COVERT CLOTH, smooth satin finish and good heavy weight, 56-inch, $1.50 yd.
ENGLISH COVERT SUITING, thoroughly shrunk, suitable for travelling suits, 52-inch, $1.00 to 1.25 yd.
ENGLISH AND GERMAN HOMESPUN SUITING, in all the newest weaves and shades, 52 to 54-inch, 65c to $1.25 yd.
ENGLISH FRIEZE SUITING, in smooth weaves, also rough finish, 54-inch, 85c to $1.25 yd.

Evening Wear Dress Materials.

FRENCH CASHMERE, in cream and light shades, 40-inch, 25c; 44-inch, 35c yd.
FRENCH HENRIETTA, silk finish, in cream and light shades, 44-inch, 50c yd.
NUN'S VEILING, in all the evening shades, with fancy figures, 30-inch, 35c yd.
BRILLIANTINE LUSTRES, in cream and white, 40-inch, 25c; 42-inch, 35c; 44-inch, 50c; 46-inch, 75c yd.
CREAM SERGES, in coating twills and cheviots, 40-inch, 35c; 44-inch, 50c; 46-inch, 75c; 50-inch. $1.00; cream cashmere serge, 44-inch, 50c yd.
AMAZON AND LADIES' CLOTH, in cream only, 52-inch, $1.00, 1.25 yd.
BEDFORD CORD, in cream only, 42-inch, 50c; 44-inch, 65c; 46-inch, 85c yd.
CHILDREN'S CLOAKINGS, in cream, honeycomb cloth, all pure wool, 50-inch, $1.00 yd.
FANCY DRESS MATERIALS, suitable for dresses or blouses, including figured lustres, dotted henriettas, albatross, and amazons, embroidered with silk, in the newest designs and colorings, 40 to 44-inch, 50c, 75c, 85c yd.
GLORIA SILK, in plain colors and all the leading shades, suitable for waists or blouses, 48-inch, 85c yd.

Priestley's and Salt's Serges.

Quality and color guaranteed. Goods shrunk and sponged, if desired, free of charge.

PRIESTLEY'S ALL-WOOL DRESS AND COATING SERGE, in navy and black only, 42 to 44-inch, 35c, 50c, 65c yd.
PRIESTLEY'S CAMPBELL TWILL DRESS SERGE, smooth finish, in navy and black only, 42-inch, 35c, 50c, 65c; 46-inch, 75c, 85c yd.
PRIESTLEY'S SOFT ROUGH FINISH SERGE, navy, 48-inch, 75c, $1.00 yd.
PRIESTLEY'S ESTAMINE SERGE, soft woolly finish and shower proof, navy, 40-inch, 25c; 41-inch, 35c; 42-inch, 50c; 48-inch, 75c yd.
SALT'S COATING TWILL DRESS SERGES, soft woolly finish, navy, 50-inch, 85c, $1.00, 1.25 yd.
SALT'S CHEVIOT DRESS SERGE, smooth soft finish, good suiting weight, navy, 52-inch, $1.00 yd.
SALT'S EXTRA SPECIAL COATING DRESS SERGE, superior finish, fine clear twill, black and navy, 52-inch, 65c yd.

French Serges.

FRENCH COATING DRESS SERGE, smooth finish, colors of fawn, brown, navy, red, 42-inch, 35c yd.
FRENCH COATING DRESS SERGE, fine twill, in leading shades, 42-inch, 50c yd.
FRENCH FLORENTINE SERGE, in cashmere twill, in navy and black only, 44-inch, 50c yd.

Poplinettes and Satin Cloths.

FRENCH POPLIN, in all-wool and leading shades, 45-inch, 50c, 75c, $1.00 yd.
FRENCH POPLINETTE, newest novelty, in light weight dress material, 44-inch, 85c yd.

PARISIAN CORD SUITINGS, very suitable for medium weight dress suitings, nice smooth finish and all the leading shades, 48-inch, 85c, $1.00 yd.
PRIESTLEY'S SATIN CLOTH, in navy, royal, brown, fawn, green, pearl, grey and red, 44-inch, 50c, 75c yd.

Cashmeres, Lustres, Cravenettes and Nun's Veilings.

FRENCH CASHMERE, all pure wool, in all shades, 40-inch, 25c; 44-inch, 35c yd.

FRENCH HENRIETTA, in silk finish, full range of shades, 46-inch, 50c, 75c yd.

BRILLIANTINE OR LUSTRE, in leading shades, 42-inch, 35c; 44-inch, 50c.

IMPERIAL CRAVENETTE, in medium and dark grey and navy, 60-inch, $1.00 yd.

NUN'S VEILING, in colors of navy, brown, green, 60-inch, $1.00 yd.

Moreen Skirtings.

PRIESTLEY'S BLACK MOREEN SKIRTINGS, 38-inch, 35c, 50c yd.
PRIESTLEY'S COLORED MOREEN SKIRTING, in new shades, 38-inch, 35c, 50c yd.

Low-priced Dress Goods.

AMAZON SUITING, extra quality and value, in variety of shades, 48-inch, 25c yd.
ENGLISH COVERT SUITING, suitable for tailored suits, 52-inch, 35c yd.
ENGLISH COVERT SUITINGS, broadcloth finish, in good variety of leading shades, 52-inch, 50c yd.

Plaids and Checks.

SHEPHERD'S PLAIDS, in black and white, 40-inch, 25c, 35c; 42-inch, 50c yd.
SCOTCH TARTANS AND FANCY PLAIDS, assorted colors, 38-inch, 25c; 42-inch, 50c yd.
SCOTCH TARTANS, heavy quality, 50-inch, 75c yd.
FANCY BLACK WOOL AND MOHAIR DRESS MATERIAL, 40-inch, 25c yd.
FANCY TWEEDS, in mixed colorings, 44-inch, 25c yd.

Silks and Satins.

Our assortment of plain and novelty silks surpasses in variety and richness any former collection we have ever shown. The combinations and colorings are more beautiful and varied than ever. Description cannot convey any adequate idea of the richness of quality of these goods. They require to be seen and handled to be fully appreciated

Black Silks and Satins.

Samples sent on application.

BLACK PEAU DE SOIE, pure silk, double face, 21-inch, 75c, 85c yd.
BLACK PEAU DE SOIE AND IMPERIAL LUXOR, BONNET'S make, all pure silk, reversible, wear guaranteed, 22-inch, $1.00, 1.25; 23-inch, $1.50, 1.75, 2.00 yd.
BLACK SATIN DUCHESSE, all pure silk, soft finish, 21-inch, $1.00; 22-inch, $1.25 yd.
BLACK IMPERIAL DUCHESSE, pure silk, very best French make, dye and wear guaranteed. 24-inch, $1.50, 1.75, 2.00 yd.
BLACK SATIN MERVEILLEUX, pure silk, bright rich finish, suitable for dresses and waists, 20-inch, 50c; 21-inch, 65c, 75c, 85c; 22-inch, $1.00 yd.
BLACK GROS-GRAIN, all pure silk, fine grain, 21-inch, 75c, 85c; 22-inch, medium grain, $1.00; 23-inch, $1.25, 1.50 yd.
BLACK SILK BENGALINE, medium cord, reversible, 21-inch, 75c yd.
BLACK SILK POPLIN, extra wearing quality, medium cord, reversible, very best French make, 22-inch, $1.00, 1.25; 23-inch, $1.50 yd.
BLACK SURAH SILK, pure silk, fine and medium twills, 21-inch, 50c, 65c; 22-inch, 75c, 85c; 23-inch, $1.00 yd.
ROYAL ARMURE, all pure silk, specially adapted for mourning wear, 21-inch, $1.00, 1.25 yd.
BLACK SILK AND SATIN BROCADES all new and exclusive designs, very best French maker's goods, 21-inch, 65c, 75c; 22-inch, 85c, $1.00; 22-inch, extra weight, $1.25; 23-in., $1.50, 2.00 yd.

BLACK FAILLE FRANCAISE, all pure silk, medium cord, 21-inch, 75c, 85c; 22-inch, $1.00, 1.25; 23-inch, $1.50 yd.
BLACK ONDINE CORD, dress silk, a heavy, fancy cord, 21-inch, 85c yd.
BLACK SILK FACONNE, new fancy cord, for skirts and trimmings, 21-inch, $1.00 yd.
Write for samples, stating price and make desired.
BLACK TAFFETA DRESS AND LINING SILK, from the very best manufacturers, all pure silk, 21-inch, 50c, 65c; 23-inch, 75c, 85c, $1.00, 1.25 yd.

Black Satin.

Write for samples. State price.

BLACK SATINS.

VICTORIA SATIN, special, 23-inch, 35c yd.
BLACK VICTORIA SATINS, listed below. Special attention of customers is directed to these satins, which are manufactured exclusively for us and are the best that can be procured in these lines, excelling all others in wear. Note this fact: **all are Yarn Dyed.** To know their values notice that color of edge corresponds with color of edge catalogued. We recommend the blue and pink edge to any one wanting a 50c or 65c a yd satin as more than ordinary in quality and value combined. **Order Samples.**

VICTORIA SATIN.

PINK EDGE, black Victoria satin, heavy durable quality, for trimmings, linings or blouses, special, 24-inch, 50c yd.
BLUE EDGE, heavy black Victoria satin, a beautiful rich trimming or lining for fur garments or jackets, special, 24-inch, 65c yd.
TERRA-COTTA EDGE, black Victoria satin, heavy fine bright finished quality, for all purposes, special, 24-inch, 75c yd.
GREEN EDGE, black Victoria satin, a model weight of rich superior finish, for trimming or lining purposes, 25-inch, special, 85c yd.
MAUVE EDGE, black Victoria satin, strikingly bright, soft rich pile and heavy weight, 25-inch, special, $1.00 yd.
RED EDGE, very best quality black Victoria satin for purposes requiring an excellent material, 25-inch, $1.25 yd.

Fancy Black and White Silks.

Samples sent on request; state style and price desired.
TAFFETA SILK, in fancy black and white checks, 20-inch, 50c, 65c, 75c yd.
STRIPED TAFFETA, in black and white, 21-inch, 75c yd.
BLACK AND WHITE BROCADES, in a good range of new designs, 21 inch, 75c, 85c, $1.00; 22-inch, $1.25, 1.50 yd.
BLACK AND WHITE STRIPED SATIN MERVEILLEUX, 21-inch, 85c, $1.00 yd.

Fancy Waist and Dress Silks.

Write for samples, stating color and price desired.
FANCY STRIPED WAIST SILKS, in a good range of colorings, 20-inch, 35c yd.
TAFFETA SILK, fancy stripes, in a choice range of medium colors, 20-inch, 50c, 65c yd.
TAFFETA SILK, in an excellent range of the very latest stripes, checks and fancy brocades, light, medium and dark colorings, 21-inch, 75c, 85c, $1.00 yd.
NOVELTY WAIST SILKS. These consist of the very latest New York and Parisian styles in fancy Dresdens and Louisine taffetas, all new exclusive designs, 21-inch, $1.50, 1.75, 2.00 yd.
TAFFETA SILKS, in new fancy stripes and checks, in light and dark combinations, best wearing quality, 21-inch, $1.25 yd.
SILK AND SATIN BROCADES, in a full range of evening shades, all pure silk, 21-inch, 75c, 85c, $1.00; 22-inch, $1.25, 2.00 yd.
SILK AND SATIN BROCADES, black ground, with fancy colored designs, 21-inch, 75c, 85c, $1.00, 1.50 yd.

Dress and Waist Silks.

In white, ivory and cream.

SILK BENGALINE, medium cord, 21-inch, 75c, $1.00 yd.
CRYSTALLINE CORD, a new fancy dress silk, 21-inch, 85c yd.
GROSS-GRAIN TAFFETA, pure silk, 21-inch, $1.00 yd.
TAFFETA SILK, medium weight, good wearing quality, 20-inch, 50c; 21-inch, 75c yd.
SILK AND SATIN BROCADES, an excellent range of entirely new and exclusive designs, 21-inch, 50c, 65c, 75c, 85c, $1.00; 22-inch, $1.25, 2.00 yd.

Plain Colored Silks.

TAFFETA SILK, in a complete range of all the latest colorings for fall, soft finish, special, 20-inch, 50c yd.
TAFFETA SILK, best French make, excellent wearing quality, specially recommended for waists and linings, 21-inch, 75c yd.
MOUSSELINE TAFFETA, soft rich finish, very best wearing quality, full range of colorings, 21-inch, $1.00 yd.
POPLIN CORDED DRESS SILK, good range of colorings, 21-inch, 75c yd.
SATIN MERVEILLEUX, all pure silk, soft finish, excellent wearing dress silk, 21-inch, 65c yd.

Japanese Habutai Draping Silks.

Full range of Art and Dress Colors.

When writing for samples, please state color and price.
JAPANESE HABUTAI, soft finish, 20-inch, 20c yd.

SPECIAL.

300 Pieces of Japanese Habutai Silk, in a complete range of all colors, best Japanese dye, good weight, 23-inch, 25c yd.

JAPANESE HABUTAI, Lyons' dye, taffeta finish, extra heavy weight, full range of colors, 23-inch, 35c; 27-inch, 45c yd.
JAPANESE HABUTAI, Lyons' dye, in black and white only, 27-inch, 65c; 36-inch, 85c, $1.00 yd.

Plain Colored Satins.

Full range of all colors.

Write us for samples; be sure and state color and price desired.

VICTORIA SATIN, 23-inch, 35c; 24-inch, 50c yd.
VICTORIA SATIN, extra fine quality, suitable for waists and linings, 21-inch, 65c, 85c yd.
DUCHESSE SATIN, pure silk, specially adapted for dresses and waists, wear guaranteed, 21-inch, $1.25 yd.
PEAU DE SOIE, all pure silk, very best wearing quality for dresses and waists, 21-inch, $1.00 yd.

Victoria and Duchesse Satins.

In white, ivory and cream.

VICTORIA SATIN, 24-inch, 35c, 50c yd.
VICTORIA SATIN, extra fine quality, suitable for dresses, waists and linings, 21-inch, 65c, 75c; 23-inch, 85c, $1.00 yd.
DUCHESSE SATIN, all pure silk, specially adapted for dresses, 21-inch, $1.25, 1.50; 22-inch, $2.00 yd.

Velveteens.

When writing for samples, be sure and state color and price desired.
When ordering, state whether you wish velveteen cut straight across or on the bias.
VELVETEEN, in black only, 22-inch, 25c yd.
ROYALETTE VELVETEEN, in black and colors of navy, browns, reds, greens, purple, grey and fawn, 23-inch, 35c yd.
ROYALETTE VELVETEEN, twilled back, suitable for dresses and waists, full range of colors, 24-inch, 50c yd.
ROYALETTE VELVETEEN, specially for dresses, in black and staple shades, 24-inch, 65c, 85c yd.
ROYALETTE VELVETEEN, special quality, for coats and dresses, in black only, 26-inch, $1.00, 1.25 yd.

Silk Velvets.

When ordering, state whether you wish velvet cut straight across or on bias.
SILK VELVETS, in colors of black, navy, browns, reds, greens, greys and fawn, suitable for waists and trimmings, 18-inch, 65c yd.
SILK VELVETS, in a well selected range of new fall shades, 18-inch, $1.00, 1.25 yd.
SILK VELVETS in black only, 18-inch, 50c, 75c, $1.00, 1.25 yd.
LYONS' SILK VELVET, superior quality and make, very best dye, suitable for dresses, waists and trimmings, 18-inch, $1.50, 2.00 yd.
CAPE AND MANTLE VELVET, black only, 32-inch, $1.50, 2.00, 2.50 yd.

Dress Plush.

ENGLISH SILK DRESS PLUSH, in a good range of colorings, including black, 18-inch, 75c yd.
ENGLISH SILK DRESS PLUSH, in colors of black, brown, green, blue, red and purple, 23-inch, 90c yd.

Wrapper Flannelettes.

English printed plain wrapper flannelette, large range of patterns, in check and scroll effects, all the leading colors, No. A, 26½-inch, 7c yd.
English and Canadian printed flannelettes, with a variety of patterns, in blue and black, purple and black, green and black, combination designs, fast colors, No. B, 27-inch, 8c yd.
Canadian and English plain wrapper flannelettes, assorted, in red, light blue and pink grounds, with small check, spot, stripe, and spray designs, fast colors, 27-inch, No. C, 8c yd.
Heavy English printed plain wrapper flannelettes, soft finish, large range of patterns, in royal, navy, garnet, black, mauve and light blue grounds, with combination color effects, No. D, 28-inch, 10c yd.
English and American wrapper flannelettes, cashmere twilled face and napped back, cardinal, garnet, navy, mauve and black grounds, with color combinations, fast colors, No. E, 28-inch, 10c yd.
Heavy English twilled wrapper flannelette, lightly napped face and back, soft pure finish, navy, black, light blue, pink and mauve grounds, in small broken checks and small neat patterns, very suitable for house jackets, No. F, 27-inch, 12½c yd.
American plain wrapper flannelette, in large range of colorings and designs, specially suitable for wrappers, guaranteed fast colors, No. G, 36-inch, 12½c yd.
French flanella, a cloth closely resembling a French flannel in color designs and finish, twilled, in plain and napped face, colors are navy, fawn, grey, garnet, mauve, light blue and pink, fast colors, No. H, 27-inch, 15c yd.
English flannelettes, printed both sides, in small and medium broken checks, black and red effects, fast colors, No. I, 27-inch, 8c yd.

English wrapper flannelette, printed both sides, small and medium checks and sprays, in black and red, and black and white, fast colors, No. J, 27-inch, 10c yd.

Heavy English velour flannelettes, especially desirable for morning, loose gowns and dressing sacques, etc., rich in design and color effects, No. K, 27-inch, 11c, 12½c, 15c yd.
A SPECIAL OFFER in 10-yard wrapper lengths.—These are English and American made, and come in patterns and colorings specially suitable for wrappers; the cloth is a cashmere-finished twill, guaranteed fast, No. L, 10 yds for 93c.
Flannelette skirting, large range of colors and designs, 36-inch, 12½c, 15c yd.

Sateens, Prints, Ginghams, Ducks, French Cambrics, Linings.

CANADIAN PRINT, 26-inch, in new fancy patterns, light and dark fast colors, special, 5c yd.

CANADIAN PRINTS, light and dark grounds, complete range of new patterns, 28-inch, 9c yd.

QUILTING PRINTS, new range of blocked and pieced patterns, 28-inch, 9c yd.

FINE ENGLISH PRINTS, light and dark shades, 32-inch, 12½c yd.

PLAIN CHAMBRAY, fast colors, in sky, pink, red, fawn and grey, 32-inch, 15c yd.

CANADIAN GINGHAM, fancy check, stripe effect, light and medium ground, 30-inch, special, 11c yd.

SCOTCH GINGHAM, 28-inch, plaids, check and fancy stripe effects, in the newest shades, 15c, 18c, 20c, 25c yd.

PLAIN WHITE DRESS DUCK, 28-inch, 12½c, 15c yd.

INDIGO BLUE DRESS DUCK, stripe polka dots and fancy designs, 27-inch, special, 12c yd.

INDIGO BLUE DRESS DUCK, new designs, 32-inch, 13½c yd.

DRESS SATEENS, dark and light grounds, stripes, polka dots and fancy effects, 15c, 25c yd.

FRENCH CAMBRIC, in the latest coloring and designs, for ladies' shirt waists or gents' shirts, 32-inch, 15c, 20c yd.

Muslins, Lawns, Nainsooks

WHITE VICTORIA LAWN, 45-inch, 8c yd.

WHITE VICTORIA LAWN, extra quality, smooth finish, 45-inch, 10c, 12½c, 15c yd.

WHITE INDIA LINEN LAWN, for infants' wear and children's dresses, without filling, 36-inch, 15c, 20c, 25c, 30c, 35c, 40c yd.

WHITE IRISH LINEN LAWN, for handkerchiefs and fancy work, 36-inch, 50c, 75c, $1.00, 1.25 yd.

WHITE IRISH LINEN LAWN, extra fine sheer quality, 19-inch, 75c, $1.00, 1.25; 36-inch, $1.25, 1.50, 1.75 yd.

WHITE SCOTCH NAINSOOK, free from filling, specially adapted for infants' wear, 36-inch, 12½c, 15c, 20c, 25c; 40-inch, 15c, 20c, 25c yd.

WHITE EMBROIDERY CAMBRIC, soft finish, for infants' and ladies' underwear, 40-inch, 12½c; 42-inch, 15c, 20c yd.

WHITE DIMITY MUSLIN, assorted stripes, 28-inch, 12½c, 15c; 30-inch, 20c, 25c yd.

WHITE HAIRCORD MUSLIN, for infants' dresses, 36-inch, 12½c, 15c, 20c yd.

WHITE JACONET MUSLIN, 36-inch, 12½c, 15c, 20c yd.

WHITE BRILLIANT, small designs, 30-inch, 12½c, 15c yd.

WHITE MUSLIN, fancy stripes, 27-inch, 8c; 28-inch, 10c, 12½c yd.

WHITE MUSLIN, fancy checks, 28-inch, 8c, 10c, 12½c yd.

WHITE PALE BOOK MUSLIN, 36-inch, 12½c, 15c, 20c, 25c, 30c, 35c yd.

WHITE FRENCH ORGANDIE, 66-inch, 20c, 25c, 30c, 35c, 40c, 50c to 75c yd.

WHITE SWISS DRESS MUSLIN, hand-worked spots and fancy designs, 30-inch, 15c, 20c, 25c, 30c to 50c yd.

WHITE TARLATAN, 52-inch, 12½c, 15c, 20c, 25c, 30c, 35c, 40c yd.

COLORED TARLATAN, full range of colors, 52-inch, 15c, 20c yd.

LAPPET SPOT AND FIGURED MUSLIN, 25-inch, 5c; 35-inch, 10c; 35-inch, 12½c; 45-inch, 15c yd.

LENO OR MOSQUITO NET, for candy bags, etc., 60-inch, 8c yd, or piece of 8 yds for 60c; 40-inch, 6c yd, or piece of 12 yds for 60c.

WHITE LAWN, plain hem and cluster of tucks, 36 to 40-inch, 15c, 20c, 25c, 30c yd.

WHITE LAWN, hemmed and tucked, with one row of insertion, 36-inch, 25c, 30c; two rows, 35c, 40c, 50c yd.

WHITE NAINSOOK, hemmed and tucked, suitable for infants' dresses, 36-inch, 20c, 25c, 30c yd.

WHITE NAINSOOK, hemmed and tucked, one row of insertion, 36-inch, 25c, 30c, 35c; two rows, 40c, 50c yd.

ALLOVER TUCKING for yokes, fronts and blouses, in lawn and nainsook, 22-inch, 50c, 75c, $1.00, 1.25 yd.

Black and Colored Muslin.

FANCY EMBROIDERED SWISS MUSLIN, for evening wear, in all the newest designs, pale blue, pink and silver grey ground, with black embroidered stripe and fancy knot, also pale blue, reseda, pink, mauve and silver grey, with white stripe and fancy knot, 44-inch, $1.50 yd.

FANCY EMBROIDERED SWISS MUSLIN, in black, white, pink, sky, ecru, mauve and mazarine, blue ground, with black and white fancy scroll, stripe and figured patterns, 44-inch, $1.75, 2.00, 2.25 yd.

PLAIN COLORED SILK ORGANDIES, best French make, in all the leading shades, 48-inch, 25c, 35c, 50c yd.

SILK ORGANDIE, in black and white only, 48-inch, 30c, 35c, 50c, 65c yd.

PLAIN COLORED COTTON ORGANDIES, in all the leading shades, 66-inch, 40c yd.

Waist and Skirt Linings.

Fast Colors, Superior Qualities.

25-INCH CAMBRIC SKIRT LINING, in all colors, 5c yd.

35-INCH SILESIA SKIRT LINING, in black, brown, slate and fawn, 8c yd.

38-INCH SILESIA SKIRT LINING, in all staple shades, 10c yd.

36-INCH SILESIA SKIRT LINING, in all staple shades, 12½c yd.

36-INCH FAST BLACK LINENETTE SKIRT LINING, 10c yd.

45-INCH FAST BLACK LINENETTE SKIRT LINING, 12½c yd.

36-INCH CROWN PERCALINE WAIST AND SKIRT LINING, in all colors, 12½c, 15c yd.

36-INCH CROWN PERCALINE NUBIAN FAST BLACK WAIST AND SKIRT LINING, 12½c, 15c yd.

36-INCH NUBIAN FAST BLACK PERCALINE WAIST LINING, 20c, 25c yd.

36-INCH SILESIA WAIST LINING, in all staple colors, 12½c, 15c yd.

40-INCH SILESIA WAIST LINING, fine and soft finish, in black, brown, slate, cream and white, 20c yd.

36-INCH SPUN-GLASS LINING, for organdies and evening dresses, including fast black, 25c yd.

36-INCH REVERSIBLE WAIST LINING, fast black on one side, fancy color on the other, 20c, 25c yd.

Canvas and Haircloths.

30-INCH HARD BOOK MUSLIN, black and white, 6c yd.

25-INCH GRASS CLOTH, in black, white and grey, 8c yd.

25-INCH PURE LINEN DRESS CANVAS, in natural black and white, 10c, 12½c, 15c yd.

25-INCH FRENCH ELASTIC TAILORS' CANVAS, natural color, 20c yd.

25-INCH FRENCH ELASTIC SHRUNK CANVAS, natural color, 20c yd.

36-INCH MILITARY COLLAR CANVAS, natural color only, 20c yd.

25-INCH AMERICAN COLLAR STIFFENING, in black and white, 20c yd.

34-INCH WIGAN, in black and white, 10c yd.

18-INCH HAIRCLOTH, in black and grey, 25c yd.

18-INCH HAIRCLOTH, in grey only, 35c yd.

18-INCH FRENCH HAIRCLOTH, in black, white and grey, 35c yd.

Farmer Satins and Sateens

38-INCH ROMAN SATIN, permanent silk finish, in 40 different shades, including fast black, 25c yd.

54-INCH MERCERIZED - FINISH ROMAN SATIN, in all the leading shades, including fast black, 50c yd.

31-INCH MERCERIZED - FINISH DRESS SATEENS, in fast black, 12½c, 15c, 20c yd.

31-INCH MERCERIZED-FINISH DRESS AND LINING SATEENS, all colors, 12½c, 15c, 20c yd.

COMPLETE LINING SETS.

When ordering give number of set and color required in lining, other trimmings will be sent to match.

Lining Set No. 1

6 yds cambric lining, 5c (skirt)	$0 30
2 " linen canvas, 10c (skirt)	0 20
4 " velveteen binding, 4c (skirt)	0 16
2 " silesia waist lining, 12½c (waist)	0 25
1 set dress bones (waist)	0 05
1 pair dress shields (waist)	0 08
1 single belting (waist)	0 03
1 double belting (skirt)	0 03
1 card hooks and eyes (waist)	0 02
2 spools sewing silk, 5c	0 10
2 " silk twist, 2c	0 04
2 " sewing cotton, 4c	0 08
	$1 34
Linings for waist	$0 55
" " skirt	0 79
	$1 34

Lining Set No. 2 superior quality.

4½ yds double-fold silesia or linenette, 10c (skirt)	$0 45
2 " best linen canvas, 12½c (skirt)	0 25
4 " Brush binding, 6c (skirt)	0 24
2 " percaline or silesia waist lining 15c (waist)	0 30
1 set waist steels (waist)	0 12
1 pair dress shields, size 2 (waist)	0 15
1 single belting (waist)	0 03
1 double belting (skirt)	0 03
1 card hooks and eyes	0 02
2 spools sewing silk, 5c	0 10
2 " silk twist, 2c	0 04
2 " sewing cotton, 4c	0 08
	$1 81
Linings for waist	$0 75
" " skirt	1 06
	$1 81

Lining Set No. 3—linings required for tailor-made suits.

2½ yds silk-finished Roman satin, 38 inches wide, 25c yd; or 1¼ yds 54 inches wide, 50c yd (jacket)	$0 63
1 yd soft tailor's canvas (jacket)	0 20
4½ yds silesia or percaline, 12½c (skirt)	0 57
2 " linen canvas, 12½c (skirt)	0 25
4 " Brush binding, 10c (skirt)	0 40
¼ oz sewing silk black only, (jacket)	0 18
2 spools cotton (skirt)	0 08
Belting for skirt	0 04
2 sheets wadding (jacket)	0 05
	$2 40
Jacket	$1 06
Skirt	1 34
	$2 40

If jacket is to be tight fitting, 3 yards of featherbone will be required, at 12c yd—36c extra to above suggestion.

Turkey Red Cambrics, Jeans.

29-INCH TURKEY RED CAMBRIC, plain and twill, 10c, 12½c, 15c, 20c yd.

30-INCH WHITE AND DOVE CORSET JEANS, for children's waists, 15c, 20c yd.

54-INCH WHITE AND DOVE COUTIL, 50c yd.

28-INCH WHITE SATIN JEAN, extra fine, 50c yd.

Suiting, Tailors' Trimmings.

54-INCH ITALIAN COAT LINING, superior quality, black only, 35c yd.

54-INCH ITALIAN COAT LINING, mercerized finish, navy, cardinal, greens, fawn, browns, myrtle, old rose and black, 50c yd.

54-INCH ITALIAN TWILL COAT LINING, black only, 35c, 50c yd.

54-INCH ITALIAN COAT LINING, black only, 65c, 75c, 85c yd.

40-INCH MOHAIR SLEEVE LINING, 50c yd.

38-INCH FANCY STRIPE SLEEVE AND VEST LINING, 10c, 12½c, 15c, 20c, 25c yd.

36-INCH JEAN POCKETING, in black and drab, 20c yd.

34-INCH LINEN HOLLAND, in black, cream and slate, 20c yd.

DRESS TRIMMINGS.

THIS season we show a larger and more complete range of Dress Trimming Braids, Gimps, etc., than ever. Here you have the novelties and choicest patterns selected from the trimming centres of London, Paris and New York. When ordering, give price and number of pattern, we will then send nearest design.

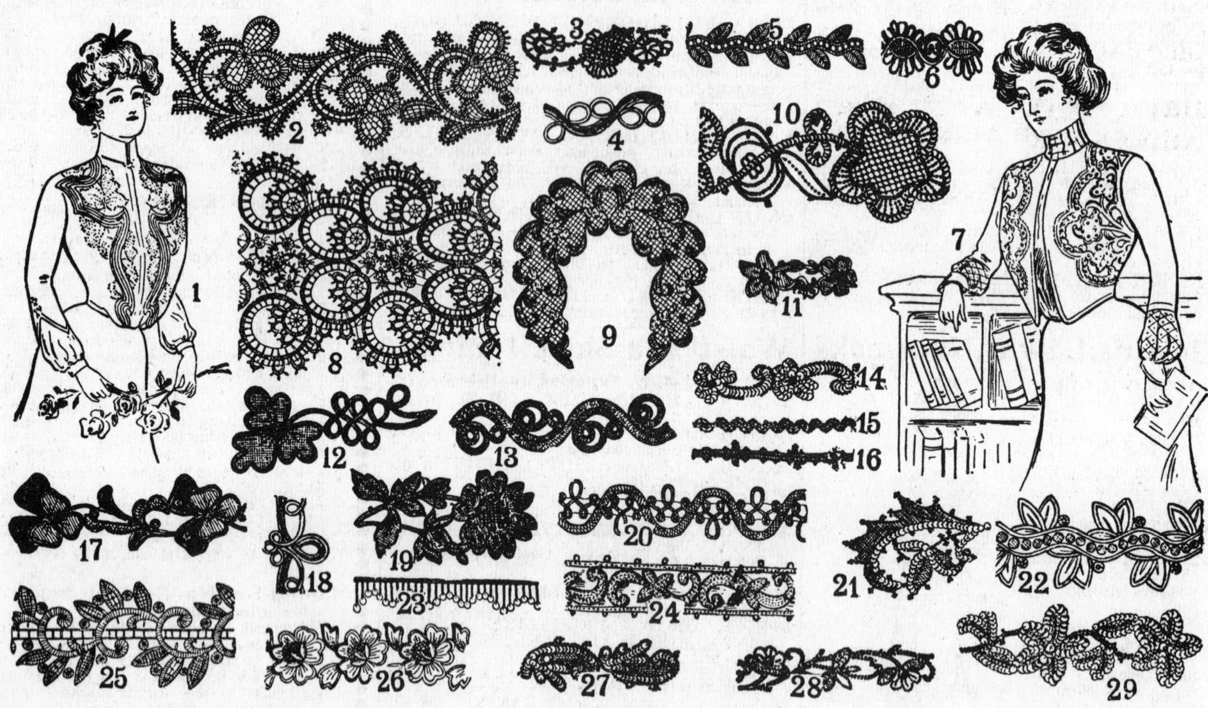

1. Black steel, cream, black and gold revers, in beaded or silk, $1.00 to 4.00 each.
2. Cream, black and colored silk applique, 75c, $1.00 yd.
3. Black jet, 60c yd.
4. Black, white and colored silk gimp, 20c yd.
5. Cream, black or colored silk applique, 35c yd.
6. Colored and black silk gimps, 20c yd.
7. Boleros, cream, black, cream and gold combined, $3.00 to 7.00 each.
8. Cream or black silk applique, $1.50 yd.
9. Persian shaded silk collar, $5.00 each.
10. Black, black and steel sequin, $1.50 yd.
11. Colored, cream and black silk applique, 75c yd.
12. Black silk passementerie, 50c to $1.25 yd.
13. Black mohair braid passementerie, 40c to 75c yd.
14. Black sequin passementerie, 65c to $1.50 yd.
15. Narrow black jet, black silk and colored silk gimp, 5c to 10c yd.
16. Colored bead and black jet, 25c yd.
17. Black and gold, cream and gold passementerie, $1.50 to 2.00 yd.
18. Black silk gimp, 35c to 50c yd.
19. White, black and colored silk applique, $1.00 to 1.50 yd.
20. Silk gimp, in black, cream or colors, 20c to 30c yd.
21. Black, black and steel sequin, $1.25 to 2.00 yd.
22. Silk applique, in black and white, 75c to $1.00 yd.
23. Black, black and steel, white pearl fringe, 40c to $1.25 yd.
24. Persian band, 65c to $1.50 yd.
25. Silk applique, cream, black and colors, $1.00 yd.
26. Colored silk applique, 85c yd.
27. Black, black and steel sequin or jet, 65c to $1.00 yd.
28. Cut steel passementerie, 65c to $1.00 yd.
29. Black sequin or jet passementerie, 85c to $1.50 yd.

BRAIDS AND GIMPS.

Woollen, Cotton, Tinsel Braids and Dress Laces.

BLACK MOHAIR MILITARY BRAID, ⅛-inch, 2c; ¼-inch, 3c; ⅜-inch, 4c; ½-inch, 5c; ⅝-inch, 6c; ¾-inch, 7c; 1-inch, 8c; 1⅛-inch, 10c; 1¼-inch, 12½c; up to 2½-inch, 25c yd.

BLACK WORSTED MILITARY BRAID, ⅛-inch, 2c; up to 2½-inch, 20c yd.

BLACK LOOP EDGE BRAID, ½-inch, 10c, 12½c yd.

BLACK MOHAIR RUSSIA BRAID, ⅛ to ¼-inch, 3c, 4c, 5c, 6c, 7c yd.

BLACK MOHAIR TUBULAR BRAID, ¼ to ⅜-inch, 5c, 6c, 7c, 8c, 10c, 12½c yd.

BLACK WORSTED TUBULAR BRAID, ¼-inch, 3c, 4c, 5c; ⅜-inch, 6c, 7c, 8c, 10c yd.

BLACK MOHAIR BINDING BRAID, ¼-inch, 4c, 5c; ½-inch, 6c, 7c, 8c; ¾-inch, 8c, 10c yd.

BLACK SILK BINDING BRAID, ¼-inch, 4c, 5c; ⅜-inch, 6c, 7c; ½-inch, 8c, 9c; ¾-inch, 10c yd.

BLACK WORSTED SOUTACHE BRAID, ⅛-inch, 1c, 2c, 3c, 4c yd.

COLORED WORSTED SOUTACHE BRAID, ⅛-inch, 1c yd, or 10c doz yds.

BLACK OR COLORED SILK SOUTACHE BRAID, ⅛-inch, 3c yd, or 30c doz yds; also 5c yd, or 50c doz yds.

BLACK AND GOLD (mixed) BRAID, ¼-inch, 5c, 10c, 12½c; ½-inch, 15c, 20c, 25c yd.
CREAM WOOLLEN RUSSIA BRAID, ⅛-inch, 1c, 1½c, 2c yd.
CREAM WOOLLEN HERCULES BRAID, ⅛ inch, 1c; ¼ inch, 2c; ⅜-inch, 3c; ½-inch, 4c; ¾-inch, 5c; up to 1½-inch, 10c yd.
WHITE COTTON TRIMMING BRAIDS, ⅛-inch, 1c; ¼-inch, 2c; ⅜-inch, 3c; ½-inch, 4c; up to 1½-inch, 7c yd.
SILVER OR GOLD TINSEL BRAID (flat), ⅛-inch, 2c; 3-16 inch, 3c, 4c yd; ¼-inch, 5c; ⅜-inch, 6c, 7c; ½-inch, 10c; up to 2-inch, 50c, 65c yd.
GOLD OR SILVER SOUTACHE BRAID, ⅛-inch, 3c, 4c, 5c yd.
COLORED MILITARY BRAID, ¼-inch, 2c, 3c; up to 2-inch, 10c, 12½c yd.
BLACK AND COLORED SILK DRESS OR SHIRT LACES, 54 inches long, 8c each, or 2 for 15c.

Black Silk and Bead Gimps and Appliques.

BLACK BEADED GIMPS, ¼-inch, 3c to 15c; ½-inch, 5c, 8c, 10c, 15c to 35c; ¾-inch, 10c to 40c, 1-inch, 12½c to 75c; 1½-inch, 15c to $1.25; 2-inch; 75c to $2.00.
DULL JET, for mourning, 10c, 12½c, 15c, 20c to $1.25 yd.
BLACK SEQUIN GIMPS, ¼-inch, 10c, 12½c, 15c, 20c; ½-inch, 15c, 20c, 25c; ¾-inch, 30c, 35c, 40c; 1-inch, 50c, 65c, 75c; 1½ to 2-inch, 85c, $1.00, 1.25, 1.50, 2.00; 3-inch, $3.00 yd.
BLACK JET INSERTIONS, 1-inch, 20c to 60c; 1½-inch, 50c to $2.00 yd.
BLACK JET AND STEEL (combined) GIMPS, ½-inch, 20c, 25c; 1-inch, 50c, 65c, 75c yd.
BLACK JET FRINGE, 1-inch, 40c; 1½-inch, 50c; 2½-inch, 75c; 3-inch, $1.00; 4-inch, $1.25, 1.50 yd.
BLACK SEQUIN FRINGE, ¾-inch, 25c; 1½-50c, 75c; 2-inch, 85c, $1.00.
BLACK SEQUIN AND CUT STEEL PASSEMENTERIE, can be separated, 1½ and 2-inch, $1.25, 1.50 yd.
BLACK SILK GIMPS, ¼-inch, 5c; ½-inch, 8c, 10c to 35c; ¾ to 1½-inch, 10c to $1.50 yd.
BLACK MOHAIR GIMPS, ½-inch, 15c, 20c; ¾ to 1-inch, 25c, 30c, 35c to 50c; 1½ and 2-inch, 60c, 85c; 3-inch, 75c, $1.00 yd.
BLACK TAFFETA SILK APPLIQUE, 1-inch, 50c, 75c; 1½-inch, $1.00, 1.25; 2-inch, $1.50, 2.00 yd.
BLACK SILK APPLIQUE, ½-inch, 25c, 30c, 35c, 40c; ¾-inch, 40c, 50c; 1-inch, 65c, 75c; 1½-inch, 85c, $1.00, 1.25; 2-inch, $1.50, 2.00.
BLACK AND GOLD SILK PASSEMENTERIE, 1½ and 2-inch, $1.00, 1.25, 1.50, 2.00 yd.
BLACK AND GOLD BEAD PASSEMENTERIE, 75c, $1.00 yd.
BLACK AND WHITE MIXED SILK PASSEMENTERIE, ¾-inch, 35c; 1-inch, 40c, 50c; 1½-inch, 75c, $1.00 yd.

Colored Beaded, Silk and Mohair Gimps.

COLORED BEADED GIMPS, ¼-inch, 10c, 15c; ½-inch, 15c to 35c; ¾-inch, 35c to 50c; 1-inch, 40c to 60c; 1½-inch, 75c to $1.50 yd.
CUT STEEL GIMPS, ¼ inch, 10c, 12½c to 20c; ½-inch, 25c to 35c; ¾-inch, 25c to 40c; 1-inch, 40c to 75c; 1½ and 2-inch, 85c to $1.50.
WHITE AND GOLD SILK APPLIQUE, ¾-inch, 75c, 85c; 1 and 1½-inch, $1.00, 1.25 yd.
COLORED SILK GIMPS, ¼-inch, 5c, 8c; ½-inch, 8c, 10c, 12½c; ¾-inch, 15c to 35c; 1 and 1½-inch, 40c to 50c yd.
COLORED MOHAIR BRAID PASSEMENTERIE, ½-inch, 15c, 20c to 35c; 1½ and 2-inch, 30c, 35c to 50c yd.
CREAM SILK GIMPS, ¼-inch, 5c, 8c; ½-inch, 10c, 12½c; 1-inch, 15c to 25c yd.

Evening Wear Trimmings.

WHITE TAFFETA SILK, embroidered in blue or gold, 18 inches, suitable for fronts or yokes of waists, $5.50 to 7.00 yd.
BLACK OR WHITE TAFFETA SILK, embroidered in silk braid, 18 inches wide, $5.00, 6.00, 7.00 yd.
CREAM OR WHITE SILK APPLIQUE, ½-inch, 25c, 30c, 35c; ¾ and 1-inch, 40c, 50c, 65c, 75c, $1.00; 1½ and 2-inch, $1.25, 1.50, 2.00; 2½-inch, $2.50 yd.
WHITE TAFFETA SILK APPLIQUE, 1-inch, 50c, 75c, $1.00; 1½ and 2-inch, $1.50, 2.00, 2.50 yd.
SILK APPLIQUE, in all leading shades, ½-inch, 30c, 35c, 40c, 50c; 1-inch, 50c, 75c; 1½ to 2-inch, $1.00 to 2.00; 4-inch, $2.50 yd. (Can be separated in sections.)
GOLD OR SILVER TINSEL GIMPS, ½-inch, 5c, 8c, 10c, 12½c; ¾-inch, 15c; 1-inch, 15c, 20c yd.
CREAM OR WHITE SILK FRINGE, 3-inch, 50c, 75c, $1.00 yd.
PEARL AND BEAD FRINGE, 1-inch, 40c; 1½-inch, 85c, $1.25 yd.
BLACK SILK FRINGE, 2½-inch, 50c; 3-inch, 75c; 4-in., $1.00, 1.25; 5 to 6-in., $1.50 to 2.00 yd.
WHITE BEADED GIMPS, narrow widths, 10c, 12½c, 15c, 20c yd.
PEARL AND BEAD GIMPS, narrow widths, 20c to 40c; 1-inch, 40c to 75c; 1½-inch, 75c to $2.00 yd.
GOLD INSERTIONS, ½-inch, 15c, 20c; ¾-inch, 25c, 30c yd.
PERSIAN BAND TRIMMINGS, 1-inch, 65c, 75c; 1½ and 2-inch, 85c, $1.00, 1.25 yd.
WHITE SEQUIN GIMPS, ½-inch, 15c, 20c, 25c; 1-inch, 40c, 50c, 60c; 1½-inch, 75c, $1.00 yd.

Ornaments and Garnitures.

White pearl and bead garnitures, 65c, 75c, $1.00 to 3.50 each.
BLACK JET GARNITURES, 75c, $1.00, 1.25, 1.50, 2.00 to 3.50 each.
BLACK JET REVERS, $1.00, 1.25, 1.50 up to 3.50 pair.
CREAM OR BLACK LACE BOLEROS, $2.00, 2.50, 3.00, 3.50, 4.00, 5.00 each (suitable for wearing over silk, muslin or woollen waists).
BLACK ZOUAVE JACKETS, for front of waists only, in silk or jet, $3.00, 4.00 pair.
CUT STEEL REVERS, $1.50, 2.00 pair.
REVERS AND COLLAR COMBINED, in rich Persian shades, cream and gold, black and gold, $5.00, 6.00 each.
GOLD CLOTH, 18 inches wide, $4.50 yd.
CREAM CLOTH APPLIQUE, 35c, 45c, 60c yd.
BLACK AND WHITE MOHAIR PASSEMENTERIE, 25c, 35c, 40c, 50c, 60c yd.

Skirt Bindings, Belting, Collar Canvas and Dome Fasteners

Duxbak, black only, waterproof, brush binding, 1-inch wide, 10c yd.

Victoria brush binding, with heavy velveteen edge, 1½-in. wide, 8c yd, or 90c dozen yds.

"Hercules" Amazon brush binding, pure wool, all colors, 6c yd, or 65c dozen yds.
"Leader" brush binding, pure wool, all colors, 4c yd, or 40c doz. yds.

S. H. & M. bias velvet, with brush edge, skirt binding, all colors, 10c yd, $1.00 doz. yds.

Colored worsted skirt braids, 1c yd, or 12c dozen yds.
Black worsted skirt braids, 1c, 2c, 3c, 4c, 5c yd.
Prussian binding, for seam binding, in black, grey, white, fawn, brown, 2c yd, 20c dozen yds.
Corticelli mohair skirt protector in bunches of 5 yds, black only, 25c bunch.
Corticelli worsted skirt protector in bunches of 5 yds, colors and black, 15c bunch.

Redfern corded velveteen binding, heavy quality, 1¾-inch, all shades, 7c yd, 75c dozen yds.
Bias velvet binding, in all colors, 1⅝-inch, 4c yd, or 40c dozen yds.
Black corduroy velvet binding, 1⅝-in., 5c yd.

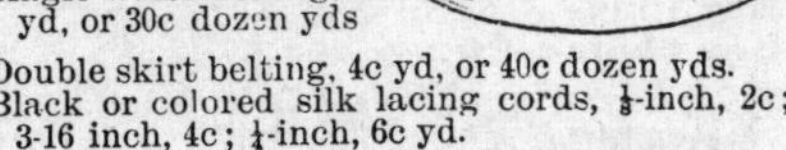

Vorwerk collar stiffener, shaped ready for collars and cuffs, in black or white, 1½-in., 8c; 2-in., 10c; 2½-in., 12½c; 3-inch, 18c yd.
Single waist belting, 3c yd, or 30c dozen yds 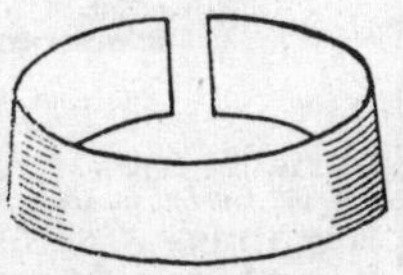
Double skirt belting, 4c yd, or 40c dozen yds.
Black or colored silk lacing cords, ⅛-inch, 2c; 3-16 inch, 4c; ¼-inch, 6c yd.

Featherbone Stock Foundation Collars.

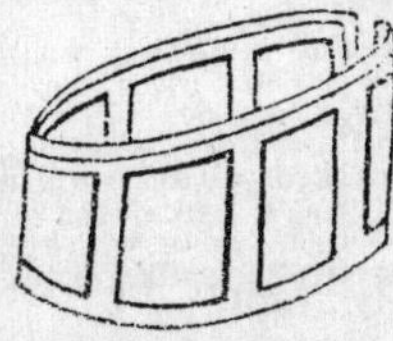

Featherbone stock foundation collars, in black or white, light weight, in two shapes, all plain, same width all round, and as cut, deeper at sides than front, for covering with silk or other materials, sizes 12½, 13, 13½, 14, 14½-in., 15c ea.
Silk featherbone collars, round shape, transparent, in black or white, sizes 12½, 13, 13½, 14, 14½-inch, 35c each.

Dome fasteners, in black and white, 8c dozen.
Eye-glass cord, black only, 5c yd.

Real Fur Trimming.

Best quality only. Wider widths than here quoted will be charged in proportion. We do not send samples of these goods owing to their expensive character.

Thibet, black, 1-inch, 65c yd.
" white, 1-inch, 65c yd.
Angora, black, ¾-inch, 30c yd.
" white, ½-inch, 20c; ¾-inch, 25c; 1-inch, 30c yd.
Opossum, black, 1-inch, 35c yd.
Wool seal, 1-inch, 40c yd.
Australian opossum, 1-inch, 40c yd.
Iceland lamb, 1-inch, 30c yd.
Black French coney, 1-inch, 25c.
Sable, No. 1, $1.50 yd; No. 2, $1.00 yd.
Grey lamb, 1-inch, 50c yd.
Persian lamb, 1-inch, $1.50 yd.
Nutria, 1-inch, 50c yd.
Beaver, 1-inch, $1.10 yd.
Ohio sable, 1-inch, 60c yd.
Raccoon, 1-inch, 60c yd.
Bear, 1-inch, $2.00 yd.
Mink, 1-inch, $2.50 yd.
Black astrachan, 1-inch, 45c yd.

Imitation Fur Trimming.

Imitation beaver, 1-inch, 15c, 20c; 1½-inch, 25c, 30c, 35c yd.
Imitation white fur trimming, 15c, 20c, 25c; 1½-inch, 40c, 50c yd.
Imitation black astrachan, 1-inch, 15c, 20c; 1½-inch, 25c, 30c, 35c yd.
Lambs' wool, tinted, in white and grey, 25c yd.
White lambs' wool, ½-inch, 15c; 1-inch, 20c yd, for trimming children's bonnets and cloaks.
Swansdown trimming, for children's cloaks and bonnets, also used for opera cloaks, ½-inch, 25c; ¾-inch, 35c; 1-inch, 50c yd.

Smallwares and Notions.

Button Hooks.

C201. Steel, with wood or bone handle, 5c, 10c each; steel combination hook and shoe horn, 10c each.

C202. Glove button hooks, pearl or bone handle, 10c each.

Boot and Shoe Laces.

C203. Shoe laces, mohair, ½ inch wide, 27 inches long, black or tan, 3 pair for 5c; finer quality, 2 pair for 5c; in silk, 5c, 10c pair; same style, mohair, 45 inches long, black or tan, 3 pair for 10c.

C204. Boot laces, mohair, 36 inches long, extra strong, black, 5c, 7c doz; better quality, black or tan, fine or heavy quality, 42 inches long, 10c doz; same style, 52 inches long, suitable for bicycle boots, 2 pair for 5c.

C205. Boot laces, mohair, best quality, banded spiral ends, black or tan, ladies' or gents' sizes, 2 pair for 5c.

C206. The "Johnston" boot lace, a mixture of Egyptian corded thread and woollen yarn, ladies' or gents', black or tan, 2 pair for 5c.

C207. Paton's wool boot lace, ladies' or gents', black or tan, 3 pair for 10c.

C203. Leather boot laces, 36 inches long, single tag, 8c doz; double tag, 10c doz; spiral twist ends, 2 pair for 5c; imitation porpoise, 5c pair; real porpoise, 8c pair; "White Whale," extra strong, 10c pair.

Boot Buttons—C209. Assorted sizes, 2 boxes for 5c.

Automatic Buttons — C210. Can instantly replace a missing button, 8c doz; better quality, 10c doz. (see cut).

C211. Bees' universal button fasteners, for fastening all buttons that can be attached with needle and thread, 1 doz. fasteners in package, 5c (see cut); with 1 doz pant buttons, 10c.

Binding—C212. Prussian binding for seams, black, 15c doz; white and drab, 20c doz; in silk glaced, white or black, 30c doz yds.

C213. Silk Italian ferret, for binding flannel, black and white, 4c yd, 40c doz; colors, 5c yd, 50c doz yd.

Glove Laces—C214. Silk glove laces, assorted browns and black, 5c pair.

Corset Busks.—C215. Misses' size, jean, white or drab, 4 hooks, 5c pair. Ladies' size, jean, drab or white (5 hooks), same style, cork back, straight, 8c pair; spoon, 10c pair; best sateen-covered cork back, in black or buff (5 hooks), 13-inch, straight, 10c pair; 12-inch (4 hooks), same colors, 10c pair.

C216. The "Duplex" lock corset steel, cannot come unclasped, 10c pair.

C217. The "F.P." waterproof corset steel, superior finish and stitching, black, white or drab, 10c pair. The "Tricora," same style, cork back, 12½c pair.

C218. Kid-covered corset busks, 10c, 12½c, 15c pair.

C219. Side steels, uncovered, 4 for 5c; sateen covered, 20c doz; kid covered, 30c, 40c, 60c doz.

Corset Shields—C220. "Venus" corset shield, prevents corset breaking at waist or hips, 25c pair.

Corset Laces—C221. Round elastic, black or white, 2½ yds, 2 for 5c; flat elastic, 3 for 10c, 5c each; round, satin, 10c each.

C222. Round or flat cotton, 2½ yds, black or white, 4 for 5c; glazed cotton, flat, black, white or drab, 3 for 5c; linen, 2 for 5c.

Chalk—C223. Tailors' marking chalk, black, white or colors, 5c doz.

Cuff holders—C224. The "Washburne," cuff holder, 10c pair; the "Magnet," 10c pr; the "Wizard" 10c pair; the "Derby," 10c pair (see cut).

Crochet hooks—C225. Steel, 2 for 5c, 5c each; wire, reversible, 2 for 5c; bone, 2 for 5c, 5c each; bone, 8 inches long, 5c; 10 inches long, 10c.

Darners—C226. Enamelled stocking darners, 5c each.

Dress Weights—C227. Made of lead, assorted sizes, 10c doz.

Emery Bags—C228. For polishing needles (see cut), 5c, 10c, 15c ea.

Hooks and Eyes.

C229. Swan Bill, black, 6 cards for 5c; white and yellow brass, 3 cards for 5c.

C230. Improved safety, black or white, 4 cards for 5c; better quality, 2 cards for 5c.

C231. Washable brass safety hook and eye, black or white, 5c card; better quality, 8c card.

C231½. The "Francis" hook and eye, black or white, 10c card.

C232. The "Corono" invisible hook and eye, black or white, 5c card.

C233. The "Brownie," extra small, rust-proof hook and eye, used on collars, blouses, etc., black or white, 8c card.

C234. "Peet's" invisible eyes, black or white, 2 doz for 5c.

C235. Pant hooks and eyes, black or white, 3 doz for 10c.

C236. Vest buckles, japanned, 10c doz.

C237. The ball-and-socket garment fasteners; dressmakers recommend them for plaquets, etc., silvered or japanned, 8c doz; small size, better quality, 15c doz. See cut C237.

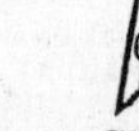

C237.

Initial Letters—C238. For marking linen, etc., 4 doz for 5c, or 15c gross (see cut).

Key Rings—C239. In steel, 3c, 5c each.

Key Chains—C240. In steel, 10c each.

Mending Wool—C241. "Diamond" quality, made by J. & J. Baldwin, 27 yds on card, in black, white, tan, grey and natural shades, 3 cards, 5c; 17c doz.

C242. Ball mending wool, fine worsted yarn, black only, 2 balls 5c.

Mending Cotton — C243. On cards, black, white or tan, 4 cards, 5c; on spools, black or white, 2 for 5c; in silk, black only, 2 cards, 5c.

Meshes—C244. In bone, for netting, all sizes, 4c each, 3 for 10c.

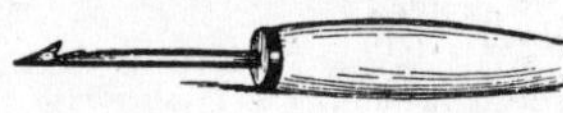

Mat hooks—C245. With wood handle, 5c each (see cut).

Needles.

C246. Best quality, Abel Morrell's, all sizes, also assorted, 5c paper; cheaper quality, 2 papers 5c.

C247. "Diamond" sewing needles, specially tempered for Canadian trade, all sizes, 5c paper.

C248. Scientific needles, tapering from the centre, sews easily, all sizes, 5c paper.

Darning Needles—C249. Same quality as our best sewing needles, assorted sizes, 5c paper.

C250. Glove needles, 10c paper.

C251. Between (or tailors') needles, 5c paper.

C252. Chenille needles, 10c paper.

C253. Straw (milliners') needles, 5c paper.

C254. Packing needles, 5c each.

C255. Self-threading needles, 5c paper.

C256. Upholsterers' needles, 5c each.

C257. Machine needles **(always send name and sample of needles required)**, 20c doz.

C258. Netting needles, all sizes, 5c each.

C259. Steel knitting needles, all sizes, 3c set.

C260. Rubber and bone knitting needles, 10c pair; wood, 5c pair.

C261. Embroidery needles, 5c pkg.

C262. Carpet needles, 10c paper.

Needle Cases.

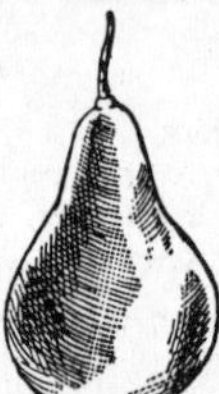

C263. An assortment of English sewing needles and darning needles, neatly arranged, leather-finished case, price according to number of needles, 15c, 25c, 35c, 50c each.

Artificial Fruit—C264. Perfect imitation of assorted fruits, such as peaches, pears, bananas, apples, plums, etc., used for pincushion or decorative purposes, 5c each, 50c doz.

Pin Department.

Hat Pins—C265. English steel hat pins, glass tops, 6 or 7 inches long, black or white, 5c dozen.

C266. Small fancy gilt lace pins, assorted designs, 2 for 5c; with white and colored unbreakable pearl tops, 10c dozen (see cut).

Sheet Pins—C267. 200 adamantine pins, on sheet, 1c paper; English brass pins, "Diamond" brand, 200 assorted pins, 2 papers for 5c; 250 on sheet, 3c paper; 360 on sheet, 5c paper; 150 extra large size pins, 5c paper.

C268. The "Challenge" brass pin, 360 on sheet, extra strong, 5c paper; Taylor's "Queen's Own" brass pins, sizes 1 to 10, 5c paper; The "Ne Plus Ultra" best quality heavy wire brass pins, 360 on sheet, 10c paper; best English steel pins, 360 on sheet, 10c paper.

Bulk Pins—Pins catalogued by the pound come in pound boxes only.

C269. Adamantine, 20c lb; mixed brass, 35c lb; small brass, 40c lb.

C270. Small brass, 15c ¼-lb box; extra small brass ribbon pins, in ¼-lb boxes, 25c.

C271. Steel mourning pins, in boxes, ½-oz. box, 5c; 1-oz box, 10c.

C272. "Pyramid" pincushion, consisting of 365 pins, put up in a useful form for office or toilet use, 10c.

Toilet Pins—C273. Small berry pins, in black, white or assorted, 2 for 5c.

C274. A tablet containing an assortment of toilet and berry pins, glass tops, black or white, 5c card.

C275. Black or white veiling pins, assorted sizes from 1½ to 2½ inches, also 2½ to 3½ inches, 2 cards for 5c.

C276—Toilet pins, black or white, sizes 2½, 3, 3½, 4 and 4½ inches long, all one size on card, 2 for 5c.

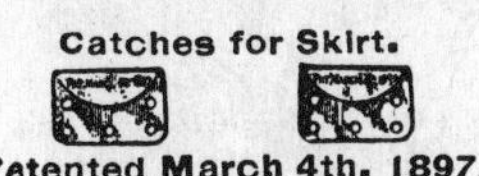

C277. Pin cubes, containing 96 pins in all, black and white assorted, or black, white and colored, 5c each; larger size, 10c each (see cut).

Belt Supporters and Holders.

Catches for Skirt.

Patented March 4th, 1897.

Supporter.

Gairs' Queen Skirt Support—C278. Prevents skirt from sagging, and shirt waist from slipping up. Pins and hooks are discarded. Full directions with each, 1 belt and 6 catches (enough for 3 dresses), 25c; extra holders, 10c doz.

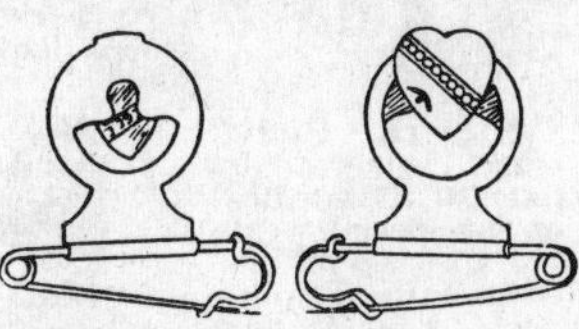

C279. The **All-ways Ready** shirt waist holder and skirt supporter, requires no preparation of shirt waist or skirt before wearing. It holds both firmly together in perfect position, and leaves the waist-line smooth (see cut), 25c each.

C280. Fancy metal belt holders, black, silver or gilt, 2 for 5c; better quality, 5c.

Back View. Front View.

C281. The "Gem" belt holder is made to fasten to button on back of waist, made in pretty design, black, silver, gilt or oxidized, 10c each (see cut).

Safety Pins—C282. Lindsay safety pins, sizes 2, 2½, 3, 2 dozen for 5c; The "Columbia" (see cut), nickel-plated, protected points, 3 sizes, 5c dozen; the "Victoria," heavier wire, guarded spring, 8c dozen; the "Clinton," extra strong wire, black or white, small size, 8c dozen; medium size, 8c dozen; large size, 10c dozen.

C283. The "Stronghold" safety pin, with small catch in the pin which prevents it from coming unclasped under any strain, made in 3 sizes, 10c dozen.

C284. Safety-pin book, with two doz. small, medium and large silvered safety pins, 10c book.

C285. Lindsay blanket pins, 3c, 4c, 5c each.

C286. The "Climax" pin book case, consisting of 2 dozen assorted sizes in black and white "Climax" safety pins, also 6 dozen best brass pins, put up in a neat paper book, 10c.

C287. **Skirt yokes**, assorted colors, woven in one piece, with lining and buttonholes, 12c each.

C288. **Stilettos**, in bone, 2 for 5c.

C289. **Tailors' Sewing Wax**, 5c each.

C290. **Button Moulds**, assorted sizes, 2 doz. for 5c.

Thimbles—C291. White metal, 10c doz.; aluminum, 1c each; heavier metal, 2 for 5c; best quality aluminum, 5c each; steel, 2 for 5c; better quality, 5c each; steel, enamel lined, 2 for 5c; white metal, enamel lined, 2 for 5c; celluloid, 2 for 5c; silver finish, 5c each, better quality, extra heavy, 10c.

C292. The "Iles," solid nickel thimble, armored with ebony, which protects the finger from contact with metal, 10c each.

C293. "Iles" Ivorine thimbles, puncture proof, 5c each.

C294. Tailors' steel thimbles, 2 for 5c; better quality, 5c each.

These thimbles come in four sizes: misses', small women's, women's, and large women's. Please state size when ordering.

Finger Shields—C295. In celluloid, to protect the forefinger from the thimble or needle, 2 for 5c.

C296. Cotton tape measures, 60 inches long, figured both sides (correct measure), 2 for 5c; better quality, linoleum, double-tipped, English standard measure, will not stretch, 5c, 8c, 10c each.

C297. Tailors' tape measures, stitched edge, 60 inches long, ⅝-inch wide, single-tipped, 5c each; better quality, fine sateen, 10c, 15c, 20c each.

C298. Spring tape measures, 36 inches long, 5c each; better quality, 10c, 15c, 20c; 40 inches long, 25c; with fine steel wire, best English make, 40 inches long, 40c each; 60 inches long, 75c each; 78 inches long, $1.25 each.

C299. Tape measures for carpenters' or contractors' use, brass bound cases, cotton tape, 25 ft., 25c; 50 ft., 35c; 75 ft., 50c; 100 ft., 75c each.

Tie Clips—C300. The "Au fait" tie holder, for holding the tie in place on shirt or blouse fronts (see cut), 5c each. The "Washburn" tie holder, nickel plated, very neat and strong, 5c each.

C301. **Display** clasps, made of steel, 3 for 5c.

Tatting Shuttles—C302. In white bone or black rubber, extra smooth finish, 10c each.

C303. Bobbins, made of bone, for winding silk, 2 for 5c.

Victoria Plaiter—C304. Used by leading dressmakers and milliners to make all kinds of trimmings, in plain or fancy patterns; no lady should be without one, 10c each.

Pinking Irons—C305. Assorted sizes (see cut), 10c each.

The Swiss Darner—C306. With this machine a large darn can be made in much less time than in the old way. The darn is woven right into the cloth, leaving no lumps or botches in the garment. It mends table cloths, curtains, and fine silks equally as well, and is so simple a child can use it, 20c each.

Tapes—

C307. Bunched tape, assorted widths, 12 pieces, all white or all black, or mixed white and black, 5c, 10c bunch (see cut.)

C308. Twilled cotton tape, black, white or drab, narrow, medium or wide widths, 5c roll of 12 yds.

C309. Blocked tape, assorted widths, white cotton, 2 for 5c; linen, 3 for 5c.

Tracers—C310. Best steel teeth, sharp and perfect, 5c, 10c, 15c, 25c ea (see cut).

Splashers—C311. Made of wood splints, decorated, used on wall behind washstand, 8c, 10c, 15c, 25c each.

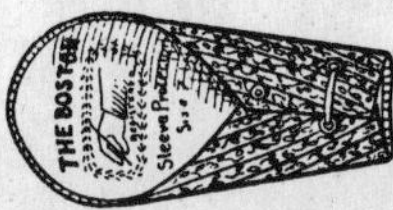

C312. **Sleeve Protectors**—The "Boston" sleeve protector protects the sleeves when working, keeps light material from being soiled, assorted patterns, small, medium and large, 15c pair (see cut).

C313. Rubber sleeves, soft as sateen, but **much** superior, 25c pair.

Vapor Bath Cabinets.

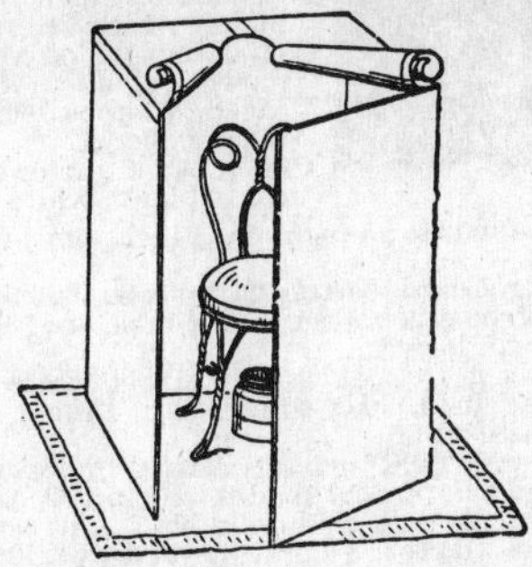

Now acknowledged to be a household necessity. Doctors recommend them. Their largely increased sale is sufficient testimony of their worth.

C314. Vapor bath cabinets, made by a reliable manufacturer especially for us, single drill, rubber lined, best material used in construction, steel or wood frame, is 30 inches square and 42 inches high, alcohol heater, lamp, etc., supplied with each cabinet, usually sold at $6.50, our special price, $4.75.

C315. Same style cabinet, with double thickness of cloth, made of antiseptic germ-proof material, will not break or crack easily, trimmings are japanned and will not rust, regular price, $12.50; our special price, $8.25.

Face Steamers—C316. For vapor bath, 75c ea.

Woodenware.

C317. Towel rings, 4-inch or 6-inch in diameter, colors blue, white, pink, yellow and oak, 5c each.

C318. Towel racks, 3 bars, same colors, 5c each.

C319. Towel racks, 18-inch bar, with three rings and brass chain holder attached, same colors, 15c each.

C320. Glove or stocking darners, assorted colors, 5c each.

C321. Enamelled match-holders, special, 5c each.

C322. Enamelled tooth-brush holders, 5c each.

Match Strikers—C323. Patriotic match strikers, with picture of British lion under the ensign, with the words, "Strike me and I'm your match," 5c each.

Piano Cleaner.

C324. For dusting and cleaning piano keys, can be used with wood alcohol, enamel wood back, 25c; ebony back, fancy handle, 35c; ebony back, with silver mounting, 50c (see cut).

Elastics.

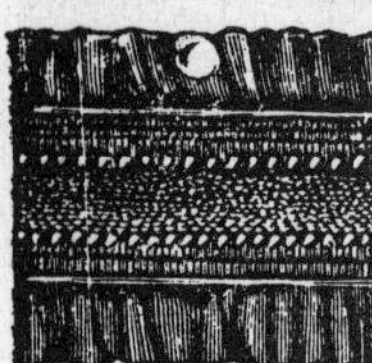

C325. Fancy colored garter elastic, extra strong and durable, special, 5c yd.
C326. French cotton garter elastic, ⅝-inch wide, plaid patterns, 8c yd.
C327. Fancy frilled cotton garter elastic, satin faced, a good strong elastic, 10c yd.
C328. Cotton garter elastic, in black, white and grey, ½-inch, 4c; ⅝-inch, 5c; ¾-inch, 6c; ⅞-inch, 8c yd.
C329. Mercerized cotton garter elastic, black, extra strong web, ½-inch, 5c; ⅝-inch, 7c; ¾-inch, 8c; ⅞-inch, 10c yd.
C330. Silk garter elastic, in black, white and colors, ½-inch, 10c; ⅝-inch, 12½c; ¾-inch, 15c; ⅞-inch, 20c yd.
C331. Fancy silk garter elastic, pure silk, assorted colors, new shades, 20c, 25c, 30c yd.
C332. Narrow silk elastic, in black and white, 6 cord, 2 yds 5c; 8 cord, 4c yd, 3 yds, 10c; 10 cord, 4c yd.
C333. Round silk elastic, black and white, small, medium and large sizes, 3 yds, 5c.

Arm Bands.

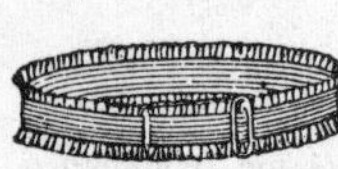

C334. Wool-covered round elastic arm bands, very easy to wear, assorted, plain colors, 5c pair; silk-covered, 10c pair.
C335. Flat silk elastic arm bands, assorted, plain colors, 10c pair.
C336. Cotton elastic arm bands, assorted, plain colors, 5c pair.
C337. Patent ventilated arm bands, fine nickelled steel wire, assorted sizes, 12½c pair.
C338. Fancy frilled elastic arm bands (see cut), 25c pair.
C339. Sleeve holders, metal catches, silk elastic, 10c pair.

Gents' Garters.

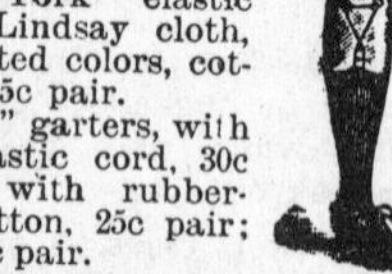

C340. Men's "New York" elastic garters (see cut), Lindsay cloth, tipped clasp, assorted colors, cotton, 25c pair; silk, 35c pair.
C341. Gent's "Boston" garters, with satin web and elastic cord, 30c pair; plain web with rubber-tipped fastener, cotton, 25c pair; best quality silk, 45c pair.

Ladies' Garters.

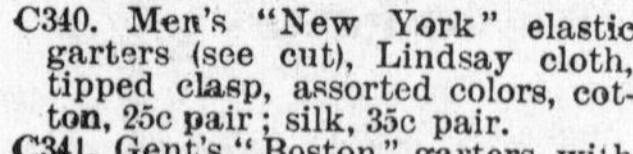

C342. Ladies' frilled cotton elastic garters, assorted colors, 10c, 15c pair; silk-covered elastic, assorted colors, 25c, 35c pair; pure silk elastic, 50c, 75c pair.
C343. Fancy garter buckles, 10c, 15c, 25c pair.

Garter Lengths.

C344. Garter lengths, ¾-yd lengths, fancy cotton elastic, 5c; frilled cotton, silk faced, 10c; silk frilled elastic, 15c, 20c, 25c.

Boys' or Girls' "Suspender Waists."

C345. Holds children's clothing together (see cut). Does not bind the waist, but rather clings to it; may be worn with skirt, waist or blouse, the buttons are placed for trousers or drawers. When ordering state age of child. Sizes for children from 2 to 10 years, 25c each.

Ladies' Side Supporters.

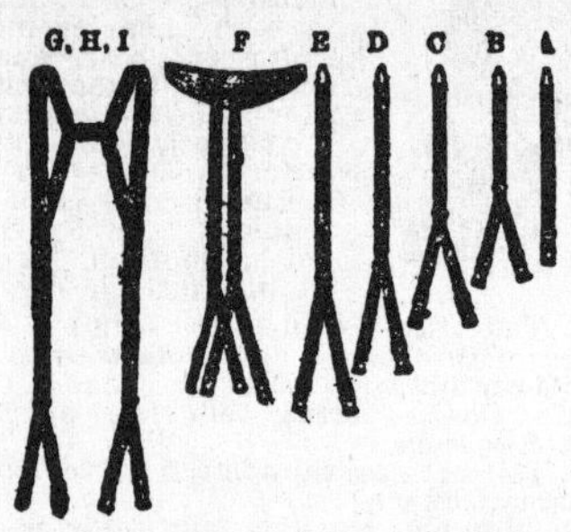

C346. The "Diamond" rubber-tipped button fastener, extra strong lisle web, made especially for us.
(B) Babies', double strap, cotton, 10c pair.
(C) Misses', double strap, cotton, 12½c pair.
(E) Ladies', double strap, cotton, 15c pair.

The "Flexo" rubber-tipped supporter, best quality lisle elastic. The button is so constructed that it will not tear the hose.

C347. Babies', double strap, cotton, 15c pair.
Children's, double strap, cotton, 20c pair.
Ladies', double strap, cotton, 20c pair.
(F) Ladies', plain belt supporters, 25c pair.

Lindsay Felt Finish Supporter.

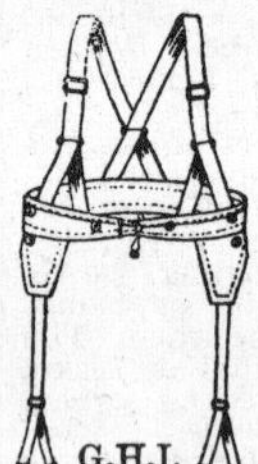
G.H.I.

C348. (A) Babies', single strap, cotton, 12½c pair.
(B) Babies', double strap, cotton, 15c; silk, 30c pair.
(D) Misses', double strap, cotton, 20c; silk, 35c pair.
(E) Ladies' double strap, cotton, 20c; silk, 45c pair
(F) Ladies', plain belt supporters, cotton, 30c; with satin belt and silk elastic, assorted colors, 75c; side supporters, white only, with combination belt, cotton, 35c pair.

GHI. Shoulder brace and hose supporter combined, Lindsay fastener, black or white, ladies', 35c pair; misses', 30c pair; child's, 25c pair.

NOTE.—Silk supporters come in black, white and plain colors.

C349. Ladies' non-elastic garment suspenders, white, 20c pair.

C350. Ladies' fancy frilled elastic side garters, silk faced, assorted colors (see cut C350), 25c pair; silk elastic, assorted colors, 35c pair; pure silk elastic, nickelled buckle, 65c pair.

C350.

C351. "Hook-on" supporter. It hangs from the corset (see cut C351). The natural position for a supporter to hang. Keeps the corset from protruding in front. In cotton, black or white, 25c pair; better quality, 35c pair; four straps, best lisle web, 50c pair; with silk frilled elastic ends, 50c pair; same style, four straps, $1.00 pair.

C351.

C352 The "Marloe" hose supporter, same style as the "Hook-on" with different clasp, in cotton, 35c pair; in cotton frilled elastic, assorted colors, 25c pair; in silk frilled elastic, 50c, 75c, $1.00 pair.

C353. The new "Cast Off" corset supporter, can be adjusted or removed without unfastening the corset, cannot become unfastened accidently, silk finished elastic, assorted colors, 35c pair; pure silk elastic, 75c pair.

354.

C354. The new "Foster" abdominal hose supporters, gives the wearer that straight military front effect so much desired at present, it has a front pad and supporting bands which push back the entire abdomen, giving the wearer a correct standing position, in black or white, ¾-inch lisle elastic, 50c; ⅞-inch elastic, 60c; colored frilled elastic, 75c; extra heavy and wide elastic, $1.25 pair. (See cut 354.)

C355. Children's knee-protectors, stockinette or leather, 25c pair (see cut).

C355.

Shoulder Braces.

Ladies'—C356. Dr. Grey's supporting shoulder brace, in small, medium and large sizes (see cut), $1.00 pair.

Gents'—C357. Dr. Grey's shoulder brace, supports the back from the hips to the shoulder, desirable for men or boys. Made in three sizes, boys', men's and young men's. Always give height and waist measure (see cut), $1.75 per pair.

English Military Brace.—C358. Strengthens and supports the shoulders, back, sides, chest and stomach, and imparts to the wearer an appearance of ease and grace, ladies' or gents', 75c each.

The "Natural Body" Brace—C359. Endorsed by leading men of the medical profession for special weaknesses and diseases of women. It is a natural uplifting support, applied where it is needed. Write for pamphlet giving full description, also directions for measurement. As they have to be made after order is received, it will take about 10 days to fill orders.

Made in three qualities, special line at $6.00; better quality webbing and metal trimmings, $7.50; fine silk webbing, $10.00.

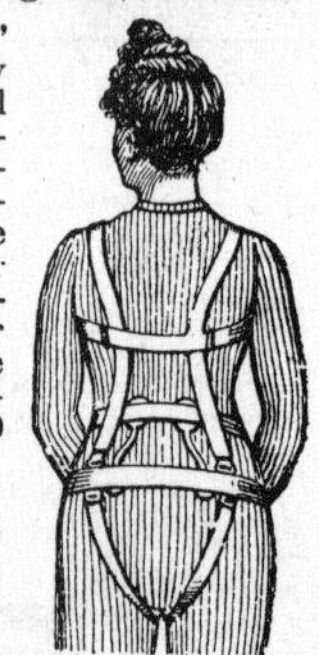

Beads.

C360. Assorted beads, put up in a gauze bag or glass-covered box, 2 for 5c.
C361. Bead necklaces, in white and colored, 10c, 15c, 20c each.

Souvenir Buttons.

C362. Souvenir buttons of His Majesty King Edward VII., from a famous photograph (this must not be confused with cheap lithographed buttons), 5c each.
C363. Cabinet photographs of King Edward VII., taken from the photograph by Lafayette, copyrighted, a handsome picture, 25c each.

Gauze Fans.

C701. Gauze fans, beautiful decorations, polished handles, in pink, blue, white, black, 50c, 75c, $1.00 each.

C702. Gauze fans, hand-painted floral decorations, all new designs, in pink, blue, white, black, $1.25, 1.50, 1.75, 2.00, 2.50, 3.00, 3.50, 4.00, 4.50, 5.00 each.

Feather Fans.

C703. Feather fans, "Marguerite" style, feathers both sides, bone handles, in white, pink, blue and black, 50c, 75c, $1.00 each.

C704. Ostrich feather fans, best quality feathers, price according to number and quality of feathers, also style of handles, $3.50, 4.00, 4.75, 5.50, 6.50, 7.00, 8.00 each.

Braids.

C111. Vandyke or rick-rack braid, 12 yds to bunch, in white, sizes 1, 2, 5c bunch; sizes 3, 4, 5, 6, 10c bunch; same braid, with picot edge, sizes 1, 5c bunch; sizes 2, 3, 4, 5, 10c bunch (see cut).

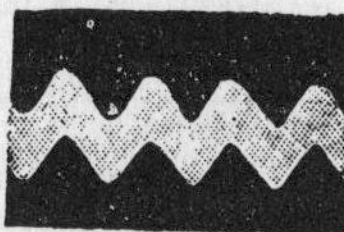

C112. Novelty or anti-macassar braid, size 0, 20c doz yds; size 1, 25c doz yds; size 2, 30c doz yds (see cut).

C113. Novelty insertion, 25c, 30c, 35c doz yds.

C114. Feather-edge braid, in white only, sizes 0, 20c doz; size 1, 25c doz; size 2, 30c doz; size 3, 35c doz yds (size of cut is 0).

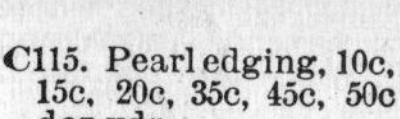

C115. Pearl edging, 10c, 15c, 20c, 35c, 45c, 50c doz yds.

C116. Battenburg lace braid, in cream or white, sizes 4, 5, 10c doz yds; sizes 6, 8, 10, 15c doz yds; finer quality, sizes 1, 2, 20c doz yds; size 3, 25c doz yds; black silk Battenburg, 35c, 45c, 50c doz yds.

C117. Fancy Battenburg braid, size 3, in cream and white, 35c doz yds.

C118. Gordon braid, in white only, sizes 0, 1, 2, 3, 10c doz yds.

C119. Star braid, white only, for braiding or trimming, 5c bunch of 12 yds.

C120. Honiton braid, English make, according to size and quality, in white, 45c, 50c, 60c, 75c, 95c, $1.20, 1.50, 1.80 doz yds (size of cut is 50c doz yds); in cream, 45c, 50c, 65c doz yds; in black silk, 65c, 75c doz yds.

C121. Honiton insertion, in white, 20c, 25c, 30c, 35c, 45c, 50c, 65c, 75c, 95c, $1.20 doz yds; in cream, 25c, 30c doz yds; in black silk, 50c per doz yds.

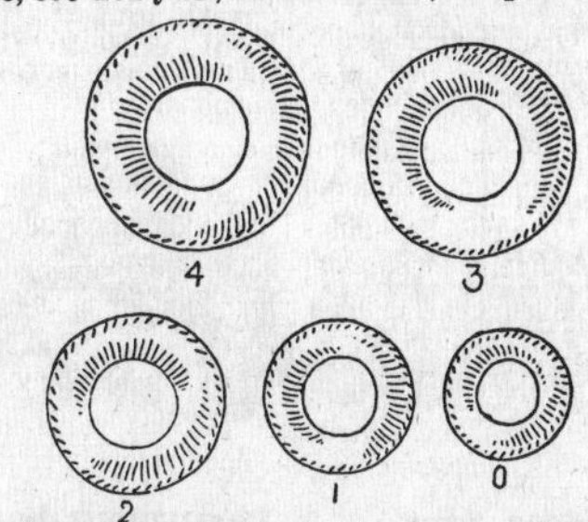

C122. Battenburg rings, in white or cream, assorted sizes, 3c per doz; in silk, black, white, or cream, sizes 0, 1, 2, 10c per doz.

C123. Honiton or Battenburg lace thread, sizes 30 to 200, 4c ball, 3 for 10c; size 300 to 1,500, 5c ball; in cream, 60 to 200, 4c ball, 3 for 10c; 300 to 1,000, 5c ball.

C124. Coronation braid, in white, red, orange, navy, black and green, 15c bunch of 9 yds.

C125. Tinsel thread, used in making Battenburg and point lace, etc., 8c skein.

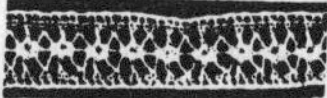

C126. French insertion, assorted patterns, cream or white, 3c yd, 35c doz yds.

C127. French insertions, new and pretty patterns, cream or white (see cut), 50c per doz yds.

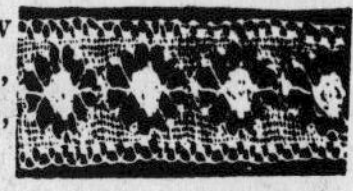

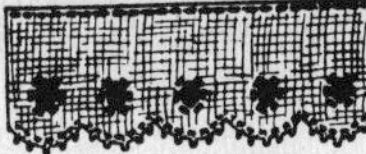

C128. New French edging, cream or white, 45c doz yds; in silk, black or white, 75c doz yds.

C129. Duchess braid (see cut) cream or white, 45c doz yds; black or white silk, 95c doz yds.

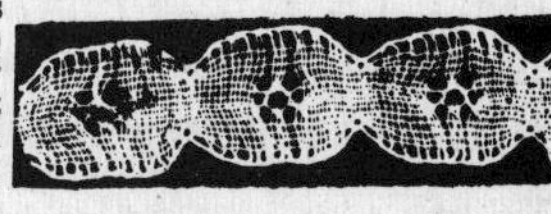

C130. Black silk insertion, French patterns, 50c, 95c doz yds.

C131. Finishing braid, white and colors, 10c bunch of 12 yds; finer quality in white, 12½c, 15c, 20c bunch of 12 yds.

Battenburg Designs.

They are stamped on colored cambric. The braid is intended to be stitched on, and each pattern can be used many times. Doileys, 5c, 8c, 10c each; cosies, 10c, 12½c, 15c each; handkerchiefs, 10c, 12½c, 15c each; centre-pieces, 12½c, 15c, 20c each; cushion tops, 15c, 20c, 25c each; lace, 10c, 15c each; table covers, 35c, 45c, 50c; tie ends, 8c, 10c each; yokes, 25c each; sailor collars, 20c, 25c each; stock collars, 8c, 10c each; bolero jackets, 25c, 35c, 40c each; tray cloths, 20c each; curtains, 40c each; sideboard scarfs, 20c, 40c each.

NOTE.—A complete illustrated Catalogue of Battenburg and Honiton lace, braids, designs, threads, etc., will be forwarded on application.

WOOLS AND YARNS.

Berlin Wools.

C621. Berlin wools, 4 and 8 fold, in a beautiful range of colors, also black and white, 5c skein.

C622. Shaded Berlin, 4 and 8 fold, 7c skein.

C623. Zephyr, or 2 fold Berlin, black, white and colors, 6c skein.

C624. Andalusian, in black, white and colors, 6c skein.

C625. "**Southdown Floss**" is a 2-ply wool, very fleecy, adapted for ladies' and children's garments, in cream, white, pink, blue, black, cardinal, grey, yellow, and mauve, full oz for 7c.

C626. Wave Crest "**Diamond Floss**" a 2-ply vest wool, very soft, suitable for fancy garments and underwear, colors white, pink, blue, cardinal, green, mauve, yellow and black, 7c skein.

C627. "**Diamond Pompadour**" wool, in white, blue, pink, cardinal, black, a silk and woollen mixture for edging garments, 12c ball.

C628. "**Diamond**" ice wool, in white, cream, pink, blue, black, cardinal and mauve, 12c ball.

C629. "**Diamond**" Angora wool, in grey, white and black, 12c ball.

C630. "**Wyvern**" vest wool, in pink, blue, and white, 9c skein, $1.40 lb.

C631. "**Lady Betty**" vesting wool, white only, 12½c skein, $2.00 lb.

Fingering Yarns.

We sell 16 skeins of yarn for a pound; this will average from 15½ to 16½ ozs.

C632. Canadian wheeling yarn, 3-ply, white, black and greys, 37c lb; colors, 45c lb; 2-ply, black, white, greys and colors, 45c lb.

C633. "**Halifax**" worsted knitting yarn, a pure worsted yarn, extra strong and durable, in black, white and greys, special price, 50c lb.

C634. **Eaton's Scotch** fingering yarn, white, black, grey and drab, 5c oz, 65c lb; pink, blue, cardinal, navy and heather mixture, 75c lb.

C635. "**Diamond Scotch**" fingering, in black only, special, 75c lb.

Wools.

C636. "**Our Best**" Scotch fingering, black only, fine and strong, our special line, 4 ozs for 25c, $1.00 lb.

C637. "**Blarney**" fingering, in black, greys, cardinal and heather, noted for its wearing qualities, 4 ozs for 25c, $1.00 lb.

C638. **Baldwin's "Bee Hive"** fingering, 3-ply, in black, white and greys, 6c skein, $1.12 lb of 16 ozs.

C639. **Baldwin's "Bee Hive"** fingering, 4-ply, in black, greys and colors, 7c oz, $1.12 lb of 15 ozs.

C640. **Baldwin's "Bee Hive"** fingering, 5-ply, in black, white and greys, 9c skein, $1.12 lb of 16 ozs.

C641. **Baldwin's "Bee Hive,"** fingering, 6-ply, in cardinal, grey and black, extra strong and fleecy, 12c skein, $1.15 lb. of 16 ozs.

C642. "**Diamond Saxony**" knitting wool, an extra high grade of fingering, in black, white, greys and colors, 7c skein, $1.12 lb.

C643. "**Queen Diamond Saxony,**" a finer grade than "Saxony," 8c skein, $1.25 lb.

C644. Ball mending wool, fine and strong, black only, 2 balls for 5c.

NOTE.—For other mending wool, see **Diamond** page 75.

Real Hair Goods

How to Order Ready-Made Hair Goods.

Choose the style required and the No. Send a sample of the hair, *not from the ends*, but from the roots, close to the scalp, as the ends of the hair as a rule are lighter than the roots, hence a bang or a switch would not match the roots if as light as the ends. It is preferable to have the artificial hair always a shade darker, as it naturally gets lighter with wear.

Hair Switches.

Weight.	Length.	Price.
1½-oz.	16-inch	$1.00
2-oz.	18-inch	1.50
2-oz.	20-inch	2.00
2½-oz.	22-inch	3.25
2½-oz.	24-inch	4.00

Wavy Switches.

Weight.	Length.	Price.
2-oz.	22-inch	$4.00
2-oz.	24-inch	5.00

We also carry a line of switches, superior quality of hair than above, prices as follows—

Weight.	Length.	Price.
1½-oz.	16-inch	$1.75
2-oz.	18-inch	2.50
2-oz.	20-inch	3.25
2¼-oz.	22-inch	4.25
2½-oz.	24-inch	5.50

Above prices are for common colors only. Other shades, such as drab, blonde, auburn, silver and grey will cost extra, from 50c upwards. We can also make extra lengths from 26 to 28 inches, price according to weight and shade of hair. Send sample for estimate.

Bangs.

No. 1. Parisian bang switches, prices according to color, length of hair, etc., $5.00 to $12.00.

No. 2.

No. 2. Trilby bang, as cut, $2.50 to $6.00, according to size and shade.

No. 1.

No. 3.

No. 3 represents ladies' wig, light weight. These wigs can be dressed high or low. and made with gauze or hair-lace parting, straight or natural curly hair, from $12.00 to 25.00.

No. 4. **Waved Bang.**

No. 4. Waved bangs, with short curly hair, $4.00 to $8.00; with long hair, as cut, $5.00 to $10.00, according to length and shade.

No. 5. **Pompadour Bang.**

No. 5. Pompadour bang, easily adjusted, the latest style, $2.50 to $5.00.

Plain front pieces, for elderly ladies, $3.50 to $10.00.

Chignons.

No. 6. No. 7.

No. 6. Chignons, curly hair, $2.60 to $5.00.

No. 7. Made with two 24-inch long single strands, with curly ends, on a frame, very easy to dress. Straight hair, as cut No. 7, $6.50 to $8.75.

No. 7½. Chignons, wavy hair, as cut No. 7, $8.00 to $9.75.

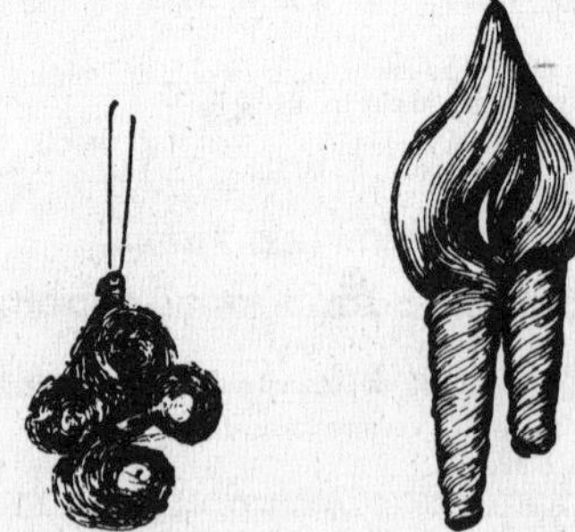

No. 8. **Curls.** No. 9. **Curls.**

No. 8. Pin curls, as cut, 40c each; grey, 60c each.

No. 9. Curls, made of natural curly hair, with loop or pin, $1.50.

No. 10. Long curls, easily attached to back head dress, 50c, 75c, 85c; grey, 75c, $1.00, 1.25.

NOTE.—When ordering toupee or wig follow carefully instructions for measurements given below. State where parting is wanted, also send sample where possible.

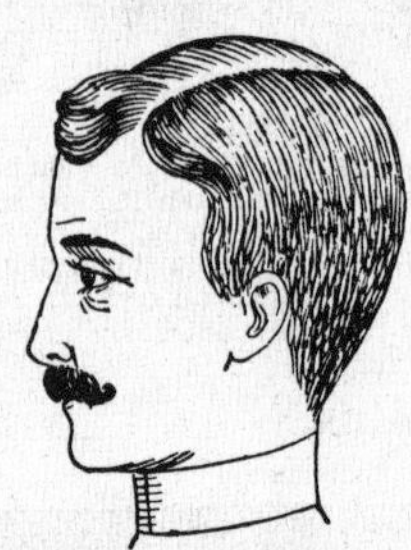

No. 11. Gent's wigs, straight or curly hair, with gauze under parting, $7.25 to $12.00; with hair lace under parting, ventilated, $15.00 to $25.00 each.

No. 11. **Gents' Wigs.** No. 12. **Toupees.**

No. 12. Toupees, with gauze under parting, $6.00 to $8.00; with hair lace under parting, $8.50 to $15.00; all hair lace, $20.00 to $25.00.

Theatrical Hair Goods.

No. 1. Moustaches, 15c, 25c, 50c each; side whiskers, 40c to 75c pair; full beard, 80c to $1.50; chin beards, 25c to 75c, according to size.

We will be pleased to quote prices on any, thing in theatrical hair goods.

Measurement Charts.

FOR TOUPEE.—Cut a piece of paper exact size and shape of bald spot, also measure around the head, and mark on paper where parting is wanted. Always send sample, and state whether straight or wavy hair is wanted.

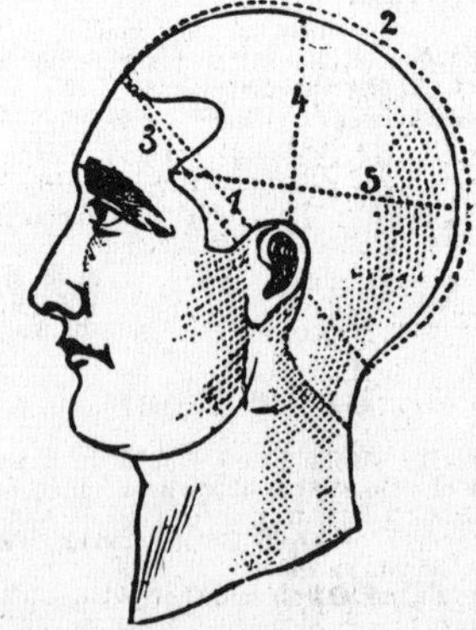

To Measure for a Wig.

No. 1.—Around the head - - .... inches.
No. 2.—From the hair on forehead to the pole of neck - .... inches.
No. 3.—From ear to ear across the crown - - - - - - - .... inches.
No. 4—From ear to ear over top of the head - - - - - .... inches.
No. 5.—From temple to temple around back of the head - .... inches.

The above are the measurements required for both ladies' and gents' wigs. Fill in the spaces.

NOTE.—As all real hair goods have to be made after order is given, it will take from three to six days to fill it. When goods are to be sent separate always enclose enough for postage.

HAIR GOODS.

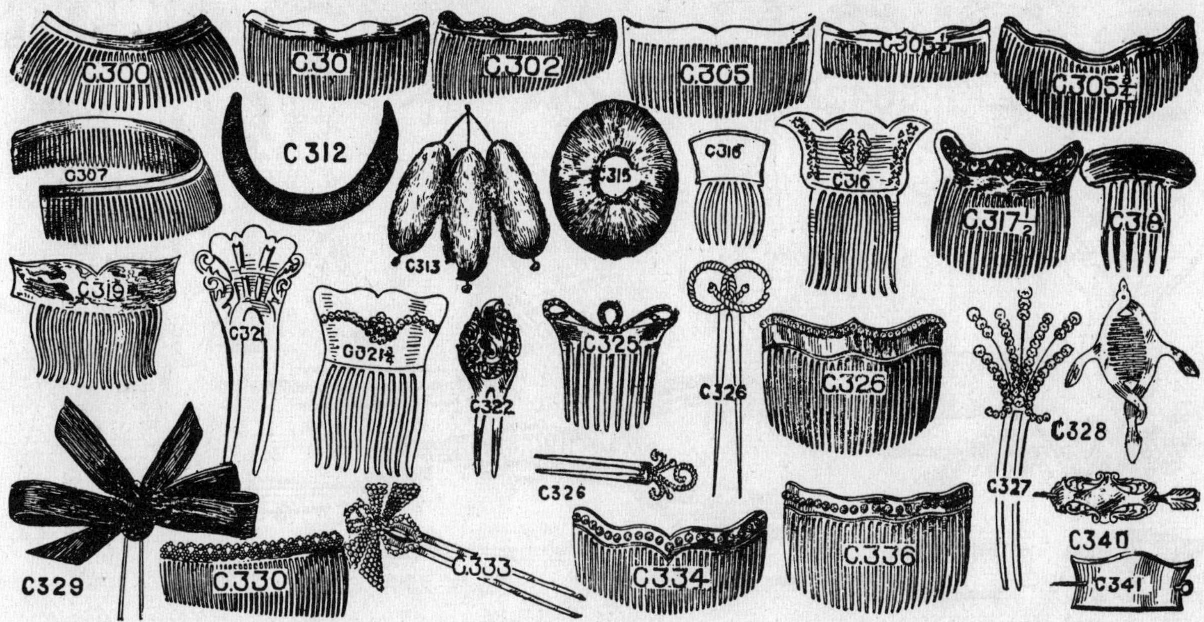

Side Combs.

C300. Side combs, shell, amber or black, curved top, special, 5c pair; heavier shell, straight or curved, 10c, 15c, 20c (see cut); extra heavy top, straight or curved, 25c, 30c pair.

C301. Side combs, superior quality and finish, extra heavy tortoise shell coloring, heavy top (see cut), 35c, 50c, 60c, 75c pair.

C302. Side combs, with white stone settings, American make, stones will not easily fall out, 35c, 50c, 75c pair; with best rhinestone settings, Parisian designs (see cut), $1.00, 1.25, 1.50, 1.75, 2.00 pair.

C303. Side combs, real tortoise shell, $2.25, 2.50, 2.75, 3.00 pair.

C304. Side comb sets, consisting of one pair side combs and puff comb, fancy shape, in shell, 50c, 60c set; in black, with jet beaded border, 50c, 60c, 75c set.

Pompadour Combs and Pads.

C305. **Chignon** or puff combs (see cut), can be worn front or back, 15c; heavier shell, 20c, 25c; same style, longer (these combs are very popular at present and are used for the present style of coiffure (see cut C305½), 20c, 25c; same style, with heavy plain shell, curved top (see cut C305¾), 35c, 40c, 50c each; with rhinestone setting, $1.50, 1.75, 2.00.

C306. **Bang** or puff combs, with brilliant settings, shell or amber, 75c, $1.00.

C307. **Pompadour** combs, shell, special line at 10c; better quality, shell, amber or black, 15c; larger size (see cut), 20c, 25c; better quality, extra heavy top, 30c, 35c, 40c, 50c; with rhinestone setting, $3.00.

C308. Combination side comb and hair band, for misses or ladies, plain band, 20c; fancy band, 25c.

C312. **Pompadour pads,** made of fine covered wire, in blonde, black and brown (see cut), 6 and 8-inch, 13c; 12 and 15-inch, 20c; 18-inch, 25c.

C313. **Frizzettes,** or hair pads, assorted browns (see cut), set of 3 for 10c; white or grey, 12½c; same style, single pad, assorted colors, 8 and 10-inch, 15c; 12, 14 and 16-inch, 20c; 18 and 20-inch, 25c.

C315. Wire hair frames, imitation hair covered, assorted browns, blonde or black, oval or round shape (see cut), 5c, 7c each.

Empire Combs and Fancy Pins.

C316. Shell back combs, plain or fancy top (see two cuts), 10c, 15c, 20c; heavier quality shell, low plain top (see cut C319), 25c, 35c, 40c, 50c.

C316½. Back combs and side combs, with plain gold-filled bands on top, latest Parisian novelty, 75c, $1.00.

C317. Parisian empire combs, tortoise shell colorings, low or high top, plain or fancy, 25c, 30c, 40c; same style, better quality, more fancy in design (see cut C317½), 50c, 65c, 75c; in real tortoise shell, plain or fancy, $2.75, 3.50, 4.75, 5.00 each.

C318. Plain tuck combs for elderly ladies, 10c each (see cut C318).

C319½. We carry a line of cheaper back combs at 5c each; these we do not recommend.

C321. 2-prong shell pins, fancy top (see cut), 10c, 15c, 20c, 25c; better quality, Parisian design, shell, black or amber (see cut C322), 50c each; with fancy brilliant tops (see two cuts C326 of stick pins), $1.00, 1.25, 1.50; with movable top, to be set high or rest flat on the hair (see cut C327), very pretty, $1.25, 1.50, 1.75.

C321½. Fancy brilliant pin with movable top, set with osprey, $1.00, 1.75, 2.00.

C321¾. Shell back combs, brilliant settings (see cut), 75c, $1.00; low top, best quality stones (see cuts C325 and C326 of back combs), $1.25, 1.50; high top, Parisian designs, $1.50, 1.75, 2.00, 2.25.

C328. The "Fin de Siecle" hair comb, does away with the use of hairpins (see cut), 25c, 50c each.

C329. **Velvet bow** for hair dressing (see cut), 25c; with black and colored velvet, very pretty, 50c.

Cut Steel Ornaments.

C330. Side combs, with cut steel trimmings, small size, 75c, $1.00; large, curved (see cut), $1.50, 2.00 pair.

C331. Shell back combs, with cut steel mountings, $1.00, 1.50, 2.50.

C332. Puff combs, steel trimmings, style of C305, 75c.

C333. Stick pin, movable top, fancy steel designs (see cut), 35c, 50c, 75c, $1.00; larger top, $1.75, 2.00.

Jet Ornaments.

C334. Black side combs, beaded border (see cut), 35c, 40c, 50c pair.

C335. Black jet back combs, fancy beaded design, 50c, 60c, 75c.

C336. Jet puff or bang combs (see cut), beaded design, 40c, 50c, 60c, 75c each.

C337. Real French jet side combs, 75c, $1.00, 1.25, 1.75; same style, in puff comb, $1.00, 1.25, 1.50; in fancy stick pins, pretty tops, $1.50, 2.25, 3.00.

C338. Real cut jet back combs, $1.50, 2.00.

Hair Fasteners and Binds.

C340. Celluloid braid pins, fancy design (see cut C34), 5c, 10c, 15c, 20c, 35c; in plain (see cut C341), 10c, 15c each.

C341. The "New Century" hair retainer, for holding the fine loose hairs away from the neck, also acts as a hair ornament, 50c.

C342. Hindes' patent hair binds (see cut C373), 10c each.

C312½. Celluloid hair clasps, for binding the hair (see cut C374), 10c each.

HAIR GOODS.

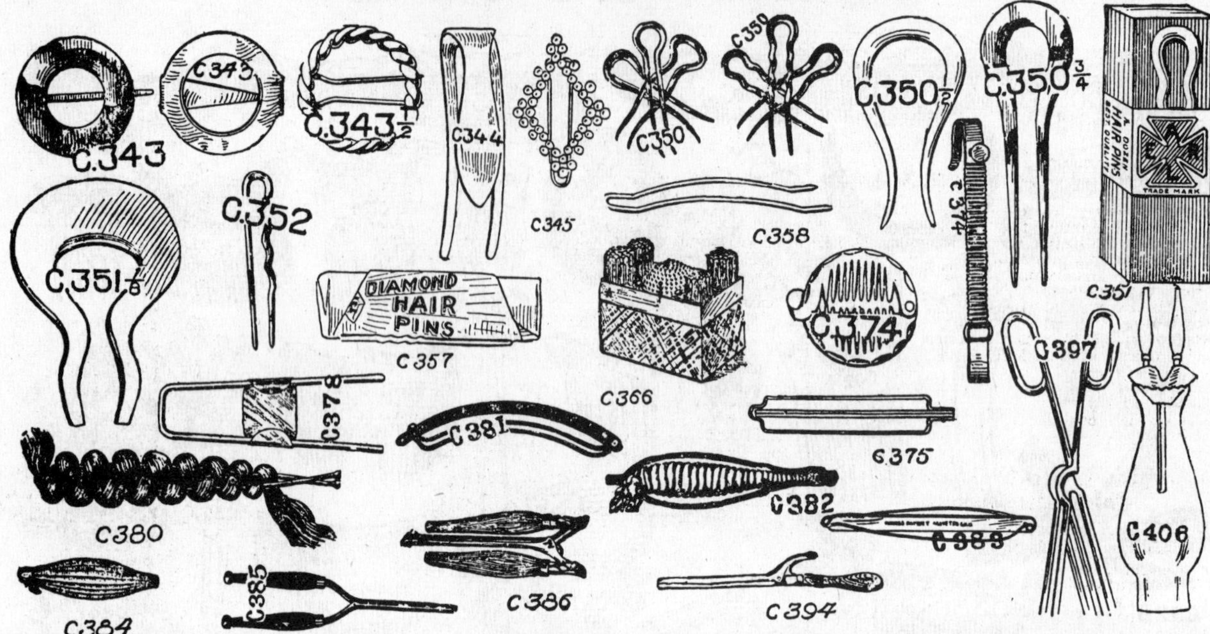

Hair Brooches and Ornaments.

C313. **Shell** hair clasps, for holding stray hairs at the back, oval or round shape (see two cuts, No. C343), 10c; also in fancy shapes, such as horseshoe, crescent, wish-bone, etc., 10c, 15c each.

C313½. **Gilt** hair clasps, latest New York style, in rope design (see cut), also in plain assorted shapes, 10c, 15c, 20c, 25c; gold filled, 50c, 75c.

C345. **Pressed steel** hair brooches (see cut), assorted designs, 25c, 35c, 50c; genuine French cut steel hair brooches, beautiful designs, 75c, $1.00, 1.50.

C347. **Fancy jet** hair or neck brooches, 35c, 50c, 75c, $1.50.

C344. Coiffure pins, for holding stray hair (see cut), 5c, 10c each.

Hair Pins.

C350. **Bone** hair pins, black, amber or shell, crimped, waved or straight (see cuts), 15c, 20c, 25c, 30c, 35c, 40c, 50c doz; with large round top (see cut C350½), 40c, 50c doz; larger size, heavier top (see cut C350¾), 5c, 8c, 10c each; extra large size (see cut C351⅛), 15c each.

C351. **"Earl brand"** hair pins, a special line we recommend for smooth finish, in crimped, waved or straight, all colors, medium size (see cut), 20c box of 1 doz; larger size, heavier shell, 25c box of ½-doz.

C352. Bone hair pins, with a straight and crimped pin (see cut), does not pull the hair or fall out easily, medium size, 20c doz; large size, 40c doz.

C353. **Rubber** hair pins, shell or black, crimped, waved or straight, 12½c, 20c, 25c doz; same style as C350½, 40c doz.

C354. **Wire** hair pins, "Hindes" ball point, put up in boxes of 18 pins, 2 for 5c; 50 pins, assorted, 5c box; 100 pins, assorted, 10c.

C357. The "**Diamond**" English hair pin (see cut), crimped or straight, 2½ to 3½ inches long, extra heavy wire, 2 pkgs for 5c; "Onduleur," better quality, not so heavy, best japanned, 3 pkgs for 10c.

C358. The "**Scientific**" hair pin, fastens the hair securely (see cut), 4c pkg, 3 for 10c.

C360. 100 best japanned hair pins, put up in a flat box, assorted styles and sizes, special, 5c box.

C361. Ball point hair pins, waved or straight, a special line, French japanned, 3 pkgs for 5c.

C362. **Gilt** hair pins, invisible, 25 pins in a box, 5c box; large size, crimped or plain, 18 pins for 5c.

C363. **Invisible** hair pins, best japanned, 50 pins in a box, 1½ to 2½ inches long, 2 for 5c.

C364. Steel point hair pins, 5c box.

C366. Unique hair pin cabinets (see cut), consists of 125 assorted hair pins, also toilet pins, 10c box; same, without toilet pins, consisting of 80 pins, put up in fancy paper or wooden cabinet, 5c.

Hair Nets.

C370. Invisible cotton, assorted browns and black, 2 for 5c; cotton and silk mixture, 5c; silk, 10c; real hair, 5c, 10c each; real hair, grey mixture, 15c each, 2 for 25c; pure white, 20c each.

C371. Front or bang nets, assorted browns or black, small size, 5c; large size, 10c; grey mixture, 15c; pure white, 20c.

Hair Curlers.

C375. In steel, no heating necessary (see cut), 5c doz.

C376. Hair wavers, made of lead, with woven cover, 5c, 10c doz.

C378. Waving pins, for waving the hair (see cut), 7c doz; better quality, 10c doz.

C380. "La Donna," French crimping pins, no heat necessary (see cut), 7c doz.

C381. Hindes' patent hair wavers, for making large waves (see cut), 25c box of 3 curlers.

C382. "Onduleurs" produces a natural and wavy appearance to the hair (see cut), 20c box of 5 curlers.

C383. Same style, with celluloid or steel centre bar (see cut), 20c box of 5 curlers.

C384. **Kid-covered** hair curlers (see cut), with sheepskin cover, 5c, 8c, 10c, 12½c, 15c doz, according to length; best quality and stitching, French kid, leather cover, 10c, 12½c, 15c, 20c, 25c doz.

Curling Tongs and Waving Irons.

C385. Curling tongs, double handle, small size, 3c; medium size, oak handle, 5c pair; large size, oak handle, 8c pair; nickel-tipped handle, medium size (see cut), 10c pair.

C385½. Curling tongs, nickel-plated rod and tipped handles, hand polished, rosewood finish, 12½c pair; large size, oak or polished walnut handles, 12½c pair; extra large size, for making large curls, 25c pair.

C386. Curling irons, folding handle, convenient to carry (see cut), oak handles, 8c pair; walnut handles nickel plated, chased rod and joints, put up in separate box, 25c pair.

C387. Gents' moustache curlers, 5c pair; nickel-tipped handles, 8c pair.

C388. "Grace Darling" curling iron, highly ornamented, spring will not weaken, as the heat cannot affect it, price according to size, 12½c, 15c, 20c, 25c pair.

C389. Curling tongs, imitation ebony handles, tubular rod and clamp, which prevents the heat going into the handles, tapered rod, 20c pair; with folding handles, 25c pair.

C394. The "Cute" curling iron, nickel plated, single oak handle (see cut), 10c pair.

C397. Waving irons, used for waving or crimping the hair (see cut), 5 prongs, 15c pair; large size, 20c pair; with wood handles, 20c pair; with folding wood handles, 25c pair.

C398. Lamp chimney stove for warming food, boiling water, etc., made of cast-iron, 5c each; the "Tip Top," also used for heating curlers, made of bright brass, 9c each.

C398½. Peerless lamp chimney, for heating tongs, also with removable top for warming food, heating water, etc., 20c each.

C399. Nicols' patent curling iron heater, will not blacken the tong while heating, 12½c each.

C406. The "Common Sense" curling iron heater (see cut), prevents chimney from being blackened while heating curlers, 5c each.

C407. Alcohol lamps, for heating curling iron, handy for travelling, 25c, 35c, 50c, 75c each.

Cloth Department, Shawls, Etc.

Mantle Cloths for Winter Wear.

54-inch English beaver cloth, black and navy, 75c yd.
54-inch English beaver cloth, black, navy, royal blue, fawn, brown and green, $1 00, 1.25, 1.50 yd.
54-inch all-wool beaver cloth, black, navy, fawn and brown, $2.00 yd.
54-inch all-wool frieze, black, navy, fawn, brown, green and Oxford grey, 75c yd.
54-inch genuine Harris Rockwood frieze, 28 oz., pure all-wool, colors black, navy, brown, green, grey and Oxford grey, $1.25 yd.
54-inch heavy all-wool cheviot, medium grey and Oxford grey, $1.00 yd.
54-inch heavy all-wool check-back tweeds, in Oxford grey only, $1.25 yd.
54-inch heavy plaid-back cheviots for golf capes, $1.50, 2.00 yd.
54-inch fancy all-wool tweeds for children's ulsters, $1.00 yd.
54-inch boucle curl cloth, in black and navy, $1.00 yd.

Light and Medium Weight Cloths for Ladies' Wear.

54-inch English cheviot mixtures, heavy weight, colors black, navy, fawn, brown, green, grey and Oxford, 60c yd.
54-inch fine all-wool English cheviot serges, 75c, $1.00, 1.25 yd.
50-inch broadcloth, colors black, navy, fawn, brown, cardinal and green, $1.25 yd.
50-inch German covert cloth, colors fawn, castor, brown, royal, black and navy, $1.40 yd.
52-inch satin-finished Venetian twill cloth, shades fawn, castor and black, $2.00 yd.

Astrachan Curl Cloth, etc.

48-inch black Astrachan curl cloth, $1.50, 2.00, 2.50, 3.00, 3.50, 4.00 yd.
48-inch grey Astrachan curl cloth, $3.00 yd.
48-inch cream Astrachan curl cloth, $3.00 yd.
48-inch cream bearskin cloth, $1.50, 2.00, 2.50 yd.

Silk Sealettes.

Black seal sealettes, 48 inches wide, $2.50, 3.00, 3.50, 4.00, 5.00, 6.00 yd.
Alaska sealette, seal brown, 48 inches wide, $2.50, 3.50, 5.00, 7.50 yd.

Matelasse Mantle Cloths.

50-inch black brocaded mantle cloths, $2.00 2.50, 3.00, 3.50, 4.00 yd.

Fascinators.

Ice wool fascinators, in white, black, sky and pink, 50c each.
Ice wool fascinators, in white or black, 65c, 75c each.

Infants' Sacques.

Style A. Infants' hand-made zephyr wool sacques, in all white, and white with blue or pink, 50c, 75c; with silk edging, $1.00.

Style B. Infants' hand-made zephyr wool sacques, empire style, in all white, and white with pink or blue trimming, 75c, $1.00.

Priestley's Cravenette Waterproof Cloth.

60-inch cravenette cloth, in black and navy, all-wool, $1.00 yd.
60-inch cravenette covert cloth, shades fawn, blue, Oxford grey and bronze, $1.25 yd.
56-inch cravenette cloth, all-wool, heavy quality, in black and navy, $1.50 yd.
56-inch cravenette covert cloth, heavy make and finest all-wool, $2.00, 2.50 yd.

Men's and Boys' Suitings.

27-inch Halifax tweed, 25c, 30c yd.
27-inch fancy tweeds, 30c, 35c, 40c, 50c, 60c yd.
27-inch striped panting tweeds, 30c, 35c, 50c, 60c yd.
27-inch navy blue serge, 30c, 35c, 50c yd.
28-inch English worsted trouserings, small neat designs, $1.00, 1.25 yd.
54 inch English serges, all-wool, shades black and navy, 75c, 85c, $1.00, 1.25, 1.50 yd.
56-inch English worsted serge suitings, colors black and navy, $1.50, 2.00, 2.50 yd.
56-inch English Clay worsteds, colors navy and black, $1.50, 2.00, 2.50 yd.
53-inch English black Venetian worsted, $1.50, 2.00, 2.50, 3.00 yd.
56-inch English Clay mixture worsteds, in grey shades, $1.50, 2.00, 2.50 yd.

Samples of any of these cloths can be had for the asking.

Shawls.

Ice wool shoulder shawls, in white or black, 50c, 65c, 75c, 85c each.
Knitted silk shawls, in black or white, $2.00, 2.50, 3.00, 3.50 each.
Honeycomb shawls, colors white, black, cardinal, grey, pink and sky, 45 inches square, 50c each.
Honeycomb shawls, with plain centre, colors white, black, cardinal, grey, pink and sky, 48 inches square, 75c each.
Honeycomb shawls, colors white, black, cardinal, grey, pink and sky, 58 inches square, $1.00 each.
Honeycomb shawls, in white, black, cardinal and grey, 62 inches square, $1.25, 1.50 each.
White honeycomb shawls, with silk border, $1.00, 1.25, 1.50, 2.00, 2.50 each.
Black melton cloth shawls, 50c, 75c, 85c, $1.00, 1.25, 1.50, 2.00 each.
Velvet shawls, assorted colors, $1.25, 2.00 each.
Heavy reversible shawl wraps, $1.50, 2.00, 2.50, 3.00, 4.00 each.

Measurement Diagram for Suits, Jackets and Skirts.

FRONT AND BACK.—1. All around neck, over dress collar, at bottom of collar.
1 to 2. From bottom of collar to waist line, not too long.
3. Bust measure, all around body, under arms, not too tight. (Take your bust measure well up under the arms around largest part of bust.)
3 to 4. Measurement across bust from armhole to armhole at largest part of bust.
5 to 6. Length of sleeves, inside seam.
7 to 8. Under arm to waist line, not too long. (This measurement should be taken along the line directly underneath the arm.)
8. Size of waist all around.
9 to 10. Length of back from bottom of collar to waist line, not too long.
11 to 12. Across back.
13. Hip measure, around body six inches below waist, not too tight.

Skirt.

14 to 15. Length in front from bottom of skirt belt to desired length.
16 to 17. Length on side from bottom of skirt belt to desired length.
18 to 19. Length in back from bottom of skirt belt to desired length.
(Be careful to have these measurements accurate when ordering suits or skirts.)

Take measurements carefully, and write them down plainly. Be sure to use an accurate tape measure. Do not make any allowance for seams.
When taking measurements, tie a cord around your waist in order that you may see exactly where your waist line is.
Pay particular attention to measurement 9 to 10, which gives the length of back from bottom of collar band to the waist line.
In taking your bust measure, have tape placed around your bust well up under the arms, around largest part of the bust. Do not take the bust measure too tight.

White Embroideries.

B5. 2½-inch, work 1¼-inch wide, 5c yd.

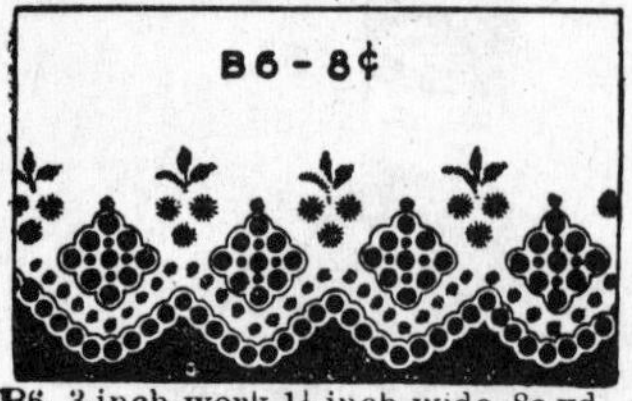

B6. 3-inch, work 1½-inch wide, 8c yd.

B7. 4-inch, with 2-inch work, 10c yd.

B8. 5-inch, with 2½-inch work, 12½c yd.

Cambric edgings, 1 to 2½-inch, work ½ to 1½-inch wide, 5c yd; 2 to 4-inch, work 1 to 2-inch, 8c yd; 2 to 5-inch, work 1 to 2½-in, 10c, 12½c, 15c, 20c yd.

Cambric insertions, 8c, 10c, 12½c, 15c, 20c yd.

Nainsook embroideries, 1 to 7-inch, 5c to 50c yd.

Nainsook insertions, 10c to 30c yd.

B8—12½¢

Swiss embroideries, 2½ to 5½-inch, 8c to 30c yd.

Swiss insertions, 10c to 20c yd.

Cambric flouncing embroidery for skirts, 8 to 10-in, 25c, 30c, 35c, 40c yd.

Cambric, nainsook, Swiss flouncing, for children's dresses, 22 to 27-inch, 35c, 50c, 65c, 75c yd.

Cambric, nainsook skirting, 44-inch, suitable for infants' long robes, 50c, 65c, 75c to $1.65 yd

Allovers, cambric and nainsook, 20-inch, 35c, 50c, 75c, $1.00, 1.50, 2.00, 2.25 yd.

Allover tucking, 20-inch cambric, 50c yd; 18-inch nainsook, 65c yd.

B358.

B358. Plantagenet frillings, white, for trimming underwear, 5c, 8c, 10c, 12½c, 15c, 20c yd.

Infants' Bibs and Feeders.

Quilted bibs, cambric, 5c each.

Fine cambric quilted bibs, with lace or embroidery trimming, new patterns, at 7c each, or 4 for 25c; 9c each, or 3 for 25c; 10c, 12½c, 15c, 20c each; and a special line at 18c each, or 3 for 50c.

Fine quilted cambric bibs, trimmed with neat embroidery, 25c each.

Silk-faced quilted bibs, lace and embroidery trimming, 9c each, or 3 for 25c; 10c, 12½c, 15c, 18c, 20c each.

Japanese silk quilted bibs, with fancy embroidered design, trimmed with lace or silk embroidery, 25c, 35c, 50c, 75c, 85c, and a special line, 65c each.

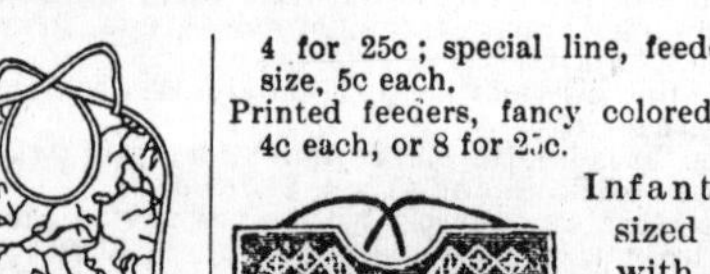

Fine hand-made mull bibs, quilted and embroidered, with fancy edges, 35c each, or 3 for $1.00; also same style, 25c, 50c each.

Oilcloth feeders, 5c each.

Oilcloth feeders, larger size, 7c each, or 4 for 25c; special line, feeders, large size, 5c each.

Printed feeders, fancy colored designs, 4c each, or 8 for 25c.

Infants' large sized feeders, with fringed and hem-stitched ends, 15c each.

Also a large variety of figured feeders, in crash and linen, 9c each, 3 for 25c; 10c, 12½c each.

Silk Chiffons, Frillings and Ruchings.

B83. Double edge shirred silk ribbon, ⅜ inch wide, in black, white, cream and all the leading shades, special, 5c yd.

B84. Double edge shirred silk chiffon ruching, ½ inch wide, in black, white, cream, rose, sky, and all the leading shades, 10c yd.

B85. Double edge shirred silk chiffon, 1 inch wide, in black, white, cream, rose, sky, and all the leading shades, 15c yd.

B86. Double edge chiffon ruching, suitable for dress trimmings and finishing yokes, in black, white, cream, and all the leading shades, 35c yd.

B88. Fancy chiffon frillings, in black, white, cream and colors, 15c, 20c, 25c yd.

B89. Something new in lisse frillings, in black, white and cream, 15c, 20c, 25c, 35c yd.

B90. Widows' lisse borderings, in black and white, 15c, 20c, 25c, 35c yd.

Widows' lisse borderings, in double row, 30c yd.

Double ruching for babies' bonnets, in white and cream, 30c yd.

B91. 1-inch muslin frilling, double row, suitable for nurses' caps, in white and cream, 5c yd, or 55c doz yds.

Also tourists' silk cord frilling, in white and cream, 5c yd, or 55c doz yds.

3-inch double ruching, in lisse and chiffon, suitable for neck ruffs and cape trimmings, in black only, 50c, 65c, 75c, $1.00 yd.

B93. 6-inch silk chiffon band, with satin edges, in black, white, cream, mais, sky, pink, Nile, heliotrope and cardinal, 8c yd.

B94. 14-inch silk chiffon, with satin-striped edges, in black and ivory only, 25c yd.

B95. 41-inch silk chiffon, in black, white, cream, mais, rose, sky, Nile, helio, and all the leading shades, special, 35c yd.

B96. 48-inch silk mousseline de soie, in black, white and cream only, 65c yd.

B96X. 46-inch pure silk chiffon, in black, white and cream only, 50c yd.

B97. 4-inch plaited chiffon, in black, white, cream, pink, sky, 12½c yd.

B98. 14-inch plaited chiffon, in black, white, cream, pink, sky, 25c yd.

B99. 22-inch plaited chiffon, in black, white and cream only, 35c yd.

We carry an extensive range of chiffon silk-embroidered laces, in fancy evening shades, embroidered in white on sky, pink, Nile and ivory, 3-inch, 15c; 5-inch, 20c yd.

Also 18-inch fancy embroidered chiffon allovers, in black and white, also two-tone effects, in fancy Persian designs, the very newest thing for yokes, fronts, sleeves, etc., $2.75, 3.00, 3.50, 3.75, 4.00, 4.50, 5.00, 5.50, 6.00, 6.50 yd.

FANCY NECKWEAR

We do not exchange fancy neckwear or linen collars that have been soiled or buttoned on.

B1. Ladies' chiffon jabot, lace trimmed, cascade effect, very dainty, 35c.

B2. Net tie, 9 inches wide and 2 yds long, white or cream, ends finished with tucks and lace, 50c, 65c.

B3. Chiffon jabot, in black or ivory, trimmed with silk lace (see cut), 35c.

B4. Fancy chiffon stock, with heavy cascade of plaited chiffon and ruched edge—a new piece of neckwear and very effective, in black, white, sky, pink and turquoise (see cut), $2.00.

B5. Ladies' golf stock, white pique stock, with tie of colored chambray, 50c.

B6. Fancy neck scarf, 1¾ yds long, embroidered edges and fancy ends, cream or ivory (see cut), 65c, 75c, $1.00.

B7. Chiffon scarfs, 1½ and 2 yds long, in ivory or black, with Luxieul and Battenburg ends, 65c, 85c, $1.00, 1.25, 1.50, 2.00.

B8. Taffeta silk corded collar, feather boned, with hemstitched edges, may be fastened in a variety of ways, similar to cut, all colors, 85c.

B9. Featherboned silk collar, same as B8, but with row of hemstitching through centre, $1.00.

B12. Ladies' sixfold satin stock collar, best quality, plain round shape, as cut B15, in black, white, cream, pink, cardinal and sky, 25c.

B13. Satin stock collar, with fancy turnover flap, colors as B12, 25c.

B15. Four-fold satin stock, colors as B12, 15c.

B16. Ladies' children or men's Windsor ties, pure silk, in tartans, and fancy plaids, including McKenzie, Forbes, Royal Stewart, Victoria, McDuff, Gordon, Hunting Stewart, also plain colors, with hemstitched ends, in white, black, pink, cardinal, sky and heliotrope, 25c.

Cheaper lines, in plain colors and fancy plaids and polka dots, 12½c, 15c.

B17. Ladies' fancy stock and tie, in flowing end shape, taffeta silk, in all the new colors, trimmed with silk applique or plaited chiffon, $1.50, 2.00.

B18. Lace scarfs, in cream or white, 1½ yds long, 3 to 5 inches wide, 15c, 25c, 35c, 50c, 85c.

B19. Fancy sailor collar, satin ribbon, with heavy guipure lace, $1.50.

B20. Ladies' fancy chiffon front, for wearing with Eton jacket, trimmed with lace and velvet baby ribbon (see cut), $1.75.

B21. Ladies' fine sailor collars, with revers, in batiste and guipure, in cut-out effect, for wearing with jacket, $1.00, 1.50, 2.00.

B22. Ladies' silk Windsor scarfs, 2 yds long, with fringed ends, black, white, pink, cardinal and sky, 50c.

B23. Ladies' shield bow, for wearing with stand-up turndown collar, all the leading colors, fancy plaids and polka dot, in silk and satin, see cut, 15c.

B24. Ladies' lawn bows, with square or pointed ends, silk stitched, 3 for 25c.

B25. Ladies' white lawn strings, 2 for 5c, 25c doz.

B26. Ladies' string ties, in silk or satin, stripes, plaids, or polka dots, 15c.

B27. Bolero or Zouave jacket, being very much worn for fall, good effects, in heavy guipure lace, $1.50, 2.00, 2.50; Battenburg and gold braid effects, $4.00, 5.00, 6.50.

B28. Fancy fichu, silk or chiffon, with lace or chiffon trimming, long or short ends, all colors, see cut, $1.50 to 3.00.

B29. New stock collar, covered with guipure lace, trimmed with velvet baby ribbon, all colors, $1.00.

B48. Fine embroidered tab collars, as cut, white only, 10c, 15c, 20c, 25c, 35c.

B49. Ladies' featherbone foundation, for wearing under ribbon, cool, light, sizes 12½ to 14½, white or black (see cut), 15c.

B49X. Ladies' transparent foundation silk featherbone, covered with chiffon, in black or white, size 12½ to 14½, 35c.

B30. Cambric collar, 4-ply, 2¼-inch (as cut B32), 10c each.

B31. Linen collar, 4-ply, 1¾-inch (as cut B32), 12½c each.

B32. Linen collar, 4-ply, 2¼-inch (as cut), 12½c each.

B34. Linen collar, stand-up, with 2½-inch turn-down, 4-ply (as cut B35), 12½c each.

B35. Linen collar, stand-up, with 2¾-inch turn-down, 4 ply (as cut), 12½c.

708. Linen collar, plain stand-up, with round corners, 4-ply, 2¼-inch (as cut), 15c each.

B50. Linen collar, stand-up, with 2¾-inch turn-down square corners, 4-ply (as cut), 12½c each.

B51. Linen collar, stand-up, with 3-inch turn-down, round corners, 4-ply (as cut), 12½c each.

B53. Linen collar, clerical shape, with high back, front 2¼-inch; back, 2¾-inch, 4-ply (as cut), 12½c each.

9010. Cambric cuff, with round corners, 1 button, 2½-inch wide (as cut), 15c pair.

INO. Linen cuff, square corners, 2 buttons, 4-ply, 3-inch wide, 20c pr.

B80. Boys' Eton collars, up-to-date, linen, front 2 inches, back 3 inches, square corners, 15c each.

B81. Boys' Eton collars, round corners, 2-inch back, 2½-inch front (as cut), 12½c each.

B82. Ladies' linen chemisettes, in white only, 25c each.

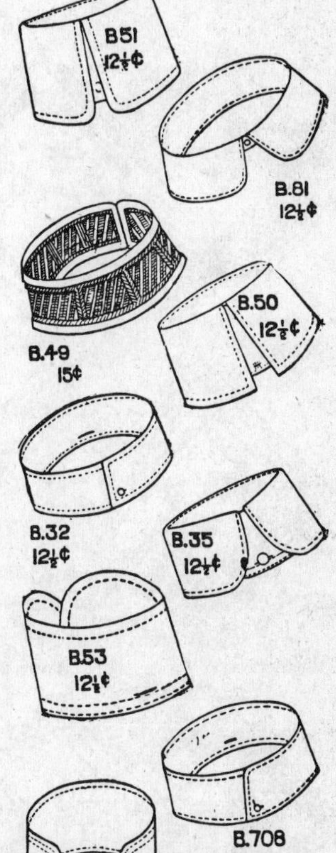

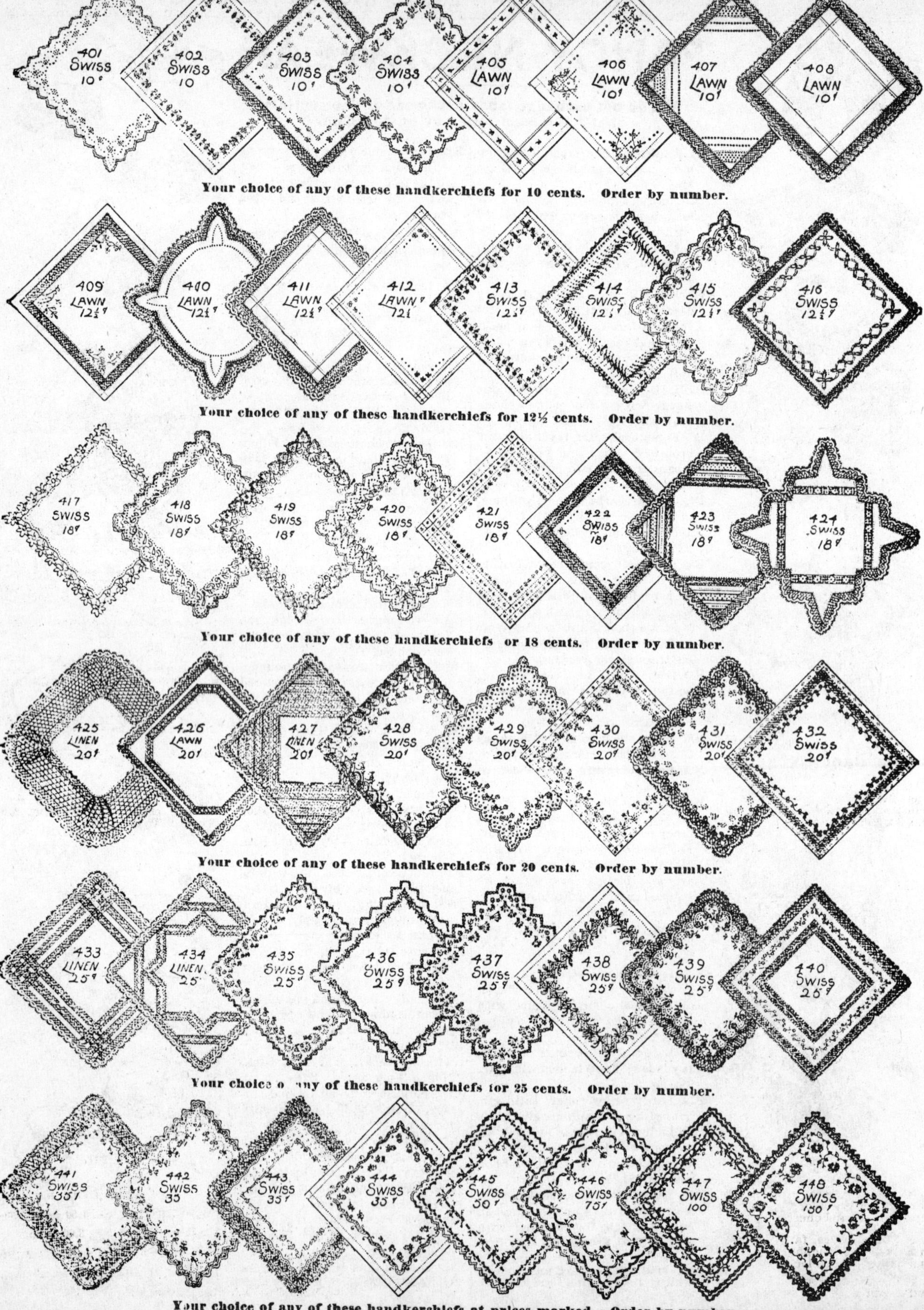

Your choice of any of these handkerchiefs for 10 cents. Order by number.

Your choice of any of these handkerchiefs for 12½ cents. Order by number.

Your choice of any of these handkerchiefs or 18 cents. Order by number.

Your choice of any of these handkerchiefs for 20 cents. Order by number.

Your choice o any of these handkerchiefs for 25 cents. Order by number.

Your choice of any of these handkerchiefs at prices marked. Order by number.

HANDKERCHIEFS.

Cotton Handkerchiefs.

101. Children's handkerchiefs, 6 in fancy box, 15c box.

10X. 3 neat lace-trimmed lawn handkerchiefs, in fancy box, 25c.

102. Children's plain white hemmed Irish lawn, also colored borders, 20c, 24c, 30c doz.

103. Ladies' plain white hemstitched Irish lawn, also colored borders, 8 for 25c; 6 for 25c; 4 for 25c.

104. Ladies' plain white hemstitched and initialled Irish lawn, 4 for 25c; 3 for 25c.

105. Ladies' Irish lawn hemstitched, black bordered, 6 for 25c; 4 for 25c.

106. Men's tape-bordered Irish lawn, large size, 8 for 25c; 6 for 25c; extra large, 4 for 25c.

107. Men's plain white hemstitched Irish lawn, also colored borders, 4 for 25c; 3 for 25c.

108. Men's colored handkerchiefs, red and white, also blue and white, 6 for 25c; 4 for 25c; 3 for 25c; 2 for 25c, and 10c each.

109. Nurses' kerchiefs, extra large hemstitched squares, 18c, or 3 for 50c, and 25c each.

Linen Handkerchiefs.

110. Handkerchief centres, pure Irish linen, 8 and 9 inches square, ½-inch hemstitch, 3 for 25c; 2 for 25c; finer line, 9 x 9 inches, 15c each.

111. Ladies' 12-inch fine Irish linen, hemstitched, ¼ and ½-inch hems, 3 for 25c, 10c, 12½c, 15c each, or $1.70 per doz; 18c each, or 3 for 50c; 20c each, or $2.25 doz. Finest linen made.

112. Ladies' full size pure Irish linen, hemstitched, wide and narrow hems, 4 for 25c, 3 for 25c, 10c, 12½c each; finer lines, 15c each, or $1.70 doz; 18c each, or $2.00 doz; 20c each, or $2.25 doz; 25c each, or $2.75 doz.

113. Ladies' extra fine sheer linen, hemstitched, ¼ and ½-inch hems, 12½c, 15c, 18c, 20c, 25c, 35c each.

114. Ladies' hemstitched and initialled fine Irish linen, 2 for 25c, 18c each, or $2.00 doz; 25c each, or $2.75 doz. See cut B218.

115. Men's hemstitched pure Irish linen, wide and narrow hems, 10c, 12½c, 15c each, or $1.70 doz; 18c each, $2.00 doz; 20c each, or $2.25 doz; 25c each, or $2.75 doz; 35c each, or $4.00 doz.

116. Men's hemstitched extra large fine Irish linen, wide and narrow hems, 30c each, or $3.40 doz; 35c each, or $4.00 doz; 45c each or $5.00 doz; 60c each, or $6.75 doz.

117. Men's initialled fine Irish linen hemstitched handkerchiefs, 25c each, or $2.75 doz; 35c each, or $4.00 doz. See cut B226.

118. Men's tape border pure Irish linen, medium size, 4 for 25c, 3 for 25c, 12½c, 15c each, or $1.70 doz; 18c each, or $2.00 doz; 20c each, or $2.25 doz; 25c each, or $2.75 doz; 30c each, or $3.40 doz; 35c each, or $4.00 doz.

119. Men's large size pure Irish linen, tape borders, 2 for 25c, 15c each, or $1.70 doz; 18c each, or $2.00 doz; 20c each, or $2.25 doz; 25c each, or $2.75 doz; 35c each, or $4.00 doz; extra large, 18c each, or $2.00 doz; 20c each, or $2.25 doz; 25c each, or $2.75 doz; 35c each, or $4.00 doz.

Mourning Handkerchiefs.

120. Ladies' pure Irish linen, with neat black borders, also men's, 12½c, 15c, or $1.70 doz; 18c each, or $2.00 doz; 20c each, or $2.25 doz; 25c each, or $2.75 doz.

Fancy Handkerchiefs.

121. Swiss, with neat embroidered edges, also hemstitched and embroidered and lace trimmed, 3 for 25c; 10c, 12½c, 15c; 18c each, or 3 for 50c; 20c, 25c; 35c each, or 3 for $1.00.

122. Swiss handkerchiefs, embroidered in black, 12½c, 15c; 18c each, or 3 for 50c; 20c, 25c each.

123. Linen, embroidered in black, 35c each, or 3 for $1.00; 50c each.

124. Linen, embroidered in white, 35c each, or 3 for $1.00; 50c, 65c, 75c, 85c each.

125. Embroidered linen, extra fine, $1.00, 1.25, 1.50, 1.75, 2.00 each.

126. Embroidered, with neat guipure edges, very fine, 65c, 75c, 85c, $1.00, 1.75, 2.00, 3.50 each.

Real Lace Handkerchiefs.

127. Maltese, deep lace edge, 65c, $1.00, 1.25, 1.50, 2.00, 2.25, 2.50, 3.00 each.

128. Honiton, $1.50, 2.00, 2.50, 3.00, 3.50, 4.00, 4.25, 5.00 each, and upwards.

129. Brussels point, $10.00, 15.00, 20.00, 25.00 each, and upwards.

130. Maltese lace silk, 25c, 35c, 50c, 65c, 75c, 85c, $1.00, 1.25, 1.50, 2.50 each.

Silk Handkerchiefs.

Plain cream Japanese, hemstitched, pure silk, 10c, 15c, 20c; large size, special, 25c each.

Plain cream hemstitched Japanese pure silk, also twilled, 50c, 75c, $1.00 each, extra heavy.

Ladies' embroidered cream silk, neat patterns, 50c, 65c, 75c, 85c, $1.00 each.

Men's tape border Japanese pure silk, large size, 25c, 35c, 65c each.

Men's tape bordered initialled Japanese pure silk, extra large and heavy, 65c each.

Black hemstitched Japanese pure silk, 25c, 35c, 50c, 75c each.

Brocaded silk handkerchiefs, cream, 25c, 35c, 50c, 65c, 75c; extra heavy, $1.00, 1.25, 1.50 each.

Brocaded silk handkerchiefs, in colors, 25c, 35c, 50c, 65c, 75c each; extra heavy, $1.00, 1.25, 1.50 each.

Japanese paper table napkins, 25c, 35c, 45c, 50c per hundred.

MUFFLERS.

144. Cotton mixture, plain cream, also plain with colored polka dot, fancy stripes and checks, 15c, 20c.

145. Cotton mixture, fancy colored, in polka dots, shepherd's checks and broken plaids, 15c, 20c, 25c, 35c.

146. Cashmere all-wool plain cream, and cream with colored polka dot and fancy light stripes, 25c, 35c, or 3 for $1.00.

147. Colored cashmere, all wool, in light and dark colors, plaids and polka dots, also fancy silk mixtures, 35c, 50c, 75c.

148. Cashmere, pure wool, in shepherd's plaids, black and white check, 25c, 35c, 50c.

149. Colored silk, large size, brocaded, fancy stripes and plaids, newest designs, 75c, $1.00, 1.25, 1.50 each; extra heavy, $2.00, 2.25, 2.50, 3.00 each.

150. Black silk mufflers, hem-stitched, twilled, also black and white shepherd's plaid, with tape bordered edge, 75c, $1.00, 1.25, 1.50 each.

151. Cream brocaded silk mufflers, large size, 75c, $1.00, 1.50 each; extra heavy, $2.00, 2.50, 3.00 each.

152. Cream Japanese pure silk, hemstitched, twilled, extra large size, 75c, $1.00 each.

LADIES' NIGHT GOWNS.

54, 56, 58 AND 60 INCHES LONG.

50. Cotton, Mother Hubbard, frill of cotton 35c
51. Cotton, yoke of 4 clusters tucks, 2 rows insertion, revers each side, frill on neck and down front 50c
52. Fine cotton, yoke of insertion, revers of embroidery, frill of embroidery down front, 75c; E. L. S..................$1.00
53. Fine cotton, 4 rows insertion, 4 clusters tucks, double frill of embroidery 88c
54. Fine cotton, yoke solid tucking, finished with frill of fine embroidery, $1.00; E. L. S.................................$1.25
55. Fine cotton, Empire style, trimmed with lace insertion and frill........$1.25
56. Fine cambric, Empire front, 3 rows insertion and embroidery, revers solid tucking, fine embroidery, $1.50; E. L. S.$2.00
57. Fine nainsook, round yoke of 2 rows insertion, puffing and frill of embroidery $1 75
58. Fine nainsook, Empire style, fancy front of insertion and lace, revers of insertion tucks and lace $2.00
59. Fine cambric, collar of insertion, finished with fine embroidery, ribbon and embroidery on neck, $2.25; E. L. S...$2.85
60. Fine nainsook, yoke of 2 clusters tucks and 4 rows insertion, ribbon beading across front, finished with frill of fine valenciennes lace, frill of lace on neck and down front $2.50
61. Nainsook, Empire style, 2 rows insertion, beading ribbon, insertion and frill of wide embroidery down each side..$2.50
62. Nainsook, fancy pointed yoke of solid tucking, finished with insertion, wide frill of embroidery and ribbon, neck of beading ribbon and embroidery, tucked back, $2.75; E. L. S............ $3.50
63. Nainsook, Empire front, round neck of valenciennes insertion, beading and ribbon, wide frills of lawn, with insertion and valenciennes lace............. $4.00

LADIES' FLANNELETTE GOWNS.

SIZES 54, 56, 58, 60 INCHES. Extra large sizes 10 per cent. extra.

75. Striped flannelette, Mother Hubbard yoke of 1-inch tucks, turn-down collar, front finished with braid 39c

76. Striped flannelette, Mother Hubbard yoke, turn-down collar, finished with frilling 50c

77. Striped flannelette, Mother Hubbard yoke, turn-down collar, finished with frill of goods, frilling down front and on sleeves 55c

78. Striped flannelette, Mother Hubbard yoke, turn-down collar, finished with frill of goods edged with fine torchon lace 65c

79. Striped flannelette, extra good quality, front finished with tucks, turn-down collar, frilling on collar and 2 rows down front 75c

80. Plain shades, white, pink and blue, front tucked, turn-down collar, frilling of goods on sleeves, collar, and 2 rows down front......75c

81. Plain shades, Mother Hubbard yoke, collar finished with frill of goods, 2 rows of frilling down front, double yoke in back...........85c

82. Plain shades, Empire style, front finished with tucks and frilling, silk flossed, fancy collar of tucking, finished with frilling, silk flossed, box-plaited back $1.00

83. Plain shades, Mother Hubbard yoke, turn-down collar, finished with handsome silk embroidery, same shades as flannelette, pearl buttons $1.15

84. Plain shades, Mother Hubbard yoke, handsomely trimmed with frilling of goods, hemstitched and flossed with silk, turn-down collar, flossed with silk, pearl buttons $1.25

85. Plain shades, front tucked with clusters of tucking, turn-down collar, with silk flossing and frilling edged with fine torchon lace, front elaborately trimmed with two frills, edged with fine torchon lace and silk flossing $1.25

86. Plain shades, front tucked with fine tucking, collar finished with silk flower, hemstitched, frill of goods edged with torchon lace, front finished with 2 rows of frilling edged with fine torchon lace, silk hemstitching on centre piece, box-plaited back $1.50

87. Plain shades, front tucked, sailor collar, finished at corners with silk flossing, frill of goods edged with fine torchon lace and handsomely flossed with silk flossing, front prettily trimmed with frilling, lace and silk flossing, pearl buttons $1.50

88. Plain shades, front tucked in clusters, finished with straps of hemstitching, frill of silk embroidery round neck and down front, pearl buttons $1.50

89. Plain shades, Mother Hubbard yoke, neck, front and sleeves finished with wide silk embroidery, pearl buttons $1.55

90. Plain shades, front tucked with cluster tucks, turn-down collar, finished with flossing and pretty silk embroidery, front with 2 rows of silk flossing and silk embroidery, pearl buttons $1.65

91. Plain shades, Empire style, front finished with beading, ribbon and silk embroidery, collar finished with cluster of tucks and frill of wide silk embroidery $1.75

92. Plain shades, front of clusters of tucks, double frill of silk embroidery down front, sailor collar, finished with frill of silk embroidery, double frill on sleeves $2.00

LADIES' SKIRTS.

100. White cotton, deep hem, 1 cluster tucks, 38 and 40 inches **25c**

101. White cotton, umbrella frill, 2 clusters tucks, 38 and 40 inches **50c**

102. White cotton, 1 cluster tucks, deep flounce of embroidery, 38 and 40 inches **75c**

103. White cotton, umbrella frill, finished 1 cluster tucks and wide frill of embroidery and braid, 38 and 40 inches **1.00**

104. White cotton, very fine, deep umbrella frill of hemstitched tucking, 38 and 40 inches **1.10**

105. Fine cotton, wide umbrella frill of 3 clusters of tucks and wide flounce of embroidery, dust frill, 38 and 40 inches **1.25**

106. Fine cotton, wide frill, finished with cluster of solid tucking and frill of extra fine embroidery under frill, 38 and 40 inches **1.50**

107. Fine cambric, umbrella frill, 1 row of valenciennes insertion and frill of lace, dust frill, 38, 40 and 42 inches..... **1.75**

108. Fine cambric, wide umbrella frill, 3 clusters tucks, 2 rows fine valenciennes insertion. frill of lace, dust frill, French band, 38, 40 and 42 inches **2.25**

109. Fine cambric, deep umbrella frill of lawn with hemstitched tucks, flounce of fine embroidery, dust frill, 38, 40 and 42 inches **2.50**

110. Fine cambric, wide umbrella frill, finished with 2 rows of extra fine valenciennes insertion and frill of lace under frill, French band, 38, 40 and 42 inches **2.75**

111. Fine cambric, 2 rows fine insertion, cambric frill, finished with fine embroidery, dust frill, 38, 40 and 42 inches. **3.50**

112. Fine cambric, umbrella frill of lawn, valenciennes insertion and tucks down frill, 1 row of valenciennes insertion and deep edge of lace around skirt, dust frill, 38, 40 and 42 inches **4.50**

113. Fine cambric, wide umbrella frill, 1 row of fine valenciennes insertion across top of frill, insertion down frill, finished at bottom with wide flounce of very fine lace, dust frill, 38, 40 and 42 inches . **4.25**

LADIES' DRAWERS AND CHEMISES.

E. L. S. means Extra Large Size.

Drawers.

25 and 27 inches.

150. White cotton, 1 cluster tucks, frill of lace 12½c
151. White cotton, 1 cluster tucks, wide frill of cambric 25c
E. L. S. 35c
152. Cotton, 1 cluster tucks, umbrella frill, with hemstitched tucks 35c
153. Fine cotton, 1 cluster tucks, wide frill of embroidery 39c
E. L. S 50c
154. Fine cotton, hemstitched tucking, frill of embroidery 50c
E. L. S 65c
155. Fine cotton, umbrella frill, cluster tucks, frill of lace 50c
E. L. S 65c
156. Fine cambric, umbrella frill, finished with row insertion, frill of embroidery 75c
157. Cambric, 1 row valenciennes insertion, frill of valenciennes lace 85c
158. Cambric, umbrella frill, finished cluster of hemstitched tucks, wide embroidery 1.00
159. Cambric, row fine insertion, with ribbon frill, extra fine embroidery 1.50

Flannelette Drawers.

Sizes 30, 32, 34 inches long.

175. Striped flannelette, elastic at knee 22c
176. Fancy striped flannelette, elastic at knee, silk embroidered 28c
177. Heavy flannelette, in light and fancy stripes, elastic at knee 35c
178. Same as 177, silk embroidered 38c
179. English flannelette, fancy stripes, elastic at knee, edge of lace 45c
180. Plain flannelette, colors white, pink, blue, elastic at knee 35c
181. Same as 180, silk embroidered 43c
182. Plain English flannelette, elastic at knee, edge of lace 45c
183. English flannelette, plain color, white only, finished cambric embroidery 50c
184. Same as 183, finished with Swiss silk embroidery 55c
185. Grey union flannel drawers, elastic at knee 55c
186. Grey all-wool flannel, elastic at knee 68c
187. Same as 186, heavily silk embroidered 75c
188. Fine red flannel, elastic at knee, silk embroidered 1.00

Chemises.

200. White cotton, lace on neck and arms 12½c
201. White cotton, frill of cambric on neck, arms and down front 28c
202. Fine cotton, finished with frill of fine embroidery 43c
203. Fine cotton, front of tucking insertion and embroidery 50c
204. Cambric, pointed front of 1 row lace insertion and frill of lace, with ribbon 85c
205. Cambric, front of insertion and embroidery, arms and neck trimmed with embroidery 1.00
206. Cambric, long chemise, finished with insertion lace and ribbon, frill finished with edge of lace 1.75
207. Cambric yoke, finished with 2 rows lace insertion, 3 rows beading, frill of lace top and bottom of yoke, frill at bottom finished with tucks and lace 2.25
225. Flannelette chemise, fancy stripes in pink and white, blue and white, frill around neck 25c
226. Flannelette chemise, plain colors, pink, white and blue, button front, frill around neck and down front 35c

CORSET COVERS AND SETS.

Corset Covers.

32 to 40 inches.

250. White cotton, high neck, close fitting ... 9c
251. White cotton, square neck, finished with edge of lace 22c

252. Fine cotton, pointed yoke of fine embroidery 25c

253. Cotton, low neck, French front, embroidery on neck and arms 35c

254. Cotton, French style, full front, trimmed on neck and arms with frill and edge of lace 40c

255. Fine cotton, yoke of insertion and tucks, finished with edge of embroidery around yoke and on arms 50c

256. Cambric, French style, front of tucks, finished with beading, baby ribbon and fine embroidery 65c

257. Nainsook, 3 rows beading, 2 rows lace insertion, frill of lace on neck and sleeves, French style 75c

258. Nainsook, full front, hemstitched tucks, beading ribbon and lace on neck 85c

259. Fine cambric, front tucked, square neck, 2 rows insertion, fine embroidery around neck and arms 1.00

260. Nainsook, front of fine valenciennes lace, beading ribbon and frill of lace around neck, ribbon at waist 1.25

261. Nainsook, French style, 4 rows fine insertion, frill of embroidery on neck and sleeves 1.50

Flannelette Corset Covers.

275. Fancy stripes, pink and white, blue and white, high neck, plain 18c

276. Plain colors, pink, white, and blue, high neck 22c

Bridal Sets.

Set 300. Fine cotton. **Gown**, 54 to 60 inches, sailor collar style, front tucked and lace finished, collar of wide lace. **Corset cover**, 32 to 40 inches, tucked front, square yoke of insertion and lace, arms trimmed with lace. **Drawers**, 25 and 27 inches, umbrella frill, finished with lace. Three pieces complete 2.50

Set 301. Cambric. **Gown**, round neck of lace insertion beading and frill of lace. **Drawers**, umbrella frill, valenciennes insertion, frill of lace. **Corset cover**, pointed neck of beading ribbon and frill of valenciennes lace. Three pieces complete 4.00

Set 302. Fine cambric. **Gown**, Empire style, front of 1 row beading, 2 rows insertion, frill of embroidery, collar of 2 rows insertion, frill of fine embroidery. **Corset cover**, pointed neck, finished with 2 rows insertion, 1 row beading and ribbon, frill of fine embroidery on neck and arms. **Drawers**, beading and ribbon, frill of extra fine embroidery. Three pieces complete 6.50

Ladies' Aprons and Children's Pinafores.

Aprons.

350. Lawn, finished with hem and band 15c
351. Lawn, 3 1-inch tucks, wide hem and sashes 25c
352. Fine lawn, fine tucking, band and sashes 30c
353. Fine lawn, fine tucking, band and sashes extra wide 40c
354. Fine lawn, ½-inch tucks down side and across bottom 35c
355. Fine lawn, 2 rows fine insertion, band and sashes 50c
356. Fine lawn, 1 row wide insertion down side and across bottom 50c
357. Lawn, front of 1 row insertion and frill of embroidery, bib finished 2 rows insertion and frill of embroidery 28c
358. Lawn, deep hem, bib of insertion and tucks, revers of insertion and embroidery.38c
359. Lawn, bib of extra fine tucks, insertion and embroidery, skirt finished with deep hem and tucks 50c
360. Fine lawn, bib of tucks, insertion and embroidery, revers of fine insertion and embroidery, skirt finished deep hem and 1 row insertion 75c
361. Fine lawn, bib of tucks, insertion and embroidery, revers of fine insertion and embroidery, skirt finished with tucks, insertion and deep hem $1.00
362. Heavy plain linen, pocket hem and band 25c
363. Heavy linen, fancy striped border, hem and sashes 35c
364. Fine linen, yoke band, bib finished with rows fancy braid 35c
365. Blue colored Holland, pocket bib, finished with braid 35c
366. Heavy linen, wide hem, bib and straps over shoulders 45c
367. Black sateen, finished with hem, band and sashes 25c
368. Black sateen, better quality, with pocket, band and sashes 35c
370. Gingham, band and sashes, 20c; better quality 28c
371. Gingham, with bib and straps over shoulders 35c
375. Dusting caps, made of print, dark colors 15c
376. Night caps, fine cambric, tucks and frill 35c
377. Fine lawn, insertion frill, finished with fine lace 50c

Pinafores.

Sizes	1,	2,	3,	4,	5,	6,
Ages	2,	4,	6,	8,	10,	12 years.

400. Lawn, Mother Hubbard, frill of lawn...28c
401. Lawn, Mother Hubbard, frill of lawn and edge of embroidery 40c
402. Lawn, Mother Hubbard yoke, edge of lawn finished with frill of embroidery.....50c
403. Lawn, yoke of insertion and frill of embroidery 50c
404. Lawn, insertion across front, lapels of insertion and edge of lace 65c
405. Lawn, Mother Hubbard yoke, band of insertion and lace at neck, frill of lawn edged with lace 75c
406. Boys' overalls, 1 to 4 years, gingham, edged with lace 50c
407. Print or gingham pinafores, Mother Hubbard, finished with self frills 35c

6

CHILDREN'S UNDERWEAR.

Gowns.

Sizes 1, 2, 3, 4, 5, 6, 7, 8, 9, 10,
Ages 1½, 2½, 4, 5½, 7, 8½, 10, 12, 14, 16 years.

500. Cotton, Mother Hubbard, tucks and lace trimmed, sizes 1 to 4, 28c; 5 to 8, 33c; 9 to 10, 35c
501. Cotton, yoke of tucks, frill of cambric, sizes 1 to 4, 35c; 5 to 8, 43c; 9 to 10 ....47c
502. Cotton, yoke of insertion, tucks and frilling, 1 to 4, 38c; 5 to 8, 48c; 9 to 10 ....50c

Flannelette Gowns.

505. Striped flannelette, frill on neck and front, 1 to 4, 33c; 5 to 8, 38c; 9 to 10 ....45c
506. Striped flannelette, sailor collar, trimmed frill of self on collar and down front, 1 to 4, 37c; 5 to 8, 45c; 9 to 10 ....50c
507. Striped flannelette, style as 506, only better quality, 1 to 4, 50c; 5 to 8, 58c; 9 to 10 ......65c
507½. Striped flannelette, same as 507, only silk flossed, 1 to 4, 55c; 5 to 8, 65c; 9 to 10 ....75c
508. Plain flannelette, white, pink and blue, sailor collar, frill on collar and front, 1 to 4, 50c; 5 to 8, 58c; 9 to 10 ....65c
509. Plain flannelette, same as 508, only silk flossed, 1 to 4, 55c; 5 to 8, 65c; 9 to 10 ......75c
510. Plain flannelette, pink, white and blue, sailor collar, frill of self and edge of lace, 1 to 4, 65c; 5 to 8, 75c; 9 to 10......................85c
511. Fancy striped flannelette sleeping suits, button back, sizes 1 to 4 only 45c
512. Grey flannel sleeping suits, button back, sizes 1 to 4 only..............................85c

Drawers.

Sizes 1, 2, 3, 4, 5, 6, 7, 8,
Ages 2, 4, 6, 8, 9, 10, 12, 14 years.

550. White cotton, tucks and hem, sizes 1 to 4, 11c; 5 to 8.......................................12c
551. White cotton tucks and cambric frilling, sizes 1 to 4, 17c; 5 to 8 ....20c
552. White cotton tucks, embroidery frill, sizes 1 to 4, 27c; 5 to 8 ....32c
553. Fine cotton, umbrella frill, insertion tucks and lace frill, sizes 5 to 8...........................65c
560. Fancy striped flannelette, elastic at knee, sizes 1 to 4, 17c; 5 to 8 ....19c
561. Fancy striped flannelette, silk flossing, embroidery, sizes 1 to 4, 20c; 5 to 8 ....23c
562. Striped flannelette, best quality, elastic at knee, sizes 1 to 4, 22c; 5 to 8 ....28c
563. Same as 562, only silk flossed, sizes 1 to 4, 25c; 5 to 8..30c
564. Plain flannelette, pink, white and blue, elastic at knee, sizes 1 to 4, 23c; 5 to 8......28c
565. Plain flannelette, same as 562, silk flossed, sizes 1 to 4, 25c; 5 to 8 ....30c
566. Plain flannelette, pink, white and blue, elastic at knee, finished with edge of lace, sizes 1 to 4, 30c; 5 to 8 ....35c

Misses' Skirts.

Sizes 18 to 36 inches.

600. White cotton, 1 cluster tucks, deep hem, 18 to 24, 24c; 26 to 30, 26c; 32 to 36 ....28c
601. White cotton, 1 cluster tucks, frill of cambric, 18 to 24, 35c; 26 to 30, 40c; 32 to 36.....45c
602. Cotton, cambric frill, hemstitched tucks, 18 to 24, 60c; 26 to 30, 70c; 32 to 36..........80c
603. Cambric, umbrella frill, tucks and lace frill, 18 to 24, 80c; 26 to 30, 90c; 32 to 36 ..$1.00
604. Cambric, 2-cluster tucks, frill of embroidery, 18 to 24, 65c; 26 to 30, 75c; 32 to 36.....85c
605. Cambric, 2-cluster hemstitched tucks, frill fine embroidery, 18 to 24, $1.00; 26 to 30, $1.10; 32 to 36 ....$1.25
606. Fancy striped flannelette, with hem, 18 to 24, 25c; 26 to 30, 30c; 32 to 36.................35c
607. Striped or plain flannelette, striped fancy colors, plain pink, white and blue, frill of goods, 18 to 24, 28c; 26 to 30, 33c; 32 to 36 ..38c

Childs' Skirts.

1 to 4 years.

650. Cotton, waist, tuck and hem 30c
651. Cambric, 1 cluster tucks, frill of cambric 45c
652. Cambric, 1 cluster tucks, frill of embroidery 55c
653. Cambric, wide frill, with tuck, insertion and embroidery 85c
654. Fancy striped flannelette, with hem 30c
655. Plain flannelette, pink, white and blue..30c
656. Plain flannelette, same as 655, silk flossed 35c
657. Plain white flannel, silk embroidered ..65c
658. Plain white flannel, with hem 50c

Infants' Slips.

700. Night slip, cotton, cambric frill..........45c
701. Night slip, cotton, tucked yoke, cambric frilling 50c
702. Slip, cambric yoke of tucks and insertion, embroidery on neck and sleeves............75c
703. Slip, cambric, front of solid tucking and embroidery..85c
704. Slip, cambric, yoke of tucks, insertion and embroidery, insertion in skirt $1.15
705. Slip, nainsook, square yoke of 4 clusters tucks, 3 rows valenciennes insertion, frill edged with valenciennes lace, skirt finished deep hem and valenciennes insertion ..$1.25
706. Slip, nainsook, yoke of wide and narrow insertion, embroidery frill on neck, skirt finished with insertion $1.50
707. Slip, nainsook, pointed yoke, extra fine solid tucking, finished with frill of embroidery, skirt 2 clusters tucks, frill of wide embroidery $1.50
708. Slip, cambric, yoke of tucks, insertion and embroidery, tucks, insertion and embroidery on skirt...$1.50
709. Slip, lawn, yoke of tucks, insertion and lace, skirt finished with 7 clusters tucks, 5 rows valenciennes insertion and frill of lace. ..$2.50
710. Slip, lawn, yoke of 4 rows valenciennes insertion, fine nainsook beading, frill of lace, skirt finished 3 rows insertion, 2 rows beading and frill of lace...............................$2.75
711. Slip, lawn, yoke of 3 rows valenciennes insertion, frill of lace, insertion and lace on sleeves, skirt finished with 4 clusters tucks, 3 rows valenciennes insertion and frill of lace $3.50
712. Slip, fine lawn, yoke of tucks, Swiss and lace insertion, frill of lace, skirt finished 4 rows lace insertion, 2 rows Swiss insertion, 3 clusters tucks and frill of lace..............$3.75
713. Slip, striped flannelette, pink and white, blue and white.....................................55c
714. Slip, white flannelette, tucked front, frill on neck and sleeves 65c
Same, silk embroidered 75c

Long Skirts.

725. Nainsook, 2 clusters tucks, 1 row insertion, frill of embroidery $1.50
726. White flannel, deep hem, neatly silk embroidered...$1.50

Barrowcoats.

750. White flannelette, bound with silk braid.75c
750½. White flannel, bound with silk braid.$1.10

Head Shawls.

775. White flannel, embroidered 35c
776. White flannel, as cut 50c
777. White flannel, embroidered edges and corner 75c
778. White flannel, elaborately embroidered $1.00

Shirts.

779. Cambric, lace trimmed 12½c

Diapers.

780. White cotton, embroidery trimmed 25c
781. White cotton, as cut, embroidery frilling.38c
782. Rubber diaper, sizes 16 to 24 ....35c
783. Stockinette diaper, with buttons, sizes 16 to 24 ....50c
784. Stockinette, with buttons, Canfield, sizes 16 to 24 ....65c

Bibs.

785. Stockinette, with ties, Canfield..... ....30c
786. Stockinette, square, with ties............35c
787. Stockinette, large, with ties at waist and neck 50c

Sheets.

790. Stockinette carriage sheet, 18 x 24.......75c
791. Rubber crib sheet, 27 x 38..............$1.00
792. Stockinette crib sheet, 27 x 38 .... 1.25
793. Stockinette bed sheet, 37 x 60............2.50

Aprons.

794. Rubber, 36 inches long, check $1.15
795. Stockinette, 36 inches long 1.25

No. 1000. INFANTS' OUTFITS. No. 1001.

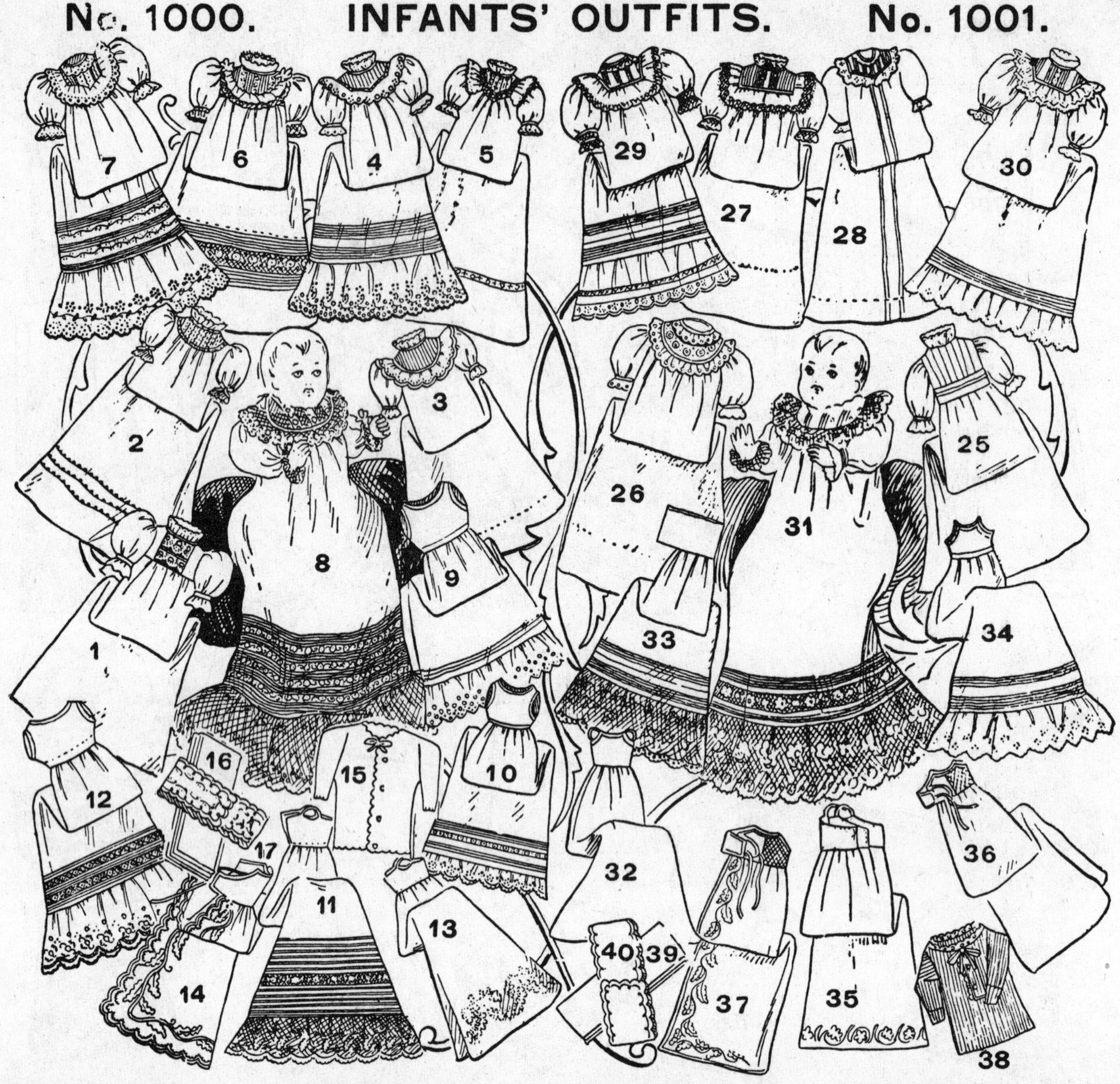

Outfit No. 1000.

1. 1 cambric night slip, front of embroidery, finished around neck and sleeves with embroidery $0 65
2. 1 cambric slip, yoke of hemstitched tucks, embroidery on neck and sleeves 0 75
3. 1 cambric slip, front of solid tucking and embroidery ... 0 85
4. 1 cambric slip, yoke of tucks and embroidery, skirts finished with tucks and embroidery 1 25
5. 1 nainsook slip, yoke of fine hemstitch tucks and insertion, embroidery over shoulder on neck and sleeves, insertion on skirt 1 50
6. 1 nainsook slip, yoke of insertion, tucks, frill of lace around yoke on neck and sleeves, skirt finished with insertion and tucks 1 85
7. 1 nainsook slip, yoke of insertion, with fine embroidery around yoke, neck and sleeves, skirt finished 3 clusters tucks, 2 rows insertion, frill embroidery 2 57
8. 1 lawn slip, yoke of 4 rows valenciennes insertion, fine nainsook beading, frill of lace, skirt of 4 rows insertion, 5 clusters tucks, frill of lace . $4 25
9. 1 skirt, cambric, 1 cluster tucks, frill embroidery 0 90
10. 1 skirt, cambric, 1 row insertion, 2 clusters tucks, frill of embroidery 1 10
11. 1 skirt, cambric, 2 clusters wide tucks, 1 row lace insertion, frill of lace 1 25
12. 1 skirt cambric, 2 rows insertion, 5 clusters tucks, frill of embroidery 1 25
13. 2 white flannel skirts, silk embroidered ($1.50) 3 00
14. 2 white flannel barrowcoats, silk embroidered ($1.50) 3 00
15. 2 vests, all wool, button front, white (30c) 0 60
16. 12 napkinettes, white canton flannel 1 50
17. 4 bands, white flannel, silk embroidered (20c) 0 80

34 pieces $27 25
Each garment separately at prices quoted, or outfit complete for **$25.50.**

Outfit No. 1001.

25. 1 nightslip, cambric, embroidery trimmed.. .... $0 60
26. 1 slip, cambric, yoke of insertion and embroidery.. .. 0 65
27. 1 slip, cambric, yoke of insertion, tucks, frill of lace around yoke and neck $0 85
28. 1 slip, cambric, pointed yoke of insertion, tucks and embroidery 1 00
29. 1 slip, cambric, yoke of insertion, frill of lace around yoke, insertion and lace on sleeves, tucks on skirt, frill finished with insertion and lace 1 15
30. 1 slip, cambric, yoke of tucks, insertion and embroidery, frill of embroidery and tucks on skirt 1 25
31. 1 slip, nainsook, yoke of insertion and tucks, lace around yoke, insertion, tucks and lace on skirt 2 00
32. 1 skirt, flannel, white, deep hem 1 00
33. 1 skirt, cambric, 2 clusters of tucks and frill of lace 1 00
34. 1 skirt, cambric, tucks and embroidery 0 85
35. 1 skirt, white flannel, silk embroidered 1 25
36. 1 barrowcoat, white flannel, silk braid binding 1 10
37. 1 barrowcoat, white flannel, silk embroidered 1 25
38. 2 vests, fine, all wool, button front, (25c) 0 50
39. 12 napkinettes, white canton flannel $1 50
40. 4 flannel bands, silk embroidered (15c) 0 60

30 pieces $15 55
Separately at prices quoted or complete for **$14.50.**

Outfit No. 1002.

41. 1 slip, cotton, cambric frill.. $0 45
42. 1 slip, cotton, tucked yoke, cambric frilling 0 50
43. 1 slip, fine cotton, embroidery trimmed 0 50
44. 1 slip, fine cambric, embroidery on neck and sleeves 0 60
45. 1 long skirt, cotton, tucks and hem 0 40
46. 2 long skirts, striped flannelette, deep hem (50c) 1 00
47. 2 barrowcoats, fancy striped flannelette (50c) 1 00
48. 2 bands, white flannel, silk embroidery (15c) 0 30
49. 6 napkinettes, bleached canton flannel 0 60
50. 2 cambric shirts, lace trimmed (12½c) 0 25

19 pieces $5 60
$5.00 complete, or separately at prices quoted.
Other outfits, **$10.00** and **$13.50.**

Vests and Drawers.

28 to 38 inches.

800. Vests, heavy cotton, natural...12½c
801. Vests, heavy ribbed cotton, natural color, button front 15c
802. Vests, extra heavy ribbed natural cotton 25c
802½ Drawers to match 802 ....25c
803. Vests, ribbed merino, style as 802, natural color, 39c ; drawers........45c
804. Vests, same quality as 803, color white, 45c ; drawers...............50c
805. Vests, heavy ribbed fine quality merino, natural color, 50c ; drawers.55c
806. Vests, best quality ribbed wool and cotton, button front, ribbons, long sleeves, natural color, 60c ; white, 65c ; drawers, natural color, 70c ; white..75c
808. Vests, ribbed all wool, white and natural, 75c ; drawers 85c
809. Vests, same quality as 808, black, 85c ; drawers......................$1.00
810. Vests, heavy ribbed Swiss all wool, ribbon trimming, white and natural, 75c ; drawers to match 85c
811. Vests, fine heavy ribbed all wool, button front, silk embroidery, ribbons, natural, 90c ; white, $1.00 ; drawers, natural, $1.00 ; white $1.10
812. Vests, extra heavy Swiss ribbed all wool, button front, neatly trimmed, white and natural, $1.15 ; drawers.$1.25
813. Heavy ribbed Swiss all-wool vests and drawers, 40, 42, 44 inches, button front, long sleeves, natural colors.$1.00
814. Vests, heavy ribbed merino, 40, 42, 44 inches, button front, natural colors, 65c ; drawers............................75c
815. Ribbed silk and cotton vests, pink, blue and white, no sleeves, 45c ; short sleeves, 50c ; long sleeves..........75c
816. Ribbed all-silk vests, pink, blue and white, no sleeves, $1.00 ; short sleeves, $1.25 ; long sleeves $1.75
820. Fancy ribbed vests, embroidered front, no sleeves, low neck, pink, white, blue, $1.25, 1.50, 2.00 to ...$3.75
825. Ribbed merino nursing vests, natural.. ....50c
826. Ribbed merino corset covers, natural, 25c ; better quality wool, white and natural 50c

Seal-lined Underwear.

200. Heavy ribbed vests and drawers, soft fleece lined, white, natural, ecru 45c
204. Heavy ribbed merino vests and drawers, soft fleece lined, fancy button front, cream and natural...... 65c
206. Heavy ribbed vests and drawers, wool fleece lined, fancy button front, white $1.00

---

830. Plain vests and drawers, heavy cotton, button front..................35c
831. Plain merino vests and drawers, same as 830 ....50c
832. Shetland wool vests and drawers. fine quality, natural color 55c
833. Natural wool vests, button down or across front, drawers............75c
834. Natural wool vests, heavy quality, button front, long sleeves, drawers ankle length $1.00
835. Natural wool vests, heavy, imported, long sleeves, button front, $1.00 ; drawers, $1.15 ; better quality, vests, $1.25 ; drawers $1.35

"Stuttgarter" Underwear

220. Vests and drawers, fine natural wool, button front, ankle length, $1.25 ; better quality, white and natural, vests, $1.65 ; drawers........$1.75
220. Combination suits, natural wool, $2.50 ; better quality, fine Australian wool, white and natural..........$2.75

Woolsey Brand.

836. Heavy natural wool vests, fine quality, imported, white and natural, $1.65 ; drawers, $1.75 ; combination suit...............................$2.75

Combination Suits.

850. Heavy ribbed merino, natural..$1.00
851. Heavy ribbed wool, style as 852, natural...............................$1.50
852. Heavy ribbed Swiss wool, natural and white $1.75
853. Heavy ribbed all wool, fine quality, button front, ankle length, long sleeves, white and natural.................$2.00
854. Heavy ribbed Swiss all wool, fine quality, white and natural $3.00
855. "Knit-to-fit," heavy merino, perfect fitting, white and natural $3.50
855. "Knit-to-fit," finest Australian wool, perfect shape, white and natural, $3.75 ; better quality $4.00
856. Heavy natural wool, button across or down front $1.50
857. Imported natural wool, button down front, long sleeves, ankle length, $2.00 ; better quality $2.50
858. Scotch wool, full fashioned, natural $3.00
882. Ribbed bands, all wool, white and natural 25c
882½. Ribbed bands, finest wool, white and natural 50c
880. Chamois vest, covered fine quality red felt, elastic at side, no sleeves, 32-inch, $1.50 ; 34-inch, $1.65 ; 36-inch, $1.85 ; 38 and 40-inch $2.00
881. Chamois vests, lined with fine red flannel, same style as cut, no sleeves, all sizes, $2.50 ; long sleeves......$3.00
883. Chest protectors, covered fine quality felt, size 1, 50c ; 2, 75c ; 3 ....95c
884. Black equestrienne tights, wool, 90c ; better quality, $1.15 and $1.50

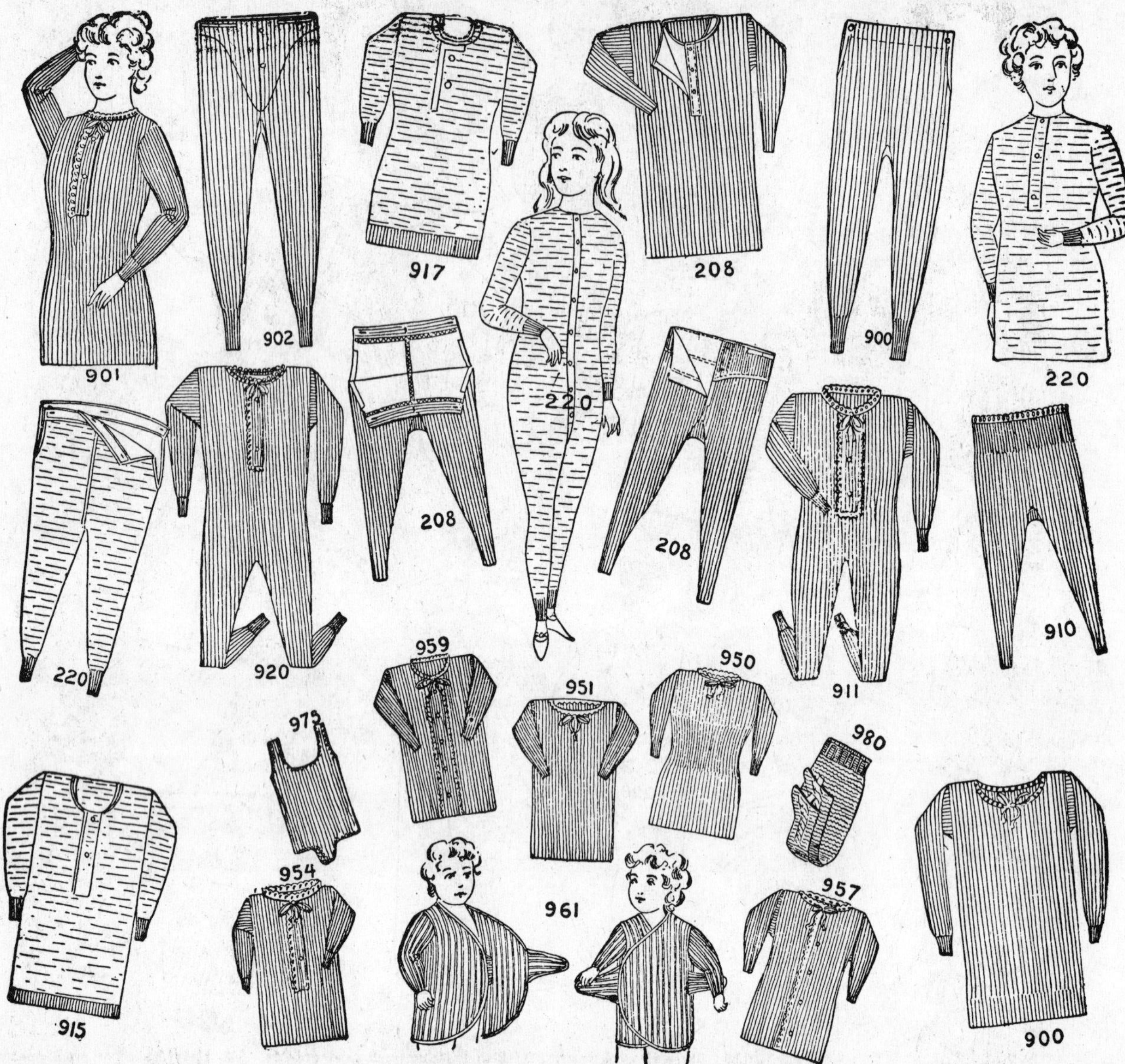

Children's Underwear.

Sizes 1, 2, 3, 4, 5, 6, 7,
Ages 2, 4, 6, 8, 10, 12, 14 yrs.

899. Ribbed wool and cotton vests, long sleeves, girls', drawers to match—
1, 2, 3, 4, 5, 6, 7,
12½c, 15c, 18c, 20c, 22c, 25c, 28c.

900. Ribbed merino vests, natural, girls', drawers to match—1, 2, 25c; 3, 4, 33c; 5, 6, 40c.

901. Ribbed merino vests, button front—1, 2, 30c; 3, 4, 37c; 5, 6, 45c.

902. Boys' ribbed merino vests, button front, long sleeves, drawers to match—1, 2, 25c; 3, 4, 33c; 5, 6, 40c.

904. Swiss all-wool vests, as 900, white and natural, girls', drawers to match—1, 2, 35c; 3, 4, 45c; 5, 6, 55c.

905. Same as 904, only button front—1, 2, 40c; 3, 4, 50c; 5, 6, 60c.

906. Ribbed all-wool vests, as style 900, girls' drawers to match—

	1,	2,	3,	4,	5,	6,
Natural,	35c,	35c,	45c,	45c,	55c,	55c.
White,	40c,	40c,	50c,	50c,	60c,	60c.

907. Heavy ribbed all-wool, style as 901—

	1, 2,	3, 4,	5, 6,
Natural,	40c,	50c,	60c.
White,	45c,	55c,	65c.

908. Heavy Scotch wool vests, boys' and girls', natural, button front, drawers to match—1, 2, 65c; 3, 4, 75c; 5, 6, 85c.

Seal Lined Underwear.

Vests 12 to 32 in., Drawers 20 to 32 in.

208. Ribbed, fleeced lined boys' and girls' vests, natural, button front, long sleeves, drawers to match—

12	14	16	18	20	22	24	26	28	30	32
20c	20c	25c	25c	30c	30c	35c	35c	40c	40c	45c

220. Stuttgarter girls' vests and drawers, fine natural wool, drawers ankle length—

20,	22,	24,	26,	28,	30,
90c,	90c,	90c,	$1.10,	1.10	1.10.

220. Girls' Stuttgarter combination suits, same quality as vests—20, 22, 24, $1.25; 26, 28, 30, $1.50.

915. Plain wool and cotton vests and drawers, boys' and girls', natural color—1, 2, 25c; 3, 4, 33c; 5, 6, 38c.

916. Plain merino vests and drawers, boys' and girls', button front, long sleeves—1, 2, 35c; 3, 4, 45c; 5, 6, 55c.

917. Plain natural wool vests and drawers, boys' and girls', drawers ankle length—1, 2, 45c; 3, 4, 55c; 5, 6, 65c.

910. Black tights and drawers—1, 2, 60c; 3, 4, 70c; 5, 6, 80c.

Combination Suits.

920. Ribbed wool and cotton, long sleeves, ankle length, natural—1, 2, 65c; 3, 4, 75c; 5, 6, 85c.

921. Heavy ribbed merino, same as 911, natural—1, 2, 95c; 3, 4, $1.10; 5, 6, $1.25.

911. Heavy Swiss ribbed all-wool, lace ribbon trimmed—

	1, 2,	3, 4,	5, 6,
Natural,	$1.00,	1.15,	1.25.
White,	1.10,	1.25,	1.35.

Knit-to-fit Combination Suits.

922. Finest ribbed merino, finished seams, natural and white—1, 2, 3, 4, $2.25; 5, 6, 7, 8, $2.50.

923. Finest ribbed, all wool, white and natural—1, 2, 3, 4, $2.50; 5, 6, $3.00; 7, 8, $3.25.

Infants' Underwear.

Sizes	1,	2,	3,	4,
Ages	3,	6,	12,	18 months.

950. Zephyr wool, shaped, ribbon around neck, white, 1 to 4, 18c.

951. Ribbed merino, closed front, natural, 1, 10c; 2, 12½c; 3, 15c; 4, 18c.

952. Ribbed merino, same as 951, white, better quality—1, 12½c; 2, 15c; 3, 18c; 4, 20c.

953. Ribbed all-wool, same as 951, white—1, 20c; 2, 20c; 3, 25c; 4, 25c.

954. Ribbed merino, half-open front, natural—1, 18c; 2, 18c; 3, 22c; 4, 22c.

955. Ribbed merino, style as 954, better quality, white—1, 20c; 2, 20c; 3, 25c; 4, 25c.

956. Ribbed, all wool, style as 954, white—1, 25c; 2, 25c; 3, 30c; 4, 30c.

957. Ribbed merino, all open front, white—1, 25c; 2, 25c; 3, 30c; 4, 30c.

958. Ribbed, all wool, all open front, white—1, 30c; 2, 30c; 3, 35c; 4, 35c.

959. Fine ribbed Swiss all-wool, button down front, neatly trimmed, white, sizes 1, ?, 35c; 3, 4, 40c.

960. Fine ribbed imported, all-wool, style as 959, better quality, white, sizes 1, 2, 50c; 3, 4, 60c.

961. Reuben vests, all-wool, white—1, 25c; 2, 30c; 3, 35c; 4, 40c.

962. Reuben vests, all-wool, finest quality, white—1, 35c; 2, 40c; 3, 45c; 4, 50c.

975. Infants' bands, white, 25c; better quality, 35c.

980. Overalls, all-wool, with or without feet, white and black, 6 months to 2 yrs, 50c; 3 and 4 yrs, 65c; better quality, 75c, 85c.

Acme Corsets.

11. Jean throughout, lace-trimmed, medium length, 2 side steels, white and drab, 18 to 30 .... 28c

13. Jean with sateen strips, boned bust, medium length, embroidery, white and drab, 18 to 30, 35c

15. Coutil, with sateen strips, straight front, boned bust, lace and baby ribbon, white and drab, 18 to 30.............................. 50c

19. Sateen, single strips, filled with fine tempered steel wire, lace top and bottom, short hip, white, drab and black, 18 to 30 .... 75c

21. Nursing, coutil, steel wire filling, embroidery trimmed, white and drab, 19 to 30 .... 75c

29. Misses' corset, coutil, 2 side steels, lace edging, white and drab, 19 to 26..................... 35c

31. Misses' coutil, sateen stripping, 2 side steels, embroidery trimming, white and drab, 19 to 26 .... 50c

35. Ladies' fine sateen, single strip, medium length, filled with fine wire, lace and baby ribbon, white and drab 18 to 30 ...... 1.00

74. Straight front, coutil with sateen strips, lace and baby ribbon, steel wire filling, white, drab and black, 18 to 30 .... 75c

83. Empire, fine sateen, single strip, lace and baby ribbon, white, drab and black, 18 to 24 .... 75c

90. Empire, made of jean, with sateen strip, lace and baby ribbon, white and drab, 18 to 24..50c

91. Straight front, English coutil throughout, filled with fine steel wire, single strips, baby ribbon and lace at top, finished with tab for hose supporter, white and drab, 18 to 30...1.00

B. & C. Corsets.

200. Straight front, heavy jean, drab, white or black, girdled and lace-trimmed, 18 to 30, 1.00

201. Same, steel boned, tan jean 1.00

207. Same, featherbone-filled, drab only 1.00

208. Straight front, "hip-spring," non-stretchable jean, steel-boned, white or drab 1.00

211. Straight front, "hip-spring," in fine coutil, white or drab 1.25

202. Straight front, jean, sateen strips, drab only, 18 to 30 .... 75c

204. Straight front, drab only, 18 to 26........ 50c

215. Straight front, short girdle, drab jean, 18 to 26 .... 50c

Kabo Bust Perfector, drab and white jean or summer net, 18 to 26 .... 1.00

Kabo Corsets.

605. Short length, 10-inch clasp with 5 hooks, 3 lower hooks in close relation, white batiste, 18 to 30.. 1.25

603. Same as 605, only medium length 1.25

611. Fine non-stretchable jean, low-cut bust, 10-inch clasp, satin ribbon trimmed, drab, black and white, 18 to 30.............................. 1.25

604. Fine, low bust, sateen, 10-inch clasp, good long skirt, white, drab and black, 18 to 30.. 1.75

608. 11½-inch clasp, long skirt, non-stretchable jean, handsomely trimmed, black, white and drab, 18 to 30 .... 1.25

806. Medium length, trimmed with broad lace and silk embroidered, French coutil, white, drab and black, 18 to 26.... .... 2.25

804. Drab and white French coutil, black, in English sateen, medium length, low dip bust, 10-inch clasp, lace-trimmed and embroidered at gores, 18 to 26.. 2.75

803. Medium length, coutil of extreme fineness, buttonholed by hand, flossed and trimmed handsomely low cut, white and drab only, 18 to 26.. 3.75

805. Medium length, diamond sateen, low-cut bust, lace-trimmed, embroidered and buttonhole stitched at gores, four-hook clasp, black only, 18 to 26.. 4.00

811. Long skirt, finest French coutil, in white and drab, diamond sateen in black, satin ribbon trimmed and flossed, gores buttonhole stitched, for stout figures, 18 to 30 .... 5.00

W. B. Corsets.

660. Coutil, 3-bone, strips sateen, short hip, trimmed top and bottom with lace and baby ribbon, white, drab, black, sizes 18 to 30..$1.00
533. Nursing, jean, strips sateen, edge silk embroidery, white, drab, sizes 18 to 30........$1.00
115. Fine batiste, light and durable, single strips, short hip, trimmed top and bottom with baby ribbon, white, sizes 18 to 26...$1.25
701. Erect Form, the latest straight-front corset, bias cut, made of jean, gored hip, perfect in shape, colors drab, white and black, sizes 18 to 26 ....$1.25
937. Bias cut, gored over hip, fine sateen, elegant shape, white, drab and black, sizes 18 to 30 ....$1.25
705. Erect Form, fine light batiste, same style as 701, white only, sizes 18 to 30........ $1.25
702. Erect Form, same style as 701, only made of fine sateen, lace trimmed, white, drab and black, sizes 18 to 26.........................$2.00
108. Heavy coutil, suitable for stout figures, 3-bone strip. spoon clasp, drab, black and white, sizes 19 to 36..................................$2.00
963. Erect Form, French coutil, short waist, gored hip and bust, lace trimmed, white, drab and black, sizes 18 to 26 ....$2.00
965. Erect Form, batiste, short, fine lace trimming, gored hips and bust, white only, sizes 18 to 26 ....$2.25
962. Erect Form, same style as 701, only made of French coutil, lace trimmed, white, drab and black, sizes 18 to 30 ....$2.50

631. "La Vida," new short Parisian model, perfect fitting, diamond sateen, white, drab and black, handsome lace trimming, short cutaway hip, French bust, graceful, all whalebone, sizes 18 to 30 ....$6.00

R. & G. Corsets.

297. Heavy jean, with coutil strip, short over hip, lace trimmed, white, drab and black, sizes 18 to 30 ....$1.00
601. Straight front, coutil, lace top and bottom, bias cut, white, drab and black, sizes 18 to 30 ....$1.25
397. Coutil, single strips of sateen, lace and baby ribbon, elegant shape, short hip, white, drab and black, sizes 18 to 30 ....$1.25
53. Nursing, medium waist, single strips of sateen, white and drab, sizes 18 to 30 ....$1.25
497. Fine sateen throughout, 3-bone strip, short hip, lace at top and bottom, white, drab and black, sizes 18 to 30..............................$1.60
511. Straight front, bias cut, gored hips, lace top and bottom, medium low bust, sizes 18 to 30, French coutil, white, $2.25; fine sateen, black $2.50
3. Batiste, empire style, lace and drawing ribbon, 11 inches long in front, 10-inch clasp, white, pink and blue, sizes 18 to 22 ....$1.25

La Grecque Ribbon Corsets.

303. Straight front, stylish shape, full bust, 7-inch length of waist, an elegant fit, color white, with pink, white and blue ribbons, sizes 18 to 30...$2.00

305. Same as 303, only 1 inch shorter from waist line up, sizes 18 to 30........................$2.00

P. N. Corsets.

441. Heavy jean, long waist, silk embroidered, white, drab and black, sizes 18 to 30..... $1.00
493. Heavy jean, sateen strips, 2 side steels, zone waist, white, drab and black, sizes 18 to 30 ....$1.25
458. High bust, coutil, sateen strips, straps over shoulders, white, drab and black, sizes 18 to 30 ....$1.25
724. Coutil, in white and drab, sateen, in black, straight front, medium waist, bias cut, satin trimming, 4-hook clasp, sizes 18 to 30 ....$1.25
908. Heavy coutil, in white and drab, sateen, in black, bias cut, gored hip and bust, satin binding, medium form, sizes 18 to 30 ....$1.75
454. Heavy jean, abdominal, elastic and lacing on hip, for large people, drab, sizes 20 to 30, $1.75; 1 to 36.......................................$2.00
593. Fine brocaded sateen, white and black, trimmed top and bottom with satin, silk embroidery, medium and long form, straight front, sizes 18 to 26 ....$3.50

F. P. Corsets.

Abdominal, heavy jean, spoon clasp, sidelacing, for stout ladies, drab, sizes 20 to 30, $1.50; sizes 31 to 36 ....$1.75

Nemo.

Self Reducing, made of imported French coutil, long and short waist, white, drab and fast black sateen, sizes 18 to 36 ....$3.00

Acme Waists.

911. Misses' waist, 7 to 12 years, fine sateen, laced back, button front, fine corded, white and drab, sizes 20 to 26.......................65c

900. Child's waist, white and drab, soft jean, sateen strips, corded, 4 to 7 years, sizes 20 to 26........35c

901. Child's waist, soft jean, button back, color white, 1 to 4 years, sizes 20 to 26 ....20c

902. Child's waist, 4 to 7 years, soft jean, button back, white and drab, sizes 20 to 26.....................25c

903. Child's waist, 4 to 10 years, fine cambric, full front, white, sizes 20 to 26...............................35c

904. Boys' waist, 4 to 7 years, soft jean, button front, white and drab, sizes 20 to 26.....................25c

910. Child's waist, soft sateen, small cording, drab and white, 2 to 6 years, sizes 20 to 26...............45c

912. Ladies' waist, fine sateen, medium form, long waist, button front, white and drab, sizes 19 to 30..$1.00

916. Misses' waist, 12 to 17 years, coutil, with sateen strips, lace and baby ribbon, steel clasp front, button on side, lace back, colors white and drab, sizes 20 to 26..........85c

Ferris Waists.

223. Misses' or young ladies' waist, fine sateen, plaited bust, 13 to 15 years, white and drab, sizes 20 to 26 ....$1.25

603. Equipoise waist, fine twill cotton, color white, sizes 20 to 30 .....$2.25

220. Ladies' waist, sateen, medium form, long waist, button front, white, drab and black, sizes 19 to 30 ....$1.25

319. Ladies' waist, fine sateen, full bust, steel front, white, drab and black, sizes 19 to 30............$1.25

230. Ladies' long waist, fine sateen, lace on hip, white, drab and black, sizes 19 to 30 ....$1.50

215. Misses' waist, 7 to 12 years, laced back, button front, sateen, white and drab, sizes 20 to 26 ....$1.15

212. Child's waist, 4 to 6 years, sateen, white and drab, sizes 20 to 26 .$1.00

229. Child's waist, 1 to 4 years, fine sateen, white and drab, sizes 20 to 26 ....65c

250. Infants' waist, fine soft material, color white, sizes 20 to 26 ....50c

B. & C. Waists.

130. Comfort waist, sateen, open or closed hip, white and drab, sizes 18 to 30................................$1.00

320. Wright's bust form, slender figure, white and drab, jean, summer net..................................$2.25

176. Sahlin form, jean, white and drab, $1.25 ; better quality $1.75

Bustles and Dress Forms.

68. Lennox form, tempered wire 45c
69. Grace form, white wire 35c
70. Hygeia dress forms, oval in shape, light and comfortable 50c
71. Braid wire forms, covered with knitted lace 50c
72. Imperial hip bustle, made of finest tempered wire, black and white ...60c
73. Combination hip, light and **graceful,** fine tempered wire............ ...60c
76. Royal hip, fine tempered **wire, white** and black 45c
77. La Belle, white tempered **wire, covered,** white and black 38c
78. Queen, 2-roll, fine tempered **wire**..40c
79. Queen, 3-roll, fine wire 45c
80. Princess, perfect shape, **fine tempered** wire 35c
81. The Gem, fine white wire 25c
82. The Beauty, fine tempered **wire**..22c
83. Empire, best tempered wire......35c
84. Feather filled, color black........15c
85. Featherbone, haircloth covered...50c
86. Featherbone, white, grey, **black**..50c
87. Featherbone bust forms 45c
88. Acme belt supporter 20c
89. Peerless distender 35c
90. Antiseptic hygienic towels, No. 1, 25c ; No. 2, 35c ; No. 3..... ....50c
91. Straight front distender, netting, lace trimmed 25c
92. Straight front **distender, fine quality** net, lace trimmed 35c

Art Needlework.

No. 1. Jewel case, silk, embroidered top of white linen or bolting silk, silk and lace frill, each $1.50

No. 2. Fancy silk head rest, any shade, crochet top, silk puffing, satin ribbon frill, $2.00; more elaborate, each .. $2.50

No. 3. Oblong pincushions, hand-embroidered linen top, rich satin ribbon frill, assorted shades, 12-in, $1.50; 15-in, $1.75; 18-in, $2.00; 24-in, $3.00; 27-in, each $3.25

No. 4. Heart-shaped shaving case, embroidered linen front, tissue pad, razor pocket, satin ribbon trimming, ea .. $1.50

No. 5. Round shaving case, like No. 4, $1.50; with more embroidery work, and better ribbon, each $2.00

No. 6. Dainty tinsel pinballs, ribbon trimming, 40c; larger, each 75c

No. 7. Shaving case, embroidered linen front, tissue pad, razor pocket, satin ribbon bows and hanger, each, $1.50; more elaborate $1.75

No. 8. Photo frame, three openings, embroidered on white linen, assorted floral designs desired, glass and brass corners, $2.50; more elaborate, each .. $3.00

No. 9. Sofa cushion, hand-embroidered top, maple leaf (as cut), or other floral designs, two shades of ribbon, frill, good form, each, $5.00; tinted "maple leaf" top only, each 40c

No. 10. Tea cosy, fine art sateen, double silk puffing, "Russian down" form, $1.00, 1.25; better quality sateen, each .. $1.50

No 11. Knitted tea cosy, double Berlin wool, in pink, blue, yellow and green, bow of ribbon, each $1.25

No. 11A. Knitted corn cob tea-pot holder, assorted shades, ribbon trimming, each 20c

No. 12. Bangle board for keys, button-hooks, etc., silk puffing, lace frills, trimmed with baby ribbon, each ... 75c

No. 13. Silk brush and comb cases, silk and lace frill, rich satin ribbon trimming, assorted shades, $1.50; more elaborate each, $2.00 .... $2.25

No. 14. Dainty baby basket, silk lining, assorted shades, pockets and pincushion, each $2.75

No. 14A. Fancy baskets, assorted styles and sizes, bows of ribbon, suitable for hair receiver, jewel case, etc., each, 40c to $1.25

No. 15. Linen teapot holder, butterfly design, shaded silk embroidery, silk pad, double frill, each 75c

No. 16. Set (5) crochet dinner mats, $1.75; finer quality in set, $2.00 .... $2.25

No. 17. Hanging pincushion, egg-beater design, padded, large bows of ribbon, each, 40c; more elaborate, each 50c

No. 18. White linen photo frames, three openings, floral embroidery, glass and gilt moulding, each, $3.00; more elaborate, each $3.50

No. 19. Sofa cushions, lithographed tops, in beautiful colorings and designs (as cut, or others), good form, shades of satin ribbon, frill, each, $4.50; "Minuet" top only (as cut), each 60c

No. 20. Match receiver, assorted baby ribbon trimming, each 40c

No. 21. White linen photo frame, embroidered, any floral design, with glass, brass corners, each, $1.50; with gilt moulding, each $2.00

No. 22. White linen watch pockets, raised embroidery, floral design, silk puffing, baby ribbon, each 65c

No. 23. Tea cosy, hand-embroidered, linen sides, floral designs, buttonhole edge, double silk puffing, each, $3.50; more elaborate, $4.00 .... $4.50

No. 24. White linen tie or handkerchief cases, raised embroidery, floral designs, finished double frill of silk and lace, $1.50; more elaborate, $2.00; embroidered on bolting cloth, $2.25; more elaborate, each $2.50

No. 25. Hand-embroidered book-marks, white linen on satin ribbon, each .. 50c

No. 26. Towel rings, large bows of satin ribbon, any shade, each, 85c $1.00

No. 27. Hanging pin ball, flag top and row of pins all around, ribbon trimmed, each, 50c; hanging key rack, with flag top, each 50c

No. 27A. Hanging pincushion, biscuit design, bows of narrow ribbon, each, 40c

No. 27B. White linen pin balls, embroidered in raised designs, pins all around (as cut No. 27), needle case on back, each 60c

No. 28. White linen photo frame, embroidered in pretty floral designs, glass, brass corners, each $2.25

No. 29. Sofa cushion, tinted and embroidered top, basket of violets (as cut), or other designs, two shades of ribbon frill, good forms, each, $5.50; with heavier worked tops, $6.00, 6.50 each; tinted "basket of violets," top only (as cut), each 50c

No. 29A. Silk sofa pillow, Battenburg lace top, ribbon frill, each, $3.50 ... $4.00

No. 30. Silk tea cosy, three large puffings, Battenburg lace sides, each $2.50; finer lace sides $3.50

No. 31. Silk bangle board, applique of lace, brass hooks, bows of baby ribbon, each 50c

No. 32. Whisk holder, embroidered on colored linen, bows of satin ribbon, each $1.25

For Additional Prices see Opposite Page.

Embroidery Silks, Cushion Cords, etc.

Belding, Paul & Co.'s Wash Embroidery Silks.

B. & P. filo floss, all shades, 4c skein, 45c doz.
B. & P. royal floss, all shades, 4c skein, 45c doz.
B. & P. twisted silk, all shades, 4c skein, 45c doz.
B. & P. rope embroidery silk, all shades, 4c skein, 45c doz.
B. & P. Sicilian embroidery silk, all shades, 4c skein, 45c doz.
B. & P. Dresden silk, plain or shaded, 4c skein, 45c doz.
B. & P. Honiton or etching silk, 3c skein, 30c doz.
Filoselle, all colors, 5c skein, 50c doz.
Britannia crochet silk, all shades, 5c spool.
Daisy embroidery or crochet silk, all shades, 25-yd spool, 10c.
Mayflower crochet silks, all shades, 15c spool.
Peerless crochet wash silks, all shades, ½-oz spool, 25c each.
Belding's crochet or knitting wash silks, all shades, ½-oz spool, 45c ea.
Belding's purse twist, in navy, red, brown, steel grey, dark grey and black shades, ½-oz spool, 50c each.
Belding's books, showing lines of shadings on colored plate, 10c each.
Belding's skein holders for embroidery silk, will hold 1 doz skeins, 4c each.

(See Cut on opposite page.)

No. 33. Padded comb and brush tray, large crochet rings, wide satin ribbon, quite new for dresser, each, $1.50; better trimming, each $1.75
No. 34. Pincushion, fancy ribbon top, any two shades, silk and lace frill, each, $1.75
No. 35. Hand-embroidered doylies, fine white linen, assorted floral designs, 9 x 9 inch, each, 60c, 75c; 12 x 12, 75c .. $1.00
No. 36. Whisk holder, raised embroidery, floral designs, lace frill, all shades, 75c each; better trimming $1.00
No. 37. Large pincushion, hand-embroidered top, silk and lace frill, large bow satin ribbon, each, $1.50; better trimming $2.00
No. 38. Crochet hair receiver, pineapple design, silk lining, ribbon bows, each, 50c
No. 39. Hairpin glass, flowers and clusters of baby ribbon, each, 35c; better trimming 50c
No. 40. Hand-embroidered centre-pieces, buttonhole edge, new rose, violet, carnation and other floral designs, each, $2.50, 3.00, 3.50; more elaborately worked, each, $4.00, 4.50 .... $5.00
No. 41. Black handkerchief crochet pocket, silk rings, silk puffs and narrow ribbon bows, all black, each $1.00
No. 42. Round pincushion, all shades of silk, lace top, silk and lace frill, each, $1.50; embroidered top, ribbon frill, $2.00
No. 42A. Embroidered hat bands, satin ribbon, any shade, each 75c

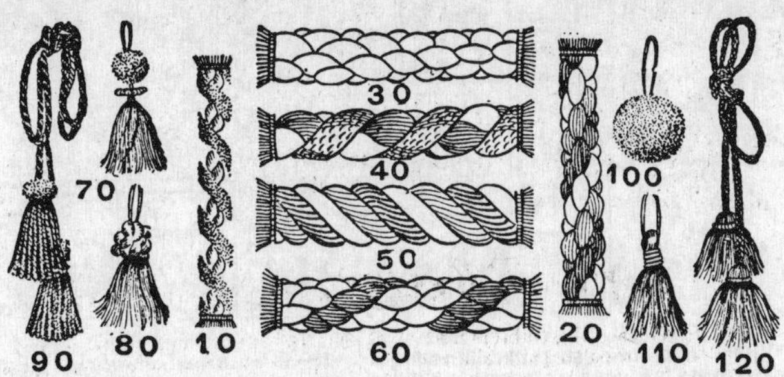

Steel Beads, Penelope Canvas, Sheet Celluloid, Bolting Cloth.

Silver steel beads, for making purses, in bunches of 12 strands, sizes 7, 8, 15c bunch; sizes 9, 10, 18c bunch.
Penelope canvas, used for Ottoman covers, slippers, wool work, fancy work, etc., 27 inches wide, 25c yd.
Sheet celluloid, in green, pink, white and blue, 18 inches wide, per sheet of ⅞-yd, 75c; per ½-yd, 25c.
Silk bolting cloth, as used for fancy work, 20 inches wide, $1.00 yd; 40 inches wide, $2.00 yd.

Bath and Dressing Robe Girdles.

No. 65. Heavy cotton girdles, in white, red, pink, brown, grey, blue, navy and black, with heavy tassel, 2 yds long, 35c each.
No. 120. Heavy woollen girdles (as cut), in white, red, pink, brown, grey, blue, navy and white, also black, with heavy tassel, 2 yds long, 50c each.
No. 90. Heavy silk girdles (as cut), plaited, very solid, with heavy tassel, well covered, in colors as No. 120, 2¼ yds long, $1.00 each.
No. 95. Woollen neck cords to match girdles, colors as No. 120, 15c each.

Silk Tassels and Pom-poms.

No. 100. Pure silk pom-poms (as cut), all shades, 10c doz.
No. 70. Pure silk tassels (as cut), all shades, 15c doz.
No. 110. Pure silk tassels (as cut), all shades, 18c doz.
No. 80. Pure silk tassels (as cut), all shades, 25c doz.
No. 85. Pure silk tassels, as cut No. 70, only much better quality of silk, all shades, 50c doz.
No. 99. Pure silk pom-poms, for cushion corners, all shades, 15c pair; 90c doz.

Cushion Cords.

Write for samples.

No. 10. Fancy chenille cord for fancy work (as cut), in all shades, 5c yd.
No. 20. Silk cushion cord (as cut), plaited, very solid and extra well covered, all art colors and combinations, 15c yd.
No. 30. Mercerized cushion cord (as cut), well covered, ⅜-inch thick, all variegated shades, 12½c yd.
No. 40. Heavy plaited silk cord (as cut), guaranteed, well covered, new combination colors, 25c yd.
No. 50. Our special "mercerized" or imitation silk cord (as cut), in cushion and drapery size, in all plain and combination colors, well covered, 10c yd.
No. 60. Heavy silk cushion cord (as cut), in all plain and combination colors, guaranteed well covered, and plaited solid, 20c yd.
Silk cord and tassel for cushions, 3 yds long, to go around and tie at one corner, 75c each.

Embroidery Cottons, Linens, Tinsel Thread, etc.

White linen floss, in sizes 0 and 00, 4c skein, 48c doz.

Barbour's white linen floss, sizes 1, 2, 3, 4, star, 20c doz.

White Moravian cotton, as used for padding raised embroidery work on linens, also for initialing, sizes 7, 8, 9, 5c spool.

Turkey red tracing cotton, sizes 8, 10, 12, 14, 20c doz.

White, sky, pink and yellow marking cotton, 20c doz.

Japanese gold thread, for working on silk drapes, cushions, etc., 5c, 8c, 10c, 12½c, 15c, 18c bunch.

Tinsel thread, used extensively for fancy work, etc., 8c skein.

Embroidery needles, assorted, Nos. 7, 8, 9, 10, 5c doz.

Silver thread, as used for fancy work, 8c skein.

Tinted Table Covers, Scarfs, Centres and Doylies.

Art table covers, of cotton duck material, in white only, tinted in assorted colors and floral designs for outlining—
Sizes 30 x 30, 19c; 36 x 36, 29c each.

Art centrepieces and doylies, of same material, tinted as above, for outlining—
Sizes 12 x 12, 7c; 18 x 18, 12½c each.

Art scarfs, of cotton duck material, tinted in neat floral designs, for toilet covers or sideboards—
Sizes 16 x 45, 19c; 16 x 65, 25c each.

With knotted fringe—
Sizes 16 x 50, 25c each.

Art table covers, assorted floral designs, tinted on corners for outlining, fringed—
Size 33 x 33, 35c each.

With knotted fringe—
Size 36 x 36, 60c each.

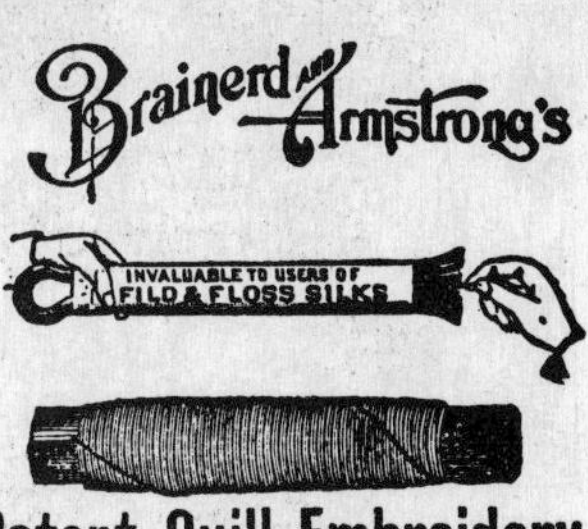

Patent Quill Embroidery

B. & A. quill embroidery silk, all shades, for patch work, etc., 1c each, 10c doz.
B. & A. twisted embroidery silk, all shades, 4c skein, 48c doz.
B. & A. Honiton or buttonhole silk, in patent holders, 4c skein, 45c doz.
B. & A. filo floss, all shades, in patent holders, 5c skein, 50c doz.
B. & A. Roman floss, all shades, in patent holders, 5c skein, 50c doz.
B. & A. white Caspian floss, in patent holders, 5c skein, 50c doz.
Corticelli crochet silk, all shades, ½-oz spool, 25c each.
B. & A. crochet or knitting silk, all shades, ½-oz spool, 45c each.
Corticelli glove-mending silks, in plait of assorted shades, 25c each.
Corticelli home needlework books, containing items from the best authors on needlework, with colored plates, 10c each.

Duchess Embroidery Hoops.

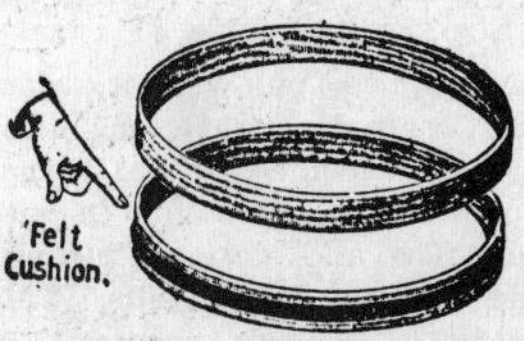

The Duchess embroidery hoop does not require any winding, as the felt cushion on the inside hoop gives the proper tension to hold either light or heavy material tightly and without injury, none better, sizes 5 and 6 inches, 10c set, or package of half dozen, 55c.

Pin Cushion and Tea Cosy Forms.

Pin cushions, in round, square or heart shapes, assorted sizes, 10c ea.
Pin cushion forms, oblong, well made—
Size 4 x 12, 10c.
4 x 15, 12c.
4 x 18, 15c.
4 x 24, 18c.
4 x 27, 20c.
4 x 36, 25c.
Tea cosy forms, white cambric covered, well filled, size 12 x 14 inches, Russian down, 25c; mixed down, 35c, No. 1 down, 50c each.
Head rest forms, well filled with Russian down, size 11 x 14, 20c.

Pillow Tops.

20th Century Pillow Top.

The 20th century pillow top is an elaborate design, lithographed on white sateen, in the centre are grouped the representative soldiers of the allied powers, each holding the flag of his country. At the top surmounting the whole design is a portrait of King Edward VII., with the flags of England and United States gracefully festooned behind. In the two upper corners are designs suggestive of the passing of the old century and the dawn of the new. In the lower corners two vignettes showing types of the soldiers who fought in South Africa and the Philippines, the one a Strathcona horseman, the other a trooper of the American army. This top must be seen to be appreciated—
20 x 20, our special price, 25c each.

Tinted pillow tops, on art ticking, beautiful designs and colorings, may be worked solid, short and long stitched or outlined. We always have a large selection of these—
Size 22 x 22, 40c, 50c, 60c each.

Lithographed pillow tops, beautifully colored, on art ticking, no embroidery required, quickly made and durable, may be had in assorted colors and designs, including the "Minuet," "Angelus," "May Queen," "Queen Louise," and others—
Our special price, 60c each.

Gibson pillow tops, tinted on ecru art duck, for outlining in black silk, no color is used; these are reproductions from the original C. D. Gibson drawings, assorted designs—
Top only, 50c; top and back, 65c.

Satin cushion tops, Japanese, hand embroidered with silk and gold thread, in assorted designs, all the newest shades—
22 x 22, $1.00, 1.25, 1.50, 1.75, 2.00.

Plush cushion tops, in assorted colors, will make up a beautiful cushion—
Size 18 x 18, 25c each.

Skeleton cushion slip of fancy cretonne material, in choice colors and designs, finished with 3½-inch frill, already for form—
Special, 29c each.

Cushion backs of colored art ticking and other material, colors green, red and ecru, 15c each.

Stamped Linens.

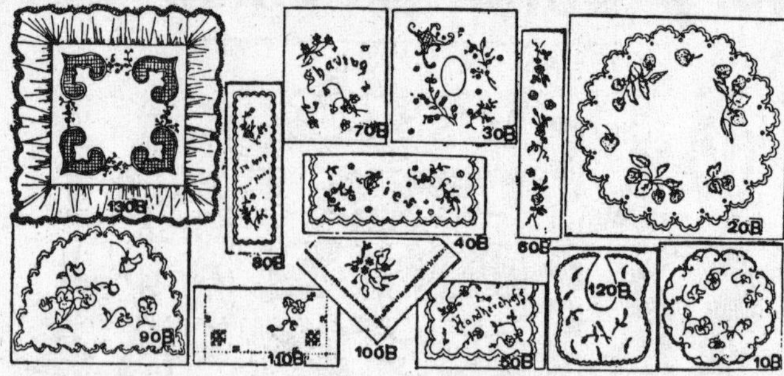

When ordering stamped linens please state as near as possible the design required.

The linen we use for stamping purposes is manufactured especially for us with round even thread and has that soft needle finish.

No. 10B. Stamped linen doylies with buttonhole edge, new designs, including pansies, violets, roses, carnations, maiden hair fern, etc.—
Size 4 x 4, 2c, 3c.
" 6 x 6, 3c, 5c.
" 8 x 8, 5c, 7c.
" 9 x 9, 5c, 8c, 10c.
" 12 x 12, 10c, 12½c.

No. 20B. Stamped linen centrepieces, in new conventional, floral and fruit designs, with buttonhole edge—
Size 15 x 15, 12½c, 15c.
" 18 x 18, 15c, 20c.
" 20 x 20, 20c, 25c.
" 22 x 22, 25c, 30c, 35c.
" 24 x 24, 35c, 40c, 50c.

No. 30B. Stamped photo frames, on white linen, in new designs—

1 opening, 15c; 2 openings, 20c; 3 openings, 25c each.

No. 40B. Stamped tie cases, on white linen, in neat floral designs, buttonhole edge, 20c each.

No. 50B. Stamped handkerchief or glove cases, buttonhole edge, floral designs, 20c.

No. 60B. Stamped linen pieces for oblong pin cushion tops, small floral designs, 12 and 15-inch, 10c; 18 and 24-inch, 15c; 27 and 36-inch, 20c ea.

No. 70B. Stamped linen pieces for shaving cases, neat designs, square, round and heart shape, 10c each.

No. 80B. Stamped linen book-marks, assorted flowers, buttonhole edge, 5c each.

No. 90B. Stamped linen tea cosy sides, new floral and honiton designs, buttonhole edge, for two sides, 20c, 25c.

No. 100B. Stamped centre-pieces, with hemstitched border, neat designs, 25c, 30c, 35c, 40c, 50c each.

No. 110B. Stamped linen tray cloths, hemstitched and openwork corners, new designs—
Size 18 x 27, 30c, 35c, 40c, 50c.
" 20 x 30, 35c, 40c, 50c, 60c each.

Without openwork corners—
Size 18 x 27, 25c, 30c, 35c, 40c.
" 20 x 30, 29c, 35c, 40c, 50c each.

No. 120B. Stamped linen baby bibs, in neat floral designs, with buttonhole edge, 12½c, 15c each.

No. 130B. Stamped cambric pillow covers, with 3½-inch frill and fancy openwork, as shown in cut, already for form, neat floral patterns for embroidering, quite suitable for baby carriages, special, $1.00 each.

No. 140B. Stamped bread cloths, on white linen, assorted designs, medium size, 15c; large size, 20c ea.

No. 145B. Stamped cotton pillow shams, new designs, assorted, size 36 x 36, 19c pair; better quality of cotton, 25c pair.

No. 150B. Stamped linen pillow shams, hemstitched border, $1.00, 1.20, 1.50, 1.75 pair.

No. 155B. Stamped damask tray cloths, fringed and full bleached, sizes 18 x 27, 20c; 20 x 30, 25c each.

No. 160B. Baby's white flannel head shawl, stamped with pretty borders for buttonhole edge, and design in corners, sizes 27 x 27 and 36 x 36, 75c each.

No. 165B. Stamped hemstitched linen tea cloths with openwork corners, assorted designs, size 36 x 36, 75c, 85c, $1.00, 1.25, 1.50 each; without openwork, 60c, 65c, 75c, 85c, $1.00 ea.

No. 170B. Stamped scarfs, hemstitched border, assorted designs—
Size 18 x 54, 60c, 65c, 75c, 85c, $1.00 ea.
18 x 72, 75c, 85c, $1.00, 1.25, 1.50 ea.

No. 175B. Stamped denim art ticking, Holland or crash cushion tops, in conventional Bulgarian and floral designs, size 20 x 20, top only, 20c; top, back and frill, 50c each.

Laundry or Soiled Linen and Shoe Bags.

No. 15.

No. 5. Laundry bags, with drawing string, fancy applique work on side, white only, size 17 x 28, 15c each.

No. 10. Laundry or soiled linen bags, finished with drawing string, floral design on side, colors assorted, size 18 x 28, 20c each.

No. 15. Laundry bags, plain white, finished with cord and tassel, stamped as shown in cut, size 19 x 29 inches, 25c each.

No. 20. Plain white laundry bags, with pink or blue top, finished with cord and tassel, stamped, size 20 x 30 inches, 30c each.

No. 25. Laundry bags, in colored and plain white linen, finished with drawing string, with word "Linen" and design embroidered on, size 18 x 28 inches, 35c each.

No. 30. Laundry bags, of colored art ticking, with white sateen top, cord and tassel, the word "Laundry" and design appliqued on good strong bag, size 19 x 31 inches, 65c each.

No. 35. Shoe pockets, of assorted colored material, to hang on wall, 2 pockets, 12½c; 4 pockets, 20c; 6 pockets, 30c each.

No. 40. Stocking bag, colored material, something very useful, 29c each.

No. 45. Brush and comb bags, colored material, to hang up, 12½c each.

Japanese Silk Drapes, Covers and Scarfs.

Japanese silk drapes, suitable for mantel or piano, heavy knotted silk fringe, assorted in shades of crimson, olive, Nile, gold, blue, pink and white, embroidered with gold thread, in new designs—
Size 23 x 90, $1.50, 1.75, 2.00.
" 25 x 90, $1.75, 2.00, 2.25, 2.50, 3.00.
" 27 x 99, $2.50, 2.75, 3.00, 3.50, 3.75, 4.00, 5.00 each.

Japanese silk drapes, in above shades, embroidered with gold thread—
No. 10. Size 23 x 90, $1.75.
" 27 x 99, $1.98 each.

Mantel or piano drapes, best Japanese silk, knotted fringe, embroidered with gold thread, above colors—
No. 20. Size 25 x 95, $2.25.
" 27 x 100, $2.50 each.

Japanese silk drapes, knotted fringe, choice designs, richly embroidered with silk and gold thread, above colors—
No. 30. Size 27 x 99, $2.75.
" 27 x 103, $3.25 each.

Best quality Japanese silk drapes, heavy knotted fringe, heavily embroidered with silk and gold, above colors—
No. 40. Size 27 x 100, $3.50.
" 27 x 108, $4.50 each.

Japanese silk table covers, with knotted fringe, the shades are olive, crimson, Nile, blue, pink and gold, embroidered with silk and gold thread—
36 x 36, $1.35, 1.75, 2.00, 2.50 each.

Japanese silk chair, picture or easel scarfs, embroidered with gold thread in assorted designs, knotted fringe on both ends, same shades as drapes—
Size 13 x 36, 25c, 35c.
" 15 x 40, 45c, 50c, 60c.
" 18 x 45, 65c, 75c, 85c, $1.00 ea.

HOSIERY DEPARTMENT.

Table of Hose Sizes.

			Sizes	
Infants'	Size	Shoe Worn	0, 1, 1½, 2, 2½, 3, 3½, 4, 4½, 5	1 to 2 years.
"	"	Hose "	4, 4, 4, 4½, 4½, 4½, 4½, 5, 5, 5	
Misses'	"	Shoe "	5, 5½, 6, 6½, 7, 7½, 8, 8½, 9, 9½, 10, 10½	2 to 7 yrs.
"	"	Hose "	5, 5½, 5½, 5½, 6, 6, 6, 6½, 6½, 7, 7, 7	
Misses'	"	Shoe "	11, 11½, 12, 12½, 13, 13½, 1, 1½, 2, 2½	7 to 15 yrs.
"	"	Hose "	7½, 7½, 7½, 8, 8, 8, 8, 8½, 8½, 8½	
Ladies'	"	Shoe "	2½, 3, 3½, 4, 4½, 5, 5½, 6, 6½, 7.	
"	"	Hose "	8½, 8½, 8½, 9, 9, 9½, 9½, 10, 10, 10.	

Be sure in ordering Hose to use this table, it will save mistakes, and you will be sure to get correct size. Hose wears longer when the right size.

The following lines of hosiery may be had in sizes 8½, 9, 9½, 10.

Cashmere Hose.

B200. Ladies' plain black cashmere hose, full fashioned, double sole, heel and toe, high spliced, Eaton's special 25c hose.

B201. Ladies' medium and heavy weight, fine black cashmere hose, full fashioned double sole, heel and toe, this is a wearer, 35c, or 3 pair for $1.00.

B202. Ladies' plain black cashmere hose, full fashioned, double sole, heel and toe, our special 45c, or 3 pair for $1.25.

B203. Ladies' extra fine plain black cashmere hose (Llama make), fashioned throughout, 50c pair.

B204. Ladies' finest Indiana cashmere hose, full fashioned. This hose is made of very soft and durable yarns, 65c, or 2 pair for $1.25.

Outside Sizes.

B205. Ladies' outside sizes cashmere hose, full fashioned, double sole, heel and toe; this hose is made with extra wide leg, 50c, 65c a pair, or 2 pair for $1.25.

Opera-Length Hose.

B206. Ladies' opera-length hose, full fashioned; this hose is made with extra long leg, very warm and comfortable for fall and winter wear, 65c, 75c pair.

Colored Cashmere Hose.

B207. Ladies' cashmere hose, in tan, cardinal and cream, full fashioned, double sole, heel and toe, 35c pair.

Embroidered Hose.

B208. Ladies' plain black cashmere hose, full fashioned, double heel and toe, and made with colored embroidered fronts, in very newest designs, embroidered in white, sky, heliotrope and red, 35c, 50c, 65c, 75c, $1.00 pair.

B209. Ladies' fancy colored stripes in cashmere hose, in very pretty designs and colors, 50c pair.

Ribbed Cashmere Hose.

B210. Ladies' ribbed black plaited hose; this stocking has a little cotton which will keep it from shrinking and is warranted to wear, 18c or 3 pair for 50c, also 20c a pair.

B211. Ladies' 2/1 ribbed black cashmere hose, seamless feet; this hose is made from pure cashmere yarn and we think it is the best stocking in the market for so little money, special, 25c pair.

B212. Ladies' 2/1 ribbed black cashmere hose, full fashioned, double sole, heel and toe, fine soft yarn, 35c, or 3 pairs for $1.00.

B213. Ladies' 1/1 ribbed black cashmere hose, full fashioned, double sole, heel and toe, high spliced, 35c pair.

B214. Ladies' 2/1 ribbed black cashmere hose, full fashioned, double sole, heel and toe, heavy weight, 45c, or 3 pair for $1.25.

B215. Ladies' 1/1 ribbed black cashmere hose, full fashioned, double sole, heel and toe, this is a very fine make, 45c, or 3 pair for $1.25.

B216. Ladies' 2/1 ribbed black cashmere hose, full fashioned, double sole, heel and toe; this hose is made from best English spun yarn, 50c; 65c, or 2 pair for $1.25.

Misses' and Boys' Ribbed Cashmere Hose.

B217. Misses' and boys' ribbed plaited cashmere hose; this hose is made with a little cotton, but we think it will wear better for this—
4½, 5, 5½, 6, 6½, 7, 7½, 8, 8½,
12½c, 12½c, 15c, 15c, 15c, 20c, 20c, 20c, 20c,

B218. Misses' and boys' 2/1 ribbed pure cashmere hose, made with heavy 6-fold knee—
4½, 5, 5½, 6, 6½, 7, 7½, 8, 8½,
15c, 15c, 20c, 20c, 25c, 25c, 25c, 25c, 25c.

B219. Misses' and boys' 2/1 ribbed and 1/1 ribbed black cashmere hose, full fashioned, double sole, heel and toe, high spliced ankles—
4½, 5, 5½, 6, 6½, 7, 7½, 8, 8½,
20c, 20c, 25c, 25c, 30c, 30c, 30c, 35c, 35c.

B220. Boys' and misses' 2/1 ribbed full fashioned cashmere hose, made with double knee—
5, 5½, 6, 6½, 7, 7½, 8, 8½,
25c, 30c, 30c, 35c, 40c, 45c, 50c, 50c.

B221. Misses' and boys' 1/1 ribbed black cashmere hose, double knee, sole and heel—
5, 5½, 6, 6½, 7, 7½, 8, 8½,
25c, 30c, 30c, 35c, 40c, 45c, 50c, 50c.

B222. Boys' and misses' heavy 6-fold knee, fashioned throughout—
5, 5½, 6, 6½, 7, 7½, 8, 8½,
30c, 35c, 35c, 40c, 45c, 45c, 50c, 50c,
9, 9½, 10,
50c, 50c, 50c.

Misses' Plain Cashmere Hose.

B223. Misses' plain black cashmere hose, full fashioned, double sole, heel, toe and knee—
4, 4½, 5, 5½, 6, 6½, 7,
12½c, 12½c, 15c, 15c, 20c, 20c, 25c,
7½, 8, 8½,
25c, 25c, 25c.

B224. Misses' full fashioned fine plain black cashmere hose, made with double knee, heel and toe—
4, 4½, 5, 5½, 6, 6½, 7,
15c, 15c, 20c, 20c, 25c, 25c, 30c,
7½, 8, 8½
30c, 35c, 35c.

B225. Children's plain black cashmere hose, full fashioned, made with heavy double knee, heel and toe—
4, 4½, 5, 5½, 6, 6½, 7,
20c, 20c, 25c, 25c, 30c, 30c, 35c,
7½, 8, 8½,
35c, 40c, 40c.

Colored Cashmere Hose.

B226. Children's plain cashmere hose, fashioned throughout, in tan, cardinal and cream colors—
4, 4½, 5, 5½, 6, 6½, 7,
15c, 15c, 20c, 20c, 25c, 25c, 30c,
7½, 8, 8½,
30c, 35c, 35c.

Ladies' Lisle Hose.

These hose can be had in the following sizes, 8½, 9, 9½.

B227. Ladies' plain black lisle thread hose, fast black, full fashioned, 35c, 45c, 50c pair.

B228. Ladies' black lisle hose, with lace ankle, 35c, 50c, 75c pair.

B229. Ladies' brilliant lisle hose, in cream, white, sky and pink, $1.00 pair.

B230. Ladies' plain lisle hose, in white, cream, heliotrope, pink and sky, 35c pair.

B231. Ladies' white and cream lisle hose, 50c pair.

B232. Ladies' white and cream lisle hose, with lace ankle, 35c, 50c pair.

Silk Hose.

B233. Ladies' plain black silk hose, 75c, $1.00, 1.50, 2.00, 2.50, 3.00 pair.

B234. Ladies' black silk hose, lace ankles, in assorted patterns, $1.00, 1.25 pair.

B235. Ladies' plain silk hose, in pink, white, cardinal, sky, cream and gold, $1.00.

Lace Silk Hose.

B236. Ladies' black silk lace hose, in assorted patterns, $2.50, 3.00, 3.50, 4.50, 5.00.

Ladies' Cotton Hose.

B237. Ladies' black cotton hose, full fashioned, double sole, heel and toe, 12½c, 18c, 25c, 35c pair.

B238. Ladies' fleece-lined cotton hose, 25c, 35c pair.

B239. Ladies' colored cotton hose, in white, pink, sky, cream, red, grey, heliotrope, 25c pair.

Ladies' Wool Hose.

B240. Ladies' wool hose, plain, medium weight, 15c, 25c pair.

B241. Ladies' fine plain wool hose, made with cashmere finish and seamless feet, 35c, or 3 pair for $1.00.

B242. Ladies' ribbed wool hose, medium weight, 20c, 25c, 35c, or 3 pair for $1.00.

B243. Ladies' fine lamb's wool hose, ribbed, seamless and fashioned, medium and heavy weight, 50c, 65c pair.

Misses' Wool Hose.

B244. Misses' plain wool hose—
5, 5½, 6, 6½, 7, 7½, 8, 8½,
10c, 10c, 12½c, 12½c, 15c, 15c, 20c, 20c.

B245. Misses' ribbed wool hose—
5, 5½, 6, 6½, 7, 7½, 8, 8½,
15c, 15c, 20c, 20c, 20c, 25c, 25c, 25c.

B246. Misses' heavy ribbed wool hose—
5, 5½, 6, 6½, 7, 7½, 8, 8½,
20c, 20c, 25c, 25c, 25c, 30c, 35c, 35c.

B247. Misses' medium weight ribbed wool hose, fashioned—
5, 5½, 6, 6½, 7, 7½, 8, 8½,
25c, 25c, 30c, 30c, 35c, 35c, 45c, 50c.

B248. Misses' 2/1 ribbed heavy knit wool hose; this is a regular winter stocking—
5, 5½, 6, 6½, 7, 7½, 8, 8½,
25c, 25c, 30c, 30c, 35c, 35c, 45c, 50c.

Boys' Wool Hose.

B249. Boys' heavy ribbed wool hose—
6, 6½, 7, 7½, 8, 8½, 9, 9½, 10,
15c, 15c, 15c, 15c, 20c, 20c, 20c, 20c, 20c.

B250. Boys' medium weight, black ribbed wool hose, fine soft make—
6, 6½, 7, 7½, 8, 8½, 9, 9½, 10,
15c, 15c, 20c, 20c, 20c, 25c, 25c, 25c, 25c.

B251. Boys' medium weight worsted hose; this is a wearer, our special—
7, 7½, 8, 8½, 9, 9½, 10,
25c, 25c, 25c, 25c, 25c, 25c, 25c.

B252. Boys' heavy ribbed wool hose—
8½, 9, 9½, 10,
35c, 35c, 35c, 35c or 3 pair for $1.00.

B253. Boys' heavy worsted hose, ribbed—
6, 6½, 7, 7½, 8, 8½, 9, 9½, 10,
25c, 25c, 25c, 30c, 30c, 35c, 35c, 35c, 35c.

B254. Boys' extra heavy worsted, made from English yarn, with fashioned leg and seamless feet—
6, 6½, 7, 7½, 8, 8½, 9, 9½, 10,
35c, 35c, 45c, 45c, 50c, 50c, 50c, 50c, 50c.

B255. Boys' heavy lamb's wool hose, ribbed, soft make, made very durable and comfortable for winter wear—
5, 5½, 6, 6½, 7, 7½, 8,
25c, 30c, 30c, 35c, 40c, 45c, 50c,
8½, 9, 9½, 10,
60c, 60c, 60c, 60c.

B256. Boys' extra heavy ribbed wool hose; this hose is made from 5-ply yarn and can be put on the needles and refooted—
6, 6½, 7, 7½, 8, 8½, 9, 9½, 10,
35c, 40c, 50c, 60c, 60c, 65c, 75c, 75c, 75c.

B257. Boys' Irish knit hose, wide rib, a splendid wearer for school—
6, 6½, 7, 7½, 8, 8½, 9, 9½, 10,
25c, 25c, 30c, 30c, 30c, 35c, 35c, 35c, 35c.

B258. Boys' Irish knit worsted hose, wide rib, medium weight; this is an excellent wearing stocking, and soft finish—
6, 6½, 7, 7½, 8, 8½, 9, 9½, 10,
30c, 30c, 35c, 40c, 45c, 50c, 50c, 60c, 60c.

B259. Boys' wide ribbed and extra heavy English wool hose—
5, 5½, 6, 6½, 7, 7½, 8,
30c, 30c, 35c, 35c, 40c, 40c, 45c,
8½, 9, 9½, 10, 10½, 11,
50c, 50c, 50c, 50c, 50c, 50c.

Over-Stockings.

B260. Ladies' and misses' over-stockings—
5½, 6, 6½, 7, 7½, 8,
25c, 25c, 30c, 30c, 35c, 35c,
8½, 9, 9½, 10,
40c, 45c, 50c, 50c.

B261. Ladies' and misses' over-stocking, shaped legs—
5½, 6, 6½, 7, 7½, 8, 8½,
30c, 35c, 35c, 40c, 40c, 50c, 55c,
9, 9½, 10, 10½,
60c, 65c, 75c, 75c.

Infants' Cashmere Socks.

B262. Infants' half length cashmere socks, in black, tan and cream, with ribbed top—
4, 4½, 5, 5½, 6, 6½, 7,
15c, 15c, 15c, 15c, 20c, 20c, 20c.

B263. Infants' three-quarter length cashmere socks, in tan, cream and black—
4, 4½, 5, 5½,
20c, 20c, 20c, 20c.

Infants' Bootees.

B264. Infants' bootees, in fancy colors, also plain white, 10c, 15c, 20c pair.

B265. Infant's hand-made bootees, in cream and light fancy shades, 25c, 50c pair.

Cashmere Socks.

These socks can be had in the following sizes, 10, 10½, 11.

B266. Men's black cashmere socks plain seamless feet, 18c, or 3 pair for 50c, and 20c pair.

B267. Men's plain black cashmere socks, double sole, heel and toe, fine soft finish, special, 25c pair.

B268. Men's extra fine plain black cashmere socks, double sole, heel and toe, 35c, or 3 pair for $1.00.

B269. Men's heavy-weight black cashmere socks, double sole and heel, high spliced, 35c, or 3 pair for $1.00.

B270. Men's extra fine plain black cashmere socks, double sole and fine soft finish, 45c, or 3 pair for $1.25.

Embroidered Socks.

B271. Men's black cashmere socks, embroidered in very pretty designs and colors, 35c, 50c pair.

Silk Socks.

B272. Men's black silk socks, 75c pair.

Men's Ribbed Cashmere Socks.

B273. Men's ribbed black cashmere socks, very special, 25c pair.

B274. Men's extra heavy, also medium weight, fashioned, double sole, heel and toe, 35c, or 3 pair for $1.00; 45c pair, or 3 pair for $1.25; 50c pair.

Men's Wool Socks.

B275. Men's heavy-weight ribbed black wool socks, soft finish and very durable, 25c, 35c pair.

B276. Men's worsted socks, ribbed, black, an excellent wearer and very warm for winter, 35c, 45c, 50c pair.

B277. Men's dark and medium grey wool socks, ribbed 25c, 35c; 45c pair, or 3 pair for $1.25.

B278. Men's Irish knit socks, in black and grey colors, 35c, 45c, 50c pair.

B279. Men's mixed union socks, 9c, or 3 pair for 25c.

B280. Men's heavy and medium weight wool socks, 10c pair.

B281. Men's medium weight wool socks, in light and dark grey, also in fawn, 12½c pair.

B282. Men's extra heavy wool socks, 12½c, 15c ; 18c or 3 pair for 50c.

B283. Men's extra heavy ribbed wool, soft and warm, suitable for street-car men and teamsters, 20c pair.

B284. Men's heavy wool socks, extra warm and soft inside, 20c, 25c pair.

B285. Men's extra long and legging socks, very heavy and tufted inside, suitable for wearing with rubber and felt boots, 50c pair.

Men's and Ladies' Umbrellas.

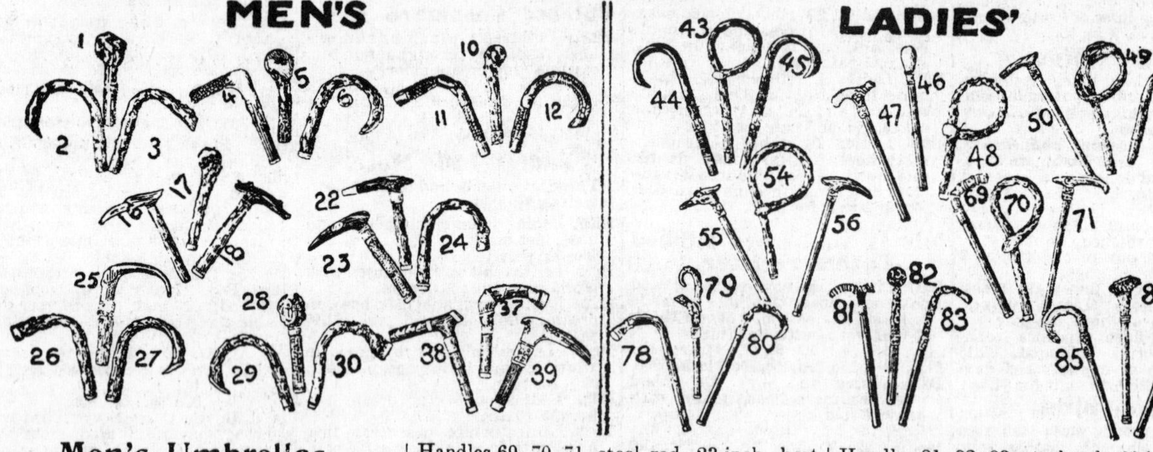

Men's Umbrellas.

Handles 1, 2, 3, wood rod, 25-inch, Austria cloth, 50c.

Handles 4, 5, 6, steel rod, 25-inch, Austria cloth, 75c.

Handles 1, 2, 3, steel rod, 25-inch, gloria cloth, special, $1.00.

Handles 10, 11, 12, steel rod, 27-inch, gloria cloth, extra large size, $1.50.

Handles 16, 17, 18, steel rod, 25-inch, best gloria cloth, $1.50.

Handles 22, 23, 24, steel rod, 25-inch, taffeta silk, cased, $2.00.

Handles 25, 26, 27, steel rod, 25-inch, fine taffeta silk, cased, $2.50.

Handles 28, 29, 30, steel rod, 25-inch, best taffeta silk, cased, $3.00, 4.00.

Handles 37, 38, 39, steel rod, 25-inch, twill silk, tape edge, cased, $5.00, 6.50.

Ladies' Umbrellas.

Handles 43, 44, 45, steel rod, 22-inch, Austria cloth, 50c, 65c.

Handles 46, 47, 48, steel rod, 23-inch, Austria cloth, 75c.

Handles 49, 50, 51, steel rod, 23-inch, fine gloria silk mix, special, $1.00.

Handles 54, 55, 56, steel rod, 23-inch, fine gloria silk mix, $1.25.

Handles 54, 55, 56, steel rod, 23-inch, best gloria silk mix, $1.50.

Handles 69, 70, 71, steel rod, 23-inch, taffeta, silk cased, $2.00.

Handles 69, 70, 71, steel rod, 23-inch, best taffeta, silk cased, $2.50.

Handles 78, 79, 80, steel rod, 23-inch, twill silk, silk cased, $3.50.

Handles 81, 82, 83, steel rod, 23-inch, twill silk, silk cased, $4.00.

Handles 84, 85, 86, steel rod, 23-inch, twill silk, tape edge, silk cased, $5.00, 7.50.

MEN'S CANES.

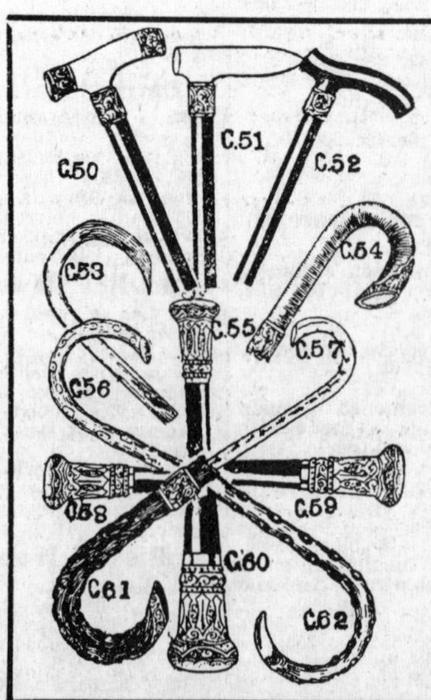

C57. Men's Congo and cherry crook canes, 25c.

C56 and C53. Men's Congo crook, silver trimmed, 50c.

C62. Men's Congo crook, 75c, $1.00.

C54. Men's cherry crook, 75c, $1.00.

C61. Men's Congo crook, $1.25, 1.50, 2.50.

C51. Men's canes, of Congo cherry, ebony and Bangor wood, $2.50, 3.00, 3.50, 4.00.

C52 and C50. Men's canes, in ebony, Malacca, Palmyra woods, horn and ivory handles, sterling and gold-plate trimmed, $3.50.

Gold-Headed Canes.

Gold-headed canes with ebony sticks, as cut C55, ⅞-inch, $5.75; cut C58, 1-inch, $7.25; cut C59, 1¼-inch, $8.75; cut C60, 1½-inch, $9.75.

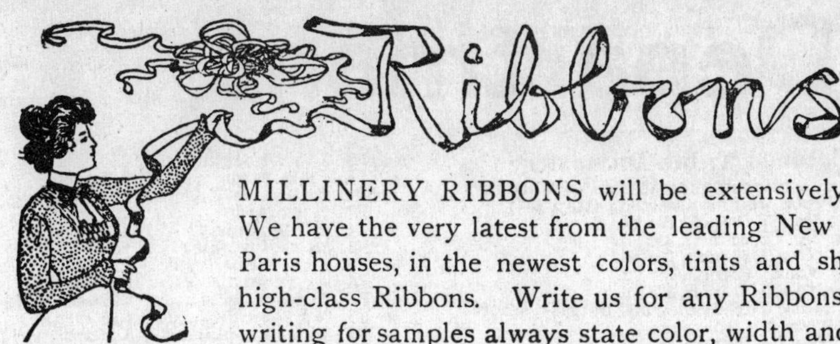

MILLINERY RIBBONS will be extensively used this season. We have the very latest from the leading New York, London and Paris houses, in the newest colors, tints and shades, in staple and high-class Ribbons. Write us for any Ribbons you need. When writing for samples always state color, width and price you wish to pay.

Fancy and Plain Neck Ribbons.

Duchesse satin, the best possible ribbon you can get to wash, 4⅜ inches wide, just the width for neckwear, in the following colors: White, cream, mais, rose, coral, turquoise, sky, new blue, navy, Nile, cardinal, mauve, black, grey, fawn, brown; the last three tints are the very latest for fall wear, millinery and dress bows.
Our leader, every thread silk, 28c per yd.

Liberty satin, this make of ribbon is satin both sides, but very soft for neck wear, rich, all silk, and comes in all the tints, colors and shades for fall wear, as above—
5-inch, special, 30c per yd.

Fancy ribbon, soft quality, plain, raised effect, with cord edge, in colors such as white, cream, mais, yellow, light blue, pink, old rose, turquoise, navy, cardinal, lilac—
3-inch, 12½c per yd.

Fancy ribbon, plain pattern, fancy edge, nice medium quality, for children's wear, in bright colors only, such as lilac, cardinal, navy, turquoise, old rose, pink, sky blue, yellow, mais, cream and white—
4-inch, 15c per yd.

Fancy ribbon, white ground, nice pattern, in plain white, mais and white, sky and white, rose and white, old rose and white and turquoise and white—
4½-inch, 19c per yd.

Fancy ribbon, taffeta, with satin stripe, beautiful rich quality for neckwear (New York pattern), in white, cream, sky, rose, turquoise, cardinal, lilac—
4-inch, 25c per yd.

Fancy taffeta ribbon, raised effect (New York pattern), very latest tints, for waist bows, etc—
4-inch, 25c per yd.

Plain taffeta ribbon, with white stripe on edge (Paris pattern), in mais, rose, sky, Nile, turquoise, lilac, navy and plain white—
4½-inch, 25c per yd.

Fine taffeta ribbon, with plain white edge, colored centre, such as lilac, rose, sky, Nile, turquoise, mais, cream and plain white; this is one of the New York new effects for neck bows, waist bows, hat bows, etc., satin stripe—
4-inch, 25c per yd.

1032. **Faille ribbon**, all silk, our leader, all colors—
½, ⅞, 1½, 2, 2¾ inches wide,
3c 5c 8c 12½c 15c per yd.

1075. **Gros-grain ribbon**, pure silk, all colors—
⅝, 1, 1½, 2⅛, 3⅛ inches wide.
5c 7c 10c 15c 20c per yd.

1050. **Satin ribbon**, for fancy work, all colors—
⅞, 1⅛, 2, 2⅞ inches wide.
3c 5c 8c 12½c per yd.

1040. **Doub'e-faced satin**, our best French make, 60 different colors—
¼, ⅜, ¾, 1, 1½, 2¼, 3 inches wide.
3c 4c 5c 7c 10c 15c 20c per yd.

1045. **Duchesse sat n and faille**, washable, all colors, for neckwear—
1, 1½, 2, 3¼, 4¼ inches wide.
7c 10c 15c 20c 28c per yd.

1080. **Fine taffeta ribbon**, pure silk, washable, all colors, for neckwear—
3⅛-inch, 18c; 4¼-inch, 25c yd.

1093. **Heavy taffeta ribbon**, for millinery purposes, latest colorings—
4-inch, 20c; 5-inch, 25c yd.

1094. **Colored moire ribbon**, soft quality, all colors, for children's wear—
¾, 1⅛, 1⅞, 2½ inches wide.
3c 5c 8c 12½c per yd.

1092. **Colored moire ribbon**, very special, all the new colorings—
4 inches wide, 22c yd.

1095. **Fine taffeta ribbon**, for dress trimmings, white only—
½, 1, 1⅝, 2⅛, 2⅞ inches wide.
3c 5c 8c 11c 15c per yd.

1014. **Black faille ribbon**, satin edge, all silk—
½, 1, 1½, 2, 2⅞ inches.
3c 5c 8c 12½c 15c yd.

1015. **Black gros-grain**, rich heavy quality, French make—
⅝, ⅞, 1¼, 1⅝, 2⅛, 2¾, 3⅛, 4¼ inches.
5c 7c 10c 12½c 15c 20c 25c 30c yd.

1016. **Black gros-grain**, plain pearl edge, mourning ribbon—
½, 1, 1½, 2¼, 2⅞, 3¼, 4¼ inches.
4c 7c 10c 15c 20c 25c 30c yd.

1018. **Black moire taffeta ribbon**, fine make—
⅝, 1, 1⅝, 2⅛, 2⅝, 3, 3½, 4¼, 5, 5½ inches.
3½c 5c 10c 12½c 15c 18c 20c 25c 30c 35c yd.

1019. **Black peau de soie**, dull finish mourning ribbon—
⅝, 1, 1⅞, 2¼, 3, 4⅛ inches.
5c 7c 12½c 15c 20c 30c yd.

1020. **Black duchesse satin**, soft make, all silk, satin face—
½, 1, 1¾, 2⅛, 2⅝, 3⅛, 4¼ inches.
4c, 8c 15c 18c 20c 25c 30c yd.

1021. **Black duchesse satin ribbon**, all silk, satin face—
3⅛-inch, 20c; 4¼-inch, 28c yd.

1022. **Black double-faced satin ribbon**, good black—
⅝, 1, 1½, 2, 2½, 3 inches.
3c 5c 7c 10c 12½c 15c yd.

1023. **Black double-faced satin ribbon**, French make—
½, ¾, 1, 1⅜, 1¾, 2¼, 3, 4¼ inches.
4c 6c 8c 10c 15c 18c 25c 35c yd.

1024. **Black double-faced satin ribbon**, heavy quality, for streamers—
3½, 4½, 5, 6 inches wide.
18c 25c 30c 35c yd.

1025. **Black crape ribbon**, for mourning, our best—
1¾, 2⅛, 2½, 3 inches wide.
12½c 15c 20c 25c yd.

1026. **Black taffeta ribbon**, very fine, for trimming—
½, 1, 1⅝, 2⅛ inches wide.
3c 5c 8c 11c yd.

1027. **Black faille ribbon**, plain edge, for mourning—
1, 1½, 2⅛, 2⅞, 4 inches wide.
7c 10c 15c 20c 25c yd.

1028. **Black taffeta ribbon**, for dress trimming, plain edge—
⅝, 1, 1¾, 2⅛, 2½, 3, 4, 4⅞, 5¼ inches.
3½c 5c 8c 10c 12½c 15c 20c 25c 30c yd.

1029. **Black velvet ribbon**, linen back, woven edge, for skirt trimming—
⅛, ¼, ⅜, ½, ⅝, ⅞, 1⅛, 1⅜, 1⅝, 2⅛, 2⅞ inches.
2½c 3c 4c 5c 6c 8c 10c 12½c 15c 18c 25c yd.

1037. **Black velvet ribbon**, linen back, woven edge, for waist trimming, in pieces of 17¾ yards—
⅛, ¼, ⅜, ½ inches wide.
40c 50c 70c 85c per piece.

1038. **Black velvet ribbo n**, satin back, French make—
⅛, ¼, ⅜, ½, ¾, ⅞, 1, 1¼, 1½, 2, 2¼, 2¾, 3¼ in.
3½c 5c 6c 7c 9c 12½c 14c 16c 18c 25c 30c 35c 40c yd.

1039. **Black velvet ribbon**, satin back, best make, special, in pieces of 17¾ yards—
⅛, ¼, ⅜, ½ inches wide.
60c 85c $1.00 1.20 per piece.

1035. **Velvet ribb n**, satin back, all colors, woven edge, pieces of 17¾ yds—
⅛-inch, 50c; ⅜-inch, 70c per piece.

1036. **Velvet ribbon**, satin back, all colors, our best make—
1-inch, 15c; 2-inch, 30c per yd.

Baby ribbons come in the following colors: Cream, mais, yellow, orange, Nile, full Nile, medium green, dark green, coral, old rose, turquoise, lilas, violet, pink, deep rose, cerise, bright red, medium red, sky, new blue, dark blue, national blue, navy, black and white.

1041. **Baby ribbon**, satin faced, faille back, all colors, for fancy work—
⅛-inch, 1½c per yd.

1042. **Baby ribbon**, satin faced, faille back, all the above colors—
⅜-inch, 2c per yd.

1043. **Baby ribbon**, satin faced, cord edge, all colors—
¼-inch, 3c per yd.

1044. **Baby ribbon**, moire effect, all silk, new colorings—
¼-inch, 3c per yd.

1045. **Double-faced satin**, splendid quality, all the new colors—
¼-inch, 3c per yd.

1046. **All-silk faille**, with satin edge, all colors—
¼-inch, 3c per yd.

1047. **Fine faille**, plain edge, very special, all colors—
⅜-inch, 3c per yd.

1048. **Fine faille**, satin edge, extra quality, about 60 colors—
½-inch, 3c per yd.

1049. **Black belting**, heavy quality—
1½, 2, 2½ inches wide,
12½c 15c 20c per yd.

1051. **Black and colored belting**, rich quality—
2-inch, 20c per yd.

Linen Department.

Bleached Linen Table Damasks.

Fine bleached union table damasks, in assorted patterns—
No. E1, 54-inch, 25c yd.
No. E2, 60-inch, 35c yd.
No. E3, 64-inch, 40c yd.

Full bleached, satin-finished table damasks, all pure linen, choice patterns—
No. E4, 64-inch, 40c yd.
No. E5, 65-inch, 45c yd.
No. E6, 68-inch, 50c yd.

Fine bleached all pure linen damasks, superior quality, rich satin finish, choice new patterns, grass bleached—
No. E7, 72-inch, 50c yd.
No. E8, 72-inch, 60c yd.
No. E9, 72-inch, 65c yd.

Superior satin-finished double damasks, soft grass bleached, select and exclusive designs, best Irish and Scotch makes, pure linen—
No. E10, 72-inch, 75c yd.
No. E11, 72-inch, 85c yd.
No. E12, 72-inch, $1.00 yd.

Extra fine double damasks, pure Irish linen, choice new patterns, soft grass bleached—
No. E13, 72-inch, $1.10 yd.
No. E14, 72-inch, 1.25 yd.
No. E15, 72-inch, 1.35 yd.
No. E16, 72-inch, 1.50 yd.

Extra heavy double damasks, full bleached, choice patterns, guaranteed all linen—
No. E17, 90-inch, $1.10 yd.
No. E18, 90-inch, 1.25 yd.
No. E19, 90-inch, 1.35 yd.
No. E20, 90-inch, 1.50 yd.

Special narrow width, full bleached damasks, guaranteed all linen—
No. E21, 36-inch, 40c yd.
No. E22, 54-inch, 50c yd.

Extra specials in full-bleached damasks, guaranteed all linen, Irish and Scotch makes, grass bleached, good patterns—
No. E23, 61-inch, 39c yd.
No. E24, 64-inch, 48c yd.
No. E25, 66-inch, 58c yd.
No. E26, 72-inch, 73c yd.
No. E27, 72-inch, 83c yd.

Bleached Damasks, with Napkins to Match.

Fine bleached satin-finished damasks, guaranteed pure Irish linen, choice patterns—
No. E28, 70-inch, 50c yd.
¾ x ¾ napkins, $1.35 doz.
No. E29, 72-inch, 75c yd.
¾ x ¾ napkins, $2.25 doz.

Extra fine full bleached double damasks, with soft satin finish, guaranteed all linen, specially selected patterns—
No. E30, 72-inch, $1.00 yd.
¾ x ¾ napkins, $3.00 doz.
No. E31, 72-inch, $1.10 yd.
¾ x ¾ napkins, $3.50 doz.
No. E32, 72-inch, $1.35 yd.
¾ x ¾ napkins, $3.50 doz.

Cream or Half-Bleached Table Damasks.

Cream or half-bleached union table damasks, Irish and Scotch makes, large range of new patterns—
No. M1, 56-inch, 20c yd. No. M4, 60-inch, 27c yd.
No. M2, 59-inch, 23c yd. No. M5, 64-inch, 30c yd.
No. M3, 60-inch, 25c yd. No. M6, 70-inch, 33c yd.
No. M7, 72-inch, 35c yd.

Half-bleached all pure linen damasks, large assortment of new patterns—
No. M8, 56-inch, 25c yd. No. M11, 66-inch, 35c yd.
No. M9, 60-inch, 27c yd. No. M12, 70-inch, 40c yd.
No. M10, 62-inch, 30c yd. No. M13, 72-inch, 45c yd.

Fine half-bleached damasks, guaranteed all linen, medium and heavy qualities, choice patterns—
No. M14, 64-inch, 30c yd. No. M16, 72-inch, 40c yd.
No. M15, 66-inch, 35c yd. No. M17, 72-inch, 45c yd.
No. M18, 72-inch, 50c yd.

Extra heavy half-bleached damasks, all linen, Irish and Scotch makes—
No. M19, 57-inch, 35c yd. No. M22, 66-inch, 50c yd.
No. M20, 64-inch, 40c yd. No. M23, 66-inch, 60c yd.
No. M21, 64-inch, 45c yd. No. M24, 70-inch, 65c yd.

Superior quality half-bleached double damasks, guaranteed all linen, choice new patterns—
No. M25, 72-inch, 60c yd. No. M27, 72-inch, 75c yd
No. M26, 72-inch, 65c yd. No. M28, 72-inch, 85c yd.
No. M29, 72-inch, $1.00 yd.

Colored Table Damasks.

Turkey on white table damasks, guaranteed fast colors, good weight, assorted patterns—
No. C1, 52-inch, 29c yd.
No. C2, 56-inch, 35c yd.
No. C3, 58-inch, 40c yd.
No. C4, 62-inch, 45c yd.
No. C5, 72-inch, 50c yd.

Extra quality, Turkey on white damask, assorted patterns, fast colors—
No. C6, 58-inch, 35c yd.
No. C7, 62-inch, 45c yd.
No. C9, 62-inch, 50c yd.

Turkey on green table damasks, guaranteed fast colors, choice floral patterns—
No. C10, 52-inch, 30c yd.
No. C11, 56-inch, 35c yd.
No. C12, 58-inch, 40c yd.
No. C13, 66-inch, 45c yd.
No. C14, 72-inch, 60c yd.

Linen Damask Table Cloths.

Fine bleached union damask tablecloths, finished with border all around—
No. E1, 2 x 2 yds, $1.00.
No. E2, 2 x 2½ yds, $1.25 each.

Full bleached all pure linen satin damask tablecloths, bordered all around, new assorted patterns—
No. E3, 2 x 2½ yards, $1.50
No. E4, 2 x 2½ " 1.65
No. E5, 2 x 2½ " 1.75
No. E5, 2 x 3 " 2.00
No. E6, 2 x 2½ " 1.85
No. E6, 2 x 3 " 2.25 each.

Fine full bleached double damask tablecloths, guaranteed all linen, bordered all around, choice assorted patterns—
No. E7, 2 x 2 yards, $1.85
No. E7, 2 x 2½ " 2.25
No. E7, 2 x 3 " 2.75
No. E8, 2 x 2½ " 2.75
No. E8, 2 x 3 " 3.25 each.

Extra fine full bleached double damask tablecloths, bordered, pure Irish linen, specially selected patterns—
No. E 9, 2 x 2½ yards, $2.00
No. E 9, 2 x 3 " 2.50
No. E 9, 2½ x 3 " 3.50
No. E 9, 2½ x 3½ " 4.00
No. E10, 2 x 2½ " 2.50
No. E10, 2 x 3 " 3.00
No. E10, 2½ x 3 " 4.00
No. E10, 2½ x 3½ " 4.50
No. E11, 2 x 2½ " 3.00
No. E11, 2 x 3 " 3.50
No. E11, 2½ x 3 " 4.50
No. E11, 2½ x 3½ " 5.25
No. E12, 2 x 2½ " 4.00
No. E12, 2 x 3 " 4.75
No. E12, 2½ x 3 " 6.00
No. E12, 2½ x 3½ " 6.50
No. E12, 2½ x 4 " 7.50 each.

Superior satin-finished double damask tablecloths, guaranteed pure Irish linen, choice selected patterns—
No. E13, 2 x 2½ yards, $3.75
No. E13, 2 x 3 " 4.50
No. E13, 2½ x 3 " 5.00
No. E13, 2½ x 3½ " 6.00
No. E13, 2½ x 4 " 7.00
No. E14, 2 x 2½ " 4.25
No. E14, 2 x 3 " 5.00
No. E14, 2½ x 3 " 6.50
No. E14, 2½ x 3½ " 8.00
No. E14, 2½ x 4 " 9.00
No. E15, 2 x 2½ " 5.50
No. E15, 2 x 3 " 7.00
No. E15, 2½ x 3 " 8.50
No. E15, 2½ x 3½ " 10.00
No. E15, 2½ x 4 " 12.00 each.

Damask Cloths, with Napkins to Match.

These are all assorted in choice range of floral and conventional patterns, guaranteed all pure linen, with rich satin finish. Numbers marked thus * are double damask.

No. F1 2 x 2½ yards......... $1.75 each.
" F1 3/4 x 3/4 napkins.... 2.00 doz.
" F2 2 x 2 yards......... 1.85 each.
" F2 2 x 2½ yards......... 2.25 each.
" F2 2 x 3 yards......... 2.75 each.
" F2 3/4 x 3/4 napkins..... 2.75 doz.
" F3 2 x 2½ yards......... 2.00 each.
" F3 2 x 3 yards......... 2.50 each.
" F3 5/8 x 5/8 napkins..... 1.50 doz.
No. F3 3/4 x 3/4 napkins..... 2.50 each.
" *F4 2 x 2½ yards......... 2.25 each.
" *F4 2 x 3 yards......... 2.75 each.
" F4 2½ x 3 yards......... 3.50 each.
" *F4 2½ x 3½ yards......... 4.00 each.
" *F4 3/4 x 3/4 napkins.... 2.75 doz.
" F5 2 x 2½ yards......... 2.50 each.
" F5 2 x 3 yards......... 3.00 each.
" F5 2½ x 3 yards......... 3.75 each.
" F5 2½ x 3½ yards......... 4.25 each.
" F5 3/4 x 3/4 napkins.... 3.00 doz.
" *F6 2 x 2½ yards .... 2.75 each.
" F6 2 x 3 yards......... 3.25 each.
" F6 3/4 x 3/4 napkins..... 3.25 each.
" *F7 2 x 2½ yards....... 3.50 each.
" F7 2 x 3 yards......... 4.00 each.
" F7 2½ x 3 yards......... 5.00 each.
" F7 2½ x 3½ yards........ 6.00 each.
" F7 3/4 x 3/4 napkins.... 4.25 doz.
" *F8 2 x 2½ yards......... 4.00 each.
" F8 2 x 3 yards......... 4.50 each.
" F8 2½ x 3 yards .... 6.00 each.
" F8 2½ x 3½ yards....... 6.50 each.
" F8 2½ x 4 yards....... 7.50 each.
" *F9 3/4 x 3/4 napkins .... 4.50 doz.
" F9 2 x 2½ yards......... 4.25 each.
" F9 2 x 3 yards......... 5.00 each.
" F9 2½ x 3 yards......... 6.50 each.
" F9 2½ x 3½ yards......... 7.00 each.
" F9 2½ x 4 yards......... 8.00 each.
" *F9 3/4 x 3/4 napkins.... 6.00 doz.
" F10 2 x 2½ yards......... 5.00 each.
" F10 2 x 3 yards......... 6.50 each.
" F10 2½ x 3½ yards......... 8.00 each.
" F10 2½ x 4 yards......... 9.00 each.
" F10 2½ x 4½ yards......... 10.00 each.
" F10 3/4 x 3/4 napkins ..... 8.00 doz.

Satin Damask Table Napkins.

The following is a guide as to actual size in inches of our napkins: ⅝ x ⅝ measure 16, 18 and 20 inches square; 16-inch, from 50c to 85c doz; 18-inch, from $1.00 to $1.50 doz; 20-inch, from $1.25 to $4.00; ¾ x ¾ napkins measure 22, 23, 24 and 25 inches square; 22-inch, from $1.25 to $1.75 doz; 23-inch, from $1.50 to $2.50 doz; 24-inch, from $1.75 to $3.50 doz; 25-inch, from $2.50 to $8.00 doz.

We do not sell less than ½-doz napkins.

Fine bleached, linen damask table napkins, in assorted patterns—
No. N1, ⅝ x ⅝, 50c No. N5, ⅝ x ⅝, $1.00
No. N2, ⅝ x ⅝, 60c No. N6, ⅝ x ⅝, 1.15
No. N3, ⅝ x ⅝, 75c No. N7, ⅝ x ⅝, 1.25
No. N4, ⅝ x ⅝, 85c doz. No. N8, ⅝ x ⅝, 1.35 doz.

Full-bleached satin-finished double damask table napkins, guaranteed all pure linen, choice patterns—
No. N 9, ⅝ x ⅝, $1.50 No. N12, ⅝ x ⅝, $2.00
No. N10, ⅝ x ⅝, 1.65 No. N13, ⅝ x ⅝, 2.25
No. N11, ⅝ x ⅝, 1.75 doz. No. N14, ⅝ x ⅝, 2.50 doz.

Extra fine pure linen double damask table napkins, superior quality, rich satin finish—
No. N15, ⅝ x ⅝, $3.00
No. N16, ⅝ x ⅝, 3.50 doz.

Full bleached all pure linen damask table napkins, with satin finish assorted patterns—
No. N18, ¾ x ¾, $1.25 No. N22, ¾ x ¾, $1.75
" N19, ¾ x ¾, 1.35 " N23, ¾ x ¾, 1.85
" N20, ¾ x ¾, 1.50 " N24, ¾ x ¾, 2.00
" N21, ¾ x ¾, 1.65 doz. " N25, ¾ x ¾, 2.25 doz.

Fine bleached Irish linen double damask table napkins, superior quality and finish, assorted in floral patterns—
No. N26, ¾ x ¾, $2.50 No. N29, ¾ x ¾, $3.25
" N27, ¾ x ¾, 2.75 " N30, ¾ x ¾, 3.50
" N28, ¾ x ¾, 3.00 doz. " N31, ¾ x ¾, 4.00 doz.

Extra fine superior quality full bleached double damask table napkins, soft grass bleached, exclusive patterns—
No. N36, ¾ x ¾, $4.50 No. N42, ¾ x ¾, $8.00
" N37, ¾ x ¾, 5.00 " N43, ¾ x ¾, 8.50
" N38, ¾ x ¾, 5.50 " N44, ¾ x ¾, 9.00
" N39, ¾ x ¾, 6.00 " N45, ¾ x ¾, 10.00
" N40, ¾ x ¾, 6.50 " N46, ¾ x ¾, 12.00 doz.
" N41, ¾ x ¾, 7.00 doz.

Underlay or Silence Cloth.

Silence cloth, for using under damask cloths, heavy weight and soft, pure finish—
54-inch 50c
56 " 65c
64 " ....75c yd.

Quilted table padding, with tape-bound edges, extra heavy and washable—
60-inch...........85c yd.
54-inch...........75c yd.

Fancy Linen Department.

Battenburg Lace Centres, Scarfs, Tray Cloths, Tea Cloths, Doylies, etc.

Battenburg lace doylies, round and square, new designs—
Size 5 x 5 inches, 8c, 10c, 12½c each.
" 7 x 7 " 15c, 20c, 25c "
" 9 x 9 " 25c, 30c, 35c "
" 12 x 12 " 40c, 50c "
" 14 x 14 " 65c, 75c "

Battenburg or renaissance lace centrepieces in all the newest designs, size 19 x 19 inches, 75c, 85c, $1.00, 1.25, 1.50, 1.75 each.

Battenburg centrepieces, with linen centre and deep border of hand-made renaissance lace, new designs, size 19 x 19 inches, $1.00, 1.25, 1.50, 1.75 each.

Battenburg tray cloths in all lace, also with linen centre and deep border of Battenburg lace, size 20 x 30 inches, $2.00, 2.50, 3.00, 3.25 each.

Battenburg sideboard or dresser scarfs, all lace or with linen centre and border of hand-made Battenburg lace, choice new designs—
Size 20 x 54, $3.00, 3.50, 4.00, 4.50, 5.00 each.
" 20 x 72, 4.00, 4.50, 5.00, 6.00, 7.00 "

Battenburg tea cloths and pillow shams, all lace, also with linen centre and wide edge of Battenburg lace, choice new designs—
Size 32 x 32, $2.50, 3.00, 3.50, 4.00 each.
" 36 x 36, 3.50, 4.00, 4.50, 5.00 "

Taoro Hand-Drawn Linens and Rueda Lace Goods.

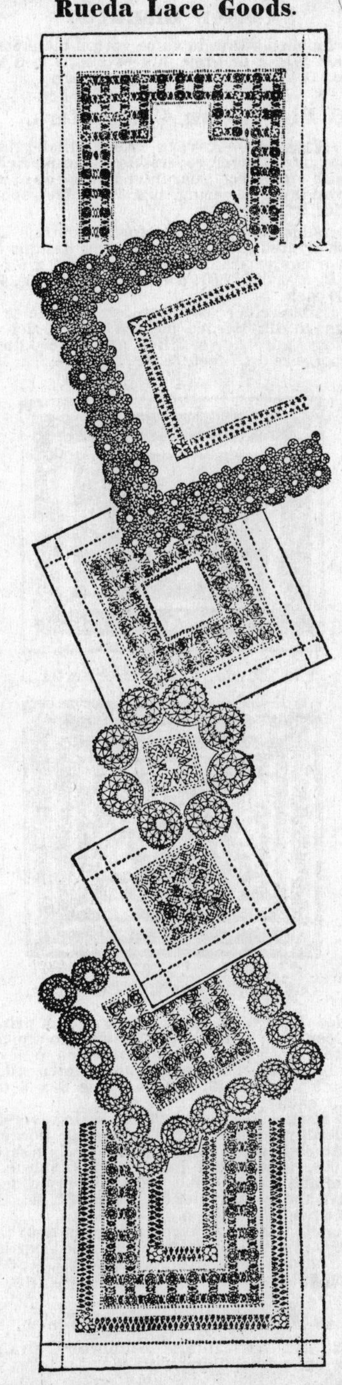

Taoro hand-drawn linens are made from the celebrated **Old Bleach Linens**, by the natives of Teneriffe. The work is beautifully fine and perfect in the smallest detail. The patterns are new and dainty. Designs as shown in above cut in the following sizes:

Doylies hemstitched and drawn—
6 x 6 in., 20c, 25c each. 8 x 8 in., 35c each.
10 x 10 inches. 45c each.

Doylies, lace edge—
6 x 6 inches, 30c each. 7 x 7 inches, 45c each.
9 x 9 " 60c " 12 x 12 " 85c "

Tray cloths hemstitched and drawn work, 20 x 30 inches, $1.75, 2.00 each.

Tray cloths lace edge and drawn work, 20 x 30 inches, $2.25, 3.25 each.

Scarfs and tea cloths hemstitched and drawn—
18 x 54 inches, $2.50, 2.75, 3.25, 3.75 each.
18 x 72 " 3.25, 4.00, 4.25 "
36 x 36 " 2.75, 3.00, 3.50, 5.00 "

Hemstitched and Drawn Linens.

Hemstitched Irish linen doylies and centrepieces with fancy drawn work—
Size 7 x 7 inches, 8c, 10c each.
" 9 x 9 " 10c, 12½c, 15c each.
" 12 x 12 " 15c, 20c, 25c "
" 18 x 18 " 20c, 25c, 30c "
" 20 x 20 " 25c, 30c, 35c, 40c each.

Hemstitched plain Irish linen tray or carving cloths—
Size 18 x 27 inches, 20c, 25c, 35c, 40c, 50c each.
" 20 x 30 " 25c, 30c, 40c, 50c, 60c "

Hemstitched plain Irish linen tray or carving cloths, with fancy drawn-work corners and sides—
18 x 27 in., 20c, 25c, 30c, 35c, 40c, 50c, 75c, $1.00 ea.
20 x 30 " 25c, 30c, 40c, 50c, 75c, 85c, $1.00, 1.25 ea

Hemstitched plain Irish linen tray cloths with drawn work and embroidered designs—
Size 18 x 27 inches, 40c, 50c, 65c each.
" 20 x 30 " 65c, 75c, 85c, $1.00 each.

Hemstitched plain Irish linen sideboard or dresser scarfs, with open work—
Size 20 x 54 inches, 40c, 50c, 60c, 75c, 85c each.
" 20 x 72 " 50c, 60c, 75c, 85c, $1.00 "

Hemstitched plain Irish linen pillow shams, superior quality, with drawn work, size 32 x 32, $1.00, 1.25, 1.50, 1.75, 2.00 per pair.

Hemstitched plain Irish linen 5 o'clock tea cloths, open work, size 36 x 36 inches, 50c, 65c, 75c, 85c, $1.00 each.

Hemstitched hand embroidered 5 o'clock tea cloths in assorted designs, size 36 x 36 inches, $2.50, 3.00, 3.50, 4.00 each.

Damask Tray, Tea and Sideboard Cloths.

Bleached linen damask tray cloths, fringed, new assorted patterns, all linen—
Size 18 x 27 inches, 12½c.
" 20 x 30 " 15c, 20c each.

Fine bleached German damask tray cloths, tied fringe, large range of new patterns, all linen—
Size 18 x 27 inches, 17c, 25c each.
" 20 x 30 " 20c, 33c "

Fine bleached German damask tray cloth, tied fringe and fancy open work, all linen, choice new patterns—
Size 18 x 27 inches, 20c, 23c each.
" 20 x 30 " 25c, 27c "

Hemstitched German damask tray cloths, all pure linen, superior quality and finish—
Size 18 x 27 inches, 20c, 23c, 25c, 30c, 35c each.
" 20 x 30 " 27c, 30c, 33c, 35c, 40c, 45c "

Hemstitched German damask tray cloths, new designs, with open work, all linen, superior quality—
Size 18 x 27 inches, 29c, 35c, 50c each.
" 20 x 30 " 33c, 40c, 50c, 60c, 65c "

Sideboard scarfs, full bleached damask, long knotted fringe, all linen—
Size 18 x 50 inches, 30c, 33c each.
" 16 x 68 " 35c, 40c "

Extra super all pure white wool blankets, absolutely free from grease, fine soft finish, at 47½c a pound, or—

Lbs.	Size.	Price per pair.
6,	60 x 80,	$2.85
7,	64 x 84,	3.33
8,	68 x 88,	3.80
9,	70 x 90,	4.28
10,	72 x 92,	4.75

Fine extra super all pure white wool blankets, absolutely free from grease, fine soft finish, at 50c a pound, or—

Lbs.	Size.	Price Per pair.
6,	60 x 80,	$3.00.
7,	64 x 84,	3.50.
8,	68 x 88,	4.00.
9,	70 x 90,	4.50.
10,	72 x 92,	5.00.

Fine pure all-wool white Saxony blankets, thoroughly cleansed and scoured, soft and lofty in finish, a superior blanket in every way, at 55c a pound, or—

Lbs.	Size.	Price Per pair.
7,	64 x 84,	$3.85.
8,	68 x 88,	4.40.
9,	70 x 90,	4.95.
10,	72 x 92,	5.50.

Extra fine pure all-wool Saxony blankets, soft lofty finish, at 60c pound, or—

Lbs.	Size.	Price Per pair.
7,	64 x 84,	$4.20.
8,	68 x 88,	4.80.
9,	70 x 90,	5.40.
10,	72 x 92,	6.00.

Extra superfine all pure wool Saxony blankets, guaranteed absolutely pure, fine lofty finish, at 75c a pound, or—

Lbs.	Size.	Price per pair.
8,	68 x 88,	6.00.
9,	70 x 90,	6.75.
10,	72 x 92,	7.50.

Fine white wool crib blankets, soft pure finished goods, $1.00, 1.25, 1.50, 1.75, 2.00, 2.50 pair.

Grey Blankets.

Grey union blankets, soft finish, a 25c a pound, or—

Lbs.	Size.	Price per pair.
5,	56 x 74,	$1.25.
6,	60 x 80,	1.50.
7,	64 x 84,	1.75.
8,	68 x 88,	2.00.

Dark grey union blankets, soft finish, at 27½c a pound, or—

Lbs.	Size.	Price per pair.
5,	52 x 72,	$1.38.
6,	56 x 74,	1.65.
7,	58 x 78,	1.93.
8,	60 x 80,	2.20.

Super grey union blankets, fine soft finish, at 30c a pound, or—

Lbs.	Size.	Price per pair.
5,	52 x 72,	$1.50.
6,	56 x 74,	1.80.
7,	60 x 80,	2.10.
8,	64 x 84,	2.40.

Extra fine grey union blankets, fine soft finish, at 35c a pound, or—

Lbs.	Size.	Price per pair.
5,	52 x 72,	$1.75.
6,	56 x 74,	2.10.
7,	60 x 80,	2.45.
8,	64 x 84,	2.80.
9,	70 x 90,	3.15.
10,	72 x 90,	3.50.

Fine unshrinkable silver grey blankets, soft finish, at 37½c a pound, or—

Lbs.	Size.	Price per pair.
5,	56 x 74,	$1.88.
6,	60 x 80,	2.25.
7,	64 x 84,	2.63.
8,	68 x 88,	3.00.

Extra fine all-wool steel grey blankets, special soft pure finish, at 40c a pound, or—

Lbs.	Size.	Price per pair.
6,	60 x 80,	$2.40.
7,	64 x 84,	2.80.
8,	68 x 88,	3.20.
9,	70 x 90,	3.60.
10,	72 x 90,	4.00.

Extra super all-wool silver grey blankets, soft and lofty finish, solid blue borders, 45c a pound, or—

Lbs.	Size.	Price per pair.
7,	64 x 82,	$3.15.
8,	68 x 86,	3.60.
9,	70 x 90,	4.05.
10,	72 x 92,	4.50.
12,	72 x 92,	5.40.

Cotton Blankets.

Soft finished swansdown or cotton blankets, in plain white or grey, 10/4 or single bed size, 65c; 11/4 or double bed size, 85c pair.

Eiderdown Comforters.

Cur Leader.—A very fine English-printed sateen comforter, reversible patterns, rich in finish and effect, guaranteed pure down, with down-proof covering, size 6 x 6 feet, special price, $6.00 each.

Reversible eiderdown comforters, of fine English-printed sateen, entirely new designs and colorings, guaranteed down-proof, 5 x 6 feet, $4.50, 5.00, 6.00, 7.00; 6 x 6 feet, $5.00, 6.00, 7.00, 8.00 each.

Reversible eiderdown comforters, choice designs in silk-finished printed sateen, rich colorings, pure down filling, guaranteed down-proof, size 6 x 7 feet, $6.50, 7.00, 8.00 each.

Cut showing Framed Comforter.

Cut showing Bordered Comforter.

Choice designs in French down-proof printed sateen reversible eiderdown comforters, framed or bordered in plain sateen, fancy or plain backs, guaranteed pure down filling, size 5 x 6 feet, $7.50 each. Size 6 x 6 feet, $8.50 each.

New designs in French-printed satin reversible eiderdown comforters, framed or bordered with plain satin, fancy printed or plain sateen backs, guaranteed pure down filling, color combinations in blue, bronze, crimson, gold, olive and copper, size 5 x 6 feet, $12.50. Size 6 x 6 feet, $15.50 each.

Reversible eiderdown comforter, as above, all satin top and back, fancy stitched patterns and corded edge, size 5 x 6 feet, $17.00; 6 x 6 feet, $20.00 each.

Wadded Comforters.

No. 2. Printed cambric comforters, straight sewing, white filling, size 48 x 69 inches, 85c each.

No. 3. Printed art cambric comforters, straight sewing, white filling, size 54 x 70 inches, $1.00 each.

No. 4. Reversible art cambric comforters, straight sewing, white filling, size 60 x 70 inches, $1.10 each.

No. 5. Reversible printed art cambric comforters, straight sewing, white filling, size 70 x 72 inches, $1.25 each.

Turkey Chintz Comforters.

English printed Turkey red plain chintz top comforters, plain linings, fancy stitching and white filling, size 72 x 72 inches, $1.25, 1.50, 1.75 each.

Heavy twill Turkey and English chintz top comforters, plain linings, fancy stitching and white filling, size 72 x 72 inches, $1.50, 1.75, 2.00 each.

Fancy Reversible Comforters.

Reversible comforters of printed art silkalines, fancy stitching and pure white carded cotton filling, size 60 x 72 inches, $1.25, 1.39, 1.50 each. Size 72 x 72 inches, $1.39, 1.50, 1.75 each.

Reversible comforters of printed art sateens, fancy stitched patterns, pure white carded cotton filling, size 60 x 72 inches, $1.75, 2.00 each. Size 72 x 72 inches, $2.00, 2.25, 2.50, 2.75, 3.00 each.

Quilted Mattress Protectors.

Washable sanitary mattress protectors, made of heavy white cotton, wadded and quilted, bound all round, size 25 x 27 inches, 40c; 40 x 35 inches, 70c; 40 x 76 inches, $1.40; 50 x 76 inches, $1.65; 60 x 76 inches, $1.85 each.

Washable sanitary mattress protector, bound on two edges, per yard, 50-inch, 75c; 60-inch, 85c.

White and Colored Quilts.

Approximate sizes—
For 9/4 read 57 x 78 inches.
For 10/4 read 64 x 86 inches.
For 11/4 read 74 x 95 inches.
For 12/4 read 82 x 104 inches.

Fine white crochet quilts, Canadian makes, soft finish, pearled edges, new designs, 11/4 size, 75c, 85c, $1.00, 1.10 each.

American crochet quilts, full-bleached, new designs, hemmed ready for use, 11/4 size, $1.00, 1.25, 1.50, 1.75 each.

American full back Marseilles quilts, in all the newest designs, soft finish and full bleach, hemmed ready for use, 11/4 size, $2.00, 2.25, 2.50, 2.75, 3.00, 3.50 each.

English fine white honeycomb quilts, fringed ends and sides, new designs, sizes 10/4, 65c, 75c, 85c, $1.00; 11/4, $1.00, 1.25, 1.50, 1.75, 2.00, 2.50 ea.

English colored honeycomb quilts, in blue and pink, guaranteed fast colors, size 11/4, $1.25 ea.

Fine satin white quilts, best English makes, full bleached, very rich in finish, new designs in Roman and scroll patterns, sizes 9/4, $1.25, 1.50; 10/4, $1.50, 1.75, 2.00; 11/4, $1.50, 1.75, 2.00, 2.25, 2.50, 2.75, 3.00, 3.50, 4.00; 12/4, $2.75, 3.50, 4.50 each.

English Alhambra colored quilts, all patterns, in red and white, blue and white, and chintz, all fast colors, size 10/4, 75c, 85c; 11/4, $1.00, 1.25, 1.35, 1.50, 1.75, 2.00 each.

Pillow Cases.

Pillow cases of good bleached cotton, 2½-inch plain hem, sizes 42 x 36, 45 x 36 inches, 25c, 30c pair.

Pillow cases of specially selected cottons, finished with 3 tucks and 2½-inch hem, sizes 42 x 36, 45 x 36 inches, 35c pair.

Pillow cases of soft finished cotton, with cambric frill and 2½-inch hem, sizes 42 x 36, 45 x 36 inches, 40c pair.

Pillow cases of fine cotton, finished with cambric frill and cluster of 4 tucks, sizes 42 x 36, 45 x 36 inches, 40c pair.

Pillow cases of selected cotton, deep embroidery frill and cluster of 3 tucks, 2½-inch hem, sizes 42 x 36, 45 x 36 inches, 50c pair.

Hemmed Sheets.

Ready-made sheets of best standard sheeting, 2-inch top and 1-inch bottom hems.

Plain bleached sheets—
64 x 90 inches, 95c, $1.05, 1.15 pair.
72 x 90 inches, $1.05, 1.15, 1.25, 1.35, 1.55 pair.
80 x 90 inches, $1.15, 1.25, 1.35, 1.55, 1.75 pair.

Twill bleached sheets—
64 x 90 inches, $1.05, 1.15, 1.25 pair.
72 x 90 inches, $1.15, 1.25, 1.35, 1.55, 1.75 pair.
80 x 90 inches, $1.25, 1.35, 1.55, 1.75, 2.00 pair.

Unbleached plain sheets—
64 x 90 inches, 75c, 85c pair.
72 x 90 inches, 85c, 95c, $1.05 pair.
80 x 90 inches, 95c, $1.05, 1.15 pair.

Unbleached twill sheets—
64 x 90 inches, 85c, 95c pair.
72 x 90 inches, 95c, $1.05, 1.15, 1.25 pair.
80 x 90 inches, $1.05, 1.15, 1.25, 1.35 pair.

Flannel Department.

Grey Union Flannels.

Unshrinkable grey union flannel, in light and dark shades, plain and twill, 25-inch, 9c, 10c yd.

Heavy unshrinkable grey union shirting flannel, soft pure finish, light and dark shades, plain and twilled, 25-inch, 12½c; 27-inch, 15c yd.

Fine pressed finished grey union flannel, unshrinkable, light and dark shades, plain and twill, 28-inch, 18c yd.

All-Wool Grey Flannels.

All-wool grey flannel, thoroughly scoured, light and dark shades, plain and twilled, 26-inch, 16c; 27-inch, 19c; 28-inch, 20c yd.

Heavy all-wool grey flannel, clear pure make, thoroughly scoured, light and dark shades, in plain and twill, 26-inch, 18c yd; 28-inch, 22c; 32-inch, 25c yd.

OUR SPECIAL all-wool grey flannel, manufactured of pure yarns, and recommended by us as a thoroughly reliable shirting and underwear flannel, light and dark shades, plain and twill, 27-inch, 25c yd.

Extra heavy grey flannel, guaranteed entirely free from grease, smooth soft finish, light and dark shades, plain and twill, 28-inch, 25c; 32-inch, 30c yd.

Extra superfine all-wool grey flannel, manufactured from fine wools, guaranteed absolutely pure, soft smooth finish, light and dark shades, plain and twill, 27-inch, 28c; 28-inch, 30c; 32-inch, 35c yd.

Special all-wool flannel, thoroughly scoured, pressed finish, light and dark shades, plain and twill, 32-inch, 28c yd.

Homespun and Kersey Flannels.

Kersey union flannel, heavy twill, in grey, and black or brown mixtures, 27-inch, 20c yd.

Extra heavy all-wool Kersey twill flannel, for men's heavy shirts, etc., unshrinkable, grey shades only, 27-inch, 25c, 30c yd.

Canadian homespun flannel, guaranteed al pure wool, unshrinkable, assorted check patterns, in black and red, and black and white, also plain grey and navy, 28-inch, 35c yd.

Navy Blue Flannels.

Canadian heavy plain and twilled navy blue flannel, unshrinkable, used for men's working shirts, 25-inch, 15c; 27-inch, 17c yd.

Medium quality navy blue union flannel, unshrinkable, plain and twill, 25-inch, 17c; 27-inch, 19c yd.

Special make fine navy blue wool flannel, indigo dye, in plain or twill, 27-inch, 25c yd.

Super all-wool navy blue flannel, guaranteed fast dye, soft pressed finish, plain or twill, 28-inch, 30c yd.

Superfine navy blue flannel, made from best quality Pacific wool, guaranteed pure indigo dye, pressed finish, plain or twill, 28-inch, 35c yd.

Extra fine all pure wool navy blue flannel, made of fine Cape wool, warranted pure, fast color, plain or twill, 28-inch, 40c yd.

Specially manufactured fine all-wool navy blue flannel, unshrinkable, in plain only, 32-inch, 28c, 35c, 40c yd.

Scotch and English Shirting Flannels.

Heavy wool mixed shirting flannels, Scotch manufacture, very strong and serviceable, thoroughly shrunk, medium grey and fawn combinations, choice dark patterns, all fast colors, 29-inch, 25c, 30c, 35c, 40c yd.

Best all-wool Scotch and English shirting flannels, made of fine long staple yarns, warranted qualities, choice patterns, dark and medium grey and fawn combinations, 29-inch, 40c, 45c yd.

Extra heavy twill shirting flannels, absolutely pure and thoroughly shrunk, large range of patterns, in grey and fawn stripes, fast colors, 29-inch, 30c yd.

"Glen cloth," an extra fine lightweight Scotch pure all-wool flannel, guaranteed unshrinkable, special soft finish, choice designs in checks and stripes, light grey, blue and fawn colorings, 30-inch, 45c yd.

Scotch all-wool tartan shirting flannels, white and black, red and black and fancy patterns, in medium and small solid and broken checks, 28-inch, 30c yd.

Military shirting flannels, English and Scotch makes, dark greys, in plain and with small pin and medium stripes, warranted unshrinkable, 30-inch, 40c yd.

Fine twilled military flannels, Scotch make, heavy quality, soft pure finish, warranted unshrinkable, in plain grey and narrow stripe patterns, 30-inch, 45c, 50c yd.

Special soft Canadian make of military flannels, extra fine stock, medium and dark grey and fawn, 27-inch, 25c, 30c yd.

Ceylon Flannels.

Fine quality pure Ceylon flannels, cream shades, guaranteed unshrinkable, 28-inch, 20c, 25c, 30c yd.

Fancy stripe Ceylon flannels, choice patterns, in cream, blue and fawn grounds, 28-inch, 15c, 20c, 25c yd.

Extra fine quality Scotch Ceylon flannels, fast colors, cream, pink and blue grounds, with combination stripes, 31-inch, 30c yd.

Extra heavy Scotch Ceylon flannels, guaranteed unshrinkable, fast colors, cream, fawn, pink and blue, combination check, 34-inch, 30c yd.

Scarlet and Natural Flannels.

Scarlet Yorkshire flannels, warranted all pure wool, soft finish, good clear color, 20-inch, 15c; 22-inch, 20c; 25-inch, 25c; 28-inch, 30c; 30-inch, 35c; 31-inch, 40c; 32-inch, 45c, 50c yd.

Fine all-wool natural color sanitary flannels, guaranteed thoroughly shrunk, soft pure finish, 26-inch, 30c; 28-inch, 35c; 30-inch, 40c; 31-inch, 45c yd.

4/4 natural flannels, heavy quality of fine English sanitary flannel, all pure wool and unshrinkable, soft finish, 36-inch, 40c, 45c yd.

Cream Flannels.

Fine cream Ceylon flannels, guaranteed unshrinkable, soft pure finish, 28-inch, 20c, 25c, 30c yd.

Fine French plain flannel, made of extra fine yarns, soft smooth finish, all pure wool and warranted unshrinkable, 26-inch, 25c; 31-inch, 30c, 35c, 40c, 45c, 50c; 36-inch, 40c, 45c, 50c, 60c yd.

French cream twill flannel, all pure wool and unshrinkable, soft finish, good clear color, 27-inch, 25c; 31-inch, 30c, 35c, 40c, 45c, 50c yd.

English Saxony flannels, soft pure make, warranted pure all wool, cream shade, 25-inch, 25c; 27-inch, 30c; 30-inch, 35c; 31-inch, 40c, 45c; 32-inch, 50c yd.

Opera and French Printed Flannels.

Plain color fine twill opera flannels, soft in texture and thoroughly fast in color, in black, garnet, cardinal, navy, pink and sky, 27-inch, 30c, 35c yd.

French twill printed all-wool flannels, specially designed for children's wear, colors pink, navy, sky, scarlet, cream, cardinal, with small polka dot, small and medium stripes, all fast colors, 27-inch, 35c yd.

French printed twill flannels, soft finish pure all-wool fabric, largely used for tea gowns, wrappers, sacques, waists, etc., latest designs and colorings, 27-inch, 40c yd.

Fine French all-wool twill flannel, with small design worked in colored silk, spots in grey, blue, mauve, cardinal, garnet and black, 27-inch, 50c yd.

Eiderdown Flannels.

Plain wool eiderdown flannel, for children's cloaks and ladies' home sacques, etc., heavy soft and downy fleece, colors cream, fawn, red, cardinal, sky, grey, navy and pink, 54-inch, 65c yd.

Extra fine quality plain wool eiderdown flannel, soft and pure in finish, colors cream, scarlet, cardinal, grey, sky, pink and royal blue, 52-inch, 85c yd.

Ripple eiderdown flannel, special quality, soft finish, colors scarlet, cardinal, cream, fawn, grey and sky, 52-inch, 85c yd.

Wavelet eiderdown flannel, a soft downy fabric, with pretty ripple effect, rich clear colorings, cream, pink, sky, scarlet, cardinal and grey, 52-inch, $1.00 yd.

White and Dyed Flannelettes.

Dyed flannelettes, plain cloth, fast colors, cream, pink, blue and white, 25-inch, 6c; 28-inch, 7c; 30-inch, 8c; 34-inch, 10c, 12½c yd.

Dyed flannelettes, twill cloth, soft finish, 28-inch, 8c; 34-inch, 10c, 12½c yd.

Fine English dyed flannelettes, superior qualities in twills, extra soft in texture and pure in finish, clear color, warranted fast dyes, white, cream, sky and pink, 31-inch, 8½c; 32-inch, 10c, 12½c; 36-inch, 15c, 20c yd.

Special make English dyed plain flannelettes, soft velvety finish, warranted pure, rich colorings, in white, cream, pink and sky, 32-inch, 12½c; 36-inch, 15c yd.

English grey and natural flannelettes, fine sanitary cloth, soft finish, 32-inch, 12½c, 15c yd.

English unbleached flannelettes, soft pure finish, well napped, 31-inch, 8c; 32-inch, 10c; 33-inch, 12½c yd.

Heavy unbleached flannelettes, soft well napped makes, 32-inch, 12½c, 15c; 36-inch, 18c yd.

Fine English white flannelettes, best qualities, extra pure cloths, full bleached, soft lofty finish, 32-inch, 8½c, 10c, 12½c; 36-inch, 18c yd.

Striped Flannelettes.

30-inch striped flannelettes, soft pure finished cloth, small and medium stripes, in almost all colorings, 5c yd.

32-inch heavy pure finished flannelette, large assortment of colorings, in small and medium stripes, guaranteed fast dyes, 6½c, 7c yd.

17 yards heavy Canadian flannelette, 32 inches wide, assorted stripes, in pink and blue combinations, fast colors, for $1.00.

14 yards pure finished flannelette, 33-inch, heavy quality, in light and medium combination stripes, fast colors, for $1.00.

33-inch pure finished striped flannelette, light and medium shades, fast colors, 8c yd.

34-inch heavy pure finished flannelette, assorted, in light and medium colors, small and medium stripes, 8½c yd.

36-inch soft finished flannelette, medium and wide stripes, fast colors, 10c yd.

32-inch English made flannelette, assorted colorings, large and small stripes, soft pure finished cloth, fast colors, 8½c yd.

33-inch fine English striped flannelette, large range of patterns, pinks, blues, greys, fast colors, 10c yd.

33-inch very fine English flannelette, soft extra pure make, choice range of new and fancy stripe patterns, warranted fast colors, 12½c yd.

35-inch heavy English soft-finished striped flannelette, medium and light colors, suitable for skirtings, night gowns, etc., 10c yd.

35-inch specially manufactured fine finished striped flannelettes, English made, wide and medium stripes, in pink, blue and fawn combinations, 12½c yd.

36-inch English flannelette, choice patterns, light and medium colors, guaranteed fast, 15c yd.

36-inch extra heavy English double-warp flannelette, new stripe patterns, very strong shirting cloth, fast colors, 18c yd.

36-inch extra fine English flannelettes, specially selected designs and colorings, guaranteed fast, 20c, 25c yd.

32-inch superior quality English twilled flannelette, fancy stripe patterns, well-assorted colors, 10c yd.

33-inch fine twilled English flannelette, new stripes, medium and light colorings, absolutely pure finish, heavy quality, 12½c yd.

36-inch extra fine English twilled flannelette, choice patterns, in medium and light colors, best English make, fast colors, 15c yd.

27-inch Angola shirting flannelettes, assorted patterns, in dark grey, red and fawn checks, 7c yd.

28-inch Angola shirting flannelettes, dark colorings, combinations of greys and browns, all fast colors, 8c, 10c, 12½c yd.

English Ceylon-finished and Silk Stripe Flannelettes.

Fine Ceylon-finished striped flannelettes, neat patterns, in cream, light blue, grey, pink, brown and natural combinations, 28-inch, plain and twill, 15c yd.

English Ceylon-finished stripe flannelettes, medium weights, assorted patterns and colorings, 33-inch, 10c, 12½c yd.

Fine Scotch and English flannelettes, with fancy-woven silk stripes, one of the prettiest cloths made for fine neglige shirts and specially suited for ladies' and children's fine wear, assorted colors, striped, in cream and light natural grounds and various combinations, all fast colors, 28-inch, 12½c, 15c, 18c, 20c, 25c yd.

Boots and Shoes.

We Invite You to order from this Catalogue freely and with absolute confidence; be assured you will be highly pleased. All our Footwear is thoroughly examined by competent inspectors before being shipped, and are guaranteed as represented or money refunded. In ordering, note carefully the sizes as given, state sample number wanted and give size of boot required.

Ladies' Boots.

10. Oil buff, rather heavy, with nailed soles, sizes 3 to 7,

95c.

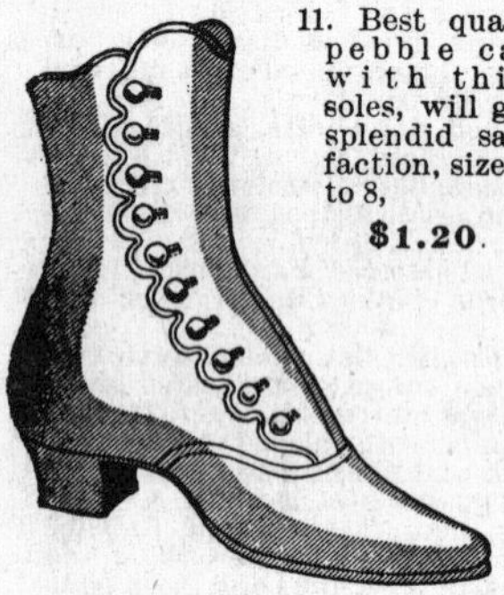

11. Best quality pebble calf, with thick soles, will give splendid satisfaction, sizes 2½ to 8,

$1.20.

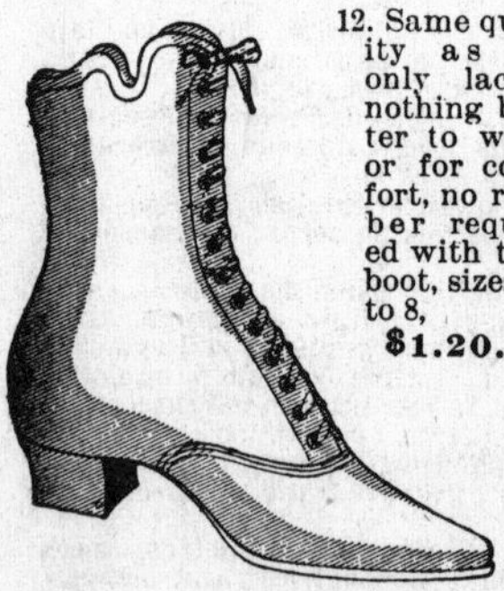

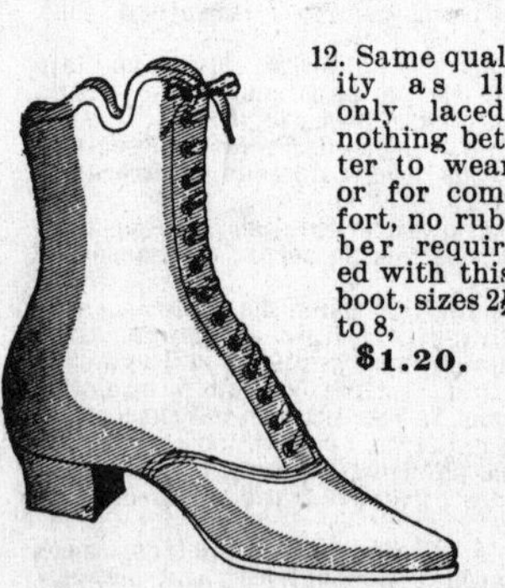

12. Same quality as 11, only laced, nothing better to wear or for comfort, no rubber required with this boot, sizes 2½ to 8,

$1.20.

13. Oil pebble leather, suitable for skating or walking, sewed soles, regulation style, great value, sizes 2½ to 7,

$1.25.

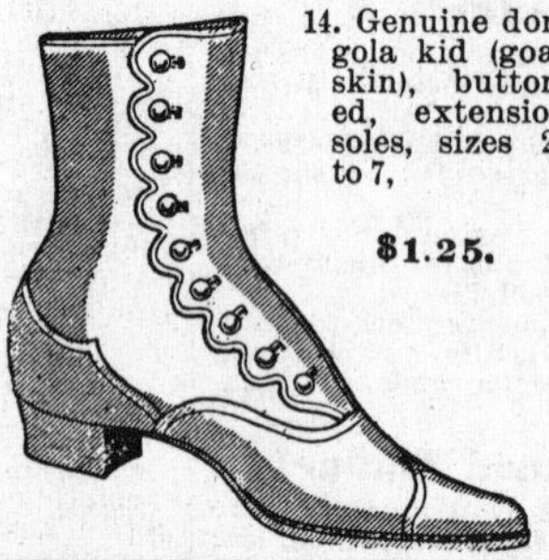

14. Genuine dongola kid (goat skin), buttoned, extension soles, sizes 2½ to 7,

$1.25.

15. Same quality as 14, only laced, sizes 2½ to 7,

$1.25.

16. Glazed kid, buttoned, extension soles, neat and durable, the best boot made for the price, sizes 2½ to 7,

$1.50.

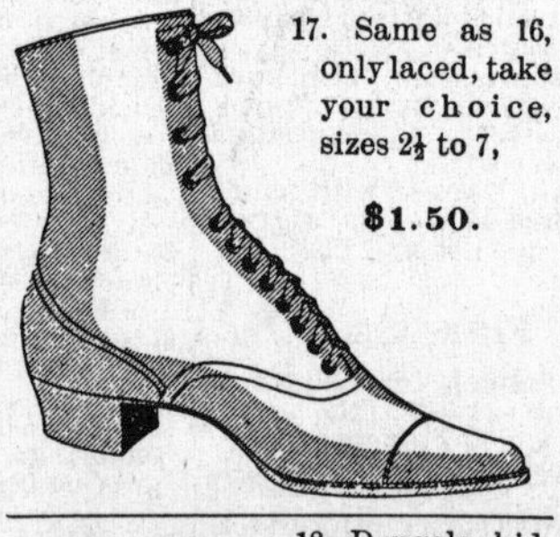

17. Same as 16, only laced, take your choice, sizes 2½ to 7,

$1.50.

18. Dongola kid, buttoned, with plain wide toe, low heel, common-sense shape, will fit a fat foot, sizes 2½ to 8... **$1.45**

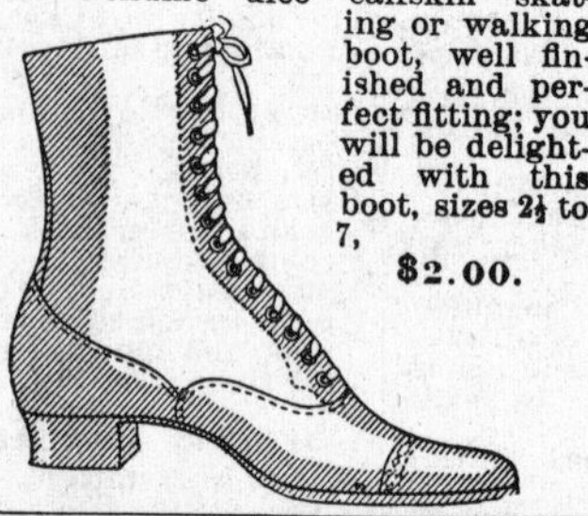

19. Genuine dice calfskin skating or walking boot, well finished and perfect fitting; you will be delighted with this boot, sizes 2½ to 7,

$2.00.

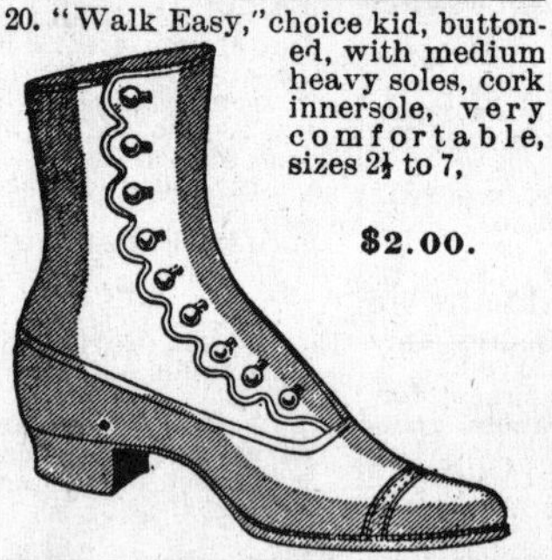

20. "Walk Easy," choice kid, buttoned, with medium heavy soles, cork innersole, very comfortable, sizes 2½ to 7,

$2.00.

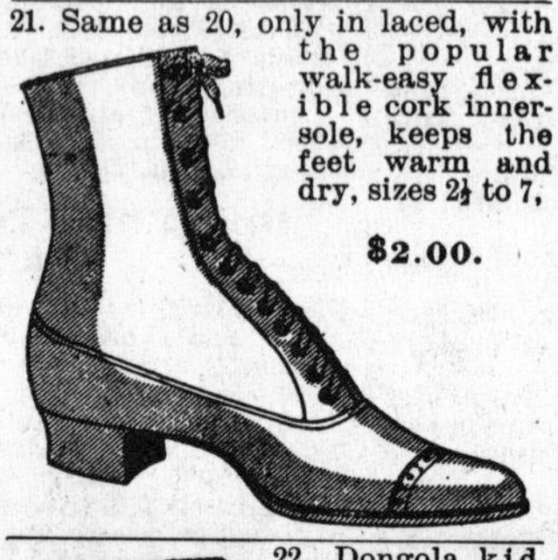

21. Same as 20, only in laced, with the popular walk-easy flexible cork innersole, keeps the feet warm and dry, sizes 2½ to 7,

$2.00.

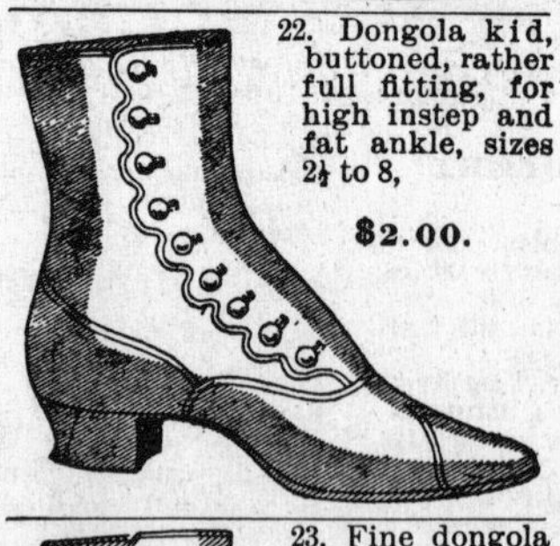

22. Dongola kid, buttoned, rather full fitting, for high instep and fat ankle, sizes 2½ to 8,

$2.00.

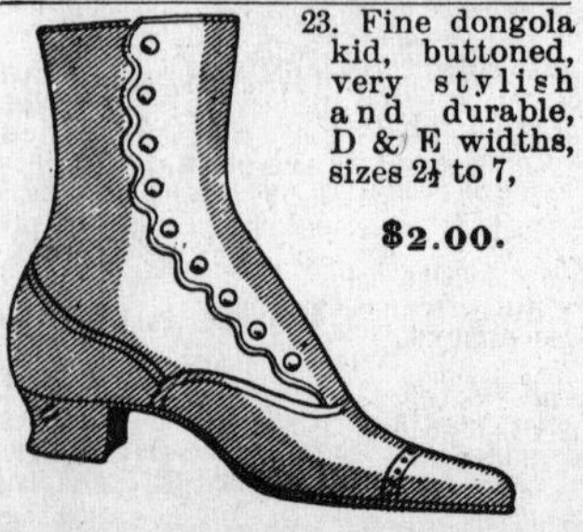

23. Fine dongola kid, buttoned, very stylish and durable, D & E widths, sizes 2½ to 7,

$2.00.

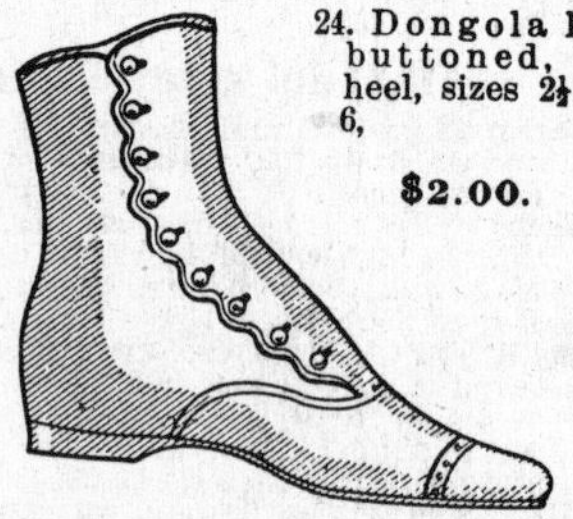

24. Dongola kid buttoned, no heel, sizes 2½ to 6,

$2.00.

25. Same style and quality as 24, in laced, sizes 2½ to 6............**$2.00**

A new boot, "The American Girl," all the rage in the United States; a perfect beauty. Our arrangements with the manufacturer make it possible for us to sell this boot in this country for $2.50. We always buy and sell in the interests of our customers. You never pay us more than others ask, generally less.

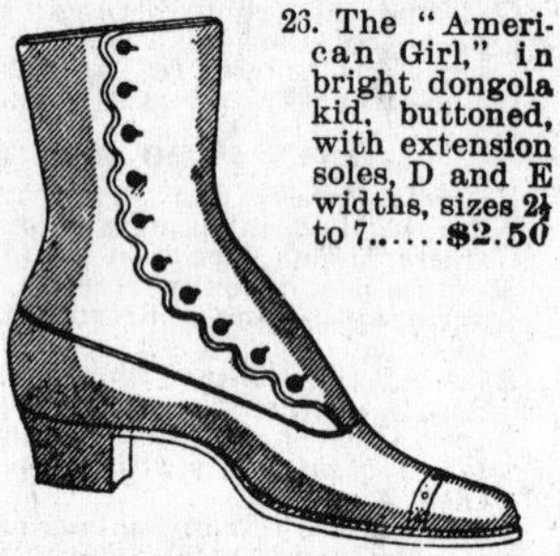

23. The "American Girl," in bright dongola kid, buttoned, with extension soles, D and E widths, sizes 2½ to 7.....**$2.50**

27. Same as 26, only laced, American Girl, a regular beauty, sizes 2½ to 7,

$2.50.

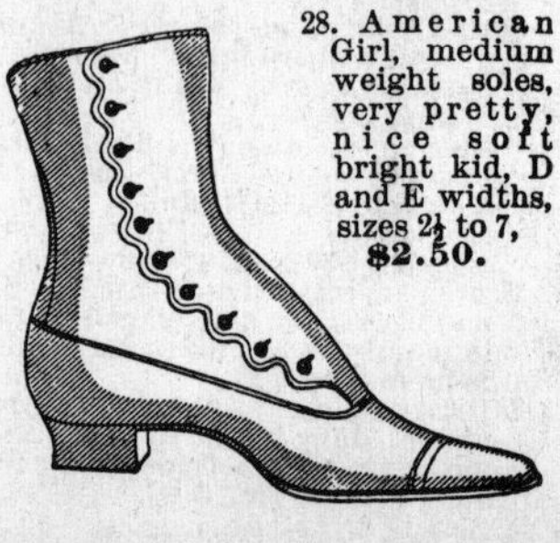

28. American Girl, medium weight soles, very pretty, nice soft bright kid, D and E widths, sizes 2½ to 7,

$2.50.

29. Same as 28 in laced, D and E widths, sizes $2\frac{1}{2}$ to 7, **$2.50.**

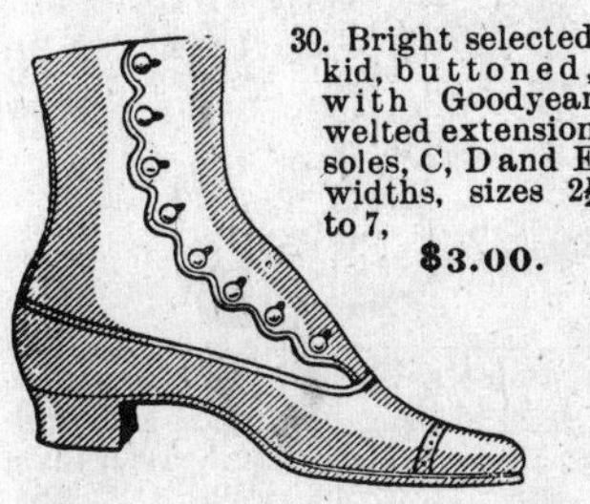

30. Bright selected kid, buttoned, with Goodyear welted extension soles, C, D and E widths, sizes $2\frac{1}{2}$ to 7, **$3.00.**

31. Same as 30, only laced, sizes $2\frac{1}{2}$ to 7............................**$3.00**

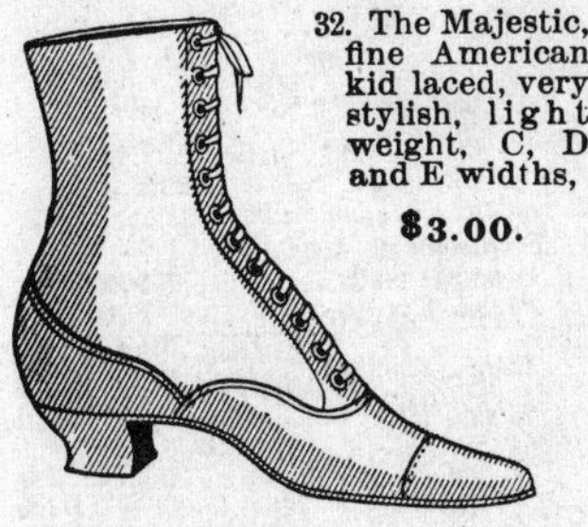

32. The Majestic, fine American kid laced, very stylish, light weight, C, D and E widths, **$3.00.**

We take pleasure in introducing a well-known boot in New York State, the "La Chic," perfection of high grade footwear.

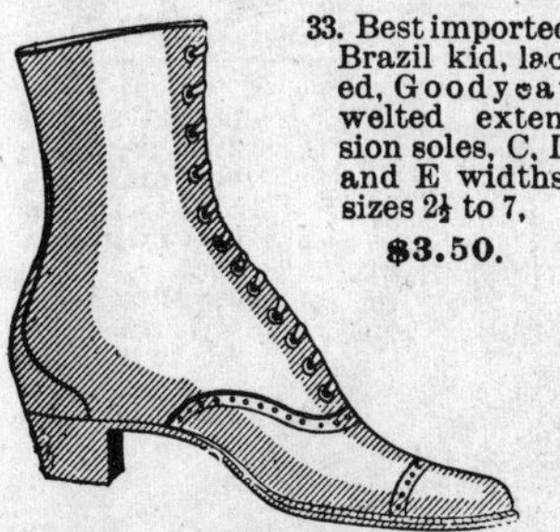

33. Best imported Brazil kid, laced, Goodyear welted extension soles, C, D and E widths, sizes $2\frac{1}{2}$ to 7, **$3.50.**

34. Same as 33, in buttoned...**$3.50**

35. "La Chic," patent calfskin, very stylish, best quality, but not guaranteed, B, C, D and E widths, sizes $2\frac{1}{2}$ to 7. **$3.50.**

36. Extra choice imported diamond black kid, laced, Goodyear welted extension or light turned flexible soles, state which you prefer; C, D and E widths, sizes $2\frac{1}{2}$ to 8, nothing better at $5.00. Our price, **$4.00.**

Ladies' Elastic Side Boots.

37. The old reliable prunella, with low heels and wide, rather heavy soles, sizes 3 to 8....................**95c**

38. Same style as 37, only better quality, with turn flexible soles, sizes 3 to 8 ....**$1.2**

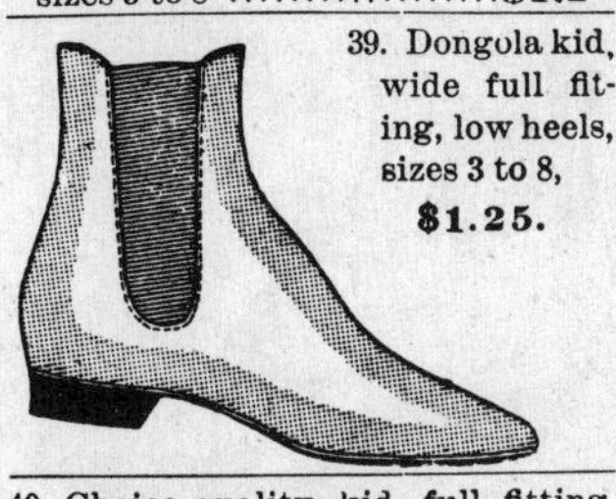

39. Dongola kid, wide full fitting, low heels, sizes 3 to 8, **$1.25.**

40. Choice quality kid, full fitting, a great favorite with all who want comfort and wear, sizes 3 to 8, **$1.95.**

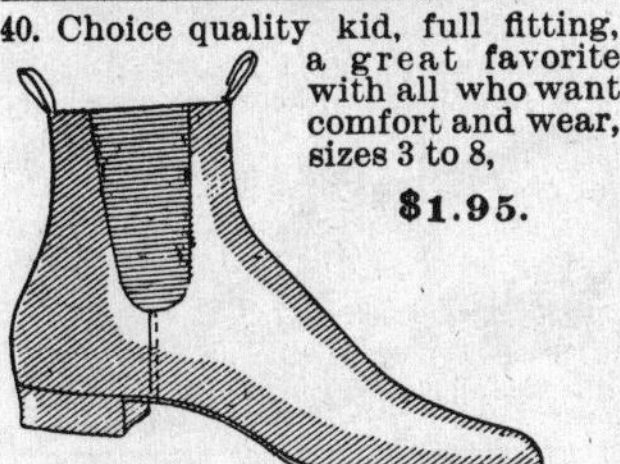

41. Fancy kid, durable and neat, medium, full fitting, sizes $2\frac{1}{2}$ to 7, **$2.00.**

Ladies' Felt Boots and Slippers.

Our felt will be found superior in quality to anything we have ever offered, having been made especially for our trade. Order early while the assortment is complete, we do not guarantee to keep up sizes later than January 1st, but will endeavor at any time to fill order.

42. Best quality, all wool felt, elastic sides, with medium heavy soles, will give perfect satisfaction, sizes 3 to 8, **$1.00.**

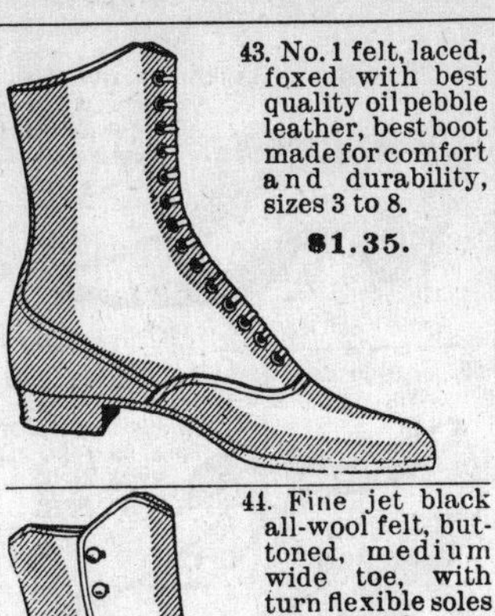

43. No. 1 felt, laced, foxed with best quality oil pebble leather, best boot made for comfort and durability, sizes 3 to 8. **$1.35.**

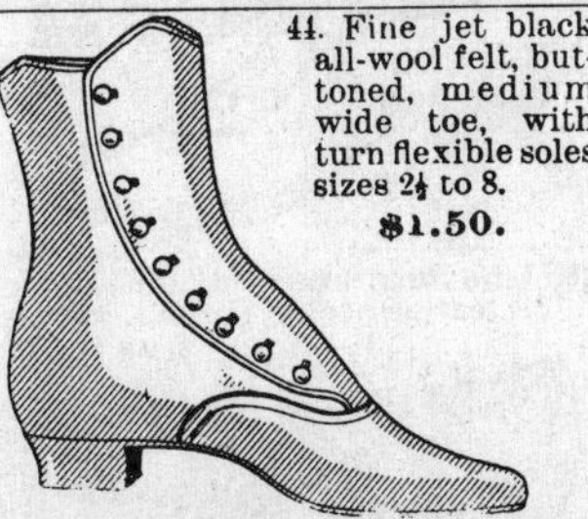

44. Fine jet black all-wool felt, buttoned, medium wide toe, with turn flexible soles sizes $2\frac{1}{2}$ to 8. **$1.50.**

45. Fine black all-wool Juliet, with turn flexible soles, neat and very comfortable, sizes $2\frac{1}{2}$ to 7, **$1.25**

46. The favorite No. 1 felt, rather full fitting, with medium weight soles, great value, sizes $2\frac{1}{2}$ to 8, **$1.00**

47. Superior double weight, hard to wear out, felt house boots, warm lined, the best boot of the kind ever made, sizes 3 to 8, no $\frac{1}{2}$ sizes, **$1.00**

48. Old ladies' thick felt house boots, low heels, wide soles, solid comfort, style, unlined, sizes 3 to 8, no $\frac{1}{2}$ sizes, **85c.**

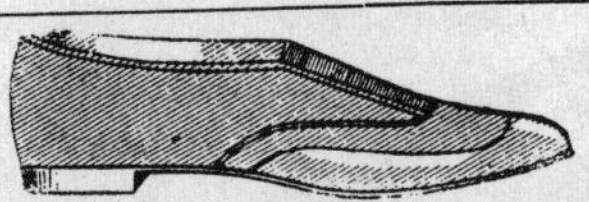

49. Felt buskin, foxed with leather, elastic over the instep, low heels and wide soles, sizes 3 to 8, no $\frac{1}{2}$ sizes............................**85c**

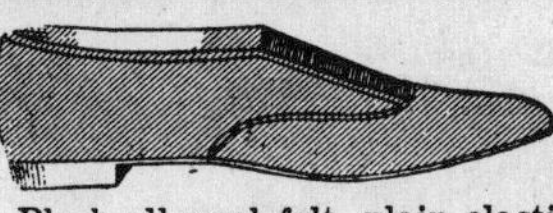

50. Black all-wool felt, plain elastic over the instep, sizes 3 to 8, no $\frac{1}{2}$ sizes............................**75c**

51. 52. 53.

51. Black English felt slippers, fancy design, with thick wool soles, covered with leather, sizes 3 to 7, no $\frac{1}{2}$ sizes............................**50c**

52. Black or wine-colored English felt all-wool slippers, with thick felt soles, suitable for bedroom or hospital wear, sizes 3 to 8, no $\frac{1}{2}$ sizes............................**40c**

53. Black English felt slippers, with thick grey felt soles, sizes 3 to 8, no $\frac{1}{2}$ sizes **25c**

54. The improved double Berlin hand-made crochet slipper, with best quality of lambs' wool soles, colors black, blue and red only, sizes 3 to 7, no $\frac{1}{2}$ sizes, **$1.00.**

Ladies' Slippers.

Always kept in stock.

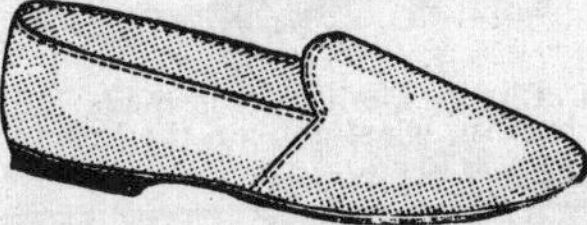

55. Heavy leather kitchen slipper, sizes 3 to 7, no $\frac{1}{2}$ sizes **35c**

56. Prunella buskin, elastic over the instep, sizes 3 to 7, no $\frac{1}{2}$ sizes **40c.**

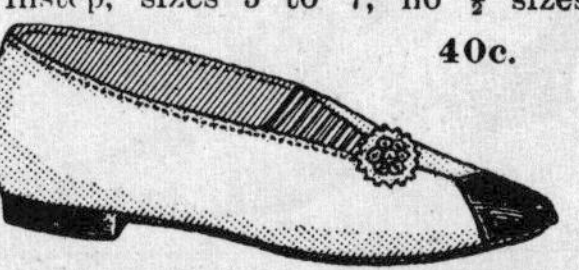

57. Fancy carpet, sewed soles, sizes 3 to 7, no $\frac{1}{2}$ sizes................**50c**

58. Best imported repp carpet slippers, nothing equals it for wear and comfort, foxed with leather, sizes 3 to 7, no $\frac{1}{2}$ sizes, **85c.**

59. One-strap genuine glazed dongola kid, with medium heavy soles, sizes 2½ to 7, **95c.**

60. Snowflake white kid sandal, high heel, flexible soles, sizes 2½ to 7, **95c.**

61. Same style as 64, Dongola kid, buskin with elastic over the instep, turn flexible soles, kid lined, sizes 3 to 8, no ½ sizes, ...**$1.00**

62. Our Leader, glazed kid, one strap, with hand-turn soles, sizes 2½ to 7, **$1.00.**

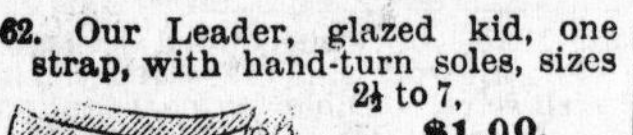

63. Snowball, white kid, with plain satin ribbon bow, superior quality, American make, sizes 2½ to 7, **$1.20.**

64. Choice quality hand-made kid, buskin, elastic over the instep, sizes 2½ to 8..................**$1.25**

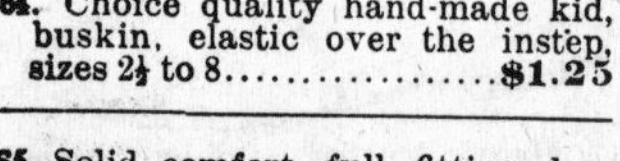

65. Solid comfort, full fitting, low heels and wide soles, sizes 2½ to 8........ **$1.25**

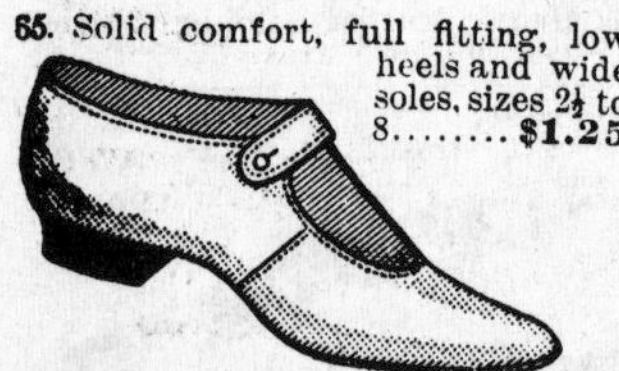

66. Bright kid sandal, with flexible soles, neat and durable, sizes 2½ to 7, **$1.25.**

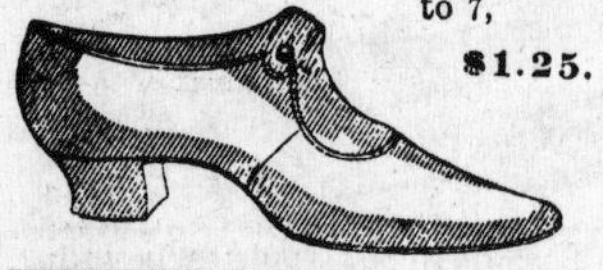

67. Fine glazed kid, with strap and bow flexible sole, kid-lined, sizes 2½ to 7, **$1.50.**

68. Two-strap, buttoned over the instep, perfect fitting, sizes 2½ to 7, **$1.50.**

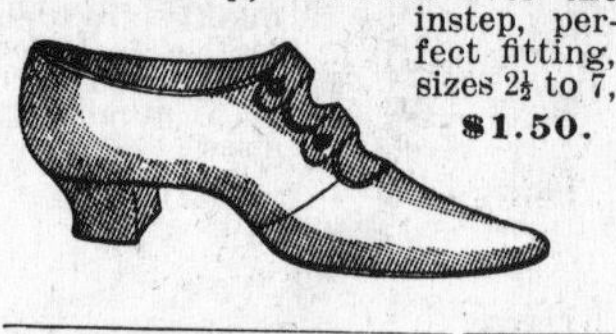

69. Choice selected Brazil kid one strap, white kid-lined, full fitting, suitable for a fat foot, sizes 2½ to 7, **$1.75.**

70. Fine American kid, hand-made, low leather heel, C, D and E widths, sizes 2½ to 7, **$2.00.**

71. American patent leather vamp, very neat, C, D and E widths, sizes 2½ to 7, **$2.00.**

72. Two-strap imported kid, hand turn flexible sole, perfect-fitting, C, D and E widths, sizes 2½ to 7, **$2.00.**

73. Two-strap, choice kid, black beaded vamp and straps, a beauty, B, C, D and E widths sizes 2½ to 7, **$2.50.**

74. One strap, 3 buttoned, best kid, with genuine patent calfskin vamp, hand-turn soles, best slippers made in America, B, C, D and E widths, sizes 2½ to 7. **$3.00.**

75. One strap, 3 buttoned, extra fine American kid, jet black, beaded vamp and strap, very swell, nothing better at $5.00; B, C, D and E widths, sizes 2½ to 7. **$3.00.**

Ladies' Oxford Shoes.

76. Fine jet black kid, white kid-lined, flexible soles, a great favorite, D and E widths, sizes 2½ to 7, **$2.00.**

78. Bright dongola kid, warranted to wear well, turn flexible soles, D and E width, sizes 2½ to 7, **$1.50.**

79. Solid comfort style, low heel and wide soles, plain wide toe, sizes 2½ to 8, **$1.25.**

80. Genuine dongola kid, best value in Canada, turn flexible soles, perfect fitting, sizes 2½ to 7 **$1.25.**

81. Real goat kid, flexible soles, kid-lined, sizes 2½ to 7, **$1.00.**

82. The favorite heavy leather outdoor shoe, sizes 3 to 8, no half sizes, **75c.**

Misses' and Children's Boots and Slippers.

83. Best quality, glazed dongola kid, buttoned, with medium heavy soles, sizes 11 to 2, **$1.50.**

84. Same as 83, only laced **$1.50**

85. The favorite, dice calfskin, superior quality, will give excellent wear,
Sizes 11 to 2 ..**$1.50**
" 8 to 10½ **1.25**

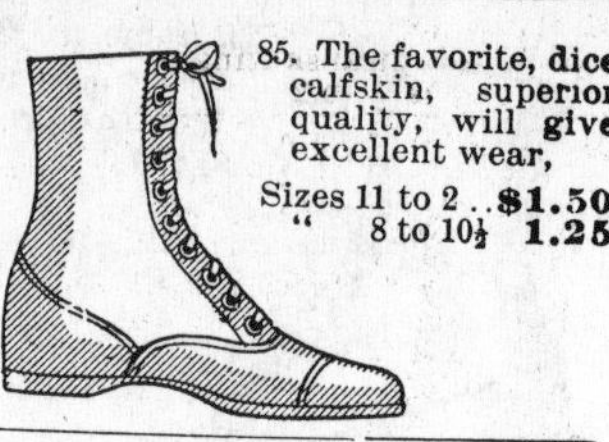

86. Same as 85, only buttoned,
Sizes 11 to 2 ....**$1.50**
" 8 to 10½ **1.25**

87. Genuine goat kid, glossy black, soft finish, great value,
Sizes 11 to 2....**$1.25**
" 8 to 10½.. **1.00**
" 5 to 7½.. **0.85**

88. Same as 87, in laced, sizes from 11 to 2 only **$1.25**

89. Box calfskin, a little heavier than goatskin, suitable for school wear,
Sizes 11 to 2 ..**$1.25**
" 8 to 10½. **1.00**
" 5 to 7½.. **0.95**

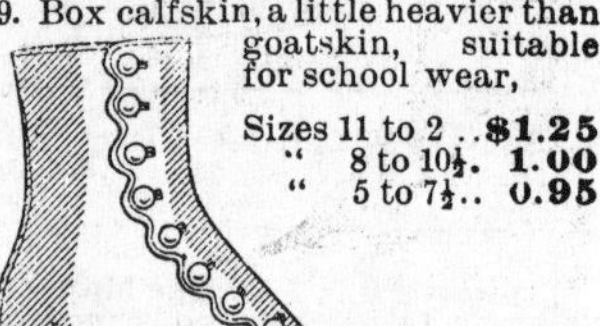

90. Same as 89, only laced,
Sizes 11 to 2 ....**$1.25**
Sizes 8 to 10½....... **1.00**

91. Iron-clad, heavy oil pebble grain leather, will stand rough wear,
Sizes 11 to 2.**$1 20**
" 8 to 10½ ..**95c**
" 5 to 7½ ..**75c**

92. Oil pebble, laced, solid and reliable; you make no mistake in buying this boot.
Sizes 11 to 2 .... **$1.00**
" 8 to 10½ **85c**

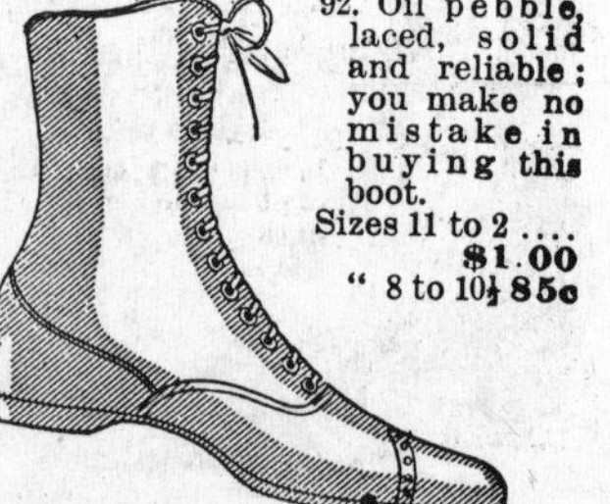

93. Same as 92, only buttoned,
Sizes 11 to 2 ....**$1.00**
" 8 to 10½ **85c**
" 5 to 7½ **75c**

94. Oil pebble, buttoned, with heel,
Sizes 11 to 2.**$1.00**

95. Same as 94, only laced, with heel; a capital skating or walking boot, sizes 11 to 2 .... **$1.00**

96. Little gents' dice calfskin, laced, just like papa's boots, only spring heel,

Sizes 8 to 10½..**$1.20**
" 11 to 13....**1.50**

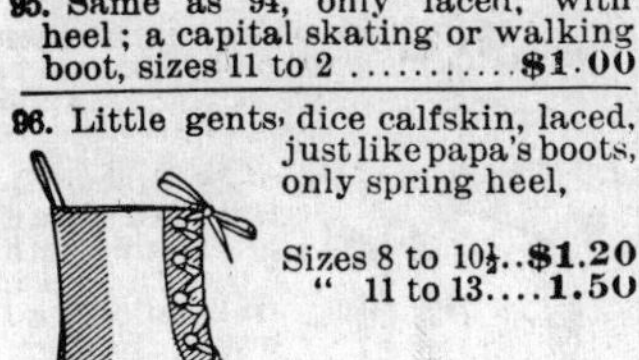

97. Little gents' iron-clad heavy soles, hard to wear out, with heel, sizes 8 to 10½,

95c.

98. Children's genuine dongola kid, buttoned, McKay sewed, spring heels,

Sizes 8 to 10½..**$1.25**
" 5 to 7½...**1.00**

99. Same as 98, only laced,
Sizes 8 to 10½ **$1.25**
" 5 to 7½ **1.00**

100. Best quality fine diamond black American kid, buttoned, turn, flexible soles, spring heels,

Sizes 4 to 8..**$1.25**
" 8½ to 11 ..**1.50**

101. Fine kid, with flexible soles, full fitting, suitable for fat baby, wedge heel,

Sizes 4 to 8...**$1.00**
" 2 to 5, no heel.....**85c**

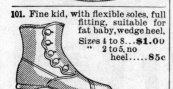

102. Pretty red kid, laced, very stylish, best American make, sizes 4 to 8,

$1.75.

103. Extra choice, American kid, fine and perfect fitting, sizes 2 to 5,

$1.00.

104. Red kid, fine American make, turn flexible leather soles, sizes 2 to 5,

$1.00.

105. Fat ankle, full fitting and durable soft kid, wedge heel, sizes 3 to 7. **75c**; 2 to 5, no heel, ... **65c**

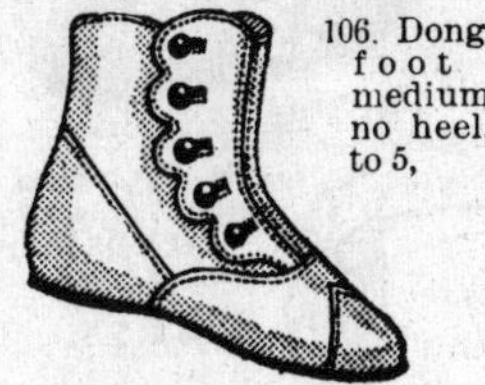

106. Dongola kid, foot form, medium fitting, no heel, sizes 2 to 5,

65c.

107. Genuine goat kid, improved quality, turn flexible leather sole, no heel, sizes 2 to 5, **40c.** wedge heel, sizes 3 to 7,

50c.

Infants' Soft Kid Sole Boots and Moccasins.

108. Extra choice kid, American make, black, chocolate, pink, white and blue, sizes 1 to 4....**60c**

109. Pink, white, blue, tan, black and red kid, sizes 1 to 4,

45c.

110. 3-buttoned, soft sole, in black or chocolate color only, sizes 1 to 4.**25c**

111. Chocolate colored kid moccasins, sizes 1 to 4,

20c.

112. Children's slippers, dongola kid, turn flexible soles, neat and durable, sizes

11 to 2..**$1.25**
8 to 10½ **1.00**
5 to 7½ **85c**

113. Genuine goat kid, soft and durable, suitable for boys or girls, sizes

11 to 2........**$1.25**
8 to 10½..... **1.00**
5 to 7½..... **85c**

114. White kid, turn flexible soles,
Sizes 11 to 2..**$1.00**
" 8 to 10½.. **90c**
" 4 to 7½.... **85c**

115. Best quality all-wool thick felt, in black and red color only,
Sizes 11 to 2..... **75c**
" 6 to 10..... **60c**
Not kept in stock after January 1st.

116. English velvet, fancy binding, thick felt soles. Not kept in stock after January 1st.
Sizes 11 to 2 ....**40c**
" 7 to 10 ....**35c**

117. The reliable fancy carpet, will give great wear, sizes
11 to 2......**45c**
7 to 10.....**35c**

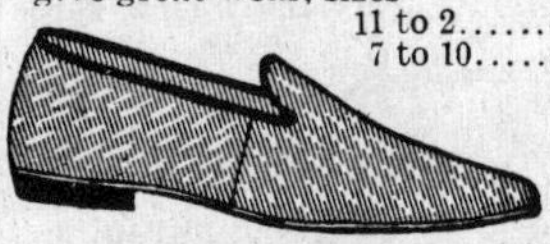

Men's Boots.

118. Medium heavy weight and will surprise you the wear they will give, sizes 6 to 10, **$1.00**

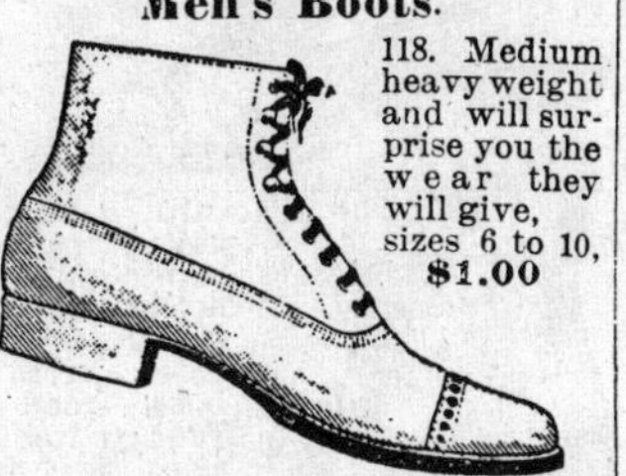

119. Heavy black buff, with thick soles, sizes 6 to 10.......**$1.25**

120. The favorite oil buff, with heavy soles, neat and durable,

Sizes 6 to 10,
$1.50

121. Something new, medium heavy Canadian leather, comfortable and durable, sizes 6 to 11,

$1.75

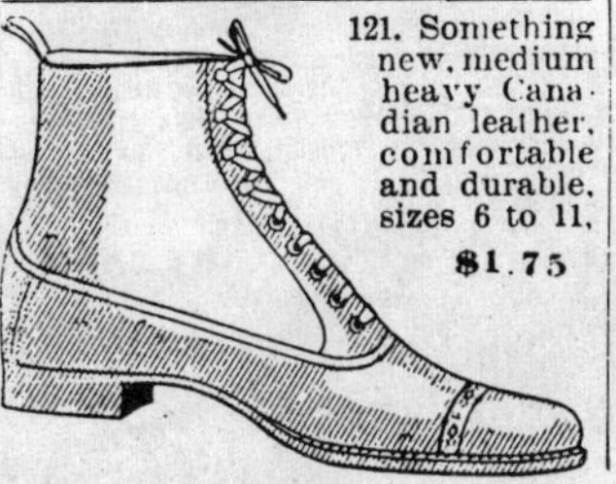

122. Heavy weight, full fitting, black smooth buff, great value,

Sizes 6 to 11,

$1.75

123. Solid comfort, glazed goat-skin, full fitting, for fat feet,
Sizes 6 to 11,

$2.00

124. The "Walk Easy" boot, dice calfskin, with flexible cork inner-sole, McKay

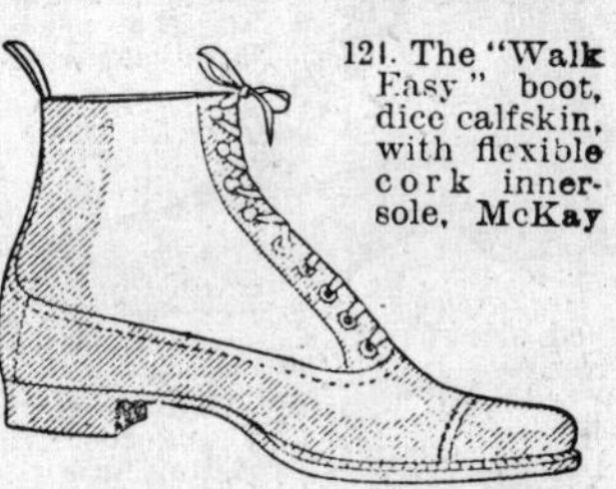

sewn soles, full fitting, sizes 6 to 11 ....**$2.00**

125. The "Walk Easy," same as 124, only medium fitting, suitable for young men, sizes 6 to 11, **$2.00**

126. The "Walk Easy," dice calfskin, elastic side, sizes 6 to 11,

$2.00

127. Fine, light weight, elastic side, with thin flexible turn soles, for dress or evening wear, sizes 6 to 10, **$2.50**

128. The fat man's friend, medium heavy, soft leather, wide plain toe, sewn soles, sizes 6 to 12, **$2.50**

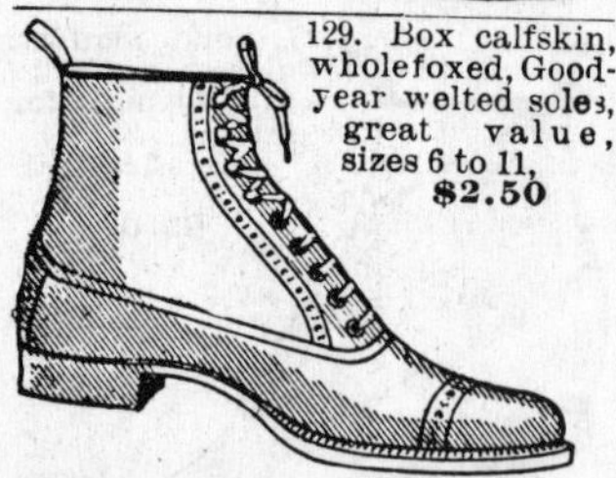

129. Box calfskin, whole foxed, Goodyear welted soles, great value, sizes 6 to 11, **$2.50**

130. Box calfskin, rather heavy, with leather lining, nothing like it in Canada at the price, Goodyear welted, sizes 6 to 11 .... **$3.00**

131. Genuine glazed kangaroo, soft and durable, with Goodyear welted heavy soles, sizes 6 to 11, **$3.00**

132. Same as 131 only laced, the usual price of kangaroo is $4.00, our price, sizes 6 to 11 .... **$3.00**

133. Kangaroo, same shape as 129, with medium heavy Goodyear soles and toe cap, sizes 6 to 11 .... **$3.00**

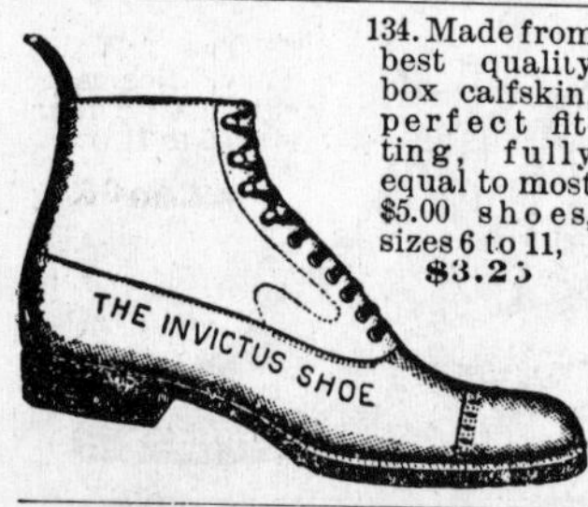

134. Made from best quality box calfskin, perfect fitting, fully equal to most $5.00 shoes, sizes 6 to 11, **$3.25**

135. Patent velour calf, the best leather made, but not guaranteed, turn flexible soles, very swell for fine wear, sizes 6 to 10 .... **$[illegible].75**

136. Same style as 134, with leather lining, sizes 6 to 11 .... **$3.50**

137. The Packard shoe, heavyweight, genuine box calfskin leather lined, Goodyear welted soles, sizes 6 to 11, **$4.00.**

138. The Packard shoe, best quality Brazil kid, white kid lining, goodyear welted soles, sizes 6 to 11, **$4.00.**

139. The police heavy box calfskin, EE width, very full fitting, three soles, leather-lined, best boot made for comfort and durability, sizes 6 to 12, **$4.00.**

140. The Packard, patent velour calfskin, nothing better, a very stylish up-to-date dress boot, goodyear welted soles, sizes 6 to 11. **$4.50.**

Workingmen's Heavy Boots.

141. Split cow hide, for rough wear, sizes 6 to 11, **90c.**

142. Genuine oil grain leather, hard to wear out, sizes 6 to 11, **$1.50.**

143. Heavy-weight, dirt proof and durable, sizes 6 to 11, **$1.25.**

144. Iron-clad, heavy soles, dirt proof, sizes 6 to 11, **$1.75.**

145. The Farmer's Delight, kip, full fitting and a great value, bellows tongue, sizes 6 to 11, **$2.00.**

146. Genuine English kip, the Digger's Delight, heavy, with smooth oil finish, this is the boot to buy, sizes 6 to 11, **$2.50.**

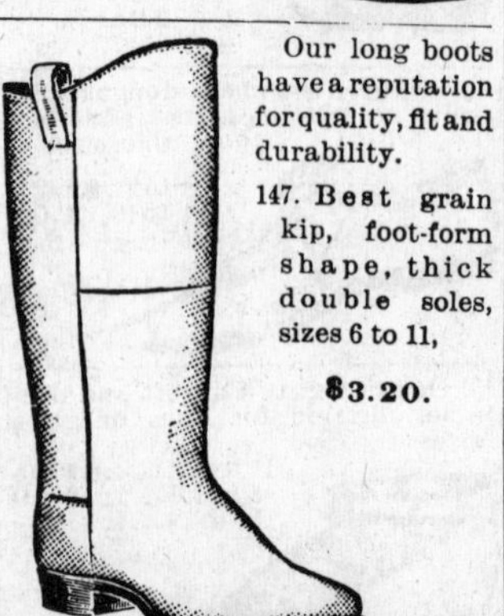

Our long boots have a reputation for quality, fit and durability.

147. Best grain kip, foot-form shape, thick double soles, sizes 6 to 11, **$3.20.**

148. Heavy cowhide long boot, good value, sizes 6 to 11 .... **$2.50**

149. The Captain riding boot, French calfskin, regulation style, sizes 6 to 10 .... **$3.75**

150. The Miner's Stand-by, best quality imported grain kip, with double soles, well-nailed all over bottom, dirt proof, sizes 6 to 11, **$3.75.**

Hockey Boots.

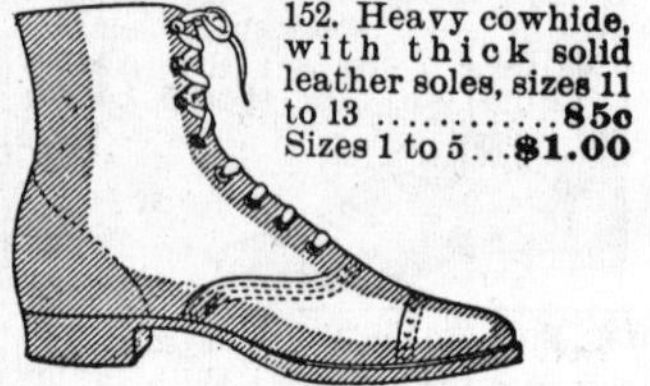

151. Men's dark tan pebble calf, very popular and durable, not kept in stock after February 1st, sizes 6 to 10, **$1.95.**

Boys sizes, 1 to 5 .... **$1.50**
Youths' sizes, 11 to 13 .... **$1.35**

Boys' Boots.

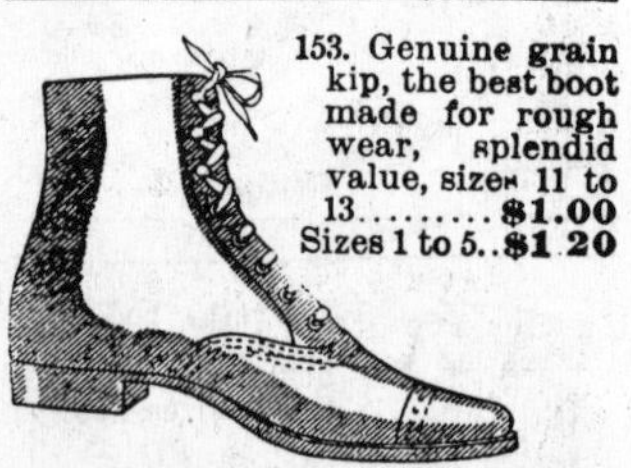

152. Heavy cowhide, with thick solid leather soles, sizes 11 to 13 .... **85c**
Sizes 1 to 5 ... **$1.00**

153. Genuine grain kip, the best boot made for rough wear, splendid value, sizes 11 to 13 .... **$1.00**
Sizes 1 to 5 .. **$1.20**

154. Black, smooth buff, heavy weight, soft uppers,
Sizes 11 to 13 .. **$1.15**
" 1 to 5. **1.25**

155. Dice calfskin, medium weight, for best wear,
Sizes 11 to 13 .. **$1.25**
" 1 to 5 .. **1.50**

156. Heavyweight oil buff, neat and durable,
Sizes 11 to 13 ....$1.25
Sizes 1 to 5 1.50

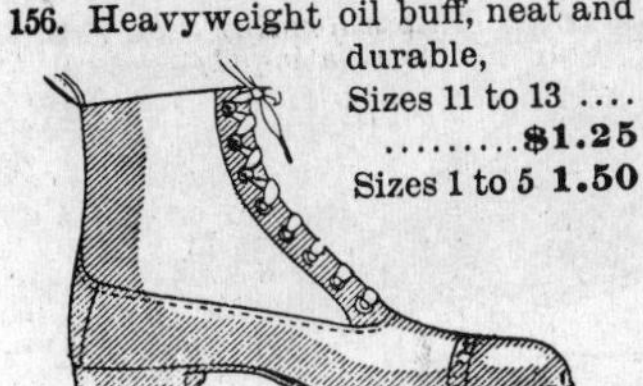

157. Box calfskin, neat and dressy, suitable for best wear, McKay sewn soles,
Sizes 11 to 13½ $1.75
Sizes 1 to 5½ 2.00

Men's and Boys' Oxford Shoes for Evening Wear.

158. Patent leather, best American make, but not guaranteed, flexible turn soles, sizes 5 to 10......$2.50

159. Extra choice, bright dongola kid, with flexible soles,
Sizes 6 to 11 .... $1.90
" 1 to 5 .... 1.50
" 11 to 13 .... 1.35

160. Glazed kid, soft and durable and easy on the feet, sizes 6 to 11,
$1.50.

Men's Slippers.

161. Genuine dongola kid, will not crack or hurt the feet, comfort style, turn flexible soles, sizes 5½ to 11,
$2.00.

162. Best American tan or black dongola kid, lined flexible soles, sizes 5 to 11,
$1.75.

163. Tan or black kid, Hamlet style, high vamp, very pretty, sizes 6 to 11,
$1.50.

164. Dice calfskin, a little heavier than kid, quite a favorite, sizes 6 to 11,
$1.25.

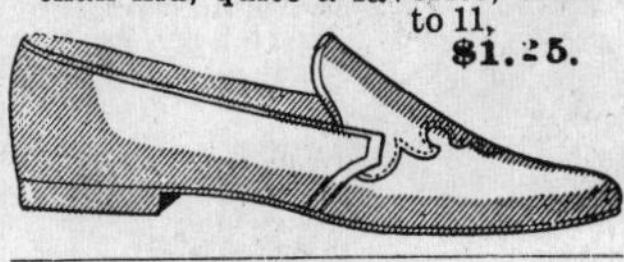

165. Dongola kid, flexible soles, easy to put on, sizes 6 to 11,
$1.25.

166. Tan or black, imitation of pigskin, a fine looking slipper, sizes 6 to 11,
$1.00.

167. Best imported German, fancy repp, foxed with leather, best wearing slipper made in Canada, sizes 6 to 11,
$1.00.

168. Same quality as 167, only plain, no foxing, sizes 6 to 11.........85c

169. The improved black velvet, with fancy vamp, nothing to equal it at the price, sizes 6 to 11,
65c.

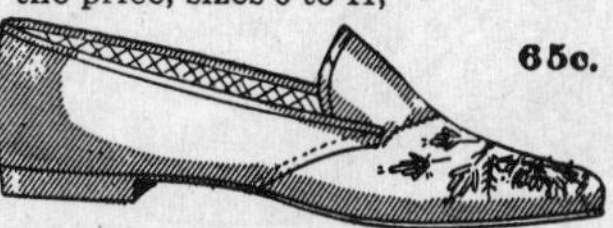

Men's Felt Slippers.

Not kept in stock after January 1st.

170. English Brussels carpet, with thick felt soles, covered, warm and durable, sizes 6 to 11 ....60c

171. Best quality home-made black wool felt, with extra thick sole, no cold feet with this line, sizes 6 to 11 ....50c

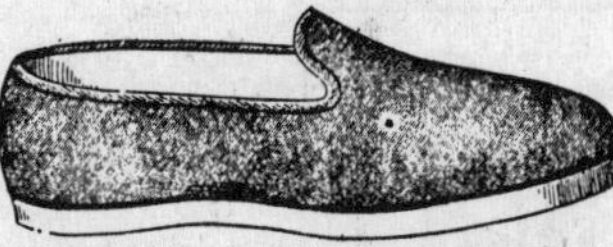

172. Black felt, with wool sole, medium heavy, second quality, sizes 6 to 11..............................25c

Boys' Slippers.

173. Pebble-grain calfskin, will give excellent wear, leather lined,
Sizes 11 to 13.......... $1.00
" 1 to 5.... .... .. 1.20

Gymnasium Shoes.

Best quality, blue canvas tops and rubber soles; it pays to buy the best.

174. Men's sizes, 6 to 11 ....60c
Boys' " 1 to 5 ....50c
Youths' " 11 to 13 ....45c

Moccasins.

175. Men's best quality genuine elk skin, wax sewn, very popular, sizes,
7 to 11..$1.25
3 to 6...1.00

176. Ladies' or boys' elk, with fancy front, sizes 3 to 6, 85c. Girls or boys,
11 to 2...75c
7 to 10...60c
3 to 6...50c

177. Babies' soft and warm, sizes 1 to 4,
25c.

Shoe Packs.

178. Best quality, tan color, oil finish, high cut, waterproof, sizes 6 to 12,
$2.00.

179. Tan color, oil finished, sizes, 6 to 12,
$1.25.

Men's heavy stockings, to be worn with lumberman's rubbers.

180. Extra heavy, best quality imported wool, double-knitted very popular in the North-West; sizes, small, medium and large,
75c.

181. All wool, black, medium weight, comes over the knee and ties with cord; sizes small, medium and large,
50c.

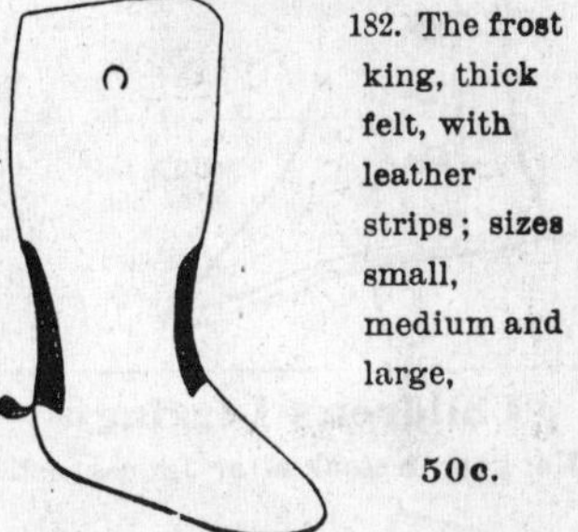

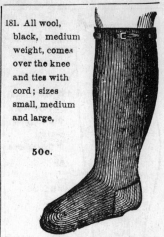

182. The frost king, thick felt, with leather strips; sizes small, medium and large,
50c.

183. Boys' black wool knitted stockings, same as 182, small, medium and large 40c

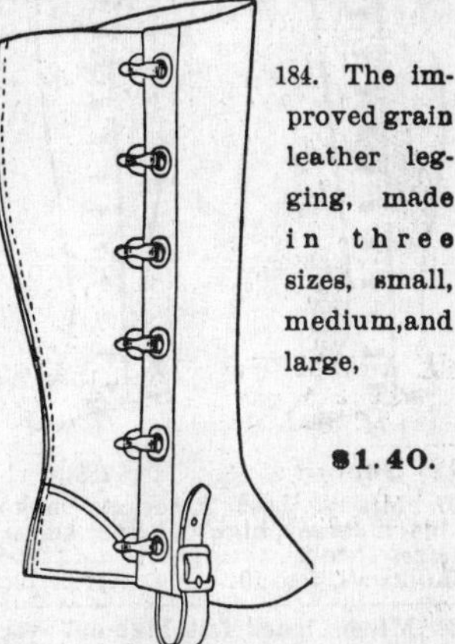

184. The improved grain leather legging, made in three sizes, small, medium, and large,
$1.40.

Ladies' Leggings.

3 to 7, no half sizes. Not kept in stock after Feb. 1st.

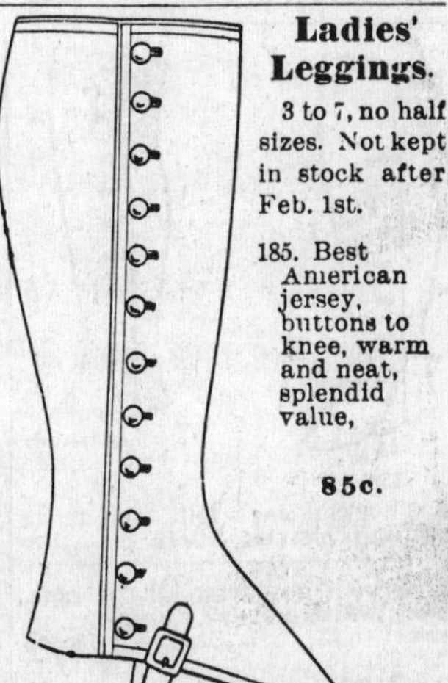

185. Best American jersey, buttons to knee, warm and neat, splendid value,
85c.

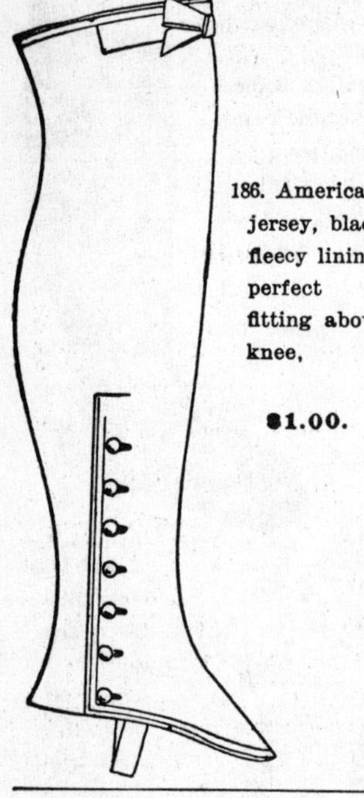

186. American jersey, black fleecy lining, perfect fitting above knee,

$1.00.

Children's Leggings.

Not kept in stock after January 1st.

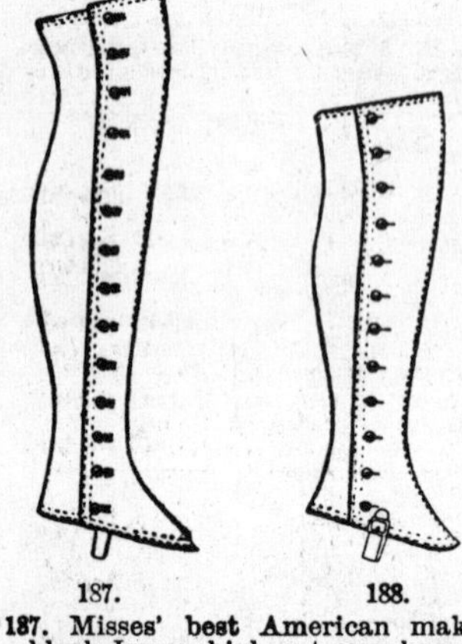

187. 188.

187. Misses' best American make black Jersey, high cut over knees, sizes 11 to 2.................85c
Children's, 5 to 10.................75c

188. Misses' black felt, high cut over knee, sizes 11 to 2.................65c

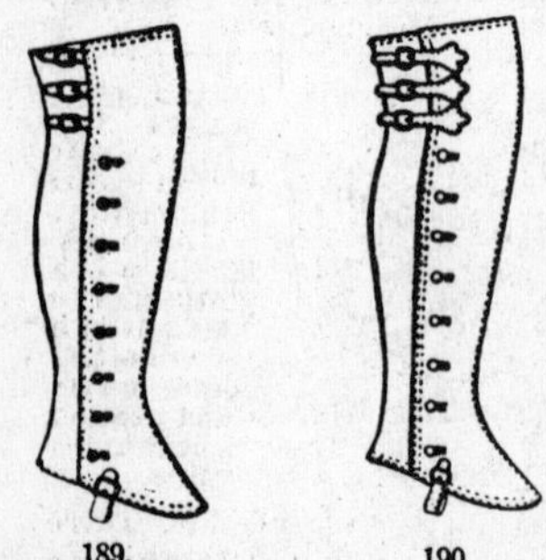

189. 190.

189. 3-buckle black felt, well made and durable, sizes 3 to 10 ....50c

190. Brown goatskin, all the rage, neat, warm and and durable.
Sizes 11 to 13.....................$2.00
" 6 to 10 .... 1.75
" 3 to 5..................... 1.50

Ladies' Overgaiters.

3 to 7, no half sizes.

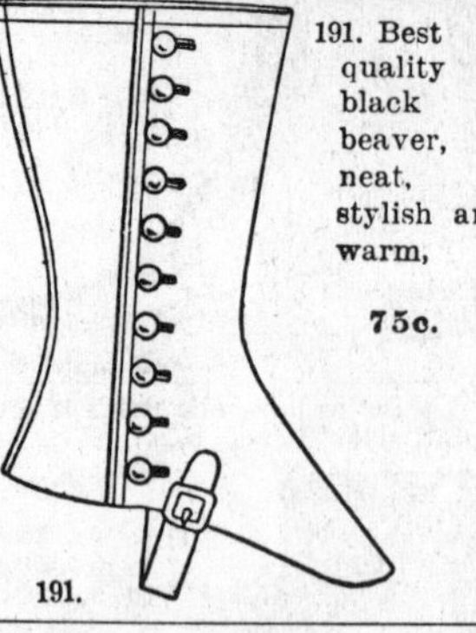

191. Best quality black beaver, neat, stylish and warm,

75c.

191.

192. All-wool black felt, American make, our leader, same style as 191 ....50c

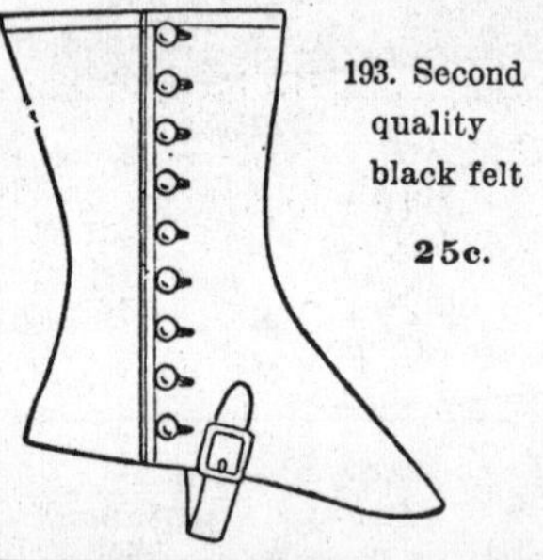

193. Second quality black felt

25c.

The improved and only genuine cardigan all-wool knitted stocking complete to toe, covered with the best quality rubber.

194. Ladies' sizes, with heel, 2½ to 8 ....$1.15
Girls' sizes, heel or spring heel, sizes 11 to 2 ....$1.00
Children's, spring heel, sizes 6 to 10½ ....90c.

Rubbers and Overshoes.

Our rubber footwear is very popular in all parts of the Dominion. We have a reputation for keeping only the best in quality, fit and styles. Order early and be prepared for the first cold snap, which may save you a doctor's bill.

Ladies'.

Sizes 2½ to 8.

195. The favorite, perfect fitting, with rolled edge to protect side, manufacturer's list price, 65c; our price 50c

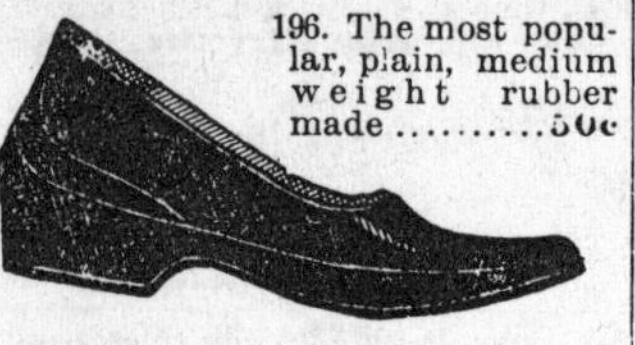

196. The most popular, plain, medium weight rubber made 50c

197. Same as 196, with fleecy wool lining 60c

198. Storm style; you should have a pair for rainy days.........0c

199. Same as 198, only with fleecy wool lining.................. ...6[illegible]c

200. Our "Leader," best value in Canada, plain, full fitting.....35c

201. Same as 200, only with wool lining, not kept in stock after February, 1st 45c

202. The ideal low-cut overshoe, best quality jersey waterproof cloth, manufacturer's price, $1.05; our price 85c

203. Best quality black all-wool felt overshoes, manufacturer's list price, $1.70; our price.......
.........$1.25

204. Fine jersey waterproof cloth, fleecy lined..........
.... $1.50

205. Extra fine jet black jersey cloth, waterproof, with buckles, fleecy wool lined $1.75

Misses' and Children's.

206. Same quality as 204, with heel, sizes 11 to 2.................$1.35

207. Same as 206, only spring heel,
Sizes 11 to 2 .... $1.35
Sizes 6 to 10½ $1.25

208. Plain, medium heavy, best rubber made, spring heel.
Sizes 11 to 2.......35c
" 4 to 10½.......25c

209. Same as 208, only with heel, sizes 11 to 2 ....35c

210. Plain, best quality, same as 209, only wool lined, with heel, sizes 11 to 2 ....40c

211. First quality, same as 208, only wool lined, for spring heel boots, sizes 11 to 2 ....40c
" 6 to 10½ 35c

212. Storm style, same as 198, with heel, sizes 11 to 2..............40c

213. Storm style, same as 212, for spring heel boots, sizes 11 to 2..40c
Sizes 6 to 10½ 35c

Men's and Boys' Rubbers and Overshoes.

214. Plain, rather heavy, with thick soles, sizes 6 to 11....50c
" 1 to 5 ....45c
" 11 to 13....40c

215. The old reliable, plain and heavy, will outwear any other rubber made, sizes 6 to 12...70c
" 1 to 5....60c
" 11 to 13..50c

216. Same as 215, only wool lined, sizes 6 to 12.........................75c
" 1 to 5.........................65c
" 11 to 13.........................60c

217. Extra heavy, patrol style, with rolled edge, hard to wear out, sizes 6 to 13 ....$1.00

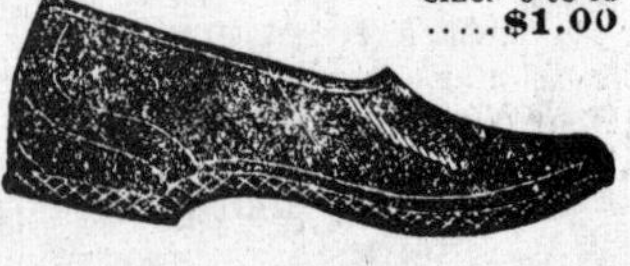

218. Storm style, manufacturer's price, $1.00; our price, sizes 6 to 11.....75c

219. Storm style, same as 218, only wool-lined 90c

220. Medium weight, stiff heel, perfect fitting, narrow, medium or round toe,

75c.

221. Blizzard style, fine Jersey waterproof, with best quality rubber soles, wool-lined, sizes 6 to 11, manufacturer's price, $1.35; our price **$1.00.**

222. Jersey arctic, wool-lined, sizes 6 to 12. $1.25
Boys', 1 to 5 .... 1.15
Youths', 11 to 13.... 1.00

223. The best snow excluder, Jersey waterproof, closed sides, heavy rubber soles and heels, will give great wear, wool-lined,
Sizes 6 to 12 ...... $1.50
Boys', 1 to 5 .... 1.25

224. Fine Jersey waterproof cloth, best made in America, fleecy wool lining, medium weight, sizes 6 to 11, **$1.50.**

225. Frost King, 2 buckles, Jersey waterproof, with closed rubber sides, great value, sizes 6 to 12, manufacturer's price, $2.25; our price, **$1.75.**

226. King of Winter, the Manitoba favorite, heavy waterproof cloth, thick wool lining, double soles and heels, manufacturer's price, $2.75; our price,
Sizes 6 to 13 ...... $2.25
Boys', 1 to 5 .... 2.00

227. Extra choice fine all-wool Jersey waterproof cloth, medium weight, sizes 6 to 11, manufacturer's price, $2.65; our price **$2.00.**

Rubbers to be worn with Stockings.

228. Armor proof, made of an extra quality of duck, specially manufactured for the purpose, strongest rubber made in Canada, sizes 6 to 12, manufacturer's price, $2.80; our price **$2.25.**

229. Pure gum, 2 buckles, with heavy soles and solid heels, sizes 6 to 12, manufacturer's price, $2.45; our price, **$2.00.**

230. One buckle, pure gum, warm, lined, something new, sizes 6 to 12, **$1.75.**

231. One buckle, armor proof, made from best quality duck, sizes 6 to 12, **$1.50.**

232. North-west, one buckle, great value,
Sizes 6 to 12............... $1.25
" 1 to 5 .... 1.00
" 11 to 13............... 95c

Rubber Boots.

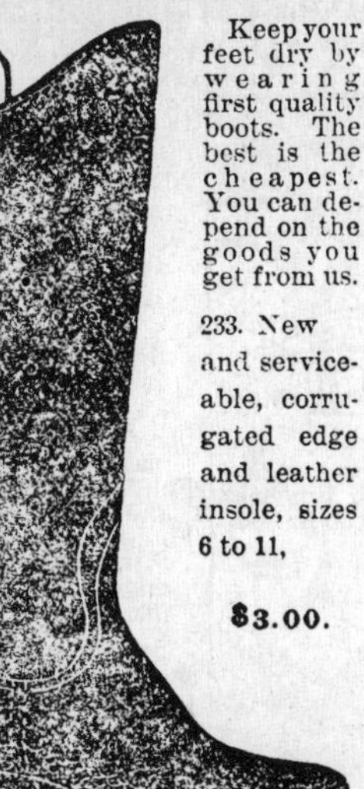

Keep your feet dry by wearing first quality boots. The best is the cheapest. You can depend on the goods you get from us.

233. New and serviceable, corrugated edge and leather insole, sizes 6 to 11, **$3.00.**

234. The reliable, extra dry, dull finish, felt lined, heavy soles and heels,
Sizes 6 to 11 .... $2.75
" 1 to 5 .... 2.40

235. Medium weight, pure rubber, felt lined, very popular and satisfactory, sizes 6 to 11 ....$3.00

236. Best quality, hip style, dull finish, felt-lined, hard to wear out, sizes 6 to 11, manufacturer's price, $5.55; our price..............$4.25

237. Ladies' medium light weight pebble leg boot, bright finished, fleecy wool lining, worth their weight in gold to any lady.
Sizes 3 to 7 .... $1.75
" 11 to 2 .... 1.45
" 6 to 10............ 1.20

Lamb's Wool Soles for Bedroom Slippers.

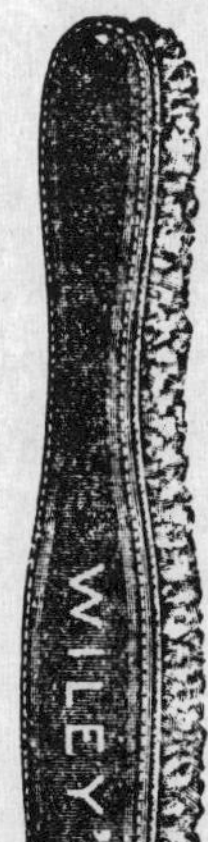

238. Capital, no binding, stitch to edge of sole, men's sizes, 6 to 11............... 30c

239. Ladies', sizes 3 to 7............... 20c

240. Girls', sizes 11 to 2 .... 20c

241. Children's, sizes 2 to 10 .... 15c

242. Ladies' eclipse, no binding, leather soles, sizes 3 to 7.... .... 25c

243. Ladies' bound, black or tan binding, sizes 3 to 7.. 15c

244. Men's cork insoles, for putting inside boots, sizes 6 to 11............... 8c

245. Ladies' cork soles, sizes 3 to 7........ 7c

Neverbreak
TRADE MARK.

Laces, finest and strongest mohair lace in the world—

246. Men's black or tan, one yard long, 2 pair for......... ......5c

247. Ladies' black or tan, 1¼ yds long, 2 pair for...................... 5c

248. Black or tan flat low shoe lace, ¾-yds long, 3 pair for 5c

249. Leather laces, round, 1 yard long, 3 pair for................... 5c

250. Men's porpoise, very strong, pair.......................... 7½c

251. Best leather lace, 1 yard long, pair........................ 5c

Sundries.

252. Wire button hooks, 6 for 5c
253. Shoe lifts, each 5c
254. Black boot buttons, 6 doz for 5c
255. Half-circle heel plates, 2 pair for 5c

256. Perfumed powder for sweating or tired feet, package.......... 10c

Shoe Dressings.

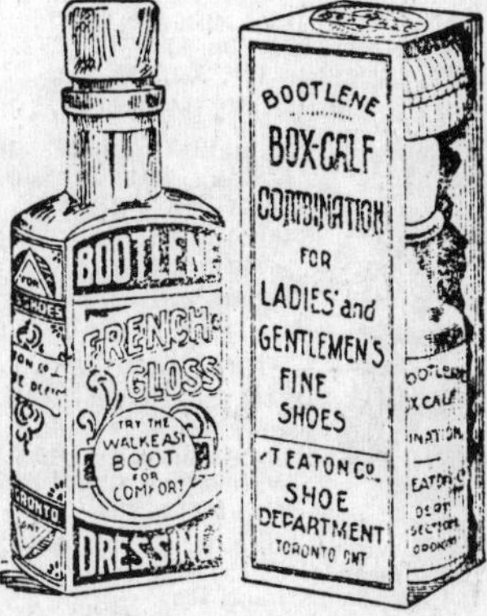

257. 258.

257. Bootlene, for ladies' and children's boots, apply with sponge attached to cork, self shine, best value in Canada, large size bottle 10c

258. "Bootlene" combination box of paste and bottle of cleaner, for ladies' and gent's kid, box calf, or patent leather boots, keeps the leather soft, rub to a shine with cloth, our special, black or tan. 10c

259. Paste blacking, for men's and boys' boots, shine with brush. This blacking lasts longer and puts a better shine on than any cheap large size boxes, besides preserving the finest leather; try it once and you will use no other. 5c

260. Bootlene paste for ladies' or gents kid, box calf or patent leather boots, shine with cloth, same as used with combination, black or tan, state which you prefer, per box.. 5c

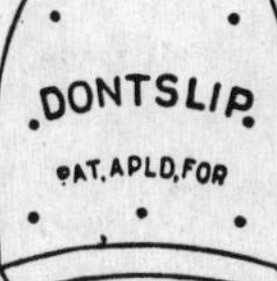

261. The Don't Slip rubber heels, pure rubber, ladies sizes, 2 to 7; men's 6 to 11, per pair.. 25c

Ebony moustache brushes, 40c.
" shaving brushes, 60c, 75c, $1.00, 1.25.
" tooth brushes, 25c, 35c, 40c.
" nail files, 20c.
" cuticle knives, 20c.
" corn knives, 20c.
" baby brushes, 40c and 60c.
Combs to match ebony goods at 25c, 35c, 50c, 60c, 75c, $1.00.

Cheaper black combs match as well, but have a bright polish which the above have not.

Cloth Brushes.

CLOTH. CLOTH.

Our styles and prices in cloth brushes are many. We have the ordinary cloth brushes, without handles, in all styles and at the following prices:
Cloth brushes, 30c, 40c, 50c, 60c, 75c, $1.00, 1.25.
Handled cloth, 30c, 60c, 75c, $1.00, 1.75, 2.00.
Hat brushes, 15c, 20c, 35c, 50c, 75c.
Bath brushes, 35c, 40c, 50c, 60c, 75c, $1.25.
Bonnet brushes, 20c, 50c, 75c.
Silver brushes, 15c, 20c, 25c, 40c.

Whisks.

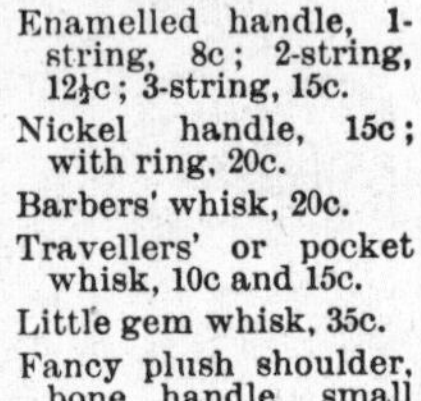

Enamelled handle, 1-string, 8c; 2-string, 12½c; 3-string, 15c.

Nickel handle, 15c; with ring, 20c.

Barbers' whisk, 20c.

Travellers' or pocket whisk, 10c and 15c.

Little gem whisk, 35c.

Fancy plush shoulder, bone handle, small whisk, 25c; medium, 30c; large, 35c.

Plain whisk, bone handle, 20c and 25c.
Long handle whisk, 10c.
Whisk, two string, 10c.

Nail Brushes.

Nail brushes, bone back, 10c, 15c, 20c, 25c, 30c, 35c, 40c, 50c, $1.00.

Wood back nail brushes, 10c, 15c, 25c, 30c, 35c, 40c, 50c, 75c, $1.00, 1.25.

Nail scrubs, fibre, wood back, 2 for 5c, 5c and 3 for 5c.

Ebony nail brushes, 25c, 35c, 60c, 75c, $1.00.

Tooth Brushes.

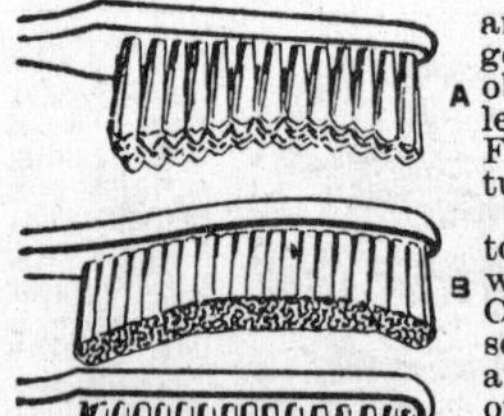

Our tooth brushes are exceptionally good value, and are obtained from the leading English and French manufacturers.

In ordering our 25c tooth brushes, say which shape, A, B, C, or D, and whether serrated or plain, and whether a lady's or gentleman's size. When over 10c, say whether hard, medium or soft bristle is required. We do not exchange tooth brushes, except for faulty manufacture. The prices are as follows: 5c, 10c, 15c, 20c, 25c, 30c, 35c, 40c.

Ebony tooth brushes, 25c, 35c, 40c.
Tooth brushes not exchanged.

Shaving Brushes.

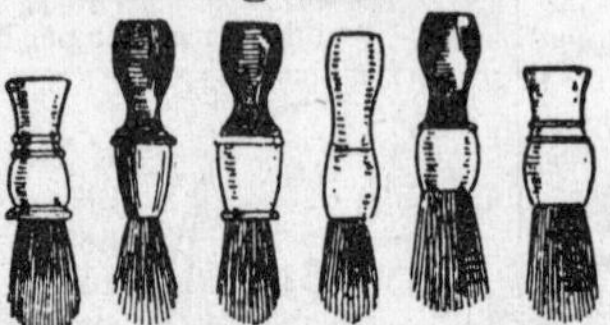

Shaving brushes, bristle, 10c, 15c, 20c, 25c.
Shaving brushes, badger hair, bone handle, 35c, 50c, 60c, 75c, $1.00.
We do not exchange bath or shaving brushes.

Mirrors.

Triple mirrors, 25c, 50c, 75c, $1.00, 1.25, 1.50, 1.75, 2.00, 2.50, 3.00, 3.50, 4.00, 5.00.

Shaving mirrors, one side magnifying, the other plain, 50c, 75c, $1.00, 1.50, 2.00, 2.50, 3.00, 3.50.
Folding shaving mirrors, in a variety of styles and sizes, from $1.25, 1.50, 1.75, 2.00.
Folding wire handle, square stand mirrors, all sizes, bevelled edge, wood back, plate mirror, 10c, 15c, 20c, 25c, 30c, 35c, 40c, 50c, 60c, 75c, $1.00, 1.15, 1.25, 1.50.

Square or oval hand mirrors, all sizes, both bevelled edged, plate, crystal white glass, ¾-white bevelled plate, plain or shock glass, at following prices:
Crystal white plate glass, bevelled edge, oval or square, mahogany wood back, mirror, according to size, 20c, 25c, 30c, 35c, 50c, 65c, 75c, $1.00, 1.25, 1.50.

Crystal white, oval or square, olive wood back hand glass, bevelled edge, according to size, 25c, 30c, 35c, 50c, 75c, $1.00.
Oval or square wood handle hand glass, plain glass, 7½c, 10c, 12½c, 15c, 20c, according to size.
Metal frame stand mirrors, 5c, 10c, 15c, 20c, 25c, 30c, 35c.
Small magnifying mirror, metal rim, round, 5c.
Black back, imitation ebony, oval and square shape hand mirrors bevelled edge, 25c, 40c, 50c, 60c.
Stand mirrors, wire handle, square, 40c, 50c, 60c, 75c.
Imitation ebony, round hand mirrors, 75c, $1.00, 1.25; also in green and antique oak, at same prices.
Ebony mirrors (see Ebony Goods).

Combs.

(Combs not exchanged.)

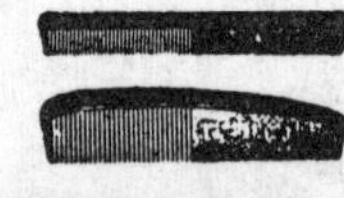

Pocket combs, 5c, 10c, 15c, 20c.
Rubber dressing combs, 5c, 10c, 12½c, 15c, 20c, 25c, 30c, 35c, 40c, 50c, 60c.
Horn dressing combs, 5c, 10c, 15c, 20c, 25c, 35c, 50c, 65c.
Celluloid dressing combs, 10c, 15c, 25c, 35c, 50c, 60c, 75c.

Fine combs, "rubber," 5c, 10c, 15c, 20c, 25c.
Fine ivory combs, 10c, 15c, 20c, 25c, 35c, 50c, 75c.

Fine combs, "horn," 5c, 10c, 15c.
Circular combs, 5c, 10c, 12½c, 15c, 20c.

Candies and Table Sundries.

Table Sundries.

Crackers

(Tom Smith's English).

1070. Somebody's Luggage, 12 crackers in box, 15c.
800. Containing 12 crackers, with hats, caps, toys, etc., 15c.
900. Christmas Gnomes, and contains toys, jewels, headdresses, children's mottoes, 12 crackers, 20c.
931. Japanese puzzles, 12 crackers, 20c.
861. Children's box of 12 jewel crackers, 20c.
930. 12 crackers, with hats, caps, toys, masks and children's mottoes, 20c.
832. Scottish crackers (12 crackers), 25c.
932. 12 crackers, containing miniature toys, mottoes, etc., 25c.
802. Box of 12 crackers, gems, jewels, headdresses, 25c.
863. Box of jewel crackers for boys and girls (12 crackers), 25c.
902. Box of 12 crackers with caps and puzzles, 30c.
763. Box of 12 puzzle crackers, 35c.
806. Box of 12 native Japanese crackers, 35c.
1112. Box of 12 Santa Claus toy crackers, 35c.
908. Box of 12 Tom Smith's Christmas conundrum crackers, 40c.
867. Box of 12 Tom Smith's jewel crackers, 40c.
868. Box of 12 Tom Smith's toy crackers, trumpets, monkeys, watches, etc., etc., 50c.
768. Larks!!! 12 crackers for boys, 50c.
939. Box of 12 crackers, containing dolls, fans, whistles, squeakers, etc., etc., 50c.
740. Gatling gun repeating crackers, 3 only monster crackers, having six charges, 50c.
940. Box of fairy jewel crackers, 60c.
843. Tom Smith's cinematograph crackers (12), 65c.
810. What's Inside? 12 Oriental crackers, 65c
712. 12 crackers, cannonade of toys, 65c.
874. 12 crackers, Kurio from Klondike, 65c.
873. Box of 12 musical toy crackers, 75c.
849. Japanese village (12 crackers), 75c.
815. Home Comforts, domestic crackers for adults (12 crackers in box), $1.00.
950. Panorama of British Heroes (12 crackers in box), $1.00.

Santa Claus surprise stockings at 12½c, 20c, 45c, 75c and $1.00 each.

Candies.

Chocolates.

Chocolates, vanilla flavor, 30c lb.
" raspberry flavor, 30c lb.
" nougat, 30c lb.
" walnut cream, 30c lb.
" nectar " 30c lb.
" orange " 30c lb.
" lemon " 30c lb.
" black currant cream, 30c lb.
" maple, 30c lb.
" cocoanut, 30c lb.
" strawberry, 30c lb.
" pineapple, 30c lb.
" ginger, 30c lb.
" coffee, 30c lb.
" dipped ginger, 40c lb.
" " pineapple, 40c lb.
" fine flavor, well assorted, 25c lb.
" caramels, best, 35c lb.
" " good, 15c lb.
" Globe, vanilla flavor, 20c lb.

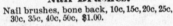

Regal chocolate drops, 20c lb.
Chocolate dates, 20c lb.
Chocolate almonds, 40c and 60c lb.
" cinnamon crisps, 30c lb.

Boxes of Candy.

1-lb box, fine bon-bons and chocolates, 30c.
½-lb " " " " 15c.
1-lb " finest " " 40c.
½-lb " " " " 20c.
1-lb " fine chocolates, 30c.
1-lb " finest " 40c.
½-lb " fine " 15c.
½-lb " finest " 20c.
Fancy boxes, filled with candy, at 15c, 20c, 25c, 30c, 35c, 50c, 60c, 75c, $1.00.
Cream almonds, 20c and 30c lb.
Cream burnt almonds, 25c lb.
Sugared almonds, 25c lb.
Lady caramels, 20c lb.
Bon-bons, assorted flavors, 20c lb.
Bon-bons, finest assorted flavors, 40c lb.
Marshmallow drops, best, 20c lb.
Rock candy, white and pink, 20c lb.
Buttercups, nut centres, best, 20c lb.
" " " good, 15c lb.
Salted almonds, 75c lb.
Crystallized ginger, 30c lb.
Spiced gum drops, extra quality, 40c lb.
Tom Thumb mixture, well flavored, 20c lb.
Cupid's whispers, conversation lozenges, 20c lb.
Gem gum drops, 20c lb.
Crystallized Santa Clara figs, 20c lb.
Peppermint lozenges, 15c lb.
" shrimps, 15c lb.
Nut cream, 15c lb.
Maple walnut bon-bons, 12½c lb.
Conversation lozenges, 15c lb.
Chocolate drops, assorted flavors, 15c lb.
Pearls (highly perfumed lozenges), white rose, red rose, musk, wintergreen, chocolate, violet, XXX mint, either assorted or straight, 30c lb.
Cheapest mixed candy, 7c and 8c lb.
Cream mixture, a well assorted mixture, suitable for Xmas trees, etc., this can be done up in ½ and 1 lb. folding boxes, 10c lb.
Silvered nuts, etc., for decorating cakes, etc., 10c oz.; $1.50 lb.
Carraway comfits, smooth, 30c lb.
Carraway comfits, assorted colors, rough, 30c lb.
Silver cachous, 10c oz.; $1.50 lb.
Sugar-coated licorice pellets, 20c lb.

English Candies.

Gibson's cough drops, 25c lb.
" horehound drops, 25c lb.
" mixed fruits, 25c lb.
" lime fruit tablets, 25c lb.
" Any of the following drops: lemon, vanilla, chocolate, malt, strawberry, plum, raspberry, pineapple, black currant, tip top, butterscotch, 25c lb.
Gibson's XXX mints, 50c lb.
Gibson's curiously strong mints, 80c lb.
" cayenne lozenges, 5c oz.; 80c lb.
" black currant lozenges, 5c oz.; 80c lb.
" Coltsfoot stick, 40c lb.
" " drops, 40c lb.
" linseed, licorice and chlorodyne cough lozengers, 5c oz.; 50c lb.
Pascall's lemon barley sugar stick, in small screw top bottles, 20c; large, 35c.
Pascall's raspberry barley sugar stick, bottle, 20c.
Pascall's mixed fruit barley sugar stick, 20c lb. bottle.
Pascall's golden maltex, 15c, 25c, 35c and 50c bottle.
Callard & Bowser's butterscotch, 10c and 20c packet.
Callard & Bowser's assorted taffy, 10c and 20c packet.

Taffies.

Maple cream, 15c and 20c lb.
" butterscotch, 15c and 20c lb.
Cocoanut cream, pink and white, 15c lb.
Walnut bar, 20c lb.
" rock, 15c lb.
Almond rock, 20c lb.
Cocoanut rock, 15c lb.
Everton rock, 15c lb.
Peanut crisp, 15c lb.
Butter taffy drops, 20c lb.
Peanut squares, 15c lb.

Photographic Department.

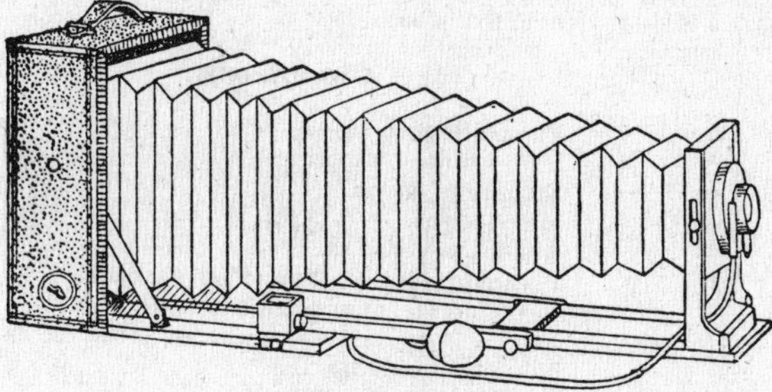
Tele-Photo Cycle Poco C.

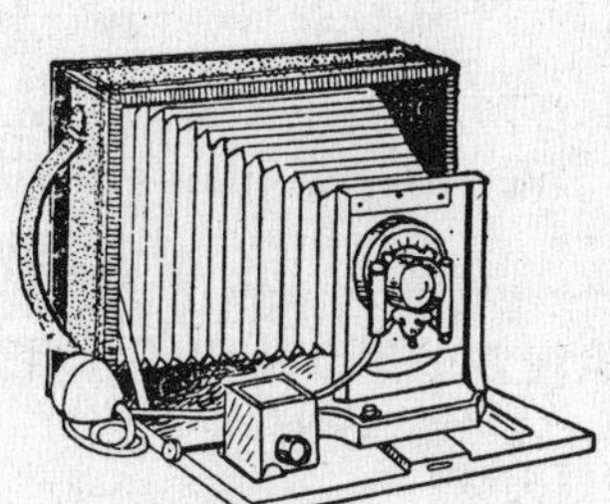
Cycle Poco, No. 1.

Cycle Poco No. 3.

Cameras and Photographic Supplies.

Tele-photo Cycle Poco C, is designed especially for lenses with more than one focus, and with the extreme length of draw, all regular lenses now on the market can be used with double and triple focus. The bed is made in three sections, each supplied with rack and pinion focusing attachment. The box is mahogany, covered with morocco grain leather, bellows is of red russia leather, rising and falling front, reversible back, having swing-back attachment or movement. The complete camera is fitted with the Auto shutter, with finger and pneumatic release, setting itself automatically on either time or instantaneous exposure. This shutter is fitted with the Tele-photo three-focus lens. One double plate-holder and sole leather carrying case accompanies each camera. Size, 4 x 5, $30.00; 5 x 7, $35.00; plate-holder, 4 x 5, 75c; 5 x 7, $1.00.

Tele-Photo Cycle Poco B is a long focus instrument, having the Auto shutter, working automatically at any desired speed. The lens is the Tele-Photo Poco three-focus lens, the front lens of which can be removed and the back combination used alone when taking objects at a distance, whereby the image is nearly doubled in size. Then the swings and combinations allow of the pictures being taken in almost any position. An olive color sole-leather carrying case, with one double plate-holder, with each camera. Price, 4 x 5, $32.00; 5 x 7, $37.00; 6½ x 8½, $53.00. Plate-holders, 4 x 5, 75c; 5 x 7, $1.00; 6½ x 8½, $1.50.

Cycle Poco No. 1 is, without a doubt, the finest camera of the season for cyclists and tourists. It is such a splendid instrument for carrying around, being unique in its completeness. This camera has all the adjustments of the less compact cameras. It is fitted with the Auto shutter, with Iris diaphragm, and the celebrated Rochester symmetrical lens, which is rectilinear and free from distortion. It is enclosed in a sole-leather carrying case, having a second compartment for plate-holders; the 4 x 5 will carry 5 double plate-holders, while the other sizes will contain four. Each camera is provided with one double plate-holder. Price, 4 x 5, $25.00; 5 x 7, $28.00; 6½ x 8½, $42.00. Double plate-holders, 4 x 5, 75c; 5 x 7, $1.00; 6½ x 8½, $1.50.

Cycle Poco No. 2 is one of the most popular cameras which we sell, having all the features of a first-class camera that are essential, viz: rising front, two tripod plates for horizontal or vertical pictures, rack and pinion, reversing finder and level, Unicum shutter with Iris diaphragm, with finger and pneumatic release bulb and hose attached. The shutter is fitted with the high-grade Rochester symmetrical lens. An olive-brown carrying case for camera and plate-holders, along with one double plate-holder, completes this outfit. Price, complete as above, 4 x 5, $20.00; 5 x 7, $24.00. Extra plate-holders as No. 1.

Cycle Poco No. 3 is a first-class camera and very popular. The rack and pinion are not on this camera, nor is the lens quite as good as No. 2, but is a good lens for all that. It is complete with Unicum shutter, 1 double plate-holder and combination carrying case. Extra plate-holders are the same as for No. 1. Price, 4x5, complete, $14.00; 5 x 7, $19.00.

Cycle Poco No. 4 is a new style of camera, meeting requirements hitherto not provided for. It combines the principal features of the No. 4, having rapid rectilinear lens with the Gem shutter. This can also be obtained with single achromatic lens. Each camera is complete in carrying case, sectioned for camera on one end and plate-holder on the other. One double plate-holder goes with each camera. Price, complete with rapid rectilinear lens, 4 x 5, $11.00; 5 x 7, $15.00.

Cycle Poco No. 5. We expect that this will be the greatest seller we will handle this year. The camera is made with reversible back, allowing change from vertical to horizontal without changing the focus when once obtained. A rising and falling front, as well as rack and pinion for focusing. There is also a view finder and level, and a popular Unicum shutter with Iris diaphragm, finger and pneumatic release, all classes of action; ball or instantaneous exposure, and speed of shutter from 1-100 to 1 second, as well as bulb and time exposure. A rapid rectilinear lens, of double combination and exceptional quality for its class, is fitted to this shutter. A double plate-holder and combination case accompanies each camera. Extra plate-holders as No. 1. Price, 4 x 5, $15.00; 5 x 7, $20.00.

Poco Folding Camera, Series A, has all the movements that are at all required for the highest grade of photography. The lens is the high-grade Rochester symmetrical, perfectly rectilinear and free from distortion. One double plate-holder accompanies each camera. Price, 4 x 5, $25.00; 5 x 7, $28.00; 6½ x 8½, $42.00; 8 x 10, $53.00.

Double plate-holders, 4 x 5, 75c; 5 x 7, $1.00; 6½ x 8½, $1.50; 8 x 10, $1.75.

Wide angle lens, 4 x 5, $6.00; 5 x 7, $7.00; 6½ x 8½, $10.50; 8 x 10, $14.00.

Cartridge roll holders, 4 x 5, $5.00; 5 x 7, $6.50.

Sole leather carrying case, 4 x 5, $2 25; 5 x 7, $3.00; 6½ x 8½, $3.50; 8 x 10, $4.75.

Poco Folding Camera, Series B, complete with Rochester symmetrical lens, Unicum shutter and Iris diaphragm, 1 double plate holder. Price, 4 x 5, $17.50; 5 x 7, $23.00.

Poco Folding Camera, series C, is a good camera, having Unicum shutter, Iris diaphragm and rapid rectilinear lens, complete with 1 double plate-holder. Price: 4 x 5, $14.00; 5 x 7, $17.50. Rack and pinion extra, $2.25; either size to order.

The Cyclone Junior and Senior Cameras are fitted with a high-grade Mensicus combination lens of universal focus, requiring no focusing attachment. One double plate-holder is included with the camera. Price: 3½ x 3½, $3.50; 4 x 5, $4.75.

Pony Premo B, 3¼ x 4¼, $22.00; 4 x 5, $22.00; 5 x 8, $28.00.

Pony Premo No. 3, 4 x 5, $15.00.

Pony Premo No. 4, 4 x 5, $20.00; 5 x 7, $25.00.

Blair Camera Company's Weno Hawk-eyes are exceptionally good value in film cameras—

The Weno Hawk-eye, 3½ x 3½, $5.00. Sunlight film, 6 exposures, 30c; 12 exposures, 60c. Carrying case, $1.25.

Weno Hawk-eye, 4 x 5, $8.00. Sunlight film, 6 exposures, 45c; 12 exposures, 90c. Leather carrying case, $1.50.

Hawk-eye, Junior, 4 x 5, $8.00. Sunlight film, 6 exposures, 45c; 12 exposures, 90c. Leather carrying case, $2.00.

The Tourist Hawk-eye, 3½ x 3½, $6.00. Special Sunlight film, 6 exposures, 30c; 12 exposures, 60c.

The Tourist Hawk-eye camera, 4 x 5, $8.00. Special film, 6 exposures, 45c; 12 exposures, 90c. Carrying case, 3½ x 3½, $1.25; 4 x 5, $1.50.

No. 3 Folding Weno Hawk-eye, 3¼ x 4¼, with double rapid rectilinear lens, $15.00; with single lens, $13.50. Sunlight film, 6 exposures, 35c; 12 exposures, 70c.

Stereo Weno Hawk-eye, $25.00.

For further information for any special camera, we will be pleased to give the very fullest information. All cameras are carefully tested before leaving the counter. Should a defect in workmanship be discovered, inform us immediately as to nature; add whether box, etc., had been received in perfect order.

PHOTOGRAPHIC SUNDRIES.

DRY PLATES.

THE PRICE IS FOR 1 DOZEN PLATES.

	2½x2½	3¼x3¼	3½x3½	3¼x4¼	4x5	4¾x6½	5x7	5x8	6½x8½	8x10
New York Record	22c	30c	30c	35c	50c	65c	80c	$1.00	$1.50	$2.25
" Crescent	22c	....	30c	35c	50c	....	80c	....	....	....
" Harvard	22c	....	30c	35c	50c	....	80c	....	....	....
Lumiere (extra rapid)	....	....	....	45c	70c	....	$1.00	....	1.55	....
Standard	....	....	30c	35c	50c	65c	80c	....	....	....
" Non-halation	....	....	....	....	60c	....	90c	....	....	....
" Orthochromatic	....	....	....	....	60c	....	90c	....	....	....
Hammer	....	....	35c	45c	65c	85c	$1.10	....	....	....
Orthonon	....	....	....	55c	80c	90c	1.40	...	$2.00	....
Transparency	....	40c	....	45c	65c	....	1.10	....	....	....

DEVELOPING AND TONING TRAYS.

Celluloid, 3¼ x 4¼, 13c; 4 x 5, 15c; 5 x 7, 20c; 5 x 8, 25c; 8 x 10, 40c.

Composition trays, 3¼ x 4¼, 13c; 4 x 5, 15c; 5 x 7, 20c.

Xylonites, with lifter, 3¼ x 4¼, 25c; 4 x 5, 30c; 4¾ x 6½, 35c.

PHOTOGRAPHIC PAPERS.

By the Gross or Packet. A few of the smaller sizes of some papers have 2 dozen sheets in a packet.

	3¼ x 4¼	3½ x 3½	3⅞x5½	4 x 5	4 x 6	4¾x6½	5 x 7	6½x8½	8 x 10	20x24
Velox, Glossy or Mat ....gross	$1.50	$1.50	$2.00	$2.00	$2.00	....	$3.50	....	....	....
Velox, Glossy or Mat..........doz	15c	15c	25c	25c	25c	35c	35c	60c.	80c	....
Velox Special.gross	... .	....	....	$2.00	....	....	$3.50	....	....	....
" " doz	....	....	....	25c	....	35c	35c	....	....	....
Argo Carbon .gross	....	$1.15	....	$1.50	....	....	$3.00	....	....	....
Portrait Mat...doz	....	15c	....	15c	....	....	30c	....	....	....
Disco ....gross	....	$1.10	....	$1.20	....	....	$2.25	....	....	....
" ....doz	2 doz., 20c	2 doz., 20c	....	2 doz., 25c	....	....	30c	....	....	....
Albuma ......gross	$1.15	$1.15	$1.35	$1.25	....	....	$2.65	....	....	..
" ....doz	2 doz., 20c	2 doz., 20c	20c	2 doz., 25c	....	....	30c	....	....	$3.00
Etching Mat, Heavy ....doz	30c	30c	....	40c	....	....	60c	90c	....	....
Thin Smooth Etching Mat ......doz	25c	25c	....	35c	....	....	45c	75c	....	....
French Satin, jun., tins of 25 sheets..	20c	20c	....	25c	....	....	40c	....	....	....
Nepera Bromide.... .... doz	15c	15c	....	25c	...	....	35c	60c	80c	....
Cyko Mat ....gross	$1.10	$1.10	....	$1.50	....	....	$3.00	....	....	....
" Portrait ..doz	15c	15c	....	15c	....	....	30c	50c	....	....
Water Tone ....doz	35c	35c	....	35c	....	....	60c	....	....	..
Helio Glossy	$1.10	$1.10	....	$1.20	....	....	$2.25	....	....	....
Gelatine Paper	2 doz., 20c	2 doz., 20c	....	2 doz., 25c	....	....	25c	....	....	....

Developers (Liquid).

Pyro developers, 2 solutions for 25c.

Eikonogen and Hydrochinone, 16-oz bottle for 30c.

Metol Bicarbonate, 16-oz bottle for 30c.

Metol and Quinol, 8-oz bottle for 15c.

Pyro and Metol developer, 3 solutions, for 25c.

Developers (Dry).

Metol, box of 10, $1.40, or 15c each.

Eikonogen Hydrochinone, box of 10 for $1.40, or 15c each.

Metol and Quinol tubes for Velox Paper, box of 5 for 75c, or 15c tube.

Toning Solutions.

Gold toning solution, 30c, 60c.

Gold and acid solution, 30c, 60c.

Platinum solution, 60c.

Toning and fixing solution, 25c.

Toners (Dry).

No. 1 Tone and finish cartridge, 10 for $1.40, or 15c each.

No. 2 Tone and finish cartridge, 10 for $2.75, or 30c each.

Reducing and Intensifying Solutions, etc.

Agfa intensifier, 4-oz bottle, 60c.

Agfa reducer, 4-oz bottle, 75c.

Intensifying solution, 2 bottles, 30c.

Reducing solution, 2 bottles, 30c.

Acid fixing bath, 15c.

Chemicals.

Pyrogallic acid, 30c oz.

Hydrochinone, 40c oz.

Eikonogen, 40c oz.

Metol, 75c oz.

Amidol, 65c oz.

Platinum chloride, 15 gr. tubes, 60c each.

Gold chloride, pure, 15 gr. tubes, 60c each.

" " and sodium, 15 gr. tubes, 35c ea.

Sulphite of soda, 15c lb.

Hyposulphite of soda, 5c lb.

Carbonate of soda, pure, 25c lb.

Sal soda, 3 lbs for 5c.

Bromide of potassium, 5c oz.

Carbonate of potash, 20c lb.

Borax, powdered, 7c lb.

Red prussiate of iron, 10c oz.

Acetate of soda, 10c oz.

Tripods.

2-length folding, $1.25.

3-length folding, $2.00.

4-length folding, $2.50.

Films in Rolls of 12 Exposures.

Pocket kodak size, 25c roll.

Folding pocket kodak, 40c roll.

Bulls' Eye or Bullet, No. 2, 60c; No. 4, 90c.

No. 4 Cartridge kodak films, in rolls of six exposures, half the price of the rolls of 12 exposures. Price 90c, roll of 12 exposures.

Printing Frames.

Wood—

3¼ x 4¼, or smaller, 15c; 4 x 5, cabinet, 20c; 5 x 7, 25c each.

Metal—

3½ x 3½, or 3¼ x 4¼, 25c; 4 x 5, 30c; 5 x 7, 35c each.

Higgins' photo mounting paste, 15c, 25c, 50c bottle.

Ladies' and Gentlemen's Watches.

REMEMBER we guarantee every Watch we sell to give satisfaction. Every Watch is thoroughly examined by our expert watchmaker before the guarantee is written. ☞When ordering be sure to mention number and page. Watches are subject to advance in price without notice. We always carry every grade of the well-known Waltham Watch in every style of case.

NOTE.—All Watches marked "R" will pass railway inspection.

The wonderful success we have met with in handling our special "London" watch leads us to again place before you these special points of excellence we claim for it:—**1st.** It is made from the finest materials and by the best workmanship of modern science. **2nd.** It in every way merits the term "perfect time-keeper" that is often applied to it by those who carry it. The lowest grade easily runs within a minute a month. **3rd.** It is of the thinnest, newest model, pendent set in all sizes and styles, and every part is interchangeable.

Chatelaine Watches for Ladies.

HALF OPEN FACE.

Sterling silver case, plain polished or engine turned.

W100. Silver case and genuine American movement, $5.25.
W101. Above case and London 7-jewelled nickel movement, $7.90.
W102. Above case and London 15-jewelled nickel movement, $9.50.
W103. Above case and Waltham 7-jewelled movement, $7.90.
W104. **Special**, solid nickel case, plain, genuine American movement, same size as cut, $3.85.

Ladies' 14k Gold-Filled Chatelaine Watches.

HALF OPEN FACE.

Same size as cut above and guaranteed to wear 25 years. Plain, engine turned or handsomely engraved.

W105. Above case and London 7-jewelled nickel movement, $11.35.
W106. Above case and London 15-jewelled nickel movement, $12.75.
W107. Above case and Waltham 7-jewelled nickel movement, $10.90.
W107½. Above case and 15-jewelled Waltham movement, $14.75.

Ladies' 14k Solid Gold Hunting Watches, 0 Size.

14k solid gold, heavy weight, of the very best make, can be had perfectly plain polished, engine turned or handsomely engraved.

W108. Above case and London 7-jewelled movement, $22.00.
W109. Above case, with London 15-jewelled nickel movement, Breguet hairspring, $23.25.
W110. Above case, with London 15-jewelled nickel movement, gold settings, patent regulator and Breguet hairspring, $25.75.
W111. Above case, with London special fine nickel adjusted 17-jewelled movement, gold settings, patent regulator, $29.25.
W112. Above case with a 7-jewelled nickel Waltham movement, $22.25.
W113. Above case, with a 15-jewelled nickel Waltham movement, $25.50.
W114. Above case and 16-jewelled nickel "Lady Waltham" movement, $26.50.
W115. Above case and Waltham 17-jewelled Riverside movement, $35.50.

Ladies' 18k Solid Gold Hunting Watches, 0 Size.

Hunting case, size as above cut, plain polished, engine turned or artistically engraved.

W116. Above case and London 15-jewelled nickel adjusted movement, jewels in gold settings, $29.25.
W117. Above case and London 17-jewelled adjusted nickel movement, very finely finished for accurate time, $32.25.
W118. Above case, with Waltham 15-jewelled nickel movement, $28.75.
W119. Above case and 16-jewelled nickel Waltham movement, $30.25.
W120. Above case and Waltham 17-jewelled Riverside movement, $39.50.

REMEMBER—We guarantee satisfaction in every case.

Ladies' 14k Gold-Filled Hunting Case, 0 Size.

We always carry the newest and best filled cases that money can procure. Ladies' 14k gold-filled small-sized case, guaranteed for twenty-five years; plain, engine turned or engraved.

W121. Above case, with London 7-jewelled movement, $13.00.
W122. Above case, with London 15-jewelled nickel movement, $14.25.
W123. Above case, with highest grade London 17-jewelled fine nickel adjusted movement, $19.85.
W124. Above case, with Waltham 7-jewelled movement, $12.50.
W125. Above case, with 15-jewelled nickel Waltham movement, $16.00.

Ladies' Silver Hunting Case, 0 Size.

Above case can be had plain polished or engine turned.

W126. Above case and 7-jewelled London nickel movement, $9.25.
W127. Above case and 15-jewelled London nickel movement, $10.25.
W128. Above case and 7-jewelled Waltham movement, $9.50.
W129. Above case and 15-jewelled Waltham movement, $12.85.

Any of above silver cases engraved, $1.00 extra.

Ladies' 14k Diamond-Set Case, 0 Size.

HUNTING CASE.

Ladies' 14k plain polished solid gold case, set with real diamonds.

W130. Above case and London 15-jewelled nickel adjusted movement, patent regulator and Breguet hair-spring, $43.75.
W131. Above case and highest grade London movement, having 17 ruby jewels, gold settings, $47.50.
W131½. Above case and 7-jewelled nickel Waltham movement, $41.75.
W132. Above case and 16-jewelled Waltham movement, $45.50.
W133. Above case and 17-jewelled Waltham Riverside movement, $54.25.

Gun-metal Chatelaine Watches, Plain.

OPEN FACE.

W134. Black gun-metal case and genuine American movement, $5.25.
W135. Gun-metal case and London 7-jewelled movement, $7.75.
W136. Gun-metal case and London 15-jewelled nickel movement, $9.00.
W137. Gun-metal case and 7-jewelled nickel Waltham movement, $8.25.
W138. Gun metal case and 15-jewelled nickel Waltham movement, $11.75.

Ladies' Diamond-Set Watches, 6 Size.

Hunting Case.

Ladies' 14k solid gold, plain polished case, set with genuine diamonds.

W139. Above case and 15-jewelled nickel London movement, $44.75.

W140. Above case and 17-jewelled nickel London adjusted movement, $51.00.

W140½. Above case and 7-jewelled Waltham movement, $41.50.

W141. Above case and 15-jewelled Waltham movement, $45.75.

W142. Above case and 16-jewelled nickel Waltham movement, $49.00.

W143. Above case and Waltham Riverside 17-jewelled nickel movement, $59.00.

Ladies' Monogram Watches.

Raised Gold Monograms.

Ladies' 14k solid gold, plain hunting case, with a raised gold monogram, any initials.

W144. The above case fitted with London 15-jewelled nickel movement, $30.00.

W145. Above case, with London 15-jewelled fine nickel movement, patent regulator and Breguet hairspring, $32.25.

W146. Above case, with the highest grade London 17 jewelled adjusted fine nickel movement, $36.00.

W147. Above case with a 15-jewelled Waltham movement, $32.50.

W148. Above case with the fine "Royal" 16-jewelled Waltham movement, $33.25.

W149. Above case, with "Riverside" 17-jewelled nickel Waltham movement, adjusted, jewels in gold settings, patent regulator, Breguet hairspring and finely finished throughout, $43.25.

> Plain case without monogram $2.50 less than above prices.

Ladies' 14k Solid Gold Hunting Case, 6 Size.

Ladies' 14k solid gold hunting case watches, regular size, good substantial weight and well made. Plain engine-turned or handsomely engraved.

W150. Above case, with 7-jewelled London nickel movement, $23.00.

W151. Above case, with a London 15-jewelled nickel movement, $24.25.

W152. Above case, with London 15-jewelled nickel movement, patent Breguet hairspring and regulator, $26.75.

W153. Above case, with London 17-jewelled fine nickel adjusted movement, jewels in gold settings, patent Breguet hairspring and regulator, and finely finished, for perfect time, $30.55.

W154. Above case and 7-jewelled Waltham movement, $21.00.

W155. Above case, with 15-jewelled Waltham movement, $24.75.

W156. Above case, with 16-jewelled fine nickel "Lady Waltham" movement, $28.50.

Ladies' 10k Solid Gold Hunting Case, 6 Size.

Ladies' 10k solid gold hunting case watches, regular size, plain polished, engine-turned or engraved.

W157. Above case and 7-jewelled nickel London movement, $18.50.

W158. Above case and 15-jewelled nickel London movement, $19.85.

W159. Above case and 17-jewelled adjusted nickel London movement, $25.85.

W160. Above case and 7-jewelled Waltham movement, $18.75.

W161. Above case and 15-jewelled Waltham movement, $20.75.

W162. Above case and 16-jewelled Waltham nickel movement, $23.75.

Ladies' 14k Gold-Filled Watches.

Ladies' hunting case 14k gold-filled watches, regular size, and guaranteed to wear 25 years, can be had plain polished, engine-turned to a shield, or handsomely engraved.

W163. Above described case, fitted with London nickel 7-jewelled movement, $12.50.

W164. Above case, fitted with London 15-jewelled nickel movement, $13.60.

W165. Above case, fitted with London 17-jewelled adjusted movement, made of fine nickel, gold settings and beautifully finished, for accurate time, $19.60.

W166. Above case, with Waltham 7-jewelled movement, $10.90.

W167. Above case, with a 15-jewelled Waltham movement, $13.50.

W168. Above case, with Waltham 16-jewelled nickel movement, named "Lady Waltham," $16.35.

W169. Above case, with 16-jewelled nickel Waltham movement, patent regulator and Breguet hairspring, $18.50.

Ladies' Sterling Silver Hunting Case Watches.

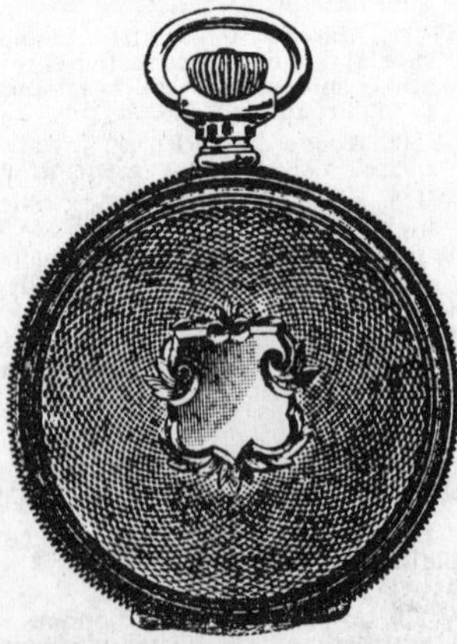

Ladies' silver hunting case watches, made in plain polished or engine-turned.

W170. Silver case and genuine American movement, $5.75.

W171. Silver case and 7-jewelled nickel London movement, $8.25.

W172. Silver case and 15-jewelled nickel London movement, $9.50.

W173. Silver case and 7-jewelled Waltham movement, $8.50.

W174. Silver case and 15-jewelled Waltham movement, $10.25.

> Engraved case for any of above, $1.00 extra.

Nurses' Watches.

SAME SIZE AS CUT.

Full open face with seconds hand, sterling silver case.

W175. Above case, and London 7-jewelled nickel movement, $7.25.

W176. Above case and London 15 jewelled movement, exposed winding wheels, $8.50.

W177. Above case and London 17-jewelled adjusted movement, with ruby jewels in settings, $14.00.

Gun-Metal Cases.

W178. Gun-metal case and London 7-jewelled nickel movement, $6.75.

W179. Gun-metal case and London 15-jewelled movement, $7.85.

W180. Gun-metal case and London 17-jewelled movement, $14.25.

14k Gold Filled.

Guaranteed to wear 25 years.

Open Face, back view.

Open-face, plain, engine-turned or engraved.

W181. Above case and London 7-jewelled nickel movement, $10.25.

W182. Above case and London 15-jewelled movement, $11.35.

W183. Above case and London 17-jewelled adjusted movement, $17.75.

14k Solid Gold Case.

Plain polished, engine-turned or engraved.

W184. Above case and London 7-jewelled nickel movement, $24.50.

W185. Above case and London 15-jewelled movement, $25.75.

W186. Above case and London 17-jewelled adjusted movement, $32.25.

The New 12-Size Gentlemen's Watches.

Open Face.

The new 12-size up-to-date gentleman's watch, light in weight, thin in model, perfectly made, an ideal gentleman's watch, 14k gold-filled case, guaranteed to wear 25 years, perfectly plain, engine turned or handsomely engraved.

W187. The above case and London 7-jewelled movement, $13.85.
W188. Above case, with London 15-jewelled adjusted nickel movement, patent regulator and Breguet hairspring, $17.50.
W189. Above case, with highest-grade London 17-jewelled nickel adjusted movement, $20.50.
W190. Above case and 7-jewelled Waltham nickel movement, $13.75.
W191. Above case, with Waltham 15-jewelled nickel movement, $16.75.
W192. Above case, with "Royal" Waltham 17-jewelled nickel movement, $21.25.

Hunting Case, $2.00 extra.

Open-face gun metal or silver cases for above watch, $5.50 less.
W193. Special gun metal case and genuine American movement, $2.75.
W194. Special silver case, with genuine American movement, $4.25.

12-Size, 14k Solid Gold Hunting or Open-Face Case.

W195. Above case and 15-jewelled nickel London movement, $36.50.
W196. Above case and 17-jewelled nickel London movement, $42.50.
W197. Above case and 7-jewelled Waltham movement, $34.50.
W198. Above case and 15-jewelled nickel Waltham movement, $37.75.
W199. Above case and 17-jewelled nickel Waltham movement, $45.75.

Gentlemen's 14k Solid Gold 16-Size Presentation Watches.

Hunting or Open Face.

14k solid gold case, hinged back and front, thin model, made in plain polished or engine turned.

W200. Above case and London 15-jewelled movement, jewels in settings, $37.75.
W201. Above case and London 17-jewelled adjusted movement, patent regulator and Breguet hairspring, $43.75.
W202. Above case and London new model, 17-jewelled, adjusted to heat, cold and all positions, damaskeened plates, and in every respect a perfect time-piece, $56.50.
W203. Above case and Waltham 15-jewelled nickel movement, $40.50.
W204. Above case and 17-jewelled Riverside Waltham movement, $52.50.

Gents' 14k Gold-Filled Watches.

16-Size, Open Face.

14k gold-filled case, warranted 25 years, stem wind and stem set, screw back and bezel, plain, engine-turned or engraved.

W205. The above described case, fitted with London 7-jewelled nickel movement, $11.75.
W206. Above case, fitted with London 15-jewelled nickel movement, $13.00.
W207. Above case, fitted with London 17-jewelled nickel adjusted movement, $19.75.
W208. Above case, with 7-jewelled Waltham movement, $12.25.
W209. Above case, with 15-jewelled Waltham movement, patent Breguet hairspring, $16.00.
R210. Above case and new 16-size, 23-jewelled, Vanguard Waltham movement, suitable for railway men, $40.00.

NOTE.—Hunting cases for above movements, $3.00 extra.

Gents' 10k Gold-Filled Watches

16 Size.

10k gold-filled case, warranted 20 years, screw back and bezel, stem wind and stem set, plain, engine turned or engraved.

W211. Above described case, fitted with London 7-jewelled nickel movement, $9.50.
W212. The above described case, fitted with London 15-jewelled movement, $10.75.
W213. Above case, fitted with London 17-jewelled nickel adjusted movement, $17.50.
W214. Above case fitted with 7-jewelled Waltham movement, $9.75.
W215. Above case, with 15-jewelled Waltham movement, $13.25.
W216. Above case, with 17-jewelled Waltham movement, $16.25.
W217. Above case, and Riverside 17-jewelled nickel Waltham movement, $24.75.

NOTE.—Hunting cases for above, $2.00 extra.

Watches for Young Men and Boys.

All Open Face.

W218. The "Eaton" Dollar watch, nickel case, $1.00.
W219. Very reliable strong dust-proof American watch, stem wind and set, $1.25.
W220. Nickel case and genuine American movement, very reliable, $2.00.
W221. Nickel case, small size, genuine American movement, $3.00.
W222. Gun-metal case and genuine American movement, small size, $3.00.

Sterling Silver 16-Size Open-Face Watches.

Solid silver case, screw back and bezel, thick glass, stem wind and set, engine-turned or perfectly plain polished.

W223. Above case and genuine American movement, $4.25.
W224. Above case, fitted with London 7-jewelled nickel movement, $7.00.
W225. Above case, with London 15-jewelled nickel movement, $8.25.
W226. Above case, with London 15 jewels, in gold settings, nickel movement, patent regulator, and Breguet hairspring, beautifully finished, $10.00.
W227. Above case, with London 17-jewelled nickel movement, patent regulator, and Breguet hairspring, and highly adjusted for accurate time, $15.00.
W228. Above case, fitted with 7-jewelled Waltham movement, $5.25.
W229. Above case, with 15-jewelled nickel Waltham movement, Breguet hairspring, $10.00.
W230. Above case, with 17-jewelled nickel Waltham movement, patent Breguet hairspring and regulator, finely adjusted to heat, cold and all positions, $16.50.
R231. Above case and Waltham 16-size 23-jewelled Vanguard movement, suitable for railway purposes, $35.00.

Gentlemen's Gun-Metal Watches.

Same size as cut above, plain cases.

W232. Gentlemen's gun-metal case, with genuine American movement, $2.50.
W233. Above case, with London 7-jewelled movement, $6.50.
W234. Above case, with London 15-jewelled movement, $7.50.
W235. Above case, with Waltham 7-jewelled movement, $7.00.
W236. Above case, with 15-jewelled Waltham movement, $10.75.

Gentlemen's Nickel-Cased Watches.

W237. Solid nickel case, plain, with genuine American movement, very reliable, $2.00.
W238. Nickel case and London 7-jewelled movement, $5.50.
W239. Nickel case and London 15-jewelled movement, $6.75.
W240. Nickel case and Waltham 7-jewelled movement, $6.35.

NOTE.—All 16-size London movements have exposed winding wheels, and are of the thinnest model.

Gentlemen's 14k Gold-Filled Cases, 18 size.

Open Face.

14k open-face gold-filled case, stem-wind and stem-set, screw back and screw bezel, dust proof, strong glass. This case is guaranteed to wear and give satisfaction for 25 years, and is plain, engine-turned or engraved.

W241. Above case, with London 7-jewelled nickel movement, $11.85.
W242. Above case, with London 15-jewelled nickel movement, exposed winding wheels and jewels in settings, $13.00.
W243. Above case, with London 15-jewelled nickel movement, exposed counter-sunk winding wheels, Breguet hairspring and patent regulator, jewels in settings, $14.75.
W244. Above case, with 17-jewelled nickel London adjusted movement, $19.65.
W245. Above case, with highest grade London 17-jewelled movement, adjusted to temperature and positions, new patent regulator, $31.65.
W246. Above case, with 7-jewelled Waltham movement, $11.40.
W247. Above case, with 15-jewelled Waltham movement, $13.85.
W248. Above case, with 17-jewelled P. S. Bartlett Waltham movement, patent regulator and hairspring, $15.50.
W249. Above case, with 17-jewelled nickel Waltham movement, patent Breguet hairspring, adjusted to heat, cold and all positions, $18.25.
R250. Above case, and 17-jewelled, "Canadian Railway Time Service" Waltham movement, $20.25.
R251. Above case, with 17-jewelled Appleton, Tracy & Co. nickel Waltham movement, $23.50.
R252. Above case and "C.P.R." Waltham movement, 17 fine ruby jewels, $20.50.
R253. Above case, with "New Model," 21-jewelled "Crescent Street" Waltham movement, $29.00.
R254. Above case and 21-jewelled Vanguard Waltham movement, $34.00.
R255. Above case and 23-jewelled Vanguard movement, the new and finest Waltham movement made, $40.25.

NOTICE TO RAILWAY MEN.

We always carry in stock a full line of Railway Watches and can supply them in any case desired. All watches marked "R" will pass railway inspection. We specially recommend the well-known Waltham watch for this purpose.

NOTE.—Hunting cases for above movements, $3.00 extra.

Gentlemen's 10k Gold-Filled Cases, 18 size.

10k open face, gold-filled case, stem-wind and set, screw back and bezel, dust-proof, strong glass, guaranteed to wear 20 years. Made in plain polished, engine-turned, or engraved.

W256. The above case, with London 7-jewelled nickel movement, $9.50.
W257. Above case, with London 15-jewelled nickel movement, exposed winding wheels, and jewels in settings, $10.75.
W258. Above case, with London 15-jewelled nickel movement, jewels in settings, exposed counter-sunk winding wheels, patent Breguet hairspring and regulator, $12.50.
W259. Above case, with London 17-jewelled nickel adjusted movement, $17.35.
W260. Above case, with the highest grade London movement, new patent regulator and 17 jewels in gold settings, $29.50.
W261. Above case, with 7-jewelled Waltham movement, $8.85.
W262. Above case, with 15-jewelled nickel Waltham movement, $11.25.
W263. Above case, with 17-jewelled P. S. Bartlett Waltham movement, patent regulator and hairspring, $12.75.
W264. Above case, with 17-jewelled nickel Waltham movement, Breguet hairspring and patent regulator, $15.25.
R265. Above case and 17-jewelled "Canadian Railway Time Service" Waltham movement, $17.50.
R266. Above case and 17-jewelled "C.P.R." Waltham movement, ruby jewels in gold settings, $17.75.
R267. Above case, with Appleton, Tracy & Co. nickel 17-jewelled Waltham movement, $21.00.
R268. Above case, with Crescent Street "New Model" 21-jewelled Waltham movement, $26.50.
R269. Above case and Vanguard 21-jewelled Waltham movement, $32.00.
R270. Above case and the new 23-jewelled Vanguard movement, $37.50.

Note.—Hunting cases for above movements, $3.00 extra.

The new 23-jewelled Vanguard movement has 23 diamond, ruby and sapphire jewels set without shellac, in raised gold settings, exposed pallets and solid gold patent micrometric regulator. It is the very finest 18-size Waltham movement made.

Gentlemen's Open-Face Silver Watches.

3-oz. solid silver, gold inlaid, locomotive, stag, woodchopper, steamboat, race horse or horse and sulky.

W271. The above case, with London 7-jewelled nickel movement, $9.90.
W272. Above case, with London 15-jewelled nickel movement, $11.25.
W273. Above case with London 15 jewels in settings nickel adjusted movement, $12.90.
W274. Above case, with London 17-jewelled nickel adjusted movement, $17.75.
W275. Above case, with highest grade 17-jewelled nickel adjusted London movement, $29.75.
W276. Above case, with 7-jewelled Waltham movement, $9.25.
W277. Above case, with 15-jewelled nickel Waltham movement, $12.00.
W278. Above case, with 17 jewels in settings, P. S. Bartlett Waltham movement, patent regulator and hairspring, $13.75.
R279. Above case and "C.P.R." Waltham movement, patent regulator, Breguet hairspring and 17 ruby jewels in settings, $18.50.
R280. Above case and Appleton, Tracy & Co. Waltham new model movement, $22.00.
R281. Above case, with new model "Crescent Street" nickel Waltham movement, $27.50.
R282. Above case and 21-jewelled "Vanguard" Waltham movement, $32.50.
R283. Above case and new 23-jewelled "Vanguard" Waltham movement, $38.25.

Gentlemen's 3-oz. Open Face Solid Silver Plain Case.

W284. 3-oz. silver case, with London 7-jewelled nickel movement, $8.90.
W285. Above case, with London 15-jewelled nickel movement, $10.25.
W286. Above case, with London 15 jewels in settings, nickel adjusted movement, $11.90.
W287. Above case, with London 17-jewelled nickel adjusted movement, $16.75.
W288. Above case, with highest grade 17-jewelled nickel adjusted London movement, $28.75.
W289. Above case, with 7-jewelled Waltham movement, $8.50.
W290. Above case, with 15-jewelled nickel Waltham movement, $11.00.
W291. Above case, with 17 jewels in settings, P. S. Bartlett Waltham movement, patent regulator and hairspring, $12.75.
R292. Above case, and Appleton, Tracy & Co. Waltham movement, $21.00.
R293. Above case, with new model "Crescent Street" nickel Waltham movement, $26.50.

All Railway Watches are marked thus "R."

Gentlemen's Solid Silver Medium-Weight Case, 18 Size.

Open Face.

Solid silver case, medium weight, screw back and bezel, dust proof, thick glass, and in every way first-class.

W294. Above case and London 7-jewelled movement, $7.25.
W295. Above case and London 15-jewelled movement, $8.75.
W296. Above case and London 15-jewelled movement, nickel, patent regulator, $10.25.
W297. Above case and London 17-jewelled movement, nickel, patent regulator, adjusted, jewels in settings, $15.25.
W298. Above case, with 7-jewelled Waltham or Elgin movement, $7.25.
W299. Above case, with 15-jewelled nickel Waltham movement, $9.50.
W300. Above case, with 17-jewelled P. S. Bartlett adjusted Waltham movement, $11.00.
W301. Above case, with 17-jewelled nickel adjusted Waltham movement, $14.00.

Gentlemen's Solid Nickel Watches, 18 size.

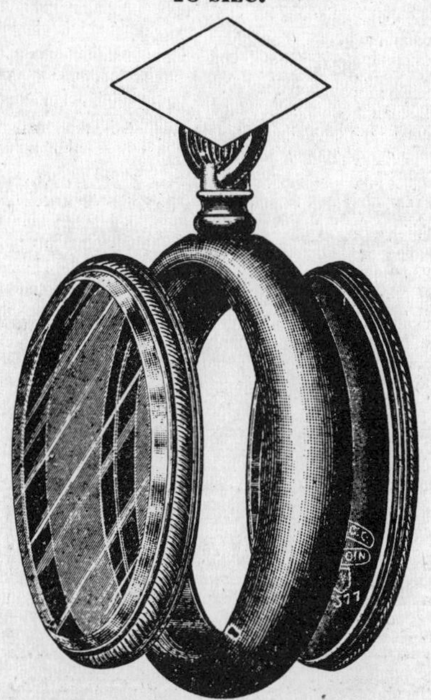

Solid nickel case, screw front and back, dust proof, thick glass, stem-wind and stem-set.

W302. Above case, with London 7-jewelled movement, $5.50.
W303. Above case and London nickel movement, 15 jewels in settings, patent hairspring, $6.75.
W304. Above case and London 15-jewelled nickel movement, patent regulator and Breguet hairspring, jewels in gold settings, $8.50.
W305. Above case and London 17-jewelled, in settings, nickel finely adjusted movement, $13.50.
W306. Above case, fitted with genuine Waltham 7-jewelled movement, $5.25.
W307. Above case, fitted with 15-jewelled Waltham movement, $7.75.
W308. Above case, fitted with P. S. Bartlett 17-jewelled adjusted Waltham movement, $9.25.
R309. Above case, fitted with an Appleton, Tracy & Co. 17 ruby-jewelled adjusted nickel Waltham movement, $17.50.
R310. Above case and "C.P.R." nickel adjusted movement, 17 ruby jewels, $14.25.
R311. Above case and new model "Crescent Street" Waltham movement, 21 fine ruby jewels in gold settings, $23.00.
R312. Above case and 21-jewelled nickel "Vanguard" Waltham movement, $28.25.
R313. Above case and 23-jewelled Waltham Vanguard movement, $34.25.

Gentlemen's 14k Solid Gold Presentation Watches.

18-Size, Open Face.

14k solid gold case, hinged back and front, the new up-to-date thin model, made in plain, polished or engine-turned. Can be supplied plain with engraved monogram, $2.00 extra.

W314. Above case and London 15-jewelled movement, jewels in settings, patent regulator and Breguet hairspring, $45.00.
W315. Above case and London 17-jewelled movement, jewels in settings, compensating balance, patent regulator, $59.50.
W316. Above case and new model 17-jewelled London movement, adjusted to heat, cold and all positions, new patent regulator, $63.00.
W317. Above case and 15-jewelled Waltham movement, nickel, Breguet hairspring, $44.75.
R318. Above case with 21-jewelled nickel "Crescent Street" Waltham movement, jewels in gold settings, patent regulator, Breguet hairspring, $60.25.
R319. Above case and the highest grade Waltham movement, Vanguard, having 23 jewels, $71.95.

NOTE.—Hunting cases for above watches no extra charge.

STERLING SILVER NOVELTIES.—925/1000 Fine.

N1, N2, N3. Sterling silver shoe horn, stocking-darner, ink blotter, also nail file, buttonhook, cuticle, ink eraser, nail brush, tooth brush, curling tongs, seal, table bell, paper knife, 50c each.

N1, N2, N3. Same assortment, with larger and heavier sterling silver handles, new grey finish, very rich design, $1.00.

N1, N2, N3. Same assortment, with smaller handle, bright finish, 25c, 35c.

N4. Pocket comb, in silver case, $1.25.

N5. Tie clip, 20c.

N6. Emery ball, silver top, 25c.

N7. Manicure scissors, bright finish, $1.00; other patterns, $1.25, 1.50, 1.75, 2.25; with amethyst settings, $2.00.

N7A. Embroidery scissors, bright finish, 75c, $1.00, 1.25, 1.50; work scissors, larger, $1.50, 1.75, 2.25.

N8. Tape measure, silver case, $1.25.

N8½. Sterling silver thimbles, plain and fancy patterns, 25c, 35c, 50c, 75c; also tailors' thimbles, plain, 25c, 35c.

NOTE.—Thimbles come in four sizes, misses', small women's, women's and large women's. Please state size when ordering.

N9. Ink stand, $3.00; other designs, $1.50, 2.00, 2.50, 3.00, 4.00, 10.00.

N10 and N11. Child's brush and comb set, grey finish, in fancy lined case, $3.25; in bright finish, different pattern, $1.50, 3.00; four pieces, brush, comb, rattle and powder box, in satin-lined leather case, $8.50.

N12. Cloth brush, grey finish, $3.00; different designs, bright finish, $3.00, 4.50, 5.00.

N13. Nail polisher, grey finish, $2.00; others in bright finish, $1.00, 1.50, 1.75.

N14. Hand mirror, grey finish, $5.50; different pattern, larger, $10.00; other designs, bright finish, $7.00, 10.00, 12.50.

N15. Hair brush, grey finish, $3.00; others in bright finish, $3.00, 4.50, 5.75.

N16. Hat brush, grey finish, $1.75; different pattern, $2.25; bright finish, $1.00, 1.50.

N17. Comb, sterling back, grey finish, $1.50; others in bright finish, 50c, 75c, $1.00, 1.25.

N18. Whisk, grey finish, $1.50; different patterns, bright finish, 75c, $1.00, 1.50, 2.00, 2.75.

N19. Match safe, grey finish, $2.50; other scenes, as golf, sailing, hunting, baseball, etc., $2.50; different, bright finish, $1.00, 1.25, 1.50; souvenir of Toronto, Canada, Ontario, British, maple leaf or fleur-de-lis, $1.75.

N20. Stamp box, bright finish, 75c; different pattern, 50c; heavier, plain satin finish, $1.25.

N21. Valise tag, 60c.

N22. Umbrella clasp, 15c, 25c.

N23. Pomade jar, 35c; others, 50c, 75c, $1.25.

N24. Puff box, $2.00; large, different pattern, $2.50, 3.00, 3.50, 4.50.

N25. Shaving brush, $2.00; others, 75c, $1.25, 1.75, 3.25; with amethyst setting, $2.25.

N26. Coat hanger, 60c; hat marker, same style, 40c.

N27. Napkin ring, $2.00; narrower, $1.50; wider, $2.25; other designs, 50c, 75c, $1.75; plain, satin finish, $1.25, 1.75.

N28. Child's cup, $6.00; other patterns, $5.00, 5.50.

N29. Tooth brush bottle, 35c.

N30. Tooth powder bottle, 35c.

N31. Smelling salts bottle, glass, with sterling top, 35c; different styles, 50c, 75c, $1.00, 1.25, to 2.50; all silver, fancy pattern, with chain attached, $1.50, 2.75.

N32. Bonnet brush, $1.50; others in different designs, $1.00, 2.25, 3.00; with amethyst setting, $2.00; larger, $3.25.

N33. Souvenir spoon, sterling silver, gold plated, with Toronto, Dominion, British or Ontario coat-of-arms or maple leaf on handle, with views of new City Hall, Parliament Buildings, University College, Metropolitan Church or St. Michael's Cathedral in bowls, tea size, $1.50; coffee size, $1.00.

N34. Souvenir coffee spoon, sterling silver, gold plated, same coats-of-arms as N33, with new City Hall, Parliament Buildings, University College or Toronto harbor in bowls, $1.00.

N35. Silk elastic garters, assorted colors, with sterling buckles, $1.25; with stone settings in buckles, $2.50 pair.

N36. Silver pencil, adjustable, 75c; others, 35c, 50c, $1.00, 1.25, 1.75, 2.25.

N37. Toothpick, adjustable, similar to cut, with jewel setting in end, 35c, 50c, 75c.

N38. Silver pencil holder, $1.25; smaller, 50c.

NOTE.—Engraving ordinary script letters on any of above goods, 3c per letter; old English letter, 5c per letter. Engraving monogram on seals, 1 letter, 35c; 2 letters, 50c; 3 letters, 75c.

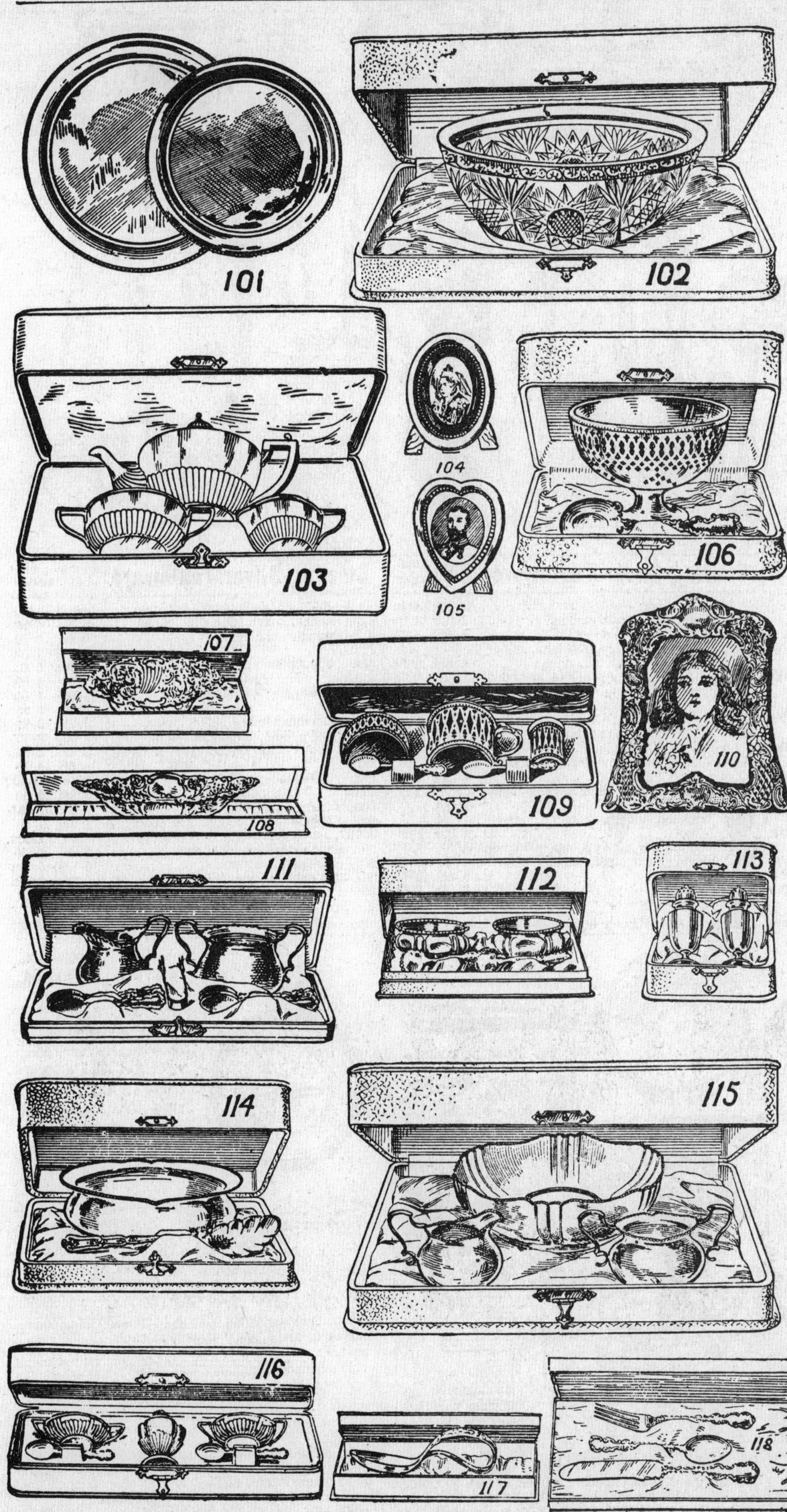

Fancy Sterling Silver Sets.

Every Piece Guaranteed 925/1000.

101. Sterling silver salver, heavy weight, 4-inch in diameter, $3.00 ; 6-inch, $5.25 ; 8-inch, $10.80; 9-inch, $15.00; 10-inch, $18.00; 12-inch, $24.00.

102. Genuine cut glass 9-inch berry or salad bowl, sterling silver rim, in handsome leatherette case, satin lined, $16.50; without case, $15.00; salad servers, Louis XV. pattern, $8.50 extra.

103. 3-piece sterling silver tea set, made in heavy weight only, teapot 5½ inches high with ebony handle, $19.00; cream pitcher, 3½ inches high, gold lined, and sugar bowl, 2¾ inches high, gold lined, $17.75 pair; complete in leather case, velvet lined, $40.00 ; without case, $36.50.

104. Sterling silver photo frame, 3 inches high, $1.00; 6½ inches, $3.00.

105. Sterling silver photo frame, 3 inches high, $1.00; larger, 4-inch, $1.50; 4¾ inches high, 3¾ inches wide, $2.50.

106. Sterling silver saw pierced sugar, jelly, honey or marmalade bowl, 5½ inches in diameter, 4½ inches high, removable blue glass inner dish, complete with spoon in leatherette case, satin-lined, $14.75; without case, $13.75.

107. Sterling silver bon-bon or almond dish, 3½ inches in diameter, in case, $1.90; 5 inches in diameter, in ivorine satin-lined case, $4.75.

108. Sterling silver bon-bon or almond dish, 7 inches long, in ivorine case, satin lined, $5.25; 4 inches long, in case, $1.90.

109. Sterling silver saw pierced blue glass lined pepper, salt and mustard set, with sterling spoons, complete in handsome leather case, velvet lined, $12.25; pair of salts with spoons, ivorine case, $4.75; pair pepper shakers, in ivorine satin-lined case, $5.50; mustard pot with spoon, $5.25.

110. Sterling silver photo frame, leather back and support, 7 x 5 inches, $4.25.

111. Sterling silver dessert set, gold lined, cream jug and sugar bowl with sugar tongs and ½ dozen coffee spoons, complete, in leatherette case, satin lined, $19.75; sugar bowl and cream jug only, $15.75.

112. Pair of sterling silver salts and spoons, in ivorine satin-lined case, $7.00.

113. Sterling silver pepper and salt shakers in leatherette case, satin lined, $6.75.

114. Sterling silver berry bowl, 6 inches in diameter, gold lined, with sterling fruit spoon, complete in leatherette case, satin lined, $18.00.

115. Sterling silver berry set, gold lined; bowl 7½ inches in diameter, cream 2½ inches high, sugar 2½ inches high, complete in handsome leatherette case, satin lined, $31.20; cream and sugar only, $12.00; berry bowl only, $18.25.

116. Sterling silver pepper and salt set, with salt spoon, in leather case, velvet lined, $11.25; pair of salts and spoons only, in leather case, $8.50; pair of salt shakers only, in leather case, $8.25; pair of salts and mustard pot, in leather case, $15.75; mustard pot only, $5.25.

117. Child's sterling silver pap spoon, with cupid embossed on handle, in ivorine case, $2.00; without case, $1.75; similar, $1.25.

118. Sterling silver child's set, knife, fork and spoon, in ivorine satin-lined case, $4.50; larger size, $5.50.

119. Carving knife, fork and steel, with sterling silver handles, in satin-lined leatherette case, $9.50.

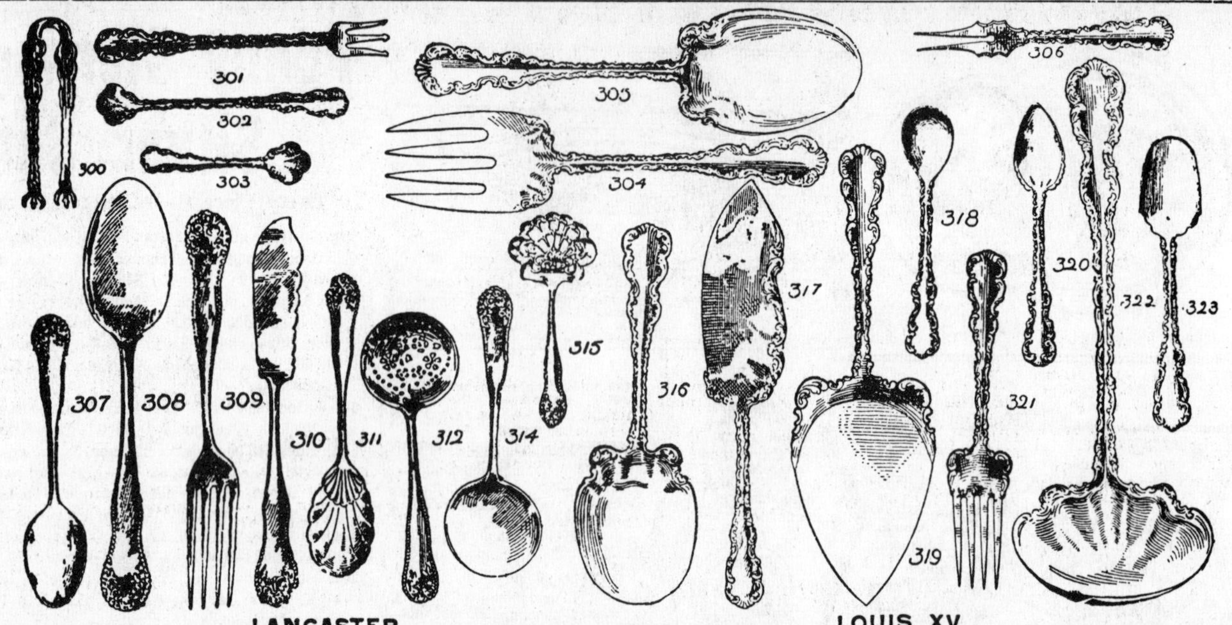

Sterling Silver Tableware	Louis XV.	Lancaster
925/1000 Fine, Fully Guaranteed.	Doz.	Doz.
307. Coffee spoons, pattern on front only, gilt bowl	$ 3 20	......
307B. Coffee spoons, standard weight..	5 25	$6 00
307C. " " " " gilt bowl	6 25	7 00
307D. Teaspoons, medium size	6 50	......
307E. Teaspoons, medium size, standard weight	7 50	8 00
307F. Teaspoons, large size, standard weight	9 50	10 25
308. Dessert spoons, regular size, standard weight	16 50	18 00
308B. Table spoons, regular size, standard weight	22 50	24 75
309. Dessert forks, regular size, standard weight	16 50	18 00
309B. Table forks, regular size, standard weight	22 50	24 75
	Each.	Each.
310. Butter knife, medium size	1 75	2 00
310B. " " " " heavier	2 25	......

Sterling Silver Tableware	Louis XV.	Lancaster
925/1000 Fine, Fully Guaranteed.	Each.	Each.
311. Sugar spoon, silver bowl	1 00	1 35
311B. " " heavier, gilt bowl...	1 50	1 75
312. Sugar sifter, regular size, silver bowl	2 25	2 75
312B. Sugar sifter, regular size, gilt bowl	2 50	2 75
312C. " " smaller size, gilt bowl	1 00	......
312D. " " cream ladle or bon bon scoop, gilt bowls	0 85	......
314. Cream ladle, regular size, silver bowl	2 25	2 25
314B. Cream ladle, regular size, gilt bowl	2 50	2 75
314C. Cream ladle, smaller size, gilt bowl	1 00	......
315. Bon-bon or candy scoop, silver bowl	1 00	1 50
315B. Bon-bon or candy scoop, gilt bowl	1 00	1 75
316. Berry spoon, large size, silver bowl	4 75	5 00
316B. " " " " gilt "	5 25	5 75
316C. " " smaller silver "	3 25	3 50
316D. " " " " gilt "	3 75	4 00

Sterling Silver Tableware	Louis XV.	Lancaster
925/1000 Fine, Fully Guaranteed.	Each.	Each.
317. Ice cream and jelly slice, silver....	6 50	6 50
318. Egg spoon, silver	0 90	0 90
318B. " " gilt	1 00	1 00
319. Pie knife, silver bowl	5 00	5 50
319B. " " gilt bowl	5 50	5 50
320. Orange spoon, silver bowl	1 00	1 00
320B. " " gilt "	1 35	1 35
321. Cold meat fork	3 75	3 75
322. Soup ladle, large size, silver bowl	9 00	9 50
322B. Gravy or sauce ladle, silver bowl.	3 50	3 75
322C. " " " gilt "	3 75	3 75
323. Cheese scoop	1 50	......
323B. " " larger	2 25	2 50
300. Sugar or bon-bon tongs, gold tips	1 00	1 35
301. Pickle forks	1 25	1 50
301B. Oyster forks	1 00	1 00
302. Mustard spoon, gilt bowl	1 00	1 00
303. Salt spoon, silver	0 75	0 75
304. 305. Salad spoon and salad fork, set	9 00	9 00
306. Fruit fork	1 00	1 00

Note.—Engraving on Jewellery, Watches, Rings and Silverware, per letter : Script, 3c. Old English or Script entwined, 5c.

Optical Goods.

No. 180. Opera glasses, French manufacture, Japanned mounts and draws, morocco covered body, fitted with finest quality lens, put up in soft crushed leather case with handle, $6.00; larger size, $8.00.

No. 181. Opera glasses, finished in goldfish, mother-of-pearl and gold-plated mounts, with detachable extension handle, finest quality French lens, very handsome design, in plush bag, $15.00.

No. 182. Same glass, without handle, in black, mother-of-pearl and gilt mounts, in leather case, $8.00, 10.00.

No. 183. Telescopes, 10, 14, 16 and 21-line glasses, in sewn morocco and japanned, 2 to 4 draw, with shade, in leather sling case, $4.75, 5.50, 6.25, 11.00; also 15, 17, 19-line glass, in sewn morocco, with 3 polished brass draws, in case, $3.75, 6.00, 7.75.

No. 184. Marine and field glasses, 19, 21 and 24-line glasses, with flat top, large eye, sewn morocco, with shades, in solid leather sling case, $9.00, 11.00, 13.00 and 18.00.

No. 185. Reading glasses, nickel-plated band, with black ebony wood handles, 2½-inch, 25c; 2½-inch, 35c; 3-inch, 60c; 3¼-inch, 75c; 3½-inch, 85c; 4-inch, $1.00; 5-inch, $1.25.

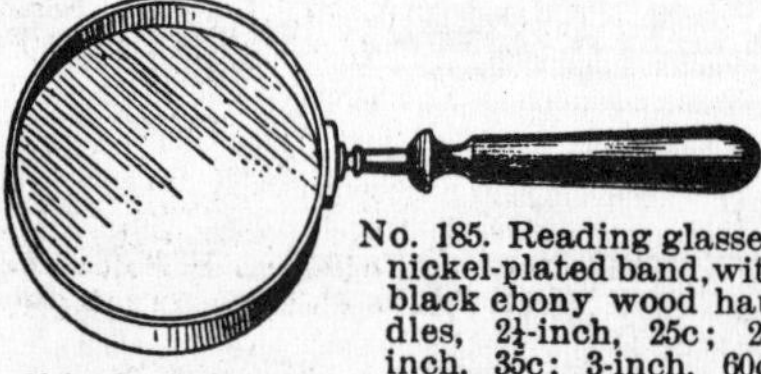

No. 186. Botany glasses, nickel-plated or gutta percha case, 1 lens, 15c; 2 lenses, 25c; 3 lenses, 35c; 2 lenses, larger size, 40c and 50c; 3 lenses, larger size, 60c and 75c.

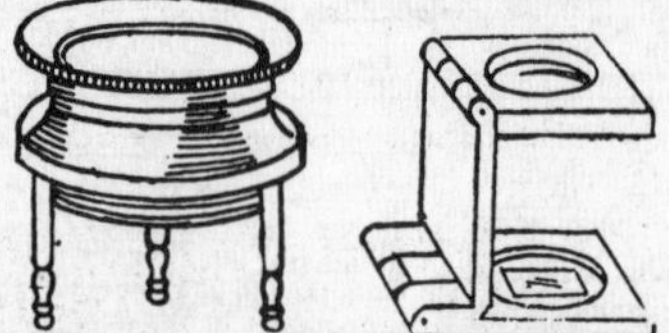

No. 187. No. 188.

No. 187. Tripods, in solid brass case, fitted with finest quality adjustable lenses, as cut, 40c, 60c.

No. 188. Linen tester, solid, polished brass folding case, fitted with strong magnifying lens, as cut, 40c.

No. 189. Compasses, gun-metal finished case, open face, 15c, 25c, 35c; nickel finish or polished brass case, open face, 20c, 25c, 35c, 50c; nickel finish, hunting case, 35c, 50c, 75c, $1.00; same case, with jewel-set needle, $2.25.

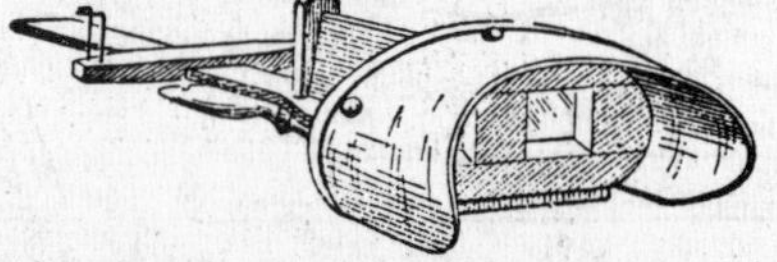

No. 190. Stereoscopes, polished wood, 25c, 50c: better quality, 85c; views, 4c each.

No. 191. Eye-glass chains, in 10k gold-filled solid links, with hook and snap, as cut, 75c; solid gold, same style, $2.75.
Black silk eye-glass guard, 5c, 10c, 15c.
Hooks, gold filled, 25c each.
Hooks, black enamelled, 10c each.

GUARANTEED ACCURATE CLOCKS.

K1.

K1. Alarm clocks, genuine "Seth Thomas" movement, nickel finish, 4½-in. dial, with second hand, as cut K1, $1.15.

K2. Same movement, without alarm, 90c.

K3. Genuine American nickel-finish alarm clock, 3½-in. dial, 75c.

K4. Genuine American nickel-finish alarm clock, 4-in. dial, extra quality, $1.00.

K5.

K5. Intermittent "can't sleep" alarm clock, American movement, nickel finish, 4-in. dial, alarm on back, rings 5 times with one winding, ringing altogether about 5 minutes, design as cut K5, $1.65.

K6. Small bedroom clock, 1-day, nickel or gilt finish, 2½-in. dial, $1.00.

K7. Same style, with alarm, $1.75.

K8.

K8. Alarm clock, nickel finish, gilt front and handle, fitted with American movement, long alarm attachment on bottom, $2.00.

K9. Similar style, 6½ in. high, with musical alarm attachment which plays 20 minutes and which also acts as an alarm, $2.75.

K10.

K10. Fancy gold-plated clock, embossed burnished finish, cream porcelain finish dial, fitted with an American movement, design as cut, $2.25.

Similar design, smaller size, $1.75.

K11.

K11. Fancy clock for mantel or boudoir use, ormulu gilt finish, guaranteed 24k gold-plate, hand-burnished cream porcelain dial, fitted with an American movement. One-day time, $6.50; 8-day time in same case, $7.50.

K12.

K12. Fancy clock for mantel or boudoir use, cupid design, richly finished in ormulu gold, guaranteed 24k gold-plate, hand-burnished finish, cream porcelain dial, fitted with an American movement, as cut, $7.50.

K13. Design without cupids and base, $2.75.

Similar designs, same finish and movement, $2.00, 2.50, 3.25, 4.25, 5.25.

K14. Large sizes in cupid design, 10 to 12 in. high, $14.50, 16.50, 20.00.

K14½. Design as cut K10, with 24k gold-plated finish and porcelain dial, $4.50.

K15.

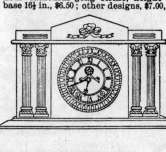

K15. Alarm clock, metal case, in enamelled, oxidized and bronze finish, fitted with an American movement, long alarm attachment on bottom, design as cut K15, $1.25.

K17.

K17. Mantel clock, polished adamantine finish on wood, neatly carved, gilt finish trimmings, 8-day movement, hour and half-hour cathedral gong strike, white dial, height 11 in., base 12½ in., handsome design, $4.75; other similar designs in larger sizes, $5.50, 5.75, 6.00.

K16.

K16. One-day time, long-alarm clock, in metal case, oxidized copper finish, in fancy ornamental design, height 10 in., 4½-in. dial, the alarm rings about 20 minutes with one winding, but can be switched off at pleasure, $3.00.

K18.

K18. Polished wood clock, adamantine finish, with gilt trimmings and feet, nicely carved, 8-day movement, hour and half-hour cathedral gong strike, height 11 in., base 16½ in., $6.50; other designs, $7.00, 7.50.

K19.

K19. Dining-room clock, in old oak finish, neat design, fancy dial, fitted with eight-day American movement, hour and half-hour cathedral gong strike, 14 to 16 in. high, $3.75.

K20. Similar design in walnut finish, $3.75.

K21.

K21. Wall clock, in oak or walnut finish, 32 in. long, regulator style, 12-in. dial, 8-day movement, $6.25; with calendar, $6.75.

K22. Drop octagon wall clock in oak or walnut finish, 8-day time, visible pendulum, 21½ in. long, dial same style as cut K31, $4.25; calendar and 12-in. dial, $5.25.

K23. Genuine weight regulator, American movement, one of our best timepieces, $14.00.

K24.

Mantel clocks, height 22 in., in oak or walnut finish, gilt decorated glass—

K24. 1-day, strike	$2 25
K25. 1-day, strike, alarm	2 60
K26. 8-day, strike	2 60
K27. 8-day, strike, alarm	3 00
K28. 8-day, cathedral gong strike	3 00
K29. 8-day, cathedral gong strike, alarm	3 25

There is a cheaper grade of these clocks, but we do not handle them and highly recommend above styles.

K30.

K30. Enamelled iron mantel clock, well polished, gold-plated trimmings, cream porcelain dial, fitted with a visible escapement. 8-day movement, hour and half-hour cathedral gong strike, 15 in. wide, $9.50.

K31. Same design and movement, without visible escapement, $8.90.

K32. Similar designs in enamelled iron clocks, some with feet, $6.50, 7.00, 7.75. Fancy designs, $10.00 and 15.00.

K33.

Mantel clocks, with thermometer and barometer attachment, in oak or walnut finish—

K33. 8-day, half-hour strike	$3 00
K34. 8-day, half-hour strike, alarm	3 25
K35. 8-day, half-hour gong strike	3 25
K36. 8-day, half-hour gong strike, alarm	3 50

140
141
142
143
144
145
146
147
148
149
150
151
152
153
154
155
156
157
158
159
160
161
162
163
164
165
166
167
BREAD
168
169
170
171
172
173
174
175

FINE QUALITY OF SILVERWARE.

140. Cheese dish, satin engraved lid on bright burnished plate, with rococo border, four fancy embossed feet, satin-finished base, bright burnished around knob, $4.00.

141. Tea set, five pieces, coffee pot, tea pot, sugar bowl and gold-lined spoon-holder and cream jug, hand burnished, fancy embossed feet, handles and spout, with steel-grey finished border and trimmings, newest design, 5 pieces complete, $42.50. (See cut of teapot, No. 141.)

142. Tea set, four pieces, tea pot, sugar bowl, cream jug and spoon-holder, satin engraved, bright cut, cream jug and spoon-holder gold lined, fancy embossed feet and handles, rococo border, bright burnished lid, $8.75; including extra tea pot, $12.75; same design in bright burnished finish, $10.50; five pieces, $15.00. (See cut of teapot, No. 142.)

143. Butter dish, bright burnished base and rim, embossed feet, rococo border and fancy twisted handles, satin engraved lid and fancy knob, as cut, $3.50; same design without bale, $3.00; other similar designs, in satin finish, $2.25, 2.50 and 7.00.

144. Smoking set, bright burnished finish, gold lined, satin-finished tray with shot bead border, $3.25; similar design, rococo border, $5.00.

145. Childs' mugs, satin finished, bright cut, engraved, gold lined, fancy handle, as cut, $1.85; plainer design, small size, 60c; medium size, 75c; large size, $1.00; other designs, $1.50 and 2.00.

146. Fern pot, fancy filigree design, embossed feet and handles, bright burnished, removable inner dish, as cut, $3.75; similar design, without handles, but with extra earthen pot, $4.00; plainer design, $2.75.

147. Syrup jug, finished with tray to match, neatly engraved, with rococo border, jug has bright burnished lid, fancy embossed feet, handles and spout, $3.00; other designs, $3.25, 6.00.

148. Card receiver, on bright burnished stand, rococo border on base and top, satin-finish centre, handsomely carved, silver lined, $2.25; gold lined, $2.75.

149. Dinner castor, handsome embossed design, fancy handle and revolving stand fitted with 5 square-shaped bottles, cut glass pattern and engraved, 12 inches high, $5.25; same design bottles, fitted on high revolving stand, satin engraved around centre, $4.25; similar design, fitted with round-shaped bottles, $3.35; other plain designs, special plate, round shaped bottles, $2.25.

150. Tea service, including tea pot, sugar bowl, cream pitcher, spoon-holder, and 12-inch waiter to match, bright burnished finish, pearl bead border, embossed handles and spout, spoon-holder and cream jug gold-lined, new design, as cut No. 150, special price, complete, $17.00; 4-piece set without waiter, as cut No. 150, $12.00.

151. Pickle cruet, embossed stand, shot bead trimming on handle, tongs on side, fitted with gilt decorated glass bottle, colored glass, bright burnished lid with fancy knob, design as cut No. 151, $2.25; design with crystal bottle and fancy stand, $1.50; other designs, $1.85, 2.50.

152. Dessert set on fancy stand, sugar bowl, cream jug and spoon, fancy shaped handle, spoon-holder on side, satin finish, neatly engraved on sides and stand, cream jug and bowl of spoon gold lined, four fancy embossed feet, bright burnished lid and edges, $4.38.

153. Breakfast cruet, wishbone design, bright burnished base, fancy handle, "Wave Crest" ware bottles, with silver-plated tops, $2.00.

154. Toast rack, bright burnished embossed feet, plain handle, six partitions, $2.50.

155. Salt and pepper sifters, in bright and satin finish, neatly carved, salt sifter has gold-plated top to prevent rust, glass lined, in neat satin-lined box, convenient for mailing, $1.75; smaller size, $1.25 and 1.50.

156. Saltcellar, white or colored glass, cut glass pattern, embossed stand, fancy handle and spoon on side, neat design, as cut No. 156, $1.50.

157. Tea set, five pieces, coffee pot, tea pot, sugar bowl, gold-lined cream pitcher and spoon-holder, pearl bead border, fancy embossed feet, handles and spouts, bright burnished finish, new design, $25.00; with ebony handles on tea and coffee pots as cut, $27.50; same design, with flat base instead of feet, $22.50; with ebony handles, $25.00; waiter to match with rococo border and ebony handles, satin shield on centre, $19.00; without ebony handles, $17.00.

158. Salad or nut bowl, burnished finish outside, gold lined inside, fancy pattern border, embossed feet, handsome design, as cut, $6.50; other designs, $4.50, 5.75, 7.50, 13.00.

159. Shaving mug and brush, fancy embossed design, satin-finish base, gold-lined cup, fine hair brush with silver-plated handle to match cup, $3.00.

160. Biscuit jar, glass bowl, cut glass pattern, fitted with silver-plated top, bright burnished lid, fancy knob, $1.00.

161. Sugar bowl and spoon-holder combined, satin finish, fancy design, bright finished base and lid, with ornamental bird knob, embossed handles, rack for holding twelve spoons around bowl, $3.00; with plain spoons attached, $4.75; heavier weight spoons, plain, $5.35; fancy pattern spoons, $6.00.

162. Coffee set, 4-piece, including coffee pot, gold-lined sugar bowl and cream pitcher, on 11-inch waiter, shot bead trimming, bright burnished finish, design, as cut, $11.00; other design in fluted pattern, $23.00.

163. Baking or pudding dish, large size, bright burnished finish, fancy embossed feet and handles, rococo border around lid and rim, separate fine porcelain-lined dish inside, fitted with extra rim, fancy embossed feet, ornamented knob, as cut, $5.75; smaller size without extra rim, satin finished and engraved, $3.75; other designs, with extra rim, $5.00, 5.50 and 9.00.

164. Tilting water pitcher, satin engraved, heavily embossed handle and base, fitted with gold-lined goblet on projected stand, very beautiful design, $10.50; same design with two goblets, $13.50; fancy embossed design, handsomely engraved, fitted with two goblets, $22.00; water pitcher, separate, same design as cut on stand, porcelain lined, $6.50; heavier design and fancy finish, $13.50.

165. Bon-bon dish, bright burnished finish, gold lined, shot bead border, new design, as cut 175; other designs, silver lined, $1.50; gold lined, $1.75.

166. Napkin ring, satin engraved, rococo edge, chicken and wishbone design, with the words "A Sterling Wish" or "Best Wishes" engraved on side, $1.25.

167. Bread tray, bright burnished finish border, fancy open-work design ends, the word "bread" neatly engraved in centre, rich pattern, as cut, $3.50; other designs with rococo border, and the word "bread" engraved on centre, satin finish, $2.25; bright burnished finish on border, $2.50; similar design, embossed ends and centre, $1.50.

168. Crumb tray and scraper, satin finished, with shot bead trimming, fitted with secure ebony wood handles, as cut, $2.75.

169. Napkin ring, new design, bright burnished finish, shot bead border, as cut, $1.00.

170. Napkin ring, barrel design, engraved to imitate barrel, satin finish, leaf design holder, as cut, 60c; other designs, 75c, 85c, $1.00.

171. Biscuit jar, "Wave Crest" ware, bowl in fancy tinted colorings of pink, blue and yellow, bright burnished lid, with scalloped border and shot bead trimming, fancy cord handle, neat design, $4.00.

172. Cake basket, round shape, fancy embossed in flower leaf design, fancy pattern handle, strongly made, design as cut, $5.00; square shape, rococo border, silver lined, $4.75; gold lined, $5.50; other designs, $6.00, 9.50.

173. Dessert set, 2-piece set, in satin-lined case, sugar bowl and cream pitcher, both pieces gold lined, fancy pattern, bright burnished finish, fancy border, embossed handles, $5.50; similar design, shot bead border, sterling silver pattern, $4.75; in solid leather case, $6.50.

174. Berry dish, with fancy stand, bright burnished base, embossed feet, shot bead trimming on handle, fitted with tinted opal-ware glass dish, very pretty, $3.00; other designs, with gold decorated dishes in floral design, with heavier stand, $5.50, 6.50, 7.50.

175. Egg set, six cups and spoons, broken egg pattern, bright burnished base, satin-finished inside, plain bright burnished handle, with receptacle for six spoons, cups and bowl of spoons gold lined, $6.50; four cups and spoons, $5.50; two cups and spoons, $3.50.

176. Waiters and Trays.—(*a*) 6-inch card tray, with shot bead border, satin finished, with shield in centre, $1.75; plain satin finished, without shield, $1.50; (*b*) round shaped waiter, with fancy border, handsomely engraved, 12-inch, $3.50; 15-inch, $4.50; (*c*) 14-inch waiter, to match No. 142 tea set, with fancy handles, satin shield on centre, $5.00; (*d*) larger sizes, 17-inch, $10.00; 20-inch, $14.00.

Hat Pins, Neck and Hair Brooches.

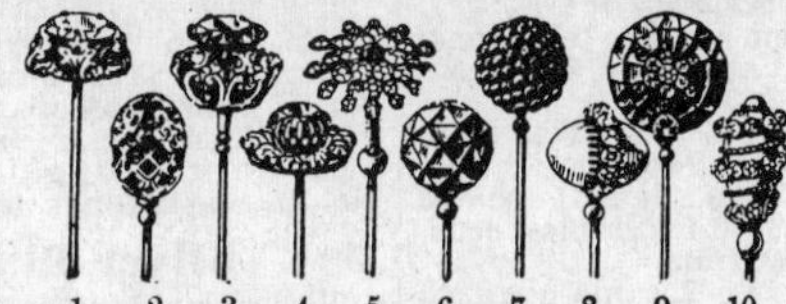

Fancy hat pins, large colored stone settings (see cut No. 1), 5c each; better quality, also in fancy enamel tops, 10c each (see cuts Nos. 2 and 3); with fancy colored stone settings, 15c, 20c, 25c (see cut No. 4).

Fancy hat pins, colored stone settings, movable tops (see cut No. 5), 10c, 15c, 25c, 35c each.

Fancy cut glass top hat pins, assorted colors (see cut No. 6), 25c each.

Fancy jet hat pins, French designs (see cut No. 7), 25c, 35c, 50c each.

Fancy hat pins, large colored brilliants, assorted colors, set with small white stones, Parisian designs (see cuts Nos. 8 and 9), 50c, 75c; with gold-plated tops, set with white and colored brilliants (see cut No. 10), $1.00, 1.25, 1.50, 1.75, 2.00 each.

No. 14. Contingent button hat pin, gold-plated, small or large (as cut No. 14), 5c each.

No. 15. Maple leaf brooch or hat pin, set in hard enamel, sterling silver, 50c; smaller size, 25c; metal, gold-plated, 15c.

No. 16. Coat-of-arms hat pin or brooch (Toronto, Dominion, British or Ontario), in sterling silver, 50c; smaller size, 25c; metal, gold-plated, 15c.

No. 17. Royal arms brooch or hat pin, sterling silver, gold-plated, hard enamelled in proper colors, 75c; larger size, $1.00.

Patriotic Hat Pins and Brooches.

No. 11. Flag brooch or hat pin, in colored enamel finish, with Canada or Toronto (as cut No. 11), sterling silver, 25c.

No. 12. Flag brooch or hat pin, with coat-of-arms and ensign, hard enamel finish (as cut No. 12), gold-plated, 15c.

No. 13. Maple leaf brooch or hat pin, with or without word Canada, hard enamelled, sterling silver (as cut No. 13), 25c; large size, 50c; gold-plated, 15c each.

Neck and Hair Brooches.

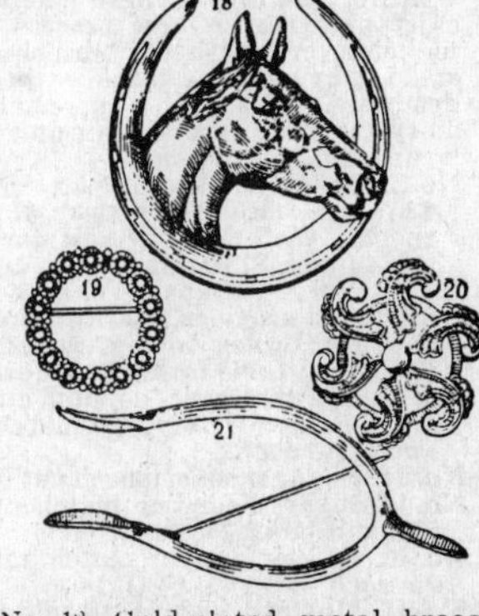

No. 18. Gold-plated metal brooch, with horse's head in horseshoe (as cut No. 18), 25c; without horse's head, 15c.

No. 19. (A) Gold-plated brooch, set with white or colored brilliants, for neck or hair use (as cut No. 19), 35c; (B) with two rings joined together, 35c; (C) with white settings, better finish, 50c; (D) with white or colored brilliants, assorted designs, 25c; (E) also a cheaper line, which we do not guarantee, ring or horseshoe designs, in white or colored settings, 10c each; (F) fine quality all white brilliant set tings, assorted designs, as star, crescent, anchor, circle and oval shapes, 75c; (G) bow of brilliants, $1.00.

No. 20. Black enamelled neck or hair brooch (as cut No. 20), 35c; similar design, 10c.

No. 21. Silver or gold-plated neck or hair brooch, in wishbone design (as cut No 21), 15c.

SILVER-PLATED FLATWARE

ENGRAVING on Jewellery, Watches, Rings, and Silverware, per letter: script, 3c; Old English or script entwined, 5c; large block monogram, $1.00.

Our Silver-plated Flatware is made by Rogers & Bros., of Waterbury, Conn.; Wm. Rogers, of Wallingford, Conn., and other well-known makers. These goods are guaranteed by the makers to be A1, plated on 18 per cent. nickel silver.

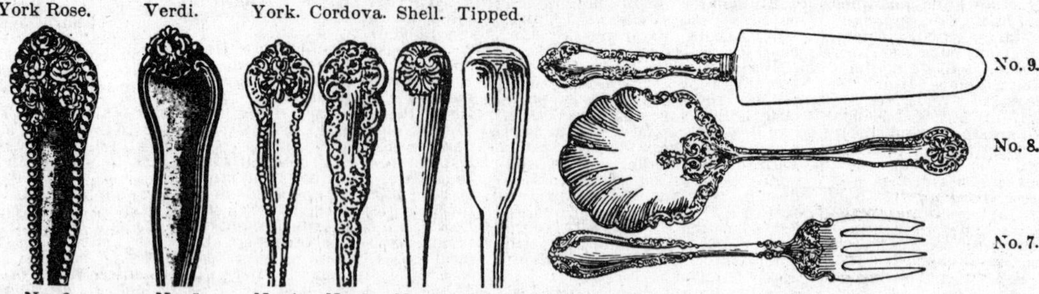

No. 1. Tipped pattern, A1 plate, warranted to wear from 4 to 6 years; teaspoons as cut No. 1, $1.69 doz; dessert spoons and forks, $2.69 doz; tablespoons and forks, $2.97 doz.

No. 2. Fancy pattern, same quality teaspoons; $1.83 doz; dessert spoons and forks, $2.83 doz; tablespoons and forks, $3.63 doz.

No. 3. Tipped pattern, A1 plate, heavier base and warranted to wear from 7 to 9 years; teaspoons as cut No. 1, $2.23 doz; dessert spoons, $3.73 doz; dessert forks, $3.73 doz; tablespoons, $4.63 doz; table forks, $4.63 doz.

No. 4. Shell pattern, as cut No. 2, same quality; teaspoons, $2.43 doz; dessert spoons, $3.87 doz; dessert forks, $3.87 doz; tablespoons, $4.83 doz; table forks, $4.83 doz.

No. 5. Cordova pattern, as cut No. 3, same quality; teaspoons, $3.00 doz; dessert spoons, $4.60 doz; dessert forks, $4.60 doz; tablespoons, $5.50 doz; table forks, $5.50 doz.

No. 6. York pattern, as cut No. 4, same quality; teaspoons, $3.00 doz; dessert spoons, $5.20 doz; dessert forks, $5.20 doz; tablespoons, $6.00 doz; table forks, $6.00 doz.

Quality of flatware as cuts Nos. 5 and 6, have attained the highest reputation with competent judges because of its superior design, finish and wearing qualities. These goods are scientifically plated by a new process on high grade nickel silver and being burnished by hand instead of by machine, it makes them particularly desirable to those who appreciate nice goods. They are extra heavy plate and warranted to wear from 10 to 12 years.

No. 7. Teaspoons, Verdi pattern as cut No. 5, $3.75 doz; dessert spoons, $7.00 doz; tablespoons, $7.50 doz; dessert forks, $7.00 doz; table forks, $7.50 doz.

No. 8. York Rose pattern, as cut No. 6, same quality, teaspoons, $3.75 doz; dessert spoons, $7.00 doz; tablespoons, $7.50 doz; dessert forks, $7.00 doz; table forks, $7.50 doz.

No. 9. Butter knives, to match cut No. 1, 35c ea.

No. 10. Butter knives, to match cuts Nos. 3 and 4, 50c each.

No. 11. Sugar spoons, match cut No. 1, 35c each.

No. 12. Sugar spoons, to match cuts Nos. 3 or 4, 50c; gilt bowl, 75c each.

No. 13. Pickle fork, to match cuts Nos. 3 or 4, 50c each.

No. 14. Mustard spoons, to match cuts Nos. 3 or 4, 35c each.

No. 15. Salt spoons, to match cuts Nos. 3 or 4, 25c each.

The following goods are put up in neat satin-lined cases.

No. 16. Berry spoons, as cut No. 8, $1.50; with gilt bowl, $2.00.

No. 17. Berry spoons, pattern same as cut No. 7, $1.50; gilt bowl, $1.75 each.

No. 18. Berry spoons, pattern same as cut No. 9, $1.50; gilt bowl, $1.75 each.

No. 19. Pie servers, as cut No. 9, $2.00 each.

No. 20. Pie servers, same pattern as berry spoon, cut No. 8, $2.50.

No. 21. Pie knive, fancy pattern handle, $1.50; gilt blade, $2.00 each.

No. 22. Cold meat fork, as cut No. 7, $1.00; gilt tines, $1.25.

No. 23. Cold meat fork, pattern as berry spoon cut No. 8, small, 75c; larger size, $1.00; with gilt tines, $1.50.

No. 24. Gravy ladle, to match cuts Nos. 3 and 4, $1.25; gilt bowl, $1.75.

No. 25. Cream ladle, to match cuts Nos. 3 and 4, 85c; gilt bowl, $1.25.

No. 26. Oyster ladle, to match cuts Nos. 3 and 4, $2.50.

No. 27. Soup ladle, to match cuts Nos. 3 and 4, large size, $3.00; small size, $2.50.

No. 28. Cheese scoops, to match cut No. 9, $1.00.

No. 29. Tomatoes or cucumber servers, to match cut No. 9, $1.50; gilt bowl, $1.75.

No. 30. Sugar tongs, to match cut No. 9, 85c.

Silver-Plated Knives.

Silver-plated knives, warranted 12 dwt. Rogers' make, hand burnished on heavy steel blades.

No. 31. Plain handle, dessert size, $3.75 doz; table size, $4.00 doz.

No. 32. Shell pattern handle, dessert size, $4.50 doz; table size, $5.00 doz.

No. 33. Hollow handle, plain bright finish, dessert size, $5.50 doz; table size, $6.00 doz; knives, fancy pattern, hollow handles, soldered with sterling silver, cannot tell them from solid silver, dessert size, $9.50 doz; table size, $11.50 doz.

No. 34. Silver-plated knives, with 6 dwt. of silver on the dozen, will wear for about six years, table and dessert sizes, $2.25 doz.

No. 35. Silver-plated knives, 2 dwt., table and dessert sizes, $1.20 doz.

Child's Sets.

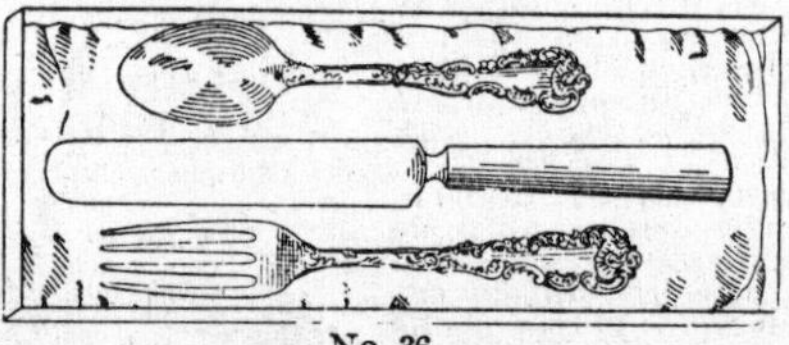

No. 36.

No. 36. Child's knife, fork and spoon, as cut No. 36, $1.00; with knife same pattern as fork and spoon, $1.35.

No. 37. Child's knife, fork and spoon, silver plated, fancy pattern, with steel knife, 25c; A1 silver-plate, 50c.

Pearl Goods.

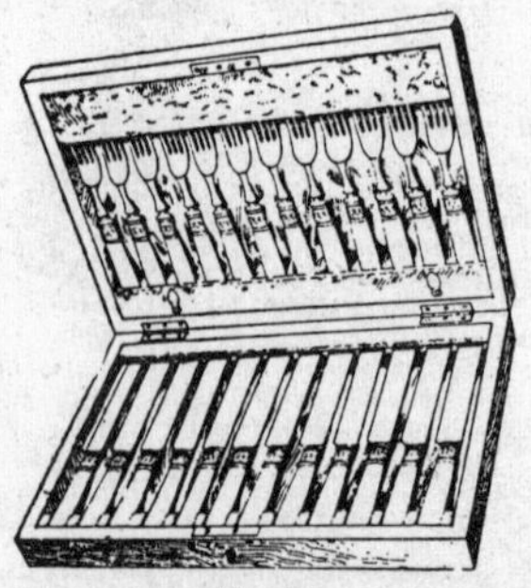

No. 38.

No. 38. Pearl set, in handsome solid oak plush-lined case, fitted with 12 knives and 12 forks, English electro-plate, sterling silver ferrules, fine quality pearl handles, dessert size, $18.50.

No. 39. Pearl set, table size, knives and forks, sterling bolster, $26.50.

No. 40. Pearl set, Waterloo bolster, with extra large pearl handles, $28.50.

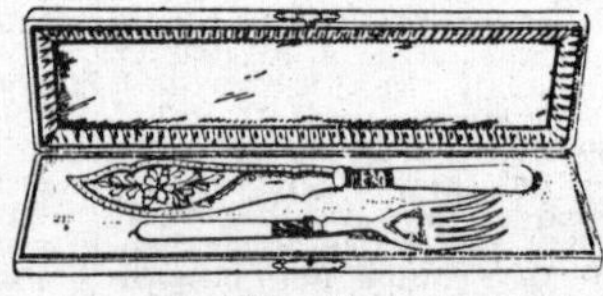

No. 41.

No. 41. Pearl handle fish carvers, in leatherette plush-lined case, English electro-plate, sterling silver ferrules, $5.00; same quality, with ivory handles, $3.50; same quality, with celluloid handles, $3.00.

No. 42. Pearl handle cake knife, saw on back of blade, English electro-plate, fancy engraved blade, silver ferrule, $1.50 each.

No. 43.

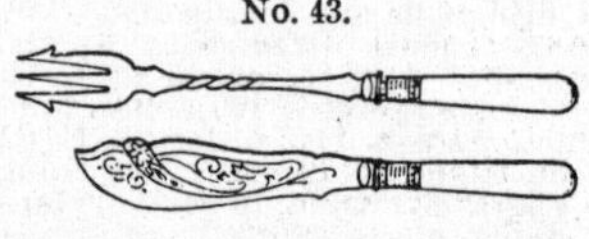

No. 44.

No. 43. Pearl handle pickle forks, same quality, as cut No. 43, 50c, 75c.

No. 44. Pearl handle butter knives, English electro-plate, fancy engraved blades, as cut No. 44, 50c, 75c, $1.00.

White Metal.

White metal is the cheapest line of flatware we sell, which we recommend as the best white metal goods made. They will wear white and not turn brassy.

No. 45. Teaspoons, 25c doz; large size, 35c doz; dessert spoons, 55c doz; dessert forks, 55c doz; tablespoons, 65c doz; table forks, 65c doz.

Nickel Silver.

These goods are warranted to wear white and not turn brassy.

No. 46. Teaspoons, tipped pattern, 50c doz; medium size, 65c doz; large size, 75c doz; dessert spoons, $1.25 doz; dessert forks, $1.25 doz; tablespoons, $1.50 doz; table forks, $1.50 doz.

Steel Table Cutlery.

Such well-known makers as Joseph Rodgers & Sons, John Derby & Sons, and George Butler, all of Sheffield, need no recommendation from us, as they are all so well-known.

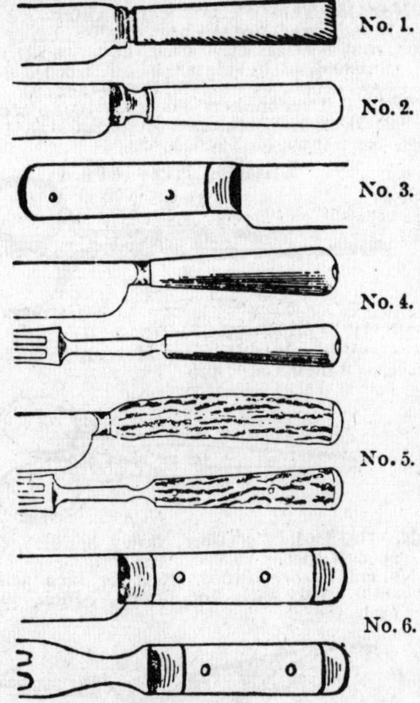

No. 47. Knives only, large size, square ivory handles, as cut No. 1, riveted, hand-forged steel blades, table, $7.50 and 11.00 doz.; dessert size, $5.00 and 7.50 per doz.

No. 48. Knives only, square celluloid handles, as cut No. 1, hand-forged steel blades, table size, $2.75 and 4.75 doz; dessert size, $2.25 and 3.75 doz.

No. 49. Knives only, square celluloid handles, table, $2.00 doz; dessert, $1.50 doz.

No. 50. Knives only, round celluloid handles, as cut No. 2, hand-forged steel blades, table size, $2.50 and 4.50 doz; dessert size, $2.00 and 3.50 doz.

No. 51. Knives only, round celluloid handles, table, $3.25 doz; dessert, $2.75 doz.

No. 51½. Knives only, round buffalo horn handles, as cut No. 4, bolster ends, table, $3.00 doz; dessert, $2 50 doz.

No. 52. Knives only, square buffalo horn riveted handles, table, $3.25 doz; dessert, $2.90 doz.

No. 53. Knives only, stag horn handles, as cut No. 5, bolster ends, table, $2.75 doz; dessert, $2.25 doz.

No. 54. Knives only, rosewood and ebony handles, as cut No. 3, single bolster, securely riveted, table or dessert size, 75c doz.

Knives and Forks.

No. 55. Knives and forks, polished buffalo horn handles as cut No. 4, forged steel blades, table size, for 12 knives and 12 forks, $4.90; dessert size, for 12 knives and 12 forks, $4.50.

No. 56. Different make in same style, table, for 12 knives and 2 forks, $3.25; dessert, for 12 knives and 12 forks, $2.75.

No. 57. Knives and forks, stag horn handles, as cut No. 5, rivet and bolster, hand-forged steel blades, table, 12 knives and 12 forks, $4.30; dessert size, $3.80.

No. 58. Different make in same style, table, 12 knives and 12 forks, $3.00; dessert, $2.75.

No. 59. Knives and forks, rosewood, or ebony handles, as cut No 6, double bolster, 12 knives and 12 forks, table, $3.50; dessert size, $3.00.

No. 60. Knives and forks, rosewood, ebony or white bone handles, securely riveted, single bolster, fine quality steel blade, 12 knives and 12 forks, $2.50; dessert, $2.30.

No. 61. Knives and forks, rosewood or ebony handles, as cut No. 3, single bolster, finely tempered steel blade and steel fork, table size, 12 knives and 12 forks, $1.50.

No. 62. Knives and forks, rosewood or ebony handles, as cut No. 3, single bolster, securely riveted, table size, 12 knives and 12 forks, $1.00.

Carving Sets.

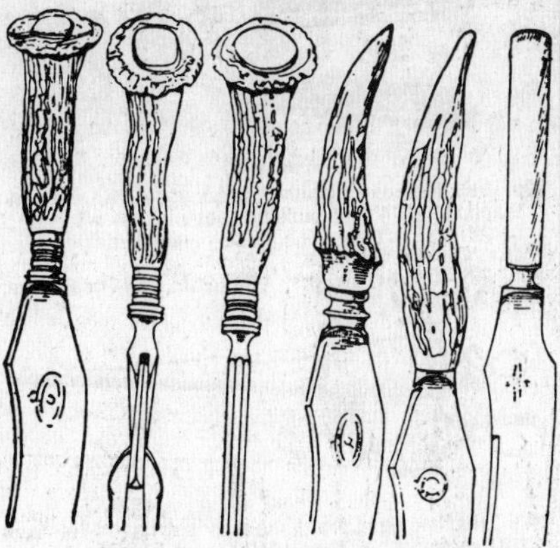

No. 1. No. 2. No. 3. No. 4.

No. 63. 3-piece carving set, fancy stag horn handle, with silver ferrule and tip, hand-forged blade, knife guard on fork, 8-inch steel to match, as cut No. 1, complete, $3.50.

No. 64. Carving knife and fork, as cut No. 1, without steel, $2.25.

No. 65. 3 piece carving set, pointed stag horn handles, as cut No. 2, fitted with 9-inch hand-forged steel blade, fork and 8-inch steel to match, $3.00.

No. 66. Carving knife and fork, as cut No. 2, without steel, $2.00.

No. 67. 3-piece carving set, pointed stag horn handle, as cut No. 3, fitted with finest Cavendish 9-inch steel blade, patent knife rest on fork, script steel to match, complete, $3.85.

No. 68. Carving knife and fork, as cut No. 3, without steel, $2.50.

No. 69. 3-piece carving set, white celluloid, round or square handles, as cut No. 4, to match knives No. 48, 8-inch steel blade, patent knife rest on fork, script steel to match, complete, $2.35.

No. 70. Carving knife and fork, as cut No. 4, without steel, $1.75.

No. 71. Carving knife and fork, finest quality, square ivory handles, to match No. 47 table knives, hand-forged steel blade, $3.75; steel to match, $1.25.

No. 72. Carving knife and fork, stag horn handles, 9-inch forged steel blade, 75c; steel to match, 25c.

No. 73. Carving knife and fork, stag horn handles, forged steel blade, $1.75.

No. 74. Carving knife and fork, stag horn handle, forged steel blade, 8-inch, $1.00; 9-inch, $1.25; steel to match, 25c.

No. 75. Butcher's steel, stag horn handle, brass mounted, with steel swivel, fitted with 11-inch steel, 75c; with round buffalo horn handle, $1.00.

No. 76. Steels, with stag horn handles, 25c, 35c, 40c, 50c.

No. 77. Carving set cases, covered with dark red or dark green leather, lined with fine quality satin, made up to fit 2-piece carver, $1.00; 3-piece, $1.25.

No. 77½. Leatherette-covered case, 85c.

No. 78.

No. 78. Butcher knives, riveted rosewood handle, forged steel blade, 6½-inch, 30c; 7-inch, 35c; 8-inch, 40c; 9-inch, 50c; 10-inch, 60c; 12-inch, 90c each.

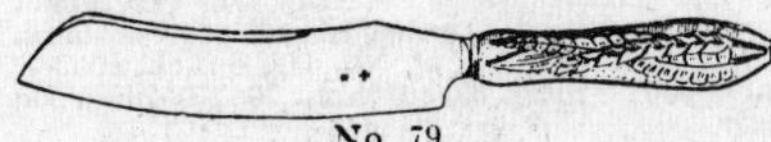

No. 79.

No. 79. Bread knife, as cut No. 79, hand-carved wood handle, forged steel blade, 6½ inch, 35c; 7½-inch, 50c.

No 80.

No. 80. Bread knife, as cut No. 80, saw blade, steel or wood handle, 50c.

No. 81. Bread knife, wire handle, saw edge, steel blade, 10c.

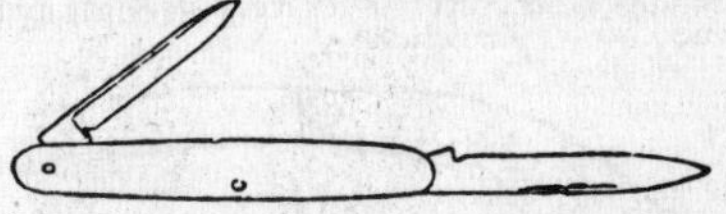

No. 82.

No. 82. Paring knife, as cut No. 82, polished wood handle, with fine steel blade, 5c, 10c.

Pocket Cutlery.

Our pocket cutlery is selected from the best stocks of English and German manufacturers.

No. 83. Ladies' penknives, pearl handle, bolster or plain ends, 2 blades, 25c; 3 blades, 35c; with bone handle, same style, 2 blades, 15c.

No. 84. Ladies' penknives, same quality, plain pearl handle, plate on side, 2 blades, 25c.

No. 85. Ladies' penknives, 2 blades and nail file on back, neat design in pearl handles, 50c.

No. 86. Gents' pocket knives, same as cut, with stag-horn and bone handles, strongly made, 40c; with bolster, 35c, 50c.

No. 87. Gents' pocket knives, with pearl handles, 2 and 3 blades, 50c, 75c.

No. 88. Gents' pocket knives, horn handles, 35c; pearl, 50c; with pearl or ivory handles, 3 blades, 75c, $1.00, 1.25.

No. 89.

No. 89. Pocket knives, shaped horn handle and shaped blades, plate on side, well made, brass lined, 60c.

No. 90. Jack knife, two blades, buffalo horn handle, fitted on finely tempered Sheffield steel blade, 1 blade, 35c; 2 blades, as cut, 45c.

No. 90.

No. 90½. Men's jack knives, with horn handles, 25c; with stag, bone and buff handles, 40c.

No. 91. Men's jack knives with stag horn and bone handles, 1 blade, 15c, 30c.

No. 91½. Men's jack knives, with bolster ends, made especially for farm use, 40c.

No. 92. This knife is specially made for cattlemen's use, as the steel is of extra quality and will therefore hold an edge longer than the ordinary knife, $1.00.

No. 93. Combination knife, best quality steel, with 2 blades, saw, corkscrew, hoof hook, gimlet, awl, screw-driver, tweezers, sliver hook, plate on side, stag horn handles, $1.50.

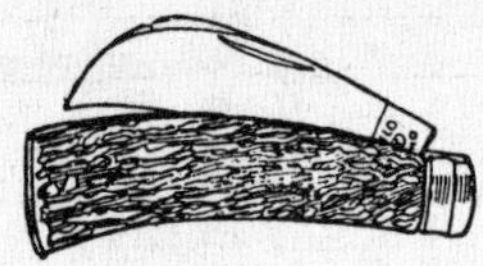

No. 94. Pruning knife, shaped blade and handle, as cut, best quality heavy Sheffield steel blades, stag horn handle, very strongly made, 65c; larger size, $1.00.

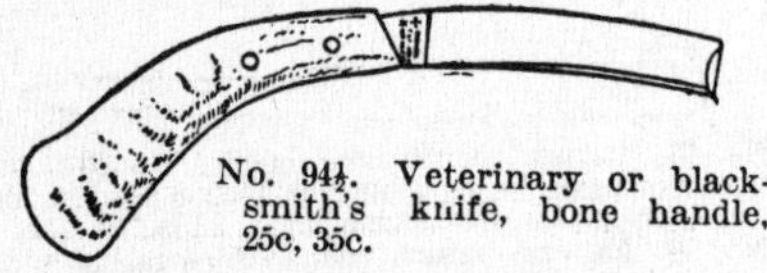

No. 94½. Veterinary or blacksmith's knife, bone handle, 25c, 35c.

Razors and Supplies.

You can rely upon getting a good razor if you send to us, as we handle only those made by the best makers.

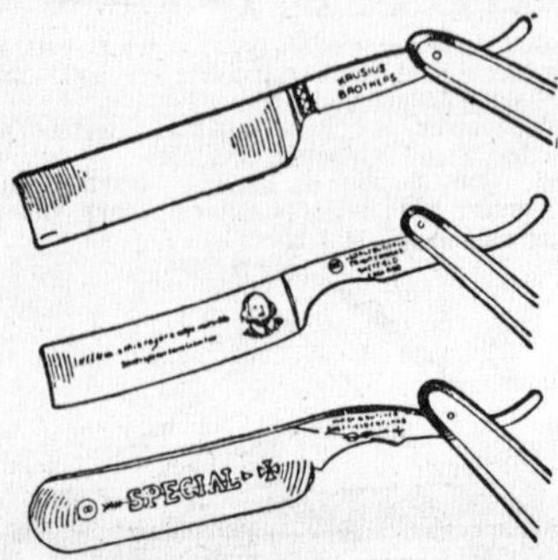

No. 95. No. 96. No. 97.

No. 95. The razor we recommend for easy shaving is the K. B. extra, which is made of the finest razor steel and is specially tempered. It is full hollow ground in ⅝ and ¾-inch blade, as cut No. 95, with black celluloid handle, $1.00; ivory handle, $1.50.

No. 95½. K. B. extra, made expressly for barbers' use, with black celluloid handle, $1.25; ivory handle, $1.75.

No. 96. George Butler & Co. need no recommendation from us, as they have 100 years' experience in manufacturing razors, and make one of the best Sheffield razors sold, ⅝ and ¾-inch blade, black celluloid handle, as cut No. 96, $1.25; ivory handle, $2.00.

No. 97. Wade & Butcher's famous razors are manufactured from the finest razor steel, and have always given perfect satisfaction; full hollow ground blade. ⅝ and ¾-inch, fitted on celluloid handle, as cut No. 97, $1.00; ivory handle, $1.50.

No. 98. The "Gem" safety razor, improved, is a great invention, which renders shaving an easy luxury and totally obviates all danger of cutting the face. The blades are made of the finest steel and are fully concave ground; blades easily removed, and when placed in the handle, which accompanies each razor, can be honed and sharpened as easily as an ordinary razor, $1.50; extra blades for "Gem," $1.00; stropping machines for "Gem," $1.00; strop for safety razor, 50c.

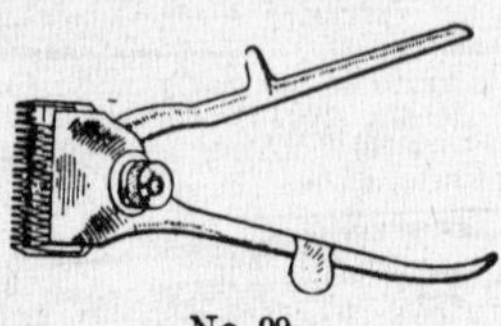

No. 99.

No. 99. Hair clippers, fine quality steel, nickel-plated, fitted with adjustable invisible springs, corrugated bottom plate, as cut 99, $1.50; without corrugated back, $1.00.

No. 100. Hair clippers, invisible springs, ball-bearings, $1.75.

No. 101. Hair clippers, best quality made, nickel-plated, corrugated back, invisible springs, $2.15.

No. 102.

No. 102. Horse clippers, solid steel, finely polished, highly tempered steel plates, with ball bearings, fitted with ebony wood handle, as cut No. 102, $2.00.

No. 103. Other makes, without ball bearings, $1.25, 1.75.

No. 104.

No. 104. Swing strop, specially prepared leather top, canvas back, solid leather handle, as cut No. 104, 50c.

No. 105. Single swing strop, fine quality leather, 20c; wider size, 25c.

No. 106. Double swing strop, with canvas back and leather top, 35c.

No. 107.

No. 107. Four-sided strop, solid leather, with hone, criterion and finish sides, enamelled wood handle, with screw adjustment, 50c.

No. 108. Four-sided strop, different style, 25c.

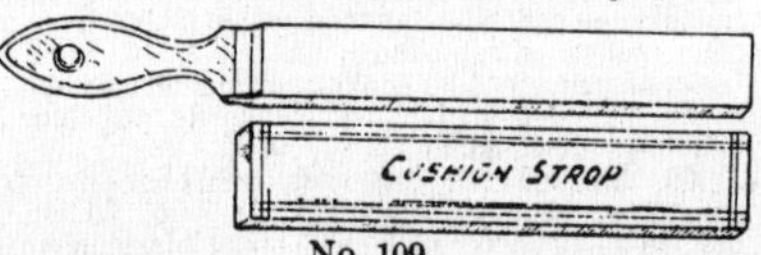

No. 109.

No. 109. Cushion strop, composition and finish sides, paste cup in handle, as cut No. 109, 75c.

No. 110.

No. 110. Pulley razor strop, manufactured from the finest quality leather, with canvas back, adjustable to any length, packed in neat box, with hook, as cut, 110, $1.25.

No. 111. Same style, without canvas back, 85c.

Scissors.

Our stock of scissors is selected from the world's best manufacturers. Such well-known shears as the Heinisch, which have been on the market for over seventy-five years; also the well-known Bailey shear and also the Weiss shear, which have attained the highest reputation for quality and finish.

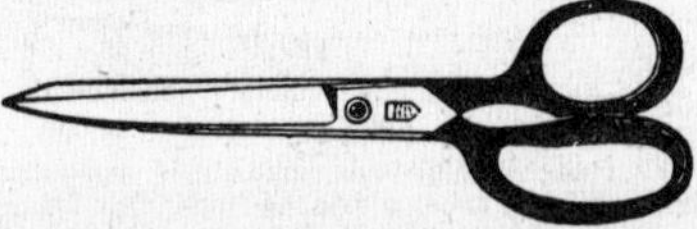

No. 112.

No. 112. Dressmakers' shears, in Heinisch make, japanned handles, nickel-plated blade, finely finished, as cut No. 112, 6-inch, 40c; 7-inch, 50c; 8-inch, 60c; 9-inch, 70c; 10-inch, 90c pair.

No. 113. Tailors' bent handle trimmers, same make, 10-inch, $1.00; 12-inch, $1.25 pair.

No. 114.

No. 114. Bailey's well-known shears need no recommendation from us; they were awarded the medal at Paris in competition with the world; they are forged from the best English steel, as cut No. 114, 6-inch, 35c; 7-inch, 43c; 8-inch, 50c; 9-inch, 60c; 10-inch, 75c.

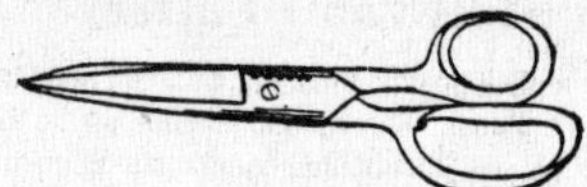

No. 115.

No. 115. The Weiss shears, which we fully recommend, are the best quality, being made from best selected steel, and are all finely-finished, nickel-plated, as cut No. 115, 6-inch, 45c; 7-inch, 55c; 8-inch, 70c; 9-inch, 85c.

No. 116. Dressmakers' shears, silver-plated, K. & B. make, stamped Rogers, 6 and 7-inch, 25c; 8-inch, 35c; 9-inch, 45c.

Ladies' Scissors.

No. 117. Ladies' scissors, K. & B. make, solid steel, highly finished and tempered, 5-inch, 55c; 6-inch, 65c; 7-inch, 75c.

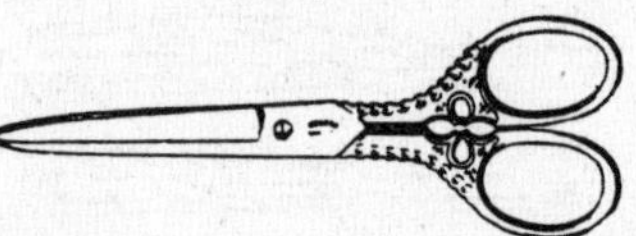

No. 118. Ladies' scissors, fancy handles, 5 and 5½-inch, 25c.

No. 119. Ladies' fancy work or lace scissors, solid steel, with fine points, 3-inch, 40c; 4-inch, 45c.

No. 120. Ladies' fancy work or lace scissors, solid steel, in swan shape design, fine points, as cut, 3-inch, 45c; 4-inch, 50c.

No. 121. Ladies' fancy work or lace scissors, with fine points, 3-inch, 15c; 4-inch, 25c; fancy handles, 35c.

No. 122. Pocket scissors, silver plated, for clerk use especially, 4-inch, 25c; 5-inch, 35c.

No. 123. Folding pocket scissors, solid steel, in neat leatherette case, as cut, 25c; similar, 35c.

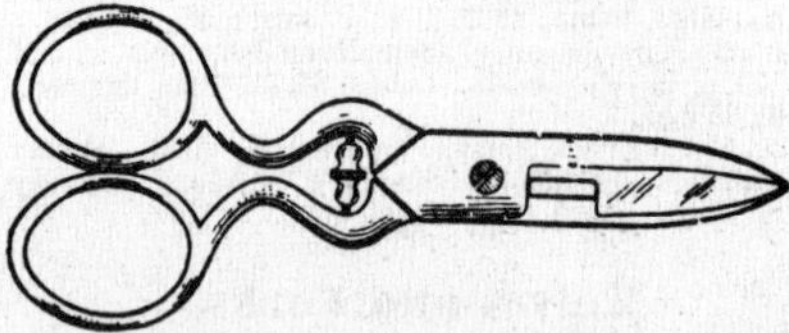

No. 124. Buttonhole scissors, silver plated, patent extension, solid steel, 35c.

No. 125. Buttonhole scissors, silver plated, different pattern, 10c; patent extension, 25c.

Manicure Scissors.

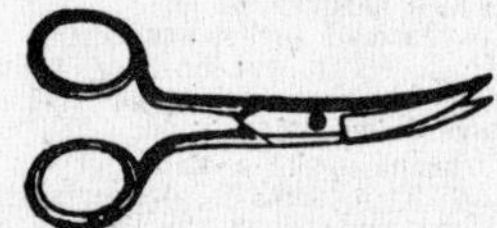

No. 126. Manicure scissors, silver plated solid steel, file on back of blade, 50c.

No. 127. Manicure scissors, different make, 35c.

Barbers' Shears.

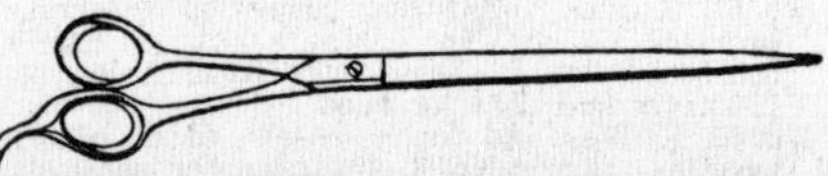

No. 128. Finest quality barbers' shears, double shear steel, highly tempered, nickel or japanned handle, Heinisch or Bailey make, 7½-inch, 65c; 8-inch, 75c.

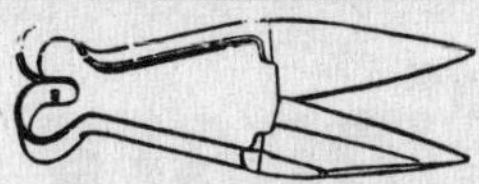

No. 129. Sheep shears, double spring, polished, Sheffield blade, finely tempered, as cut, 6½-inch, 75c; single spring, 6½-inch, 50c.

Salt and Pepper Shakers and Napkin Rings.

No. 130.

No. 131.

No. 130. Salt and pepper shakers, silver plated, nicely chased, as cut, No. 130, 30c pair; smaller size, same height, 25c pair.

No. 131. Napkin ring, silver plated, neat pattern, nicely chased, as cut No. 131, 15c each.
No. 132. Narrower size, same quality, 10c each.
No. 133. Wider size, better quality, 25c each.

Salad Sets.

No. 134. Salad sets, made from selected polished olive wood, plain pattern, as cut, 25c, 35c.
No. 135. Fancy carved handle, 75c, $1.00.

Table and Hand Bells.

No. 136.

No. 137.

No. 136. Table touch bell, silver plated, strongly made, as cut No. 136, 25c.

No. 137. Table touch bell, shape as cut No. 137, loud clear ring, 35c.

No. 138. Hand or call bells, highly polished bell metal, secure enamelled wood handle, 2½-inch, 15c; 3-inch, 25c; 3½-inch, 40c; 4-inch, 55c; 5-inch, 85c; 6-inch, $1.00.

No. 139. Same bell, fine nickel-plated finish, 2½ inch, 20c; 3-inch, 30c; 3½-inch, 50c; 4-inch, 75c; 5-inch, $1.00; 6-inch, $1.20.

PHONOGRAPHS AND GRAPHOPHONES.

The Standard phonograph is an ideal talking machine, made of iron, steel and brass, with nickelled gears and mandrel. It is black enamelled with gold striped finish, encased in a handsome oak dust-proof carrying case. It is a noiseless running machine and can be operated by a child. Weighs about 17 lbs; size is 9 x 12 inches by 9½ inches high. It will record, reproduce, and has an attachment for shaving records. Outfit includes recorder, reproducer, shaving knife, a two way bearing tube, a 14-inch polished brass horn, a camel's hair chip brush, an oil can, a winding crank and an oak carrying case. Complete (as cut) as above quoted, $20.00.

The Gem, a smaller size phonograph, taking the same records, and will answer successfully for the parlor or for home use. It is complete with a recorder, reproducer, 11-inch japanned horn, brush, oil can and neat oak carrying case. Size 8 x 10 inches, and weighs about 10 lbs, easy to operate and carry, $10.00.

The Home phonograph, larger size than the Standard, but taking the same records; will run more records per one winding, size 8 x 16 inches by 12 inches high, $30.00.

Columbia Graphophone (type AT) is of medium size and weight, made so as to last a lifetime. It has adjustable case, hardened steel-bushed bearings and a good machine for home entertainment, easy to operate. Price, including recorder, reproducer, 14-inch horn, and ornamental hand cabinet, $18.00. Records to fit all above machines, 50c each or $5.00 per doz. See list.

Phonographs and graphophones taking the larger records for concert purposes and called the Grand type, at $50, $75 and $100. Records to fit concert machine, $1.00 each.

Write for small catalogue giving full description of graphophones and phonographs, but always state, when ordering, whether it is a phonograph or graphophone you desire and the type or name of the machine. We highly recommend the phonograph.

Phonograph and Graphophone Supplies.

Horns.

We recommend hammered brass horns, with spun bells, as they give best production when used with talking machines, 14-inch, 65c; 18-inch, $1.50; 24-inch, $2.25; 30-inch, $3.50; 36-inch, $5.00; 42-inch, $8.00; 48-inch, $10.00; 56-inch, $12.00.

Japanned horns, 10-inch, 20c; 14-inch, 30c; 26-inch, 75c.

Stands and Cranes.

Excelsior combination folding horn stand, can be folded into box 24 inches long and 2½ x 2½ inches square, easy to carry, also to put up and take down, $1.50.

Extension horn crane, can be used on standard phonograph, for horns 18 to 30 inches, $1.50.

Crane to support 18-inch brass horn for Gem phonograph or type AT Columbia graphophone, 50c.

Carrying Cases.

Canvas-covered box, with pegs for 12 small cylinders, 50c; for 24 small cylinders, $1.00.

Glass for reproducers, 35c, put in free of charge.

Sapphire points for reproducers or recorders, $2.00.

Write for catalogue of parts and full list of supplies.

RECORDS.

We reserve the right to substitute where the customer does not give second choice.

It is always best to give two lists.

Following are some of the popular selections, write for latest and complete list. 50c each, or $5.00 per doz. Blank records, $2.50 doz.

Band Records.

1. Pan-American Exposition March.
2. Bridal March, from "Lohengrin."
3. Anvil Chorus, from "Il Trovatore."
4. Selections from "Robin Hood."
5. Overture to Poet and Peasant.
6. Lost Chord.
7. Marching Home from the War.
8. Ireland's Well-known Melodies.
9. Night Alarm (descriptive).
10. Jolly Coppersmith (descriptive).

Orchestra Selections.

11. Commercial Travellers' March, with Singing.
12. Selections from "The Burgomaster."
13. Barn Dance.
14. March, from "A Runaway Girl."
15. Medley, Overture (descriptive with songs).
16. Down on the Suwanee River (descriptive).
17. At the Circus.
18. Down on the Old Plantation.
19. Musquito Parade.

Solos.

20. At the Pan-I-Marry-Can (comic).
21. Rocked in the Cradle of the Deep.
22. Soldiers of the Queen.
23. Holy City.
24. The Palms.
25. My Department Store Girl.
26. The Choir Invisible (sacred).
27. I Want To Go To-morrow (comic).
28. Just Because You Made Those Goo-Goo Eyes.
29. And the Parrot Said (comic).
30. Handicap March Song.
31. Killarney.
32. When Johnnie Comes Marching Home.
33. Florida Flo (comic love).

Duets and Quartettes.

34. The Lord is My Shepherd.
35. Corn Bread (a recipe).
36. Medley of College Songs.
37. Vesper Service.
38. I Never Trouble Trouble Until Trouble Troubles Me.

Humorous Selections.

39. Jim Lawson's Horse Trade With Deacon Weatherspoon.
40. Shultz on the Automobile.
41. A Meeting of the Ananias Club at Pumpkin Centre.
42. Casey at the Telephone.
43. Pumpkin Centre Railroad.
44. The Lightning Rod Agent.

Speeches and Orations.

45. The 23rd Psalm and Lord's Prayer.
46. Talmage on Infidelity.
47. Sheridan's Ride.
48. Hamlet's Soliloquy.

Whistling and Laughing Songs.

49. The Laughing Coon.
50. Turkey in the Straw.

(Send for complete list of 2,000 records.)

Books, Music and Stationery.

Allow 5c for registering books worth $1.00 or over.

WE carry a full line of the popular magazines, all at prices below the average. Estimates furnished to Mechanics' Institutes, Public Libraries and Sunday Schools on any books not mentioned in this Catalogue. When ordering books, we would be pleased if our customers would state whether we may substitute other titles in case those ordered are not in stock at the time the order is received.

Postage paid on all printed books in this list ordered through our Mail Order Department, except those which are marked postage extra. **While we prepay postage on some books, we never pay registration.** *The cost of registering is 5 cents for parcels weighing 5 lbs. and under.* (*See paragraph 8 on 2nd page of cover.*)

BIBLES, PRAYER AND HYMN BOOKS.

FAMILY BIBLES CAN ONLY BE SHIPPED BY EXPRESS.

BIBLES.

Bibles and Testaments.

Sizes and Names of Type.

Pearl type is this size.
Ruby type is this size.
Nonpareil type is this size.
Emerald type is this size.
Minion type is this size.
Brevier type is this size.
Bourgeois type is this size.
Long Primer type is this size.
Small Pica type is this size.
Pica type is this size.

Sizes of Books.

16mo is—7 inches x 5 inches.
24mo is—4 " x 5½ "
32mo is—4¾ " x 2¾ "
8vo is—6¾ " x 6 "

Family Bibles.

Covers with padded sides and round corners, gold edges marriage. certificates, family records, illustrations and colored maps.
Grained calf binding, with 48 illustrations, concordance, $3.25.
French morocco, pronouncing dictionary of Scripture names, $3.75.
French morocco, gold back and side titles, $4.25.
French morocco, treatises on Bible subjects, etc, $5.00.
French morocco, and new version New Testament, Smith's Bible dictionary, $6.00.

Bagster's (Teacher's) Bibles.

Morocco yapped.

Minion, 8vo, $1.00.
Long primer, 8vo, linen lined, $1.25.
Minion, kid lined, silk sewn, $2.25.

Revised Bibles (Reference).

Pearl, 16mo, cloth, red edges, 35c.
Bourgeois, 8vo, cloth, red edges, $1.25.
Bourgeois, 8vo, morocco, gilt, $1.50.
Bourgeois, 8vo, " yapped, $1.75.

Bibles (Oxford Edition).

Pearl, 24mo, cloth, gilt, maps, 25c.

Morocco yapped binding:
Pearl, 32mo, leather, gilt, maps, 50c.
Diamond, 32mo, pocket size, 75c.
Ruby, 16mo, reference maps, 75c.
Diamond, 32mo, kid lined, $1.00.
Ruby, 24mo, kid lined, refs., $1.00.
Minion, 16mo, teachers', $1.00.
Ditto, kid lined, $1.25.
Long primer, 16mo, $1.50.
Emerald, 16mo, teachers', $1.50.
Emerald, 16mo, kid lined, refs., $1.50.
Ruby, ditto, teachers', $1.75.
Emerald, 16mo, India paper, $1.75.
Emerald, 16mo, kid lined, teachers', $2.00.
Minion, 8vo, kid lined, concordance, $3.00.
Longprimer, 8vo, silk sewn, teachers', $3.75.
Minion, 8vo, kid lined, teachers', $4.00.

Pulpit Bibles.

French morocco, raised panel, antique, gilt edges, extra large type, 13½ x 11 inches, $8.25.

Prayer Books.

25c, 30c, 35c, 50c, 75c, $1.00.

Prayers and Hymns.

25c, 35c, 50c, 85c.
Large type, 75c, $1.00, 1.25.

Prayers and Hymns.

In cases.

75c, 90c, $1.00, 1.25, 1.50, 1.75, 2.00.

Hymn Books, A. and M.

35c, 50c, 60c.
Large type, cloth, 70c.
Large type, leather, $1.25, 1.40.

Hymns Ancient and Modern, with Music.

Cloth, 65c; leather, $1.00, 1.25.
Large type, cloth, $1.25; leather, $1.85.

Catholic Prayer Books.

Cloth, 15c, 35c; leather, 50c, 65c, 75c, $1.00, 1.25.

Testaments.

Small Size.

Cloth, 10c, 15c.
Leather, 25c, 35c, 50c, 65c, $1.00.
Marked Testaments, 10c, 20c, 45c, 50c.

Presbyterian Book of Praise.

(Words only.)

Black cloth, red edges, 10c.
Paste grain, limp, gilt edges, 35c.
French turkey grain, padded, 60c.
Paste grain, padded, gilt line, 75c.
Arabian morocco, yapped, leather-lined, gilt edges, $1.00.
Alaska seal, limp, silk-sewn, $1.50.
Levant morocco, yapped, $2.00.

Long Primer 24mo.

Larger size, 6 x 3⅞ x ¾ inches.

Black cloth, red edges, 30c.
Paste grain, limp, gilt edges, 75c.
Rutland, limp, red and gilt edges, $1.00.
French seal, yapp, round corners, red under gilt edges, $1.25.
Rutland morocco, limp, $1.50.
Levant morocco, yapp, India paper, $4.00.

The Large Type Edition.

Pica, 8vo. On ordinary paper.
Size, 7½ x 4⅞ x 1 inch.

Black cloth boards, red edges, 60c.
Paste grain, boards, gilt edges, $1.25.
Seal, yapp, red and gilt edges, $2.25.

Presbyterian Book of Praise, with Tunes.

Emerald type.

Black cloth, boards, red edges, 60c.
Superior cloth, leather back, 90c.
Paste grain, limp, gilt edges, $1.25.
Seal, yapp, round corners, linen lined, gilt edges, $2.25.
Alaska seal, limp, leather lined, $4.00.

Large Type Edition.

Long Primer, 8vo.
Size, 9 x 6 x 1 inch.

Black cloth, boards, red edges, 90c.
Cloth, leather back, $1.25.
Alaska seal, limp, leather lined, silk sewn, India paper, $5.00.

Bibles and Presbyterian Hymn Books Combined.

Size, 5⅝ x 3¼ x 1 inch, pearl type.
Rutland, yapp, r/c, red under gilt edges, 70c.
Paste grain, yapp, padded, 90c.
Size, 5½ x 3½ x 1 inch, Ruby type.
French Rutland, yapp, r.c, 80c.
Size, 6 x 4 x 1¼ inches, Ruby type.
French Rutland, yapp, round corners, $1.00.
Seal, yapp, red under gilt edges, $1.50.

On Oxford India Paper.

Size, 5¾ x 4 x ¾ inch.

Aleutian seal, yapp, $2.25.
Alaska seal, yapp, silk sewn, $3.00.
Emerald, morocco, yapped, ref., India paper, $3.75.
Diamond, morocco, yapped, kid-lined, size, 5 x 3 in, $1.75.
Diamond, morocco, yapped, silk sewn, size, 5 x 3 in, $2.50.

Methodist Hymn Books.

Size, 6 x 4¼ x ½ inch, Pearl type.
Cloth, sprinkled edges, 25c.
Roan, " " 40c.
French morocco, limp, flaps, 75c.
Persian morocco, limp, r.g. edges, leather lined, $1.35.
Size, 7⅜ x 5¼ x ⅝ inch, Brevier type.
Cloth, sprinkled edges, 55c.
French morocco, limp, gilt edges, $1.10.
Size, 6½ x 4¼ x 1½ inches, Small Pica.
Cloth, sprinkled edges, 75c.
French morocco, yapped, $1.35.
Persian morocco, kid lined, round corners, red under gold, $1.85.

India Paper Edition.

Old People's Size—Pica type.
Size, 7¾ x 5¼.

Egyptian seal, yapped, round corners, red under gold, leather lined, $2.75.

Methodist Hymn and Tune Book.

Size 7½ x 5¾ inches.

Cloth, plain edges, 90c.
Morocco, yapped, gold edges, $1.85.
Egyptian seal, yapped, India paper, $2.75.

Methodist Hymn Books and Bibles, Combined.

Reference Bible, ruby type; hymns, 32mo, pearl type—
No. 01. French morocco, flaps, $1.35.
No. 02½. Persian morocco, flaps, gilt edges, $2.50.
Reference Bible, nonpareil type, India paper; hymns, brevier type, size 7 x 5 x ¼ inch; French morocco, limp, yapped edges, $3.50.

Sacred Songs and Solos

750 pieces, Sankey's, music and words—
HH 1. Cloth limp, 65c.
HH 2. Board cover, music, 85c.
FF 1. Cloth limp, large type, $1.00.
FF 2. Cloth boards, large type, $1.15.
FF 3. Bevelled boards, gilt $1.35.
AA2. Words only, 90c per doz.
BB 1. " " 12½c each.
EE1. " " large type, 60c each.

888 pieces by Ira D. Sankey.

AN1. Words only, 10c each.
HN1. Cloth, limp, music, $1.00.
FN1. Cloth, limp, music, $1.25.
FN2. Board cover, music, $1.40.

New Songs and Solos.

Price per single copy—
Canadian Hymnal, words only, 12c.
Canadian Hymnal, revised and enlarged, with music, 50c.
Finest of the Wheat, Nos. 1 and 2, 35c each; 1 and 2 combined, 60c.
Triumphant Songs (board covers), Nos. 1, 2, 3, 4, 5, 35c each; Nos. 1 and 2 combined, 55c.
Sacred Songs, No. 1, 35c; No. 2, 30c.
Songs of Salvation, 25c.
Pentecostal Praises, by W. J. Kirkpatrick and H. L. Gilmour, 35c.
Sifted Wheat, by Gabriel, 35c.
The Seed Sower, by A. F. Myers, 35c.
Songs for Young People, by E. O. Excell, 25c.

Sunday School Lessons.

Notes on the International S. S. Lessons. By Peloubet, $1.00.
Hulburt's Notes on S.S. Lessons, $1.00.
The Gist of the Lessons. A concise exposition of the International Sunday School Lessons for 1901, 25c.

Bible Commentaries.

Matthew Henry's Commentary, 6 vols, cloth, $8.00.
Clark's Commentary, 6 vols, $10.00.
Cruden's Complete Concordance, cloth cover, 75c.

Standard Sets.

Dickens, Charles, bound in cloth, complete in 15 vols, $4.75.

Dickens, Charles, bound in silk cloth, gilt titles, illustrated, complete in 15 vols, $6.75.

Dickens, Charles, bound in silk cloth, gilt tops and titles, illustrated edition, complete in 15 vols, $8.25.

Dickens, Charles, bound in ½ calf, gilt top and titles, complete in 15 vols, $15.00.

Ruskin's library edition, illustrated with all of the wood engravings in the text and all the full-page plates, plain and colored, of the London editions, printed from large, clear type, with all the notes, cloth cover, gilt top, 13 vols, $12.00.

Scott's Waverley Novels, bound in cloth, complete in 12 vols, $4.25.

Scott's Waverley Novels, bound in silk cloth, gilt titles, complete in 12 vols, $6.25.

Scott's Waverley Novels, bound in ½ calf, gilt tops, illustrated edition, complete in 12 vols, $15.00.

Thackeray's Novels, bound in cloth, complete in 10 vols, $2.50.

Thackeray's Novels, bound in cloth, gilt decorations, 10 vols, $4.50.

Thackeray's Novels, bound in silk cloth, illustrated edition, complete in 10 vols, $5.25.

Eliot's Works, bound in cloth, complete in 6 vols, $1.50.

Eliot's Works, bound in silk cloth, gilt titles, complete in 6 vols, $2.75.

Eliot's Works, bound in silk cloth, gilt tops and titles, complete in 8 vols, $5.00.

Conan Doyle, 6 vols, cloth, $1.00.

Edna Lyall, 6 vols, cloth, $1.00.

Smiles, 4 vols, silk cloth, $1.25.

Ruskin, 4 vols, cloth, $1.00.

Works of William Shakespeare.

Handy volume Shakespeare, bound in maroon cloth, 15 vols, $3.00.

"Bedford" edition of Shakespeare's works, 12 vols, handsomely bound in leather, good clear type, put up in a neat leather case, $9.50.

Shakespeare's dramatic and poetical works, complete in 39 vols, handy vol. size, limp cloth binding, gilt top and frontispiece, $7.00.

Same edition, paste grain leather, gilt top, $11.50.

Temple edition of Shakespeare, containing notes, each play bound in separate volumes, complete in 40 vols, cloth cover, 30c vol, or $10.50 set; leather cover, 45c vol, or $16.50 set.

Sets of Historical Works.

Parkman, complete in 12 vols, $15.00
Napier's Peninsular War, 5 vols, $2.50.
Green's England, bound in buckram cloth, 16 mo, 5 vols, $1.00.
Green's History of England, 4 vols, cloth, $2.50.
Gibbon's Rome, 5 vols, cloth, $2.50.
History of Peru, Prescott, 2 vols, cloth, $1.00.
History of Mexico, Prescott, 2 vols, cloth, $1.00.
Ferdinand and Isabella, Prescott, 2 vols, cloth, $1.00.

The Excelsior 2 Vol. Sets.

Cloth binding. Publisher's price, $1.50; our price, 75c per set.
The Wandering Jew. Eugene Sue.
Life of Christ. Farrar.
French Revolution. Carlyle.
History of Our Own Times. McCarthy.
Essays. Emerson.
Les Miserables. Hugo.

Uniform 5 Vol. Edition Sets.

Cloth binding. Publisher's price, $3.00; our price, $1.50.
Macaulay's England.
Cooper's Sea Tales.
Cooper's Leather Stocking Tales.
Conan Doyle.
Marie Corelli.
Rosa Carey.
Hawthorne.

Popular 5 Vol. Sets.

Printed on good paper, durably bound in fine book cloth, titles stamped in gold, special price, 90c, postpaid—
Hall Caine.
Rosa Carey.
Cooper's Sea Tales.
Cooper's Leather Stocking Tales.
Marie Corelli.
Hawthorne.
Macaulay's History of England.

POETS.

Cabinet Poets.

Crown 8vo.

Cloth, regular price, 70c: our price 40c.

Burns.	Byron.
Browning, Mrs EB	Cowper.
Coleridge.	Keats.
Goldsmith.	Longfellow.
Hemans, Mrs.	Moore.
Milton.	Scott.
Shelley.	Wordsworth.
Shakespeare.	Whittier.

Large crown 8vo.

Elegantly printed in large, clear type.

Cloth, gilt, regular price, $1.25; our price, 75c.

Byron.	Burns.
Browning, Mrs EB	Hemans, Mrs.
Longfellow.	Milton.
Moore.	Shelley.
Scott.	Shakespeare.
Wordsworth.	Whittier.

Padded leather edition, regular full gilt edges, price, $1.50; our price, $1.00.

Burns.	Byron.
Browning, Mrs EB	Cowper.
Campbell.	Keats.
Hemans, Mrs.	Longfellow.
Milton.	Moore.
Shelley.	Shakespeare.
Scott.	Whittier.
Wordsworth.	

Padded Morocco edition, full gilt edges, regular price, $1.75; our price, $1.50.

Burns.	Byron.
Browning, Mrs EB	Hemans, Mrs.
Longfellow.	Moore.
Milton.	Shakespeare.
Scott.	Wordsworth.
Whittier.	

Albion Poets.

Elegantly printed in large, clear type.

Large crown 8vo.

Padded Nubian, regular, $3.00; our price, $2.00.

Burns.	Byron.
Longfellow.	Moore.
Milton.	Shakespeare.
Scott.	Whittier.
Wordsworth.	

Padded Morocco edition, full gilt edges with photos. Regular, $3.00; our price, $2.50.

Mrs. Browning.	Wordsworth.
Whittier.	Longfellow.
Scott.	Shakespeare.
Burns.	

Miniature Edition of the Poets.

Size 4 x 5 inches. Padded Leather, Price, 60c.

Longfellow.	Scott.
Mrs. Browning.	Wordsworth.

Poems by Whitcombe Riley.

CLOTH.

Riley's Love Lyrics, $1.10.
Afterwhiles, $1.10.
A Child World, $1.10.
Armazindy, $1.10.
Rhymes of Childhood, $1.10.
Neighborly Poems, $1.10.
Green Fields and Running Brooks, $1.10.
Old Fashioned Roses, $1.50.

E. W. Wilcox's Poems.

Poems of Pleasure, cloth, 35c.
Poems of Passion, cloth, 35c.
Maurine, cloth, 35c.

Poems by Eugene Field.

With Trumpet and Drum, cloth, 85c.
Love Songs of Childhood, cloth, 85c.
A Little Book of Western Verse, cloth, $1.10.
Second Book of Western Verse, cloth, $1.10.
Lullaby Land, cloth, $1.25.

Havergal's Poems.

Padded leather, complete in 1 vol, $2.50.

Robert Browning's Complete Poetical Works.

Camberwell Edition, edited by C. Porter and H. A. Clarke, the only fully annotated, line-numbered edition, 12 vols, cloth, gilt top, boxed, $7.50.
R. Browning, complete in 1 vol, maroon cloth, $2.50.
R. Browning, cloth cover, 85c.

Shakespeare's Poems.

Cloth cover, good clear type, 45c.
Shakespeare's Poems, large cloth edition, good clear type, 75c.

Tennyson's Poems.

Cloth, gilt top, $1.00.
Paste grain, limp leather, $1.25.
Padded, grain leather, $1.50.
" morocco " $2.00.
Limp leather, complete edition, $2.25.
Padded leather, complete edition, $2.50.
Padded morocco leather, illustrated, complete edition, $3.00.
Tree calf, complete edition, illustrated, $3.50.

Arch. Lampman's Poems.

Cloth cover, $1.85.

Thoughts: A beautiful book of choice quotations, printed on antique paper, illustrated with portraits, cloth, $1.25.

The Dodge Classics.

These are little gems of artistic skill. The bindings are of the finest imported art leathers, finished in "suede" style, flexible covers, boxed, regular price, $1.50; our price, $1.25.
Barrack Room Ballads. Kipling.
Borrowings: Quotations.
Favorite Poems.
Fifty Songs of Love. Selected Poems.
Friendship and other Essays. Emerson.
Rubaiyat of Omar. Khayyam.
Christmas Carols, Ancient and Modern. Edited, with notes, by Joshua Sylvestre. 12mo, cloth, with cover in two colors and gilt, photogravure frontispiece and five illustrations, 85c.
Friendship. Two Essays on Friendship by Ralph Waldo Emerson and Marcus Tullius. Cicero. Beautifully printed on Stratford deckle edge paper, 16mo, cloth, with specially designed title page and end papers, full gilt, 85c.

RECENT PUBLICATIONS.

Uncle Terry. Chas. C. Munn. Paper, 65c; cloth $1 20
The Master Christian. Corelli. Paper, 65c; cloth 1 10
The Farringdons. Fowler. Paper, 65c; cloth 1 25
To Have and To Hold. Mary Johnston. Paper, 65c; cloth 1 20
Prisoners of Hope. By Mary Johnston. Paper, 65c; cloth. 1 20
Biography of a Grizzly. E. S. Thompson. Cloth 1 25
Joan of the Sword Hand. S. R. Crockett. Paper, 65c; cloth 1 10
A Treasury of Canadian Verse. By Theodore H. Rand. Cloth 1 15
Janice Meredith. Ford. Paper, 65c; cloth 1 20
Richard Carvel. Churchill. Paper, 65c; cloth 1 10
Via Crucis. Crawford. Paper, 65c; cloth 1 25
The Man from Glengarry. By Ralph Connor. Paper, 65c.; cloth 1 10
Sky Pilot. Ralph Connor. Cloth 0 90
Black Rock. " Cloth 0 90
The Habitant. By Drummond. Cloth, 90c; cloth, gilt top, ills. 2 00
David Harum. By E. N. Westcott. Paper, 65c; cloth 1 10
Kit Kennedy. By S. R. Crockett. Paper, 65c; cloth 1 10
In the Palace of the King. Crawford. Paper, 65c; cloth 1 10
Tommy and Grizel. By J. M. Barrie. Paper, 65c; cloth 1 10
Eben Holden. By Bacheller. Paper, 65c; cloth 1 10
The Great Boer War. Conan Doyle. Paper, 65c; cloth ... 1 25
Winsome Womanhood. By Margaret E. Sangster 1 10
Babs the Impossible. By Sarah Grand. Cloth 1 20
Quincy Adams Sawyer and Mason's Corner Folks. (A picture of New England Home Life.) By Chas. Felton Pidgin. Paper, 65c; cloth 1 20
Lords of the North. By A. C. Laut. Paper, 65c; cloth 1 10
Richard Yea and Nay. By Maurice Hewlitt. Paper, 65c; cloth 1 00
Edward Blake. By Sheldon. Paper, 23c; cloth 0 45
Born to Serve. By Sheldon. Paper, 23c; cloth 0 45
The Crisis. By Winston Churchill. Paper, 65c; cloth 1 00
Graustark. By G. B. McCutcheon. Paper 65c; cloth 1 10
The Puppet Crown. By H. MacGrath. Paper, 65c; cloth 1 10
A Daughter of New France. By M. C. Crowley, paper, 65c; cloth 1 10
The Eternal City. By Hall Caine. Paper, 65c; cloth 1 25
Queen Victoria, Her Life and Times. By Author of "Grace Darling." 1819-1901. Cloth cover, with 35 illustrations .. 0 45
The Life of Queen Victoria. By G. Barnett Smith. 1819-1901. Cloth cover, fully illustrated. 0 90
Cinderella. By S. R. Crockett. Paper, 65c; cloth 1 10

MISCELLANEOUS.

Victorian Literature: Sixty Years of Books and Bookmen. By Clement Shorter. Cloth 0 70
The Reader's Handbook of Allusions. Ref. Plots and Stories. By Dr. Brewer. Cloth, 1,500 pages $1 90
Life of John G. Paton. Cloth 0 45
Mackay of Uganda. Cloth 0 45
The Canadian Lawyer, a handy book for business men, farmers, mechanics, etc 1 25
Cruden's Concordance. Cloth. 0 75
Scottish Clans. Cloth 0 75
Looking Forward. By J. R. Miller. Cloth 0 65
Friendship. By Black. Cloth. 0 65
Dict. of Phrase and Fable. By Dr. Brewer. ½-leather bound 1 35
The Nuttall Encyclopædia of Universal Information. Being a concise and comprehensive dictionary of general knowledge. Edited by Rev. Jas. Wood. Cloth cover 0 75
Christmas in French Canada. By Louis Frechette. Cloth, fully illustrated 1 80
A Short Introduction to the Literature of the Bible. By R. C. Moulton, M. A., in maroon silk cloth 0 85
Tennyson: His Art in Relation to Modern Life. By Stoffard A. Brooke. Silk cloth 1 40
Wit and Humor: Compilations of some of the best specimens of wit and humor contained in the English language. Irish, English, Scotch, American (2 vols.). Handsome cover design in gold, 16mo, cloth, price, each 0 45

Large Illustrated Editions.

The Queen's Empire. A Pictorial and Descriptive Record, illustrated from photos. Size 9½ x 12 inches, bound in red silk cloth. Over 300 illustrations. In 2 vols., 1897 and 1899 editions (post, 20c extra), each 2 25
The Queen's London. A Pictorial and Descriptive Record of the Great Metropolis in the Year of Her Majesty's Diamond Jubilee. Size 9½ x 12 inches, bound in red silk cloth. Over 600 illustrations (post, 20c extra) 3 50
The Paris Salon of 1900. Being a reproduction of 95 famous paintings printed on fine plate paper. Size 11 x 13 inches (post extra) 0 75
London: Historic and Social. By Claude de la Roche Francis. Illustrated with 50 full-page photogravures from original negatives. 2 vols., crown 8vo, cloth gilt, gilt top, boxed, price 4 25
Ireland: Historic and Picturesque. By Chas. Johnstone. Illustrated with 25 full-page photogravures and a map, crown, 8vo, cloth, gilt, gilt top, boxed, price 2 75
Scotland: Historic and Picturesque. By M. H. Lansdale. Illustrated with 50 full-page photogravures and a map. 2 vols. Crown 8vo, cloth, gilt, gilt top, boxed, price 4 25
Heroes of the United Service (Army and Navy). By Mrs. Valentine. With colored front and title page, and 16 full-page plates, crown quarto, cloth, gilt edges (post 15c extra) 1 25
Toronto Illustrated. 47 views. Size of book, 9½ x 6 inches. Fancy paper binding, 25c; cloth 0 35

Out-of-Door Books.

On Birds, Flowers, Trees, Insects, etc.

Bird Neighbors. An introductory acquaintance with 150 of our common birds, containing 52 colored plates. Cloth 2 10
Mooswa. By A. W. Fraser. Illustrated by A. Heming 1 25
Game Birds and Birds of Prey. By Neltje Blanchon (companion book to Bird Neighbors). Cloth, illustrated $2 10
Bird Portraits. By Ernest Seton-Thompson, with descriptive text by Ralph Hoffmann. Size 8¾ x 12 inches. Fully illustrated 1 35
Wild Animals I Have Known. By E. S. Thompson. Cloth. Fully illustrated 1 75
Trail of the Sand Hill Stag. By E. S. Thompson. Cloth. Fully illustrated 1 25
The Biography of a Grizzly. By E. S. Thompson. Cloth. Fully illustrated 1 25
A Woman Tenderfoot. By E. S. Thompson. Cloth. Fully illustrated 1 75
The Butterfly Book. By W. J. Holland, LL.D. Illustrated in colors. Cloth 2 75
A Guide to the Wild Flowers. By A. Lounsberry. With 64 colored and 100 black and white plates, and 44 diagrams by Mrs. E. Rowan, with an introduction by Dr. N. L. Britton. Cloth 2 35
A Guide to the Trees. By Alice Lounsberry. With 64 colored and 164 black and white plates, and 55 diagrams by Mrs. E. Rowan, with introduction by Dr. N. L. Britton. Cloth 2 35
Nature's Garden. By Neltje Blanchon. Its 32 superb colored plates and many black and white illustrations are all from photographs. A fascinating book, bringing out in a wonderful way the relations between plants and their insect visitors. 7¾ x 10⅜. Illustrated. Cloth 2 75
The Popular Natural History. By Rev. J. G. Wood. With 600 illustrations and colored plates. Cloth cover, gilt edge. 1 25
Young Folks' Natural History, comprising descriptions of animal life, birds, reptiles, etc. By Chas. C. Abbott, M.D. Cloth cover. Illustrated 0 65
Natural History. By Miles. Containing short anecdotes of nature, habits, manners, etc., of birds, animals, fishes, etc. Cloth. Fully illustrated 1 00

Popular Works of History.

A Popular History of Greece, from the Earliest Period to the Incorporation with the Roman Empire. By D. Rose. Cloth cover, illustrated 1 00
A Popular History of France, brought down to the First Years of the present Republic. By H. W. Dulcken, Ph.D. Cloth cover, illustrated 1 00
A Popular History of Rome, from the Foundation of the City, B.C. 753, to the Fall of the Western Empire, A.D. 476. By D. Rose. Cloth cover, illustrated 1 00
A Popular History of England, from the Earliest Period to the Diamond Jubilee of Queen Victoria in 1897. By H. W. Dulcken, Ph.D. Cloth cover, illustrated 1 00
History of Our Own Times from 1880 to Diamond Jubilee. By Justin McCarthy. Cloth. 1 50
General Lord Roberts; 41 Years in India. Complete in 1 vol; cloth 2 35
Constitutional History of England. By Hallam. Cloth 1 10
A History of Canada. By Charles G. D. Roberts. Cloth 1 90
Canada (Story of Nation Series). Cloth 1 25
South Africa (Story of Nation Series). Cloth 1 25
Lord Clive. The foundation of British rule in India. By Sir Alex. J. Arbuthnot. Cloth cover, etching frontispiece .. 0 75
Sir Walter Raleigh. The British Dominion of the West. By Martin A. S. Hume. Cloth cover, etching frontispiece .. $0 75
John and Sebastian Cabot. The Discovery of North America. By C. R. Beazley. Cloth cover, etching frontispiece 0 75

Our Historical Studies for Children. Cloth, 50c.

The Children's Study of Ireland. By R. B. O'Brien.
The Children's Study of Scotland. By Mrs. Oliphant.
The Children's Study of Germany. By K. E. Kroeker.
The Children's Study of Greece. By A. Zimmern.
The Children's Study of Rome. By Mary Ford.
The Children's Study of England. By F. E. Cooke.
The Children's Study of Canada. By J. N. McIlwraith.
Little Arthur's History of England. By Lady Calcott. New edition, with 36 illustrations. Cloth, 40c.

The World Library.

Regular price, $1.25; our price, 85c.

Plutarch's Lives.
Whiston's Josephus.
Hume's Essays.
Adam Smith's Wealth of Nations.
Hallam's Europe.
Essays. Thomas de Quincey.
Locke's Human Understanding.
Emerson's Works.
Bartlett's Familiar Quotations.
Crabb's English Synonyms.
Millman's History of Jews.
The Conquest of Mexico. By Prescott.
The Conquest of Peru. By Prescott.
Gems of English Poetry.

Large Type Edition of Popular Works. Complete in 1 Vol.

Price, 65c each.

Les Miserables. By Victor Hugo.
The Mysteries of Paris. Eugene Sue.
Charles O'Malley. By Charles Lever.
Count of Monte Cristo. Dumas.
The Wandering Jew. Eugene Sue.

Theological and Religious Works.

Works by Ralph Waldo Trine.

CLOTH.

The Greatest Thing Ever Known 0 25
What All the World's a Seeking 0 90
In Tune with the Infinite 0 90

Works by N. D. Hillis.

CLOTH.

A Man's Value to Society 0 90
The Investment of Influence .. 0 90
Great Books as Life Teachers. 0 90
The Influence of Christ in Modern Life 1 25

Daily Cheer for All the Year. Selected and arranged by Virginia Reed. Cloth cover. Size 4 x 6½ 0 45

The Works of Prof. Henry Drummond.

CLOTH.

Drummond's Address $0 25
The Ascent of Man 0 95
The Ideal Life 1 00
The Life of Henry Drummond. By Geo. Adam Smith. Illustrated 1 90
The New Evangelism 1 00

Ian Maclaren's Works.

CLOTH.

Beside the Bonnie Brier Bush $0 90
The Days of Auld Lang Syne 0 90
Afterwards 1 00
Kate Carnegie 1 00
The Cure of Souls 1 00
The Mind of the Master 1 00

Works of F. B. Meyer, B.A.

CLOTH.

Regular price, 90c; our price, 65c.

Elijah: And the Secret of His Power.
Joseph: Beloved, Hated, Exalted.
The Life and Light of Men; Expositions of John I: 12.
The Bells of Is; or, Voices of Human Need and Sorrow.
Joshua: And the Land of Promise.
Moses: The Servant of God.
Jeremiah: Priest and Prophet.
Israel: A Prince with God.
The Way Into the Holiest.
Paul.
David.

The Blessed Life Series. By F. B. Meyer.

BOARDS, 25c each.

The Shepherd Psalm.
Christian Living.
Present Tenses of Blessed Life.
Future Tenses of Blessed Life.
Key Words of the Inner Life.
Calvary to Pentecost.

The Spirit-Filled Life Series.

CLOTH, 25c each.

The Spirit-Filled Life. By Rev. John MacNeil.
The Christian's Secret of a Happy Life. By H. W. Smith.
A Castaway, and Other Addresses. By Rev. F. B. Meyer.
In Christ. By Rev. A. J. Gordon.
Absolute Surrender. By Rev. Andrew Murray.
The Overcoming Life. By D. L. Moody.

Works by Rev. Andrew Murray.

CLOTH.

With Christ	$0 35
Abide in Christ	0 35
Like Christ	0 35
Holy in Christ	0 35
The Spirit of Christ	0 35
The Master's Indwelling	0 35
Jesus Himself	0 25
Love Made Perfect	0 25

The Moody Library.

BOARDS, 25c each.

The Way to God and How to Find It.
Sowing and Reaping.
Pleasure and Profit in Bible Study.
Sovereign Grace.
Secret Power.
The Life of D. L. Moody. By W. R. Moody and A. P. Fitt, with introduction by Rev. F. B. Meyer. Cloth cover, 25c.

Devotional Series.

Full white vellum, handsome design in gold and colors, with mezzo-tint inlaid effect, gold tops, boxed. Regular price, 50c; our price, 25c.

Abide in Christ. Murray.
Beecher's Addresses.
Best Thoughts. Henry Drummond.
Bible Birthday Book.
Brook's Addresses.
Changed Cross.
Coming to Christ. Havergal.
Daily Food for Christians.
Drummond's Addresses.
Evening Thoughts. Havergal.
Gold Dust.
Imitation of Christ. A. Kempis.
John Ploughman's Pictures. Spurgeon.
John Ploughman's Talk. Spurgeon.
Kept for the Master's Use. Havergal.
Line Upon Line.
Manliness of Christ. Hughes.
Morning Thoughts. Havergal.
My King and His Service. Havergal.
Natural Law in the Spiritual World. Drummond.
Peep of Day.
Precept Upon Precept.
Prince of the House of David. Ingraham.
Shepherd Psalm. Meyer.
Steps Into the Blessed Life. Meyer.

Chas. M. Sheldon's Works.

Paper covers, 10c each; cloth, 25c each. Paper covers, 2c each extra for postage.

In His Steps.
Robert Hardy's Seven Days.
Redemption of Freetown.
His Brother's Keeper.
Overcoming the World.
Crucifixion of Phillip Strong.
Richard Bruce.
The Twentieth Door.
Miracle at Markham. Paper, 23c; cloth, 45c.
Born to Serve. Paper, 23c; cloth, 45c.
John King's Question Class. Paper, 23c.

Sabbath Library of Books

Paper Covers, 5c each. Postage Extra.

Chonita.
The Days of Mohammed.
A Devotee and a Darling.
Kohath Sloane. J. McNair Wright.
Out of the Triangle. M. E. Banford.
A Double Story. Geo. MacDonald.
Titus. F. M. Kingsley.
Ten Nights in a Bar-Room. Arthur.
The Wrestler of Philippi.
A Star in Prison. A. M. Wilson.
Paula Clyde. K. W. Hamilton.
Intra Muros. Mrs. R. R. Springer.
The Young Ditch Rider.
Ruby. A. Lilie Riley.
In League with the Powerful. By E. D. Bigham.
Marti: a Story of the Cuban War.
Ti: a Story of San Francisco's Chinatown.
For the Sake of a Name. Grinnell.

Medical Books.

Gardner's Household, Medicine and Sick Room Guide. Cloth	$2 00
The Doctor at Home and Nurse's Guide Book. By Geo. Black, M.B. Cloth cover. Illustrated	0 85
Physical Life of Woman. By Napheys. Cloth	0 80
The Transmission of Life. Dr. Napheys. Cloth	0 80
Tokology. Alice B. Stockham Cloth	2 25
Nursing. By S. V. Levis. Cloth	0 40
Mother, Baby and Nursery. "A Manual for Mothers." By T. Tucker, M.D. Cloth cover. Illustrated	0 50
Dr. Chase's Recipes; or, Information for Everybody. An invaluable collection of over 1,000 practical recipes. Illustrated, revised and enlarged in 1900, price	0 85

Books on Etiquette.

Manners for Men. By Mrs. Humphrey. Board cover, 25c.
Manners for Women. 25c.
A Word to Women. 25c.
Etiquette. By Agnes H. Morton. Cloth, 40c.
Letter Writing. By Agnes H. Morton. Cloth, 40c.
Ideals for Girls. By Rev. H. W. Haweis, M.A. Cloth, 60c.

Popular Hand-Books.

Practical Palmistry. By Henry Frith. Cloth, 40c.
Dancing. By Marguerite Wilson. Cloth, 40c.
Dick's Quadrill, Call Book. Paper, 45c.
Brisbane's Golden Ready-Reckoner. Board cover, 30c.
Brain and Body. By Dr. Andrew Wilson. Cloth, 35c.
Health Exercises, home gymnastics without the use of appliances, with numerous illustrations. Cloth, 25c.
Advice to Single Women Regarding Their Health, etc. By H. Brown. Cloth, 35c.
Things Worth Knowing. By J. W. Bechtel. Cloth, 40c.
The Concise Ready-Reckoner and Interest Tables, with valuable tables of weights and measures. By A. W. Thomas. Cloth, 35c.
Modern Hoyle, 25c.
Bridge Whist. By L. Leigh, formerly editor of *Whist Opinion*. Cloth, 85c.
Toronto Views. Cloth, 35c; paper, 25c.

Cook Books.

Mrs. Beeton's Book of Household Management. Cloth	$1 75
Century Cook Book	1 90
Home Cook Book	0 50
Dr. Chase's New Receipt Book	0 50
Mrs. Rorer's Cook Book	1 45
The Galt Cook Book	1 00
The White House Cook Book	1 00
Mrs. Beeton's Cook Book, 320 pages, with 21 full-page plates	0 30
365 Breakfast Dishes. A Breakfast Dish for Every Day in the Year. A compilation from Mrs. Lincoln, Mrs. Lemcke, *Table Talk*, *The Boston Cooking School Magazine*, and others. 16mo. Cloth	0 45
365 Dessert Dishes. A Dessert Dish for Every Day in the Year. Selected from Marion Harland, Mrs. Lincoln, *Table Talk*, *Good Housekeeping*, and others. Cloth	0 45

Elocution Books.

Not Exchanged.

Young Folk's Recitations, 15c.
Shoemaker's Best Selections, Nos. 1 to 26, 25c each.
Wilson's Recit. and Dialogues, 25c.
Dick's Comic Dialogues, 25c.
Choice Dialogues, 25c.
Young Folk's Dialogues, 25c.
McBride's Choice Dialogues, 25c
Kavanaugh's New Speeches and Dialogues for Children, 25c.
Young Folks' Entertainments, 25c.
Humorous Dial. and Dramas, 25c.
Holiday Selections, 25c.
Temperance Selections, 25c.
Young People's Speaker, 15c.
Entertainments for Young People 25c.
Good Humor, 25c.
Choice Dialect Reading and Recitations, 25c.
Classic Dialogues and Dramas, 25c.
School-day Dialogues, 25c.
Ideal Drills. By M. Morton, 25c.
Tableaux, Charades and Pantomimes, 25c.

Birthday Books.

Birthday Text Books. Cloth, 10c.
" " " 20c.
" " " Paste grain leather, 45c; padded, 50c.
Birthday Text Books. Half cloth, gilt top, fancy design, 25c.

Standard Library.

Popular works selected from some of the world's greatest authors. Well printed on extra laid paper, trimmed edges, and bound in maroon silk ribbed cloth, with back stamp and gold top.

Regular price, $1.00; our price, 45c.

Ardath. Marie Corelli.
Æsop's Fables.
Adam Bede. Geo. Eliot.
Bleak House. Dickens.
Bride of Lammermoor. Scott.
California and Oregon Trail. Parkman.
Child's History of England. Dickens.
Data of Ethics. Spencer.
Daniel Deronda. Eliot.
David Copperfield. Dickens.
Dombey & Son. Dickens.
Donovan. Edna Lyall.
First Violin. Jessie Fothergill.
French Revolution. Carlyle.
Felix Holt. Eliot.
Hardy Norseman. Lyall.
Harold. Lytton.
Heart of Midlothian. Scott.
Heir of Redcliffe. Yonge.
Hypatia. Kingsley.
Ivanhoe. Scott.
In the Golden Days. Lyall.
Jane Eyre. Bronte.
John Halifax. Mulock.
Knight Errant. Lyall.
Life of Christ. Farrar.
Lorna Doone. Blackmore.
Little Dorrit. Dickens.
Martin Chuzzlewit. Dickens.
Mill on the Floss. G. Eliot.
Middlemarch. Eliot.
Nicholas Nickleby. Dickens.
Our Mutual Friend. Dickens.
Oliver Twist. Dickens.
Old Curiosity Shop. Dickens.
Pickwick Papers. Dickens.
Quentin Durward. Scott.
Scottish Chiefs. Porter.
Silas Marner. Eliot.
Silence of Dean Maitland. Grey.
Tale of Two Cities. Dickens.
Talisman. Scott.
Thelma. Corelli.
Tom Brown's School Days. Hughes
Tom Brown at Oxford.
Uncle Tom's Cabin. Stowe.
Vendetta. Corelli.
Vanity Fair. Thackeray.
Waverley. Scott.
Wormwood. Corelli.
What's Mine's Mine. Macdonald.
Westward, Ho! Kingsley.

Our New Green Library.

Bound in silk cloth, gilt top, gilt titles.

Regular price, 50c; our price, 25c

Sir Walter Scott—
Abbott. Monastery.
Kenilworth. Woodstock.
Ivanhoe. Old Mortality.
Talisman. Rob Roy.
Waverley. Guy Mannering.
Bride of Lammermoor.
Fair Maid of Perth.
Scott's Poetical Works.
Heart of Midlothian.
Fortunes of Nigel.
Peveril of the Peak.
Quentin Durward.

Lord Lytton—
Alice. Harold.
Last Days of Pompeii.
Ernest Maltravers.
Last of the Barons.

Charles Dickens—
Oliver Twist. Dombey & Son.
Little Dorrit. Bleak House.
Nicholas Nickleby.
Christmas Tales.
Martin Chuzzlewit.
Barnaby Rudge.
Old Curiosity Shop.
Pickwick Papers.
David Copperfield.

Charles Kingsley—
Alton Locke. Hypatia.
Westward, Ho!

Innocents Abroad. Mark Twain.

Grace Aguilar—
Vale of Cedars. Days of Bruce.
Home Influence.
Mother's Recompense.
Woman's Friendship.

Captain Marryatt—
Peter Simple. Poor Jack.
Masterman Ready.
Mr. Midshipman Easy.
Jacob Faithful.
Japhet in Search of a Father.

E. P. Roe—
Knight of the 19th Century.
From Jest to Earnest.
Opening a Chestnut Burr.
Barriers Burned Away.
Without a Home.

Evans Wilson—
Infelice. St. Elmo. Beulah.
Macaria. Vashti.
At the Mercy of Tiberius.

James Grant—
Romance of War. Jane Seton.
Adventures of an Aide-de-camp.

Mrs. Craik—
Ogilvies. John Halifax.
Olive. Head of the Family.

W. M. Thackeray—
Vanity Fair. Pendennis.
Esmond.
Samuel Lover—
Handy Andy. Rory O'More.
Irish Legends and Stories.
Aunt Jane's Hero. E. Prentiss.
Stepping Heavenward. E. Prentiss.
W. H. Ainsworth—
Guy Fawkes.
Tower of London.
Windsor Castle.
Old St. Paul's.
Lamplighter. M. S. Cummins.
Mabel Vaughan. M. S. Cummins.
W. H. G. Kingston—
Swiss Family Robinson.
Peter the Whaler.
Mark Seaworth.
Valentine Fox. H. Cockton.
Sylvester Sound. H. Cockton.
Rev. Ingraham—
Prince of House of David.
Throne of David.
Pillar of Fire.
Tom Cringle's Log. Michael Scott.
Ben-Hur. Lew Wallace.
Melbourne House. Susan Warner.
Little Women and Good Wives. Miss Alcott.
Burns' Poems.
Byron's Poems.
Longfellow's Poems.
Shakespeare's Works.
Uncle Tom's Cabin. H. B. Stowe.
Adventures of Robin Hood. John B. Marsh.
Adam Bede. Geo. Eliot.
Helen's Babies. Habberton.
Miss Wetherell—
Daisy. Daisy in Field.
Say and Seal. Golden Ladder.
Wych Hazel. My Desire.
Nobody. End of a Coil.
Diana. Stephen, M.D.
Gold of Chickaree.
Wide, Wide World.
Ellen Montgomery's Bookshelf.
Two School Girls.
Letter of Credit.

Oxford Library.

Printed from large type on good paper, bound in fine cloth, gilt tops.

Regular price, 70c; our price, 25c.

Aunt Diana. Carey.
Alice. Lytton.
Arundel Motto. Mary Cecil Hay.
Antiquary. Scott.
By Order of the King. Victor Hugo.
Bondman. Hall Caine.
California and Oregon Trail. Parkman.
Charles O'Malley. Lever.
Conquest of Peru. Prescott.
Child's History of England. Dickens.
Donovan. Edna Lyall.
Dombey & Son. Dickens.
Don Quixote. Cervantes.
Education. Spencer.
First Violin. Jessie Fothergill.
Fifteen Decisive Battles. Creasy.
Frederick the Great and His Court. Muhlbach.
Green Mountain Boys. Thompson.
Guy Mannering. Scott.
Hypatia. Kingsley.
History of a Crime. Victor Hugo.
Hardy Norseman. Edna Lyall.
Holy Roman Empire. Bryce.
Ivanhoe. Scott.
In the Golden Days. Lyall.
It is Never Too Late to Mend. Reade.
Jane Eyre. Bronte.
John Halifax. Mulock.
Kenilworth. Scott.
Knight Errant. Lyall.
Les Miserables. Victor Hugo
Lamplighter. Miss Cummins.
Last Days of Pompeii. Lytton.
Lorna Doone. Blackmore.
Life of Christ. Farrar.
" " Geikie.
Mary St. John. Carey.
Middlemarch. Eliot.
Mill on the Floss. "
Mr. Midshipman Easy. Marryat.
Mysteries of Paris. Eugene Sue.
Not Like Other Girls. Carey.
Oliver Twist. Dickens.
Old Curiosity Shop. Dickens.
Only the Governess. Carey.
Origin of Species. Darwin.
Our Bessie. Carey.
Pilgrim's Progress. Bunyan.
Pride and Prejudice. Jane Austin.
Plutarch's Lives.
Queenie's Whim. Rosa Carey.
Romola. Geo. Eliot.
Robinson Crusoe. Defoe.
Scottish Chiefs. Porter.
Six to Sixteen. Ewing.
Swiss Family Robinson. Wyss.
Tale of Two Cities. Dickens.
Thelma. Corelli.
Tom Brown's School Days. Hughes.
Tom Brown at Oxford. Hughes.
Uncle Tom's Cabin. H. B. Stowe.
Wee Wifie. Rosa Carey.
We Two. Edna Lyall.
Won by Waiting. Edna Lyall.
Wide, Wide World. E. Wetherell.
Wandering Jew. Eugene Sue.

Library of Useful Stories.

A very useful series of small manuals on subjects of common interest. Small 8vo, 30c each.

Story of the—
Plants. Grant Allen.
Electricity. J. Munro.
Solar System. G. F. Chambers.
Stars. " "
Piece of Coal. E. A. Martin.
Earth's Atmosphere. D. Archibald.
Germ Life. H. W. Conn.
Earth. H. G. Seeley.
Life in the Seas. S. J. Hickson.
British Race. John Munro.
Photography. A. T. Story.

The Aetna Series.

Attractively bound in best silk-finished cloth, stamped from new and original designs, in ink and genuine gold.

Publisher's price, 50c; our price, 19c

Adam Bede. George Eliot.
Æsop's Fables.
Andersen's Fairy Tales. H. C. Andersen.
Our Mutual Friend. Dickens.
Rienzi. Lytton.
Scottish Chiefs. Porter.
Ships that Pass in the Night. Beatrice Harraden.
A Terrible Temptation. Chas. Reade.
Tour of the World in Eighty Days. Jules Verne.
Arabian Nights Entertainments.
Ardath. Marie Corelli.
Beyond Pardon. Bertha M. Clay.
Child's History of England. Charles Dickens.
Deerslayer, The. J. F. Cooper.
Donovan. Edna Lyall.
Dora Thorne. Bertha Clay.
Duke's Secret. " "
East Lynne. Mrs. H. Wood.
Grimms' Fairy Tales. Brothers Grimm.
Handy Andy. Samuel Lover.
Hardy Norseman. Edna Lyall.
Ivanhoe. Sir Walter Scott.
Jane Eyre. Charlotte Bronte.
John Halifax. Miss Mulock.
King Solomon's Mines. H. Rider Haggard.
Knight-Errant. Edna Lyall.
Last Days of Pompeii. Bulwer Lytton.
Lamplighter. Marie Cummings.
Last of the Mohicans. J. Fenimore Cooper.
Micah Clarke. A. Conan Doyle.
Mysterious Island. Jules Verne.
Oliver Twist. Charles Dickens.
Pathfinder. J. Fenimore Cooper.
Pioneers, The. J. Fenimore Cooper.
Prairie, The. " "
Robinson Crusoe. Daniel Defoe.
Romance of Two Worlds. Marie Corelli.
Sign of the Four. Conan Doyle.
Swiss Family Robinson.
Spy, The. J. Fenimore Cooper.
Tale of Two Cities. Charles Dickens.
Thelma. Marie Corelli.
Tom Brown's School Days. Thomas Hughes.
Twenty Thousand Leagues Under the Sea. Jules Verne.
Vendetta. M. Corelli.
We Two. Edna Lyall.
Wee Wifie. Rosa Carey.
When a Man's Single. J. M. Barrie.
White Company, The. A. Conan Doyle.
Wormwood. Marie Corelli.
Woman Against Woman. Mrs. M. Holmes.
Window in Thrums. J. M. Barrie.
Wife in Name Only. B. M. Clay.
Count of Monte Cristo. Dumas.
First Violin. Jessie Fothergill.
Harry Lorrequer. Chas. Lever.
Lover or Friend. Rosa N. Carey.
Deemster. Hall Caine.
Hypatia. C. Kingsley.
Jess. Rider Haggard.
Mary St. John. Rosa Carey.
Only the Governess. Rosa Carey.
Princess of the Moor. E. Marlitt.
Samantha at Saratoga. M. Holley.
Not Like Other Girls. Rosa Carey.
Thaddeus of Warsaw. Jane Porter.
Tom Brown at Oxford. Hughes.
Treasure Island. R. L. Stevenson.
Wooed and Married. Rosa Carey.
What's Bred in the Bone. Grant Allen.

Illustrated Vade Mecum Series.

Each volume contains illuminated title and portrait of author and illustrations in monochrome tints. Full cloth, ivory finish, ornamental inlaid back and side, boxed.

Publisher's price, 40c; our price, 25c

Ethics of the Dust. John Ruskin.
Pleasures of Life. Sir John Lubbock.
Twice Told Tales. Nathaniel Hawthorne.
Bacon's Essays.
Representative Men. Ralph Waldo Emerson.
The Light of Asia. Sir Edwin Arnold.
The Lays of Ancient Rome. T. B. Macaulay.
Thoughts of Marcus Aurelius.
Imitation of Christ. Thos. à Kempis.
Addresses. Henry Drummond.
Reveries of a Bachelor. Ik Marvel.
Dream Life. Ik Marvel.
Sartor Resartus. Thomas Carlyle.
Heroes and Hero Worship. Thomas Carlyle.
My Point of View. Selections from Drummond's Works.
Sketch Book. Washington Irving.
Kept for the Master's Use. Frances Ridley Havergal.
Lucile. Owen Meredith.
Lalla Rookh. Thomas Moore.
Lady of the Lake. Sir Walter Scott.
Marmion. Sir Walter Scott.
Evangeline. Henry W. Longfellow.
The Queen of the Air.
Greek Heroes. Charles Kingsley.
A Wonder Book. Nathaniel Hawthorne.
Undine. Fouque.
Addresses by Phillips Brooks.
Balzack's Shorter Stories.
The Crown of Wild Olives. John Ruskin.
Natural Law in the Spiritual World. Henry Drummond.
Cranford. Mrs. Gaskell.
Window in Thrums. J. M. Barrie.
Rab and His Friends. John Brown.
Tales From Shakespeare. Chas. and Mary Lamb.
Discourses of Epictetus.
Best Thoughts. Henry Dummond.
Bible Birthday Book.
Drummond's Addresses.
Shepherd Psalm. Meyer.
Steps into the Blessed Life. Meyer.
Brooks' Addresses.
John Ploughman's Pictures.
Uncle Tom's Cabin. Harriet Beecher Stowe.
Abbe Constantine. Ludovic Halevy.
Confessions of an Opium Eater. Thos. DeQuincey.
Poems. Lowell.
Morning Thoughts. Frances Havergal.
John Ploughman's Talk. Spurgeon.
Adventures of a Brownie. Mulock.
Blithedale Romance. Hawthorne.
Vicar of Wakefield.
Prince of House of David.
Jessica's First Prayer.
Changed Cross.
Bab Ballads. W. H. Gilbert.
Childe Harold. Byron.
Coming to Christ. F. R. Havergal.
Christian Life.
Daily Food for Christians.
Pathway of Promise.
Pathway of Safety. Ashton Oxenden.
Magic Nuts. Molesworth.
School for Scandal. Sheridan.
Water Babies. Kingsley.
Christie's Old Organ. Walton.
Dog of Flanders. Ouida.
Tanglewood Tales.

Pocket Library.

Imperial 32mo, cloth. Price, 20c each.

Bret Harte's Poems.
Goldsmith's Vicar of Wakefield.
Hood's Serious Poems.
Moore's Irish Melodies.
Fifty Bab Ballads.
Poems by E. Barrett Browning.
Milton's Paradise Lost.
Scott's Lady of the Lake.
Book of Wit and Humor.
Will Carleton's Farm Ballads.
Longfellow's Dante—Inferno.
" " —Paradiso.
" " —Purgatorio.
Autocrat of the Breakfast Table. O. W. Holmes.
Professor at the Breakfast Table. O. W. Holmes.
Poet at the Breakfast Table. O. W. Holmes.
Evangeline and Miles Standish. Longfellow.
Tales from Shakespeare.

Sterling Series.

An attractive line of standard authors of the world. Bound in assorted colors of cloth.

Regular price, 25c; our price, 15c.

Abbe Constantine. Ludovic Halevy.
Adventures of a Brownie. Miss Mulock.
Alice in Wonderland. L. Carroll.
Autocrat of the Breakfast Table. O. W. Holmes.
Bacon's Essays.
Browning's, Robert, Poems.
Confessions of an Opium Eater. De Quincey.
Cranford. Mrs. Gaskell.
Crown of Wild Olives. J. Ruskin.
Discourses of Epictetus.
Drummond's Addresses.
Ethics of the Dust. J. Ruskin.
Heroes and Hero Worship. Thomas Carlyle.
House of Seven Gables. Nathaniel Hawthorne.
Idle Thoughts of an Idle Fellow. J. K. Jerome.
Imitation of Christ. Thomas à Kempis.
Lalla Rookh. Thomas Moore.
Lamb's Tales from Shakespeare.
Queen of the Air. J. Ruskin.
Rab and His Friends. Dr. J. Brown.
Rasselas. Samuel Johnson.
Reveries of a Bachelor. Ik Marvel.
Representative Men. R. W. Emerson.
Sartor Resartus. Thomas Carlyle.
Sketch Book. Washington Irving.
Story of an African Farm. Olive Schreiner.
Ten Nights in a Bar-Room. T. S. Arthur.
Emerson's Essays, Vol. I.
" " Vol. II.
Through the Looking Glass. Lewis Carroll.
Vicar of Wakefield. Goldsmith.
Water Babies. Charles Kingsley.

Boys' and Girls' Library Books.

Annie S. Swan Series.

CLOTH.

A Victory Won $0 85
A Bitter Debt 0 85
Elizabeth Glen, M.B. 0 85
A Stormy Voyager 0 85
Mrs. Keith Hamilton 0 85
The Ne'er-do-Weel 0 85
Wyndham's Daughter 0 85
A Son of Erin 0 85
Burden Bearers 0 85
Briar and Palm 0 75
Sheila 0 75
Maitland of Laureston 0 75
St. Vedas 0 75
Who Shall Serve 0 75
A Lost Ideal 0 75
The Guinea Stamp 0 75
The Gates of Eden 0 75
A Better Part 0 65
Ayres of Studleigh 0 60
Carlowrie 0 35
Kinsfolk 0 35
Homespun 0 35
Mistaken and Marion Forsyth ... 0 35
Thomas Dryburgh's Dream 0 35
Robert Martin's Lesson 0 35
The Secret Panel 0 35
Wrongs Righted 0 35
Hazel and Sons 0 35
Twice Tried 0 35
Sundered Hearts 0 35
Shadowed Lives 0 35
Ursula Vivian 0 35
A Divided House 0 35
A Vexed Inheritance 0 35

Works by Emma Jane Worboise.

Handsomely bound in cloth.
Price, 75c each.

Thorneycroft Hall.
Millicent Kendrick.
Margaret Torrington.
The Fortunes of Cyril Denham.
Singlehurst Manor.
Overdale.
Mr. Montmorency's Money.
Nobly Born.
Chrystabel.
Canonbury Holt.
The House of Bondage.
Emilia's Inheritance.
Oliver Westwood.
Lady Clarissa.
Grey House at Endlestone.
The Brudenells of Brude.
The Heirs of Errington.
Wraleigh Trust.
Esther Wynne.
His Next of Kin.
Evelyn's Story.
The Lillingstones.
Campion Court.
Sir Julian's Wife.
Lottie Lonsdale.
Heart's-ease in the Family.
Our New House.
Maude Bolingbroke.
Amy Wilton.
Helen Bury.

Pansy Books.

CLOTH.
Regular price, 70c; our price, 55c.

Judge Burnham's Daughters.
Aunt Hannah, Martha and John.
John Remington, Martyr.
Miss Dee Dunmore Bryant.
Stephen Mitchell's Journey.
Wanted.
Twenty Minutes Late.
What They Couldn't.
Making Fate.
Overruled.
As In a Mirror.
Yesterday Framed in To-Day.

Alcott Series.

CLOTH.
Regular price, 70c; our price, 45c.

Little Men.
Little Women.
Under the Lilacs.
Jimmy's Cruise in the *Pinafore*.
Jack and Jill.
Eight Cousins.
Dred.
Silver Pitchers.
Rose in Bloom.
Old-fashioned Girl.
Lulu's Library.
Spinning-wheel Stories.
Shawl Straps.
Aunt Jo's Scrap Bag.
We and Our Neighbors.
Work and Beginning Again.
Jo's Boys, $1.15.

The Star Series.

Regular price, 70c; our price, 40c.
CLOTH

Drayton Hall. Alice Gray.
Golden Ladder. E. Wetherell.
What She Could. "
Wych Hazel. "
Gold of Chickaree. "
The Letter of Credit. "
The End of a Coil. "
Ben Hur. Lew Wallace.
A Daughter of Fife. A. E. Barr.
Between Two Loves. A. E. Barr.
Say and Seal. E. Wetherell.
Without and Within. W. Jay.
Diana. E. Wetherell.
My Desire. "
Nobody. "

The Chimes Series.

Stories for Girls. By Mrs. Marshall.

Illustrated. In new and attractive binding. Cloth, price, 50c.

Silver Chimes; Story for children.
Daphne's Decision.
Cassandra's Casket.
Poppies and Pansies.
Rex and Regina.
Dewdrops and Diamonds.
Heather and Harebell.
The Roses of Ringwood.
In the Purple.
Eastward Ho!

Agnes Giberne's Stories for Girls.

Illustrated. Handsomely bound in green and gold. Price, 50c.

Enid's Silver Bond.
St. Austin's Lodge.
The Dalrymples.
No. 3 Winnifred Place.
Least Said, Soonest Mended.
Sweetbriar.
Aimee.
The Andersons.
Miss Con; or, All Those Girls.
Kathleen.
Coulying Castle.

Works by Ethel Turner.

Cloth, gilt. Price, 60c each.

"Miss Ethel Turner is Miss Alcott's true successor. The same healthy spirited tone is visible which boys and girls recognized and were grateful for in 'Little Women' and 'Little Men,' the same absence of primness, and the same love of adventure."—*The Bookman.*

The Camp at Wandinong. Illustrated by F. Ewan and others.
Miss Bobbie. Illustrated by Harold Copping.
The Little Larrikin. Illustrated by A. J. Johnson.
Seven Little Australians. Illustrated by A. J. Johnson.
The Family at Misrule (sequel to above). Illustrated by A. J. Johnson.
The Three Little Maids.

Books by Laura F. Richards.

CLOTH.

Captain January $0 45
Rosin, the Beau 0 45
Melody 0 45
Marie 0 45

Books by the Author of "Probable Sons."

Teddy's Button. Cloth......... $0 45
Probable Sons. Board cover .. 0 30
The Odd One. Cloth " 0 45
A Thoughtless Seven " " 0 45
On the Edge of the Moor. " .. 0 85
Dwell Deep. Board " 0 65
Eric's Good News. " " 0 30
Bulbs and Blossoms " " 0 45
A Puzzling Pair. Cloth " 0 45
His Big Opportunity 0 65

Books by Kate Douglas Wiggin.

CLOTH.

The Birds' Christmas Carol.... 0 50
Timothy's Quest 0 90
Story of Patsy 0 60
Rita 0 90
Penelope's Irish Experiences .. 1 10
Penelope's Experiences in Scotland 1 10
Cathedral Courtship in England. Cloth 1 10

The Fairy Library.

Ornamental cloth, extra illustrated.
Price, 50 cents.

Golden Fairy Book (profusely illustrated.) By various Authors.
The Blue Fairy Book (profusely illustrated). By Andrew Lang.
The Red Fairy Book (profusely illustrated). By Andrew Lang.
The Green Fairy Book (profusely illustrated). By Andrew Lang.
The Yellow Fairy Book (profusely illustrated). By Andrew Lang.

Henty Books for Boys.

CLOTH, ILLUSTRATED.
Regular price, $1.75; our price, $1.00.

At the Point of the Bayonet. } New,
Through Harad to Cabul. } 1901.
With Roberts to Pretoria }
Out with Garibaldi. }
In the Irish Brigade. } New 1900.
With Buller in Natal. }
Both Sides of Border.
At Aboukir and Acre.
Thro' Russian Snows.
On the Irrawaddy.
Wulf the Saxon.
March on London.
With Frederick the Great.
No Surrender. A Tale of the Rising in La Vendée.
Won by the Sword. A Tale of the Thirty Years' War.
A Roving Commission; or, Thro' the Black Insurrection of Hayti.

Henty Books.

Regular price, $1.00; our price, 70c.

Bonnie Prince Charlie.
By England's Aid.
By Pike and Dyke.
In Freedom's Cause.
The Young Carthaginians.
The Dragon and the Raven.
With Clive in India.
With Lee in Virginia.
Captain Bayley's Heir.
The Lion of the North.
Under Drake's Flag.
In the Reign of Terror.
True to the Old Flag.
With Wolfe in Canada.
By Right of Conquest.
St. George for England.
The Bravest of the Brave.
For Name and Fame.
The Cat of Bubastes.
For the Temple.
The Lion of St. Mark.
By Sheer Pluck.
A Final Reckoning.
Facing Death.
Maori and Settler.
One of the 28th.

Henty Books.

Price, 25c.

Among Malay Pirates.
The Boy Knight.
Colonel Thorndyke's Secret.
The Cornet of Horse.
The Golden Canon.
Jack Archer.
Rujub the Juggler.
The Young Midshipman.

Standard Books for Boys.

Handsome cloth binding, 8vo, fully illustrated.
Regular 75c, for 50c.

Dick Cheveley. By W. H. G. Kingston.
Heir of Kilfinnan. By W. H. G. Kingston.
Off to the Wilds. By G. Manville Fenn.
The Two Supercargoes. By W. H. Kingston.
Under the Meteor Flag. By Harry Collingwood.
The Voyage of the Aurora. By Harry Collingwood.
Ben Burton; or, Born and Bred at Sea. By W. H. G. Kingston.
The Three Deserters. By M. T. H. Perelaer.
Lost in Africa. By F. Winder.
A Thousand Miles in the Rob Roy Canoe. By John MacGregor.
Blacks and Bushrangers. By E. B. Kennedy.
Sir Ludar. By Talbot Baines Reed.
The Black Bar. By G. Manville Fenn.
Cæsar Cascabel. By Jules Verne.
Tribulations of a Chinaman. By Jules Verne.
With Axe and Rifle.

Boys' and Girls' Library Books.

Adrift in the Pacific.
Abandoned. Verne.
The Secret of the Island. Verne.
The Archipelago on Fire. Verne.
Winning His Spurs. Henty.
Snowshoes and Canoes.
The Marvellous Country.
Hans Brinker; or, the Silver Skates. By Mrs. Dodge.
The Silver Cañon. A Tale of the Western Plains.
Adventurers of Great Hunting Grounds of the World.

The Lily Series and Youths' Library.

Well printed on good paper, each volum illustrated and attractive.y bound in cloth, gilt. Price, 35c each.

At the Mercy of Tiberius. A. J. Evans Wilson.
Adam Bede. Geo. Eliot.
Ben Hur. Lew Wallace.
Beulah. A. J. Evans Wilson.
Cross Triumphant. Florence Kingsley.
Daisy. E. Wetherell.
Daisy in the Field. E. Wetherell.
Danesbury House. Mrs. Wood.
A Humble Enterprise. Ada Cambridge.
Holiday House. C. Sinclair.
Melbourne House. E. Wetherell.
Uncle Tom's Cabin. H. B. Stowe.
Wide, Wide World. E. Wetherell.
Prince of the House of David. Rev. J. H. Ingraham.
The Throne of David. Rev. J. H. Ingraham.
Standish of Standish. Jane G. Austin.
What Katy Did at Home and at School. Susan Coolidge.
Macaria. A. J. Evans Wilson.
Prisoners of the Sea. F. M. Kingsley.
What Katy Did Next. Susan Coolidge.
Vashti. A. J. Evans Wilson.
Infelice " " "
St. Elmo " " "
A Humble Enterprise. Ada Cambridge.
John Halifax, Gentleman. Mrs. Craik.
The Pillar of Fire. Rev. J. H. Ingraham.
Mabel Vaughan. Miss Cumming.
From Log Cabin to White House. W. M. Thayer.
Robinson Crusoe. D. Defoe.
Grimm's Fairy Tales.
The Swiss Family Robinson.
Anderson's Popular Tales.
Boy's Own Sea Stories.
Scottish Chiefs. Jane Porter.
Romance of Navigation. H. Frith.
Westward Ho. Charles Kingsley.
Frank Allreddy's Fortune. Capt. F. Fox.
The Last of the Barons. Bulwer Lytton.
Harold. Bulwer Lytton.
The Heroes. Charles Kingsley.
The Beachcombers. G. Bishop.
Ministering Children. Miss Charlesworth.
Monica. E. E. Green.
Coral Island. R. M. Ballantyne.
Martin Rattler. " "
Willis, the Pilot (Sequel to Swiss Family Robinson).
Young Fur Trader. R. M. Ballantyne.
Peter the Whaler. W. H. Kingston.

Boys' and Girls' Library.

Written by our most popular authors in literature for Sunday School and Home Reading. Printed on calendered paper, bound in best cloth, each volume illustrated.

Price 35c per volume.

Ship Daphne. Rev. T. S. Millington.
Faith White's Letter Book.
Graham McCall's Victory. Grace Stebbing.
Ingleside. Mrs. Leslie.
Hunted and Harried. R. M. Ballantyne.
Head of the Firm. E. M. Vittum.
Not Forsaken. Agnes Giberne.
The Old Barracks. E. Kelly.
Old Red House. Mrs. Grosvenor.
The Orient Boys. Mrs. Keene.
Opposite the Jail. Mary A. Denison.
Sequel to Opposite the Jail. Mary A. Denison.
Chew Alley. Mrs. C. E. K. Davis.
Into the Highways. Mrs. C. E. K. Davis.
Led by Love. N. A. Paull.
Kept from Idols. M. A. Denison.
Life in a Nutshell. A. Giberne.
Lyle Macdonald. Mrs. Keene.
Life Tangles. A. Giberne.
Peep Behind the Scenes. Mrs. Walton.
Great Mistake. Rev. T. S. Millington.
King's Servants. Hesba Stretton.
Mark Steadman.
Max Victor's School-days. S. S. Pugh.
Medoline Selwyn's Work. Mrs. J. J. Colter.
John and the Demijohn. J. McN. Wright.
Ten Millions. Mrs. M. Leslie.
Benjamin's Bounty. Emma Marshall.
A Vanished Hand. Sara Doudney.
A Great Indiscretion. E. E. Green.
Ethel's Triumph. Mary Denison.
Mildred Kent's Hero. Mrs. J. J. Colter.
Child of the Barracks. Mrs. M. Leslie.
Both Sides of the Street. W. S. Walker.
This and That. Mrs. M. Leslie.
Miss Nettie's Girls. C. Evelyn.
Who is My Neighbor? Lady Hope.
What's in a Name? Sara Doudney.
Up Hill. E. S. Phelps.
Her Husband's Home. E. E. Green.
Aunt Rebecca's Charge. A. C. W.
The Viking Heir. Mrs. S. F. Keene.
The Great Salterns. Sara Doudney.
Up to Fifteen.
After Years. G. Gaylord.
Chauntry's Boy. A. Robbins.
My Lady. J. M. Drinkwater.
Peter Killip's King. Hesba Stretton.
Faithful Son. G. E. Sargent.
Little Meg's Children. Hesba Stretton.
Cost What It May. E. E. Hornibrook.
Marcus Stratford's Charge. E. E. Green.
The Poor Clerk. G. E. Sargent.
Wood Island Light. Jas. Otis.
Boys of the Central. I. T. Thurston.
Kent Fielding's Ventures. I. T. Thurston.
Sara, a Princess. Fanny E. Newberry.
Don Malcolm. I. T. Thurston.
Captain Russell's Watchword. Mrs. H. S. Grosvenor.
Joint Guardians. E. E. Green.
Mountain Patriots: a Story of Reformation in Savoy.
Culm Rock. G. Gaylord.
Old Manor House: Sequel.
The Story of the White Rock Cove.
Susan Osgoode's Prize.
Jessie's Work. M. E. Shipley.
Drifted Ashore. E. E. Green.
Shadows. Mrs. O. F. Walton.
Peter the Apprentice: an Historical Tale of Reformation in England.
Countess Maud. E. S. Holt.

Young People's Library.

Publisher's price, 50c; our price, 30c.

A new series of choice literature for children, selected from the best and most popular works. Handsomely printed on fine super-calendered paper from large clear type and profusely illustrated by the most famous artists, making the handsomest and most attractive series of juvenile classics before the public. In a uniform size—square 16mo.

The Adventures of Robinson Crusoe. (70 illustrations.)
Alice's Adventures in Wonderland. (42 illustrations.)
Through the Looking Glass and What Alice Found There. (50 illustrations.)
Josephine, Empress of France. (40 illustrations.)
Marie Antoinette, Queen of France. (41 illustrations.)
Queen Elizabeth of England. (49 illustrations.)
William the Conqueror of England. (43 illustrations.)
Alfred the Great, of England. (40 illustrations.)
Cyrus the Great, Founder of Persian Empire. (40 illustrations.)
Darius the Great, King of Medes and Persians. (34 illustrations.)
Xerxes the Great, King of Persia. (39 illustrations.)
Alexander the Great, King of Macedonia. (51 illustrations.)
Julius Cæsar, the Roman Conqueror. (44 illustrations.)
The Story of Exploration and Adventure in Africa.
Bunyan's Pilgrim's Progress. (46 illustrations.)
Child's History of England. (80 illustrations.)
Æsop's Fables. (62 illustrations.)
Christopher Columbus and the Discovery of America. (70 illustrations.)
Swiss Family Robinson. (50 illustrations.)
Gulliver's Travels. (50 illustrations.)
Mother Goose's Rhymes, Jingles and Stories. (234 illustrations.)
The Story of the Frozen Seas. (70 illustrations.)
Wood's Natural History. (80 illustrations.)
Arabian Nights. (110 illustrations.)
Lives of Presidents of United States.
Black Beauty. Anna Sewell.
Flower Fables. Louisa M. Alcott.
Aunt Martha's Corner Cupboard. Mary and E. Kirby.
Water Babies. Charles Kingsley.
Andersen's Fairy Tales. (80 illustrations.)
Child's Life of Christ. (49 illustrations.)
Child's Story of the Bible. (72 illustrations.)

Dainty Series.

Choice gift books for children, bound in half-white vellum, illuminated floral sides, gold stamping, with numerous half-tone illustrations, quarto.

Regular price, 50c; our price, 25c.

A Princess's Token. By E. E. Green.
King's Sons. By G. M. Fenn.
Silver Buckle. By M. N. Crumpton.
Dickens' Children Stories.
Children's Shakespeare.
A Golden Apple. By L. T. Meade.
Young Robin Hood. By G. Manville Fenn.
Honor Bright. By Mary C. Rowsell.
Voyage of the "Mary Adair." By Francis E. Crompton.
Kingfisher's Egg. By L. T. Meade.
Tattine. By Ruth Ogden.
Doings of a Dear Little Couple. By Mary D. Brine.
Our Soldier Boy. By G. M. Fenn.
Christmas Fairy. By John Strange Winter.
Molly, the Drummer Boy. By H. T. Comstock.
Little Skipper. By G. Manville Fenn.
Big Temptation. By L. T. Meade.
The Rose Carnation. By F. E. Crompton.
Little Gervaise. By John Strange Winter.
Rose, Tom and Ned. By Mrs. D. P. Sanford.

Boys' and Girls' Series.

Printed on fine plate paper, cloth covers, 19c each.

Taken or Left. By Mrs. Walton.
Aunt Selina's Legacy. By Emma Leslie.
Effie Patterson's Story. By L. L. Rouse. A Tale of the Covenanters.
Poppy's Presents. By Mrs. O. F. Walton.
Audrey; or, Children of Light. By Mrs. O. F. Walton.
Two Secrets, and A Man of His Word. By Hosba Stretton.
Pretty Miss Hathway. By Emma Leslie.
Sandy Jim; or, The Message of a Rose. By H. S. Streatfeild.
Christie, the King's Servant. By Mrs. O. F. Walton. A Sequel to Christie's Old Organ.
The Captain of the Eleven, and other Stories. By K. Shirley Plant.
Harry Lester's Revenge. By Alice Lang.
Vera's Christmas Guests. By K. T. Sizer.
The Mysterious House. By Mrs. O. F. Walton.
Three Little Great Ladies. By W. Percy Smith.
Effie's Temptation. By Annette Whymper.
Donald and His Friends. By Sarah Gibson.
Christie's Old Organ. By Mrs. O. F. Walton.
Tom Larkins; or, The Boy Who Was No Good. By C. A. Burnaby.
Little Peter, the Ship Boy. By W. H. G. Kingston.
Bravely Borne; or, Archie's Cross.
Little Faith; or, The Child of the Toy Stall. By Mrs. O. F. Walton.
Granny's Hero. By Salome Hocking.
How Little Bessie Kept the Wolf from the Door. By Mrs. Coates.
Under the Old Roof. By Hesba Stretton.
The Elder Brother. By Eglanton Thorne.
Pansy. A Story for Little Girls.
Jessica's First Prayer. By Hesba Stretton.
Saved at Sea. By Mrs. Walton.
No Place Like Home. By Hesba Stretton.
Alison's Ambition. By Mary Hampden.

Golden Silence Series.

19c each.

Morag: A Tale of Highland Life. By Mrs. Milne Rae.
Michael's Treasures. By Mrs. Marshall.
The Three Little Spades. By Susan and Anna Warner.
Little Bricks. By Darley Dale.
Effie's Friends; or, Chronicles of the Woods and Shore.
Matthew Frost. By Mrs. Marshall.
My Lady Bountiful. By Mrs. Marshall.
Three Paths in Life. A Tale for Girls.
Stillafont Abbey. By Emma Marshall.
Susy's Sacrifice.
Kenneth Forbes.
Pat's Inheritance. By Mrs. Marshall.
Nature's Gentleman. By Mrs. Marshall.
The Bride's Home. By Mrs. Marshall.
Miles Murchison. By Miss Giberne.
Footsteps of Fortune. By Esme Stuart.
My Grandmother's Pictures. By Mrs. Marshall.
High and Lowly. A Tale of Hearts and Homes. By Ellen L. Davis.
Peter Pengelly. By Rev. J. Jackson Wray.
Nellie Graham. By Ella Stone.
Jack Horner the Second. By Rev. J. Jackson Wray.
A Sunbeam's Influence. By Lady Dunboyne.
Three Little Sisters. By Mrs. Marshall.
Three Little Brothers. By Mrs. Marshall.
The Christmas Stocking of Karl Krinken.
When I Was Young. By Mrs. Marshall.
Golden Silence. By Mrs. Marshall.
Lettice Lawson's Legacy. By Mrs. Marshall

Boys' and Girls' Library Books.

Sir Benjamin's Bounty. By Mrs. Marshall.
Master Martin. By Mrs. Marshall.
Kitten Pilgrims. By R. M. Ballantyne.
Geoffrey Hallam; or, The Clerk of the Parish. By J. Jackson Wray.
A Song of Sixpence for the Bairns. By J. Jackson Wray.
Daisy of Old Meadow. By Agnes Giberne.
Old Umbrellas. By Agnes Giberne.

Pansy Books.

Regular price, 35c; our price, 19c.

Four Girls at Chautauqua.
Little Fishers and Their Nets.
Three People.
Echoing and Re-echoing.
Christie's Christmas.
Divers Women.
Spun from Fact.
The Chautauqua Girls at Home.
The Pocket Measure.
Julia Reid.
Wise and Otherwise.
The King's Daughter.
Links in Rebecca's Life.
Interrupted.
An Endless Chain.
Ester Reid.
Ester Reid yet Speaking.
The Man of the House.
Ruth Erskine's Crosses.
Household Puzzles.
Mabel Wynn; or, Those Boys.
Modern Prophets.
The Randolphs.
Flower of the Family.
Pillar of Fire.
Throne of David.
Prince of the House of David.
Naomi.
Mrs. Solomon Smith Looking On.
From Different Standpoints.
A New Graft on the Family Tree.
Profiles.
Sidney Martin's Christmas.
Tip Lewis and His Lamp.
Eighty-seven.
Anna Lee.
Daisy.
Fair God.
Good Wives.
The Hall in the Grove.
John Ward.
Jessamine.
Sevenfold Trouble.
What Katy Did at School.
Queechy.
What Katy Did.
Mabel Vaughan.
Old Helmet.
Ben Hur.
Aunt Jane's Hero.
Basket of Flowers.
One Common-place Day.
That Lass o' Lowrie's. Burnett.
Mansfield Park. Austin.
Sense and Sensibility. Austin.
Faith Gartney. Whitney.
Patience Strong. Whitney.
Gayworthys. Whitney.
Pride and Prejudice. Austin.

The Elsie Books.

19c each.

By Martha Finley—
Elsie Dinsmore.
Elsie's Holidays at Roselands.
Elsie's Girlhood.
Elsie's Womanhood.
Elsie's Motherhood.
Elsie's Children.
Elsie's Widowhood.
Grandmother Elsie.
Elsie's New Relations.
Elsie at Nantucket.
The Two Elsies.
Elsie's Kith and Kin.
Elsie's Friends at Woodburn.
Christmas with Grandma Elsie.
Elsie and the Raymonds.
Elsie Yachting.
Elsie's Vacation.
Elsie at Viamede.
Elsie at Ion.
Elsie at the World's Fair.
Elsie's Journey on Inland Waters.
Elsie at Home.

E. P. Roe's Works.

Cloth, 19 cents.

An Original Belle.
An Unexpected Result.
Barriers Burned Away.
Driven Back to Eden
A Day of Fate.
The Earth Trembled.
Found Yet Lost.
A Face Illumined.
From Jest to Earnest.
His Sombre Rivals.
He Fell in Love With His Wife.
Knight of the Nineteenth Century.
Miss Lou.
Near to Nature's Heart.
Opening a Chestnut Burr.
Taken Alive.
Without a Home.
What Can She Do.
A Young Girl's Wooing.

Prizes for Young People.

Cloth Covers, illustrated editions, 19c each.

Wonderful Stories for Children. Hans Andersen.
Fairy Grandmother, a London Waif.
The Children of Melby Hall. McKean.
Mark Westcroft Cordwainer. Potter.
A Humble Heroine. L. E. Tiddeman.
Baby John. Author of "Laddie."
The Green Casket. Mrs. Molesworth.
The Bewitched Lamp. "
Little Mary. L. T. Meade.
The Little Knight. Edith C. Kenyon.
Wilfrid Clifford. E. C. Kenyon.
Zoe. Author of "Laddie."
Uncle Sam's Money Box. Mrs. S. C. Hall.
Grandmamma's Pockets. Mrs. S. C. Hall.
Ernest's Golden Thread.
Their Happiest Xmas.

Every Boy's Library.

Regular price, 35c; our price, 19c.

English at the North Pole. Verne.
Five Weeks in a Balloon. "
Round the World in Eighty Days. "
Robinson Crusoe.
Lamb's Tales from Shakespeare.
Adventures in Africa.
The Original Robinson Crusoe.
Great Scholars.
The Ice Desert. Verne.
Mysterious Document. "
Round the Moon. "
Field of Ice. Verne.
Nansen and the Frozen North.
General Gordon.
Swiss Family Robinson.
England's Essayists.
Great Novelists.
Vicar of Wakefield.
Uncle Tom's Cabin.
Masters in History.
Masterman Ready.
Mission Scenes in Africa.
Life of Nelson.
Doctor's Birthday.
John Bright.
Brilliant Speakers.
Adventures in India.
Among the Cannibals.
From the Earth to the Moon.
On the Track.
The Pirates of the Mississippi.
Adventures of 3 Englishmen and 3 Russians.
From Log Cabin to White House.
Ernie Elton, the Lazy Boy.
Ernie Elton, at School.
Walter's Friend.

The Evans-Wilson Books.

Regular price, 35c; our price, 19c.

Infelice. St. Elmo.
Vashti. Macaria.
Inez. Beulah.
At the Mercy of Tiberius.

Splendid Lives Series.

12mo. Cloth. Portraits and illustrations. 19c each.

Alexander MacKay, Missionary Hero of Uganda.
Sir Samuel Baker. His Life and Adventures.
The Story of Garfield. Farm Boy, Soldier and President.
The Story of David Livingstone. WeaverBoy, Missionary, Explorer.
The Story of Florence Nightingale. the Heroine of the Crimea.
The Story of President Lincoln. Ploughboy, Statesman, Patriot.
The Story of Victoria, R. I. Wife, Mother, Queen.
The Story of Albert the Good. (Prince Consort.)
George Washington. Soldier, Statesman, Patriot.
Martin Luther. The Hero of the Reformation.
The Life of Frances Willard.
John Bunyan.
Oliver Cromwell.
James Gilmour.
Tennyson. The Story of His Life. E. J. Cuthbertson.
Wallace and Bruce. Heroes of Scotland. Mary Cochrane.
Wm. Shakespeare. The Story of his Life and Times. E. J. Cuthbertson.
Queen Victoria. The Story of Her Life and Reign.
Lord Shaftesbury and Geo. Peabody. Being tke Story of Two Great Public Benefactors, with Portraits.
William I., Emperor, and His Successors. Mary Cochrane.
Thos. Alva Edison. The Story of His Life and Inventions. E. C. Kenyon.
The Story of Watt and Stephenson.
General Gordon and Lord Dundonald. The Story of Two Heroic Lives.
The Story of Nelson and Wellington.
Livingstone and Stanley. The Story of the Opening up of the Dark Continent.
John Bright: His Life and Opinions.
Columbus and Cook. The Story of Their Lives, Voyages, etc.
The Story of Napoleon Bonaparte.

Ballantyne's Books for Boys.

Regular price, 35c; our price, 19c.

Away in the Wilderness.
Fast in the Ice.
Chasing the Sun.
Sunk at Sea.
Lost in the Forest.
Over the Rocky Mountains.
Saved by the Life Boat.
The Cannibal Islands
Hunting the Lions.
Digging for Gold.
The Battle and the Breeze.

The Pioneers.
Wrecked but Not Ruined.
Martin Rattler.
The Coral Islands.
Fur Trade.
Peter the Whaler.
Ungara.

Little Stories for Children.

CLOTH.
Regular price, 20c; our price, 15c.
CLOTH.
Regular price, 15c; our price, 10c.
CLOTH.
Regular price, 10c; our price, 7c.

Magazines.

From December 1st to February 1st there is such a rush of subscriptions that publishers are necessarily more or less delayed in entering subscriptions and mailing their first numbers. Please order early, and thus prevent complaints.

Subscriptions for English magazines do not take effect for 5 weeks after ordering.

Please state when ordering with what month you wish your subscription to begin.

Prices quoted on application for any of the English or American magazines not mentioned.

The prices are subject to change.

Estimates given to Public Libraries on application.

In ordering single numbers of any magazine, postage is required.

List of 5c Magazines.

	Per Year.
Black Cat	$0.50
Nickell	0.50
Ladies' World	0.40

List at 10c.

Modern Culture	1.00
Pearson, American edition	1.00
Weldon's Ladies' Journal	1.00
Elite Styles	1.00
Munsey's	1.00
Argosy	1.00
McClure's	1.00
Ladies' Home Journal	1.00
Cosmopolitan	1.00
Strand	1.15
Harper's Bazaar	1.00
Pulpit	$1.00
Wide World	1.15
Success	1.00
Harmsworth	1.20
Ladies' Magazine	1.00

Miscellaneous.

St. Nicholas	2.75
Outing	2.75
Nineteenth Century	4.35
Harper's Monthly	3.75
Etude, new subscribers	1.20
Etude, renewals	1.40
Literary Digest, new subs.	2.75
Literary Digest, renewals	3.00
Sunday Strand	2.00
Weldon's Bazaar of Children's Fashions	0.35
Family Herald	1.65
Review of Reviews, English	1.80
Review of Reviews, American	2.25
Young Ladies' Journal	3.25
Illustrated London News, reprint, weekly	5.75
Illustrated London News, weekly—English edition	9.25
Graphic	9.25
Ladies' Pictorial	8.75
Canadian Magazine	2.25
Boys' Own Paper, monthly	1.50
Girls' Own Paper, monthly	1.50
Pall Mall Magazine	3.50
The Illustrated Milliner	2.75
Weldon's Home Dressmaker	0.35
Scribner's	2.90
Art Amateur	3.60
North American Review	4.35
Lady's Realm	2.00

Chambers' $2.25
Cassell's 1.35
Leisure Hour 1.50
Outlook 2.90
Windsor 2.00
Trained Nurse 2.00
Woman at Home 2.00
Forum 2.75
Girls' Realm 2.00
Captain 1.75
Sunday at Home 1.50
Black and White (American Reprint), weekly 5.75
Truth 2.50
Bon-Ton 3.40
Art-de-la-Mode 3.40
Costume Royal 3.40
Toilettes 2.40
Our Home, weekly $1.75
Pearson's, English edition 2.00

Xmas Numbers of Illustrated Magazines for 1901.

Ready about December 10. Price, 35c, postage extra.

Illustrated London News.
Black and White.
Lady's Pictorial.
Holly Leaves.
Graphic.
Pear's Pictorial.
Art Annual, 65c (postage extra).

Christmas Books

Annuals and Illustrated Editions of Gift Books.

Chums, an Illustrated Annual for Boys, 1901, cloth $1 75
Girl's Own, 1901, cloth 1 75
Boys' Own, 1901, cloth 1 75
Sunday at Home, 1901, cloth 1 75
Leisure Hour, 1901, cloth 1 75
Quiver, 1901, cloth 1 75

The Girls' Realm Magazine, complete for one year (post, 25c. extra) 1 00
The Windsor Magazine, bound for 6 months (post, 15c extra). 0 75
The Captain, an illustrated magazine for boys, cloth covers, in 2 vols. (post, 15c each extra), each 0 75
Good Words Magazine, bound in cloth, gilt title, fully illustrated (post, 10c extra) 0 50
Sunday Magazine, bound in cloth, gilt title, fully illustrated (post, 10c extra) 0 50
Penny Magazine, bound in cloth, illustrated (postpaid) .. 0 40

Bible Talks in Simple Language, especially adapted to the young, with 250 engravings, cloth cover $0 65
Grandfather's Bible Stories, large cloth edition, fully illustrated 0 95
Travels and Adventures, size 6½ x 9, cloth cover, fully illustrated 0 60
Twenty Little Maidens, being twenty stories of twenty different little maidens, cloth cover, fully illustrated 0 65
Helen's Babies. By John Habberton. With original illustrations by Miss Sara Crosby. Large edition, cloth covers .. 1 00
Young Folks' Uncle Tom's Cabin, large cloth edition, fully illustrated 0 85
The True Mother Goose. With pictures by Blanche McManus, and border in color .. 0 85
Told in the Twilight. Stories to tell to children, with pictures in color by Blanche McManus. Cloth 0 65
Black Beauty. By A. Sewell. Cloth 0 45
Beautiful Joe. By Marshall Saunders. Linen cloth, 30c; cloth, illustrated 0 50
The Tale of Pierrot and His Cat. By F. A. Evans (a favorite story-teller for children. With color sketches by A. R. Wheelan 1 25
The Legend of St. Mark: Sunday Morning Talks to the Children. By Rev. Jno. Byles. Cloth cover 0 50

Toy and Picture Books.

5 cents.

Little Animal Series, 3 kinds, assorted.
Young America Series, 4 kinds, assorted.
Santa Claus Series, 4 kinds, assorted.
Topsy Series, shaped, 4 kinds assorted.

10 cents.

Mother Goose Series, 3 kinds, assorted.
Ten Little Niggers, shaped.

LIMP COVER PICTURE BOOKS. POSTPAID.

2 cents.

Hop-o'-My-Thumb Series, 6 kinds, assorted.

3 cents.

Red Riding Hood Series, 6 kinds, assorted.
Comic Animal Series, 4 kinds, assorted.

15 cents.

Little Pig Series, 3 kinds, assorted.
Slovenly Peter Series, 4 kinds, assorted.
Jack and Jill Series, 3 kinds, assorted.
Tom Thumb Series, 3 kinds, assorted.
Little Soldier Boys.
Pretty Picture A.B.C.

20 cents.

By Land and Water.
Royal Mother Goose, 3 kinds, assorted.
The Night Before Christmas.

25 cents.

Red Riding Hood.
Four-footed Friend.
Domestic Animals.
Wild Animals.
Big Animal Picture Book.
Country Joys.
Christmas, ABC, and Picture Book.

Linen Picture Books.

Postpaid.

5 cents.

Pleasure Series, four kinds, assorted.

10 cents.

Little Animal Series, 3 kinds, assorted.

15 cents.

Kriss Kringle Series, 4 kinds, assorted.

20 cents.

Child's First Book.
Three Kitten Series, 3 kinds, assorted.
Puss in Boots Series, 3 kinds, assorted.

25 cents.

Gems from Mother Goose Series, 4 kinds, assorted.
Comical Pets, A B C.
Visit of St. Nicholas.

35 cents.

Four-footed Friends.
One, Two, Three, Four.
Big Animal Picture Book.

Painting Books.

Postpaid.

5 cents.

Our Little One's Painting Books, 6 kinds, assorted.
Object, 4 kinds, assorted.

10 cents.

Little Folks, 3 kinds, assorted.
Object, 4 kinds, assorted.

15 cents.

New Palette, 2 kinds, assorted.
Floral, 3 kinds, assorted.

20 cents.

Little Artist, 3 kinds, assorted.

25 cents.

Ideal, 2 kinds, assorted.

Board and Cloth Covered Picture Books

Postage Extra.

5 cents.

Baby Bunting series, 4 kinds, assorted. Postage, 2c extra.

10 cents.

Play Room Series, 6 kinds, assorted. Postage, 3c extra.
My New Picture Book. Postage, 3c extra.

15 cents.

Sunbeam Series, 4 kinds, assorted. Postage, 4c extra.
Stories from the Bible. Bible Stories.

20 cents.

Sunny Hour Series, 4 kinds, assorted. Postage, 4c extra.
Cinderella Series, 6 kinds, assorted. Postage, 4c extra.
Walks and Talks in the Zoo. Postage, 4c extra.
Fun on the Farm. Postage, 4c extra.

25 cents.

Storyland, 4 kinds, assorted. Postage, 8c extra.
Five Little Peppers. Postage, 4c extra.

50 cents.

(Postage, 10c extra.)

Our Darlings, board and cloth cover, 12 colored illustrations.

Young Folks' Companion, over 200 illustrations.
Chatterbox for 1900, board cover, fully illustrated.
Little Folks' Annual, fully illustrated
Chatterbox for 1901, colored illustrations, board covers, 75c; cloth cover, $1.00.

35 cents.

Young America Series, 4 kinds, assorted. Postage 10c extra.

40 cents.

Boys' Book of Adventure. Postage, 10c extra.

45 cents.

(Postage, 10c extra.)

The following line of board Juvenile Books is without an equal in this class of publications. The books are well printed and bound in the best possible manner, the covers are lithographed in ten colors, and profusely illustrated.

True Stories of Famous Men and Women.
Delightful Stories of Persons and Things.
The Animal World in Picture and Story.
A Story of the World and its People.
Bible Heroes.

School Books for 1902.

Order all School Supplies through our Mail Order Department. Prices will be given on all books not in this list at shortest notice. Postage paid on school books ordered through our Mail Order, excepting Scribblers, Exercise, Copy, Drawing and Blank Books. When ordering books, give name of Author and Publisher when possible.

Dictionaries.

Concise Imperial Dictionary and Encyclopædia of Knowledge, revised and enlarged, making this an unabridged edition. As the addition to this work makes it so much larger than the former size, the carriage will be extra, cloth, $1.35; half morocco, $2.00.
Student's Standard, $2.25.
Nuttall's Pronouncing, with appendix, 75c.
Chamber's Etymological, 90c.
Webster's English, half leather, $2.25.
" " with Walker's key, $1.00.
Webster's English, 10c, 20c, 35c, 65c.
Handy Vest Pocket Dictionary, leather, 20c; cloth, 13c.
French-English, leather, 35c.
German-English, leather, 35c.
Cassell's French, German, Latin, $1.00 each.
Routledge's French, German, Latin, 40c each.
Liddell & Scott's Greek Lexicon, $1.60

Arithmetics—

New Public School, 20c.
High School, 48c.
Key to High School, $1.50.
Kirkland & Scott's (Revised), 24c.
Hamblin Smith's, 48c.
Prize Problems, 16c.
MacLean's Hints on Teaching Arithmetic, 40c.

Algebras—

High School, Part I., 60c.
" " Part II., $1.20.
Hamblin Smith's, 48c.
McLellan's Elements, 60c.
Todhunter's, for Beginners, 48c.
C. Smith's Elementary, 80c.
Hall and Knight's Elementary 80c.
Hall and Knight's Higher, $1.60.
Treatise on Algebra. C. Smith, $1.60.

Agriculture—
Public School, by Mills & Shaw, 32c
" " " C. C. James, 25c.
Manitoba Course, Part I., 30c.
" " Part II., 40c.

Book-keeping—
High School Text-book (McLean's), 50c.
Book-keeping and Précis Writing, 52c.
Copp, Clark Book-keeping Blank, No. 14, 20c; No. 8, 30c; No. 9, 40c.
Blank, No. G11, 20c; postage 5c extra.

Botany—
Spotton's High School, 80c.
" " " Part II., 48c.
Spotton's High School, Manitoba edition, 80c.
Spotton's Botanical Note Book, Part I., 40c; postage 5c extra.
Spotton's Botanical Note Book, Part II., 48c; postage 5c extra.

Chemistry—
Remsen Advanced, $3.15.
Remsen, Briefer, $1.35.
High School, 40c.
Advanced, 40c.
Kirkland's Experimental, 48c.
Chemical Note Book, 20c; postage 5c extra.

Composition—
Composition from Models, 60c.
English Composition, Welsh, 48c.
Practical English and Composition, 40c.
Strang's English Composition, 20c.
Sykes' Elementary English composition, 35c.

Copy Books—
Public School Vertical. By Newland & Rowe. Nos. 1, 2, 3, 4, 5, 6, 6c each; postage 1c extra.
Public School Vertical. By Casselman. Nos. 1, 2, 3, 4, 5, 6, 6c each; postage 1c extra.
Business Forms, Vertical, No. 7, 8c; postage 2c extra.

Drawing Books—
High School Drawing, Nos. 1, 2, 3, 8c each; postage 2c extra.
Public School Drawing, Nos. 1, 2, 3, 4, 5, 4c each; postage 1c extra.

English Literature—
Palgrave's Golden Treasury, 40c.
Palgrave's Children's Treasury. Parts I. and II. combined, 40c.
Selections for 1901-1902, by Alexander, cloth, 45c; paper, 28c.

Rolfe's Edition of Shakespeare's Plays, paper cover, 40c each; cloth, 65c each—
Richard II.
Macbeth.
Merchant of Venice.
King Lear.
Julius Cæsar.
As You Like It.
Milton's Minor Poems.—Comus, Sonnets, etc., edited by Rolfe, 40c.
Clarendon Press Edition Julius Cæsar, 28c.

French—
La Poudre, 20c.
High School French Grammar and Reader, 80c.
Exercises in French Prose (Squair and Cameron), 60c.
Le Roman d'un jeune Homme pauvre, 56c.
Madame Therese, 48c.
Colomba, Prosper Mérimee, Notes by Cameron, 40c.
La Joie Fait Peur, Mme. Emile de Girardin, by L. J. V. Gerard, 20c.
High School French Reader, new edition, 40c.

German—
Germelshausen, 24c.
High School German Grammar with Reader, 80c.
High School German Reader, new edition, 40c.
Baumbach Der Schwiegersohn, 48c.
Elz Er ist nicht eifersüchtig, Wichert, Post Festum, with notes by Vander Smissen, 48c.
Das Kalte Herz, 80c.
Leander's Traumaurian, 80c.
Horning's Exercises in German Prose Composition 48c.
Ebner Eschenbach's Die Frieherren Von Gemperlein, 24c.
Wilkelmi, Einer muss heiraten, 40c.

Greek—
Homer's Iliad, Book I., 28c.
Elementary Greek Prose Composition (Fletcher and Nicholson), $1.00.
Goodwin's Greek Grammar, $1.65.
White's Beginner's Greek, $1.20.
Demosthenes' Pro Pharmione, $1.60.
Xenophon Anabasis, Book I, 28c.
Homer's Odyssey, XIII. to XVIII., 80c.
Lysias Orationes. By Shuckburgh, 80c.
Lysias Epitaphios. By Snell, 56c.
Lucian, Charon, notes by Heitland, 40c.
Lucian, Vera Historia, notes by Jerram, 32c.

Geography—
Public School Geography, 60c.
High " " 80c.
Modern " Atlas, 60c.
Frye's Complete Geography, $1.60.
Frye's Primary Geography, 75c.
Cornell's First Steps, 45c.
" Primary Geography, 60c.
Moir's Map Geography for junior pupils, 20c.
Geography of British Colonies. By Dawson and Sutherland, 70c.
New Canadian Geography, 85c.

Geometry—
McKay's Euclid, complete, 60c.
McKay's Euclid, Books I., II., III., 40c.
Todhunter's Euclid, complete, 60c.
Todhunter's Euclid, Books I. II., III., 32c.
Hill's Lessons in Geometry, 70c.
Public School Euclid and Algebra, 20c.
Hamblin Smith's Geometry, 75c.
Todhunter and Loney's Euclid, Books I to IV, 60c.
Todhunter and Loney's Euclid, complete, 80c.

Grammars—
High School, 60c.
Public School, 20c.
Modern English Grammar, by Buehler, 65c.
English Grammar and Composition, by G. H. Armstrong, 20c.

History—
Green's Short History of the English People, $1.20.
High School History of Greece and Rome, 60c.
High School History of England and Canada, 52c.
Public School History of England and Canada, 24c.
Jeffers' History of Canada, 24c.
English and Canadian History Notes, 20c.
Topical Studies in Canadian History, by Nellie Spence, 28c.
New School History of Canada. By W. H. P. Clements, 40c.
Weaver's Canadian History, 40c.
Little Arthur's History of England, 40c.
Moir's British History Notes, 12c.
Creighton's History of Rome, 24c.
Fyffe's History of Greece, 24c.
Tait's Analysis of Green's England, 80c.
Smith's Smaller History of Rome, $1.10.
Oman's History of Greece, $1.30.
Pelham's Outlines of Roman History, $1.20.

Hygiene—
Public School Physiology, 20c.
Physiology, Health Series, No. 1, 24c; No. 2, 40c.

Latin—
Cæsar—With Notes by Henderson or Robertson—
Bellum Britannicum, 40c.
" Gallicum, II., III., IV., 60c.
" " IV., 40c.
" " V., 40c.
" " V., VI., 60c.
Kelly's Key to Cæsar, 40c.
Dr. Giles' Interlinear Key to Cæsar, 72c.
Henderson and Fletcher's Latin Prose Composition, $1.00.
First Latin, with Reader, 80c.
Latin Reader, 40c.
Primary Latin Book and Reader, by Robertson and Carruthers, new edition, 80c.
Primary Latin Reader, by Robertson and Carruthers, 40c.
Cicero in Catilinam, 48c.
Cicero, Pro Archia, 56c.
Virgil's Æneid, Book II.—Notes by Henderson and Hagarty, 28c.
Virgil's Æneid, Book II.—Notes by Rev. A. J. Church, 35c.
Kelly's Key to Virgil's Æneid, 40c.
Dr. Giles' Interlinear Key to Virgil's Æneid, 72c.
Horace Odes—
Books I., II., III., IV., 28c each.
Livy, XXI., 28c.

Music—
Educational Music Course, Books I. and II., 8c each; III. and IV., 12c each.
High School Music Reader, 60c.

Physics—
High School Physical Science, Part I., 40c; Part II., 60c.
Supplement to High School Physical Science, 28c.
Introduction to Physical Science, 85c.
Physical Science Note Book, 20c, post 5c extra.

Reading Books—
Modern Phonic Primer, 12c.
Ontario First Primer, 8c.
" Second Primer, 12c.
" " Reader, 18c.
" Third " 24c.
" Fourth " 32c.
Companion to Fourth Reader, 40c.
High School Reader, 48c.
Notes to High School Reader, 40c.
Wells' & Sykes' Notes to High School Reader, 25c.
Canadian First Primer, 6c.
" Second " 8c.
" New First Book, 20c.
" Second Reader, 24c.
" Third " 32c.
" Fourth " 40c.
" Fifth " 48c.

20th Century Edition—
Canadian First Primer, 12c.
" First Reader, 28c.
" Second " 32c.
" Third " 32c.
" Fourth " 40c.

Spelling Books—
High School Word Book, 40c.
Public School Word Book, 24c.
Practical Speller, 20c.

Trigonometry—
Hamblin-Smith's, 60c.
Locke's Trigonometry, 80c.
Hall and Knight's Elementary, 80c.
High School Trigonometry, $1.15.

Zoology—
Colton's Practical Zoology, 75c.
High School Zoology, 60c.

Mythology—
Bullfinch's Age of Fable, or Beauties of Mythology. Klapp, $1.10.
Murray's Manual of Mythology, revised. W. H. Klapp, $1.10.

Shorthand—
The Phonographic Teacher, 15c.
Key Phonographic Teacher, 15c.
Manual of Phonography, 45c.
Phonographic Reader, 15c.
" Reporter, 50c
" Dictionary, $1.25.
" " pocket edition, 65c.
Complete Phono. Instructor, $1.25.
Key to complete Phonographic Instructor, 40c.

Teachers' Aids—
Fitche's Lectures on Teaching, 80c.
McLellan's Applied Psychology, 80c.
Sinclair's First Year at School, 40c.
Steps in the Phonic System, 40c.
Millar's School Management, 80c.
Houghton's Physical Culture, 40c.
How Canada is Governed. Bourinot, 90c.
Quick's Educational Reformers, $1.25.
Psychology. Baldwin. $1.25.
Education of Man. Froebel, $1.25.
Education from a National Standpoint, $1.25.
Psychology of Number. McLellan and Dewey, $1.25.
Parker's How to Study Geography, $1.25.
Froebel's Educational Laws for Teachers. By Hughes, $1.25.
Teaching Language Arts. Hinsdale, 85c.
Education of the Greek People. Davidson, $1.25.
Old Regime in Canada, under Louis XIV. Parkman, $1.25.
Mottoes and Commentaries of Froebel's Mother Play. Susan E. Blow, $1.25.
Songs and Music of Froebel's Mother Play. Blow, $1.25.
Winners in Life's Race. A. B. Buckley, $1.25.
Life and Her Children. A. B. Buckley, $1.25.
Principles and Practice of Teaching. By Johonnot, $1.25.
La Salle. By Parkman, $1.25.
Methods in Teaching. By J. J. Tilley, $1.25.
History of Education. By Painter, $1.25.
Study of the Child. By Taylor, $1.00.
Canadian Citizenship. By Millar, 50c.
Infant Mind. By Preyer, 85c.
Outline Study of Man. By Mark Hopkins, $1.00.
Symbolic Education. By Blow, $1.25.
The Study of Children. By Francis Warner, $1.10.
Intellectual and Moral Development of the Child. By Compayre, $1.25.
History of Education. By Levi Seeley, $1.10.
Anglo-Saxons and Others. By Aline Gorren, $1.10.
The Art of Study. By Hinsdale, 85c.
Teaching of Elementary Mathematics. By D. E. Smith, 85c.
Animal Life. By Jordan and Kellogg, $1.05.

School Maps.

Size 4 x 5 feet, beautifully colored, mounted on cloth rollers, and varnished. Express extra.

Dominion, $3.25. Hemispheres, $3.25.
Ontario, $3.25.
Europe, $3.25. Mercator's World, $3.25.
Asia, $3.25.
Africa, $3.25. England, $3.25.
Scotland, $3.25.
North America, $3.25. Ireland, $3.25.
Australia, $3.25.
South America, $3.25. United States, $3.25.

Numeral frames, size 8 x 11, 100 balls, 35c. Size 9 x 12, 144 balls, 50c.

"Excelsior" Globes.

Express Extra.

Globe, 6-inch, plain, height 10 inches, wood stand, 90c.
Globe, 9-inch, plain, height 16 inches, bronze stand, $3.75.
Globe, 9-inch, meridian, height 17 inches, bronze stand, $4.75.
Globe, 12-inch, plain, height 20 inches, bronze stand, $5.00.
Globe, 12-inch, meridian, height 21 inches, bronze stand, $6.25.
Globe, 12-inch, plain, height 24 inches, on bronzed plain iron stand, with incline axis, $7.50.
Globe, 9-inch, complete stand, with nickel meridian divided into half-degrees, horizon and hour circle, height 19 inches, $9.00.
Globe, 12-inch, complete, height 18 inches, $8.75.

Atlases.

Imperial Atlas, cloth cover, 65c.
Dominion and Ontario County Atlas, 10c.
Home Reference and Pocket Atlas of the World, containing 46 full-page colored maps, showing every line of railroad and all important cities and towns, size 5½ x 7 inches, 15c.

CHRISTMAS CARDS.

Postpaid.

These goods ready November 1st.

We have a large and beautiful assortment of Cards. Booklets. Calendars, etc. In ordering from price list, our best judgment will be used in selecting these goods.

Christmas cards, in packages of 1 doz, 10c, 15c, 25c, 35c, 50c package.

Fancy leaflet Christmas cards, 10 in box, 25c, 35c, 50c a box.

Fancy leaflet Christmas cards, handsome designs, 3c, 5c, 8c, 10c, 12½c, 15c, 20c, 25c each.

SCRIPTURE TEXT CARDS.

Fancy text cards for Sunday Schools, 12 cards in package, 5c, 8c, 10c pkg.

Fancy illuminated text cards for decoration, embossed, 5c, 8c, 10c, 12½c, 15c, 20c, 25c each.

Doll Sheets.

(To be cut out.)

Our Little Pets.
Children From Many Lands, 5c sheet.

Dressing Dolls.

Colonial Belles.
Dolls for all Seasons.
Our Pets, 10c pkg.

Booklets.

Fancy booklets, in packages of 1 doz, 25c pkg.

5 cents.

Booklets, 5 assorted titles.

8 cents.

15 assorted titles.

Kitty's Greeting.
Serving Others.
Sunrise.
Evening Prayer, etc.

10 cents.

10 assorted titles.

Thoughts and Greetings.
The Message of Flowers.
Christmas Music.
Faith, Hope, Charity, etc.

12½ cents.

8 assorted titles.

The Christmas Holly.
The Lord is My Shepherd.
The Beatitudes, etc.

15 cents.

14 assorted titles.

Christmas Merriment.
Sweet Memories.
Gliding Time.
Village Blacksmith, etc.

20 cents.

5 assorted titles.

Softly Now the Lights.
God be With You.
The Heavenly Guest.

25 cents.

I Heard the Voice.
Soldiers of Christ.
Psalm of Life.

30 cents.

5 assorted titles.

Heaven Light.
Christmas Wishes.
Lead, Kindly Light.

40 cents.

5 assorted titles.

Gray's Elegy.
Links of Friendship
Friendship's Message.

$1.00

Gleanings from the Poets.

CALENDARS.

Postpaid.

Block calendars, for fancy work, 1c, 2c, 3c each.

Block calendars, with monthly pad, 10c each.

Block calendar, with leaf and quotations for every day of the year, 20c, 30c each.

Fancy pocket calendars, 3c, 5c each.

Fancy booklet, calendars, 20c, 25c, 40c, 50c each.

Fan-shaped calendars, 15c, 20c, 35c, 50c each.

Drop Calendars.

5 cents.

7 assorted titles.

8 cents.

I Need Thee.
Day Unto Day.
Bible Gems.
Sweet Peeping Faces.
Doggie.

10 cents.

Loving Messages.
Bright Flowers.
Joyful Years, etc.

12½ cents.

10 assorted titles

Sacred Reveries.
Divine Message.
The Medallion Calendar.
Spring Voices, etc.

15 cents.

8 assorted titles.

The Gem.
Pansy Calender.
Feathered Folks.
Bird and Cat Calendar, etc.

20 cents.

9 assorted titles.

Garlands of Thought.
Fleeting Days.
Hopeful Days.
Cat Calendar, etc.

25 cents.

10 assorted titles.

Divine Light.
Heavenly Light.
The Blossoming Year.
Gem Calendar.
Garlands of Daisies, etc.

30 cents.

Little Messengers, novelty drop.

35 cents.

Floral Calendar.
The Sportsman.

40 cents.

American Beauties.
The Ivy Gem.
Art and Nature.

50 cents

7 assorted titles.

Garland Calendar.
Feathered Favorites.
Peace.
Heavenly Light, etc.

75 cents.

Pansy-land.
Quiet Resting Place.
Fan-shaped calendar, 20c, 25c, 35c, 50c, 75c.

Overturn Calendars.

5 cents.

Assorted floral designs, etc.

10 cents.

10 assorted titles.

Remembrance.
Abide With Me.
Forget-me-not.
Days of Fortune, etc.
Ever True, novelty.

12½ cents.

Heavenly Praise.
Golden Truths.
Scripture Melody.

15 cents.

6 assorted titles.

Little Charmers.
Cross of Christ.
The Twenty-third Psalm.

20 cents.

5 assorted titles.

Spring Charmers.
Sunny Memories.
Faithful Promise, etc.

25 cents.

8 assorted titles.

Memory Gems.
Glad Tidings.
Joy Bells.
Home Pets, etc.

30 cents.

Fleeting Year.
Nature's Gems.
Primroses and Violets.
Thro' the Seasons.
My Times are, etc.

35 cents.

6 assorted titles.

Violets.
Century Bells, novelty.
Christmas Chimes, novelty.
Under the Mistletoe "

40 cents.

Words of Wisdom.
Christian Graces.
Day Unto Day.
Sunshine in all Seasons.

50 cents.

14 assorted titles.

A Violet Offering Wreath, novelty.
Season's Greeting.
Little Gems, novelty.
Christmas Cheer.
Violets Blue, etc.

60 cents.

He Calleth for You.
Fine Art.
Pleasant memories.

75 cents.

7 assorted titles.

Light of the World.
Fra Angelico.
Heavenly Guidance.
Happy Days, etc.

85 cents.

10 assorted titles.

Beauty's Crown.
Longfellow.
Forget-me-not.
Floral Calendar.
The Ideal, etc.

$1.00.

Nature's Haunts.
In Days of Old.

$1.25.

Gems of Beauty.

$1.35.

The Beauty Calendar.
The Bachelor.
Sports and Pastimes.

$1.50.

The Elite.
The Murillo.

$1.75.

Fleet-Footed Friends.

Photo Frames.

Our leading novelty, an artistic line of picture frames, with removable calendars, embossed with daisies, roses, violets, etc, 25c.

Miscellaneous Novelties.

Card blotters, size 6 x 8, with calendar attached, 20c each.

Satin bookmarks, in assorted colors, printed with favorite poems, etc., 25c each.

Bookmarks, hand painted on ivorine, mounted on ribbon, or all ribbon, size 2 x 12, 50c each.

Banners, printed on heavy satin ribbon, delicate shades, size 5 x 12, with selections from different poets (in box), 50c each.

Wall Roll. Links of light containing 31 lines, with different quotations for every day of the month, size 13 x 20 inches, 60c each.

Office Diaries for 1902.

Postage extra.

Long cap, ½ bound, marble sides, 13 x 4¼, 50c.

Broad 4to, 3 days to page, ½ bound, marble sides, 50c.

Broad 4to, 2 days to page, ½ bound, marble sides, 65c.

Broad 4to, 1 day to page, ½ bound, marble sides, $1.10.

Broad 4to, 2 days to page, cloth sides, 75c.

Cap folio, 2 days to page, cloth sides, extra, 13 x 8¼, $1.25.

Scribbling diary, cap folio, week to page, Sunday, 13 x 8, 40c.

Pocket diaries, 15c, 20c, 25c, 35c, 50c, to $1.00 each.

Fancy Ink Bottles and Stands.

Postage Extra.

Heavy glass ink bottles, 10c, 15c, 25c, 35c, 45c, 50c each.

Safety travelling ink wells, in leather, 25c, 35c, 45c, 50c each.

Fancy ink stands, gold mounted, 50c to $2.00 each.

Fancy inkstands, in bronze, 25c, 50c, 65c, 90c to $1.50 each.

Fancy blotters, imitation leather cover, 25c each.

Leather writing portfolios, 75c, $1.00, 1.25, 1.50, 2.00, 2.50 to 5.00 each.

Desk pads, leather corners, 2 ft x 1 ft 7 inches, $1.00; 1 ft 7 inches x 1 ft, 75c; 1 ft 2 inches x 8½ inches, 50c ea.

Scrap Albums.

Postage Extra.

Scrap albums, bound in cloth, 35c, 45c, 60c, 65c, 75c each.

Scrap albums, board cover, 25c each.

Postage Stamp Albums.

Postage Extra.

Scott's International Stamp Album, bound in cloth, gilt decorations; this album contains spaces for all varieties ever issued by any nation; portraits of rulers; flags, arms of every nation, together with valuable information regarding their size, population, capitals, etc., illustrated with over 4,000 engravings, $3.50 each.

Scott's International Stamp Album, containing spaces for every known issue by any nation, also blank pages for future issues, advanced 1901 edition, giving color, date of issue and value of stamps, $2.50 each.

Scott's International Stamp Album, bound in boards, half cloth, containing 4,000 engravings, complete advanced edition up to 1901, giving value, color and date of issue, $1.50 each.

Also we have in stock Scott's complete catalogue of stamps, 60c each.

Stamp hinges or stickers, 10c per 1,000.

The International Postage Stamp Album, published in three languages, providing for 11,082 postage stamps, cards, envelopes, etc., with 1 map, $1.00 each.

The International Stamp Album, containing 3,330 spaces for all varieties of postage stamps, and giving date of issue, value and color of each stamp, illustrated with 1,816 engravings of stamps, 78 of arms, 105 watermarks, 43 portraits of regents, 50c each.

Illustrated Postage Stamp Album, containing 2,139 engravings of stamps, 79 arms and 49 portraits, 35c each.

Illustrated Postage Stamp Album, containing 1,860 engravings of stamps, 57 watermarks, 69 arms and 24 portraits, 25c each.

Unmounted Photo Albums.

Postage Extra.

Unmounted photo books, bound in cloth, size 6 x 7 inches, 25c; 8 x 9 inches, 40c each.

Star plain leaf albums for unmounted photographs, in full cloth binding, colors black or drab, containing 25 leaves, size 5½ x 7 inches, 45c each.

In imitation seal grain leather binding, colors blue, green and red, size 5½ x 7 inches, containing 25 leaves, 65c each.

In imitation seal grain leather, colors black, red and green, size 5½ x 7 inches, containing 50 leaves, 75c each.

In full cloth binding, colors black or drab, size 7 x 10 inches, containing 50 leaves, 90c each.

In imitation seal grain leather, colors red, green or black, size 7 x 10 inches, containing 25 leaves, 90c each.

In imitation seal grain leather, colors red, green or black, containing 50 leaves, size 7 x 10 inches, $1.15 each.

In full seal leather binding, size 5½ x 7 inches, colors black or red, containing 50 leaves, $1.15 each.

In full seal grain leather binding, size 7 x 10 inches, colors black or red, containing 50 leaves, $1.65 each.

Deckle albums for unmounted views, size 8 x 10 inches, 65c; 11 x 13, 90c each.

Photo Albums.

Postage Extra.

Leather album, gilt or floral decorations, containing 14 cabinets and 16 visites, 50c each.

Leather album, containing 24 cabinets and 16 visites, spring clasp, 75c each.

Celluloid album, with or without floral decorations, containing 24 cabinets and 16 visites, 75c each.

Leather albums, containing 25c abinets and 16 visites, spring clasp, $1.00 each.

Celluloid albums, with plush, containing 20 cabinets and 15 visites, $1.00 each.

Leather albums, in the long shape, containing 24 cabinets and 16 visites, $1.25 each.

Leather albums, in either long or square shape, with or without floral decorations, containing 24 cabinets and 16 visites, $1.50 each.

Celluloid albums, plush back, gilt decorations, containing 24 cabinets and 16 visites, $1.50 each.

Leather albums, with floral decorations, leather cover, containing 28 cabinets and 16 visites, $2.00 each.

Leather albums, raised leather decorations, containing 24 cabinets and 16 visites, $2 50 each.

Leather albums, containing 32 cabinets and 16 visites, $3.00 each.

Leather albums, with gilt or raised leather decorations, containing 28 cabinets and 16 visites, $4.00 each.

Stationery.

POSTAGE EXTRA.
For postage add 5c for each quire of paper, and 4c for each package of envelopes.
These goods go far cheaper by sending with other goods by express or freight.

Whiting's linen or vellum paper, in cream or blue, pkg of 5 quires, 25c; envelopes to match, 5c.

No.			Paper per Quire.	Envelopes per pkt.
28	Crane's extra superfine,	60 lb. white wove,	18c	18c.
63	" parchment vellum,	70 " cream,	20c	20c.
65½	Hurd's Irish linen	54 " "	10c	10c.
	Whiting's French Organdie, grey and blue Lakewood,		20c	20c.
	Whiting's French Organdie, grey and blue Vassar,		15c	15c.
194	Hurd's satin wove,	60 lb, cream,	10c	10c.
391	Crane's superfine,	60 " pink,	15c	15c.
413	" Venetian repp,	60 " "	18c	18c.
194	" satin wove.	miniature,	10c	10c.
711	" linen lawn, Dresden white Douglas,		20c	20c.
711	" " "	" Astoria.	15c	15c.
	Eatonia note, fine vellum, plain,		5c	5c.
303	Note paper, cream, ruled, or plain (5-quire, 25c),		5c	5c.
125½	Hurd's Egyptian linen,	12 lb, cream,	8c	10c.
404	Note, commercial, ruled or plain,		6c	7c.
	London Grey paper, 8vo and billet sizes,		7c	8c.
	Silurian (mottled grey), 8vo, plain and billet		5c	5c.
	Foreign note paper,		5c	10c.
	Mourning note, 8vo, plain, narrow, middle broad, extra broad and double broad,		7c	8c.
	London grey, black bordered, as above,		10c	10c.

Fancy Papeteries.

Postage Extra.

Fancy boxes of stationery, in newest shapes and tints, 15c, 20c, 25c, 35c, 50c, 75c, $1.00, 1.25, 1.50 each.

Typewriting Papers and Supplies.

Postage extra.

Heavy linen laid, $1.00 per ream; 5c quire.
Berkshire linen wove, 75c per ream.
Extra super wove, 60c per ream.
No. 1 Carbon paper, $4.25 per 100 sheets, or 60c doz.
Ribbons, all colors, 80c each, postpaid.

Foolscap paper, 10c quire.
Legal Cap, 15c quire.
Sermon paper, 8c quire; 35c package
Paper wrappers, 50 in book, 12½c.
Butter paper, 50c ream.
Music paper, 35c quire.
Blotting paper, 2 sheets for 5c, or 50c quire.

Envelopes.

Envelopes, No. 4, square, good paper, 250 in box, 25c box.
" " 7, white wove, good paper, 500 in box, $1.00 per 1,000.
" " 7, " " " " 500 " 70c per 1,000.
" " 7, " " " " 2c pkg, 40c box of 500.

Printing.

Envelopes, per 250, $1.00; per 500, $1.15; per 1,000, $1.25.
Letterheads, size 11 x 8, printed and padded complete, per 100, $1.40; per 500, $1.95; per 1,000, $2.65.
Billheads, size 8 x 5, printed and padded, per 100, $1.10; per 500, $1.80; per 1,000, $2.00.

Card Engraving.

With your order for Note Paper and Envelopes, send us your Initial (single letter), which you can have embossed, in any of three styles, viz., Script, Old English or Rustic letters, for 7 cents per quire and 7 cents per package for envelopes. This quotation is for 1 package of paper (5 quires) and three packages of envelopes. Smaller quantities will be 10 cents per quire and 10e per package for envelopes.

Postage, 1 cent per oz. extra.

Crest, $2.25.
Crest and motto, $4.00 to 6.00.

Engraving—
Card plate, name only, 50c.
Card plate, Mr. and Mrs., name only, 65c.
Each additional name, 50c.
Day or address, each 25c.

Gents' superfine thick or thin visiting cards (50 in box), 10c box.
Ladies' superfine thick or thin visiting cards (50 in box), 15c and 20c box.

Mrs. Smith

7 Elm St. *Friday*

James Smith

Lithographing 50 cards from plate, ladies' or gents' (not including cards), 35c; 100 cards, 70c.

Embossing—
Under 5 quires, 12½c per quire.
From 5 quires to ½ ream, 9c per quire.
Envelopes, 9c per package.

Gold stamping—
30c per quire; $4.50 per ream.
Plates and dies delivered to customers.

Monograms, two or three letters, $2.00.

Wedding cabinets, containing not less than 50 complete invitations, including printing, $2.50, 2.75 each (printing only, $1.25 each). We do not print less than 50 invitations.
Quotations for engraving wedding invitations given on application.
You can have your name printed almost as good as engraving. We do not engrave or print less than 50 cards.

Robert G. Rawes

50 cards (cards and name printed), ladies' or gents', 50c; 100 cards, 90c.
Postage on 50 cards, 5c extra; on 100 cards, 10c extra.

Wedding cake boxes, 3½x2½-in, 40c doz
" " " 4½x2-in, 50c "

Invitation Cards.

Plain invitation cards, 60c per 100.
Printed at-home cards, $1.00 per 100.
Envelopes to match, 20c per 100.

Tissue Papers.

Fine crepe tissue, in all shades, 10c roll.
Plain tissue paper, white, 15c quire; colored, 20c quire.
Shelf paper, perforated and scalloped, in pink, blue, green, yellow and white, 10 yards in piece, 5c.
Fancy crepe paper for lamp shades, 25c roll.
Eaton's royal wax, box of 5 sticks, assorted, 20c box, or 5c stick
Letter seals for wax, 15c each.

Writing Tablets.

Postage on tablets, 1 cent per oz.

	Each	Postage extra.
Writing tablets, 80 sheets, small, ruled or plain, blotter cover,	5c	6c.
" 100 " " " " " " "	7c	8c.
" 100 " " " " card cover and blotter	10c	10c.
" 100 " large, " " blotter cover,	15c	18c.
" 100 " " " " India linen, blotter cover	13c	14c.
" 100 " " plain Oxford linen, card cover and blotter,	20c	16c.
" 100 " " plain linen,	25c	14c.
" 80 " " plain olde parchment bond, white,	25c	12c
" 80 " " overland white,	25c	14c.
" 80 " " parchment cream,	25c	18c.
" 80 " " bond white,	25c	14c.
" 60 " " silurian grey,	15c	10c.

Exercise Books and Scribblers.

	Each.	Postage extra.
Exercise books, 84 pages, fine manilla cover, 2 for 5c	..	3c ea
Exercise books, 84 pages, press board cover	5c	4c
" " 150 " cloth cover	10c	6c
¼ bound, good paper, marginal line board	10c	8c
½ leather bound, good paper, marginal line,	25c	12c
Scribblers, 200 pages, press board cover (3 for 5c)	2c	4c
Scribblers, 300 pages, press board cover,	5c	9c
Reporters' note book, press board cover, oblong, 152 pages, 2 for 5c	..	3c
Reporters' note book, press board cover, oblong, 164 pages	5c	3c

Day Books, Journals, etc.

Postage extra.

Calf, half rough sheep, well bound, 20c per 100 pages; smallest size, 200 pages.
Counter books, from 5c to 25c, best value.
Pass books, 2 for 5c, 5c and 10c each.
500 page letter copying books, 90c.
1000 " " " " " 1.35.
Duplicate or triplicate order books, 40c each.
Refiles for order books, 20c pad.
Weekly, fortnightly or monthly time-books, 5c each.
Index books, size 4 x 13, 10c each.
Broad index books, 8½ x 13, 20c each.
Housekeeping expense book, 15c and 25c each.
Portfolio and desk blotting book, 5c and 10c book.

Leather Covered Memos.

Vest Pocket Memos, open at side or end, 10c.
Vest Pocket Memos, with or without indexed, 2½ x 5½, 15c.
Memos, 3 x 5, open at side or end, 15c.
Memos, indexed, 3 x 5, 15c.
Memos, 4 x 6, open at side or end, 20c
Memos, 4 x 6, indexed, 25c.
Address Books, indexed, 30c, 35c, 45c.
Russian Leather, with clasp, open at end, 3 x 5 and 3½ x 5¾, $1.00 and $1.25.

Billheads and Blanks.

Billheads, pads of 100 sheets, 10c; post., 11c.
Receipt blanks, 5c, 8c, 10c pad.
Promissory note blanks, 10c for 50 blanks.
Board files, size 9 x 14¼, 25c and 35c each.
Shannon board files, complete, with perforator and index, $1.00.
Indices for board files, 4c each.
Bill file hooks, 8c and 10c each.
Bill stick files, 8c and 10c each.
Bill clips, 5c, 10c, 12½c, 15c, 25c each.
Pen racks, 10c each.
Stephen's qt bottle writing fluid, 70c.
" pt " " 45c.
" ½ pt " " 25c.
" ¼ pt " " 10c.
Stephen's copying inks, 25c, 50c, 75c bottle.
Red inks, 5c, 10c bottle.
Mucilage, 5c, 10c, 15c bottle.
Paste, 5c bottle.
Paste in tubes, 5c, 10c tube.
Le Pages liquid glue, 8c, 10c bottle.
" " " in tins, 15c. 25c, 45c tin.
2½ oz letter balances, 15c.
4 " " " " 25c.
8 " " " " 35c.
12 " " " " 50c.
18 " " " " 65c.

Postage paid on the following:

Lead Pencils—
Plain cedar, 5c doz.
Pearl cedar, rubber tips, 10c doz.
Johann Faber's medium grade, 10c doz.
Faber's hexagon pencils, 10c doz.
Faber's pencils, H or HB, 20c doz.
Faber's pencils, all grades, 30c doz.
Faber's, graded, hexagon, 60c doz.
Rubber tips, at 20c, 25c and 30c doz.
Lyra graphite drawing pencils in HB, H, 2H and 3H, compressed lead, 10c each, 3 for 25c.
Colored pencils, 20c doz, or 3 for 5c.
Colored pencils, 60c doz, or 5c each.
Copying pencils in wood, for writing on glass or metal, 4c each.
Indelible copying pencils, in wood, 2 for 5c and 5c each.
Carpenters' pencils, 30c and 60c doz.
Pencil protectors, with inserted rubber tips, 2 for 5c.
Faber's pocket pencils, with nickel pencil protectors, 5c each.
Johann Faber's dermatograph pencil, for writing on the skin, 10c ea.
Slate pencils (in wood), 10c doz.
Programme pencils, assorted colors, 20c doz.
Tassels for pencils, 10c doz.

Gold Pencils and Pens—
Postpaid.
Solid gold pencils, chased or plain, $2.00, 2.50, 3.00, 3.50 each.
Pearl-handled pens, solid gold points, $1.00, 1.25, 1.50, 2.00, 2.50.
Fancy pocket pencils, 10c, 25c, 50c, 75c each.

Paper Cutters—
Pearl blades with sterling silver handles, 25c, 35c, 50c, 75c, $1.00 each.
Hard rubber paper cutters, 15c ea.
Sterling silver pencil holders, 75c, $1.00.

Pen Holders—
Faber's reversible, hard rubber, 15c, 20c, 25c each.
Faber's hard rubber holders, 12½c, 15c each.
Cork handles, 8c each.
Cork holder, with wood handle, 5c, 7c each.
Faber's enamelled cedar sticks, 5c each.
Red and black, swell holders, 30c doz.
Plain cedar, swell holders, 20c doz.
Accommodation pen holders, 5c doz.
Mapping pens (6 pens and 1 holder on card), 5c card.

Pens—
292 Eaton's, 25c gross.
292 Gillott's, 45c "
404 " 45c "
303 " 90c "
Eaton's J, 30c gross.
Mitchell's J, 75c "
Gold J, 75c "
Eaton's Falcon, 30c gross.
Esterbrook's Falcon, 75c gross.
Bank of Montreal, 30c gross.
Bank of England, 30c "
G pens, 30c gross.
Blackstone, Esterbrook, 90c gross.
Judge's quill, " 90c "
Chancellor, " 90c "
Spencerian, No. 1, 90c gross.
Relief, Esterbrook, 90c gross.
Myers' vertical writer, 45c gross.
Ball pointed pens (2½ doz in box), 20c per box.
Waverley pens, box of 1½ doz, 10c.
Pickwick pens, box of 1½ doz, 10c.

Fountain Pens—
Postpaid.
Waterman's Ideal fountain pens, $2.50, 3.50 and 4.00 each; gold mounted, $5.00.
Paul E. Wirt's gold mounted fountain pens, $2.75 and 3.25 ea.
Wirt's No. 1, fine, medium or stub points, $1.50.
Britannia fountain pen, $1.25.
Eagle fountain pen, $1.00.

Thumb tacks, 15c and 20c doz.
Paper fasteners, No. 1, 10c gross.
" No. 2, 15c "
Eagle compass and divider, 25c each.
Compasses, with pencils attached, 10c each.
Compass sets, at 25c, 35c, 50c set.
Rulers, 15-inch, brass edge, 19c each.
Rulers, 12-inch, brass edge, 8c each.
Rulers, 12-inch, plain edge, 5c each.
Rulers, 12-inch, plain edge, 2c each.
Jensin's marking ink, requires no heating, 20c bottle.
Melanye marking ink, requires no heating, 20c.
Payson's indelible marking ink, 20c bottle.
Pencil sharpeners, 3c and 8c each.
Faber's brass pencil sharpener, with reversible knife, 15c each.

Rubber Bands—
Thread, No. 9, 12, 15,
10c, 10c, 10c box.
⅛-inch, 0¼, 00¼, 000¼,
8c, 10c, 15c doz.
¼-inch 0¼, 00¼, 000¼, 0000¼,
12½c, 15c, 20c, 25c doz.
Per pound, boxes, $3.00, all sizes or assorted.
Assorted boxes Faber's bands, 25c box.
Colored oil mapping crayons, 5c and 8c box.
Colored pencils, in wood, 6 in box, 5c.

Rubber Erasers—
Bevel, 1c, 2c, 3c and 5c each.
Circular, 5c each.
Circular eraser, with brush, 8c ea.
Ink and pencil, 8c each.
E. Faber's kneaded eraser, 5c and 8c each.
Typewriter's erasers, 5c and 8c each.

Postage extra on the following:

Slates, bound, 5 x 7, 8c; 6 x 9, 10c; 7 x 11, 12c each.
Slate pencils in boxes of 100, each, 10c box.

White chalk, 10c box.
Colored chalk, 30c and 60c gross box.
Blackboard erasers, 7c and 9c each.
Rubber stamps, made to order, with name or name and address, 50c and 75c each.
Stamping outfits at 25c, 75c each.
Self-inking stamp-pads, 20c, 25c each.

Pencil Boxes.

Postage Extra.

Pencil cases, 5c, 10c, 15c, 20c, 25c each.
Pencil cases, filled with pens, pencils, etc., 25c each.

SCHOOL BAGS.

Postage extra on the following sundries:

Sheepskin bags, 25c, 30c, 35c, 40c, 45c each.
Canvas bags, 35c, 45c each.
Grain leather bags, with strap or handle, in tan, olive or black, 75c each.

Music Books.

NOT EXCHANGED. POSTAGE EXTRA.

INSTRUMENTAL.

Universal Piano Folio, latest collection of Standard Piano Solos, 62 pieces, board covers, 60c; post., 15c extra.

Coronet Folio, 49 pieces, for piano or organ, 50c; post., 10c extra.

Imperial Folio, 63 pieces, piano or organ, 50c; post, 10c. extra.

Royal Crown Folio, 71 pieces, piano or organ, 50c; post., 10c extra.

Royal Folios of Music, Nos. 1, 2 and 3, for piano or organ, each 50c; post., 10c.

Royal March and Two-Step Folio, a collection of 32 popular marches and two-steps, 40c; post., 5c extra.

Royal Pearls, easy for piano or organ, 40c; post., 9c extra.

Ruby Series, easy, 10 books, each, 20c; post., 3c extra.

Superb Folio, popular selections for piano, 50c; post., 9c extra.

Church Voluntaries for Organ or Harmonium, containing 48 select voluntaries, 50c; post., 5c extra.

Ten Church Voluntaries for Organ or Harmonium, new, 25c; post., 3c extra.

Wicken's College Album, containing waltzes, schottisches, polkas, lancers, two-steps, etc., 25c; post., 4c extra.

Wicken's College Album, very easy pieces, piano or organ, for little players, 25c; post., 4c extra.

Classic Folios, Vols. 1, 2 and 3, three collections of good classical music, each $1.00; post., 10c extra.

Balmoral Reel Book, contains over 100 Highland schottisches, reels, strathspeys, 50c; post., 5c extra.

VOCAL.

The Universal Song Folio, just published, containing 83 of the most popular songs and duets, board covers, 60c; post., 11c extra.

Globe Song Folio, largest collection of standard songs, paper cover, 60c; post., 12c extra.

Century Folio, choice collection of standard vocal and instrumental music, paper cover, 65c; post., 12c extra.

New Songs of University of Toronto, paper cover, 70c; post., 7c extra; cloth, 95c; post., 15c extra.

Favorite Song Folio, Nos. 1, 2, 3, 4, 5, and comic, each containing between 70 and 75 popular songs. 35c each; post., 7c extra.

American Song Folio, words and music, 50c; post., 10c extra.

Gems of Scottish Song, 215 Scotch songs, with portrait of Burns, 90c; post., 15c extra.

110 Scotch Songs, popular Scottish songs, with music, 50c; post., 5c extra.

Royal Song Folio, contains 107 songs, 50c; post., 10c extra.

University of Toronto Song Book, contains 148 choruses, glees, etc., paper, 75c; post., 7c extra; cloth, $1.00; post., 12c extra.

Canadian Patriotic Songs, including "The Land of the Maple," 25c; post., 2c extra.

Superb Song Folio, containing 54 new songs, with music, 50c; post., 10c extra.

120 Scotch Songs, a new collection, 50c; post., 5c extra.

Cheerful Voices, 27 action and primary songs, 40c; post., 5c extra.

Sacred Song Folio, 57 popular sacred songs, 50c; post., 5c extra.

Francis & Day's Comic Annual for 1902, contains 17 comic songs, 35c; post., 4c extra.

Merry Little Tunes - Children's Nursery Rhymes, music and words, 25c; post., 3c extra.

INSTRUCTION BOOKS.

Bellak's New Method for Piano, paper cover, 25c; post., 3c extra; board cover, 40c; post., 6c extra.

Bellak's Improved Piano Method, No. 2, paper cover, 30c; post., 3c extra; board cover, 40c; post., 6c extra.

Bellak's Ideal Method for Piano, paper cover, 35c; post., 3c extra; board cover, 50c; post., 6c extra.

Gurlitt's Pianoforte Method, paper, 60c; post., 4c extra; boards, 75c; post., 6c extra. Foreign and American fingering.

Richardson's New Method for Piano, board cover, $1.25; post., 10c extra.

Sydney Smith's Method for Piano, board cover, 65c; post., 8c extra; paper cover, 50c; post., 4c extra.

Wicken's Rapid Method for Piano, 50c; post., 5c extra. Foreign and American fingering.

Bellak's Improved Organ Method, No. 2, paper, 30c; post., 3c extra; board, 40c; post., 6c extra.

Getz's Organ Method, paper, 35c; post., 5c; boards, 45c; post., 7c extra.

Louis Plaidy's Technical Studies, foreign and American fingering, 65c; post., 8c extra.

Czerny's 101 Preparatory Studies, Books 1 and 2 combined, 40c; post., 5c extra.

Matthews' Graded Studies, 10 books, each 75c; post., 5c extra.

Pipe Organ Method, by Dr. Stainer, 50c; post., 5c extra.

Otto Langey's Methods for all String and Brass Instruments, 75c; post., 7c extra.

Winner's Violin and Guitar Methods, each, 25c; post., 3c extra.

Winner's Banjo, Accordion, Concertina, Cornet, Flute, Fife, Clarionet Methods, each, 30c; post., 3c extra.

Violin, A Complete Instructor, by Tours, 50c; post., 5c extra.

Vocal Method, by Bassini, $1.00; post., 5c extra.

" " by Randegger, $1.00; post., 5c extra.

We can supply best vocal or instrumental music books as soon as published.

We carry in stock a complete collection of the

Schirmer Library of Musical Classics.

The most carefully prepared edition of the classics published. Tastefully and strongly bound, and lying flat when opened.

Our prices on these books are 40 per cent. lower than publisher's. Add 10 per cent. to publisher's price for postage.

A Few of the more Popular.

When ordering, mention No. of volumes.

No. of Vol.	TITLE.	Pub. Price	Our Price	Postage
15	Bach, 21 short Preludes and 6 Fugues, paper........	60c	36c	06c
16	Bach, 2 and 3-part Inventions (Wm. Mason), paper ..	60	36	05
1 & 2	Beethoven Sonatas (Bulow-Tebert), 2 vols., paper, each	1 50	90	25
530	Biehl, Elements of Piano Playing, Op. 30.	60	36	03
135	Bertini, 12 little Pieces and Preludes, paper..........	40	24	03
136	" Op. 100, 25 Easy Studies Without Octaves...	40	24	03
137	" Op. 29, 24 Studies............	40	24	03
138	" Op. 32, 24 Studies (a sequel to Op. 29)	40	24	03
27	Chopin, Waltzes.	50	30	08
28	" Mazurkas	1 00	60	14
30	" Nocturnes............	75	45	14
29	" Polonaises............	75	45	14
31	" Ballads and Impromptus.	75	45	14
40	Clementi, 12 Sonatinas, Op. 36, 37, 38	50	30	06
153	Czerny, Op. 139, 100 Progressive Studies without Octaves............	50	30	05
378	Czerny, Op. 261, Exercises in Passage Playing	50	30	05
161	" Op. 299, The School of Velocity, complete ...	60	36	05
148	" Op. 636, Preliminary School of Fingering ..	50	30	05
146	Czerny, Practical Method for Beginners............	50	30	05
154	" The Art of Finger Dexterity, complete......	1 25	75	07
325	Gurlitt, Album for the Young	75	45	04
176	Heller, Op. 45, 25 Melodious Studies	1 00	60	09
178	" Op. 47, 25 Studies from Rythm and Expression	1 00	60	09
170	Herz, Scales and Exercises............	50	30	04
317	Kohler, Op. 50, First Studies	50	30	04
318	" Op. 157, The Easiest Studies............	50	30	04
52 & 53	Kuhlau, Sonatinas, 2 vols., each	50	30	04
341	Liszt, Consolations and Liebestraume....	50	30	04
310, 311, 312	Loeschhorn, Op. 65, for beginners, Vogrich, 3 books, each	50	30	04
58	Mendelssohn, Songs without Words............	1 00	60	12
65	Mozart, 19 Sonatas (Lebert)	2 00	1 20	28
75	Schubert, Impromptus and Moments Musicals......	1 00	60	14
90	Schumann, Album for the Young, Op. 68, and Scenes from Childhood, Op. 15	50	30	04
91	Schumann, Album for the Young. 43 pieces, Op. 68 ..	40	24	03
51	Sonatina Album, 30 Sonatinas and pieces (Kohler)...	75	45	10

Publications for Four Hands.

No. of Vol.	TITLE.	Pub. Price	Our Price	Postage
371	Album. By Haydn, Mozart and others	75	45	07
372	" Four hands, by modern composers	60	36	05
186	Diabelli, Melodious Pieces on 5 notes, Op. 149........	50	30	04
188	Diabelli, Pleasures of Youth, 6 Sonatinas on 5 notes, Op. 163............	50	30	04

Violin Studies.

No. of Vol.	TITLE.	Pub. Price	Our Price	Postage
306	Kayser, Op. 20, Elementary Studies, 3 books, each...	50	30	04
230	Kreutzer, 42 Studies (E. Singer)	50	30	04
487	Mazas, Book I., Special Studies	60	36	07
364	Schradieck, Scale Studies............	75	45	07
297	Pleyel, Op. 8, 6 little duets for 2 violins............	50	30	04

Vocal Studies.

No. of Vol.	TITLE.	Pub. Price	Our Price	Postage
242	Concone, Op. 9, 50 lessons	50	30	04
247	" " 17, 40 " for Contralto............	50	30	04
248	" " 17, for Bass	50	30	04

Peters' Edition of Musical Classics.

35 per cent. off publisher's price, adding 10 per cent. off marked price for postage.

Complete Vocal Scores of Florodora, San Toy, Princess Chic, Burgomaster, Singing Girl, Runaway Girl, etc., etc., $1.85; post., 10c extra.

Theoretical Works.

Dr. Stainer's Harmony and Composition, 50c; post., 5c extra.

Text Book, by Banister, $1.00; post., 8c extra.

Musical Catechism, by Jousse, 8c; post., 3c extra.

Rudiments of Music, Cummings, 25c; post., 3c extra.

History of Music, Hunt, $1.00; post., 6c extra.

Musical Forms, Pauer, 50c; post., 5c extra.

Counterpoint and Double Counterpoint, Dr. Bridge, 50c; post., 5c extra.

Sheet Music.

SHEET MUSIC.

Lithographed on good paper with attractive title pages. Any selection in this list 5c a copy; regular price 10c.

(1c per copy extra for postage.)

Sheet Music and Music Books Not Exchanged.

VOCAL.

Answer.
Baby on the Wall.
Ben Bolt; or, Don't you Remember
Bonnie Banks of Loch Lomond.
Guide us, Guard us.
I Heard the Voice of Jesus Say.
If You Love Me Darling, Tell Me with Your Eyes.
Kiss and Let's Make Up.
My Old Kentucky Home.
My God and Father While I Stray.
Song That Reached My Heart.
There'll Come a Time.
Volunteer Organist.
Won't You Come to My Tea-Party
Yes, I'll be Your Sweetheart.

INSTRUMENTAL.

Aunt Ann's Antics, Cake Walk and Two-Step.
Blue Bells of Scotland, Variations.
Campbells are Coming "
Dance of the Brownies.
Dreamland Waltz.
High School Cadets, March.
Liberty Bell.
Manhattan Beach.
Marjorie Skirt Dance.
Narcissus.
Princess Bonnie Waltz.
Princess Royal Schottische.
Rastus on Parade, Cake Walk.
Star of the Sea.
Washington Post, March.
Wedding of the Lily and the Rose.

WE HAVE A GOOD STOCK OF 5c and 10c MUSIC —ASK FOR LIST.

10c, 3 FOR 25c } Publisher's Price, 25c.

VOCAL.

Choir Boy.
Coon, Coon, Coon.
Everything at Reilly's Must be Done in Irish Style.
I'd Like to Hear that Song Again.
Indeed.
I've a Longing in my Heart for You, Louise.
I'm Glad I Met You, Mary.
Last Roll Call.
Maple Leaf Forever.
Mother of the Girl I Love.
O Promise Me. DeKoven.
On the Old Missouri Shore.
Picture No Artist Can Paint.
Strike Up the Band, Here Comes a Sailor.

INSTRUMENTAL.

Alabama Camp Meeting.
Coon Hollow Capers, March, Two-Step.
Daughter of the Regiment, March, Two-Step.
Departure, March, Two-Step.
Love's Confession, Waltzes.
March to Pretoria.
Purple Lady, Waltzes.
Salome, Intermezzo.
Topsy's in Town, Two-Step.
When Knighthood was in Flower, Waltzes.

We carry a complete Stock of Music.

Some of the More Popular Selections.

Add 1c extra for postage to each of the following.
When ordering, please state what voice songs are required for.

VOCAL.

Title.	Composer.	Publisher's Price.	Our Price.
Always, 2 keys	Horwitz & Bowers	50	23
Asleep in the Deep, Bass and Baritone	Lambe & Petrie	50	23
Asthore, C, D, E, F, G	Trotere	60	35
Ave Maria, Cavalleria Rusticana, F, E flat, and C	Mascagni	60	25
Absence Makes the Heart Grow Fonder		50	23
Because, 2 keys	Bowers	50	23
Bird in a Gilded Cage	Von Tilzer	50	23
Calvary, C	Rodney	50	30
Calvary, A, D	Rodney	60	35
Chinee Soge Man, from San Toy		60	35
Come Love, Go Love, from Princess Chic		50	30
Creole L ve Song	E. B. Smith	50	25
Daddy, F, A	Behrend	40	25
Day by Day		50	23
Dolly Gray	Barnes	50	23
Don't You Cry, Ma Honey, E, G	A. W. Noll	50	25
Dre m, D flat, E, F, A flat	Bartlett	50	25
Dream of Paradise, E flat, F, G, A flat	Gray	60	35
Ev'ry Race has a Flag but the Coon		50	23
Fairies	Dolores	50	30
Fatal Rose of Red		50	23
Forgotten, F, A flat	Eugene Cowles	50	25
Gift, The, C, E flat	F. Behrend	75c.	45c.
Gipsy Love Song, from Fortune Teller		50	30
Good-Bye, E flat, F, G, A flat	Tosti	60	35
Guard While I Sleep	Warrington	25	15
Girl I Loved in Sunny Tennessee	Carter	50	23
Greeting to the King	Godfrey	50	23
Good-Bye, Dolly Gray		50	23
Heavenly Song, The, A and B flat, G, C	Gray	60	35
Holy City, A, B and D flat, C	Adams	75	45
I Love You, Dear, and Only You, from Burgomaster, C, F		50	25
I Can't Tell Why I Love You, But I Do	Edwards	50	23
I Want to Go To-morrow	Sully	50	23
I 'Aint Goin' to Weep No More	Von Tilzer	50	23
In the House of Too Much Trouble		50	23
In Old Madrid, A, B flat, C	Trotere	50	30
Just Because She Made Dem Goo-Goo Eyes		50	23
Kangaroo Song, from Burgomaster		50	25
Little Black Me	Chattaway	50	23
Lovelight In Your Eyes, from Princess Chic		50	30
Love's Old Sweet Song, E flat and F	Molloy	50	30
Lost Chord, F and A flat	Sullivan	50	30
Mamie, Don't You Feel Ashamie?		50	23
Mandy Lee	Chattaway	50	23
My Little Georgia Rose		50	23
My Wild Irish Rose		50	23
My Tiger Lily		50	23
My Rainbow Coon		50	23
My Dinah		50	23
My Blushing Rosie		50	23
My Moonbeam Babe		50	23
Never Alone (sacred)	Bullock	35	20
Palms, The, flat, B flat, C	Faure	50	30
Plains of Peace, D, F, G	Barnard	75	45
Pliny		50	23
Quiller Has the Brain, from Foxy Quiller		50	30
Recessional, The	De Koven	60	35
Rosary, The	Nevin	50	30
Rhoda, from San Toy		50	30
She Rests By the Suwanee River		50	23
She was Bred in Old Kentucky		50	23
Sing Me a Song of the South		50	23
Sleep, Little Baby of Mine, G, E	Dennée	50	35
Spider and the Fly		50	23
Sweet Annie Moore		50	23
Soldiers in the Park, from Runaway Girl		60	35
Stein Song, B flat, D	Bullard	50	25
Tell Me, Pretty Maiden, from Florodora		60	35
War Is A Bountiful Jade, from Princess Chic		50	30
When Reuben Comes To Town		50	23
When the Harvest Days Are Over		50	23
When You were Sweet Sixteen		50	23
Where the Sweet Magnolias Bloom		50	23

These are only a few of the more popular pieces.

INSTRUMENTAL.

Title.	Composer.	Publisher's Price.	Our Price.
Alice of old Vincennes, Waltzes		50c	23c
Ave Maria, from Cavalleria Rusticana		60	25
Blumenlied, Flower Song	Lange	50	20
Bunch of Blackberries, Two-Step	Holzmann	50	23
Charge of the Light Brigade	Paull	50	23
Chariot Race, Ben Hur	Paull	50	23
Colored Major, Two-Step	Henry	50	23
Coontown Revels, Rag Time Cake Walk		50	23
Dawn of the Century, March	Paull	50	23
Dream of Spring, Waltz	Ollerenshaw	60	35
Eli Green's Cake Walk	Koninsky	50	23
El Capitan March	Sousa	50	30
Frangesa March and Two-Step		50	30
Georgia Camp-Meeting, Cake Walk		50	23
Happy Hours in Coontown, Two-Step		50	23
Hail to the Spirit of Liberty, March	Sousa	50	30
Hands Across the Sea, March	Sousa	50	30
Hunky Dory, Two-Step		50	23
Invincible Eagle, March	Sousa	50	30
Kangaroo, Two-Step from Burgomaster		50	25
Man Behind the Gun, March	Sousa	50	30
Mendelssohn's Wedding March		50	10
Minuet, opus 14, No. 1	Paderewski	60	35
Mosquitoes on Parade, Two Step		50	23
Myosotis, Waltz		60	35
My Tiger Lily, Two-Step		50	23
Peace Forever, March		50	23
Pretoria, March	Hughes	50	23
Queen's Defenders, March and Two-Step	Musgrave	50	23
San Toy, March and Two Step		50	30
San Toy, Waltzes		75	45
Singing Girl Waltzes		75	45
Simple Aveu (Simple Confession)		50	30
Smoky Mokes, Cake Walk		50	23
Soldiers in the Park, March		60	35
Viola Waltzes	Gustin	50	23
Whistling Rufus	Mills	50	23
Zenda Waltzes	Witmark	50	23

We have the latest and most popular selections.

Butterick Patterns and Books.

A full stock of Butterick Patterns always on hand. Orders filled at once.

In sending for children's patterns, *always* send age, and for ladies' patterns always send bust measure under arm, and waist measure.

Descriptions and prices of all patterns we sell are contained in the following **FASHION BOOKS:**

DELINEATOR, 15c copy; $1.00 Year. Postpaid.

The Glass of Fashion Up-to-Date, issued monthly, 7c a copy, or 60c a year.

Metropolitan Catalogue of Fashions, published quarterly for Spring, Summer, Autumn, and Winter, 25c copy. If ordered by mail, 10c extra for postage.

Bicycle Fashions, 5c copy.

Character and Unique Fashions, 5c copy.

Metropolitan Art Series.

50c copy. Postpaid.

The Art of Modern Lace-Making.
The Art of Crocheting.
The Art of Knitting.
The Art of Drawn Work.
The Art of Garment-cutting, Fitting and Making.
Drawing and Painting.
Masquerades and Carnivals.
Wood-carving and Pyrography, or Poker Work.
Tatting and Netting.
Fancy and Practical Crochet Work.
Fancy and Practical Knitting.
Studies in Modern Lace-Making.

Metropolitan Pamphlet Series.

15c copy. Postpaid.

Uses of Crepe and Tissue Papers.
Smocking, Fancy Stitches Cross-Stitch and Darned Net Designs.
Mother and Babe: Their Comfort and Care.
Women's Clubs and Societies.
Child Life: Physical and Mental Development.
The Perfect Art of Canning and Preserving.
The Correct Art of Candy-Making at Home.
Dainty Desserts, Plain and Fancy.
Extracts and Beverages.
Bees and Bee-keeping.
Nursing and Nourishment for Invalids.
Tableaux, Charades and Conundrums.
Fancy Drills for Evening Entertainments.
The Perfect Art of Modern Dancing.
Wedding and Wedding Anniversaries.
A Manual of Lawn Tennis.
Dogs, Cats and other Pets.
Health—How to be Well and Live Long.
Birds and Bird-keeping.
The Decorative Art of Burnt Work.
Mothers, Sons and Daughters.

The Metropolitan Book Series.

Published by the Butterick Publishing Co. (Limited)

$1.00 copy. Postpaid.

Good Manners.
Social Life.
Home-making and Housekeeping.
The Pattern Cook Book.
Beauty: Its Attainment and Preservation.
The Delsarte System of Physical Culture.
Needle Craft.
Needle and Brush.
Kindergarten Papers.

Metropolitan Handy Series.

25c copy. Postpaid.

Recitations and How to Recite.
The Dining-Room and Its Appointments.
Venetian Iron Work.
Artistic Alphabets for Marking and Engrossing.
The Home: Its Selection, Management and Preservation.
Social Evening Entertainments.
Parlor Plants and Window Gardening.
Day Entertainments and other Functions.
Employments and Professions for Women.
Pleasant Pastimes for Children.
Pretty Pursuits for Children.
Art and Ecclesiastical Embroidery.
How Health Promotes Beauty.
Women's Colleges and College Life in America and Great Britain.
Modern Life in England and America.
Butterick's Correct Cookery.

No. 4794.

No. 4794. LADIES' DOUBLE-BREASTED JACKET, to be made with or without cuffs, and with the side-back seams terminating at plaits in the skirt or continued to the bottom. 1¾ yard 54 inches wide. 9 sizes; 30 to 46 inches bust. Price, 20 cents.

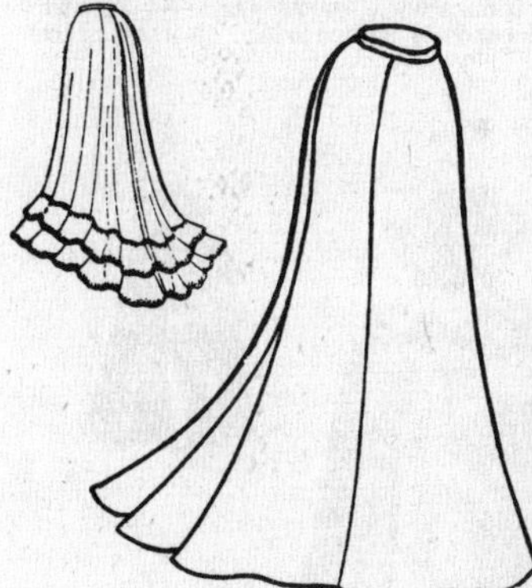

No. 4851.

No. 4851. LADIES' FIVE-GORED SKIRT, with ripple habit back; to be in sweep or round length, with one or two circular flounces or without any, and to be made with the conventional or decided dip at the top. It measures about 4½ yards at the foot in the medium sizes. The skirt with flounces, 14⅝ yards 20 inches wide, or 7 yards 50 inches wide without flounces, 8¼ yards 20 inches wide, or 4½ yards 50 inches wide. 9 sizes; 20 to 36 inches waist, 37 to 58½ inches hip. Price, 25 cents.

No. 4872.

No. 4872. LADIES' WAIST OR BODICE, with Garibaldi or plain sleeves. 1½ yard 44 inches wide, or 1⅜ yards 50 inches wide, each with 1¼ yard of satin 20 inches wide, for the vest, back-yoke, collar, puffs and wristbands, and ⅜ yard of dotted net, 45 inches wide for covering them. 8 sizes; 30 to 44 inches bust. Price, 20 cents.

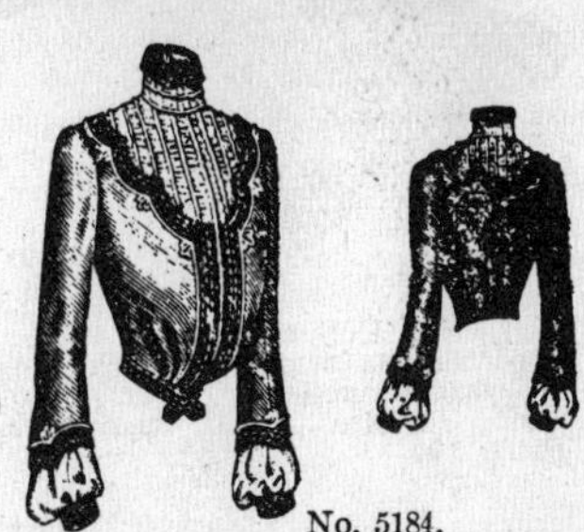

No. 5184.

No. 5184. LADIES' FANCY WAIST OR BODICE, with Garibaldi or two-seam sleeves. 30 to 42 inches bust; 7 sizes. It requires for full fronts, full back and over-sleeves, 3 yards of material 20 inches wide, or 1⅝ yard 44 inches wide, each with one yard of material 18 inches wide for collar, back yoke and yoke-vest, ⅞ yard in the same width for the puffs, and ⅜ yard of velvet (bias) for belt strap bands, turnovers, and to trim, for a lady of 34 inches bust measure. Price, 20 cents.

No. 4675.

No. 4675. LADIES' SLIGHTLY FLARED SEVEN-GORED SKIRT, with inverted box-plait at the back. (To be made with a short sweep or in round length, with or without the circular band flounce, and with the conventional or decided dip at the top.) The skirt measures about 4 yards; and the flounce about 4½ yards at the foot in the medium sizes. The skirt with the flounce of goods with figure or nap, 4½ yards; without figure or nap, 4¼ yards, each 52 inches wide. The skirt without the flounce, 4 yards with figure or nap; without figure or nap, 3½ yards, each 52 inches wide. 9 sizes; 20 to 36 inches waist, or 37 to 58½ inches hip. Price, 25 cents.

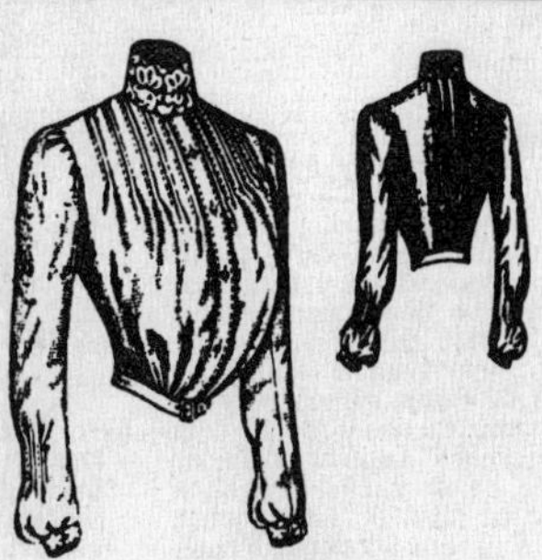

No. 5094.

No. 5094. LADIES' SHIRT WAIST OR BLOUSE, with tucked or plain Bishop sleeves, and to be made with or without fitted body and sleeve linings. For 34 inches, 2⅝ yards 36 inches wide. 9 sizes; 30 to 46 inches bust. Price, 20 cents.

No. 4402.

No. 4402.

No. 4402. LADIES' JACKETS, to have the fronts closed at the centre or over-lapped in double-breasted fashion or worn open. (Known as the *jacket sans revers.*) 4¾ yards 20 inches wide, or 3¼ yards 27 inches wide, or 2 yards 44 inches wide, 1⅝ yard 54 inches wide. 9 sizes; 30 to 46 inches bust. Price, 20 cents.

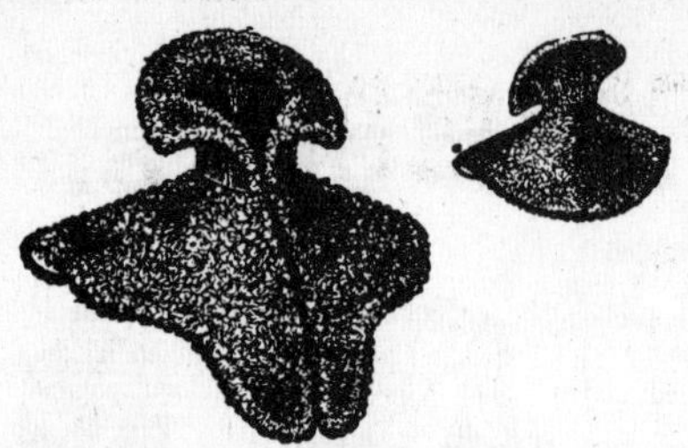

No. 3331

3331. Ladies' Collarette. For medium size, 1¾ yard 20 inches wide, or 1¼ yard 30 inches wide, or ⅝ yard 40 inches wide, or ⅜ yard 54 inches wide. 3 sizes, small, medium and large. Price, **10c.**

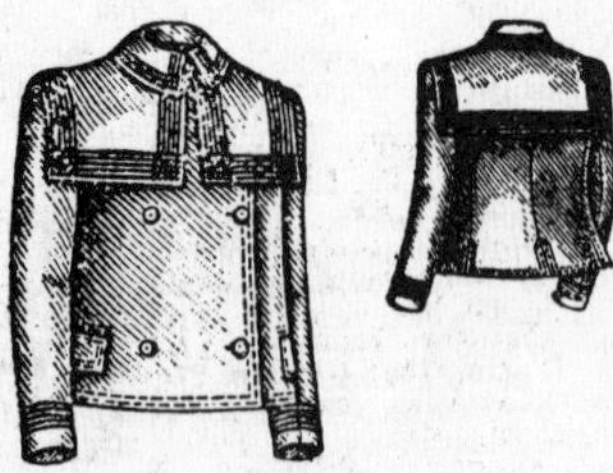

No. 3769.

3769. Child's Double-Breasted Jacket, with sailor collar (known as the sacque reefer), 3 yards 20 inches wide, or 2⅛ yards 27 inches wide, or 1⅝ yards 36 inches wide, or 1⅛ yards 54 inches wide. 8 sizes; 1 to 8 years. Price, **15c.**

No. 4581

4581. Ladies' Double-Breasted Coat or Jacket, with Medici-flare or military turn-down collar. 5 yards 20 inches wide, or including for strappings, 2½ yards 54 inches wide, with ⅞ yards of satin 20 inches wide for inlaying the collar and revers. 8 sizes, 30 to 44 inches, bust. Price, **20c.**

No. 5172

5172. Ladies' Jacket, with square or round lower front corners; to be worn open or snugly closed with visible buttons or a fly. For 34 inches, 2⅞ yards 27 inches wide, or 1¾ yards 44 inches wide, or 1½ yard 54 inches wide. 8 sizes, 32 to 46 inches, bust. Price, **20c.**

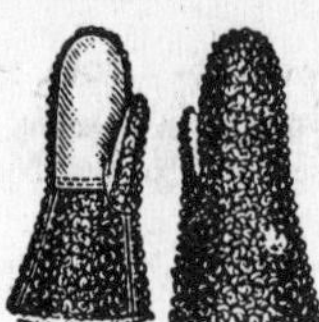

1260. Pattern for a Gauntlet Mitten, 5 sizes. Hand measures, 5 to 9 inches. Any size, **10c.**

No. 1260

No. 4479

4479. Little Girls' or Boys' Long Coat, with short body and having the skirt gored at the side seams. (To be made with one or two capes.) 5¾ yards 20 inches wide, or 4¼ yards 27 inches wide. 7 sizes, ½ to 6 years. Price, **15c.**

No. 4495.

4495. Girls' Dress, with five-gored skirt, to have an inverted box-plait or gathers at the back. 5⅛ yards 20 inches wide, or 2⅞ yards 36 inches wide, or 2¼ yards 44 inches wide, each with ½ yard of silk tucking for the yoke and collar, and ½ yard velvet for the wristbands, belt, shoulder straps and yoke ornaments. 8 sizes, 5 to 12 years. Price, **20c.**

5353.

5353. Girls' double-breasted long coat, with separate or permanent cape and hood, either of which may be omitted, 5 to 12 years; 8 sizes. This pretty coat may be stylishly made up in blue cloth, with a self-colored satin lining for the hood. It will also develop effectively in tan cloth, with plaid satin for the hood lining. It requires 5¼ yards of goods 27 inches wide, or 3¼ yards 44 inches wide, or 2⅝ yards 54 inches wide, each with ½ yard of silk 20 inches wide for lining the hood, for a girl of 9 years. Price, **20c.**

2243. Ladies' and Misses' Fancy Muff, one size. Price, **10c.**

No. 4609

4609. Misses' Double-Breasted, semi-fitted box-coat or jacket, with notched shawl-collar. For 13 years, 5½ yards 20 inches wide, or 4 yards 27 inches wide, or 2⅜ yards 44 inches wide, or 2 yards 54 inches wide. 5 sizes, 13 to 17 years. Price, **20c.**

No. 4884

4884. Ladies' Golf Cape, with removable hood and a flare, aiglon, or turn-down military collar, with or without a centre-back seam, and in either of two lengths. The long cape has a sweep of about 3½ yards in the medium sizes. 2⅞ yards 54 inches wide. 9 sizes, 30 to 46 inches, bust. Price, **20c.**

No. 4861

4861. Girls' Jacket, with fly closing, automobile back, Abbe sailor collar, and sleeves box-plaited or gathered at the top. 3 yards 27 inches wide, or 1¾ yard 44 inches wide, or 1⅜ yard 54 inches wide. 10 sizes, 3 to 12 years. Price, **20c.**

GROCERY DEPARTMENT.

PRICES SUBJECT TO CHANGE.

Our Grocery Department is very complete, and the highest standard of quality is maintained. You will always receive carefully selected goods. It is a good plan to make up an order once a month (or you and your neighbors together), and include what groceries you need. We can then ship by freight, and the charges will be very low.

Arrowroot.

Keen's West India, ½-lb tins, 15c tin.
" " in bulk, 25c lb.

Baking Powders.

BRAND.

Pure cream of tartar baking powder. We guarantee this baking powder to contain nothing but pure cream of tartar and sufficient soda to get all its rising qualities, and the smallest quantity of dried flour to preserve its strength, 1-lb tin, 25c; ½-lb tin, 15c.

Pure gold, 4-oz tin, 10c; 6-oz tin, 15c; 8-oz tin, 20c; 12-oz tin, 30c; 16-oz tin, 40c.
Cleveland, 4-oz tin, 15c; 6-oz tin, 20c; 8-oz tin, 25c; 12-oz tin, 39c; 16-oz tin, 49c.
Royal, 4-oz tin, 15c; 6-oz tin, 22c; 8-oz tin, 28c; 12-oz tin, 40c; 16-oz tin, 50c.
Dr. Price's, 6-oz tin, 22c; 12-oz tin, 40c; 16-oz tin, 50c; 2½-lb tin, $1.25.
Cook's Friend, 20c pkt.
Jersey cream, 1-lb tin, 25c.
Ocean wave, 1-lb tin, 25c.
Royal standard, 1-lb tin, 12½c; 25 lbs, $2.75.
Snowflake, 1-lb tin, 10c; 3 pkgs for 25c; 25-lb box, $2.00.

Baking Soda, etc.

Bicarbonate soda, 3 lbs 10c.
Baking Soda (Cow Brand), ½-lb pkg, 5c; 1-lb pkg, 10c.
Yeast cakes, royal, 4c pkg.
" Fleischmann's, 2c pkg.

Barley.

Finest pearl, 5c lb.
Finest pot, 4 lbs for 10c.
Robinson's patent (see Drug Catalogue).
Barley, flaked, 6 lbs for 25c.

Beans.

Finest hand-picked beans, 3 lbs for 10c, $1.90 bush.
Finest Lima beans, 7c lb.
Flaked beans, 12½c pkg.

Beef Extracts.

Armour's, 25c, 45c jar.
Johnston's, 25c, 45c jar.
Bovril (see Drug Catalogue).

Blue.

Keen's Oxford, 1-lb pkg, 18c; ¼-lb, 5c.
Reckitt's, 4c pkg.
Parisian, ¼-lb, 4c.

Bird Seed and Gravel.

Cottam's bird seed, 1-lb pkts, 3 for 25c; ½-lb pkt, 5c.
Hemp, bulk, 5c lb.
Canary, bulk, 5c lb.
Millet, bulk, 5c lb.
Rape, bulk, 7c lb.
Mixed, bulk, 5c lb.
Gravel, 4c pkg.

Bathbrick.

Powdered bathbrick, 10c pkg.
Brick, 5c each.

Butter.

Selected creamery, Danish brand—
1-lb blocks, 5-lb crocks, 7-lb " } At lowest market prices.
We guarantee this brand of butter as strictly first-class, and receive our supply daily.
Choicest dairy butter—
1-lb blocks, 5-lb crocks, 15-lb pails, 50-lb tubs } At lowest market prices.

Biscuits.

Abernethy, 11c lb.
Arrowroot, 14c lb.
Apple blossom, 15c lb.
Animal, 15c lb.
Assorted sandwich, 15c lb.
Brown meal, 9c lb.
Butter crackers, 8c lb.
Canada mixed, 15c lb.
Captain, 12c lb.
Cheese, 15c lb.
Cottage, 11c lb.
Cracknel, 25c lb.
Cape, 10c lb.
Cream sodas, 3-lb tin, 28c.
Chocolate flakes, 30c lb.
Cafe noir (small), 20c lb.
Cafe-au-lait, 20c lb.
Florence, 30c lb.
Fig bar, 13c lb.
Finger creams, 25c lb.
Grenville, 14c lb.
Ginger nuts, 13c lb.
Graham wafers, 11c lb.
" " 2-lb box, 23c.
Ginger bread, 11c lb.
" " fruit, 11c lb.
Honeymoon, 14c lb.
Household, 14c lb.
Jam-jams, 14c lb.
Jelly wafers, 14c lb.
Jubilee, 15c lb.
Jamaica, 10c lb.
Kennel, 6c lb.
Lemon sandwich, 15c lb.
Lemon biscuit, 12c lb.
Lemon snaps, 11c lb.
Lunch biscuit, 6c lb.
Lady fingers, 35c lb.
Lily drops, 25c lb.
Marshmallow wafers, 14c lb.
" fingers, 15c lb.
Moss chocolate, 17c lb.
Milk, 15c lb.
Mexican, 15c lb.
Maple cream, 15c lb.
Maizena wafers, 12c lb.
Macaroons, 45c lb.
" Spanish, 50c lb.
Molasses snaps, 8c lb.
Napoleon, 15c lb.
Niagara, 15c lb.
Oswego, 18c lb; 1-lb tin, 25c.
Oatmeal wafers, 12c lb.
Pilot, 9c lb.
Pineapple wafers, 14c lb.
People's mixed, 12½c lb.
Rusk's, 18c lb.
Rice cake, 11c lb.
Reception wafers, 12c lb.
Salt wafers, 12c lb.
Sea biscuit, 7c lb.
Shrewsbury bar, 15c lb.
Snowflake, 12c lb; 1-lb tin, 25c.
Soda biscuit, 8c lb; 3-lb package, 23c.
Sultana, 14c lb.
School cake, 13c lb.
" " fruit, 13c lb.
Social tea, 18c lb; 1-lb tins, 25c.
C. B. & Co.'s cream sodas, 3-lb tins, 28c.
C. B. & Co.'s sodas, 3-lb package, 23c.
T. B. & C. Co.'s cream sodas, 3-lb tin, 28c.
T. B. & C. Co.'s sodas, 3-lb package, 23c.
Canada Biscuit Co.'s sodas, 3-lb package, 23c; cream sodas, 28c.
Tea, 13c lb.
Village, 6c lb.
Vanilla wafers, 15c lb.
Wine, 11c lb.
Water-fine, 18c lb.

Candied Peel.

Finest Lemon, 15c lb.
Orange, 15c lb.
Citron, 20c lb.
Mixed peel, 18c lb.
Mixed peel, ½ lb box, 10c; 1 lb box, 20c.
Choice lemon and orange, 12½c lb.
Choice citron, 17c lb.

Capers.

C. & B. Capot, 10c, 15c bottle,
C. & B. Nonpareil, 12½c, 20c bottle.

Catsup.

Our own make tomato catsup, (E) brand.
Pint bottle, 15c.
Half pint bottle, 10c.
Pint gem jar, 15c.
Quart jem jar, 25c.
One gallon jar, $1.00.
Epicure tomato catsup, 15c bottle.
Snider's tomato catsup, 27c bottle.
Columbia tomato catsup, 25c bottle.
Club tomato catsup, 10c btl.
Delhi tomato catsup, 2 lb. cans, 7½c.
C. & B. mushroom catsup, 18c, 30c bottle.
C. & B. walnut catsup, 18c, 30c bot.

Chutney.

C. & B. India mangoe chutney, 18c, 35c bottle.
C. & B. Bengal Club chutney, 18c, 35c bottle.
Heinz's tomato chutney, 20c bottle.

Cocoa.

Bensdorp's, ¼-lb tin, 23c; ½-lb. tin, 43c; 1-lb. tin, 80c.
Van Houten's ¼-lb tin, 23c; ½-lb tin, 43c; 1-lb. tin, 80c.
Walter Baker's, ⅛-lb. tin, 15c; ½-lb tin, 27c.
Cowan's essence, ½-lb tin, 20c.
Cowan's perfection, ½-lb tin, 25c.
Epp's, ¼-lb tin, 10c.
Webb's, ¼-lb tin, 10c.
Cadbury's, 3-oz package, 14c.
London pearl, 25c lb.
Soluble cocoa, 12½c lb.
Pure unsweetened cocoa in bulk, 50c lb.
Condensed cocoa in milk, 25c tin.
Finest cocoa nibs, 40c lb.
Cocoa shells, 3c lb.
Rich's powdered cocoa shells, 5c pkg.

Chocolates.

Aldon's unsweetened rock chocolate, ½-lb bar, 20c.
Baker's pure chocolate, ½-lb bar, 25c.
Cowan's chocolate, ½-lb bar, 20c; ¼-lb bar, 10c.
Sweetened—
Baker's German sweet chocolate, 2-oz cake, 5c; ¼-lb cake, 10c.
Paramont vanilla chocolate, 15c bar.
Cadbury's chocolate, ¼-lb bar, 12½c; ½-lb. bar, 25c.
Atkinson's ¼-lb cake, 10c.

Cream and Milk.

We receive cream fresh daily.
Pint bottles, 20c.
10-oz bottles, 12c.
Reindeer Brand condensed cream, 15c tin.
Highland Brand condensed cream, 20c tin.
Oak Tree Brand condensed cream, 12½c tin.
Owl Brand condensed milk, 12½c tin, or $1.50 doz.
Eagle Brand condensed milk, 25c tin, or $2.75 doz.
Reindeer Brand condensed milk, 15c tin, or $1.75 doz.
Nestles' Brand condensed milk, 22c tin, or $2.50 doz.
Viking Brand condensed milk, 5c, 15c tin.
Oak Tree Brand condensed milk, 12½c tin.

Cheese.

Prices subject to market fluctuations.
Prime September, 14c lb.
Canadian cheese, 12½c lb.
Canadian cheddar, 15c lb.
Canadian Stilton, 17c lb.
English " 35c lb.
Switzer cheese, 40c lb.
Roquefort cheese, 45c lb.
Neufchatel cream cheese, 5c each.
McLaren's Imperial cheese, 5c, 10c, 20c, 40c, 80c jar.
McLaren's Roquefort cheese, 25c jar.
Miller's paragon cheese, 10c, 20c jar.

Corn Starch, etc.

London corn starch, 5c pkg.
St. Lawrence corn starch, 8c pkg.
Puddine (assorted flavors), 9c pkg.
Tapine (assorted flavors), 9c pkg.
Quick tapioca, 9c pkg.

Coffee.

ROASTED, WHOLE OR GROUND.

We keep a full assortment of the different kinds of coffee obtained direct from the different markets of the world, which we roast and grind daily. We feel sure that we can satisfy the most particular coffee drinkers. We recommend the following blends, put up in 1-lb cans:

Java, fancy brown Mandehling, 50c lb; or 10 lbs, $4.75.
Finest Old Government Java and Arabian Mocha coffee, 40c lb.
Finest Mocha and Java, with chicory, 35c lb; 10 lbs for $3.25.
Finest Maricabo and Java, with chicory, 30c lb; 10 lbs for $2.75.
Finest Maricabo and Santos, with chicory, 25c lb; 10 lbs for $2.25.
Finest Santos and Jamaica, with chicory, a good blend, 20c lb; 10 lbs, $1.75.

We can give the following coffees, whole or ground, at the following prices:

Arabian Mocha, 40c lb.
Old Government Java, 40c lb; 10 lbs, $3.75.
Plantation Ceylon, 40c lb; 10 lbs, $3.75.
Maricabo, No. 1, 30c lb; 10 lbs, $2.75.
Maricabo, No. 2, 25c lb; 10 lbs, $2.25.
Jamaica, 25c lb; 10 lbs, $2.25.
Santos, 20c lb; 10 lbs, $1.85.
Rio, 25c lb; 10 lbs, $2.25.

By ordering your coffee from us you can always depend on getting the finest coffees obtainable, as we take special care in the blending of the different lines.

Finest German chicory, 12½c lb.
Dandelion coffee, ground, 1-lb tin, 25c; ½-lb tin, 13c.
Chase & Sanburn's (Seal brand) coffee, 40c lb can.
Faust blend coffee, 45c 1-lb can.
Moja coffee, 40c 1-lb can.
Crosse & Blackwell's coffee essence, 17c, 28c bottle.
Symington's coffee essence, pure, 18c, 35c bottle; with chicory, 15c, 30c bottle.
Reindeer brand condensed coffee and milk, No. 1, 30c; No. 2, 27c; No. 3, 22c; No. 4, 19c tin.
Cereal coffee, 15c lb can.
New cereal coffee, 1-lb package, 20c; ½-lb package, 10c.
Shredded wheat drink, 1-lb pkg, 20c.
Rokco (cereal drink), 1-lb package, 12½c; 2-lb package, 20c.
Caramel cereal coffee, 20c pkg.

Celery Salt.

Pure gold, 12c bottle.
Horton Cato Co.'s, 10c bottle.

Cereals.

Farinosa, 14c pkg.
McIntosh Swiss food, 14c pkg.
McIntosh Jersey oats, 14c pkg.
Quaker oats, 12c pkg.
Pettijohn's breakfast (food wheat), 12c pkg.
Beaver oats, 10c pkg.
Lauhoff's flaked rice, 12½c pkg.
Lauhoff's flaked peas, 12½c pkg.
Lauhoff's flaked beans, 12½c pkg.
A D C flaked rice, 10c pkg.
Cook's flaked rice, 18c pkg.
Hominy, 12c pkg.
Malt health food, 15c pkg.
Cream of wheat, 20c pkg.
Shredded wheat biscuits, 15c pkg.
Granose flakes, 15c pkg.
" biscuit, 15c pkg.
Granola, 12c pkg.
Grape nuts, 15c pkg.
Ralston's hominy grits, 2-lb pkg, 15c.
" health oats, 2-lb pkg, 15c.
" barley food, 2-lb pkg, 15c.
" breakfast food, 2-lb pkg, 15c.
Ireland's desiccated wheat, 10c pkg.
Fine macaroni (imported), 1-lb pkg, 10c.
Vermicelli, 1-lb pkg, 12½c.
Hecker's farina, 1-lb pkg, 10c.
" glutine, 2-lb pkg, 12c.
Finest gold-dust cornmeal, 25c stone; in bbls of 196 lbs, $3.00.
Standard oatmeal, 35c stone.
Granulated oatmeal, 35c stone.
Finest rolled oats, 35c stone; in bbls of 180 lbs, $4.25.
Finest rolled wheat, 40c stone; in bbls of 100 lbs, $2.70.
Finest wheatlets, 45c stone.

Cocoanut.

Desiccated, 15c lb.
Featherstrip, 20c lb.

Currants.

Owing to the uncertainty of the crops, we cannot quote prices on currants. We will have the finest quality at the very lowest prices. At present we quote—

Finest Vostizza, 15c; choice, 12½c lb.
Filiatra currants, 10c lb.

Curry Powder.

C & B, 12c, 15c, 25c, 45c bottle; bulk, 35c lb.

Dates.

Sair, 5c lb.
Hallowee, 7c lb; 1-lb package, 9c.
Fard dates, 15c lb.

Extracts and Essences.

	1 oz	2 oz.	4 oz.	8 oz.	16 oz.
Lemon....	5c	10c	20c	35c	65c
Vanilla...	5c	10c	20c	40c	80c
Ratafia	5c	10c	20c	..	..
Orange..	10c	20c	..	..	..
Clove.....	5c	10c	..	..	..
Cinnamon	5c	10c	..	..	..
Ginger...	8c	15c	..	..	..

Powders, assorted flavors, 10c tin.

Flour.

Diamond (E) Brand pure whole wheat flour, made from selected wheat and specially ground by ourselves, 7 lb pkg, 20c; 14 lb package, 35c; ⅛ barrel, 55c; 1 barrel, $4.25.
Blue seal brand, finest family flour, 24½-lb sack, 50c.
Blue seal brand, do, stone (14 lbs), 30c.
Finest blue seal family flour, per bbl, $4.00.
Green seal brand, finest pastry flour, 24½-lb sack, 60c; stone (14 lbs), 40c; per bbl, $4.80.
Graham flour, 30c stone.
Prof. Hart's whole wheat flour, 40c stone.
Ralston's self-rising buckwheat flour, 2-lb pkg, 12½c.
Ireland's self-rising buckwheat flour, 2-lb pkg, 10c.
Tip-top pastry flour, 65c ½ bag.
Manitoba patent flour, $4.85 per bbl.
Hungarian flour, $4.85 per bbl.
Ogilvie's whole wheat, ½-bag, 70c.
Wright's perfected flour, 65c ½-bag.

Fruits, Dried.

Apricots, 12½c, 15c lb.
Peaches, 12½c lb.
Apples, 9c lb, or 50-lb box, $4.17.
Cooking figs, 5c lb.
Pears, 15c lb.
Silver plums, 15c lb.
Table Figs—
No. 1 Star, 10c; No. 2, 12½c; No. 3, 15c; No. 4, 20c; No. 5, 25c.

Fruits, Canned

Canned goods are put up in 1-pound, 2-pound and 3-pound size cans, which are not always the actual weight, as some goods are much heavier than others, and this term is only used to distinguish the different sizes.

We guarantee every tin.

Bartlett pears, 2-lb can, 15c.
Blue Damson plums, 2-lb can, 10c.
Lombard plums, 2-lb can, 10c.
Blueberries, 2-lb can, 9c.
Strawberries, 2-lb can, 15c.
Raspberries, 2-lb can, 15c.
Peaches, 2-lb can, 15c; 3-lb can, 25c.
" (pie), 3-lb can, 12c.
Republic sliced pineapple, 2-lb can, 25c.
Columbian brand Bahama sliced pineapple, 2-lb can, 25c.
Morton's whole pineapple, 3-lb can, 25c.
Apples, gallon tins, 20c.

Fruits, in glass.

Dunbar's figs (in cordial), 70c bottle.
Peaches, Reid Murdock's, 80c bottle.
Strawberries, Reid Murdock's, 80c bottle.
Pears, pickled, Reid Murdock's, 75c bottle.

Fruits, Fresh.

Fresh fruits supplied in season and always at lowest market prices.

Apples, oranges, lemons, pineapples, watermelons, bananas, cranberries, strawberries, Malaga grapes, etc., etc.

Fish, Canned.

Albert's sardines, ½-lb tin, with key, 12½c.
Albert's sardines, ½-lb tin, with key, 22c.
La Pilote Brand—finest French sardines, ¼-lb tin, with key, 10c.
Sportsman sardines, with key, 12½c tin.
Domestic sardines, 5c tin.
Lobster, ½-lb flats, 17c; 1-lb flats, 30c tin.
Soft shell crabs, 35c tin.
Finest shrimps, 15c tin.
Pink salmon, tall tins, 10c.
Red salmon, " 15c.
Horse shoe salmon, tall tins, 16c.
Clover leaf salmon, flat tins, 18c.
Domestic finnan haddie, 10c tin.
Golden " " 10c tin.
Halibut steak, 10c tin.
Tunny fish, 10c tin.
Morton's—
Preserved bloaters, 15c tin
Kippered herring, 18c tin.
Herring, in tomato sauce, 18c tin.
Fresh herrings, 10c tin.
Meyers'—
Anchovy paste, 10c tin.
Lobster paste, 10c tin.
Kipper paste, 3 tins, 20c.
Morton's bloater paste, 3 tins, 20c.
C. & B.'s anchovy paste, 18c, 35c pot.
" " essence, 18c, 30c bottle.

Gelatine.

Lady Charlotte (red or white), 7c per pkg.
Cox, 10c pkg.
Knox's, 12c pkg.
Knox's acidulated, 14c pkg.

Ginger.

Cheloong, preserved ginger, 25c 1-lb jar.
Jamica whole root, 20c, 35c lb; ground, 25c, 35c lb.
Cochin, whole, 20c; ground, 20c.

Honey.

Small jars, 10c; pint gem jars, 20c; quart gem jars, 40c; 5-lb pail, 60c each.
Pure clover honey in comb, 20c section.

Horse Radish.

Small bottle, 9c each.
Horse radish and mustard (Williams Bros.), 12c bottle.
Heinz evaporated horse radish, 25c per bottle.

Icings.

Pink, chocolate, lemon, almond, kernaline, white and canary, 10c package, or $1.15 per doz.
Dr. Clarke's chocolate icing, 15c package.
Icing sugar, 7c lb.

Jellies.

Crosse & Blackwell's—
Calves' foot, plain, 35c, 60c bottle.
" " 25c jar.
Port wine, 25c jar.
Champagne, 25c jar.
Orange, 25c jar.
Lemon, 25c jar.
Vanilla, 25c jar.
Black currant and red currant, 30c jar.
Batger's Nonpareil, any of the following flavors: Lemon, orange, vanilla, raspberry, strawberry, sherry, cherry, port wine, pints, 10c; quarts, 20c package.
Pure Gold jelly powders, orange, lemon, pineapple, raspberry, strawberry, vanilla, madeira, cherry, calves' foot, etc., 9c package.
McLaren's jelly powders, raspberry, strawberry, cherry, orange, lemon, vanilla, pineapple, calves' foot, etc., 9c package.

Jams.

THE T. EATON CO.'S FINEST HOME-MADE JAMS, CANNED FRUITS, ETC.

Our jams are put up from finest fruits and Extra Standard granulated sugar, 1 lb fruit to 1 lb of sugar, labelled Diamond (E) Brand.

Strawberry jam, pint gem jars, 20c; quarts, 30c; ½-gallons, 50c; 5-lb pails, 45c.
Finest raspberry jam, in pint gem jars, 20c; quart gem jars, 30c; ½-gallons, 50c; 5-lb pails, 45c.
Raspberries (canned), in pint gem jars, 20c, or $2.15 doz; quarts, 30c, or $3.00 doz; ½-gallons, 45c, or $5.00 doz.
Strawberries (canned), pint gem jars, 20c, or $2.15 doz; quarts, 30c, or $3.00 doz; ½-gallons, 45c, or $5.00 doz.
Peach jam, pint gem jars, 20c; quarts, 30c; ½-gallons, 50c; 5-lb pails, 45c.

Peaches (canned), pint gem jars, 20c, or $2.15 doz; quarts, 30c, or $3.00 doz; ½-gallons, 45c, or $5.00 doz.

Plum jam, pint gem jars, 20c; quarts, 30c; ½-gallons, 45c; 5-lb pails, 40c.

Plums (canned), pint gem jars, 20c, or $2.15 doz; quarts, 30c, or $3.00 doz; ½-gallons, 45c, or $5.00 doz.

Black currant jam, pint gem jars, 20c; quarts, 30c; ½-gallons, 50c.

Jams in small jars with patent top, Diamond (E) Brand, 15c each.

Lard.

In 3-lb pails, 35c each.

In 20-lb pails, $2.40 each.

Macaroni.

French, 10c package.

Vermicelli, 12½c package.

Marmalade.

Orange marmalade, our own make, Diamond (E) Brand, small glass jars, 15c each; quart gem jars, 30c; 5-lb pails, 45c; 7-lb pails, 65c.

Crosse & Blackwell's orange marmalade, 1-lb glass jar, 14c each.

Robertson's Scotch marmalade, 1-lb jars, 15c.

Keiler's Dundee marmalade, 1-lb jars, 19c.

Meats, Canned.

Corned beef, 1-lb tin, 15c; 2-lb tin, 30c.

Chipped beef, ½-lb tin, 15c; 1-lb tin, 30c.

Lunch tongue (Armour's), 1-lb tin, 40c.

Lunch tongue (Armour's), 1½-lb tin, 80c.

Roast beef, 1-lb tin, 15c.

" " 2-lb tin, 30c.

Pig's feet (Armour's), 30c tin.

Vienna sausage, 12½c tin.

Boneless chicken, Delhi, 22c; Strathroy, 20c tin.

Boneless turkey, Delhi, 22c; Strathroy, 20c tin.

Boneless duck, Delhi, 22c; Strathroy, 20c tin.

Meats, Cooked.

We cook our own meats and can guarantee finest quality.

(SLICED.)

Spiced beef ham, 25c lb.

Cooked ham, 30c lb.

" shoulder, 24c lb.

Dried beef, 25c lb.

Head cheese, 10c lb.

" shapes, 8c lb.

Bologna, our own make, 10c lb.

Meats, Fresh.

Our beef is the choicest quality and from our own farms.

Choice sirloin roast
" rib roast
" shoulder roast
" porterhouse steak
" round steak
" sirloin steak
" lamb
" veal
" corned beef
" roast pork
" pork-loins, finest cut
" tenderloin
— All at lowest market prices.

Meats, Jellied.

Jellied pork tongue, 25c lb.

" ox tongue, 30c lb.

" tenderloin, 25c lb.

" veal, 25c lb.

Jellied hocks, 15c lb.

" turkey, 30c lb.

Ham, chicken and tongue sausage, 10c each.

White pudding, 10c lb.

Black pudding, 10c lb.

Weinerwurst, 12c lb.

Our pork is pea fed, supplied from our own farms, and guaranteed to be of the highest quality.

Meat, Pickled.

Hams, 13c lb. Shoulders, 10c lb.

Backs, 14c lb. Sides, 13c lb.

Pickled jowls, 5c lb.

" hocks, 5c lb.

" ox tongue, 45c each.

Meats, Potted.

Ham, tongue, beef, devilled ham and tongue, ¼-lb, 5c tin.

Meyers'—
Chicken and tongue, 3 tins for 25c.
Turkey and tongue, 3 tins for 25c.
Ham and chicken, 3 tins for 25c.
Ham and tongue, 3 tins for 25c.

Morton's ham and chicken, 10c tin.

Morton's ham and tongue, 10c tin.

Ham, veal and cottage loaf, 25c tin.

Chicken soup, 15c tin.

Meats, Salted.

Long clear (dry salt), 12c lb.
Backs " 12c lb.
Sides " 12c lb.
Shoulders " 11c lb.

Meat, Smoked.

MEATS SUBJECT TO MARKET FLUCTUATION.

We feed the hogs on our own farms, cure our meats on our own premises, and guarantee finest quality.

Finest sugar-cured backs, select smoked, 16c lb.

Sides, select smoked, 14c lb.

Hams, select smoked, 15c lb.

Shoulders, select smoked, 11c lb.

Rolls, select smoked, 12½c lb.

Mincemeat.

Whetley's condensed, 10c pkg.

Mustard.

Keen's D. S. F., 1-lb tin, 40c; ½-lb tin, 23c; ¼-lb tin, 12c.

Keen's, 1-lb jar, 25c; 4-lb jar, 80c.

Williams Bros.' prepared mustard, 12c bottle.

William Bros.' prepared mustard and horse radish, 12c bottle.

Domestic, 5c, 10c jar.

Crosse & Blackwell's prepared mustard, 25c jar.

Bulk mustard, 20c lb.

Mushrooms.

French, 22c tin; in glass, 40c.

Nuts.

When placing your order with us, you can always depend on getting the very best quality, as we import the choicest and best nuts. New nuts we expect to arrive 1st of November. Walnuts about 1st of December.

Almonds, finest soft shell, 17c lb.

" hard shell, 12c lb.

Filberts (Sicily), 12c lb.

" good, 10c lb.

Walnuts, Grenoble, 15c lb; Marabot, 12½c lb; Cornes, 10c lb.

Pecans, large, 17c lb.

Finest mixed nuts, 14c lb.

Shelled walnuts, Grenoble, 28c lb.

Float almonds, finest, 40c lb.

" " good, 35c lb.

Peanuts (we roast these fresh daily), 10c quart.

Oil (Lucca).

Crosse & Blackwell's, 12½c, 20c bottle.

Olives.

Spanish manzanilla, 15c bottle.

" queen olives, 30c, 40c bottle.

Stuffed olives, 15c, 20c, 30c bottle.

Heinz's olives, 20c bottle.

Olives, in bulk, $1.10 gallon.

" " 30c quart jem jar.

" " 20c pint jem jar.

Pepper.

Whole white pepper, 35c lb.
Ground " 35c lb.
Extra fine " 40c lb.

Whole black pepper, 25c lb.
Ground " 25c lb.

Cayenne pepper, 35c lb.

Chillies, dried, 35c lb.

Poultry.

Turkeys, ducks, chickens, etc., all at lowest market prices.

Prunes.

California, 90 to 100 prunes to lb, 6¼c lb; 50-lb boxes, $3.07.

California, 80 to 90 prunes to lb, 3 lbs 20c; 50-lb boxes, $3.25.

California, 60 to 70 prunes to lb, 3 lbs, 25c; 50-lb boxes, $4.00.

California, 50 to 60 prunes to lb, 10c lb; 50-lb boxes, $4.50.

California, 30 to 40 prunes to lb, 12c lb; 25-lb boxes, $2.75.

French prunes, 5c lb.

Pickles.

Crosse & Blackwell's—

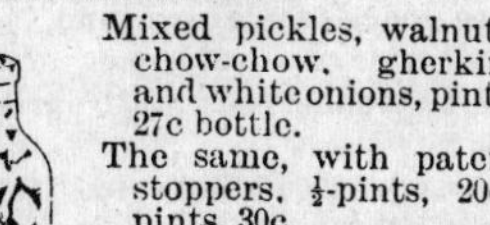

Mixed pickles, walnuts, chow-chow, gherkins and white onions, pints, 27c bottle.

The same, with patent stoppers, ½-pints, 20c; pints, 30c.

Soho sweet pickles, ½-pints, 20c.

Cashmere pickles, ½-pint, 50c.

Capers, nonpareil, 2-oz bottle, 12½c; 4-oz bottle, 20c.

Capers, Capot, 2-oz bottle, 10c; 4-oz bottle, 15c.

Mushroom catsup, 18c, 30c bottle.

Walnut catsup, 18c, 35c bottle.

Anchovy essence, 18c, 35c bottle.

Bengal club chutney, 15c, 35c bottle.

India mangoe chutney, 18c, 35c bottle.

C. & B.'s prepared mustard, 25c stone jar.

C. & B.'s malt vinegar, reputed pint, 10c.

C. & B.'s malt vinegar, imperial pint, 15c.

C. & B.'s malt vinegar, reputed quart, 20c.

C. & B.'s malt vinegar, imperial quart, 25c.

Colonel Skinner's mangoe relish, 35c bottle.

Captain White's Oriental relish, 30c bottle.

Lutz & Schramm's tomato preserves, 30c.

Heinz's—
Gherkins, extra spiced, per quart, 20c.
Sweet mixed pickles, per quart, 35c.
Mixed pickles, gherkins or chow, 15c bottle.
Sweet or sour midgets, 14-oz bottle, 30c.
India relish, 35c bottle.
Tomato chutney, 20c bottle.
Manzanilla olives, 20c bottle.
Evaporated horse radish, 25c bottle.
Red pepper sauce, 20c bottle.

Mrs. E. G. Kidd's pin-money pickles—
Bur-cucumber pickles, pints, 40c.
Cucumber " " 40c.
Mixed " " 40c.
Melon mangoe, 55c.

Williams Bros. & Charbonneau—
Sweet mixed pickles, pint bottles, 25c each.
East India relish, ½-pint bottles, 12½c each.
Chow-chow, ½-pint bottles, 12½c each.
White onions, ½-pint bottles, 12½c each.
Chilli sauce, ½-pint bottles, 15c each.

Morton's mixed pickles, chow-chow, gherkins and white onions, 20c bottle.

White & Co.'s imported mixed or chow-chow pickles, 20c bottle.

Gillard's relish, 35c bottle.

Lytle's sterling mixed pickles, and chow-chow, 30c, 20c, 15c bottle.

Mixed pickles, 10c, 15c bottle.

Mixed pickles, in gallon jars, 50c.

Horse radish, ½-pint bottle, 9c.

Paprika (Hungarian sweet pepper), 20c bottle.

Peas.

Split, 2½c lb.

Flaked, 10c package.

Canned. (See Vegetables.)

Raisins.

Owing to the uncertainty of the crops we cannot quote definitely the prices on raisins, but you may depend on getting the very best quality at very lowest prices.

At present we quote—

Selected Valencia seeded raisins, 1-lb package, 10c; 28-lb box, $2.50.

Selected Valencia, 3 lbs for 25c; 28-lb box, $2.20.

Fine off stalk, 7c lb; 28-lb box, $1.90.

Choice muscatel, 12c lb.

Sultana, choice, 15c lb.

Table raisins (22-lb boxes), 12½c lb, or $2.50 box; 15c lb, or $3.00 box; 20c lb, or $4.00 box.

Rennet—C. & B.'s essence, 15c bottle.

Rice.

Fine Rangoon rice, 6 lbs, 25c; 50 lbs, $2.00.

Finest Patna rice, 6c lbs; 50 lbs, $2.85.

Crystal Japan rice, 3 lbs 20c; 50 lbs, $3.50.

Fancy Japan rice, 3 lbs 25c; 50 lbs, $4.00.

Carolina rice, 11c lb.

Rice flour, 7c lb.

Salt.

Finest Windsor table, 5-lb bag, 5c.

Windsor table salt, 50-lb bag, 45c.

Coarse salt, $1.40 bbl.

Cerebos salt, 12c tin.

C. & B. fine table salt, 10c bottle.

Celery salt, 10c, 12c bottle.

Sardines. (See Canned Fish.)

Seasoning.

Sage, savory, thyme, mint, mixed herbs, marjoram, basil, parsley, in bottles, 10c.

Pure Gold seasonings, in package, 5c.

" " assorted, in tins, 10c.

Starch.

Canada laundry, 5c lb.

Ivory gloss, 1-lb package, 8c.

No. 1 white, 3-lb box, 20c.

Ivory gloss, 6-lb tin, 48c.

Celluloid, 1-lb package, 10c.

Ivorine, 1-lb package, 9c.

Silver brilliant (cold water starch), 5c package.

St. Lawrence corn, 1-lb package, 8c.

London corn, 1-lb package, 5c.

Sauces and Salads.

Anchovy sauce, 18c, 35c bottle.

Chilli sauce, 15c bottle.

Red pepper (Heinz's), 20c bottle.

Anglo-American sauce, 5c bottle.

Patterson's sauce, 10c bottle.

Holbrook's sauce, 15c and 40c bottle.

Lea & Perrin's sauce, 34c, 60c, $1.00 bottle.

Mrs. Holbrook's German salad, 35c bottle.

Cucumber salad, 35c bottle.

Holbrook's sauce, 15c, 40c bottle.

Patterson's sauce, 10c bottle,

Anglo American sauce, 5c.

Lea & Perrins' sauce, 34c, 60c, $1.00 bottle.

Yorkshire relish, 20c bottle.

Oscar's Waldorf sauce, 75c bottle.

Columbia salad dressing, 30c.

Gold Medal salad dressing, 25c.

"My Wife's" salad dressing, 35c.

Snider's salad dressing, 20c, 35c.

Royal, 25c, 45c bottle.

Sago.

Pearl, 5c lb.

Soups.

Van Camp's tomato, consomme, mock-turtle and bouillon, 12½c tin.

Anderson's (Monk brand) tomato, vegetable, ox-tail, mock-turtle, celery, etc., 10c tin.

Mullen, Blackledge's red letter soups, assorted, 10c tin.

Columbia, ox-tail, mock-turtle, tomato, mulligatawny, bouillon, consomme, 30c tin.

Snider's tomato, 30c tin.

Delhi chicken, 15c tin.

Aylmer chicken, 15c tin.

Sugars.

Extra standard granulated, 20 lbs, $1.00; per cwt., $4.85.

Fine yellow sugar, 22 lbs, $1.00; per cwt., $4.25 (about 300 to 350 lbs to a barrel).

Fine fruit sugar, 7c lb.

Icing sugar, 7c lb.

Paris lumps, (Redpath's), 7c lb.

Syrups.

Redpath's golden syrup, 2-lb tin, 12c.

Molasses, 30c gallon; in quart gem jars, 12c; ½-gallon gem jars, 18c.

Dark syrup, 45c gallon; in quart gem jars, 13c; ½-gallon gem jars, 20c.

Finest golden syrup, 55c gallon; ½-gallon, 22c; quart gem jar, 15c.

Honey drip syrup, 2-gallon pail, $1.35.

Maple syrup, 1/6 gallon tins, 25c.

Barbados molasses, 50c gallon.

We make an extra charge of 10c gallon for containers for syrups and molasses.

Spices.

Our spices we guarantee strictly pure.

Finest Zanzibar cloves, whole, 20c; ground, 25c lb.

Finest cassia (cinnamon), ground, 25c lb.

Finest cinnamon (pure), whole, 25c, 35c, 60c lb; ground, 25c, 35c, 60c lb.

Finest allspice, whole, 15c lb; ground, 20c lb.

Finest cochin ginger, whole, 20c; ground, 25c lb.

Finest Jamaica ginger, whole or ground, 35c lb.

Finest mace, whole or ground, 7½c oz.

Finest celery seed, 30c lb.

Finest cayenne, pods, 35c lb; ground, 35c lb.

Finest mixed pudding spice, 25c lb.

Finest " pickling, ground, 25c lb; whole, 20c lb.

Finest bay leaves, 15c lb.

Finest coriander seed, 15c lb.

Finest carraway seeds, 15c lb.

Finest nutmegs, 5c oz; whole, 75c lb; ground, 7c oz.

White pepper, whole or ground, 35c, 40c lb.

Finest Singapore black pepper, whole or ground, 25c lb.

Finest turmeric, 20c lb.

C. & B. curry powder, 1-oz bottle, 12c; 2-oz, 15c; 4-oz, 25c; 8-oz, 45c.

Curry powder, in bulk, 35c lb.

Celery salt, 12c bottle.

Tapioca, finest pearl, 5c lb.

Teas.

(Our own importations).

We are direct importers of teas, and pay special attention to the blending of different lines. You can save money by buying direct from us.

India Black Teas.

Finest golden-tip Pekoe, 75c lb.

Finest orange broken Pekoe, 50c lb; 10 lbs, $4.75; or original chest of about 50 lbs, 45c lb.

Assam broken Pekoe, fine, rich and mellow, 50c lb; 10 lbs, $4.75; by the chest, 45c lb.

Assam Pekoe, strong, full-flavored, 35c lb; 10 lbs, $3.25; or in chest of about 50 lbs, 30c lb.

Fine India Pekoe Souchong, 25c lb; 10 lbs, $2.30; or in original chest of about 50 lbs, 23c lb.

Good India Souchong, 20c lb.

Ceylon Black Teas.

Golden tip orange Pekoe, 75c lb.

Golden tip Ceylon broken Pekoe, 50c lb; or in chests of about 50 lbs, 45c lb.

Ceylon orange Pekoe, 40c lb.

Pekoe, a good rich liquoring tea, 35c lb; by chest of 50 lbs, 30c lb.

Souchong, a good liquoring tea, 25c lb; or chest, about 50 lbs, 23c lb.

China Black Teas.

Moyune, Ping Sue and Canton teas, 20c, 25c, 30c, 35c lb; or 25c and 35c in chest lots of 50 lbs, 23c lb, and 30c lb, respectively.

Green Teas.

Young Hyson, 25c lb; 10 lbs, $2.30; 35c lb, 10 lbs, $3.25.

Uncolored Japan, 20c, 25c, 35c lb; 10 lbs, $3.25; or 25c and 35c in chest lots of about 50 lbs, 23c lb, and 30c lb, respectively.

Basket-fired Japan, 50c lb; 10 lbs, $4.50.

Black Teas, Blended.

Assam broken Pekoe, together with orange Pekoe and Ceylon golden-tip Pekoe, a very fine-flavored rich liquoring tea, 50c lb; 10 lbs, $4.75; or 50-lb chest, 45c lb.

This tea should not be drawn more than five minutes, then poured off the leaves.

Assam Pekoe and Ceylon, together with orange Pekoe, is a fine full-flavored strong tea, 35c lb; 10 lbs, $3.25; or in chest of about 50 lbs, 30c lb.

India, Ceylon and China blend is the finest 25c tea sold, strong and well flavored, 10 lbs, $2.30; in original chest of 50 lbs. 23c lb.

Mixed Teas.

Our mixed teas are invariably one part green and three parts black; but we will blend in any other proportion you may order.

Finest mixed black and green tea, 45c lb; in chest of 50 lbs, 40c lb.

Fine mixed black and green tea, 35c lb; in chest of 50 lbs, 30c lb.

Good mixed black and green tea, 25c lb; in chest of 50 lbs, 23c lb.

Mixed black and green tea, 20c lb.

Vinegar.

Crosse & Blackwell's pure malt, reputed pints, 10c; imperial pints, 15c; reputed quarts, 20c; imperial quarts, 25c.

C. & B.'s crystal vinegar, 25c bottle.

" Tarragona vinegar, 18c, 30c bottle.

Wilson's pure malt vinegar, reputed pints, 15c.

XXX white wine vinegar, 30c gal.

Cider vinegar, 30c gallon.

English malt vinegar, 65c gallon.

Canadian malt vinegar, 55c gal.

We make an extra charge for jars to contain vinegar in bulk.

Vegetables, Canned.

Corn, 8c tin; 2 doz in case, $1.80.

Peas, 7½c tin; 2 doz in case, $1.80.

Peas (extra sifted), 10c tin; 2 doz in case, $2.20.

Beans, 8½c tin; 2 doz in case, $2.00.

Beans, white wax, 8½c tin; 2 doz in case, $1.80.

Pumpkin, 7½c tin; 2 doz in case, $1.80.

Tomatoes, 8½c tin, or case of 2 doz, $1.90.

Pork and beans, 9c tin.

Asparagus, 20c tin.

Beets, 3-lb cans, 10c.

Epicure beans in tomato sauce, 10c tin.

French peas, petit pois, 12½c tin; fine, 15c tin; extra fine, 18c tin.

French peas, in glass, 30c.

" beans " 27c.

" mushrooms, in glass, 40c.

" " 25c a tin.

Heinz's beans in tomato sauce, 16c tin; 3 lb tin, 25c.

Yeast.

Royal, 4c package.

Fleishmann's, 2c cake.

Write us for anything you need in groceries and do not see catalogued.

Trunks and Bags.

Prices on this page subject to change without notice.

108. Barrel top, metal covered, hardwood slats, good lock and spring clasps, tray and covered hat box, 28-inch, $1.25 ; 30-inch, $1.80 ; 32-inch, $2.10 ; 34-inch, $2.40 ; 36-inch, $2.70.

24. Barrel top, metal covered, iron-covered bottom, iron-bound corners, good lock and spring clasps, tray and covered hat box, 28-inch, $2.15 ; 30-inch, $2.40 ; 32-inch, $2.65 ; 34-inch, $2.90 ; 36-inch, $3.15.

105. Saratoga style, embossed metal covered, iron-covered bottom, iron corner clamps, hardwood slats, fall-in tray, covered boot and hat boxes, 28-inch, $3.00 ; 30-inch, $3.25 ; 32-inch, $3 50 ; 34-inch, $3.75 ; 36-inch, $4.00.

106½. Canvas-covered trunk, flat top, metal-bound corners, iron-covered bottom, with tray and covered hat box, 28 inch, $2.30 ; 30-inch, $2.60 ; 32-inch, $2.90 ; 34-inch, $3.20 ; 36-inch, $3.50.

102½. A square canvas-covered trunk, hardwood slats, iron-bound corners, iron-covered bottom, deep tray with covered hat box, 30-inch, $4.00 ; 32-inch, $4.25 ; 34-inch, $4.50 ; 36-inch, $4.75.

104. Same as No. 102½, with extra heavy mountings, 30-inch, $4.50 ; 32-inch, $4.85 ; 34-inch, $5.20 ; 36-inch, $5.50 ; 40-inch, $6.00.

38. Same as No. 104, with an extra dress tray and bound hardwood slats, linen lined, 32-inch, $5.75 ; 34-inch, $6.25 ; 36-inch, $6 75 ; 40-inch, $8.00.

38. Special, same as No. 38, with two heavy leather straps around, 32-inch, $6.75 ; 34-inch, $7.25 ; 36-inch, $7.75 ; 40-inch, $9.00.

61. Steel bound, hand riveted, linen lined, two trays, double steel hinges and Yale lock, 32-inch, $8.10 ; 34-inch, $8.70 ; 36-$9.30 ; 40-inch, $11.50. The 40-inch size has 2 outside straps.

103. Square canvas trunk, extra heavy brass bound, hinges and mountings riveted on by hand, 2 outside straps, full linen lined, two trays, Yale lock, 30-inch, $7.75 ; 32-inch, $8.25 ; 34-inch, $9.00 ; 36-inch, $9.75 ; 40-inch, $11.25.

102. Same trunk as No. 103, with following extras: Each slat is iron wrapped at ends under clamps ; it is fitted up with extra deep trays, parasol, glove boxes, etc., 30-inch, $8.50 ; 32-inch, $9.00 ; 34-inch, $10.00 ; 36-inch, $11.00 ; 40-inch, $12.00.

7. Heavy canvas-covered square trunk, extra heavy brass corners, with rubber cushion bumpers, the bottom is sheet-iron, covered with three heavy hardwood slats, large and strong casters, heavy brass mountings riveted on by hand, double strap steel hinges, sliding handles, four steel dowels on lid, one at each end, two in front ; three-lever lock, two heavy outside straps all around, heavy Irish linen lined, one dress tray and one large top tray, with deep covered hat, parasol and glove boxes, etc. ; a first-class trunk in every way, made to stand any kind of hard usage, 32-inch, $11.00 ; 34-inch, $12.00 ; 36-inch, $13.00 ; 40-inch, $15.00.

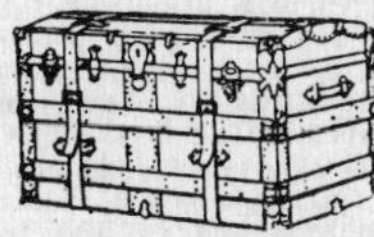

26. Square packing trunk, metal covered, no tray, 28-inch, $1.40 ; 32-inch, $1.65 ; 36-inch, $1.90 ; 40-inch, $2.15.

163. Solid sole leather trunk, heavy capped corners, riveted and hand sewn, sliding handles, brass lock with leather flap, linen lined, 33-inch, $34.00 ; 36-inch, $36.50.

151. Basket trunk, enamelled cloth covered, leather binding, hand sewn, heavy leather capped corners, linen lined, tray with deep covered hat box, leather pocket in lid, two outside leather straps around, heavy wood slats on bottom, good brass lock with leather shield, 30-inch, $18.50 ; 33-inch, $20.00 ; 36-inch, $22.00.

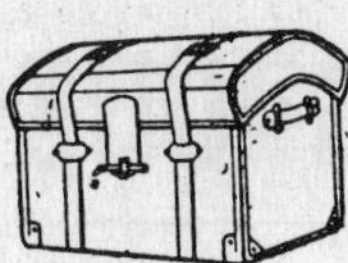

222. Basket stateroom trunk, enamelled cloth covered, edges and corners leather bound, hand sewn, linen lined, brass lock and sliding handles, 30-inch, $16.50 ; 33-inch, $17.75 ; 36-inch, $19.00.

107. Stateroom trunk, canvas covered, steel bound, hardwood slats, iron-covered bottom, shallow tray, with covered boxes, 32-inch, $3.30 ; 34-inch, $3.60 ; 36-inch, $3 90.

108. Canvas-covered stateroom trunk, extra heavy brass mounted, leather bound, iron-covered bottom, 2 outside straps, tray and covered boxes, linen lined, 32-inch, $6.25 ; 34-inch, $6.50 ; 36-inch, $6.75 ; 40-inch, $7.25.

109. Steamer trunk, waterproof canvas covered, heavy ½-inch hardwood slats, iron-wrapped ends under clamps, heavy brass clamps and corner bumpers, three 7-inch strap hinges, iron-covered bottom with three slats, all edges solid leather bound, Yale lock and steel spring clasps, two heavy straps all around, 32-inch, $8.50 ; 34-inch, $9.00 ; 36-inch, $9.75 ; 40-inch, $10.50.

108B. Enamelled cloth-covered stateroom trunk, extra heavy brass mounted, leather bound, iron-covered bottom, two outside straps, linen lined, tray with covered boxes, color black, 32-inch, $7.25 ; 34-inch, $7.50 ; 36-inch, $7.75 ; 40-inch, $8.25.

156. Leather stateroom trunk, regulation depth, linen lined, heavy capped corners, brass lock and sliding handles, 33-inch, $25.00 ; 36-inch, $28.00.

300. Black "Pacific" bag, 14-inch, 55c ; 16-inch, 60c ; 18-inch, 70c ; 20-inch, 80c ; 22-inch, 90c ; 24-inch, $1.00.

333. Gladstone style, pebble grain leather, linen lined, japanned frame, brass lock and mountings, 16-inch, $2.00 ; 18-inch, $2.30 ; 20-inch, $2.60 ; 22-inch, $2.90 ; 24-inch, $3.20.

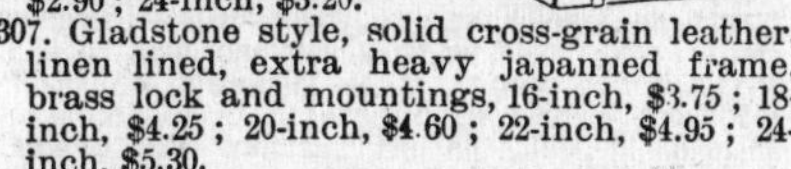

307. Gladstone style, solid cross-grain leather, linen lined, extra heavy japanned frame, brass lock and mountings, 16-inch, $3.75 ; 18-inch, $4.25 ; 20-inch, $4.60 ; 22-inch, $4.95 ; 24-inch, $5.30.

127. Same as No. 307, but with leather lining, 18-inch, $6.50 ; 20-inch, $7.00 ; 22-inch, $7.50 ; 24-inch, $8 00.

268. Leather club bag, linen lined, japanned frame, brass mountings, 10-inch, 85c ; 12-inch, $1.10 ; 14-inch, $1.35 ; 16-inch, $1.60 ; 18-inch, $1.85.

285. Solid leather club bag, black, brown or olive, linen lined, brass lock and trimmings, 10-inch, $1.75 ; 12-inch, $2.00 ; 14-inch, $2.25 ; 16-inch, $2.50 ; 18-inch, $2.75.

295. Same as No. 286, but 3 inches deeper, 14-inch, $2.85 ; 16-inch, $3.15 ; 18-inch, $3.45.

287. Cross-grain leather, leather lined, japanned frame, brass mountings, 14-inch, $2.85 ; 16-inch, $3.15 ; 18-inch, $3.45.

289. Same bag as No. 287, but with full leather lining and leather-covered frame, leather-covered steel handle with strap attachments, 12 inch, $3.40 ; 14-inch, $3.70 ; 16-inch, $4.00 ; 18-inch, $4.30.

290. A genuine cross-grain bag, ladies' style, leather lined, leather covered frame, solid brass mounted, this makes a very nobby bag, in either olive or tan color, 14-inch, $4.00 ; 16-inch, $4.35 ; 18-inch, $4.70.

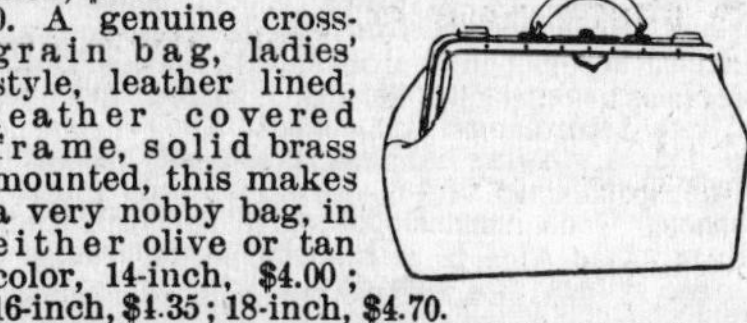

297. Genuine alligator club bag, leather lined, leather covered frame, solid brass mounted, 12-inch, $4.75 ; 14-inch, $5.35 ; 16-inch, $6.00 ; 18-inch, $6.75.

226. Lawyer's brief bag, hand sewn, black pebble grain leather, leather lined, solid brass mountings, 16-inch, $4.35 ; 18-inch, $4.75.

259. Surgical bag, chamois lined, 16-inch, $4.50 ; 18-inch, $4.75.

226. Special, same as No. 226, but in a nice colored tan buff leather, 16-inch, $4.75 ; 18-inch, $5.00.

273. Cabin bag, in brown or olive color, solid leather, leather covered frame and lining, solid brass mountings, 14-inch, $6.25 ; 16-inch, $6.75 ; 18-inch, $7.25.

126. Paris bag, solid leather, hand sewn, olive or brown, leather lined, leather covered frame, brass lock and mountings, 16-inch, $9.25 ; 18-inch, $9.75.

126½. Solid leather English travelling bag, two large outside straps, leather covered hand-sewn frame, linen lined, heavy leather capped corners, solid brass lock and mountings, 18-inch, $12.00 ; 20-inch, $13.00 ; 22-inch, $14.00 ; 24-inch, $15.00 ; 26-inch, $16.00.

261. Salisbury style bag, solid leather, linen lined, brass lock and mountings, two outside straps, 16-inch, $3.20 ; 18-inch, $3.50.

125. Gent's Victoria club bag, deep style, solid leather, leather lined, leather covered frame, hand sewn, smooth or pebble leather, brown or olive, solid brass lock and mountings, 14-inch, $6.50 ; 16-inch, $7.00 ; 18-inch, $7.50.

209. English kit bag, solid leather, hand sewn, leather covered frame, smooth or cross-grain leather, brown or olive, leather lined, and solid brass lock and mountings, 18-inch, $13.00 ; 20-inch, $14.00 ; 22-inch, $15.00.

157½. Leather suit case, linen lined, brass lock and mountings, 22-inch, $4.75 ; 24-inch, $5.00 ; 26-inch, $5.50.

159. Leather suit case, same as No. 157½, but 1½ inches deeper, 22-inch, $6.00 ; 24-inch, $6.50 ; 26-inch, $7.00.

159. Special, same as No. 159 with two straps around, 22-inch, $6.50 ; 24-inch, $7.00 ; 26-inch, $7.50.

158. Solid leather suit case, linen lined, flap in lid for shirts, solid brass mountings, 22-inch, $7.00 ; 24-inch, $7.50 ; 26-inch, $8.00.

158½. Same as No. 158, but 1½ inches deeper, 22-inch, $8.00 ; 24-inch, $8.75 ; 26-inch, $9.50.

158L. Same as No. 158, with leather lining, 22-inch, $8.50 ; 24-inch, $9.00 ; 26-inch, $9.50.

105H. Hat trunk, black enamelled cloth or grey canvas covered, hardwood slats, iron-covered bottom, leather handles, brass mountings, and good lock, size 18 inches square, fixtures for five hats, also glove tray, $6.00.

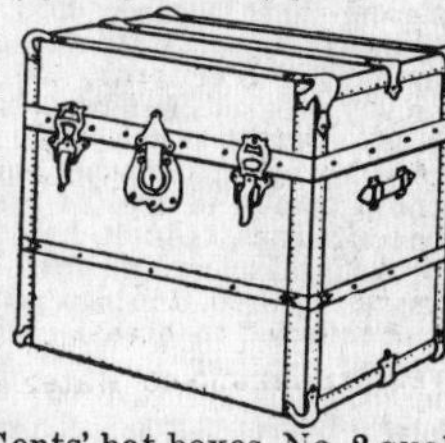

171. Gents' hat boxes, No. 2 quality plush lined, $4.00 ; No. 1 quality plush lined, $5.75.

171D. No. 1 quality plush lined, double, will hold two hats, $7.50.

191. Heavy canvas telescope bag, leather capped corners, riveted edges, 14-inch, 45c ; 16-inch, 55c ; 18-inch, 65c ; 20-inch, 80c ; 22-inch, $1.00 ; 24-inch, $1.10 ; 26-inch, $1.25.

193. Leather bound canvas telescope bag, riveted edges, three outside straps, 16-inch, $1.00 ; 18-inch, $1.25 ; 20-inch, $1.50 ; 22-inch, $1.75 ; 24-inch, $2 00 ; 26-inch, $2.25.

198. A canvas telescope, leather bound, and capped corners, wood support in bottom, 16-inch, $1.75 ; 18-inch, $2.00 ; 20-inch, $2.25 ; 22-inch, $2.50 ; 24-inch, $2.75 ; 26-inch, $3.00.

194. Canvas covered telescope suit case, leather bound and capped corners, handle on side, 16-inch, $1.00 ; 18-inch, $1.25 ; 20-inch, $1.50 ; 22-inch, $1.75 ; 24-inch, $2.00 ; 26-inch, $2.25.

English sole-leather portmanteaus, solid and bellows top, 24-inch, $20.00, 21.00 respectively.

Shaw straps, 10c, 15c, 20c, 25c, 45c each.

Gladstone bag straps, ¾-inch, 15c ; ⅞-inch, 20c ea.

Shoulder straps, with snaps and swivels, ⅝-inch, 20c ; ¾-inch, 25c ; 1-inch, 30c each.

Fibre lunch boxes, 10c, 15c, 20c each.

Folding lunch boxes, 25c each.

Address tags, leather, with strap to buckle, valise size, single space, 5c ; trunk size, double space, 10c each.

HARNESS AND HORSE GOODS DEPARTMENT.

We carry in stock harness suitable for the track, gentlemen's light driving, Surrey, English coupe, light and heavy express, dump cart, light double driving harness, medium double driving harness, double coach, double democrat, double lumber, double knockabout or plow harness—in fact, we carry every kind of harness that is ever called for in the ordinary way, also all the parts necessary to repair your old harness. If you require anything in the harness or horse goods line that you do not see in our Catalogue, write us, clearly explaining what is wanted, and we will be pleased to furnish prices, or any other information which you may require.

Single Strap Single Driving Harness.

No. 102½. Bridle, ⅝ inch, with boxed loop cheeks, good front and rosettes, over check; lines, 1 inch russet or black hand parts; breast collar, straight wide strap; traces, 1⅛-inch double and stitched ends; saddle, strap style, with large and fancy housing, skirts of saddle are doubled and stitched, strap bellybands, good strong shaft tugs with boxed loops; breeching seat single strap, wide; hip strap, ⅝-inch with boxed loops; side straps, ⅞-inch stuffed crupper, a good strong harness, suitable for any kind of light usage, nickel trimmings, very special at **$9.00** set.

No. 105. Bridle, ⅝ inch, box loops, fancy scrolled blinds, good chain front and rosettes, over check; lines, 1 inch, all black or half russet; breast collar, wide single strap, well curved out, and felt lined, with box loops; traces, 1⅛-inch, doubled and stitched at ends, buckled to breast collar; saddle, swinging bearer style, 3-inch tree, full padded patent leather skirts, leather lined, 1-inch sewed bearers, good strong shaft tugs and belly bands; breeching, 1⅛-inch body; hip strap, ⅝ inch; side straps, ⅞-inch, stuffed crupper. Nickel trimmings and neatly creased, **$10.00** set.

No. 113. Bridle, ⅝-inch with boxed loops, folded crown, patent leather blinds, round stays, chain front and crystal rosettes, over or side check; lines, 1⅛-inch, half russet or all black; breast collar, well shaped, with boxed loops; traces, 1⅛-inch, doubled and stitched at ends, and buckled to breast collar; saddle, 3-inch, patent leather jockeys and skirts, Boston metal loops, full padded, No. 1 quality, 1-inch sewn bearers, good strong shaft tugs with boxed loops, sliding belly bands; breeching, 1⅛-inch seat, ⅝-inch hip straps, boxed loops, ⅞-inch side straps, scalloped back strap with stuffed crupper—

With nickel trimmings........**$13.50 set**
With solid nickel trimmings.. **15.50** "
With genuine rubber.......... **18.00** "

The stock in No. 113 is well finished all the way through, made smooth, with rounded edges, and is a splendid looker.

No. 80. **Our Farmers' Special.** This is a real good, strong and good-looking harness, at a very reasonable price. Bridle, ⅝-inch, boxed loop cheeks, neat scrolled patent leather blinds, round stays, over checks, good metal front and rosettes; lines, 1-inch, half russet or all black; breast collar folded, wide, with layer and boxed loops; traces, 1⅛-inch, doubled and stitched, to buckle to breast collar; saddle, 3-inch, full padded, patent leather skirts and jockeys leather lined, 1-inch sewed bearers and shaft tugs, two belly bands to slide; breeching, folded seat with layer, ⅝-inch hip strap, ⅞-inch side straps, stuffed crupper, nickel trimmings, $12.00 a set.

No. 108. **Our Klondike Harness.** This harness is made of selected stock and well finished all through. Bridle, ⅝-inch, boxed loops, fancy scrolled patent leather winkers, with round stays, good chain front and crystal rosettes, over or side check; lines, 1⅛-inch, with steel spring billets, half russet or all black; breast collar folded and with wide layer, three rows of stitching, boxed loops; traces, 1⅛-inch, double and stitched, buckled to breast collar; saddle, 3-inch tree, patent leather skirts and jockeys, full padded and leather lined, first quality sewed bearers and shaft tugs, folded belly band, with sulky hitch to slide; breeching, 1¾-inch folded seat, with wide layer and three rows of stitching, ⅝-inch hip straps, boxed loops, ⅞-inch side straps, scalloped back strap, stuffed crupper, with nickel trimmings, **$14.00** set; with solid nickel trimmings, **$15.50** set; with genuine rubber trimmings, **$18.00** set.

No. 875. Bridle, ⅝-inch, boxed loop cheeks, large English blinds, round stays, side check, English chain front and rosettes; lines, 1-inch body part, with 1¼-inch folded russet hand parts, and with spring steel billets; breast collar, wide fold with scalloped and raised layer, boxed loops; traces, 1¼-inch double and stitched, raised, to buckle to breast collar; saddle, 3½-inch, patent leather skirts and jockeys full padded and leather lined, first quality sewed bearers and shaft tugs, belly bands folded and with sulky hitch; breeching, folded seat with scalloped and raised layer, with 3 rows of stitching, ¾-inch double and stitched hip straps, boxed loops, 1-inch side straps, scalloped back strap with stuffed crupper sewed on. A very suitable harness for gladstone or phaeton. Solid nickel trimmings, **$22.00** set.

No. 106. Collar and hame surrey harness. We believe this to be the greatest value ever offered in this kind of harness. It is all cut from good stock, well-finished, and is a very strong as well as a handsome harness. Bridle ⅝-inch, boxed loop cheeks, large round corner patent leather blinds, with round stays, fancy chain front and rosettes, side check, Liverpool bit, nose band, medium weight patent leather collar, full nickel hames; traces, 1¼-inch, double and stitched; lines, 1⅛-inch all black or half russet; saddle, 4-inch, full patent leather skirts and jockeys, full leather lined, 1⅛-inch, sewed bearers to slide, sewed shaft tugs; breeching, 1¾-inch fold, with scalloped and raised layer, ⅝-inch double hip straps, boxed loops, 1-inch side straps, stuffed crupper, nickel trimmings, **$21.00** set.

No. 155. A similar harness to No. 106, but much finer gotten up, and made of specially selected stock. This harness is made in right up-to-date style and is a **beauty**, solid nickel or brass trimmings, **$29.00** set.

Light Double Driving Harness.

No. 36. A very stylish harness and a winner at the price. Bridles, ⅝-inch, boxed loop cheeks, neat patent leather blinds, and over or side checks, fancy chain fronts and rosettes; collars half patent, hames full nickel, hame tugs 1⅛-inch, with boxed loops; traces, 1⅛-inch, double and stitched; pole straps, 1⅛-inch; martingales, 1-inch; light coach pads, with neat housings; lines, all black or half russet; back straps scalloped, stuffed cruppers, nickel trimmings, **$25.00** set.

No. 36½. Same as No. 36, but with genuine rubber trimmings all through, and full patent leather collars, **$31.50.**

No. 140. Double carriage harness, similar to No. 36, but much better and heavier, solid nickel trimmings, **$37.50** set.

Collars and Hames.

Half patent light buggy collar, with iron buggy hames, black, with nickel terrets and draft eyes, hame tugs with box loops attached, $4.50.

Half patent light buggy collar, with full nickel buggy hames and hame tugs, $4.75.

Full patent buggy collar, medium weight, with close plate buggy hames, double draft, solid nickel buckles, and boxed loops on hame tugs, complete, $7.75.

In case you want any of above collars and hames put on single breast collar harness we allow—

For No. 102½	harness	breast collar,	$1.50
" 105	"	"	1.75
" 113	"	"	2.00
" 80	"	"	1.50
" 108	"	"	2.00
" 875	"	"	2.25

Team Farm Harness.

No. 1. Bridles, ¾-inch harness leather blinds, or open bridles if desired, round stays and side checks, stiff or jointed bits; lines, ⅞-inch, full length, good heavy stock, with snaps; collars, (No. 5) a good strong work collar, open tops, cloth or leather faced; hames, wood, high top, steel bound; hame tugs, 1½ x 18 inches, buckling to trace, with double grip trace buckle, the best heavy harness trace buckle in use; traces, 1½ inch x 6 feet, 3-ply leather, iron cockeyes at ends; martingales, 1½-inch, pole straps, 1½ inch, with snaps; back bands, padded, leather lined, and have fancy housings, hooks and terrets, back straps, hip straps and cruppers, complete with snaps and chain spreaders, **$25.00** set.

No. 2. A similar harness to No. 1, with following changes: hame tugs, traces, pole straps, martingales are 1¾-inch, lines 1-inch, price, complete, **$26.00.**

For putting on heavy double hip strap breechings on Nos. 1 or 2 team harness, we charge $4.25 extra.

For taking off back bands, and putting heavy crotch breechings on Nos. 1 and 2, we charge $1.00 extra.

If you do not require collars on above team harness, take off $4.00 from price.

No. 3. Special Team Harness. This is a hand-sewn harness cut from first-class stock and is gotten up expressly for our trade. Some of our customers have occasionally written asking for something better than the ordinary farm harness. The combined features of good workmanship, good material and good appearance will be found in Nos. 3 and 6 special, and we look for big things from it. Description of set: Bridles, ⅞-inch cheeks, boxed loops, patent leather winkers, good fronts, rosettes, face pieces, round side checks, stiff or jointed bits; lines, first quality, 1-inch, wit snaps; collars, cork lined, thong sewn, leather faced; hames, steel bound, high top, staple; hame tugs, 3-ply x 1½ inch, with double grip buckles, martingales 1½-inch, pole straps 1½-inch, with iron slides and snaps; traces, 3-ply x 1½-inch with cockeyes, back bands padded and with large fancy housings, also hooks and terrets, belly bands heavy folded, back straps, hip straps and cruppers; trimmings, XC plate all through, complete with snaps and spreader chains, **$28.50.**

No. 6. Special Team Harness. A similar harness to No. 3, but much heavier, the changes are as follows: Hames are heavy No. 10 bolt, steel bound, hames tugs are 3-ply x 1¾-inch; traces are 1¾-inch, 3-ply; breast straps and martingales are 1¾-inch; all complete with snaps, spreaders and slides, per set, **$30.00.**

For putting on heavy double hip strap breechings on Nos. 3 and 6 team harness, we charge $4.25 extra.

For taking off back bands, and putting heavy crotch breechings on Nos. 3 and 6, we charge $1.00 extra.

If you do not want collars on Nos. 3 or 6, take off $4.50 from price.

Our No. 1 **Special Truck Harness.** We do not believe this harness can be equalled for the money outside this store; it is a hand-sewn harness and suitable for extra heavy work. Bridles, ⅞-inch, boxed loop cheeks, choice of patent leather blinds or pigeon wing blinds on bridles, round side checks, good fronts and rosettes, stiff or jointed bits; lines 1¼-inch heavy stock, good length with snaps; collars, heavy Scotch, open tops, long straw, cloth or leather faced; hames, No. 10 Concorde bolt, steel clad; hame tugs and traces, 1¾-inch, 3-ply; martingales and breast straps, 2-inch with snaps and slides; breeching seat, heavy fold with wide layer; hip straps double 1-inch, crotch straps 1-inch, running to market tug and then to hame, same as cut, side straps, 1-inch, with snaps running under horse to martingales, price of this splendid harness, **$32.25.**

HARNESS PARTS.

TRACES.

All traces 6 feet long, unless specified otherwise.

Single strap buggy traces, 1⅛-inch, $1.50; 1¼-inch, $1.85 pair.

Double and stitched buggy traces, 1⅛-inch, $1.65; 1¼-inch, $2.10 pair.

Double and stitched buggy traces, 6 ft. 6 inches, 1⅛-inch, $2.00; 1¼-inch, $2.50 pair.

Team harness traces, 3-ply with cockeyes, 1½-inch, $6.00; 1½-inch, $7.50; 1¾-inch, $8.75, set of four.

3-ply, 2-in. wide, with 15-in. steel heel chains, made for bolt hames only, $10.75 set of four.

Single-ply traces, 2½ inches wide, with 3-ply points, with either hooks or toggles, $8.50 per set of four.

Bridles.

The bridles under this heading are the same as on our sets, for full description of bridle see corresponding number on set.

No. 1. Team bridles, blind, $3.75 pair.
No. 1. Team bridles, open, $3.15 pair.
No. 1. Team bridles, with pigeon wing blinds, instead of square blinds, $3.90 pair.
No. 3. Team bridles, blind, $4.35 pair.
Team show bridles, ⅞-inch cheeks, with large patent leather blinds, metal fronts and rosettes, ring nose band, round check reins, extra heavy and showy, price per pair, $7.00.
No. 105. Buggy harness bridle, over check, nickel, $2.25 each.
No. 113. Buggy harness bridle, over check, in nickel, $2.50; in solid nickel, $3.00; in genuine rubber, $3.45 each.
No. 108. Bridle, over check, in nickel, $2.50; in solid nickel, $3.00; in genuine rubber, $3.50.

For putting on side check instead of over check, 25c extra, any of above buggy harness bridles made open instead of blind at same price.

No. 155. Harness bridle, nickel or brass, $4.00 each; in solid nickel, $5.00 each.

Riding Bridles.

No. 1. Single rein riding bridle, full cheek bit, $1.35 each.
No. 2. Double rein riding bridle, Pelham chain curb bit, a neat strong bridle, $2.80 each.
No. 4. Western riding bridle, good stock and well made, without bit, 90c each.
No. 7½. Cowboys or stockman's bridle, extra heavy stock, well finished, without bit, $2.00 each.

Breechings.

No. 105. Buggy harness breeching, nickel, complete, $3.00.
No. 108. Buggy harness breeching, nickel, complete, $3.35.
No. 1. Single work harness breeching, XC plate, $2.85; nickel or brass, $3.25.
No. 1. Team pad breechings, to be used with back bands, $5.75 per set.
No. 2. Team crotch breechings, to be used without back bands, $6.25 set.

Stirrup Straps.

Good solid stock to buckle, 1-inch, 75c pair; 1¼-inch, $1.00 pair.

Martingales.

Single buggy harness martingales, white rings, 65c each.
Single buggy harness martingales, rubber rings, 75c each.
Double buggy harness martingales, nickel buckles, ⅞-inch, 60c each; 1-inch, 65c each; 1-inch with patent leather frog, 85c each.
Team work harness martingales, good heavy stock, 1¼-inch, 35c; 1½-inch, 45c; 1¾-inch, 55c; 2-inch, 75c each.
Team work harness check reins, round, 50c; flat, 45c each.
Buggy harness over checks, nickel, 60c each; genuine rubber, 75c each.
Buggy harness, side checks, nickel, 60c each; genuine rubber, 75c each.

Bridle Fronts or Brow Bands.

Team fronts, solid leather, 10c, 12c each.
Nickel or brass team fronts, 20c each.
Light driving harness fronts, neat assortment of chains, etc., nickel, 15c each.
The handy reversible front, nickel, 18c each.
The "basket" front, stylish, 25c each.
Medium and heavy English style chain fronts, 30c, 35c, 50c each; in leather, 30c each.

Housings.

Plain felt gig saddle housings, 20c each.
Wide felt express housings, 35c, 50c each.
All felt team pad housings, 50c pair.
Fancy imitation patent leather top gig saddle housings, felt lined, 20c, 35c each.
Patent leather housings, fancy edge felt lined, 40c each.
Patent leather housings, plain, beaded edge, very stylish, 50c each.
Patent leather "basket" housing, 65c each.
Breast collar housings, patent leather, shaped, 65c each; straight, 50c each; all felt, 35c each.

Bridle Parts.

Team bridle crowns, 25c each.
" " throat latches, 20c each.
" " cheeks for open bridles, $2.00 set.
Buggy harness bridle crowns, 20c, 25c each.
" " " throat latches, 15c.
Team bridle cheeks, with blinds attached, $3.70 set.
Light harness round cheeks, nickel, 50c pair; genuine rubber, 85c pair.
Light harness boxed loop cheeks, with neat blinds attached, nickel, $1.25 pair.

Rosettes.

Team harness rosettes, 2¼-inch nickel or brass, 15c pair.
Light nickel rosettes, for light harness, 15c pair.
Fancy assorted glass rosettes, horse and dog heads, and floral designs, 20c pair.
Glass rosettes, plain, 15c pair.
Imitation rubber rosettes, 25c pair; genuine rubber, 50c, 75c pair.

Team Lines.

No 1 Team lines, cut from good heavy selected stock, ⅞-inch, $2.45; 1-inch, $2.65; 1⅛-inch, $3.00; 1¼-inch, $3.50 set.
Single driving lines, all black or half russet, 1-inch, with loop, $1.25 pair; 1-inch, to buckle, $1.45 pair; 1⅛-inch, with steel billet, $1.65 pair; 1¼-inch, with steel billet, $2.00 pair.
Single driving lines, 1-inch body part with 1¼-inch folded russet hand parts; this makes a nice driving line (a sure grip), and is especially suited for ladies' use, $2.65.
Double driving lines, black or half russet, $3.00; full russet, $3.50 pair.
Rope plow lines with handles and snaps, hemp, 20c; cotton, 25c pair.
Leather loop hand pieces, for driving lines, 75c pair.
Team belly bands, folded, heavy, 55c each.
Buggy harness belly bands, straps, 50c; folded, 70c pair.
Sulky hitch belly bands, 80c each.
Shaft tugs, suitable for Nos. 102½, 105, 113, 80, 108 harness, nickel, 55c; solid nickel, 75c; genuine rubber, $1.25 pair.
Suitable for Nos. 875, 106, 155 harness, nickel, $1.00; solid nickel, $1.25 pair.

Gig Saddles.

No. 102½. Harness saddles, $2.25 each.
No. 1. Plain strap saddle, $1.85 each.
No. 105. Harness saddle, $3.00.
No. 113. " " nickel, $3.50; solid nickel, $4.00; genuine rubber, $5.00.
No. 106. Harness saddle, nickel, $5.50.
Team back bands, well padded and have large fancy housings, hooks and terrets, XC plate, $4.00 pair.

Turf and Interfering Boots.

We quote the lines most in use. We carry a complete line of these goods; if you do not see what you want, write us.

Ankle boots, solid leather, 15c each.
" " " felt lined, 20c each.
" " " zinc " 25c "
" front or hind, calf skin wrapper, $1.00 pair.
Front shin and ankle boots, with elastic, $2.00 pair.
Hind shin and ankle boots, $2.50 pair.
Knee boots, $2.50 pair.
Knee and arm boots, $3.00 pair.
Shoulder straps, 75c pair.
Scalpers, $1.35 pair.
Cornets "
Bell quarter boots, $2.50 pair.
Hinged " " "
Pacing " one piece or two piece, $2.50 pair.
Stationery quarter boots, $2.50 pair.
Trotting balls, 35c per string.
Speeding hobbles, $5.00 set.
Bandages, derby, 50c, set of four.
Newmarket bandages, superior quality and extra long, $1.50, set of four.
We do not break sets of bandages.

Sweat Collars.

No. 1 quality white drill sweat pads, brown backs, hair stuffed, large and extra quality, 35c each.
No. 1 quality all-felt sweat pads, 4 springs, heavy felt, 65c each.
Heavy white duck feed bags, ventilated, 75c each.
Leather pipes for chain traces, 50c each.
Cruppers, for buggy harness, nickel buckles, 25c each.
Cruppers for team harness, XC plated buckles, large, 25c each.

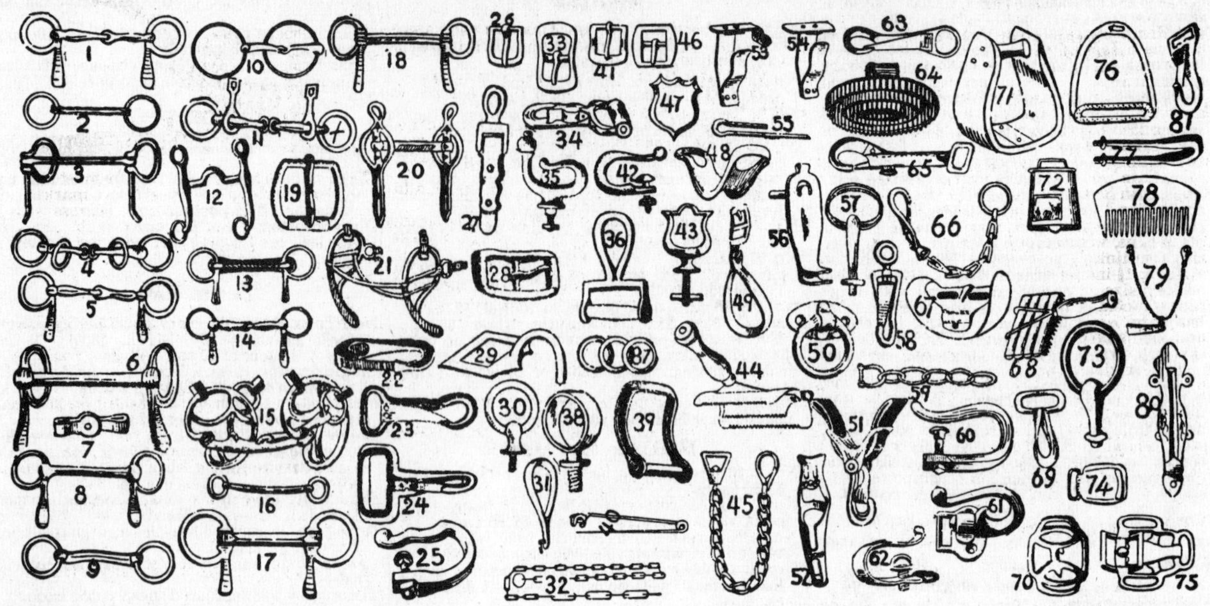

No. 1. Nickel-plated half-cheek snaffle bit, jointed, 20c; in imitation rubber, 25c each.
No. 2. Double-twisted wire scissors bit, severe, 20c each.
No. 3. Solid bar, half-cheek snaffle bit, nickel-plated, stiff or jointed, 30c each.
Full-cheek riding bridle bits, stiff or jointed, 15c each.
No. 4. Four ring Wilson bit, in fine XC plate, 20c each; nickel-plated, 50c each.
No. 5. Nickel-plated half-cheek Dexter bit, heavy, jointed, 35c each.
No. 6. Forged-steel Dexter bit, half-cheek, stiff, an extra good bit for the money, $1.00 each.
No. 7. Steel chain repair links, to rivet, absolutely unbreakable, 4c each or 45c doz.
No. 8. Nickel-plated, half-cheek Dexter bit, stiff, 35c each.
No. 9. Rubber-covered mouth team bit, 25c each.
No. 10. Nickel-plated racing bit, large loose rings, jointed, 50c each.
No. 11. The old familiar Rockwell bit, in fine XC plate, 20c; nickel-plated, 50c each.
No. 12. Port riding bit, nickel-plated, without curb chain, 65c each.
No. 13. Flexible rubber half-cheek bit. This bit has a steel chain running through centre, as shown in cut, 50c each.
The Columbia, a similar bit to No. 13, 35c each.
No. 14. Common team bits, XC plated, stiff or jointed, plain ring ends, 8c each.
No. 15. The Imperial bit. This bit positively cures tongue lolling and prevents side-pulling. It will control the most vicious horse, and can instantly be changed to suit the most tender mouth. In fine XC plate, $1.00 each; nickel-plated, $1.50.
No. 16. Steel over-check bit, 10c each.
No. 17. Solid leather mouth bit. This is one of the best bits in use to-day for tender or sore mouths, 65c each.
No. 18. Nickel-plated, double bar, half-cheek snaffle bit, stiff only, 30c each.
No. 19. Single bar, common roller buckle, XC or japanned, ⅝-inch, 10c; ¾-inch, 12c; ⅞-inch, 15c; 1-inch, 18c; 1¼-inch, 20c; 1½-inch, 25c; 1¾-inch, 30c doz.
No. 20. The Liverpool curb bit. Complete with chain curb, nickel-plated, $1.00; solid nickel, $1.75 ea.
No. 21. The famous Jay-Eye-See bit, is considered one of the most effective bits for use on vicious and unruly horses, XC plated, 50c each.

No. 22. Bit snaps, for use on halter bridles, 4c each or 45c doz.
The favorite bit snap, opens at both ends, 3c each or 30c doz; larger size, 5c each.
No. 23. German snaps, 1-inch, 2 for 5c, or 25c doz; 1½-inch, 5c each, 50c doz; 1¾-inch, 6c each, 65c doz; 2-inch, 8c each or 90c doz.
No. 24. Champion snaps, 1-inch, 2 for 5c, or 25c doz; 1½-inch, 5c each, 50c doz; 1¾-inch, 6c each, 65c doz; 2-inch, 7c each or 75c doz.
No. 25. Gig saddle hook, nickel or brass, 10c each; $1.00 doz.
No. 26. Single-bar harness buckle, nickel, wire pattern, ½-inch, 15c; ⅝-inch, 20c; ¾-inch, 25c; ⅞-inch, 35c; 1-inch, 50c doz.
No. 27. Clip cockeyes, for repairing traces, 8c each or 90c doz.
No. 28. Double bar buckle, with roller, XC or japanned, ½-inch, 10c; ⅝-inch, 12c; ¾-inch, 15c; ⅞-inch, 18c doz.
No. 29. The "Simple" trace carrier, XC plated, 5c pair; 50c doz pairs.
No. 30. Gig saddle terret, wire patterns, nickel or brass, 12c each or $1.25 doz.
No. 31. Chapman side-check swivel, nickel, 15c pair or $1.50 doz pairs.
No. 32. Steel trace chains, length 7 ft, 60c; 7½ ft, 75c pair.
No. 33. Fancy double bar buckle, nickel or brass, ⅝-inch, 7c; ¾-inch, 8c; ⅞-inch, 9c; 1-inch, 10c; 1¼-inch, 25c each.
No. 34. Breast strap roller snaps, 1¼-inch, 20c; 1½-inch, 22c; 2-inch, 25c each.
No. 35. Gig saddle post hook, very stylish, in wire or band pattern or C shape, as desired, nickel, 25c each or $2.75 doz; in XC plate or japan, 10c each.
No. 36. Screw cockeye, 1¼-inch, 4c each or 45c doz; 1½-inch, 5c each or 50c doz; 1¾-inch, 5c each or 50c doz.
No. 37. Martingale or spread rings, composition, in red, white or blue, 5c each or 50c doz.
Large wooden rings, in red, white or blue, 5c each, 50c doz.
Celluloid rings, white only, inside measure, 1½-inch, 25c each; 1¾-inch 30c each; 2-inch, 35c each; 2¼-inch, 45c each.
No. 38. Gig saddle terret, band pattern, nickel or brass, 12c each or $1.25 doz; XC plate, 5c each, or 50c doz.
No. 39. Screw bale or hame tug loops for double-grip trace buckles, 7c each or 75c doz.
No. 40. Large safety-pins for horse blankets, 5c each or 50c doz.
No. 41. Single-bar harness buckle, nickel, band pattern, ½-inch, 15c; ⅝-inch, 20c; ¾-inch, 25c; ⅞-inch, 35c; 1-inch, 50c doz.
No. 42. Gig saddle-hook, wire pattern, nickel or brass, 12c each or $1.25 doz.
No. 43. Fancy terrets, very neat, 10c each, $1.00 doz; oval shaped terrets and hooks, japanned, 5c each.
No. 44. Steel cattle comb, 12c each.
No. 45. Stallion lead chain, all steel, snap and swivel, length 18-inch, 35c each.
Steel leading chain, ring and swivel snap, heavy, length 18-inch, 20c each.
No. 46. Fancy double-bar buckle, flat or band style, in brass only, ⅞-inch, 6c; 1-inch, 7c; 1½-inch, 15c each.
No. 47. Fancy ornaments, shield-shape, brass only, ⅞-inch, 5c each or 50c doz; 1-inch, 6c each or 65c doz; 1¼-inch, 7c each or 75c doz; 1½-inch, 8c each or 85c doz; 1¾-inch, 10c each or $1.00 doz; plain nickel spots, ½-inch and ⅝-inch, 1c each or 10c doz; ¾-inch and ⅞-inch, 2c each or 20c doz.
No. 48. Breast strap slides or irons, 1¼-inch, 5c each or 50c doz; 1½-inch, 7c each or 75c doz; 2-inch, 10c each or $1.00 doz.
No. 49. Flexible side-check swivels, for team harness, in fine XC plate or japanned, 5c pair or 50c doz pairs; nickel-plated, for buggy harness, 20c pair.
No. 50. Drop terret, XC plate or japanned, 8c each or 85c doz.
No. 51. The combined breast strap, slide and snap, a very convenient and durable article, 1¼ and 1½-inch, 25c each.
No. 52. Common whip socket, japanned, 5c each or 50c doz.
No. 53. Anti-rattler and bolt holder, steel, 15c pair or $1.75 doz pairs.
No. 54. Anti-rattler, 10c pair or $1.00 doz pairs.
No. 55. Hame clips, 3c each or 30c doz.
No. 56. Tongues for repairing double-grip buckles, easily put on, XC or japanned, 5c each or 50c doz.
No. 57. Hame line rings, with washers, 5c each or 50c doz.
No. 58. Round-eye swivel snap, steel, ¾-inch eye, 4c each or 40c doz.
No. 59. Heel chains for team traces, 1½-inch, 20c each; 1¾-inch, 25c each; 2-inch, 30c each.
No. 60. Gig saddle hook, band pattern, nickel or brass, 12c each or $1.25 doz.
No. 61. Drop hook, XC or japanned, 8c each or 85c doz.
No. 62. "Syracuse" pad hook for team harness, XC plated, 7c each or 75c doz; japanned, 5c each or 50c doz.
No. 63. Round-eye German snaps, ½-inch, 2 for 5c or 25c doz; ⅝-inch, 2 for 5c or 25c doz; ¾-inch, 3c each or 30c doz.
No. 64. "Horse's Friend" curry-comb, 15c each.
No. 65. Bolt snap, 1-inch, 3c each or 30c doz; 1½-inch, 5c each or 50c doz; 1¾-inch, 6c each or 65c doz; 2-inch, 8c each or 85c doz.
No. 66. Steel spreader or rein chain, ring and swivel snap, 8c each or 85c doz; 4-ring spreader straps, composition ring, 90c pair; 3-ring spreader straps, celluloid rings, $2.00 pair; 4 rings, $2.50 pair.
No. 67. Zinc collar top pad, two sizes, without straps, 25c and 30c each; straps for zinc collar pads, 16c pair.
No. 68. Curry combs, 5 bars, closed back, 6c; 6 bars, closed back, 15c; 6 bars open back, 10c; 6 bars, open back, with mane comb, 18c each.
No. 69. The "Gem" snap, 1-inch, 4c each or 40c doz; 1½-inch, 6c. each or 65c doz; 1¾-inch, 7c each or 75c doz; 2-inch, 10c each or $1.00 doz.
No. 70. Trace-carrier, to sew on or to rivet, very strong, 5c each or 50c doz.
No. 71. Wooden stirrups, 25c pair.
Wooden stirrups, galvanized iron bound, 2½-inch wide, $1.00 pair.
Same, only brass bound, $1.25 pair.
No. 72. Cow bells, height 4½-inch, 20c; 5½-inch, 25c; 6½-inch, 35c each. Sheep bells, 10c and 15c each.
No. 73. Hame breast-strap rings, with washers, 5c each or 50c doz.
No. 74. Buckle shields or keepers, nickel or brass, ⅝ and ¾-inch 8c each, or 85c doz; ⅞ and 1-inch, 10c each or $1.00 doz.
Patent wire shields, in nickel or imitation rubber, ⅝-inch size, 3c each; ¾-inch size, 4c each; ⅞-inch size, 5c each.
No. 75. The double-grip trace buckle, the strongest and handiest trace buckle on the market to-day, in fine XC plate or nicely japanned, 1¼-inch, 10c; 1½-inch, 12c; 1¾-inch, 15c each.
No. 76. Stirrup irons, XC plated, 25c; nickel plated, light, 75c; heavy, 95c pair.
No. 77. Hame staples with washers, 3c each or 30c doz.
No. 78. Horse mane or tail comb, made of horn, very strong, 10c each.
No. 79. Heavy breast chains, snap on one end to shorten chain if necessary, each chain tested, 75c pr.
No. 80. Combined whip and line holder, 35c.
No. 81. All steel snaps, 1-inch, 2 for 5c, or 25c doz; 1½-inch, 5c each or 50c doz; 1¾-inch, 6c each or 65c doz.
Curb chains, nickel, 35c; solid nickel, 50c each.

Snaps.

The Merritt breast strap buckle snap, strong buckle attached to snap, to use for making breast straps out of old traces, etc., 1¼-inch, 25c pair.
Heavy stallion bits, stiff, 25c each.
Hanoverian curb bits (no chain), in fine XC plate, 25c each; nickel plated, $1.25 each.
Steel chain calf ties, 15c each.
Steel chain cow ties, 20c each.
Steel chain bull ties, extra strong, 35c each.
Steel chain halter shanks, 20c each.
"Dominion" cow tie stall fixture, 15c each.
Steel picket chains, 20-ft, $1.00 each.
Picket pins, with swivel, 20c each.
Cold shut links, for repairing chain, 1-inch size, 3c doz; 1⅜-inch size, 5c doz; 1½-inch size, 8c doz; 1¾-inch size, 10c doz: 2-inch size, 15c doz.
Assorted cold shut repair links, for farmers' or trappers' use, per box, 25c.
One ring swivel, ¾-inch rings, 36c doz.
Two ring swivel, ¾-inch rings, 60c doz.
Two ring swivel, 1-inch rings, 84c doz.
Harness rings, XC plate, ⅞-inch, 5c doz; 1-inch, 6c doz. Japanned (light), 1½-inch, 10c doz; 1¾-inch, 11c doz; 2-inch, 12c doz. Japanned (heavy), 1½-inch, 15c doz; 1¾-inch, 18c doz; 2-inch, 25c doz.
The old reliable "lock" snap, 1-inch, 5c each; 1½-inch, 8c each; 1¾-inch, 10c each.

Tethering Hobbles.

Tethering hobbles, extra heavy stock, 75c pair.

Kicking straps, 1¼-inch, $1.15 each; 1½-inch, $1.25.

Weight straps, 1-inch x 7 ft., 35c each; 1-inch x 12 ft., 65c each; 1¼-inch x 7 ft., 45c each; 1¼-inch x 12 ft., 75c each.

Hames.

No. 8. Concorde bolt hames, steel bound, varnished, set for 2 horses, $2.00.
No. 10. Bolt hames, extra heavy steel bound, set for 2 horses, $2.50.
No. 2. Hook hames, steel bound, steel hooks. $1.50, set for 2 horses.
No. 3. Hook hames, heavy steel bound, steel hocks, $1.70, set for 2 horses.

Hames, with Hame Tugs attached.

No. 1. Team harness hames, with 1½-inch hame tugs attached, ready for use, $6.00 for set, 2 horses.

No. 2. Team harness hames, and hame tugs, $6.25 set.

Japanned buggy hames, nickel trimmings, with hame tugs attached, $2.00; full nickel, $2.25; full brass, $2.00 pair.

When ordering hames, give size of collar they are to be used with.

Breast Collars.

Complete with neck straps.

No. 105. Harness breast collar, nickel buckles, $1.75 each.
No. 113. Harness breast collar, nickel, $2.00 each,
No. 108. Harness breast collar, nickel, $2.00; solid nickel, $2.25 each.
Heavy express or working breast collar, felt lined, double neck strap, felt lined, 1¼-inch or 1½-inch buckles, $2.85 each.
No. 35½. Double harness breast collar, with pole strap irons, all complete, $5.50 per set.
Breast straps for carriage harness, nickel or brass buckles, 1⅛-inch, 60c each.
For team harness, 1½-inch, 45c; 1¾-inch, 55c; 2-inch, 75c each.
Team breeching side straps, heavy stock, good length, ⅞-inch, 35c; 1-inch, 40c each.
Single harness breeching or side strap, ⅞-inch, 20c; 1-inch, 25c; 1⅛-inch, 30c; 1¼-inch, 35c each.
Twin neck yoke breeching straps, 1¼-inch, $2.50 set of 4; 1½-inch, $3.00 set of 4.
Hame straps, ⅝-inch and ¾-inch, 8c; ⅞-inch, 9c; 1-inch, 10c; 1⅛-inch, 12c; 1¼-inch, 14c each.
Hitch or tie reins, with snap, ⅝-inch, 20c; ¾-inch, 22c; ⅞-inch, 25c each.
Halter shanks, 1-inch, 22c; 1⅛-inch, 25c; 1¼-inch, 30c each.

Collars.

Be sure and measure your horse collar from inside of top to inside of bottom.
No. 1. Scotch collars, long straw, open or closed top, leather or cloth faced, $2.85 each.
Full Scotch, high tops, 1 row cane, $8.75; 2 row cane, $10.00; 3 row cane, extra high and heavy, $11.25 pair.
For pipe in any Scotch collar add $1.00 to price.
No. 5. Short straw collars, cloth or leather faced, open tops, the best work collar on the market for the money, $2.00 each.
Our No. 13 cork lined, thong sewed collar, a very popular work collar and one that will give grand satisfaction, open top, leather faced only, $2.25 each.
No. 35½. Half patent buggy collar, light, $2.50 each.
No. 37. Full patent buggy collar, light, $3.25 each.
No. 155. Half patent coupe or surrey collar, medium weight, $3.00 each.
No. 160. Full patent coupe or surrey collar, medium, $3.75 each.

Halters.

Riveted halters, good strong shanks, 1-inch, 65c; 1¼-inch, 75c each.
Sewed halters, extra heavy, well selected stock and well sewn, 1-inch, 90c each.
Our leader, 1¼-inch sewed halter, specially selected stock, strong shank, an A1 heavy halter, which we do not believe can be easily duplicated at the price, $1.15 each.
1-inch sewn halter, with shank, colt size, 90c.
Adjustable web halters, rope shank, heavy web, 25c each.
Rope neck halter, ring and snap, 10c each.

Horse Dandy Brushes.

No. 54. Whisk, dandy, 15c.
No. 50. Superior whisk, a splendid brush for the money, 25c each.
No. 52. Superior whisk, large size, something extra in a dandy brush. 35c each.
No. 53. Superior English, best quality, well filled, warranted, 45c each.

Horse Body Brushes.

No. 44. Leather back, yellow bristles, 25c each.
No. 45. Leather back, fine quality of yellow bristles, good strap, 50c each.
No. 140. Leather back, best quality bristles, filled, strong strap, $1.00 each.
No. 46. Wooden back, mixed hair and bristles, 25c each.
No. 47. Similar brush to No. 46, only larger and better filled, 35c each.
No. 48. Wooden back, bristle filled, a good strong brush, 50c each.
No. 60. Wooden back, superior quality of bristles, extra strong leather strap on back, $1.15 each.

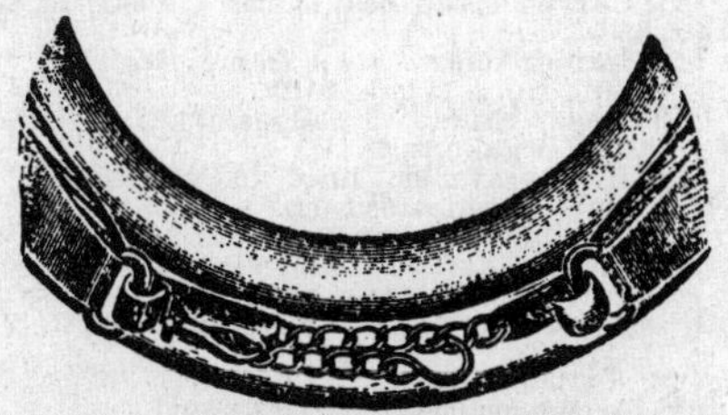

The success hame fastener, stronger and better than a dozen hame straps, and twice as handy, 35c each.

Washers.

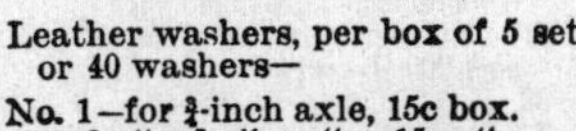

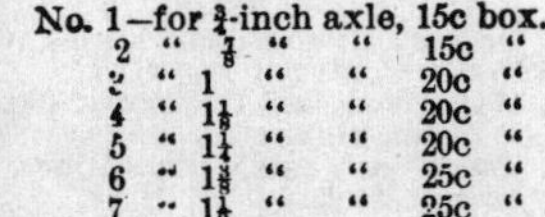

Leather washers, per box of 5 sets, or 40 washers—

No. 1—for ¾-inch axle, 15c box.
2 " ⅞ " " 15c "
3 " 1 " " 20c "
4 " 1⅛ " " 20c "
5 " 1¼ " " 20c "
6 " 1⅜ " " 25c "
7 " 1½ " " 25c "

Coil axle washers, can be cut to fit any size axle, 5 coils or 100 washers in each box, 25c box.

The farmer's friend. One of the most useful and money saving devices on the market. You can repair any part of your harness with it in a very short time; price, 35c each. Rivets for above, 2 packages, assorted sizes, for 15c.

Whips.

Buggy whips, 6-ft. straight, 15c, 25c, 35c, 50c, 75c, $1.00, 1.50 each.
Team whips, one piece, 25c, 35c, 75c, $1.00, 1.25 each.
Hickory stocks, with loop, 10c each.
Leather covered black-snake stocks, 50c each.
Genuine horse hide whip lashes, 3 ft, 10c; 4 ft, 15c; 5 ft, 20c; 6 ft, 25c each.
Genuine buckskin lashes, 5 ft, 30c each.
Solid rawhide riding whip, with hand loop, 25c each.
Imitation holly lash whips, 50c each.
Genuine " " $1.00, 1.50, 2.00, 2.50 each.

Harness Polish, Soap, Oils, etc.

Alligator harness oil, pints, 25c; quarts, 35c.
F. Miller's harness oil, superior quality, pints, 35c; quarts, 50c.
Axle oil, 25c pint.
Harness soap, in bars, 18c, 20c; in tin boxes, 10c, 20c each.
Peerless hoof ointment, best healing remedy known, 20c box.
Diamond axle grease, 5c box.
Mica axle grease, tin, 10c; 3-lb pail, 25c.
F. Miller's carriage top dressing, ½-pint tins, 30c.

Horse Blankets.

We do not sell horse blankets by the pair, prices quoted is for single blanket.

Unlined jute stable blankets, good quality striped jute, medium size, shaped and strapped, 40c, 65c, 85c each.

Our special lined stable blanket, good quality striped jute, ¾-lined with wool, medium size, shaped and strapped, very special, 85c each.

Our blizzard, full lined, stable blanket, heavy quality of jute and kersey wool quilted in lining, well shaped and strapped, size 72 x 72 inches, $1.10 each.

The Prairie. Heavy full-lined jute stable blanket, broken check pattern, full lined and quilted with a good quality of wool lining, full size, shaped and strapped, $1.35 each.

Our Klondike Blanket. Heavy quality of striped jute, lined all through with a good quality of Kersey wool quilted in, well strapped and shaped, full size, $1.65 each.

Our heavy stallion blanket, made specially for large horses or stallions, extra heavy quality of striped jute and lined all through with a superior quality of wool (quilted in), size 76 x 84 inches, shaped and strapped, $1.75 each.

Manitoba Blanket. First quality materials are used in the make up of this blanket; it is good looking and a great wearer, made of extra strong jute, full lined and quilted with wool, and all bound with fancy binding, size 72 x 74 inches, our price for this splendid blanket, $2.00 each.

(Can't come off.)

Stay-on blankets, fitted with surcingles to snap, made of heavy jute, and with heavy wool lining quilted in, full size, well shaped, $1.50 each.

Stay-on blankets, made of heavy brown duck, heavy lining quilted in, 2 surcingles to snap, well shaped and good size, $2.50 each.

Kersey Horse Blanket. The famous Kersey blanket, neat stripe, strong and warm, shaped and bound, full size, $1.15 each.

Saxony Kersey, full size, extra heavy, strong and warm, good size, shaped and bound, $1.35 each.

The favorite Kersey blanket, plain brown color, bound with fancy red binding, large size, very warm and a good looker, one of our most popular lines, well shaped and strapped, $2.25 each.

Superior English Kersey blankets, in fawn or blue color, well bound, extra quality, large size, well shaped and strapped, $3.25 each.

Surcingles or Blanket Girths

No. 1. Made of strong jute, good strap and buckle, not padded, 15c each.
No. 2. Strong webbing strap and buckle, not padded, 25c each.
No. 3. Padded surcingle, made of jute, good pad, strap and buckle, 25c each.
No. 4. Padded, good strong web, soft pad, buckle and strap, 35c each.
No. 5. Heavy surcingle, made of extra heavy web, large soft pad, heavy strap and buckle, large size only, 50c each.

Woollen Horse Blankets.

(For outdoor or street use.)

No. 0. All-wool shaped horse blanket, medium size, neat red and black check, with strap and buckle, $2.25 each.
Nos. 1, 2, 3. The favorite, all-wool, shaped and strapped, in a good range of colors, in blue and black, green and black, and red and black, medium size, $2.50 each.
No. 4. All-wool blanket, bound with fancy braid, plain colors in either fawn or plain blue medium size, shaped and strapped, $2.50 each.
No. 5. Sandow, pure all-wool street blanket, plain dark blue color, with wide braid binding, size 80 x 86 inches, shaped and strapped, a strong and stylish looking outdoor blanket, $6.00 each.

Square Street Blankets.

No. 6. Woollen blanket, plain grey with red and blue stripes, with strap and buckle, size 80 x 80 inches, a good servicable blanket, $2.25 each.
No. 7. All-wool blanket, 80 x 80 inches square, neat red and black check, with straps, $3.00 each.
No. 8. All-wool square street blanket, with straps, neat broken blue check, size 80 x 80 inches, $3.00 each; size 90 x 90 inches, $3.50 each.
No. 9. English fawn street blankets, square, no straps, a first-class blanket, size 80 x 80 inches, $3.50 each; size 90 x 90 inches, $4.75 each.
No. 10. All pure wool cooler, neat blue check on white ground, size 90 x 100 inches, a very popular blanket among turf men, $3.00 each.

Horse Rain Covers.

These covers are made of heavy oiled duck, and are very st ong; they come in three sizes, and are fitted complete with straps.
Loin covers, $1.50 each.
Hame covers, covering horse from collar to tail, $2.00 each.
Breast covers, covering horse all over, reaching well up the neck and buckling around in front of breast, also hav.ng a place for high top hames, $2.25 each.
Rubber horse covers, covering horse all over, $3.50 and 4.00 each.

Sleigh Bells and Chimes.

Back Bells.

No. 1. 12 nickel bells, plain, 40c each.
No. 2. 12 nickel bells, felt lined strap, 85c each.
No. 3. 12 nickel bells, felt lined straps, with ornaments, $1.00 each.

Body Bells.

No. 4. 30 nickel bells, plain leather strap, $1.00 each.
No. 5. 40 nickel bells, plain leather strap, $1.25 each.
No. 6. 50 nickel bells, plain leather strap, $1.50 each.
No. 7. 60 nickel bells, plain leather strap, $1.85 each.
No. 9. 50 nickel bells, extra finish black strap, $2.75 each.
No. 10. 50 brass bells, extra finish russet leather strap, $2.75 each.
No. 11. 24 nickel dome-shape bells, plain strap, 85c each.
No. 12. 24 nickel dome shape bells, strap felt lined, $1.00 each.

Shaft Gongs.

All nicely nickel plated, and on iron straps.
(Set means for both shafts.)

No. 15. 2 bells on each strap, 24c per set.
No. 16. 3 bells on each strap, 40c per set.
No. 17. 3 bells on each strap, 60c per set.
No. 18. 4 bells on each strap, nice tone, $1.00 per set.
No. 19. 4 bells on each strap, nicely tuned, $1.25 per set.

Saddle Chimes.

No. 1. 1 large gong, outside chain hammers, nickel plated, very neat, $1.00 each.
No. 2. 2 medium size open gong, with one large closed gong in centre, with outside chain hammers, very stylish, nickel plated, $3.00 ea.
No. 3. Large coach saddle chime, 3 large open gongs, tuned, strong frame, nickel plated, a beauty, $3.50 each.
Common strap collar belts, 7c each.
Large stamped team belts, nickel plated, 15c ea.

Air-Cushion Rubber Horse-Shoe Pads.

(Pads sold by the pair only.)

This pad overcomes every objection to driving horses on hard and slippery streets and roads, reducing concussion to the minimum; it cures or relieves all lameness produced or aggravated by jarring on the hard roads.

Prices, sizes 1, 1½, 2, 2½, 3, 3½, 4, $1.10 pair; 4½, $1.30 pair; 5, $1.40 pair; 5½, $1.65 pair; 6, $1.75 pair.

Household Furnishings.

FOR ILLUSTRATIONS SEE OPPOSITE PAGE.

1. Canadian washer, $3.50; reacting, $5.00.
2. Self-wringing mop, 25c; diamond mop stick, 10c; mop cloths, 10c.
3. Wooden wash tubs, 50c, 60c, 70c, 80c; fibre tubs, 80c, 95c, $1.15, 1.30; fibre pails, 32c, 40c; wooden pails, 15c, 17c.
4. Folding tub stands, $1.00; folding ironing boards, $1.25; linen covered and varnished, $1.75.
5. Clothes lines, cotton or hemp, 50 ft, 15c; 75 ft, 20c; 100 ft, 25c; manilla, 5c, 10c; wire, 50 ft, 20c; 100 ft, 35c.
6. Clothes pegs, 5 doz for 5c.
7. The Dowswell washer, $3.50.
8. Leader churn, No. 1, 9 gals, $3.75; No. 2, 15 gals, $4.00; No. 3, 20 gals, $4.75.
9. Queen mangle, three maple rollers, casters, folding table, best English steel springs, $15.00.
10. Wash board, Globe, 15c; solid back, 20c; toy wash boards, 10c; pastry boards, 25c; bosom boards, shaped neck, 10c; sleeve boards, 10c; skirt boards, 25c, 35c, 50c; bosom and sleeve boards, 35c.
11. Wringers, Royal Dominion, $2.50; Leader, $3.00; Paragon, with ball bearings, $3.45.
12. Clothes horse, folding, 4 ft, 35c; 5 ft, 45c; extension, 4 ft, 75c; 5 ft, 90c; 6 ft, $1.00.
13. Butter ladles, 5c, 8c.
14. Table mangles, $7.00.
15. Salt boxes, 10c.
16. Butter moulds, ½ and 1-lb, 20c.
17. Clothes arm, 5 arms, 15c; towel arm, 3 arms, 10c, 15c.
18. Coffee mill, 25c, 50c, 75c.
19. Butter moulds, oblong, ½ and 1-lb, 25c.
20. Maple bowls, 10c, 20c, 35c, 50c.
21. Carved bread boards, 35c, 45c, 65c, 75c, $1.25, 1.50.
22. Leader churn, steel frame. No. 1, 9 gals, $4.00; No. 2, 15 gals, $4.25.
23. Dash churns, 5 gallons, $1.25; 7 gallons, $1.50; 10 gallons, $1.65.
24. Knife trays, 10c; lined and varnished, 15c.
25. Butter spades, 5c each.
26. Window cleaners, 9-inch, 25c; 12-inch, 35c.
27. Step ladder with pail rack, 5 ft, 50c; 6 ft, 60c; 7 ft, 75c; pine, extra strong, with pail rack and extra spreader, 5 ft, 90c; 6 ft, $1.10; 7 ft, $1.35.
28. Knife board, 15c.
29. Wood spoons, 4c, 5c, 6c, 8c.
30. Hunter's axe handle, 7c; axe handles, 10c, 15c; adze handles, 15c; pick handles, 15c; broad axe handles, 15c; D spade and fork handles, curved and straight, 25c; hammer handles, 5c. All made of second growth hickory.
31. Platform scales, weighing to 600 lbs, $12.00; to 1,200 lbs, $14.75.
32. Butter spades, 5c.
33. Grocers' or household scales, weighing 4 lbs, $2.50; weighing 10 lbs, $3.75.
34. Happy medium bucksaws, 40c.
35. Wooden knives, 5c.
36. Spice cabinets, glass jars, $1.50; with drawers, $1.25.
37. Folding coat and hat rack, 10 pegs, 15c; 13 pegs, 30c.
38. Champion scales, weighing from 1 oz to 240 lbs, $5.00.
39. Stable brooms, best quality cane, hardwood handles, 50c, 60c, 70c; split cane, 50c, 60c; bass, 85c.
40. Shoe brush, 15c, 25c.
41. Hat and coat hooks, 4 pegs, 25c; 6 pegs, 35c.
42. Towel rollers, 15c, 20c, 25c.
43. Bamboo hat and coat hooks, 15c, 20c; white enamelled, 25c.
44. Sink brush, 10c.
45. Stove mit, with dauber, 15c.
46. Stove dauber, 5c, 7c, 12c.
47. Crumb brush, 15c, 35c, 45c.
48. Banister brushes, bristle and fibre, 20c, 25c, 35c, 40c; whisk root, 25c.
49. Shoe daubers, 5c, 10c, 15c, 20c.
50. Window brushes, grey bristles, 25c, 35c, 45c; 10 ft handles for above, 15c.
51. Wool dusters, 20c.
52. Stove brushes, 10c, 15c, 30c; best quality bristles, 25c, 50c.
53. Double banister brushes, 35c, 45c, 50c.
54. Scrub brushes, green corn, 6c; whisk root, 8c, 10c, 15c, 20c, 25c; white fibre, 10c, 25c.
55. Bottle brush, 5c.
56. Shoe brush, plain, with top-knot dauber, 15c; handled, with top-knot dauber, 10c, 15c, 20c, 25c, 30c, 35c, 50c.
57. Heather sink scrubs, 5c.
58. Hearth dusters, japanned handles, 25c.
59. Wool wall dusters, with handle, 50c.
60. Dish mop, 5c.
61. Feather dusters, turkey, 25c, 35c, 45c, 50c, 65c; ostrich feathers, large size, $1.00, 1.15, 1.35.
62. Silver brushes, 20c, 25c.
63. Silver brushes, 25c, 35c.
64. Hair brooms, handles included, 55c, 75c, 90c, $1.00, 1.25.
65. Table scrub fibre, 5c.

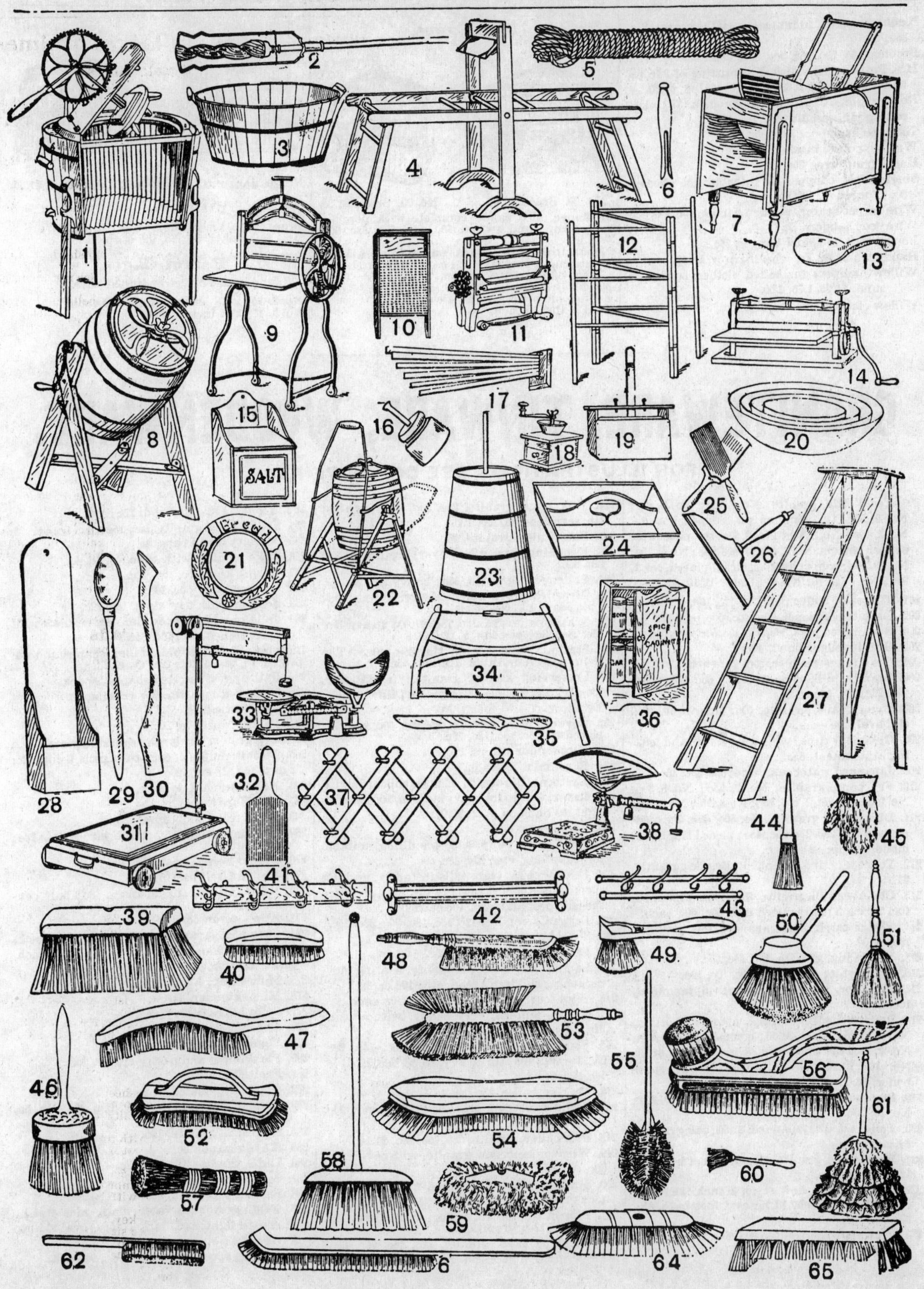
SALT
Bread
SPICE CABINET

Blackening kits, in imitation leather cases, 25c, 35c.
Brooms, 15c, 20c, 25c, 30c, 35c, 40c.
Mrs. Potts' irons, polished, consisting of 3 irons, handle and stand, 89c; nickel plated, $1.00.
Rolling pin, 5c; enamelled handles, 7c; glass rolling pin, can fill with ice, 50c.
Tooth picks, box of 1,000, 5c.
Wooden potato masher, 5c.
Henis' fruit press, 30c.
Single meat chopper, 5c; double, 10c; heavy, 20c; forged steel, 25c.
Wire carpet beater, wooden handle, 10c.
Wire coat hangers, 3c.
Belmar suit and skirt hanger, 25c.
Handy truck, $2.00; wheelbarrow, $2.50.
Willow hampers for soiled clothes, square or round, $1.25, 1.75, 2.00.
Willow clothes baskets, 55c, 65c, 75c.

Bird Cages.

No. 30. Brass, $2.40.

No. 00. Brass, $1.35.

Japanned bird cages, complete with perches, feed cups and swing, 55c, 65c, 75c, 85c, 90c, $1.10.
No. 00. Brass bird cages, our special, a large sized cage, very strong, neat design, with scalloped edge around bottom, $1.35.
No. 30 Brass cages, $2.40, 2.75.
Adjustable brass guards, 45c each.
Opal baths, 5c each.

No. 10. Japanned, 75c. No. 20. Japanned, $1.35.

Opal feed cups, 10c each.
Nests, 6c each.
Brass chain, 10c yard.
Bronze bracket, 5c, 12c, 15c each.

Parrot Cages.

Round, made of heavy tinned wire.

No. 2. 15¾ x 23½ inches high, $5.25 each.
No. 3. 17½ x 25 inches high, $5.75 each.

GRANITEWARE, TINWARE, WOODENWARE.

FOR ILLUSTRATIONS SEE OPPOSITE PAGE.

200. Tea kettle, granite, No. 7, 75c; No. 8, 80c; No. 9, 95c; tin, common pit, copper bottom, No. 7, 40c; No. 8, 45c; No. 9, 50c; tin, patent pit copper bottom, No. 7, 55c; No. 8, 65c; No. 9, 75c; No. 10, 80c; copper kettles, nickel-plated, No. 7, 90c; No. 8, $1.10; No. 9, $1.20; No. 10, $2.00.
201. Tin tea or coffee pot, 12c, 14c, 16c.
202. Granite coffee pot, 35c, 40c, 50c, 60c, 65c.
203. Granite tea pots, 30c, 35c, 40c, 50c, 60c, 65c ea.
204. Granite sugar bowl, 40c.
205. Granite tea steeper, 20c, 25c each.
206. Granite milk can, 35c, 45c, 60c, 75c; tin, 20c, 22c, 28c, 30c each.
207. Dinner pails, granite, 50c; tin, round, 15c; tin, oval, 18c each.
208. Creamery cans, with gauge, tap and locking attachment, 65c.
209. Japanned water cans, zinc rose, 25c, 35c.
210. Fry pans, granite, No. 7, 25c; No. 8, 30c; No. 9, 35c; steel, No. 7, 25c; No. 8, 30c; No. 9, 35c.
211. Dish pans, granite, 45c, 50c, 60c, 70c, 80c; pressed tin, 28c, 33c, 35c, 45c; pieced tin, handmade, 12c, 15c, 20c each.
212. Toilet jar, tin, japanned, 25c, 45c; granite, $1.15.
213. Chamber pail, granite, $1.00; tin, japanned, 40c, 50c each; galvanized iron, 50c, 60c each.
214. Water carrier, tin japanned, oak grained, 75c, $1.00.
215. Water jug, granite, 45c, 55c, 65c.
216. Mug, white granite, 8c, 9c, 10c, 12c.
217. Cuspidor, granite, 30c, 40c; tin, japanned, 10c, 15c.
218. Boilers, medium, tin, copper pit bottom, No. 8, $1.25; No. 9, $1.50; common pit bottom, No. 7, heavy, $1.00; No. 8, 90c; No. 9, $1.10; No. 10, $1.50; No. 8, nickel-plated copper boiler, $3.00; No. 9, $3.50.
219. Steamers, No. 7, 20c; No. 8, 22c; No. 9, 25c; No. 10, 30c.
220. Toilet set, tin, japanned, $1.60; oak grained, $1.85.
221. Roast pans, granite, 45c, 50c; sheet iron, 10c, 12c, 15c and 18c.
222. Infants' bath, new style, 28-inch, $1.10; 32-inch, $1.35; 40-inch, $1.75; oval foot bath, 65c, 80c.
223. Wash bowls, granite, 16c, 18c, 22c, 28c, 33c, 35c; tin, 8c, 10c, 15c.
224. Milk pans, granite, 25c, 30c, 35c; pressed tin, seamless, 8c, 10c, 12c.
225. Butter dish, granite, 25c.
226. Kneading pans, with cover, granite, $1.35; tin, 85c.
227. Cullenders, granite, 35c; heavy tin, 20c.
228. Measures, government stamped, ½-pk, 30c; ¼-pk, 35c; 1-pk, 60c; 2-pk, 75c.
229. Water pails, granite, 75c, $1.00; heavy tin, 22c, 28c, 33c; pieced tin, 12c, 18c.
230. Strainer pails, pieced tin, 35c, 40c. The Gem, with removable strainer, 65c.
231. Preserving kettles, granite, 24c, 28c, 32c, 36c, 42c, 50c, 60c, 75c, 90c; pressed tin, 12c, 16c, 20c, 28c, 30c.
232. Covered pails, granite, 22c, 25c, 30c, 40c, 45c; pieced tin, 8c, 10c, 12c, 15c.
233. Victor flour sifters, 12c.
234. Egg timer, 25c each.
235. Lanterns, lift or tilt, 45c; dashboard, with reflector, 65c; extra heavy lantern, 90c; search light, to hang on post, $2.00.
236. Comb case, 15c.
237. Small spirit lamp, asbestos filling, suitable for travelling, etc., 25c, 35c, 50c.
238. Dead shot rat trap, kills instantly, nothing suspicious about it to scare the rats, they are the cheapest and best, 10c each.
239. Frypan, steel, 10c, 12c, 15c, 18c, 20c, 22c, 25c.
240. Set skewers, 15c.
241. Fancy wire toast rack, 35c.
242. Lamp attachments, handy for heating curling tongs, children's food, etc., 10c each.
243. Wire toaster, wooden handle, 10c each.
244. Candle lantern, very handy, without candle, 13c each.
245. Saucepans, lipped, granite, 10c, 14c, 20c, 25c, 30c, 35c, 40c; tin, heavy, 6c, 8c, 10c, 12c, 14c, 16c, 22c, 24c.
246. Tin rice boiler, 25c.
247. Berlin saucepan, granite, with cover, 30c, 40c, 50c, 60c, 70c.
248. Rice boiler, granite, 55c, 75c, 95c, $1.15.
249. Windsor saucepan, granite, with cover, 20c, 30c, 40c, 50c.
250. Straight saucepan, pieced tin, 8c, 10c, 12c, 15c; granite, 30c, 33c, 42c, 50c, 55c, 75c each.
251. Dipper, tin, pieced, 5c, 10c; extra heavy tin, seamless, 17c; granite, 25c.
252. Pudding pans, granite, 12c, 16c, 20c, 25c; tin, seamless, 4c, 6c, 8c, 10c.
253. Flour sieves, tin band, 12c each.
254. Jelly plates, granite, 12c, 15c; tin, 5c, 6c.
255. Novelty bread pans, 6c.
256. Cake moulds, with tube, 4c, 5c, 6c.
257. Paring knife, 5c, 10c, 12c.
258. Cake moulds, 20c, 25c.
259. Jelly moulds, new style, 18c, 22c.
260. Jelly moulds, copper rim, 35c, 40c, 45c; all copper, tinned, 65c, 75c, 85c.
Individual jelly moulds, fancy shapes and designs, 5c, 6c, 7c, 10c, 12c, 15c each.
261. Patty pans, assorted shapes, 9c doz.
262. Thumb scoops, tin, 5c; granite, 9c.
263. Candlestick, 5c.
264. Pastry brush, 7c, 10c.
Nutmeg grater, 3c; large vegetable grater, 5c.
265. Biscuit, muffin or corn-cake pans, 6-cup, 12c; 8-cup, 15c; 12-cup, 20c.
266. Asbestos mats, 3c each.
267. (See Hardware.)
268. Knife trays, embossed, 22c.
269. Machine oilers, 7c; large size drip, 10c; long spout, 15c.
270. Dinner horns, japanned, 10c.
271. Broilers, self basting, 35c.
272. Dustpans, tin, 5c; japanned, 8c; half covered, 15c.
273. Apple corer, 5c.
274. Cash box, japanned, with tray, good lock, 8-inch, 80c; 9-inch, 90c; 10-inch, $1.00; 11-inch, $1.10; 12-inch, $1.35.
275. Mouse trap, 4-hole, 5c.
276. Milk skimmer, 3c.
277. Spice boxes in tray, 25c.
278. (See nickel-plated ware.)
279. Edgar nutmeg grater, 10c.
280. Pie crimper and pastry cutter, 5c.
281. Fruit fillers, 6c.
282. (See nickel-plated ware.)
283. Funnel, granite, 10c, 12c, 15c, 20c; tin, 5c, 7c, 8c, 10c.
284. Soap dish, granite, 14c.
285. Stove scraper, 6c.
286. Ladle, granite, 12c; tin, 8c.
287. Soap dish, tin, 9c.
288. Basting spoon, tin, 4c, 5c.
289. Folding wooden table mats, nice finish, alternate light and dark colors, oval shape, 35c set of 3; oblong shape, 25c set of 3.
290. Basting spoon, granite, 7c, 8c, 9c each.

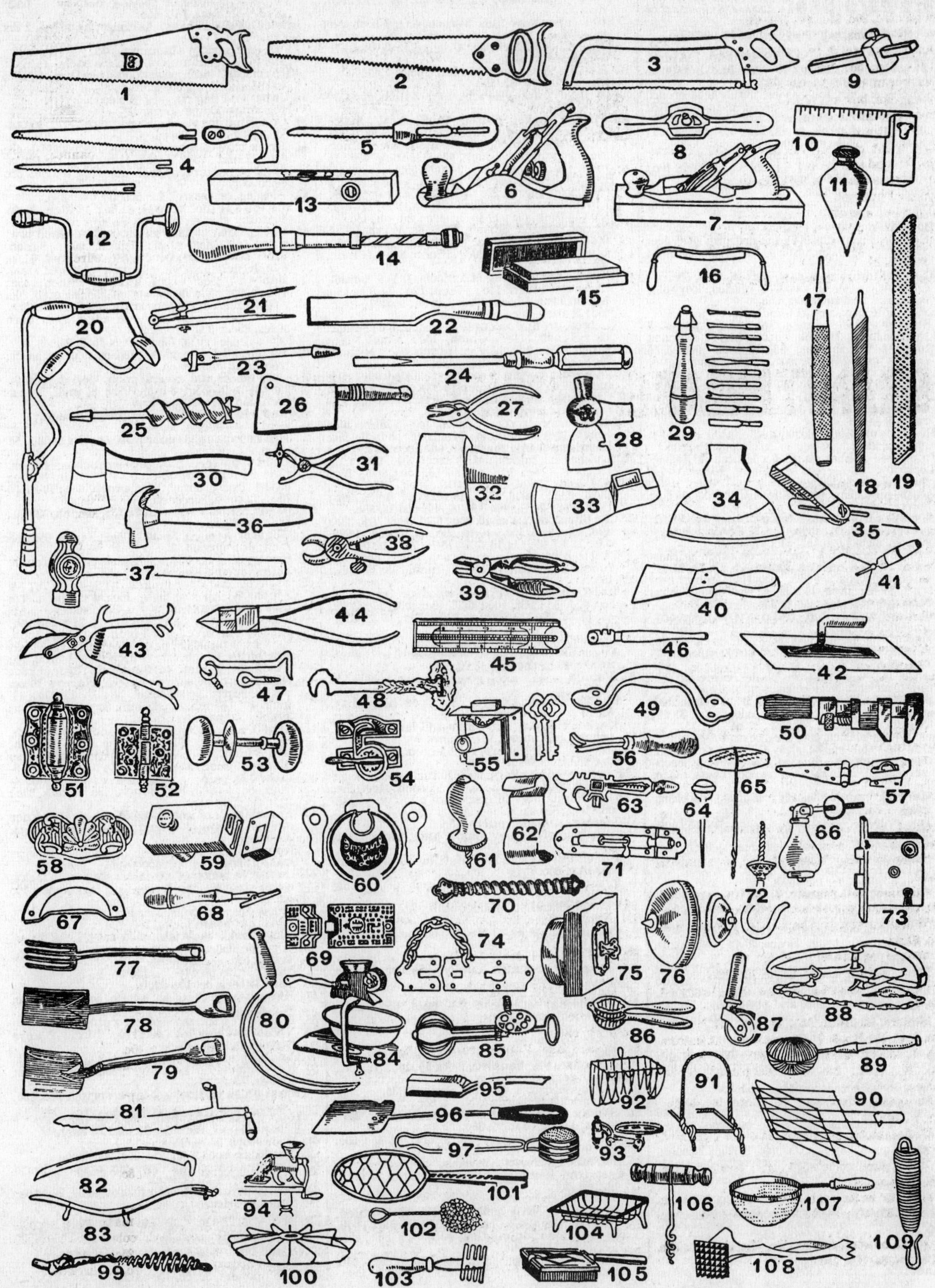

Hardware Dept. *All Prices Subject to Change Without Notice*

(For illustrations see opposite page.)

1. Henry Disston's saws, the D8 brand, 18-inch, $1.25; 22-inch, $1.50; 24-inch, $1.65; 26-inch, either cross-cut or rip, $1.75.
Shurley & Dietrich's saws, maple leaf brand, 18-inch, 85c; 20-inch, $1.00; 22-inch, $1.15; 24-inch, $1.25; 26-inch, $1.50; 28-inch, $1.60; 10-inch stiff back saws, 85c; 12-inch, $1.00; 10-inch hack saws, 25c.
Extension hack saw frames, $1.35.
Star hack saw blades, 8-inch, 8c; 9-inch, 10c; 10-inch, 12c; 12-inch, 15c.
Scroll saws, 10c doz.
Cast steel family saws, 20-inch, 40c; 24-inch, 50c; 26-inch, 65c.
Boys' 12-inch saws, 15c.
2 S. & D. 18-inch double edge pruning saw, 50c.
3. 22-inch S. & D. butcher saws, $1.25; 24-inch, $1.35.
14-inch family meat saw, 40c; 16-inch, 50c.
4. Disston's nest of saws, 3 blades, keyhole, compass, and pruning, 85c.
5. Key-hole saw, metal handle, 25c.
6. Stanley's iron planes, smoothing plane, 8 inches long, 1¾-inch cutter, $1.90; 9 inches long, 2-inch cutter, $2.15; jack plane, 14 inches long, 2-inch cutter, $2.35; fore plane, 18 inches long, 2⅜-inch cutter, $3.00; jointer plane, 22 inches long, 2⅜-inch cutter, $3.50.
Duplex rabbet plane and fillister, iron stock and fence, 8½ inches long, 1½-inch cutter, $1.50.
Rabbet and block plane, detachable side, 7 x 1¾-inch, $1.25.
Improved rabbet plane, 8 x 1¼-inch, $1.15.
Tonguing and grooving plane, ¾-inch to 1¼-inch board, $2.50 each.
Adjustable circular plane, either concave or convex, $3.00.
Sargent's iron planes, smoothing, 9 x 2, $1.75; jack, 14 x 2, $2.00; fore, 18 x 2⅜, $2.65; jointers, 22 x 2⅜, $2.90; jointer, 24 x 2⅝, $3.40.
7. Stanley wood bottom planes, same adjustment as iron ones, smoothing, 8 x 1¾, $1.25; smoothing, 8 x 2, $1.25; handled smoothing, 9 x 2, $1.65; jack, 14 x 2⅛, $1.65; fore, 20 x 2⅜, $1.85; jointer, 26 x 2⅝, $2.10.
Stanley make, but different adjustment, smoothing plane, 8 x 1¾, $1.00; handled smoothing plane, 10 x 2⅛, $1.25; jack plane, 15 x 2⅛, $1.25; fore, 20 x 2⅜, $1.35; jointer, 26 x 2⅝, $1.65.
Sargent's wood bottom planes, same adjustment as the iron ones, smoothing, 8 x 1¾, $1.00; smoothing, 8 x 2, $1.25; handled smoothing, 9 x 2, $1.50; jack, 15 x 2, $1.25; fore, 20 x 2⅜, $1.50; jointer, 26 x 2⅝, $1.75.
Iron block planes, 15c, 25c, 35c and 50c each.
8. Double iron spoke shave, 25c; single iron, 15c; 2½-inch beechwood, 25c; 3-inch beechwood, 30c; 2½-inch beechwood, brass plate, 35c.
9. Marking gauge, 5c, 15c; mortise marking gauge, 25c, 35c.
10. Try squares, wood arm, 4½-inch, 20c; 6-inch, 25c; 7½-inch, 30c; 9-inch, 35c.
Disston's iron arm try squares, 4½-inch, 20c; 6-inch, 25c; 8-inch, 30c.
Steel squares, 14 x 24, 75c, $1.00.
11. Plumb bobs, 10c, 15c each.
12. Boys' brace, 15c each.
10-inch braces, without ratchet, 35c, 50c, 65c;
Miller Falls' ball-bearing brace, $1.50.
Ratchet braces, 85c, $1.00, 1.35.
Ball-bearing ratchet brace, $1.75; with gun metal finish, $2.00.
13. 18 to 24-inch spirit levels, 35c; 24-inch spirit level and plumb, 50c; 24-inch spirit level and plumb, adjustable, brass mounted, $1.25.
12-inch boxwood level and plumb, 65c, 75c; 18-inch, $1.00; 24-inch, $1.25; 12-inch mahogany and brass level and plumb, 75c.
Pocket level, 10c.
14. Yankee spiral ratchet screw-driver, right hand only, $1.15, 1.35, 1.50; right and left hand, $1.85 each.
15. Oil stones, in neat wooden case, 15c, 40c.
Small pen-knife stones, 5c; large size, 10c.
Deer lick oil stones, 30c; lily white and rosy red Washita oil stones, 55c, 65c, 70c; extra fine and large, $1.00.
Razor hones, 15c, 25c, 50c, 75c, $1.25, 1.75 each.
Kitchen sandstones, set in case, 10c each.
Round knife stones, 15c each.
Whet stones, 4c, 7c each.
16. 9-inch draw knife, P. S. & W. make, 65c each.
17. Flat bastard files, 4-inch, 12c; 5-inch, 13c; 6-inch, 14c; 8-inch, 18c; 10-inch, 24c; 12-inch, 30c; 14-inch, 45c; 15-inch, 55c.
Mill bastard files, 4-inch, 9c; 5-inch, 10c; 6-inch, 12c; 8-inch, 14c; 10-inch, 19c; 12-inch, 25c; 14-inch, 35c; 15-inch, 40c.
6-inch wood rasp, 22c; 8-inch, 30c; 10-inch, 40c.
Slim taper saw files, 3½-inch, 5c; 4-inch, 5c; 4½-inch, 6c; 5-inch, 7c; 6-inch, 9c.
Taper files, 3½-inch, 5c; 4-inch, 6c; 4½-inch, 7c; 5-inch, 8c; 6-inch, 10c.
19. Heller's horse rasp, 15-inch, 70c.
20. Corner brace, $3.00.
21. Wing dividers, 6-inch, 20c; 8-inch, 25c; 10-inch, 45c.
22. Firmer socket chisel, P. S. & W. make, bevelled edge, gun metal finish, guaranteed, ⅜-inch, 30c; ½-inch, 32c; ⅝-inch, 35c; ¾-inch, 38c; ⅞-inch, 40c; 1-inch, 42c; 1¼-inch, 45c; 1½-inch, 48c; 1¾-inch, 50c; 2-inch, 55c.
Broad's firmer socket chisels, ⅛-inch, 22c; ¼-inch, 22c; ⅜-inch, 22c; ½-inch, 25c; ⅝-inch, 28c; ¾-inch, 30c; ⅞-inch, 30c; 1-inch, 35c; 1¼-inch, 38c; 1½-inch, 40c; 1¾-inch, 42c; 2-inch, 45c.
Firmer tanged chisels, P. S. &. W. make, ⅜-inch, 22c; ¼-inch, 24c; ½-inch, 25c; ⅝-inch, 27c; ¾-inch, 29c; ⅞-inch, 30c; 1-inch, 34c; 1¼-inch, 45c.
Broad's firmer tanged chisels, ⅛, ¼, 5/16-inch, 10c each; ⅜-inch, 11c; ½-inch, 12c; ⅝-inch, 13c; ¾-inch, 14c; ⅞-inch, 16c; 1-inch, 18c; 1¼-inch, 25c; 1½-inch, 30c; 1¾-inch, 35c.
Gouges, ground on outside, ⅛-inch, 10c; ¼-inch, 12c; ⅜-inch, 14c; ½-inch, 15c; ⅝-inch, 18c; ¾-inch, 20c; ⅞-inch, 22c; 1-inch, 25c; 1¼-inch, 30c; 1½-inch, 35c; 2-inch, 45c.
Clark's expansion bit cuts, from ½-inch to 1½-inch, $1.00; from ⅞-inch to 3-inch, $1.50 each.
24. Challenge screw-drivers, extra strong, 6-inch, 35c; 8-inch, 45c.
Ideal screw-drivers, 2-inch, 7c; 3-inch, 10c; 4-inch, 12c; 5-inch, 15c; 6-inch, 18c; 8-inch, 25c; handles not included in measurement.
25. Auger bits, good quality steel, 3/16, 15c; 4/16, 15c; 5/16, 15c; 6/16, 15c; 7/16, 15c; 8/16, 15c; 9/16, 16c; 10/16, 17c; 11/16, 18c; 12/16, 20c; 13/16, 22c; 14/16, 25c; 15/16, 27c; 16/16, 30c; 18/16, 38c; 20/16, 40c; 22/16, 45c; 24/16, 50c.
Car bits, 4/16, 25c; 5/16, 25c; 6/16, 38c; 7/16, 39c; 8/16, 40c; 9/16, 45c; 10/16, 50c; 11/16, 55c; 12/16, 60c; 13/16, 65c; 14/16, 70c; 15/16, 75c; 16/16, 80c.
Centre bits, ½-inch, 8c; ¾-inch, 8c; ⅞-inch, 9c; 1-inch, 10c; 1¼-inch, 11c; 1½-inch, 12c; 1¾-inch, 15c.
Twist drills, for either wood or iron, 2/32, 8c; 3/32, 8c; 4/32, 10c; 5/32, 12c; 6/32, 15c; 7/32, 18c; 8/32, 20c; 10/32, 25c; 12/32, 30c; 16/32, 35c.
Gimlet bits, 7c, 10c each.
Screw-driver bits, 10c, 15c each.
Auger bit sets, in neat wood case, 9 to the set, $1.85; 13 to the set, $3.00.
26. Family meat axe, good quality steel, 35c each.
Butchers' meat axe, 75c, $1.00; extra quality, $1.75.
Market cleaver, extra fine and large, $2.00.
27. 4-inch Lodi pliers, 5c; 5-inch, 8c.
5-inch flat nose pliers, 10c; 5-inch, good quality, 20c.
8-inch fencing pliers, 25c; 10-inch, 35c.
5-inch round nose pliers, 10c; 5-inch, steel, 30c.
5½-inch long nose pliers, extra quality, polished steel, 65c each.
6-inch gas burner pliers, 15c.
5½-inch steel burner pliers and wire cutter, 25c.
5½-inch burner and side cutting pliers, extra quality, 65c.
9-inch pipe pliers, 50c; 6½-inch adjustable pipe pliers, 75c.
28. Shingle hatchet, good quality steel, 40c, 50c each.
Cast iron claw hatchets, 15c each.
Lathing hatchets, 75c each.
29. Tool sets, 10 tools in neat, plain handle, 50c set; mahogany handle, 65c set; better quality, $1.00.
30. Hunter's axe, 45c each.
31. Revolving belt punch, 4 cuts, 65c each; single cut, 25c each.
No. 3 Straight belt punch, 6c; No. 5, 7c; No. 7, 8c; No. 10, 10c.
32. Eagle axes, handled, 3½ to 4½ lbs, 95c.
Gatineau axes, handled, 3½ to 4½ lbs, 75c.
Boys' axe, good quality, 60c.
33. Warnock's adze, 4½-inch blade, $1.35.
34. Warnock's bench axe, No. 4, 85c; No. 6, $1.15.
35. Sliding T bevels, 6-inch, 20c; 8-inch, 25c; 10-inch, 30c; 12-inch, 35c.
36. Solid steel carpenters' hammers, 35c, 45c, 60c.
Maydole claw hammers, $1.00, 1.25.
Bell face hammers, 40c each.
Cast iron hammers, 12c; cast iron, nickel plated, 20c.
Tack hammers, 5c, 8c.
37. Machinists' ball pein hammers, handled, ¾-lbs, 45c; 1-lb, 50c; 1¼-lb, 55c; 1½-lb, 60c; 1¾-lb, 65c; 2-lbs, 70c; unhandled, ¾-lb, 35c; 1-lb, 40c; 1¼-lb, 45c; 1½-lb, 50c.
Riveting hammers, 35c, 40c, 45c, 55c, 65c, handled.
Tinners' pæning or setting hammers, nandled, 1-lb, 50c; ¾-lb, 45c.
Bricklayers' adze eye hammer, handled, 2 lbs '0c.
Farriers' adze eye hammer, 50c.
Shoemakers' hammers, 35c, 45c each.
Upholsters' hammers, good quality steel, 50c; extra quality, $2.00 each.
38. Japanned hog ringers, 10c each.
Hog rings, 10c package.
39. Combination glass cutter, pliers, etc., 10c ea.
40. Wall scrapers, 15c each.
41. Brick trowel, 9½-inch, 25c; Johnston's 11-inch, 65c; 12 inch, 75c; Rose's, 11-inch, $1.50; Philadelphia pattern, 5½-inch pointing trowel, 30c each.
42. Plasterers' trowel, for family use, 25c.
Disston's 11-inch trowel, $1.35; 12-inch, $1.50.
43. Pruning shears, 30c, 50c, $1.00 each.
44. 8-inch side-cutting pliers, full polished jaw, extra quality, $1.25; 7-inch, 90c; 8-inch, $1.00; 6-inch, 65c; 7-inch, nickel plated, $1.00; 8-inch, polished, 90c; 4½-inch, polished steel, side cut, 25c; extra quality, 5-inch, 55c; 6-inch, 60c; 5-inch, japanned, 25c; 5½-inch, 30c.
45. 2 ft 4-fold carpenters' rule, 8c, 15c, 20c, 25c, 45c; brass bound on one edge, 25c; both sides, 35c.; 3 ft 4-fold, 20c.
2 ft caliper rule, 75c; 1 ft 4-fold, 25c.
46. Wooden handle glass cutter, 10c, 15c each; iron handle, 5c each.
47. Gate hooks and eyes, 1½-inch, 12c doz; 2-inch, 15c; 2½-inch, 20c; 3-inch, 25c; 3½-inch, 30c; 4-inch, 35c; 5-inch, 45c doz.
4 and 5-inch hooks with staples, 5c each.
48. Bird cage hooks, 5c, 8c, 15c.
49. Heavy japanned door pull, 5c; light, 3c, 5c each.
50. Ladd's pattern monkey wrenches, 6-inch, 35c; 8-inch, 35c; 10-inch, 40c; 12-inch, 45c; extra strong, 6-inch, 55c; 8-inch, 65c; 10-inch, 75c; 12-inch, 85c each.
10-inch Stillson wrench, $1.75; 14-inch, $2.00; 18-inch, $2.50.
Alligator wrench, 5½-inch, 20c; 9-inch, 65c; 10-inch, double end, 75c.
51. Spring hinges, 10c pair; screws, 2c; double acting spring hinges, 25c pair.
52. Figured cast door hinges, 3 x 2½-inch, 7c; 3 x 3-inch, 8c; 3½ x 3½-inch, 10c; 4 x 4-inch, 12c pair; screws extra.
Loose pin butts, 2½ x 2-inch, 5c; 2½ x 2½-inch, 5c; 3 x 2½-inch, 6c; 3¼ x 3-inch, 8c; 3½ x 3½-inch, 10c; 4 x 4-inch, 12c pair; screws extra. Narrow butts, 1-inch, 2c; 1¼-inch, 2c; 1½-inch, 2c; 2-inch, 3c; 2½-inch, 4c; 3-inch, 5c; 3½-inch, 6c; 4-inch, 8c pair; screws extra. Narrow brass butts, ¾-inch, 2c; ⅞-inch, 3c; 1-inch, 3c; 1¼-inch, 4c; 1½-inch, 5c; 2-inch, 8c; 2½-inch, 10c; 3-inch, 15c pair.
Light T hinges, 3-inch, 5c; 5-inch, 6c; 8-inch, 10c pair; heavy T hinges, 5-inch, 12c; 6-inch, 18c; 8-inch, 20c; 10-inch, 25c pair; light strap hinges, 3-inch, 5c; 4-inch, 5c; 5-inch, 6c; 8-inch, 12c pair; corrugated steel hinges, 4-inch, 8c; 5-inch, 10c; 6-inch, 12c; 8-inch, 20c; 10-inch, 25c pair.
53. Porcelain door knobs, white or black, either mortise or rim, 10c each; nickel mountings, 25c each.
Bronze knobs, 45c each.
Brass-finished knobs, 75c each.
54. Cast sash locks, 6c, 7c each; steel sash locks, extra strong, small size, 7c; large size, 10c each.
55. Brass drawer locks, 35c, 40c.
Brass cupboard locks, 18c, 20c.
Chest locks, 10c each.
Spring chest locks, 40c each.
Trunk locks, 15c each.
Small brass box locks, 15c each.
56. Tack lifters, 5c, 10c each.
57. Hinge hasp, 2-inch, 4c; 3-inch, 5c; 6-inch, 10c; straight hasp with staples, 3c, 5c, 12c.
58. Brass and oxidized drawer pulls, 5c each.
59. Night latches, 35c, 40c, 75c, $1.35; 2 keys with each lock.
Pin tumbler night latch, with 3 keys, $1.50.
60. Keystone padlocks, 4-lever, 35c; 6-lever, 50c; 8-lever, 75c.
Brass-finish padlocks, 2 keys, spring, 10c, 12c, 15c, 25c.
Heavy black japanned, one key, 15c.
Yale padlocks, 65c, 75c, $1.15, 1.65 each.
61. Door stops, 3c each.
62. Moulding hooks, 5c, 10c, 20c, 25c doz.
63. Combination corkscrew, can opener, knife sharpener, etc., 5c each.
64. White porcelain head picture nails, 20c doz; fancy, 30c doz.
65. Gimlets, 5c, 7c, 10c.
66. Ebony drop drawer pulls, 5c each; ring drawer pulls, 3c each.
67. Black japanned drawer pulls, 12c doz.
Berlin bronzed, 24c doz.
68. Can openers, 5c, 8c, 10c each.

69. Berlin bronzed cupboard turns, 5c; with white knobs, 6c each.
70. Door springs, 10c, 15c each; extra heavy, 20c each.
Torey door spring, 20c each.
71. 4-inch barrel bolts, 5c; 5-inch, 7c; 6-inch, 10c; 3-inch tower bolts, 4c; 4-inch, 5c; 3-inch bronze barrel bolts, 12c; 4-inch, 15c.
72. 3-inch chandelier hooks, 5c, 7c; 6-inch, 10c; 9-inch, 10c each.
73. Mortise locks, 15c, 25c, 35c.
Inside mortise set brass-finished knobs, 75c set; outside mortise sets, brass knobs and escutcheon plate, $2.50 set.
4-in rim knob locks, 15c, 20c, 30c; 5-in, 50c; carpenters' locks, 50c; rim latches, 15c, 20c each.
74. Chain door fasteners, 15c, 25c, 50c each.
75. Rotary electric stroke door bells, nickel plated bells and brass plates, 85c; bronze finish, 65c.
Lever door bells, 50c each.
76. Push button door bells, $1.35.
77. Steel garden forks, 65c each.
78. Steel spades, 75c each.
79. Square mouth shovels, 85c; D handle, round shovel, 75c; long handle, 75c each.
Ditching spades, 95c; post-hole spades, 95c ea.
D handle scoops, $1.00, 1.15.
80. Grass hooks, 25c each.
81. Electic hay knife, 95c each.
82. Scythes, 85c each.
83. Snaths, 65c each.
84. Raisin seeder, 10c.
85. Dover egg beater, 9c, 20c.
86. Lemon squeezer, 15c.
87. Lignum vitæ casters, 10c; iron casters, 10c; iron bed casters, 10c; lignum vitæ bed casters, 35c; steel ball-bearing plate casters, 20c, 35c; ball-bearing shank casters, 20c, 35c set.
88. Gopher or ground hog traps, No. 0, no chain, 12c; No. 1, no chain, 15c; No. 1, with chain, 20c; No. 1½, with chain, 35c.
89. Wire skimmer, 5c; 7-inch, 7c.
90. Light wire toasters, 5c, 6c, 8c, 10c, 12c, 15c; heavy, 18c, 20c, 22c; extra heavy, broiler or toaster, 30c, 35c, 40c, 45c, 50c.
91. Brass-finished plate easels, 10c, 15c, 20c, 25c, 50c; cup and saucer easels, 10c, 15c, 25c; photo easels, 15c, 25c; plaque easels, 18c, 20c, 25c, 30c, 40c each.
92. Sponge racks, 10c, 15c, 25c, 30c each.
93. Flower pot brackets, single, 15c; double, 30c.
94. Empire meat chopper, $1.50, 2.00, 2.50 each.
Ideal food chopper, $1.25, 2.25.
Sausage filler, for Empire meat chopper, $3.50.
95. Short handle fire shovel, 4c; long handle, 10c each.
96. Cake turners, 5c, 7c, 8c each.
97. Soap saver, 8c, 15c each.
99. Alaska stove lifter, 10c; wood handle, 5c; all iron, 3c each.
100. Tea pot stands, 5c, 10c.
101. Surprise egg beaters, 2c, 5c each.
102. Wire dish cloths, 5c, 10c.
103. Wire potato mashers, 3c, 10c each.
104. Wire soap dishes, 5c, 10c; for bath, 15c.
105. Corn popper, 10c.
106. Cork screw, 5c, 10c, 15c, 25c, 35c each.
107. Wire bowl strainers, 4c, 6c, 8c, 10c, 12c, 15c, 25c; extension strainers, 35c, 50c, 75c; tea strainers, 2 for 5c, 5c, 10c each.
108. Steak pounder, 15c.
109. Bird cage spring, 5c; with chain, 15c.
Nickel-plated knurled nail sets, 10c; blued and knurled, 8c.
Centre punches, 5c each.
Cold chisels, 15c, 25c.
Tape measures, 25 feet, 25c; 50 feet, 35c; 66 feet, 65c, 75c; steel wired 50 feet tape line, $1.50; 66 feet, $2.00; 100 feet, $2.50.
File handles, 3c each.
Brad awls, 3c each.
Carpenters' chalk, red, white and blue, 3 for 5c.
Saw set, the perfect, 50c; cross-cut saw set, 65c each.
Champion saw jointer, 20c each.
Putty knives, 20c each.
Socket chisel handles, 5c; leather head, 7c; tanged, 5c, 10c each.
Jack plane handles, 4c.
Fore " " 6c.
Hand saw " 10c each.
Disston's saw filer's vise, 85c.
Vises, small japanned, 15c.
1½-lb vise, steel jaws, 75c; 2½-lb, $1.00; 4-lb, $1.25 each.
Adjustable washer cutter, 50c each.
Boker's hand vise, 60c each.
Reamer bits, square, ½-inch, 10c; half round, ½-inch, 10c.
Countersink bits, ½ to ⅝-inch, 10c.
Rose counter sink bits, 10c each.
Carpenter's tool baskets, lined, 40c, 50c each.
Copper soldering irons, 25c, 50c each.
Solder, 5c, 10c, 20c, 35c per stick.
Farriers' pincers, 14-inch, $1.00 each.
Tinsmiths' snips, 35c, $1.65 each.
Yankee reciprocating drill, $2.75.
6-inch inside or outside calipers, 15c; wing calipers, 30c each.
Automatic drill, 10 bits in handle, $1.75 each.
Steel wire on spools, 4c; covered wire, 5c spool; brass or copper, 8c spool.
Brass curtain rings, ⅛-inch, 2c doz, 15c gross; ¼ and ⅜-inch, 2c doz, 20c gross; 7/16, ½, ⅝-inch, 3c doz, 30c gross; ¾-inch, 4c doz, 40c gross; ⅞-inch, 5c doz, 50c gross; 1-inch, 7c doz, 75c gross.
Draping hooks, 5c, 8c doz.
Picture wire, 5c, 10c, 15c, 25-yd package.
Steel wire shelf brackets, very strong and light, 4 x 5, 5c pair; 5 x 7, 8c pair; 6 x 8, 10c pair; 7 x 9, 12c pair; 8 x 10, 15c pair; 10 x 12, 18c pair.
Black japanned thumb latch, 5c; Berlin bronzed, heavier, 10c.
Japanned clothes line hooks, 5c each.
Clothes line pulleys, 8c each.
Bull snap, with chain, 40c.
Bull rings, copper, 20c each.
Brass sash lifts, 8c each; heavy, 12c each; Berlin bronzed, 18c, 24c doz.
Twine boxes, to hang, 15c.
Sand paper, 1c sheet; emery cloth, 5c.
Steel screw hooks, from 3c to 30c doz.
Screw eyes, from 2c to 8c doz.
Cornice hooks, from 4c to 12c doz.
Flat head wood screws, ⅜-inch, all sizes, 10c gross; ½-inch, 10c, 12c, 14c gross; ⅝-inch, 10c, 12c, 14c gross; ¾-inch, 10c, 12c, 14c, 15c gross; ⅞-inch, 10c, 12c, 14c, 15c, 16c gross; 1-inch, 12c, 14c, 15c, 18c, 19c, 25c gross; 1¼-inch, 15c, 16c, 18c, 19c, 22c, 27c gross; 1½-inch, 16c, 19c, 20c, 25c, 28c gross; 1¾-inch, 19c, 20c, 22c, 23c, 26c, 31c gross; 2-inch, 20c, 22c, 23c, 25c, 27c, 37c, 45c gross; 2½-inch, 29c, 32c, 40c, 52c gross; 3-inch, 44c, 48c, 59c gross.
Butter triers, 4-inch, 25c; 18-inch, 75c.
Machinists' steel scale up to 64ths, 6-inch, 25c, 50c; 12-inch, 25c, 35c, 75c.

INCUBATORS.

With each incubator we furnish a book of instructions, suggestions from which, coupled with experiments and common sense, should make you an expert in raising chickens by machinery; however, we do not guarantee this.

The Prairie State Incubators are all self-regulating, and all except the Baby, No. 1, is fitted with an automatic turning tray.

The Prairie State Baby Incubators, are built in two sizes, respectively, 50-egg size, and 100-egg size. It has the same system of ventilation used in our standard machine, with the same automatic regulator, heater and lamps. All metal parts are of brass and galvanized iron. The principal difference between our Baby and B machine, is the thickness of the case. **We will not exchange Incubators.**

Prairie State "B" Incubator.

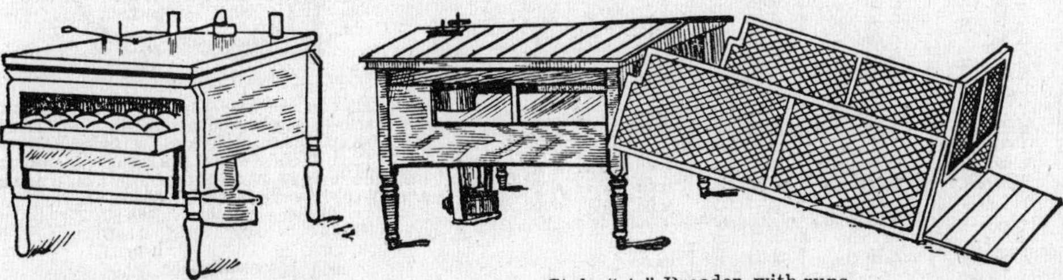

Prairie State "Baby" Incubator.

Style "A," Brooder, with runs.

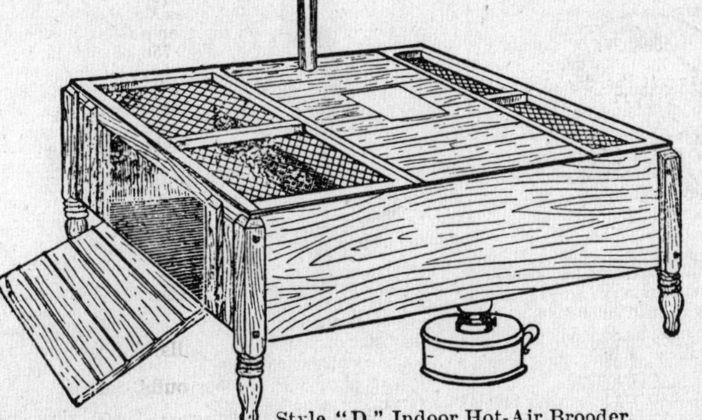

Style "D," Indoor Hot-Air Brooder.

Incubators.

	Dimensions.	Capacity.	Weight, Crated (about)	Price.
No. 1. Baby,	14½ x 24,	50-eggs,	45 lbs	$7.25
No. 2. Baby,	19½ x 31,	100-eggs,	70 lbs	12.00
No. 1. B,	27 x 37,	150-eggs,	150 lbs	18.00
No. 2. B,	27½ x 47,	210-eggs,	195 lbs	26.00

Brooders.

Style "A," hot air, self-regulating, with runs

	Dimensions.	Capacity.	Weight, Crated (about)	Price.
No. 1.	24 x 38,	100-eggs,	100 lbs	$16.25
No. 2.	28 x 33,	200-eggs,	120 lbs	22.00

Style "D," Hot Air, Indoor Brooders.

	Dimensions.	Capacity.	Weight, Crated (about)	Price.
No. 1.	24 x 35,	80-eggs,	60 lbs	$8.25
No. 2.	26 x 35,	125-eggs,	85 lbs	10.50

CROCKERY, CHINA AND GLASSWARE DEPARTMENT.

ORDER from the following list as much or as little as you require. Should you want samples of any of the Dinnerware, buy one piece of anything you desire to see, and when it is returned we will refund the money, less the charges.

Dinner and Tea Set Compositions.

40-piece tea sets: 12 tea plates, 12 cups and saucers, 2 cake plates, 1 slop bowl, 1 cream jug.

44-piece tea set: 12 tea plates, 12 cups and saucers, 2 cake plates, 1 teapot, 1 sugar bowl, 1 slop bowl, 1 cream jug.

56-piece tea set: 12 tea plates, 12 cups and saucers, 12 fruit dishes, 2 cake plates, 1 teapot, 1 sugar bowl, 1 slop bowl, 1 cream jug.

100-piece dinner set: 12 tea plates, 12 dinner plates, 12 soup plates, 12 fruit dishes, 12 individual butters, 12 cups and saucers, 3 platters, 1 gravy boat, 1 baker, 2 covered vegetable dishes, 1 pickle, 1 teapot, 1 sugar bowl, 1 slop bowl, 1 cream jug.

112-piece dinner set, same as 100-piece set, with 12 extra breakfast plates.

125-piece dinner set, same as 100-piece set, with following extras: 12 breakfast plates, 1 platter, 1 soup tureen complete, 1 sauce tureen complete, 1 salad, 1 casserole, 1 jug.

ORDER WHAT YOU WISH FROM THE FOLLOWING LIST.

PIECES OF DINNER-WARE.	No. 10.	No. 11.	No. 12.	No. 13.	No. 14.	No. 15.
Plates, fruit, 5-inch....	$0 55 doz.	$0 85 doz.	$0 90 doz.	$1 00 doz.	$2 25 doz.	$1 35 doz.
" tea, 6-inch	0 70 "	1 00 "	1 20 "	1 25 "	2 75 "	1 65 "
" breakfast, 7-inch	0 85 "	1 20 "	1 35 "	1 35 "	3 00 "	1 90 "
" dinner, 8-inch ..	1 00 "	1 40 "	1 50 "	1 50 "	3 50 "	2 50 "
" soup, 7-inch	0 85 "	1 20 "	1 35 "	1 35 "	....	....
" " 8-inch	1 00 "	1 40 "	1 50 "	1 50 "	3 50 "	2 50 "
Fruit dishes	0 40 "	0 60 "	0 65 "	0 85 "	1 65 "	1 35 "
Butter pats	0 30 "	0 40 "	0 40 "	0 60 "	1 00 "	0 60 "
After dinner coffees ...	....	....	....	....	....	2 00 "
Teacups and saucers ..	1 00 "	1 65 "	1 65 "	1 60 "	4 20 "	2 65 "
Breakfast cups&saucers	....	....	....	....	....	2 65 "
Platters, 9-inch	....	....	....	....	0 65 ea.	....
" 10-inch	0 20 ea.	0 30 ea.	0 30 ea.	0 50 ea.	0 85 "	0 75 ea.
" 12-inch	0 30 "	0 50 "	0 50 "	0 60 "	1 10 "	0 95 "
" 14-inch	0 45 "	0 75 "	0 75 "	0 75 "	1 40 "	1 10 "
" 16-inch	0 70 "	1 00 "	1 10 "	1 00 "	2 75 "	1 50 "
" 18-inch	1 00 "	1 40 "	1 60 "	1 50 "	3 75 "	2 75 "
Soup tureen, complete..	2 25 "	3 00 "	3 75 "	3 50 "	†3 50 "	†2 25 "
Sauce " "	0 65 "	1 00 "	1 00 "	1 25 "	*1 75 "	*0 85 "
Gravy boat	0 20 "	0 30 "	0 30 "	0 25 "	1 50 "	0 75 "
Baker	0 20 "	0 30 "	0 30 "	0 35 "	1 10 "	0 55 "
Salad	0 45 "	0 85 "	0 85 "	1 00 "	1 35 "	1 10 "
Covered vegetable	0 50 "	0 85 "	0 85 "	1 00 "	2 25 "	1 50 "
Casserole	0 50 "	0 85 "	0 85 "	1 00 "	2 25 "	1 50 "
Butter dish	....	....	0 65 "	....	....	....
Pickle	0 15 "	0 20 "	0 20 "	0 25 "	....	0 30 "
Teapot	0 35 "	0 45 "	0 50 "	0 35 "	1 35 "	0 55 "
Sugar bowl	0 25 "	0 35 "	0 40 "	0 30 "	0 85 "	0 40 "
Slop bowl	0 10 "	0 15 "	0 15 "	0 20 "	0 35 "	0 25 "
Creamer	0 15 "	0 20 "	0 20 "	0 20 "	0 50 "	0 30 "
Jug, size 6	....	....	....	....	1 35 "	....
" " 12	....	....	....	....	1 10 "	....
" " 24	0 20 "	0 25 "	0 25 "	0 30 "	0 85 "	0 85 "
Bone dishes	....	1 00 doz.	....	0 85 doz.	....	....
Oatmeal	0 65 doz.	1 00 "	1 00 doz.	1 20 "	2 40 doz.	1 65 doz.
Cake plates	0 15 ea.	0 20 ea.	....	0 25 ea.	0 50 ea.	0 50 ea.
Celery dishes	....	....	....	....	0 85 "	0 55 "
Bread and butter plates	....	....	0 25 ea.	....	....	....
Notched casserole, with ladle	1 35 "	1 85 "	1 75 "	2 25 "	....	....

*No ladle. †No stand.

No. 10. Upper Hanley's King's border, in brown or green, semi-porcelain, decorated, for ordinary wear surpasses anything we have seen. Prices as per list, or for complete sets, as—

40-piece tea set	.... $2.25.
44 " "	.... 2.85.
56 " "	.... 3.25.
100 " "	.... 8.25.
112 " "	.... 9.10.
125 " "	.... 14.15.

No. 11. Meakin's Gloriana pink, is a very dainty pattern, the floral decoration being interlaced with a fine vine pattern with gold tracings. Prices as per list, or in complete sets, as—

40-piece tea set	......$3.35.
44 " "	...... 4.15.
56 " "	...... 4.75.
100-piece dinner set	.. 12.35.
112 " "	.. 13.55.
125 " "	.. 20.90.

No. 12. Dunn Bennit's Ladysmith, printed in a neat green and black pattern, filled in with neat floral designs, heavy gold tracings. Prices as per list, or in complete sets, as—

40-piece tea set	......$3.70.
44 " "	...... 4.60.
100-piece dinner set	.. 13.00.
112 " "	.. 14.35.
125 " "	.. 22.65.

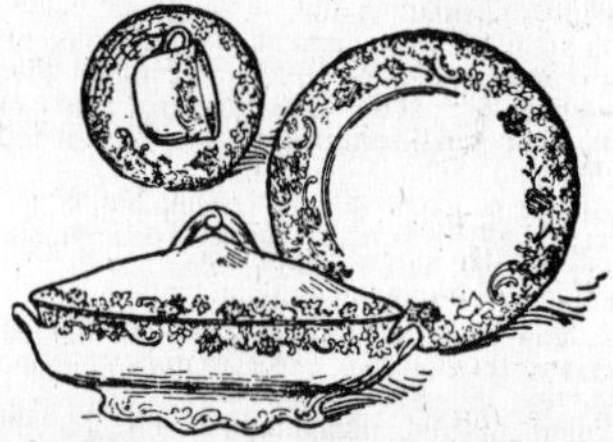

No. 13. Doulton's Albermarle pattern, in a dark blue or pink and green decoration, filled-in colors with heavy gold lines, an exceedingly pretty pattern—

40-piece tea set	$3.75.	100-piece dinner set	$13.55.
44 " "	4.40.	112 " "	14.90.
56 " "	5.25.	125 " "	23.45.

No. 14. Haviland's fine French china, in four decorations, embossed and scalloped, Louis XVI. shape, beautifully gold stippled handles and edges, decorated in pink apple blossoms, blue, heliotrope, pink floral border on tinting, a very select set of dishes—

40-piece tea set	......$8.80.
44 " "	......11.00.
56 " "	......12.65.
100-piece dinner set	..32.00.
112 " "	..35.00.
121 " "	..48.70.

No. 15. Ohme's fine German china, extra smooth finish, deep scalloped edges, handsomely embossed, pretty floral design, neat gold lines on edges—

40-piece tea set	......$5.85.
44 " "	...... 6.80.
56 " "	...... 7.15.
100-piece dinner set	....20.90.
112 " "	....22.80.

No. 3. Fine English China tea sets, consisting of 44 pieces, prettily decorated in blue or pink with gold lines, newest style cups and unique-shaped teapot. Composition: 12 tea plates, 12 cups and saucers, 2 cake plates, 1 teapot, 1 sugar bowl, 1 slop bowl, 1 cream jug. Price, complete, $5.50.
No. 4. Similar set to No. 3, but with filled-in colors and gold lines, $6.50 per set.
No. 5. Similar to No. 3, with filled-in colors and heavy gold stippled edges, $8.50 per set.

No. 1. Fine English china tea sets, very thin, white with gold lines and sprig in centre $2.80 for 40 pieces.

No. 2. Semi-porcelain tea sets, with gold band and sprig in centre, $2.39 for 40 pieces.

We also have a nice collection of tea sets at $10.00, 15.00 and 25.00 set.

Brown Rockingham Ware.

No. 1. Teapots, 10c, 15c, 18c, 20c, 22c each.
No. 2. Jugs, 6c, 7c, 9c, 12c, 15c, 20c each.
No. 3. Oblong or oval bakers, 6c, 7c, 8c, 10c, 12c, 15c, 20c each.
No. 4. Mixing bowls, 3c, 5c, 7c, 10c, 12c, 15c, 20c, 25c each.
Rockingham ware teapots, individual, 8c each.
Round bakers, 7c, 8c, 10c, 12c each.
Lipped bowls, 15c, 20c, 25c, 30c each.
Pie plates, 9-inch, 5c; 10-inch, 7c each.
Best English jetware teapots, decorated, flowers and gold lines, 25c, 30c, 35c, 50c each.
Individual teapots, undecorated, 15c each.
Teapot stands, 15c each.
Jugs, 20c, 25c, 30c each.
Rockingham ware bed pans, 65c each.
Caneware bed pans, 50c each.

Stoneware.

Butter pots, with cover, 1-gal., 25c; 1½-gal., 30c; 2-gal., 40c; 3-gal., 50c; 4-gal., 60c; 5-gal., 75c; 6-gal., 90c each.
Open cream pots, 1-gal., 20c; 2-gal., 30c; 3-gal., 40c; 4-gal., 50c each.
Dutch crocks, 5-lb., 8c; 10-lb., 12c; 15-lb., 18c ea.

Should you require butter pots without covers deduct 5c from 1 and 1½ gals; 10c ea. up to 4 gals., over 4 gals., 15c each.

Cane Ware, White Lined.

Round bakers, 10c, 12c, 15c each.
Mixing bowls, 10c, 12c, 15c, 20c, 25c each.

Ironstone China.

The goods quoted below are manufactured by J. & G. Meakin, which is a sufficient guarantee of their quality.

In Crown and Astro we carry a full line, but in Wheat pattern we only carry cups and saucers, fruit plates, tea plates, breakfast plates, dinner plates, soup plates, 7 and 8-inch. Prices as follows:

Cups and saucers, 75c doz.
Fruit plates, 5-inch, 45c doz.
Tea plates, 6-inch, 55c doz.
Breakfast plates, 7-inch, 65c doz.
Dinner plates, 8-inch, 75c doz.
Soup plates, 7-inch, 65c doz; 8-inch, 75c doz.
Round fruits, 30c doz.
Individual butter pats, 25c doz.
Bowls, 6c, 8c, 10c each.
Covered vegetable dishes, 45c each.
Gravy boats, 15c each.
Platters, 3-inch, 5c; 4-inch, 6c; 5-inch, 7c; 6-inch, 8c; 7-inch, 9c; 8-inch, 10c; 10-inch, 15c; 12-inch, 25c; 14-inch, 35c; 16-inch, 55c; 18-inch, 75c.
Scalloped bowls, 8c, 10c, 12c, 18c, 22c each.
Oval bakers, 2½-inch, 6c; 3-inch, 7c; 4-inch, 8c; 5-inch, 9c; 6-inch, 10c; 7-inch, 12c; 8-inch, 15c; 9-inch, 20c.
Jugs, 10c, 15c, 20c, 25c, 30c and 45c each.
Individual creams, 5c each.
Ice jugs, 30c each; with bar to hold in ice, 35c each.
Jugs for toilet sets, 35c each.
Basins for toilet sets, 35c each.
Chambers for toilet sets, 30c each.
Covered chambers, 45c each.
3-piece toilet sets, $1.00 per set.
Covers of chambers, 15c each.
Slop jars, no covers, 75c each.
Slop jars, covered, 90c each.
Soap dishes, 25c each.
Soap slabs, 5c each.

English China, White and Gold.

Gold band and sprig cups and saucers, tea size, $1.20 doz; coffee size, $1.65 doz.
Tea plates, $1.00 doz.
Fruit or bread and butter plates, 85c doz.
Bowls, 15c each.
Bread plates, 15c each.
Cream pitchers, 15c each.

Semi-Porcelain, White and Gold.

White, with gold lines and sprig.

Semi-porcelain cups and saucers, tea size, $1.10.
Fruit plates, 5-inch, 65c doz.
Tea plates, 6-inch, 85c doz.
Breakfast plates, 7-inch, $1.00 doz.
Dinner plates, 8-inch, $1.20 doz.
Soup plates, $1.20 doz.
Bowls, 7c, 9c, 12c each.
Bakers, 25c, 30c each.
Vegetables, 75c each.
Platters, 10-inch, 30c; 12-inch, 45c; 14-inch, 65c; 16-inch, 90c.
Gravy boat and stand, complete, 45c ea.
Sauce tureen, 4 pieces, complete with ladle, 95c.
Soup tureen, 4 pieces, complete with ladle, $3.00.
Notched casserole, $2.00 each.
Butter pats, 40c doz.
Sauce dishes, 45c doz.
China egg cups, white and gold lines, 20c doz.
Soup ladles, 45c each.
Sauce ladles, 25c each.

Toilet Sets.

10-piece toilet sets, in pink, brown or blue, underglaze decorations, printed in one pattern only, $2.00 per set.
10-piece toilet sets, same decorations, same as above cut, but with large, rolled edge basin, $2.25 set.

10-piece toilet sets, in pink, blue or pearl, underglaze decorations, with gold tracings, rolled edge basin, $3.50 and 3.75 per set.

10-piece toilet sets, with filled-in colors and heavy gold stippled edge, $4.50.
Also a fine collection of toilet sets, in a large variety of shapes and designs, at $5.00, 6.00, 8.00 to 12.00 per set.

German China Fruit Sets.

Fine German china fruit sets, consisting of 12 fruit nappies and 1 large bowl, floral decorations and gold lines, $1.10, 1.35, 1.85 set.

Miscellaneous China.

Low candlesticks, 15c each.
Candlesticks, figure attached, 15c, 20c each.
Butter pats, 40c, 50c, $1.00 doz.
Nest eggs, 25c doz.
Bisque match holders, 10c, 15c each.
Bisque figures, 35c each.
Pin trays, 15c, 25c each.
Haviland china, salad or fruit bowls, 50c, 75c, $1.00, 1.25 each.

German china salad or fruit bowls, scalloped edges, 35c, 50c each.
China toothpick holders, 10c each.
French and German china fruit dishes, 85c, $1.00, 2.50 doz.
Biscuit jars, 50c, $1.25 each.
Cheese dishes, $1.00, 1.25, 2.00 each.
Fancy teapots, 75c, $1.00, 1.25 each.
Muffin dishes, $1.00 each.
Marmalade jars, $1.00 each.
Fancy bread or cake plates, perforated handles, 50c each.
Children's white china mugs, floral decorations, 5c, 10c, 15c each.
Spit cups, loose top, plain, 25c; decorated, 35c each.
Invalid cups, boat shaped, 15c each.
Invalid cups, cup shaped, 25c each.
Shaving mugs, gold edge, beautifully decorated, 10c, 15c, 25c each.

China Tea Sets.

China tea sets, consisting of sugar bowl, cream jug, spoon-holder and butter dish, with heavy gold lines and colored decorations, 60c, 75c, $1.00 set.

Fancy Plates and Cups and Saucers.

Fine French china cups and saucers, gold stippled on handles and edges, prettily decorated in natural flowers, 20c, 25c, 35c each; plates to match above, 20c, 25c each.
Fine German china cups and saucers, gold lined and floral decorations, 50c, 65c each.
Plates to match above, 25c, 50c each.
Cups and saucers, assorted sizes and colors, 10c, 15c, 20c, 25c, 35c, 50c, 65c each.
A fine collection of odd china plates, with gold tracing, 10c, 15c, 25c, 50c, 75c, $1.00 and 1.25 each.

Jugs.

Majolica jugs, holding 1½ pint, 10c; 2 pints, 15c; 2½ pints, 20c. All wine measure.
Semi-porcelain decorated, plain print, 3 sizes, 12c, 15c and 18c; fancy shape, 15c, 18c, 20c each.

Cuspidors.

Fine china cuspidors, tinted in pink, brown and green, with white and gold scalloped border, 50c each.
Floral decoration, satin finished, solid ground, a perfect beauty, 75c each.

Porridge Sets.

Consisting of plate, jug and bowl, gold lined, natural colors, 25c, 35c, 50c, per set.

Table Glassware.

Tea set, consisting of sugar bowl, cream jug, butter dish and spoon holder, 25c set.
Butter dishes, plain, 10c each, cut glass patterns, 20c each.
Sugar bowls, with cover, 20c each.
Spoon holders, 15c each.
Vinegar bottles, 15c, 20c, 25c each.
Syrup pitchers, spring top, nickelled, 25c, 35c each.
Finger bowls, 20c; genuine cut glass, 25c, 50c, 65c each.
Glass cruets, 4 bottles, 50c, 75c; 3 bottles, 25c; 2 bottles, 15c each.
Olive dishes, with handle, 10c, 15c each.
Water jugs, 25c, 35c each.
Cream jugs, 10c, 15c each.
Mustard pots, 12c each.
Low fruit dishes, 15c, 20c, and 25c each.
Pickle jars, 15c each.
Salts and peppers, colored and decorated, 10c, 15c each.
Lemonade sets, 6 glasses, 1 large tankard with embossed tray, $1.25.
Individual salts or celery dips, 25c doz.
Table salts, open, 5c each.

Crystal Glassware.

Our Crystal Glassware is as brilliant as cut glass, and is of the finest quality.

No. 600. Cake stand, 11-inch 55c
No. 601. Salts and peppers 5c
No. 602. Cracker jars, each 35c
No. 603. Hotel sugar bowls and covers 15c
No. 604. Toothpick holders, each 5c
No. 605. Individual cream jugs, each 8c
No. 606. Candlesticks, each 35c
No. 607. Pitchers, ½-gallon size, each 50c
No. 608. Tumblers, 8c; with gold, each 15c
No. 609. Sugar bowls and covers, individual, each 8c
No. 610. Goblets, each 8c
No. 611. Fruit comports, 9-inch, each 45c
No. 612. Oil or vinegar bottles, each 25c
No. 613. Hotel cream jugs, each 15c
No. 614. Footed bowls, 9-inch, each 50c
No. 615. Nappy, 7-inch, 20c; 8-inch, each 25c
No. 616. Berry bowls, oval, each 25c
No. 617. Celery trays, each 35c
No. 618. Shakers, salt and pepper, silver-plated top, each 15c
No. 619. Molasses cans, plated top, each 35c
No. 620. Pickle jars and covers, each 20c
No. 621. Tea sets, crystal, 75c; with gold on edges, each $1.25
No. 622. Wine glasses, each 5c
No. 623. Water bottles, each 50c
No. 624. Tankard jugs, ½-gallon size, 50c; with gold on edges, each $1.00
No. 625. Footed jelly bowls, 5-inch, each 15c
No. 626. Cake salvers, 9-inch, each 35c
No. 627. Tall celery, 20c; with gold, each 35c
No. 628. Custard, each 8c
No. 629. Comports, 4½-inch, each 5c
No. 630. Handled nappies, 5-inch, 10c; 6-inch, each 15c
No. 631. Ice cream nappies, 6-inch, each 6c
No. 632. Plates, 5-inch, each 8c

Tumblers and Stem Goods.

No. 1. Heavy, 50c doz.
No. 2. " 75c doz.
No. 3. " decorated, $1.20 doz.
No. 4. Heavy, 8c each.
No. 5. " 9c each.
No. 6. " 5c each.
No. 7. Light, decorated, 20c each.
No. 8. Light, decorated, 18c each.
No. 9. Light, decorated, 18c each.
No. 10. Light, decorated, 15c each.
No. 11. Light, decorated, 15c each.
No. 12. Light, plain cordial glass, ¾-oz, or 1-oz, $1.50 doz.
No. 13. Light wine glass, 2-oz or 2½-oz, $1.65 doz.
No. 14. Light wine glass, 3-oz, $1.65 doz, or claret, 4-oz, $1.80 doz.
No. 15. Light champagne glass, 5-oz, $1.80, or goblet, 7-oz, $2.00 doz.
No. 16. Light champagne glass, 9-oz, or 11-oz, $2.00 doz.
No. 17. Light, heavy bottom, 10c each.
No. 18. Light, heavy bottom, 5c each.
No. 19. Heavy, 60c doz.
No. 20. Light, 60c doz.
No. 22. " 60c doz.
No. 23. " 72c doz.
No. 24. " 60c doz.
No. 25. " 60c doz.
No. 26. " 96c doz.
No. 28. Light, ground bottom, 50c doz.
No. 29. " 35c doz.
No. 30. " will not nest, 81c doz.
No. 31. " 60c doz.
No. 32. " needle etched, $1.25 doz.
No. 33. " engraved, $1.00 doz.
No. 34. " " 1.00 doz.
No. 35. " " 1.00 doz.

Lamp, Gas and Electric Fixtures.

PRICES SUBJECT TO CHANGE WITHOUT NOTICE.

Hall and Hanging Lamps.

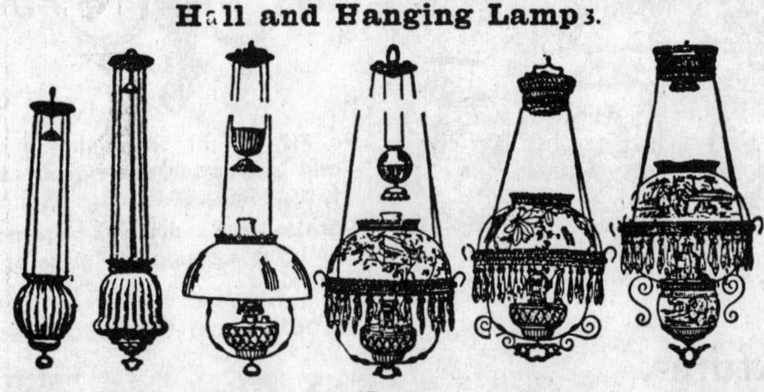

No. 1 No. 2 No. 3 No. 4 No. 5 No. 6

Above cut represents six o our very best lamps. They are very serviceable, as well as ornamental.

No. 1. Hall lamp, gilt lacquered chain and mountings, rose or ruby globe, $1.65.

No. 2. Hall lamp, larger size, gilt lacquered chain and mountings, rose or ruby, $2.50.

No. 3. Hanging lamp, glass fount, large-sized burner, 14-inch plain opal dome-shaped shade, weight balance, brass mountings, $2.25; with decorated shade, $2.50.

No. 4. Hanging lamp, glass fount, brass mountings, weight balance, decorated shade, 30 prisms, $4.30.

No. 5. Hanging lamp, glass fount, with fine gilt lacquered frame, decorated and tinted shade, spring balance, $5.40.

No. 6. Hanging lamp, polished bronze metal, rich gold finish, improved spring extension, length closed, 36 inches, extends to 72 inches, removable oil pot, handsome bisque-finished 14-inch dome, shade and fount to match, hand-decorated, centre draught burner, 75 candle-power, can be lighted without removing chimney, 30 crystal prisms, $6.80.

Hall Lamps.

With gilt lacquered chain and mountings, chimney and burner, complete, and very handsome globes, $2.00 each.

Fancy brass frames, large fancy globes, large burner and chimney, $3.50, 4.00, 4.50, 5.00 each.

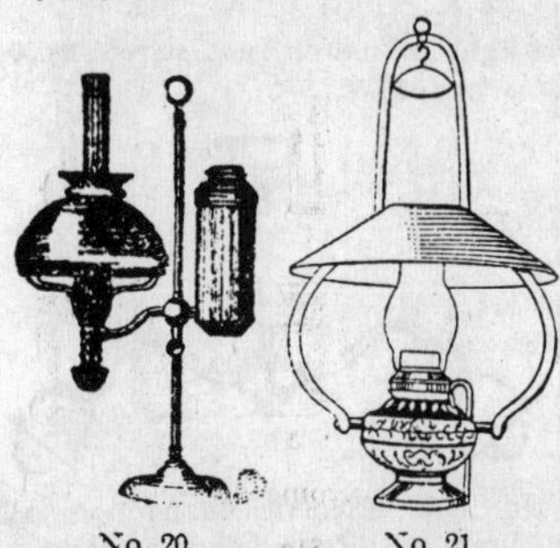

No. 20. No. 21.

No. 20. Student's lamp, nickel plated, centre-draft burner, removable fount, adjustable green shade, $4.25 each.

Sewing or reading lamp, brass, centre draft, circular burner, white shade, $1.95; decorated shade, $2.10 each.

No. 21. Mammoth lamp for store or hall, brass fount, centre-draft burner, 300 candle power, complete with tin shade, $3.75.

No. 21½. Mammoth lamp, with 14 inch opal dome shade, $4.20.

Spring extension for above, $1.50 each extra.

Banquet Lamps.

No. 22. No. 23.

No. 22. Embossed brass, with openwork foot, guaranteed centre-draft burner, complete, with new device for lighting, $1.75, 2.00 each.

No. 23. Banquet lamp, cupid pedestal, fount not detachable, silver or gilt figure, ornamental foot, centre-draft burner, complete with chimney, $2.50 each.

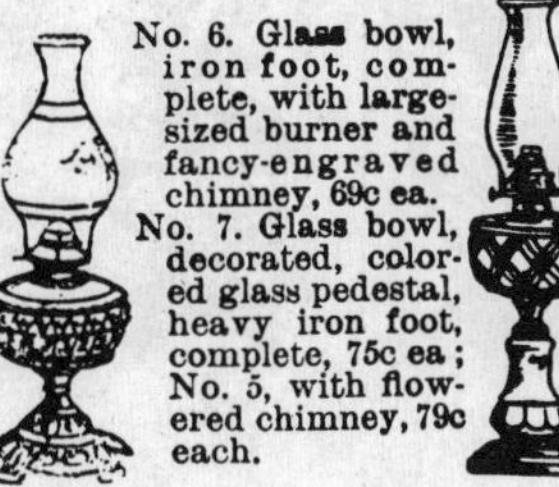

No. 6. Glass bowl, iron foot, complete, with large-sized burner and fancy-engraved chimney, 69c ea.

No. 7. Glass bowl, decorated, colored glass pedestal, heavy iron foot, complete, 75c ea; No. 5, with flowered chimney, 79c each.

No. 6. No. 7.

Bracket Lamps.

No. 8.

Bracket lamps, complete, same as cut No. 8, 65c each.

Lamp brackets like above, less lamp and reflector, 10c, 15c, 30c each.

Fancy lamp bracket, solid brass, as cut No. 9, single swing, extends 12 in., without burner or glass, $1.00 each.

No. 9.

Double swing, extends 18 inches, $1.25 each.

Lamp Globes.

This style of shade has driven silk shades entirely out of the market, and we have some very pretty decorations at prices ranging from 75c, $1.00, 1.25 to 7.00 each.

Lamp Shades.

7-inch decorated dome, 35c each.

10-inch dome shades, for vase lamps, plain white opal, 35c; with hand decorations, 50c each.

14-inch dome shades, for hanging lamps, plain white opal, 50c; with hand decorations, fired, 75c, 85c, $1.00 each.

Stiff paper shades, for glass lamps, 5c, 10c each.

Folding paper lamp shades, in pink and green, complete with wire holder, 15c each.

Lamp Fittings.

Burners, A or medium size, 7c each; B or large size, 9c each; Duplex, single, will fit B size collar, 15c each; Duplex, double, will fit B size collar, 25c each.

Lantern burners, 7c each.

Lantern burners, to fit tubular lantern, 12c each.

Candle wick, 5c ball.

Wick, best quality, A or B size, 3c yd; D size, best quality, 5c yd; wick for banquet lamps, 5c each; students' lamps, 2 for 5c; night lamps, 2 wicks for 1c; mammoth lamps, 10c each.

Chimneys, finest lead flint glass, crimped top, A or medium size, 4c each; B or D size, 6c each.

Globe chimney, to fit A burner, 8c each.

Globe chimneys, engraved, for B burner, 10c each.

Lamp glasses, for hall lamps, medium size, 5c; large size, 7c.

Lamp glass, to fit banquet lamp, 10c; to fit student's lamp, 7c; to fit Duplex burner, 10c; small size, for night lamps, 2c each.

Auer light chimney, 10c each.

Mammoth glasses, 25c each.

Lantern globes, lead flint, 8c each.

Red lantern globes, 25c each.

Wire frames for silk lamp shades, made in hexagon shapes, with turned-up points, 14-inch, 15c; 16 inch, 15c; 18-inch, 20c; 20-inch, 25c each.

Brass rings, to fit on banquet lamps to hold shade, 10c each.

Prisms, 4c each.

Candle shades, fancy stripes and colors, 15c to 50c each.

Holders for same, 5c each.

Reflectors, glass, 6-inch, 15c; 8-inch, 20c; 10-inch, 25c each.

Glass Lamps.

No. 1. No. 2. No. 3. No. 4. No. 5. No. 6. No. 7. No. 8. No. 9. No. 10. No. 11.

No. 1. Complete, with B burner, chimney and wick, 25c each.

No. 2. Complete, with self-filling cap, B burner, chimney and wick, 30c each.

No. 3. Complete, with self-filling cap, handle, B burner, chimney and wick, 35c each.

No. 4. Complete, with handle, A burner, chimney and wick, 20c each.

No. 5. Complete, with handle, A burner, chimney and wick, 25c each.

No. 6. Complete, with A burner, chimney and wick, 25c each.

No. 7. Complete, with A burner, chimney and wick, 30c each.

No. 8. Complete, with B burner chimney and wick, 35c each.

No. 9. Complete, with B burner, chimney and wick, 40c each.

No. 10. Complete, with B burner, chimney and wick, 45c each.

No. 11. Same as No. 10, but with climax burner, 51c each.

Vase Lamps.

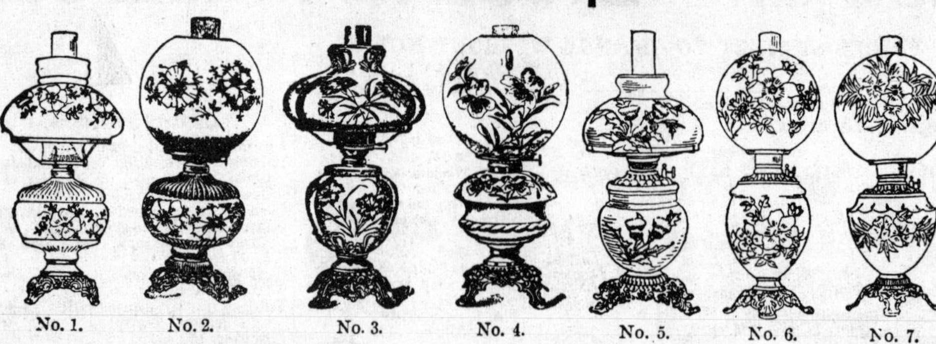

No. 1. No. 2. No. 3. No. 4. No. 5. No. 6. No. 7.

No. 1. Brass foot, large-sized burner, 7-inch dome shade, decorated to match fount, tinted in pink or green, complete with chimney and wick, $1.00 each.

No. 2. With 6-inch globe, tinted in pink and green, $1.25.

No. 3. With 10-inch fluted dome shade, climax burner and chimney, $1.75.

No. 4. With 8-inch globe, climax burner, tinted and decorated with neat floral design, $2.00.

No. 5. Large-sized bowl and 10-inch shade, lift-out fount, circular burner, tinted in pink and blue, $3.00.

No. 6. With 10-inch globe and bowl to match, circular burner, 28 inches high, tinted in pink and yellow, $4.50.

No. 7. With 10-inch globe, bowl to match, circular burner, 24 inches high, in pink and yellow, hand-painted decorations, $4.00.

Prices on this page subject to change without notice.

Piano Lamps.

All gilt, onyx top, patent extension rod, with automatic fastener, removable fount, round plain legs, complete with chimney, $8.50 each.

Brass table, onyx top, removable fount, cast bowl and legs, $12.00, 15.00, 20.00 each.

Wrought iron piano lamp, extension rod, removable founts, circular burner, automatic stop, complete with chimney, special, $8.50, 10.00, 12.00 each.

Brass Tables.

No. 1. Plain polished legs, onyx 8 x 8, $5.00, 6.00, 7.00.

No. 2. Square polished legs, fancy shaped onyx 8 x 8, ornamental lower shelf, $8.00.

No. 3. Heavy cast legs, lacquered, large onyx, very ornamental, $10.00.

Also a variety of designs with two pieces of onyx, cast legs, ornamental lower shelf, from $12.00 to 50.00 each.

Gas Fixtures.

Length of pendants and gasoliers, 30 or 36 inches.

Our Gas and Electric Fixture Department is one of the finest in Toronto. We are always pleased to furnish estimates and prices of any goods not quoted below for private or public buildings.

Gas Wall Brackets.

No. 7. No. 8. No. 4. No. 5.

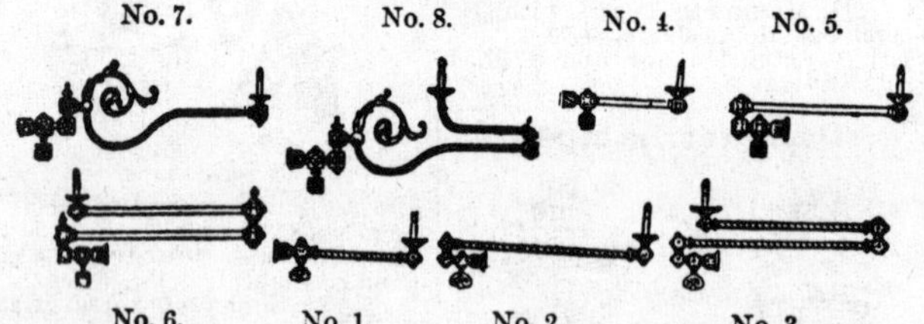

No. 6. No. 1. No. 2. No. 3.

Rope pattern—
No. 1. Stiff, 25c.
No. 2. Single swing, 40c.
No. 3. Double swing, 60c.

Square and polished—
No. 4. Stiff, 50c.
No. 5. Single swing, 70c.
No. 6. Double swing, $1.00.

Square and fancy—
No. 7. Single swing, $1.25.
No. 8. Double swing, $1.65.

Hall Lights.

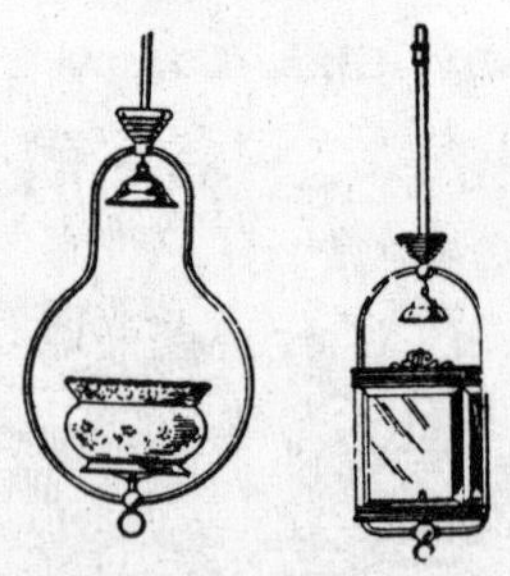

No. 1. No. 2.

No. 1. Fancy brass trimmings, complete with fancy colored globe, $2.10, 2.50, 2.75, 3.00 each.

No. 2. Square lantern, best British plate glass, bevelled edges, an ornament to any hall, $4.50, 5.00, 6.00 each.

Pendants and Chandeliers.

(Prices quoted do not include globes.)

1-light pendant, 60c.

2-light chandeliers, plain, all brass, complete with rings, $1.25.

2-light chandelier, fancy twisted ball and curved arms, $1.75; 3-light, $2.25.

2-light chandeliers, solid brass, complete with rings, prettily curved arms, $2.00; 3-light, $2.75.

2-light chandelier, fancy body and canopy, $2.50; 3-light, $3.25.

No. 812. 2-light chandelier, heavy cast body, arms, and ribbon taps, $5.00; 3-light, $6.00.

We also have a most complete stock of fixtures, ranging in price up to $35.00.

Acetylene Gas Burner.

This cut represents our "Crescent" burner. It gives as good, if not better, satisfaction than other burners which cost you more money; ¼, ½, ¾ and 1 foot sizes, 20c each.

Globe holders, 8c each.

Argand burners, 25c ea.

Lava gas tips, 15c doz.

Gem self-lighting gas burners, 35c each.

¼-inch L cocks, 20c each.

⅜-inch " 25c "

Electric and Combination Fixtures.

Prices quoted do not include globes.

Our stock of electric fixtures is complete. Should you desire something in that line, not quoted below, write us for prices. When prices of combination or straight electric fixtures or brackets are quoted "wired" they include wire, sockets and shade holders (not the shades).

Electric fixtures required more than 36 inches long, 40c per foot extra.

No. 1200. 2-light electric chandelier, plain body, rope, spiral, and curved arms, not wired, $2.00; wired, $2.75.

3-light to match, not wired, $2.50; wired, $3.50.

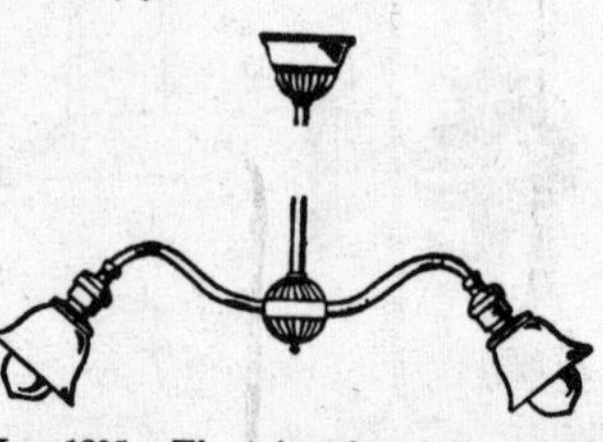

No. 1205. Electric chandelier, all brass, with fancy body and canopy, length 36 inches, spread 20 inches—

2-light,	not wired, $2.50;	wired, $3.25.
3 "	" 3.10;	" 4.10.
4 "	" 3.70;	" 5.20.

No. 1207. Electric chandelier, fancy arms and body, twisted stem, length 36 inches, spread 20 inches—

2-light, not wired, $5.00; wired, $5.75.
3 " " 6.00; " 7.00.
4 " " 7.00; " 8.25.

No. 814. 2-light electric chandelier, heavy cast body and arms, same as cut of gas fixture No. 812, not wired, $5.00; wired, $5.75.

3-light to match, not wired, $6.00; wired, $7.00.

No. 812.

No. 815. One light electric ceiling fixture, spun brass top, finished in rich gold lacquer or black, wrought iron, complete with 6-inch opalescent globe, wired, $1.50. With 8-inch opalescent globe, wired, $1.75.

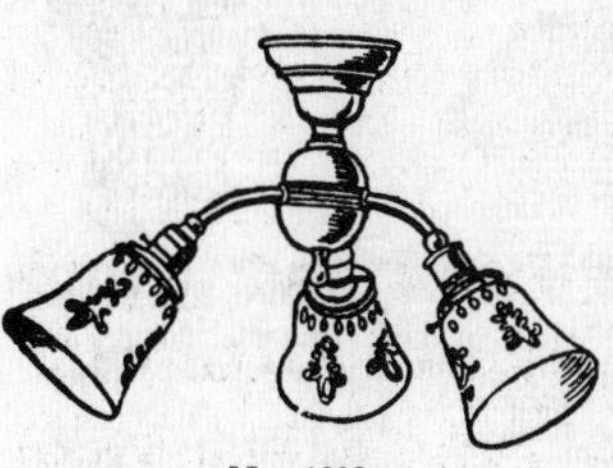

No. 1203.

No. 1208. 3-light ceiling cluster, not wired, $2.25; wired, $3.25.

No. 1209. 3-light electric ceiling cluster, heavy cast brass body and arms, finished in ivory and gold lacquer, not wired, $6.00; wired, $7.25.

No. 1210. 3-light ceiling cluster, spun brass canopy and curved arms, not wired, $7.00; wired, $8.25.

No. 1211. Electric newel post fixture, height 26 inches, not wired, $2.65; wired, $3.00.

No. 1212. Gas newel post fixture, same as No. 1211, $2.65 each.

No. 1211.

Electric portable or table lamp complete, with 6-inch green shade, white inside 10-foot cord and plug attachment, $2.80.

Electric table lamp, slate base, 10-foot cord, plug attachment and 10-inch white shade, $1.80; with green shade, $2.20.

Electric Brackets.

Prices quoted do not include globes.

No. 77. No. 75.

No. 77. Extends $3\frac{1}{2}$ inches, not wired, 18c; wired, 45c.

No. 75. Extends 9 inches, not wired, 25c; wired, 55c.

No. 63.

No. 63. Extends $5\frac{1}{2}$ inches, not wired, 30c; wired, 60c.

No. 60. Extends 9 inches, not wired, 30; wired, 60c.

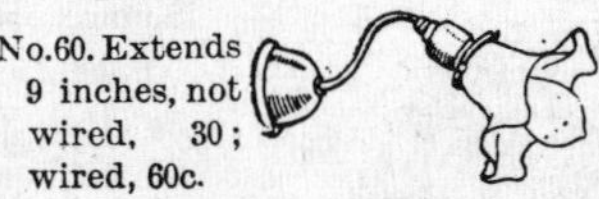

No. 60.

No. 67. Extends 9 inches, not wired, 45c; wired, 75c.

No. 57. Extends 10 inches, not wired, $1.00; wired, $1.30.

Electric Fittings.

Edison's sockets (fibre lined), with key, 20c; keyless, 19c ea.

Thompson & Houston (fibre lined), with key, 20c; keyless, 19c ea.

Shade holders, $2\frac{1}{4}$-inch, 5c; $3\frac{1}{4}$-inch, 8c each.

Wall receptacles, Edison or T. & H., 20c each.

Insulating tape, $1.50 per lb.

Incandescent electric lamps, Edison or T. & H. base, 8, 10 or 16 candle power, 25c; 32 candle power. 35c.

Edison Base.

T. & H. Base.

Above we show cuts of Edison and T. & H. bases. When ordering, be sure and specify style and voltage required.

Gas and Electric Globes.

Gas globes fit 4-inch holder. Electric shades fit $2\frac{1}{4}$-inch holder.

No. 120.

No. 120. Electric shade, flat white opal, 6-inch diameter, 10c each.

No. 121.

No. 140E.

No. 121. Electric shade, white opal, corrugated, 10c each.

No. 140E. Electric globe, flaming top, imitation cut glass, 15c each.

No. 140. Gas globe, to match above, 15c each.

No. 122.

No. 390E.

No. 122. Electric shade, engraved pattern, scalloped top, 25c each.

No. 123. Gas globe, to match above, 30c each.

No. 390E. Colored electric shade, fancy scalloped top, in red, yellow and blue, 50c each.

No. 390. Gas globe, to match above, 60c each.

No. 124. Electric shade, lily shape, in white red and green, 35c each.

No. 126. Electric shade, fern pattern, and scalloped edges, 50c each.

No. 124.

No. 127. Gas globe to match, 50c ea.

No. 125.

No. 125. Electric shade, rose shape, in white, red, blue, yellow and pink, 65c each.

No. 128. Electric shade, tulip shape, in red, pink and green, 65c each.

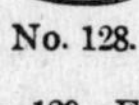

No. 128.

No. 129. Electric shade, fancy scalloped edges, in red, pink and green, 65c each.

No. 129.

No. 130. Electric ball, twisted opalescent, takes $3\frac{1}{4}$-inch holder, 6-inch diameter, 50c; 8-inch diameter, 75c each.

No. 130.

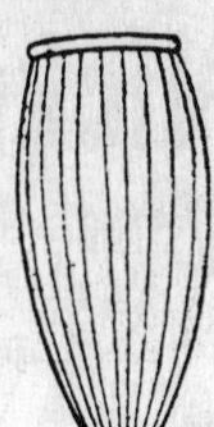

Electric stalactite opalescent, fits $3\frac{1}{4}$-inch holder, 25c each.

Electric drop-light shade, green grass, white inside, $2\frac{1}{4}$ x 6, 40c; $2\frac{1}{4}$ x 10, 65c each.

Electric Motors and Fans

The usefulness of this little motor is unlimited. It can be utilized for operating fans, model ships, trains, mechanical toys, etc.

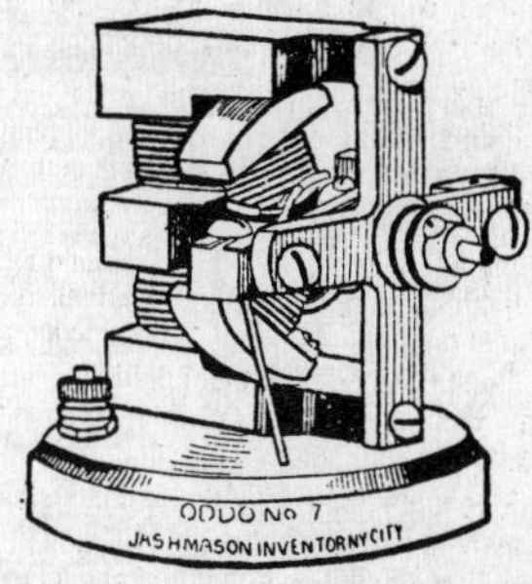

Oddo, No 7. This little motor is 3 inches high, well-made, and nicely finished, with one cell of a good battery it will revolve 1,500 times a minute, $1.00.

Oddo, No. 3. This motor is larger and more powerful than No. 7, and weighs $2\frac{1}{4}$ lbs, $2.00.

Oddo, No. 4, is one size larger than No. 3, stands $4\frac{1}{2}$ inches high and weighs $5\frac{1}{4}$ lbs, $4.00.

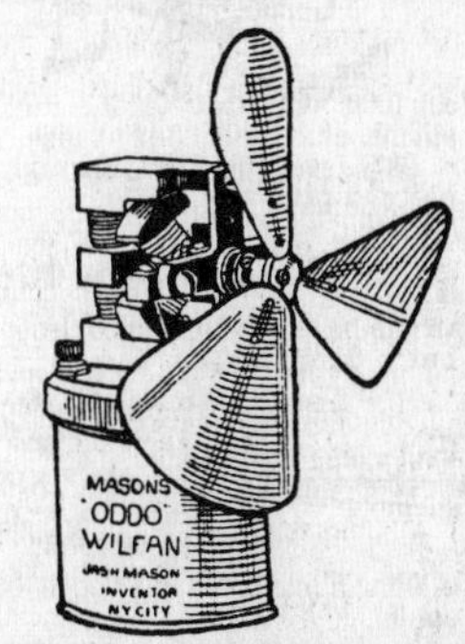

Wilfan, No. 99. The above cut represents one of the most useful articles in the electrical line; it is No. 7 motor, mounted on a stand, complete with a 6-inch fan, $1.75.

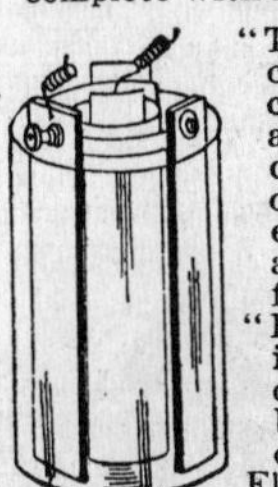

"Type H. Cell." This cell is designed for constant work, such as running motors or fans; it is easily cared for and is not expensive to operate, $1.25; including formula.

"Redalite" for charging cells, a dry coarse powder, 1 lb box will do five charges, 20c per lb.

Flexible cord for connecting motors and batteries, 6c per yd.

Nickel-PLated Ware.

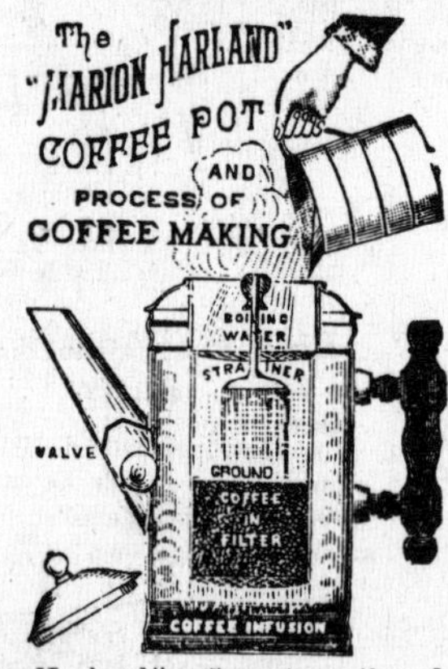

"Marion Harland" coffee pots, well made, strong and handsomely nickel-plated parts, cannot possibly get out of order, 1 pint size, 85c; 1 quart size, $1.10; 2 quart size, $1.25; 3 quart size, $1.75; 4 quart size, $2.00.

No. 259. 5 o'clock kettle and stand, wrought iron stand, brass kettle and lamp, complete, $4.00.

No. 2005. Brass kettle and brass stand, complete, $2 00.

Dewey kettle and stand, 85c.

No. 1009. Chafing dish, nickel-plated, nickel stand, complete, 3-pint size, $5.00.
No. 1008. Chafing dish, wrought iron stand, complete, 2-pint size, $3.50.

Bath-Room Fittings.

Canvas bath seats, adjustable to any width of bath, $1.25, 1.50 each.

Nickel-plated towel bars, $1.00, 1.25, 1.50, 1.60.

No. 420. Nickel-plated glass holders, complete with glass, $1.00 each.

No. 920. Nickel-plated tooth brush holder, $1.65 each.

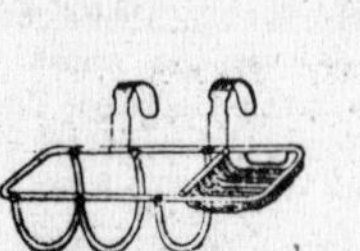

No. 5.

No. 3.

Soap and sponge racks, nickel-plated, to hang over bath, No. 5, $1.25; No. 6, $1.30; No. 1, $1.50; No. 3, $1.60.

No. 100. Sponge holders, nickel-plated, to fasten on wall, $1.50 each.

No. 23.

Nickel-plated soap dishes, 75c, $1.00 each.

No. 23. Soap dish, to hang on bath, $1.30.

No. 24. Soap dish, to hang on bath, 75c.

Three Fall and Winter Specials.

Nickel-plated towel bar, 35c each.

Nickel-plated soap dish, 50c each.

Nickel-plated soap dish, with drainer, 25c each.

No. 114. Solid brass, nickel-plated crumb tray and scraper, ebony handle, $2.50.
No. 14. Solid brass, nickel-plated crumb tray and scraper, $1.75.
No. 15. Crumb tray and brush, nickel finish, $1.00.
No. 16. Crumb tray and brush, nickel finish, 65c.
No. 3. Crumb tray and scraper, nickel-plated, 65c.
No. 2. Crumb tray and scraper, brass, 65c.
No. 1. Crumb tray and scraper, tin, nickel-plated, 35c.
No. 278. Japanned crumb tray and brush, 25c, 50c, 65c.

No. 282. Nickel-plated trays, round, 10c, 15c, 25c, 30c, 35c, 40c, 65c each.
Oval, 50c, 65c, 75c each.

Square, 12-inch, 35c; 14-inch, 50c; 16-inch, 65c; 16-inch, $1.00; 18-inch, 1.25 each.

Nickel plated glass-holder, 35c each.

No. 9. Nickel-plated cuspidors, 20c, 35c, 75c each.

No. XX. Copper, nickel-plated, tea and coffee pots, 25c, 35c, 40c, 50c, 60c, 70c, $1.25, 1.50, 3.00 each.

FANCY BASKETS.

Assortments of baskets are soon broken, so that we will substitute unless told not to.

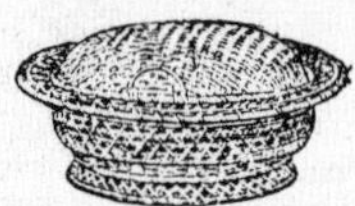

Covered work baskets, square or round, 50c, 65c, 75c each.

Without cover, 20c, 25c, 30c, 50c each.

Square, open work basket, unlined, 15c, 25c, 35c, 50c, 75c ea.

Square open work basket, lined, 15c, 25c, 35c each.

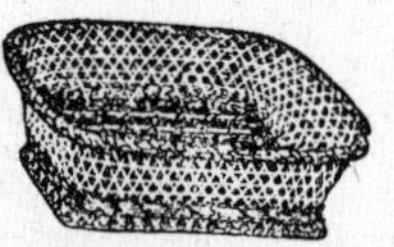

Baby linen baskets, 55c, 65c, 80c, 90c each.
Scrap baskets, 25c, 35c, 50c, 75c, $1.00, 1.25, 1.50 ea.
Bon-bon baskets, covered, 15c, 20c, 25c; very fine, 50c, 75c, $1.00; small fancy, odd shapes, 10c, 15c, 20c each.
Fancy flower baskets, long handles, 65c, 75c, $1.00, 1.75 each.
Fancy flower baskets, covered, very pretty, 50c, 75c, $1.00, 1.75, 2.25, 2.75, 3.00 each.

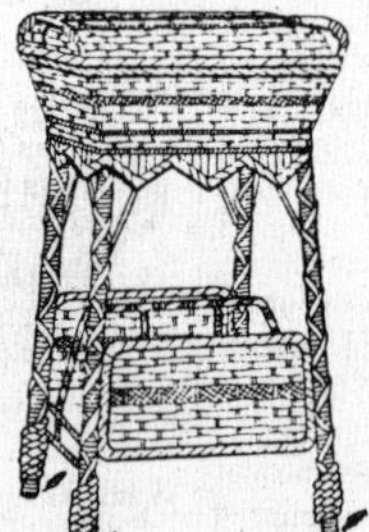

Stand baskets, square, with cover and handle, tray on bottom of stand (see cut), $2.50 each.

Smaller sizes, $1.75, 2.00 each.

Oblong stand baskets, side handles (as per cut), $2.25 each.
Smaller sizes, $1.50, 2.00 each.

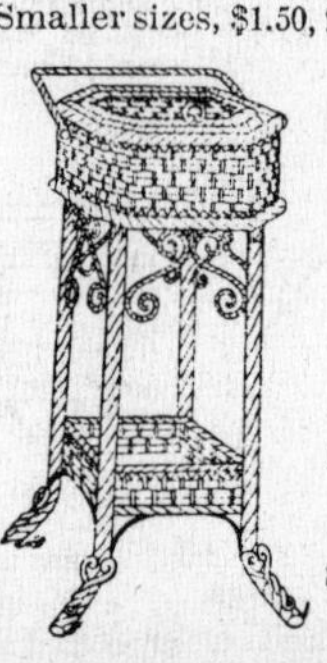

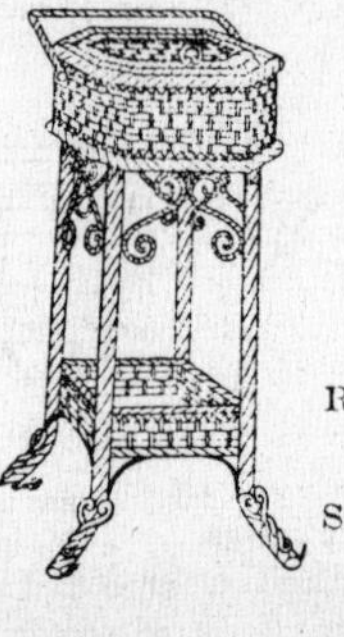

Round stand baskets, covered (see cut), $2.00 each.

Smaller sizes, 75c, $1.00, 1.50 each.

MUSICAL GOODS.

MUSICAL GOODS NOT EXCHANGED.

Band Instruments.

For other instruments not quoted here write us, describing fully the instrument needed.

"Sterling" Cornets.

These are made after the instructions of a well-known Toronto musical house, are easy to blow, well in tune, good models, strongly made.

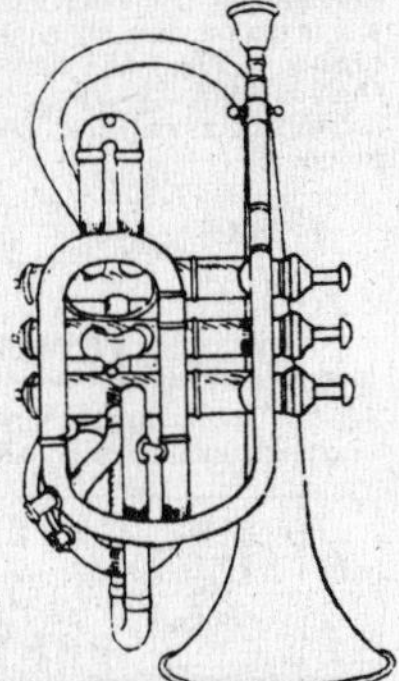

No. 13. B♭ cornet, brass, light action, German silver piston valves and water key, $9.00.

No. 14. B♭, similar to No. 13, but nickel-plated, $11.50.

No. 17. B♭ cornet, brass, light action, German silver piston valves, double water key, $12.50.

No. 19. B♭, similar to No. 17, but triple silver-plated, $20.00.

Ideal Mandolins.

Ideal mandolins are of Canadian manufacture, and will, of course, stand our climatic changes much better than foreign importations.

No. 1. Seven ribs, walnut and maple, rosewood finger-board, pearl position dots, inlaid guard-plate, nickel-plated tail piece, $3.50.

No. 2. Nine ribs, mahogany and walnut, rosewood finger-board, pearl position dots, inlaid guard-plate, nickel-plated tail piece, $6.00.

No. 3. Nine ribs, mahogany, rosewood finger-board, pearl position dots, inlaid around sound-hole, celluloid guard-plate, nickel-plated tail piece, $7.50.

Imperial Mandolins.

Imperial mandolins are neither cloth nor paper pasted on the inside, but are constructed on scientific principles, every instrument stamped "Imperial, warranted."

No. 4. Nine bird's-eye maple and rosewood strips, with five colored strips between rosewood cap and side strips, mahogany neck, oval ebony finger-board, pearl position dots, German silver frets, colored wood inlaid around sound hole, inlaid celluloid guard plate, ebony bridge, nickel-plated tail piece, $9.75.

No. 6. Eleven rosewood strips, rosewood cap and side strips, mahogany neck, head veneered with rosewood, oval ebony finger-board, oblong sound hole, pearl position dots, German silver frets, bevelled top, braced, imitation ivory edges, inlaid celluloid guard-plate, ebony bridge, nickel-plated tail piece, patent machine head, full French polished, $15.00.

Mandolin Strings.

Mandolin strings, E and A, are 3c each, or 2 for 5c; D and G, covered strings, 5c each; the full set of 8 strings for 20c.

Banjos.

No. 5. 16 nickel-plated brackets, nickel-plated rim, wood lined, polished walnut neck, German silver raised frets, calfskin head, nickel-plated tail piece, 11-inch rim, 18-inch finger-board, $5.00.

No. 8. 38 nickel-plated professional brackets, nickel-plated rim, wired edge, highly polished walnut neck, raised German silver frets, inlaid with fancy design of celluloid, calfskin head, imitation ivory pegs and tail piece, 11-inch rim, 18-inch finger-board, $7.50.

No. 101. German silver rim, wired edge, grooved hoop, cherry neck, highly polished, veneered finger-board, inlaid pearl position dot, 20 nickel-plated brackets, $10.00.

Genuine Stewart banjo, 20 professional brackets, polished mahogany neck, N. P. rim, "The Student," $12.00.

Banjo Strings.

1st, 2nd, 3rd and 5th strings, Padua smooth finish, 5c each.

4th string, covered on finest Chinese silk, 5c each.

Banjo strings, Imperial quality, the finest made—

1st, 2nd, 3rd and 5th strings, 10c each.

4th, finest silk centred, covered with silver wire, 10c each.

Guitars.

The cheapest, most attractive and best-selling styles of guitars ever put on the market.

No. 309. Standard size, imitation mahogany sides and back, colored front, fancy inlaid around sound-hole, imitation ebony finger-board and bridge, pearl position dots, imitation cherry neck, American machine head, $4.00.

No. 104. Small, concert size, imitation rosewood sides and back, fancy-colored strip down the back, French polished colored front, fancy sound hole, rosewood finger-board and bridge, position dots, imitation mahogany neck, American make, patent head, $5.00.

No. 111½. Standard size, fine imitation rosewood back and sides, highly polished, fancy strip down back, celluloid bound edges front and back, colored front, fancy ornamental sound-hole, rosewood finger-board and bridge, position dots, imitation mahogany neck, American patent machine head, $6.00.

No. 1. Imperial, antique oak, highly polished mahogany neck, rosewood finger-board and bridge, pearl position dots, inlaid sound-hole, $9.00.

No. 1½. Similar to No. 1, but in concert size, $10.00.

No. 2. Imperial guitar, rosewood, highly polished, similar to No. 1, standard size, $12.00; concert size, $15.00.

No. 4. Standard size, rosewood sides and back, mahogany neck, two rings of colored wood inlaid around sound-hole, fine colored wood inlay and imitation ivory binding around front edge, fancy strips of inlaying down the back and across side under the end pin, ebony finger-board and bridge, head of neck veneered with rosewood, $20.00.

Guitar Strings.

1st, 2nd, 3rd, gut, Padua smooth finish, transparent; 4th, 5th, 6th, Chinese silk centre, covered with silver wire, 10c each, or 50c the set of six strings.

Autoharps.

Full instructions, a book of music, two picks, and tuning key accompany each instrument, which is done up in a nice case. These instruments are manufactured of the very choicest hardwood, with California cedar tops, which give them a most beautiful and musical quality of tone.

No. 10. 3 bars, producing 3 chords, $1.95.

No. 20. 4 bars, producing 4 chords, $2.15.

No. 25. 5 bars, producing 5 chords, $2.50.

No. 30. 6 bars, producing 6 chords, concert size, $4.00.

No. 35. 10 stops, producing 10 chords, new covered bar system, a most beautiful instrument, $5.00.

Autoharp strings, plain wire, 5c each; covered strings, 10c each, or per complete set, $1.00. In ordering sets give number of strings required.

Prices on this page subject to change without notice.

Violins.

These prices do not include bows.

No. 18. Red or brown shaded, $1.00.

No. 10. Hopf, brown varnish, polished, better quality, $2.00.

No. 33. Conservatory model, amber color, nicely shaded, fine finish, the best violin on the market for the money, $3.00.

No. 100E. Stradivarius model, dark amber, shaded, good tone, ebony trimmings, $4.00.

No. 178. Stainer model, bright reddish brown, highly flamed and polished, very fine finish and trimmings, $5.00.

No. 886. Paganini concert violin, amber shaded, highly polished, fine tone and finish, $7.00.

No. 313. Conservatory Stradivarius, brown and amber shaded, fine trimmings, well made and good tone, a splendid instrument, $10.00.

No. 893. Wieniawski violin, D'Artist, dark shaded, engraved on head, elegantly finished and fine tone, $12.00.

No. 206. Celebrated Duerer violin, Stradivarius model, brown amber varnish, fine tone and finish, $15.00.

Violins above $3.00 furnished in ½ or ¾ size.

Violin Bows.

No. 18. Maple red, black frog, bone button, 25c.

No. 151. Brazil wood, ebony frog, pearl slide, full German silver lined, 50c.

No. 136½. Brazil wood, polished, ebony frog, pearl slide, German silver button and tip, 75c.

No. 145. Brazil wood, octagon polished stick, ebony frog, pearl eye, German silver trimmed, German silver button, leather winding, $1.00.

No. 800. Pernambuco, polished stick, fine ebony polished frog, with pearl eye, full German silver mountings, ivory tip, leather winding, $1.25.

No. 199B. Pernambuco, polished, round stick, fine ebony frog, full German silver trimmed, pearl eye, fine quality, $1.50.

No. 246. Pernambuco, ebony frog, full German silver trimmed, pearl slide and eye, fine quality, $2.00.

Bows, for ½ and ¾ size violins, same numbers and prices as above.

Violin Fittings.

Bridges—
Maple, 3 scrolls, Panpi, 3c each.
Maple, 3 scrolls, Bausch, 4c each.
Flamed maple, 3 scrolls, Aubert, 5c each.
Flamed maple, 3 scrolls, Vuillaume, 8c each.
Pegs—
Boxwood, black, 5c each.
Ebony, polished, Bausch model, pearl dot, 7c each.
Rosewood, polished, German model, pearl dot, 10c each.
Tail pieces—
Imitation ebony, inlaid with pearl eye, 8c each.
Imitation ebony, inlaid pearl shield, 15c each.
Ebony, inlaid, 3 pearl flowers, 25c each.
Ebony, highly polished, inlaid with 5 pearl flowers, German silver saddle, 40c each.
No. 11. Chin rests, ebony, with hook, 25c each.
No. 13. Chin rests, ebony, engraved, with German silver tightener, 50c each.
No. 14. Chin rests, ebony, engraved, with 2 German silver tighteners, 75c each.
No. 22. Gutta percha, nickel plated, velvet shoulder rest, improved model Becker, $1.25.
Resin, conservatory, 5c, 10c, 15c each.
Mutes, ebony, 10c; brass, 10c.
Tuning forks, A or C, 10c each.
Combination pitch pipes, A and C, 20c each.

Violin Strings.

E, A and D, Padua finish, smooth, transparent, 10c each.
G. American stretched, made with care, 10c ea.
Imperial violin strings, superior satin finish, the finest string made—
E, A and D strings, 20c each.
G strings, covered with pure silver wire, 30c each.

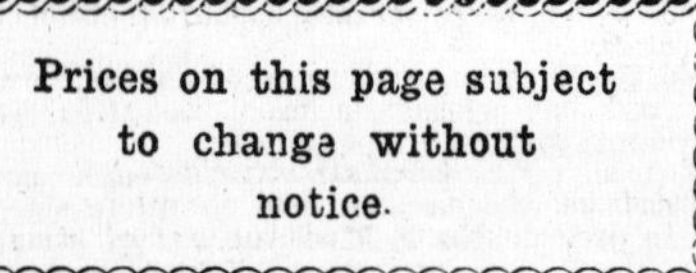

Accordions.

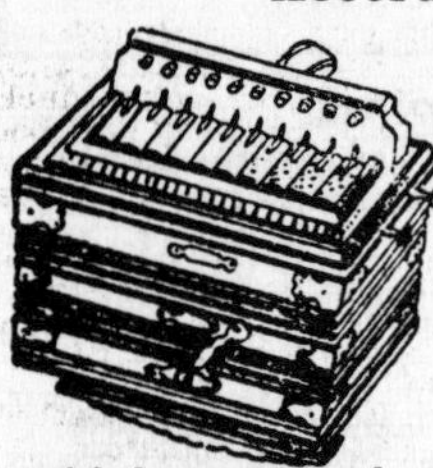

No. 65. Miniature size, ebonized frame, open action, nickel keys, one set of reeds, $1.25.
No. 122. Ideal miniature size, ebonized frame, open action, nickel keys, two stops, two sets of reeds, $2.00.
No. 195½. Ideal, ebonized mouldings double bellows, nickel corners and clasps, German silver reeds, open nickel keys, fancy gilt borders, $2.50.
No. 173. Imperial, small size, 10 keys, 2 stops, 3 bass keys, $3.50.
No. 3. Imperial, regular size, ebonized moulding, white enamelled panels, nickel mouldings and nickel protectors, simplex action, bass valves, 8-fold double bellows, leather straps, 10 keys, 2 stops, extra broad steel reeds, $5.00.
No. 1442. Imperial, regular size, ebonized moulding, depressed keyboard, artistically decorated frames, nickel corners and clasps, double bellows, leather bound, two sets of steel bronze reeds, patent vox humana attachment, $5.00.
A collection of high-class accordions, ranging in prices from $7.00 to 14.00 each.

Blow Accordions.

No. 21. Ten nickel keys, 2 brass keys, wood case, nickel corners, nickel extension, bell and cord, with tassels, 85c each.
No. 22. Ten nickel keys, 2 brass keys, nickel case, with 4 fancy bugles, and nickel extension bell, $1.00.
No. 23. Ten nickel cylinder keys, ebonized wood case, with silver moulding around keyboard, adjustable mouth piece, $1.50.

Concertinas, 20 Keys.

No. 1. 20 keys, imitation rosewood, single reed, good quality, $1.00.
No. 21. 20 keys, rosewood, German silver inlaid edges, handsome bellows, double reeds, $2.00.
No. 139. 20 keys, mahogany, ivory keys, imitation leather bellows, Anglo style, $2.50.
Collection of extra quality concertinas, $4.00, 5.00.
Mandolin picks, 7c each.
Autoharp picks, 10c each.
Music stands, "Ideal," umbrella, japanned, $1.00 each.
Metronomes, $3.00; with bell, $3.75.
Nickel-plated music stands, $2.35.

Tambourines.

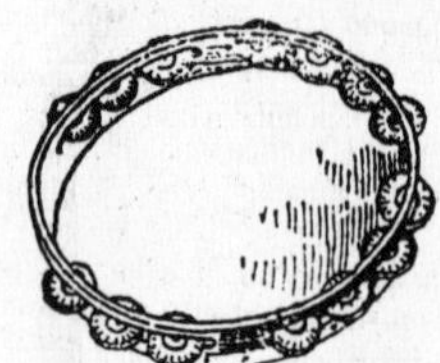

No. 1. 8-inch maple rim, plain calf head, 3 sets of brass jingles, 50c.
No. 3. 10-inch maple rim, fancy painted rim, calf head, 6 sets German silver jingles, Salvation Army style, 75c.
No. 6. 10-inch maple rim, fancy painted, calf head, 1 row, 14 sets of German silver jingles, skeleton model, $1.50.

Flutes.

No. 1. Key of D, cocoa wood, German silver tipped, with one key, $1.75.
No. 4. Key of D, Grenadella or cocoa wood, German silver tipped, with slide cork joints, and 4 keys, $3.25.
No. 6. Key of D, Grenadella or cocoa, German silver tipped, with slide, six keys, $3.75.
No. 7. Key of D, Grenadella or cocoa wood, with slide, German silver tipped, cork joints, with eight keys, $5.00.
No. 11. Similar to No. 7, but a much finer instrument, with an ivory head, $12.00.
No. 1. B or C, black, German silver ferrules, 25c.
No. 5. B or C, ebony, German silver ferrules, 75c.
No. 24. B or C, metal, nickel plated, professional model, full bore, raised embouchure plate, easy flowing, $1.00.

Wood Flageolets with Piccolo Heads.

No. 1. Cocoa wood, black, 1 German silver key, and tipped, with piccolo head, $2.75.
No. 3. Grenadella or cocoa wood, 6 German silver keys, and tipped, $4.00.

Instrument Cases.

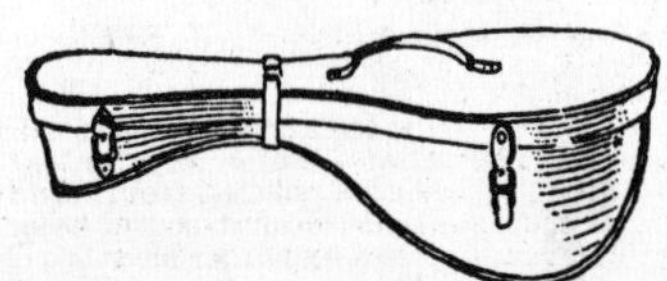

No. 3. Mandolin case, made of canvas, leather bound, flannel lined, $1.75.
No. 6. Black or orange pebbled leather, all hand sewn, embossed, flannel lined, $5.00.

Banjo and Guitar Cases.

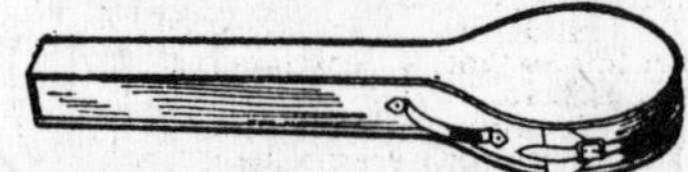

No. 45. Canvas-covered banjo case, leather bound, $1.75.

No. 3. Canvas-covered guitar case, leather binding, open at end, full flannel lined, $1.75.
No. 9. Leather guitar case, in black or orange, pebbled, hand sewn, flannel lined, open at end, embossed, made in both standard or concert size, $6.00.

Violin Cases.

No. 2. Violin case, wood, black, swell top, hooks, no lock, $1.25.
No. 3. Same as No. 2, with lock, $1.50.
No. 8. Wood, swell top, curved sides, spring clasp lock, full flannel lined, nickel clasps and handle, $3.75.
No. 9. Canvas, slate color, leather bound, flannel lined, $1.75.
No. 15. Exposition shape, black, smooth leather covered, velvet lined, embossed patent nickel catches, $6.00.

Mouth Organs.

We do not exchange mouth organs.

The mouth organs we sell are manufactured by M. Hohner, in Germany. They are without doubt the finest and best goods of the kind that are made. They are all perfectly tuned and noted for correctness of scale, and can always be depended upon. Our cheapest mouth organ is 20c. We have come to the conclusion that a strictly first-class and perfectly tuned harmonica cannot be furnished under that price.

No. 0. Ten double holes, brass plates, nickel covers, superior quality, 20c.

No. 1. "Capetown to Pretoria," nickel plated, twenty reeds, put up in neat lidded case, 25c.
No. 1½. Hohner's organ pipe harp, a new novelty, ten single holes, sweet tone, 25c.
No. 3. Up-to-Date, has ten double holes, put up in handsome case, 50c.
No. 10. Marine Band, concert size, for professional use, ten double holes, forty reeds, rich powerful tone, 75c.

No. 5. Midget, Hohner's smallest-size mouth organ, can be covered with one hand, 3 inches long, single reeds, finely nickel-plated, 25c.

No. 6. Grand Symphony, a splendid instrument for professional or amateur players, 20 reeds, put up in neat satin lined case, 25c.
No. 8. Ten single holes, finely nickel plated, rounded covers, put up in handsome satin-lined case, 35c.
No. 9. Special, ten double holes, forty reeds, finely nickel plated, bevelled edge covers, extra sonorous tone, a grand instrument, 50c.

All our musical instruments are carefully examined before shipment, and guaranteed to be in perfect condition when leaving us.

Sporting Goods, Guns, Revolvers and Ammunition

ALL PRICES SUBJECT TO CHANGE WITHOUT NOTICE.

Footballs.

Finest quality materials only are used in the manufacture of our football covers and bladders, and as they are thoroughly tested before leaving us, we will not under any circumstances replace these goods.

Rugby or Association covers—No. 3, $1.00; No. 4, 1.10; No. 5, 1.25; No. 6, 1.50 each.

Bladders for Rugby or Association footballs—No. 3, 50c; No. 4, 65c; No. 5, 75c; No. 6, 75c each.

Footballs Complete.

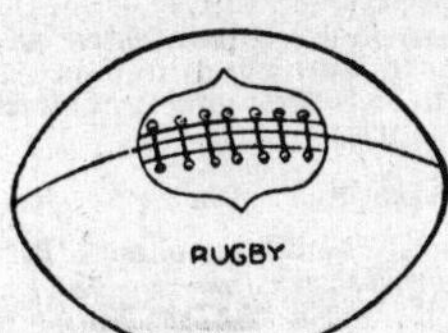

Rugby or Association—

No. 3, $1.50 each.
No. 4, 1.75 "
No. 5. 2.00 "
No. 6, 2.25 "

Football Shin Guards.

Boys' size, no ankle pads, 30c pair; with ankle pads, 75c pair.

Men's size, no ankle pads, 40c pair; with ankle pads, 90c pair.

Basket Ball Goods.

The Spalding official basket ball, officially adopted for use in all match games. The cover is well made of the finest and most carefully selected pebble grain leather; the bladder is made specially for this ball, of extra heavy and purest para rubber. Each, $5.00.

The Spalding regulation basket ball, regulation size, fine leather cover, capped ends, $3.25.

Practice ball, selected leather cover, regulation size, $2.00.

Spalding official basket ball goals, complete with ring, wall brackets and net, $5.00 pair.

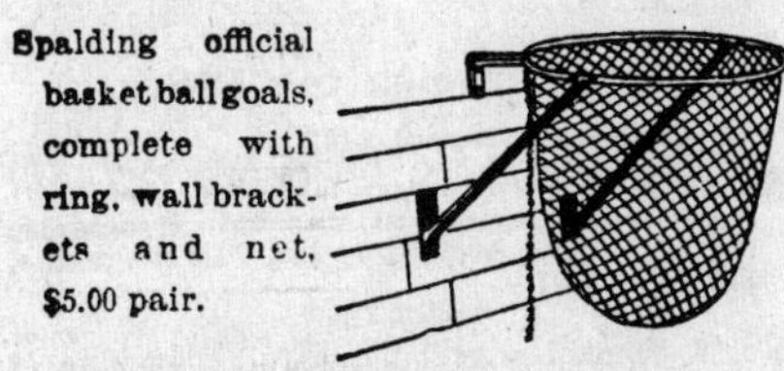

Indoor Baseball.

Spalding's indoor baseballs, horsehide covers, adopted by the National Association of Indoor Baseball Leagues, every ball guaranteed to last a game.

No. 1. Official, 95c each.

Indoor baseball bats, No. 0, 65c each.

Striking Bag Gloves.

No. 14. Made of claret-colored kid, padded back, safety grip, 75c pair.

No. 15. Made of wine-colored kid, short palm, lightly padded over knuckles, with grip in palm, 50c pair.

Boxing Gloves.

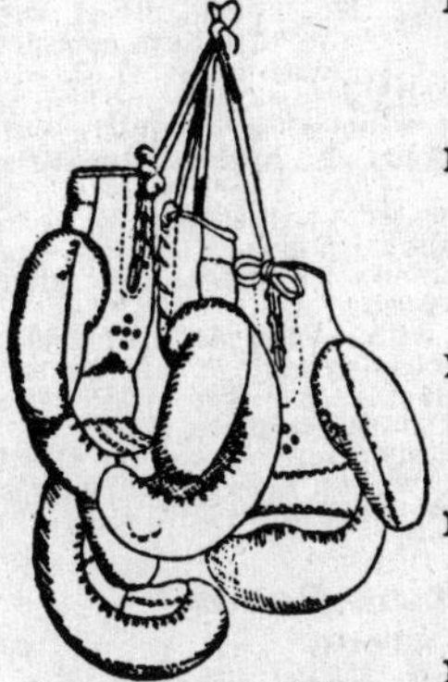

No. 1. Boys' boxing gloves, gold tan leather, elastic wrist, filled with hair, $1.25.

No. 3. Boys' Corbett style, wine color, elastic wrist, and filled with good quality curled hair, $1.65 set.

No. 2. Men's gloves, made of gold tan kid, elastic wrist, full size, hair-filled, $1.50 set.

No. 4. Made of wine-colored kid, laced wrist, and filled with curled hair, $2.00 set.

No. 5. Made of brown Yucatan kid, with safety grip, Corbett pattern, laced wrist, and filled with curled hair, $2.50 set.

No. 6. Made of wine-colored kid, Corbett pattern, padded wrist, safety grip laced and filled with good quality curled hair, $3.25 set.

No. 7. Made of fine quality green kid, California thumb side pad, padded wrist, laced, safety grip, and filled with superior quality curled hair, Fitzsimmons' style, $4.50 set.

No. 7. Made of the finest imported tan kid, Corbett style, padded wrist, safety grip, 4, 5, 6, 7 oz, $6.00 set.

Striking Bags.

Single End.

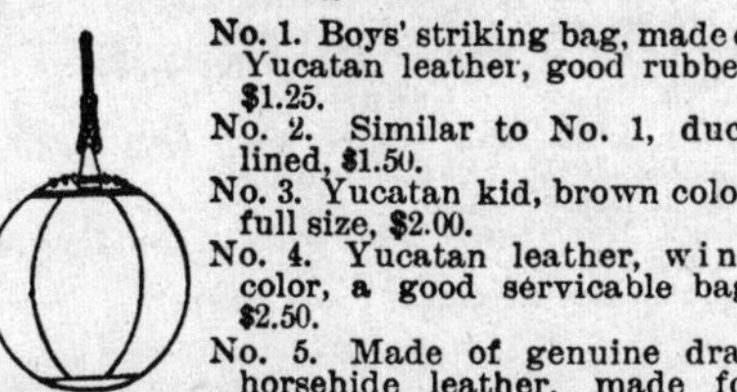

No. 1. Boys' striking bag, made of Yucatan leather, good rubber, $1.25.

No. 2. Similar to No. 1, duck lined, $1.50.

No. 3. Yucatan kid, brown color, full size, $2.00.

No. 4. Yucatan leather, wine color, a good servicable bag, $2.50.

No. 5. Made of genuine drab horsehide leather, made for heavy work, $3.75.

No. 6. Made of pearl-colored Angora goat skin, lined with heavy twilled duck; this is one of the strongest and best bags that can be found anywhere, and is especially adapted for gymnasium and heavy work, $5.00.

Double End.

No. 7. Boys' size, made of Yucatan leather, good rubber, $1.50.

No. 8. Same as No. 7, only duck-lined, $1.75.

No. 9. Yucatan leather, brown color, full size, $2.50.

No. 10. Made of wine-colored Yucatan leather, a very popular bag, $2.75.

No. 11. Yucatan leather, wine color, a strong durable bag, $3.00.

No. 12. Made of fine Benton tan kid, very strong, light and durable, $3.50.

No. 13. Made of genuine horsehide, drab color, a good heavy work bag, $4.25.

NOTE.—All our striking bags are fitted complete with rope, elastic cable, screw eyes, etc., and put up in neat cardboard box. Rubber in Nos. 1, 2, 7, 8, not guaranteed.

Golf Clubs.

Morristown iron or wooden golf clubs, in either ladies' or gents' sizes, 85c each.

Golf Balls.

The Wonder, 20c each; $2.25 dozen.
The Ocobo, 25c each.
The Silvertown, 30c each.
The O.K. Silvertown, 25c each.
The A1 Black, 25c each.
The Eureka, 25c each.
Pierce's golf enamel, 40c tin.
Paper tees, 15c per box of 25.
Rubber tees, 2 for 15c.
Heavy rubber tees, 15c each.
Ball cleaners, 20c each.
Score books, 10c each.

Bar Bells and Wands.

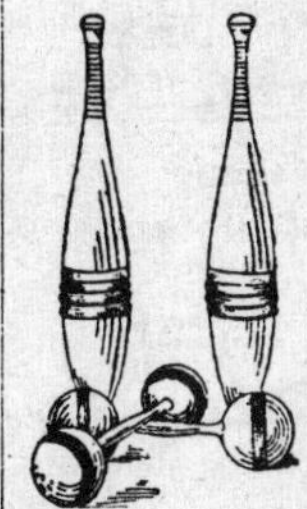

Bar bells and wands, made of choice selected hardwood, well finished. Bar bells, 35c; wands, 10c each.

Indian Clubs and Dumb Bells.

Made of choice hardwood, nicely turned and well finished.

Clubs—
$\frac{3}{4}$-lb, 15c; 1-lb, 20c; $1\frac{1}{2}$-lb, 30c; 2-lb, 40c; 3-lb, 50c pair.

Dumb Bells—
$\frac{3}{4}$-lb, 30c; 1-lb, 35c; $1\frac{1}{2}$-lb, 45c; 2-lb, 50c pair.

Caddy Bags.

No. 1. Made of heavy 10-oz duck, leather reinforced top and bottom, ball pocket, strap leather sling, 5-inch ring, wood bottom, $1.25.

No. 2. Similar to No. 1, but has 4-inch ring, gilt buckles and studs, $1.50.

No. 3. Made of 14-oz brown duck, leather reinforced top and bottom, oak tanned strap leather sling, brass buckles and studs, 4-inch ring, pocket, $1.75.

No. 4. Made of extra heavy 20-oz brown duck, leather reinforced top and bottom, strap leather sling, brass trimmings, 4-inch ring, $2.00.

No. 5. Made of smooth Benton tan bag leather, light brown color, full leather bottom, gilt trimmings, 4-inch oval ring, long pocket, $2.75.

No. 6. Made of the best oak tan tourist leather, 4-inch oval ring, sole leather bottom, hand sewn, brass trimmed detachable sling, in neat colors, $4.00.

No. 7. Made of russet strap leather, pigskin pebbled, soft finish, 4-inch oval ring, sole leather bottom, hand sewn, brass trimmings, an A1 bag, $4.50.

Folding pocket cups, a very handy article for bicyclists, campers or tourists, in two sizes, small 20c, large 25c each.

Waterproof match boxes, guaranteed to be absolutely water tight and moisture proof, 35c each.

Safety pocket axe, very strong and durable, with selected hickory handle, $1.50 each; with 11-inch steel handle and hard rubber grip, $2.50 each.

China carpet bowls, a very interesting parlor game, $1.50 per set.

Ankle and wrist supports, made of No. 1 stock, soft and pliable, just the thing for athletes, etc.; wrist supports, 15c and 20c each; ankle supports, 20c pair.

Hockey Sticks and Pucks.

Small boys' hockey sticks, 10c each.
Boys' No. XXX elm, and No. 1 ash sticks, 10c each.
Youths' size, narrow blade, 15c each.
Men's No. IX ash, 25c.
Men's No. XXX elm, 20c.
Men's second growth ash, 35c.
Goal sticks, elm, wide blade, 35c each.
Hockey pucks, boys' size, 15c each; **men's size,** 20c each.

Skates.

All genuine Starr skates, manufactured by the Starr Manufacturing Co., of Dartmouth, N.S., have been the leading skates for Canada for years, and as usual, we intend carrying a complete line for the coming season.

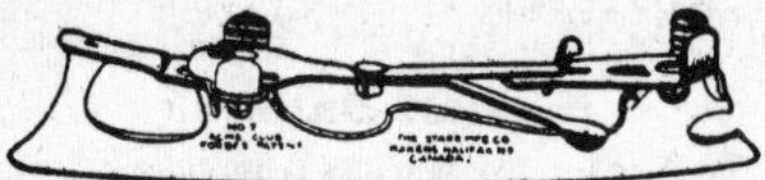

No. 90. Genuine Starr acme, sizes 7½ to 12, 45c pair.

No. 25. Acme, full nickel plated and highly finished, sizes 8½ to 12, $1.15 pair.

Boys' hockey, made of good quality steel, proportioned to stand extra rough usage, sizes 8 to 10½, 45c pair.

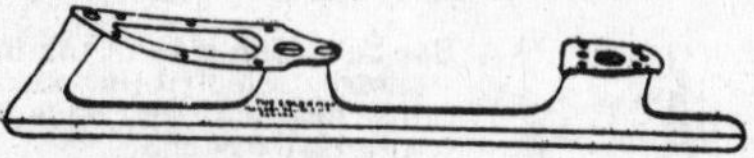

The Starr Hockey Skate.

No. 20. Starr hockey, light and strong, sizes 8½ to 12, $1.00 pair.

No. 25. Starr hockey skate, polished steel, with puck stop, $1.45 pair.

The Micmac.

No. 10. Quality, a first-class skate in every particular, no puck stop, sizes 10, 10½, 11, 11½, 12, $2.65 pair.

The Chebucto.

No. 7 quality, Chebucto polished steel, sizes 9½ to 12, $1.75 pair.

No. 10 quality, full nickel plated, sizes 9½ to 12, $2.25 pair.

The Chebucto is a first-class and up-to-date skate in every respect.

Ladies' Beaver.

No. 25. Ladies' Beaver flanged runner, extremely light in weight, very strong, and unapproachable for beauty of design, full nickel plated, sizes 9, 9½, 10, 10½, $1.45 pair.

The Fisher Tube Skate.

Made of the finest quality of crucible cast steel, hardened and tempered, highly polished and nickel plated, making a very handsome and strong skate. Suitable for either pleasure or racing.

The Fisher tube hockey skate, sizes 10½, 11, 11½, 12, $5.00.

The Fisher racing skate, 14 or 16-inch blade, sizes 10½, 11, 11½, nickel plated, $5.00.

NOTE.—The above price is for the Skates only and does not include the boots.

Whitely Exercisers.

Made in three weights; light, medium and heavy. Plainly state which you want when ordering.

The Whitely Exerciser, the most popular exerciser on the market, simple and durable, can be operated in any room, only weighs 2 lbs.

No. 0 style, fitted with wood pulleys, complete with chart, $1.50.

No. 1 style, fitted with adjustable cone-bearing pulleys, which are noiseless, complete with chart, and Anderson's "Physical Education," $2.25 each.

No. 2 style, decorated, adjustable noiseless cone-bearing pulleys, polished handles, complete with Anderson's "Physical Education" and chart, $3.25 each.

No. 3 style, fitted with nickel-plated, noiseless adjustable cone-bearing pulleys, silk covered cable, cork handle grips, Anderson's "Physical Education" and chart, complete, $4.00.

If you have a Whitely Exerciser and the elastic in it is worn out, we can give you elastic at 5c a foot for light weight, and 10c a foot for heavy weight.

Fencing Goods.

Foils.

No. 2. Solingen foil, corded grip, open steel guard, $1.25 pair.

No. 1. Solingen foil, same as No. 2, but with better quality blade, $1.50 pair.

The France foil, fancy corded grip, with brass guard, $2.00 pair.

Klingenthal foil, leather handle, wired, fancy brass guard and casting, best quality Klingenthal blade, $2.75 pair.

Blades.

Solingen blades, 35c each.
Paris blades, 50c each.
Klingenthal blades, 50c each.

Masks.

With ear and head pads, $1.25 and $1.75 each.

Plastrons.

No. 1. Gents' size, well padded and quilted, for protection of chest, $2.00 each.

No. 1. Ladies', similar to No. 1 gents'; $2.00 each.

Gauntlets.

No. 1. Men's, tan colored kid, well padded, patent leather cuff, $1.00 each.

No. 1. Ladies', $1.00 each.

No. 2. Men's gauntlets, without padding, 75c each.

Rubber tips for end of blade, 5c each.

Guns and Ammunition

Write for Special Catalogue.

Single-Barrel Shot Guns.

No. 1. Single-barrel breech-loading gun, pistol grip stock, rebounding lock, rolled steel barrel, bored for black powder, weight about 7 lbs, 12 and 16 gauge, $6.50.

No. 2. Single-barrel gun, with automatic ejector, rebounding lock, pistol grip stock, decarbonized steel barrel, taper choke bored and shot for pattern, case hardened frame, bored for black or nitro powder, 12 and 16 gauge, weight about 7 to 7½ lbs, $9.00.

Double-Barrel Shot Guns.

No. 3. Double barrel, semi-machine made, steel barrels, back action, rebounding lock, extension rib, top lever action, solid plungers, patent fore-end, polished walnut pistol grip stock, weight 6½ to 8½ lbs, 12 and 16 gauge, $10.00.

No. 4. Double barrel, top lever action, laminated steel barrels, extension matted rib, double bolt, circular hammers, bar rebounding locks, left barrel choked, English walnut pistol grip stock, rubber heel and pistol butt plate, 12 and 16 gauge, $14.00.

No. 5. Same as No. 4, with Damascus pattern barrels, Greener cross bolt, choke bored, 12 and 16 gauge, 6½ and 8½ lbs, $15.75; 10-inch gauge, 9½ lbs, $16.75.

No. 6. Laminated steel barrels, engraved bar, rebounding locks, extension matted rib, Greener cross bolt, Deeley & Edge patent fore-end, circular hammers, left barrel choked, 12 and 16 gauge, $19.50.

No. 7. Model 1897, Winchester repeating shot gun, in 12 gauge, $25 00.

No. 8. The Ithaca, quality A, genuine English stub twist barrel, black walnut stock, pistol grip, checkered, automatic compensating fore-end, reinforced frame, narrow skeleton rib, double thick nitro breech, extra low circular hammer, rebounding locks, weight about 7½ to 8 lbs, 12 and 16 gauge, $27.50.

No. 9. Ithaca, quality B, fine Damascus steel barrels, double thick nitro breech, reinforced frame, narrow skeleton rib, automatic compensating fore-end, extra low circular hammer, rebounding locks, black walnut stock, full pistol grip nicely checkered and engraved, 12 and 16 gauge, weight about 7½ lbs, $40.00.

No. 10. Ithaca, quality 1P, hammerless, fine English stub twist barrels, double thick nitro breech, reinforced frame and stock fastening, narrow skeleton rib, automatic compensating fore-end, black walnut stock, pistol grip, nicely checkered, 12 and 16 gauge, $35.00.

No. 11. Ithaca, quality No. 1½, hammerless, Damascus barrels, double thick nitro breech, reinforced frame and stock fastening, narrow skeleton rib, automatic compensating fore-end, black walnut stock, full pistol grip nicely checkered, 12 and 16 gauge, $45.00.

All Ithaca guns are choke bored, tested and guaranteed. A record and guarantee tag is attached to each. There is no stronger or closer shooting gun on the market.

Rifles.

No. 12. Flobert rifles, 22-calibre, shoots B.B. caps, 22 short or long, $3.25.

No. 13. Same as No. 12, but 32-calibre, $3.75.

No. 14. Model 1900, Winchester take-down, 22-calibre, single shot, $5.00.

No. 15. Davenport Brownie, take-down, automatic ejector, 22 short or long, $7.25.

No. 16. Steven's favorite take-down, in 22, 25 and 32-calibre, with open sights, $6.75; with combination front and Vernon rear sights, $9.50.

Winchester Repeating Rifles.

Model 1892.

No. 16. 24-inch round barrel, full magazine, 14 shot, weight about 6½ lbs, $15.00; octagon barrel, weight about 6¾ lbs, $16.50.

Model 1894.

No. 17. 26-inch barrel, full magazine, 9 shot, weight about 7½ lbs, round barrel, $15.00; octagon barrel, weight about 7½ lbs, $16.50.

Model 1894.

No. 18. Smokeless, 26-inch octagon barrel, full magazine, 9 shot, weight 7½ lbs, very effective on large game with soft point bullets, $20.00.

No. 19. Shoots black powder and lead bullets or smokeless powder and soft point bullets, 26-inch round barrel, weight about 7½ lbs, 6 shot, $18.50; 26-inch octagon barrel, weight about 8½ lbs, 6 shot, $20.00.

Model 1895.

No. 20. Sporting rifle, 30 U.S. Army, 28-inch round nickel steel barrel, 8½ lbs, 6 shot, shoots smokeless soft point or regular army ammunition, $25.00.

Marlin Repeating Rifles.

Model 1893.

No. 21. 26-inch round barrel, 10 shot, weight 7½ lbs, full magazine, $17.00; 26-inch octagon barrel, 10 shot, weight 7¾ lbs, full magazine, $18.00.

Model 1893.

No. 22. Smokeless, soft point, full magazine, 10 shot, weight 7⅞ lbs, $20.00; 26-inch octagon barrel, $21.00.

Savage Repeating Rifles.

No. 23. 26-inch round barrel, 6-shot, 303-calibre, weight about 7½ lbs, $25.00.

No. 24. 26-inch, ½-octagon or full octagon barrel, weight about 7¾ lbs, 6-shot, 303-calibre, $26.50.

With No. 1 Lyman ivory bead, front sight and Savage combination rear sight, $4.00 extra.

No. 6 reloading tool, will reload No. 2 cartridges and No. 6 miniature, $2.50 per tool.

No. 2 expanding nickel jackets soft point bullets, 303 calibre, 25 in box, 35c per box.

No. 6 miniature, nickel jacket bullets, 303 calibre, 50 in box, 50c per box.

Double-Action Revolvers.

Double Action, I. J. Model, 1900.

No. 25. Rim fire, 22-calibre, $2.25.
No. 26. Central fire, 32-calibre, $2.50.
No. 27. Central fire, shoots S. & W. cartridges, 38 calibre, $2.50.

Iver Johnson double-action automatic safety hammer and hammerless revolvers, 5-shot, 3-inch barrels—

No. 27. 32-calibre, safety hammer, nickel plated, $4.75.
No. 28. 32-calibre, safety hammer, blued, $5.25.
No. 29. 32-calibre, safety, hammerless, nickel plated, $5.75.
No. 30. 32-calibre, safety, hammerless, blued, $6.25.
No. 31. 38-calibre, safety hammer, nickel plated, $4.75.
No. 32. 38-calibre, safety hammer, blued, $5.25.
No. 33. 38-calibre, safety, hammerless, nickel plated, $5.75.
No. 34. 38-calibre, safety, hammerless, blued, $6.25.
No. 35. 38-calibre, safety hammer, 6-inch blued barrel, $7.00.
No. 36. 38-calibre, safety, hammerless, 6-inch blued barrel, $7.50.

Smith & Wesson revolvers, double action, automatic shell extractor, 5-shot, rubber stock, blued finish—

No. 37. 3½-inch barrel, 32-calibre, $14.25.
No. 38. 6-inch barrel, 32-calibre, $15.75.
No. 39. 4-inch barrel, 38-calibre, $16.00.
No. 40. 6-inch barrel, 38-calibre, $17.25.

Smith & Wesson Hammerless.

No. 40½. 32-calibre, 3½-inch barrel, $15.75.
No. 41. 38-calibre, 4-inch barrel, $17.50.
No. 42. 38-calibre, 6-inch barrel, $18.50.

Reloading Tools.

No. 43. Best steel wad cutters, in 10, 12, 14, 16-gauge, 15c.
No. 44. Cleaning rods, for 22 and 32, 10c.
No. 45. Recappers, in 10, 12, 16-gauge, 15c.
No. 46. Eureka shell closers, 10, 12, 16-gauge, 35c.
No. 47. Shell extractors, 5c.
No. 48. Cleaning rods, 10, 12, 16-gauge, 35c.
No. 49. Reloading sets, complete, 10, 12, 16-gauge, $1.00.
No. 50. Reloading sets, for 32 and 38 S. & W. and 44 and 40 Winchester, $2.50.
No. 51. Reloading sets, for 38-55, 38-72, 30-30 and 30 army, 1895 models, $3.00.

Hunting Knives and Axes.

No. 52. Best Sheffield steel, 75c, $1.00, 1.25.
No. 53. Marbel's hunting knives, $2.25.
No. 54. Duck decoys, 75c.
No. 55. Duck calls, 25c.

Rim Fire Cartridges.

B.B. caps, per box of 100, Dominion, 15c; U.M.C., 20c.
C.B. caps, per box of 100, Dominion, 25c; U.M.C., 30c.

50 in box.
22 Cal. short, Dominion, 15c; U.M.C., 18c.
22 " long, Dominion, 18c; U.M.C., 20c.
22 " long rifle, Dominion, 20c, U.M.C., 25c.
25 " Stevens, U.M.C., 50c.
32 " short, Dominion, 30c; U.M.C., 35c.
32 " long, Dominion, 35c; U.M.C., 40c.
38 " U.M.C., 55c.

Centre Fire Revolver Cartridges.

32 S. & W. short, 50 in box, Dominion, 50c; U.M.C., 55c.
32 Colts short, 50 in box, Dominion, 50c; U.M.C., 55c.
32 Colts long, 50 in box, Dominion, 55c; U.M.C., 60c.
38 S. & W. long, 50 in box, Dominion, 60c; U.M.C., 70c.
38 Colts short, 50 in box, Dominion, 60c; U.M.C., 70c.
38 Colts long, 50 in box, Dominion, 65c; U.M.C., 75c.
38 Winchester and Marlin, 50 in box, Dominion, 70c; U.M.C., 90c.
44/40 Winchester and Marlin, 50 in box, Dominion, 70c; U.M.C., 90c.
44 British bulldog, 50 in box, U.M.C., 75c.
45 Colts, 50 in box, U.M.C., $1.00.

Loaded Shells.

Dominion trap shells, 10 and 12 gauge, $1.75 per hundred or 45c per box of 25.

Union Metallic, New Club Shell.

16 gauge, $2.00 per hundred, or 50c per box of 25.
12 " 2.10 " " 53c " "
10 " 2.20 " " 55c " "
10 gauge, B.B. shot, $2.40 per hundred, or 60c per box of 25.

Primers, Dominion, all sizes at 43c per box of 250. Primers, Union Metallic, all sizes at 50c per box of 250. Muzzle-loading gun caps, 7c per box of 100.

Black edge wads, 16, 14 and 12 gauge, 20c per 250; 10 and 8 gauge, 25c per box of 250.

Cardboard wads, 16, 14 and 12 gauge, 20c per 1000; 10 and 8 gauge, 25c per 1000.

Empty shot shell, U. M. C. Union shell, same quality as New Club, $1.00 per 100.

Dominion trap shell, 16, 14, 12 and 10 gauge, 85c per 100.

Brass shells, solid head, $4.75 per 100, or $1.20 per box of 25.

Sporting Cartridges.

25/20 Winchester, 50 in a box, 90c.
25/20 Marlin, 50 in a box, 90c.
25/20 Stevens, 50 " 90c.
25/25 " 20 " 55c.
32/40 Winchester, Marlin and Ballard, 20 in a box, 65c.
38/55 Winchester & Marlin, 20 in a box, 80c.
38/56 " " " 80c.
38/72 " " " 80c.
40/60 " " " 80c.
40/60 Marlin, 20 in a box, 80c.
40/65 Winchester, 20 in a box, 80c.
40/72/330 " model 1895, 20 in a box, 80c.
40/82/260 " " 1896, " " 80c.
44/40 Winchester & Marlin, 50 in a box, 90c.
44/60/395 Sharp & Remington, 20 in a box, 90c.
45/60 Winchester, 20 in a box, 80c.
45/75 " " " 80c.
45/85/285 Marlin, 20 in a box, 80c.
45/90 Winchester, " " 80c.

Smokeless Sporting Cartridges.

30/30 Winchester, model 1894, 20 in a box, 90c.
30/30 Marlin, model 1893, 20 in a box, 90c.
30 U. S. Army (soft point), Winchester, model 1895, 20 in a box, $1.20.
303 Savage, model 1899, 20 in a box, $1.00.
303 (No. 6 minature nickel bullet), 20 in a box, 85c.
38/55 Winchester, 20 in a box, $1.00.
38/55 Marlin, " " 1.00.
38/72 Winchester, " " 1.00.

A more complete list will be sent on application.

Wheel Goods, Toys and Sleighs.

Girls' Tricyles.

With plush upholstered seats.

No. 18. For girls 2 to 4 years, iron tires, $4.00; rubber tires, $6.65.
No. 20. For girls 3 to 5 years, iron tires, $5.35; rubber tires, $8.00.
No. 1. For girls 4 to 7 years, iron tires, $6.65; rubber tires, $11.35.
No. 2. For girls 7 to 10 years, iron tires, $8.00; rubber tires, $12.75.
No. 3. For girls 10 to 15 years, iron tires, $9.50; rubber tires, $14.00.

Velocipedes.

(The Strongest Made).

When ordering velocipedes take inside measurement of child's leg.

No. 1H. Leg 16 in., iron tires, $2.00; rubber tires, $4.00.
No. 2H. Leg 18 in., iron tires, $2.30; rubber tires, $4.60.
No. 3H. Leg 20 in., iron tires, $2.60; rubber tires, $5.20.
No. 4H. Leg 22 in., iron tires, $2.90; rubber tires, $5.80.
No. 5H. Leg 24 in., iron tires, $3.20; rubber tires, $6.40.

The new chain cycle, for boys or girls from 4 to 9 years, latest safety style, 3 wheels, $4.50.

Toy Carts.

Sheet steel bodies, painted red with black striping, steel wheel and axle—
No. 0. 35c each.
No. 1. Body 6 x 10 in., wheel, 7 in., 45c each.
No. 2. Body 8 x 12 in., wheel 9 in., 65c each.
No. 02. Wooden body and wheels, 18c each.

Toy Wheelbarrows.

Sheet steel bodies, painted in red with black striping, steel wheel and axle.
No. 5. Barrow, 40c each.
No. 6. Barrow, box 9 x 12 in. high, 50c each.
No. 7. Barrow, same as No. 6, but well braced, 60c each.
No. 8. Barrow, 11 x 14½ x 5½ in. high, 70c each.
No. 9. Barrow, 13 x 16 x 6 in. high, 80c each.
Our "Pet" all-wood barrow, 20c each.

Wooden Box Waggons.

Hardwood body with steel axle and wheels.

No. 14. Size of box 9 x 18 in., $1.00.
No. 14½. " " 10 x 20 in., 1.15.
No. 15. " " 11 x 22 in., 1.25.
No. 16. " " 12½ x 25 in., 2.00.
No. 17. " " 14 x 28 in., 2.25.

Steel body waggons, neatly painted and with strong steel axles and wheels.

No. 04. Size of box 9 x 18 in., $1.00.
No. 03. " " 10 x 20 in., 1.15.
No. 02. " " 11 x 22 in., 1.25.
No. 0. " " 12 x 24 in., 1.75.
No. 1. " " 13 x 26 in., 2.00.
No. 2. " " 14 x 28 in., 2.25.
No. 3. " " 15 x 30 in., 2.65.

Shoo-Fly Rockers.

A very pleasing toy, dapple grey horses, hardwood rockers, nicely finished, in two sizes, small, 75c; large and heavy, 90c.

Delivery Waggon.

No. 18. Handsomely finished, size of box 18 x 30 x 6 in., extra heavy gear, diameter of wheels 14 in., $5.00.

Dog Sulky.

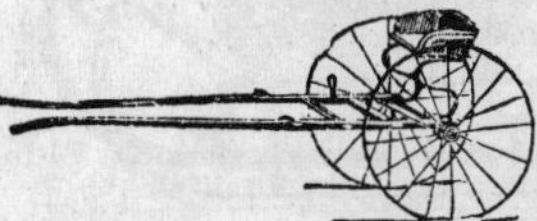

Nicely painted in red, strong shafts, springs best quality steel, steel axle and wheels, whip socket, foot rests, etc., No. 1, with 22 in. wheels, $3.50; No. 2, with 28 in. wheels, $5.00.

Canopy Top Spring Waggon.

Same as cut, $5.75; with handle to pull waggon, $5.00.

Bent-Rail Waggons.

Nicely varnished, with black striping, steel axles and wheels—

No. 1. Body 10 x 20 in., $1.00.
No. 1½. Body 11 x 22 in., $1.25.
No. 2. Body 12 x 25 in., $1.75.
No. 7. Hardwood platform, turned steel railing, $2.40; with fenders, $2.65.

Boy's Truck.

No. 13. Body made of hardwood, size 14 x 28 in., diameter of wheels 9 in., handsomely painted in red and varnished, patent all iron gear, steel wheels. Letters G.T.R. on side if desired, $2.25.

Buckboard Waggon.

No. 11. Made of hardwood, varnished, with slat bottom, foot and back rail, steel gear, body 13 x 31 in.: wheels, front 10 in., back 14 in., single seat, $2.25.
No. 12. Buckboard, same as No. 11, but having two seats and no back rail, $2.50.

Sleds.

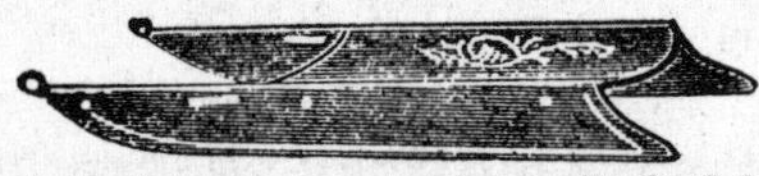

No. 1. Boys' sled, maple runners, nicely finished and painted, size 10 x 28 in., 15c each.
No. 2. Size 10 x 33 in., 20c each.
No. 3. Size 10 x 37 in., 25c each.

The Victor, maple runners with hand holes, and spring steel runners, size 10½ x 33 in., 40c.
The Sport, size 10½ x 44 in., 55c each.

The Racer, size 15 x 44 in., steel spring runners, side hand rails, a fast strong sled, 65c each.

Cutters.

The Leader, size 11 x 28 in., 2 knees, nicely painted, 45c each.
The Canada, size 13 x 32 in., 2 knees, 55c each.
The Comfort, size 13 x 32 in., with railing, 65c.
The bent rail, size 11 x 28 in., with railing, 60c.
The Nonpareil, size 13 x 36 in., 3 knees, bronze swan's necks, 90c each.
The Stanley, size 16 x 38 in., 3 knees, with braced side hand-rail, swan's necks, $1.25 ea.

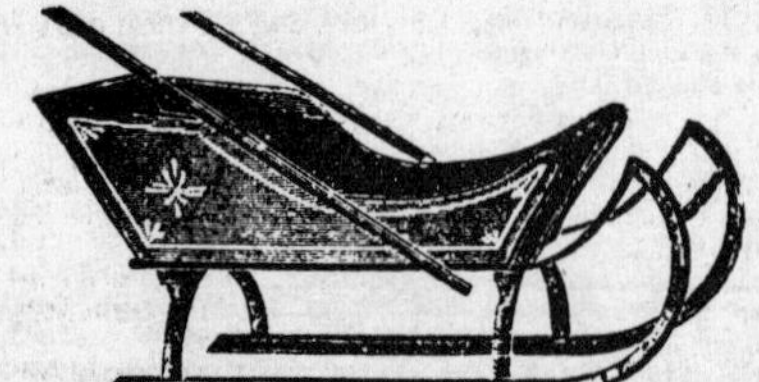

The Popular baby sleigh, solid wooden box, reversible handles to draw or push, box 30 in. long, $1.00 each.

Toys, Dolls and Games.

As these lines of goods are for the holiday trade only, we will not under any circumstances exchange Toys, Dolls or Games.

We will, "unless told not to" substitute any line we are sold out of.

Dressed dolls, jointed body, bisque head, assorted fancy dresses, with hat to match, also shoes and stockings. This doll can be undressed, solid or movable eyes, 25c, 50c, 75c, $1.00, 1.50, 2.00, 2.50 up to 8.50 each.

Undressed kid body dolls, with bisque heads, curly hair, solid or movable eyes. The most serviceable doll made, 15c, 25c, 35c, 50c, 75c, $1.00, up to $7.00 each.
Undressed jointed dolls, with bisque heads and curly hair, 10c, 25c, 50c, 75c each.
Eaton's beauty, $1.00, 1.50, 2.00 up to 6.00 each.
Nigger dolls, 20c, 25c, 50c and $1.00 each.
Pa, Ma, speaking dolls, 25c each.
Nankeen dolls, 5c, 10c, 15c, 25c each.
Rubber dolls, 15c, 25c, 50c, 65c each.
Miniature dressed dolls, 20c, 25c, 50c each.
Metal headed dolls, unbreakable, 50c each.

Drums.

All our drums have calfskin head, complete with sticks, 25c, 35c, 50c, 75c, $1.00 each.
Shell drums, complete with polished sticks, etc., $1.00, 1.25, 1.50, 1.75, 2.00 each.

Pianos.

Our pianos are of the best American manufacture, and are first class in every respect, 25c, 50c, $1.00, 2.00 up to 7.00 each.

Toy guns, shoots sticks, 15c, 25c, 35c, 50c, 75c, $1.00.

Wooden horses on stands, 25c, 50c, 75c, $1.00 up to 2.50.

Wooden horses and carts, 25c, 50c, 75c, $1.00 ea.

Mechanical toys, 15c, 25c, 50c each.

Doll Heads.

When ordering doll heads, send measure across from shoulder to shoulder, price according to size required.
Bisque doll heads, solid eyes, 10c, 12c, 15c, 20c, 25c, 35c, 50c, 65c, 75c ea.
Movable eyes, 15c, 20c, 25c, 30c, 40c, 50c, 60c, 70c, 85c, $1.00 each.

China heads, 5c, 6c, 7c, 8c, 9c, 10c, 12c, 15c each.

Metal, unbreakable brass heads, 15c, 20c, 25c, 30c, 40c, 50c, 65c, 75c each.

Dolls' wigs, good hair, 25c, 35c, 50c, 65c, 75c ea.
" slippers, 5c, 10c, 20c pair.
" boots, 20c, 25c, 35c pair.
" stockings, 5c, 10c, 25c pair.
" gloves, 20c, 35c pair.
Toy dishes, 5c, 10c, 15c, 20c, 25c up to $1.00 set.

Tool chests, not cheaply gotten up, each piece being a practical piece in itself, and all made of good material, 25c, 50c, 75c, $1.00, 1.25, 1.50 up to 4.50 set.
Horns, nickel-plated, 25c, 35c, 50c each.
Blackboards, 25c, 50c, 75c, $1.00, 1.50, 2.00.
Magic lanterns, with assorted views, 35c, 50c, 75c, $1.00, 1.50, 1.75, 2.00, 2.50, up to 14.00.

We keep separate slides, send us size required, price according to size.

Banks.

Iron combination safes, 25c, 50c, 75c, $1.00 each.

Iron Toys.

We keep a large and well selected assortment of iron toys, ranging in prices from 10c to $2.00, including fire engines, hook and ladders, sulky, phaetons, coupes, passenger trains, buckboards and delivery waggons.

Swinging Horses

range in price from $3.00 to 18.00.

Games.

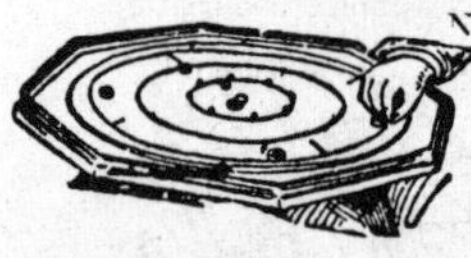

No. 1. Crokinole board, 90c.
No. 2. Special crokinole board 65c.
Improved crokinole board, 65c.

Game of Fort, with cue, 60c.

Wood chess, at 35c, 50c and 65c set.
Bone chess, at 65c, $1.00, 1.35, 1.75, 2.00 and 2.50 a box, standard size.

Dominoes, 25c, 50c, 75c box.
Checker men, 5c, 10c, 15c, 20c, 25c box.
Checker boards, from 5c to $1.00 each.
Card games at 10c each: Authors, Nations, Lost Heir, Old Maid and Snap.
Card games at 25c each: Lost Heir, Donkey Party, Parcheesi, Halma.
Games at 35c and 50c: Parcheesi and Halma.

NOTE.—A Christmas Supplement will be issued about October 15th. Write for one.

STOVES AND RANGES.

Royal Alexandra.
Showing draw-out duplex grate, draw-out oven-**rack**, interior of oven and drop hearth-plate.

No. 2. Royal Alexandra, square, 8/18, six 8-inch covers, wood, $30.00; duplex grate, coal or wood, $32.00. 9/20, six 9-inch covers, wood, $33.50; duplex grate, coal or wood, $36.00.

No 3. Royal Alexandra with reservoir, 8/18, six 8-inch covers, wood, $35.00; duplex grate, coal or wood, $37.00. 9/20, six 9-inch covers, wood, $39.00; duplex grate, coal or wood, $41.50.

No. 4. Royal Alexandra, square top and high shelf, 8/18, six 8-inch covers, wood, $33.50; duplex grate, coal or wood, $35.50. 9/20, six 9-inch covers, wood, $37.00; duplex grate, coal or wood, $39.50.

The Royal Alexandra, a twentieth century name and a twentieth century range.

This is positively the finest range on the market. It has the drop hearth-plate, draw-out duplex grate, draw-out oven-rack, accurately proportioned fire-box, full size square oven, extra large water reservoir and is so proportioned that the designs and ornamentations are shown off to the best possible advantage.

We positively guarantee this range to be perfect in every part.

No. 5. Royal Alexandra, with reservoir and high shelf, 8/18, six 8-inch covers, wood, $38.50; duplex grate, coal or wood, $40.50. 9/20, six 9-inch covers, wood, $42.50; duplex grate, coal or wood, $45.00.

No. 6. Royal Alexandra, square top and high closet, 8/18, six 8-inch covers, wood, $37.75; duplex grate, coal or wood, $39.75. 9/20, six 9-inch covers, wood, $41.25; duplex grate, coal or wood, $43.75.

Water front in No. 8 or 9, $3.25.

Thermometer in No. 8 or 9, $1.50.

High shelf on No. 8 or 9, $3.5..

High closet on No. 8 or 9, $7.75.

Coal linings in addition to the wood linings, $5.00.

Length of fire box for wood—
No. 8/18 is 20½ inches.
No. 9/20 is 22½ inches.

Dimensions of oven—
No. 8/18, 18½ x 18½ x 12 inches.
No. 9/20, 20½ x 20½ x 13 inches.

The Alexandra stoves are the finest made and for bakers are head and shoulders over all competitors.

No. 7. Royal Alexandra, reservoir and high closet, 8/18. six 8-inch covers, wood, $42.75; duplex grate, coal or wood, $44.75. 9/20, six 9-inch covers, wood, $46.75; duplex grate, coal or wood, $49.25.

Eaton's Gothic, for Coal or Wood.

Eaton's Gothic, with High Shelf.

One of the newest cast stoves on the market, massive base, most approved duplex grate, will burn either coal or wood, or can be fitted for wood only. This is a medium priced cast range, and except in very large kitchens, or for very large families, will do the work of any stove made

No. 8/18. Square, coal or wood, six 8-inch cooking holes, size of oven 18 x 18 x 11, $20.00.

No. 8/18. Extended oven with reservoir, coal or wood, six 8-inch cooking holes, size of oven 18 x 18 x 11, $25.00.

No. 9/18. Square, coal or wood, four 9-inch and two 7-inch cooking holes, size of oven 18 x 18 x 11, $21.50.

No. 9/18. Extended, oven with reservoir, coal or wood, four 9-inch and two 7-inch cooking holes, size of oven 18 x 18 x 11, $26.50.

High shelf extra, $3.50; oven thermometer, extra, $1.50.

In ordering this stove be sure to state whether you want it for coal or for wood. If fitted for wood it takes a stick 18 inches long.

Heaters.

Our base burner is a beauty. It is most elaborately and handsomely nickel-plated, and the mica surface being very extensive gives it a most beautiful appearance when lighted; this is a self-feeder, so constructed that it takes care of the fire for a wonderfully long period.

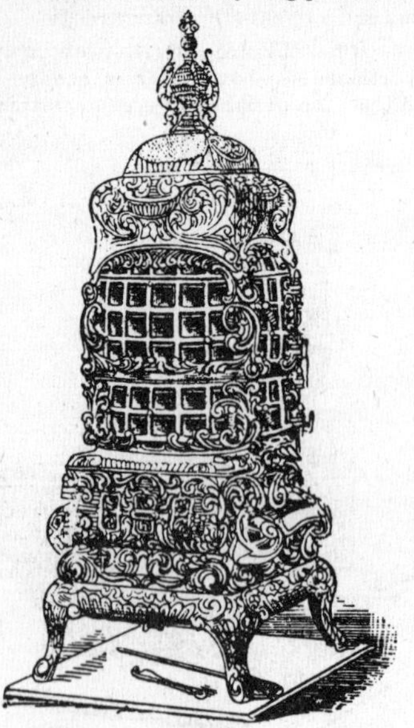

Heater.

Heater with Oven.

No. 611.	11-inch fire pot	$21.50
No. 613.	13-inch "	26.50
No. 614.	14-inch "	28.50
No. 613.	With oven, 10 x 15 x 10 special	29.75

Oxford Air Blast.

For Wood.

It burns knots, chunks, chips, trash and anything that will go into a 13-inch opening at the top; no fire can fall from it; the ashes need removing only once in a long time, one or two knots or chunks will run it twelve hours in cold weather.

One size only, for 24-inch wood, $5.00.

Cook Stove, the "Oxford Don," for Wood Only.

Oxford Don, Square.

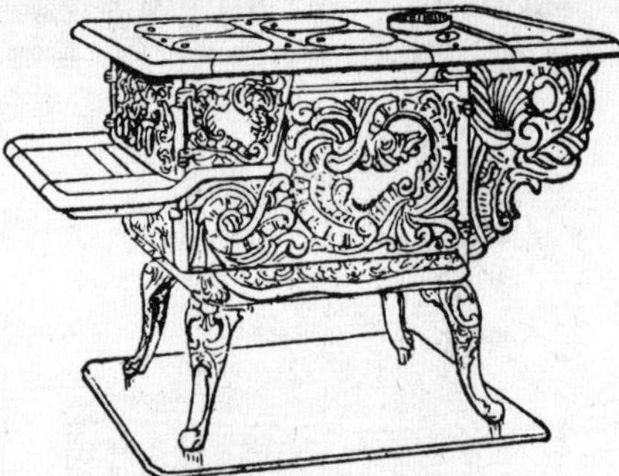

Oxford Don, Extended.

	Cooking holes.	Oven dimensions.	Length of fire box.	Price.
No. 7/16. Square,	four 7-inch	16 x 13½ x 10	18-inch	$9.00
No. 8/18. "	" 8-inch	18 x 14½ x 10½	20-inch	11.00
No. 9/22. "	" 9-inch	22 x 18½ x 11¾	25-inch	13.00
No. 9/22. Extended,	" 9-inch	22 x 18½ x 11¾	25-inch	17.50

The above is a first-class plain wood cookstove, and when utility only is required, it certainly fills the bill.

OXFORD BOX STOVE.

No. 125. For 25-in. wood, two 8-inch cooking holes, $6.00.
No. 128. For 28-in. wood, two 8-inch cooking holes, $7.25.
No. 131. For 31-in. wood, two 9-inch cooking holes, $8.00.

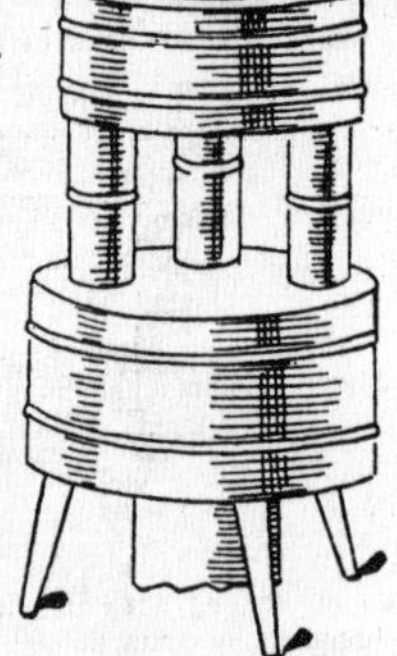

TWO-STORY DRUM.

Made of heavy sheet-iron, turns a cold room into a comfortable one, without extra fire, made for 7-inch pipe, $2.25 each.

Evening Light.

A sheet-iron stove for wood. Very ornamental and a good heater—
No. 26. For 26-inch wood, $11.50.
No. 28. For 28-inch wood, $12.50.

The Wasp. This is a small office or bedroom heater and is very powerful—

No. 5. Diameter of pot, 10 inches; height, 25 inches, $4.50.

No. 6. Diameter of pot, 11 inches; height, 27½ inches, $5.00.

GO-CARTS.

For Other Lines Write Us

No. 208. Wicker body, adjustable back and front, moving independently, takes the place of a cheap carriage, without parasol or cushion, $5.30; with parasol and rod, $6.95; complete with parasol and cushion, $7.80.

Rubber-tired wheels on go-carts, small size, $1.10 per set extra; large size, $1.60 per set extra.

Sleigh runners for baby carriages, $1.00 pair.

BABY CARRIAGES.

No. 650. One of our prettiest designs, cut does not do it justice, upholstering, parasol, finish and style the very latest, reed body, 16th century finish, retinned wheels and gearing, RMEF parasol, price only $17.90.

For Go-Carts see page 207.

No. 610. Reed body, 16th century finish, large size, fancy front, braided around edge, plush roll, upholstered in Derby cloth, Roman satin parasol, with one frill, $7.50.

Carriage Wheels.

Rubber-tired wheels on baby carriages, small size rubber, $1.60 per set extra.

Large-sized rubber tires, $2.00 per set extra.

C. Our Leader. Reed body, heavy roll around back, curved front, upholstered in plush, MEH parasol, $11.00.

We have carried this carriage for years. We have tried our best to beat it, but we cannot. The parasol has two frills instead of one, as shown in the cut.

WESTERN SADDLES.

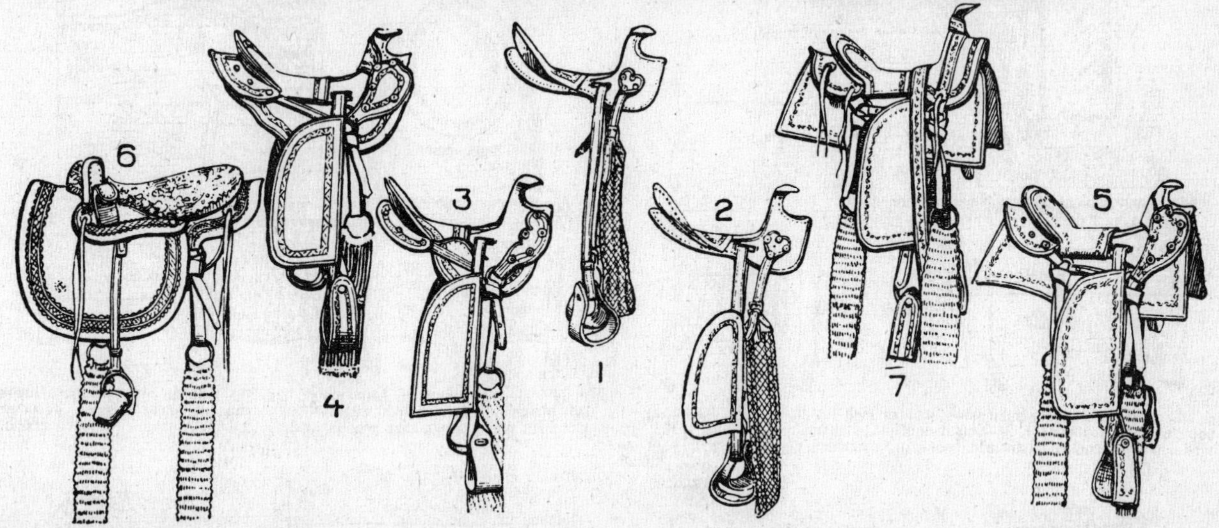

WE do not always carry these saddles in stock, therefore you will kindly allow from ten to twelve days to have them made to order. If you do not see the kind of saddle you want write us, explaining what is wanted.

1. Saddle, made on a 13 inch rawhide-covered tree, leather seat, good girth to buckle, $2.50.
2. Similar to No. 1, but with fenders, $3.25.
3. 14-inch rawhide-covered tree, leather seat, fenders and cotton hair cinchas, $5.25.
4. Men's Mexican saddle, 15-inch rawhide-covered Morgan tree, good wooden stirrups, 1½-inch stirrup leathers, fenders, wool-lined skirts, cotton or hair cinchas, 1-in. latigoes, $8.
5. Men's Mexican saddle, 15-inch rawhide-covered Morgan tree, good wood stirrups, 1½-inch stirrup leathers, large fenders, wool-lined skirts, cotton or hair cinchas, $10.50.
6. Cow-girl or ladies' western saddle, made on a Morgan tree, cloth or leather seat as desired, padded bars, cotton or hair cincha rigged, leaping horn, 1-inch latigoes, slipper stirrup, the regulation western side-saddle, $12.75.
7. Men's "Jackson" saddle, rawhide-covered tree, steel fork (guaranteed), wool-lined skirts, large fenders, wooden stirrups, 1½-inch stirrup leathers, laced or to buckle, 1-inch latigoes, cotton or hair cinchas, $12.75.

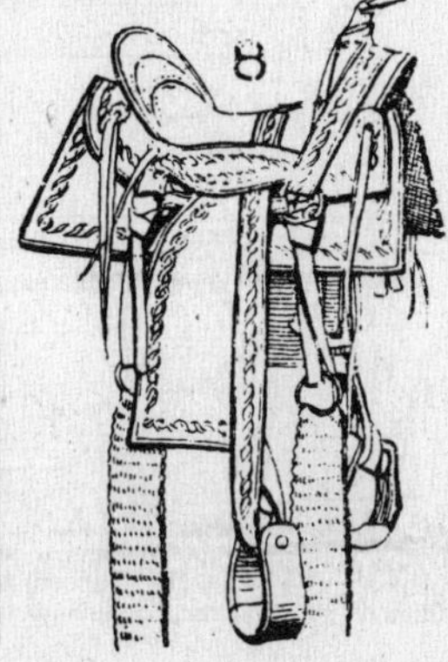

8. Men's Mexican saddle, California tree, guaranteed steel fork, 3-inch block stirrups, 1½-inch stirrup leathers, laced or to buckle, wool-lined skirts, 25 x 13 inches; latigoes, 1½-inch; cotton or hair cincha rigged, the best saddle ever offered for the money, $17.00.

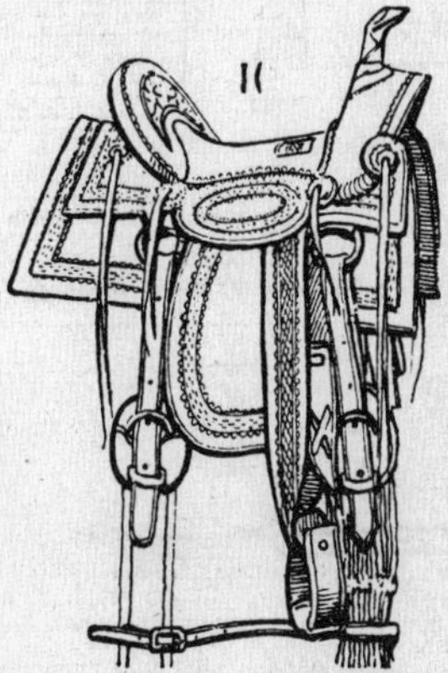

10. Cowboys' "Favorite," made on best rawhide-covered steel fork tree, any pattern, skirts wool lined, 27 x 15 in.; covered rings, 3 in. zinc-bound stirrups, 2½-in. stirrup leathers, best white California cinchas, back cincha web or hair as preferred, latigoes 1½-in. rim on cantle, weight about 32 lbs., $35.00.

BEDROOM SUITES.

No. 432. Bedroom suite, hardwood, golden finish, neatly carved, cheval style bureau, with 14 x 24-inch shock mirror, washstand 24 inches wide, bedstead 4 ft 2 in wide, 5 ft 4 in high $8.9
Same suite, with bevel-plate mirror $9.50

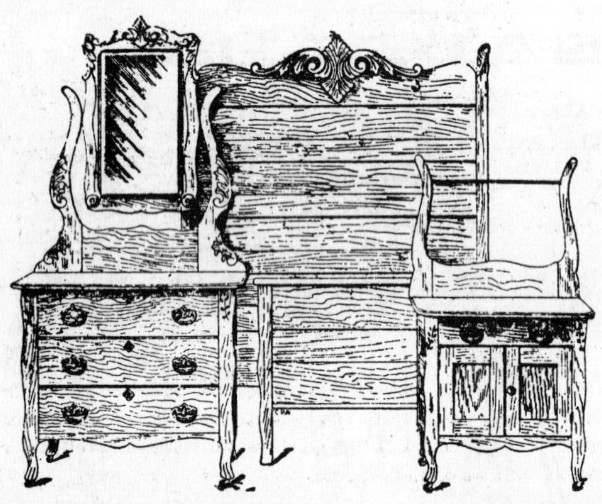

No. 139. Bedroom suite, hardwood, golden oak finish, bureau has shaped top and legs, with 14 x 24-inch bevel-plate mirror, bedstead 4 ft 2 in. wide, washstand with double doors and drawers, complete with castors $10.25

No. 143. Bedroom suite, golden oak finish, neatly carved and well finished, bureau with swell-shaped top, fitted with 20 x 24-inch bevel-plate mirror, bedstead 4 ft 2 in. wide, large size washstand $11.50

No. 436. Bedroom suite, elm, golden oak finish, richly carved, new design, bureau with shaped top, bevel-plate mirror 20 x 24 inches, combination washstand to match bedstead, 4 ft 2 in. wide $12.25

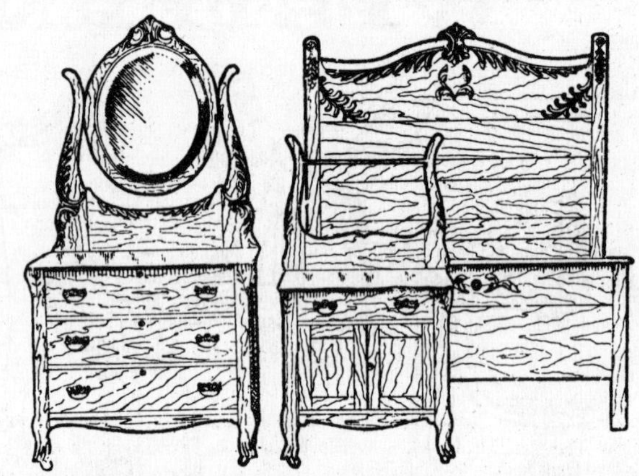

No. 149. Bedroom suite, hardwood, golden finish, bureau has shaped double top, fitted with 20 x 24-inch oval shaped plate mirror, bedstead 4 ft 2 in. wide, large size washstand to match $12.45

No. 31½. Bedroom suite, elm, golden oak finish, neatly carved; this suite is well made, having solid corner posts in bureau and stand, hardwood, drawer sides, bureau has 20 x 24-inch bevel-plate mirror, combination washstand, bedstead 4 ft 2 in. wide $12.60

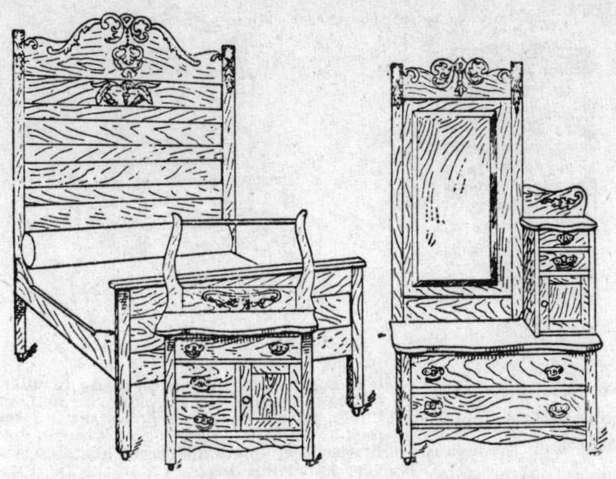

No. 440. Bedroom suite, hardwood, rich antique finish, neatly carved, cheval-shaped bureau with shaped top, fitted with 18 x 36-inch bevel-plate mirror, combination washstand, bedstead 4 ft. 2 in. wide....$14.50

No. 440½. Same suite as No. 440, but made in solid oak, rich golden finish $17.50

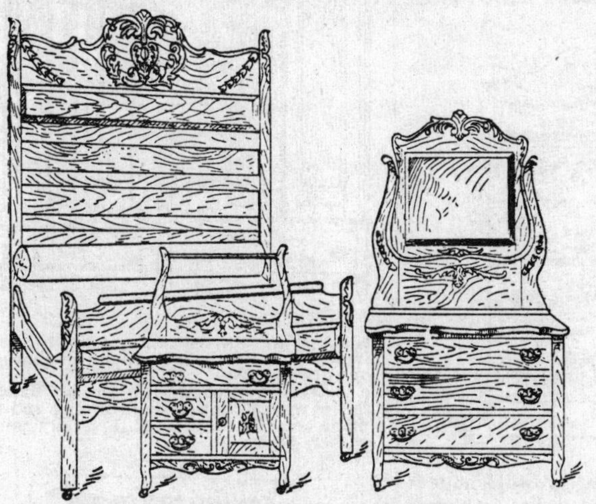

No. 444. Bedroom suite, made of selected ash, golden finish, neatly carved, bureau 40 in. wide, with shaped top, fitted with 20 x 24-inch bevel-plate mirror, combination washstand, bedstead 4 ft. 2 in. wide $14.25

Same suite, made of birch, mahogany finish 15.00

Same suite, made of solid oak, golden finish 16.50

No. 454 Bedroom suite, solid quartered oak, hand-carved and polished, bureau 44 in. wide, shaped top, 24 x 30-in. British bevel-plate mirror, bedstead 4 ft. 6 in. wide, large combination washstand $28.50

No. 420. Bedroom suite, oak, rich golden finish, carved and well finished, bureau has shaped top and swell top drawers, with 22 x 28-inch shaped British bevel-plate mirror, combination washstand, bedstead has quartered oak panels, 4 ft. 2 in. wide................................$26.25

No. 417. Bedroom suite, made of select quarter-cut oak, golden finish, hand-carved and polished, large size bureau, shaped top and drawer front, fitted with 24 x 30-inch British plate shaped bevelled mirror combination washstand to match, bedstead 4 ft. 4 in. wide $32.50

No. 442. Bedroom suite, made in select quarter-cut oak, rich golden finish, highly polished and neatly hand-carved, bureau 47 inches wide, with shaped top and swell- op drawers, fitted with 28 x 40-inch shaped British bevel-plate mirror, large combination washstand to match, bedstead 4 ft. 6 in. wide $38.00

Separate Bureau and Washstand, suitable to go with Brass or Iron Bedsteads, etc.

No. 79. Bureau and washstand, made in solid oak, golden finish, neatly hand carved; bureau has shaped top, 44 inches wide, fitted with 24 x 30-inch fancy shaped British bevel-plate mirror, large size combination washstand to match, $21.50.

Bureau and washstand, as cut No. 432, with bevel mirror, $7.50; as cut No. 139, $8.00; as cut No. 143, $9.25; as cut No. 149, $10.25; as cut No. 31½, $10.35; as cut No. 436, $10.00; as cut No. 440, $12.00; No. 440½, oak, $14.50; as cut No. 444, ash, $12.00; mahogany finish, $12.25; oak, $13.25; as cut No. 420, $21.25; as cut No. 454, $23.00; as cut No. 417, $27.00; as cut No. 442, $31.50.

Separate Wooden Bedsteads.

No. 81. Bedstead, single size, complete with castors, $2.25; double size, complete with castors, $2.25.

Odd bedstead, double size, hardwood, golden finish, $2.75; in solid oak, $3.50.

Folding Mantel Beds.

Folding beds, strongly made, with double-woven wire spring mattress attached, inside measure 4 ft. x 6 ft., length over all 6 ft. 8 in., closes up with mattress and bed clothes, made in hardwood, golden oak finish, $5.60; ash, $6.25; oak, $7.25.

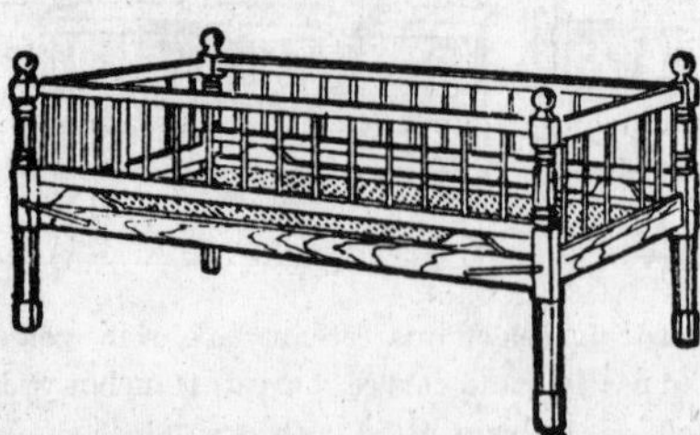

No. 21. Child's folding cot, hardwood, antique finish, with woven-wire spring bottom, size 2 ft. 4 in. wide, by 4 ft. 6 in. long, $2.90.

Chiffonnieres.

No. 88. Chiffonniere, elm, antique finish, 36 inches wide, 18 inches deep, 56 inches high, with 5 large drawers, $6.50.

No. 88½. Same as No. 88, with 14 x 24-inch bevel-plate mirror, $8.50.

No. 88.

No. 365.

No. 365. Chiffonniere, in quarter-cut golden oak and mahogany finish, neatly carved and polished, 31 inches wide, 72 inches high, with 16 x 16 inch shaped British bevel mirror, $14.25.

No. 5. Five-drawer bureau, hardwood, antique finish, 42 inches wide, 54 inches high, well made and finished, $6.75.

No. 7. Seven-drawer bureau, hardwood, golden oak finish, 45 inches wide, 57 inches high, large and roomy, $8.50.

Photos and description of other lines of Chiffonnieres will be sent on application. Kindly state kind of wood, and about price you wish to pay.

No. 6. Ladies' dressing table, made in quarter-cut oak or curly birch, golden or mahogany finish, richly carved and polished, 3 feet 3 inches wide, fitted with 22 x 24-inch shaped British bevel-plate mirror. This table is of a very handsome design and of the finest workmanship, $19.50.

No. 115. No. 2.

No. 115. Wardrobe, ash, antique finish, 3 feet 9 inches wide, 7 feet 5 inches high, double doors and drawer, $9.50.

No. 2. Wardrobe, hardwood, antique finish, 49 inches wide, 87 inches high, strong and well made, can be shipped K.D., easily put together, $11.50.

No. 92. Bedroom table, hardwood, antique finish, strongly made, 20 x 28-inch top, shaped legs and drawer, $1.40.

Same table, made in solid oak, golden finish, $1.75.

No 36. Bedroom commode, box shape, 17 x 17 in. square outside measure, 13 x 12 in. square inside measure, made of ash, antique finish $2.00

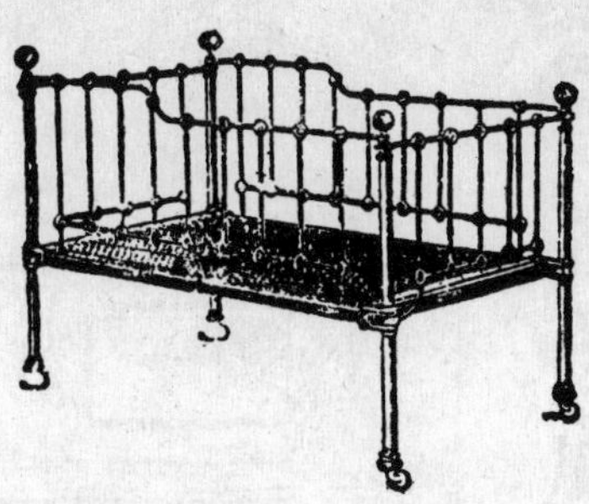

No. 0411. Iron cot, white enamel finish, with woven-wire spring bottom attached, 2½ x 4½ ft.. $5.65

No. 0611. Iron cot, best white enamel finish, with spring bottom and drop sides (as shown in cut), brass rails, knobs and caps, 2 ft. 6 in. by 4 ft. 6 in. long, $8.25; similar cot, without brass rail.................................$7.00

No. 541. Iron cot, white enamel finish, with brass rails around top, brass knobs and caps, with woven-wire spring bottom attached, 2½ x 4½ ft....................................$9.25

Mixed mattresses, to fit any of above cots, specially made, $1.25, 1.50; best sateen ticking $1.75

Cradles.

Children's willow cradles, hood tops $1.40

Children's reed cradles, hood tops..$1.90 and 2.25

Pillow Sham Holders.

Sham holder, double size, to fit any wooden bed, double spring brackets 25c

Sham holder, japanned brackets, to fasten on with screws 30c

Tarbox sham holder, to fasten on centre of bed back of pillows, does not fold the shams, "lifts straight up" 60c

Mattresses.

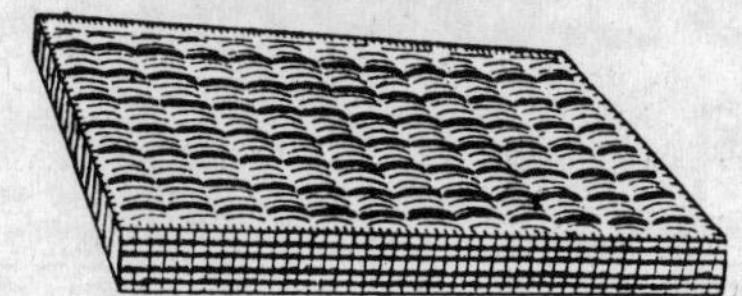

No. 1. Mixed mattresses, seagrass and wool both sides, in sizes 2 ft. x 4 ft., 2 ft. 6 in. x 4 ft. 6 in., $1.25; 3 ft. x 6 ft., $1.90; 3 ft. 6 in. x 6 ft., to 4 ft. 6 in. x 6 ft.........................$2.00

No. 1S. Mixed mattresses, seagrass centre, and white cotton tops both sides, covered in extra heavy ticking, well made, sizes 3 ft. x 6 ft., $2.40; 3 ft. 6 in. x 6 ft., $2.65; 4 ft. to 4 ft. 6 in. x 6 ft......................................$2.90

No. 3S. Mixed mattress, covered with sateen ticking, extra well made, well filled with seagrass and white cotton tops both sides, 3 ft. x 6 ft., $2.75; 3 ft. 6 in. x 6 ft., $3.00; 4 ft. to 4 ft. 6 in. x 6 ft............................. .....$3.25

No. 3G. Same filling as No. 3S, but with best quality sateen ticking in any of above sizes, extra 25c

Fibre and white cotton mattresses, covered in heavy twill ticking, closely tufted, sizes 3 ft x 6 ft., $4.00; 3 ft. 6 in. to 4 ft. 6 in. x 6 ft.....$4.50

Fibre and hair mattresses, covered in best heavy twill ticking, 3 ft. x 6 ft., $5.00; 3 ft. 6 in. x 6 ft., $5.50; 4 ft. to 4 ft. 6 in. x 6 ft $6.00

Coir hair mattress. This is a new filling for mattresses, which we now use very extensively. It is a vegetable fibre, free from odor. It does not pack or become lumpy, and we highly recommend it as being next in quality to curled hair, 3 ft. x 6 ft., $5.75; 3 ft. 6 in. x 6 ft., $6.00; 4 ft. to 4 ft. 6 in. x 6 ft. $6.75

Hair mattresses, HB quality, 3 ft. x 6 ft., $6.50; 3 ft. 6 in. x 6 ft., $7.50; 4 ft. to 4 ft. 6 in. x 6 ft. $8.50

Hair mattresses, No. 3, black hair, 3 ft. x 6 ft., $8.75; 3 ft. 6 in. x 6 ft., $9.60; 4 ft. to 4 ft. 6 in. x 6 ft....................................$12.50

Hair mattresses, No. 2, grey or black, 3 ft. x 6 ft., $11.00; 3 ft. 6 in. x 6 ft., $12.80; 4 ft. to 4 ft. 6 in. x 6 ft $16.00

Hair mattresses, best black or white drawings, 3 ft. x 6 ft., $19.00; 3 ft. 6 in. x 6 ft., $23.60; 4 ft. to 4 ft. 6 in. x 6 ft.........................$27.50

Mixed mattresses, made in two parts, 35c extra; over 6 ft. long, 25c extra.

When ordering mattresses, state exact size required. For double size we always send 4 ft. 2 in. x 6 ft.

Woven Wire Spring Mattresses.

No. 20. Spring mattress, heavy hardwood frame, double weave, with cable and copper wire supports, all sizes $1.40

No. 19. Woven-wire spring mattress, with 6 lock weave bands and 2 copper wire edge supports, heavy hardwood frame, all sizes $1.50

No. 23. Woven-wire mattress, well made, very closely woven top, and reinforced with 9 lock weaves, bands and side supports; this we recommend...$2.00

No. 33. Hercules spring, heavy hardwood frame, closely woven fabric, with 22 patent interlacing wires, all sizes............................$1.65

No. 226. Hercules woven-wire spring, heavy hardwood frame, close-woven fabric, with 36 patent interlacing wires, any size $2.25

No. 11. Hercules woven-wire spring, guaranteed not to sag, any size.......................$3.25

No. 25. Woven-wire spring, extra heavy hardwood frame, well finished, with closely-woven fabric (double weave), with 10 very strong lock bands and side supports, guaranteed not to sag $2.50

Springs require to be one inch narrower and one inch shorter than bedstead to fit properly. When ordering double size we always send 4 ft. 1 in. wide by 5 ft. 11 inches long.

Bed Pillows.

No. W. Pillows, wool filled, covered in special ticking, size 20 x 26 in., pair 75c

No. H & T. Pillows, filled with mixed hen and turkey feathers, heavy ticking covered, pair $1.10

No. H. Pillows, all good clean hen and chicken feathers, size 20 x 26 in., pair..............$1.25

No. L. Pillows, filled with good mixed feathers, linen covered, size 21 x 27 in., 7 lbs, pair...$1.65

No. G. & D. Pillows, mostly all new duck feathers, size 21 x 27 in., 6 lbs, pair $2.00

No. G. & D. Pillows, goose and duck feathers, soft and light, pair..........................$2.50

No. G. Pillows, filled with all new goose feathers, covered in blue stripe linen ticking, size 22 x 28 in., 5 lbs, pair $3.35

6 lbs, pair...$4.00

No. D. Pillows, down filled, sateen or linen ticking covered, pair.........................$5.50

Ostermoor Patent Felt Mattresses.

Equal to any all-hair mattress, and only half the cost. The Ostermoor patent elastic felt mattress is made of the purest selected cotton. By a certain process this cotton is rendered absolutely dry and non-absorbent. After this it is formed into light, airy, fibrous sheets, so closely interlaced as to secure uniform thickness, softness and elasticity. That is why physicians endorse its use, and also the reason why so many of the best and largest hospitals are equipped with the Ostermoor patent elastic felt mattress. All the Ostermoor mattresses are 6 ft. 2 in. long. They are covered with a superior quality fancy striped sateen ticking. Our prices are:

2 ft. 6 in. wide, 25 lbs, each ....$ 9.50
3 ft. wide, 30 lbs, each........................ 11.00
3 ft. 6 in. wide, 35 lbs 12.50
4 ft. wide, 40 lbs 14.00
4 ft. 6 in. wide, 45 lbs.......................... 15.00

If made in two parts, the cost will be 75c extra.

Mail orders filled promptly.

SIDEBOARDS.

No. 370. Sideboard, hardwood, antique finish, neatly carved with shaped double top, 46 in. wide, 14 x 24 in. bevel-plate mirror, with 2 small drawers and double door cupboard....$8.00
Same sideboard, with carved panel back in place of mirror................$6.50

No. 372. Sideboard, hardwood, dark antique finish, with shaped double top, 46 in. wide, 14 x 24 in. bevel-plate mirror, 1 large and 2 small drawers, and double cupboard, well made and finished $9.35

No. 474. Sideboard, made of selected ash, golden finish, richly carved, top 48 in. wide, 81 in. high, 15 x 26 in. plate mirror, 2 small and one large drawer, large roomy cupboard, doors are panelled instead of plain as shown in cut $12.50
Same sideboard made of oak, golden finish $16.75

No. 374. Sideboard, made of ash, golden finish, neatly carved, fitted with 16 x 28 in. bevel-plate mirror $10.75
Same sideboard, in solid oak, golden finish $13.00

No. 379. Solid oak sideboard, massive design, richly carved, golden finish, shaped top, 48 in. wide, swell shaped drawers, 18 x 36 in. wide, bevel-plate mirror $17.00

No. 364. Sideboard, solid oak, golden finish, elaborately carved and polished, swell-shaped top and front, 4 ft. 4 in. wide, with 18 x 36 in. shaped British bevel-plate mirror $21.00

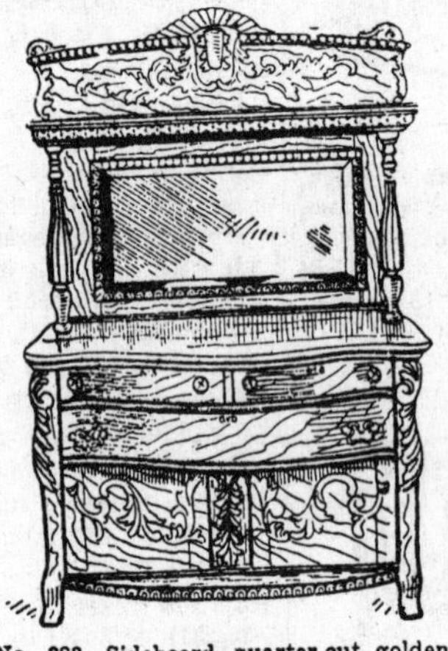

No. 383. Sideboard, quarter-cut golden oak, richly carved and polished, shaped top 4 ft. 4 in. wide, swelled front, 18 x 36 in. British bevel-plate mirror, 1 drawer lined $24.50

No. 465. Sideboard, quarter-cut oak, golden polished finish, heavily carved, 48 in. wide, shaped top and drawer, 18 x 34 in. British bevel-plate mirror, 1 large and 3 small drawers, 1 lined for cutlery $24.00

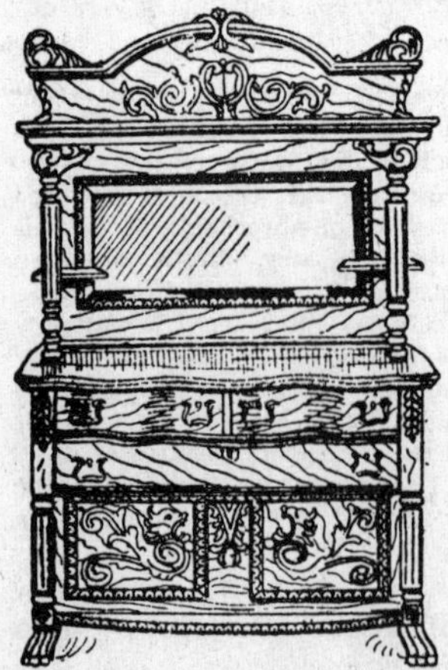

No. 384. Sideboard, made of select quarter-cut golden oak, heavily hand carved and polished, 4 ft. 6 in. shaped top, 18 x 40 in. British bevel plate mirror $27.50

No. 1102. Sideboard, made of the finest quarter-cut oak, golden finish, beautifully hand carved and polished, 50 in. wide, 20 x 32 in. British plate mirror.. ....$27.75

No. 1308. Sideboard, massive design, made of best selected quarter-cut oak, richly hand carved and polished, 4 ft. 7 in. wide, shaped top and centre drawer, 20 x 36 in. British bevel-plate mirror... ....$38.00

No. 476. Sideboard, made of selected quarter-cut oak, rich golden finish, hand carved and polished, 4 ft. 6 in. wide, shaped top and swell drawer, 20 x 36 in. British plate bevelled mirror. $32.50

No. 289. Extension table, hardwood, golden finish, top 40 inches wide, with heavy rim and strongly braced legs, extending to 6 ft. long. $4.20; extending to 8 ft. long $4.75

No. 272. Extension table, hardwood, golden finish. 42 x 42 in. top, 5 heavily-turned and fluted legs, strongly braced, extending to 8 ft. long $6.60

Same table, in solid oak 8.75

No. 278. Extension table, hardwood, golden oak finish, round top, 44 inches in diameter, extending to 8 feet long $8.75

Same table in solid oak, golden finish, extending to 8 feet long $10.75

No. 360. Corner china closet, quarter-cut golden oak, hand-carved and polished, 34 inches wide, 71 inches high, swell-shaped door, shelves and inside well-finished in quartered oak $17.00

No 297. Extension table, hardwood, dark antique finish, top size when closed 42 x 42 in., has 5 heavy turned and fluted legs, which are fastened to top with patent blocks, and can be shipped at a very low freight rate; extending to 6 ft. long, $5.15; extending to 8 ft. long.$5.85

No. 93. Extension table, selected ash, golden finish, top size 3 ft. 8 in. wide, extending to 8 ft. long, with handsome turned and fluted legs, strongly braced, leaves are cleated, which prevents warping, $8.00; extending to 10 ft. long............$9.00

No. 280. New colonial extension table, quarter-cut golden oak polished, top size 44 inches, extending to 8 feet long............$13.75

Extending to 10 feet long............$15.75

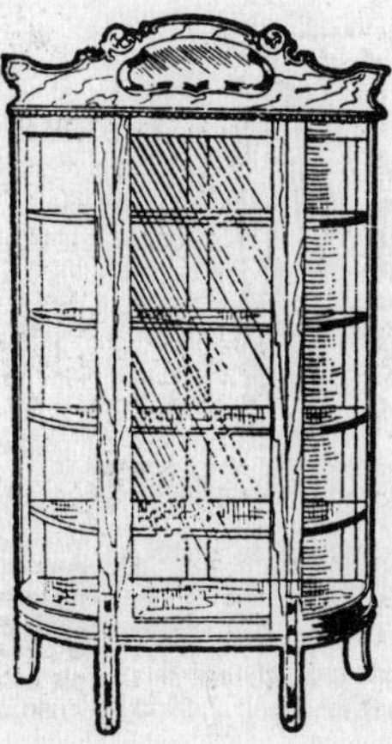

No. 379. China cabinet, select quarter-cut oak, golden polish finish, 39 in. wide, 72 in. high, top fitted with 6 x 16 in. fancy-shaped British plate bevelled mirror, circular-shaped ends........$18.00

No. 87S. Extension table, hardwood, imitation oak finish, heavy well-braced legs, with fancy embossed carving, top 42 in. wide, extending to 8 ft. long............$6.50

Same table, made in solid oak 8.25

No. 279. Extension table, solid oak, golden finish, polished top 44 x 44 in., has 5 heavy fancy turned and fluted legs, strongly made, extending to 8 ft. long, $9.85; extending to 10 ft. long $11.50

Same table, made in choice quarter-cut golden oak, extending to 8 ft. long, $11.25; extending to 10 ft. long $13.00

No. 227. Extension table, solid oak, rich golden color, highly polished, top 48 x 48 inches, 5 massive legs, extending to 8 feet long...$13.75

Extending to 10 feet long............ 16.50

Same table in choice quarter-cut golden oak, extending to 8 feet long............$15.75

Extending to 10 feet long............ 18.25

Same table, with round top, quartered oak, extending to 8 feet long $18.00

Extending to 10 feet long 20.75

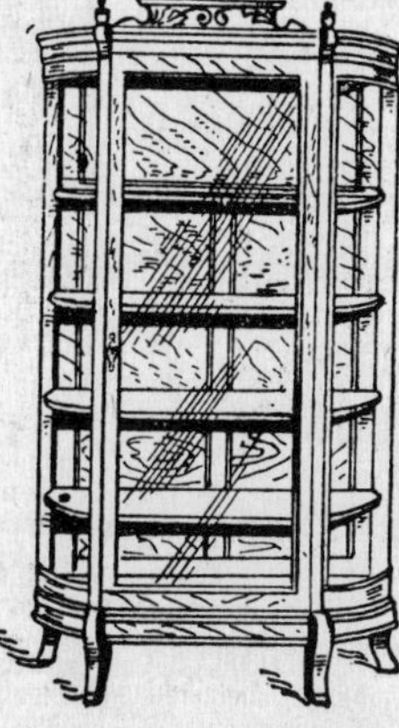

No. 384. China cabinet, quarter-cut oak, golden finish, polished bent glass ends and front, 3 feet 2 inches wide, 5 feet 6 inches high........$25.00

No. 12. Chair, hardwood, antique finish, strongly made, each 35c

No. 6. Chair, hardwood antique finish, shaped wood seat, strongly made, brace arms, each..............40c

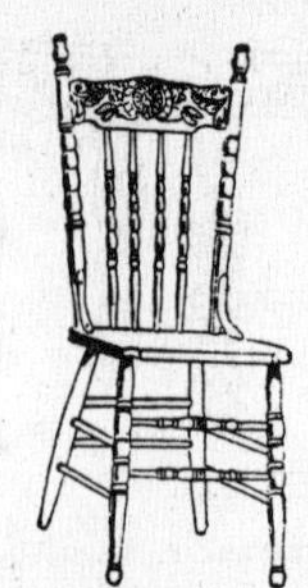

No. 70. Chair, hardwood, golden oak finish, impervious veneered seat, brace arms, each 48c

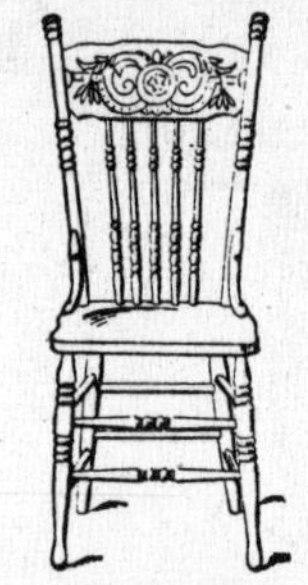

No. 40. Chair, hardwood, antique finish, back is neatly carved, with fancy turned spindles, solid shaped wood seat, brace arms, each...50c

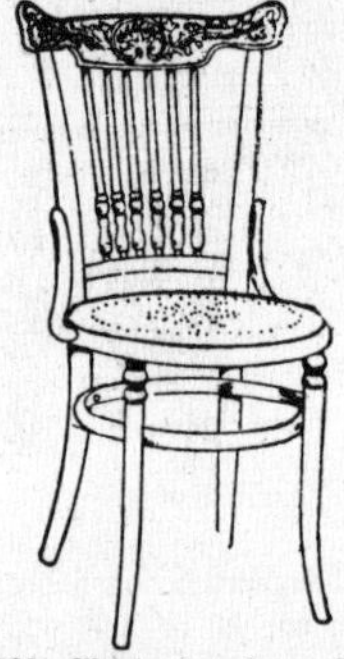

No. 720. Chair, hardwood, antique finish, embossed carved back, brace arms, perforated or impervious veneered seat, legs are strongly bolted to rim and rung, and is shipped K. D., ea. 80c

No. 700. Chair, hardwood, antique finish, handsomely carved, with impervious veneered seat, strongly made, each 77c

Same chair, with cane seat, each 95c

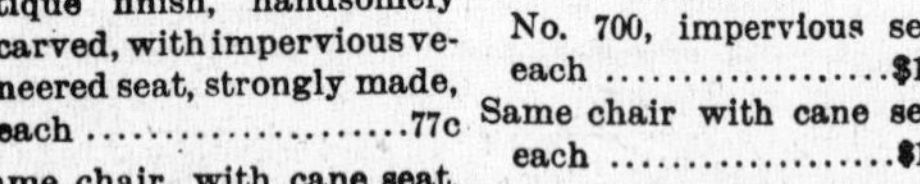

No. 702. Arm chair to match No. 700, impervious seat, each $1.27

Same chair with cane seat, each $1.40

No. 841. Chair, hardwood, antique finish, embossed carved slat back, brace arms, cane seat, each $1.00

No. 843. Arm chair to match No. 841, each..........$1.65

No. 314. Chair, solid oak, quarter-cut back slats, very comfortable, saddle-shaped seat, each $1.50

Arm chair to match..... 2.45

No. 6. Dining-room chair, solid oak or walnut frames, polish finish, with fancy embossed leather cobbler-shaped seat, each $1.65

Same chair, with seat upholstered genuine leather, colors green or maroon, each...................$2.00

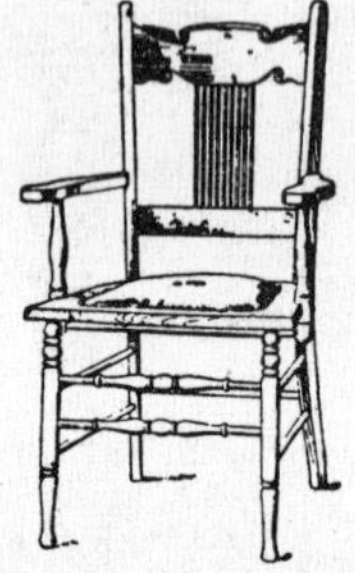

No. 6A. Arm chair, to match No. 6, with embossed leather cobbler-shaped seat, each $2.15

With genuine leather upholstered seat, each $2.55

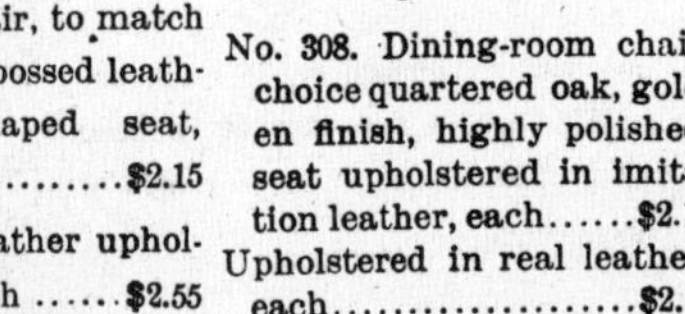

No. 308. Dining-room chair, choice quartered oak, golden finish, highly polished, seat upholstered in imitation leather, each......$2.10

Upholstered in real leather, each....................$2.70

No. 308A. Arm chair to match No. 308, seat upholstered in imitation leather, ea...$3.40

Upholstered in real leather, each $4.20

No. 306. Dining-room chair, quarter-cut oak, polished, seat upholstered in best quality leather, each...$2.70

No. 306A. Arm chair to match No. 306..........$4.35

No. 38. Dining-room chairs, in solid quarter-cut oak, antique or golden finish, hand carved and polished, with solid leather cobbler seats, each.....................$2.90

Upholstered spring seat, in best leather, each......$4.65

No. 38A. Arm chair to match No. 38, with cobbler seat, each....................$4.25

With upholstered spring seat, in best leather, each...$6.25

No. 32. Dining-room chair, quarter-cut oak frame, polish finish, hand carved, upholstered in real leather spring seats, padded back, shaped legs; this is a very pleasing design, also made in solid walnut frames.$5.75

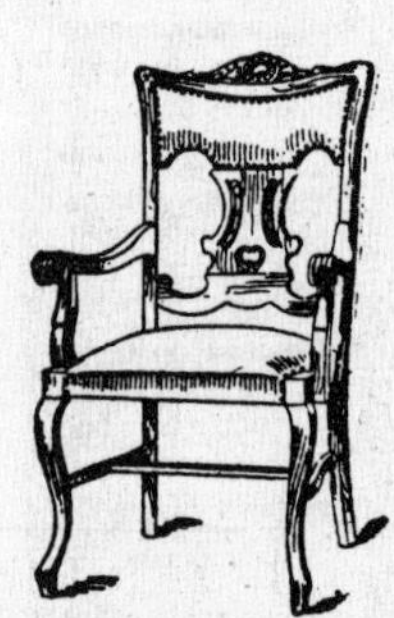

No. 32A. Arm chair, to match No. 32, large and comfortable, each..............$7.25

No. 36. Lounge, hardwood frame, golden finish, neatly carved, upholstered spring seat, covered in heavy satin russe $3.95

Same lounge, upholstered in heavy tapestry $4.75

No. 30. Lounge, hardwood, antique-finished frame, upholstered spring seat, in satin finished tapestry $4.10

Upholstered in extra heavy satin-faced tapestry..........................$4.90

Upholstered in extra heavy figured velours $5.75

No. 15. Couch, all-over upholstered and fringed both sides the same, a new and very comfortable design, good spring seat, well upholstered in French tapestry covering, colors Nile, blue, reseda, terra cotta and crimson $4.85

Same couch, upholstered in fancy figured velours, fringe to match, olive, myrtle, tobac, golden brown and red $6.45

No 19. This couch is our most popular shape, has beautiful sloped head, upholstered with a fine grade of satin-faced tapestry, spring seat, fringed all around $7.90

Upholstered in figured velours $9.00

No. 92. Bed couch, heavy hardwood frame, back can be lowered level with seat, forming a double bed, there is also a wardrobe or box underneath seat for storing bed clothes, etc., upholstered with springs all over, and deeply tufted, in heavy tapestry covering $13.50

Upholstered in figured velours $14.75

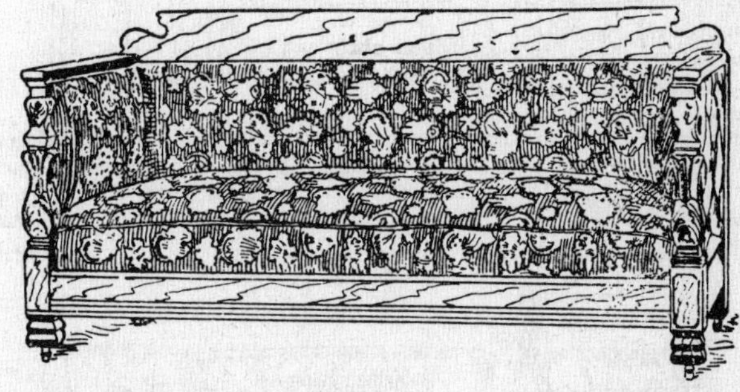

No. 190. Davenport sofa, quarter-cut oak, golden-finished frame, hand carved and polished, 76 inches long, 31 inches deep, 37 inches high, upholstered spring back and spring-edge seat, buttoned band, in extra heavy figured velour covering..$32.50

No. 263. Morris reclining chairs, golden oak frame, with patent adjusting rod, reversible cushions covered in fancy figured velours or English tapestry $7.00

No. 213. Morris reclining chair, in solid oak or mahogany-finished frame, polished, spring seat, upholstered in heavy figured velour, brass adjusting rod $6.75

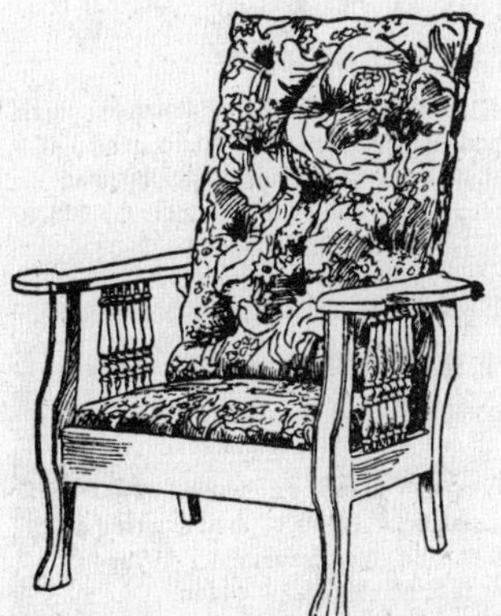

No. 201. Morris chair, golden oak or mahogany finish, polished, heavy shaped legs and arms, spring seat, reversible back cushion, all moss filled, covered in heavy figured velour $10.50

Upholstered in real leather $15.00

No. 203. Morris chair, golden oak, massively carved and polished, upholstered spring seat, reversible cushion back, covered in fancy figured velour $14.75

Upholstered in real leather....$19.00

No. 10. Parlor suite, the most reliable on the market, in solid walnut or mahogany finished frames, neatly carved and polished, 5 pieces (sofa, arm chairs, arm rocker and 2 reception chairs), upholstered in heavy tapestry covering, silk plush trimmed, good spring seats and plain back........$19.75

Upholstered in fancy figured velour........$21.00

Upholstered in black haircloth........$23.50

No. 11. Parlor suite, upholstered on same frames as No. 10, with first-class upholstering throughout, spring seats and edges double stuffed and tufted backs—

Upholstered in heavy figured velour........$29.50

Upholstered in silk tapestry........$31.00

No. 247. Parlor suite, 3 pieces (as cut), frames are well made, mahogany finish, highly polished, upholstered in silk tapestry, good spring seats, colors Nile, green, reseda, olive, terra cotta, rose, pink and old gold........$26.00

Upholstered in high-grade silk tapestry........$28.75

No. 761. Parlor suite, 3 pieces (as cut), mahogany-finished frames, with genuine inlaid lines, highly polished, upholstered in high-grade silk tapestry. This makes an elegant 3-piece suit, and upholstered in first-class style........$31.00

PRICES AND DESCRIPTIONS.

Prices and descriptions of other higher-priced suites on application.

We will send samples of coverings used on parlor suites, lounges, easy chairs, etc., on application. Always state price of article you require. Parlor suites can be upholstered in different colors on separate pieces, if so selected, at the same price.

As rugs for Nos. 15 and 2½ suites and rug lounges are made in squares, special sizes to fit, we cannot cut off samples.

We upholster all our own goods and guarantee all work to be first-class, new, fresh and clean. It usually takes from two to three days to make up parlor suites when special colors or coverings are required.

No. 40. Parlor suite, 3 pieces, mahogany finished frames, hand carved and highly polished, thoroughly well made, upholstered in fine silk tapestry, in colors olive, Nile, green, rose, light blue, golden brown, spring seat and edges, buttoned back and bands........$36.00

No. 5. Parlor suite, stuffed over, 5 pieces (sofa, arm chair, arm rocker and 2 ladies' chairs), spring seats and edges, large and comfortable, seats are double-stuffed, well upholstered in heavy figured velour, fringed to match........$34.50

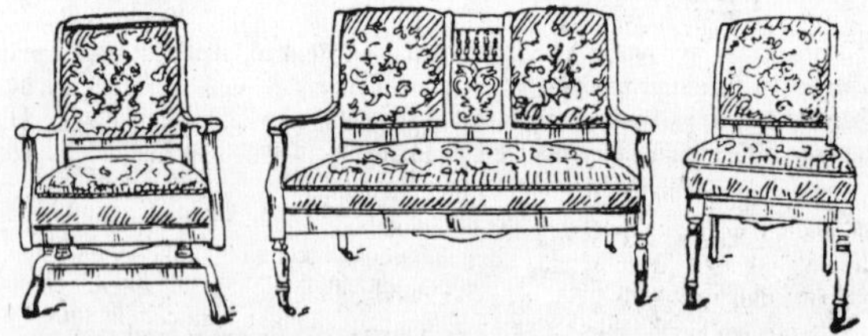

No. 2½. Parlor suite, solid walnut frames, 5 pieces (sofa, arm chair, arm rocking chair and 2 reception chairs), upholstered in best English Wilton rugs, silk plush bands, double-stuffed, spring seat and edges, ...$35.00

Upholstered in satin-faced tapestry........$27.50

No. 15. Parlor suite, 5 pieces, allover upholstered in best Wilton rugs, silk plush trimmed, fringed to match, consisting of sofa, arm chair, arm rocker and 2 reception chairs, spring seats, backs and edges, ...$55.00

In separate pieces: sofa, $18.50; arm rocker, $12.50; arm chair, $12.00, and reception chairs, each........$6.50

No. 416. Five-piece parlor suite, birch, mahogany finish, elaborately hand carved and highly polished, shaped arms strongly braced, suite consists of sofa, arm chair, arm rocker, and two reception chairs, well upholstered with spring seats and edges, double-stuffed, upholstered in fine silk tapestry........$57.50

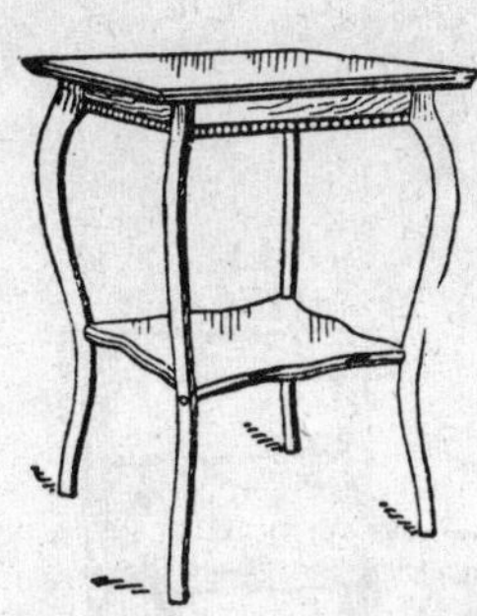

No. 81. Table, hardwood, antique finish, 16 x 16-inch top, shaped legs and shelf 85c
22 x 22-inch top, shaped legs and shelf $1.10

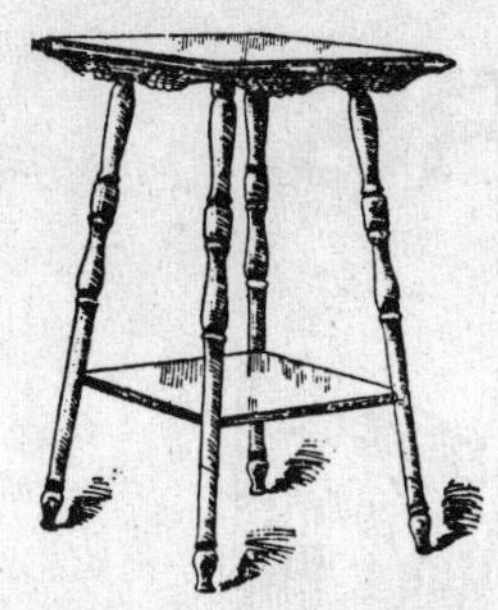

No. 100. Parlor table, with quartered oak top and shelf, or birch, mahogany finish, polished, 18 x 18-inch top, fancy turned legs, can be shipped K.D.................$1.10

No 447. Parlor table, in solid oak or mahogany finish, 24 x 24-inch top, with fancy turned legs and brass claw feet......................$2.00

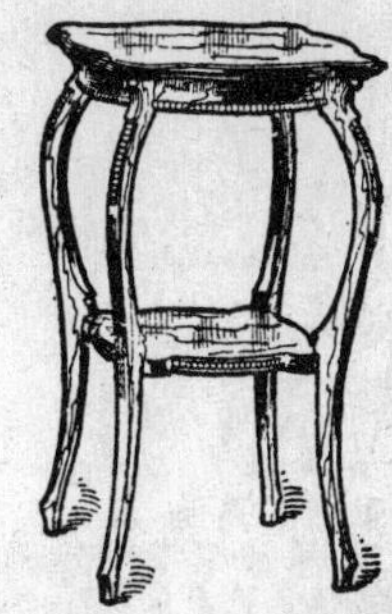

No. 395. Parlor table, quarter-cut golden oak and birch, mahogany finish, 16½ x 16½-inch top, highly polished, a very handsome table $2.65

No. 499. Parlor table, quartered oak, golden finish or curly birch, mahogany finish, polished, 24 x 24-inch shaped top and shelf, can be shipped K. D..................$2.95

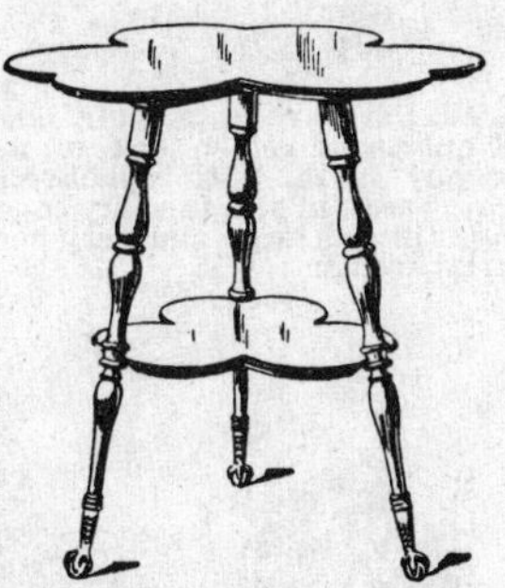

No. 114. Parlor table, in quarter-cut oak and birch, mahogany finish, 25 x 25-inch fancy shaped top, and shelf, well polished $3.35

No. 325. Parlor table, quarter-cut oak, golden finish or birch, mahogany finish, highly polished, 23 x 23-inch top...................$3.25

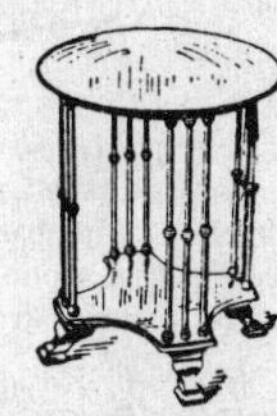

No. 84. Jardiniere stand, in quarter-cut golden oak, or mahogany finish, 15 x 15-inch round top, highly polished, 20 inches high......$2.35

No. 424. Jardiniere stand, quarter-cut oak, or birch, mahogany finish, top 16 x 16 inches, 17½ inches high 95c

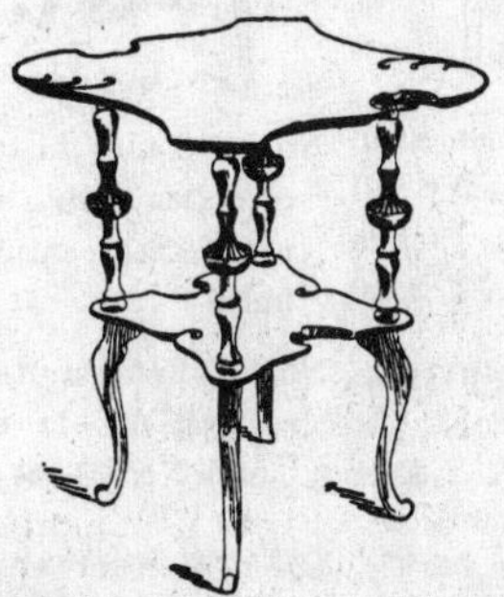

No. 252. Parlor table, quartered oak or mahogany, hand carved and polished, 24 x 24-inch fancy shaped top and shelf, with brass beading on edges; this is a high-grade table in every particular............$5.75

No. 82. Tea table, make in quartered oak, golden finish or mahogany, new design, top is 24 x 24 inches, height 24 inches...............$4.75

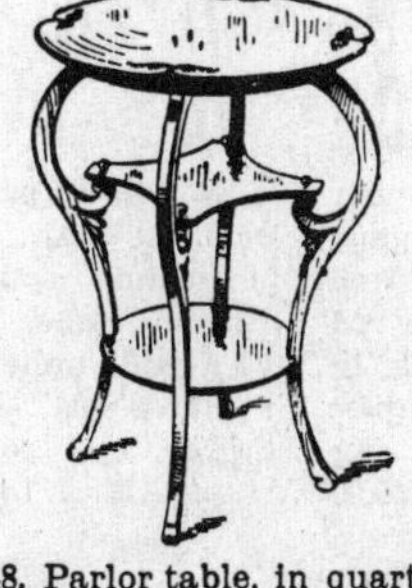

No. 148. Parlor table, in quarter-cut oak, rich golden finish or mahogany, highest polish finish, with 20 x 20-inch top, 2 shelves; this is one that will always please you $1.95

No. 345. Jardiniere stand, quarter-cut oak, or mahogany finish, 22 inches high, 15 x 15-inch top...$2.75

No. 1047. Library table, quartered oak, golden finish, highly polished, 26 x 48-inch top, with fancy shaped legs, neatly hand-carved....$9.25

No. 71. Library table, made of select quarter-cut oak, rich golden polish finish, top size 28 x 48 inches, heavy shaped cross-banded rim, fancy turned and fluted legs, with brass claw feet $14.00

CHAIRS.

No. 82. Large arm chair, so id oak frame, carved and polished, shaped legs, good spring seat, back and arms are deep tufted, upholstered in real leather, colors green or maroon $26.50

No. 930. Arm chair, quarter-cut oak, golden finish or mahogany, highly polished. This chair is beautifully shaped and very comfortable, has full spring seat and back, with heavy roll head rest, upholstered in best leather................$21.50

Rocker to match $22.50

No. 999. Parlor rocking chair, made of quartered golden oak or mahogany finish, with upholstered spring seat, in silk tapestry covering ; this is a large and very comfortable chair..................$9.25

No. 92. Parlor rocking chair, rich mahogany finish, very highly polished, spring seat, upholstered in best silk tapestry.........$11.75

No. 220. Arm rocking chair, in curly birch, mahogany finish, richly polished, upholstered in fine silk tapestry $9.00

No. 233. Arm chair, curly birch, rich mahogany finished frame, well polished, fancy carved back, upholstered in extra quality silk tapestry covering, spring seat..............$9.00

No. 232. Ladies' parlor reception chair, birch, mahogany-polish finished frame, neatly carved, upholstered spring seat, in silk tapestry covering $6.90

No. 0114. Rattan reception chair, in 16th century finish, a very handsome design, ...$5.20

No. 053. Rattan arm chair, with heavy roll edge, strongly made $5.00

No. 0103. Rattan rocking chair to match No. 053 ....$5.10

No. 038. Fancy rattan reception chair, natural or 16th century finish $4.45

No. 077. Fancy rattan rocking chair to match No. 038..$4.50

No. 558. Rocking chair, solid quarter-cut oak and mahogany finish, neatly carved back, solid leather lap-over cobbler seats.........$4.75

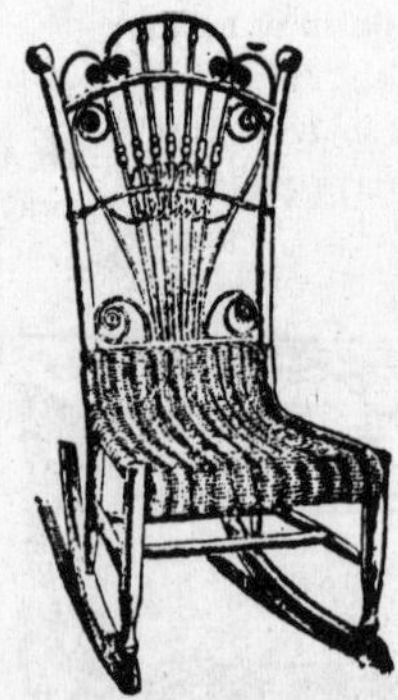

No. 5539. Ladies' rattan rocking chair, 16th century finish $2.00

Reception chair to match $2.00

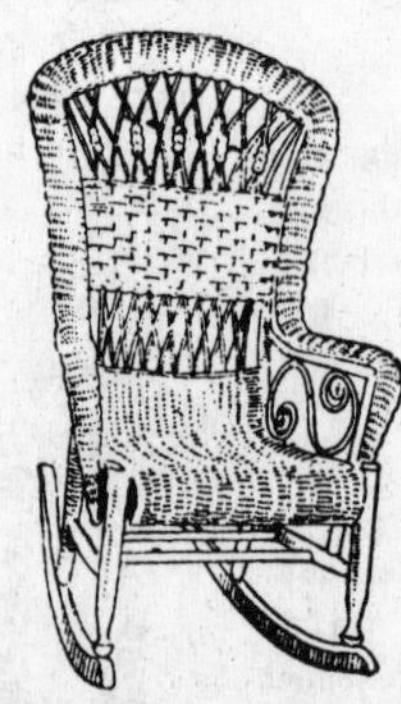

No. 5546. Ladies' large rattan arm rocking chair, 16th century or natural finish $3,65

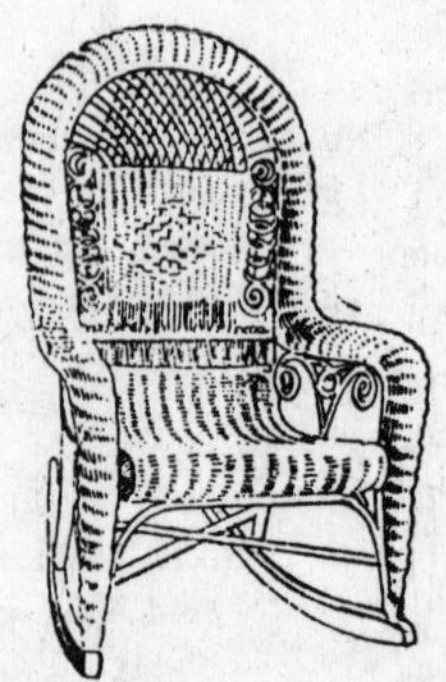

No. 5603. Large rattan arm rocker, with heavy roll edge and seat, 16th century or natural finish.........$5.25

No. 5617. Gents' large-size arm rocking chair, natural or 16th century finish ... $7.75

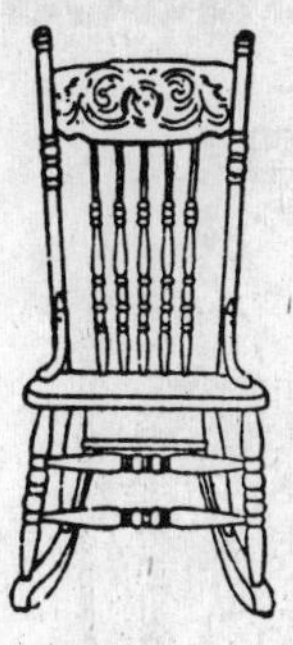

No. 35. Rocking chair, hardwood, antique finish, embossed, carved high back, shaped wood seat 85c

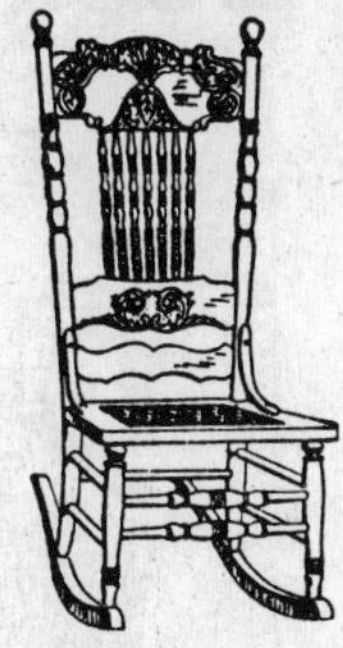

No. 705. Rocking chair, hardwood, antique finish, neatly carved, high back, with fancy turned spindles, cane seat......$1.25
Same with impervious veneered seat............$1.10

No. 309. Rocking chair, golden elm, high back, neatly carved, solid wood seat $1.00

No. 22. Rocking chair, antique finish, large size, high back............$1.25
Also larger size, with roll seat..................$1.55

No. 310. Arm rocking chair, elm, golden oak finish, large and comfortable...........$1.50

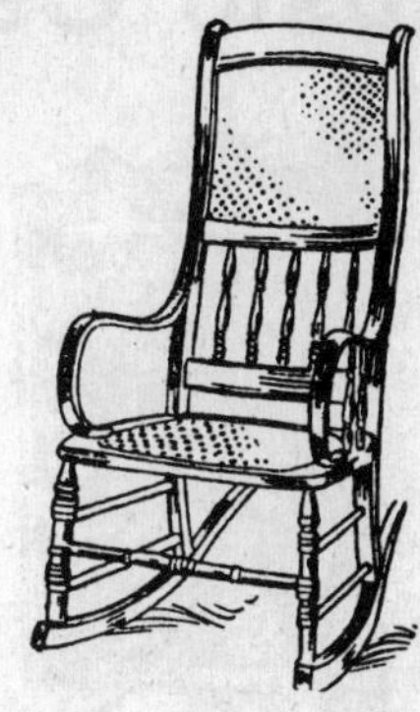

No. 110. Rocking chair, hardwood, antique finish, high back, bent arms, extra comfortable, with perforated seat and back....$1.75
Cane seat and back......$2.00

No. 2. Rocking chair, solid oak or mahogany-finished frames, neatly carved and polished, solid leather cobbler-shaped seats $1.90

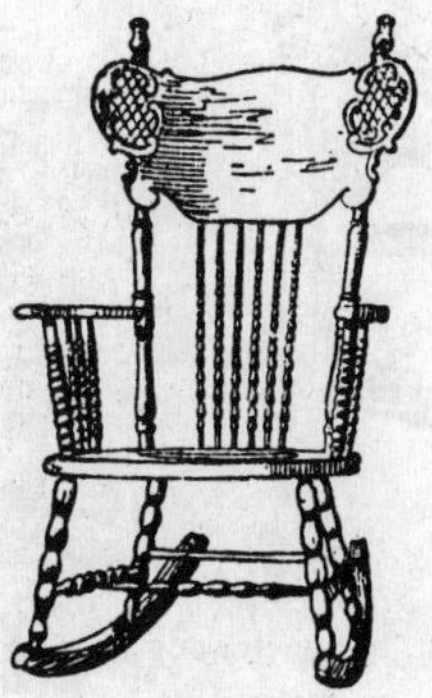

No. 67. Rocking chair, solid oak or mahogany-finished frame, carved and polished, with embossed leather cobbler-shaped seat .$2.75

No. 506. Rocking chair, solid oak or birch, mahogany finish, well carved and polished, embossed leather cobbler-shaped seat....$3.50

No. 4. Rocking chair, larger size, strongly made, shaped arms, in quarter-cut oak and curly birch, mahogany finished, solid and embossed leather cobbler-shaped seats......$3.90

No. 82. Arm rocking chair, made of solid quarter-cut oak, golden finish or mahogany finish, highly polished..................$9.00

No. 59. High chair, hardwood, antique finish, with shaped wood seat 95c

No. 700. High chair, hardwood, antique finish, shaped seat, ...$1.15

No. 702. High chair, solid oak, antique gloss finish, cane seat.........$1.65

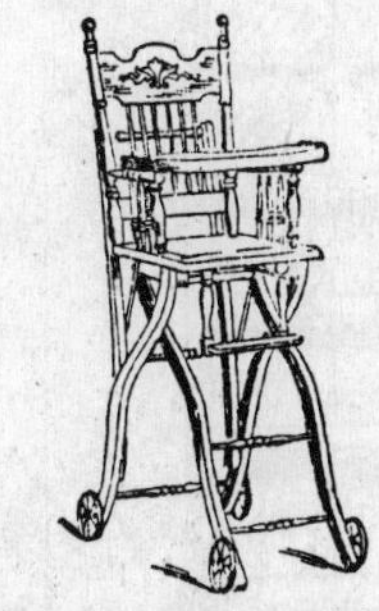

No. 571. Combination high chair, hardwood antique finish, cane seat, with wheels, can be lowered down to make a carriage $2.25

No. 5330. Rattan high chair, in 16th century finish, swing table, closely woven seat, strong and durable....$2.75

No. 47. Child's kindergarten chair, hardwood, painted red or blue, 12 in. high to seat............39c

No. 42. Child's commode chair, bow back, assorted colors............59c

No. 41. Child's commode chair, square back, lighter make 45c

No. 45. Child's rocking chair, hard wood antique finish, strongly made...60c

No. 1. Child's willow commode chair, enclosed stand, with table $1.00

No. 37. Large size bedroom commode chair, high back, with arms, light finish...........$2.00

Music Cabinets, Writing Desks, Bookcases.

No. 209. Music cabinet, in quarter-cut oak and imitation mahogany, 40 inches high, 18 inches wide, 13 inches deep $3.90

No. 275. Parlor cabinet, in birch, mahogany fine polish finish, 34 inches wide, 60 inches high, cabinet in centre, with bent glass door and lined shelves, 3 fancy-shaped British bevel-plate mirrors $23.75

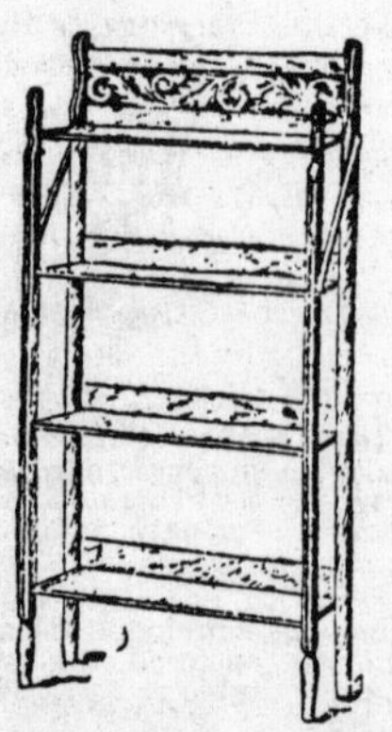

No. 1. Folding bookshelf, antique finish, 27 inches wide, 54 inches high $1.45

No. 613. Music cabinet, birch, mahogany finish, highly polished, inside neatly fitted with shelves, 6 x 16-inch British bevel mirror $10.00

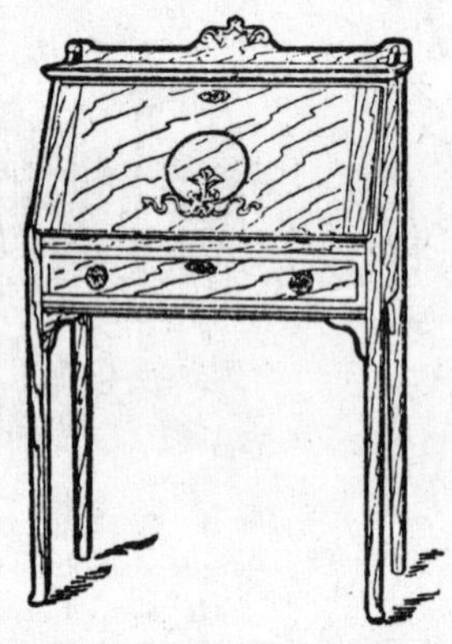

No. 310. Ladies' writing desk, made of oak, golden finish or birch mahogany finish, highly polished, neatly carved, 28 inches wide, 44 inches high $5.50

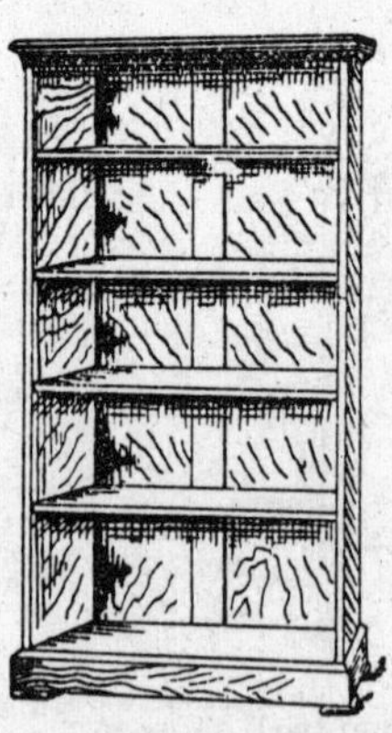

No. 175. Bookshelf, made in choice ash, golden finish, 30 inches wide, 57 inches high, movable shelves $4.50

Same bookshelf, in solid oak....$5.25

No. 192. Music cabinet, solid quarter-cut oak or mahogany finish, polished, 30 inches high, 18 x 24-inch top $7.25

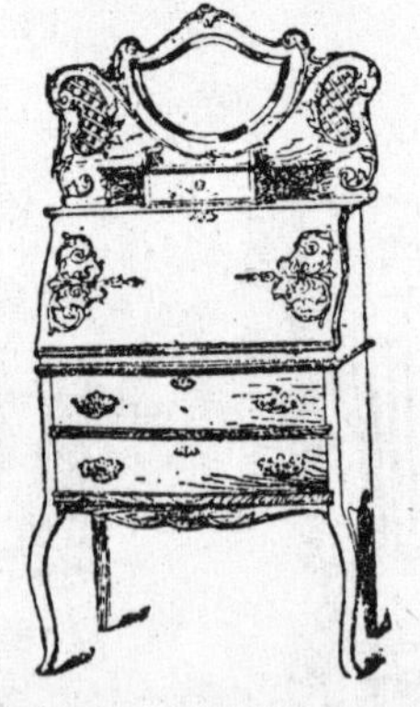

No. 313. Ladies' desk, in quarter-cut oak, golden finish, or mahogany, hand-carved and polished, 30 inches wide, 60 inches high, with 10 x 16-inch British bevel mirror $17.25

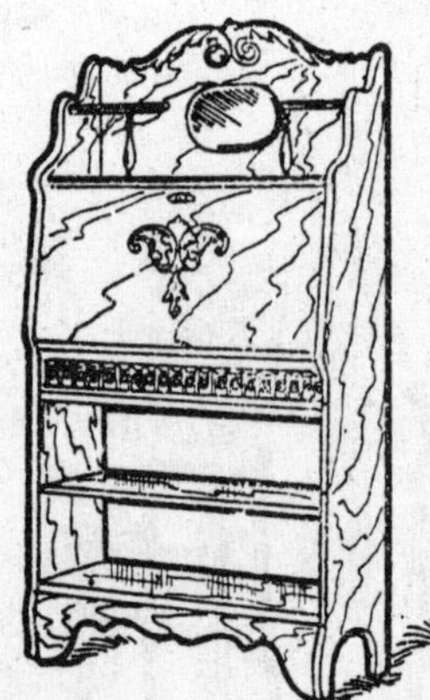

No. 101. Ladies' secretary, select ash, golden finish, neatly carved and well made, 30 inches wide, 60 inches high, large size drawer, top fitted with $6\frac{1}{2}$ x $10\frac{1}{2}$-inch plate mirror $6.90

Same secretary, made in solid oak $8.25

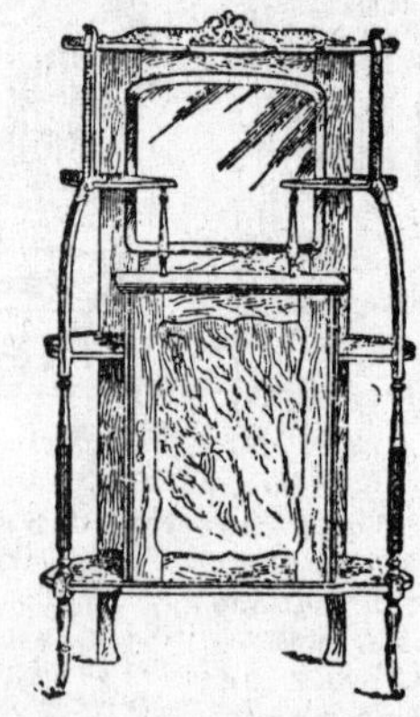

No. 273. Parlor and music cabinet combined, rich mahogany finish, 43 inches wide, 58 inches high, 16 x 18-inch British bevel-plate mirror $14.75

No. 318. Combination secretary and bookcase, quarter-cut golden oak and birch, mahogany finish, extra well polished and hand carved, 41 inches wide, 70 inches high, fitted with 14 x 16-inch shaped British bevel-plate mirror............$18.50

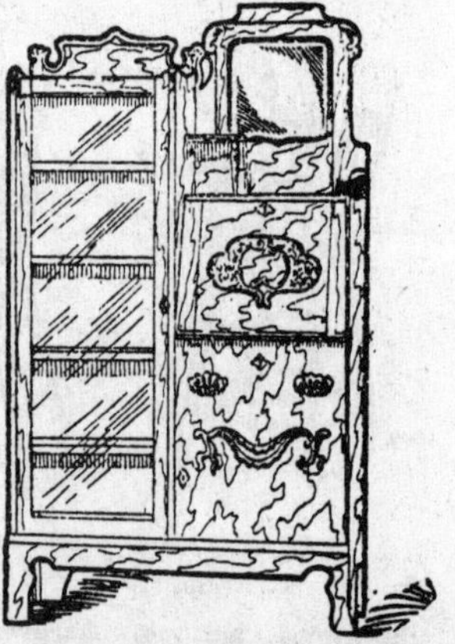

No. 331. Combination bookcase and secretary, quarter-cut golden oak, neatly carved, 38 inches wide, 66 inches high, 12 x 12-inch British bevel mirror..................$13.50

No. 1. Student's easy chair, hardwood frames, golden oak finish, spring seat, upholstered in satin-finished tapestry, $4.45 ; with sleepy hollow seat, $4.20 ; upholstered in heavy tapestry, with spring seat $5.25 ; upholstered in heavy tapestry, sleepy hollow seat. $5.00

No. 2. Student's easy platform rocking chair, hardwood, oak finish, spring seat, upholstered in satin-finished tapestry, $5.25 ; upholstered in satin-finished tapestry, hollow seat, $5.00 ; upholstered in heavy tapestry, hollow seat, $5.85 ; upholstered in heavy tapestry, spring seat, ...$6.10

No. 427. Hanging hall rack, quartered golden oak, 24½ inches high, 32 inches long, 12 x 20-inch bevel-plate mirror, 4 branch hat and coat hooks......$3.25

No. 327. Hanging hall rack, made of highly polished quarter-cut oak, neatly carved, size 32½ x 28 inches, fitted with 12 x 20-inch bevel-plate mirror, very artistic design...$3.75

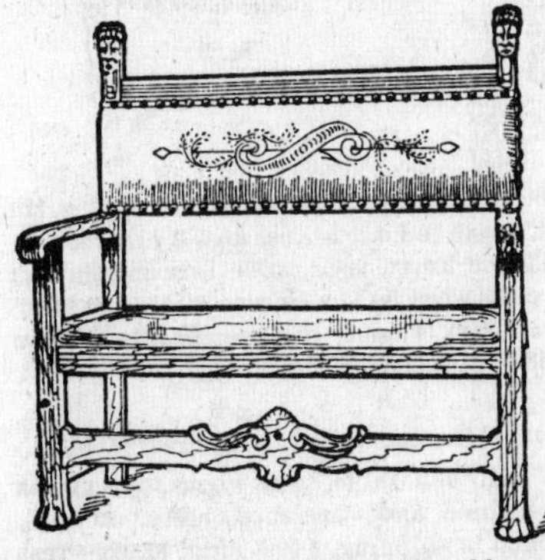

No. 304. Hall settee, quarter-cut golden oak, polished, heavy shaped seat, 42 inches wide, heavily hand carved back, upholstered in leather.................................$12.50

No. 411. Hall settee, quarter-cut golden oak, or Flemish oak, 39 inches long...............$5.50

No. 304½.

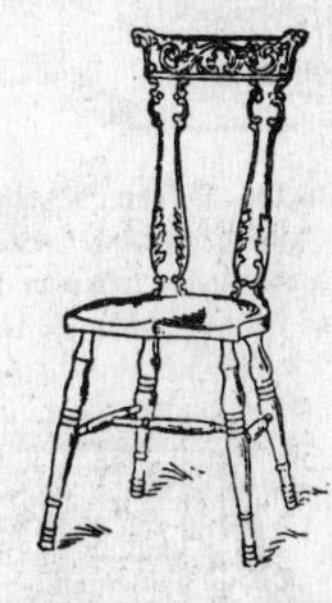

No. 327.

No. 304½. Hall chair to match No. 304 settee $6.90

No. 327. Hall chair, quarter-cut oak, golden finish, polished saddle-shape seat $3.00

No. 185. Hall rack, solid quarter-cut oak, polished, 82 inches high, 39 inches wide, fitted with 12 x 20 inch bevel-plate mirror, box seat and lid $8.25

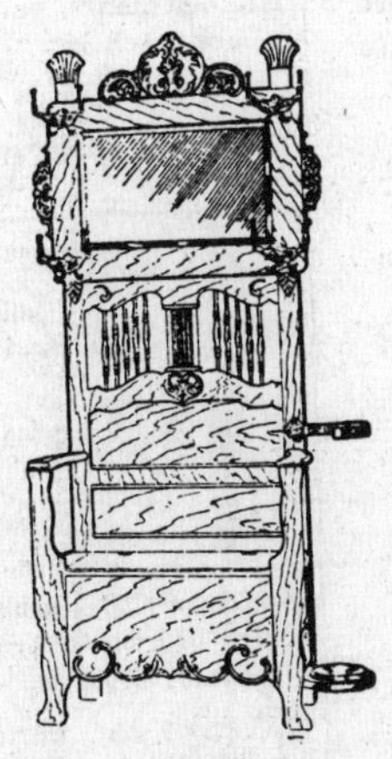

No. 135. Hall rack, quarter-cut oak, golden polish finish, neatly hand carved, 40 inches wide, 79 inches high, with 14 x 24-inch bevel-plate mirror............$11.25

Wernicke Elastic Book Case.

The Wernicke Elastic Book Case consists of a series of small compartments, each ingeniously designed to interlock with another in vertical and horizontal arrangement. These, with suitable tops and bases, are the "units" of the system, and are of different depths and heights to suit all sizes of books. They are made in a variety of grades to suit all requirements. The front of each compartment is provided with a dust-proof glass door, which, at its upper corners, hangs on movable pivots, so that it opens outward and upward and can be pushed back over top of the books entirely out of the way.

No. 1.

No. 1. This cut illustrates a base, with compartment and top units, showing the divided shelf construction, whereby vertical expansion with stability, economy of space and good appearance are made possible.

No. 2. This cut shows a double section arrangement of six door units, with "Export" tops and bases. The cases are an ornament in any home or office. Small enough for ten or large enough for 10,000 books. Always complete, but never finished.

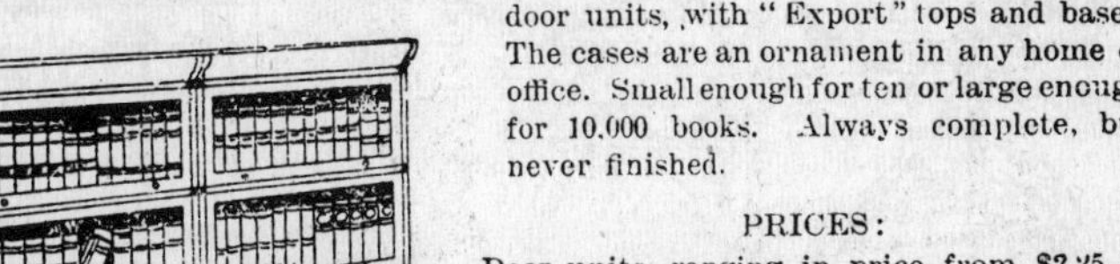

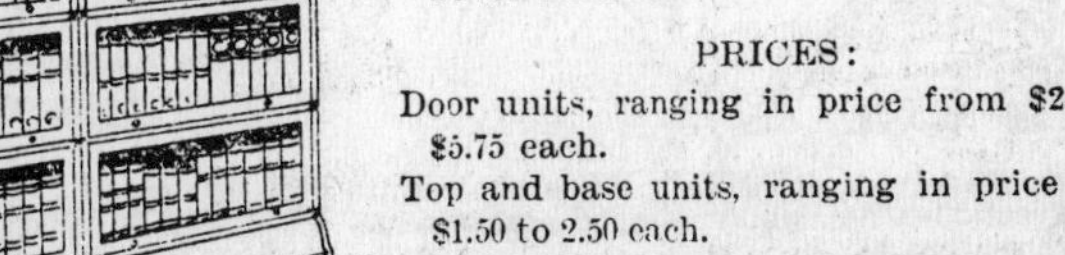

No. 2.

PRICES:

Door units, ranging in price from $2.25 to $5.75 each.

Top and base units, ranging in price from $1.50 to 2.50 each.

Write us for Special Catalogue, which fully describes the Wernicke Elastic Book Case, with price list.

No. 456. Office desk, made of choice ash, antique finish, 30 x 48-inch top, separate lock on each drawer, and cupboard fitted for books, $9.50.

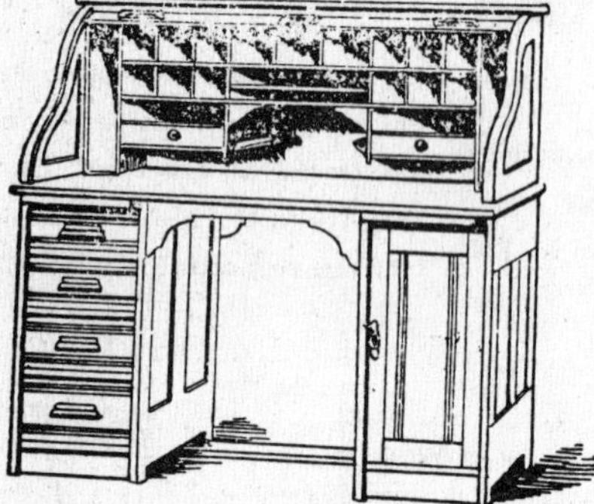

No. 106. Office roll-top desk, well made of solid oak, polished, with solid oak writing bed, automatic drawer locks, slides on each side, 48 inches wide, 30 inches deep, 50 inches high. $15.90

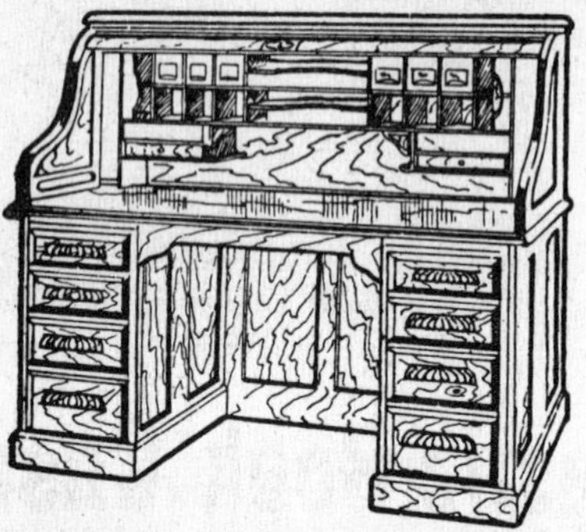

No. 104. Office roll-top desk, made in solid oak, golden polish finish, quarter-cut oak writing bed, 50 inches wide, 30 inches deep, 50 inches high, drawers lock automatically, slide on each side, top neatly fitted with pigeon-holes, with 6 enclosed wooden document boxes, ...$20.00

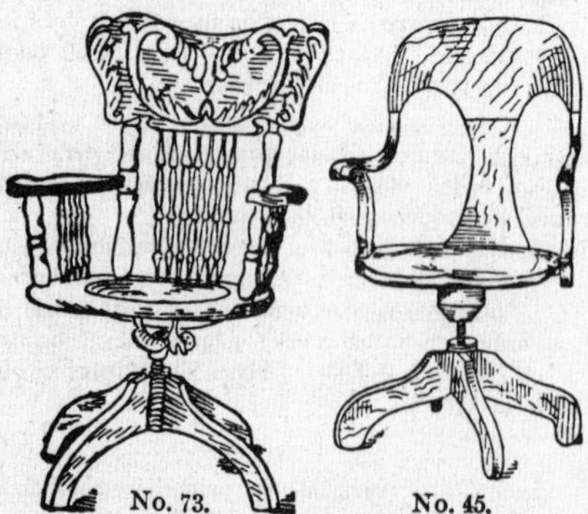

No. 73. No. 45.

No. 73. Revolving and tilting office chair, solid oak, solid leather cobbler-shaped seat, size 15-inch seat, $5.50.

No. 45. Office chair, made of select quarter-cut oak, golden finish, highly polished saddle-shaped seat, $7.25.

Kitchen Furniture.

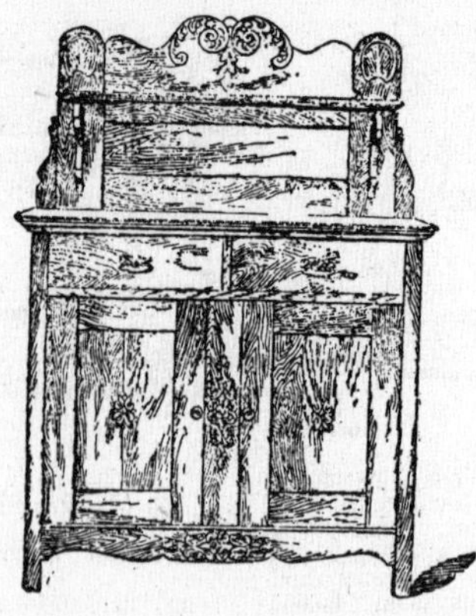

No. 275. Kitchen cupboard, elm, golden oak finish, 3 feet 10 inches wide, 5 feet 5 inches high, cupboard with 2 doors and shelf, 2 drawers and top shelf, $5.95.

No. 2. Kitchen cupboard, with glass doors on top, made of hardwood, golden oak finish, 3 feet 6 inches wide, 7 feet 2 inches high, $8.90.

No. 4. Kitchen cupboard, with double glass door top, 2 drawers and cupboard, with shelf 50 inches wide, 7 feet 6 inches high, hardwood, golden finish, $9.75.

No. 13. Table, hardwood, golden oak finish, top 24 x 36 inches, legs bolted on, can be shipped K.D.; with drawer, $1.60; without drawer, $1.40.

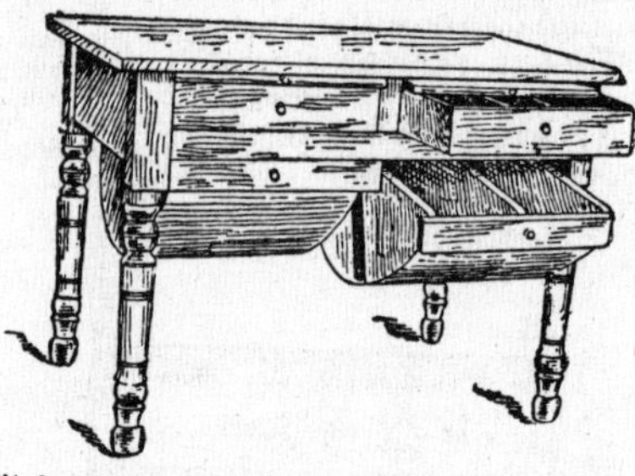

Kitchen cabinet, has 2 capacious flour bins, tin lined, made to hold 50 lbs, also 2 large drawers, 1 fitted for spices, 1 for cutlery and linens; above drawers is 1 large-size sliding baking-board. Top is made of clean basswood, size 28 x 48 inches, heavy turned legs, oil finished, $5.50.

Kitchen tables, unpainted, with drawer, $1.40.

No. 00. Kitchen table, basswood top, maple legs, stained and varnished, bolted-on legs, detached in shipping, 4 feet long, $1.95; 4 feet 6 inches long, $2.20; 5 feet long, $2.30.

Fall-leaf table, antique and dark finish, bolted legs, $2.90.

Kitchen chairs, double rungs, strongly made, not painted, each 32c.

Kitchen chairs, painted yellow, square or bow back, each 35c.

Office Furniture.

No. 17. Writing table, made of golden ash, top size 30 x 60 inches, covered with imitation leather, $7.00.

No. 81. Stool, antique finish, hardwood, 24 inches high, wood seat, 50c; 32 inches high, wood seat, 65c; 24 inches high, perforated seat, 60c; 32 inches high, perforated seat, 75c; 24 inches high, cane seat, 65c; 32 inches high, cane seat, 85c.

No. 84. Office stool, similar to No. 81, fitted with revolving seat and screw, raising from 35 inches to 40 inches, perforated seat, $1.60; raising from 35 inches to 40 inches, cane seat, $1.65.

HEAVY TAPESTRY CURTAINS.

No. 400. Tapestry curtains, 40 inches wide, 3 yds long, figured allover patterns, in full range of colorings, pair 1.75
48 inches wide, 3 yds long, pair 2.75

No. 558. Tapestry curtains, 36 inches wide, 3 yds long, reversible designs, colors olive, crimson, rose, green and blue, pair 2.25

No. 581. Tapestry curtains, 50 inches wide, 3 yds long, combination colors, green, rose, blue, olive and crimson, pair 3.00

No. 577. Heavy tapestry curtains, width 50 inches, length 3 yds, self colors, olive, green, blue, rose and crimson, per pair 4.50

No. 592. Heavy Ottoman tapestry curtains, width 50 inches, length 3 yds, repp effect, colors green, rose, golden brown and crimson, pair 5.00

No. 589. Heavy tapestry curtains, width 50 inches, length 3 yds, rich combination colors, green, olive, golden brown, rose, gold and crimson, pair ... 6.00

No. 549. Heavy tapestry curtains, 50 inches wide, 3 yds long, reversible designs, colors crimson, olive, blue, golden brown, rose and green, pair 7.50

No. 587. Heavy tapestry curtains, width 50 inches, length 3 yds, self colors, crimson, rose, olive and green, pair 9.00

No. 301. Tapestry curtains, mercerized, equal in effect to silk curtains, very stylish, colors blue, olive, Nile, tan and crimson, pair 12.00

No. 981. Chenille curtains, 3 yds. long, 34 in. wide, fancy dado and fringe top and bottom, in crimson, blue, terra cotta, brown, olive, bronze, electric, myrtle and fawn, pair... **2.50**
38 in. wide, pair **3.00**

No. 960. Chenille curtains, with deep fancy broken dado, and heavy knotted fringe top and bottom, in crimson, terra cotta, myrtle, tan, light blue, dark green, reseda, old red, bronze and olive, 48 in. wide, 3 yds. long, pair **5.00**

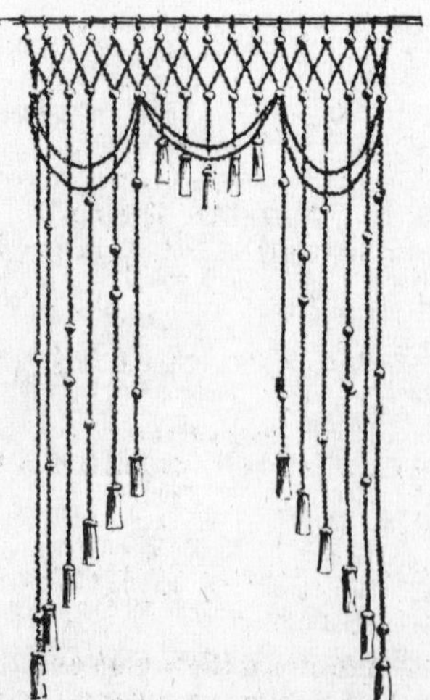

No. 100. Rope portieres, made of 3-ply tinsel cord, in colors to match surroundings, with sliding tassels, size 6 x 8 feet, ½-in. cord, $3.00; 7 x 8 feet, ⅝-in. cord, each $4.50, 5.50 and... **6.00**

No. 952. Chenille curtains, 42 in. wide, 3 yds. long, deep fancy floral dado and fringe top and bottom, in blue, crimson, terra cotta, myrtle, olive, fawn, bronze and reseda, pair, ... **3.75**

Prices of Chenille, Tapestry and Silk Portieres.

Plain Shiela curtains, 48 inches wide, 3 yds long, extra heavy quality, with heavy knotted fringe on both ends, colors all-red, empire, olive, reseda, brown and rose, per pair **8.50**

Heavy arch portieres, with deep fancy dado and fringe top and bottom, in crimson, terra cotta, fawn, electric, rose and bronze, 3½ yds long, 68 in. wide, per pair........ **8.50**

Extra heavy tapestry curtains, with deep fancy knotted fringe top and bottom, in repp and real tapestry effects, 50 in. wide and 3 yds long, in a variety of new patterns and colors, per pair, $5.00, 6.00, 7.00, 9.00........ **10.00**

Heavy Oriental Bagdad curtains, in a variety of new combinations, 48 in. wide, 3 yds long, fringed top and bottom, per pair, $..50, 5.00, 6.50 .... **7.75**

Heavy tapestry curtains, 50 inches wide, 3 yds long, in rich Turkish and Oriental designs, reversible, in combination colors, per pair, $8.50, 9.50........ **10.00**

Tapestry couch covers, for loose throws, fringed all round, reversible patterns, in Oriental or Bagdad effects, each $2.50, 4.50, 5.50 .... **6.50**

Japanese rice portieres, size 3½ x 9 feet, each $1.00, 1.25........ **1.50**

Japanese, rattan and bead portieres, in fancy patterns and rich colors, each $1.00, 1.50, 2.25 .... **3.75**

Reed Portieres.

Japanese string portieres, size 3 feet 6 inches by 9 feet, made in a vast assortment of Oriental colors, designs and qualities, suitable for doors, etc.

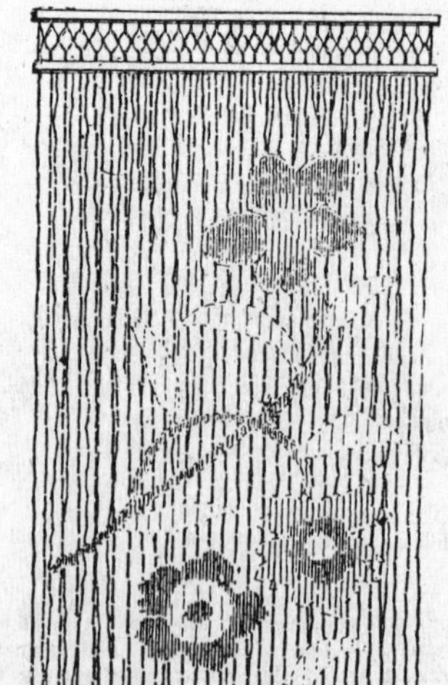

Rice quality, each........ **1.00, 1.25**
Reed quality, each........ **75c, 1.00**
Reed and bead quality, each .... **1.25 to 5.00**
Glass, all bead quality, each........ **6.00**

No. 985. Chenille curtains, 3 yds. long, 44 in. wide, with deep fancy dado and fringe top and bottom, in crimson, terra cotta, myrtle, brown and olive, dark blue and fawn, pr.. **4.60**
3½ yds. long, pair........ **4.75**

No. 1321. Chenille curtains, 48 in. wide, 3 yds long, in self colors, knotted fringe top and bottom and one side, colors red, crimson, terra cotta, brown, myrtle, olive, electric and rose, pair........ **5.50**

No. 107. Rope portieres, made of 3-ply ⅞-in. tinsel cords, size 7 x 8 feet long, made in any combination of colors, with sliding tassels, each $8.00 .... **10.00**

UPHOLSTERY, CURTAIN MATERIALS.

Heavy tapestry, satin finish, for coverings or curtains, 48 in. wide, new patterns, colors crimson, blue, olive, green, brown and golden brown, 40c yd.

Heavy cotton French tapestry, strong and durable, suitable for coverings or curtains, 50 in. wide, in fancy stripes and floral designs, in bronze, olive, electric, blue, terra cotta, crimson and golden brown, 45c, 50c yd.

Heavy American and French cotton tapestries, satin finish, 50 in. wide, rich effects, for furniture coverings, in combination colorings, crimson, dark blue, light blue, olive, bronze, terra cotta, gold and brown, 60c, 75c yd.

Fancy silk-striped tapestries for curtains and draperies, 50 in. wide, in combinations of cream, Nile and old red; cream, electric, blue and old red; coral, cream, pink and Nile, 65c, 75c, $1.00, 1.25 yd.

Fancy figured Florentine tapestries, in small and medium patterns, for draperies, curtains and upholstery purposes, 50 in. wide, self colors, blue, reseda, Nile, red, olive and salmon, $1.25 yd.

Heavy French tapestry, for furniture coverings and portieres, 50 in. wide, in rich effects and combination colors, olive and ecru; bronze, Nile and ecru; blue, green, gold and ecru; old red, cream, ecru and olive, $1.00 yd.

Heavy French and Gobelin tapestries, 50 in. wide, real tapestry effects, rich combination colorings, in green, blue, olive, bronze and old red, $1.25, 1.50, 1.75 yd.

Silk-faced tapestry, 50 in. wide, new choice designs, in blue, olive, green and red, $1.50, 1.75, 2.00 yd.

This cut represents a tapestry subject, used for screens, cushions or framing, size 24 x 24 in., $1.25 each.

Different prices and sizes as follows: 12 x 18 in., 50c; 18 x 18 in., 35c, 45c, 50c; 20 x 20, 50c, 75c; 24 x 24, 50c, 65c, 75c, $1.00, 1.25 each.

This cut illustrates a fancy iron lantern with colored glass sides, handsome designs, very strong well-made goods, being very latest idea for halls, smoking rooms, Moorish rooms or Turkish divans. The bracket is separate from the lantern, but it adds very much to the appearance of each to have both.

No. 135. Fancy iron lanterns with colored glass, in entirely new designs, can be used for halls, Moorish rooms or Turkish divans, $3.50 each.

Other styles and sizes, in iron and brass, $1.50 to 10.00 each.

Bracket, $1.50 each.

Heavy Wilton coverings for upholstering, 50 in. wide, blue, green, terra cotta, $2.00, 2.50 yd.

Fine silk tapestry, reversible, for fine upholstery and silk draperies, 50 in. wide, in a variety of entirely new designs, in olive, electric, crimson, blue, bronze, Nile, $1.25, 1.65, 2.00 yd.

Fine French and American silk tapestry, for fine upholstering and over draperies, 50 in. wide, in very choice designs and newest colors, olive, terra cotta, gold, blue, bronze and green, $2.50, 2.75, 3.00, 3.50 yd.

Extra fine French and American all-silk tapestry, newest designs and colors, coral, Nile, pink, blue and mode, $4.00, 5.00, 6.50 yd.

Fancy Draping Silks.

Fine silk drapery materials, soft finish, light weight, for arches or mantels, 50 in. wide, reversible, new designs and colorings, electric, gold, Nile, terra cotta, olive, old red and bronze, 75c, $1.00, 1.25, 1.50 yd.

Fine soft silk-finished drapery materials, 50 in. wide, for all styles of drapes, colors olive, red, blue, rose, terra cotta and green, 35c, 40c, 50c yd.

Art Drapery Serges.

Plain art drapery serges, 50 in. wide, in crimson, blue, gold, terra cotta, slate, olive, steel, 40c yd.

This cut represents a large tapestry subject, used especially for screens, wall panels, and for filling in cosy corner backs, size 4 ft. 2 in. 6 ft. 8 in., $6.50 each.

A full range of other designs in all sizes, ranging in prices from $2.50, 3.50, 5.00, 6.50 to 50.00 ea.

Cut No. 1 represents a piece of cuff armor, and is used as a wall decoration, being greatly in demand for halls, libraries, smoking rooms, dens, etc., $4.00 each.

Other different styles, from $3.25, 4.50, 5.00 to 20.00 each.

Cut No. 2 represents a piece of hat hook armor, and is very useful as well as a decoration for halls, dens, etc., $1.50 each.

We also have a larger and more fancy piece at $2.00.

All-Wool Damasks.

Figured all-wool damasks, 45 in. wide, for coverings, curtains and draperies, crimson, maroon, 40c; 50 in. wide, extra heavy, 65c yd.

Repps.

All-wool repps, in crimson and maroon, 48 in. wide, 75c, $1.00 yd.

Furniture Plushes.

Silk plush (Lister's), 24 in. wide, in a full range of new colors, 95c yd.

Plain mohair plush, 24 in. wide, in crimson, $1.00 yd.

Heavy velvet mohair plush, 24 in. wide, in crimson, $1.35, 1.75, 2.00 yd.

Plushette, 50 in. wide, in crimson, blue, gold and olive, 60c yd.

Linen velours, for drapes, portieres and upholstery, 50 in. wide, colors electric, old red, Nile, terra cotta, blue, bronze, rose, steel, 75c, $1.00, 1.10 yd.

Best French linen velours, deep nap, silk effects, colors terra cotta, Nile, electric, coral, bronze, gold and blue, 50 in. wide, $1.25 yd.

Heavy reversible plain linen velours, for portieres and draperies, 51 in. wide, rich effects in bronze, terra cotta, Nile, copper, blue, salmon, $1.75 yd.

Baize.

Green baize, 36 in., 30c; 52 in., 50c; 72 in., 65c yd.
Red baize, 36 in., 30c; 52 in., 50c; 72 in., 65c yd.

Felt Cloth.

All-wool felt cloths, 72 in. wide, for table covers, fancy work, scarfs, etc., in light and dark shades of crimson, blue, terra cotta, gold, brown, emerald, olive, bronze, black, fawn, rose, 65c yd.

Extra heavy felt cloth, 72 in. wide, in white and other colors, 75c yd.

Haircloth Seating for Furniture Coverings.

Haircloth, 14 in., 40c; 16 in., 45c; 18 in., 50c; 20 in., 55c; 24 in., 70c; 27 in., 85c; 30 in., $1.15. Prices subject to change.

Imitation leather, 50 in. wide, for upholstery purposes, in dark green and brown, 55c yd.

Pantesote, in dark green and brown, 54 in. wide, $1.75 yd.

WHITE DOWN CUSHIONS.

(Covered in white cambric.)

Odorless and Pure.

Comfort, 18 x 18 inches, 25c each.

Russian Down.

16 x 16 inches	30c each.	22 x 22 inches,	65c each.
18 x 18 "	40c "	24 x 24 "	75c "
20 x 20 "	50c "		

No. 1 Quality.

16 x 16 inches,	40c each.	22 x 22 inches,	90c each.
18 x 18 "	50c "	24 x 24 "	$1 10 "
20 x 20 "	75c "		

Fine Quality.

16 x 16 inches,	65c each.	22 x 22 inches,	$1 25 ea.
18 x 18 "	75c "	24 x 24 "	1 50 "
20 x 20 "	$1 00 "		

Extra Fine Quality.

16 x 16 inches,	75c each.	22 x 22 inches,	$1 50 ea.
18 x 18 "	90c "	24 x 24 "	1 85 "
20 x 20 "	$1 25 "		

Cushion Slip Covers.

Made of art silkaline, art cretonnes or sateens, in light or dark colors, with 3½-inch double frill, 18 x 18-inch, each 30c.

NEW DRAPERY DESIGNS.

Estimates for all styles of Drapery furnished on application. Send for samples of materials.

This cut represents a drapery for an opening between two rooms, showing one curtain and one-half of the drapery on either side. This is considered very effective, and can be made to look pretty with any priced materials, the goods used in this drape being 1 pair of portieres, 7 yards of overdrapery at 50c a yard; 10½ yds of fringe, 25c yd; 2 short poles, say 3 feet long each, 2 large brass rings and 2 pair of loops. Send for samples.

This cut represents a drapery for a mantel, and can be made from any soft-finished material. Articles required: 4 yards of single width, or 2½ yards of 50-inch goods, 6 yards of fringe, 2 medium-sized curtain rings and 1½ pair of loops.

This cut shows an arch draped without curtains. A drapery of this style will take about 1¼ yards of material to 1 foot of space. It will take 3 yards more fringe than material, allowing it to go on both ends; other fixings required, 1 large ring, 1 short pole and 1 pair of loops.

This cut shows a cosy corner, fitted up with Oriental hangings. The articles required for fitting up being 1 seat covered with Oriental tapestry, 1 tapestry panel for background, 2 Bagdad curtains, 9 to 12 yards of striped Oriental drapery goods, 2 spear heads and poles, 10 to 12 yards of turkey red for shirring the back, cushions, and one small lantern.

Screens, Sweepers, Fringes, Loops, etc.

Screens.

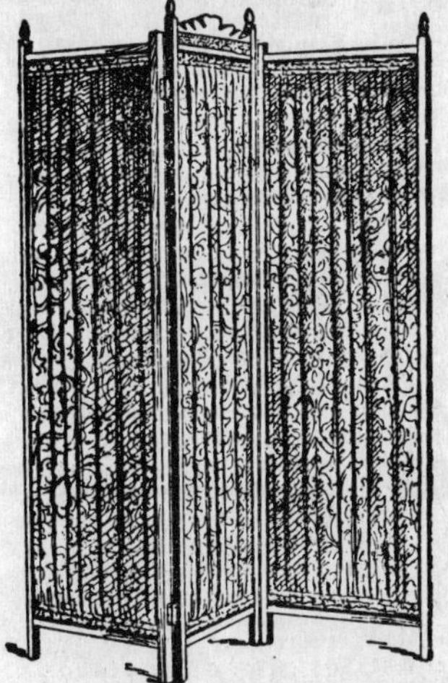

No. 111. Fancy folding screens, 3 panels, each 20 x 66 inches, solid oak frame, strong and durable, filled with figured art silkaline, in assorted colors, $1.95 each; frame only, $1.25

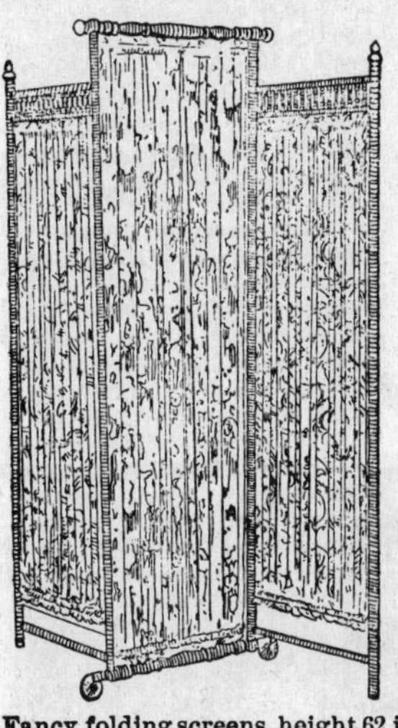

No. 303. Fancy folding screens, height 62 inches, centre panel 17 x 58, sides 17 x 48, solid oak or mahogany finish, filled with figured art silkaline, assorted colors, $2.95 ea; frame only, $2.00.

No. 0628. Fancy fire screens, single panel, size 24 x 28 inches, frame oak or mahogany, filled with fancy tapestry subject, $2.95 each; frame only, $1.75.

Bissell's "Champion" carpet sweepers, highly-finished woods, in assorted colors, japanned, $1.50; nickel, $1.75 each.

Bissell's "Brunswick" sweepers, durable and finely finished, in assorted woods, $2.00 each.

Bissell's "Grand Rapids" sweepers, cyclo bearings, mahogany and antique oak finish, $2.75 ea.

Bissell's "Gold Medal" carpet sweepers, highly finished wood, nickel trimmings, latest improvements, $3.25 each.

Drapery Fringes.

No. 651. Cotton tassel fringe, full line of colors to match muslin, per yd......................5c

No. 700. Cotton tassel fringe, assorted colors, to match curtain materials, 4½ inches deep, per yd 15c

No. 146. Silk tassel fringe, in colors to match, muslins and silks, 1½ inches deep, per yd...10c

No. 474. Silk drapery fringe, assorted colors, to match muslins and silks, 2¼ in. deep, yd., 20c

No. 601. Silk drapery fringe, in colors to match silks and drapery materials, 3 in. deep, yd, 35c

Rug Fringes.

No. 40. Rug fringe, double headed, 4½ inches deep, per yd 13c
Rug fringes, in assorted colors, per yd., 8c, 13c, ...25c

Furniture Fringes.

No. K84. Furniture fringe, wool, silk covered cord and tassel, 7 inches deep, per yd., 35c, per doz. (24 yd. pieces).......................$4.00
Cotton furniture fringes, per yd 15c
Worsted and silk furniture fringe, 7½ inches deep, per yd., 35c, 50c, 75c $1.35

Silk Curtain Loops.

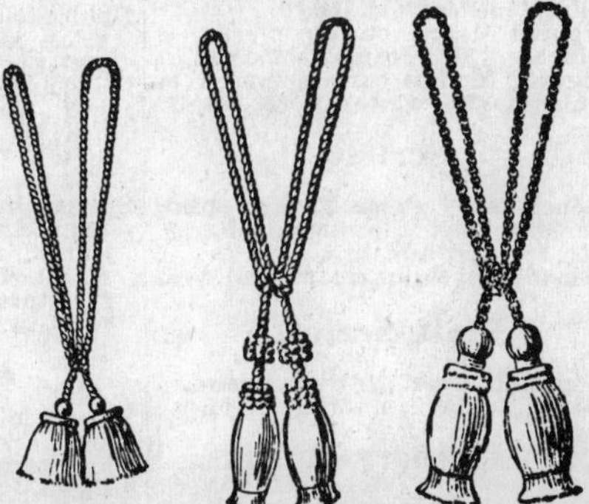

No. 872. No. 208. No. 203.

No. 872. Silk sash curtain loops, 13 inches long, in a full range of colors, per pair 25c
No. 208. Silk curtain loops, 16 inches long, in combination colors, per pair.................50c
No. 203. Silk curtain loops, 21 inches long, in combination colors, per pair 75c
Prices of silk curtain loops, per pair, 13c, 25c, 35c, 50c, 75c, $1.00, 1.25, 1.50, 2.00..............$2.50

Cotton Curtain Loops.

Cotton curtain loops, white or cream, per pair, 8c, 10c, 12c, 15c, 20c..................................25c

Chenille Curtain Loops.

No. 23. Chenille loops, 20 inches long, in crimson, blue, electric, terra cotta, bronze, olive, gold, fawn and rose, per pair.....................25c
No 21. Chenille loops, 24 inches long, full range of colors, per pair 50c
Worsted loops for tapestry curtains, in a full range of colors and combinations, per pair, 25c 50c

Sash Curtain Nets.

Swiss Irish point sash curtain nets, white or ivory, 27 to 30 inches wide, single borders, 30c, 35c, 40c, 45c, 50c, 65c yd; double borders, 30 inches wide, 50c, 65c yd.
Panel sash nets, Irish point, imitation of renaissance, white or ivory, 18 inches wide, 35c, 40c, 50c yd; 30 inches wide, 65c, 85c, $1.00 yd.
Tambour sash curtain nets, 27 to 30 inches wide, white only, 30c, 35c, 40c, 50c yd.
Brussels sash curtain nets, 27 to 30 inches wide, white only, 35c, 40c, 45c, 50c, 65c, 75c, 85c yd.
Frilled Brussels sash nets, 30 inches wide, white, frilled on both sides, 75c, $1.00 yd.
Real renaissance sash nets, 27 to 30 inches wide, ivory color only, panel designs, $2.00, 2.50, 3.00, 3.50 yd.
Swiss tambour sash curtain muslins, 30 inches wide, 15c, 18c, 20c and 25c yd.
Frilled curtain muslins, with spot pattern (small and medium), 30 inches wide, 20c, 25c yd.
Nottingham lace curtain nets, white or ecru, 30 and 36 inches wide, 10c, 13c, 15c yd; 45 inches wide, 20c, 25c yd; 50 inches wide, 20c, 25c, 30c, 40c yd.

White Curtain Muslins.

White figured and spot curtain muslins, small, medium and large spots, and a variety of new figured patterns, 36 inches wide, 12½c, 15c yd.
White coin spot muslins, 45 inches wide, in small, medium and large spots, 18c, 20c, 22c yd.
White figured curtain muslins, 45 inches wide, a variety of new patterns, 25c yd.
White curtain muslins, with colored coin spots, 45 inches wide, 20c yd.

White Muslins.

Frilled on both sides, in coin spots, stripes and fancy patterns, 48 inches wide, 35c, 40c yd; frilled on one side, 25c, 35c yd.

Madras Curtain Muslins.

Figured cream Madras curtain muslin, 27 inches wide, 15c yd.
Figured Madras curtain muslin, 45 inches wide, cream, 22c, 25c yd.
Figured Madras curtain muslin, 54 inches wide, white, 40c, 45c yd.

Scrims.

36-inch fancy stripe curtain scrim, cream only, in assorted patterns, 5c, 8c yd; white, 5c, 10c yd.
40-inch fancy scrim, cream, 10c, 13c yd.

Plain Scrims.

38-inch plain scrim, cream, 12½c yd.
42-inch plain cream scrim, 20c yd.

Art Drapery Muslins.

Figured art drapery muslin, a large assortment of new patterns and colors, 30 inches wide, 6c, 8c yd; 36 inches wide, 10c, 12½c, 15c yd.
Figured art silkaline, 36 inches wide, a large assortment of new floral patterns and colors, 12½c, 15c yd.
Bordered art muslin, 45 inches wide, 12½c yd; 50 inches wide, 15c yd.

Japanese Crepe Cloths.

Japanese gold-figured crepe cloth, 25 inches wide, a large variety of patterns and colors, 10c yd; 30 inches, 12½c yd.

Art Drapery Silks.

A large variety of the latest designs and colors in China and Florentine drapery silks, figured, 32 inches wide, 65c, 85c yd.

Furniture Cords and Gimps.

Silk cord, 4c, 7c yd; 45c and $1.00 a piece of 18 yds.

Furniture Gimps.

Cotton, 1c yd, or $1.20 gross.
Silk, 2c yd, or $2.20 gross.
" 3c yd, or $4.00 "
" 5c yd, or $6.50 "
Heavy cotton cord for edging curtains and cushions, assorted colors, 12½c yd.
Silk cord, assorted colors, 20c yd.

Webbing.

Furniture webbing, 2½-inch, 2½c yd; $1.25 a piece about 65 yds.

Cretonnes, Denims, Sateens, etc.

Our collection of the above goods for this season includes the best qualities and the newest and most handsome patterns of English and American manufacture, the color combinations being simply perfect from the cheapest to the most expensive. To insure satisfaction when ordering, please specify as nearly as possible the colors required. The following ground colors make up some of our stock: Crimson, maroon, olive, fawn, terra cotta, black, blue, electric and myrtle, with rich combinations of other colors combined.
English twilled cretonnes, 27 in. wide, 6c; 29 in. wide, 8c; 30 in. wide, 10c, 12½c, 15c yd.
Extra heavy crepe cretonnes, 30 in., 12½c, 15c; 30 in., 18c, 20c yd.
Extra heavy English cretonnes, soft finish, in combinations, 30 in. wide, 10c, 12½c, 15c, 20c yd.
Heavy English reversible crepe-finished cretonnes, 30 in. wide, 15c, 20c yd.

Bordered and Reversible Cretonnes, Suitable for Curtains, etc.

Double-fold reversible cretonnes, colors same as single width, with pretty combination borders—
40 inches wide, 15c, 18c yd.
42 " " 20c, 25c "
44 " " 25c, 30c "
48 " " 25c, 30c, 35c yd.
52 " " 35c, 40c yd.
Special heavy American art cretonne, in the very newest designs, soft pure finish, rich combination of colors, suitable for draperies, furniture covering, etc., 36 in. wide, 20c yd.

Art Denims.

Heavy plain colored denims, in light and dark blue, myrtle, moss, yellow, terra cotta, red, 36 in. wide, 25c yd.
Genuine printed American denims, in the above colored grounds, in the very newest designs and combinations of colors for this season, used largely for cushions, table covers, curtains, furniture and floor coverings, 36 inches wide, 35c yd.

Villa Cloth.

Villa cloth, self-colors, 36 inches wide, suitable for cushions or drapery purposes; colors garnet, rose, blue, orange, crimson, moss green, 20c yd.
Art ticking, self-colors, twilled, soft finish; colors gold, Nile, slate, fawn, pea-green; 36 inches wide, 30c yd.
Art ticking, floral designs, light grounds, 36 inches wide, in a full range of new colors and patterns, 30c yd.

Art Sateens.

Figured art sateens, English, French and American manufacture. The following colors will be a guide of what we carry in stock in all qualities: crimson, maroon, olive, fawn, blue, electric, Nile, myrtle, rose, pink, terra cotta and black, with rich combinations of other colors.

30 inches wide, 12½c, 15c, 20c, 25c yd.

Fine English art sateen, 31 inches wide, beautiful rich soft finish, choice designs, 25c, 30c, 35c, 40c yd.

Turkey Chintz.

Chintz, Turkey red, used principally for comforter covering, in a big range of all new and well selected patterns, 10c, 12½c, 15c yd.
Special Turkey chintz, 36 inches wide, in a range of new designs, fast colors, 12½c yd.

FLAGS.

BRITISH ENSIGN.

Length.	Width.		Price.
1 ft. 6 in. x	0 ft. 9 in......	each	$0.40
2 ft. 3 in. x	1 ft. 1 in......	"	0.50
2 ft. 6 in. x	1 ft. 3 in......	"	0.60
3 ft. 0 in. x	1 ft. 6 in......	"	0.75
3 ft. 6 in. x	1 ft. 9 in	"	1.00
3 ft. 0 in. x	2 ft. 0 in	"	1.15
4 ft. 6 in. x	2 ft. 3 in	"	1.25
5 ft. 0 in. x	2 ft. 6 in	"	1.50
6 ft. 0 in. x	3 ft. 0 in......	"	2.00
7 ft. 6 in. x	3 ft. 9 in......	"	2.75
9 ft. 0 in. x	4 ft. 6 in......	"	3.50
10 ft. 6 in. x	5 ft. 3 in......	"	4.25
12 ft. 0 in. x	6 ft. 0 in......	"	5.00
13 ft. 6 in. x	6 ft. 9 in......	"	6.75
15 ft. 0 in. x	7 ft. 6 in	"	8 50
18 ft. 0 in. x	9 ft. 0 in......	"	12.50
21 ft. 0 in. x	10 ft. 6 in......	"	15.00
24 ft. 0 in. x	12 ft. 0 in......	"	17.50

(British Ensigns made of Wool Bunting.)

UNION JACK.

Length.	Width.		Price.
1 ft. 6 in. x	0 ft. 9 in......	each	$0.40
2 ft. 3 in. x	1 ft. 1 in......	"	0.50
2 ft. 6 in. x	1 ft. 3 in......	"	0.60
3 ft. 0 in. x	1 ft. 6 in......	"	0.75
3 ft. 6 in. x	1 ft. 9 in......	"	1.00
4 ft. 0 in. x	2 ft. 0 in......	"	1.15
4 ft. 6 in. x	2 ft. 3 in......	"	1.25
5 ft. 0 in. x	2 ft. 6 in......	"	1.50
6 ft. 0 in. x	3 ft. 0 in......	"	2.00
7 ft. 6 in. x	3 ft. 9 in......	"	3.00
9 ft. 0 in. x	4 ft. 6 in......	"	4.00
10 ft. 6 in. x	5 ft. 3 in......	"	5.50
12 ft. 0 in. x	6 ft. 0 in......	"	7.50
13 ft. 6 in. x	6 ft. 9 in......	"	9.00
15 ft. 0 in. x	7 ft. 6 in......	"	10.50
18 ft. 0 in. x	9 ft. 0 in......	"	14.00
21 ft. 0 in. x	10 ft. 6 in......	"	17.50
24 ft. 0 in. x	12 ft. 0 in......	"	21.00

(Union Jacks made of Wool Bunting.)

CANADIAN FLAG.

Length.	Width.		Price.
3 ft. 0 in. x	1 ft. 6 in......	each	$1.50
4 ft. 6 in. x	2 ft. 3 in......	"	2.50
6 ft. 0 in. x	3 ft. 0 in......	"	3.00
7 ft. 6 in. x	3 ft. 9 in......	"	4.00
9 ft. 0 in. x	4 ft. 6 in......	"	5.00
10 ft. 6 in. x	5 ft. 3 in......	"	6.00
12 ft. 0 in. x	6 ft. 0 in......	"	7.50
13 ft. 6 in. x	6 ft. 9 in......	"	9.50
15 ft. 0 in. x	7 ft. 6 in......	"	11.00
18 ft. 0 in. x	9 ft. 0 in......	"	14.75
21 ft. 0 in. x	10 ft. 6 in......	"	18.00
24 ft. 0 in. x	12 ft. 0 in......	"	22.00

(Canadian Flags made of Wool Bunting.)

Cotton Flags.

(Mounted on sticks.)

Canadian Ensigns and Union Jacks—

Sizes					
Sizes 3 x 2	inches,	$0.06	a doz.,	½c	ea.
" 6 x 4	"	0.12	"	1c	"
" 8 x 6	"	0.20	"	2c	"
" 12 x 8	"	0.35	"	3c	"
" 20 x 15	"	0.75	"	7c	"
" 24 x 18	"	1.00	"	10c	"
" 28 x 20	"	1.65	"	15c	"
" 36 x 21	"	2.00	"	20c	"

Soft Finish Cotton Flags.

Union Jack (Unmounted)—

Sizes					
Sizes 14 x 10	inches,	$0.40	a doz.,	4c	ea.
" 17 x 15	"	0.60	"	6c	"
" 20 x 13	"	0.70	"	7c	"
" 29 x 16	"	1.00	"	10c	"
" 27 x 25	"	1.25	"	12½c	"
" 35 x 23	"	1.50	"	15c	"
" 50 x 36	"	3.25	"	30c	"
" 72 x 40	"	7.00	"	65c	"
" 72 x 50	"	8.00	"	75c	"
" 90 x 70	"	19.00	"	$1.75	"

Canadian Ensigns (Unmounted)—

Sizes					
Sizes 13 x 9	inches,	$0.35	a doz.,	3c	ea.
" 29 x 16	"	1.00	"	10c	"
" 35 x 22	"	1.50	"	15c	"

Silk Flags.

UNION JACKS, BRITISH ENSIGNS, CANADIAN AND AMERICAN (SILK.)

Size.	Each.	Size.	Each.
3 x 2 in..	$0.02	18 x 18 in..	$0.55
6 x 4 in..	0.04	20 x 20 in..	0.65
8½ x 6 in..	0.08	24 x 24 in..	0.75
12 x 8 in..	0.12½	36 x 23 in..	0.85
16 x 10½ in..	0.20	32 x 48 in..	1.25
18 x 12 in..	0.25	60 x 35 in..	2.00
23 x 16 in..	0.35		

ROYAL STANDARD.

20 x 20 in..$0.85   24 x 24 in..$0.95

SCOTCH AND IRISH.

6 x 4 in..	$0.04	18 x 12 in..	$0.25
12 x 8 in..	0.12½	36 x 23 in..	0.85

For other sizes in Bunting, Silk, and Cotton Flags, ask for prices.
Wool Bunting, 18 inches wide, in red, white or blue, 20c yd.

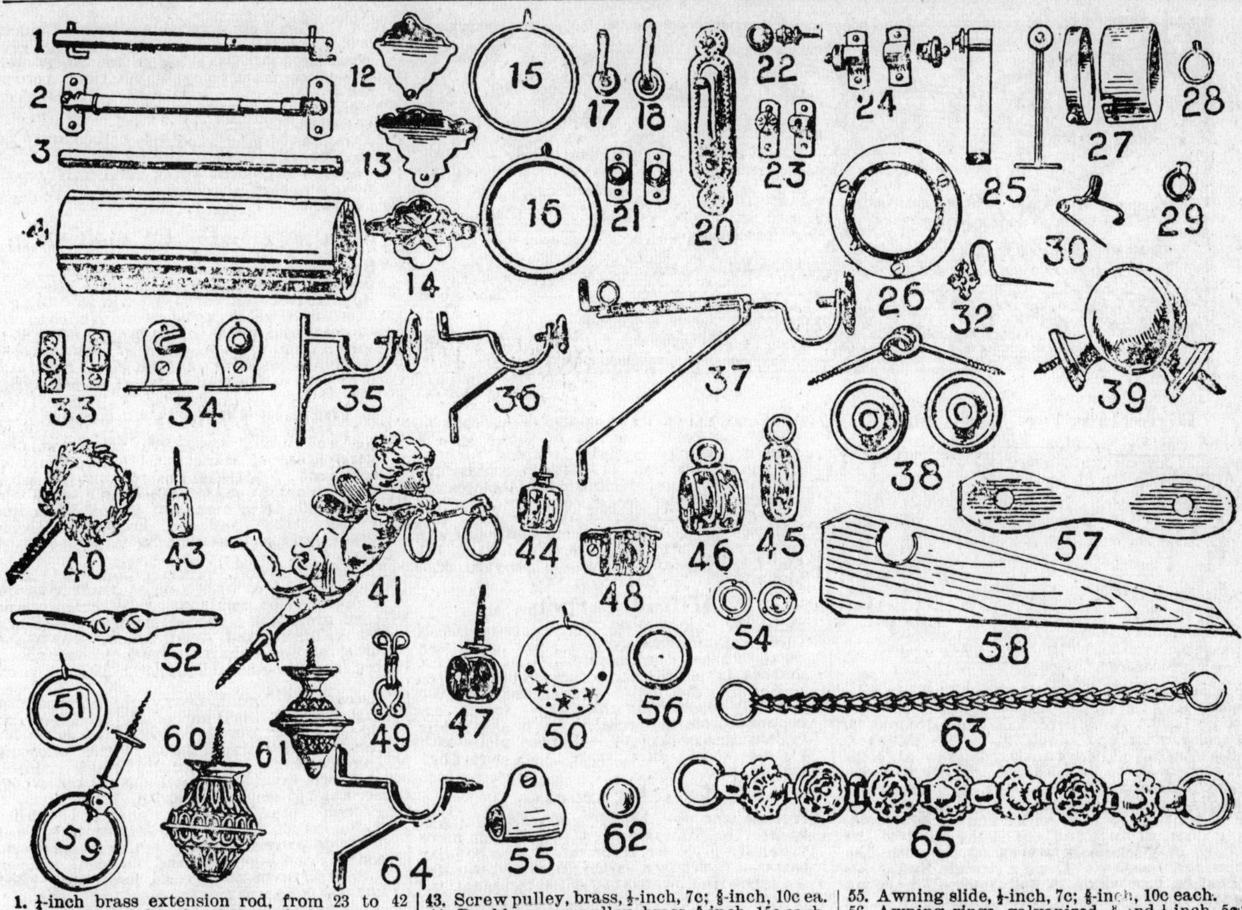

1. ½-inch brass extension rod, from 23 to 42 inches, with brackets, 10c each.
2. 5/16-inch extension rod, 14 to 24 inches, with brackets, 12c; 24 to 44-inch, 15c each.
3. ¼-inch brass rod, 4c ft.
4. ⅜-inch brass rod, 6c ft.
5. 5/16-inch brass-cased tubing, 7c ft.
6. ⅜-inch " " 8c ft.
7. ½-inch " " 10c ft.
8. ¾-inch " " 13c ft.
9. 1-inch " " 20c ft.
10. 1½-inch brass tubing, 25c ft.
11. 2-inch " 35c ft.
12. Brass or nickel stair plates, 12½c doz.
13. " " " 15c doz.
14. " " " 20c doz.
15. American pole rings, 1½-inch, 12c; 2-in, 18c doz.
16. English pole rings, ½-inch, 12c; ¾-inch, 13c; 1-in., 15c; 1¼-in., 18c; 1¾-in., 20c; 2¼-in., 30c doz.
17. Tassel hooks, 3c pair.
18. " 5c pair.
19. " 10c pair.
20. " 12c pair.
21. Vestibule sockets, ¼-inch, 3c; ⅜-inch, 5c pair.
22. Vestibule sockets, ¼-inch, 8c; ⅜-inch 10c; ½-inch, 15c pair.
23. Vestibule brackets, ¼-inch, 5c; ⅜-inch, 7c pr.
24. Vestibule brackets, ¼-inch, 7c; ⅜-inch, 10c; ½-inch, 15c pair.
25. Extension vestibule brackets, ¼ and ⅜-inch, 15c pair.
26. Pole sockets, 1½-inch, 7c; 2-inch, 10c pair.
27. Pole sockets, ¾-inch, 12c; 1-inch, 13c; 1½-inch, 15c; 2-inch, 25c pair.
28. Vestibule rings, ⅜-inch, 5c; ½-inch, 8c doz.
29. Vestibule rings, ⅜-inch, 8c; ½-inch, 10c doz.
30. Drapery pins, 3c doz, 25c gross.
31. Drapery pins, solid brass, 4c doz, 35c gross.
32. Gordon drapery pins, 12½c doz.
33. Roller brackets for inside shades, 3c pair.
34. Roller brackets, 3c pair.
35. Pole brackets, English brass, ¾ and 1-inch, 12c; 1½-inch, 15c; 2-inch, 18c pair.
36. Pole brackets, American brass, 1 and 1½-inch, 12c; 2-inch, 15c pair.
37. Pole extension brackets, 1-inch, extends from 4 to 7 inches, 18c; 1½ and 2-inch, from 4 to 7 in., 18c; 1½ and 2-inch, from 7 to 12 in., 25c pr.
38. Pole joints (2 links and 4 caps), 1½-inch, 15c; 2-inch, 20c pair.
39. Pole joints, 1½-inch, 30c; 2-inch, 40c pair.
40. Drapery ornament (wreath), 15c each.
41. " " (cupid), $2.00, 2.50, 3.50, 4.00, 5.50 each.
43. Screw pulley, brass, ½-inch, 7c; ⅝-inch, 10c ea.
44. Double screw pulley, brass, ⅝-inch, 15c each.
45. Swivel awning pulley, galvanized, ¾-inch, 4c; 1-inch, 5c each.
46. Double swivel awning pulley, galvanized, 1-inch, 5c; 1½-inch, 8c each.
47. Screw stop pulley, ¾-inch, 5c each.
48. Corner stop pulley, ¾-inch, 5c each.
49. Tent hook and eye, galvanized, 15c doz.
50. Crescent shade pull, 1c each.
51. Ring shade pulls, 1c, 2c, 5c each.
52. Line cleat, 4½-inch, 5c; 8-inch, 8c each.
54. Grommets (tent), 3c, 4c, 5c, 15c doz.
55. Awning slide, ½-inch, 7c; ⅝-inch, 10c each.
56. Awning rings, galvanized, ⅜ and ½-inch, 5c; 1-inch, 7c doz.
57. Toggles, for guy ropes, 20c doz.
58. Tent pins, 10-inch, 20c; 15-inch, 25c doz.
59. Brass drapery ring, extends 6 inches, with 6 inch ring, $1.00 each.
60. Brass pole end, 1½-inch, 10c pair.
61. Brass pole end, 1-inch, 13c pair.
62. Drugget pin, ⅝-inch, 10c; ¾-inch, 12c doz.
63. Curtain chains, 12c pair.
64. Pole bracket, 1½-inch, 5c pair.
65. Curtain chains, 25c pair.

Send for Descriptive PRICE LIST, showing different styles of Tents, Flags and Awnings.

WALL TENT.

Length and width.	Height.	Height of wall.	Prices without poles and pins. 8 oz. Ducks.	10 oz. Ducks.	12 oz. Ducks.	Poles and pins extra.	Length and width.	Height.	Height of wall.	Prices without poles and pins. 8 oz. Ducks	10 oz. Ducks	12 oz. Ducks	Poles and pins extra.
7x 7 ft.	7 ft.	2 ft.	$6.25	$7.25	$8.50	$1.25	12x12 ft.	9 ft.	3½ ft.	$15.50	$18.50	$21.50	$2.00
7x 9½ "	7 "	2 "	7.25	8.25	10.00	1.35	12x14 "	9 "	3½ "	17.00	19.00	23.00	2.25
8x12 "	7½ "	3 "	10.50	11.50	13.50	1.75	12x16 "	9 "	3½ "	19.00	21.00	25.50	2.25
9x12 "	8 "	3 "	11.00	12.00	15.00	1.75	14x14 "	10 "	4 "	20.50	22.50	27.50	2.25
10x12 "	8 "	3 "	12.00	13.75	16.50	1.75	14x16 "	10 "	4 "	22.00	24.50	30.00	2.50
10x14 "	9 "	3 "	14.00	16.00	19.50	2.00							

If higher walls are required add 5 per cent. for each additional 6 inches.

Directions for Measuring.

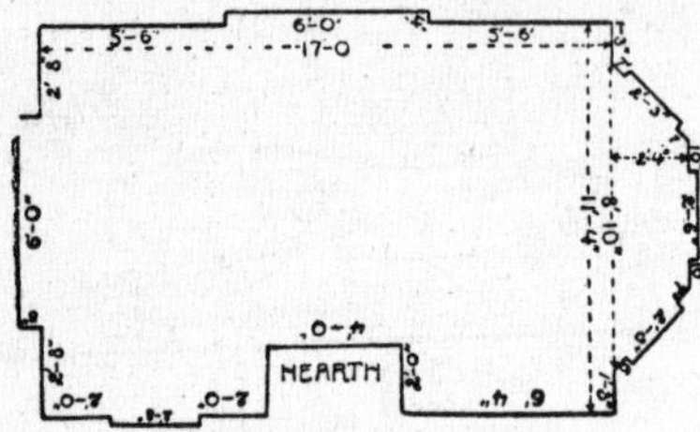

You cannot be too particular in taking measurements for carpets, especially so if they are to be bordered, as bordered carpets cannot be turned under, and should fit exact. (Make no allowances.) Always draw a diagram of rooms if carpets are to be bordered. It is not necessary to draw to a scale. Give all measures on all lines exact to $\frac{1}{2}$ inch, al-o the total length and width of room in centre and through folding doors (if any), and see if the total of the short or broken measures agree with the through measures. Draw a straight line across jogs and bay windows, and you will have an accurate base to work from. Locate all doors and jogs and give the depth of each, so we can sew on carpet or filling for same if desired; also designate front of rooms and state which way you wish breadths to run. When the room is of such a size as to require a fraction of a breadth (in addition to the full breadths used) we will be obliged to piece it in one or two places, unless you are willing to pay for a full breadth. In such cases state same on your order, and we will send balance of the breadth with the carpet. If for several connecting rooms, make a plan of same all on one sheet. By being careful in taking measures and seeing that they prove before sending in the order, you will perhaps save the delay of our sending back the plan for remeasurements, as we will not cut the carpets unless the measures prove correct.

In measuring circular or winding stairs, always measure on wall or long side.

NOTE.—When ordering carpets not estimated on by us, allow at least one yard extra for waste in matching pattern on each room. If carpet can be cut with less waste, money will be refunded. Delay in despatch will be avoided by carefully carrying out above instructions.

Carpet Sample Department.

Samples showing qualities and colors of any line of goods in this department, with the exception of rugs, squares and crumbcloths, will be cheerfully sent upon application. As these samples are valuable to us, we would ask that they be returned after inspection. Mark the pattern you select on pin ticket attached, and give number of same on order sheet to prevent any misunderstanding.

Prices for Sewing Carpets.

Sewing all carpets, 3c yard, with an additional charge of 5c for each mitre on bordered carpets.

Axminster Carpets.

English Axminster carpets. Our range of these strictly high-grade carpets for this season excels by far any of our previous efforts. Everything that is newest and most artistic in design from the looms of the most noted makers in England are represented, beautiful conventional and geometrical designs in dainty self-colored effects of blues, greens, rose or chintz, specially adapted for fine drawing, reception or sitting rooms and the rich Oriental designs with the heavier coloring of reds, greens, blues, etc., for the dining-room, library, smoking room, den, hall or stairs, with $\frac{5}{8}$ borders and $\frac{3}{4}$ stairs to match, splendid values, per yard, $1.25, 1.50 and 2.00. 4/4 stairs to match, per yard, $2.50 and 3.50.

Wilton Carpets.

English Wilton carpets—our importations of these well-known floor coverings have been on an unusually large scale, all that is newest and best in designs and color combinations to be found in the British markets are here. We specially recommend this carpet for its exceptional wearing quality for banks, public halls, offices or private residences, made with $\frac{5}{8}$ border and $\frac{3}{4}$ stair to match, per yard, $1.25 1.50 and 2.00.

Velvet Carpets.

For those who wish the rich effect of the Axminster or Wilton carpet at a much more moderate price we recommend this popular carpet. We show a large range of beautiful designs with all the latest color combinations of greens, blues, terra cotta, crimson, fawn and ecru shades with $\frac{5}{8}$ borders and $\frac{3}{4}$ stairs to match, great values, per yard, $1.00 and 1.15.

English Brussels.

English Brussels carpets. We desire to draw special attention to our range of these popular carpets, as the greatest of care has been paid to their selection; it contains the best that time, money or long experience could buy from the leading English makers, the designs being especially handsome with all the latest color combinations, suitable for any room or hall, with $\frac{5}{8}$ borders and $\frac{3}{4}$ stairs to match, exceptional values, per yard, 75c, 90c, $1.00, 1.15 and 1.25.

Tapestry Carpets.

Our importation of these goods for this season is particularly attractive, special attention having been paid to their selection, which show a marked improvement in style, finish and general effect, which represents the production of the leading British manufacturers, especially in the three best grades which for effective design and color combinations equals the best Brussels, with $\frac{5}{8}$ border and $\frac{3}{4}$ stair to match, 55c, 65c, 80c per yard.

Cheaper grades of tapestry carpet, 30c, 35c, 40c, 45c, 50c per yard.

Mottled tapestry carpets at 25c per yard.

Tapestry Stair Carpets.

27-inch, 35c, 40c, 45c, 50c, 55c, 65c, 80c yard.
22 " 30c, 35c, 40c, 50c yard.
18 " 25c, 30c, 35c yard.

Information, estimates and quality samples sent on application.

Ingrain Carpets—All Wool.

Our stock of reversible ingrain carpets contains a full range of the best English and domestic made goods, in beautiful designs and color combinations, suitable for sitting rooms, bedrooms or halls, and shrewd buyers tell us that nowhere else can they find the same great values.

"Victorian" brand, best 3-ply reversible all-wool carpets, full 36 inches wide, a splendid range of choice patterns with the newest colorings of olive green, sage, terra cotta, crimson, fawn and ecru, per yard, $1.00.

Best English 2-ply reversible all-wool, 36 inches wide, specially recommended for its great wearing qualities, a big range of new up-to-date designs and color combinations at 85c per yard.

"Venice" brand best Canadian 2-ply all-wool carpets at 75c per yard.

"Trafalgar" brand, superfine 2-ply all-wool carpet, 36 inches wide, a large assortment of new designs and colorings of maroon, olive, brown, fawn and ecru shades, excellent value at 65c per yard.

Ingrain Carpets—All-wool Filling.

"Brunswick" brand, a cotton warp, best wool filled carpet, made 36 inches wide, the finest imported Scotch yarns used in the filling of this carpet, which can be recommended to hold its color and wear well, a large and well assorted range of choice patterns with new color combinations of green and ecru, fawn and brown, blue and white, etc., at 55c per yard.

Ingrain Carpets—"Union."

"Nassau" brand, best extra super union reversible carpet, 36 inches wide, a splendid assortment of artistic designs, in the latest color combinations of green and terra, maroon and ecru, ecru and green, fawn and brown, green and red, brown and wood shades, an excellent wearing carpet, per yard, 45c.

Omdurman brand, super union carpets, 36 inches wide, a large range of effective designs, in color combinations of crimson and ecru, green and ecru, red and green, fawn and black, brown and wood, black, brown and blue, maroon and ecru, a splendid floor covering for bedrooms and upper halls, per yard, 40c.

"Kitchener" brand, heavy union carpet, 36 inches wide; this is one of our most popular lines; we carry in these goods an extensive range of attractive designs in the following color combinations, sage and brown, crimson and ecru, fawn and green, brown and wood, ecru and green, per yard, 30c.

"French" brand, special line, good quality union carpet, 36 inches wide, a large range of up-to-date designs, in colors of sage and green, maroon and sage, ecru and maroon, crimson and red, fawn and green, fawn and wood shades, per yard, 25c.

Also a complete range of church carpets. Samples sent on application.

Hemp Carpets.

Fancy stripes, 32-inch, 10c; 33-inch, $12\frac{1}{2}$c; 34-inch, 15c; 35-inch, 18c yard.

Heavy fancy stripes, $35\frac{1}{2}$-inch, 20c, 25c; 54-inch, 38c; 72-inch, 50c yard.

Fancy floral designs, reversible patterns, 33-inch, 15c; $35\frac{1}{2}$-inch, 20c; 36-inch, 25c; 54-inch, 38c; 72-inch, 50c yard.

Hemp Stair Carpets.

Fancy stripe, 18-inch, 8c, 10c, 15c; 22-inch, $12\frac{1}{2}$c, 15c, 20c yard.

China and Japanese Mattings.

China and Japanese mattings in great variety, in plain white and fancy checks, inlaid designs and fancy colored and damask patterns. These goods are in great demand for bedrooms, dining-rooms and upper halls, being neat in appearance and more durable than carpet at the same price.

China mattings, jointed every two yards at back, in fancy check patterns, 36 inches wide, 10c, $12\frac{1}{2}$c yard.

Jointless China mattings, in plain white and fancy checks, 15c, 20c, 25c yard.

Damask patterns, extra heavy, jointless and reversible, 30c yard.

Japanese cotton warp mattings, jointless and reversible, inlaid and fancy carpet and other patterns, 15c, 20c, 25c, 30c, 40c yard

Cocoa Mattings.

Natural color in all the standard widths.

No. 5. 18-inch, 22½c; 27-inch, 35c; 36-inch, 42½c yard.

No. 9. 18-inch, 27½c; 27-inch, 42½c; 36-inch, 52½c yard.

No. A. Calcutta hard twist, 18-inch, 35c; 27-inch, 52½c; 36-inch, 65c yard.

Wider widths, up to 72 inches, made to order in quantities of not less than 20 yards, at proportionate prices.

String Mattings.

Heavy string mattings, fancy patterns, 36 inches wide, 25c, 35c yard.

Extra heavy quality, plain, 27-inch, 25c; 36-inch, 35c yard.

Plain centre, with fancy border, or in fancy check patterns, 18-inch, 18c; 22-inch, 23c; 27-inch, 27c; 36-inch, 35c yard.

Zinc and Rubber Matting Ends.

Zinc ends for cocoa and other mattings, with copper rivets to fasten, 18-inch, 13c; 27-inch, 18c; 36-inch, 25c each.

Knapp's patent rubber binding, 2 inches wide, for cocoa and other mattings, in 18-inch, 27-inch, 36-inch, 54-inch, 72-inch lengths, 20c foot.

4-inch heavy webbing, for binding mattings, 4c yard.

Stair Pads, Carpet Lining and Felt Paper.

Best quality novelty stair pads, for 36-inch carpet, $1.50 doz; for 27-inch carpet, $1.00 doz; for 22-inch carpet, 90c doz.

Best underlaid felt carpet lining, taped both sides, 36 inches wide, 7c per yard.

Superior carpet lining, 5c yard.

Standard carpet lining, 4c yard.

Felt paper (16 ozs. to yard), 3c yard.

Linoleums and Floor Oilcloths.

Inlaid linoleums, 2 yards wide, is specially recommended for any place where there is hard wear, such as public offices, banks, dining-rooms or hall, owing to the colors going right through to the canvas, making it give almost endless wear; a complete, range of new floral, blocks, tile and parquetry designs from the most celebrated makers in the world, Stains, Greenwich, Deutsche, Barry, Ostlere and others, best qualities, $1.10, 1.25, 1.35 square yard.

No. 2 quality inlaid linoleum, in similar designs, 90c square yard.

Printed linoleums, 2 and 4 yards wide, best English and Scotch makes, floral, blocks and inlaid effects, patterns painted over hard cork composition, suitable for kitchens, dining-rooms, lower halls, bathrooms, etc., 50c, 60c square yard.

Linoleums, 2 yards wide only, floral, block and inlaid designs, 35c, 40c, 45c square yard.

Plain Brown Linoleums.

2 and 4 yards wide.

No. 1 quality, 90c square yard; 6-inch border to match (key pattern), 25c lineal yard; 9-inch border to match (key pattern), 35c lineal yard.

No. 2 quality, 75c square yard; 6-inch key border, 20c lineal yard; 9-inch key border to match, 30c lineal yard.

No. 3 quality, 55c per square yard; 6-inch key border to match, 15c lineal yard; 9-inch key border to match, 25c lineal yard.

Plain Cork Carpet.

A thicker form of linoleum, suitable for nurseries, school rooms, offices, public buildings, or any place where it is desirable to lessen noise; 2-yard widths only.

No. 1 quality, $1.00 square yard; 9-inch key border to match, 35c lineal yard.

No. 2 quality, cork carpet, 75c square yard; 9-inch key border to match, 25c lineal yard.

No. 3 quality cork carpet, 65c square yard.

Passage and stair linoleums, key borders and plain centres, 18-inch, 20c, 25c; 22-inch, 25c, 32c; 27-inch, 30c, 38c; 36-inch, 40c, 50c yard.

Stair Linoleums.

Best quality stair linoleum, made very pliable to bend over steps, plain centre with scroll border, 18-inch, 50c; 22-inch, 60c; 27-inch, 70c; 36-inch, $1.00; 45-inch, $1.25 yard.

Floor Oilcloths.

Our large range of patterns in these goods excels anything we have ever shown before.

	36-in.	45-in.	54-in.	72-in.	90-in.	
No. 1.	40c,	50c,	60c,	80c,	$1.00	yard.
" 2.	30c,	38c,	45c,	60c,	75c	"
" 3.	25c,	32c,	38c,	50c,	..	"

Floor oilcloth, 3 and 4 yards wide, 45c and 55c square yard.

Passage and stair oilcloths, floral and small neat patterns, with fancy borders, 18-inch, 11c and 16c yard; 22-inch, 13c, 19c yard; 27-inch, 16c, 24c yard.

Oilcloth mats, bordered, light and medium colors—

Size,	36 x 36 inches,	40c each.
"	36 x 54 "	60c "
"	45 x 45 "	65c "
"	54 x 54 "	90c "
"	54 x 72 "	$1.20 "
"	72 x 72 "	1.60 "
"	72 x 90 "	2.00 "
"	90 x 90 "	2.50 "

Brass and Zinc Oilcloth Bindings.

Zinc binding, including corners and nails, 4 yds, 12½c; 5 yds, 15c; 6 yds, 20c; 8 yds, 25c.

Brass binding, 4 yards, 20c; 5 yards, 25c; 6 yards, 30c; 8 yards, 40c.

Corrugated rubber stair treads, for hotels and public buildings, cut any size to order. Write for samples and estimates.

Corrugated rubber matting, 36 inches wide, ¼ inch thick, $2.00 yard.

NOTE.—Estimates and samples of Linoleums and Oilcloths sent on application.

Carpet Squares and Rugs.

Every season finds these goods more popular and in greater demand, especially when used with hardwood floors or fancy parquetry borders; they make a very artistic and sanitary floor covering. Our stock was never so complete in all lines as it is this season. Cuts showing designs and color combinations of Axminster rugs sent on application.

Axminster carpet squares, best quality, woven all in one piece, with 18-inch border, made from the finest English worsted yarns, a splendid range of handsome Oriental, medallion and floral designs, with exquisite color combinations of green, blue, rose, crimson and chintz shades, suitable for drawing-rooms, dining-rooms, libraries, reception rooms or dens, in the following sizes, always kept in stock—

Size	6 ft. 6 inches	x	9 ft. 8 inches,	$20.00 each.
"	7 " 6 "	x	10 " 3 "	25.00 "
"	8 " 3 "	x	11 " 6 "	30.00 "
"	8 " 8 "	x	10 " 10 "	30.00 "
"	9 " 10 "	x	13 " 1 "	40.00 "
"	10 " 11 "	x	14 " 3 "	50.00 "

Axminster rugs, in a special quality, made from a softer yarn, but an excellent wearing carpet, artistic designs and color combinations, in the following sizes—

Size	9 ft. 0 inches	x	12 ft. 0 inches,	$35.00 each.
"	10 " 6 "	x	13 " 6 "	47.50 "
"	12 " 0 "	x	15 " 0 "	55.00 "

Axminster rugs, second quality, a well assorted range of the newest designs and color combinations—

Size	6 ft. 6 inches	x	9 ft. 8 inches,	$13.50 each.
"	7 " 6 "	x	10 " 3 "	16.75 "
"	8 " 3 "	x	11 " 6 "	20.00 "
"	8 " 8 "	x	10 " 10 "	20.00 "
"	9 " 0 "	x	12 " 0 "	25.00 "
"	9 " 10 "	x	13 " 1 "	27.50 "
"	10 " 11 "	x	14 " 3 "	35.00 "

When writing for cuts of these rugs please state size wanted.

English Wilton Carpet Squares.

These squares are made in a special heavy quality, with 22-inch interwoven borders, a large assortment of beautiful designs, in the leading color combinations of crimson, greens, blues, browns and oak shades—

Size	9 ft. 0 inches	x	10 ft. 6 inches,	$19.00 each.
"	9 " 0 "	x	12 " 0 "	22.50 "
"	11 " 3 "	x	13 " 6 "	31.00 "

Velvet Carpet Squares.

Velvet pile carpet squares, made by the famous house of John Crossley & Sons, Ltd., Halifax, all woven in one piece, with 22-inch interwoven border, a splendid range of artistic designs and color combinations from the leading designers in England—

Size	4 ft. 6 inches	x	6 ft. 6 inches,	$5.50 each.
"	5 " 3 "	x	7 " 6 "	9.00 "
"	6 " 6 "	x	9 " 8 "	13.50 "
"	7 " 5 "	x	10 " 10 "	18.00 "
"	8 " 9 "	x	11 " 0 "	23.50 "
"	9 " 7 "	x	12 " 6 "	30.00 "

Brussels Squares.

Heavy English Brussels carpet squares, with 22-inch interwoven border, recommended for their great wearing qualities, a splendid range of choice designs, with colorings of crimson, blue, brown, terra, green and oak—

Size	9 ft. 0 inches	x	10 ft. 6 inches,	$14.00 each.
"	9 " 0 "	x	12 " 0 "	16.00 "
"	11 " 3 "	x	12 " 0 "	20.00 "
"	11 " 3 "	x	13 " 6 "	22.50 "
"	11 " 3 "	x	15 " 9 "	26.25 "

Tapestry Carpet Squares.

Best quality tapestry carpet squares, with 18-inch interwoven borders, Brussels patterns and colors—

Size	3 x 3	yards,	$9.00 each.
"	3 x 3½	"	10.25 "
"	3 x 4	"	11.50 "
"	3 x 4½	"	13.00 "
"	3½ x 4	"	14.00 "
"	3½ x 4½	"	15.50 "
"	4 x 4	"	15.00 "
"	4 x 4½	"	17.50 "

Second quality tapestry carpet squares—

Size	3 x 3	yards,	$6.00 each.
"	3 x 3½	"	7.00 "
"	3 x 4	"	8.00 "
"	3½ x 3½	"	8.00 "
"	3½ x 4	"	9.50 "
"	4 x 4	"	10.75 "
"	4 x 4½	"	12.00 "
"	4 x 5	"	13.75 "

Ingrain Carpet Squares.

Best 2-ply all-wool carpet squares, "Sackville" brand, woven in one piece, with 18-inch inter-

woven border, a splendid range of good designs, including some very effective medallions, in colors of green, blue, terra-cotta, crimson, brown, fawn and ecru mixtures—

Size, 2½ x 3	yards,	$6.00 each.
" 3 x 3	"	7.25 "
" 3 x 3½	"	8.50 "
" 3 x 4	"	9.50 "
" 3½ x 4	"	11.25 "
" 4 x 5	"	16.00 "

"Brunswick" carpet squares, best all-wool filling, cotton warp, colors as fast as all-wool, specially adapted for bedroom carpets, a well-assorted range of up-to-date designs and color combinations, in the following sizes—

Size 2½ x 3	yards,	$4.50 each.
" 3 x 3	"	5.50 "
" 3 x 3½	"	6.25 "
" 3 x 4	"	7.25 "
" 3½ x 4	"	8.50 "
" 4 x 5	"	12.00 "

"Omdurman carpet squares, extra super union quality, everything that is newest and best in designs and colorings is represented in our range of these squares—

Size 2½ x 3	yards,	$3.00 each.
" 3 x 3	"	3.50 "
" 3 x 3½	"	4.25 "
" 3 x 4	"	4.75 "
" 3½ x 4	"	5.50 "
" 4 x 5	"	8.00 "

Reversible linen crumb cloths, in floral and block patterns, with appropriate borders, in two qualities, as follows:
Size in feet and inches.

Size	Black pattern on white ground	Brown pattern on white ground.
5/7 x 6/10,	$1.25 each.	$1.00 each.
5/7 x 8/7	1.50 "	1.25 "
7/ x 8/7	2.00 "	1.75 "
7/ x 10/	2.25 "	2.00 "
8/6 x 10/	2.75 "	2.50 "
8/6 x 11/6	3.25 "	3.00 "
10/ x 11/6	3.75 "	3.50 "

Door Mats.

Sheepskin mats and rugs, crimson—

Size 10 x 33	inches,	50c each.
" 12 x 35	"	75c "
" 15 x 36	"	$1.00 "
" 17 x 38	"	1.35 "
" 21 x 45	"	1.65 "

Double door sizes—

16 x 56	inches,	$2.00 each.
18 x 60	"	2.50 "
18 x 69	"	2.90 "
Hearth rug, 30 x 60	"	5.00 "

These mats can be made in white, cream, orange, green, or any other color desired, except black, at same price as crimson. Six to ten days required to fill orders for special colors and double door sizes.

Axminster door mats, fringed all round, a large assortment of choice patterns and color combinations, size 14 x 30 inches, 75c each.

Ornamental Parquet Floors and Borders.

Nothing can compare with parquetry wood-flooring for beauty, cleanliness, and utility. It is not, as many people suppose, a temporary floor covering to be laid down and taken up at pleasure, but is a permanent new floor on top of the old one. A floor so covered will last for generations, and although the initial expense may be somewhat greater than carpet, the facility with which the rooms can be cleaned and the beauty and durability of the floor more than compensate for this increase.

Field Patterns.

No. 1. Oak, maple, mahogany and dark oak, 36c square foot.
No. 2. Oak, maple and dark oak, 42c square foot.
No. 3. Light and dark oak, 35c square foot.
No. 4. Oak, maple, mahogany and dark oak, 60c square foot.
No. 5. Oak, mahogany, 25c square foot.
No. 6. Light and dark oak, 35c square foot.

Border Patterns.

No. 7. 17 inches wide, light and dark oak, 75c lineal foot.
No. 8. 12 inches wide, oak, walnut and mahogany, 65c lineal foot.
No. 9. 22 inches wide, oak, maple and rosewood, $2.00 lineal foot.
No. 10. 10 inches wide, light and dark oak, 30c lineal foot.
No. 11. 15 inches wide, oak, maple and dark oak, 60c lineal foot.
No. 12. 22 inches wide, dark oak and maple, $1.10 lineal foot.

Roll goods (sometimes called wood carpet) are stripes of white quarter-cut oak, usually 1⅜ inches wide, 5/16 inch thick, firmly glued on canvas and rolled in lengths of 4 yards by 36 inches wide, $1.20 per yd.

For price of filler wax and floor finish, see Catalogue for Paints. Catalogues showing designs of floors and borders, and estimates furnished on application.

Plain Durries and Felt for Rug Surrounds.

Plain durries, all-wool, 36 inches wide, best English make, in shades of green, terra cotta, crimson and blue, $1.00 per yd.

Plain felt, special heavy quality, 50 inches wide, in shades of old gold, green, blue, terra cotta, crimson and olive, 80c yd.

Hearth Rugs.

Best quality English Wilton or Dag-Dag rugs, made by John Crossley & Sons, Halifax, England, fine soft all-wool pile, Persian and floral designs, in very rich blending of colors—

Size 13 x 30 inches, fringed ends, $1.25 each.
" 13 x 36 " " " 1.50 "
" 18 x 36 " " " 1.90 "
" 18 x 36 " " sides, 2.25 "
" 36 x 36 " " ends 3.75 "
" 27 x 54 " " " 4.25 "
" 36 x 63 " " " 6.25 "
" 36 x 72 " " " 7.25 "

Real mohair rugs, plain effects, in crimson, robin's egg, old gold, wine and green shades—

Size 36 x 72 inches, $7.25 each.
" 27 x 64 " 5.00 "
" 18 x 54 " 3.25 "
" 15 x 32 " 1.50 "
" 12 x 30 " 1.15 "

"Toreador," extra heavy English Axminster rugs, in rich dark and medium shades—

Size 36 x 72 inches, $6.00 each.
" 24 x 36 " 2.75 "

"Excelsior" rugs, heavy English Axminster quality, light, medium and dark shades, Persian and floral designs—

Size 32 x 64 inches, $4.00 each.
" 36 x 72 " 5.00 "
" 54 x 84 " 9.00 "

Kidderminster rugs, a good English Axminster rug, with fringed ends, in light, medium or dark shades—

Size 27 x 60 inches, $2.50 each.
" 32 x 66 " 3.00 "
" 33 x 74 " 3.75 "

Reversible Smyrna rugs, Tecumseth quality, this rug has become very popular on account of its rich appearance and great durability, our range is exceptionally strong in handsome Oriental, medallion and floral effects—

16 x 32 in. door mat, fringed ends, 95c each,
21 x 45 " bureau rug fringed ends, $1.75 each.
26 x 54 " hearth rug, fringed ends, 2.00 "
30 x 60 " " " " " 2.50 "
36 x 72 " " " " " 4.00 "

Reversible Smyrna hall runners, in Oriental designs and colorings—

Size 2 ft. 6 inches x 9 ft. 0 inches, $6.00 each.
" 2 " 6 " x 12 " 0 " 8.00 "
" 3 " 0 " x 9 " 0 " 6.75 "
" 3 " 0 " x 12 " 0 " 9.00 "

Outside Door Mats.

Best English fancy cocoa mats—

Size 16 x 27 inches, $1.75 each.
" 18 x 30 " 2.25 "
" 20 x 33 " 2.75 "
" 22 x 36 " 3.25 "
" 24 x 39 " 3.75 "

Outside door mats, cocoa, plain brush, medium quality—

No. 1. Size 14 x 24 inches, 35c each.
" 2. " 16 x 27 " 45c "

Plain brush, heavy quality—

No. 1. Size 14 x 24 in., 60c; extra heavy, 75c each.
" 2. " 16 x 27 " 75c; " 90c "
" 3. " 18 x 30 " 90c; " $1.15 "
" 4. " 20 x 33 " $1.15; " 1.40 "
" 5. " 22 x 36 " 1.40; " 1.65 "
" 6. " 24 x 39 " 1.65; " 2.00 "
" 7. " 26 x 42 " 2.00; " 2.25 "

Heavy brush mat, with iron scraper—

No. 2. Size 16 x 27 inches, $1.00 each.
" 3. " 18 x 30 " 1.25 "

Brush vestibule mats, with fancy wool borders—

No. 2. Size 16 x 27 inches, $1.25 each.
" 3. " 18 x 30 " 1.50 "
" 4. " 20 x 33 " 1.75 "
" 5. " 22 x 36 " 2.00 "

Larger sizes, suitable for churches or public buildings, in heavy brush quality, made to order at 33c square foot; extra heavy quality, 40c square foot.

Rubber door mats, fancy moulded patterns—

Size 17 x 31 inches, $1.65 each.
" 18 x 36 " 2.00 "

Reversible steel wire door mats—

No. 1. Size 16½ x 24 inches, $1.25 each.
" 2. " 18 x 28 " 1.50 "
" 3. " 20 x 30 " 1.75 "
" 4. " 22 x 36 " 2.00 "

Oriental Rugs.

A beautiful range of Turkish and Persian rugs, in the following well-known makes: Oushak, Shiraz, Boukhara, Anatolian, Geundge, Kara-bagh, Kazak, and Ghurdes, both antique and modern, many of which are rare specimens of the Oriental art and used in rooms or halls laid with parquetry flooring, they are especially effective and artistic, in sizes from 2/11 x 5/3 to 12/0 x 15/2, ranging in price from $5.00 to 175.00 each.

PICTURE DEPARTMENT.

Imitation pastels, colored fruit and landscape subjects, framed in fancy color and gilt mouldings, size 11 x 14, 1-inch moulding, 25c; 16 x 20, 2-inch moulding, 50c; 20 x 24, 3-inch moulding, 75c each.

Yard pictures, size 8 x 36, colored flower and fruit subjects, framed with 1-inch white enamel and gilt, and 1-inch plain gilt mouldings, 75c each.

English colored chromos (as cut), size 20 x 28, good assortment of landscape and water scenes, framed in 3½-inch fancy gilt and colored mouldings, $1.00 each.

English strip etchings, size 12 x 22, pretty landscape scenes, framed with 1-inch oak moulding, 50c each.

Artist-signed etchings (as cut), size 17 x 26, framed with 2-inch fancy oak moulding, and steel lining, $1.00; framed with 1½-inch polished ivory moulding, 75c each.

Sepia colored etchings, choice selection of American landscape and water scenes, 3-inch Flemish brown moulding, with gilt strap inside, size 12 x 18, $1.75; 14 x 25, $2.25 each.

Photogravures, platinum and sepia colored, size 15 x 20 and 16 x 22, choice landscape, marine and figure subjects, framed with 3-inch black and wax brown Florentine frames, burnished tips and solid corners, $3.50 each.

Standard American artotypes, large assortment of figure, landscape and marine subjects, size 11 x 14, framed in 1-inch oak mouldings, 25c; 16 x 20, framed in 2-inch fancy oak moulding, with steel lining, 95c; 20 x 24, framed with 2½-inch oak moulding, with steel lining, $1.35; 22 x 28, framed in 3-inch fancy polished oak moulding, with steel lining, $2.00 each.

Steel engravings (framed as cut), marine and figure subjects, ranging in size from 20 x 24 to 24 x 30, framed with 3-inch polished oak and figured steel lining; such subjects as, The Shores of Old England; A Lady in Waiting; Grace Darling; Dawn of Love; The Reaper; Spaniel and Pheasant; $3.25 each.

Steel plate engravings (framed as cut), with 3-inch fancy grey black bog oak moulding with gold burnished tips, ranging in size from 24 x 36 to 30 x 42; selected subjects, such as, Stag at Bay; Highland Solitude; Plunge for Life; Wounded Hound; No Thoroughfare; Haying Time; There's Many a Slip; Departure and Return of Life Boat; $4.75 each.

Steel plate engravings, good selection of religious, military, marine and landscape subjects, sizes ranging from 22 x 27 to 30 x 40, framed with fancy walnut, oak and gilt mouldings, 3 and 4 inches wide, with 1-inch steel or gilt lining, $5.00, 5.50, 6.00, 7.50, 10.00 and 12.00 each.

Colored steel-plate engravings, choice and new military, figure and landscape subjects (sizes and complete description sent on application) framed to suit pictures, with heavy fancy oak and gilt Florentine mouldings, with gilt linings, $13.50, 15.00, 18.00, 20.00, 24.00 and 25.00 each.

Berlin Photochromes (colored photographs, framed as cut), size 11 x 14, mounted with dark grey, black, brown and green mats, large range of subjects, comprising points of interest and historical places in England, Ireland, Scotland and America, framed with 1½-inch fancy reeded moulding, finished in gilt, russet, black and green colors, with fancy brass corners, 95c each.

Hand-colored pastels, landscape and water scenes, size 12 x 20, fitted with gilt mats, framed with 1-inch gilt moulding and brass corners, $2.25; 14 x 17, gilt mat with oval opening, framed with 1-inch gilt moulding and brass corners, $2.75; 16 x 24, olive and grey mats, framed with 2-inch gilt moulding and brass corners, $4.50; 18 x 26, gilt mat, oval opening, framed with 2-inch burnished gilt moulding, with solid brass burnished corners, $7.50 each.

Genuine water colors, artist signed, pretty landscape and water scenes, mounted with 3-inch gilt mats, framed with 1½-inch gilt moulding with fancy brass corners, size 14 x 22, $3.50 each.

European oil paintings, size 9 x 11, choice figure and landscape subjects, framed with 3-inch high back gilt moulding, solid corners, $5.00 each.

Perry pictures and colored prints (framed as cut), in 8 inch circle frame with 4½-inch opening, finished in bone, black and brown wax, good assortment of French figures and heads, 35c each.

Aquarelle etchings (as cut), dainty colored heads and figures, framed in fancy bone black frames, square outside, with oval centre and gilt bead around the inside, size 5½ x 6½, complete with easel backs, 25c each.

Fancy table medallions, gilt frames, fancy brass corners, large assortment of figure subjects, size 6 x 8, 30c, 50c each.

Table medallions (as cut), photo colored, burnished gilt frames, neat brass corners, large assortment of subjects, size 7 x 9, 65c each.

Table medallions, size 8 x 10, plain and colored, large assortment of the newest subjects, gilt frames, with relief corners, 80c, $1.00 each.

Fancy table medallions (as cut), choice collection of head and figure subjects, handsomely colored, 1-inch gilt frame, with overlaid corners, size 11 x 14, $1.25 each.

Fancy table medallions, in a large variety of styles and subjects, sizes 10 x 13 and 11 x 14, solid brass and burnished corners, $1.75, 2.25, 2.75, 3.25 each.

Wall medallions, plain and colored, in a variety of designs, ranging in size from 13 x 17 to 16 x 20, framed with fancy gilt mouldings, projecting and overlaid corners, $2.25, 3.25, 3.50, 4.25, 5.00, 6.00, 7.50, 10.00 each.

Carbon and platinotype pictures, heads and fancy figure subjects, oval and oblong shapes, framed with black, grey and Flemish brown mouldings, $3.50, 4.00, 5.00, 7.50 each.

Genuine English carbon photographs, framed, as cut, size 14 x 17, famous subjects, such as Head of Christ, Gleaners, Angels' heads, Broken Pitcher, Rembrandt and Lorna Doone, framed in 3-inch brown wax frame, with gold burnished tips, $4.50 each.

Photos Enlarged.

No. 1204. Gold frame, Astrical design (as cut), 3 inches wide, with heavy gold burnished scroll pattern on outside edge and fancy gold burnished corners, suitable for watercolors and portraits, size 16 x 20, $3.00; 20 x 24, $3.25; 22 x 28, $3.50 each. This frame can be had in any size desired, price according to size; allow about ten days for making odd sizes.

Photos enlarged in crayon, water colors, sepia, and pastel. It takes from 6 to 10 days to enlarge photos. When ordered with other goods we will hold orders, unless otherwise instructed. All photos sent to be enlarged will be taken care of and returned with the enlargement.

Enlarged crayons, 16 x 20, $1.15; 18 x 22, $1.45; 20 x 24, $1.70; 22 x 27, $2.00 each.

Water colors, mounted on stretchers, 16 x 20, $2.00; 18 x 22, $2.50; 20 x 24, $2.75; 22 x 27, $3.00 each.

Enlargements made in sepia, same price as water colors.

Pastels, mounted on stretchers, 16 x 20, $2.75; 18 x 22, $3.25; 20 x 24, $3.75; 22 x 27, $4.25 each.

Pastels, very best finish, 16 x 20, $4.50; 18 x 22 $5.00 each.

Picture Framing

Our assortment of sample mouldings comprises the newest patterns, colors and finish. All kinds of frame moulding can be cut and mitred for any size picture ready to be put together, thus making smaller parcels and saving freight.

Four days are required for making complete frames. When ordering with other goods please state if we may hold them and ship with frames, or ship separately.

To find length of moulding required for frame, measure the four sides of picture, and allow eight times the width of moulding for waste in mitring. We do not send out samples of frame mouldings.

The following is a list of prices for frames cut and mitred any size, or put together, without glass; all of the sizes given can be shipped at once from the mouldings illustrated below:

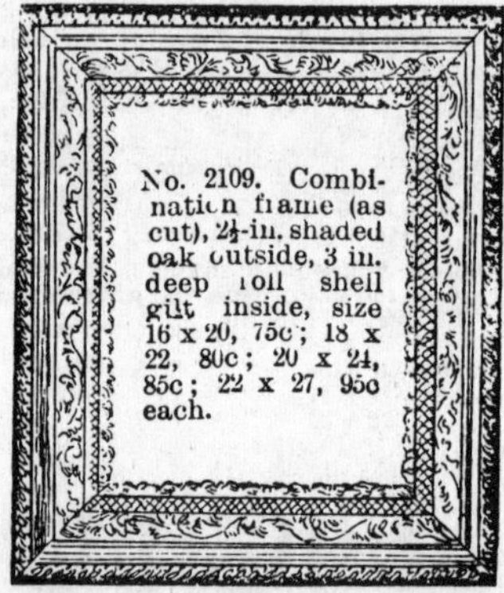

No. 2109. Combination frame (as cut), 2½-in. shaded oak outside, 3 in. deep roll shell gilt inside, size 16 x 20, 75c; 18 x 22, 80c; 20 x 24, 85c; 22 x 27, 95c each.

No. 2150. Combination frame (as cut), 5 in. wide, 2-in. green, bronze and gold outside, 3-in. deep roll shell gilt inside with 1-in. burnished line in centre, size 16 x 20, $1.20; 18 x 22, $1.30; 20 x 24, $1.40; 22 x 27, $1.50 each.

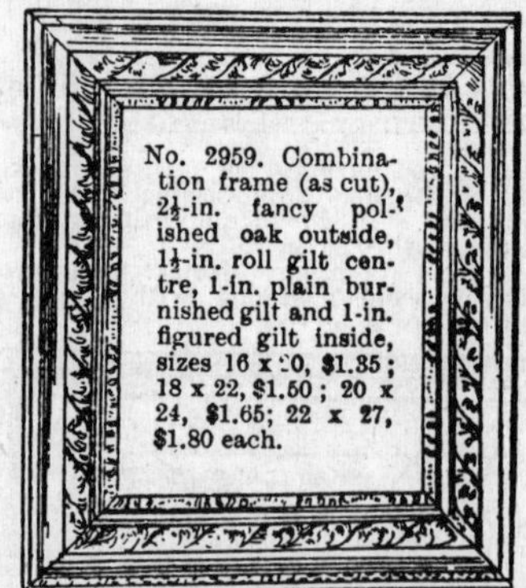

No. 2959. Combination frame (as cut), 2½-in. fancy polished oak outside, 1½-in. roll gilt centre, 1-in. plain burnished gilt and 1-in. figured gilt inside, sizes 16 x 20, $1.35; 18 x 22, $1.50; 20 x 24, $1.65; 22 x 27, $1.80 each.

All the above frames have been specially selected for enlarged portraits in crayon, water color, sepia and pastel.

Glass for above frames, 16 x 20, 15c; 18 x 22, 20c; 20 x 24, 25c; 22 x 28, 30c each.

1-inch oak, antique and plain, 3c foot; carved, 4c foot; 1½-inch, plain or shaded, 4c foot; carved, 6c foot; 2-inch, plain or shaded, 6c foot; carved, 8c foot; 2½-inch, plain or shaded, 7c foot; carved, 10c foot; 3-inch plain or shaded, 9c foot; carved, 14c foot; 4-inch, plain or shaded, 12c foot; carved, 18c foot.

Linings suitable for the same, in steel or gilt, ½-inch, 3c; ¾-inch, 4c; 1-inch, 5c foot.

Bone black and grey black mouldings, plain, 1-inch, 4½c; 1½-inch, 5c; 2-inch, 6c; 2½-inch, 7c; 3-inch, 8c foot.

Bone black and grey black mouldings, carved, with gilt ornament, 1-inch, 8c; 2-inch, 9c; 2½-inch, 12c; 3-inch, 18c foot.

Dark green mouldings, plain, ½-inch, 4c; 1-inch, 5c; 2-inch, 6c; 2½-inch, 8c; 3-inch, 9c foot.

Dark green mouldings, carved, with gilt ornament, ½-inch, 7½c; 1-inch, 10c; 2-inch, 13c; 2½-inch, 15c; 3-inch, 18c foot.

Imitation mahogany, with gilt ornament, 1-inch, 7½c; 1½-inch, 10c; 2-inch, 15c; 2½-inch, 18c foot.

Fancy colored mouldings, in gilt and white, pink, gilt and white; blue, gilt and white; green, gilt and white; and olive green and gilt, 1-inch, 5c; 1½-inch, 6c; 2-inch, 7c; 2½-inch, 8c; 3-inch, 9c; 4-inch, 11c foot.

Flat or shell gilt mouldings, 1-inch, 4c; 1½-inch, 5c; 2-inch, 6c; 2½-inch, 7c; 3-inch, 8c; 4-inch, 10c foot.

Plain gilt mouldings, with ornamented edge, suitable for oil paintings, 1½-inch, 12c; 2-inch, 15c; 2½-inch, 18c; 3-inch, 23c; 4-inch, 30c foot.

Fancy Florentine mouldings, with open-work edge, in gilt, or olive green and gilt, 1-inch, 10c; 1½-inch, 12c; 2-inch, 14c; 2½-inch, 18c; 3-inch, 25c foot.

Ebony, black and brown wax mouldings, with gold burnished tips, 1-inch, 12c; 2-inch, 15c; 2½-inch, 18c; 3-inch, 20c foot.

Unframed Pictures, Sheet Form.

Imitation pastels (colored), large selection of religious, landscape and water subjects, size 11 x 14, 5c; 16 x 20, 10c; 20 x 24, 25c each.

Standard American artotypes, figure, landscape and marine subjects, size 11 x 14, 7c; 16 x 20, 15c; 20 x 24, 25c; 22 x 28, 45c each.

English photogravures, choice heads, figures, landscape and hunting scenes, size 14 x 17, 35c; 16 x 20 to 18 x 24, $1.00; 24 x 36 to 30 x 40, $6.00 each.

Engravings, figure, landscape and marine, subjects, size 14 x 16 to 18 x 24, 75c; 22 x 28 to 24 x 30, $1.50; 24 x 32 to 30 x 40, $2.00 each.

English strip etchings, pretty landscape and water scenes, size 12 x 22, 13c; 14 x 28, 20c; 20 x 24, 50c; 20 x 30, 75c each.

English carbon pictures, copies of famous paintings, size 8 x 10, 75c; 10 x 13, $1.25; 14 x 17, $2.00 each.

Imitation platinum pictures, pretty heads, figure and landscape subjects, size 11 x 14, 10c; 14 x 17, 13c; 14 x 28, water and lanscape scenes only, 28c each.

Artotype picture of the late Queen Victoria, copied from her latest photograph, size 18 x 24, 40c each.

Cabinet photographs, size 4½ x 6½, King Edward VII., Queen Alexandra, late Queen Victoria, Duke and Duchess of Cornwall, 25c each.

Photo Frames.

Photo bracket (as cut), in white enamel or polished oak, fitted with white or dark grey mats, with oval or square openings and top shelf for bric-a-brac, size 8 x 16, 3 openings, 75c; 8 x 21, 4 openings, $1.25 each.

We have a large and varied stock of the latest designs in photo frames in all sizes.

Miniature photo frames, in bronze, with burnished tips, oval and square shapes, with easel backs, 25c, 35c, 40c, 50c each.

Cabinet photo frames, in bronze, with burnished tips, fancy Florentine designs, 65c, 75c, $1.00, 1.25, 1.50 each.

Miniature photo frames, guaranteed quadruple gold plate, oval and square shapes, with easel backs, 90c, $1.15, 1.25, 1.40 and 1.75 each.

Cabinet photo frames, guaranteed quadruple gold plate, newest designs, fancy Florentine edge, oval and square shapes, $2.25, 2.50, 2.75, 3.25, 3.75, 4.25 and 4.75 each.

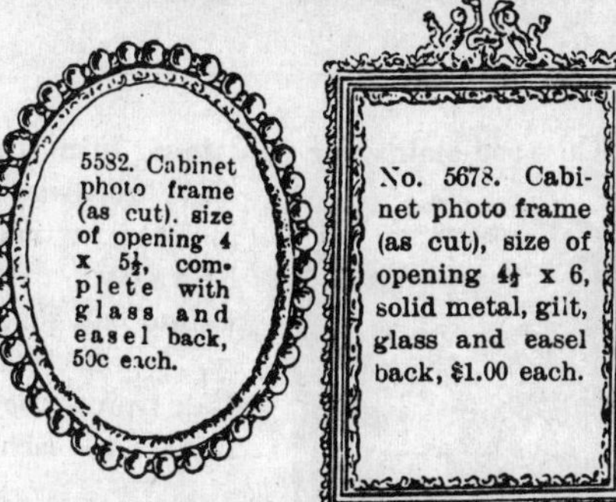

5582. Cabinet photo frame (as cut). size of opening 4 x 5½, complete with glass and easel back, 50c each.

No. 5678. Cabinet photo frame (as cut), size of opening 4½ x 6, solid metal, gilt, glass and easel back, $1.00 each.

7538. Cabinet photo frame (as cut), size of opening 5 x 7, solid metal, gilt with burnished ornaments and tips, glass and easel back, $1.35 each.

Mirrors.

No. 217. Mirrors, framed in 1-inch reeded moulding, oil finish, size 6 x 9, 12c; 8 x 10, 15c; 9 x 12, 18c; 10 x 14, 20c ea.

No. 215. Mirrors, arch top, framed with 2-inch walnut stained moulding and narrow gilt lining, size 7 x 9, 25c; 8 x 10, 30c; 9 x 12, 35c; 10 x 14, 45c; 10½ x 17, 55c; 12 x 18, 60c; 12 x 20, 65c; 13 x 22, 75c; 14 x 24, 85c each.

No. 271. Special line German plate mirrors, size 9 x 12-inch, 1-inch polished oak frame, 65c; 10 x 14, 1½-inch oak moulding, 85c; 10 x 17, 1½-inch oak moulding, $1.15; 12 x 18, 1½-inch moulding, $1.35; 12 x 20, 1½-inch moulding, $1.60; 12 x 20, bevelled, 1½-inch moulding, $1.85; 14 x 24, 2-inch moulding, $2.75; 20 x 24, 2½-inch moulding, $3.50; 18 x 36, 2½-inch moulding, $5.25; 18 x 40, 2½-inch moulding, $6.00 each.

Wall Pockets.

Bamboo wall pockets, light, durable, size 14 x 15 inches, 35c each.

Oak wall pockets, strong and well made, size 15 x 17 inches, 50c each.

Wall pockets, white enamel and gilt, imitation pastel in front, with glass, size 16 x 19½, 65c ea.

No. 24135. Wall pockets (as cut), green bronze, tipped with silver, very handsome design, pretty colored scenes in front, with glass, size 17 x 24, 75c each.

Easels.

Bamboo easels, neat and strong, 60 inches high, 50c; bamboo easels, ornamented, 66 inches high, 65c, 85c each.

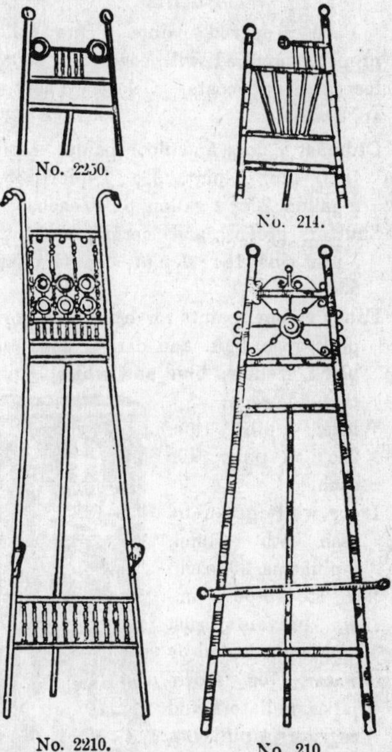

No. 2250. No. 214. No. 2210. No. 210.

No. 214. Bamboo easel (as cut), 66 inches high, pretty design and well made, 75c each.

No. 210. Bamboo easel (as cut), 66 inches high, handsome design and durable, $1.15 each.

Oak easels, plain, 60 inches high, 50c; ornamented with brass trimmings, and adjustable rests, 66 inches high, 75c, $1.25, 1.50 and 2.25 ea.

No. 2250. Oak easel (as cut), 60 inches high, polished oak, fancy top, adjustable rests, 90c each.

No. 2210. Solid polished oak easel, (as cut), 66 inches high, with fancy grill work, top and bottom, brass trimmings and adjustable brass rests, $2.00 each.

Picture Wire.

(25 yards to a coil.)

Tinned, No. 0, 4c; No. 1, 7c; No. 2, 10c; No. 3, 15c; No. 4, 20c; No. 5, 25c coil.

Gilt, No. 11, 35c; No. 12, 40c; No. 13, 50c coil.

Picture Nails

Brass-headed nails, 2½ inches long, 5c doz; porcelain slide-head nails, 15c doz; fancy colored slide-head nails, 25c doz.

Brass Moulding Hooks.

Made to fit 1-inch, 1½-inch and 2-inch mouldings, 10c, 18c, 25c, 30c, 35c and 40c doz.

Paints, Brushes and Mouldings.

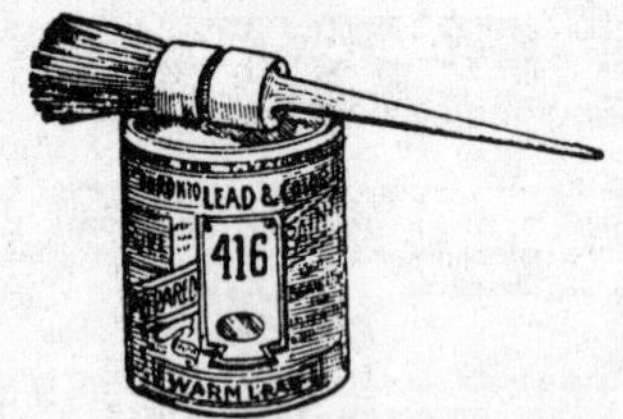

Paints.

Pure prepared paints. One gallon properly applied will cover 200 square feet with two coats. Color card sent on application.

Ordinary colors and floor paints, ½-pint tins, 11c; 1-pint, 22c; 1-quart, 35c; ½-gallon, 70c; 1-gallon, $1.40 each.

Shutter greens and vermilion colors, ½-pint tins, 18c; 1 pint, 33c; 1 quart, 50c each.

Fancy enamel paints for decorative work, pink, rose, light and dark green, red, black, yellow, blue and white, ½-pint tins, 15c each.

White, ½-pint tins, 25c; 1-pint, 45c each.

Ivory, white, green and rose bath enamel, ½-pint tins, 30c each.

"G" stovepipe enamel, prevents rust and is unaffected by water, for stovepipes, radiators and registers, ½-pint tins, 20c; 1-pint, 35c each.

No. 20. "Our Favorite" gold enamel paint, put up in boxes, with brush and liquid for mixing, small size, 18c; large size, 30c each.

No. 20.

Japanese gold paint, ready for use, with brush, 20c each.

Gold bronze, per oz, 15c; per lb, $2.00.

Aluminum and copper bronze, per oz, 20c; per lb, $2.50.

Furniture varnish, ½-pint tins, 11c; 1-pint, 18c; 1-quart, 30c each.

Oak varnish, ½-pint tins, 16c; 1-pint, 28c; 1-quart, 45c each.

White varnish, same price as the oak.

White lead, 1-lb tins, 12c; 5-lb, 55c; 12½-lb, $1.10 each.

Oil wood-stains, for re-staining furniture and woodwork, imitation mahogany, oak, walnut and cherry, ½-pint tins, 15c; 1-pint, 25c; 1-quart, 40c each.

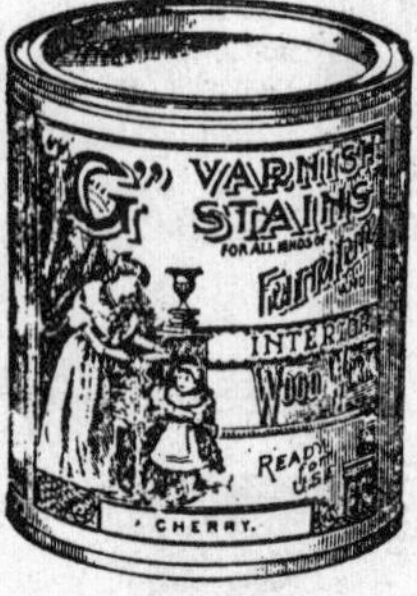

No. 21.

No. 21. Varnish stains, in imitation mahogany, rosewood, oak, walnut and cherry, ½-pint tins, 18c; 1-pint, 35c; 1-quart, 60c each.

Prepared kalsomine, blue, flesh, cream, green and terra cotta colors, 5-lb package, 20c each.

"G" furniture polish not only cleans, but gives the furniture a beautiful and lasting gloss, 4-oz bottle, 10c; 8-oz, 20c ea.

Wax and Finishes for Hardwood Floors.

Johnson's paste-wood filler, for new work only, 1 lb properly applied will cover 40 square feet. 1-lb tin, 12c; 25-lb can, $2.25 each.

Johnson's prepared wax, 1 lb will cover 300 square feet, 1 coat, put up in 1-lb, 2-lb and 5-lb tins, per lb, 45c.

Johnson's floor finish, for natural woods, 1-quart bottle, 75c.

Johnson's floor restorer, will clean and restore the finish of hardwood floors, 1-pint bottle, 75c; 1-quart bottle, $1.25.

Johnson's natural wood renower, for removing stains and discolorations, 1-quart bottle, 75c.

Steel shavings for rubbing down floors, per lb, 50c.

Johnson's weighted brushes, for polishing floors, 15-lb, $2 50; 25-lb, $3.00 each.

Brushes.

Round sash tools, tin bound, pure bristles, 9c, 12c, 18c, 25c, 35c each.

Flat sash tools, tin bound, pure bristles, 9c, 13c, 15c, 20c, 28c each.

Oval paint, pure white bristles, plain, 17c, 25c, 30c; bridled, 2/0, 40c; 4/0, 60c; 5/0, 75c; 8/0, $1.20 each.

Columbia, black, oval, plain, 25c, 27c, 35c, 60c; bridled, 5/0, $1.10; 7/0, $1.40; 8/0, $1.60; 9/0, $1.85 each.

Chiselled flat varnish, tin bound, pure white bristles, 1-inch, 12c; 1½-inch, 17c; 2-inch, 25c; 2½-inch, 30c; 3-inch, 40c each.

Standard flat paint, 30c, 35c, 40c; pure bristles, plain, 50c; bridled, 75c, $1.00 each.

Tip-top flat paint, black bristles, 45c, 55c, 80c each.

Painters' dusters, 50c, 60c each.

Paper layers, pure bristles, single thick, 10-inch, 50c; 12-inch, 75c; double thick, 10-inch, 80c; 12-inch, 95c each.

Combination paper layers, pure bristles, 12-inch, 95c each.

Kalsomine brushes, mixed, 45c, 55c, 80c, $1.25; pure bristles, $1.50, 1.75, 2.50, 2.75, 3.50, 4.00 each.

Whitewash brushes, mixed, 20c, 25c, 28c, 32c each.

Whitewash heads, mixed, pure bristles, $1.15, 1.25, 1.65 each.

Room Mouldings.

1½-inch American room moulding (as cut), blended colors, crimson and gilt; blue, cream and gilt; green, pink and gilt, 3½c foot.

1½-inch Canadian room mouldings, in fancy colors and gilt, colors to match any shade of wall paper, 3c foot.

2-inch American room moulding; blended colors, crimson, olive and gilt, green and gilt; sage, cream and gilt, 4½c foot.

2-inch Canadian room mouldings, large assortment of fancy color and gilt, to harmonize with our new shades of wall paper, 4c foot.

1-inch fancy color and gilt, blended, cream, blue, green and terra cotta, 2c and 2½c foot.

1-inch, plain burnished gilt, 3c; 1½-inch, 4c foot.

1½-inch polished antique oak, 3c foot.

Our Room Moulding Colors are fast and will not rub or run when damp. When 100 or more feet of the same pattern and color is bought we make a reduction in price of 25c per 100 feet.

INDEX.

Description and Price of Illustrations on First Page of Cover.

Lady With Cloth Suit.

Hat, velvet top, tucked chiffon and sequin facings, bird of Paradise osprey, black and white, grey and white, castor and white .... $9.00 to 11.00

No. 6173. Ladies' suit, made of fine all-wool covert coating, colors black, navy, fawn, royal and oxford, trimmed with taffeta silk straps, silk velvet collar, and taffeta vest, jacket is lined with taffeta silk, and skirt is lined with percaline and bound with velveteen.......................... $16.50

Lady With Fur Jacket.

Hat, shirred velvet facings, velvet crown with ribbon run through, fancy bird breasts, buckle ornament, navy, castor, brown, grey, and black. .... $6.80 to 8.00

Ladies' black Persian lamb jacket, 26 inches deep, best selected German dyed skins, bright full curl, lined with heavy silk backed satin, close fitting back, large Alaska sable roll collar and long revers, as cut on first page of cover........... $120.00

No. 5303. Ladies' stylish black taffeta silk skirt, made with deep ruffles and trimmed with silk velvet ribbon, has drop lining with accordion plaited silk ruffle $21.00

Men's Clothing.

Men's Fur Coats, imported English beaver cloth shell, good strong muskrat lining, medium dark Otter step collar, sleeves lined with striped satin and underlined with chamois, as cut on front page of cover $50.00

Men's and Youths' Persian lamb caps, bright German dyed skins, full even curl, as cut on first page of cover $5.00, 6.50, 8.00

INDEX.

If you do not see in this List or Catalogue the goods you require kindly write us.